American Foreign Policy
Theoretical Essays

SECOND EDITION

G. John Ikenberry
The University of Pennsylvania

HarperCollins*CollegePublishers*

Acquisitions Editor: Leo Wiegman
Project Coordination and Text Design: York Production Services
Cover Design: Scott Russo
Manufacturing Manager: Hilda Koparanian
Electronic Page Makeup: York Production Services
Printer and Binder: R. R. Donnelley and Sons Company, Inc.
Cover Printer: Color-Imetry Corp.

American Foreign Policy: Theoretical Essays, Second Edition

Library of Congress Cataloging-in-Publication Data

American foreign policy: theoretical essays / edited by G. John
    Ikenberry—2nd ed.
        p.   cm.
    Includes bibliographical references.
    ISBN 0-673-52440-X
    1. United States—Foreign relations—1945–1989—Philosophy.
I. Ikenberry, G. John.
E840.A634   1995
327.73—dc20   95-20894
                                                          CIP

95 96 97 98 9 8 7 6 5 4 3 2 1

Contents

PART Four
NATIONAL VALUES, DEMOCRATIC INSTITUTIONS, AND FOREIGN POLICY   249

PART Five
PUBLIC OPINION, POLICY LEGITIMACY, AND SECTIONAL CONFLICT   349

PART Six
BUREAUCRATIC POLITICS AND ORGANIZATIONAL CULTURE   413

PART Seven
PERCEPTIONS, PERSONALITY, AND
SOCIAL PSYCHOLOGY   513

PART Eight
THEORETICAL DEBATES AFTER THE COLD WAR   623

Preface

The purpose of this book is to provide students with representative statements of the major, contending explanations of American foreign policy. The idea is to showcase the variety of theoretical perspectives that scholars have pursued in attempting to make sense of policy. I have gathered these essays together in the hope that students will become more familiar with the avenues of inquiry that are available and the debates they engender. Left only to the textbook or the occasional popular book on the subject, students and teachers alike can all too easily overlook the very real controversies at the heart of the study of American foreign policy: What political, economic, and cultural forces shape policy? What is the realm of choice and what is the realm of necessity in making policy? What types of language and levels of analysis are most useful in our search to explain policy? My hope is that after reading the essays in this volume, the student can achieve more clarity in answering these questions.

The theoretical traditions that these essays represent are of long standing. Scholars over many generations have worked within them and drawn on many of them, although the specific formulations presented in most of the essays are quite original. Because the effort is to present theoretical approaches and not analysis of current foreign policy events, the essays themselves range in vintage as widely as they range in content. This is a virtue; it reinforces the notion that scholarly endeavor springs from theoretical traditions. We build on some and react to others. Through this process we create new traditions.

In the introduction I present an overview of the challenge of explanation in foreign policy. The problem in the study of American foreign policy is that we have too many ways of explaining policy—we have an overabundance of theory. In this essay I explore some of the methods whereby students can deal with this problem of overdetermination. Part One, "The Problem of Explanation," presents discussions of analytical choice in the study of foreign policy. These essays help us develop a set of tools to explore more specific types of explanation. Each of the following parts represents an alternative route to explanation. Taken together, the book provides a sort of compendium of maps for the study of foreign policy. It is the readers who must judge which map is most useful.

Many of the categories of explanation and some of the essays that are presented here were used in a course I taught for many years at Princeton University. Over the years this course was taught and passed along to several professors. Its organization, with a focus on explanation, was given shape by Miles Kahler and Kenneth Oye as well as myself. Its original inspiration, if oral history is correct, came from James Kurth when he taught Government 179, Comparative Foreign Policy, at Harvard. As it turns out, the teaching of American foreign policy also has its traditions.

G. John Ikenberry

Introduction

G. John Ikenberry

Few areas of American political life have attracted more commentators, critics, and interpreters than United States foreign policy. Popular views of the proper direction and aims of American foreign policy are as ubiquitous and wide-ranging as the policies themselves. Scholarly analysis of American foreign policy is no less diverse. Schools of thought that claim to explain the sources and purposes of foreign policy are scattered across the academic landscape. This is scarcely surprising. The foreign policy of the United States covers so much history and so many events that it seems capable of sustaining many interpretations, even contradictory ones, at the same time. Scholars are drawn to the study of foreign policy in efforts to develop powerful and satisfying accounts of the forces that shape policy. Yet very little agreement can be found over what those forces are and how they operate. The student of foreign policy is left with an array of historical cases and lots of theories. What is to be done?

Confronted with this predicament, happily, we can make some headway. We can begin by clarifying what exactly these theories seek to explain. A more precise understanding of the claims that a theoretical approach makes allows us to judge its plausibility; we put ourselves in a position to accept or reject the claims in the light of the historical evidence. This volume is organized so as to allow this process of clarification to take place. We are confronted with important and divergent approaches to American foreign policy. Presented with a sort of theoretical menu, we can see what each has to offer. What specifically is each theoretical approach attempting to explain? What are the forces and mechanisms at work? What explicit or implicit models of individual and state action are embedded within each approach? How generalizable are the claims? What unacknowledged normative claims linger below the surface concerning how American foreign policy is best conducted?

Coming to grips with the range of explanations for American foreign policy still leaves us with an overabundance of theory, but we can make headway here as well. In some case we are confronted with competing explanations for policy—different theories that claim to explain the same events. In circumstances such as these we need to know how to evaluate the alternatives; we need standards of judgment as we sort through the theoretical options. Which types of theories provide the most powerful and robust explanations?

In other cases we are confronted with theories that are lodged at different levels of explanation. The theories are trained on different aspects of foreign policy and are not in direct competition. Here we need to know how to provide layered analysis and to judge which levels are most enduring and fundamental. In both these cases we need a sort of methodology of choice, or a theory of theories, that provides guidance in how to deploy our analysis.

In this introduction I discuss each of these tasks—the clarification of theories and the methodology of choice. We begin this exercise with a sober appreciation of the problems of finding definitive answers to our questions. We must be willing to manage the ambiguity that is inherent in attempting to understand a seemingly unmanageable array of history that we loosely group together as American foreign policy. But the exercise is essential. Precisely because everybody has an opinion on foreign policy, we need to probe more deeply the theoretical assumptions that lie beneath the surface. At the very least we will come to a better understanding of the largely implicit theoretical commitments we often make in the heat of political debate. But we just might advance even further and cut through the welter of opinion to stake out a more systematic and reasoned set of views on American foreign policy. The absence of a systematic and reasoned set of views on foreign policy is often the first criticism we level at our political leaders. We should demand no less of ourselves.

VARIETIES OF THEORY AND LEVELS OF ANALYSIS

Part of the problem in clarifying and comparing alternative explanations of American foreign policy is that these explanations do not always seek to explain the same events. Foreign policy can be found, among other places, in the decisions of a president or secretary of state, in the policies of a government, or in the broad patterns of the nation's history. In explaining the American intervention in Vietnam, are we interested in understanding President Johnson's fateful 1965 decision to send combat troops to South Vietnam or in the larger sequence of American policy and the doctrine of containment that stretched over five administrations? Are we interested in explaining specific decisions of a single individual, or sequences of decisions that stretch over many years, or the policy outcomes of entire government bodies, such as Congress or the executive branch? The types of policy outcomes or decisions that we seek to explain may well influence what theoretical bodies of literature we want to draw on. At the same time what appear to be contradictory theoretical claims by different scholars may actually simply arise from differences in their choice of subject matter.

Levels of Analysis

In clarifying the range of foreign policy outcomes and the range of theoretical explanations many scholars have invoked the notion of levels of analysis. Kenneth Waltz, concerning himself with international politics and not foreign policy as such, has specified three "images" of international politics: the individual, the state, and the state system.[1] Each image captures a different level of causation in international relations. The first image is the individual; as a source of behavior in international politics, it brings with it the idiosyncratic features and beliefs that constitute all individuals. How do you explain why a nation goes to war? You look at the ambitions and personalities of its leaders. The second image focuses on the characteristics of the nation-state, its culture, society, and political institutions. How do you explain why a nation goes to war? You look at the forces that grow out of its democratic or authoritarian or socialist institutions. The third image is the international system. At this systemic level the concern is with the enduring patterns and structures of power within the state system. How do you explain why a nation goes to war? You look at the competitive nature of the state system and the changing balance of power. Waltz argues that this level is the most powerful as a guide to understanding international politics. The systemic level identifies the forces within which individuals and states operate; it generates constraints and imperatives to which all individuals and states, regardless of their uniquenesses, must abide.

In another classic statement of the problem, J. David Singer also distinguishes levels of analysis. In assessing the levels' descriptive, explanatory, and predictive capabilities, Singer finds that the international system level is the most comprehensive and most capable of predictive generalizations. Yet in moving to a systemic model, such theory loses the richness and specificity of analysis on the national level. At the international level states take on a certain sameness as the analysis deemphasizes national autonomy and independence of choices.[2] In the end Singer argues for a balance of systemic and national-level analysis; an exclusive preoccupation with one or the other risks an exaggeration of either similarities or differences in states.

In a further refinement Robert Jervis distinguishes between four levels of analysis: the level of decision making; the level of bureaucracy; the nature of the state and the workings of domestic politics; and the international environment.[3] Apart from the decision-making level, which delineates the realm of choice for the actor, the other levels locate features of the actor's setting. Analysis at each of these levels makes a claim: that if we know enough about the setting in which foreign policy is made—bureaucratic, national or international—we can explain and predict the actor's behavior. Yet the emphasis on one of these variables seems to diminish the importance of the others. The importance of the international setting as a force that shapes foreign policy, for example, suggests an image of foreign policy officials relatively unconstrained by their own bureaucracy or domestic political system. Likewise, if bureaucracy plays a serious role in shaping policy, this has implications for the claims we might make about the role of political parties or public opinion. Specifying levels of analysis immediately reveals the theoretical tensions.

There is no uniform method for the classification of types of theories or variables. The organization of this book goes further than do the authors just discussed in distinguishing between types of variables or levels of analysis. Several of the sections, such as those concerning economic and cultural determinants of foreign policy, fall rather easily into Waltz's second image or Jervis's national level of analysis. The categorization of variables into levels of analysis is at least initially simply a matter of theoretical housekeeping. For our purposes the levels-of-analysis exercise organizes into manageable parts the various elements of social reality that bear on the making of foreign policy.

International and Domestic Structures

Running through the discussion of levels of analysis is the issue of the primacy of one level over the others. In this there is some controversy. Kenneth Waltz, as we have noted, gives pride of place to forces that operate at the international level. An anarchic state system and a prevailing distribution of power are unrelenting forces that operate on states. To begin one's analysis with more particularistic national or individual variables is to risk missing common international forces that impose their constraints on many states. Political culture or public opinion, for example, may influence foreign policy in specific cases and at the margin, but it is the basic structure of the international system that sets the terms of the conduct of foreign policy over the long run. J. David Singer is not as insistent on leaving explanations at the international level. Theorists of foreign policy are in effect caught between Scilla and Charybdis; a proper theoretical understanding of foreign policy must avoid the dangers that emerge when we move too far in either a national or systemic direction.

There is reason to be skeptical of the strongest claims of systemic analysis that the structure of the international system *determines* foreign policy; and indeed most of the controversy is really over how theoretically privileged this level of analysis should be. Most scholars who stress the importance of systemic forces argue that it sets constraints on foreign policy rather than shapes policy in any more direct sense; it is a necessary but not sufficient component of our analysis. Waltz's theory of international politics is just that: a theory that seeks to explain recurring patterns of behavior within the international system. As Waltz notes, to explain how any single nation-state will respond to the constraints imposed by the international structure requires a theory of foreign policy.[4] The international system influences but does not determine foreign policy.

Yet even if the international system (characterized by its competitive nature and prevailing distribution of power) manifests imperatives and constraints, it is still necessary to understand how and to what extent those imperatives and constraints operate. How does a state (or individuals within it) perceive and act on forces generated within a competitive state system? The international system may well create incentives for political leaders to protect their national autonomy and security, but many foreign policy outcomes are consistent with this demand. Statesmen may be pressed to attend to the nation's survival and well-being, but the international setting does not provide unambiguous clues about how best to do so. In the same way, the specification of international constraints may leave a wide range of options open to state officials. Constraints may be more or less confining, and so we need to know under what conditions they are more and under what conditions they are less confining. A focus on constraints tells us what is not possible. If constraints are very tight, we may have most of the story. If they are loose, we are left with little guidance concerning what is still possible.[5]

If the international setting does not provide enough explanatory power, we might want to turn to national-level variables. Here we are interested in such factors as the social and economic structure of the nation and the character of its domestic politics. The variety of domestic variables that may impinge on foreign policy is huge, and many of them are organized in the sections of this book. Some theories argue for the importance of the nation's culture, its economic and class structure, or its ruling political institutions. Some make strong claims that a particular variable determines foreign policy in conjunction with other variables. When we move to this level of analysis, the types of variables that may impinge on foreign policy proliferate.

In each case we are confronted with the same issues as those that arose in our discussion of systemic theory. Each approach makes a claim about the constraints and imperatives that are imposed by a particular set of characteristics in the decision maker's domestic setting. States with the same critical domestic feature should pursue similar sorts of foreign policy when they are in similar sorts of international situations (and also act similarly when confronted with significantly different situations); states that differ in this critical domestic feature should also differ in their foreign policy, even if they are confronted with similar sorts of international situations.[6] It is here that national-level theories of foreign policy are put to the test. Revisionist historians argue that the cold war had its roots in the expansive behavior of American capitalist society. Critics of this position argue that United States policy toward the Soviet Union was motivated by geopolitical circumstances that would have been felt and acted on by American political leaders regardless of the nation's internal economic or political characteristics. History makes it very difficult to settle this controversy, but the theoretical issues at stake are clear.

Theories of foreign policy that stress the importance of domestic setting make the implicit claim that if different leaders were present in the same domestic circumstances, they would make the same choices. The stronger the claim made about the role of domestic setting, the less it is necessary to know about the activities and beliefs of the actual individuals who make decisions. But again we are confronted with theoretical challenges. Unless one takes an extreme position, the theory characterizes the domestic sources of foreign policy as constraints and imperatives that more or less shape policy. In what way do political leaders feel the pressures and constraints of culture or class or political institutions? What are the mechanisms? How do they operate? Under what conditions can they be ignored or transformed? If a particular type of domestic structure, such as class structure, is only loosely constraining, we may need to consider several sets of structures and entertain the possibility that they interact with one another. Bureaucratic politics may be magnified by the play of societal pressures, or it may insulate political leaders from the larger society. Political culture and ideals may manifest themselves most profoundly in the institutions of government that in turn help to influence the course of foreign policy.

Choice and Decision Making

When we have exhausted the explanatory power of a state's domestic and international setting, we are left with the decision makers themselves. The theories we have discussed to this point are *structural* theories. That is, they are theories that make predictions about foreign policy outcomes without reference to the cognition and actions of the actors themselves. According to these theories, setting, of whatever type, shapes policy. In their strongest form structural theories that stress domestic and international setting leave little or no room for individual beliefs, perceptions, or choices. Individuals are theoretically fungible. Substitute one individual for another, and if the setting remains the same, so too does foreign policy.

If structural theories do not satisfactorily explain foreign policy, we can turn to *decision-making* explanations of policy. Here we are interested in theories that explain policy in terms of the reasons, beliefs, and processes by which individuals make choices. Domestic and international structures may constrain and propel foreign policy, but when they leave room for meaningful choice, we need theories of individual and group decision making.[7]

The autonomy of the decision-making level remains a matter of some controversy. This issue is implicit when students of American foreign policy debate various historical "what-ifs." If Franklin Roosevelt had lived, would he have been able to prevent or moderate postwar hostilities between the United States and Soviet Union beyond the talents of an inexperienced Harry Truman? If John F. Kennedy had not been killed in Dallas, would the tragedy of Vietnam have been avoided? Alternatively, in both these cases were the evolving geopolitical circumstances or shifting international currents leading these presidents in the same direction as their successors? In the most important episodes of postwar American foreign policy, when policy was made that lasted a generation, did individuals make a difference or were they swept up in larger historical forces? These are questions about the role of the individual in history. They are questions as stimulating as they are frustrating, and we cannot provide definitive answers to them. Nonetheless, if we are prepared to grant our foreign policy leaders a realm of choice, we must equip ourselves with a means to understand their decisions.

Several literatures probe the workings of foreign policy decision making. One group of theories focuses on the manner in which government bureaucracy shapes the content of policy. The claims of this type of explanation are fourfold: the de facto power to make foreign policy is divided across the executive establishment; the various "players" in the decision-making process have different goals and interests, largely determined by their bureaucratic position ("Where a person stands depends on when he sits"); decision making is a process of bargaining and compromise; and consequently, policy is a "resultant"—it is the product of a political rather than an analytical process. The seminal statement of this approach is provided by Graham Allison, and it is included in this volume along with major statements of critique.

The implication of this body of theory, if it is to be truly taken seriously, is that policy emerges not in response to the external setting of the actors charged with making decisions but rather from within the organizations of the state itself. It is the bureaucratic interests of government officials and the distribution of power within the state that determine the substantive content of policy. If, however, those interests and configurations of power are only a reflection of larger social interests and powers, the bureaucratic approach to explanation is substantially reduced in theoretical importance. We may want to know about the details of decision making within the "black box" of government, but that process is trivial as a guide to the forces that shape policy. Alternatively, bureaucratic politics and organizational process may be decisive sources of policy in the foreign policy backwaters—in areas of least significance. We must be prepared to differentiate policies as we search for explanations.

The decision-making level has also been approached by other scholars who focus on the beliefs and cognition of top leaders. As is the case with the bureaucratic politics approach, the attention to beliefs and perceptions assumes a realm of choice in policy making. The importance of cognitive variables may emerge in several situations. We may want to focus on this aspect of decision making if there are cases in which consistent differences exist between decision makers' perceptions and reality. These may be cases of major foreign policy blunders, when officials misjudge their position or that of their adversary. Such cases may provide evidence of the role of domestic constraints or pressures, but it is equally plausible that the officials were conducting policy with an inappropriate set of beliefs. Alternatively, we may want to probe the role of perceptions and beliefs when officials placed in the same situation behave differently. In these cases officials may bring to office very different sets of beliefs about the world.[8] These types of beliefs and cognitive frameworks are explored in Part Seven of this book.

Provided with these various levels of analysis and theoretical approaches, we can explore their utility in the study of foreign policy. We can begin to appreciate the various levels of social structure and decision making that may bear on policy. At the same time it is easy to see that we are supplied with an overabundance of theory. We need further guidance in making theoretical choices. It is not enough simply to pick some theoretical approach and run with it. We need guidance in how to proceed when different approaches seem to provide equally plausible explanations—to better understand when a particular level of analysis or type of variable is most suitable in rendering an account of foreign policy. We turn to these issues now.

THE PROBLEM OF THE OVERSUPPLY OF THEORY

Of the various approaches to foreign policy in this volume, each promises to explain some aspects of American foreign policy, and at each level there is seemingly great promise. The international system can be brought to bear in explaining almost all foreign policy. Internationally generated pressures of various sorts find their way into all facets of policy making. Foreign policy also elicits strong views from many segments of society, and some types of foreign policy serve to advantage and disadvantage various societal groups. Thus, even if direct pressure by these groups is not apparent, an underlying set of societal interests may still account for patterns of outcomes. Finally, political leaders and the bureaucracy have a hand in shaping foreign policy simply by virtue of their location and formal powers. Indeed, to no one's surprise, these officials find it easy to rationalize their actions in terms of national or "state" interests. It is clear that we are left not with an absence of adequate explanations of foreign policy but with an oversupply. As James Kurth puts the issue, "[t]he problem with questions about the making of military policy, and also about the making of foreign policy, is not that there are no answers but that there are too many answers."[9] How are we to proceed?

It may not be possible to settle these theoretical controversies—to decide which theory or level of analysis is most important. But we can put ourselves in a situation to judge the merits of various approaches to foreign policy. When we are confronted with competing and seemingly coequal explanations of foreign policy, we can turn to three methods by which to adjudicate the claims: empirical, aesthetic, and analytical.

The most obvious attempt to solve the problem of overdetermination is to turn the problem into an *empirical* problem. If we are confronted, for example, with a structural account and a decision-making account of an episode in American foreign policy, we may want to investigate the recollections of the government officials themselves to see what they perceived to be their realm of choice. Stanley Hoffmann provides a structural account of American policy in the early postwar period: "When the nature of Soviet power and policy and the crumbling of British strength became obvious, the United States simply had to fill the vacuum. President Truman's freedom of choice was strictly limited; it concerned the moment and the manner in which America's taking up the challenge would be demonstrated. Even in this respect the margin of choice was narrowed by the development of the crisis in Greece in 1947. . . . Rarely has freedom been more clearly the recognition of necessity, and statesmanship the imaginative exploitation of necessity."[10] This systemic argument about the forces that drove American policy (and the various bureaucratic, economic, and cultural accounts that compete against it) can be clarified by investigating the range of options that officials themselves entertained.

There are inherent limits, however, to empirical solutions to theoretical problems. Government officials may seek to rationalize their decisions by arguing that the imperatives of geopolitics left them no choice; or they may take credit for making a choice where none really existed. Even more problematic, the theories themselves point to different types of evidence, each with its own biases. In explaining why President Kennedy chose a policy of blockade during the Cuban missile crisis, we can find evidence to support a variety of explanations. We could point to the president's individual characteristics, to political pressures of the upcoming midterm election in 1962, or to the international balance of power. There is evidence that would seem to suit each type of explanation. Adjudication the claims of various theories by strict reference to the historical "facts" runs into the same problem we have with the theories themselves: there is an overabundance, not a paucity, of empirical evidence. Empirical investigations may give us some help, but they do not resolve the problems of the oversupply of theory.

A second approach to the problem of competing explanations could be called the *aesthetic* solution. Competing theories are judged in terms of basic standards of theoretical rigor. These standards, as Harry Eckstein argues, include regularity (does a theory involve claims to "rulefulness" with statements of causation and probability?); reliability and validity (does the theory provide a set of conditions that if repeated would produce the same outcome?); foreknowledge (does the theory provide statements of anticipated outcomes in areas currently unknown?); and parsimony (how wide a range and number of phenomena can the theory order and how simple are the theoretical constructs it uses to do so?)[11]

From the standpoint of these elements of rigor, the theories in this volume present different strengths and weaknesses. Systemic theory, with its attention to international structural variables, is attractive for its parsimony. If we want to explain general characteristics of American foreign policy over long stretches of time, this is a good place to begin. Yet international-level theory, as we have already noted, posits constraints and imperatives on actors; it does not provide the basis for predicting specific outcomes. Systemic theory may still provide the most powerful explanation of foreign policy in some circumstances, yet its parsimony is often purchased at the price of less specificity in the outcomes it can explain. Other structural theories that specify the setting within which actors make decisions also suffer from problems of this sort. Theories that rely on political culture or ideology, although less parsimonious than systemic theory, also tend to have a huge variety of outcomes that are consistent with their predictions. Theories that are lodged at the decision-making level rely on variables that tend to come and go with the individuals themselves; patterns and regularities in foreign policy are tied closely to sets of intervening conditions. At the same time decision-making theories may be able to capture more of the richness and critical detail of foreign policy.

It is clear that no one theory or set of variables can be the most important in all situations. Consequently, our efforts are probably not best served by seeking to find one approach that triumphs over the rest. The importance of a set of variables varies with the cases we are seeking to understand. This leads to a final method for dealing with the problem of the oversupply of theory—what we can call the *analytical* approach. Here the efforts are not to choose between the contending explanations as such, but to draw on each in various ways. This can be done in two ways. One approach is eclectic. In this we simply pick and choose from the various approaches in fashioning plausible accounts of American foreign policy. This approach appears reasonable at first glance, particularly because the types of policies we might wish to explain vary so enormously. Nonetheless, this ad hoc approach has flaws, as James Kurth criticizes: "It is intellectually unsatisfying and even self-abnegating. Further, it suffers from what might be called the nth + 1 problem. Given n theories, the simple eclectic will accept them all and equally, for he has no standards with which to discriminate among them. But suppose someone offers another explanation, the nth + 1 theory. The simply eclectic must accept this theory too. And the same is true for the nth + 2, nth + 3. . . ."[12]

The analytical solution, however, does not need to be eclectic. Rather than simply picking and choosing elements of the various approaches, this approach can involve the development of more overarching propositions that bring the various theories together in comprehensive ways. In effect what this final approach attempts to do is to develop "metatheory" that incorporates the several types of variables into larger-scale frameworks. An exercise of this sort is all the more useful when we note that many of the theories are not strictly speaking alternative and co-equal. The explanatory usefulness of a variable, as we have argued, may depend on what level of generality we wish to locate our analysis. The international system may influence the general contours of American foreign policy, but domestic and decision-making variables are necessary to explain more specific aspects. Or it may be, as Robert Jervis argues, that the importance of variables at each level may vary with the stages of decision: "domestic politics may dictate that a given event be made the occasion for a change in policy; bargaining within the bureaucracy may explain what options are presented to the national leaders; the decision maker's predisposition could account for the choice that was made; and the interests and routines of the bureaucracies could explain the way the decision was implemented."[13]

Another way to make sense of the multitude of variables and levels is to pose their significance as conditional propositions. Thus, we can argue that systemic-level variables are most important during times of international crisis. It is at these moments that government officials are most attentive to the constraints and opportunities of the international system and most willing to ignore domestic political pressures. In the absence of a foreign policy crisis, domestic politics or the working of bureaucracy are more likely to come into play. One can also develop contingent propositions that relate variables to different types of foreign policy issues. Foreign economic policy may be subject to greater domestic pressures than military policy.[14] Doubtless there are many other ways to develop contingent propositions of this sort that link sets of variables with divergent aspects of American foreign policy. In the end we are still left with an overabundance of theory, but we now have methods with which to cope with the many possibilities.

CONCLUSION

The choices we make about how to probe the workings of American foreign policy carry with them normative implications. This is not evident at first glance. Discussions of theory, and even more so "metatheory," seem to be far removed from our own views about the conduct of foreign policy. Yet the link exists. In his essay in Part One, James Kurth observes that the conclusions we draw on the theory of foreign policy tell us, when we turn to policy advocacy, what needs to be reformed. If we conclude that high levels of military spending and an expansionary foreign policy are rooted in the very nature of the American capitalist system, as Marxists and others have argued, the agenda for change is profound indeed. If such policies are propelled by more transient sets of institutions or ruling coalitions, reform would lead in a different direction. Our theories give us guidance when we want to talk about improving American foreign policy.

Those who argue that the international system is an overpowering force in shaping foreign policy are faced with their own moral questions. If foreign policy officials are the faithful stewards of the balance of power, who is to be judged accountable? Robert Jervis poses this issue:

When all people would respond the same way to a given situation, it is hard to praise or blame the decision maker. Thus, those accused of war crimes will argue that their behavior did not differ from others who found themselves in the same circumstance. And the prosecution will charge, as it did against Tojo and his colleagues, that "These defendants were not automatons; they were not replaceable cogs in a machine. . . . It was theirs to choose whether their nation would lead an honored life . . . or . . . would become a symbol of evil throughout the world. They made their choice. For this choice they must bear the guilt."[15]

Our theories tell us who should be held accountable in the conduct of foreign policy. Is the president in control or is he the hostage of a massive federal bureaucracy? Do our democratic institutions shape foreign policy or is it guided by the hidden hand of class interests?

We may have to live with the fact that our answers to these questions are not definitive. The drawing of satisfying theoretical conclusions about the sources and purposes of American foreign policy is a complicated affair; we are left with a certain amount of theoretical ambiguity. We can remember Albert Einstein's advice that "if you wish to describe truth, leave elegance to the tailor." At the very least we can begin by being more theoretically self-conscious about our arguments and opinions. This book seeks to array the relevant literatures so as to allow such a process to go forward.

NOTES

1. Kenneth N. Waltz, *Man, the State, and War* (New York: Columbia University Press, 1959).
2. J. David Singer, "The Level-of-Analysis Problem in International Relations," in Klaus Knorr and Sidney Verba, eds., *The International System: Theoretical Essays* (Princeton: Princeton University Press, 1961).
3. Robert Jervis, *Perception and Misperception in International Politics* (Princeton: Princeton University Press, 1976), Chapter 1.
4. Kenneth N. Waltz, *Theory of International Politics* (Reading, Mass.: Addison-Wesley, 1979). Chapter 6, "Anarchic Orders and Balances of Power," reprinted in this book as Chapter 4.
5. For a very insightful discussion of the nature of constraints and determinants see Arthur A. Stein, "Structure, Purpose, Process, and Analysis of Foreign Policy: The Growth of Soviet Power and the Role of Ideology," in Roman Kolkowicz, ed., *The Roots of Soviet Power: Domestic Determinants of Foreign and Defense Policy* (Boulder: Westview Press, 1989).
6. See Jervis, *Perception and Misperception in International Politics*, p. 22.
7. See Stein, "Structure, Purpose, Process, and the Analysis of Foreign Policy."
8. Jervis, *Perception and Misperception in International Politics*, p. 29.
9. James R. Kurth, "A Widening Gyre: The Logic of American Weapons Procurement," *Public Policy* XIX (Summer 1971), reprinted as Chapter 1 of this book.
10. Stanley Hoffmann, "Restraints and Choices in American Foreign Policy," in Stanley Hoffmann, *The State of War: Essays on the Theory and Practice of International Politics* (Praeger Publishers, 1965).
11. Harry Eckstein, "Case Study and Theory in Political Science," in Nelson Polsby and Fred Greenstein, eds., *Handbook of Political Science* (Reading, Mass.: Addison-Wesley, 1975), vol. 2, p. 88.

For discussion of the scientific method as it relates to the study of Soviet foreign policy, see Jack Synder, "Richness and Rigor, and Relevance in the Study of Soviet Foreign Policy," *International Security,* vol. 9, no. 3 (Winter 1984/85).

12. James R. Kurth, "United States Policies and Latin American Politics: Competing Theories and Comparative Analyses," unpublished paper, 1972.
13. Jervis, *Perception and Misperception in International Politics,* p. 17.
14. See Barry B. Hughes, *The Domestic Context of American Foreign Policy* (San Francisco: W.H. Freeman and Company, 1978), Chapter 7.
15. Jervis, *Perception and Misperception in International Politics,* pp. 15–16.

PART
One

THE PROBLEM OF EXPLANATION

T he following three essays examine the general analytical problems of explaining foreign policy. James R. Kurth, focusing on weapons procurement, outlines the competing explanations of American military policy. The problem of explanation, Kurth argues, is not that there are no answers but that there are too many answers. At the same time each explanation—for example, economic theory or bureaucratic theory—carries with it a distinctive normative agenda for reform. Yet the ability to arrive at determinate causal explanations of foreign policy is elusive. By focusing on specific case studies, Kurth demonstrates how the "thicket of theories" can be cut away to yield a clearer sense of explanation.

John Odell is interested in explaining American foreign economic policy, particularly monetary policy. His chapter is an effort to survey the competing theories that make claims about the sources of foreign economic policy change. These factors include the international market and power conditions, interest group politics, and internal government bargaining. Odell also pays attention to the role of "ideas"—by which he means the substantive policy beliefs of top policy makers and advisers. Odell's goal is both to specify the rival approaches to explaining foreign economic policy and to determine which approaches are most useful in analyzing concrete historical cases.

Ole Holsti is interested in facilitating exchange between diplomatic historians and political scientists, which he does by offering a map of the various schools of thought in the professional study of international relations and foreign policy.

Holsti's survey begins by examining theories of the international system: classical realism and its modern variations, global society and complex interdependence, and Marxism. Holsti moves on to examine various models of foreign policy decision making: bureaucratic politics, group dynamics, and individual decision making. Holsti argues that systemic and decision-making approaches each have advantages and limitations, and a satisfying explanation may need to work within both traditions. At the same time, it is important to clearly specify the outcome that one wants to explain; this also determines which model is most useful.

A Widening Gyre: The Logic of American Weapons Procurement

James R. Kurth

I. THE MAKING OF MILITARY POLICY: A THICKET OF THEORIES

In the wake of the Vietnamese War and under the threat of a costly and dangerous Soviet-American arms race, basic questions are being asked about the making of American military policy. Why does the United States buy a costly anti-ballistic missile system (ABM) despite expert testimony that it will not work and despite urgent pleas to "reorder national priorities" toward domestic problems of the 1970s? Why does the United States deploy multiple independently targeted reentry vehicles (MIRV) despite expert testimony that they will re-create "the reciprocal fear of surprise attack" and "the delicate balance of terror" of the 1950s and despite a Senate plea to postpone their deployment?[1] And what will be the consequences of such weapons systems for U.S. strategic doctrines?

The problem with questions about the making of military policy, and also about the making of foreign policy, is not that there are no answers but that there are too many answers. Around ABM, or around MIRV, or around nearly every significant military policy, there has grown up a cluster of competing explanations, a thicket of theories, which prevents us from having a clear view of the making of that policy. For example, does MIRV result from rational calculation about Soviet threats or from reckless pursuit by weapons scientists of technological progress for its own sake, or from resourceful efforts by weapons manufacturers and by their allies in the military services to maintain production and profits, or from some combination of these factors? Today men debate and denounce each other over such competing explanations of military policies.

Of course, some would quickly prune away some explanations as obviously being mere brambles. They might say of the effect of a hypothetical cause what Robert Dahl has said of the power of a hypothetical act:

> Suppose I stand on a street corner and say to myself, "I command all automobile drivers on the street to drive on the right side of the road"; suppose further that all the

James R. Kurth, "A Widening Gyre: The Logic of American Weapons Procurement," *Public Policy* XIX (Summer 1971). Reprinted by permission. Brief quotes from Robert S. McNamara, *The Essence of Security,* Harper & Row, Publishers, Inc., 1968, pp. 57 and 60.

drivers actually do as I "command" them to do; still most people will regard me as mentally ill if I insist that I have power over automobile drivers to compel them to use the right side of the road.[2]

But when we turn from traffic to politics, as we know from Dahl's own efforts to analyze power, the difference between madmen or mad theories and rules of the road or rules of political behavior is no longer so obvious to so many objective observers.

II. COMPETING EXPLANATIONS OF MILITARY POLICIES

Let us distinguish five major competing explanations of American military policies: the strategic, the technocratic, the bureaucratic, the democratic, and the economic.[3]

1. The Strategic Theory

This explanation emphasizes the international system and America's security and status within it as the determinant of military policies. Until recently this approach probably was the most common among scholars: Balance of power theory, game theory, bargaining theory, and analyses of the reciprocal dynamics of arms races are all variations on the strategic theme. Leading strategic theorists of American military policies are Thomas Schelling, Henry Kissinger, and Herman Kahn.[4] And of course strategic arguments remain the chosen rationales of policy makers, for example in presentations to Congress by the current administration, such as President Nixon's "U.S. Foreign Policy for the 1970s" and Secretary of Defense Laird's annual defense report.

2. The Technocratic Theory

This explanation emphasizes the technical interests of weapons scientists as the determinant of military policies. It argues that a weapons system is developed because, as J. Robert Oppenheimer put it about an H-bomb design, it is "technically so sweet."[5] Leading technocratic theorists are Ralph Lapp and for the most part Herbert York.[6] Among policy makers, the Defense Department's director of science and engineering, John Foster, has asked, "By what mechanisms does our society select the goals and opportunities which our research and development community will pursue?" His answer: "Many are pursued because they are possible or because they are exciting."[7]

3. The Bureaucratic Theory

This explanation sees military policies as the outcomes of competition between bureaucracies, especially the army, navy, and air force. As such, it is a form of interest-group theory with a shift in locus from Congress to the executive and a shift in content from "low politics" to "high politics." Leading bureaucratic theorists of American military policies are Samuel Huntington, Warner Schilling, and for the most part John Kenneth Galbraith.[8] Closely related to this explanation from bureaucratic politics is the explanation from the bureaucratic process; this explanation sees military policies as the outputs of processes and standard operating procedures *within* bureaucracies. Graham Allison's work is an explicit illustration of the bureaucratic or organizational process explanation as well as the bureaucratic politics explanation.[9]

4. The Democratic Theory

Another possible explanation of military policies would emphasize the political system as the determinant. Here, congressional and presidential elections would be central, and relatedly, pork-barrel politics and corporate campaign contributions. At present, however, no one has systematically emphasized electoral politics as the major determinant of military policies, although Bruce Russett has done statistical analysis along these lines, and many journalists have made fragmentary observations.[10]

5. The Economic Theory

This explanation emphasizes the economic system as the determinant of military policies, for example, the role of industrialism, capitalism, and the great corporations. In a less sweeping but more frequent formulation of the economic theory, the emphasis is on one section of the economy, the aerospace industry. Leading economic theorists of American military policies are Gabriel Kolko, Harry Magdoff, and the late Paul Baran.[11]

The bureaucratic and economic explanations in combination yield, of course, the theory of the military-industrial complex, which in its pure form argues that the military and industry are roughly equal in their influence on policy outcomes. This argument has often been advanced by journalists. Some give equal weight to a third element in the complex, the major military committees of Congress.

In normal times, this rather dry recital of competing explanations of military policies would have only descriptive value; at the present time, however, when men debate "the need to reorder national priorities" and fear the risks and burdens of a new arms race, the different theories have different implications for action, have prescriptive value.

Let us imagine men who find fault with American military policies and who hope to contribute to their correction. For them each of the major theories or explanations has a different prescriptive implication.

1. The strategic theory: individual reasoning with the leading policy makers.
2. The technocratic theory: procedural reform of research and development.
3. The bureaucratic theory: bureaucratic reorganization.
4. The democratic theory: electoral or constitutional reform.
5. The economic theory: industrial reorganization or even social revolution.

Consequently and generally, the prescriptive implications become successively more radical.[12] Each theory permits but does not prescribe the corrective or preventive prescription of the theories listed before it in the above order; given one particular theory, the preceding prescriptions may be helpful but will not be sufficient for the correction or prevention of a military policy. Conversely, assuming norms of economy of effort and economy of effect, each theory proscribes the prescriptions of the theories listed after it; given one particular theory, the succeeding prescriptions will not be necessary for the correction or prevention of a military policy. In brief, each theory precludes the sufficiency of the ones before it, and each precludes the necessity of the ones after it.

Given this array of competing explanations and the corresponding array of correcting prescriptions, how should we choose among them? Immediately we confront two very serious problems.

One problem is what we can call the problem of alternative causes or the problem of *a posteriori* overdetermination. For nearly any interesting military policy (or indeed for any interesting policy generally), we can discover or invent, *a posteriori*, several alternative explanations and sometimes even all of the explanations above, each of which is logically and plausibly a sufficient explanation for the policy, is exhaustive and therefore will seem an exclusive explanation for the policy.

I would argue especially that nearly any military policy can be explained or rationalized in terms of the international system, in strategic terms. Further, not only can most military policies be internationalized, but most can also be bureaucratized, democratized, economized, and even technocratized. But even this is not all. For the bureaucratic theory and the economic theory really are variations on a theme of rational policy making, of "the strategy of conflict," with the locus of the rationality shifted from the level of the unitary, rational actor within the international system to the level of the unitary bureau within the bureaucratic system or the unitary corporation within the economic system. Theories of rational interest can be attacked at these lower levels just as theories of a rational or national interest can be attacked at the highest level. Thus, the bureaucratic and the economic theories can themselves be bureaucratized and economized and so on downward through the bureaucratic or corporate hierarchies *ad infinitum.*

In brief, *a posteriori,* the military policy is overdetermined by several alternative and analytically coequal explanations. The logical dynamic of the process of discovering or inventing alternative causes is to equalize explanations, to destroy degrees of validity among them, while not destroying the explanations themselves. We are left entangled within the thicket of theories.

For example, this condition of overdetermination with several coequal explanations characterizes each of the most important cases of American weapons procurement in the 1960s: the massive missile build-up of the Kennedy administration, the TFX or F-111 fighter-bomber, the C-5A jumbo transport, the MIRV, and the ABM.

The second problem is more familiar and is the reverse of the first. It is what we can call the problem of alternative consequences or the problem of *a priori* underdetermination, and it concerns the combination of explanation and prediction rather than explanation alone. No one major explanation or causal theory or even a combination of them is sufficient for confident *a priori* prediction of a military policy; one "cause" can yield several different, alternative, even opposite, policies or "consequences." This is largely true even if we attempt what might be called "retroactive prediction," i.e., if we pick an historical case, take several alternative explanations, and try to imagine ourselves predicting the historical event before it actually occurred. A *priori,* the military policy is underdetermined by an explanation or explanations which yield several alternative and analytically coequal consequences. An example would be trying to predict the outcome of the ABM debate during any time in 1966–1969.

At any rate, today many men seem to resolve the question of selection by a leap of faith. We probably are entering into an era of multiple and competing explanations of U.S. military policy, or of any U.S. policy, each rooted in faith and each immune from being disproven by evidence or by logic. In this situation the process of argument and the fuel of passion probably will lead to reinforcing and rigidifying the competing theories rather than dissolving them in a great empirical and pragmatic consensus. The epistemological contract shall be broken, and the intellectual union based on common standards of evidence shall be dissolved. In its place shall be constructed great and grand alternative *Weltanschauungen,* and each shall expand and link up with analogous theories of other political and social phenomena, such as foreign policy. Around these *Weltanschauungen* shall cluster men who are at once intellectual and faithful; together they may recapitulate the great conflicting ideological movements of an earlier Europe. And, some might add, in a distant future they may even recapitulate the syndicates and the *Lager* of interwar Europe, those states within and against the state, and the dissolution of the epistemological contract will have led to the dissolution of the social contract.

This essay is an effort to cut away at the thicket of theories. In it we will examine the four major cases of American weapons procurement of the 1960s and 1970s, that is, of the period covering the Kennedy, Johnson, and Nixon administrations. There are (1) the massive build-up of Minuteman and Polaris missiles; (2) MIRV; (3) aircraft procurement, in particular the F-111 fighter-bomber, the C-5A jumbo transport, and the B-1 large bomber; and (4) ABM.[13]

III. THE MISSILE BUILD-UP: QUANTITATIVE CHANGE

The first important case of American weapons procurement in the 1960s was the massive build-up of Minuteman and Polaris missiles from 1961 to 1964. This case is also the simplest to examine and explain: A decision was made during a relatively limited time and for a merely quantitative change.

Because Minuteman and Polaris were invulnerable and thus second-strike weapons, they had a generally stabilizing impact on the strategic balance between the Soviet Union and the United States. As such, a strategic explanation of the U.S. build-up, focusing on international stability, might seem quite sufficient. However, even Secretary of Defense McNamara in 1967 retrospectively criticized as excessive the *degree* of the U.S. expansion and its effect on the Soviets:

> Our current numerical superiority over the Soviet Union in reliable, accurate and effective warheads is both greater than we had originally planned and more than we require. . . . Clearly, the Soviet build-up is in part a reaction to our own build-up since the beginning of the 1960s.[14]

Why did the United States deploy as many missiles as it did? McNamara's own explanation, like almost all official explanations, is a strategic one; but it stresses his lack of accurate information.

> In 1961 when I became secretary of defense, the Soviet Union possessed a very small operational arsenal of intercontinental missiles. However, they did possess the technological and industrial capacity to enlarge that arsenal very substantially over the succeeding several years. We had no evidence that the Soviets did plan, in fact, fully to use that capability. But, as I have pointed out, a strategic planner must be conservative in his calculations; that is, he must prepare for the worst plausible case and not be content to hope and prepare merely for the most probable.
>
> Since we could not be certain of Soviet intentions, since we could not be sure that they would not undertake a massive build-up, we had to insure against such an eventuality by undertaking ourselves a major build-up of the Minuteman and Polaris forces. Thus, in the course of hedging against what was then only a theoretically possible Soviet build-up, we took decisions which have resulted in our current superiority in numbers of warheads and deliverable megatons. But the blunt fact remains that if we had had more accurate information about planned Soviet strategic forces, we simply would not have needed to build as large a nuclear arsenal as we have today.
>
> Let me be absolutely clear. I am not saying that our decision in 1961 was unjustified; I am saying that it was necessitated by a lack of accurate information.[15]

But McNamara's account does not explain why the U.S. ordered a massive build-up all at once instead of ordering part of the build-up at first and delaying the rest of it until more information became available.

An alternative explanation emphasizing bureaucratic politics is given by Schlesinger in his account of the drawing-up of the Kennedy administration's first full defense budget in the fall of 1961:

> The budget . . . contemplated a sizable increase in missiles; and the White House staff, while favoring a larger Minuteman force than the original Eisenhower proposal, wondered whether the new budget was not providing for more missiles than national security required. But the President, though intimating a certain sympathy for this view, was not prepared to overrule McNamara's recommendation. As for the secretary, he did not believe that doubling or even tripling our striking power would enable us to destroy the hardened missile sites or missile-launching submarines of our adversary. But he was already engaged in a bitter fight with the Air Force over his effort to disengage from the B-70, a costly, high-altitude manned bomber rendered obsolescent by the improvement in Soviet ground-to-air missiles. After cutting down the original Air Force demands considerably, he perhaps felt that he could not do more without risking public conflict with the Joint Chiefs and the vociferous B-70 lobby in Congress. As a result, the President went along with the policy of multiplying Polaris and Minuteman missiles.[16]

A similar account is given by David Halberstam, one which, however, emphasizes more the power of Congress:

> In 1961 some White House aides were trying to slow the arms race. At that point the U.S. had 450 missiles, and McNamara was asking for 950, and the Chiefs were asking for 3000. The White House people had quietly checked around and found that in effectiveness the 450 were the same as McNamara's 950.

"What about it, Bob?" Kennedy asked.

"Well, they're right," he answered.

"Well, then, why the 950, Bob?" Kennedy asked.

"Because that's the smallest number we can take up on the Hill without getting murdered," he answered.[17]

In summary, the massive build-up of Minuteman and Polaris missiles resulted from a decision made for a merely quantitative change and during a relatively limited time. It is best explained by bureaucratic politics: bargaining among different actors within the executive branch over the share and degree of incremental change, with allies within Congress playing a supporting role. But, as we shall see in section V, the missile build-up also can be fitted into a broader economic analysis.

IV. MIRV: INNOVATIVE CHANGE

The Minuteman and Polaris build-up was the first important case of American weapon procurement in the 1960s. But the most important case, because of its potentially destabilizing impact on the strategic balance between the Soviet Union and the United States, was MIRV.[18]

With its high accuracy in targeting, its high number of warheads, and its high immunity to aerial surveillance, MIRV readily and reasonably can provoke a Soviet fear of an American first strike against Soviet land-based, even hardened, missiles, and it will provoke the Soviets into acquiring their own MIRVs, perhaps leading again to "the reciprocal fear of surprise attack" and "the delicate balance of terror." In the face of these foreseen strategic risks, the procurement of MIRV seems both momentous and dangerous.

Why did the United States develop and deploy MIRV? The official explanation is again a strategic one, and the usual argument has been that MIRV is needed to penetrate Soviet ABM systems. But this does not explain why highly accurate, as opposed to merely multiple, warheads are needed. Nor does it explain why the U.S. continued to develop MIRV in the mid-1960s after the Soviets limited their development of ABM. A more accurate strategic explanation, suggested by the following censored congressional testimony, would argue that MIRV was developed in order to increase the U.S. capability to destroy Soviet missiles, and in effect to give the U.S. a first-strike capability.

> *Question (by Senator Mike Mansfield, Democrat from Montana):* Is it not true that the U.S. response to the discovery that the Soviets had made an initial deployment of an ABM system around Moscow and probably elsewhere was to develop the MIRV system for Minuteman and Polaris?
>
> *Answer (by Dr. John S. Foster, director of defense research and engineering):* Not entirely. The MIRV concept was originally generated to increase our targeting capability rather than to penetrate ABM defenses. In 1961–1962 planning for targeting the Minuteman force it was found that the total number of aim points exceeded the number of Minuteman missiles. By splitting up the payload of a single missile (deleted) each (deleted) could be programmed (deleted) allowing us to cover these targets with (deleted) fewer missiles. (Deleted.) MIRV was originally born to implement the payload split-up (deleted). It was found that the previously generated MIRV concept could equally well be used against ABM (deleted).[19]

Although McNamara had rejected a first-strike targeting doctrine, the Air Force commanders, formally his subordinates, had not. They preferred a first-strike doctrine, with its double implication that the United States could *win* a war with the Soviet Union and that the Air Force would have the prime role in doing so, to a second-strike doctrine, which implied that the U.S. could only *deter* a war and that the Air Force would be only an equal of the navy in the task. Against McNamara, the Air Force commanders could not achieve an official first-strike targeting doctrine for the United States; with MIRV, however, they could achieve a real first-strike targeting capability for the Air Force.[20]

The research and development of MIRV was of course highly classified so that knowledge of it would be kept from the Soviets. But the effect was also to keep knowledge of MIRV from Congress and the public. Nor, in the early phases of the program, did Defense officials have any need to build support in Congress and the public for large expenditures of funds. As a result, the MIRV program faced no political opposition, and it progressed in accordance with technical and bureaucratic procedures of research and development internal to different organizations within the Defense Department. By the time the existence and implications of MIRV became public knowledge, it had already been tested, the production of Minuteman III and Poseidon missiles had already commenced, and the conversion of Polaris-launching submarines into Poseidon ones had already begun.[21] Given this momentum generated by initial technocratic interests and by internal bureaucratic processes, the MIRV program could have been brought to a halt after 1968 only if the president or leading members of Congress had been willing to expend an extraordinary amount of political capital. Further, once the U.S. had successfully tested MIRV, the Soviets could not be sure that the U.S. had not also deployed it. The Soviets probably then felt themselves compelled to test and deploy their own MIRV; the Soviet program, in turn, reinforces the pressures behind the American one.

In summary, MIRV resulted from developmental procedures for an innovative change, over a relatively lengthy time, but within a relatively limited circle of organizations. It is best explained by bureaucratic processes: bureaucratic doctrines, bureaucratic standard operating procedures, including in this case normal procedures for the research and development of technocratic interests, and bureaucratic programs for organizational preservation and growth. But, again, as we shall see in the next section, MIRV also can be fitted into a broader economic analysis.

V. AIRCRAFT PROCUREMENT: RENOVATIVE CHANGE

In contrast to missile procurement, the two major cases of manned aircraft procurement in the 1960s were less important strategically but more debated politically. These were the F-111 fighter-bomber and the C-5A jumbo transport.[22] Both aircraft became famous, even notorious, because of financial troubles ("cost overruns"), mechanical failures, and Congressional investigations. Further, in June 1970 the air force awarded a contract to produce prototypes of a new, large, manned bomber, the B-1, which begins anew the numbering of the bomber series and which would go into operational deployment in the late 1970s. By that time, given the efficiency of strategic missiles and antiaircraft missiles, the new B-1 would seem to be about as useful and about as obsolete as the first B-1 of the 1920s.

Why did the United States buy such aircraft? There are, of course, the official, strategic explanations: The F-111 is needed for a variety of tasks, such as tactical bombing, strategic bombing, and air defense; the C-5A is needed for massive airlifts of troops and supplies; and the B-1 is needed for strategic bombing and postattack reconnaissance. But these explanations neglect the fact that the respective tasks can be performed by a variety of ways and weapons, and that these particular manned aircraft are not clearly the most cost-effective (to use McNamara's own proclaimed criterion) way to do so.

There are, also, the possible bureaucratic explanations: The F-111 was needed by the Tactical Air Command to preserve its power and prestige within the overall balance of the military bureaucracies; the C-5A was needed similarly by the Military Airlift Command; and the B-1 is desired by the aging commanders of the Air Force and of the Strategic Air Command within it, who look back with nostalgia to their youth and to the manned bomber in which they rode first to heroic purpose and then to bureaucratic power. But these explanations are not fully satisfactory: Neither the Tactical Air Command nor the Military Airlift Command is the strongest organization within the air force (the strongest is the Strategic Air Command), and probably neither of them could achieve such expensive programs as the F-111 and C-5A without allies. And even the powerful commanders of the air force and the Strategic Air Command could not achieve the B-1 on the basis of nostalgia alone, especially in a period of unusually sharp criticism of military spending and after the predecessor of the B-1, the B-70, had been canceled as obsolescent by McNamara several years before.

An alternative explanation, more economic in emphasis and more general in scope, can be constructed by drawing some relations between two variables: (1) military and military-related aerospace systems, and (2) aerospace corporations which produce military and military-related airframes, missiles, and space systems, or what I shall call for short military airframe production lines.

The major military aerospace systems produced in the 1960s were the following: the B-52, B-58, and B-70 large bombers; the Minuteman and Polaris missiles and their MIRV successors or follow-ons, Minuteman III and Poseidon; the F-111 and F-4 fighter-bombers; and the C-141A and C-5A transports. In addition, there was the military-related Apollo moon program. Major military aerospace systems for the 1970s, in addition to Minuteman and Poseidon, are the Undersea Long-Range Missile System (ULMS), which will be a follow-on to Poseidon; the B-1, which can be seen as a long-delayed follow-on to the canceled B-70; and the F-14 and F-15, which will follow the F-4.[23] In addition, the Johnson and Nixon administrations programmed the SST, a supposedly commercial aircraft which under a new and unique arrangement would have been financed almost entirely by the U.S. government, but which was canceled by Congress in 1971.[24]

These various aerospace systems can be grouped into six functional categories or production sectors: (1) large bombers, (2) missile systems, (3) fighter-bombers, (4) military transports, (5) commercial transports, and (6) space systems.

The major military airframe production lines in the 1960s were the following five: (1) Lockheed, (2) General Dynamics, (3) Boeing, (4) McDonnell Douglas, and (5) North American Rockwell.[25] Further, if we analytically split the largest, Lockheed, into its two main military divisions, Lockheed–Missiles and Space, located in California, and Lockheed-Georgia, there were six major production lines.

We can chart the major military and military-related aerospace systems according to the production lines to which the U.S. government awarded the contract and according to the years when major production phased in or out or is scheduled to do so.[26] Some interesting patterns result. (See Table 1.1.)

About the time a production line phases out a major government contract, it phases in a new one, usually within a year. Further, in most cases, the new contract is for a system which is similar while superior to the system being phased out; that is, the new contract is a follow-on contract. (The exceptions are the SST and Apollo; the B-1 is a follow-on, one step removed, to the B-70.) At the end of the 1960s, a seventh major production line emerged. Grumman at the beginning of the decade was a minor production line with annual military sales of some $300 million. In the early 1960s, it was awarded two large subcontracts, once for the rear fuselage of the F-111 and one for elements of the Apollo moon program. In 1968 Grumman neared $1 billion in annual military and space sales. As the phase-out of the two large subcontracts approached, the navy awarded Grumman in January 1969 the prime contract for the F-14, with a prospective value of $9 billion.

A large and established aerospace production line is a national resource—or so it seems to many high officers in the armed services. The corporation's managers, shareholders, bankers, engineers, and workers, of course, will enthusiastically agree, as will the area's congressmen and senators. The Defense Department would find it risky and even reckless to allow one of only six or seven large production lines to wither and die for lack of a large production contract. There is at least latent pressure upon it from many sources to award a new, major contract to a production line when an old major contract is phasing out. Further, the disruption of the production line will be least and the efficiency of the product would seem highest if the new contract is structurally similar to the old, in the same functional category or production sector, that is, is a follow-on contract. Such a contract might be seen as a renovative change: It renovates both the large and established aerospace corporation that produces the weapons system and the large and established military organization that deploys it.

This latent constraint or rather compulsion imposed on weapons procurement by industrial structure might be called the follow-on imperative and contrasted with the official imperative. The official imperative for weapons procurement might be phrased as follows: If a military service needs a new weapons system, it will solicit bids from several competing companies; ordinarily, the service will award the contract to the company with the most cost-effective design. The follow-on imperative is rather different: If one of the seven production lines is opening up, it will receive a new major contract from a military service; ordinarily, the new contract will be structurally similar to the old, i.e., a follow-on contract. Relatedly, the design competition between production lines is only a peripheral factor in the award.

Table 1.1 MILITARY AEROSPACE SYSTEMS AND MAJOR PRODUCTION LINES

	General dynamics	Boeing	Lockheed M & S	Lockheed-Georgia	McDonnell Douglas	North-American Rockwell
1960	B-58	B-52 Minuteman	Polaris	C-130	F-4	B-70
1961–1962	B-58 out F-111 in	B-52 out Minuteman build-up	Polaris build-up	C-141A in		
1963–1964						B-70 out Apollo in
1965–1966			Polaris out Poseidon in	C-141A out C-5A in		
1967–1968		Minuteman out Minuteman III in				
1969–1970				C-5A out ?	F-4 out F-15 in	Apollo out B-1 in
1971–1972 1973–1974	F-111 out ?	Minuteman III out SST in?	Poseidon out ULMS in?			

More precisely, we might conceive of two forms of this imperative: (1) the strong form or the follow-on imperative proper, which asserts that if one of the seven production lines is opening up, it will receive a new major contract from a military service, *and* the new contract will be structurally similar to the old; and (2) the weak form or what might be called the prop-up imperative, which merely asserts that if one of the seven production lines is opening up, it will receive a new major contract from a military service and predicts nothing about structure.

The follow-on imperative proper would have predicted and can perhaps explain the production line and the product structure of seven out of the ten major contracts awarded from 1960 to 1970: (1) Minuteman III follow-on to Minuteman, (2) Poseidon follow-on to Polaris, (3) C-141A follow-on to C-130, (4) C-5A follow-on to C-141A, (5) F-15 follow-on to F-4, (6) F-111 after B-58, a somewhat less certain case, (7) B-1 delayed follow-on to B-70.

In regard to the remaining three contracts, Apollo, F-14, and perhaps the SST, the production line which would receive the contract would have been suggested by the expected opening up of that particular line while the other production lines were otherwise engaged.

The imperatives of the industrial structure are reinforced, not surprisingly, by the imperatives of the political system, as would be suggested by a democratic explanation. Four of the production lines are located in states which loom large in the Electoral College: California (Lockheed–Missiles and Space and North American Rockwell), Texas (General Dynamics), and New York (Grumman). The three others are located in states which in the 1960s had a senator who ranked high in the Senate Armed Services Committee or Appropriations Committee: Washington (Boeing, Henry Jackson), Georgia (Lockheed-Georgia, Richard Russell), and Missouri (McDonnell Division of McDonnell Douglas, Stuart Symington).

The chart indicates that there has been considerable pressure on the Nixon administration. In 1969–1970 the administration confronted two impending phase-outs, the F-4 Phantom program of the McDonnell division of McDonnell Douglas and the Apollo program of North American Rockwell; it resolved the problem in the easiest and most incremental way, by a follow-on contract, the F-15, to the McDonnell division in December 1969 and by a delayed follow-on, the B-1, to North American Rockwell in June 1970. Seen in this perspective, the other competitors for the F-15 (Fairchild Hiller and North American Rockwell) and for the B-1 (General Dynamics and Boeing) were never really in the running.

In summary, the F-111, C-5A, and B-1 each resulted from a contract cycle of small but successive decisions made for a renovative change, over a relatively lengthy time, and among a relatively large circle of actors. These cases of aircraft procurement are best explained by bureaucratic-corporate alliances, otherwise known as military-industrial complexes.

The chart also indicates that the pressure on the Nixon administration will be especially intense in the future. In the next year or two, two other production lines will open up, General Dynamics and Lockheed-Georgia. The latter is the largest industrial enterprise in the Southeastern United States.[27] How will the administration fill the contract gap?

The problem becomes especially acute because of the recent evolution of the six functional categories or production sectors. The aerospace systems within them or follow-on contracts are of course becoming progressively more complex and expensive, but they are also becoming progressively more dangerous (MIRV), or damaging (SST and B-1), or at best dubious (F-14, F-15, C-5A, and the space program).

In confronting its contract dilemmas, the Nixon administration seems to have chosen a combination of half measures and extreme measures. For a stop-gap and the short run, Lockheed and General Dynamics have been awarded new but smaller contracts in other production sectors, such as antisubmarine warfare. But for a cure-all and the long run, the Nixon solution for the plight of the aerospace industry probably will be those endlessly expensive contracts in that endlessly expansive production sector of missile defense—the ABM.

VI. ABM: REDISTRIBUTIVE CHANGE

The ABM is, in many ways, the superlative case among our four cases of weapons procurement. In regard to the probable cost of the completed system, at least $10 billion, it is the most expensive. In regard to the length of time that the system has been an issue (programs date back to 1955), it is the most extensive. In regard to the scope of actors participating in the decision-making process, it is the most inclusive. And in regard to the heat of the public debate over procurement, it is the most intensive.[28]

Why did the U.S. buy the ABM? More specifically, why did the Johnson administration in September 1967 propose the Sentinel ABM, and why did the Nixon administration in March 1969 and since propose the Safeguard ABM? The official strategic explanations have been many and varied. McNamara in 1967 argued that the ABM was needed to protect cities from China. Nixon and Laird in 1969 argued that it was needed to protect Minutemen from the Soviet Union. More recently they have extended the proposed protection to some cities again. All of the justifications have been questioned by many strategists, scientists, and congressmen; the most decisive refutation is simply the argument that the ABM will not work, especially given the ease with which the Soviets could overload the system with a dense attack.

Bureaucratic explanations are possible but not very plausible. The army sees the ABM as its way to get again into the missile programs, from which it has been excluded while the air force has had Minuteman and the navy has had Polaris and Poseidon, and thus as its way to restore the bureaucratic balance of power. But this had been the case for almost a decade before 1967. Little had come of it, although Congress in 1966 had voted funds to prepare ABM production, which the Johnson administration had refused to spend. Further, within the army, the air defense and missile defense organizations are not the dominant organizations; the large-scale deployment of ABM will redistribute bureaucratic power within the army.

A democratic explanation is also possible, and, for the 1967 decision, more plausible. President Johnson feared being vulnerable in the approaching election to charges from the Republicans that he has neglected the nation's security. John Kennedy in 1960 charged a "missile gap"; Lyndon Johnson in 1967 feared an "ABM gap."[29] But in 1969 the Nixon administration faced quite different political problems. The next presidential election was far away, Congress had to be pressured by the administration to approve ABM, the reverse of the situation two years before (in the Senate in 1969, an amendment to prevent deployment was defeated by only two votes), and within the public there was much more criticism of ABM. Why, then, did the Nixon administration go ahead with ABM, albeit under a different rationale and under a different name?

What about economic explanations? One argument would be that Nixon was aware of impending difficulties in the aerospace industry and that he saw ABM contracts as increasing his options and instruments with which to manage these difficulties. The initial contract for the main missile of the ABM system, the Spartan, had been awarded to the healthiest of the production lines, McDonnell Douglas. But as the ABM system is expanded, major subcontracts could go to other production lines as they open up and when contracts are needed: to General Dynamics as it phases out the F-111, to Lockheed-Georgia as it phases out the C-5A, and perhaps to Boeing as it phases out Minuteman III and is unable to phase in the SST. Such thoughts were suggested in the preceding discussion of the follow-on imperative.

Another economic argument would be that Nixon was aware of impending difficulties not only in the aerospace industry but in the economy generally and that he saw ABM contracts as increasing his options and instruments with which to manage this larger recession. The ABM will benefit not only many aerospace firms but also corporations beyond the aerospace sector of the economy. Major ABM contracts have been awarded to corporations whose major production is not aerospace, such as Western Electric, a subsidiary of AT&T, and General Electric;[30] the large-scale production of ABM will redistribute economic benefits from military contracts within the economy just as the large-scale deployment of it will redistribute bureaucratic power within the army. And to some extent it will be redistribution upward. The five major aerospace corporations (Lockheed, General Dynamics, Boeing, McDonnell Douglas, and North American Rockwell) normally rank between twentieth and fiftieth (by annual sales) in the *Fortune* directory of the 500 largest industrial corporations. But Western Electric and General Electric are normally among the top ten.[31]

Thus, a new aerospace production sector, missile defense, is being created and added on to the six sectors already established. At the same time, new aerospace production lines, Western Electric, General Electric, and perhaps others, are being created and added on to the seven lines already established. The ABM might be used to resolve the current dilemmas of the aerospace industry or of the general economy, but it would do so only by expanding the number of production lines and thus only by insuring that the next set of dilemmas would have to be resolved on an even grander and more expensive scale.

More generally, the above discussions of aircraft procurement and the ABM suggest that the early 1970s will see expansion in the number of production sectors, in the number of production lines, in the costs of weapons systems, and in the dangers and damages that they bring; weapons procurement will feature wider and wider scope, higher and higher costs, greater and greater risks, and less and less control by the president, by Congress as a whole, and by the people they are supposed to represent. "Turning and turning in the widening gyre, the falcon cannot hear the falconer."[32]

VII. MODES OF CHANGE AND MODES OF CAUSATION

Can we find any general pattern in these four cases of weapons procurement? The preceding accounts have suggested four modes of change—quantitative, innovative, renovative, and redistributive—and four modes of causation—bureaucratic politics, bureaucratic processes, bureaucratic-corporate alliances, and the economic system. In this section, we will review these modes of change, putting the quantitative last so as to make the order analytical rather than historical.

1. Innovative Change

An innovative change is the development, production, and deployment of a weapons system in which both the technical advances and the strategic implications are unfamiliar and far-reaching. Indeed, the strategic implications will seem strange and fearsome. MIRV has already been discussed under the heading of innovative change, but ABM is an innovative change along with being a redistributive one. Other major innovative changes since the Second World War have been the H-bomb, the ICBM, and the Polaris missile system. In the case of MIRV, the innovative system was not only unfamiliar; in the early stages of research and development, it was also inexpensive.

Because an innovative change is unfamiliar and sometimes inexpensive, it normally begins not in a decision at the higher levels of policy making and budget making but in technical and organizational procedures for research and development. At this initial point, some sort of technocratic explanation seems best. The director of defense research and engineering, John Foster, has described the process as follows:

> Now most of the action the United States takes in the area of research and development has to do with one or two types of activities. Either we see from the field of science and technology some new possibilities, which we think we ought to exploit, or we see threats on the horizon, possible threats, usually not something the enemy has done but something we have thought ourselves that he might do, we must therefore be prepared for. These are the two forces that tend to drive our research and development activities.[33]

Thus, a strategic consideration of a rather remote sort is also present. Once the new weapons system reaches a later phase, a stronger strategic imperative enters into the picture. It will now seem plausible that the Soviet Union is also secretly developing the system. At the same time, there is not yet any certainty about how the system will work and what it will do. A Defense Department planner will think that he must be, in McNamara's words, "conservative in his calculations; that is, he must prepare for the worst plausible case and not be content to hope and prepare merely for the most probable."[34] Such calculations, which are made in some degree about any weapons system, will be especially compelling when the system is both fearsome and cheap. Thus, there will be great pressure within the Defense Department to continue with its development.

During this phase, moreover, high secrecy and low expense continue to keep the system out of public debate, and it will face no significant opposition from Congress or even from other bureaucracies until development is near or at completion. Bureaucratic momentum, propelled by procedures for weapons testing and programs for bureaucratic growth, is sufficient to bring the innovation to full development. To reach this point, an explanation emphasizing bureaucratic process seems best.

Bureaucratic momentum alone, however, does not seem sufficient to explain the expensive jump from research and development to production and deployment. The combination of bureaucratic momentum and strategic fears may be sufficient to do so, although the evidence is unclear. The four innovative systems that have been widely deployed and strategically crucial—H-bomb, ICBM, Polaris, and MIRV—have been not only technically and strategically innovative, but also bureaucratically and economically renovative. More generally, as an innovative change moves beyond development to production and deployment, it follows one of two paths and becomes a change that is either renovative as well as innovative or redistributive as well as innovative. The following discussions of renovative change and redistributive change suggest the characteristics of each path.

2. Renovative Change

The pure form of renovative change is the production and deployment of a weapons system whose technical characteristics are generally familiar, whose strategic implications are generally minor, whose production renovates an established aerospace corporation, and whose deployment renovates an established military organization. Good examples are the F-111, C-5A, B-1, F-14, and F-15.

Weaker forms of renovative change lack one or more of the features of the pure form. The most relevant is a form we have already suggested, a combination of innovative and renovative change: the development, production, and deployment of a weapons system whose technical characteristics and strategic implications are generally unfamiliar and far-reaching, whose production renovates an established aerospace corporation, and whose deployment renovates an established military organization. The best example is MIRV: Here, the reentry vehicles or MIRVs proper are innovative, while the carrier vehicles or Minuteman III and Poseidon are renovative. Other examples, which fit the category less perfectly, are the H-bomb, ICBM, and Polaris.

Because a renovative change, by definition, involves large-scale production and deployment, economic costs will be relatively high. If the strategic threat posed by similar Soviet weapons is relatively low, as it is in the pure form of renovative change, then the combination of high cost and low threat forces the nurturing military organization to mobilize its allies in the congressional committees and the aerospace corporations in order to make the jump from research and development to production and deployment. At the same time, the high economic cost, i.e., large contract awards, invites these allies in their own interest to push for the renovation. Such bureaucratic-corporate alliances for renovation, or military-industrial complexes, become even more natural, if not powerful, in times of budgetary stringency.

In contrast, if the strategic threat and associated strategic fears are high, as they are in the form of renovative change which is also innovative, then these fears can be a substitute for allies under certain conditions; bureaucratic-corporate alliances can be rendered unnecessary by bureaucratic-strategic anxieties. Whether this happens seems to be a function of the relative bureaucratic power of the nurturing military organization.

If the organization is the dominant one within a military service (for example, the Strategic Air Command within the air force), then the combination of bureaucratic momentum and strategic fears will be sufficient to propel the jump from research and development to production and deployment. The ICBM and MIRV are examples of innovative changes that smoothly moved into renovative ones, and they did so under the shelter of SAC.[35] If, however, the organization is a subordinate one within a military service (for example, the submarine forces within the navy and the Air Defense Command within the army), a jump to large-scale production and deployment will also be a redistribution of relative bureaucratic power within the military service, and additional forces will be needed to propel the jump. The critical variable now seems to become the organization's allies in Congress and in the corporations.

If the major contractors for the new system are established aerospace corporations, among the seven major production lines (for example, Lockheed for the Polaris missile), then the combination of (subordinate) bureaucratic momentum, strategic fears, and corporate influence will be sufficient to propel the jump, although only after considerable bureaucratic conflict and delay. The Polaris is an example. If, however, the major contractors are corporations whose main production is not aerospace (for example, Western Electric and General Electric for ABM), a jump to large-scale production and deployment will be not only a redistribution of relative bureaucratic power within the military service but also a redistribution of relative economic power within the economic system, and still more forces will be needed to propel the jump.[36] This brings us to a discussion of redistributive change proper.

3. Redistributive Change

A redistributive change is the production and deployment of a weapons system whose production redistributes the relative economic rewards among industrial sectors.[37] Such changes are rare. The ABM has been the only major example since the Second World War, although the war itself brought several redistributive changes, including the build-up of the military aircraft industry and the A-bomb. Moreover, such changes are complex. In the case of the ABM, the cost of the program is unusually high, the scope of its consequences unusually wide, and the variety of plausible explanations unusually rich.

Given the historical rarity and the analytical complexity of redistributive change, any effort to determine its causes and conditions would be more speculative than conclusive and in any case would be beyond the scope of this essay. I shall confine myself to a few suggestions.

In redistributive change, the critical forces needed to propel the jump from research and development to production and deployment have to be both unusual in kind and general in scope, although not necessarily so unusual and so general as the Great Depression and the Second World War, which had so much to do with earlier redistributive changes such as the build-up of the military aircraft industry and the A-bomb. For the contemporary period, there seem to be two possibilities.

Presidential Elections   As already suggested, a president will fear being vulnerable in an approaching election to charges of neglect of the nation's security. Kennedy in 1960 charged a "missile gap"; Johnson in 1967 feared an "ABM gap." Electoral considerations probably were the major cause of the Johnson administration's Sentinel ABM system, announced in September 1967. In general, presidents will seek to avoid a gap-trap.

Economic Recessions   Policy makers could try to blunt a recession and to manage the economy with large-scale and widespread military contracts, which might be redistributive in nature. Or they could try to prevent the collapse of several failing aerospace corporations, turning the redistributive change toward a renovative one, but one in multiple form. Economic considerations probably were the major cause of the Nixon administration's Safeguard ABM system.

4. Quantitative Change

A quantitative change is the simplest change of all, a mere change in the numbers of a highly familiar weapons system.

Each military service wants more of what it already has or is scheduled to get. The services compete with each other and with other bureaucracies over their share of the budget. The particular quantity bought of a weapons system will be the outcome of a complex bargaining process of negotiating, logrolling, and trading, such as the trade-off between the Minuteman build-up and the B-70 cancellation. Quantitative disputes, being about merely numerical changes and highly familiar weapons, are especially amenable to bargaining and to precise compromises and trade-offs. The bargaining ordinarily takes place among actors within the executive branch; it is, as Huntington long ago pointed out, "executive legislation."[38] Although each service has its own allies in Congress and among the corporations beyond, these normally play only a supporting role.

Yet in a sense quantitative change is the extreme, simplest form of renovative change: With more of the same produced and deployed, both the military organization and the aerospace corporation enjoy renovation with a minimum of unsettling innovation. It would seem natural, then, for bureaucratic-corporate alliances to form and push for quantitative changes as well. And in a period of opposition to the military among members of Congress and of more stringent budget making within the executive, such alliances for quantitative changes will be more natural and more necessary than before.

VIII. THE FUTURE OF AMERICAN WEAPONS PROCUREMENT

What are the implications of this analysis of past military policies for future ones? The internal dynamics of the aerospace industry and of the general economy may move weapons procurement in a widening gyre, but perhaps congressional opposition or public opinion will impose limits on movement in this direction and encourage alternative paths. Congress has already rejected the Nixon administration's proposal to continue the SST program. However, it will probably accept the administration's proposal that the federal government guarantee $250 million in bank loans to Lockheed.

In the debates over military policies and changing priorities, several alternative paths for the major production lines have been proposed.

1. Convert production lines from aerospace to nonaerospace production. Mass transportation and waste disposal systems are the alternatives most often proposed. The normal experience of aerospace corporations with such conversions, however, has been quite limited in scope or in success, and their executives generally take a pessimistic view of the possibilities.[39] Significant progress down this path in the 1970s is unlikely.
2. Convert production lines from military aerospace to nonmilitary aerospace production. Here, commercial aircraft is the alternative. Again, the actual experience with such conversions is not encouraging, and even suggests that the cure is worse than the disease.

   Thus, General Dynamics in the early 1960s entered the commercial aircraft market with the Convair 880, only to lose so much money that the F-111 contract was needed to save the corporation from bankruptcy. Similarly, Lockheed in the early 1970s entered the market with the L-1011, only to drive Rolls Royce into bankruptcy and consequently Lockheed itself into a position in which only government guarantees of bank loans would save it from bankruptcy. If Congress rejects the Nixon administration's proposal for such guarantees, however, it will greatly increase the probability that the administration will award a large-scale follow-on contract for the ULMS to Lockheed, which produces Poseidon in California as well as the L-1011. It is most unlikely that Congress will refuse to approve such an important weapons system. Similarly, Congress's cancellation of the SST program greatly increases the probability that the administration will award a large-scale follow-on contract for a super-MIRV, now being planned, to Boeing, producer of Minuteman III as well as the SST. Again, it is most unlikely that Congress will refuse to approve.

There seem to be structural limits on conversion to nonmilitary aerospace production. The number of major production lines for commercial transports seems to be limited to two (Boeing with its 700 series and McDonnell Douglas with its DC series); improvements which are both economically sound and ecologically safe seem to be limited to the airbus (the Boeing 747 and the McDonnell Douglas DC-10). Significant progress down this second path in the 1970s is also unlikely.

3. Collapse production lines from seven into a smaller number. A persuasive case can be made that the United States needs only three production sectors for new aerospace systems (missile systems, particularly submarine-launched ones, fighter-bombers, and perhaps space systems) and two for carrying on existing systems (military transport and commercial transports). If so, then the United States needs only three or four major production lines.

   The most attractive candidates for preservation would be Boeing (strong in missile systems and commercial transports), McDonnell Douglas (fighter-bombers and commercial transports), and one of the two Lockheed lines, either Lockheed–Missiles and Space (submarine-launched missile systems) or Lockheed-Georgia (military transports). Consequently, the other Lockheed plant would be shut down, as would be the General Dynamics plant in Fort Worth, Texas. North American Rockwell would shrink from a major to a minor production line, specializing in a minimal space program, and Grumman would return to being a minor production line.

   Yet Lockheed-Georgia is the largest industrial enterprise in the Southeastern United States. As for Lockheed in California, President Nixon has said,

   > We need a strong airframe producer like Lockheed in Southern California. And if we can save the company and frankly help it toward better management, we will do so.[40]

And a year or so from now, he will probably say the same thing about General Dynamics in Texas. More generally, the shutting down of any one of the major production lines would mean the direct liquidation of some fifty thousand jobs and a local economic depression. It probably would mean also the bankruptcy of the corporation, the liquidation of hundreds of millions of dollars in loans from the major U.S. banks, and the risk of a credit crisis and stock market decline comparable to that of May and June of 1970.[41] The shutting down of any two of the major production lines, not far apart in time, probably would generate one of the biggest shocks to the American financial system since the Great Depression. Given these costs and risks, it is unlikely that any administration will permit the shutting down of two production lines or even one, if it can prevent it. Further, given the ease with which an administration can point to a Soviet strategic threat and the ease with which it can embarrass a congressman who fails to perceive it, it is unlikely that Congress will reject administration proposals for strictly military systems.

4. Constrict production lines from $1 billion or more each in annual weapons sales to a smaller amount. Relatedly, a major weapons system would be

shared between production lines, much as, in the case of the F-111, General Dynamics produced most of the airframe, but Grumman produced the rear fuselage. This approach, which is the most promising of the four, would permit Congress to decrease the funding of weapons procurement by the incremental method which is so congenial to it. And to some extent constriction is already being carried out, with employment at some production lines in 1971 having declined 15 percent to 30 percent since the peak year of 1968.[42] Of course, this approach would permit incremental increases in funding too, and the bases for powerful bureaucratic-corporate alliances and for renewed expansion of weapons procurement in the future would remain.

Whatever the possibilities of control of weapons procurement in the coming decade, there is a need to control the strategic consequences of missile and aircraft procurement in the decade that is past. An incident during the Six Day War of 1967 suggests the problems in strategic control, the ease of strategic escalation, and the size of the strategic stakes. Israeli forces mistakenly attacked the *Liberty,* a U.S. Navy communications ship. Several months later, Secretary of Defense McNamara testified about the incident: "I thought the *Liberty* had been attacked by Soviet forces. Thank goodness, our carrier commanders did not launch directly against the Soviet forces who were operating in the Mediterranean at the time."[43]

In the years to come there will be deployed MIRVs and super-MIRVs along with bombers and fighter-bombers. They may some day mean fears or fire for many men. But for now they mean jobs for workers, profits for businessmen, and power for bureaucrats. And to weapons engineers and scientists, they mean problems that are "exciting" and solutions that are "technically so sweet."

NOTES

1. The phrases are the titles of two well-known strategic analyses written in the late 1950s: the first is Chapter 9 in Thomas C. Schelling, *The Strategy of Conflict* (Cambridge, Mass.: Harvard University Press, 1960); the second an article by Albert Wohlstetter in *Foreign Affairs.* 37 (January 1958). On the characteristics of ABM and MIRV, as well as other strategic systems, see Ian Smart, *Advanced Strategic Missiles: A Short Guide* (Adelphi Papers, No. 63; London: Institute for Strategic Studies, December 1969). On the strategic implications of accurate MIRVs, see especially *Strategic Survey 1969* (London: Institute for Strategic Studies, 1970), pp. 30–33.
2. Robert A. Dahl, "The Concept of Power," in J. David Singer (ed.), *Human Behavior and International Politics* (Chicago: Rand McNally, 1965), p. 374.
3. Although other, hypothetical theories could be considered (for example, one emphasizing national character or national style), the five theories listed are the ones which are best represented in writings on military policy.
4. Thomas C. Schelling, *op. cit.,* and *Arms and Influence* (New Haven, Conn.: Yale University Press, 1966); Henry A. Kissinger, *Nuclear Weapons and Foreign Policy* (New York: Harper, 1957) and *The Necessity for Choice* (New York: Harper, 1961); Herman Kahn, *On Thermonuclear War* (Princeton, N.J.: Princeton University Press, 1960) and *On Escalation* (New York: Praeger, 1965).

5. Quoted in Warner Schilling, "Scientists, Foreign Policy, and Politics," *American Political Science Review*, LVI (June 1962), p. 294.
6. Ralph E. Lapp, *Arms Beyond Doubt: The Tyranny of Weapons Technology* (New York: Cowles Book Co., 1970); Herbert York, *Race to Oblivion: A Participant's View of the Arms Race* (New York: Simon and Schuster, 1970).
7. Quoted in Lapp, *op. cit.*, pp. 22, 23.
8. Samuel P. Huntington, *The Common Defense* (New York: Columbia University Press, 1961); Schilling, *op. cit.* and "The Politics of National Defense: Fiscal 1950," in Warner R. Schilling, Paul Y. Hammond, and Glenn H. Snyder, *Strategy, Politics and Defense Budgets* (New York: Columbia University Press, 1962); John Kenneth Galbraith, *How to Control the Military* (New York: New American Library, 1969).
9. Graham T. Allison, "Conceptual Models and the Cuban Missile Crisis," *American Political Science Review* 63 (September 1969), 689–718.
10. Bruce M. Russett, *What Price Vigilance? The Burdens of National Defense* (New Haven, Conn.: Yale University Press, 1970).
11. Gabriel Kolko, *The Roots of American Foreign Policy* (Boston: Beacon Press, 1969); Harry Magdoff, "Militarism and Imperialism," *American Economic Review*, 60 (May 1970), 237–242; Paul A. Baran and Paul M. Sweezy, *Monopoly Capital* (New York: Modern Reader, 1968), Chapter 7.
12. Some would argue, however, that technocratic values are rooted deep in American society and national character, and therefore that a technocratic theory has much more radical implications than mere reform of procedures for research and development.
13. The missile build-up, MIRV, and ABM are defined as major cases because of their impact on the strategic balance between the superpowers. Aircraft procurement is defined as a major case because of the great expenditures on and debate over the F-111, C-5A, and B-1 programs (eventually $5 billion to $10 billion each). A longer analysis would also examine the major cases of nonprocurement, that is, the B-70 and Skybolt. On these two cases, see Alain C. Enthoven and K. Wayne Smith, *How Much is Enough? Shaping the Defense Program, 1961–1969* (New York: Harper and Row, 1971), pp. 243–262; and James M. Roherty, *Decisions of Robert S. McNamara: A Study of the Role of the Secretary of Defense* (Coral Gables, Fla.: University of Miami Press, 1970).
14. Robert S. McNamara, *The Essence of Security* (New York: Harper and Row, 1968), pp. 57, 60.
15. *Ibid.*, pp. 57, 58.
16. Arthur M. Schlesinger, Jr., *A Thousand Days* (Boston: Houghton Mifflin, 1965), pp. 499, 500.
17. David Halberstam, "The Programming of Robert McNamara," *Harpers* 232 (February 1971), 54.
18. For detailed discussion of the MIRV case, see York, *op. cit.*, pp. 173–187; and Lapp, *op. cit.*, pp. 17–34.
19. Quoted in *ibid.*, p. 21.
20. On the nuclear strategies of McNamara and the Air Force, see Enthoven and Smith, *op. cit.*, pp. 163–196; and William W. Kaufmann, *The McNamara Strategy* (New York: Harper and Row, 1964), Chapter 2.
21. See the discussion of MIRV before the Congressional Conference on the Military Budget and National Priorities (March 28 and 29, 1969), especially the statements by Jeremy J. Stone, George W. Rathjens, Leonard Rodberg, and Congressman Robert L. Leggett, Democrat from California, in Erwin Knoll and Judith Nies McFadden (eds.), *American Militarism 1970* (New York: Viking Press, 1969), pp. 70–82.
22. For a detailed analysis of the F-111 case, see Robert J. Art, *The TFX Decision: McNamara and the Military* (Boston: Little, Brown, 1968). For a critical account of the C-5A

case, see Berkeley Rice, *The C-5A Scandal* (Boston: Houghton Mifflin, 1971); a more sympathetic account is Harold B. Meyers, "For Lockheed, Everything's Coming Up Unk-Unks," *Fortune* 80 (August 1, 1969), 71–81, 131–134.

23. For descriptions of the aerospace systems and contract awards of the 1960s and 1970s, see *The 1970 Aerospace Year Book* (official publication of the Aerospace Industries of America, Inc.; Washington, D.C.: Books, Inc., 1970); and various editions of *Jane's All the World's Aircraft* (New York: McGraw-Hill).

24. For a discussion of the financing of the SST, see George Eads and Richard R. Nelson, "Governmental Support of Advanced Civilian Technology: Power Reactors and the Supersonic Transport," *Public Policy* XIX (Summer, 1971).

25. Each of these five received $1 billion or more in military or space "prime contract awards" both in any one year during the 1960s and on the average over the decade. Statistics are given in Ralph E. Lapp, *The Weapons Culture* (Baltimore: Penguin, 1969), pp. 192, 193; and William Simon Rukeyser, "Where the Military Contracts Go," *Fortune* 80 (August 1, 1969), 74. (McDonnell Douglas and North American Rockwell were formed in the mid-1960's from mergers of major production lines, McDonnell and North American, with other corporations.)

    The five production lines, interestingly, were also the top five American corporations in terms of the number of retired colonels or navy captains employed in 1969, and the only corporations with 100 or more such employees. For the figures and an analysis of them, see Adam Yarmolinsky, *The Military Establishment: Its Impacts on American Society* (New York: Harper and Row, 1971), pp. 60–66.

26. See various editions of the *Aerospace Year Book, op. cit.,* and *Jane's All the World's Aircraft, op. cit.*

27. Berkeley Rice, "What Price Lockheed?" *New York Times Magazine* (May 9, 1971), 24.

28. For detailed analysis of the ABM case, see Aaron Wildavsky. "The Politics of ABM." *Commentary* 48 (November 1969), 55–63; and Abram Chayes and Jerome B. Wiesner (eds.), *ABM: An Evaluation of the Decision to Deploy an Anti-ballistic Missile System* (New York: New American Library, 1969).

29. See the account in Lapp, *Weapons Culture, op. cit.,* pp. 150, 151.

30. General Electric is normally among the top six military contractors in terms of the value of prime contract awards, but these normally add up to only about 18 percent of its annual sales. See Rukeyser, *op. cit.,* p. 74.

31. See *Fortune* 83 (May 1971), 172, and earlier issues of the directory.

32. William Butler Yeats, "The Second Coming."

33. Quoted in Lapp, *Arms Beyond Doubt, op. cit.,* p. 4.

34. McNamara, *op. cit.,* p. 58.

35. With ICBM, bomber generals in SAC initially resisted the shift from bombers to missiles.

36. With ABM, however, one of the seven major production lines, McDonnell Douglas, is the subcontractor which is producing the Spartan missile.

37. From a different perspective, Theodore Lowi has analyzed the difference between regulatory, distributive, and redistributive policies in his "American Business, Public Policies, Case-Studies, and Political Theory," *World Politics* 16 (July 1964), 690–715.

38. Huntington, *op. cit.,* pp. 146–166.

39. On efforts at conversion to nonaerospace production, see Gilbert Burck. "Famine Years for the Arms Makers," *Fortune* 83 (May 1971), 163–167, 242–248; "Aerospace Tries to Pick up the Pieces," *Business Week* (December 12, 1970), 48–53; and "Aerospace: The Troubled Blue Yonder," *Time* (April 5, 1971), 76–82.

40. *New York Times* (May 2, 1971), p. 2.

41. On the credit crisis, see Carol J. Loomis, "The Lesson of the Credit Crisis," *Fortune* 83 (May 1971), pp. 141–143, 274–286.

42. "Aerospace: The Troubled Blue Yonder," *op. cit.*, p. 77. Boeing's employment has declined by some 60 percent, but most of the layoffs have been from work on commercial aircraft.
43. Quoted in Joseph C. Goulden, *Truth is the First Casualty: The Gulf of Tonkin Affair in Illusion and Reality* (Chicago: Rand McNally, 1969), p. 102. See also William H. Honan, "Russian and American Pilots Play 'Chicken,'" *New York Times Magazine* (November 22, 1970), pp. 25–27, 103–116.

Explaining Change in Foreign Economic Policy

John S. Odell

The facts of foreign economic policy will not organize themselves. Commentators on them normally reach for one or two major conceptual tools for sifting through the evidence and identifying possible explanatory factors. Often, to no one's surprise, the commentator finds that his or her chosen tool provides the best explanation, even though significant rival explanations were not even considered.

For the serious observer, the challenge is to select and sharpen a few approaches that will identify key forces that move policies, and to ascertain which are more and less useful in analyzing concrete cases. Here let us consider five perspectives on foreign economic policy. Each stresses a different general explanatory factor, and with varying degrees of precision each sets up expectations about the content of new policy. Versions of each approach have been used before, though often haphazardly and separately. Nonetheless, illustrations will show that certain historical events have been viewed from several contrasting angles. These five are selected for dealing with U.S. international monetary policies of the 1960s and 1970s. But none of the tools is limited in principle to the United States or to international monetary matters.

The five approaches are presented in such a way as to make each as powerful as seems reasonable and to highlight the contrasts among them, contrasts deriving from substantial intellectual traditions. Most of them have had strong or extreme advocates, but the purpose here is not to create straw men to be demolished in later chapters. A strong statement of the core ideas is valuable, in the first place, because there are cases for which such formulations turn out to be valid. Furthermore, if in analyzing other policies it is necessary to qualify the argument or to blend several

"Explaining Change in Foreign Economic Policy," from John S. Odell, *U.S. International Monetary Policy: Markets, Power, and Ideas as Sources of Change* (Princeton: Princeton University Press, 1982).

approaches together, that particular modification or blending may not be the most persuasive application of the basic approaches when one turns to still other cases. Hence, an interest in developing analytical tools of wider relevance suggests the value of keeping in mind a sharp image of the core ideas of each perspective.

The five approaches are rivals in that they identify factors which can and do vary independently of each other. This does not mean that the respective explanatory factors do not influence each other at all, as will become clear. Nor does it mean that they are mutually exclusive. In explaining U.S. international monetary policy in the 1960s and 1970s, none of them is sufficient by itself and none can be rejected as entirely worthless. But the conclusion will not be that they are equally valuable or powerful. The cases to be analyzed indicate the relative strengths and weaknesses of each.

The most widely influential framework for viewing U.S. foreign policy, at least on political-military issues, is the traditional *realpolitik* perspective, which emphasizes the security and power of the state. But discussions of international monetary affairs, including American policy, are often couched in a quite different framework. Most commentators familiar with this arcane subject are educated and experienced not nearly as much in the language of world politics as in the language of markets. These two approaches are not contradictory or mutually exclusive in every application, but their roots and implications are markedly different in critical respects. Let us first consider in turn these approaches emphasizing international conditions. The market approach will be introduced first, because power thinking in the economic realm has often arisen as a reaction to it.

INTERNATIONAL MARKET CONDITIONS

Content of the Perspective

An international market approach for explaining policy change is found more often in the popular press and in other less formal writing than in scholarly literature. For example, one of the purest specimens is the *Economist's* account of the 1967 devaluation of sterling:

> The devaluation of the pound sterling last weekend was not caused by any bankers' ramp, or wickedness by speculators, or even any sudden upsurge in either the incompetence or the revived common sense of the present British Government. It was the inexorable pressure of facts alone that caused Mr. Wilson and Mr. Callaghan to eat so many of their past words, and any dangers that now beset Britain or the international monetary system arise mainly from the fact that their meal has been so unconscionably long delayed. It has been clear for some years that sterling has been overvalued in relation to the main trading currencies of continental Europe and Japan. . . . The truth is that the men responsible for managing Britain's affairs in the last three years honestly have not understood that the level of a currency, like the tide on King Canute's beach, really does not depend on what anybody, even a Chancellor of the Exchequer, says it is. It depends on a whole series of adamantine forces which can be readily analysed by the application of either ordinary common sense or scientific techniques.[1]

This approach identifies international market conditions as the chief, or a major, source of change in policy content. For present purposes, the conditions of greatest interest are supplies and demands for currencies in the markets for foreign exchange. Underlying the foreign exchange markets are the state of payments balances, which in turn depend on trends or cycles in relative prices, incomes, and national money stocks.

This approach focuses attention on these "underlying" international economic conditions and on the behavior of markets. In general, a market explanation for policy change claims that international market conditions changed so as to make it economically irrational for a government to continue prevailing policy, and it was for this reason that the government yielded and adopted a new policy more in conformity with market signals. Market conditions would have made such a change likely, regardless of other conditions also present.

This perspective has its roots in the classical liberal tradition of Hume, Smith, Ricardo, Cobden, and Mill and in the notion of the self-regulating market. In this well-known conception, a large set of small buyers and sellers engaging in unregulated exchange gives rise to natural forces pressing toward equilibrium and efficient allocation of resources. If an item demanded by buyers is in short supply, its price will rise, calling forth reallocation of resources and increased production and trade; conversely, surpluses lead to price declines. If prices are allowed to remain flexible, their movements will signal how resources should be shifted among different activities so as to reduce imbalances and produce the largest possible bundle of those goods and services currently demanded by families and firms. The strong implication is that government intervention in private exchange, beyond minimal policies necessary to enhance the self-regulation mechanism, is irrational. If governments interfere with the market, in many circumstances they will only make their people worse off. Policies departing further from laissez faire than minimal intervention are therefore always in danger of sinking under the weight of efficiency costs.

This core idea of the efficient, self-regulating market then becomes the basis for an explanation of policy change, and it sets up some expectations about the content of new policy. The analyst of government policy who uses this core idea monitors not interstate power structures, nor which party is in power, but monitors instead the relevant markets, through the lenses of neoclassical liberalism. A market imbalance is a clue to expect some shift in policy involving either a lesser degree of government intervention or a change in the form of intervention to perfect the market. One such change might be to make regulations less restrictive. Another would be to move a controlled price up or down as indicated by excess demand or supply, respectively. Another might be to organize greater interstate policy coordination, or to create supranational institutions, in order to widen the market. From the perspective of the market analyst, the efficiency incentives presented by changed market conditions are likely to make for such a policy shift, at least in the long run, regardless of domestic politics, or the ideology or skill of the rulers, or domination by foreign governments. Modern uses of this type of policy explanation all recognize that the institutional heritage in virtually every state establishes a backdrop of extensive government participation in and regulation of economic activity. Viewing such a world through the concepts of the liberal tradition then sets up a rationale for expecting and explaining policy changes in the direction of laissez faire.

What is here characterized as a market perspective on foreign economic policy is not the same as liberal economics. The central task of economics as a discipline is not to explain government behavior, but rather to explain trade flows, the commodity composition of trade and production, financial flows, price movements, and so on. A liberal economist qua economist views an exchange rate as a price in a market, not as a feature of government behavior. For the classical political economists of the early nineteenth century, the political organization of the world recedes into a dim background.

Individual economists, however, do sometimes step outside the conventional boundaries of their discipline. They offer explanations of government policy, as well as prescriptions. On those occasions it is not surprising that, when asking themselves why a government acted as it did or how it is likely to act in the future, they reach for—among other things—the familiar concept of the self-regulating market. If the economics tradition as such has any implication for government behavior, the most obvious is that governments, if rational, will yield to market forces, at least "in the long run." The efficiency costs of defying the market are one force continuously tending to push policy in the direction indicated by market conditions.

The Case of the United States

Finally, among the industrial countries the United States is widely regarded as the one in which liberal laissez-faire ideology is held most widely and strongly. Therefore, evidence that the U.S. government responds to market forces as indicated in this perspective would be less compelling support for the power of the perspective than would be evidence from a nation like France. Conversely, evidence showing that even the United States resists market pressures would constitute a telling limitation on the scope of the perspective.

INTERNATIONAL SECURITY AND POWER STRUCTURE

In contrast to the market perspective, and sometimes in reaction against it, the traditional *realpolitik* worldview sees a world not of markets but of states. The decisive fact about international relations since the seventeenth century, from this perspective, is that the world is essentially anarchic, consisting of sovereign states interacting under no higher authority. Each state must be the protector of its own integrity. In the modern period, no state, not even the most powerful, has ever eliminated all potential external threats to its security. This perspective explains the foreign policies of states according to the imperatives of such an international system. The fundamental objective of any state must be survival, and deriving from that is the urge to accumulate and preserve the state's power and to limit the power of its rivals. The state's relative position is more significant than its absolute strength. This traditional perspective emphasizes the zero-sum nature of international relations.

For present purposes, the core idea of this approach is that shifts in the international distribution of power, and the behavior of rival states in the struggle for influence, are the dominant forces producing major changes in foreign economic policies. This perspective orients the analyst toward external political compulsion and competition arising in interstate relations, rather than international markets, domestic politics, government organization, or leaders' beliefs.

Elements of Power

This approach includes several more specific propositions, which are discussed below. But since the meaning of power is often unclear, it may be helpful first to identify the national capabilities that are likely to make the greatest differences in the net influence a state has on the behavior of other states on monetary issues. Four elements are likely to account most for these differences. The four elements are listed here and then developed with examples below and in Chapters 3, 4, and 5.

The State's Share of World Military and Productive Capabilities   Some theorists regard the military or overall power structure as the key determinant of international relations. Others emphasize that behavior on some issues departs significantly from what would be expected from the distribution of military forces, productive capacity, and general spending power. International monetary relations are more affected by the general international power structure than some have claimed. There seems to be a significant fungibility of military and general resources into the monetary issue area. Even so, changes in the general structure need not be the most important source of policy change in a given case. Structures, by definition, tend not to change rapidly.

The State's Share of International Transactions   States accounting for relatively small shares of world exports, imports, or credit have lesser means with which to reward or punish other states, and therefore their wishes are less likely to be complied with. Similarly, we may suppose that a given state's international monetary policies will be more responsive to a second state that accounts for a large share of its national transactions than to a third that accounts for less. The large trader or large lender affects commercial conditions in other countries willy-nilly, whether or not its government deliberately manipulates transactions.

The Self-Sufficiency or Openness of the Economy   A more closed or self-sufficient economy is more immune to disturbances in the world economy and to other states' influence attempts. Conversely, the economy whose international transactions are large relative to total national activity finds it more costly to resist foreign influence attempts. Thus its net interstate influence is less.

Ability to Finance or Eliminate Payments Deficits   The strictly monetary elements of power may also be important. There are a variety of subdimensions here, having unknown weights. Large international reserves, relative to the state's international transactions, give a country in deficit the ability to postpone complying with foreign demands to change its policies. Larger reserves may also support larger lending to other countries (and greater ability to block credit flows). But reserves are not the only means of financing deficits. The greater the country's ability to raise loans abroad, the greater its financing ability. Countries operating international currencies derive some access to short-term credit by this means. Furthermore, as C. Fred Bergsten points out, countries differ in their ability to eliminate payments deficits at relatively low cost. The country for which adjustment through internal measures is less onerous thereby enjoys a way to escape from the need to borrow abroad and submit to foreign influence. Bergsten is referring to the country's ability to reduce inflation relative to the cost in terms of unemployment, and to the leverage of domestic income and price changes over changes in the external accounts. Another monetary dimension is relevant for a reserve-currency country that seeks to maintain convertibility of its currency into its own reserves. Its ability to defend convertibility is greater to the extent that the ratio of its reserves to its liquid liabilities to foreign governments is higher. The more that foreign claims rise relative to the reserve backing, the more difficult it will be to deter foreign governments from converting, other things being equal.

Security, Balance, and Realignment

The most familiar hypothesis from this perspective directs attention to the distribution of military capabilities among states. It holds that the more balanced the power structure, the more stable it is likely to be, in the sense either of peace or the preservation of the sovereignty of the major actors. This is so because a state situated in a more balanced structure is presented with incentives to restrain its quest for gain at the expense of the others.

Shifts in the military power structure are expected to touch off shifts in state policy, sometimes producing realignments that establish a new equilibrium to constrain the newly strengthened state or alliance. Such realignments may involve foreign economic policies as well as other policies. Thus one hypothesis suggested by the power-structure perspective is that a fall in a state's relative military capabilities (or a rise in external security threat) leads that state to change its foreign economic policies so as to strengthen a military-political alliance or to weaken an adversary, at some point and to some degree. These policies can be quite surprising to an international market analyst.

This mode of explanation has been used often by historians. A classic example was France's policy of directing heavy loans to tsarist Russia, beginning in the 1890s, as well as to southern European countries that were hardly attractive credit risks. The French were responding to the rise of German power with the startling Dual Alliance, cemented with financial ties, and with links to lesser states for the same reasons.

One interpretation of changes in British international monetary policies during the 1930s is another clear example of this mode of explanation. In September 1936, the major financial powers—the United States, Britain, and France—announced the Tripartite Monetary Agreement, a modest step away from the ruins of the 1933 London Economic Conference and toward coordinated stabilization of exchange rates. As Benjamin Rowland reads the evidence, the lack of an agreement before 1936 was partly due to larger political rivalries between Washington and London. The British government refused to meet American demands to give up the empire as long as the isolationist United States was not prepared to make any reliable political commitments to stand behind Britain in a conflict. But in March 1936 came Hitler's bold remilitarization of the Rhineland. The German threat to the security of the Western democracies increased, and the Western governments responded with changes in foreign monetary policies, retreating toward the alliance they later formed. The U.S. Treasury had already been thinking of a monetary agreement to protect U.S. trade in the event of a French devaluation.

> Eagerness to take a strong stand against the Germans and fear that an economic crisis might drive France to embrace fascism were two potent political reasons which now joined Morgenthau's economic calculations. . . . In Britain, too, the overriding motive for stabilization was concern over the deteriorating political situation. The decision to cooperate was not one that Britain reached with any great enthusiasm. It sprang, instead, from a failure of alternatives. . . . Britain dropped her objections to a measure of stabilization as she would later cease to resist a degree of trade liberalization, less from the intrinsic economic merits of following such a policy than from a growing fear of alienating the United States.[2]

Hegemony

A power perspective leaves us with ambiguities, however, no less than a market perspective does. Power analysts have long been divided. A second, contrary hypothesis holds that imbalanced systems are more stable than balanced ones. Here, a shift toward a more equal structure is said to widen incentives for the state to engage in *de*stabilizing behavior. For the military-political realm, A.F.K. Organski presents evidence in support of such a "hegemony" theory of stability.[3]

In the realm of foreign economic polices, the most influential statement of a hegemony theory has come from Charles Kindleberger.[4] His thesis is that an international economic system is likely to remain open and stable only if it is structured around a single country able to lead and manage it. Openness and stability are international public goods, benefits that accrue to all members whether or not they pay their share of the costs of providing the goods. According to this theory, "leadership" is required for the provision of the collective goods. Kindleberger defines leadership as setting standards of conduct, seeking to get other states to observe them, and, especially, assuming a disproportionate share of the burden of defending the system itself in a crisis. These burdens include maintaining a relatively open market for distress goods during depressions (while others are raising tariffs), providing counter-cyclical long-term lending, and performing as lender of last resort during banking panics.

A single leader is necessary for maintaining such a system. A clearly dominant competitor will gain sufficiently from an open system to justify paying the short-range costs of acting on behalf of the system. But only such a dominant state will so act. In a large group most members will find it rational to take advantage of the "free ride." Most states are too small to undertake a stabilizing initiative that would have any effect, while some powers are nonetheless large enough for their actions to disrupt the system. In general, duopoly will be unstable, since with more than one possible leader "the buck has no place to stop."

By implication, a change in the economic power structure toward or away from single-state hegemony will lead to policy shifts, at least by the rising or declining leader. Decline causes the erstwhile leader, now unable to reap so disproportionate a share of the collective good, to cease providing the costly leadership services.

Kindleberger sees the late nineteenth-century structure as one with a single economic leader. Britain dominated industrially and financially. Its relative position explains the leaderly behavior it exhibited during that period. But by the 1920s, Britain had lost the capacity for carrying these burdens, and it therefore abandoned the earlier policies. The United States by then had the capacity but not the will. "In 1929, the British couldn't and the United States wouldn't. When every country turned to protect its national private interest, the world public interest went down the drain, and with it the private interest of all."[5]

A refinement of the economic hegemony hypothesis distinguishes between the general interstate power structure and the special power structures peculiar to particular international issues. Robert Keohane and Joseph Nye suggest that the distribution of power capabilities most relevant for a particular issue may vary independently of the distribution of general capabilities. In their formulation, incongruity between the overall power structure and the issue-specific one leads to change in the international regime for that issue. That is, the strong make the rules in their own interest, and they can be expected to change the rules when their interests change. But a state's power and interests are determined at two levels. Its general capabilities may be useful for influencing the creation of a set of issue rules, but once the rules are accepted, these general capabilities are not of much immediate use. Under a given set of rules, capabilities specific to the issue will determine relative influence and state interest. This issue-structure model suggests that it is only when a formerly hegemonic state loses its issue-specific relative power position, and hence its interest in supporting a given regime, that it will abandon its policies supporting that regime.[6]

This refinement is applied to international monetary issues by focusing on the maintenance or suspension of gold convertibility by reserve center countries. Keohane and Nye argue that the issue-structure model and structural incongruity are important for explaining Britain's suspension in 1931. In contrast to Kindleberger, they picture Britain's general capabilities as still substantial at that time. But her monetary capabilities, especially official reserves, were relatively weak. The monetary rules of the time called for convertibility and fixed rates. But for Britain, maintaining prewar parity was difficult in the 1920s, and it

> became impossible once the banking collapse of 1931 occurred. Thus Britain found that she was helpless within the old rules (because she could not change the value of the pound in terms of gold, but also could not supply sufficient gold or foreign exchange to meet the demand at the current rate). Yet Britain was still a major financial power. Thus when she went off gold and allowed the pound to float (or intervened to manipulate the float), her position immediately strengthened.[7]

This policy change was predictable, they argue, from the issue-structure model. Britain had lost her interest in the old monetary regime, yet she still had sufficient general capabilities to force a monetary rule change that supposedly was in her larger interest.

Competitive Weakness and Interventionism

Other elements of this viewpoint suggest that an increase in economic power leads to policies of greater international openness, while relative decline makes policies of greater intervention more likely. The strong economy is naturally likely to favor policies of conforming to market forces, while a less competitive one is likely to prefer resisting them, in this traditional view. Critics since Alexander Hamilton and Friedrich List have insisted that what are called markets rarely feature equal competition, but rather reflect unequal market power. Pointing out that the English had an industrial head start, List poured sarcasm on the English ideology that all would gain from laissez faire, holding—as E. H. Carr did more than a century later—that "Laissez faire, in international relations as in those between capital and labour, is the paradise of the economically strong."[8] For a weak state to forego protectionism and other interventionist policies would be to ensure permanent inferiority. Moreover, according to these critics, not only are some nations' industries more competitive than others', but what appear to be market forces are also actually shaped by government policies.

The power perspective begins with the premise that policies are most determined by the drive for gain relative to other states. The weaker competitor, seeking means for overcoming its relative weakness, is thus expected to intervene in markets more than the stronger competitor state. In the mid-nineteenth century, German and Japanese industry lagged behind British, and the German and Japanese governments followed clearly more interventionist trade and industrial policies than did the British. By implication, changes in competitive strength on the part of a single state can be expected to lead to corresponding changes in policy emphases. Broadly speaking, such patterns of change are illustrated by British decline and interventionist policies beginning in the 1930s, U.S. rise and policy liberalizations in the 1940s and 1950s, and Japanese rise and liberalization in the 1970s.

DOMESTIC POLITICS

Content of the Perspective

A third perspective for explaining changes in international economic policy content points not to the international military-political situation and not to international markets but to the domestic political scene. This perspective, like the others, has evolved into several variants, two of which are especially relevant here. First, policy content in a variety of fields may respond to shifts in the strengths of the major political parties or, between elections, to the strength of the governing party as measured by mass opinion surveys. Writing about domestic social policies, Hugh

Heclo notes that "the most pervasive tradition identifies the electoral process and party competition as central to policy formation in democratic states."[9] Rarely is it argued even with regard to domestic policy that citizens' policy opinions are transmitted directly via the party system into policy. But this perspective does suggest that the electorate exercises indirect control by setting limits on the range of policies available for consideration and by voting out administrations that fail to solve important problems.

The starkest theoretical formulation, in a work by Anthony Downs, holds that parties in and out of office formulate policies and platforms exclusively for the purpose of winning elections, tailoring the elements of the platform carefully to maximize the size of the coalition.[10] In this perspective, a change in the policy preferences of the electorate or in the popularity of the incumbent government gives rise to a political party or coalition reflecting the growing policy view, which then ousts the incumbents and enacts policies according to the direction of the electorate's change. Alternatively, these changes in public opinion are monitored by the incumbents, who change their policies accordingly.

Alternations among political parties or factions might have a significant influence on policy content even with regard to an issue on which the mass electorate had no opinions, or one which had not been salient in a recent election campaign. If the different parties' leaders and their appointees hold systematically different policy views or ideologies, then a change of party could lead to a predictable change in policy direction, whatever the forces that produced the defeat of one and the victory of the other. In the United States, the leaders of the Democratic and Republican parties distinguish themselves clearly in their ideologies regarding government involvement in economic activity. According to data from 1956 and 1968, Republican leaders' personal attitudes correspond to their popular image as the party of business, and Democratic leaders' attitudes are clearly more favorable to assertive government regulation.[11] In this important respect, the parties are not Tweedledum and Tweedledee, although the range of difference is certainly smaller than in other countries. This accounts in part for different responses to inflation, for example. Compared with the Democratic Truman administration's response to the inflation of 1950–1952, the Republican Eisenhower administration's response to the inflation of 1955–1958 involved much less use of direct controls over the economy. During the same period, an analogous difference in response was observed in nine other advanced industrial countries, in most of which conservative parties had gained control in the interim.

With reference to U.S. exchange-rate policy, a political party hypothesis would imply that Democrats will be more likely than Republicans to use controls and foreign-exchange market intervention to defend a declared parity or preferred rate. By this reasoning, Democrats would be somewhat less likely than Republicans to yield to market pressure and allow an exchange-rate change. This hypothesis has no clear implications for international liquidity policy.

A slightly different party comparison indicates the same sort of difference in exchange-rate behavior. Voters commonly believe Democrats to be freer spenders than Republicans, and have the image of Republicans as more orthodox financially, just as Democrats are often thought more likely to be "soft on Communism." On one view, these party reputations will affect policy makers. A Republican, faced with a serious payments deficit, and less vulnerable to partisan charges of financial irresponsibility, will be more likely to devalue than a Democrat, just as it was easier for Richard Nixon to go to Peking than it would have been for a Democratic President.

A second variant of the domestic-politics perspective emphasizes interest-group influence as the decisive source of policy change. Groups have more or less self-evident interests regarding a given policy issue, and group representatives articulate their respective positions. They urge policies aimed at maximizing their group's interests, and presumably the more a group would be affected by a given measure, the more intense would be its political pressure. Policy content is explained by pointing to the political coalition of groups that benefit from the mix of actual policies and by showing that these groups acted to promote those policies, either by placing sympathizers in positions of authority or by directing lobbying and publicity campaigns at officials. In general, the stronger its pressure, the more a group succeeds in bending policy in its preferred direction. A change in the policy mix is explained by a change in the mix of group interests and pressures converging on the government from the domestic political environment.

In theory, group politics could explain U.S. exchange-rate policy. A fundamental deficit in international payments and an overvalued currency hurt exporters and American producers competing with imports. In such an international financial situation, these groups have an interest in dollar depreciation, since U.S. exports would then be more competitive abroad and foreign products would be less competitive in the United States (assuming that sales are affected by relative prices). But at the same time, U.S. consumers of imported goods, tourists going abroad, and producers using imported inputs gain from an overvalued dollar; a depreciation would increase their costs. Therefore on one side U.S. farmers and producers of high-technology goods would be expected to press for a depreciation, and the textile, shoe, steel, and other industries would join in the campaign. On the other side, workers in service sectors and consumer organizations would be expected to oppose such a step, which would reduce their standard of living. The better organized forces would be expected to prevail. In the opposite situation—a payments surplus and an undervalued currency—we would expect to see the same two coalitions exerting pressure in the opposite directions.

Interest groups, however, often do not in fact express the views attributed to them in this theory. Thinking through the implications of an interest-group explanation for policy forces recognition of the complexity of the causal linkages in economics and politics. If groups find that their interests actually are multiple or uncertain, then the analyst searching only for group interests is not likely to discover an adequate explanation for policy formation and may find it necessary to turn to other variables.

Illustrations

Many examples can be cited to show that American public opinion restrains, or sometimes drives, foreign policy on political-military issues. East European immigrant voters constrained the Roosevelt administration from concluding a sphere-of-influence deal with Stalin; McCarthyist fervor delayed U.S. reconciliation with the People's Republic of China; mass protests limited or ended the campaign in Vietnam; American liberal beliefs in representative institutions and human rights burst forth during the Wilson and Carter administrations. But analysts often conclude that, even in America, public opinion is not a significant influence. Other factors would have accounted for the same policies; the public in the aggregate pays little attention to concrete issues, or is divided; the President can often shape the public opinion he hears.

In the realm of foreign monetary policy, illustrations of the first domestic political variant are scarce. In the West German election campaign of 1969, exchange-rate policy was perhaps the most salient issue dividing the main rivals. The balance of payments was in persistent surplus and the Social Democratic party campaigned for a currency appreciation to hold down inflation and cheapen imports; the incumbent government, led by the Christian Democrats, opposed it, in line with the interests of industrial exporters of the Ruhr region and farmers. The challengers were victorious, and they repegged the deutsche mark at a new higher value as their first major act.

Most past interest-group explanations of foreign economic policy pertain to trade policy. England's turn in 1846 away from the protectionist Corn Laws of 1815 resulted not only from shifts in comparative advantage and from the intellectual arguments of Ricardo and his followers, but also from a long domestic campaign by middle-class manufacturers against the agrarian landowners and shipowners who dominated Parliament. The free-trade reform did not succeed until after the electoral reform of 1832 had increased representation of the manufacturing districts in the north of England.

In the United States, the 1930 Smoot-Hawley tariff, which raised high protection even higher and spread it to many industries, is often regarded as the extreme example of successful pressure upon Congress by interest groups.[12] A study of a different type of trade-legislation politics during the 1950s, however, questions the generality of the Smoot-Hawley case. In the later instance, much of the initiative was found to originate with members of Congress themselves rather than with lobbyists. In addition, businessmen's positions on protection depended not only on what products they sold, but also on their general ideas, such as attitudes of isolationism or internationalism. Political behavior sometimes departed from simple economic self-interest.[13]

Perhaps the clearest instance of interest-group influence on U.S. monetary policy is the successful pressure by silver-mining firms for a policy of buying and monetizing more silver, begun in 1933 and maintained despite objections from other domestic groups and despite the disorder it caused in China and Mexico.[14]

During the 1920s, American bankers played a direct role in international relations in the context of the isolationist and laissez-faire policies then dominant in Washington. J. P. Morgan, Jr., Thomas Lamont, Charles Dawes, and Owen Young negotiated currency stabilization loans with foreign governments and chaired international conferences dealing with reparations. The Depression and the New Deal then brought a sharp decline in bankers' influence on policy. During the diplomacy that created the International Monetary Fund and World Bank at the end of World War II, U.S. bankers played only a small part, though they nevertheless prospered under the subsequent operation of these institutions.

Finally, according to some analysts the dominant groups in America are big banks and corporations and their Wall Street lawyers, who have little need to engage in active lobbying because they are so successful in placing their own members directly in high office.[15] In the monetary sphere, a familiar Washington generalization maintains that private bankers have a firm hold on the Treasury Department and the Federal Reserve system. Treasury Secretaries Andrew Mellon, Douglas Dillon, David Kennedy, and William Simon illustrate this maxim, which survives despite the long disconfirming case of Henry Morgenthau, as well as more recent exceptions like Henry Fowler, John Connally, and Michael Blumenthal.

Other Domestic Influences

This exposition of a domestic politics perspective has omitted several possible analytical tools, and the reasons can be identified in a few words. Some theories center on the effects of "domestic structure" for foreign policy. While the meaning of this concept is often fuzzy, it does clearly include the relatively permanent political institutions of a state as contrasted to those of other states. However useful this may be in explaining policy differences *among* states, it is obviously of less use when the subject is the changing behavior of a single state. To note that authority is fragmented under the U.S. constitution, as compared with that of Japan or France, gives few clues about which of several alternative policies regarding international liquidity or exchange rates the United States will pursue or why these policies might change. If it could be demonstrated, however, that the foreign economic policy of France or Japan is generally more coherent than that of the United States, then differences between "strong states" and "weak states" might be used to explain this difference, as opposed to explaining policy substance itself and its variations.

One change in domestic structures during the early twentieth century added an indirect constraint on international monetary policies that was fairly constant through the period after World War II. In the United States and other countries, labor was organized and incorporated into the political party system. Thereafter, the forces opposing deflationary domestic policies were clearly stronger than they had been during the gold-standard period. This means of avoiding exchange-rate changes over very long periods became more expensive politically.

Domestic structure is sometimes said to include the country's ideology, with ideology treated as one building block interlocked with others such as the nation's constitutional division of authority and the relative strengths of public and private sectors. But more discriminating analysis is possible when ideology is treated as a separate, cognitive variable. While the distribution of authority among governmental units is relatively constant, the reigning ideology may vary. Few ideologies are shared unanimously within a society, and in practice some tenets are often rejected or discounted by a substantial element of the national political elite. These people can come to office, sometimes without changes in other dimensions of domestic structure. U.S. politicians are not all equally hostile to state intervention in economic activity; French leaders are not all equally enthusiastic about it. Britain has its Wilsons and its Thatchers; China has its Mao Zedongs and its Deng Xiao-pings. When the reigning ideology changes, striking policy changes often result. In addition, the relative salience of an individual's ideological beliefs may vary, giving way, for instance, to a security fear or a domestic political calculation on particular occasions. Once the policy beliefs of incumbent decision-makers are recognized as constituting an alternative general explanatory perspective, then treating ideology as a variable cognitive element along with other beliefs becomes more appealing than considering it a fixture of domestic structure.

Another objection to the domestic-politics perspective might be that the line between domestic policy and foreign policy has become blurred in the last generation. In the monetary area, it can be argued that U.S. domestic monetary policy—credit conditions and the rate at which the Federal Reserve allows the money supply to grow—is as important to the rest of the world as the positions the Treasury Department takes in international exchange-rate negotiations. So, for that matter, are fiscal policy and all other factors that affect macroeconomic conditions within the United States. Yet domestic macroeconomic policy may be more responsive to domestic politics than external policy appears to be.

This "blurring" thesis is certainly valid. In many countries, what is nominally domestic policy has important causes and effects abroad, and what is nominally foreign policy has important causes and effects at home. A description of either without mentioning the other is likely to be deficient, although it is also true that our knowledge about these linkages and their magnitudes is not based on sufficient systematic study.

ORGANIZATION AND INTERNAL BARGAINING

A fourth analytical approach dwells on a special domestic factor, the organizational structure of the government and the internal bargaining among officials. The several versions of this familiar perspective all begin by rejecting the premise implicit in most international-level approaches, namely that governments are unitary actors. Modern governments are instead seen as huge administrative conglomerates. Different agencies are designed to perform different and sometimes conflicting national missions, and a given policy issue will always touch the concerns of several agencies. This approach expects that organizations will compete with each other for resources, and that they will typically recommend different policies or priorities. One high priority for each will be the preservation and promotion of that agency and its special mission. The first distinctive insight of this perspective is captured by the aphorism, "Where you stand depends on where you sit."

Policies are then shown to be results of bargaining among these divided officials, rather than command decisions. Even in a country with a presidential structure, like the United States, presidents are weaker in relation to their subordinates than the formal hierarchy would suggest. Fragmentation of authority gives other officials a base from which to force the President to bargain. Presidents compromise their preferred strategies in order to build support at home; other participants also accept less than they desire; policy substance then becomes an inconsistent mixture desired initially by no one. Or the President may permit or require decisions to be made at lower levels, and the bargaining occurs there. In any case, no one is really in charge. One might suppose that this view is even more valid in parliamentary structures lacking a directly elected chief executive.

A slightly different variant derives from cybernetic analogies. Here the emphasis falls less on top-level decisions and bargaining, and more on the standard operating procedures of autonomous bureaucracies in the absence of such decisions or during the intervals between them. In this conception, each organization focuses on only one or a few of the many objectives of government, and the agency develops a set of programmed responses for dealing with occasions when the "critical variables" it monitors move outside their acceptable ranges. Just as a thermostat monitors temperature and reacts to change by activating a heating or cooling mechanism, so a nation's finance ministry monitors inflation and government budgets, and reacts to change by recommending adjustments in expenditures and taxes. Meanwhile, the foreign ministry may be monitoring alliance cohesion and foreign requests for economic assistance, and making commitments accordingly. It is assumed that top leaders are unable to impose more than occasional, loose coordination on the conglomerate, and that otherwise each agency will push "policy" in the direction indicated by its own program. This variant's core implication, then, is that policy substance as a whole will appear partially self-contradictory.

Related is the claim that the established bureaucratic machinery limits the choices of senior policy makers. They may fail to consider policies that would have been expected on other grounds, because they rely on information collected and processed by official bureaucracies, which have an interest in shaping reports so they do not reflect unfavorably on the organizations. Whether or not agencies distort information flows, a limited inventory of policy instruments available at a given time may bias choice away from responses that would have been expected on other grounds. It is further argued that when leaders are able to order a preferred new measure, the machine may later distort this policy by delaying or by using delegated discretion more in keeping with old routines.

This organization perspective is narrower than the notion of "bureaucratic politics" has often been in practice. If defined broadly enough, it could "explain" every case, but at the risk of tautology. Some observers have stretched the notion to cover situations in which leaders' "stands" differ but for reasons unrelated to their organizational positions. Some have exaggerated the influence of "pulling and hauling" among bureaucrats on policy content by overlooking rival hypotheses, such as the ideas and influence of the President himself. Internal struggle does produce compromised policy in some cases, but in others in which such struggle is ended by a President persuaded to adopt one player's view and reject the rest, the decisive variable is the President's thinking, not the organizational structure or process. Sometimes "bureaucratic politics" is stretched to include incumbents' attitudes and the arrival of new incumbents while organizational structures remain unchanged. But to confound structural change with personnel turnover is to risk confused analysis. The two can vary independently. Since a sharply defined perspective does help explain some important cases, it is important not to dull the edge of this analytical tool.

Many of the best-documented instances of U.S. bureaucratic politics arise in the military realm or in the intersection of military and economic affairs—such as setting military strategy and the national budget in the late 1940s, responding to Soviet missiles in Cuba in 1962, and deploying the anti-ballistic missile in the late 1960s. If these instances were reinterpreted in light of the foregoing distinctions, it could be shown that even there, the influence of organization and internal bargaining was less—and the role of the President and policy ideas was greater—than has sometimes been thought.

In foreign economic policy, a bargaining process in which the President is forced to accept a compromise recurs on issues involving legislation and congressmen as well as bureaucrats—foreign economic assistance, for example. Loose coordination and diverging agencies played their part in the "Great Food Fumble" of 1972, according to I. M. Destler. In that year, huge and initially secret Soviet grain purchases from U.S. companies contributed to sharp food price inflation for Americans and increasing burdens on the developing countries that relied on U.S. foreign aid. Washington's policies in 1972 seemed almost designed to exacerbate these problems. For weeks after it was evident that these sales were driving up prices, the government continued export subsidies encouraging further sales, at great cost to the Treasury. Not until six months later were changes made in the acreage policies that were holding down grain supplies. Destler's explanation is that food policy was largely left to the Secretary of Agriculture, who was pursuing a predictably narrow strategy of increasing U.S. farmers' prices and exports. President Nixon and his National Security Adviser, Henry Kissinger, were also using grain trade to help improve relations with the Soviet Union. The Council of Economic Advisers and others charged with inflation policy did not participate heavily enough or early enough to avert the "fumble." The following year, U.S. policy lurched in the other direction, with an export embargo on U.S. soybeans for anti-inflation reasons, damaging farm and foreign policy interests.[16]

In the monetary field, Richard Gardner points to "defective liaison" between the Treasury and State Departments in explaining the creation of the Bretton Woods institutions, particularly their limited funds when compared to the magnitude of the reconstruction needs that became apparent after 1944. Treasury planning concentrated on monetary stabilization, to the relative neglect of the problem of immediate postwar reconstruction. State Department officials warned that the plans of Harry White, deputy to the Treasury Secretary, were based on the unrealistic assumption that reconstruction would somehow be taken care of, but their own plans for a separate solution to that problem were hampered by Treasury's jurisdictional supremacy.[17] Treasury has maintained that supremacy over other agencies on international monetary matters down to the present time.

A third variant of this approach emphasizes "transgovernmental relations," or direct contacts between middle- and lower-level bureaucrats in different countries and international organizations, far removed from close control by chief executives and cabinets. Specialists dealing with the same problem develop a common expertise and to some extent similar priorities vis-à-vis other functional areas. Engaging in frequent international policy coordination, it is said, these officials develop a transnational camaraderie that can lead to less conflicting policy. Students of common markets report that this sense of professional comradeship produces more flexible bargaining and more extensive coordination than would have been the case among governments operating as unitary actors.

Transgovernmental effects may also operate through coalitions formed by bureaucrats from various governments and international secretariats, through which an American official obtains the support of foreign officials (or vice versa) to influence the policy process in the U.S. or its outcome. For example, the official U.S. position in the United Nations Conference on the Law of the Sea in Geneva was to oppose broadening the jurisdiction of coastal states over the continental shelf and to defend traditional freedom of the seas. Meanwhile, however, delegates from the Interior Department joined oil companies and others from foreign countries in a coalition lobbying for broader jurisdiction. Thus, considering agencies as actors on the world stage introduces complex possibilities for policy change not suggested by the other two variants.

The most obvious sites for transgovernmental relations involving U.S. monetary policy are the meetings of financial officials at the International Monetary Fund and the central bankers' confidential gatherings at the Bank for International Settlements in Basel, Switzerland. Speaking before the 1971 annual meeting of the IMF Board of Governors, Britain's Chancellor of the Exchequer, Anthony Barber, hinted at a transnational sense of comradeship when he joked:

> Whatever differences we Finance Ministers may have, to be together with one's fellow sufferers and far away from one's spending colleagues at home is a most agreeable experience which only we can share![18]

Coordination among central bankers independently of their national governments was most consequential during the 1920s. During the 1950s and 1960s, notable communication occurred among the financial bureaucrats of 11 major financial nations, but it did not significantly modify governments' monetary policies. Robert Russell finds also that, while central banks successfully coordinated foreign-exchange market interventions and arranged short-term credit facilities, the formation of transgovernmental coalitions did not have much effect on national economic policies.[19] In one exceptional case, the West German Economics Ministry hinted, at a meeting of a committee of the Organization for Economic Cooperation and Development, that a favorable recommendation from the committee would aid the Ministry on a matter already rejected by the German cabinet. The committee made the recommendation, and the German cabinet later accepted it.

These variants of an organization perspective do not tell us what the content of policy is likely to be. They do identify conditions that could impose a drag on any policy change. If prevailing policy is a bargained package, then an attempt to modify one element will risk disturbing all the other elements and the advocates of each, including those not especially concerned about the specific problem at issue. Even though external conditions may change, a corresponding policy element may not change if it is embedded in an internal package. If prevailing policy is the product of standard operating routines, then a new situation is likely to evoke first an attempt to apply a standard response, not to create a new one. If existing routines prove ineffective, the next likely response would be an incremental modification. Organizational considerations as such do not prepare the observer to expect sharp shifts of policy direction, as long as the organizational structure remains basically unchanged.

Implicit in the three variants, finally, is the proposition that a change in that structure may cause a change in policy content. Following this logic, one presidential commission after another in the United States has proposed to solve policy problems by means of organizational reforms, whether dismantling or creating agencies or White House posts, transferring authority from one agency to another, or rearranging responsibilities for coordination. Interest groups have also urged structural changes to bring about policy more favorable to them. Farmers' complaints, for instance, led in 1962 to the transfer of responsibility for trade negotiations from the Department of State to a new office, the Special Representative for Trade Negotiations.

IDEAS

Content of the Perspective

Each of the approaches discussed thus far identifies an element of the policymaker's situation as an influence on policy content. But according to many commentators, behavior depends not on reality but on how reality is perceived and interpreted. A fifth and final perspective, then, focuses attention on the substantive ideas held by top policy makers and advisers as decisive or necessary elements of explanation. The core claim of this cognitive approach is that changes in reigning ideas help produce changes in policy content.

Before this approach is elaborated, some important assumptions and distinctions should be noted. One key assumption is that ideas, while affected by interests, are not simply determined by them. Ideas have more complex origins, and they can have independent effects on policy content. Thus, theories relying on interests alone will be inadequate for predicting or explaining policy changes. It is also assumed that, while generalizing about such matters is difficult, attention to policy ideas need not be an entirely ad hoc exercise. Some cognitive approaches to policy formation have made systematic use of cognitive psychology, emphasizing the effects of recurring cognitive processes on policy. The present perspective takes account of this line of analysis, but goes beyond it. The central emphasis here is on the content of ideas rather than on cognitive processes. Efforts to discover patterns in cognitive content are only beginning, but the results are promising.

The claim that ideas matter may seem perfectly obvious to some. A cognitive perspective could be stated so strongly, in fact, as to be a truism. That is, one could deny that behavior has any meaning at all except in the terms through which the actor himself understands it; one could build an explanation insisting on "act meaning" to the complete exclusion of "action meaning," to use Abraham Kaplan's terms.[20]

Every policy change would be explained by describing the beliefs, perceptions, and values of the policy makers at the time of decision. Such an epistemology seems too extreme; it implies rejection of much persuasive social science and may impose unnecessary burdens on investigators. It undoubtedly conveys an exaggerated impression of the policy maker's actual room for maneuver. The cognitive perspective used here follows instead the more conventional social-science assumption that behavior has meaning given it by the analyst's theory as well as "act meaning." Behavior is a product of some combination of environmental and internal factors.

An emphasis on ideas often elicits skeptical materialist counterarguments. Analysts of foreign policies have been reluctant to embrace this approach, for historical and other reasons. In principle, explanations focusing on situational factors could be more persuasive than one using a cognitive approach, to the point that the latter would be unnecessary. It may be that a given international security threat or international market imbalance would have evoked the same response from any state in that situation, regardless of the national culture or the outlooks of particular leaders. In that case, we would expect to find evidence of very little disagreement among the state's leaders. If the beliefs and perceptions of the leaders are in this sense virtually determined by the external situation, then a cognitive perspective is superfluous. If policy content seems to vary regularly with the political party in control of the government, a domestic political explanation would be appropriate, whether or not the covariation is recognized by decision makers. If leaders' views tend to differ regularly by organizational position, then a case fitting this pattern can more properly be explained by an organization perspective than by a cognitive approach. If we can assume that a satisfactory explanation can always be provided by one or more of the situational approaches, then investigators can avoid the task of gathering detailed evidence on the beliefs, perceptions, and priorities of top leaders. Such research is costly in time and effort, yet making inferences about motives and perceptions without collecting evidence and cross-checking and interpreting it introduces substantial risks of bias. In the absence of direct or indirect evidence, claims about motives and perceptions must be regarded as intelligent speculation at best. So the advantage of the foregoing perspectives is not a trivial one.

We know from considerable research, however, that many cases of foreign policy do not fit such patterns. All but the most extreme policy situations seem highly complex and uncertain; policy makers typically disagree among themselves as to diagnosis and prescription, or later analysts uncover evidence and reasoning that support more than one plausible interpretation of the national interest. Conflicting schools of thought cutting across interest groups, political parties, and bureaucracies are often evident. Policies sometimes seem to vary to a greater extent with the rotation of these schools of thought through the offices of government than with other variables. The cognitive analyst may argue that for a given case, a change in reigning ideas would have made a greater difference for policy content than conceivable changes in other factors. Situational factors may explain the rejection of an old policy, the timing of a policy change, or the degree of policy coherence, but contain no explanation for the choice of a new policy from among the alternatives. Actual policy changes may come in packages, having some elements that seem virtually inevitable in the light of situational changes but other elements that require a different explanation. In Hugh Heclo's words, "governments not only 'power'; they also puzzle."[21]

It is useful to distinguish between specific beliefs and general beliefs. Specific beliefs are an individual's causal map of the immediate situation—for example, a belief that the Soviet Union erected missiles in Cuba last month because the U.S. had appeared weak last year during the Bay of Pigs incident, or that if a central bank raises its discount rate this week, the effects will include an immediate run on the nation's currency, because international markets will interpret the action in present circumstances as a sign of panic. The individual may interpret a situation by specific analogy, believing that the cause of the current episode is X because the cause of a previous episode was a comparable X. According to this perspective, identifying such specific calculations is essential for explaining why a government rejected certain courses of action in favor of others. Specificity of a belief, incidentally, does not imply idiosyncrasy. In principle, a given specific belief can be peculiar to a single individual or shared by every observer of the situation.

General beliefs, theories or ideologies for example, may play a direct role in policy formation. A theory such as Ricardian free-trade theory or Leninist imperialism theory might be applied directly and literally by a decision maker in choosing policy at a given moment. Or a new economic theory devised by a particular writer might be explicitly cited as the source of a policy experiment. Similarly, a cognitive perspective might lead to the finding that one or another ideology—a belief system claiming a very wide range of application, having a tightly interrelated internal structure, usually having an authoritative promulgation, and pointing the way to the attainment of the highest human values—has been directly applied in a given case.

More often, however, general beliefs and values have a more indirect role. They appear as predispositions that policy makers bring with them when they take office. Rather than dictating specific policy moves, these predispositions influence behavior by shaping and coloring the way new information is processed. As Robert Jervis puts this hypothesis: "Decision makers tend to fit incoming information into their existing theories and images. Indeed, their theories and images play a large part in determining what they notice."[22] A general belief or attitude may make an individual more sensitive to information supporting his predispositions than to information contradicting them. For example, Secretary of State John F. Dulles's general negative predisposition toward the Soviet government deeply colored the way he processed new specific information about Soviet foreign policy. An increase in friendly Soviet behavior was interpreted in a manner that reduced dissonance and preserved Dulles's predisposition and the stability of his hard-line policy. To take another example, this perspective might hypothesize that persons educated primarily in economic theory and those educated primarily in diplomatic history tend to develop different predispositions concerning foreign economic policy. In any given international power or market situation, and regardless of their bureaucratic location, the former will be predisposed to notice the efficiency costs of a given policy option more than the implications for political allies and security, and the latter vice versa.

If predispositions reduce the range of policy options considered seriously, they provide the analyst with a way of grouping individual policy participants into "schools of thought" in advance, provided information is available, thus reducing the range of policies most likely to be adopted by a given administration or set of leaders. The limits of this relationship between predispositions and an individual's specific diagnosis of a situation are difficult to specify, however. Although "barefoot empiricism" seems impossible to find in policy-making, there is also evidence of careful consideration of discrepant information under some conditions. And minds do change.

Policy debates sometimes turn less on the nature of the facts, or beliefs about them, than on the question of which facts are to be considered most important. Some changes in U.S. international monetary policy may be traced to changes in belief content from one period to the next, while others may reflect instead changes in the *relative salience* of different cognitions, all of which are acknowledged as valid by all. Salience can be defined as the prominence of a cognition in an individual's awareness. Individuals A and B may favor different policies not because A doubts the validity of B's argument that a given policy would have a certain desirable effect X, but because A, though agreeing with that argument, cares little about X and cares very much about Y instead. During the 1960s, some Americans believed that Communism in North Vietnam had been oppressive, proving the wisdom of U.S. military intervention that would have the effect of defeating Hanoi. To other Americans, the sins of Saigon were more salient, leading them to oppose U.S. policy that supported the South Vietnamese government.

The individual's belief salience ordering may vary with the situation; he may ignore each wheel until it squeaks. In other cases, his analytical emphasis may be more predictable, shaped by professional experience. Relative salience may also reflect values. For example, some leaders place a higher value on reducing unemployment than on reducing inflation, if forced to choose. Some give priority to enhancing international alliance cohesion over providing additional help to national business. The higher value can be expected to concentrate thinking more on the effects of a policy for that value than on its other effects. Leaving aside relative salience, the very content of a causal belief may of course be penetrated by an obvious or hidden value premise as well. In the monetary arena, one hears such value-laden beliefs as "the international use of the dollar gives America an inordinate privilege in the monetary system," or "the currency was undermined by excessive wage increases."[23]

One further clarification is crucial. It would be a mistake to understand this intellectual perspective as simply an argument that the idiosyncrasies of individual leaders are important in history. This perspective includes but is not limited to that form of argument. Ideas vary in the breadth of their acceptance. Some cultural assumptions are shared by an entire nation. Some ideological tenets are believed by a majority, while a given economic theory may be accepted only by a minority. Probably very few effective policy ideas are truly peculiar to a single individual. Some may be, and in some cases a cognitive perspective might find that an idiosyncrasy was decisive in producing a particular policy direction. But the emphasis is on ideas, regardless of how widely they are shared. To use individual leaders' beliefs as evidence is not necessarily to claim that policy would have been different without those particular individuals. The usual claim, rather, is that policy would have been different unless *some* member of the same school of thought had been making policy.

To summarize, a cognitive perspective claims that the content of reigning ideas has independent effects on policy content. The core claim is not construed so broadly as to be valid by definition. Distinctions are made between specific beliefs and general beliefs, and among beliefs according to their relative salience. The emphasis is on ideas, not idiosyncrasies.

But can the approach be elaborated further, and can it help the observer anticipate future policy changes? Does it explain how change takes place, or which new ideas are more likely and less likely to prevail? For that matter, where do policy ideas come from? Obviously, such questions will not be resolved in any single study. But a few hypotheses can be suggested.

Sources of Policy Ideas

Class   One source of beliefs and predispositions is social class. Officials and potential leaders differ in previous occupation and income level. By one classic hypothesis, the governing elite's social class indicates the range of policy ideas to be expected, particularly on some economic issues. Class-based interpretations have had very little to say about international monetary policies, however. For reasons discussed below, this connection is largely left for other investigations.

Generation   Members of a given age cohort share a common historical experience during the stage of life when individuals often form their fundamental substantive beliefs and values. The generational background of leaders and potential leaders may give loose clues as to which predispositions are more likely, and which policy options are least likely to be taken seriously.

Professional Education and Training   Impressionistic evidence suggests that individuals' policy predispositions are correlated with their university background or occupational experience. Admittedly, careful study might show that there is no simple or direct connection between studying at the University of Chicago or Cambridge University, or working for years in a central bank, on the one hand, and policy predispositions on the other. But such considerations might help narrow the range of policy ideas to be expected in a government.

Conditions and Directions of Change

A proposition of cognitive psychology holds that established beliefs, whatever their sources, shape perceptions of new information so as to help maintain those prior causal beliefs and preferences. Basic orientations toward international politics and toward economic problems tend to group themselves into recognizable schools of thought, some schools containing distinct sub-schools. Consequently, when adherents of a different ideology or school of thought come to office (or are ousted), an analyst could expect policy change toward (or away from) that school's characteristic prescription. Personnel change is one mechanism of change in governing ideas. Of course, incumbents sometimes change their minds, or form specific beliefs for the first time, while in office. One circumstance in which cognitive change is more likely is a vivid event that is clearly inconsistent with established beliefs.

Culture and Ideology   New policy ideas that are more consonant with the nation's culture or with a major ideology are more likely to spread and affect policy than those that are more dissonant or alien.

Simplicity   New ideas expressed in clear, simple terms are more likely to spread than those expressed only in a highly complicated form or that are more difficult to grasp.

Association   Ideas associated psychologically with negative symbols, such as past policy disasters, are less likely to be accepted in the present or future than proposals free of such coloration or associated with positive symbols, like prestigious thinkers or famous universities.

Organization   Those policy options promoted by organizations through active public campaigns and mass media are more likely to be adopted and to influence policy content than schemes which are not.

Illustrations

The cognitive approach as defined here is not common, but isolated explanations of this type are scattered through the literature of policy history and analysis. Typically, little effort is made to evaluate rival hypotheses. To judge from the following examples, this approach may be as applicable to security policies as to economic ones.

Ideological predispositions have an independent importance for policy in the United States, according to Anthony King. He confronts the question of why the direct operating role of government in the United States is so strikingly different from what it is in three European countries and Canada. He finds that the contrast cannot be explained by differences in the countries' elites, differences in mass demands for state activity, different interest-group strength, or unique political institutions. King concludes that the most satisfactory explanation lies in Americans' distinctive beliefs and assumptions about government.[24]

During the mid-nineteenth century, free-trade policies spread across Europe. These changes had many causes, Charles Kindleberger points out, but he finds that the most satisfactory explanation is that "Europe as a whole was motivated by ideological considerations rather than economic interests."[25] During the 1830s, economic liberalism "burst forth as a crusading passion."[26] Many British landlords themselves finally agreed to repeal of the Corn Laws. "Manchester and the English political economists persuaded Britain, which persuaded Europe—by precept and example."[27]

Other examples point to the beliefs of a particular generation in history, beliefs shared almost universally among the informed public of a given era. After World War I, Britain pushed sterling back up to its prewar parity. This policy is puzzling from a mercantilist perspective. Given its declining economic power and payments problems, a mercantilist Britain determined to expand exports would have adopted an *under*valued currency. William Adams Brown, Jr., accounts for the paradox with a cognitive factor. After the war, certain widely-held "concepts of normal" obscured the true breakdown of the prewar gold standard, he shows. Prices in different countries had diverged, and pent-up demand and capital movements were to put additional unanticipated pressure on the "normal" currency parities implied by prewar legislation. Brown traces the return to parity in 1925 basically to "moral considerations, combined with faith in the mechanisms of the pre-war gold standard system based upon long experience. The British paper pound was a promise to pay a certain weight of gold, and this promise had to be redeemed."[28] In 1925, it was expected, falsely, that the return to gold would set in motion corrective international forces that had traditionally adjusted payments imbalances. In a similar vein, Charles Kindleberger attributes policy responses in the Great Depression a few years later to widespread "economic illiteracy."[29]

But analysts have also identified ideas shared less widely during a given era. Nations become divided into rival schools of thought when interpreting national interests, both military and economic. Replacing one school with another would have been expected to produce policy change. During the 1930s, for instance, American officials who agreed about German strength and hostility were divided in their beliefs about international conflict. Some believed that American refusal to join Europe in the League of Nations had prevented war. Others believed that isolation, given German strength and hostility, was encouraging war. If the isolationist view had been replaced by the alternative view, U.S. policy would have been different.

During the origins of the Cold War, Washington was divided between the traditional "universalist" school and the "sphere of influence" school. A later shift in U.S. military doctrine, to cite a final security example, came about when President Kennedy brought into office the strategists who had been criticizing Eisenhower's doctrine of "massive retaliation" and who then proceeded to substitute their idea of "flexible response."

Certain "lessons" of the past have affected economic as well as security policies.[30] Richard Gardner maintains that U.S. economic planning for the post-World War II period was deeply imprinted with three lessons American leaders drew from World War I peacemaking experience. The unpreparedness of the U.S. delegation to Paris, the American failure to join the League, and poor handling of economic problems had all led to subsequent breakdown of the international order. Gardner also credits a resurgence of liberal thinking in Britain for the collaboration that produced the Bretton Woods institutions.[31]

In economics, Keynesianism was doubtless the most influential school of thought created during the first half of the twentieth century. The process through which its distinctive ideas penetrated and changed American macroeconomic policy is what Herbert Stein calls "The Fiscal Revolution in America." The revolution is symbolized by the contrast between the policies of 1931 and 1962. In both years, unemployment was a problem and a federal budget deficit was in prospect. President Hoover recommended a tax increase; President Kennedy proposed a tax reduction. Stein summarizes in the following way his explanation for the eventual adoption of the principle of compensatory fiscal policy, particularly deliberate budget deficits:

> The policy changed because the view of the economic and political world changed, and the view changed partly because the facts changed [the budget became a much larger influence in the national economy]. . . .The way we thought about the facts also changed. This was partly the result of experience [namely, proof after 1929 that depressions could last a long time, and repeated experiences of budget deficits without

collapse]. But changes in the factual situation and accumulating experience seldom lead unequivocally to particular changes in policy. The facts and the experience have to be interpreted in some way. In part the fiscal revolution was propelled by the development of new ideas with which to understand the facts, new or unchanged, and the experience.[32]

A Keynesian school had coalesced in the United States in the late 1930s, and by the 1950s Keynesianism dominated professional economics. Eisenhower's 1958 deficit helped to undermine further the "budget balancing religion" among businessmen and other laymen. By 1962, the inflation problem was less salient to the authorities, who feared deterioration in output and employment.

By the late 1970s, economists and the public agreed in recognizing what had come to be called stagflation as the central macroeconomic problem. But on the question of how much stimulus, if any, the government should inject, there was, as Marina Whitman observed in 1977,

> a wide range of disagreement among reasonable and honest people. . . . How one answers it depends partly on one's diagnosis of what caused the problem in the first place. . . . Competing explanations of what has caused the current stagflation generate very different prescriptions for the conduct of macroeconomic policy during the current stage of recovery.[33]

In some cases, policy change reflects ideas shared by only a small circle. The New Deal devaluation of the dollar, as one illustration, is another puzzling shift, from the standpoint of international power and market conditions. In 1933, the United States was arguably the dominant world monetary power, and it had had a trade surplus for years. On these grounds one would have expected an effort to lead a multilateral response to the depression, or at least not the unilateral competitive depreciation that broke up the London Economic Conference. The evidence suggests the influence of domestic political changes and the flow of new ideas into Washington—generally, a belief in the merits of greater government management of money, and specifically, one professor's theory.

During 1933 and early 1934, the United States embargoed payments of gold to Americans and to foreign countries, first in March 1933 as an emergency measure, then in April as a definite but defensive abandonment of the gold standard. Later in the year, the dollar was actively pushed downward by means of gold purchases, and in January 1934 the dollar was fixed again at $35 an ounce—a very large devaluation.

At the time of Roosevelt's inauguration in 1933, domestic banks were in crisis, and during that year, farmers and other domestic forces desperate for a recovery of prices were active in Congress and elsewhere. "The dead weight of debts contracted at higher price levels threatened to collapse the whole economy,"[34] and furthermore, much of the initial New Deal legislation was seen as deflationary. The Committee for the Nation agitated for monetary inflation and devaluation. The external trade balance, however, was not in deficit, high tariff protection already having been enacted.

After shoring up the banks, Roosevelt moved from one monetary experiment to another with the problem of domestic prices uppermost in his mind. He told a press conference in April that he had little idea where his monetary policy would lead; he could plan only one move at a time and then watch what happened. Many of his advisers were taken by surprise by his 20 April decision abandoning the gold standard temporarily. Roosevelt professed fears of a foreign run on the gold reserves, but the stocks were sufficient for normal demands, unlike British stocks in September 1931. To explain his decision, he referred reporters to an article by Walter Lippmann. Lippmann had argued that since 1931 no nation had been able both to maintain internal prices and to keep up the value of the currency abroad; the automatic gold standard could depress internal prices.

By the time of Roosevelt's brusque July message to the London Economic Conference rejecting international currency stabilization, he was developing an interest in managed money, and particularly in the theories of Professor George Warren, an agricultural economist at Cornell. Warren's maverick idea was that the supply and demand for gold were the most important determinants of commodity prices. Therefore, by devaluing the dollar and pushing up the price of gold, the government could raise farm prices directly. Roosevelt's close friend, Henry Morgenthau, Jr., had studied under Professor Warren. Morgenthau introduced the two and presented Warren's charts to Roosevelt during a Campobello vacation, and Roosevelt decided to reject his other advisers' plan for a loose international stabilization agreement.

For some weeks after the April gold embargo, the floating dollar depreciated and domestic commodity prices rose. But prices fell back again during the summer. In October, amid threats of farmers' strikes and over the protest of his more conservative advisers, Roosevelt decided to try Warren's clear-cut gold-purchase plan. He insisted that personal compassion for human suffering, not political pressure, made inaction unconscionable.

In the event, Warren's theory was discredited. By the end of January 1934, the gold price had risen about 69 percent, but wholesale commodity prices were up only slightly more than 20 percent. Roosevelt fixed the dollar and turned away from Warren's theory, without, however, abandoning his more general and more salient idea that control over money had to be wrested away from Wall Street. Referring to Roosevelt's administration, G. Griffith Johnson, Jr., concludes: "The central decisions in monetary policy must be explained in terms of the attitude of the President and the influences and opinions which have been brought to bear thereon."[35]

CONCLUSION

The major omission from this discussion of analytical approaches is the Marxist tradition. I have not presented a Marxist approach here because I doubt that it would be either necessary or convincing for explaining changes in American foreign monetary policy. There seem to have been very few efforts to apply Marx's concepts to international monetary phenomena. Marxism has certainly been used to explain relations between rich and poor nations, and to analyze the effects of transnational corporations on social conditions in both. Perhaps political economists better educated in the subtleties of Marxist analysis could produce a persuasive model that would put international monetary policies in a new light. Such an approach would probably begin by asking fundamentally different questions.

The questions asked here do not seem to demand a class-based interpretation. There is little evidence for supposing that a strictly working-class government in the United States would have designed a different international monetary policy during this period. At the same time, there is considerable evidence that informed high-income Americans were significantly divided in their preferences for policy in this field. Distinctions other than class seem more fruitful and interesting for these questions.

Nor is it clear that more structural Marxist or neo-Marxist approaches would add significantly here. One may assume that the United States is a capitalist state, regardless of the class origins of incumbent officials. Then the problem would be to show that it was the changing interests of this capitalist state that produced the observed monetary policy changes. This would not be accomplished by flights of abstraction that are not connected to concrete phenomena. But more concrete efforts seem likely—judging from available work—to lead back to the very factors with which we begin: payments imbalances ("contradictions"), political power, and ideologies and perceptions.

NOTES

1. *The Economist,* 25 November 1967, p. 825.
2. Benjamin M. Rowland, "Preparing the American Ascendency: The Transfer of Economic Power from Britain to the United States, 1933–1944," in *Balance of Power or Hegemony: The Interwar Monetary System,* ed. Benjamin M. Rowland (New York: New York University Press, 1976), pp. 207–210.
3. A. F. K. Organski, *World Politics,* 2d ed. (New York: Knopf, 1968).
4. Charles P. Kindleberger, *The World in Depression 1929–1939* (Berkeley and Los Angeles: University of California Press, 1973).
5. Kindleberger, *World in Depression,* p. 292. This hegemony theory is generalized for trade policy by Stephen D. Krasner, "State Power and the Structure of International Trade," *World Politics* 28 (1976):317–347. The theory is ambiguous as to whether hegemony facilitates stability because of the sacrifices borne by the leader, or because of the coercion exercised by the leader.
6. Robert O. Keohane and Joseph S. Nye, Jr., *Power and Interdependence: World Politics in Transition* (Boston: Little, Brown, 1977), Chapters 3 and 6.
7. Keohane and Nye, *Power and Interdependence,* pp. 139–140.
8. Carr, *Twenty Years' Crisis,* p. 60.
9. H. Hugh Heclo, *Modern Social Politics in Britain and Sweden: From Relief to Income Maintenance* (New Haven, Conn.: Yale University Press, 1974), p. 6.
10. Anthony Downs, *Economic Theory of Democracy.*
11. Herbert McClosky et al., "Issue Conflict and Consensus Among Party Leaders and Followers," *American Political Science Review* 54 (1960):406–427; John W. Soule and James W. Clark, "Issue Conflict and Consensus," *Journal of Politics* 33 (1971):72–92.
12. E. E. Schattschneider, *Politics, Pressures and the Tariff* (New York: Prentice-Hall, 1935).
13. Raymond A. Bauer, Ithiel de Sola Pool, and Lewis A. Dexter, *American Business and Public Policy: The Politics of Foreign Trade,* 2d ed. (Chicago: Aldine-Atherton, 1972).

14. Arthur W. Crawford, *Monetary Management under the New Deal* (New York: Da Capo Press, 1940, 1972), Chaps. 5, 7, and 14; Kindleberger, *World in Depression*, pp. 234–235.

15. Richard J. Barnet, *The Roots of War* (Baltimore: Penguin, 1971); Gabriel Kolko, *The Roots of American Foreign Policy* (Boston: Beacon, 1969).

16. I. M. Destler, "United States Food Policy 1972–1976: Reconciling Domestic and International Objectives," *International Organization* 32 (1978):617–654. Destler's interpretation places heavy weight on intellectual changes and lags as well as on agency interests. The treatment of the President's views and participation is sketchy.

17. Richard N. Gardner, *Sterling-Dollar Diplomacy: Anglo-American Collaboration in the Reconstruction of Multilateral Trade* (Oxford: Clarendon Press, 1956), Chap. 5.

18. International Monetary Fund, *Annual Meeting of the Board of Governors: Summary Proceedings* 1971 (Washington: IMF, 1971), p. 27.

19. Robert W. Russell, "Transgovernmental Interaction in the International Monetary System, 1960–1972," *International Organization* 27 (1973):431–464.

20. Abraham Kaplan, *The Conduct of Inquiry: Methodology for Behavioral Science* (Scranton, Pa.: Chandler, 1964).

21. Heclo, *Modern Social Politics,* p. 305.

22. Robert Jervis, "Hypotheses on Misperception," *World Politics* 20 (1968):455.

23. Fritz Machlup and Burton G. Malkiel, in *International Monetary Arrangements: The Problem of Choice* (Princeton: International Finance Section, Princeton University, 1964), attempt to sort out disagreements among economists, and they attribute some of the differences to subtly different values and different hunches about the future.

24. Anthony King, "Ideas, Institutions, and the Policies of Governments: A Comparative Analysis," *British Journal of Political Science* 3 (1973):291–313 and 409–423.

25. Charles Kindleberger, *Economic Response: Comparative Studies in Trade, Finance and Growth* (Cambridge, Mass.: Harvard University Press, 1978), p. 65.

26. Karl Polanyi, *The Great Transformation: The Political and Economic Origins of Our Time* (Boston: Beacon, 1944), p. 137.

27. Kindleberger, *Economic Response*, p. 65; see also Joseph A. Schumpeter, *History of Economic Analysis* (New York; Oxford University Press, 1954), pp. 397–398.

28. William Adams Brown, Jr., *The International Gold Standard Reinterpreted 1914–1934*, 2 vols. (New York: National Bureau of Economic Research, 1940), vol. 1, pp. 165–174, 177–178, 282–287, and 385–390. Active opinion in Britain was almost unanimous: "gold at any rate other than $4.86 was unthinkable" (D. E. Moggridge, *The Return to Gold, 1925: The Formulation of Economic Policy and its Critics* [Cambridge: Cambridge University Press, 1969], pp. 80–88). See also Stephen Clarke, *The Reconstruction of the International Monetary System: 1922 and 1933*, Princeton Studies in International Finance, No. 33 (Princeton: International Finance Section, Princeton University, 1973).

29. Kindleberger, *World in Depression*, pp. 23, 237, 297–298.

30. For lessons affecting American security policies, see Ernest R. May, *"Lessons" of the Past: The Use and Misuse of History in American Foreign Policy* (London: Oxford University Press, 1973).

31. Gardner, *Sterling-Dollar Diplomacy*, Chap. 1.

32. Herbert Stein, *The Fiscal Revolution in America* (Chicago: University of Chicago Press, 1969), pp. 4–5.

33. Marina v. N. Whitman, "The Search for the Grail: Economic Policy Issues of the Late 1970s," in *Economic Advice and Executive Policy: Recommendations from Past Members of the Council of Economic Advisers*, ed. Werner Sichel (New York: Praeger, 1978), pp. 80–81.

34. Arthur Schlesinger, Jr., *The Coming of the New Deal* (Boston: Houghton Mifflin, 1958), p. 195.
35. Schlesinger, *New Deal*; Crawford, *Monetary Management under the New Deal*; Herbert Feis, *1933: Characters in Crisis* (Boston: Little, Brown, 1966).

Models of International Relations and Foreign Policy

Ole R. Holsti

Universities and professional associations usually are organized in ways that tend to separate scholars in adjoining disciplines and perhaps even to promote stereotypes of each other and their scholarly endeavors. The seemingly natural areas of scholarly convergence between diplomatic historians and political scientists who focus on international relations have been underexploited, but there are also a few welcome signs that this may be changing. These include recent essays suggesting ways in which the two disciplines can contribute to each other; a number of prize-winning dissertations, later turned into books, by political scientists during the past decade that effectively combine political science theories and historical research and materials; collaborative efforts among scholars in the two disciplines; and the appearance of such interdisciplinary journals as *International Security* that provide an outlet for historians and political scientists with common interests.[1]

This essay is an effort to contribute further to an exchange of ideas between the two disciplines by describing some of the theories, approaches, and "models" that political scientists have used in their research on international relations during recent decades. A brief essay cannot do justice to the entire range of models that may be found in the current literature, if only because the period has witnessed a proliferation of approaches. But perhaps the models described here, when combined with citations to some representative works, will provide diplomatic historians with a useful, if sketchy, road map toward some of the more prominent landmarks in a neighboring discipline.

Because "classical realism" is the most venerable and persisting model of international relations, it provides a good starting point and baseline for comparison with competing models. Robert Gilpin may have been engaging in hyperbole when

Diplomatic History, 13,1 (Winter 1989), pp. 15–43.

he questioned whether our understanding of international relations has advanced significantly since Thucydides, but one must acknowledge that the latter's analysis of the Peloponnesian War includes concepts that are not foreign to contemporary students of balance-of-power politics.[2]

Following a discussion of classical realism, an examination of "modern realism" will identify the continuities and differences between the two approaches. The essay then turns to several models that challenge one or more core premises of both classical and modern realism. The first two challengers focus on the system level: Global-Society/Complex-Interdependence models and Marxist/World-System/Dependency models. Subsequent sections discuss several "decision-making" models, all of which share a skepticism about the adequacy of theories that focus on the structure of the international system while neglecting political processes within units that comprise the system.

Three limitations should be stated at the outset. Each of the three systemic and three decision-making approaches described below is a composite of several models; limitations of space have made it necessary to focus on the common denominators rather than on subtle differences among them. This discussion will also avoid purely methodological issues and debates; for example, what Stanley Hoffmann calls "the battle of the literates versus the numerates."[3] Finally, efforts of some political scientists to develop "formal" or mathematical approaches to international relations are neglected here; such abstract, often ahistorical models are likely to be of limited interest to historians.[4] With these caveats, let me turn now to classical realism, the first of the systemic models to be discussed in this essay.

There have always been Americans, such as Alexander Hamilton, who viewed international relations from a realist perspective, but its contemporary intellectual roots are largely European. Three important figures of the interwar period probably had the greatest impact on American scholarship: the historian E. H. Carr, the geographer Nicholas Spykman, and the political theorist Hans J. Morgenthau. Other Europeans who have contributed significantly to realist thought include John Herz, Hedley Bull, Raymond Aron, and Martin Wight, while notable Americans of this school include scholars Arnold Wolfers and Norman Graebner, as well as diplomat George F. Kennan, journalist Walter Lippmann, and theologian Reinhold Niebuhr.[5]

Although realists do not constitute a homogeneous school—any more than do any of the others discussed in this essay—most of them share at least five core premises about international relations. To begin with, they view as central questions the causes of war and the conditions of peace. They also regard the structure of the international system as a necessary if not always sufficient explanation for many aspects of international relations. According to classical realists, "structural anarchy," or the absence of a central authority to settle disputes, is the essential feature of the contemporary system, and it gives rise to the "security dilemma": in a self-help system one nation's search for security often leaves its current and potential adversaries insecure, any nation that strives for absolute security leaves all others in the system absolutely insecure, and it can provide a powerful incentive for arms races and other types of hostile interactions. Consequently, the question of *relative* capabilities is a crucial factor. Efforts to deal with this central element of the international system constitute the driving force behind the relations of units within the system; those that fail to cope will not survive. Thus, unlike "idealists" or "liberal internationalists," classical realists view conflict as a natural state of affairs rather than a consequence that can be attributed to historical circumstances, evil leaders, flawed sociopolitical systems, or inadequate international understanding and education.[6]

A third premise that unites classical realists is their focus on geographically based groups as the central actors in the international system. During other periods the major entities may have been city states or empires, but at least since the Treaties of Westphalia (1648), states have been the dominant units. Classical realists also agree that state behavior is rational. The assumption behind this fourth premise is that states are guided by the logic of the "national interest," usually defined in terms of survival, security, power, and relative capabilities. To Morgenthau, for example, "rational foreign policy minimizes risks and maximizes benefits." Although the national interest may vary according to specific circumstances, the similarity of motives among nations permits the analyst to reconstruct the logic of policymakers in their pursuit of national interests—what Morgenthau called the "rational hypothesis"—and to avoid the fallacies of "concern with motives and concern with ideological preferences."[7]

Finally, the nation-state can also be conceptualized as a *unitary* actor. Because the central problems for states are starkly defined by the nature of the international system, their actions are primarily a response to external rather than domestic political forces. At best, the latter provide very weak explanations for external policy. According to Stephen Krasner, for example, the state "can be treated as an autonomous actor pursuing goals associated with power and the general interest of the society."[8] However, classical realists sometimes use domestic politics as a residual category to explain deviations from rational policies.

Realism has been the dominant model of international relations during at least the past five decades, perhaps in part because it seemed to provide a useful framework for understanding World War II and the Cold War. Nevertheless, the classical versions articulated by Morgenthau and others have received a good deal of critical scrutiny. The critics have included scholars who accept the basic premises of realism but who found that in at least four important respects these theories lacked sufficient precision and rigor.

Classical realism usually has been grounded in a pessimistic theory of human nature, either a theological version (e.g., St. Augustine and Reinhold Niebuhr), or a secular one (e.g., Machiavelli, Hobbes, and Morgenthau). Egoism and self-interested behavior are not limited to a few evil or misguided leaders, as the idealists would have it, but are basic to *homo politicus* and thus are at the core of a realist theory. But according to its critics, because human nature, if it means anything, is a constant rather than a variable, it is an unsatisfactory explanation for the full range of international relations. If human nature explains war and conflict, what accounts for peace and cooperation? In order to avoid this problem, most modern realists have turned their attention from human nature to the structure of the international system to explain state behavior.

In addition, critics have noted a lack of precision and even contradictions in the way classical realists use such concepts as "power," "national interest," and "balance of power."[9] They also see possible contradictions between the central descriptive and prescriptive elements of classical realism. On the one hand, nations and their leaders "think and act in terms of interests defined as power," but, on the other, statesmen are urged to exercise prudence and self-restraint, as well as to recognize the legitimate national interests of other nations.[10] Power plays a central role in classical realism, but the correlation between the relative power balance and political outcomes is often less than compelling, suggesting the need to enrich analyses with other variables. Moreover, the distinction between "power as capabilities" and "useable options" is especially important in the nuclear age.

While classical realists have typically looked to history and political science for insights and evidence, the search for greater precision has led many modern realists to look elsewhere for appropriate models, analogies, metaphors, and insights. The discipline of choice is often economics, from which modern realists have borrowed a number of tools and concepts, including rational choice, expected utility, theories of firms and markets, bargaining theory, and game theory. Contrary to the assertion of some critics, however, modern realists *share* rather than reject the core premises of their classical predecessors.[11]

The quest for precision has yielded a rich harvest of theories and models, and a somewhat less bountiful crop of supporting empirical applications. Drawing in part on game theory, Morton Kaplan described several types of international systems—for example, balance-of-power, loose bipolar, tight bipolar, universal, hierarchical, and a unit-veto system in which any action requires the unanimous approval of all its members. He then outlined the essential rules that constitute these systems. For example, the rules for a balance-of-power system are: "(1) increase capabilities, but negotiate rather than fight; (2) fight rather than fail to increase capabilities; (3) stop fighting rather than eliminate an essential actor; (4) oppose any coalition or single actor that tends to assume a position of predominance within the system; (5) constrain actors who subscribe to supranational organizational principles; and (6) permit defeated or constrained essential actors to re-enter the system."[12] Richard Rosecrance, J. David Singer, Karl Deutsch, Bruce Russett, and many others, although not necessarily realists, also have developed models which seek to understand international relations by virtue of system-level explanations. Andrew M. Scott's survey of the literature, which yielded a catalogue of propositions about the international system, also illustrates the quest for greater precision in systemic models.[13]

Kenneth Waltz's *Theory of International Politics*, the most prominent effort to develop a rigorous and parsimonious model of "modern" or "structural" realism, has tended to define the terms of a vigorous debate during the past decade. It follows and builds upon another enormously influential book in which Waltz developed the Rousseauian position that a theory of war must include the system level (what he called the "third image") and not just first (theories of human nature) or second (state attributes) images. Why war? Because there is nothing in the system to prevent it.[14]

Theory of International Relations is grounded in analogies from microeconomics; international politics and foreign policy are analogous to markets and firms. Oligopoly theory is used to illuminate the dynamics of interdependent choice in a self-help anarchical system. Waltz explicitly limits his attention to a structural theory of international systems, eschewing the task of linking it to a theory of foreign policy. Indeed, he doubts that the two can be joined in a single theory and he is highly critical of many system-level analysts, including Morton Kaplan, Stanley Hoffmann, Richard Rosecrance, Karl Deutsch and J. David Singer, and others, charging them with various errors, including "reductionism"; that is, defining the system in terms of the attributes or interactions of the units.

In order to avoid reductionism and to gain rigor and parsimony, Waltz erects his theory on the foundations of three core propositions that define the structure of the international system. The first concentrates on the principles by which the system is ordered. The contemporary system is anarchic and decentralized rather than hierarchical; although they differ in many respects, each unit is formally equal.[15] A second defining proposition is the character of the units. An anarchic system is composed of similar sovereign units and therefore the functions that they perform are also similar rather than different; for example, all have the task of providing for their own security. In contrast, a hierarchical system would be characterized by some type of division of labor, as is the case in domestic politics. Finally, there is a distribution of capabilities among units in the system. Although capabilities are a unit-level attribute, the distribution of capabilities is a system-level concept.[16]

A change in any of these elements constitutes a change in system structure. The first element of structure as defined by Waltz is a quasi-constant because the ordering principle rarely changes, and the second element drops out of the analysis because the functions of units are similar as long as the system remains anarchic. Thus, the last of the three attributes, the distribution of capabilities, plays the central role in Waltz's model.

Waltz uses his theory to deduce the central characteristics of international relations. These include some non-obvious propositions about the contemporary international system. For example, with respect to system stability (defined as maintenance of its anarchic character and no consequential variation in the number of major actors) he concludes that: because the present bipolar system reduces uncertainty, it is more stable than alternative structures; interdependence has declined rather than increased during the twentieth century, a tendency that has actually contributed to stability; and the proliferation of nuclear weapons may contribute to rather than erode system stability.[17]

Unlike some system-level models, Waltz's effort to bring rigor and parsimony to realism has stimulated a good deal of further research, but it has not escaped controversy and criticism.[18] Leaving aside highly charged polemics—for example, that Waltz and his supporters are guilty of engaging in a "totalitarian project of global proportions"—most of the vigorous debate has centered on four alleged deficiencies relating to interests and preferences, system change, misallocation of variables between the system and unit levels, and an inability to explain outcomes.[19]

Specifically, a spare structural approach suffers from an inability to identify completely the nature and sources of interests and preferences because these are unlikely to derive solely from the structure of the system. Ideology or domestic considerations may often be at least as important. Consequently, the model is also unable to specify adequately how interests and preferences may change. The three defining characteristics of system structure are too general, moreover, and thus they are not sufficiently sensitive to specify the sources and dynamics of system change. The critics buttress their claim that the model is too static by pointing to Waltz's assertion that there has only been a single structural change in the international system during the past three centuries.

Another drawback is the restrictive definition of system properties, which leads Waltz to misplace, and therefore neglect, elements of international relations that properly belong at the system level. Critics have focused on his treatment of the destructiveness of nuclear weapons and interdependence. Waltz labels these as unit-level properties, whereas some of his critics assert that they are in fact attributes of the system.

Finally, the distribution of capabilities explains outcomes in international affairs only in the most general way, falling short of answering the questions that are of central interest to many analysts. For example, the distribution of power at the end of World War II would have enabled one to predict the rivalry that emerged between the United States and the Soviet Union, but it would have been inadequate for explaining the pattern of relations between these two nations—the Cold War rather than withdrawal into isolationism by either or both, a division of the world into spheres of influence, or World War III.[20] In order to do so, it is necessary to explore political processes *within* states—at minimum within the United States and the USSR—as well as *between* them.

Robert Gilpin shares with Waltz the core assumptions of modern realism, but his study of *War and Change in World Politics* also attempts to cope with some of the criticism leveled at Waltz's theory by focusing on the dynamics of system change. Drawing upon both economic and sociological theory, his model is based on five core propositions. The first is that the international system is stable—in a state equilibrium—if no state believes that it is profitable to attempt to change it. Second, a state will attempt to change the status quo of the international system if the expected benefits outweigh the costs; that is, if there is an expected net gain for the revisionist state. Related to this is the proposition that a state will seek change through territorial, political, and economic expansion until the marginal costs of further change equal or exceed the marginal benefits. Moreover, when an equilibrium between the costs and benefits of further change and expansion is reached, the economic costs of maintaining the status quo (expenditures for military forces, support for allies, etc.) tend to rise faster than the resources needed to do so. An equilibrium exists when no powerful state believes that a change in the system would yield additional net benefits. Finally, if the resulting disequilibrium between the existing governance of the international system and the redistribution of power is not resolved, the system will be changed and a new equilibrium reflecting the distribution of relative capabilities will be established.[21]

Unlike Waltz, Gilpin includes state-level processes in order to explain change. Differential economic growth rates among nations—a structural-systemic level variable—play a vital role in his explanation for the rise and decline of great powers, but his model also includes propositions about the law of diminishing returns on investments, the impact of affluence on martial spirits and on the ratio of consumption to investment, and structural change in the economy.[22] Table 3.1 summarizes some key elements of realism. It also contrasts them to two other system-level models of international relations—the Global-Society/Complex-Interdependence and the Marxist/World-System/Dependency models, to which we now turn our attention.

Just as there are variants of realism, there are several Global-Society/Complex-Interdependence (GS/CI) models, but this discussion focuses on two common denominators; they all challenge the first and third core propositions of realism identified earlier, asserting that inordinate attention to the war/peace issue and the nation-state renders it an increasingly anachronistic model of global relations.[23] The agenda of critical problems confronting states has been vastly expanded during the twentieth century. Attention to the issues of war and peace is by no means misdirected, according to proponents of a GS/CI perspective, but concerns for welfare, modernization, the environment, and the like are today no less potent sources of motivation and action. The diffusion of knowledge and technology, combined with the globalization of communications, has vastly increased popular expectations. The resulting demands have outstripped resources and the ability of existing institutions—notably the sovereign nation-state—to cope effectively with them. Interdependence arises from an inability of even the most powerful states to cope, or to do so unilaterally or at acceptable levels of cost and risk, with issues ranging from trade to AIDS, and immigration to environmental threats.

Paralleling the widening agenda of critical issues is the expansion of actors whose behavior can have a significant impact beyond national boundaries; indeed, the cumulative effects of their actions can have profound consequences for the international system. Thus, although nation-states continue to be important international actors, they possess a declining ability to control their own destinies. The aggregate effect of actions by multitudes of non-state actors can have potent effects that transcend political boundaries. These may include such powerful or highly visible non-state organizations as Exxon, the Organization of Petroleum Exporting Countries, or the Palestine Liberation Organization. On the other hand, the cumulative effects of decisions by less powerful or less visible actors may also have profound international consequences. For example, decisions by thousands of individuals, mutual funds, banks, pension funds, and other financial institutions to sell securities on 19 October 1987 not only resulted in an unprecedented "crash" on Wall Street, but also within hours its consequences were felt throughout the entire global financial system. Governments might take such actions as loosening credit or even closing exchanges, but they were largely unable to contain the effects of the panic.

The widening agenda of critical issues, most of which lack a purely national solution, has also led to creation of new actors that transcend political boundaries; for example, international organizations, transnational organizations, non-government organizations, multinational corporations, and the like. Thus, not only does an exclusive focus on the war/peace issue fail to capture the complexities of contemporary international life but it also blinds the analyst to the institutions, processes,

Table 3.1 THREE MODELS OF THE INTERNATIONAL SYSTEM

	Realism	Global society	Marxism
Type of model	Classical: descriptive and normative / Modern: deductive	Descriptive and normative	Descriptive and normative
Central problems	Causes of war / Conditions of peace	Broad agenda of social, economic, and environmental issues arising from gap between demands and resources	Inequality of exploitation / Uneven development
Conception of current international system	Structural anarchy	Global society / Complex interdependence (structure varies by issue-area)	World capitalist system
Key actors	Geographically based units (tribes, city-states, nation-states, etc.)	Highly permeable nation-states *plus* a broad range of nonstate actors, including IOs, IGOs, NGOs, and individuals	Classes and their agents
Central motivations	National interest / Security / Power	Human needs and wants	Class interests
Loyalties	To geographically based groups (from tribes to nation-states)	Loyalties to nation-state declining / To emerging global values and institutions that transcend those of the nation-state and/or to sub-national groups	To class values and interests that transcend those of the nation-state
Central processes	Search for security and survival	Aggregate effects of decisions by national and nonnational actors / How units (not limited to nation-states) cope with a growing agenda of threats and opportunities arising from human wants	Modes of production and exchange / International division of labor in a world capitalist system
Likelihood of system transformation	Low (basic structural elements of system have revealed an ability to persist despite many other kinds of changes)	High in the direction of the model (owing to the rapid pace of technological change, etc.)	High in the direction of the model (owing to inherent contradiction within the world capitalist system)
Sources of theory, insights, and evidence	Politics / History / Economics (especially "modern" realists)	Broad range of social sciences / Natural and technological sciences	Marxist-Leninist theory (several variants)

and norms that permit cooperation and significantly mitigate some features of an anarchic system. In short, according to GS/CI perspectives, an adequate understanding of the emergent global system must recognize that no single model is likely to be sufficient for all issues, and that if it restricts attention to the manner in which states deal with traditional security concerns, it is more likely to obfuscate than clarify the realities of contemporary world affairs.

The GS/CI models have several important virtues. They recognize that international behavior and outcomes arise from a multiplicity of motives, not merely security, at least if security is defined solely in military or strategic terms. They also alert us to the fact that important international processes and conditions originate not only in the actions of nation-states but also in the aggregated behavior of other actors. These models not only enable the analyst to deal with a broader agenda of critical issues but, more importantly, they force one to contemplate a much richer menu of demands, processes, and outcomes than would be derived from power-centered realist models. Stated differently, GS/CI models are more sensitive to the possibility that politics of trade, currency, immigration, health, the environment, and the like may significantly and systematically differ from those typically associated with security issues.

On the other hand, some GS/CI analysts underestimate the potency of nationalism and the durability of the nation-state. Two decades ago one of them wrote that "the nation is declining in its importance as a political unit to which allegiances are attached."[24] Objectively, nationalism may be an anachronism but, for better or worse, powerful loyalties are still attached to nation-states. The suggestion that, because even some well-established nations have experienced independence movements among ethnic, cultural, or religious minorities, the sovereign territorial state may be in decline is not wholly persuasive. Indeed, that evidence perhaps points to precisely the opposite conclusion: In virtually every region of the world there are groups which seek to create or restore geographically based entities in which its members may enjoy the status and privileges associated with sovereign territorial statehood. Evidence from Poland to Palestine, Spain to Sri Lanka, Estonia to Eritrea, Armenia to Afghanistan, and elsewhere seems to indicate that obituaries for nationalism may be somewhat premature.

The notion that such powerful non-national actors as major multinational corporations (MNC) will soon transcend the nation-state seems equally premature. International drug rings do appear capable of dominating such states as Colombia and Panama. However, the pattern of outcomes in confrontations between MNCs and states, including cases involving major expropriations of corporate properties, indicate that even relatively weak nations are not always the hapless pawns of the MNCs. Case studies by Joseph Grieco and Gary Gereffi, among others, indicate that MNC-state relations yield a wide variety of outcomes.[25]

Underlying the GS/CI critique of realist models is the view that the latter are too wedded to the past and are thus incapable of dealing adequately with change. At least for the present, however, even if global dynamics arise from multiple sources (including non-state actors), the actions of nation-states and their agents would appear to remain the major sources of change in the international system. However, the last group of systemic models to be considered, the Marxist/World-

System/Dependency (M/WS/D) models, downplays the role of the nation-state even further.

As in other parts of this essay, many of the distinctions among M/WS/D models are lost by treating them together and by focusing on their common features, but in the brief description possible here only common denominators will be presented. These models challenge both the war/peace and state-centered features of realism, but they do so in ways that differ sharply from challenges of GS/CI models.[26] Rather than focusing on war and peace, these models direct attention to quite different issues, including uneven development, poverty, and exploitation within and between nations. These conditions, arising from the dynamics of the modes of production and exchange, are basic and they must be incorporated into any analysis of intra- and inter-nation conflict.

At a superficial level, according to adherents of these models, what exists today may be described as an international system—a system of nation-states. More fundamentally, however, the key groups within and between nations are classes and their agents: As Immanuel Wallerstein put it, "in the nineteenth and twentieth centuries there has been only one world system in existence, the world capitalist world-economy."[27] The "world capitalist system" is characterized by a highly unequal division of labor between the periphery and core. Those at the periphery are essentially the drawers of water and the hewers of wood, whereas the latter appropriate the surplus of the entire world economy. This critical feature of the world system not only gives rise to and perpetuates a widening rather than narrowing gap between the wealthy core and poor periphery but also to a dependency relationship from which the latter are unable to break loose. Moreover, the class structure within the core, characterized by a growing gap between capital and labor, is faithfully reproduced in the periphery so that elites there share with their counterparts in the core an interest in perpetuating the system. Thus, in contrast to realist theories, M/WS/D models encompass and integrate theories of both the global and domestic arenas.

M/WS/D models have been subjected to trenchant critiques.[28] The state, nationalism, security dilemmas, and related concerns essentially drop out of these analyses; they are at the theoretical periphery rather than at the core: "Capitalism was from the beginning an affair of the world-economy," Wallerstein asserts, "not of nation-states."[29] A virtue of many M/WS/D models is that they take a long historical perspective on world affairs rather than merely focusing on contemporary issues. However, by neglecting nation-states and the dynamics arising from their efforts to deal with security in an anarchical system—or at best relegating these actors and motivations to a minor role—M/WS/D models lose much of their appeal. Models of world affairs during the past few centuries that fail to give the nation-state a central role seem as deficient as analyses of *Hamlet* that neglect the central character and his motivations.

Second, the concept of "world capitalist system" is central to these models, but its relevance for the late twentieth century can be questioned. Whether this term accurately describes the world of the 1880s could be debated, but its declining analytical utility or even descriptive accuracy for international affairs of the 1980s seems clear. Thus, one can question Wallerstein's assertion that "there are today no socialist systems in the world economy any more than there are feudal systems because there is only *one world system.* It is a world-economy and it is *by definition capitalist* in form."[30] Where within a system so defined do we locate the USSR or Eastern Europe? This area includes enough "rich" industrial nations that it hardly seems to belong in the periphery. Yet to place these states in the core of a "world capitalist system" would require terminological and conceptual gymnastics of a high order. Does it increase our analytical capabilities to describe the USSR and East European countries as "state capitalists?" Where do we locate China in this conception of the system? How do we explain dynamics within the "periphery," or the differences between rapid-growth Asian nations such as South Korea, Taiwan, or Singapore, and their slow-growth neighbors in Bangladesh, North Korea, and the Philippines? The inclusion of a third structural position—the "semi-periphery"—does not wholly answer these questions.

Third, M/WS/D models have considerable difficulty in explaining relations be-tween noncapitalist nations—for example, between the USSR and its East Euro-pean neighbors or China—much less outright conflict between them. Indeed, ad-vocates of these models usually have restricted their attention to West-South relations, eschewing analyses of East-East or East-South relations. Does one gain greater and more general analytical power by using the lenses and language of Marxism or of realism to describe relations between dominant and lesser nations; for example, the USSR and Eastern Europe, the USSR and India or other Third World nations, China and Vietnam, India and Sri Lanka, or Vietnam and Kam-puchea? Are these relationships better described and understood in terms of such M/WS/D categories as "class" or such realist ones as "relative capabilities?"

Finally, the earlier observations about the persistence of nationalism as an el-ement of international relations seem equally appropriate here. Perhaps national loyalties can be dismissed as prime examples of "false consciousness," but even in areas that have experienced almost two generations of one-party Communist rule, as in Poland, evidence that feelings of solidarity with workers in the Soviet Union or other nations have replaced nationalist sentiments among Polish workers is in short supply.

Many advocates of realism recognize that it cannot offer fine-grained analyses of foreign policy behavior and, as noted earlier, Waltz denies that it is desirable or even possible to combine theories of international relations and foreign policy. Decision-making models challenge the premises that it is fruitful to conceptualize the nation as a unitary rational actor whose behavior can adequately be explained by reference to the system structure—the second, fourth, and fifth realist proposi-tions identified earlier—because individuals, groups, and organizations acting in the name of the state are also sensitive to pressures and constraints other than in-ternational ones, including elite maintenance, electoral politics, public opinion, pressure group activities, ideological preferences, and bureaucratic politics. Such core concepts as "the national interest" are not defined solely by the international system, much less by its structure alone, but they are also likely to reflect elements within the domestic political arena. Thus, rather than assuming with the realists that the state can be conceptualized as a "black box"—that the domestic political processes are both hard to comprehend and quite unnecessary for explaining its external behavior—decision-making analysts believe one must indeed take these internal processes into account, with special attention directed at decision makers and their "definitions of the situation."[31] To reconstruct how nations deal with each other, it is necessary to view the situation through the eyes of those who act in the name of the nation-state: decision makers, and the group and bureaucratic-organizational contexts within which they act. Table 3.2 provides an overview of three major types of decision-making models that form the subject for the remainder of this essay, beginning with bureaucratic-organizational models.[32]

Traditional models of complex organizations and bureaucracy emphasized the positive contributions to be expected from a division of labor, hierarchy, and centralization, coupled with expertise, rationality, and obedience. Such models assumed that clear boundaries should be maintained between politics and decision making, on the one hand, and administration and implementation on the other. Following pioneering works by Chester I. Barnard, Herbert Simon, James G. March and Simon, and others, more recent theories depict organizations quite differently.[33] The central premise is that decision making in bureaucratic organizations is not constrained only by the legal and formal norms that are intended to enhance the rational and eliminate the capricious aspects of bureaucratic behavior. Rather, all (or most) complex organizations are seen as generating serious "information pathologies."[34] There is an *emphasis* upon rather than a denial of the political character of bureaucracies, as well as on other "informal" aspects of organizational behavior. Complex organizations are composed of individuals and units with conflicting perceptions, values, and interests that may arise from parochial self-interest ("what is best for my bureau is also best for my career"), and also from different perceptions of issues arising ineluctably from a division of labor ("where you stand depends on where you sit"). Organizational norms and memories, prior policy commitments, normal organizational inertia routines, and standard operating procedures may shape and perhaps distort the structuring of problems, channeling of information, use of expertise, and implementation of executive decisions. The consequences of bureaucratic politics within the executive branch or within the government as a whole may significantly constrain the manner in which issues are defined, the range of options that may be considered, and the manner in which executive decisions are implemented by subordinates. Consequently, organizational decision making is essentially political in character, dominated by bargaining for resources, roles and missions, and by compromise rather than analysis.[35]

Perhaps owing to the dominant position of the realist perspective, most students of foreign policy have only recently incorporated bureaucratic-organizational models and insights into their analyses. An ample literature of case studies on budgeting, weapons acquisitions, military doctrine, and similar situations confirms that foreign and defense policy bureaucracies rarely conform to the Weberian "ideal type" of rational organization.[36] Some analysts assert that crises may provide the motivation and means for reducing some of the non-rational aspects of bureaucratic behavior: crises are likely to push decisions to the top of the organization where a higher quality of intelligence is available; information is more likely to enter the top of the hierarchy directly, reducing the distorting effects of information processing through several levels of the organization; and broader, less parochial values may be invoked. Short decision time in crises reduces the opportunities for

Table 3.2 THREE MODELS OF DECISION MAKING

	Bureaucratic politics	Group dynamics	Individual decision making
Conceptualization of decision making	Decision making as the result of bargaining within bureaucratic organizations	Decision making as the product of group interaction	Decision making as the result of individual choice
Premises	Central organizational values are imperfectly internalized	Most decisions are made by small elite groups	Importance of subjective appraisal (definition of the situation) and cognitive processes (information processing, etc.)
	Organizational behavior is political behavior	Group is different than the sum of its members	
	Structure and SOPs affect substance and quality of decisions	Group dynamics affect substance and quality of decisions	
Constraints on rational decision making	Imperfect information, resulting from: centralization, hierarchy, and specialization	Groups may be more effective for some tasks, less for others	Cognitive limits on rationality
	Organizational inertia	Pressures for conformity	Information processing distorted by cognitive consistency dynamics (unmotivated biases)
	Conflict between individual and organizational utilities	Risk-taking propensity of groups (controversial)	Systematic and motivated biases in causal analysis
	Bureaucratic politics and bargaining dominate decision making and implementation of decisions	Quality of leadership	Individual differences in abilities related to decision making (e.g., problem-solving ability, tolerance of ambiguity, defensiveness and anxiety, information seeking, etc.)
		"Groupthink"	
Sources of theory, insights, and evidence	Organization theory	Social psychology	Cognitive dissonance
	Sociology of bureaucracies	Sociology of small groups	Cognitive psychology
	Bureaucratic politics		Dynamic psychology

decision making by bargaining, logrolling, incrementalism, lowest-common-denominator values, "muddling through," and the like.[37]

However, even studies of international crises from a bureaucratic-organizational perspective are not uniformly sanguine about decision making in such circumstances. Graham T. Allison's analysis of the Cuban missile crisis identified several critical bureaucratic malfunctions concerning dispersal of American aircraft in Florida, the location of the naval blockade, and grounding of weather reconnaissance flights from Alaska that might stray over the Soviet Union. Richard Neustadt's study of two crises involving the United States and Great Britain revealed significant misperceptions of each other's interests and policy processes. And an examination of three American nuclear alerts found substantial gaps in understanding and communication between policymakers and the military leaders who were responsible for implementing the alerts.[38]

Critics of some organizational-bureaucratic models and the studies employing them have directed their attention to several points.[39] They point out, for instance, that the emphasis on bureaucratic bargaining fails to differentiate adequately between the positions of the participants. In the American system, the president is not just another player in a complex bureaucratic game. Not only must he ultimately decide but he also selects who the other players will be, a process that may be crucial in shaping the ultimate decisions. If General Matthew Ridgway and Attorney General Robert Kennedy played key roles in the American decisions not to intervene in Indochina in 1954 or not to bomb Cuba in 1962, it was because Presidents Eisenhower and Kennedy chose to accept their advice rather than that of other officials. Also, the conception of bureaucratic bargaining tends to emphasize its non-rational elements to the exclusion of genuine intellectual differences that may be rooted in broader concerns—including disagreements on what national interests, if any, are at stake in a situation—rather than narrow parochial interests. Indeed, properly managed, decision processes that promote and legitimize "multiple advocacy" among officials may facilitate high-quality decisions.[40]

These models may be especially useful for understanding the slippage between executive decisions and foreign policy actions that may arise during implementation, but they may be less valuable for explaining the decisions themselves. Allison's study of the Cuban missile crisis does not indicate an especially strong correlation between bureaucratic roles and evaluations of the situation or policy recommendations, as predicted by his "Model III" (bureaucratic politics), and recently published transcripts of deliberations during the crisis do not offer more supporting evidence for that model.[41] On the other hand, Allison does present some compelling evidence concerning policy implementation that casts considerable doubt on the adequacy of "Model I" (the traditional realist conception of the unitary rational actor).

Another decision-making model used by some political scientists supplements bureaucratic-organizational models by narrowing the field of view to top policymakers. This approach lends itself well to investigations of foreign policy decisions, which are usually made in a small-group context. Some analysts have drawn upon sociology and social psychology to assess the impact of various types of group dynamics on decision making.[42] Underlying these models are the premises that the group is not merely the sum of its members (thus decisions emerging from the group are likely to be different than what a simple aggregation of individual preference and abilities might suggest), and that group dynamics, the interactions among its members, can have a significant impact on the substance and quality of decisions.

Groups often perform better than individuals in coping with complex tasks owing to diverse perspectives and talents, an effective division of labor, and high-quality debates centering on evaluations of the situation and policy recommendations for dealing with it. Groups may also provide decision makers with emotional and other types of support that may facilitate coping with complex problems. On the other hand, they may exert pressures for conformity to group norms, thereby inhibiting the search for information and policy options or cutting it off prematurely, ruling out the legitimacy of some options, curtailing independent evaluation, and suppressing some forms of intragroup conflict that might serve to clarify goals, values, and options. Classic experiments by the psychologist Solomon Asch revealed the extent to which group members will suppress their beliefs and judgments when faced with a majority adhering to the contrary view, even a counterfactual one.[43]

Drawing upon a series of historical case studies, social psychologist Irving L. Janis has identified a different variant of group dynamics, which he labels "groupthink" to distinguish it from the more familiar type of conformity pressure on "deviant" members of the group.[44] Janis challenges the conventional wisdom that strong cohesion among the members of a group invariably enhances performance. Under certain conditions, strong cohesion can markedly degrade the group's performance in decision making. Thus, the members of a cohesive group may, as a means of dealing with the stresses of having to cope with consequential problems and in order to bolster self-esteem, increase the frequency and intensity of face-to-face interaction. This results in a greater identification with the group and less competition within it. The group dynamics of what Janis calls "concurrence seeking" may displace or erode reality testing and sound information processing and judgment. As a consequence, groups may be afflicted by unwarranted feelings of optimism and invulnerability, stereotyped images of adversaries, and inattention to warnings. Janis's analyses of both "successful" (the Marshall Plan, the Cuban missile crisis) and "unsuccessful" (Munich Conference of 1938, Pearl Harbor, the Bay of Pigs invasion) cases indicate that "groupthink" or other decision-making pathologies are not inevitable, and he develops some guidelines for avoiding them.[45]

Still other decision-making analysts focus on the individual. Many approaches to the policymaker emphasize the gap between the demands of the classical model of rational decision making and the substantial body of theory and evidence about various constraints that come into play in even relatively simple choice situations.[46] The more recent perspectives, drawing upon cognitive psychology, go well beyond some of the earlier formulations that drew upon psychodynamic theories to identify various types of psychopathologies among political leaders: paranoia, authoritarianism, the displacement of private motives on public objects, etc.[47] These more recent efforts to include information-processing behavior of the individual decision maker in foreign policy analyses have been directed at the cognitive and motivational constraints that, in varying degrees, affect the decision-making performance of "normal" rather than pathological subjects. Thus, attention is directed to all leaders, not merely those, such as Hitler or Stalin, display evidence of clinical abnormalities.

The major challenges to the classical model have focused in various ways on limited human capabilities for performing the tasks required by objectively rational decision making. The cognitive constraints on rationality include limits on the individual's capacity to receive, process, and assimilate information about the situation; an inability to identify the entire set of policy alternatives; fragmentary knowledge about the consequences of each option; and an inability to order preferences on a single utility scale.[48] These have given rise to several competing conceptions of the decision maker and his or her strategies for dealing with complexity, uncertainty, incomplete or contradictory information, and, paradoxically, information overload. They variously characterize the decision maker as a problem solver, naive or intuitive scientist, cognitive balancer, dissonance avoider, information seeker, cybernetic information processor, and reluctant decision maker.

Three of these conceptions seem especially relevant for foreign policy analysis. The first views the decision maker as a "bounded rationalist" who seeks satisfactory rather than optimal solutions. As Herbert Simon has put it, "the capacity of the human mind for formulating and solving complex problems is very small compared with the size of the problem whose solution is required for objectively rational behavior in the real world—or even a reasonable approximation of such objective rationality."[49] Moreover, it is not practical for the decision maker to seek optimal choices; for example, because of the costs of searching for information. Related to this is the more recent concept of the individual as a "cognitive miser," one who seeks to simplify complex problems and to find shortcuts to problem solving and decision making.

Another approach is to look at the decision maker as an "error prone intuitive scientist" who is likely to commit a broad range of inferential mistakes. Thus, rather than emphasizing the limits on search, information processing, and the like, this conception views the decision maker as the victim of flawed heuristics or decision rules who uses data poorly. There are tendencies to underuse rate data in making judgments, believe in the "law of small numbers," underuse diagnostic information, overweight low probabilities and underweight high ones, and violate other requirements of consistency and coherence. These deviations from classical decision theory are traced to the psychological principles that govern perceptions of problems and evaluations of options.[50]

The final perspective I will mention emphasizes the forces that dominate the policymaker, forces that will not or cannot be controlled.[51] Decision makers are not merely rational calculators; important decisions generate conflict, and a reluctance to make irrevocable choices often results in behavior that reduces the quality of decisions. These models direct the analyst's attention to policymakers' belief systems, images of relevant actors, perceptions, information-processing strategies, heuristics, certain personality traits (ability to tolerate ambiguity, cognitive complexity, etc.), and their impact on decision-making performance.

Despite this diversity of perspectives and the difficulty of choosing between cognitive and motivational models, there has been some convergence on several types of constraints that may affect decision processes.[52] One involves the consequences of efforts to achieve cognitive consistency on perceptions and information processing. Several kinds of systematic bias have been identified in both experimental and historical studies. Policymakers have a propensity to assimilate and interpret information in ways that conform to rather than challenge existing beliefs, preferences, hopes, and expectations. Frequently they deny the need to confront tradeoffs between values by persuading themselves that an option will satisfy all of them. And, finally, they indulge in rationalizations to bolster the selected option while denigrating those that were not selected.

An extensive literature on styles of attribution has revealed several types of systematic bias in causal analysis. Perhaps the most important for foreign policy analysis is the basic attribution error—a tendency to explain the adversary's behavior in terms of his characteristics (for example, inherent aggressiveness or hostility) rather than in terms of the context or situation, while attributing one's own behavior to the latter (for example, legitimate security needs arising from a dangerous and uncertain environment) rather than to the former. A somewhat related type of double standard has been noted by George Kennan: "Now is it our view that we should take account only of their [Soviet] capabilities, disregarding their intentions, but we should expect them to take account only for our supposed intentions, disregarding our capabilities?"[53]

Analysts also have illustrated the important effect on decisions of policymakers' assumptions about order and predictability in the environment. Whereas a policymaker may have an acute appreciation of the disorderly environment in which he or she operates (arising, for example, from domestic political processes), there is a tendency to assume that others, especially adversaries, are free of such constraints. Graham T. Allison, Robert Jervis, and others have demonstrated that decision makers tend to believe that the realist "unitary rational actor" is the appropriate representation of the opponent's decision processes and, thus, whatever happens is the direct result of deliberate choices. For example, the hypothesis that the Soviet destruction of KAL flight 007 may have resulted from intelligence failures or bureaucratic foulups, rather than from a calculated decision to murder civilian passengers, was either not given serious consideration or it was suppressed for strategic reasons.[54]

Drawing upon a very substantial experimental literature, several models linking crisis-induced stress to decision processes have been developed and used in foreign policy studies.[55] Irving L. Janis and Leon Mann have developed a more general conflict-theory model which conceives of man as a "reluctant decisionmaker" and focuses upon "when, how and why psychological stress generated by decisional conflict imposes limitations on the rationality of a person's decisions."[56] One may employ five strategies for coping with a situation requiring a decision: unconflicted adherence to existing policy, unconflicted change, defensive avoidance, hypervigilance, and vigilant decision making. The first four strategies are likely to yield low-quality decisions owing to an incomplete search for information, appraisal of the situation and options, and contingency planning, whereas the vigilant decision making characterized by a more adequate performance of vital tasks is more likely to result in a high-quality choice. The factors that will affect the employment of decision styles are information about risks, expectations of finding a better option, and time for adequate search and deliberation.

A final approach we should consider attempts to show the impact of personal traits on decision making. There is no shortage of typologies that are intended to link leadership traits to decision-making behavior, but systematic research demonstrating such links is in much shorter supply. Still, some efforts have borne fruit. Margaret G. Hermann has developed a scheme for analyzing leaders' public statements of unquestioned authorship for eight variables: nationalism, belief in one's ability to control the environment, need for power, need for affiliation, ability to differentiate environments, distrust of others, self-confidence, and task emphasis. The scheme has been tested with impressive results on a broad range of contemporary leaders.[57] Alexander L. George has reformulated Nathan Leites's concept of "operational code" into five philosophical and five instrumental beliefs that are intended to describe politically relevant core beliefs, stimulating a number of empirical studies and, more recently, further significant conceptual revisions.[58] Finally, several psychologists have developed and tested the concept of "integrative complexity," defined as the ability to make subtle distinction along multiple dimensions, flexibility, and the integration of large amounts of diverse information to make coherent judgments.[59] A standard content-analysis technique has been used for research on documentary materials generated by top decision makers in a wide range of international crises, including World War I, Cuba (1962), Morocco (1911), Berlin (1948–49 and 1961), Korea, and the Middle East wars of 1948, 1956, 1967, and 1973.[60]

Decision-making approaches clearly permit the analyst to overcome many limitations of the systemic models described earlier, but not without costs. The three decision-making models described here impose increasingly heavy data burdens on the analyst. Moreover, there is a danger that adding levels of analysis may result in an undisciplined proliferation of categories and variables with at least two adverse consequences: it may become increasingly difficult to determine which are more or less important; and ad hoc explanations for individual cases erode the possibilities for broader generalizations across cases. However, several well-designed, multicase, decision-making studies indicate that these and other traps are not unavoidable.[61]

The study of international relations and foreign policy has always been a somewhat eclectic undertaking, with extensive borrowing from disciplines other than political science and history.[62] At the most general level, the primary differences today tend to be between two broad approaches. Analysts of the first school focus on the structure of the international system, often borrowing from economics for models, analogies, insights, and metaphors, with an emphasis on *rational preferences and strategy* and how these tend to be shaped and constrained by the structure of the international system. Decision-making analysts, meanwhile, display a concern for domestic political processes and tend to borrow from social psychology and psychology in order to understand better the *limits and barriers* to information processing and rational choice.

At the risk of ending on a platitude, it seems clear that for many purposes both approaches are necessary and neither is sufficient. Neglect of the system structure and its constraints may result in analyses that depict policymakers as relatively free agents with an almost unrestricted menu of choices, limited only by the scope of their ambitions and the resources at their disposal. At worst, this type of analysis can degenerate into Manichean explanations that depict foreign policies of the "bad guys" as the external manifestation of inherently flawed leaders or domestic structures, whereas the "good guys" only react from necessity. Radical right explanations of the Cold War often depict Soviet foreign policies as driven by inherently aggressive totalitarian communism and the United States as its blameless victim; radical left explanations tend to be structurally similar, with the roles of aggressor and victim reversed.[63]

Conversely, neglect of foreign policy decision making not only leaves one unable to explain the dynamics of international relations, but many important aspects of a nation's external behavior will be inexplicable. Advocates of the realist model have often argued its superiority for understanding the "high" politics of deterrence, containment, alliances, crises, and wars, if not necessarily for "low" politics. But there are several rejoinders to this line of reasoning. First, the low politics of trade, currencies, and other issues that are almost always highly sensitive to domestic pressures are becoming an increasingly important element of international relations. Second, the growing literature on the putative domain *par excellence* of realism, including deterrence, crises, and wars, raises substantial doubts about the universal validity of the realist model even for these issues.[64] Finally, exclusive reliance on realist models and their assumptions of rationality may lead to unwarranted complacency about dangers in the international system. Nuclear weapons and other features of the system have no doubt contributed to the "long peace" between major powers.[65] At the same time, however, a narrow focus on power balances, "correlations of forces," and other features of the international system will result in neglect of dangers—for example, the command, communication, control, intelligence problem or inadequate information processing—that can only be identified and analyzed by a decision-making perspective.[66]

At a very general level, this conclusion parallels that drawn three decades ago by the foremost contemporary proponent of modern realism: the "third image" (system structure) is necessary for understanding the context of international behavior, whereas the first and second images (decision makers and domestic political processes) are needed to understand dynamics within the system.[67] But to acknowledge the existence of various levels of analysis is not enough. *What* the investigator wants to explain and the *level of specificity and comprehensiveness* to be sought should determine which level(s) of analysis are relevant and necessary. In this connection, it is essential to distinguish two different dependent variables: foreign policy decisions by states, on the one hand, and the outcomes of policy and interactions between two or more states, on the other. If the goal is to understand the former—foreign policy decisions—Harold and Margaret Sprout's notion of "psychological milieu" is relevant and sufficient; that is, the objective structural variables influence the decisions via the decision maker's perception and evaluation of those "outside" variables.[68] However, if the goal is to explain outcomes, the "psychological milieu" is quite inadequate; the objective factors, if misperceived or misjudged by the decision maker, will influence the outcome. Political scientists studying international relations are increasingly disciplining their use of multiple levels of analysis in studying outcomes that cannot be adequately explained via only a single level of analysis.[69]

Which of these models and approaches are likely to be of interest and utility to the diplomatic historian? Clearly there is no one answer; political scientists are unable to agree on a single multilevel approach to international relations and foreign policy; thus they are hardly in a position to offer a single recommendation to historians. In the absence of the often-sought but always-elusive unified theory of human behavior that could provide a model for all seasons and all reasons, one must ask at least one further question: A model for what purpose? For example, in some circumstances, such as research on major international crises, it may be important to obtain systematic evidence on the beliefs and other intellectual baggage that key policymakers bring to their deliberations. Some of the approaches described above should prove very helpful in this respect. Conversely, there are many other research problems for which the historian would quite properly decide that this type of analysis requires far more effort than could possibly be justified by the benefits to be gained.

Of the systemic approaches described here, little needs to be said about classical realism because its main features, as well as its strengths and weaknesses, are familiar to most diplomatic historians. Those who focus on security issues can hardly neglect its central premises and concepts. On the other hand, modern or structural realism of the Waltz variety is likely to have rather limited appeal to historians, especially if they take seriously his doubts about being able to incorporate foreign policy into it. It may perhaps serve to raise consciousness about the importance of the systemic context within which international relations take place, but that may not be a major gain—after all, such concepts as "balance of power" have long been a standard part of the diplomatic historian's vocabulary. Gilpin's richer approach, which employs both system- and state-level variables to explain international dynamics, may well have greater appeal. It has already been noted that there are some interesting parallels between Gilpin's *War and Change in World Politics* and Paul Kennedy's recent *The Rise and Fall of the Great Powers*.

The Global-Society/Complex-Interdependence models will be helpful to historians with an interest in evolution of the international system and with the growing disjuncture between demands on states and their ability to meet them—the "sovereignty gap." One need not be very venturesome to predict that this gap will grow rather than narrow in the future. Historians of all kinds of international and transnational organizations are also likely to find useful concepts and insights in these models.

It is much less clear that the Marxist/World-System/Dependency models will provide useful new insights to historians. They will no doubt continue to be employed, but for reasons other than demonstrated empirical utility. If one has difficulty in accepting certain assumptions as *true by definition*—for example, that there has been and is today a single "world capitalist system"—then the kinds of analyses that follow are likely to seem seriously flawed. Most diplomatic historians also would have difficulty in accepting models that relegate the state to a secondary role. Until proponents of these models demonstrate a greater willingness to test them against a broader range of cases, including East-South and East-East relations, their applicability would appear to be limited at best. Finally, whereas proponents of GS/CI models can point with considerable justification to current events and trends that would appear to make them more rather than less relevant in the future, supporters of the M/WS/D models have a much more difficult task in this respect.

Although the three decision-making models sometimes include jargon that may be jarring to the historian, many of the underlying concepts are familiar. Much of diplomatic history has traditionally focused on the decisions, actions, and interactions of national leaders who operate in group contexts, such as cabinets or ad hoc advisory groups, and who draw upon the resources of such bureaucracies as foreign and defense ministries or the armed forces. The three types of models described above typically draw heavily upon psychology, social psychology, organizational theory, and other social sciences; thus for the historian they open some important windows to highly relevant developments in these fields. For example, theories and concepts of "information processing" by individuals, groups, and organizations should prove very useful to diplomatic historians.

Decision-making models may also appeal to diplomatic historians for another important reason. Political scientists who are accustomed to working with fairly accessible information such as figures on gross national products, defense budgets, battle casualties, alliance commitments, United Nations votes, trade and investments, and the like, often feel that the data requirements of decision-making models are excessive. This is precisely the area in which the historian has a decided comparative advantage, for the relevant data are usually to be found in the paper trails—more recently, also in the electronic trails—left by policymakers, and they are most likely to be unearthed by archival research. Thus, perhaps the appropriate point on which to conclude this essay is to reverse the question posed earlier: Ask not only what can the political scientist contribute to the diplomatic historian but ask also what can the diplomatic historian contribute to the political scientist. At the very least political scientists could learn a great deal about the validity of their own models if historians would use them and offer critical assessments of their strengths and limitations.

NOTES

1. See, for example, John Lewis Gaddis, "Expanding the Data Base: Historians, Political Scientists, and the Enrichment of Security Studies," *International Security* 12 (Summer 1987):3–21; John English, "The Second Time Around: Political Scientists Writing History," *Canadian Historical Review* 57 (March 1986):1–16; Jack S. Levy, "Domestic Politics and War," *Journal of Interdisciplinary History* 18 (Spring 1988):653–73; Joseph S. Nye, Jr., "International Security Studies," in *American Defense Annual, 1988–1989*, ed. Joseph Kruzel (Lexington, MA, 1988), 231–43; Deborah Larson, *Origins of Containment: A Psychological Explanation* (Princeton, 1985); Timothy Lomperis, *The War Everyone Lost–And Won: America's Intervention in Viet Nam's Twin Struggles* (Washington, 1987); Barry Posen, *The Sources of Military Doctrine: France, Britain, and Germany between the World Wars* (Ithaca, 1984); Paul Gordon Lauren, ed., *Diplomacy: New Approaches to History, Theory, and Policy* (New York, 1979); and Richard R. Neustadt and Ernest R. May, *Thinking in Time: The Use of History for Decision-Makers* (New York, 1986). Many other examples could be cited.

2. Robert Gilpin, *Change and War in World Politics* (Cambridge, England, 1981).

3. Stanley Hoffmann, "An American Social Science: International Relations," *Daedalus* 106 (Summer 1977):54.

4. The British meteorologist Lewis Fry Richardson is generally regarded as the pioneer of mathematical approaches to international relations. See his *Statistics of Deadly Quarrels* (Pittsburgh, 1960); and his *Arms and Insecurity: A Mathematical Study of the Causes and Origins of War* (Chicago, 1960). These are summarized for nonmathematicians in Anatol Rapport, "L. F. Richardson's Mathematical Theory of War," *Journal of Conflict Resolution* 1 (September 1957):249–99. For a more recent effort see Bruce Bueno de Mesquita, *The War Trap* (New Haven, 1981); and idem, "The War Trap Revisited: A Revised Expected Utility Model," *American Political Science Review* 79 (March 1985):156–77.

5. Among the works that best represent their realist perspectives are E. H. Carr, *Twenty Years' Crisis* (London, 1939); Nicholas Spykman, *America's Strategy in World Politics: The United States and Balance of Power* (New York, 1942); Hans J. Morgenthau, *Politics among Nations: The Struggle for Power and Peace,* 5th ed. (New York, 1973); John Herz, *International Politics in the Atomic Age* (New York, 1959); Hedley Bull, *The Anarchical Society: A Study of Order in World Politics* (London, 1977); Raymond Aron, *Peace and War* (Garden City, NY, 1966); Martin Wight, "The Balance of Power and International Order," in *The Bases of International Order: Essays in Honor of C. A. W. Manning,* ed. Alan James (London, 1973); Arnold Wolfers, *Discord and Collaboration* (Baltimore, 1962); Norman A. Graebner, *America as a World Power: A Realist Appraisal from Wilson to Reagan* (Wilmington, DE, 1984); George F. Kennan, *American Diplomacy, 1900–1950* (Chicago, 1951); Walter Lippmann, *U.S. Foreign Policy: Shield of the Republic* (Boston, 1943); and Reinhold Niebuhr, *The Children of Light and the Children of Darkness* (New York, 1945).

6. For useful comparisons of realism and liberalism see Joseph Grieco, "Anarchy and the Limits of Cooperation: A Realist Critique of the Newest Liberal Institutionalism," *International Organization* 42 (Summer 1988):485–507; and Joseph S. Nye, Jr., "Neorealism and Neoliberalism," *World Politics* 40 (January 1988):235–51.

7. Morgenthau, *Politics,* 7, 5.

8. Stephen D. Krasner, *Defending the National Interest: Raw Materials Investment and U.S. Foreign Policy* (Princeton, 1978), 33. Krasner's study compares realist, interest-group liberal, and Marxist theories.

9. Inis L. Claude, *Power and International Relations* (New York, 1962); James S. Rosenau, "National Interest," *International Encyclopedia of the Social Sciences,* vol. 11 (New York, 1968), 34–40; Alexander L. George and Robert Keohane, "The Concept of National Interests: Uses and Limitations," in *Presidential Decision-Making in Foreign Policy: The Effective Use of Information and Advice,* ed. Alexander George (Boulder, 1980); Ernst B. Haas, "The Balance of Power: Prescription, Concept, or Propaganda?" *World Politics* 5 (July 1953):442–77; Dina A. Zinnes, "An Analytical Study of the Balance of Power," *Journal of Peace Research* 4, no. 3 (1967):270–88.

10. Morgenthau, *Politics,* 5.

11. Richard K. Ashley, "The Poverty of Neorealism," *International Organization* 38 (Spring 1984):225–86.

12. Morton Kaplan, *System and Process in International Politics* (New York, 1957).

13. Richard Rosecrance, *Action and Reaction in International Politics* (Boston, 1963); idem, "Bipolarity, Multipolarity, and the Future," *Journal of Conflict Resolution* 10 (September 1966): 314–27; Kenneth Waltz, "The Stability of a Bipolar World," *Daedalus* 93 (Summer 1964):881–909; J. David Singer, "Inter-Nation Influence: A Formal Model," *American Political Science Review* 57 (June 1963):420–30; Bruce M. Rus-

sett, "Toward a Model of Competitive International Politics," *Journal of Politics* 25 (May 1963):226–47; Karl W. Deutsch and J. David Singer, "Multipolar Power Systems and International Stability," *World Politics* 16 (April 1964):390–406; Andrew Scott, *The Functioning of the International Political System* (New York, 1967).

14. Kenneth Waltz, *Theory of International Politics* (Reading, MA, 1979); idem, *Man, the State, and War* (New York, 1959).

15. Because Waltz strives for a universal theory that is not limited to any era, he uses the term "unit" to refer to the constituent members of the system. In the contemporary system these are states, but in order to reflect Waltz's intent more faithfully, the term "unit" is used here.

16. Waltz, *Theory*, 82–101.

17. Waltz, "The Myth of National Interdependence," in *The International Corporation*, ed. Charles P. Kindleberger (Cambridge, MA, 1970); Waltz, "The Spread of Nuclear Weapons: More May Be Better," *Adelphi Papers*, no. 171 (1981).

18. Joseph M. Grieco, *Cooperation Among Nations: Europe, America, and Non-Tariff Barriers to Trade* (Ithaca: Cornell University Press, 1990); Stephen M. Walt, *The Origin of Alliances* (Ithaca, 1987). The best single source for the various dimensions of the debate is Robert Keohane, ed., *Neorealism and Its Critics* (New York, 1986).

19. Ashley, "Poverty," 228.

20. I am grateful to Alexander George for this example.

21. Gilpin, *War and Change*, 10–11.

22. *Ibid.*, Chap. 4. Gilpin's thesis appears similar in a number of respects to Paul Kennedy, *The Rise and Fall of the Great Powers: Economic Change and Military Conflict from 1500 to 2000* (New York, 1987).

23. Robert Keohane and Joseph S. Nye, Jr., *Power and Interdependence: World Politics in Transition* (Boston, 1977); Edward Morse, *Modernization and the Transformation of International Relations* (New York, 1967); James N. Rosenau, *The Study of Global Interdependence* (London, 1980); Richard Mansbach and John Vasquez, *In Search of Theory: A New Paradigm for Global Politics* (New York, 1981); Andrew M. Scott, *The Dynamics of Interdependence* (Chapel Hill, 1982); James N. Rosenau, *Turbulence in World Politics: A Theory of Change and Continuity* (Princeton: Princeton University Press, 1990).

24. Rosenau, "National Interest," 39. A more recent statement of this view may be found in Richard Rosecrance, *The Rise of the Trading State* (New York, 1986). See also John H. Herz, "The Rise and Demise of the Territorial State," *World Politics* 9 (July 1957): 473–93; and his reconsideration in "The Territorial State Revisited: Reflections on the Future of the Nation-State," *Polity* 1 (Fall 1968):12–34.

25. Joseph Grieco, *Between Dependence and Autonomy: India's Experience with the International Computer Industry* (Berkeley, 1984); Gary Gereffi, *The Pharmaceutical Industry and Dependency in the Third World* (Princeton, 1983).

26. John Galtung, "A Structural Theory of Imperialism," *Journal of Peace Research* 8, no. 2 (1971):81–117; James Cockroft, André Gunder Frank, and Dale L. Johnson, *Dependence and Under-Development* (New York, 1972); Immanuel Wallerstein, *The Modern World-System* (New York, 1974); idem, "The Rise and Future Demise of the World Capitalist System: Concepts for Comparative Analysis," *Comparative Studies in Society and History* 16 (September 1974):387–415; Christopher Chase-Dunn, "Comparative Research on World System Characteristics," *International Studies Quarterly* 23 (December 1979):601–23; idem, "Interstate System and Capitalist World Economy: One Logic or Two?" *ibid.* 25 (March 1981): 19–42; J. Kubalkova and A. A. Cruickshank, *Marxism and International Relations* (Oxford, 1985). Debates among advocates of these models are illustrated in Robert A. Denemark and Kenneth O. Thomas, "The Brenner-Wallerstein Debates," *International Studies Quarterly* 32 (March 1988):47–66.

27. Wallerstein, "Rise and Future Demise," 390.
28. Tony Smith, "The Underdevelopment of Development Literature: The Case of Dependency Theory," *World Politics* 31 (January 1979):247–88; Aristide R. Zolberg, "Origins of the Modern World System," *ibid.* 33 (January 1981):253–81.
29. Wallerstein, "Rise and Future Demise," 401.
30. *Ibid.,* 412 (emphasis added).
31. Richard C. Snyder, H. W. Bruck, and Burton Sapin, eds., *Foreign Policy Decision-Making* (New York, 1962).
32. There are also models that link types of polities with foreign policy. Two of the more prominent twentieth-century versions—the Leninist and Wilsonian—have been effectively criticized by Waltz in *Man, the State, and War.* Although space limitations preclude a discussion here, for some recent and interesting research along these lines see, among others, Rudolph J. Rummel, "Libertarianism and International Violence," *Journal of Conflict Resolution* 27 (March 1983):27–71; Michael Doyle, "Liberalism and World Politics," *American Political Science Review* 80 (December 1986):1151–70; and Doyle, "Kant, Liberal Legacies, and Foreign Affairs," *Philosophy and Public Affairs* 12 (Winter 1983):205–35.
33. Chester Barnard, *Functions of the Executive* (Cambridge, MA, 1938); Herbert Simon, *Administrative Behavior: A Study of Decision-Making Processes in Administrative Organization* (New York, 1957); James G. March and Herbert Simon, *Organizations* (New York, 1958).
34. Harold Wilensky, *Organizational Intelligence: Knowledge and Policy in Government and Industry* (New York, 1967).
35. Henry A. Kissinger, "Domestic Structure and Foreign Policy," *Daedalus* 95 (Spring 1966):503–29; Graham T. Allison, *Essence of Decision: Explaining the Cuban Missile Crisis* (Boston, 1971); Graham T. Allison and Morton Halperin, "Bureaucratic Politics: A Paradigm and Some Policy Implications," *World Politics* 24 (Supplement 1972): 40–79; Morton Halperin, *Bureaucratic Politics and Foreign Policy* (Washington, 1974).
36. The literature is huge. See, for example, Samuel R. Williamson, Jr., *The Politics of Grand Strategy: Britain and France Prepare for War, 1904–1914* (Cambridge, MA, 1969); Paul Gordon Lauren, *Diplomats and Bureaucrats: The First Institutional Responses to Twentieth-Century Diplomacy in France and Germany* (Stanford, 1975); and Posen, *Sources of Military Doctrine.*
37. Wilensky, *Organizational Intelligence;* Theodore J. Lowi, *The End of Liberalism: Ideology, Policy, and the Crisis of Public Authority* (New York, 1969); Sidney Verba, "Assumptions of Rationality and Non-Rationality in Models of the International System," *World Politics* 14 (October 1961):93–117.
38. Charles F. Hermann, "Some Consequences of Crises which Limit the Viability of Organizations," *Administrative Science Quarterly* 8 (June 1963):61–82; Allison, *Essence;* Richard Neustadt, *Alliance Politics* (New York, 1970); Scott Sagan, "Nuclear Alerts and Crisis Management," *International Security* 9 (Spring 1985):99–139.
39. Robert Rothstein, *Planning, Prediction, and Policy-Making in Foreign Affairs: Theory and Practice* (Boston, 1972); Stephen D. Krasner, "Are Bureaucracies Important? (Or Allison Wonderland)" *Foreign Policy* 7 (Summer 1972):159–70; Robert J. Art, "Bureaucratic Politics and American Foreign Policy: A Critique," *Policy Sciences* 4 (December 1973):467–90; Desmond J. Ball, "The Blind Men and the Elephant: A Critique of Bureaucratic Politics Theory," *Australian Outlook* 28 (April 1974):71–92; Amos Perlmutter, "Presidential Political Center and Foreign Policy: A Critique of the Revisionist and Bureaucratic-Political Orientations," *World Politics* 27 (October 1974):87–106.
40. Alexander L. George, "The Case for Multiple Advocacy in Making Foreign Policy," *American Political Science Review* 66 (September 1972):751–85, 791–95.

41. David A. Welch and James G. Blight, "The Eleventh Hour of the Cuban Missile Crisis: An Introduction to the ExComm Transcripts," *International Security* 12 (Winter 1987/88):5–29; McGeorge Bundy and James G. Blight, "October 27, 1962: Transcripts of the Meetings of the ExComm," *ibid.*, 30–92.

42. Joseph de Rivera, *The Psychological Dimension of Foreign Policy* (Columbus, OH, 1968); Glenn D. Paige, *The Korean Decision, June 24–30, 1950* (New York, 1968); Irving L. Janis, *Victims of Groupthink: A Psychological Study of Foreign Policy Decisions and Fiascos* (Boston, 1972); idem, *Groupthink: Psychological Studies of Policy Decisions and Fiascos* (Boston, 1982); Margaret G. Hermann, Charles F. Hermann, and Joe D. Hagan, "How Decision Units Shape Foreign Policy Behavior," in *New Directions in the Study of Foreign Policy*, ed. Charles F. Hermann, Charles W. Kegley, and James N. Rosenau (London, 1987); Charles F. Hermann and Margaret Hermann, "Who Makes Foreign Policy Decisions and How: An Initial Test of a Model" (Paper presented at the annual meeting of the American Political Science Association, Chicago, 1987); Philip D. Stewart, Margaret G. Hermann, and Charles F. Hermann, "The Politburo and Foreign Policy: Toward a Model of Soviet Decision Making" (Paper presented at the annual meeting of the International Society of Political Psychology, Amsterdam, 1986).

43. Leon Festinger, "A Theory of Social Comparison Processes," and Solomon Asch, "Opinions and Social Pressure," in *Small Groups: Studies in Social Interaction*, ed. A. Paul Hare, Edgar F. Borgatta, and Robert F. Bales (New York, 1965); Asch, "Effects of Group Pressures upon Modification and Distortion of Judgment," in *Group Dynamics: Research and Theory*, ed. Dorwin Cartwright and A. Zander (Evanston, IL, 1953).

44. Janis, *Victims;* idem, *Groupthink.* See also Philip Tetlock, "Identifying Victims of Groupthink from Public Statements of Decision Makers," *Journal of Personality and Social Psychology* 37 (August 1979):1314–24; and the critique in Lloyd Etheredge, *Can Governments Learn? American Foreign Policy and Central American Revolutions* (New York, 1985), 112–14.

45. Janis, *Groupthink,* 260–76.

46. For a review of the vast literature see Robert Abelson and A. Levi, "Decision Making and Decision Theory," in *Handbook of Social Psychology*, 3d ed., vol. 1, ed. Gardner Lindzey and Elliot Aronson (New York, 1985). The relevance of psychological models and evidence for international relations is most fully discussed in Robert Jervis, *Perception and Misperception in International Politics* (Princeton, 1976); John Steinbruner, *The Cybernetic Theory of Decision: New Dimensions of Political Analysis* (Princeton, 1974); and Robert Axelrod, ed., *The Structure of Decision: The Cognitive Maps of Political Elites* (Princeton, 1976).

47. See, for example, Harold Lasswell, *Psychopathology and Politics* (Chicago, 1931).

48. March and Simon, *Organizations,* 113.

49. Simon, *Administrative Behavior,* 198.

50. Amos Tversky and Daniel Kahneman, "The Framing of Decisions and the Psychology of Choice," *Science* 211 (30 January 1981):453–58; Kahneman and Tversky, "On the Psychology of Prediction," *Psychological Review* 80 (July 1973):237–51; Kahneman, Paul Slovic, and Tversky, *Judgment under Uncertainty: Heuristics and Biases* (Cambridge, England, 1982).

51. Irving L. Janis and Leon Mann, *Decision Making: A Psychological Analysis of Conflict, Choice, and Commitment* (New York, 1977); Miriam Steiner, "The Search for Order in a Disorderly World: Worldviews and Prescriptive Decision Paradigms," *International Organization* 37 (Summer 1983):373–414; Richard Ned Lebow, *Between Peace and War* (Baltimore, 1981).

52. Donald Kinder and J. R. Weiss, "In Lieu of Rationality: Psychological Perspectives on Foreign Policy," *Journal of Conflict Resolution* 22 (December 1978):707–35; Ole R.

Holsti, "Foreign Policy Formation Viewed Cognitively," in Axelrod, *Structure of Decision.*

53. George F. Kennan, *The Cloud of Danger: Current Realities of American Foreign Policy* (Boston, 1978), 87–88.

54. Allison, *Essence;* Jervis, *Perception;* Seymour M. Hersh, *The Target Is Destroyed: What Really Happened to Flight 007 and What America Knew about It* (New York, 1986).

55. Charles F. Hermann, *International Crises: Insights from Behavioral Research* (New York, 1972); Margaret G. Hermann and Charles F. Hermann, "Maintaining the Quality of Decision-Making in Foreign Policy Crises," in *Report of the Commission on the Organization of the Government for the Conduct of Foreign Policy,* vol. 2 (Washington, 1975); Margaret G. Hermann, "Indicators of Stress in Policy-Makers during Foreign Policy Crises," *Political Psychology* 1 (March 1979):27–46; Ole R. Holsti, *Crisis, Escalation, War* (Montreal, 1972); Ole R. Holsti and Alexander L. George, "The Effects of Stress on the Performance of Foreign Policy-Makers," *Political Science Annual,* vol. 6 (Indianapolis, 1975); Lebow, *Between Peace and War.*

56. Janis and Mann, *Decision Making,* 3.

57. Margaret G. Hermann, "Explaining Foreign Policy Behavior Using Personal Characteristics of Political Leaders," *International Studies Quarterly* 24 (March 1980):7–46; idem, "Personality and Foreign Policy Decision Making," in *Perceptions, Beliefs, and Foreign Policy Decision Making,* ed. Donald Sylvan and Steve Chan (New York, 1984).

58. Nathan Leites, *The Operational Code of the Politburo* (New York, 1951); Alexander L. George, "The 'Operational Code': A Neglected Approach to the Study of Political Leaders and Decision-Making," *International Studies Quarterly* 13 (June 1969): 190–222; Stephen G. Walker, "The Interface between Beliefs and Behavior: Henry Kissinger's Operational Code and the Vietnam War," *Journal of Conflict Resolution* 21 (March 1977):129–68; idem, "The Motivational Foundations of Political Belief Systems: A Re-Analysis of the Operational Code Construct," *International Studies Quarterly* 27 (June 1983):179–202; idem, "Parts and Wholes: American Foreign Policy Makers as 'Structured' Individuals" (Paper presented at the annual meeting of the International Society of Political Psychology, Secaucus, New Jersey, 1988).

59. Integrative simplicity, on the other hand, is characterized by simple responses, gross distinctions, rigidity, and restricted information usage.

60. Peter Suedfeld and Philip Tetlock, "Integrative Complexity of Communications in International Crises," *Journal of Conflict Resolution* 21 (March 1977):169–86; Suedfeld, Tetlock, and C. Romirez, "War, Peace, and Integrative Complexity: UN Speeches on the Middle East Problem, 1947–1976," *ibid.* (September 1977):427–42; Theodore D. Raphael, "Integrative Complexity Theory and Forecasting International Crises: Berlin 1946–1962," *ibid.* 26 (September 1982):423–50; Tetlock, "Integrative Complexity of American and Soviet Foreign Policy Rhetoric: A Time Series Analysis," *Journal of Personality and Social Psychology* 49 (December 1985):1565–85.

61. Alexander L. George and Richard Smoke, *Deterrence in American Foreign Policy: Theory and Practice* (New York, 1974); Smoke, *Escalation* (Cambridge, MA, 1977); Glenn H. Snyder and Paul Diesing, *Conflict among Nations: Bargaining, Decision Making, and System Structure in International Crises* (Princeton, 1977); Michael Brecher and Barbara Geist, *Decisions in Crisis: Israel, 1967 and 1973* (Berkeley, 1980); Lebow, *Between Peace and War.* Useful discussions on conducting theoretically relevant case studies may be found in Harry Eckstein, "Case Study and Theory in Political Science," in *Handbook of Political Science,* ed. Fred I. Greenstein and Nelson W. Polsby (Reading, MA, 1975), 7:79–138; and Alexander L. George, "Case Studies and Theory Development: The Method of Structured, Focused Comparison," in *Diplomacy: New Approaches in History, Theory, and Policy,* ed. Paul Gordon Lauren (New York, 1979), 43–68.

62. The classic overview of the field and the disciplines that have contributed to it is Quincy Wright, *The Study of International Relations* (New York, 1955).

63. Ole R. Holsti, "The Study of International Politics Makes Strange Bedfellows: Theories of the Radical Right and the Radical Left," *American Political Science Review* 68 (March 1974):217–42.

64. In addition to the literature on war, crises, and deterrence already cited see Richard Betts, *Nuclear Blackmail and Nuclear Balance* (Washington, 1987); Robert Jervis, Richard Ned Lebow, and Janice G. Stein, *Psychology and Deterrence* (Baltimore, 1985); Lebow, *Nuclear Crisis Management: A Dangerous Illusion* (Ithaca, 1987); and Ole R. Holsti, "Crisis Decision-Making," and Jack S. Levy, "The Causes of War: A Review of Theories and Evidence," in *Behavior, Society, and Nuclear War,* vol. 1, ed. Philip E. Tetlock et al. (New York, 1989).

65. John Lewis Gaddis, "The Long Peace: Elements of Stability in the Postwar International System," *International Security* 10 (Spring 1986):99–142.

66. Paul Bracken, *Command and Control of Nuclear Forces* (New Haven, 1983); Bruce Blair, *Strategic Command and Control: Redefining the Nuclear Threat* (Washington, 1985); John D. Steinbruner, "Nuclear Decapitation," *Foreign Policy* 45 (Winter 1981–82):16–28; Sagan, "Nuclear Alerts"; Alexander L. George, *Presidential Decision-Making in Foreign Policy: The Effective Use of Information and Advice* (Boulder, 1980).

67. Waltz, *Man, the State, and War,* 238.

68. Harold and Margaret Sprout, "Environmental Factors in the Study of International Politics," *Journal of Conflict Resolution* 1 (December 1957):309–28.

69. See, for example, David B. Yoffie, *Power and Protectionism: Strategies of the Newly Industrializing Countries* (New York, 1983); John Odell, *U.S. International Monetary Policy: Markets, Power, and Ideas as Sources of Change* (Princeton, 1982); Jack Snyder, *The Ideology of the Offensive: Military Decision Making and the Disaster of 1914* (Ithaca, 1984); Vinod K. Aggarwal, *Liberal Protectionism: The International Politics of Organized Textile Trade* (Berkeley, 1985); Larson, *Origins of Containment;* Posen, *Sources of Military Doctrine;* and Walt, *Alliances.*

PART Two

INTERNATIONAL SOURCES OF FOREIGN POLICY

*P*ride of place is often given to systemic explanations of foreign policy. It is here that the structural forces of the international system shape and constrain the choices of foreign policy officials. What are the characteristics of the international system, and how does the international system actually influence foreign policy? Scholars continue to debate these questions. The most consistent advocates of systemic explanations are Realist scholars who focus on the enduring competitive nature of international politics.

Kenneth Waltz produces one of the most influential Realist analyses of international politics. In this chapter from his influential book, *Theory of International Politics,* Waltz details the essential organizational characteristics of the international system—organizational characteristics he calls anarchy. Waltz insists on fundamental distinctions between the organizing principles of domestic politics and those of international politics. Domestic politics is the realm of specialization and hierarchy. International politics takes place in a self-help system with inherent limits on the level of integration and specialization. With the anarchic nature of the international system properly understood, Waltz is able to describe recurrent types of strategies that states pursue to safeguard their security. In particular, states act to promote or ensure a balance of power. Waltz does not present a theory of foreign policy; rather he argues that the anarchic system and the distribution of power produce a certain sameness in the behavior of states. The international system does not directly shape the foreign policy of states, but it does present powerful constraints and imperatives in terms of which states are likely to abide.

Mastanduno, Lake, and Ikenberry are also interested in the constraints on state action produced by the international system. But they attempt to expand the Realist perspective by looking at the impact of both international and domestic structures on state action. In their framework, the state is a "two-sided" actor, attempting to accomplish objectives in both the international and domestic realm but constrained or empowered in one arena by its position in the other. The result is a set of hypotheses that explores the types of challenges to the state and the responses that would be expected given the structural setting of the state. Mastanduno, Lake, and Ikenberry use Realist theory as a point of departure, but they attempt to expand the variety of structural conditions that influence the actions and objectives of state officials.

Melvyn Leffler is a diplomatic historian who is interested in discovering the fundamental strategic and economic factors that shaped the American concept of national security after World War II. In effect, this essay probes the actual experience of government officials who sought to interpret and respond to the emerging postwar international structure. Leffler finds American defense planners and other officials preoccupied with preserving the geopolitical balance of power in Europe and Asia but the perceived threat to that balance came less from Soviet military capability as from the communist exploitation of widespread social and economic disarray and turmoil. The essay reveals the bureaucratic and intellectual complexities that confronted postwar planners as they attempted to create and implement an American concept of national security.

Anarchic Orders and Balances of Power

Kenneth Waltz

I

1. Violence at Home and Abroad

The state among states, it is often said, conducts its affairs in the brooding shadow of violence. Because some states may at any time use force, all states must be prepared to do so—or live at the mercy of their militarily more vigorous neighbors. Among states the state of nature is a state of war. This is meant not in the sense that war constantly occurs but in the sense that with each state deciding for itself whether or not to use force, war may at any time break out. Whether in the family, the community, or the world at large, contact without at least occasional conflict is inconceivable; and the hope that in the absence of an agent to manage or to manipulate conflicting parties the use of force will always be avoided cannot be realistically entertained. Among men as among states, anarchy, or the absence of government, is associated with the occurrence of violence.

The threat of violence and the recurrent use of force are said to distinguish international from national affairs. But in the history of the world surely most rulers have had to bear in mind that their subjects might use force to resist or overthrow them. If the absence of government is associated with the threat of violence, so also is its presence. A haphazard list of national tragedies illustrates the point all too well. The most destructive wars of the hundred years following the defeat of Napoleon took place not among states but *within* them. Estimates of deaths in China's Taiping Rebellion, which began in 1851 and lasted thirteen years, range as high as twenty million. In the American Civil War some six hundred thousand people lost their lives. In more recent history, forced collectivization and Stalin's purges eliminated five million Russians, and Hitler exterminated six million Jews. In some Latin American countries coups d'état and rebellions have been normal features of national life. Between 1948 and 1957, for example, two hundred thousand Colombians were killed in civil strife. In the middle 1970s most inhabitants of Idi Amin's Uganda must have felt the lives becoming nasty, brutish, and short, quite as in Thomas Hobbes's state of nature. If such cases constitute aberrations, they are uncomfortably common ones. We easily lose sight of the fact that struggles to achieve and maintain power, to establish order, and to contrive a kind of justice within states may be bloodier than wars among them.

If anarchy is identified with chaos, destruction, and death, then the distinction between anarchy and government does not tell us much. Which is more precarious: the life of a state among states, or of a government in relation to its subjects? The answer varies with time and place. Among some states at some times, the actual or expected occurrence of violence is low. Within some states at some times, the actual or expected occurrence of violence is high. The use of force or the constant fear of its use are not sufficient grounds for distinguishing international from domestic affairs. If the possible and the actual use of force mark both national and international orders, then no durable distinction between the two realms can be drawn in terms of the use or the nonuse of force. No human order is proof against violence.

To discover qualitative differences between internal and external affairs one must look for a criterion other than the occurrence of violence. The distinction between international and national realms of politics is not found in the use or the nonuse of force but in their different structures. But if the dangers of being violently attacked are greater, say, in taking an evening stroll through downtown Detroit than they are in picnicking along the French and German border, what practical difference does the difference of structure make? Nationally as internationally, contact generates conflict and at times issues in violence. The difference between national and international politics lies not in the use of force but in the different modes of organization for doing something about it. A government, ruling by some standard of legitimacy, arrogates to itself the right to use force—that is, to apply a variety of sanctions to control the use of force by its subjects. If some use private force, others may appeal to the government. A government has no monopoly on the use of force, as is all too evident. An effective government, however, has a monopoly on the *legitimate* use of force, and legitimate here means that public agents are organized to prevent and to counter the private use of force. Citizens need not prepare to defend themselves. Public agencies do that. A national system is not one of self-help. The international system is.

2. Interdependence and Integration

The political significance of interdependence varies depending on whether a realm is organized, with relations of authority specified and established, or remains formally unorganized. Insofar as a realm is formally organized, its units are free to specialize, to pursue their own interests without concern for developing the means of maintaining their identity and preserving their security in the presence of others. They are free to specialize because they have no reason to fear the increased interdependence that goes with specialization. If those who specialize most benefit most, then competition in specialization ensues. Goods are manufactured, grain is produced, law and order are maintained, commerce is conducted, and financial services are provided by people who ever more narrowly specialize. In simple economic terms the cobbler depends on the tailor for his pants and the tailor on the cobbler for his shoes, and each would be ill-clad without the services of the other. In simple political terms Kansas depends on Washington for protection and regulation and Washington depends on Kansas for beef and wheat. In saying that in such situations interdependence is close, one need not maintain that the one part could not learn to live without the other. One need only say that the cost of breaking the interdependent relation would be high. Persons and institutions depend heavily on one another because of the different tasks they perform and the different goods they produce and exchange. The parts of a polity bind themselves together by their differences.[1]

Differences between national and international structures are reflected in the ways the units of each system define their ends and develop the means for reaching them. In anarchic realms like units coact. In hierarchic realms unlike units interact. In an anarchic realm, the units are functionally similar and tend to remain so. Like units work to maintain a measure of independence and may even strive for autarchy. In a hierarchic realm the units are differentiated and they tend to increase the extent of their specialization. Differentiated units become closely interdependent, the more closely so as their specialization proceeds. Because of the difference of structure, interdependence within and interdependence among nations are two distinct concepts. So as to follow the logicians' admonition to keep a single meaning for a given term throughout one's discourse, I shall use *integration* to describe the condition within nations and *interdependence* to describe the condition among them.

Although states are like units functionally, they differ vastly in their capabilities. Out of such differences something of a division of labor develops. The division of labor across nations, however, is slight in comparison with the highly articulated division of labor within them. Integration draws the parts of a nation closely together. Interdependence among nations leaves them loosely connected. Although the integration of nations is often talked about, it seldom takes place. Nations could mutually enrich themselves by further dividing not just the labor that goes into the production of goods but also some of the other tasks they perform, such as political management and military defense. Why does their integration not take place? The structure of international politics limits the cooperation of states in two ways.

In a self-help system each of the units spends a portion of its effort, not in forwarding its own good, but in providing the means of protecting itself against others. Specialization in a system of divided labor works to everyone's advantage, though not equally so. Inequality in the expected distribution of the increased product works strongly against extension of the division of labor internationally. When faced with the possibility of cooperating for mutual gain, states that feel insecure must ask how the gain will be divided. They are compelled to ask not "Will both of us gain?" but "Who will gain more?" If an expected gain is to be divided, say, in the ratio of two to one, one state may use its disproportionate gain to implement a policy intended to damage or destroy the other. Even the prospect of large absolute gains for both parties does not elicit their cooperation so long as each fears how the other will use its increased capabilities. Notice that the impediments to collaboration may not lie in the character and the immediate intention of either party. Instead, the condition of insecurity—at the least the uncertainty of each about the other's future intentions and actions—works against their cooperation.

In any self-help system, units worry about their survival, and the worry conditions their behavior. Oligopolistic markets limit the cooperation of firms in much the way that international political structures limit the cooperation of states. Within rules laid down by governments, whether firms survive and prosper depends on their own efforts. Firms need not protect themselves physically against assaults from other firms. They are free to concentrate on their economic interests. As economic entities, however, they live in a self-help world. All want to increase profits. If they run undue risks in the effort to do so, they must expect to suffer the consequences. As William Fellner[2] says, it is "impossible to maximize joint gains without the collusive handling of all relevant variables." And this can be accomplished only by "complete disarmament of the firms in relation to each other." But firms cannot sensibly disarm even to increase their profits. This statement qualifies rather than contradicts the assumption that firms aim at maximum profits. To maximize profits tomorrow as well as today, firms first have to survive. Pooling all resources implies, again as Fellner puts it, "discounting the future possibilities of all participating firms." But the future cannot be discounted. The relative strength of firms changes over time in ways that cannot be foreseen. Firms are constrained to strike a compromise between maximizing their profits and minimizing the danger of their own demise. Each of two firms may be better off if one of them accepts compensation from the other in return for withdrawing from some part of the market. But a firm that accepts smaller markets in exchange for larger profits will be gravely disadvantaged if, for example, a price war should break out as part of a renewed struggle for markets. If possible, one must resist accepting smaller markets in return for larger profits. "It is," Fellner insists, "not advisable to disarm in relation to one's rivals." Why not? Because "the potentiality of renewed warfare always exists." Fellner's reasoning is much like the reasoning that led Lenin to believe that capitalist countries would never be able to cooperate for their mutual enrichment in one vast imperialist enterprise. Like nations, oligopolistic firms must be more concerned with relative strength than with absolute advantage.

A state worries about a division of possible gains that may favor others more than itself. That is the first way in which the structure of international politics limits the cooperation of states. A state also worries lest it become dependent on others through cooperative endeavors and exchanges of goods and services. That is the second way in which the structure of international politics limits the cooperation of states. The more a state specializes, the more it relies on others to supply the materials and goods that it is not producing. The larger a state's imports and exports, the more it depends on others. The world's well-being would be increased if an ever more elaborate division of labor were developed, but states would thereby place themselves in situations of ever closer interdependence. Some states may not resist that. For small and ill-endowed states the costs of doing so are excessively high. But states that can resist becoming ever more enmeshed with others ordinarily do so in either or both of two ways. States that are heavily dependent or closely interdependent worry about securing that which they depend on. The high interdependence of states means that the states in question experience or are subject to the common vulnerability that high interdependence entails. Like other organizations, states seek to control what they depend on or to lessen the extent of their dependency. This simple thought explains quite a bit of the behavior of states: their imperial thrusts to widen the scope of their control and their autarchic strivings toward greater self-sufficiency.

Structures encourage certain behaviors and penalize those who do not respond to the encouragement. Nationally, many lament the extreme development of the division of labor, a development that results in the allocation of ever narrower tasks to individuals. And yet specialization proceeds, and its extent is a measure of the development of societies. In a formally organized realm a premium is put on each unit's being able to specialize in order to increase its value to others in a system of divided labor. The domestic imperative is "specialize!" Internationally, many lament the resources states spend unproductively for their own defense and the opportunities they miss to enhance the welfare of their people through cooperation with other states. And yet the ways of states change little. In an unorganized realm each unit's incentive is to put itself in a position to be able to take care of itself, since no one else can be counted on to do so. The international imperative is "take care of yourself!" Some leaders of nations may understand that the well-being of all of them would increase through their participation in a fuller division of labor. But to act on the idea would be to act on a domestic imperative, an imperative that does not run internationally. What one might want to do in the absence of structural constraints is different from what one is encouraged to do in their presence. States do not willingly place themselves in situations of increased dependence. In a self-help system considerations of security subordinate economic gain to political interest.

What each state does for itself is much like what all of the others are doing. They are denied the advantages that a full division of labor, political as well as economic, would provide. Defense spending, moreover, is unproductive for all and unavoidable for most. Rather than increased well-being, their reward is in the maintenance of their autonomy. States compete, but not by contributing their individual efforts to the joint production of goods for their mutual benefit. Here is a second big difference between international-political and economic systems.

3. Structures and Strategies

That motives and outcomes may well be disjoined should now be easily seen. Structures cause actions to have consequences they were not intended to have. Surely most of the actors will notice that, and at least some of them will be able to figure out why. They may develop a pretty good sense of just how structures work their effects. Will they not then be able to achieve their original ends by appropriately adjusting their strategies? Unfortunately, they often cannot. To show why this is so I shall give only a few examples; once the point is made, the reader will easily think of others.

If shortage of a commodity is expected, all are collectively better off if they buy less of it in order to moderate price increases and to distribute shortages equitably. But because some will be better off if they lay in extra supplies quickly, all have a strong incentive to do so. If one expects others to make a run on a bank, one's prudent course is to run faster than they do even while knowing that if few others run, the bank will remain solvent, and if many run, it will fail. In such cases pursuit of individual interest produces collective results that nobody wants, yet individuals by behaving differently will hurt themselves without altering outcomes. These two much-used examples establish the main point. Some courses of action I cannot sensibly follow unless you do too, and you and I cannot sensibly follow them unless we are pretty sure that many others will as well. Let us go more deeply into the problem by considering two further examples in some detail.

Each of many persons may choose to drive a private car rather than take a train. Cars offer flexibility in scheduling and in choice of destination; yet at times, in bad weather for example, railway passenger service is a much-wanted convenience. Each of many persons may shop in supermarkets rather than at corner grocery stores. The stocks of supermarkets are larger, and their prices lower; yet at times the corner grocery store, offering, say, credit and delivery service, is a much-wanted convenience. The result of most people usually driving their own cars and shopping at supermarkets is to reduce passenger service and to decrease the number of corner grocery stores. These results may not be what most people want. They may be willing to pay to prevent services from disappearing. And yet individuals can do nothing to affect the outcomes. Increased patronage *would* do it, but not increased patronage by me and the few others I might persuade to follow my example.

We may well notice that our behavior produces unwanted outcomes, but we are also likely to see that such instances as these are examples of what Alfred E. Kahn describes as large changes that are brought about by the accumulation of small decisions. In such situations people are victims of the "tyranny of small decisions," a phrase suggesting that "if one hundred consumers choose option x, and this causes the market to make decision X (where X equals $100\,x$), it is not necessarily true that those same consumers would have voted for that outcome if that large decision had ever been presented for their explicit consideration."[3] If the market does not present the large question for decision, then individuals are doomed to making decisions that are sensible within their narrow contexts even though they know all the while that in making such decisions they are bringing about a result that most of them do not want. Either that or they organize to overcome some of the effects of the market by changing its structure—for example by bringing consumer units roughly up to the size of the units that are making producers' decisions. This nicely makes the point: So long as one leaves the structure unaffected, it is not possible for changes in the intentions and the actions of particular actors to produce desirable outcomes or to avoid undesirable ones. Structures may be changed, as just mentioned, by changing the distribution of capabilities across units. Structures may also be changed by imposing requirements where previously people had to decide for themselves. If some merchants sell on Sunday, others may have to do so in order to remain competitive even though most prefer a six-day week. Most are able to do as they please only if all are required to keep comparable hours. The only remedies for strong structural effects are structural changes.

Structural constraints cannot be wished away, although many fail to understand this. In every age and place the units of self-help systems—nations, corporations, or whatever—are told that the greater good, along with their own, requires them to act for the sake of the system and not for their own narrowly defined advantage. In the 1950s, as fear of the world's destruction in nuclear war grew, some concluded that the alternative to world destruction was world disarmament. In the 1970s, with the rapid growth of population, poverty, and pollution, some concluded, as one political scientist put it, that "states must meet the needs of the political ecosystem in its global dimensions or court annihilation."[4] The international interest must be served; and if that means anything at all, it means that national interests are subordinate to it. The problems are found at the global level. Solutions to the problems continue to depend on national policies. What are the conditions that would make nations more or less willing to obey the injunctions that are so often laid on them? How can they resolve the tension between pursuing their own interests and acting for the sake of the system? No one has shown how that can be done, although many wring their hands and plead for rational behavior. The very problem, however, is that rational behavior, given structural constraints, does not lead to the wanted results. With each country constrained to take care of itself, no one can take care of the system.

A strong sense of peril and doom may lead to a clear definition of ends that must be achieved. Their achievement is not thereby made possible. The possibility of effective action depends on the ability to provide necessary means. It depends even more so on the existence of conditions that permit nations and other organizations to follow appropriate policies and strategies. World-shaking problems cry for global solutions, but there is no global agency to provide them. Necessities do not create possibilities. Wishing that final causes were efficient ones does not make them so.

Great tasks can be accomplished only by agents of great capability. That is why states, and especially the major ones, are called on to do what is necessary for the world's survival. But states have to do whatever they think necessary for their own preservation, since no one can be relied on to do it for them. Why the advice to place the international interest above national interests is meaningless can be explained precisely in terms of the distinction between micro and macro theories. Among economists the distinction is well understood. Among political scientists it is not. As I have explained, a microeconomic theory is a theory of the market built up from assumptions about the behavior of individuals. The theory shows how the actions and interactions of the units form and affect the market and how the market in turn affects them. A macro theory is a theory about the national economy built on supply, income, and demand as systemwide aggregates. The theory shows how these and other aggregates are interconnected and indicates how changes in one or some of them affect others and the performance of the economy. In economics, both micro and macro theories deal with large realms. The difference between them is found not in the size of the objects of study, but in the way the objects of study are approached and the theory to explain them is constructed. A macro theory of international politics would show how the international system is moved by systemwide aggregates. One can imagine what some of them might be—amount of world GNP, amount of world imports and exports, of deaths in war, of everybody's defense spending, and of migration, for example. The theory would look something like a macroeconomic theory in the style of John Maynard Keynes, although it is hard to see how the international aggregates would make much sense and how changes in one or some of them would produce changes in others. I am not saying that such a theory cannot be constructed, but only that I cannot see how to do it in any way that might be useful. The decisive point, anyway, is that a macro theory of international politics would lack the practical implications of macroeconomic theory. National governments can manipulate systemwide economic variables. No agencies with comparable capabilities exist internationally. Who would act on the possibilities of adjustment that a macro theory of international politics might reveal? Even were such a theory available, we would still be stuck with nations as the only agents capable of acting to solve global problems. We would still have to revert to a micropolitical approach in order to examine the conditions that make benign and effective action by states separately and collectively more or less likely.

Some have hoped that changes in the awareness and purpose, in the organization and ideology, of states would change the quality of international life. Over the centuries states have changed in many ways, but the quality of international life has remained much the same. States may seek reasonable and worthy ends, but they cannot figure out how to reach them. The problem is not in their stupidity or ill will, although one does not want to claim that those qualities are lacking. The depth of the difficulty is not understood until one realizes that intelligence and goodwill cannot discover and act on adequate programs. Early in this century Winston Churchill observed that the British-German naval race promised disaster *and* that Britain had no realistic choice other than to run it. States facing global problems are like individual consumers trapped by the "tyranny of small decisions." States, like consumers, can get out of the trap only by changing the structure of their field of activity. The message bears repeating: The only remedy for a strong structural effect is a structural change.

4. The Virtues of Anarchy

To achieve their objectives and maintain their security, units in a condition of anarchy—be they people, corporations, states, or whatever—must rely on the means they can generate and the arrangements they can make for themselves. Self-help is necessarily the principle of action in an anarchic order. A self-help situation is one of high risk—of bankruptcy in the economic realm and of war in a world of free states. It is also one in which organizational costs are low. Within an economy or within an international order, risks may be avoided or lessened by moving from a situation of coordinate action to one of super- and subordination, that is, by erecting agencies with effective authority and extending a system of rules. Government emerges where the functions of regulation and management themselves become distinct and specialized tasks. The costs of maintaining a hierarchic order are frequently ignored by those who deplore its absence. Organizations have at least two aims: to get something done and to maintain themselves as organizations. Many of their activities are directed toward the second purpose. The leaders of organizations, and political leaders preeminently, are not masters of the matters their organizations deal with. They have become leaders not by being experts on one thing or another but by excelling in the organizational arts—in maintaining control of a group's members, in eliciting predictable and satisfactory efforts from them, in holding a group together. In making political decisions the first and most important concern is not to achieve the aims the members of an organization may have but to secure the continuity and health of the organization itself.[5]

Along with the advantages of hierarchic orders go the costs. In hierarchic orders, moreover, the means of control become an object of struggle. Substantive issues become entwined with efforts to influence or control the controllers. The hierarchic ordering of politics adds one to the already numerous objects of struggle, and the object added is at a new order of magnitude.

If the risks of war are unbearably high, can they be reduced by organizing to manage the affairs of nations? At a minimum management requires controlling the military forces that are at the disposal of states. Within nations, organizations have to work to maintain themselves. As organizations, nations, in working to maintain themselves, sometimes have to use force against dissident elements and areas. As hierarchical systems, governments nationally or globally are disrupted by the defection of major parts. In a society of states with little coherence, attempts at world government would founder on the inability of an emerging central authority to mobilize the resources needed to create and maintain the unity of the system by regulating and managing its parts. The prospect of world government would be an invitation to prepare for world civil war. This calls to mind Milovan Djilas's reminiscence of World War II.[6] According to him, he and many Russian soldiers in their wartime discussions came to believe that human struggles would acquire their ultimate bitterness if all men were subject to the same social system, "for the system would be untenable as such and various sects would undertake the reckless destruction of the human race for the sake of its greater 'happiness.'"[7] States cannot entrust managerial powers to a central agency unless that agency is able to protect its client states. The more powerful the clients and the more the power of each of them appears as a threat to the others, the greater the power lodged in the center must be. The greater the power of the center, the stronger the incentive for states to engage in a struggle to control it.

States, like people, are insecure in proportion to the extent of their freedom. If freedom is wanted, insecurity must be accepted. Organizations that establish relations of authority and control may increase security as they decrease freedom. If might does not make right, whether among people or states, then some institution or agency has intervened to lift them out of nature's realm. The more influential the agency, the stronger the desire to control it becomes. In contrast, units in an anarchic order act for their own sakes and not for the sake of preserving an organization and furthering their fortunes within it. Force is used for one's own interest. In the absence of organization, people or states are free to leave one another alone. Even when they do not do so, they are better able, in the absence of the politics of the organization, to concentrate on the politics of the problem and to aim for a minimum agreement that will permit their separate existence rather than a maximum agreement for the sake of maintaining unity. If might decides, then bloody struggles over right can more easily be avoided.

Nationally, the force of a government is exercised in the name of right and justice. Internationally, the force of a state is employed for the sake of its own protection and advantage. Rebels challenge a government's claim to authority; they question the rightfulness of its rule. Wars among states cannot settle questions of authority and right; they can only determine the allocation of gains and losses among contenders and settle for a time the question of who is the stronger. Nationally, relations of authority are established. Internationally, only relations of strength result. Nationally, private force used against a government threatens the political system. Force used by a state—a public body—is, from the international perspective, the private use of force; but there is no government to overthrow and no governmental apparatus to capture. Short of a drive toward world hegemony, the private use of force does not threaten the system of international politics, only some of its members. War pits some states against others in a struggle among similarly constituted entities. The power of the strong may deter the weak from asserting their claims, not because the weak recognize a kind of rightfulness of rule on the part of the strong, but simply because it is not sensible to tangle with them. Conversely, the weak may enjoy considerable freedom of action if they are so far removed in their capabilities from the strong that the latter are not much bothered by their actions or much concerned by marginal increases in their capabilities.

National politics is the realm of authority, of administration, and of law. International politics is the realm of power, of struggle, and of accommodation. The international realm is preeminently a political one. The national realm is variously described as being hierarchic, vertical, centralized, heterogeneous, directed, and contrived; the international realm, as being anarchic, horizontal, decentralized, homogeneous, undirected, and mutually adaptive. The more centralized the order, the nearer to the top the locus of decisions ascends. Internationally, decisions are made at the bottom level, there being scarcely any other. In the vertical-horizontal dichotomy, international structures assume the prone position. Adjustments are made internationally, but they are made without a formal or authoritative adjuster. Adjustment and accommodation proceed by mutual adaptation. Action and reaction, and reaction to the reaction, proceed by a piecemeal process. The parties feel each other out, so to speak, and define a situation simultaneously with its development. Among coordinate units adjustment is achieved and accommodations arrived at by the exchange of "considerations," in a condition, as Chester Barnard put it, "in which the duty of command and the desire to obey are essentially absent."[8] Where the contest is over considerations, the parties seek to maintain or improve their positions by maneuvering, by bargaining, or by fighting. The manner and intensity of the competition are determined by the desires and the abilities of parties that are at once separate and interacting.

Whether or not by force, each state plots the course it thinks will best serve its interests. If force is used by one state or its use is expected, the recourse of other states is to use force or be prepared to use it singly or in combination. No appeal can be made to a higher entity clothed with the authority and equipped with the ability to act on its own initiative. Under such conditions the possibility that force will be used by one or another of the parties looms always as a threat in the background. In politics force is said to be the ultima ratio. In international politics force serves not only as the ultima ratio but indeed as the first and constant one. To limit force to being the ultima ratio of politics implies, in the words of Ortega y Gasset, "the previous submission of force to methods of reason."[9] The constant possibility that force will be used limits manipulations, moderates demands, and serves as an incentive for the settlement of disputes. One who knows that pressing too hard may lead to war has strong reason to consider whether possible gains are worth the risks entailed. The threat of force internationally is comparable to the role of the strike in labor and management bargaining. "The few strikes that take place are in a sense," as Livernash has said, "the cost of the strike option which produces settlements in the large mass of negotiations."[10] Even if workers seldom strike, their doing so is always a possibility. The possibility of industrial disputes leading to long and costly strikes encourages labor and management to face difficult issues, to try to understand each other's problems, and to work hard to find accommodations. The possibility that conflicts among nations may lead to long and costly wars has similarly sobering effects.

5. Anarchy and Hierarchy

I have described anarchies and hierarchies as though every political order were of one type or the other. Many, and I suppose most, political scientists who write of structures allow for a greater and sometimes for a bewildering variety of types. Anarchy is seen as one end of a continuum whose other end is marked by the presence of a legitimate and competent government. International politics is then described as being flecked with particles of government and alloyed with elements of community—supranational organizations whether universal or regional, alliances, multinational corporations, networks of trade, and whatnot. International political systems are thought of as being more or less anarchic.

Those who view the world as a modified anarchy do so, it seems, for two reasons. First, anarchy is taken to mean not just the absence of government but also the presence of disorder and chaos. Since world politics, although not reliably peaceful, falls short of unrelieved chaos, students are inclined to see a lessening of anarchy in each outbreak of peace. Since world politics, although not formally organized, is not entirely without institutions and orderly procedures, students are inclined to see a lessening of anarchy when alliances form, when transactions across national borders increase, and when international agencies multiply. Such views confuse structure with process, and I have drawn attention to that error often enough.

Second, the two simple categories of anarchy and hierarchy do not seem to accommodate the infinite social variety our senses record. Why insist on reducing the types of structure to two instead of allowing for a greater variety? Anarchies are ordered by the juxtaposition of similar units, but those similar units are not identical. Some specialization by function develops among them. Hierarchies are ordered by the social division of labor among units specializing in different tasks, but the resemblance of units does not vanish. Much duplication of effort continues. All societies are organized segmentally or hierarchically in greater or lesser degree. Why not, then, define additional social types according to the mixture of organizing principles they embody? One might conceive some societies approaching the purely anarchic, of others approaching purely hierarchic, and of still others reflecting specified mixes of the two organizational types. In anarchies the exact likeness of units and the determination of relations by capability alone would describe a realm wholly of politics and power with none of the interaction of units guided by administration and conditioned by authority. In hierarchies the complete differentiation of parts and the full specification of their functions would produce a realm wholly of authority and administration with none of the interaction of parts affected by politics and power. Although such pure orders do not exist, to distinguish realms by their organizing principles is nevertheless proper and important.

Increasing the number of categories would bring the classification of societies closer to reality. But that would be to move away from a theory claiming explanatory power to a less theoretical system promising greater descriptive accuracy. One who wishes to explain rather than to describe should resist moving in that direction if resistance is reasonable. Is it? What does one gain by insisting on two types when admitting three or four would still be to simplify boldly? One gains clarity and economy of concepts. A new concept should be introduced only to cover matters that existing concepts do not reach. If some societies are neither anarchic nor hierarchic, if their structures are defined by some third ordering principle, then we would have to define a third system. All societies are mixed. Elements in them represent both of the ordering principles. That does not mean that some societies are ordered according to a third principle. Usually one can easily identify the principle by which a society is ordered. The appearance of anarchic sectors within hierarchies does not alter and should not obscure the ordering principle of the larger system, for those sectors are anarchic only within limits. The attributes and behavior of the units populating those sectors within the larger system differ, moreover, from what they would be and how they would behave outside of it. Firms in oligopolistic markets again are perfect examples of this. They struggle against one another, but because they need not prepare to defend themselves physically, they can afford to specialize and to participate more fully in the division of economic labor than states can. Nor do the states that populate an anarchic world find it impossible to work with one another, to make agreements limiting their arms, and to cooperate in establishing organizations. Hierarchic elements within international structures limit and restrain the exercise of sovereignty but only in ways strongly conditioned by the anarchy of the larger system. The anarchy of that order strongly affects the likelihood of cooperation, the extent of arms agreements, and the jurisdiction of international organizations.

But what about borderline cases, societies that are neither clearly anarchic nor clearly hierarchic? Do they not represent a third type? To say that there are borderline cases is not to say that at the border a third type of system appears. All categories have borders, and if we have any categories at all, we have borderline cases. Clarity of concepts does not eliminate difficulties of classification. Was China from the 1920s to the 1940s a hierarchic or an anarchic realm? Nominally a nation, China looked more like a number of separate states existing alongside one another. Mao Tse-tung in 1930, like Bolshevik leaders earlier, thought that striking a revolutionary spark would "start a prairie fire." Revolutionary flames would spread across China, if not throughout the world. Because the interdependence of China's provinces, like the interdependence of nations, was insufficiently close, the flames failed to spread. So nearly autonomous were China's provinces that the effects of war in one part of the country were only weakly registered in other parts. Battles in the Hunan hills, far from sparking a national revolution, were hardly noticed in neighboring provinces. The interaction of largely self-sufficient provinces was slight and sporadic. Dependent neither on one another economically nor on the nation's center politically, they were not subject to the close interdependence characteristic of organized and integrated polities.

As a practical matter observers may disagree in their answers to such questions as just when did China break down into anarchy, or whether the countries of western Europe are slowly becoming one state or stubbornly remaining nine. The point of theoretical importance is that our expectations about the fate of those areas differ widely depending on which answer to the structural question becomes the right one. Structures defined according to two distinct ordering principles help to explain important aspects of social and political behavior. That is shown in various ways in the following pages. This section has explained why two and only two types of structure are needed to cover societies of all sorts.

II

How can a theory of international politics be constructed? Just as any theory must be. First, one must conceive of international politics as a bounded realm or domain; second, one must discover some lawlike regularities within it; and third, one must develop a way of explaining the observed regularities. . . . Political structures account for some recurrent aspects of the behavior of states and for certain repeated and enduring patterns. Wherever agents and agencies are coupled by force and competition rather than by authority and law, we expect to find such behaviors and outcomes. They are closely identified with the approach to politics suggested by the rubric realpolitik. The elements of realpolitik, exhaustively listed, are these: the ruler's, and later the state's, interest provides the spring of action; the necessities of policy arise from the unregulated competition of states; calculation based on these necessities can discover the policies that will best serve a state's interests; success is the ultimate test of policy, and success is defined as preserving and strengthening the state. Ever since Machiavelli, interest and necessity—and raison d'état, the phrase that comprehends them—have remained the key concepts of realpolitik. From Machiavelli through Meinecke and Morgenthau the elements of the approach and the reasoning remain constant. Machiavelli stands so clearly as the exponent of realpolitik that one easily slips into thinking that he developed the closely associated idea of balance of power as well. Although he did not, his conviction that politics can be explained in its own terms established the ground on which balance-of-power theory can be built.

Realpolitik indicates the methods by which foreign policy is conducted and provides a rationale for them. Structural constraints explain why the methods are repeatedly used despite differences in the persons and states who use them. Balance-of-power theory purports to explain the result that such methods produce. Rather, that is what the theory should do. If there is any distinctively political theory of international politics, balance-of-power theory is it. And yet one cannot find a statement of the theory that is generally accepted. Carefully surveying the copious balance-of-power literature, Ernst Haas discovered eight distinct meanings of the term, and Martin Wight found nine. Hans Morgenthau, in his profound historical and analytic treatment of the subject, makes use of four different definitions.[11] Balance of power is seen by some as being akin to a law of nature; by others, as simply an outrage. Some view it as a guide to statesmen; others as a cloak that disguises their imperialist policies. Some believe that a balance of power is the best guarantee of the security of states and the peace of the world; others, that it has ruined states by causing most of the wars they have fought.

To believe that one can cut through such confusion may seem quixotic. I shall nevertheless try. It will help to hark back to several basic propositions about theory. (1) A theory contains at least one theoretical assumption. Such assumptions are not factual. One therefore cannot legitimately ask if they are true, but only if they are useful. (2) Theories must be evaluated in terms of what they claim to explain. Balance-of-power theory claims to explain the results of states' actions under given conditions, and those results may not be foreshadowed in any of the actors' motives or be contained as objectives in their policies. (3) Theory, as a general explanatory system, cannot account for particularities.

Most of the confusions in balance-of-power theory, and criticisms of it, derive from misunderstanding these three points. A balance-of-power theory, properly stated, begins with assumptions about states: They are unitary actors who at a minimum seek their own preservation and at a maximum drive for universal domination. States, or those who act for them, try in more or less sensible ways to use the means available in order to achieve the ends in view. Those means fall into two categories: internal efforts (moves to increase economic capability, to increase military strength, to develop clever strategies) and external efforts (moves to strengthen and enlarge one's own alliance or to weaken and shrink an opposing one). The external game of alignment and realignment requires three or more players, and it is usually said that balance-of-power systems require at least that number. The statement is false, for in a two-power system the politics of balance continue, but the way to compensate for an incipient external disequilibrium is primarily by intensifying one's internal efforts. To the assumptions of the theory we then add the condition for its operation: that two or more states coexist in a self-help system, one with no superior agent to come to the aid of states that may be weakening or to deny to any of them the use of whatever instruments they think will serve their purposes. The theory, then, is built up from the assumed motivations of states and the actions that correspond to them. It describes the constraints that arise from the system that those actions produce, and it indicates the expected outcome: namely, the formation of balances of power. Balance-of-power theory is micro theory precisely in the economist's sense. The system, like a market in economics, is made by the actions and interactions of its units, and the theory is based on assumptions about their behavior.

A self-help system is one in which those who do not help themselves or who do so less effectively than others will fail to prosper, will lay themselves open to dangers, will suffer. Fear of such unwanted consequences stimulates states to behave in ways that tend toward the creation of balances of power. Notice that the theory requires no assumptions of rationality or of constancy of will on the part of all of the actors. The theory says simply that if some do relatively well, others will emulate them or fall by the wayside. Obviously, the system won't work if all states lose interest in preserving themselves. It will, however, continue to work if some states do while others do not choose to lose their political identities, say, through amalgamation. Nor need it be assumed that all of the competing states are striving relentlessly to increase their power. The possibility that force may be used by some states to weaken or destroy others does, however, make it difficult for them to break out of the competitive system.

The meaning and importance of the theory are made clear by examining prevalent misconceptions of it. Recall our first proposition about theory. A theory contains assumptions that are theoretical, not factual. One of the most common misunderstandings of balance-of-power theory centers on this point. The theory is criticized because its assumptions are erroneous. The following statement can stand for a host of others:

> If nations were in fact unchanging units with no permanent ties to each other, and if all were motivated primarily by a drive to maximize their power, except for a single balancer whose aim was to prevent any nation from achieving preponderant power, a balance of power might in fact result. But we have seen that these assumptions are not correct, and since the assumptions of the theory are wrong, the conclusions are also in error.[12]

The author's incidental error is that he has compounded a sentence some parts of which are loosely stated assumptions of the theory and other parts not. His basic error lies in misunderstanding what an assumption is. From previous discussion we know that assumptions are neither true nor false and that they are essential for the construction of theory. We can freely admit that states are in fact not unitary purposive actors. States pursue many goals, which are often vaguely formulated and inconsistent. They fluctuate with the changing currents of domestic politics, are prey to the vagaries of a shifting cast of political leaders, and are influenced by the outcomes of bureaucratic struggles. But all of this has always been known, and it tells us nothing about the merits of balance-of-power theory.

A further confusion relates to our second proposition about theory. Balance-of-power theory claims to explain a result (the recurrent formation of balances of power) which may not accord with the intentions of any of the units whose actions combine to produce that result. To contrive and maintain a balance may be the aim of one or more states, but then again it may not be. According to the theory, balances of power tend to form whether some or all states consciously aim to establish and maintain a balance, or whether some or all states aim for universal domination. Yet many, and perhaps most, statements of balance-of-power theory attribute the maintenance of a balance to the separate states as a motive. David Hume, in his classic essay "Of the Balance of Power," offers "the maxim of preserving the balance of power" as a constant rule of prudent politics.[13] So it may be, but it has proved to be an unfortunately short step from the belief that a high regard for preserving a balance is at the heart of wise statesmanship to the belief that states must follow the maxim if a balance of power is to be maintained. This is apparent in the first of Morgenthau's four definitions of the term: namely, "a policy aimed at a certain state of affairs." The reasoning then easily becomes tautological. If a balance of power is to be maintained, the policies of states must aim to uphold it. If a balance of power is in fact maintained, we can conclude that their aim was accurate. If a balance of power is not produced, we can say that the theory's assumption is erroneous. Finally, and this completes the drift toward the reification of a concept, if the purpose of states is to uphold a balance, the purpose of the balance is "to maintain the stability of the system without destroying the multiplicity of the elements composing it." Reification has obviously occurred where one reads, for example, of the balance operating "successfully" and of the difficulty that nations have in applying it.

Reification is often merely the loose use of language or the employment of metaphor to make one's prose more pleasing. In this case, however, the theory has been drastically distorted, and not only by introducing the notion that if a balance is to be formed, somebody must want it and must work for it. The further distortion of the theory arises when rules are derived from the results of states' actions and then illogically prescribed to the actors as duties. A possible effect is turned into a necessary cause in the form of a stipulated rule. Thus, it is said, "the balance of power" can "impose its restraints upon the power aspirations of nations" only if they first "restrain themselves by accepting the system of the balance of power as the common framework of their endeavors." Only if states recognize "the same rules of the game" and play "for the same limited stakes" can the balance of power fulfill "its functions for international stability and national independence."[14]

The closely related errors that fall under our second proposition about theory are, as we have seen, twin traits of the field of international politics: namely, to assume a necessary correspondence of motive and result and to infer rules for the actors from the observed results of their action. . . . In a purely competitive economy, everyone's striving to make a profit drives the profit rate downward. Let the competition continue long enough under static conditions, and everyone's profit will be zero. To infer from that result that everyone, or anyone, is seeking to minimize profit, and that the competitors must adopt that goal as a rule in order for the system to work, would be absurd. And yet in international politics one frequently finds that rules inferred from the results of the interactions of states are prescribed to the actors and are said to be a condition of the system's maintenance. Such errors, often made, are also often pointed out, though seemingly to no avail. S. F. Nadel has put the matter simply: "an orderliness abstracted from behaviour cannot guide behaviour."[15]

Analytic reasoning applied where a systems approach is needed leads to the laying down of all sorts of conditions as prerequisites to balances of power forming and tending toward equilibrium and as general preconditions of world stability and peace. Some require that the number of great powers exceed two; others that a major power be willing to play the role of balancer. Some require that military technology not change radically or rapidly; others that the major states abide by arbitrarily specified rules. But balances of power form in the absence of the "necessary" conditions, and since 1945 the world has been stable, and the world of major powers remarkably peaceful, even though international conditions have not conformed to theorists' stipulations. Balance-of-power politics prevail wherever two and only two requirements are met: that the order be anarchic and that it be populated by units wishing to survive.

For those who believe that if a result is to be produced, someone or everyone must want it and must work for it, it follows that explanation turns ultimately on what the separate states are like. If that is true, then theories at the national level or lower will sufficiently explain international politics. If, for example, the equilibrium of a balance is maintained through states abiding by rules, then one needs an explanation of how agreement on the rules is achieved and maintained. One does not need a balance-of-power theory, for balances would result from a certain kind of behavior explained perhaps by a theory about national psychology or bureaucratic politics. A balance-of-power theory could not be constructed because it would have nothing to explain. If the good or bad motives of states result in their maintaining balances or disrupting them, then the notion of a balance of power becomes merely a framework organizing one's account of what happened, and that is indeed its customary use. A construction that starts out to be a theory ends up as a set of categories. Categories then multiply rapidly to cover events that the embryo theory had not contemplated. The quest for explanatory power turns into a search for descriptive adequacy.

Finally, and related to our third proposition about theory in general, balance-of-power theory is often criticized because it does not explain the particular policies of states. True, the theory does not tell us why state X made a certain move last Tuesday. To expect it to do so would be like expecting the theory of universal gravitation to explain the wayward path of a falling leaf. A theory at one level of generality cannot answer questions about matters at a different level of generality. Failure to notice this is one error on which the criticism rests. Another is to mistake a theory of international politics for a theory of foreign policy. Confusion about the explanatory claims made by a properly stated balance-of-power theory is rooted in the uncertainty of the distinction drawn between national and international politics or in the denials that the distinction should be made. For those who deny the distinction, for those who devise explanations that are entirely in terms of interacting units, explanations of international politics *are* explanations of foreign policy, and explanations of foreign policy *are* explanations of international politics. Others mix their explanatory claims and confuse the problem of understanding international politics with the problem of understanding foreign policy. Morgenthau, for example, believes that problems of predicting foreign policy and of developing theories about it make international-political theories difficult, if not impossible, to contrive.[16] But the difficulties of explaining foreign policy work against contriving theories of international politics only if the latter reduces to the former. Graham Allison betrays a similar confusion. His three "models" purport to offer alternative approaches to the study of international politics. Only model I, however, is an approach to the study of international politics. Models II and III are approaches to the study of foreign policy. Offering the bureaucratic-politics approach as an alternative to the state-as-an-actor approach is like saying that a theory of the firm is an alternative to a theory of the market, a mistake no competent economist would make.[17] If Morgenthau and Allison were economists and their thinking continued to follow the same pattern, they would have to argue that the uncertainties of corporate policy work against the development of market theory. They have confused and merged two quite different matters.

Any theory covers some matters and leaves other matters aside. Balance-of-power theory is a theory about the results produced by the uncoordinated actions of states. The theory makes assumptions about the interests and motives of states, rather than explaining them. What it does explain are the constraints that confine all states. The clear perception of constraints provides many clues to the expected reactions of states, but by itself the theory cannot explain those reactions. They depend not only on international constraints but also on the characteristics of states. How will a particular state react? To answer that question we need not only a theory of the market, so to speak, but also a theory about the firms that compose it. What will a state have to react to? Balance-of-power theory can give general and useful answers to that question. The theory explains why a certain similarity of behavior is expected from similarly situated states. The expected behavior is similar, not identical. To explain the expected differences in national responses, a theory would have to show how the different internal structures of states affect their external policies and actions. A theory of foreign policy would not predict the detailed content of policy but instead would lead to different expectations about the tendencies and styles of different countries' policies. Because the national and the international levels are linked, theories of both types, if they are any good, tell us some things, but not the same things, about behavior and outcomes at both levels. . . .

III

. . . Before subjecting a theory to tests, one asks whether the theory is internally consistent and whether it tells us some things of interest that we would not know in its absence. That the theory meets those requirements does not mean that it can survive tests. Many people prefer tests that, if flunked, falsify a theory. Some people, following Karl Popper,[18] insist that theories are tested only by attempting to falsify them. Confirmations do not count because among other reasons confirming cases may be offered as proof, while consciously or not, cases likely to confound the theory are avoided. This difficulty, I suggest later, is lessened by choosing hard cases—situations, for example, in which parties have strong reasons to behave contrary to the predictions of one's theory. Confirmations are also rejected because numerous tests that appear to confirm a theory are negated by one falsifying instance. . . . However, [there is] the possibility of devising tests that confirm. If a theory depicts a domain and displays its organization and the connections among its parts, then we can compare features of the observed domain with the picture the theory has limned.[19] We can ask whether expected behaviors and outcomes are repeatedly found where the conditions contemplated by the theory obtain.

Structural theories, moreover, gain plausibility if similarities of behavior are observed across realms that are different in substance but similar in structure, and if differences of behavior are observed where realms are similar in substance but different in structure. This special advantage is won: International-political theory gains credibility from the confirmation of certain theories in economics, sociology, anthropology, and other such nonpolitical fields.

Testing theories, of course, always means inferring expectations, or hypotheses, from them and testing those expectations. Testing theories is a difficult and subtle task, made so by the interdependence of fact and theory, by the elusive relation between reality and theory as an instrument for its apprehension. Questions of truth and falsity are somehow involved, but so are questions of usefulness and uselessness. In the end one sticks with the theory that reveals most, even if its validity is suspect. I shall say more about the acceptance and rejection of theories elsewhere. Here I say only enough to make the relevance of a few examples of theory testing clear. Others can then easily be thought of. . . .

Tests are easy to think up, once one has a theory to test, but they are hard to carry through. Given the difficulty of testing any theory and the added difficulty of testing theories in such nonexperimental fields as international politics, we should exploit all of the ways of testing I have mentioned—by trying to falsify, by devising hard confirmatory tests, by comparing features of the real and the theoretical worlds, by comparing behaviors in realms of similar and of different structure. Any good theory raises many expectations. Multiplying hypotheses and varying tests are all the more important because the results of testing theories are necessarily problematic. That a single hypothesis appears to hold true may not be very impressive. A theory becomes plausible if many hypotheses inferred from it are successfully subjected to tests.

Knowing a little bit more about testing, we can now ask whether expectations drawn from our theory can survive subjection to tests. What will some of the expectations be? Two that are closely related arise in the above discussion. According to the theory, balances of power recurrently form, and states tend to emulate the successful policies of others. Can these expectations be subjected to tests? In principle the answer is yes. Within a given arena and over a number of years, we should find the military power of weaker and smaller states or groupings of states growing more rapidly, or shrinking more slowly, than that of stronger and larger ones. And we should find widespread imitation among competing states. In practice to check such expectations against historical observations is difficult.

Two problems are paramount. First, though balance-of-power theory offers some predictions, the predictions are indeterminate. Because only a loosely defined and inconstant condition of balance is predicted, it is difficult to say that any given distribution of power falsifies the theory. The theory, moreover, does not lead one to expect that emulation among states will proceed to the point where competitors become identical. What will be imitated, and how quickly and closely? Because the theory does not give precise answers, falsification again is difficult. Second, although states may be disposed to react to international constraints and incentives in accordance with the theory's expectations, the policies and actions of states are also shaped by their internal conditions. The failure of balances to form, and the failure of some states to conform to the successful practices of other states, can too easily be explained away by pointing to effects produced by forces that lie outside of the theory's purview.

In the absence of theoretical refinements that fix expectations with certainty and in detail, what can we do? As I have just suggested . . . we should make tests ever more difficult. If we observe outcomes that the theory leads us to expect even though strong forces work against them, the theory will begin to command belief. To confirm the theory one should not look mainly to the eighteenth-century heyday of the balance of power when great powers in convenient numbers interacted and were presumably able to adjust to a shifting distribution of power by changing partners with a grace made possible by the absence of ideological and other cleavages. Instead one should seek confirmation through observation of difficult cases. One should, for example, look for instances of states allying in accordance with the expectations the theory gives rise to even though they have strong reasons not to cooperate with one another. The alliance of France and Russia, made formal in 1894, is one such instance. . . . One should, for example, look for instances of states making internal efforts to strengthen themselves, however distasteful or difficult such efforts might be. The United States and the Soviet Union following World War II provide such instances: the United States by rearming despite having demonstrated a strong wish not to by dismantling the most powerful military machine the world had ever known; the Soviet Union by maintaining about three million men under arms while striving to acquire a costly new military technology despite the terrible destruction she had suffered in war.

These examples tend to confirm the theory. We find states forming balances of power whether or not they wish to. They also show the difficulties of testing. Germany and Austria-Hungary formed their Dual Alliance in 1879. Since detailed inferences cannot be drawn from the theory, we cannot say just when other states are expected to counter this move. France and Russia waited until 1894. Does this show the theory false by suggesting that states may or may not be brought into balance? We should neither quickly conclude that it does nor lightly chalk the delayed response off to "friction." Instead, we should examine diplomacy and policy in the fifteen-year interval to see whether the theory serves to explain and broadly predict the actions and reactions of states and to see whether the delay is out of accord with the theory. Careful judgment is needed. For this historians' accounts serve better than the historical summary I might provide.

The theory leads us to expect states to behave in ways that result in balances forming. To infer that expectation from the theory is not impressive if balancing is a universal pattern of political behavior, as is sometimes claimed. It is not. Whether political actors balance each other or climb on the bandwagon depends on the system's structure. Political parties, when choosing their presidential candidates, dramatically illustrate both points. When nomination time approaches and no one is established as the party's strong favorite, a number of would-be leaders contend. Some of them form coalitions to check the progress of others. The maneuvering and balancing of would-be leaders when the party lacks one is like the external behavior of states. But this is the pattern only during the leaderless period. As soon as someone looks like the winner, nearly all jump on the bandwagon rather than continuing to build coalitions intended to prevent anyone from winning the prize of power. Bandwagoning, not balancing, becomes the characteristic behavior.

Bandwagoning and balancing behavior are in sharp contrast. Internally, losing candidates throw in their lots with the winner. Everyone wants someone to win; the members of a party want a leader established even while they disagree on who it should be. In a competition for the position of leader, bandwagoning is sensible behavior where gains are possible even for the losers and where losing does not place their security in jeopardy. Externally, states work harder to increase their own strength, or they combine with others if they are falling behind. In a competition for the position of leader, balancing is sensible behavior where the victory of one coalition over another leaves weaker members of the winning coalition at the mercy of the stronger ones. Nobody wants anyone else to win; none of the great powers wants one of their number to emerge as the leader.

If two coalitions form and one of them weakens, perhaps because of the political disorder of a member, we expect the extent of the other coalition's military preparation to slacken or its unity to lessen. The classic example of the latter effect is the breaking apart of a war-winning coalition in or just after the moment of victory. We do not expect the strong to combine with the strong in order to increase the extent of their power over others, but rather to square off and look for allies who might help them. In anarchy security is the highest end. Only if survival is assured can states safely seek such other goals as tranquility, profit, and power. Because power is a means and not an end, states prefer to join the weaker of two coalitions. They cannot let power, a possibly useful means, become the end they pursue. The goal the system encourages them to seek is security. Increased power may or may not serve that end. Given two coalitions, for example, the greater success of one in drawing members to it may tempt the other to risk preventive war, hoping for victory through surprise before disparities widen. If states wished to maximize power, they would join the stronger side, and we would see not balances forming but a world hegemony forged. This does not happen because balancing, not bandwagoning, is the behavior induced by the system. The first concern of states is not to maximize power but to maintain their positions in the system.

Secondary states, if they are free to choose, flock to the weaker side; for it is the stronger side that threatens them. On the weaker side they are both more appreciated and safer, provided, of course, that the coalition they join achieves enough defensive or deterrent strength to dissuade adversaries from attacking. Thus Thucydides records that in the Peloponnesian War the lesser city states of Greece cast the stronger Athens as the tyrant and the weaker Sparta as their liberator.[20] According to Werner Jaeger, Thucydides thought this "perfectly natural in the circumstances," but saw "that the parts of tyrant and liberator did not correspond with any permanent moral quality in these states but were simply masks which would one day be interchanged to the astonishment of the beholder when the balance of power was altered."[21] This shows a nice sense of how the placement of states affects their behavior and even colors their characters. It also supports the proposition that states balance power rather than maximize it. States can seldom afford to make maximizing power their goal. International politics is too serious a business for that.

The theory depicts international politics as a competitive realm. Do states develop the characteristics that competitors are expected to display? The question poses another test for the theory. The fate of each state depends on its responses to what other states do. The possibility that conflict will be conducted by force leads to competition in the arts and the instruments of force. Competition produces a tendency toward the sameness of the competitors. Thus Bismarck's startling victories over Austria in 1866 and over France in 1870 quickly led the major continental powers (and Japan) to imitate the Prussian military staff system, and the failure of Britain and the United States to follow the pattern simply indicated that they were outside the immediate arena of competition. Contending states imitate the military innovations contrived by the country of greatest capability and ingenuity. And so the weapons of major contenders, and even their strategies, begin to look much the same all over the world. Thus at the turn of the century Admiral Alfred von Tirpitz argued successfully for building a battleship fleet on the grounds that Germany could challenge Britain at sea only with a naval doctrine and weapons similar to hers.[22]

The effects of competition are not confined narrowly to the military realm. Socialization to the system should also occur. Does it? Again, because we can almost always find confirming examples if we look hard, we try to find cases that are unlikely to lend credence to the theory. One should look for instances of states conforming to common international practices even though for internal reasons they would prefer not to. The behavior of the Soviet Union in its early years is one such instance. The Bolsheviks in the early years of their power preached international revolution and flouted the conventions of diplomacy. They were saying, in effect, "we will not be socialized to this system." The attitude was well expressed by Trotsky, who, when asked what he would do as foreign minister, replied, "I will issue some revolutionary proclamations to the peoples and then close up the joint."[23] In a competitive arena, however, one party may need the assistance of others. Refusal to play the political game may risk one's own destruction. The pressures of competition were rapidly felt and reflected in the Soviet Union's diplomacy. Thus Lenin, sending foreign minister Chicherin to the Genoa Conference of 1922, bade him farewell with this caution: "Avoid big words."[24] Chicherin, who personified the carefully tailored traditional diplomat rather than the simply uniformed revolutionary, was to refrain from inflammatory rhetoric for the sake of working deals.

These he successfully completed with that other pariah power and ideological enemy, Germany.

The close juxtaposition of states promotes their sameness through the disadvantages that arise from a failure to conform to successful practices. It is this sameness, an effect of the system, that is so often attributed to the acceptance of so-called rules of state behavior. Chiliastic rulers occasionally come to power. In power, most of them quickly change their ways. They can refuse to do so and yet hope to survive only if they rule countries little affected by the competition of states. The socialization of nonconformist states proceeds at a pace that is set by the extent of their involvement in the system. And that is another testable statement.

The theory leads to many expectations about behaviors and outcomes. From the theory one predicts that states will engage in balancing behavior whether or not balanced power is the end of their acts. From the theory one predicts a strong tendency toward balance in the system. The expectation is not that a balance, once achieved, will be maintained, but that a balance, once disrupted, will be restored in one way or another. Balances of power recurrently form. Since the theory depicts international politics as a competitive system, one predicts more specifically that states will display characteristics common to competitors: namely, that they will imitate each other and become socialized to their system. . . .

NOTES

1. E. Durkheim, *The Division of Labor in Society* (New York: Free Press, 1964).
2. W. Fellner, *Competition among the Few* (New York: Knopf), pp. 35, 132, 177, 199, 217–18.
3. A. Kahn, "The tyranny of small decisions: market failures, imperfections, and the limits of econometrics." In Bruce M. Russett (ed.), *Economic Theories of International Relations* (Chicago: Markham, 1968), p. 523.
4. R. W. Sterling, *Macropolitics: International Relations in a Global Society* (New York: Knopf), p. 336.
5. P. Diesing, *Reason in Society* (Urbana: University of Illinois Press, 1962), pp. 198–204. A. Downs, *Inside Bureaucracy* (Boston: Little, Brown, 1967), pp. 262–70.
6. M. Djilas, *Conversations with Stalin* (New York: Harcourt, Brace and World, 1962), p. 50.
7. C. Barnard, "On planning for world government," in Barnard (ed.), *Organization and Management* (Cambridge: Harvard University Press, 1948), pp. 148–52. M. Polanyi, "The growth of thought in society," *Economica*, vol. 8, 1941, pp. 428–56.
8. C. Barnard, "On planning for world government," in Barnard (ed.), *Organization and Management* (Cambridge: Harvard University Press, 1948), pp. 150–51.
9. Quoted in C. Johnson, *Revolutionary Change* (Boston: Little, Brown, 1966), p. 13.
10. E. R. Livernash, "The relation of power to the structure and process of collective bargaining," in Bruce M. Russett (ed.), *Economic Theories of International Politics* (Chicago: Markham, 1968), p. 430.
11. E. Haas, "The balance of power: prescription, concept, or propaganda?" *World Politics*, vol. 5, 1953. M. Wight, "The balance of power," in H. Butterfield and Martin Wight (eds.), *Diplomatic Investigations: Essays in the Theory of International Politics* (Lon-

don: Allen and Unwin, 1966). H. Morgenthau, *Politics Among Nations*, 5th ed. (New York: Knopf, 1953).

12. A. F. K. Organski, *World Politics*, 2nd ed. (New York: Knopf, 1968), p. 292.

13. D. Hume, "Of the balance of power," in Charles W. Hendel (ed.), *David Hume's Political Essays* (Indianapolis: Bobbs-Merrill, 1953), pp. 142–44.

14. H. Morgenthau, *Politics Among Nations*, 5th ed. (New York: Knopf, 1973), pp. 167–74, 202–207, 219–20.

15. S. F. Nadel, *The Theory of Social Structure* (Glencoe, Ill.: Free Press, 1957), p. 148. E. Durkheim, *The Division of Labor in Society* (New York: Free Press, 1964), pp. 386, 418. M. Shubik, *Strategy and Market Structure* (New York: Wiley, 1959), pp. 11, 32.

16. H. Morgenthau, *Truth and Power* (New York: Praeger, 1970), pp. 253–58.

17. G. T. Allison, *Essence of Decision* (Boston: Little, Brown, 1971), and Morton Halperin, "Bureaucratic politics: a paradigm and some policy implications," *World Politics*, vol. 24, 1972.

18. K. Popper, *The Logic of Scientific Discovery* (New York: Basic Books, 1959), Chapter 1.

19. E. E. Harris, *Hypothesis and Perception* (London: Allen and Unwin, 1970).

20. Thucydides, *History of the Peloponnesian War* (New York: Modern Library, Random House, 1951), Book 5, Chapter 17.

21. W. Jaeger, *Paideia: The Ideals of Greek Culture*, vol. 1 (New York: Oxford University Press), 1939.

22. R. J. Art, "The influence of foreign policy on seapower: new weapons and Weltpolitik in Wilhelminian Germany," *Sage Professional Paper in International Studies*, vol. 2. (Beverly Hills: Sage Publications, 1973), p. 16.

23. T. H. Von Laue, "Soviet Diplomacy: G. V. Chicherin, People's Commissar for Foreign Affairs 1918–1930." In Gordon A. Craig and Felix Gilbert (eds.), *The Diplomats, 1919–1939*, vol. 1 (New York: Atheneum, 1963), p. 235.

24. B. Moore, Jr., *Soviet Politics: The Dilemma of Power* (Cambridge: Harvard University Press, 1950), p. 204.

Toward a Realist Theory of State Action

Michael Mastanduno
David A. Lake
G. John Ikenberry

INTRODUCTION

The growing interaction of international and domestic politics complicates the task of state officials seeking to realize objectives in both realms. In both the advanced industrial and the less developed worlds, the realities of interdependence dictate that the ability of governments to pursue domestic economic policies effectively is influenced and constrained by developments in the international economy. The success of domestic policy relies increasingly on the global performance of the nation-state and on the ability of state officials to secure an accommodating international environment.

It is equally evident that the realization of international objectives depends meaningfully on domestic politics and economics. Across much of the globe governments have come to rediscover the significance of the domestic economy to the pursuit of international power, and consequently have sought to restructure or revitalize the former. Gorbachev's provocative reform effort is clearly driven by such a realization, as is, arguably, the European Community's ambitious 1992 program. Two prominent members of the American foreign policy establishment recently warned that the weaknesses of the U.S. economy would be among the most critical and urgent foreign policy challenges facing the next administration (Kissinger and Vance, 1988). Likewise, scholars and practitioners alike have begun to understand that effective international economic cooperation depends not only on the external interests and actions of states, but on their ability to manage, channel, or circumvent domestic political pressures as well.

Much of the recent work in the field of international political economy has been motivated by the problems of interdependence, broadly conceived. Yet, despite the critical and growing significance of domestic and international linkages, political scientists have enjoyed only limited success in conceptualizing and explaining them. As Robert Putnam (1988:427) recently noted, "domestic politics and international relations are often somehow entangled, but our theories have not

Michael Mastanduno, David A. Lake, G. John Ikenberry, "Toward a Realist Theory of State Action," *International Studies Quarterly* 33(1989), 457–474. Reprinted with permission.

yet sorted out the puzzling tangles." Indeed, international and domestic politics remain largely separate fields of scholarly inquiry. In the former, the dominant paradigm of structural Realism has tended to abstract from domestic politics and to explain international outcomes—such as system stability, economic openness, or regime creation—as a function of international attributes, principally the distribution of power. Much of the study of domestic politics, on the other hand, still proceeds without devoting systematic attention to international relations.

To be sure, in recent years political scientists have turned their attention to different *aspects* of the relationship between international and domestic realms. The extensive literature on foreign policy studies, for example, has sought to identify the domestic sources of state behavior in the international arena. The most influential work has highlighted the importance of bureaucratic politics in the conduct of foreign policy, and the relevance of institutional networks and state-society relationships in the formulation and performance of foreign economic policy.[1] Conversely, a growing interest has recently emerged, largely among comparativists, in the international sources of domestic politics, or the "second image reversed." This literature has generated rich insights by examining how international factors such as economic size, trade dependence, and war shape domestic political structures (Gourevitch, 1978; Almond, 1985; Katzenstein, 1985; Rogowski, 1987). While each of these studies has made, and likely will continue to make, important contributions, none comes to terms with the fact that international and domestic politics are interactive. Policy made in one arena spills over into the other. Governments act at home to meet international challenges and abroad to solve domestic problems, often simultaneously. What are needed are conceptual frameworks that address not only the impact of one on the other, but the interplay between domestic and international factors.[2]

In this paper, we propose one possible framework. Because of its unique position at the intersection of the domestic and international political systems, we place the state at the center of our analysis.[3] Although interactions between international and national politics take place at many levels, our view is that the activities and choices of state officials, situated between these domains, are particularly important.[4] We assume that state officials have both international and domestic goals, and we are interested in the ways they pursue domestic goals within the international system and international goals within the domestic system.

Our analysis is embedded within the Realist tradition in the belief that international anarchy and the pursuit of national power are central to understanding both domestic and international politics. We focus on classical Realism because of the fruitful (if implicit) conception within this school of the state as an organization distinct from society and purposive in character. At the same time, we draw upon the more formal and systematic analytic approach characteristic of structural Realism.

Thus, our purpose in this paper is to lay the foundation for an explicit Realist theory of state action which bridges domestic and international politics.[5] Our task is essentially integrative. Many of the hypotheses developed below already exist in the international relations literature—often as "stylized facts." The framework set forth in this paper, however, seeks to pull together otherwise disparate strands into a coherent, theoretical whole. We proceed by positing assumptions about state objectives and deducing strategies relevant to their pursuit. First, in order to set forth the framework that follows, we examine conceptions of the state found in classical and structural Realism. Second, we present two models or "faces" of state action which relate the goals of state officials in one arena to the strategies available in pursuit of such goals in the other. Third, building upon these two models, we put forth several hypotheses which explore the types of challenges to the state that arise in one arena and may trigger responses in the second. Fourth, we introduce variations in domestic and international structures and predict the choice of strategy made by the state across venues. Finally, a concluding section examines the implications of this effort for future Realist inquiry and the study of domestic and international politics.

REALISM AND THE STATE: CLASSICAL AND STRUCTURAL

Within the Realist tradition three arguments are central (Keohane, 1983; Vasquez, 1983; Gilpin, 1984). First, the international system is dominated by sovereign nation-states, each beholden to no higher authority than itself. It is, in other words, anarchic. Second, the relations between nation-states are fundamentally competitive, although this does not preclude the possibility of cooperation in the pursuit of national interests. Finally, with a system so constituted, nation-states behave purposively in the pursuit of power and material well-being. Despite these common arguments, important differences exist among Realists, including conceptions of the state. These differences are particularly evident between the older, classical Realism and the newer, structural Realism.

Classical Realism has been concerned primarily with the sources and uses of national power in international relations. These issues lead the analyst to focus on power relations between nation-states as well as the character of government and its relation to society. Within classical Realism, exemplified in the works of Morgenthau and Carr, one can identify implicit notions of the state as an agent of the larger nation. Classical Realists frequently refer to "statesmen" who, as representatives of the nation-state, are predominantly concerned with monitoring and responding to changes in the international system. Morgenthau describes the tasks of statesmen (or "representatives of the nation") as follows: "They speak for it, negotiate treaties in its name, define its objectives, choose the means of achieving them, and try to maintain, increase, and demonstrate power" (Morgenthau, 1985:118). The lines between the state, on the one hand, and the economy and society, on the other, are not boldly or theoretically drawn in classical Realist writings. Yet an implicit notion of the state that is at once separate from and interactive with society can be detected.

There are two critical components to this implicit classical Realist conception of the state. First, as suggested above, the state is distinct from domestic society.

The concept is not simply that of "government" aggregating or responding to societal interests or demands. Rather, "statesmen" or "agents" of the nation-state are assumed to possess a realm of autonomous behavior. The state's central mission is the conduct of foreign policy, and carrying out that task is what legitimates and differentiates statesmen from the rest of society. Second, in the pursuit of foreign policy, the state must draw upon the society and economy for material resources and political support. In effect, the state's external policies depend critically on what it can extract from its domestic system. In the pursuit of foreign policy, the state finds itself giving great attention to strengthening, shaping, and developing domestic material and political resources. The sources of national power are many—political, economic, and military. The ability to project this power abroad hinges in important respects on the deftness of state officials in cultivating public opinion, educating the citizenry, and bolstering the authority of government institutions (see Morgenthau, 1985; Carr, 1962: Chapter 8). The classical Realists tell us that the state's external power position cannot be divorced from its internal situation and capabilities. The statesman must be an astute diplomat, but he must also be an able student of domestic politics.

It should be emphasized that while the classical Realists rely heavily on notions of the state and its relations to society, these notions remain implicit. There is no attempt to analyze systematically or theorize about the state's ability to marshall domestic resources or opinion. Moreover, the analysis itself is only partial. Classical Realists acknowledge that the nature of domestic politics is vital in sustaining or limiting the state's international goals. Yet they leave aside how international policies might be used in the service of the state's domestic goals.

Structural Realism represents an attempt to develop more rigorous and deductive theories about the international system and the constraints on foreign policy. Far more so than their classical counterparts, structural Realists are sensitive to the levels of analysis and the placement of their arguments within them. Their central task is to delineate the impact of the international structure on international outcomes. The structure of the international system is understood in terms of an ordering principle, such as anarchy, and a particular distribution of power. These characteristics constitute truly international sources of the behavior of nation-states. Importantly, because their concern is with the international sources of international outcomes, structural Realists tend for purposes of analysis to collapse the state and nation-state into one entity. With this merging of the two concepts, domestic politics and structures are eliminated from the approach.

Kenneth Waltz's analysis is the strongest and most prominent expression of this structural Realist approach. In constructing his international theory, Waltz evokes the analogue of the market. The international system is similar in structure to the market in that both are systems created through the actions of self-regarding actors. The system, Waltz argues, is the unintended yet inevitable and spontaneously generated outgrowth of activities by nation-states concerned fundamentally with their own survival. Different types of systems generate different international outcomes; Waltz argues, for example, that multipolar systems tend to be less stable than bipolar ones (Waltz, 1979).

Other structural Realists address more proximate international outcomes such as policy coordination and regime creation and maintenance. While motivated, perhaps, by how developments in these areas affect the domestic political economy, the focus is nonetheless on the international sources of international outcomes. The "theory of hegemonic stability," for example, represents an attempt to account for such outcomes as international economic openness and regime strength in terms of the distribution of economic capabilities among the major powers of the system. Given the power and interests of dominant states, it is hypothesized that hegemony will lead to openness and stable regimes.[6]

In their attempts to explain recurring patterns of international behavior, structural Realists, and Waltz in particular, are highly critical of reductionist approaches. Waltz concludes that "it is not possible to understand world politics simply by looking inside of states" (Waltz, 1979:65). In its pure form, however, the alternative theory constructed by structural Realism does not require scholars to look inside nation-states at all.

In summary, structural Realist theory treats the internal characteristics of nation-states as given. Changes in the behavior of nation-states and in system outcomes are explained not in terms of changes in internal characteristics of nation-states, but in terms of changes in the system itself. Because they are interested in international causes and consequences of state action, structural Realists direct us away from domestic politics and therefore do not provide us with the equipment necessary for investigating the relationship between domestic and international systems.[7] In analyzing international politics in a more systematic, self-consciously theoretical fashion, structural Realism constitutes a significant improvement over its classical predecessor. This progress, however, has been gained at the expense of some of the richness of the earlier variants of Realism. In what follows, we attempt to combine the rigor of structural Realist theory with the sensitivity to state-society relations found in classical Realism.

THE TWO FACES OF STATE ACTION

The literature on domestic strategies for the pursuit of domestic objectives, largely the purview of comparative political studies, and that on international strategies for the pursuit of international objectives, the domain of structural Realism, are already well developed. Given our particular interest in exploring the nexus between international and domestic politics, we develop two complementary models of state action. The first examines domestic strategies for the pursuit of international goals; the second, international strategies for the pursuit of domestic goals.[8] In combination, the models provide a framework for understanding why and under what circumstances state officials use their unique position, situated between domestic and international arenas, to achieve their objectives. The two models are united by the assumption that the state's ultimate goal is survival. From this we deduce more proximate international and domestic goals. Together, these constitute the *minimal* goals of the state. States do many things only tangentially related to survival. Yet any state—whether pre-capitalist, capitalist, centrally planned, relatively autonomous, or wholly autonomous from society—must assure its survival (and that of its nation-state) prior to pursuing other objectives.

International Goals and Domestic Strategies

Our first model accepts the Realist contention that the proximate international goal of any state is the acquisition of power and wealth. Power and wealth are valued because they provide the means to insure both the state's survival and to pursue other goals within an anarchic and competitive international system. Power, as Realists remind us, is a currency with which to purchase security and other valued political goods. Wealth, as Jacob Viner and others have argued, is a necessary means to power, and the two are in long-run harmony (Viner, 1948).

The concern with power and wealth creates two domestic strategies all states must pursue. First, state officials *mobilize resources* and intervene in the economy to stimulate economic growth and enhance the wealth of society as a whole. The state, in other words, performs a role in the economy similar to the "encompassing coalitions" identified by Mancur Olson (Olson, 1982). It acts, following Pareto's famous distinction, not *for* the good of the community but in the interests *of* the community.[9]

This strategy of internal mobilization can take two forms. A state can directly control and allocate production through planning, nationalization, or other means. This is particularly effective when the nation-state needs to undertake a "big push" or Great Leap Forward to catch-up with competitors who have industrialized earlier (Gerschenkron, 1962). Direct mobilization also tends to be most efficacious in the extensive growth phase of economic development. The state can also indirectly intervene in the economy to facilitate the accumulation of societal wealth.[10] It can create more efficient property rights, provide an atmosphere conducive to technological innovation, dismantle rent-seeking coalitions, or insulate itself from such coalitions (North, 1981; Olson, 1982; Rosenberg and Birdzell, 1986). Mobilization is, in an important sense, an investment in international power. By expanding wealth, the state helps create the resources necessary to sustain military expenditures, stimulate technological innovation, and otherwise expand the political and economic bases of power. But while generally beneficial, mobilization is not without costs. Direct mobilization requires an expensive administrative apparatus and, over time, introduces inefficiencies into the economy. In indirect mobilization, on the other hand, costs incurred in persuading non-state actors to expand production are probably more important. To the extent that mobilization reduces rents previously enjoyed by groups in society, it may also entail substantial domestic political costs to the state.

Second, the state *extracts resources* from society for military expenditures, foreign aid, contributions to international organizations, propaganda, and other exercises of international power. Wealth provides the basis for international power, but it is not synonymous with power. The state must convert wealth into power by taxing, requisitioning, or expropriating social resources.[11] States clearly differ in their abilities to make claims on national resources (see Lamborn, 1983). In authoritarian or totalitarian countries it is often possible to construct a command economy in which extraction occurs through the state's direct control of the means of production. Even within democratic capitalist societies, states differ in their extractive abilities. Centralized and insulated states, it is often argued, are better able to extract social wealth than decentralized and constrained states (Krasner, 1977). While the form of extraction will differ according to the strength of the state relative to its society, all states must still convert wealth into power.

Like mobilization, extraction does entail costs and may generate discontent from affected societal groups. More importantly, extraction diminishes the present and future wealth of the nation-state. Only if extracted wealth is redistributed by the state to societal groups with higher rates of marginal returns will extraction expand national wealth. Using extracted resources for international power purposes, on the other hand, consumes rather than produces wealth.

Consequently, a trade-off exists between the two strategies of mobilization and extraction. Mobilization is the creation of wealth and an investment in power. Internal extraction is the creation of power and the consumption of wealth. As extraction increases, the state is likely to redouble its efforts at mobilization, but the effectiveness of the latter may decline because 1) the sum of investable wealth is now lower and 2) incentives for future wealth creation are undermined by discouraging investment and introducing inefficiencies into the economy. These problems are less acute in direct mobilization, yet that strategy by its very nature involves the introduction of greater economic inefficiencies. Extraction is necessary but costly in its long-term effects on the nation-state's ability to compete in the anarchic international system. Therefore, states will seek an equilibrium between extraction and mobilization which satisfies their immediate power needs while enhancing the future power capabilities of the nation-state.[12]

Domestic Goals and International Strategies

As noted above, the ultimate goal of the state is assumed to be self-preservation. While the survival of the state in the international arena requires the defense of the sovereignty and territorial integrity of the nation-state, domestically it demands that the state meet and overcome challenges from, and maintain the support of, societal groups and coalitions. This is the case both for the state as an organization and for the incumbents who occupy dominant positions in the state apparatus at any given moment. In their efforts to maintain support and overcome opposition, state officials pursue two more proximate goals. First, they seek to acquire control over resources in order to coopt or coerce challengers and reward supporters. Obviously, the greater the challenges confronted by state officials to their power and authority, the more resources they will require. Second, state officials seek to preserve their legitimacy. An intangible asset of the state, legitimacy is the acceptance on the part of domestic groups of the state's claim to the exercise of decision-making authority. The greater the legitimacy enjoyed by state officials, the less they must rely upon coercive or compensatory strategies; conversely, as legitimacy wanes the need for such strategies, and thus for control of the resources associated with them, becomes more pressing.[13]

In light of their domestic goals, the two most important international strategies state officials can pursue are *external extraction* and *external validation*. External extraction refers to state efforts to accumulate resources from outside its borders that can be of use in achieving domestic objectives. It may be direct, involving the transfer of external resources to the state itself; or it may be indirect, involving the transfer of such resources to domestic society, a portion of which, in turn, the state may extract. The effective use of external extraction enhances the ability of states to meet their domestic goals by increasing the resources available for coercion or compensation. Moreover, gaining access to externally-generated resources may allow states to reduce internal extraction and thereby ease the domestic political pressure often associated with this latter strategy. Most forms of external extraction rely either overtly or covertly on coercion. Even the pursuit of free trade under American hegemony, an indirect extractive strategy which also improved the well-being of many countries, required that the United States alter the behaviors of other nation-states (Lake, 1988:50–52). Because of this reliance on coercion, relatively powerful countries are likely to be more successful in their attempt at external extraction.

External validation refers to attempts by state officials to utilize their status as authoritative international representatives of the nation-state to enhance their domestic political positions. Like external extraction, this strategy may take a variety of forms. For new states (i.e., those that have come to power in the wake of internal revolutions), external validation involves first and foremost the quest for diplomatic recognition. Gaining the recognition of the international community appears to be an exceptionally powerful means for a nascent state to establish legitimacy in the eyes of its domestic population. That the refusal or withdrawal of diplomatic recognition is one of the most potent weapons used by states, short of military intervention, to undermine the domestic political position of others serves as testimony to the importance of this form of external validation. At a more basic level, scholars have noted the relationship between the evolution of the nation-state system with its international norms of sovereignty and the consolidation of the state's claims over national territories (see Giddens, 1985; Ruggie, 1983; and Ashley, 1984). Here, the state's *sui generis* domestic position as sovereign representative of society is dependent in some sense on the recognition of other states within the international system.

It is difficult to generalize about the relationship between the pursuit of our two external strategies, extraction and validation. Clearly, they have the potential to be mutually reinforcing. By participating in international organizations, elites in developing countries may enhance both their status at home and their ability to extract resources from advanced industrialized nation-states. The potential conflicts are equally apparent. Given the widespread acceptance of national self-determination since 1945, the practice of imperialism as an extractive strategy clearly detracts from a state's efforts at external validation.

In summary, all states seeking to survive possess the international goals of power and wealth, from which the need for internal mobilization and extraction follow, and the domestic goals of control over resources and the preservation of legitimacy, which suggest the international strategies of external extraction and validation. This inventory of state goals and strategies provides systematic reasons why states, seeking to advance their own interests, will move across the domestic-international divide. The importance of these strategies and how and why they might be pursued is discussed in the following sections.

EXPLORING THE TWO FACES OF STATE ACTION: CHALLENGE AND RESPONSE

Building upon the framework developed in the last section, we now explore the types of challenges to the state arising in one arena that may trigger responses in the other arena. We consider whether and how the state will respond domestically, first, to changes in its long-term international power and, second, to changes in the immediate security threats that it confronts. Next we examine possible international responses by the state to challenges to its domestic political stability. Because we are primarily concerned here with exploring responses across arenas, we do not attempt to analyze the full range of possible responses to any particular challenge. The propositions in this section refer to the responses of states irrespective of their particular domestic or international structural positions. In the next section we develop propositions that accommodate variations in these factors.

H1: As the Long-Term Power of the Nation-State Declines, the State Will Increase Its Internal Mobilization   A detrimental shift in the power of the nation-state undermines the ability of state officials to achieve their international objectives. Faced with such a threat the state is likely to respond on both domestic and international fronts. In the domestic arena, extraction might be an effective short-run remedy, but over time it is likely to undermine the economic and political bases of national power. Thus, to the extent state officials perceive their decline of power to be enduring, they are more likely to respond in the domestic arena with mobilization rather than extraction. Mobilization, unlike extraction, has the potential to enhance the long-term power of the nation-state by stimulating economic growth and investment.

Historically, mobilization has been a common response by state leaders who fear that their national position, and thus their national security, is threatened by their relative backwardness (Gerschenkron, 1962). Stalin's strategy of rapid industrialization and the Mejii Restoration sought to enable Russia and Japan, respectively, to elevate their international ranking and prestige and to compete more effectively with the great powers of the West. More recently, the prominence that officials within the European Community have given to the ambitious 1992 liberalization reforms reflects a wide-spread concern that the nation-states of Western Europe may be in danger of falling behind the technologically more dynamic societies of America and Japan, and represents an attempt to redress this imbalance over the long term.[14] Proponents of industrial policy in the U.S. and economic reform in the Soviet Union share a similar concern over the relative economic decline of their nation-states and a belief in the desirability of alternative mobilization strategies.

Similarly, failure to pay adequate attention to internal mobilization can be costly for the nation-state. Sixteenth-century Spain paid dearly for neglecting its domestic economic base in pursuit of external extraction through the plundering of precious metals from the New World (Dehio, 1963:47). For reasons suggested below, late nineteenth-century Britain similarly relied primarily on international responses, such as portfolio investment, and thereby failed to arrest its decline. In a well-known study Robert Gilpin warned that the postwar United States, by emphasizing a strategy of foreign direct investment, risked following a similar path (Gilpin, 1975).

H2: As External Security Threats Increase, the State Will Increase Its Internal Extraction   More immediate threats to a nation-state's security arise when adversaries achieve unforeseen technological breakthroughs of military significance, or initiate direct military or economic confrontations. The immediacy of such challenges dictates that they be met, if possible, in the short-run. In such cases, extraction enjoys advantages over mobilization. Extraction allows the state to gain rapid access to society's resources, which can be used to meet the threat to national security.[15] States facing such threats may attempt mobilization yet simultaneously will be compelled to increase extraction, despite the potential long-term costs to the economy of adopting this strategy.

The most obvious examples of this domestic response involve the nation-state at war, or preparing for it. During World War II, Britain and Germany devoted half their economic resources to the military effort, obviously a far greater proportion than either state had been accustomed to committing to defense during peacetime (Knorr, 1975:47). Similarly, postwar American defense spending reached its peak as a percent of GNP during the Korean war, not only to pay for American participation but also to prepare for what many U.S. officials perceived as an imminent military conflict with the Communist world. It should also be noted that states unwilling or unable to extract in the face of perceived security threats will find their options to be severely constrained. The Johnson Administration faced this dilemma over Vietnam, and its unwillingness to raise taxes decisively shaped the manner in which it conducted the war.

H3: As Domestic Political Instability Increases, the State Will Pursue External Extraction and Validation   Political instability varies along a continuum from declining public support for state incumbents to revolutionary upheaval that threatens the integrity of the state as an organization. In response to such minor and major threats to their domestic position, states can draw upon a vast array of domestic strategies. We hypothesize that states will engage in international strategies as well, since such strategies can enhance the ability of the state to satisfy the proximate domestic goals jeopardized by instability.

External validation can enhance the legitimacy or popular support of state officials. Leaders of unstable regimes in the developing world have attempted to use the New International Economic Order (NIEO) and the international exposure associated with it to bolster their domestic status (Krasner, 1985). Similarly, President Richard Nixon attempted to neutralize the impact of Watergate by engaging in highly visible diplomatic encounters with Soviet leaders. Partly in response to the discontent generated by the socialist economic experiment, in the early 1980s French President Mitterand took a more interventionist role in foreign affairs, notably in Africa. One might argue that at that time the Libyan and Iranian regimes empowered themselves domestically by provoking and confronting the United States. Finally, and at the extreme, states may even go to war to resolve domestic political problems (see Mayer, 1969).

External extraction can be used to generate resources, which in turn can be used to reinforce the domestic position of the state. The resources provided by OPEC's dramatic reversal of the terms of trade enabled member states to reduce the burdens of domestic extraction and potentially coopt the sources of domestic discontent. Similarly, the French state has been able to extract considerable resources from the European Community through the common agricultural policy, thereby subsidizing farmers who comprise an important voting bloc (Zysman, 1978).

Because states participate in both international and domestic systems, opportunities exist for solving problems that arise in one domain by taking actions in the other. Consequently, analysis that focuses exclusively on state action in only one domain risks being misleading or incomplete. Structural Realists, for example, make a theoretical commitment to explain international outcomes by reference to characteristics of the international system. The problem here is that states may respond to international events through domestic actions or, alternatively, domestic problems may intrude on international relations in ways that are not understandable in terms of the prevailing character of the international system. If Realists are interested in explaining state action, systematic attention must be paid to interaction between systems.

INTEGRATING THE TWO FACES OF STATE ACTION: STRATEGIES AND CHOICES

Drawing upon the two previous sections, we now introduce variations in domestic and international structures and predict the choice of strategy made by states. Our approach here differs from the one used in the last section. There we examined the determinants of state action and presumed that all states would respond in similar ways to domestic and international challenges. In this section, we pose constraints on state action which differ across states. In doing so, we attempt a preliminary synthesis of the two faces of state action.

States differ in their domestic and international structural positions. Following Waltz (1979), by international structure we mean primarily the distribution of capabilities or power, defined as the ability to influence the behavior of foreign state and non-state actors. While international power is clearly a continuum, we distinguish for analytical purposes between states which are internationally "strong" or "weak."

Similarly, the structural position of a state in relation to its society varies along a continuum from decentralized and constrained by societal groups to centralized and insulated from society.[16] Important differences exist in the capacities of states to influence and shape the society and economy. In specifying the domestic structural capacities of states, scholars have focused on such institutional factors as the autonomy of administrative organizations and the presence or absence of policy tools. Again, for reasons of analytic convenience, we distinguish between "soft" (decentralized and constrained) and "hard" (centralized and autonomous) states.[17] Soft states may do little more than register the demands of societal groups or, at best, resist private demands. Hard states are able not only to resist societal forces but actively to reshape aspects of the economy and society.[18] Mixed cases exist, of course. The small European states examined by Katzenstein (1985) combine the centralized decision-making of hard states with a high degree of societal penetration characteristic of soft states—albeit societal influence channeled through centralized peak associations. The centralization of these states and societies suggests that they incline toward the hard end of our continuum. Their policy postures also tend to bear out this presupposition. While subtlety is lost with any analytic simplification, and in individual cases subtle differences may be all-important, we nonetheless believe that this distinction between soft and hard states is useful for comparative purposes.

H4: Soft States Will Rely on International Strategies to a Greater Extent Than Will Hard States. Conversely, Hard States Will Rely on Domestic Strategies to a Greater Extent Than Will Soft States   More restricted by social actors, decentralized and constrained states are less able to mobilize internally and extract resources than their hard state counterparts. Because they are limited in their ability to act at home, such states will tend to emphasize international strategies for the pursuit of state goals and ultimately for their survival. Centralized and insulated states, on the other hand, have a greater range of choice between venues. While they may still act internationally, their choice of strategy will be more weighted toward domestic strategies than in soft states.

H5: Internationally Weak States Will Emphasize Domestic Strategies More Than Will Internationally Powerful States. Likewise, Powerful States Will Emphasize International Strategies More Than Will Weak States   Weak states are more constrained in their ability to achieve their goals through international action. As a result they, more so than internationally powerful states, will focus their attention on internal mobilization and extraction. More powerful states are better equipped to extract resources from abroad, since the possession of wealth and power generally enhances their ability to accumulate further increments of it.

H6: Soft States Will Rely on Internal Extraction to a Greater Extent Than Will Hard States. Hard States Will Rely on Internal Mobilization to a Greater Extent Than Will Soft States   For reasons similar to those developed in H4, soft states are less powerful relative to society than are hard states and they implement domestic strategies with greater difficulty. They are less able to dismantle rent-seeking coalitions or insulate themselves from such groups. Enacting efficient property rights may also be difficult as groups clamor for special favors. Faced with this constraint, the state is likely to engage in greater extraction to maintain or increase its international power. In effect, the state becomes another rent-seeking actor (Krueger, 1974; Buchanan, Tollison, and Tullock, 1980; Conybeare, 1982; Olson, 1982). As we argued above, extraction is necessary for all states to convert wealth into power. Even hard states, as a result, will extract social resources. Yet because they are better able to reshape society and insulate themselves from rent-seekers, hard states will engage in internal mobilization more than will soft states.

H7: Internationally Weak States Will Emphasize External Validation More Than Will Stronger States. Internationally Powerful States Will Engage in External Extraction to a Larger Extent Than Will Weak States
External extraction often requires an ability to influence other nation-states, to get them to do what they would otherwise not do. Internationally powerful states, with more capabilities at their disposal, are better able than weak states to implement this strategy. As a result, weak states—more so than strong ones—will resort to external validation, which typically does not require coercive capabilities.

Taken together these hypotheses yield a synthesis of the relationship between domestic and international structures and strategies. The synthesis is presented in Figure 5.1.

Soft states rely on international strategies to a greater degree than do hard states (H4). If they are also internationally weak, they will emphasize domestic strategies more than do strong states (H5). Thus we can expect soft, weak states to combine a reliance on internal extraction (H6) and external validation (H7). This is the strategic mix currently employed by certain states in the developing world, and it leads to an unfortunate predicament. Plagued by the demands of rent-seeking coalitions, state elites find themselves extracting resources from domestic society

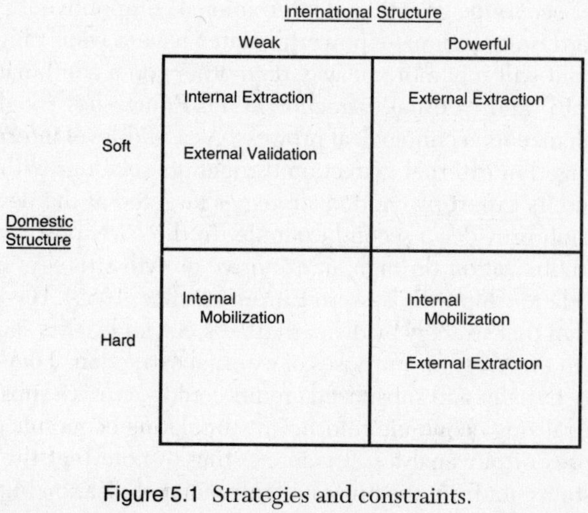

Figure 5.1 Strategies and constraints.

for redistribution to social claimants and to themselves (Bates, 1981; Levi, 1981). In seeking help from the international arena these states are forced by their subordinate position to rely primarily upon multilateral bargaining in the United Nations (such as in the NIEO) and other forms of symbolic international politics to maintain domestic legitimacy. Being ill-equipped to mobilize resources domestically or extract resources internationally, these states are compelled to pursue strategies that tend to reinforce their domestic weakness and do little to expand their international power.

Internationally powerful, soft states, such as the United States, will emphasize a strategy of international (H4, H5) extraction (H7). Throughout the post-war period, the United States has relied on a strategy of international extraction (albeit indirect) by creating and maintaining international economic regimes. American state officials constructed a free trade regime, renegotiated this regime to sanction non-tariff barriers to trade as the country's competitive position began to wane, and created an international monetary regime based upon seigniorage and the dollar (Parboni, 1981). In short, American officials convinced other states to participate in international arrangements that reinforced and enhanced the global power of the United States. Yet, as suggested by the recent tendency of the U.S. to run large budget and trade deficits and finance them with foreign capital, reliance on external extraction diminishes the incentives for state officials to engage in internal mobilization, sowing the seeds for later decline. As was the case for soft, weak states, over the long run the strategic preference of a soft, powerful state works to the detriment of its competitive position.

Hard states that are internationally weak will emphasize the domestic strategy (H4, H5) of internal mobilization (H6). Unable to coerce other nation-states, these states will turn inward and use their domestic strength to stimulate growth and the accumulation of national wealth to meet both international and domestic needs. Such a strategy characterized late nineteenth-century Japan and the Soviet Union and China in the periods after their respective revolutions. Similarly, the postwar Japanese state provided a variety of administrative and economic incentives designed to foster economic growth and international competitiveness.

Finally, hard, internationally powerful states have a wide range of strategies open to them but will rely more heavily than others on a combination of internal mobilization (H6) and external extraction (H7). France has sought to stimulate growth and enhance its technological prowess. As a mid-level international power, it has also engaged in external extraction through its relations with the European Community and its export promotion strategies targeted at the developing world. The Soviet Union provides a second example. In the early postwar period it pursued internal mobilization through an extensive growth strategy, and external extraction in its relationship with Eastern Europe (Bunce, 1985). Having reached the apparent limits of that strategy by the early 1970s, Soviet leaders sought to use economic links with the West for purposes of external extraction. They hoped, in vain, that technology transfer and subsidized credits could serve as a substitute for much needed decentralizing economic reforms in stimulating economic development.[19] For the purposes of our analysis, it is interesting to note that the current Soviet predicament stems not from the pursuit of internal mobilization but from the manner in which that strategy has been pursued. Over the long run, direct state-led mobilization has proven to be a less effective means to accumulate wealth than has indirect market-led mobilization. Not surprisingly, a central thrust of Gorbachev's current reform program involves the use of market incentives within the framework of a command economy.

In this section we have examined how variations in international and domestic structural positions combine to affect the strategic preferences of state officials. The framework put forth is more comprehensive than that found in the existing international relations literature. The "domestic structures" literature, for example, holds the international position of states constant and predicts foreign economic strategy by varying state-society relations (Katzenstein, 1978). Such an approach cannot account for differences in the strategies adopted by states with broadly similar domestic structures yet disparate international positions. Similarly, it would have difficulty explaining changes in strategy that took place in any given state over time, as its domestic structure remained the same and its international position shifted. Structural Realism, on the other hand, holds domestic structure constant and predicts strategy based on international position. Such an approach is inadequate in accounting for variations in strategy among states, or within the same state over time, when international position remains constant but state-society relations vary. By combining the two sets of variations in an integrated framework, the approach outlined above offers greater explanatory power.

CONCLUSION

A general theory of international relations, as others have noted, requires a theory of state action.[20] Realism claims to provide such a theory. Yet as we have seen, classical Realists, who appreciate the multidimensional nature of state action, fail to develop its logic in a rigorous fashion. Structural Realists, on the other hand, collapse the distinction between state and nation-state and thereby develop only part of the logic of state action. It is ironic that the Realist tradition places the state at the center of its analysis but fails to develop a comprehensive theoretical appreciation of its nature or logic. Since states are organizations that participate in both international and domestic political arenas, it is not surprising that the pursuit of goals in one arena influences actions in the other.[21] States may both respond to international events through domestic actions and attempt to solve domestic problems through international actions. This is an observation few analysts would disagree with but one which has yet to be systematically incorporated into general theories of international (or domestic) politics.

The alternative framework presented in this paper attempts to move beyond existing Realist theories. It places the state at the center of the analysis and develops a range of strategies, across domestic and international arenas, available to state officials in pursuit of their objectives. It also deduces, given the domestic and international structural position of the state, which strategy or combination of strategies the state is likely to pursue. By taking into account both the domestic and international constraints on the state, and by articulating both the domestic and international choices available to the state, we are able to provide a more comprehensive, integrated approach to the analysis of state behavior.

An adequate empirical test of the propositions generated by this approach is beyond the scope of the present paper. The illustrations provided, however, should be sufficient to indicate the potential utility of the approach. It yields insights, for example, into the problem of great-power decline. Our model suggests that soft, powerful states will be compelled, by the combined logic of their domestic and international positions, to pursue a dominant strategy of external extraction. This is so despite the fact that over the long run that strategy, when employed at the expense of internal mobilization, tends to erode the power that gave rise to it initially. The model captures the irony that states, in pursuit of wealth and power, undertake short-term strategies that diminish their long-term ability to acquire and accumulate those assets.

This approach should also prove useful in exploring the dilemmas of underdevelopment. Dependency theorists argue that underdevelopment is a function of a nation-state's international predicament—its position in the global division of labor—while their critics emphasize internal characteristics such as the strength of the state. Our approach combines the insights of the two and moves beyond each of them by positing that soft, weak states are driven to pursue strategies that ultimately perpetuate underdevelopment, while hard, weak states have the potential to extricate themselves from that condition. The latter assertion is largely consistent with the "dependent development" school, which assigns a prominent role to the state and its ability to bargain with multinationals in accounting for divergent paths of development (Evans, 1979).

Finally, the model presented here is potentially useful in anticipating the broad shifts in foreign policy that accompany changes in the structural position of a state. The Soviet Union prior to 1945 emphasized internal mobilization, while in the postwar period, as it acquired great-power status, it increased its emphasis on external extraction. Similarly, as soft states move from international weakness to strength, we would anticipate a shift from an emphasis on internal extraction and external validation to one on external extraction. In part, this consideration underlies the fear, shared by allies and adversaries, of contemporary Germany or Japan translating their formidable economic power into independent military strength. Alternatively, as weak states move from hard to soft domestically, we would expect them to place greater weight on external validation. One might explore, for example, whether the interest of the post-Facist democratic state of Spain in joining NATO and the EEC might serve as partial support for this hypothesis.

These are simply some of the issues that might be explored in the context of this model. They can be understood essentially as suggestions for further research. Scholars have been increasingly interested in the relationship between domestic and international systems. Our contention is that a focus on the state and an appreciation of its dual environment provide a basis for developing a systematic theoretical understanding of that relationship. The framework developed here also suggests that international relations scholars and practitioners alike would benefit from increased attention to state-society relations and, in particular, the ways in which the national economy is organized for the pursuit of international power.

The conduct of foreign policy depends not only on relations between nation-states but also on supposedly "domestic" politics.

NOTES

1. This is the task of the so-called "bureaucratic politics" literature that came into prominence in the late 1960s. The seminal contribution is Allison (1971) and, in the foreign economic policy literature, Katzenstein (1978).
2. Putnam's recent work (1988) is an important contribution in this regard.
3. We define the nation-state as the territorial unit. The state, in turn, is defined as politicians and administrators in the executive branch of government. Our primary focus is on the goal-oriented behavior of politicians and civil servants as they respond to internal and external constraints in an effort to manipulate policy outcomes in accordance with their preferences. An underlying presumption is that these preferences are partially, if not wholly, distinct from the parochial concerns of either societal groups or particular government institutions, and are tied to conceptions of the national interest or the maximization of some social welfare function. See Ikenberry, Lake, and Mastanduno (1988:10).
4. The major and perhaps more widely accepted alternative to the Realist, state-centered approach developed here focuses not on the state as an organization situated between the domestic and international political systems, but on social groups which define their material interests by their "international situation" and pursue their desires through the mechanism of the state. See Ferguson (1984), Gourevitch (1984), and Frieden (1988). There are many well-known problems with this society-centered alternative, including the inherent problems of choosing the appropriate level of interest aggregation and measuring the strength of various domestic groups. Given these problems, we believe it is useful to propose a state-centered approach to studying the nexus of international and domestic politics. Ultimately, the choice between alternatives will be based on their relative explanatory power.
5. It is important to underscore the partial nature of our enterprise. Because we focus only on strategies and goals which bridge the domestic-international divide, and self-consciously ignore other approaches or strategies which do not, we cannot and do not purport to have a complete theory of state action.
6. See Keohane (1980, 1984) and Krasner (1976, 1983). In *After Hegemony*, Keohane is critical of the "crude" version of hegemonic stability theory, in part for its inadequate attention to domestic politics (1984:35). His own revision and extension of the theory, however, focuses not on domestic politics but on international regimes and their functional attributes.
7. In their critical review of the regimes literature, Haggard and Simmons (1987) fault structural Realism for neglecting domestic politics. This neglect is ironic, since the early versions of what became the structural Realist literature (e.g., Keohane and Nye, 1977) were concerned with domestic politics and the impact of interdependence on it. Putnam (1988) argues that domestic politics fell out of focus as the literature came to emphasize regimes.
8. In these models, we put forth a conception of the state as an actor in both the domestic and international realms (see also Ikenberry, Lake, and Mastanduno, 1988). The notion of the state as an international actor is widely accepted, perhaps because of the collective nature of many policies in this arena. As domestic politics often focuses on distrib-

utive or redistributive issues, the role of a relatively unified and autonomous state in this realm is certainly more constrained—and may be analytically problematic. Nonetheless, we argue vigorously for the utility of our conception of the state as a domestic actor. Douglass North (1981) has examined the role of the state, often under pressure from internal and external competitors, in setting domestic property rights. Levi (1988) has used a similar framework to explore tax systems. Stepan (1978) and Trimberger (1978) provide accounts of the efforts of states to restructure their domestic societies. We believe that our own work also supports this conception. Ikenberry (1988) examines the state-led politics of American oil decontrol in the 1970s. Lake (1988) analyzes the international and, in turn, statist origins of American tariff policy in the late nineteenth and early twentieth centuries. Both of these policies deal with quintessentially "domestic" issues. Mastanduno (1988) has examined American export controls from a state-as-actor approach, a policy that more clearly bridges the domestic and international arenas. These studies do not demonstrate conclusively the utility of a conception of the state-as-actor in domestic politics, but they do suggest that the approach is plausible and analytically fruitful.

9. Pareto is cited in Krasner (1978:12).

10. This general argument is presented by Polanyi (1957).

11. A good discussion is found in Knorr (1975).

12. This dilemma is discussed in the context of statebuilding in the early modern period by Tilly (1985), Hirschman (1978), and North (1981).

13. We are referring here to the Weberian argument concerning the organization of legitimate authority. Systematic incentives exist for rulers to organize power in ways that establish or preserve the legitimacy of government institutions and decision-making. In the modern period, the state has found legal-rational authority to be the most effective method for the organization of political power. See Weber (1978, Vol. 1:212–16). For a recent discussion of this argument and its bearing on the behavior of modern state officials, see Schmitter (1985).

14. In their quest for technological parity, European Community officials have placed considerable emphasis on indirect mobilization, specifically the removal of all remaining intra-Community barriers to the free movement of labor and goods across national borders. See "A Survey of Europe's Internal Market," *The Economist,* July 9, 1988.

15. Lamborn, in his discussion of the constraints on the extractive capabilities of states, recognizes the importance of the level of perceived external threat. See Lamborn (1983:131, 137–38).

16. We have elsewhere criticized the weak state–strong state distinction as developed by Katzenstein, Krasner, and others. See Ikenberry, Lake and Mastanduno (1988:14). Foremost among our points of contention is that the concept of weakness and strength does not tell us enough about the specific sources of state power and the instruments available to any particular state. We recognize, however, that the simple dichotomy is useful for comparative purposes in a "first-cut" or preliminary explanation. Future work should, of course, seek to further refine this distinction even in its comparative usage.

17. Immanuel Wallerstein also distinguishes between strong and weak states (1974). But in doing so he fails to separate international and domestic dimensions of strength. As we note, and as critics of Wallerstein observe, the two spheres of state strength are not identical and, indeed, are frequently quite divergent (Zolberg, 1981).

18. John Zysman, who is interested in the divergent abilities of advanced industrial states to become involved in industrial adjustment, focuses on three structural elements: mechanisms of recruitment in the national civil service, the degree of centralization within government civil service, and the extent of independence from legislative oversight (Zysman, 1983:300). See also Katzenstein (1976; 1978), and Krasner (1978: Chapter

Three). The term "soft state" comes from Myrdal (1968:895–900). See also Waterbury (1985). In a similar fashion, the term "soft regime" is used by Kahler (1985:368).

19. On U.S. attempts to exploit the Soviet predicament, see Mastanduno (1985).

20. Keohane (1983) notes: "Understanding the general principles of state action and the practices of governments is a necessary basis for attempts to refine theory or to extend the analysis to non-state actors." See also Gilpin (1981:15).

21. The logic of this two-sided image is also explored in Ikenberry (1986).

REFERENCES

Allison, G. (1971) *Essence of Decision: Explaining the Cuban Missile Crisis.* Boston: Little, Brown.

Almond, G. (1985) Internal vs. External Factors in Political Development: An Evaluation of Recent Historical Research. Paper presented at the Annual Meeting of the American Political Science Association, New Orleans.

Ashley, R. (1984) The Poverty of Neo-Realism. *International Organization* **38**(2):225–86.

Bates, R. (1981) *Markets and States in Tropical Africa: The Political Basis of Agricultural Policies.* Berkeley: University of California Press.

Buchanan, J., R. Tollison and G. Tullock, eds. (1980) *Toward a Theory of the Rent-Seeking Society.* College Station, TX: Texas A&M Press.

Bunce, V. (1985) The Empire Strikes Back: The Evolution of the Eastern Bloc from a Soviet Asset to a Soviet Liability. *International Organization* **39**(1):1–46.

Carr, E. (1962) *The Twenty Years Crisis, 1919–1939: An Introduction to the Study of International Relations.* London: Macmillan & Co.

Conybeare, J. (1982) The Rent-Seeking State and Revenue Diversification. *World Politics* **35**(1):25–42.

Dehio, L. (1963) *The Precarious Balance: The Politics of Power in Europe, 1494–1945.* London: Chatto Windus.

Evans, P. (1979) *Dependent Development: The Alliance of Multinational, State and Local Capital in Brazil.* Princeton: Princeton University Press.

Ferguson, T. (1984) From Normalcy to New Deal: Industrial Structure, Party Competition, and American Public Policy in the Great Depression. *International Organization* **38**(1):41–94.

Frieden, J. (1988) Sectoral Conflict and Foreign Economic Policy, 1914–1940. *International Organization* **42**(1):59–90.

Gerschenkron, A. (1962) Economic Backwardness in Historical Perspective. In *Economic Backwardness in Historical Perspective,* edited by A. Gerschenkron, pp. 5–30. Cambridge: Harvard University Press.

Giddens, A. (1985) *The Nation-State and Violence.* Berkeley: University of California Press.

Gilpin, R. (1975) *U.S. Power and the Multinational Corporation: The Political Economy of Foreign Direct Investment.* New York: Basic Books.

Gilpin, R. (1981) *War and Change in World Politics.* Cambridge: Cambridge University Press.

Gilpin, R. (1984) The Richness of the Tradition of Political Realism. *International Organization* **38**(2):287–305.

Gourevitch, P. (1978) The Second Image Reversed: The International Sources of Domestic Politics. *International Organization* **32**(4):881–912.

Gourevitch, P. (1984) Breaking with Orthodoxy: The Politics of Economic Policy Responses to the Depression of the 1930s. *International Organization* **38**(1):95–129.

Haggard, S. and B. Simmons. (1987) Theories of International Regimes. *International Organization* **41**(3):491–517.

Hirschman, A. (1978) Exit, Voice and the State. *World Politics* **31**(1):90–107.

Ikenberry, G. J. (1986) The State and Strategies of International Adjustment. *World Politics* **39**(1):53–77.

Ikenberry, G. J. (1988) *Reasons of State: Oil Politics and the Capacities of American Government.* Ithaca: Cornell University Press.

Ikenberry, G. J., D. Lake and M. Mastanduno. (1988) Introduction: Explaining American Foreign Economic Policy. *International Organization* **42**(1):1–14.

Kahler, M. (1985) Politics and International Debt: Explaining the Crisis. *International Organization* **39**(3):357–82.

Katzenstein, P. (1976) International Relations and Domestic Structures: Foreign Economic Policies of Advanced Industrial States. *International Organization* **30**(1):1–45.

Katzenstein, P. (1978) *Between Power and Plenty: The Foreign Economic Policies of Advanced Industrial States.* Madison: University of Wisconsin Press.

Katzenstein, P. (1985) *Small States in World Markets: Industrial Policy in Europe.* Ithaca: Cornell University Press.

Keohane, R. (1980) The Theory of Hegemonic Stability and Changes in International Economic Regimes, 1967–1977. In *Changes in the International System,* edited by Ole Holsti, et al., pp. 131–62. Boulder: Westview Press.

Keohane, R. (1983) Theory of World Politics: Structural Realism and Beyond. In *Political Science: The State of the Discipline,* edited by A. Finifter, pp. 503–40. Washington: American Political Science Association.

Keohane, R. (1984) *After Hegemony: Cooperation and Discord in the World Political Economy.* Princeton: Princeton University Press.

Keohane, R. and J. Nye. (1977) *Power and Interdependence: World Politics in Transition.* Boston: Little, Brown and Company.

Kissinger, H. and C. Vance. (1988) Bipartisan Objectives for American Foreign Policy. *Foreign Affairs* **66**(5):899–921.

Knorr, K. (1975) *The Power of Nations: The Political Economy of International Relations.* New York: Basic Books.

Krasner, S. (1976) State Power and the Structure of International Trade. *World Politics* **28**(3):317–43.

Krasner, S. (1977) Domestic Constraints on International Economic Leverage. In *Economic Issues and National Security,* edited by K. Knorr and F. N. Trager, pp. 160–81. Lawrence: Regents Press of Kansas.

Krasner, S. (1978) *Defending the National Interest: Raw Materials Investments and U.S. Foreign Policy.* Princeton: Princeton University Press.

Krasner, S., ed. (1983) *International Regimes.* Ithaca: Cornell University Press.

Krasner, S. (1985) *Structural Conflict: The Third World Against Global Liberalism.* Berkeley: University of California Press.

Krueger, A. (1974) The Political Economy of the Rent-Seeking Society. *The American Economic Review* **64**:291–303.

Lake, D. A. (1988) *Power, Protection and Free Trade: International Sources of U.S. Commercial Strategy, 1887–1939.* Ithaca: Cornell University Press.

Lamborn, A. C. (1983) Power and the Politics of Extraction. *International Studies Quarterly* **27**:125–46.

Levi, M. (1981) The Predatory Theory of Rule. *Politics and Society* **10**(4):431–65.

Levi, M. (1988) *Of Rule and Revenue.* Berkeley: University of California Press.

Mastanduno, M. (1985) Strategies of Economic Containment. *World Politics* **37**(4):503–31.

Mastanduno, M. (1988) Trade as a Strategic Weapon: American and Alliance Export Control Policy in the Early Postwar Period. *International Organization* **42**(1):121–50.

Mayer, A. (1969) Internal Causes and Purposes of War in Europe, 1870–1956: A Research Assignment. *Journal of Modern History* **41**:291–303.

Morgenthau, J. (1985) *Power Among Nations.* New York: Alfred A. Knopf.

Myrdal, G. (1968) *Asian Drama.* New York: Pantheon.

North, D. (1981) *Structure and Change in Economic History.* New York: Norton.

Olson, M. (1982) *The Rise and Decline of Nations: Economic Growth, Stagflation, and Social Rigidities.* New Haven: Yale University Press.

Parboni, R. (1981) *The Dollar and Its Rivals.* New York: New Left Books.

Polyani, K. (1957) *The Great Transformation: The Political and Economic Origins of Our Time.* Boston: Beacon Press.

Putnam, R. (1988) Diplomacy and Domestic Politics: The Logic of Two-Level Games. *International Organization* **42**(3):427–60.

Rogowski, R. (1987) Political Cleavages and Changing Exposure to Trade. *American Political Science Review* **81**(4):1121–37.

Rosenberg, N. and L. Birdzell. (1986) *How the West Grew Rich: The Economic Transformation of the Industrial World.* New York: Basic Books.

Ruggie, J. (1983) Continuity and Transformation in the World Polity: Toward a Neorealist Synthesis. *World Politics* **35**(2):261–85.

Schmitter, P. (1985) Neo-Corporatism and the State. Unpublished paper.

Stepan, A. (1978) *The State and Society: Peru in Comparative Perspective.* Princeton: Princeton University Press.

Tilly, C. (1985) Warmaking and Statemaking as Organized Crime. In *Bringing the State Back In,* edited by P. B. Evans, D. Rueschemeyer, and T. Skocpol, pp. 169–91. New York: Cambridge University Press.

Trimberger, E. K. (1978) *Revolution from Above: Military Bureaucrats and Development in Japan, Turkey, Egypt and Peru.* New Brunswick: Transaction Books.

Vasquez, J. (1983) *The Power of Power Politics: A Critique.* New Brunswick: Rutgers University Press.

Viner, J. (1948) Power versus Plenty as Objectives of Foreign Policy in the Seventeenth and Eighteenth Centuries. *World Politics* **1**(1):1–29.

Wallerstein, I. (1974) *The Modern World-System: Capitalist Agriculture and the Origins of the European World-Economy in the Sixteenth Century.* New York: Academic Press.

Waltz, K. (1979) *Theory of International Politics.* New York: Wiley.

Waterbury, J. (1985) The Soft State and the Open Door: Egypt's Experience with Economic Liberalization, 1974–1984. *Comparative Politics* 18(1):65–83.

Weber, M. (1978) *Economy and Society,* edited by G. Roth and C. Wittich, vol. 1. Berkeley: University of California Press.

Zolberg, A. (1981) Origins of the Modern World System: A Missing Link. *World Politics* **35**:253–81.

Zysman, J. (1978) The French State in the International Economy. In *Between Power and Plenty: Foreign Economic Policies of Advanced Industrial States,* edited by P. J. Katzenstein, pp. 255–93. Madison: University of Wisconsin Press.

Zysman, J. (1983) *Governments, Markets, and Growth: Financial Systems and the Politics of Industrial Change.* Ithaca: Cornell University Press.

The American Conception of National Security and the Beginnings of the Cold War, 1945–1948 *

Melvyn P. Leffler

IN AN INTERVIEW with Henry Kissinger in 1978 on "The Lessons of the Past," Walter Laqueur observed that during World War II "few if any people thought . . . of the structure of peace that would follow the war except perhaps in the most general terms of friendship, mutual trust, and the other noble sentiments mentioned in wartime programmatic speeches about the United Nations and related topics." Kissinger concurred, noting that no statesman, except perhaps Winston Churchill, "gave any attention to what would happen after the war." Americans, Kissinger stressed, "were determined that we were going to base the postwar period on good faith and getting along with everybody."[1]

That two such astute and knowledgeable observers of international politics

---

*The extensive footnotes of the original article have been heavily redacted in this reprint. Interested readers should consult the original publication for the excellent detailed literature review and original research that Professor Leffler provides there.

Melvyn P. Leffler, "The American Conception of National Security and the Beginnings of the Cold War, 1945–48 *American Historical Review*, Vol. 89, no. 2 (April 1984). Reprinted by permission.

were so uninformed about American planning at the end of the Second World War is testimony to the enduring mythology of American idealism and innocence in the world of Realpolitik. It also reflects the state of scholarship on the interrelated areas of strategy, economy, and diplomacy. Despite the publication of several excellent overviews of the origins of the Cold War, despite the outpouring of incisive monographs on American foreign policy in many areas of the world, and despite some first-rate studies on the evolution of strategic thinking and the defense establishment, no comprehensive account yet exists of how American defense officials defined national security interests in the aftermath of World War II. Until recently, the absence of such a study was understandable, for scholars had limited access to records pertaining to national security, strategic thinking, and war planning. But in recent years documents relating to the early years of the Cold War have been declassified in massive numbers.

This documentation now makes it possible to analyze in greater depth the perceptions, apprehensions, and objectives of those defense officials most concerned with defining and defending the nation's security and strategic interests.[2] This essay seeks neither to explain the process of decision making on any particular issue nor to dissect the domestic political considerations and fiscal constraints that narrowed the options available to policy makers. Furthermore, it does not pretend to discern the motivations and objectives of the Soviet Union. Rather, the goal here is to elucidate the fundamental strategic and economic considerations that shaped the definition of American national security interests in the postwar world. Several of these considerations—especially as they related to overseas bases, air transit rights, and a strategic sphere of influence in Latin America—initially were the logical result of technological developments and geostrategic experiences rather than directly related to postwar Soviet behavior. But American defense officials also considered the preservation of a favorable balance of power in Eurasia as fundamental to U.S. national security. This objective impelled defense analysts and intelligence officers to appraise and reappraise the intentions and capabilities of the Soviet Union. Rather modest estimates of the Soviets' ability to wage war against the United States generated the widespread assumption that the Soviets would refrain from military aggression and seek to avoid war. Nevertheless, American defense officials remained greatly preoccupied with the geopolitical balance of power in Europe and Asia, because that balance seemed endangered by communist exploitation of postwar economic dislocation and social and political unrest. Indeed, American assessments of the Soviet threat were less a consequence of expanding Soviet military capabilities and of Soviet diplomatic demands than a result of growing apprehension about the vulnerability of American strategic and economic interests in a world of unprecedented turmoil and upheaval. Viewed from this perspective, the Cold War assumed many of its most enduring characteristics during 1947–48, when American officials sought to cope with an array of challenges by implementing their own concepts of national security.

AMERICAN OFFICIALS FIRST BEGAN to think seriously about the nation's postwar security during 1943–44. Military planners devised elaborate plans for an overseas base system. Many of these plans explicitly contemplated the breakdown of the wartime coalition. But, even when strategic planners postulated good postwar relations among the Allies, their plans called for an extensive system of bases. These bases were defined as the nation's strategic frontier. Beyond this frontier the United States would be able to use force to counter any threats or frustrate any overt acts of aggression. Within the strategic frontier, American military predominance had to remain inviolate. Although plans for an overseas base system went through many revisions, they always presupposed American hegemony over the Atlantic and Pacific oceans. These plans received President Franklin D. Roosevelt's endorsement in early 1944. After his death, army and navy planners presented their views to President Harry S. Truman, and Army Chief of Staff George C. Marshall discussed them extensively with Secretary of State James C. Byrnes.

Two strategic considerations influenced the development of an overseas base system. The first was the need for defense in depth. Since attacks against the United States could only emanate from Europe and Asia, the Joint Chiefs of Staff concluded as early as November 1943 that the United States must encircle the Western Hemisphere with a defensive ring of outlying bases. In the Pacific this ring had to include the Aleutians, the Philippines, Okinawa, and the former Japanese mandates. Recognizing the magnitude of this strategic frontier, Admiral William E. Leahy, chief of staff to the president, explained to Truman that the joint chiefs were not thinking of the immediate future when, admittedly, no prospective naval power could challenge American predominance in the Pacific. Instead, they were contemplating the long term, when the United States might require wartime access to the resources of southeast Asia as well as "a firm line of communications from the West Coast to the Asiatic mainland, plus denial of this line in time of war to any potential enemy."[3] In the Atlantic, strategic planners maintained that their minimum requirements included a West African zone, with primary bases in the Azores or Canary Islands. Leahy went even further, insisting on primary bases in West Africa itself—for example, at Dakar or Casablanca. The object of these defensive bases was to enable the United States to possess complete control of the Atlantic and Pacific oceans and keep hostile powers far from American territory.[4]

Defense in depth was especially important in light of the Pearl Harbor experience, the advance of technology, and the development of the atomic bomb. According to the Joint Chiefs of Staff, "Experience in the recent war demonstrated conclusively that the defense of a nation, if it is to be effective, must begin beyond its frontiers. The advent of the atomic bomb reemphasizes this requirement. The farther away from our own vital areas we can hold our enemy through the possession of advanced bases . . . , the greater are our chances of surviving successfully an attack by atomic weapons and of destroying the enemy which employs them against us." Believing that atomic weapons would increase the incentive to aggression by enhancing the advantage of surprise, military planners never ceased to extol the utility of forward bases from which American aircraft could seek to intercept attacks against the United States.[5]

The second strategic consideration that influenced the plan for a comprehensive overseas base system was the need to project American power quickly and effectively against any potential adversary. In conducting an overall examination of requirements for base rights in September 1945, the Joint War Plans Committee stressed that World War II demonstrated the futility of a strategy of static defense. The United States had to be able to take "timely" offensive action against the adversary's capacity and will to wage war. New weapons demanded that advance bases be established in "areas well removed from the United States, so as to project our operations, with new weapons or otherwise, nearer the enemy." Scientists, like Vannevar Bush, argued that, "regardless of the potentialities of these new weapons [atomic energy and guided missiles], they should not influence the number, location, or extent of strategic bases now considered essential." The basic strategic concept underlying all American war plans called for an air offensive against a prospective enemy from overseas bases. Delays in the development of the B-36, the first intercontinental bomber, only accentuated the need for these bases.

In October 1945 the civilian leaders of the War and Navy departments carefully reviewed the emerging strategic concepts and base requirements of the military planners. Secretary of the Navy James Forrestal and Secretary of War Robert P. Patterson discussed them with Admiral Leahy, the Joint Chiefs of Staff, and Secretary of State Byrnes. The civilian secretaries fully endorsed the concept of a farflung system of bases in the Atlantic and Pacific oceans that would enhance the offensive capabilities of the United States. Having expended so much blood and effort capturing Japanese-held islands, defense officials, like Forrestal, naturally wished to devise a base system in the Pacific to facilitate the projection of American influence and power. The Philippines were the key to southeast Asia, Okinawa to the Yellow Sea, the Sea of Japan, and the industrial heartland of northeast Asia. From these bases on America's "strategic frontier," the United States could preserve its access to vital raw materials in Asia, deny these resources to a prospective enemy, help preserve peace and stability in troubled areas, safeguard critical sea lanes, and, if necessary, conduct an air offensive against the industrial infrastructure of any Asiatic power, including the Soviet Union.

Control of the Atlantic and Pacific oceans through overseas bases was considered indispensable to the nation's security regardless of what might happen to the wartime coalition. So was control over polar air routes. Admiral Leahy criticized a Joint Strategic Survey Committee report of early 1943 that omitted Iceland and Greenland as primary base requirements. When General S. D. Embick, the senior member of that committee, continued to question the desirability of a base in Iceland, lest it antagonize the Russians, he was overruled by Assistant Secretary of War John McCloy. McCloy charged that Embick had "a rather restricted concept of what is necessary for national defense." The first postwar base system approved by both the Joint Chiefs of Staff and the civilian secretaries in October 1945 included Iceland as a primary base area. The Joint War Plans Committee explained that American bases must control the air in the Arctic, prevent the establishment of enemy military facilities there, and support America's own striking forces. Once Soviet-American relations began to deteriorate, Greenland also was designated as a primary base for American heavy bombers and fighters because of its close proximity to the industrial heartland of the potential enemy. As the United States sought rights for bases along the Polar route in 1946 and 1947, moreover, American defense officials also hoped to thwart Soviet efforts to acquire similar rights at Spitzbergen and Bear Island.

In the immediate postwar years American ambitions for an elaborate base system encountered many problems. Budgetary constraints compelled military planners to drop plans for many secondary and subsidiary bases, particularly in the South Pacific and Caribbean. These sacrifices merely increased the importance of those bases that lay closer to a potential adversary. By early 1948, the joint chiefs were willing to forego base rights in such places as Surinam, Curacoa-Aruba, Cayenne, Nounea, and Vivi-Levu if "joint" or "participating" rights could be acquired or preserved in Karachi, Tripoli, Algiers, Casablanca, Dharan, and Monrovia. Budgetary constraints, then, limited the depth of the base system but not the breadth of American ambitions. Furthermore, the governments of Panama, Iceland, Denmark, Portugal, France, and Saudi Arabia often rejected or abolished the exclusive rights the United States wanted and sometimes limited the number of American personnel on such bases. Washington, therefore, negotiated a variety of arrangements to meet the objections of host governments. By early 1948, for example, the base in Iceland was operated by a civilian company under contract to the United States Air Force; in the Azores, the base was manned by a detachment of Portuguese military personnel operating under the Portuguese flag, but an air force detachment serviced the American aircraft using the base. In Port Lyautey, the base was under the command of the French navy, but under a secret agreement an American naval team took care of American aircraft on the base. In Saudi Arabia, the Dharan air strip was cared for by 300 U.S. personnel and was capable of handling B-29s. Because these arrangements were not altogether satisfactory, in mid-1948 Secretary of Defense Forrestal and Secretary of the Army Kenneth Royall advocated using American economic and military assistance as levers to acquire more permanent and comprehensive base rights, particularly in Greenland and North Africa.

Less well known than the American effort to establish a base system, but integral to the policymakers' conception of national security, was the attempt to secure military air transit and landing rights. Military planners wanted such rights at critical locations not only in the Western Hemisphere but also in North Africa, the Middle East, India, and southeast Asia. To this end they delineated a route from Casablanca through Algiers, Tripoli, Cairo, Dharan, Karachi, Delhi, Calcutta, Rangoon, Bangkok, and Saigon to Manila. In closing out the African–Middle East theater at the conclusion of the war, General H. W. Aurand, under explicit instructions from the secretary of war, made preparations for permanent rights at seven airfields in North Africa and Saudi Arabia. According to a study by the Joint Chiefs of Staff, "Military air transit rights for the United States along the North African–Indian route were most desirable in order to provide access to and familiarity with bases from which offensive and defensive action might be conducted in the event of a major war, and to provide an alternate route to China and to United States Far Eastern bases." In other words, such rights would permit the rapid augmentation of American bases in wartime as well as the rapid movement of American air units from the eastern to the western flank of the U.S. base system. In order to maintain these airfields in a state of readiness, the United States would have to rely on private airlines, which had to be persuaded to locate their operations in areas designated essential to military air transit rights. In this way, airports "in being" outside the formal American base system would be available for military operations in times of crisis and war. Assistant Secretary McCloy informed the State Department at the beginning of 1945 that a "strong United States air transport system, international in scope and readily adapted to military use, is vital to our air power and future national security." Even earlier, the joint chiefs had agreed not to include South American air bases in their strategic plans so long as it was understood that commercial fields in that region would be developed with a view to subsequent military use.[6]

In Latin America, American requirements for effective national security went far beyond air transit rights. In a report written in January 1945 at Assistant Secretary McCloy's behest, the War Department urged American collaboration with Latin American armed forces to insure the defense of the Panama Canal and the Western Hemisphere. Six areas within Latin America were considered of special significance either for strategic reasons or for their raw materials: the Panama Canal and approaches within one thousand miles; the Straits of Magellan; northeast Brazil; Mexico; the river Plate estuary and approaches within five hundred miles; and Mollendo, Peru-Antofagusta, and Chile. These areas were so "important," Secretary of War Patterson explained to Secretary of State Marshall in early 1947, "that the threat of attack on any of them would force the United States to come to their defense, even though it were not certain that attack on the United States itself would follow." The resources of these areas were essential to the United States, because "it is imperative that our war potential be enhanced . . . during any national emergency."[7]

While paying lip service to the United Nations and worrying about the impact of regional agreements in the Western Hemisphere on Soviet actions and American influence in Europe, the Joint Chiefs of Staff insisted that in practice non-American forces had to be kept out of the Western Hemisphere and the Monroe Doctrine had to be kept inviolate. "The Western Hemisphere is a distinct military entity, the integrity of which is a fundamental postulate of our security in the event of another world war."[8] Developments in aviation, rockets, guided missiles, and atomic energy had made "the solidarity of the Hemisphere and its united support of the principles of the Monroe Doctrine" more important than before. Patterson told Marshall that effective implementation of the Monroe Doctrine now meant "that we not only refuse to tolerate foreign colonization, control, or the extension of a foreign political system to our hemisphere, but we take alarm from the appearance on the continent of foreign ideologies, commercial exploitation, cartel arrangements, or other symptoms of increased non-hemispheric influence. . . . The basic consideration has always been an overriding apprehension lest a base be established in this area by a potentially hostile foreign power." The United States, Patterson insisted, must have "a stable, secure, and friendly flank to the South, not confused by enemy penetration, political, economic, or military."[9]

The need to predominate throughout the Western Hemisphere was not a result of deteriorating Soviet-American relations but a natural evolution of the Monroe Doctrine, accentuated by Axis aggression and new technological imperatives.[10] Patterson, Forrestal, and Army Chief of Staff Dwight D. Eisenhower initially were impelled less by reports of Soviet espionage, propaganda, and infiltration in Latin America than by accounts of British efforts to sell cruisers and aircraft to Chile and Ecuador; Swedish sales of anti-aircraft artillery to Argentina; and French offers to build cruisers and destroyers for both Argentina and Brazil. To foreclose all foreign influence and to insure United States strategic hegemony, military officers and the civilian secretaries of the War and Navy departments argued for an extensive system of United States bases, expansion of commercial airline facilities throughout Latin America, negotiation of a regional defense pact, curtailment of all foreign military aid and foreign military sales, training of Latin American military officers in the United States, outfitting of Latin American armies with U.S. military equipment, and implementation of a comprehensive military assistance program.[11]

The military assistance program, as embodied in the Inter-American Military Cooperation Act, generated the most interagency discord. Latin American experts in the State Department maintained that military assistance would stimulate regional conflicts, dissipate Latin American financial resources, and divert attention from economic and social issues. Before leaving office, Byrnes forcefully presented the State Department position to Forrestal and Patterson. Instead of dwelling on the consequences of military assistance for Latin America, Byrnes maintained that such a program would be too costly for the United States, would focus attention on a region where American interests were relatively unchallenged, and would undermine more important American initiatives elsewhere on the globe. "Greece and Turkey are our outposts," he declared.[12]

The secretary of state clearly did not think that Congress would authorize funds for Latin America as well as for Greece and Turkey. Although Truman favored military assistance to Latin America, competing demands for American resources in 1947 and 1948 forced both military planners and U.S. senators to give priority to Western Europe and the Near East. In June 1948 the Inter-American Military Cooperation Act died in the Senate. But this signified no diminution in American national security imperatives; indeed, it underscored Byrnes's statement of December 1946 that the "outposts" of the nation's security lay in the heart of Eurasia.[13]

FROM THE CLOSING DAYS OF WORLD WAR II, American defense officials believed that they could not allow any prospective adversary to control the Eurasian land mass. This was the lesson taught by two world wars. Strategic thinkers and military analysts insisted that any power or powers attempting to dominate Eurasia must be regarded as potentially hostile to the United States. Their acute awareness of the importance of Eurasia made Marshall, Thomas Handy, George A. Lincoln, and other officers wary of the expansion of Soviet influence there. Cognizant of the growth in Soviet strength, General John Deane, head of the United States military mission in Moscow, urged a tougher stand against Soviet demands even before World War II had ended. While acknowledging that the increase in Soviet power stemmed primarily from the defeat of Germany and Japan, postwar assessments of the Joint

Chiefs of Staff emphasized the importance of deterring further Soviet aggrandizement in Eurasia. Concern over the consequences of Russian domination of Eurasia helps explain why in July 1945 the joint chiefs decided to oppose a Soviet request for bases in the Dardanelles; why during March and April 1946 they supported a firm stand against Russia in Iran, Turkey, and Tripolitania; and why in the summer of 1946 Clark Clifford and George Elsey, two White House aides, argued that Soviet incorporation of any parts of Western Europe, the Middle East, China, or Japan into a communist orbit was incompatible with American national security.

Yet defense officials were not eager to sever the wartime coalition. In early 1944 Admiral Leahy noted the "phenomenal development" of Soviet power but still hoped for Soviet-American cooperation. When members of the Joint Postwar Committee met with their colleagues on the Joint Planning Staff in April 1945, Major General G. V. Strong argued against using U.S. installations in Alaska for staging expeditionary forces, lest such a move exacerbate Russo-American relations. A few months later Eisenhower, Lincoln, and other officers advised against creating a central economic authority for Western Europe that might appear to be an anti-Soviet bloc.[14] The American objective, after all, was to avoid Soviet hegemony over Eurasia. By aggravating Soviet fears, the United States might foster what it wished to avoid. American self-restraint, however, might be reciprocated by the Soviets, providing time for Western Europe to recover and for the British to reassert some influence on the Continent.[15] Therefore, many defense officials in 1945 hoped to avoid an open rift with the Soviet Union. But at the same time they were determined to prevent the Eurasian land mass from falling under Soviet and communist influence.

Studies by the Joint Chiefs of Staff stressed that, if Eurasia came under Soviet domination, either through military conquest or political and economic "assimilation," America's only potential adversary would fall heir to enormous natural resources, industrial potential, and manpower. By the autumn of 1945, military planners already were worrying that Soviet control over much of Eastern Europe and its raw materials would abet Russia's economic recovery, enhance its war-making capacity, and deny important foodstuffs, oil, and minerals to Western Europe. By the early months of 1946, Secretary Patterson and his subordinates in the War Department believed that Soviet control of the Ruhr-Rhineland industrial complex would constitute an extreme threat. Even more dangerous was the prospect of Soviet predominance over the rest of Western Europe, especially France. Strategically, this would undermine the impact of any prospective American naval blockade and would allow Soviet military planners to achieve defense in depth. The latter possibility had enormous military significance, because American war plans relied so heavily on air power and strategic bombing, the efficacy of which might be reduced substantially if the Soviets acquired outlying bases in Western Europe and the Middle East or if they "neutralized" bases in Great Britain.[16]

Economic considerations also made defense officials determined to retain American access to Eurasia as well as to deny Soviet predominance over it. Stimson, Patterson, McCloy, and Assistant Secretary Howard C. Peterson agreed with

Forrestal that long-term American prosperity required open markets, unhindered access to raw materials, and the rehabilitation of much—if not all—of Eurasia along liberal capitalist lines. In late 1944 and 1945, Stimson protested the prospective industrial emasculation of Germany, lest it undermine American economic well being, set back recovery throughout Europe, and unleash forces of anarchy and revolution. Stimson and his subordinates in the Operations Division of the army also worried that the spread of Soviet power in northeast Asia would constrain the functioning of the free enterprise system and jeopardize American economic interests. A report prepared by the staff of the Moscow embassy and revised in mid-1946 by Ambassador (and former General) Walter Bedell Smith emphasized that "Soviet power is by nature so jealous that it has already operated to segregate from world economy almost all of the areas in which it has been established." While Forrestal and the navy sought to contain Soviet influence in the Near East and to retain American access to Middle East oil, Patterson and the War Department focused on preventing famine in occupied areas, forestalling communist revolution, circumscribing Soviet influence, resuscitating trade, and preserving traditional American markets especially in Western Europe. But American economic interests in Eurasia were not limited to Western Europe, Germany, and the Middle East. Military planners and intelligence officers in both the army and navy expressed considerable interest in the raw materials of southeast Asia, and, as already shown, one of the purposes of the bases they wanted was to maintain access to those resources and deny them to a prospective enemy.[17]

While civilian officials and military strategists feared the loss of Eurasia, they did not expect the Soviet Union to attempt its military conquest. In the early Cold War years, there was nearly universal agreement that the Soviets, while eager to expand their influence, desired to avoid a military engagement. In October 1945, for example, the Joint Intelligence Staff predicted that the Soviet Union would seek to avoid war for five to ten years. In April 1946, while Soviet troops still remained in Iran, General Lincoln, the army's principal war planner, concurred with Byrnes's view that the Soviets did not want war. In May, when there was deep concern about a possible communist uprising in France, military intelligence doubted the Kremlin would instigate a coup, lest it ignite a full scale war. At a high-level meeting at the White House in June, Eisenhower stated that he did not think the Soviets wanted war; only Forrestal dissented. In August, when the Soviet note to Turkey on the Dardanelles provoked consternation in American policy-making circles, General Hoyt Vandenberg, director of central intelligence, informed President Truman that there were no signs of unusual Soviet troop movements or supply build-ups. In March 1947, while the Truman Doctrine was being discussed in Congress, the director of army intelligence maintained that the factors operating to discourage Soviet aggression continued to be decisive. In September 1947, the CIA concluded that the Soviets would not seek to conquer Western Europe for several reasons: they would recognize their inability to control hostile populations; they would fear triggering a war with the United States that could not be won; and they would prefer to gain hegemony by political and economic means. In October 1947, the Joint Intelligence Staff maintained that for three years at least the Soviet Union would take no action that would precipitate a military conflict.

Even the ominous developments during the first half of 1948 did not alter these assessments. Despite his alarmist cable of March 5, designed to galvanize congressional support for increased defense expenditures, General Lucius Clay, the American military governor in Germany, did not believe war imminent. A few days later, the CIA concluded that the communist takeover in Czechoslovakia would not increase Soviet capabilities significantly and reflected no alteration in Soviet tactics. On March 16, the CIA reported to the president, "The weight of logic, as well as evidence, also leads to the conclusion that the Soviets will not resort to military force within the next sixty days." While this assessment was far from reassuring, army and navy intelligence experts concurred that the Soviets still wanted to avoid war; the question was whether war would erupt as a result of "miscalculation" by either the United States or Russia. After talking to Foreign Minister V. M. Molotov in June, Ambassador Smith concluded that Soviet leaders would not resort to active hostilities. During the Berlin blockade, army intelligence reported few signs of Soviet preparations for war; naval intelligence maintained that the Soviets desired to avoid war yet consolidate their position in East Germany. In October 1948, the Military Intelligence Division of the army endorsed a British appraisal that "all the evidence available indicates that the Soviet Union is not preparing to go to war in the near future." In December Acting Secretary of State Robert Lovett summed up the longstanding American perspective when he emphasized that he saw "no evidence that Soviet intentions run toward launching a sudden military attack on the western nations at this time. It would not be in character with the tradition or mentality of the Soviet leaders to resort to such a measure unless they felt themselves either politically extremely weak, or militarily extremely strong."

Although American defense officials recognized that the Soviets had substantial military assets, they remained confident that the Soviet Union did not feel extremely strong. Military analysts studying Russian capabilities noted that the Soviets were rapidly mechanizing infantry units and enhancing their firepower and mobility. It was estimated during the winter of 1946–47 that the Soviets could mobilize six million troops in thirty days and twelve million in six months, providing sufficient manpower to overrun all important parts of Eurasia. The Soviets were also believed to be utilizing German scientists and German technological knowhow to improve their submarine force, develop rockets and missiles, and acquire knowledge about the atomic bomb. During 1947 and 1948, it was reported as well that the Soviets were making rapid progress in the development of high performance jet fighters and already possessed several hundred intermediate range bombers comparable to the American B-29.

Even so, American military analysts were most impressed with Soviet weaknesses and vulnerabilities. The Soviets had no long-range strategic air force, no atomic bomb, and meager air defenses. Moreover, the Soviet navy was considered ineffective except for its submarine forces. The Joint Logistic Plans Committee and the Military Intelligence Division of the War Department estimated that the Soviet Union would require approximately fifteen years to overcome wartime losses in manpower and industry, ten years to redress the shortage of technicians, five to ten years to develop a strategic air force, fifteen to twenty-five years to construct a modern navy, ten years to refurbish military transport, ten years (or less) to quell resistance in occupied areas, fifteen to twenty years to establish a military infrastructure in the Far East, three to ten years to acquire the atomic bomb, and an unspecified number of years to remove the vulnerability of the Soviet rail-net and petroleum industry to long-range bombing.[18] For several years at least, the Soviet capability for sustained attack against North America would be very limited. In January 1946 the Joint Intelligence Staff concluded that "the offensive capabilities of the United States are manifestly superior to those of the U.S.S.R. and any war between the U.S. and the USSR would be far more costly to the Soviet Union than to the United States."[19]

Key American officials like Lovett, Clifford, Eisenhower, Bedell Smith and Budget Director James Webb were cognizant of prevailing Soviet weaknesses and potential American strength. Despite Soviet superiority in manpower, General Eisenhower and Admiral Forrest E. Sherman doubted that Russia could mount a surprise attack, and General Lincoln, Admiral Cato Glover, and Secretaries Patterson and Forrestal believed that Soviet forces would encounter acute logistical problems in trying to overrun Eurasia—especially in the Near East, Spain, and Italy. Even Forrestal doubted reports of accelerating Soviet air capabilities. American experts believed that most Soviet planes were obsolescent, that the Soviets had insufficient airfields and aviation gas to use their new planes, and that these planes had serious problems in their instrumentation and construction.

In general, improvements in specific areas of the Soviet military establishment did not mean that overall Soviet capabilities were improving at an alarming rate. In July 1947, the Military Intelligence Division concluded, "While there has been a slight overall improvement in the Soviet war potential, Soviet strength for total war is not sufficiently great to make a military attack against the United States anything but a most hazardous gamble." This view prevailed in 1946 and 1947, even though the American nuclear arsenal was extremely small and the American strategic bombing force of limited size. In the spring of 1948 the Joint Intelligence Committee at the American embassy in Moscow explained why the United States ultimately would emerge victorious should a war erupt in the immediate future. The Soviets could not win because of their "inability to carry the war to U.S. territory. After the occupation of Europe, the U.S.S.R. would be forced to assume the defensive and await attacks by U.S. forces which should succeed primarily because of the ability of the U.S. to outproduce the U.S.S.R. in materials of war."[20]

Awareness of Soviet economic shortcomings played a key role in the American interpretation of Soviet capabilities. Intelligence reports predicted that Soviet leaders would invest a disproportionate share of Russian resources in capital goods industries. But, even if such Herculean efforts enjoyed some success, the Soviets still would not reach the pre–World War II levels of the United States within fifteen to twenty years. Technologically, the Soviets were behind in the critical areas of aircraft manufacturing, electronics, and oil refining. And, despite Russia's concerted attempts to catch up and to surpass the United States, American intelligence experts soon started reporting that Soviet reconstruction was lagging behind Soviet ambitions, especially in the electronics, transportation, aircraft, construction machinery, nonferrous metals, and shipping industries. Accordingly, throughout the years 1945–48 American military analysts and intelligence experts believed that Soviet transportation bottlenecks, industrial shortcomings, technological backwardness, and agricultural problems would discourage military adventurism.

IF AMERICAN DEFENSE OFFICIALS DID NOT EXPECT a Soviet military attack, why, then, were they so fearful of losing control of Eurasia? The answer rests less in American assessments of Soviet military capabilities and short-term military intentions than in appraisals of economic and political conditions throughout Europe and Asia. Army officials in particular, because of their occupation roles in Germany, Japan, Austria, and Korea, were aware of the postwar plight of these areas. Key military men—Generals Clay, Douglas MacArthur, John Hilldring, and Oliver P. Echols and Colonel Charles H. Bonesteel—became alarmed by the prospects of famine, disease, anarchy, and revolution. They recognized that communist parties could exploit the distress and that the Russians could capitalize upon it to spread Soviet influence. As early as June 1945, Rear Admiral Ellery Stone, the American commissioner in Italy, wrote that wartime devastation had created fertile soil for the growth of communism in Italy and the enlargement of the Soviet sphere. MacArthur also feared that, if the Japanese economy remained emasculated and reforms were not undertaken, communism would spread. Clay, too, was acutely aware that German communists were depicting themselves and their beliefs as their country's only hope of salvation. In the spring of 1946 military planners, working on contingency plans for the emergency withdrawal of American troops from Germany, should war with Russia unexpectedly occur, also took note of the economic turmoil and political instability in neighboring countries, especially France. Sensitivity to the geopolitical dimensions of the socioeconomic crisis of the postwar era impelled Chief of Staff Eisenhower to give high priority in the army budget to assistance for occupied areas.

Civilian officials in the War, Navy, and State departments shared these concerns. In the autumn of 1945, McCloy warned Patterson that the stakes in Germany were immense and economic recovery had to be expedited. During the first half of 1946 Secretary Patterson and Assistant Secretary Peterson continually pressed the State Department to tackle the problems beleaguering occupation authorities in Germany and pleaded for State Department support and assistance in getting the Truman administration to provide additional relief to the devastated areas of Europe. On Peterson's urging, Acheson wrote Truman in April 1946, "We have now reached the most critical period of the world food crisis. We must either immediately greatly increase the exports of grain from the United States or expect general disorder and political upheaval to develop in [most of Eurasia]."[21] Forrestal had already pressed for a reassessment of occupation policies in Germany and Japan. In May, Clay suspended reparation payments in order to effect an accord on German economic unity. In June, Patterson began to support the merger of the American and British zones. The man most responsible for this latter undertaking was William Draper, Forrestal's former partner in Dillon, Read, and Co., and Clay's chief economic assistant. Draper firmly believed that "economic collapse in either [France or Germany] with probable political break-down and rise of communism would seriously threaten American objectives in Europe and in the world."[22]

American defense officials, military analysts, and intelligence officers were extremely sensitive to the political ferment, social turmoil, and economic upheaval throughout postwar Europe and Asia. In their initial postwar studies, the Joint Chiefs of Staff carefully noted the multiplicity of problems that could breed conflict and provide opportunities for Soviet expansion. In the spring of 1946 army planners, including General Lincoln, were keenly aware that conflict was most likely to arise from local disputes (for example, in Venezia-Giulia) or from indigenous unrest (for example, in France), perhaps even against the will of Moscow. A key War Department document submitted to the State-War-Navy Coordinating Committee in April 1946 skirted the issue of Soviet military capabilities and argued that the Soviet Union's strength emanated from totalitarian control over its satellites, from local communist parties, and from worldwide chaotic political and economic conditions. In October 1946 the Joint Planning Staff stressed that for the next ten years the major factor influencing world political developments would be the East-West ideological conflict taking place in an impoverished and strife-torn Europe and a vacuum of indigenous power in Asia. "The greatest danger to the security of the United States," the CIA concluded in mid-1947, "is the possibility of economic collapse in Western Europe and the consequent accession to power of Communist elements."[23]

In brief, during 1946 and 1947, defense officials witnessed a dramatic unravelling of the geopolitical foundations and socioeconomic structure of international affairs. Britain's economic weakness and withdrawal from the eastern Mediterranean, India's independence movement, civil war in China, nationalist insurgencies in Indo-China and the Dutch East Indies, Zionist claims to Palestine and Arab resentment, German and Japanese economic paralysis, communist inroads in France and Italy—all were ominous developments. Defense officials recognized that the Soviet Union had not created these circumstances but believed that Soviet leaders would exploit them. Should communists take power, even without direct Russian intervention, the Soviet Union, it was assumed, would gain predominant control of the resources of these areas because of the postulated subservience of communist parties everywhere to the Kremlin. Should nationalist uprisings persist, communists seize power in underdeveloped countries, and Arabs revolt against American support of a Jewish state, the petroleum and raw materials of critical areas might be denied the West. The imminent possibility existed that, even without Soviet military aggression, the resources of Eurasia could fall under Russian control. With these resources, the Soviet Union would be able to overcome its chronic economic weaknesses, achieve defense in depth, and challenge American power—perhaps even by military force.

IN THIS FRIGHTENING POSTWAR ENVIRONMENT American assessments of Soviet long-term intentions were transformed. When World War II ended, military planners initially looked upon Soviet aims in foreign affairs as arising from the Kremlin's view of power politics, Soviet strategic imperatives, historical Russian ambitions, and Soviet reactions to moves by the United States and Great Britain.

American intelligence analysts and strategic planners most frequently discussed Soviet actions in Eastern Europe, the Balkans, the Near East, and Manchuria as efforts to establish an effective security system. Despite enormous Soviet gains during the war, many assessments noted that, in fact, the Soviets had not yet achieved a safe security zone, especially on their southern periphery. While Forrestal, Deane, and most of the planners in the army's Operations Division possessed a skeptical, perhaps even sinister, view of Soviet intentions, the still prevailing outlook at the end of 1945 was to dismiss the role of ideology in Soviet foreign policy yet emphasize Soviet distrust of foreigners; to stress Soviet expansionism but acknowledge the possibility of accommodation; to abhor Soviet domination of Eastern Europe but discuss Soviet policies elsewhere in terms of power and influence; and to dwell upon the Soviet preoccupation with security yet acknowledge doubt about ultimate Soviet intentions.

This orientation changed rapidly during 1946. In January, the Joint War Plans Committee observed that "the long-term objective [of the Soviet Union] is deemed to be establishment of predominant influence over the Eurasian land mass and the strategic approaches thereto." Reports of the new military attaché in Moscow went further, claiming that "the ultimate aim of Soviet foreign policy seems to be the dominance of Soviet influence throughout the world" and "the final aim . . . is the destruction of the capitalist system." Soon thereafter, Kennan's "long telegram" was widely distributed among defense officials, on whom it had considerable impact. Particularly suggestive was his view that Soviet leaders needed the theme of capitalist encirclement to justify their autocratic rule. Also influential were Kennan's convictions that the Soviet leaders aimed to shatter the international authority of the United States and were beyond reason and conciliation.

During the spring and summer of 1946, defense officials found these notions persuasive as an interpretation of Soviet intentions because of the volatile international situation, the revival of ideological fervor within the Soviet Union, and the domestic political atmosphere and legislative constraints in the United States. President Truman wished to stop "babying the Soviets," and his predilection for a tougher posture probably led his subordinates to be less inclined to give the Soviets the benefit of any doubt when assessing Russian intentions.[24] Forrestal believed the Soviet communist threat had become more serious than the Nazi challenge of the 1930s; General John E. Hull, director of the Operations Division, asserted that the Soviets were "constitutionally incapable of being conciliated"; and Clark Clifford and George Elsey considered Soviet fears "absurd." A key subcommittee of the State-War-Navy Coordinating Committee declared that Soviet suspicions were "not susceptible of removal," and in July 1946 the Joint Chiefs of Staff declared the Soviet objective to be "world domination." By late 1946 it was commonplace for intelligence reports and military assessments to state, without any real analysis, that the "ultimate aim of Soviet foreign policy is Russian domination of a communist world."[25] There was, of course, plentiful evidence for this appraisal of Soviet ambitions—the Soviet consolidation of a sphere of influence in Eastern Europe; the incendiary situation in Venezia Giulia; Soviet violation of the agreement to withdraw troops from Iran; Soviet relinquishment of Japanese arms to the Chinese communists; the Soviet mode of extracting reparations from the Russian zone in Germany; Soviet diplomatic overtures for bases in the Dardanelles, Tripolitania, and the Dodecanese; Soviet requests for a role in the occupation of Japan; and the Kremlin's renewed emphasis on Marxist-Leninist doctrine, the vulnerability of capitalist economies, and the inevitability of conflict.

Yet these assessments did not seriously grapple with contradictory evidence. While emphasizing Soviet military capabilities, strategic ambitions, and diplomatic intransigence, reports like the Clifford-Elsey memorandum of September 1946 and the Joint Chiefs of Staff report 1696 (upon which the Clifford-Elsey memorandum heavily relied) disregarded numerous signs of Soviet weakness, moderation, and circumspection. During 1946 and 1947 intelligence analysts described the withdrawal of Russian troops from northern Norway, Manchuria, Bornholm, and Iran (from the latter under pressure, of course). Numerous intelligence sources reported the reduction of Russian troops in Eastern Europe and the extensive demobilization going on within the Soviet Union. In October 1947 the Joint Intelligence Committee forecast a Soviet army troop strength during 1948 and 1949 of less than two million men. Soviet military expenditures appeared to moderate. Other reports dealt with the inadequacies of Soviet transportation and bridging equipment for the conduct of offensive operations in Eastern Europe. And, as already noted, assessments of the Soviet economy revealed persistent problems likely to restrict Soviet adventurism.

Experience suggested that the Soviet Union was by no means uniformly hostile or unwilling to negotiate with the United States. In April 1946, a few days after a State-War-Navy subcommittee issued an alarming political estimate of Soviet policy (for use in American military estimates), Ambassador Smith reminded the State Department that the Soviet press was not unalterably critical of the United States, that the Russians had withdrawn from Bornholm, that Stalin had given a moderate speech on the United Nations, and that Soviet demobilization continued apace. The next month General Lincoln, who had accompanied Byrnes to Paris for the meeting of the council of foreign ministers, acknowledged that the Soviets had been willing to make numerous concessions regarding Tripolitania, the Dodecanese, and Italian reparations. In the spring of 1946, General Echols, General Clay, and Secretary Patterson again maintained that the French constituted the major impediment to an agreement on united control of Germany. At the same time the Soviets ceased pressing for territorial adjustments with Turkey. After the diplomatic exchanges over the Dardanelles in the late summer of 1946 the Soviets did not again ask for either a revision of the Montreux Convention or the acquisition of bases in the Dardanelles. In early 1947 central intelligence delineated more than a half-dozen instances of Soviet moderation or concessions. In April the Military Intelligence Division noted that the Soviets had limited their involvement in the Middle East, diminished their ideological rhetoric, and given only moderate support to Chinese communists. In the months preceding the Truman Doctrine, Soviet behavior—as noted by American military officials and intelligence analysts—hardly justified the inflammatory rhetoric Acheson and Truman used to secure congressional support for aid to Greece and Turkey. Perhaps this is why General Marshall, as secretary of state, refrained from such language himself and preferred to focus on the socioeconomic aspects of the unfolding crisis.

In their overall assessments of Soviet long-term intentions, however, military planners dismissed all evidence of Soviet moderation, circumspection, and restraint. In fact, as 1946 progressed, these planners seemed to spend less time analyzing Soviet intentions and more time estimating Soviet capabilities.[26] Having accepted the notion that the two powers were locked in an ideological struggle of indefinite duration and conscious of the rapid demobilization of American forces and the constraints on American defense expenditures, they no longer explored ways of accommodating a potential adversary's legitimate strategic requirements or pondered how American initiatives might influence the Soviet Union's definition of its objectives.[27] Information not confirming prevailing assumptions either was ignored in overall assessments of Soviet intentions or was used to illustrate that the Soviets were shifting tactics but not altering objectives. Reflective of the emerging mentality was a report from the Joint Chiefs of Staff to the president in July 1946 that deleted sections from previous studies that had outlined Soviet weaknesses. A memorandum sent by Secretary Patterson to the president at the same time was designed by General Lauris Norstad, director of the War Department's Plans and Operations Division, to answer questions about relations with the Soviet Union "without ambiguity." Truman, Clark Clifford observed many years later, liked things in black and white.

DURING 1946 AND EARLY 1947, the conjunction of Soviet ideological fervor and socioeconomic turmoil throughout Eurasia contributed to the growth of a myopic view of Soviet long-term policy objectives and to enormous apprehension lest the Soviet Union gain control of all the resources of Eurasia, thereby endangering the national security of the United States. American assessments of Soviet short-term military intentions had not altered; Soviet military capabilities had not significantly increased, and Soviet foreign policy positions had not greatly shifted. But defense officials were acutely aware of America's own rapidly diminishing capabilities, of Britain's declining military strength, of the appeal of communist doctrine to most of the underdeveloped world, and of the opportunities open to communist parties throughout most of Eurasia as a result of prevailing socioeconomic conditions. War Department papers, studies of the joint chiefs, and intelligence analyses repeatedly described the restiveness of colonial peoples that had sapped British and French strength, the opportunities for communist parties in France, Italy, and even Spain to capitalize upon indigenous conditions, and the ability of the Chinese communists to defeat the nationalists and make the resources and manpower of Manchuria and North China available to the Soviet Union. In this turbulent international arena, the survival of liberal ideals and capitalist institutions was anything but assured. "We could point to the economic benefits of Capitalism," commented one important War Department paper in April 1946, "but these benefits are concentrated rather than widespread, and, at present, are genuinely suspect throughout Europe and in many other parts of the world."[28]

In this environment, there was indeed no room for ambiguity or compromise. Action was imperative—action aimed at safeguarding those areas of Eurasia not already within the Soviet sphere. Even before Kennan's "long telegram" arrived in Washington the joint chiefs adopted the position that "collaboration with the Soviet Union should stop short not only of compromise of principle but also of expansion of Russian influence in Europe and in the Far East."[29] During the spring and summer of 1946, General Lincoln and Admiral Richard L. Conolly, commander of American naval forces in the eastern Atlantic and Mediterranean, worked tirelessly to stiffen Byrnes's views, avert American diplomatic concessions, and put the squeeze on the Russians.[30] "The United States," army planners explained, "must be able to prevent, by force if necessary, Russian domination of either Europe or Asia to the extent that the resources of either continent could be mobilized against the United States." Which countries in Eurasia were worth fighting over remained unclear during 1946. But army and navy officials as well as the joint chiefs advocated a far-reaching program of foreign economic assistance coupled with the refurbishment of American military forces.[31]

During late 1946 and early 1947, the Truman administration assumed the initiative by creating German Bizonia, providing military assistance to Greece and Turkey, allocating massive economic aid to Western Europe, and reassessing economic policy toward Japan. These initiatives were aimed primarily at tackling the internal sources of unrest upon which communist parties capitalized and at rehabilitating the industrial heartlands of Eurasia. American defense officials supported these actions and acquiesced in the decision to give priority to economic aid rather than rearmament. Service officers working on foreign assistance programs of the State-War-Navy Coordinating Committee supported economic aid, showed sensitivity to the socioeconomic sources of unrest, and recognized that economic aid was likely to be the most efficacious means of preserving a favorable balance of power in Eurasia. Because they judged American military power to be superior and war to be unlikely, Forrestal, Lovett, and Webb insisted that military spending not interfere with the implementation of the Marshall Plan, rehabilitation of Germany, and revival of Japan. "In the necessarily delicate apportioning of our available resources," wrote Assistant Secretary of War Peterson, "the time element permits present emphasis on strengthening the economic and social dikes against Soviet communism rather than upon preparing for a possibly eventual, but not yet inevitable, war."[32]

Yet if war should unexpectedly occur, the United States had to have the capability to inflict incalculable damage upon the Soviet Union. Accordingly, Truman shelved (after some serious consideration) proposals for international control of atomic energy. The Baruch Plan, as it evolved in the spring and summer of 1946, was heavily influenced by defense officials and service officers who wished to avoid any significant compromise with the Soviet Union. They sought to perpetuate America's nuclear monopoly as long as possible in order to counterbalance Soviet conventional strength, deter Soviet adventurism, and bolster American negotiating leverage. When negotiations at the United Nations for international control of atomic energy languished for lack of agreement on its implementation, the way was clear for the Truman administration gradually to adopt a strategy based on air power and atomic weapons. This strategy was initially designed to destroy the adversary's will and capability to wage war by annihilating Russian industrial, petroleum, and urban centers. After completing their study of the 1946 Bikini atomic tests, the Joint Chiefs of Staff in July 1947 called for an enlargement of the nuclear arsenal. While Truman and Forrestal insisted on limiting military expenditures, government officials moved vigorously to solve problems in the production of plutonium, to improve nuclear cores and assembly devices, and to increase the number of aircraft capable of delivering atomic bombs. After much initial postwar disorganization, the General Advisory Committee to the Atomic Energy Commission could finally report to the president at the end of 1947 that "great progress" had been made in the atomic program. From June 30, 1947, to June 30, 1948, the number of bombs in the stockpile increased from thirteen to fifty. Although at the time of the Berlin crisis the United States was not prepared to launch a strategic air offensive against the Soviet Union, substantial progress had been made in the development of the nation's air-atomic capabilities. By the end of 1948, the United States had at least eighteen nuclear-capable B-50s, four B-36s, and almost three times as many nuclear-capable B-29s as had been available at the end of 1947.

During late 1947 and early 1948, the administration also responded to pleas of the Joint Chiefs of Staff to augment the overseas base system and to acquire bases in closer proximity to the Soviet Union. Negotiations were conducted with the British to gain access to bases in the Middle East and an agreement was concluded for the acquisition of air facilities in Libya. Admiral Conolly made a secret deal with the French to secure air and communication rights and to stockpile oil, aviation gas, and ammunition in North Africa. Plans also were discussed for postoccupation bases in Japan, and considerable progress was made in refurbishing and constructing airfields in Turkey. During 1948 the Turks also received one hundred eighty F-47 fighter-bombers, thirty B-26 bombers, and eighty-one C-47 cargo planes. The F-47s and B-26s, capable of reaching the vital Ploesti and Baku oil fields, were more likely to be used to slow down a Soviet advance through Turkey or Iran, thereby affording time to activate a strategic air offensive from prospective bases in the Cairo-Suez area.

Despite these developments, the joint chiefs and military planners grew increasingly uneasy with the budgetary constraints under which they operated. They realized that American initiatives, however necessary, placed the Soviet Union on the defensive, created an incendiary situation, and made war more likely—though still improbable. In July 1947, intelligence analysts in the War Department maintained that the Truman Doctrine and the Marshall Plan had resulted in a more aggressive Soviet attitude toward the United States and had intensified tensions. "These tensions have caused a sharper line of demarcation between West and East tending to magnify the significance of conflicting points of view, and reducing the possibility of agreement on any point." Intelligence officers understood that the Soviets would perceive American efforts to build strategic highways, construct airfields, and transfer fighter bombers to Turkey as a threat to Soviet security and to the oilfields in the Caucuses. The latter, noted the director of naval intelligence, "lie within easy air striking range of countries on her southern flank, and the Soviet leaders will be particularly sensitive to any political threat from this area, however remote." Intelligence analysts also recognized that the Soviets would view the Marshall Plan as a threat to Soviet control in Eastern Europe as well as a death-knell to communist attempts to capture power peacefully in Western Europe. And defense officials were well aware that the Soviets would react angrily to plans for currency reform in German Trizonia and to preparations for a West German republic. "The whole Berlin crisis," army planners informed Eisenhower, "has arisen as a result of . . . actions on the part of the Western Powers." In sum, the Soviet clampdown in Eastern Europe and the attempt to blockade Berlin did not come as shocks to defense officials, who anticipated hostile and defensive Soviet reactions to American initiatives.

The real consternation of the Joint Chiefs of Staff and other high-ranking civilian and military officials in the defense agencies stemmed from their growing conviction that the United States was undertaking actions and assuming commitments that now required greater military capabilities. Recognizing that American initiatives, aimed at safeguarding Eurasia from further communist inroads, might be perceived as endangering Soviet interests, it was all the more important to be ready for any eventuality. Indeed, to the extent that anxieties about the prospects of war escalated in March and April 1948, these fears did not stem from estimates that the Soviets were planning further aggressive action after the communist seizure of power in Czechoslovakia but from apprehensions that ongoing American initiatives might provoke an attack. On March 14 General S. J. Chamberlin, director of army intelligence, warned the chief of staff that "actions taken by this country in opposition to the spread of Communism . . . may decide the question of the outbreak of war and of its timing." The critical question explicitly faced by the intelligence agencies and by the highest policy makers was whether passage of the Selective Service Act, or of universal military training, or of additional appropriations for the air force, or of a military assistance program to Western European countries, or of a resolution endorsing American support for West European Union would trigger a Soviet attack. Chamberlin judged, for example, that the Soviets would not go to war just to make Europe communist but would resort to war if they felt threatened. The great imponderable, of course, was what, in the Soviet view, would constitute a security threat justifying war.

Recognizing the need to move ahead with planned initiatives but fearing Soviet countermeasures, the newly formed staff of the National Security Council undertook its first comprehensive assessment of American foreign policy. During March 1948, after consulting with representatives of the army, navy, air force, State Department, CIA, and National Security Resources Board, the National Security Council staff produced NSC 7, "The Position of the United States with Respect to Soviet-Dominated World Communism." This study began with the commonplace assumption that the communist goal was "world conquest." The study then went on to express the omnipresent theme behind all conceptions of American national security in the immediate postwar years. "Between the United States and the USSR there are in Europe and Asia areas of great potential power which if added to the existing strength of the Soviet world would enable the latter to become so superior in manpower, resources, and territory that the prospect for the survival of the United States as a free nation would be slight." Accordingly, the study called, first, for the strengthening of the military potential of the United States and, second, for the arming of the non-Soviet world, particularly Western Europe. Although this staff study was never formally approved, the national security bureaucracy worked during the spring and summer of 1948 for West European unity, military assistance to friendly nations, currency reform in Trizonia, revitalization of the Ruhr, and the founding of the Federal Republic of Germany.

The priority accorded to Western Europe did not mean that officials ignored the rest of Eurasia. Indeed, the sustained economic rejuvenation of Western Europe made access to Middle Eastern oil more important than ever. Marshall, Lovett, Forrestal, and other defense officials, including the joint chiefs, feared that American support of Israel might jeopardize relations with Arab nations and drive them into the hands of the Soviet Union. Although Truman accepted the partition of Palestine and recognized Israel, the United States maintained an embargo on arms shipments and sought to avoid too close an identification with the Zionist state lest the flow of oil to the West be jeopardized. At the same time, the Truman administration moved swiftly in June 1948 to resuscitate the Japanese economy. Additional funds were requested from Congress to procure imports of raw materials for Japanese industry so that Japanese exports might also be increased. Shortly thereafter, Draper, Tracy S. Voorhees, and other army officials came to believe that a rehabilitated Japan would need the markets and raw materials of Southeast Asia. They undertook a comprehensive examination of the efficacy and utility of a Marshall Plan for Asia. Integrating Japan and Southeast Asia into a viable regional economy, invulnerable to communist subversion and firmly ensconced in the Western community, assumed growing significance, especially in view of the prospect of a communist triumph in China. But communist victories in China did not dissuade policymakers from supporting, for strategic as well as domestic political considerations, the appropriation of hundreds of millions of dollars in additional aid to the Chinese nationalists in the spring of 1948. And the American commitment to preserve the integrity of South Korea actually increased, despite the planned withdrawal of occupation forces.

The problem with all of these undertakings, however, was that they cost large sums, expanded the nation's formal and informal commitments, and necessitated larger military capabilities. Yet on March 24, 1948, just as NSC 7 was being finished, Truman's Council of Economic Advisors warned that accelerating expenditures might compel the president "to set aside free market practices—and substitute a rather comprehensive set of controls." Truman was appalled by this possibility and carefully limited the sums allocated for a build-up of American forces. Key advisers, like Webb, Marshall, Lovett, and Clifford, supported this approach because they perceived too much fat in the military budget, expected the Soviets to rely on political tactics rather than military aggression, postulated latent U.S. military superiority over the Soviet Union, and assumed that the atomic bomb constituted a decisive, if perhaps short-term, trump card. For many American policy makers, moreover, the Iranian crisis of 1946, the Greek civil war, and the ongoing Berlin airlift seemed to demonstrate that Russia would back down when confronted with American determination, even if the United States did not have superior forces-in-being.

As secretary of defense, however, Forrestal was beleaguered by pressures emanating from the armed services for a build-up of American military forces and by his own apprehensions over prospective Soviet actions. He anguished over the ex-

cruciatingly difficult choices that had to be made between the imperatives of foreign economic aid, overseas military assistance, domestic rearmament, and fiscal
orthodoxy. In May, June, and July 1948, he and his assistants carefully pondered intelligence reports on Soviet intentions and requested a special State Department
study on how to plan American defense expenditures in view of prospective Soviet
policies. He also studied carefully the conclusions of an exhaustive study of the
navy's contribution to national security undertaken by the General Board of the
navy under the direct supervision of Captain Arleigh Burke. Still not satisfied, Forrestal asked the president to permit the National Security Council to conduct another comprehensive examination of American policy objectives. Forrestal clearly
hoped that this reassessment would show that a larger proportion of resources
should be allocated to the military establishment.

The Policy Planning Staff of the Department of State prepared the initial
study that Forrestal requested and Truman authorized. Extensively redrafted it
reappeared in November 1948 as NSC 20/4 and was adopted as the definitive
statement of American foreign policy. Significantly, this paper reiterated the long-
standing estimate that the Soviet Union was not likely to resort to war to achieve its
objectives. But war could erupt as a result of "Soviet miscalculation of the determination of the United States to use all the means at its command to safeguard its
security, through Soviet misinterpretation of our intentions, and through U.S. miscalculation of Soviet reactions to measures which we might take." Immediately following this appraisal of the prospects of war, the National Security Council restated its conception of American national security: "Soviet domination of the
potential power of Eurasia, whether achieved by armed aggression or by political
and subversive means, would be strategically and politically unacceptable to the
United States."[33]

Yet NSC 20/4 did not call for a larger military budget. With no expectation that
war was imminent, the report emphasized the importance of safeguarding the domestic economy and left unresolved the extent to which resources should be devoted to military preparations. NSC 20/4 also stressed "that Soviet political warfare
might seriously weaken the relative position of the United States, enhance Soviet
strength and either lead to our ultimate defeat short of war, or force us into war under dangerously unfavorable conditions." Accordingly, the National Security
Council vaguely but stridently propounded the importance of reducing Soviet
power and influence on the periphery of the Russian homeland and of strengthening the pro-American orientation of non-Soviet nations.[34]

Language of this sort, which did not define clear priorities and which projected
American interests almost everywhere on the globe, exasperated the joint chiefs
and other military officers. They, too, believed that the United States should resist
communist aggression everywhere, "an overall commitment which in itself is all-
inclusive." But to undertake this goal in a responsible and effective fashion it was
necessary "to bring our military strength to a level commensurate with the distinct
possibility of global warfare." The Joint Chiefs of Staff still did not think the Soviets
wanted war. But, given the long-term intentions attributed to the Soviet Union and
given America's own aims, the chances for war, though still small, were growing.

Particularly worrisome were studies during 1948 suggesting that, should war occur, the United States would have difficulty implementing basic strategic undertakings. Although the armed services fought bitterly over the division of funds, they concurred fully on one subject—the $15 billion ceiling on military spending set by Truman was inadequate. In November 1948, military planners argued that the $14.4 billion budget would jeopardize American military operations by constricting the speed and magnitude of the strategic air offensive, curtailing conventional bombing operations against the Soviet Union, reducing America's ability to provide naval assistance to Mediterranean allies, undermining the nation's ability to control Middle East oil at the onset of a conflict, and weakening initial overall offensive capabilities. On November 9, the joint chiefs informed the secretary of defense that the existing budget for fiscal 1950 was "insufficient to implement national policy in any probable war situation that can be foreseen."

From the viewpoint of the national military establishment, the deficiency of forces-in-being was just one of several problems. Forrestal told Marshall that he was more concerned about the absence of sufficient strength to support international negotiations than he was about the availability of forces to combat overt acts of aggression, which were unlikely in any case. During 1948, the joint chiefs also grew increasingly agitated over the widening gap between American commitments and interests on the one hand and American military capabilities on the other. In November, the Joint Chiefs of Staff submitted to the National Security Council a comprehensive list of the formal and informal commitments that already had been incurred by the United States government. According to the joint chiefs, "current United States commitments involving the use or distinctly possible use of armed forces are very greatly in excess of our present ability to fulfill them either promptly or effectively." Limited capabilities meant that the use of American forces in any specific situation—for example, in Greece, Berlin, or Palestine— threatened to emasculate the nation's ability to respond elsewhere.[35]

HAVING CONCEIVED OF AMERICAN NATIONAL SECURITY in terms of Western control and of American access to the resources of Eurasia outside the Soviet sphere, American defense officials now considered it imperative to develop American military capabilities to meet a host of contingencies that might emanate from further Soviet encroachments or from indigenous communist unrest. Such contingencies were sure to arise because American strategy depended so heavily on the rebuilding of Germany and Japan, Russia's traditional enemies, as well as on air power, atomic weapons, and bases on the Soviet periphery. Such contingencies also were predictable because American strategy depended so heavily on the restoration of stability in Eurasia, a situation increasingly unlikely in an era of nationalist turmoil, social unrest, and rising economic expectations. Although the desire of the national military establishment for large increments in defense expenditures did not prevail in the tight budgetary environment and presidential election year of 1948, the mode of thinking about national security that subsequently accelerated the arms race and precipitated military interventionism in Asia was already widespread among defense officials.

Indeed, the dynamics of the Cold War after 1948 are easier to comprehend when one grasps the breadth of the American conception of national security that had emerged between 1945 and 1948. This conception included a strategic sphere of influence within the Western Hemisphere, domination of the Atlantic and Pacific oceans, an extensive system of outlying bases to enlarge the strategic frontier and project American power, an even more extensive system of transit rights to facilitate the conversion of commercial air bases to military use, access to the resources and markets of most of Eurasia, denial of those resources to a prospective enemy, and the maintenance of nuclear superiority. Not every one of these ingredients, it must be emphasized, was considered vital. Hence, American officials could acquiesce, however grudgingly, to a Soviet sphere in Eastern Europe and could avoid direct intervention in China. But cumulative challenges to these concepts of national security were certain to provoke a firm American response. This occurred initially in 1947–48 when decisions were made in favor of the Truman Doctrine, Marshall Plan, military assistance, Atlantic alliance, and German and Japanese rehabilitation. Soon thereafter, the "loss" of China, the Soviet detonation of an atomic bomb, and the North Korean attack on South Korea intensified the perception of threat to prevailing concepts of national security. The Truman administration responded with military assistance to southeast Asia, a decision to build the hydrogen bomb, direct military intervention in Korea, a commitment to station troops permanently in Europe, expansion of the American alliance system, and a massive rearmament program in the United States. Postulating a long-term Soviet intention to gain world domination, the American conception of national security, based on geopolitical and economic imperatives, could not allow for additional losses in Eurasia, could not risk a challenge to its nuclear supremacy, and could not permit any infringement on its ability to defend in depth or to project American force from areas in close proximity to the Soviet homeland.

To say this is neither to exculpate the Soviet government for its inhumane treatment of its own citizens nor to suggest that Soviet foreign policy was idle or benign. Indeed, Soviet behavior in Eastern Europe was often deplorable; the Soviets sought opportunities in the Dardanelles, northern Iran, and Manchuria; the Soviets hoped to orient Germany and Austria toward the East; and the Soviets sometimes endeavored to use communist parties to expand Soviet influence in areas beyond the periphery of Russian military power. But, then again, the Soviet Union had lost twenty million dead during the war, had experienced the destruction of seventeen hundred towns, thirty-one thousand factories, and one hundred thousand collective farms, and had witnessed the devastation of the rural economy with the Nazi slaughter of twenty million hogs and seventeen million head of cattle. What is remarkable is that after 1946 these monumental losses received so little attention when American defense analysts studied the motives and intentions of Soviet policy; indeed, defense officials did little to analyze the threat perceived by the Soviets. Yet these same officials had absolutely no doubt that the wartime experiences and sacrifices of the United States, though much less devastating than those of Soviet Russia, demonstrated the need for and entitled the United States to oversee the resuscitation of the industrial heartlands of Germany and Japan, establish a viable balance of power in Eurasia, and militarily dominate the Eurasian rimlands, thereby safeguarding American access to raw materials and control over all sea and air approaches to North America.

To suggest a double standard is important only insofar as it raises fundamental questions about the conceptualization and implementation of American national security policy. If Soviet policy was aggressive, bellicose, and ideological, perhaps America's reliance on overseas bases, air power, atomic weapons, military alliances, and the rehabilitation of Germany and Japan was the best course to follow, even if the effect may have been to exacerbate Soviet anxieties and suspicions. But even when one attributes the worst intentions to the Soviet Union, one might still ask whether American presuppositions and apprehensions about the benefits that would accrue to the Soviet Union as a result of Communist (and even revolutionary nationalist) gains anywhere in Eurasia tended to simplify international realities, magnify the breadth of American interests, engender commitments beyond American capabilities, and dissipate the nation's strength and credibility. And, perhaps even more importantly, if Soviet foreign policies tended to be opportunist, reactive, nationalistic, and contradictory, as some recent writers have claimed and as some contemporary analysts suggested, then one might also wonder whether America's own conception of national security tended, perhaps unintentionally, to engender anxieties and to provoke countermeasures from a proud, suspicious, insecure, and cruel government that was at the same time legitimately apprehensive about the long-term implications arising from the rehabilitation of traditional enemies and the development of foreign bases on the periphery of the Soviet homeland. To raise such issues anew seems essential if we are to unravel the complex origins of the Cold War.

NOTES

1. Kissinger, *For the Record: Selected Statements,* 1977–1980 (Boston, 1980), 123–24.
2. I use the term "defense officials" broadly in this essay to include civilian appointees and military officers in the departments of the Army, Navy, and Air Force, in the office of the secretary of defense, in the armed services, in the intelligence agencies, and on the staff of the National Security Council. While purposefully avoiding a systematic analysis of career diplomats in the Department of State, who have received much attention elsewhere, the conclusions I draw here are based on a consideration of the views of high-ranking officials in the State Department, including James F. Byrnes, Dean Acheson, George C. Marshall, and Robert Lovett.
3. For Leahy's explanation, see JCS, "Strategic Areas and Trusteeships in the Pacific," October 10, 18, 1946, RG 218, ser. CCS 360 (12-9-42), JCS 1619/15, 19; JCS, "United States Military Requirements for Air Bases," November 2, 1943; JCS, "Overall Examination of United States Requirements for Military Bases and Base Rights," October 25, 1945, *ibid.,* JCS 570/40.
4. JCS, "United States Military Requirements for Air Bases," November 2, 1943; JCS, Minutes of the 71st meeting, March 30, 1943, RG 218, ser. CCS 360 (12-9-42); Leahy,

Memorandum for the President, November 15, 1943, *ibid.;* Nimitz, Memorandum, October 16, 1946, *ibid.,* JCS 1619/16; and Joint Planning Staff [hereafter, JPS], "Basis for the Formulation of a Post-War Military Policy," August 20, 1945, RG 218, ser. CCS 381 (5-13-45), JPS 633/6.

5. JCS, "Statement of Effect of Atomic Weapons on National Security and Military Organization," March 29, 1946, RG 165, ser. ABC 471.6 Atom (8-17-45), JCS 477/10. Also see JCS, "Guidance as to the Military Implications of a United Nations Commission on Atomic Energy," January 12, 1946, *ibid.,* JCS 1567/26; and JCS, "Over-All Effect of Atomic Bomb on Warfare and Military Organization," October 30, 1945, *ibid.,* JCS 1477/1.

6. JPS, "Over-All Examination of Requirements for Transit Air Bases . . . ," January 20, 1946, RG 218, ser. CCS 360 (10-9-42), JPS 781/1; and McCloy, Memorandum to the Department of State, January 31, 1945, RG 165, OPD 336 (top secret). Also see JPS, "Over-All Examination of Requirements for Transit Air Bases," January 8, 1946; and, for the joint chiefs' view on South American air fields, see JCS, Minutes of the 69th meeting, March 23, 1943, RG 218, CCS 360 (12-9-42).

7. P&O, "The Strategic Importance of Inter-American Military Cooperation" [January 20, 1947], RG 319, 092 (top secret). Also see H. A. Craig, "Summary," January 5, 1945, RG 107, Records of the Assistant Secretary of War for Air, Establishment of Air Fields and Air Bases, box 216 (Latin America); and War Department, "Comprehensive Statement" [January 1945], *ibid.*

8. JCS, "Foreign Policy of the United States," February 10, 1946, RG 218, ser. CCS 092 United States (12-21-45), JCS 1592/2; and JCS to the Secretary of the Navy and Secretary of War, September 19, 1945, *ibid.,* ser. CCS 092 (9-10-45), JCS 1507/2. For JCS views on the Western Hemisphere, also see JCS to the Secretary of the Navy and Secretary of War, February 11, 1945, *ibid.,* ser. CCS 092 (1-18-45); JCS, "International Organization for the Enforcement of World Peace and Security," April 14, 1945, *ibid.,* ser. CCS 092 (4-14-45), JCS 1311; and JCS, "Guidance as to Command and Control of the Armed Forces to be Placed at the Disposal of the Security Council of the United Nations," May 26, 1946, *ibid.,* JCS 1670/5.

9. For Patterson's views, see P&O, "Strategic Importance of Inter-American Military Cooperation" [January 20, 1947]; and Patterson to Byrnes, December 18, 1946, RG 107, RPPP, safe file, box 3.

10. This evaluation accords with the views of Chester J. Pach, Jr.; see his "The Containment of United States Military Aid to Latin America, 1944–1949," *Diplomatic History,* 6 (1982):232–34.

11. See, for example, Craig, "Summary," January 5, 1945; JPS, "Military Arrangements Deriving from the Act of Chapultepec Pertaining to Bases," January 14, 1946, RG 218, ser. CCS 092 (9-10-45), JPS 761/3; Patterson to Byrnes, December 18, 1946; and P&O, "Strategic Importance of Inter-American Military Cooperation" [January 20, 1947].

12. Minutes of the meeting of the Secretaries of State, War, and the Navy, December 18, 1946, April 23, May 1, 1947, RG 107, RPPP, safe file, box 3; and M. B. Ridgway, Memorandum for the Assistant Secretary of War, February 1947, *ibid.,* HCPP, 092 (classified).

13. Pach, "Military Aid to Latin America," 235–43.

14. Leahy, excerpt from letter, May 16, 1944, RG 59, lot 54D394 (Records of the Office of European Affairs), box 17. For Strong's opinion, see JPS, Minutes of the 199th meeting, April 25, 1945, RG 218, ser. CCS 334 (3-28-45); and, for the views of Eisenhower and Lincoln, see Lincoln, Memorandum for Hull, June 24, 1945, USMA, GLP, War Dept. files; and Leahy, Memorandum for the President [late June 1945], *ibid.*

15. For the emphasis on expediting recovery in Western Europe, see, for example, McCloy, Memorandum for Matthew J. Connelly, April 26, 1945, HTL, HSTP, PSF, box 178; and,

for the role of Britain, see, for example, Joint Intelligence Staff [hereafter, JIS], "British Capabilities and Intentions," December 5, 1945, RG 218, ser. CCS 000.1 Great Britain (5-10-45), JIS 161/4.

16. See, for example, JIS, "Military Capabilities of Great Britain and France," November 13, 1945, RG 218, ser. CCS 000.1 Great Britain (5-10-45), JIS 211/1; JIS, "Areas Vital to Soviet War Effort," February 12, 1946, *ibid.*, ser. CCS 092 (3-27-45), JIS 226/2; and JIS, "Supplemental Information Relative to Northern and Western Europe," April 18, 1947, *ibid.,* JIS 275/1.

17. Strategy Section, OPD, "Post-War Base Requirements in the Philippines," April 23, 1945; JCS, "Strategic Areas and Trusteeships in the Pacific," October 18, 1946; MID, "Positive U.S. Action Required to Restore Normal Conditions in Southeast Asia," July 3, 1947, RG 319, P&O, 092 (top secret); and Lauris Norstad to the Director of Intelligence, July 10, 1947, *ibid.*

18. JLPC, "Russian Capabilities," November 15, 1945; and MID, "Intelligence Estimate of the World Situation for the Next Five Years," August 21, 1946, RG 319, P&O, 350.05 (top secret). For a contemporary analysis of the Soviet transport network, also see Paul Wohl, "Transport in the Development of Soviet Policy," *Foreign Affairs,* 24 (1946): 466–83.

19. JIS, "Soviet Post-War Military Policies and Capabilities," January 15, 1946, RG 218, ser. CCS 092 USSR (3-27-45), JIS 80/24; MID. "Ability of Potential Enemies to Attack the Continental United States," August 8, 1946; and P&O, "Estimate of the Situation Pertaining to the Northeast Approaches to the United States," August 12, 1946, RG 319, P&O, 381 (top secret).

20. MID, "Estimate of the Possibility of War between the United States and the USSR Today from a Comparison with the Situation as It Existed in September 1946," July 21, 1947, RG 319, P&O, 350.05 (top secret); and JIC, Moscow Embassy, "Soviet Intentions," April 1, 1948.

21. Acheson to Truman, April 30, 1946, RG 107, HCPP, general subject file, box 1. Also see McCloy to Patterson, November 24, 1945, *ibid.*, RPPP, safe file, box 4. For pressure on the State Department, see Patterson to Byrnes, December 10, 1945, RG 165, Civil Affairs Division [hereafter, CAD], ser. 014 Germany; Patterson to Byrnes, February 25, 1946; OPD and CAD, "Analysis of Certain Political Problems Confronting Military Occupation Authorities in Germany," April 10, 1946, RG 107, HCPP, 091 Germany (classified); and "Combined Food Board" file, spring 1946, *ibid.*, HCPP, general subject file, box 1.

22. William Draper, Memorandum [early 1947], RG 107, HCPP, 091 Germany (classified); and Forrestal to Acheson, January 14, 1946, ML, JFP, box 68. For Clay's initiative, see Smith, *Papers of General Lucius D. Clay,* 1:203–04, 213–14, 218–23; John F. Gimbel, *The American Occupation of Germany: Politics and the Military, 1945–1949* (Stanford, 1968), 35–91; John H. Backer, *The Decision to Divide Germany: American Foreign Policy in Transition* (Durham, N.C., 1978), 137–48; and Bruce Kuklick, *American Policy and the Division of Germany: The Clash with Russia over Reparations* (Ithaca, N.Y., 1972), 205–35. For Patterson's concerns and his support of Bizonia, see Patterson to Byrnes, June 11, 1946, RG 107, HCPP, 091 Germany (classified); Patterson to Truman, November 20, 1946, *ibid.*, RPPP, safe file, box 4; Minutes of the War Council meeting, December 5, 1946, *ibid.*, box 7; and Patterson to Palmer Hoyt, December 27, 1946, *ibid.*, box 4. For the merger of the zones, also see *FRUS, 1946,* 5:579–659; Smith, *Papers of General Lucius D. Clay,* 1:245, 248–49; and, for Draper's importance, also see Carolyn Eisenberg, "U.S. Social Policy in Post-War Germany: The Conservative Restoration," paper delivered at the Seventy-Fourth Annual Meeting of the Organization of American Historians, held in April 1981, in Detroit.

23. CIA, "Review of the World Situation as It Relates to the Security of the United States," September 26, 1947. Also see, for example, JCS, "Strategic Concept and Plan for the Employment of United States Armed Forces," Appendix A, September 19, 1945; JPS, Minutes of the 249th and 250th meetings; Lincoln to Wood, May 22, 1946, RG 165, ser. ABC 381 (9-1-45); [Giffin (?)] "U.S. Policy with Respect to Russia" [early April 1946], *ibid.*, ser. ABC 336 (8-22-43); JPS, "Estimate of Probable Developments in the World Political Situation up to 1956," October 31, 1946, RG 218, ser. CCS 092 (10-9-46), JPS 814/1; MID, "World Political Developments Affecting the Security of the United States during the Next Ten Years," April 14, 1947, RG 319, P&O, 350.05 (top secret).

24. Robert L. Messer, *The End of an Alliance: James F. Byrnes, Roosevelt, Truman, and the Origins of the Cold War* (Chapel Hill, N.C., 1982), 152–94, and "Paths Not Taken," 297–319.

25. Forrestal to Clarence Dillon, April 11, 1946, ML, JFP, box 11; Hull to Theater Commanders, March 21, 1946, RG 165, ser. ABC 336 (8-22-43); for the Clifford-Elsey viewpoint, see Krock, *Memoirs: Sixty Years on the Firing Line*, 428; and SWNCC, "Resume of Soviet Capabilities and Possible Intentions," August 29, 1946, NHC, SPD, ser. 5, box 106, A8. For the SWNCC estimate, see JCS, "Political Estimate of Soviet Policy for Use in Connection with Military Studies," April 5, 1946, RG 218, ser. CCS 092 USSR (3-27-45), JCS 1641/4; and JCS "Presidential Request for Certain Facts and Information Regarding the Soviet Union," July 25, 1946. Some of the most thoughtful studies on Soviet intentions, like that of the Joint Intelligence Staff in early January 1946 (JIS 80/20), were withdrawn from consideration. See the evolution of studies and reports in RG 218, ser. CCS 092 USSR (3-27-45), sects. 5–7.

26. Both the quantity and the quality of JCS studies on Soviet intentions seem to have declined during 1946. In "Military Position of the United States in Light of Russian Policy" (January 8, 1946), strategic planners of the Joint War Plans Committee maintained that it was more important to focus on Soviet capabilities than on Soviet intentions. During a key discussion at the White House, Admiral Leahy also was eager to dismiss abstract evaluations of Russian psychology and to focus on Russian capabilities; S. W. D., Memorandum for the Record, June 12, 1946. My assessment of the quality of JCS studies is based primarily on my analysis of the materials in RG 218, ser. CCS 092 USSR (3-27-45); ser. CCS 381 USSR (3-2-46); RG 319, P&O, 350.05 (top secret); and NHC, SPD, central files, 1946–48, A8.

27. During 1946 it became a fundamental tenet of American policy makers that Soviet policy objectives were a function of developments within the Soviet Union and not related to American actions. See, for example, Kennan's "long telegram," in *FRUS, 1946*, 4:696–709; JCS, "Political Estimate of Soviet Policy," April 5, 1946; JCS, "Presidential Request," July 25, 1946; and the Clifford/Elsey memorandum, in Krock, *Memoirs*, esp. 427–36.

28. [Giffin] "U.S. Policy with Respect to Russia" [early April 1946]. Also see Giffin, Draft of Proposed Comments for Assistant Secretary of War on "Foreign Policy," [early February 1946]; MID. "Intelligence Estimate," June 25, 1946; JPS, "Estimate of Probable Developments in the World Political Situation," October 31, 1946, RG 218, ser. CCS 092 (10-9-46), JPS 814/1; Special Ad Hoc Committee of SWNCC, "Study on U.S. Assistance to France," April 9, 1947, RG 165, ser. ABC 400.336 France (3-20-47); MID, "World Political Developments," April 14, 1947; JWPC, "The Soviet Threat against the Iberian Peninsula and the Means Required to Meet It," May 8, 1947, RG 218, ser. CCS 381 USSR (3-2-46), JWPC 465/1; and CIA. "Review of the World Situation," September 26, 1947.

29. JCS, "Foreign Policy of the United States," February 10, 1946.

30. Lincoln to Hull [April 1946], RG 59, Office of European Affairs, box 17; Lincoln, Memorandum for the Record, April 16, 1946; Lincoln to Hull, April 16, 1946, RG 165, ser. ABC 092 USSR (11-15-44); Lincoln to Cohen, June 22, 1946, *ibid.*, ABC 381 (9-1-45); Richard L. Conolly, oral history (Columbia, 1960), 293–304; Lincoln, Memorandum for Chief of Staff, May 20, 1946; and Lincoln, Memorandum for Norstad, July 23, 1946, USMA, GLP, War Department files.

31. Giffin, "Draft of Proposed Comments" [early February 1946]. Also see, for example, JCS, "Foreign Policy of the United States," February 10, 1946; [Giffin] "U.S. Policy with Respect to Russia" [early April 1946]; JCS, "Political Estimate of Soviet Policy," April 5, 1946; and Sherman, Memorandum for Forrestal, March 17, 1946, ML, JFP, box 24.

32. Peterson, as quoted in Chief of Staff, Memorandum [July 1947], RG 165, ser. ABC 471.6 Atom (8-17-45). Also see, for example, Lovett diaries, December 16, 1947, January 5, 15, 1948; Baruch to Forrestal, February 7, 1948, ML, JFP, box 78; Forrestal to Baruch, February 10, 1948, *ibid.;* and Excerpt of Phone Conversation between Forrestal and C. E. Wilson, April 2, 1948, *ibid.*, box 48.

33. NCS 20/1 and 20/4 may be found in Gaddis and Etzold, *Containment,* 173–211 (the quotations appear on page 208). Also see *FRUS, 1948,* 1:589–93, 599–601, 609–11, 615–24, 662–69.

34. Gaddis and Etzold, *Containment,* 209–10.

35. For the position of the JCS, see NSC 35, "Existing International Commitments," November 17, 1948, *FRUS, 1948,* 1:656–62. For Forrestal's view, see *ibid.,* 644–46. For background, see William A. Knowlton, Memorandum for the Chief of Staff, October 21, 1948, RG 319, P&O, 092 (top secret); for the reference to Greece, see JCS, "The Position of the United States with Respect to Greece," April 13, 1948, RG 218, ser. CCS 092 Greece (12-30-47), JCS 1826/8.

PART
Three

CAPITALISM, CLASS, AND FOREIGN POLICY

*A*merican foreign policy is conducted in the leading capitalist society. Accordingly, an important theoretical tradition has investigated the linkages between capitalism, economic interests, and foreign policy. The earliest scholarship in this area emerged in the years immediately preceding and after World War I, when Marxists and other writers probed the economic and class determinants of European imperialism and war. In the United States the tradition was invigorated again during the Vietnam War as scholars provided radical critiques of American foreign policy. Some writers have focused on the underlying structures of capitalist society and the general pattern of imperialist foreign policy. Here the linkages between capitalism and policy are deep and structural: governmental officials, whether they know it or not, act to protect and advance the interest of capitalism as a whole. The limited range of foreign policy options are generated by the system itself. Others adopt a more narrow instrumental perspective and focus on particular capitalist elites and particular policies. In this approach it is the capitalists themselves who act within the institutions of government to advance their own class interests.

James Kurth explores the political consequences of the rise of specific leading industries in Europe and the United States over the last two centuries. Kurth argues that the textile, steel, and automobile industries each came to prominence in the Western world with particular "political tendencies." Each sector, emerging in particular countries, served to strengthen, reinforce, or undermine particular social classes and political groups. The results had a profound impact on the politics and foreign policy of such countries as Britain, Germany, and the United States. The argument is that the ongoing and underlying transformations in leading industrial sectors have an indirect yet powerful influence on the political coalitions and policy orientations of the Western industrial countries. To explain politics and foreign policy, one needs to dig deep into the country's changing economic structures.

Jeff Frieden, working primarily within the instrumentalist tradition, provides an interpretation of the historic shift during the interwar period in American foreign economic policy from nationalism to internationalism. After World War I, Frieden argues, many U.S. banks and corporations saw opportunities in overseas expansion and attempted to push American policy in an internationalist direction. Other U.S. corporations saw international competition as a threat and supported the prevailing isolationist stance of government. Throughout the 1920s and early 1930s the two coalitions struggled to dominate foreign economic policy, each attaching themselves to different parts of the governmental apparatus. The standoff ended with the triumph of the internationalist wing of American capitalism, a victory made possible by the crisis of the 1930s and the destruction of foreign economic competition following World War II. Historic shifts in American foreign policy make sense, Frieden argues, only when related to the underlying struggles among competing class factions.

Fred Block is interested in the 1950 rearmament decision and its similarities with the expansion of military spending at the end of the Carter administration. Adopting a neo-Marxist perspective, Block argues that interstate "threats" can be used by state officials seeking to justify increased military spending and an expansionary foreign policy to stabilize and protect the national economy and an open world capitalist system. Block examines the historic planning document from the Truman administration, NSC-68, from this perspective. Foreign policy officials, according to Block, sought military rearmament as a way to meet critical economic objectives but felt compelled to justify increased military spending in the context of a more dramatic and sweeping "militarization" of American foreign policy.

The Political Consequences of the Product Cycle: Industrial History and Political Outcomes

James R. Kurth

THE PUBLIC POLICIES OF MAJOR INDUSTRIES: THE CONTEMPORARY CONFLICT

What explains the continuing stagnation in the industrial economies of the West? What will be the impact of such stagnation upon domestic politics and upon international relations? Are there domestic and foreign policies which the state can undertake to bring about a return to sustained economic prosperity and a recapitulation of that lost golden age of 1948–1973? These are now the central questions for scholars in the emerging field of international political economy. A recent special issue of *International Organization,* edited by Peter Katzenstein, has presented some of the most useful and sophisticated approaches to these questions and analyses of the international political economy of the West during the period of the last thirty years.[1]

These questions are, of course, also the central ones for major economic actors such as industrial corporations and financial institutions. And here we can distinguish five different answers or solutions to the problem of economic stagnation. Each is preferred and supported by a particular cluster of industries or banks, and each has particular implications for domestic and foreign policies.

The most minimal solution to economic stagnation, in the sense that it requires the least change from government policies of recent years, is the conventional Keynesian one of government–induced demand–creation. This approach is preferred by the consumer-durables industries, the most important of which is the automobile industry. A familiar variation is government spending on weapons procurement and government support of weapons exports; this approach of mutant or military Keynesianism is preferred by the aerospace industry. The two variations on a Keynesian theme, supported by the two leading industries of the long prosperity of 1948–1973 which contributed so much to the acceptance of Keynes' ideas, in turn favor the continuation of the existing system of international free trade. Unfortunately, however, these two Keynesian approaches to economic stag-

James R. Kurth, "The Political Consequences of the Product Cycle: Industrial History and Political Outcomes," *International Organization* 33,1 (Winter 1979). © 1979 by the Board of Regents of the University of Wisconsin System. Reprinted with permission.

nation are so minimal that they are already perceived by other economic sectors as inadequate for their needs.

A third approach requires greater change from past priorities: systematic restraint or reduction of industrial wages and welfare benefits, in order to increase the rate of profit and thus the amount of capital available for reinvestment in industry to make it more competitive in the world market. This approach, once known as deflation and now often associated with the ideas of Milton Friedman, is preferred by the large commercial banks heavily engaged in international operations. And, of course, this approach also favors the continuation of the existing system of international free trade.

The fourth approach would be rather more radical: it would displace the system of international free trade with one of "organized free trade," i.e., international cartels, or even with one of vigorous protection of national industries with tariffs and quotas against imports. This, its advocates claim, would permit sufficient capital formation to make the protected industries efficient once again. This approach, which has been called neomercantilism, is of course the one preferred by the oldest industries, in particular the textile, steel, and chemical industries of Europe and America.

The above four solutions focus on preservation of existing industries. A fifth, rather different approach is possible, which focuses on the creation of new industries or indeed new leading sectors whose rapid growth would lift up the entire economy behind them, much as the automobile industry did in America in the 1920s and in Europe in the 1950s–1960s. And since the nation which introduces a new industry has a natural advantage in the world market for a decade or even for a generation, industrial innovation would also favor the continuation of the system of international free trade. This approach draws upon that other great economist of the 1930s, Joseph Schumpeter, who saw the advantages of "gales of creative destruction," i.e. depressions, which pruned the economy of overinvestment in old industries and cleared the way for investment in new ones, but whose ideas were eclipsed by Keynes' during the long prosperity of 1948–1973.[2] By its nature, its advocates would be found among new, growing industries, such as telecommunications, rather than mature, established ones, and among investment banks, rather than commercial ones.

The politics of the next few years, then, will involve the conflict between these alternative solutions to economic stagnation and the conflict between the different industries that support them. But it will not be the first time that politics in major industrial countries have been shaped by the public policies of major industries and by the conflicts between them.

This essay seeks to add a historical dimension to the analysis of the political impact of different industries. It examines the political tendencies of three successive leading sectors in Europe and America over the last two centuries—textiles, steel, and automobiles. Each of these has been the largest industry for several major industrial nations in the West at one time or another. Of course, there have been other industries which have also formed major economic sectors in particular countries at particular times, for example, the chemical and electrical industries in Germany, which we will also discuss, and the aerospace industry in the United States. Nevertheless, from the overall perspective of comparative economic history, the textile, steel, and automobile industries assume an especially prominent place.

Each of these three industries has gone through what could be seen as a life cycle of growth, stagnation or saturation, and decline in the major countries of Europe and in the United States. The process has been similar to one which Raymond Vernon has analyzed in his studies of contemporary transnational enterprises and which he has termed the product cycle.[3] In Vernon's concept the product cycle consists of four phases:

1. Innovation of a product and growth of its sales in the domestic market.
2. Saturation of the domestic market and export of the product to foreign markets. Exports will go first to those countries whose demand structures (e.g., national income per capita) are most similar to that in the home country. When these markets in turn are saturated, the export drive will move on to countries whose demand structures are less similar.
3. Manufacture of the product within foreign markets, i.e., direct foreign investment. Again, investment will go first to those countries whose supply structures (e.g., factors of production) and demand structures are most similar to those in the home country and later to countries whose supply structures are less similar. Within the home country, the manufacture of the product reaches a plateau.
4. Export of the product from foreign countries into the original home market. Eventually, indeed, there will be export of the product from the latest foreign countries to manufacture it into not only the original home market but also into other foreign countries which had once been the latest manufacturers. Within the home country and these other earlier producers, the manufacture of the product goes into decline.

These four phases describe very well the life cycle of the automobile industry in the United States and in the countries in Western Europe. But the life cycles of the textile industry and the steel industry have also been variations on the same theme. The textile and steel industries rarely engaged in direct foreign investment in manufacturing, phase 3, but each passed through the other three phases. And in the steel industry there was the functional equivalent of phase 3 with *indirect* foreign investment, the financing of the foreign railroads which were the major final consumer of the home steel industry. In addition, as we shall see, the steel industry passed through its own peculiar phase, that of government procurement of its products for military purposes.

In his own work, Vernon has not extensively examined the consequences of the product cycle for major political outcomes. However, Robert Gilpin, in a major, pathbreaking book, has drawn on the concept of the product cycle, expanded it into the concept of the growth and decline of entire national economies, and analyzed the relations between this economic cycle, national power, and international politics.[4]

In this essay, we will pursue these themes of Vernon and Gilpin by examining some of the political consequences of the industrial life cycles of textiles, steel, and automobiles over the last two centuries. In general, the major consequences of the domestic growth phase of an industry have been for domestic politics, including the nature of political regimes. Conversely, the major consequences of the later phases, those of foreign exports and foreign investments, have been for foreign policies. For the textile industry and the steel industry, our focus will be on the major countries of Europe; for the automobile industry, we will widen our focus to include the United States.

Of course, many of the political outcomes that we will discuss have been enormously complex in their causes and can hardly be adequately explained by industrial factors alone. The rise of the liberal state in the nineteenth century, the "new imperialism" of the 1870s–1890s, the Anglo-German naval race before World War I, the coming to power of Hitler in 1933, and the political stability of Western democracies in the thirty years after World War II—these momentous events have each been the subject of an enormous and sophisticated historical literature, rich in an array of competing explanations, and many readers will disagree with the particular interpretation offered here. We make no claim that our analysis provides a full explanation and understanding of these historical phenomena. It is our suggestion, however, that the industrial factor has a consistency over time and a commonality over space that gives it a special value as an explanatory approach.

THE POLITICAL TENDENCY OF THE TEXTILE INDUSTRY

The Domestic Growth Phase

In almost all countries, the first stage in industrialization has been the creation of a textile industry. This has required the mobilization of relatively modest amounts of capital, modest, that is, in relation to the amount of capital already available in the country as a result of pre-industrial enterprises and also modest in relation to the amount of capital that has been needed for the creation of later industries, such as steel, railroads, chemicals, automobiles, and aerospace. Consequently, the textile industries of Europe (and also of the United States and the most advanced countries of Latin America) were created for the most part by family firms, and the industries grew through the reinvestment of their earnings. In contrast with later industries, the capital accumulation for textile industrialization could be accomplished largely without dependence upon financing from banks, the state, or foreign investors.[5]

The lack of dependence upon financing from banks had important consequences for the development of financial institutions. The financial agencies that grew up around the textile industry were clearing houses and commercial banks engaged in short-term credits to merchants. They were not investment houses and industrial banks engaged in long-term credits to industry. Those banks that did engage in long-term credits at the time did so with loans to governments, not to industries.

The lack of dependence of the textile industry upon financing from the state also had important consequences for the development of political institutions. The capital accumulation for textile industrialization could be accomplished largely without state intervention, except for the elimination of barriers to a free market within the national boundaries (e.g., internal tariffs) and for the erection of external tariffs on occasion for the protection of the "infant industry." Textile manufacturers did not want the dynastic–authoritarian state of the past, and they did not need the technocratic–authoritarian state of the future. Rather, the textile manufacturers in Europe in the first half of the nineteenth century were opposed to many of the traditional activities of the state. They did not want the internal tariffs, the consumer taxes, and the tedious regulations of the absolutist monarchies, which prevented the manufacturers from selling their goods in a nationwide market. And they did not want the local guild monopolies and local welfare systems, which also prevented them from drawing their labor from a nationwide market.[6] Similarly, the commercial banks wanted an end to restrictions on the free movement of capital. To systematically eliminate the traditional impediments to free movement of goods, labor, and capital, however, the textile manufacturers and commercial bankers needed institutionalized representation at the national center of power. To achieve this they needed "the supremacy of parliament," ideally within "the liberal state." But the textile manufacturers did not need the assistance of the state to mobilize large amounts of investment capital; nor did they yet need its assistance to demobilize large numbers of socialist workers, services that would later be performed by such diverse authoritarian governments as those of Napoleon III in France, Bismarck in Germany, Mussolini in Italy, and Primo de Rivera and Franco in Spain.

The liberal state, with parliamentary supremacy and with property suffrage, was the most finely-tuned solution to the problems of the textile industry (and of other industries producing light consumer goods such as shoes) and of commercial banking. The liberal state gave them the abolition of traditional barriers to trade; parliamentary supremacy meant that they would be represented at the center of national power; and property suffrage meant that only they and the traditional elites would be so represented. As such, there was, in the familiar phrase of Max Weber (and of Goethe before him), an "elective affinity" between the textile industry, commercial banking, and such a regime. The political theory of the coalition between the textile industry and commercial banking was summed up by Thomas Macaulay in 1830:

> Our rulers will best promote the improvement of the nation by confining themselves strictly to their legitimate duties, by leaving capital to find its most lucrative course, commodities their fair price, industry and intelligence their national reward, idleness and folly their natural punishment, by maintaining peace, by defending property, by diminishing the price of law, and by observing strict economy in every department of the state. Let the government do this, the people will do the rest.[7]

We should not overemphasize the actual consequences of this elective affinity between textiles and liberals, however, for in Europe the political impact of the textile industry varied from one country to another according to when the country industrialized and to how the industry fit into the international market.

The British Model   The connection between textile industrialization and the liberal institutions was most obvious in the first industrializer, Britain, which in the early nineteenth century was simultaneously "the workshop of the world," "the mother of parliaments," and the center of "Manchester liberalism."[8] The textile industry also had a major political impact in the second wave of industrializers, that is, France, Belgium, and Switzerland, each of which experienced rapid growth in the industry in the 1820s. The textile manufacturers were a major force in the Revolutions of 1830 in each of these three countries (as they were in the related conflict over the Great Reform Bill in Britain in 1830–1832). And they were a major force in the establishment and support of the succeeding liberal regimes: the Orleanist Monarchy in France (the "Bourgeois Monarchy" or *monarchie censitaire*), the new and similar monarchy in now-independent Belgium, and the new regimes in the most industrialized cantons of Switzerland.[9]

In Britain, France, and Belgium prior to textile industrialization, the old absolutist monarchy had been displaced and the landed aristocracy had been diminished in power by revolutionary upheavals at one time or another. This meant that the textile industry could grow up in a relatively open political space, at least compared with the countries to the East and the South, and that it was easier for it to achieve its political aims.

In addition, the textile industries in the early industrializers were relatively competitive in the international market. This was most obviously true of Britain, "the workshop of the world," but even France, Belgium, and Switzerland were successful in selected international textile markets. This meant that for textile manufacturers in these countries, there was no conflict between the economic and the political parts of liberalism, between free trade and civil liberties. Again, this made it easier for the textile industry to develop a coherent vision and then to develop, in Gramsci's sense, an ideological hegemony. The most dramatic example was the dominance of the doctrine of Manchester liberalism in Britain.

The Prussian Mutation   The political impact of the textile industry was very different in the next or third wave of industrializers, Prussia and Austria, which experienced rapid growth in the industry only in the 1840s–1850s. Here, the Napoleonic Wars had displaced neither the old landed aristocracy nor its ally, the absolutist monarchy. Accordingly, the textile industry grew up in a relatively closed political space, cramped and contained by a well-entrenched agrarian upper class.[10]

One consequence was that textile industrialization in the East (1840s–1850s) was somewhat delayed from when it might have occurred and later than that in the West (1820s–1830s, even earlier in Britain). Yet, certain social groups in the East, in particular, students, professors, and lawyers, imported liberal ideas from the West during the Napoleonic Wars and the Restoration. The result was that a gap opened up between liberalism and industrialization. In the East in the 1810s–1830s, liberalism was a movement without much of a social base—what William Langer has called "the liberalism of the intellectuals" rather than the liberalism of the manufacturers.[11] At this point liberalism outpaced industrialization.

A second, later consequence was that when textile industrialization did occur, the textile manufacturers would not be strong enough relative to the agrarian upper classes to impose their political vision on the rest of society. The new "infant industry" in the East was highly vulnerable in its domestic markets to competition from the older established textile manufacturers in the West, and accordingly the Eastern manufacturers were highly protectionist in regard to international trade policies. These features of the textile industry in the East diminished its liberal impulse and impact. The 1840s to the 1860s were the high point of liberal movements in the history of the Hohenzollern and Habsburg monarchies, yet liberal institutions never achieved the strength that they had in the West. At this point the gap between liberalism and industrialization continued but was reversed: industrialization outpaced liberalization.

Indeed, from the 1820s to the 1860s, the political economies of Britain and Prussia were almost mirror images. British textiles were competitive in the international market, while British grain was not. Conversely, Prussian grain was competitive in the international market, while Prussian textiles were not. Thus British textile manufacturers favored both free trade and liberal institutions, and British grain producers favored neither. Prussian textile manufacturers favored liberal institutions but not free trade, and Prussian grain producers favored free trade but not liberal institutions. The fact that British textile manufacturers could impose free trade upon British grain producers (the abolition of the Corn Laws in 1846) reinforced the social power of political liberals. Conversely, the fact that Junker grain exporters could impose free trade upon Prussian textile manufacturers (the low-tariff policy of the Zollverein) reinforced the social power of political conservatives. In Britain, economic liberalism worked to reinforce political liberalism; in Prussia, economic liberalism worked to undermine it.[12]

The Latin Pattern   The political impact of the textile industry was very different again in the next or fourth wave of industrializers (Italy, Spain, and Portugal). Here, textile industrialization was delayed for a generation after that of Germany and Austria, two generations after that of France, Belgium, and Switzerland, and more than three generations after that of Britain. The countries of Latin Europe are thus the first severe case of "underdevelopment" or "dependent" industrialization.[13]

But like the East, the South also imported liberal ideas from the West during the Napoleonic Wars and the Restoration. Indeed, the first use of the term "Liberal" for a political group was in Spain in 1810, in the Constituent *Cortes* at Cadiz. Unlike the East, however, the social base of liberalism in the South also included military officers and bureaucratic officials, primarily because the old legitimate monarchies at the apex of the military and bureaucratic organizations had been displaced during the Napoleonic invasions. With such a social base, Southern liberalism was stronger than Eastern liberalism, whose social base was confined to intellectuals, but weaker than Western liberalism, whose social base included textile manufacturers. However, the absence of a new cohesive industrial class, the absence of the old cohesive agrarian class, and absence of the old legitimate monarchy combined to mean that for Latin Europe this was a period when no social group could exercise political authority, a period of military coups, popular revolts, and civil wars.

When textile industrialization did occur, the textile manufacturers could grow up in rough coequality with the agrarian upper classes. And this by the mid-1870s eventually issued in political stability and a special kind of liberal state, one based on a policy of tariff protection for both textiles and agriculture, a marriage of cloth and wheat comparable to the contemporary "marriage of iron and rye" in Bismarck's Germany.[14]

The Foreign Export Phase

The British textile industry was the first to move into the second phase, the domestic stagnation phase, of the industrial life cycle. When the British textile industry reached the saturation point in its British markets and "the falling rate of profit," its natural, because minimal, response was to simply continue its old activity in a new place, i.e., it shifted from the selling of textiles in Britain to the selling of textiles in Europe. By the end of the Napoleonic Wars, 50–70 percent of British textile production each year was sold abroad. This was the motor behind the British foreign policy of free trade.

As the European market in turn became saturated, the textile industry shifted to the selling of textiles in Latin America. Here was the motor behind the British support of, and occasional intervention in, the Latin-American Wars of Independence. This combination of free trade and gunboat diplomacy would later be termed by John Gallagher and Ronald Robinson "the imperialism of free trade."[15] It probably reached its apogee in the Opium War of 1842, near the end of the severe depression of 1837–1843.[16] The transnational enterprise of this era of free trade was the trading company, the largest being the East India Company. The foreign policy of the British textile industry was summed up, again by Thomas Macaulay, in 1833:

> It would be, on the most selfish view of the case, far better for us that the people of India were well-governed and independent of us, than ill-governed and subject to us; that they were ruled by their own kings, but wearing our broadcloth, and working with our cutlery, than that they were performing their salaams to English collectors and English magistrates, but were too ignorant to value, or too poor to buy, English manufactures. To trade with civilized men is infinitely more profitable than to govern savages.[17]

The success of British textiles in the international market led to the reinforcement of the British banking system of clearing houses, commercial banks, short-term credits, and now to insurance companies and to the expansion of its operations into the world arena. This kind of banking system, with its peculiar combination of short-term time horizons and worldwide space horizons, would have important implications for British domestic and foreign policies in later years.

There was another possible response to the saturation of domestic markets, however. That was to shift investment capital into a new industry, in this case the iron and steel industry and the railroads. This British investors did in the 1840s, and the result was the British boom of the 1850s. This choice between response one and response two, between foreign expansion and technological innovation, between producing an old commodity for a new country and producing a new commodity for the old country, was a crucial one. And the same crucial choice reappears as each new leading sector reaches its eventual and inevitable maturity and decline.

The textile industries of the other major European countries reached the saturation points of their own domestic markets at various times during the last three decades of the nineteenth century. The normal response of each country was to search for new markets in underdeveloped countries, particularly in a nation's colonial territories where the products of the national textile industry had a natural or even legal (e.g., tariffs) advantage over the products of foreign competitors. This drive for new colonial markets was one of the causes of "the new imperialism" of the late nineteenth century, including "the scramble for Africa" in the 1880s. But the textile industry by itself does not explain much about colonial policy. A more powerful engine propelling the new imperialism was the domestic stagnation phase of the steel industries of Europe.

THE POLITICAL TENDENCY OF THE STEEL INDUSTRY

The Domestic Growth Phase

The second stage in the industrialization of a country normally has been the creation of a steel industry and the related creation of those industries which are the final consumers of steel—railroads, shipbuilding, and, in the twentieth century, automobiles.

The creation of a country's steel industry and its crucial consumer in the nineteenth century, the railroads, required the mobilization of far larger amounts of capital than that required in the creation of the textile industry. This distinction between the capital required for textile industrialization and that required for steel and railroad industrialization is one aspect of the distinction that Alexander Gerschenkron drew between early industrialization and late industrialization.[18] Gerschenkron argued that in the late industrializers the need to mobilize large amounts of capital led to the need for financing by large investment banks or even by the state. This in turn led the investment banks to organize industrial cartels to prevent competition between the recipients of their investments. The complex of cartelized industry and industrial banks then was well-positioned to shape state policies. Or when the state itself undertook the financing of industrialization, it led to authoritarian measures. In Gerschenkron's view it was no accident that the late industrializers, in particular Germany, Austria-Hungary, Italy, and Russia were or eventually became authoritarian states. Guillermo O'Donnell has reached similar conclusions in analyzing Latin-American countries. O'Donnell argued that in these still later industrializers the move from the consumer-goods stage of industrialization into the capital-goods stage of industrialization generates severe balance of payments problems, the need to mobilize large amounts of capital, and again the turning of economic and technocratic elites to the solution of the "bureaucratic–authoritarian" regime, as in Brazil in 1964 and in Argentina in 1966.[19]

The actual evidence for the causal connection between the steel industry and authoritarian politics is rather mixed. In the first industrializer, Britain, the mobilization of capital for the second stage of industrialization occurred without any dramatic change in financial institutions or in state intervention. Indeed, the mobilization of capital for the British iron and steel industry and for the British railroads was achieved about as easily and as incrementally as the mobilization of capital for the British textile industry. But in Britain the ease of capital mobilization for iron, steel, and railroads was itself a consequence of the prior overwhelming success of British textiles in foreign markets, which generated large profits and large amounts of capital for investment in new enterprises. From the 1820s to the 1850s, textile exports normally formed 40–60 percent of Britain's exports each year.[20]

In France, the pattern was somewhat different. After a slow growth of the iron industry and of railroads before 1848, France experienced rapid growth in these sectors in the 1850s and 1860s. It is an oft-told tale that this rapid growth required new financial institutions, such as investment banks (e.g., the Crédit Mobilier of the Pereire brothers); in turn, these new investment banks, it is said, needed the support of a strong state (i.e., the Second Empire of Napoleon III, 1852–1870) to break the power of the traditional banks.[21] Indeed, a good case can be made that the first in the endless parade of modern bureaucratic–authoritarian regimes was the French Second Empire.

The Third Republic, which replaced the Second Empire after its defeat in the Franco-Prussian War in 1870, was not an authoritarian regime. Yet in the 1880s it organized and supported, through the Freycinet Plan, another major expansion of the French steel industry and the French railroads.[22] This casts doubt on the argument that steel and railroad industrialization in France required an authoritarian regime. On the other hand, just as in Britain in the first half of the nineteenth century, so too in France in the 1880s, the export of textiles provided the capital to finance the expansion in iron, steel, and railroads. During this period, textile exports normally formed 30–50 percent of France's exports each year. In Britain, the expansion was financed by British domination of the international markets for low-price cotton goods; in France, the expansion was financed by French domination of the international market for high-quality goods, especially woolen ones. It was France's special vocation in the quality products of the last stage of the pre-industrial era which eased its transition through the *second* stage of the industrial revolution—and made it easier to do without the discipline of another authoritarian regime.[23]

In Germany, the path to steel and railroad industrialization was very different from that in either Britain or France. At the time Prussia and then Germany undertook this second stage of industrialization, it had achieved no dominance of the world market for any product of the first stage, that of textiles. Accordingly, there was an absence of large profits from foreign trade and thus of large amounts of capital to be invested in steel and railroads. There was therefore a need for new kinds of financial institutions, specifically industrial investment banks or state enterprises.[24] And there was also a relatively open space in the German financial system within which these new institutions grew and indeed reached a dominant position. As in Britain where the weakness of the agrarian elites had permitted the textile industry and commercial banking to grow up unconfined and to eventually dominate the political system, so too in Germany the weakness of the textile industry and commercial banking (itself due to the strength of the agrarian elites, the Junkers) permitted the steel industry and industrial banking to grow up unconfined and eventually to dominate.

By the end of the long prosperity of 1850–1873, sometimes known as the great railroad boom, Britain and Germany had each institutionalized the respective methods by which they had passed through the first and second stages of industrialization. Britain represented the overdevelopment of the first stage of the industrial revolution, composed of the textile industry and commercial banking. Germany represented the overdevelopment of the second stage of the industrial revolution, composed of the steel industry and industrial banking. Even more, however, Germany represented the overdevelopment of the coalition between the last stage of the pre-industrial era, that of commercialized agriculture, and the second stage of the industrial one—what was to become in 1879 the famous "marriage of iron and rye." France took a middle position between the two, having a political economy more balanced between the agricultural, the textile, and steel sectors, between domestic and foreign markets, and between commercial and investment banking.

In Britain, France, and Germany, the iron and steel industry and the railroads developed together, as a sort of "steel–rail complex." In Italy and Spain, however, this nexus was severed. The major railroads of Latin Europe were built with rails and rolling stock imported from Britain and France and were financed with capital loaned by British and French investment banks.[25] The result was railroadization without steel industrialization. Since the capital mobilization for the railroads of Latin Europe came from foreign investors rather than from the national government, from abroad rather than from above, no dramatic reorganization of the state was necessary. It is not surprising, therefore, that the construction of the railroads of Italy and Spain in the mid- and late-nineteenth century could coexist with the conservation of their liberal institutions and parliamentary systems.

Italy did construct a substantial steel industry in the 1900s, however. (Spain would not do so until after World War II.) But, as in Britain and in France in earlier times, the necessary capital mobilization in Italy was made possible by the export of textiles. In Italy's case, it was Italian domination of the international market for high-quality silk products. It was also another case where the *second* stage of the industrial revolution was financed by the achievements of the last stage of the pre-industrial era.[26]

Most later steel industrializers, such as Spain, Brazil, and Argentina, lacked the capability to dominate the international market for a particular industrial product. This led them into severe balance of payments difficulties (even though they were exporters of agricultural products), once they tried to move from the stage of textile or "import-substitution" industrialization to the stage of steel or capital-goods industrialization. The conjunction of the need to mobilize large amounts of capital and severe balance of payments deficits leading to devaluations and severe inflation created an influential constituency among economic, bureaucratic, and technocratic elites in support of an authoritarian regime. In contrast with a liberal, parliamentary system, an authoritarian regime was better able to destroy labor unions, repress wages and consumer demand, and thus squeeze capital out of the working class in order to finance the new capital-goods sector.

The Foreign Export Phase and the Naval Procurement Phase: from the Great Depression of 1873–1896 to World War I

The most pronounced impact of the steel industry upon political outcomes came, not in its phase of domestic growth, but in its phase of domestic stagnation, that is, after steel production reached saturation in its home markets, and the industry turned to foreign ones. And because the responses of Britain to this phase in the nineteenth century can be seen as prototypes of many American industrial policies in the mid-twentieth century, we shall discuss the British experience at some length.[27]

Britain   The British iron industry (it would not become a steel industry proper until the adoption of the Bessemer process in the 1860s) and the associated railroads fueled the British boom of 1851 to 1857. A brief depression from 1857 to 1859 led the British to push for a series of international treaties to promote free trade, such as the Cobden-Chevalier treaty of 1860 between Britain and France. The 1860s were relatively prosperous. During this period some banks of the City of London began the large-scale financing through bonds of railroads on the Continent, many of them built with British rails and British equipment.[28]

By the beginning of the 1870s, however, railroad-building in Britain had reached the saturation point, and to a lesser degree the same was true of Britain's railroad-building on the Continent. An economic historian (who later went on to other things) once asked "What happened when the railroads were built?"[29] His answer was "the Great Depression of 1873–1896." Although other factors also contributed to the long economic depression after 1873, such as the entry into the world markets of massive amounts of cheap grain from the American midwest, which sharply drove down European grain prices, the peaking of railroad-building in Europe was certainly a central factor.[30]

What was the response of the British steel industry and of the bond-dealing banks of the City of London to the saturation of their former markets and more generally to the Great Depression? Again, the first response was simply to continue their old activity in a new place, i.e., they shifted the building and financing of railroads from Britain and the Continent to the "regions of recent settlement" (i.e., the United States, Canada, Australia, and Argentina) and to the regions on the borders of Europe (e.g., Turkey and Egypt). In some of the latter regions, however, the inability of weak and corrupt governments to meet their bond payments led

Britain in the 1870s and 1880s into interventions and even annexations. Thus began the first steps toward "the new imperialism." Of course, the factors making for "the new imperialism" were many, and historians have developed a variety of explanations, such as strategic calculation, bureaucratic activities, and popular moods. The industrial and financial factor, however, seems to have been an especially consistent and common one.[31]

The change that took place in the minds of some industrialists, after the beginning of the depression in 1873, was registered by William Menelaus, a leading steel manufacturer, in his presidential address to the British Iron and Steel Institute in 1875:

> We have but little demand from Europe, and we seem to have lost our American market entirely. . . . We must, I think, frankly accept the position in which we are placed, and prepare to seek new markets for our produce in countries which, even if they have the will, have not yet the power to impose restrictions on our trade.[32]

In their new foreign policy, the steel industry had allies, of course, in the textile industry, who were also suffering from the depression and who were already familiar with the advantages of "the imperialism of free trade."

However, even the new overseas receptacles of British textiles and steel soon reached the saturation point or at least the law of diminishing returns. The result was a new, sharp business downturn, the depression of 1883, within the overall Great Depression of 1873–1896. Again, the minimal response was to expand the old activities into new countries, reinforcing "the new imperialism" and "the scramble for Africa" of the 1880s.

E. J. Hobsbawm summarizes this crucial choice of Britain in response to the Great Depression:

> She was too deeply committed to the technology and business organization of the first phase of industrialization, which had served her so well, to advance enthusiastically into the new and revolutionary technology and industrial management. . . . This left her with only one major way out—a traditional one for Britain, though one also now adopted by competing powers—the economic (and increasingly the political) conquest of hitherto unexploited areas of the world. In other words, imperialism.[33]

The choice was in part the result of the British banking system. The absence of strong investment and industrial banks meant that it was especially difficult for Britain to mobilize capital for long-term equity investment in new technologies and industries.

The second response of the British steel industry to the Great Depression and in particular to the depression of 1883 was the building of steamships.[34] Just as the railroads brought cheap grain and meat from the hinterlands to the ports of the regions of recent settlement, so the steamships brought them from these ports to Britain. But these receptacles, or rather vessels, of British steel, also soon reached the saturation point. The result was another sharp business downturn, the depression of 1893, within the overall Great Depression.

The third response of the British steel industry to the Great Depression, in particular to the depressions of 1883 and 1893, was again a minimal move. Having built commercial ships, it was natural enough that the next step was to build naval ships. The beginning of the depression of 1883 was followed by the "navy scare" of 1884 and by a 20 percent increase in the British naval budget in 1885, the largest increase since the Crimean War. The beginning of the depression of 1893 was followed by another navy scare of 1893–1894 and by another 20 percent increase in the British naval budget in 1894, regularized in the Spencer naval program of 1894 which laid plans for further increases in the next few years.[35] The industry journal, *Iron and Coal Trades Review*, observed in March 1895 that the effect of the Admiralty program

> has been to enable private firms to tide over without disaster periods of depression that would otherwise have been extremely trying; and, naturally, we have seen that the same policy has stimulated local and provincial interest in naval affairs to a much greater extent than was formerly the case.[36]

The use of naval procurement as countercyclical policy seems to have continued even after the end of the Great Depression in 1896. The beginning of the less severe depression of 1900–1904 was followed by another sharp increase in the naval budget in 1901, and even the decision in 1904 to build the *Dreadnought* can be interpreted as another example of Keynesianism before Keynes.

Thus it was that by the beginning of the twentieth century, Britain had abandoned its industrial vocation for an imperial one. In 1851, "the workshop of the world" had dazzled Europe with the first industrial world's fair, The Great Exhibition at the Crystal Palace. Fifty years later, the scene was just as splendid but rather different:

> Never were instruments of war so gleaming with brass, so brilliant of paintwork, so stately with ensigns and bugle-calls and white canvas. The fleet which, in 1901, King Edward VII reviewed at Spithead at the close of the Victorian era offered perhaps the most gorgeous spectacle of power Europe has ever seen: the ships were painted in black, white and yellow, and fluttered all over with signal flags and pennants, and from their topmasts flew gigantic White Ensigns and crosses of St. George, and their crews jauntily linked the decks, and their officers majestically saluted from their high bridges, and through the line of warships came the King of England in his royal yacht, the largest steam yacht in the world—standard at the mainmast, duty officers at attention on the foredeck, a wispy stream of smoke from two bright yellow funnels, and beneath the cheers of the assembled crews and the successive melodies of the battleship bands, the soft greased thump of reciprocating engines from impeccable engine-rooms below.[37]

The British steel industry now faced vigorous competition in its colonial and even home markets from the more efficient German and American steel industries. The emerging British electrical and chemical industries, underdeveloped because of the foreign orientation of the British financial system, also faced vigorous competition from their more efficient German and American counterparts, nourished and guided by investment and industrial banks. More broadly, the small island-state serving as the head of a far-flung, loosely-knit, sea-borne empire faced vigorous strategic competition from Germany and America as two great continental powers. The liberal vision of free trade and free capital movements in a world arena was nearing exhaustion, or at least bringing about the industrial and strategic exhaustion of Britain while preserving the prosperity of the City of London.

For a brief moment, British heavy industry put forward an alternative vision of the British future. It did so under the leadership of Joseph Chamberlain, a leader of the Conservative Party and a former mayor of Birmingham, the center of the British steel industry.[38] Chamberlain and his supporters proposed that Britain erect tariff walls around much of its empire and that the dominions be compensated with greater participation in political decision making in London—imperial preference and imperial federation. The result would be a British world power with industrial and strategic strength equal to or greater than that of Germany and America. And together these three great "Saxon" powers would essentially divide much of the world into three spheres of influence and would no longer pursue conflicts of interest between themselves.

The defeat of British heavy industry and of Chamberlain's vision, finalized in the Liberal electoral victory of 1906, was probably over-determined. A key role in the new imperial order would have been played by Canada. But many Canadian economic interests wanted access to cheap American capital-goods, and by this time there were some Canadian industrialists who wanted their own tariff walls against all foreign goods, including British ones. But the decisive attack on the industrial and imperial vision came from within Britain itself and was organized by the banks of the City of London which wanted to maintain the benefits from being the center of a system of free movement of goods and capital with the world as its arena. The banks were supported by many within its old ally, the textile industry, who still believed they could compete in cotton textiles. The long hegemony of the banking system in British politics meant that this particular tale of two cities, of London and Birmingham, would not have a surprise ending.

The British steel industry was not strong enough, then, to displace the liberal vision and to impose its own. It was strong enough, however, to exact compensation in the form of renewed naval procurement and to justify the grand new battleships by pointing to the German menace in the years down to 1914.

Other nations also turned to vigorous state action during the Great Depression of 1873–1896 and later, in order to maintain their steel industries and the returns to capital in them.

France   Like its British counterpart, the French steel industry also was afflicted by the Great Depression of 1873–1876. The first response was, as we have already suggested, the state-supported expansion of the French railroad network under the Freycinet Plan of 1878. A second response was similar to that of Britain, a search for overseas markets. Jules Ferry, who had long represented the iron and steel industry of Eastern France, initiated an annexationist colonial policy when he was Premier in 1881. But this colonial policy was somewhat premature and was only fitfully pursued in the 1880s, when the major thrust of state policy was the completion of the railroad network.

What happened after the French railroads were built? The depression of 1892. One response to this new downturn was the famous Méline Tariff of that year, the first high French customs barrier since before 1860. Another response was a reinvigorated colonial policy which lasted until the eve of World War I. But the most substantial response was to build and finance railroads in Russia with French equipment and capital and to buttress this grand railroad undertaking with the Franco-Russian Alliance of 1894.[39]

Germany   The German steel industry and its associated industrial banks also were afflicted by the Great Depression. But the actions of the German state not only combined the various measures of the British and the French but included some innovative measures of its own.

The first response was a minimal move, the tariff of 1879. This tariff was a central component of the coalition between German industrialists and Junker agrarians, "the marriage between iron and rye," and 1879 has been called the Second Founding of the Second Empire. In the same year, the Anti-Socialist Law was enacted. And at about the same time, the state undertook the legal enforcement of cartel agreements to limit production and maintain prices.[40]

Yet tariff and cartel protection alone could not prevent the saturation of the steel industry's German markets, and Germany also experienced the depression of 1883. Germany then turned rather tentatively to what had been the first response of Britain, a search for overseas markets. Bismarck initiated a colonial policy in 1884, one which was not vigorously sustained. Bismarck also initiated a 20 percent increase in the German naval budget in the same year. The return of depression in 1890 was followed by a 60 percent increase in the German naval budget of 1891. The Germans, like the British before them, anticipated Keynes. The depressions of 1901 and 1908 were also followed quickly by unusual increases in the German naval budget.[41] At the same time, diplomatic efforts promoted foreign railroads, especially the Baghdad Railway, which were built with German steel and capital but which posed a threat to British economic and strategic interests.

Thus, by the beginning of the twentieth century, the steel industries of both Britain and Germany were focused on the building of warships, and the Anglo–German naval race was on. As the years went on, the naval race took on a reciprocal dynamic of its own. But it is interesting to note that most major jumps in the British and the German naval budgets occurred in a year or two after a downturn in the business cycle.

The Anglo–German naval race did not in itself lead to World War I. It did, however, place a barrier to any enduring Anglo–German détente, and it did lead to the Anglo–French naval entente of 1904. All of this, in turn, loaded the dice toward the particular form the alliance system took by 1914.

One other German response to saturation in old industries was more innovative, however, and that was the creation of two new capital-goods industries, electricity and chemicals. The German industrial banks facilitated such industrial innovation. State measures also provided important support, especially the funding of technical and science education, the reform of municipal government to provide financial security for urban electric railroads and electric power systems, and, of course, military and naval procurement of explosives manufactured by the chemical industry.[42]

Italy   The Italian steel industry was largely constructed in the 1900s. Even more than the preceding steel industries it was dependent upon state contracts and guarantees. Almost immediately, it became a major force for a vigorous foreign policy to achieve railroad concessions in the Balkans (especially, and rather pathetically, in Montenegro and Albania) and in the Ottoman Empire, and a force for a major buildup of the Italian navy.[43] Indeed, in the last years before World War I, there was something of a railroad war between Italy and Austria-Hungary in the Balkans. It was this rivalry which gradually separated Italy from its cooperation with Germany and Austria-Hungary in the Triple Alliance, and it was this search for new colonial territories to the East which drove Italy into the War on the side of the Triple Entente of Britain, France, and Russia in 1915.

The Foreign Export and Military Procurement Phases Recycled: from World War I to the Great Depression of 1929

On the morrow of World War I, the steel industries of Europe and also of America, were again faced with the old problem: how to keep themselves in business, after the period of postwar reconstruction came to its inevitable end. There was a choice of several paths.

Britain   The British, in keeping with their practice of the minimal move, of muddling through, for the most part chose simply to do more of the same. They retained their overseas empire after the war, and thus they could continue to build railroads to span their colonies, steamships to service them, and warships to defend them, i.e., they could continue in each of their three responses to the Great Depression of 1873–1896. In addition, however, they at last began the transition to a new leading sector. Having based much of their earlier industrialization on textiles and having had high earnings from foreign trade and investment, the British had, more than other European countries, a consumer-oriented economy and high per capita income. Accordingly, they possessed in 1920 the second largest (after the Americans) automobile industry in the world, and this experienced a slow but steady growth during the 1920s.

France   The French recapitulated the British pattern, but in a reduced form. Before the war, their empire, their earnings from textile (especially woolen) exports, and their earnings from foreign investment had each been second only to Britain's. After the war, they too poured the output of their steel industry into more colonial railroads, steamships, and warships and also into a small automobile industry, which nevertheless was the third largest automobile industry in the world.

Germany   The Germans, having lost the war and having remained a country without a strong consumer goods sector, had in 1920 neither an overseas empire nor an automobile industry. For the German steel industry, consequently, there seemed to be only two feasible paths, and these were mutually reinforcing. One was renewed armaments production. The other was exports of steel products to markets in Eastern Europe and, relatedly, gaining control over the growing and competing steel industries of Austria, Czechoslovakia, and Poland. Throughout the 1920s, the steel industry supported those political parties which in turn supported rearmament, revision of the Treaty of Versailles, tariff barriers against Western Europe, and German domination of Eastern Europe. Its favorite political vehicle was the National People's Party, led by Alfred Hugenberg.[44] The steel industry was joined in its support by the Junker agrarians, making the National People's Party a renewal of the old marriage of iron and rye. The Junkers, imbued with military traditions and threatened by cheap grain imports from Poland, had their own reasons for rearmament, revision of Versailles, and domination of Eastern Europe.

By the 1920s, however, the German economic scene included two other leading sectors, the chemical industry and the electrical industry, and these had a very different political tendency. The German chemical industry was the second largest and the most advanced chemical industry in the world. (Its leading enterprise, I. G. Farben, was the world's largest chemical corporation and the largest corporation of any in Europe.)[45] This meant that the chemical industry had a strong interest in free trade or at least in conditions which encouraged exports. The same was true of the German electrical industry which was the largest and the most advanced electrical industry in Europe. And since the largest and best markets for chemical and electrical products were other advanced industrial economies, these two industries were vitally interested in good relations with Western Europe. This led them to support those political parties which in turn supported "fulfillment" of the Versailles Treaty and the concluding of the Locarno Treaty of 1925 between Germany and its Western neighbors. Conversely, they were basically indifferent to Eastern Europe in the 1920s (and there was never an "Eastern Locarno"). The favorite political vehicle of the chemical and industrial industries was the German People's Party, led by Gustav Stresemann.[46]

In addition to their interest in free trade, the chemical and electrical industries also had an interest in promoting mass consumption and therefore in supporting social welfare and democratic politics. I. G. Farben, encouraged by the widespread consensus among experts in the 1920s that world petroleum supplies would soon be exhausted, diverted most of its new capital investments into building enormous plants to produce gasoline from coal by a process known as hydrogenation.[47] It thus acquired a strong interest in the development of a large German automobile industry. Similarly, the German electrical industry, a producer of consumer durables and municipal electrical equipment, also had a strong interest in social welfare and municipal services. These features led the industries into supporting parliamentary coalitions which included the Social Democratic Party. In brief, then, the Weimar Republic, with its foreign policy of "fulfillment" and its domestic policy of social welfare, was in many ways based upon a coalition of chemistry, electricity, and labor in opposition to the coalition of iron and rye.[48]

The Weimar system was in an unstable equilibrium, however. Its major leader, Stresemann, died in October 1929. At the same time, the New York stock market crash marked the beginning of a new Great Depression. The American responses to the economic crisis had momentous consequences for Germany. The Smoot–Hawley Tariff of 1930 led to the raising of tariff barriers in other countries, dealing a serious blow to the free trade policies of the German chemical and electrical industries. In addition, the drying up of American loans to Germany broke a crucial link in the international economic chain which had lifted up German prosperity in the 1920s (American loans to Germany → German reparations to Britain and France → British and French imports from Germany). These two developments meant that the free trade option, the Westpolitik, of the chemical and electrical industries suddenly became far less viable. And they meant in turn that the coercive trade option, the Ostpolitik, of the steel industry suddenly became most attractive. Finally, the depression-induced sharp drop in world oil prices in 1930–1931 and the opening up of the vast East Texas oil field in 1931 meant that I. G. Farben, with its enormous investments in hydrogenation plants, was suddenly threatened by massive imports of cheap American oil, much as the Junker agrarians had suddenly been threatened by massive imports of cheap American grain sixty years before. For I. G. Farben, the only solution to the Texan problem was a German government which would be strong enough and willing enough to guarantee a market for its coal-based gasoline, by erecting tariff barriers, by granting subsidies, by buying the gasoline itself, and by legitimating the vast expenditures entailed with an ideology of economic autarky and military preparedness—i.e., the same ideology promoted by the steel industry and the grain producers.[49]

Together, these new developments in the world market propelled the chemical and electrical industries during 1932 from political opposition into political cooperation with the steel industry and the grain producers. And as the National People's Party under Hugenberg proved insufficiently popular to win the several elections of 1932, first the steel industry and then the chemical and electrical industries shifted their financial support to the National Socialist Party under Hitler.[50] With the coming to power of the Nazis in 1933, the foreign policy of the steel industry—rearmament, revision of Versailles, high tariffs, and domination of Eastern Europe—became the foreign policy of the new Germany.

Italy   The German experience had had an earlier and a simpler trial run in Italy. Of all the European steel industries before World War I, the Italian had been the most dependent upon armaments contracts. It was, therefore, unusually vulnerable to a period of peace, especially one in which the peace treaties, like Versailles, gave Italy no substantial territories on which new railroads could be laid. The inevitable postwar economic depression hit Italy in 1921 especially hard. Accordingly, the steel industrialists supported popular movements demanding revision of "the mutilated peace" and the annexation of new territories. The major such movement, the Fascists, achieved power in 1922.[51] But Italy's efforts at territorial expansion would have to wait for more than a decade until the new Great Depression produced a diplomatic constellation of the greater powers which was more favorable to Italian aims.

We have seen the range of the different countries' responses. Given the historical British response to the combination of the Great Depression of 1873–1896 and the German naval buildup of the 1890s, one might have thought that the British response to the new Great Depression and the German rearmament of the 1930s would have been similar, i.e., British rearmament. But, of course, this was not the case. Instead, the actual British response was rather like Joseph Chamberlain's program of the early 1900s, i.e., imperial preference and appeasement of the Germans.

Part of the explanation lies ironically in the continuing hegemony of the British system of commercial banks operating in a world arena, of the same City of

London that had defeated the Chamberlain program thirty years before. In "the terrible year" of 1931, there were massive runs on the pound and on the British commercial banks, and the government installed emergency capital controls. But the City of London needed to return as soon as possible to free movements of capital. The lesson that had been learned in 1931 was that the pound was now vulnerable in the face of even slight economic and political disturbances. A small sign of inflation or a small decline in the balance of trade could lead to a new run on the pound and a new financial collapse.

In domestic affairs, this meant that Britain could not increase consumer-demand to the point that the wages of skilled labor were bid up, resulting in inflation, or that more raw materials were imported, resulting in a decline in the balance of trade. Thus Britain went through the 1930s with the government making no serious efforts at eliminating unemployment through Keynesian measures promoting mass consumption.[52] In colonial affairs, the extreme sensitivity toward the balance of trade meant that orderly, predictable markets for British exports were now highly valued. Thus, the City of London was now willing to accept imperial preference, formalized in the Ottawa Agreements of 1932.

In foreign affairs, the consequences were even more momentous. Just as the wage or raw-material dynamic could be detonated by government-induced consumer spending, so could it be detonated by government-ordered defense spending, i.e., rearmament. The City of London, haunted by the ghost of 1931, imposed a low ceiling upon rearmament efforts and thus a narrow scope upon British foreign policy. In every diplomatic confrontation with Nazi Germany and Fascist Italy in the 1930s, British foreign policy was severely constrained by the immediate need to prevent a foreign exchange crisis and by the military weakness resulting from minimal rearmament efforts. When Neville Chamberlain, the son of Joseph Chamberlain, moved from being Chancellor of the Exchequer to being Prime Minister in 1937, he was determined to accept these financial realities and to act accordingly in a coherent and systematic way. The result was his foreign policy of Appeasement.[53]

These, then, were the various responses of the different European nations to the continuing problems of saturation in their steel industries in the years following World War I. There was, however, yet another possible response, and that was to develop fully a massive new leading sector, in particular the automobile industry, and to pour steel into it. And this was the path taken by the United States.

THE POLITICAL TENDENCY OF THE AUTOMOBILE INDUSTRY

The Domestic Growth Phase

The impact of an automobile industry upon an economy is so great that it is justifiable to see the creation of that industry as a new stage in the industrialization of a country.

It was the Americans, who with an almost single-minded intensity, first took this path. On the eve of the innovation of the automobile, the United States already had developed the most consumer-oriented economy and the highest per capita income in the world. It also included a large class of prosperous, independent farmers, many exporting to European markets, who were separated by long distances from their market towns and from each other and who provided a perfect market for the automobile. It is not surprising, therefore, that even before World War I, the United States possessed the largest automobile industry in the world, both in terms of absolute numbers of cars produced and in terms of cars per capita (about one car per thirty-five persons in 1914).[54]

The "start-up costs" for automobile production were actually rather low, as long as a manufacturer was interested in producing only a few cars. Thus, manufacturers of bicycles and buggies could rather easily convert to automobiles. However, the advent of mass-production and assembly-line techniques meant that success would go to companies that could raise enormous amounts of capital, either through their profits (Ford) or through outside financing. One of the heroic moments of American capitalism was the decision by the Du Ponts, who had accumulated massive profits producing munitions for World War I (and who were confronted with a massive collapse of their markets with the advent of peace), to finance a struggling automobile company, which in 1919 had little grand about it except its name—General Motors. By 1926, General Motors was the world's largest automobile company.

The boom in the American automobile industry in the 1920s fueled the more general boom in the American economy, "the New Era." As steel poured into automobiles (30 percent of American steel production went into automobiles by the mid-1920s), the steel industry was released from the need for armaments contracts. There was therefore no leading American industry with an interest in "foreign entanglements" or a "military–industrial complex." The Washington Naval Conference of 1922, with its limitation on capital ships, registered this American shift from ships to cars, from the Great White Fleet to the black Model T, from manifest destiny to consumer sovereignty. The American automobile industry provided the motor behind the foreign policy of isolationism.

By 1929, there was one automobile for every five persons in the United States and given the existing structure of the distribution of income, the domestic market seemed to have reached saturation. Production of automobiles in the United States reached a peak in the spring of 1929. The clear leveling off of this massive leading sector was a major factor in the New York stock market crash six months later and in the ensuing Great Depression in the United States.[55]

The Foreign Export Phase and the Foreign Investment Phase

By analogy with the British pattern of 1873–1896, after the railroads were built, one would expect that one response of the American automobile industry to the saturation of its domestic market would have been to expand its foreign operations, that is, the foreign export and the foreign investment phases of the product cycle. And indeed some of this occurred. The export drive of American automobiles was aborted, however, by tariff walls raised by foreign countries in response to the record-high Smoot–Hawley Tariff, imposed by the United States in 1930 under pressure from the American textile, steel, and other older industries. In regard to foreign investment, Ford had begun manufacturing operations in Britain and Germany in the early 1920s; General Motors had begun manufacturing operations in Germany in 1929. By 1936, of the cars produced in Germany, 40 percent were produced by GM's subsidiary, Opel (the largest automobile producer in Germany), and 10 percent were produced by Ford. But the real era of direct foreign investment by the American automobile industry was to come only after World War II, a war which, among other things, made the world safe for consumer sovereignty.

Europe did not really move into its "auto-industrial age"[56] until after World War II. In 1935, Britain had only one automobile per twenty persons, France one per thirty-five, Germany one per hundred, and Italy one per two-hundred. In contrast the European countries would not reach the U.S. figure of one for every five people until the 1960s.[57]

How were the large amounts of capital for automobile industrialization mobilized in Europe after World War II? One method, analogous to the capital formation for steel and railroads in Britain, France, and Italy decades before, was through the export of manufactured products developed in an earlier stage, i.e., "export-led growth." Here, an important factor was not only the high quality of the products, but the low wages of European labor (relative to the United States) in the two decades after the end of the war. No authoritarian regime was required to repress wages in Europe. The low expectations of union membership, deriving from the privation of World War II, and the political divisions in union organization, deriving from the anti-communism of the Cold War, were for many years the functional equivalent of wage-repression. The role performed in some Latin American countries by their own armies through authoritarian rule, according to the model of Guillermo O'Donnell, was performed in Europe by the ghost of the German Army and the spectre of the Russian Army.

A second method, analogous to the earlier mobilization of capital for railroads in Italy and Spain, was through the import of foreign funds. Until the mid-1950s, this involved U.S. government aid (i.e., the Marshall Plan), and from the mid-1950s until the mid-1970s it involved massive American direct investment in the European automobile industry. Even in the late 1940s, General Motors and Ford owned a large share of the European industry, and in the 1950s the American automobile industry entered into the foreign investment phase of its product cycle on a large scale. The American automobile corporations first undertook large manufacturing investment in Britain, then West Germany, and then France. Normally, when a country of more than 20 million people has reached a certain level of economic development (roughly $1,000 per capita GNP in 1965 dollars) it has developed a market in consumer durables which is large and prosperous enough to attract large-scale direct investment in manufacturing by the American automobile corporations. And since European labor was relatively self-restrained in its wage demands, the continued flow of American direct investment also did not require the labor-repressive policies of an authoritarian regime. Of course, labor-repressive policies and authoritarian regimes did not inhibit the flow of foreign direct investment in Europe either, as was demonstrated by multinational automobile corporations when they undertook large manufacturing investments in Spain as that country rolled over the $1,000 threshold in the late 1960s.

Although the automobile industries of Britain, West Germany, France, and finally Spain were built up in part with American direct investment, the automobile industry in Italy was built up independently of it. The dominant automobile corporation in Italy, Fiat, had long differed from the other European automobile corporations in that it was a giant and profitable conglomerate which produced locomotives, aircraft, and other machinery, as well as automobiles. Other Italian automobile producers were owned or financed by the state.

Britain, West Germany, France, and Italy finally entered "the auto-industrial age" in the 1950s. The automobile boom of the 1950s–1960s in these countries was at the core of their more general economic prosperity and growth at that time. As many political analysts have observed, this general economic prosperity and growth contributed to the legitimation of the European liberal-democratic systems, to the deradicalization of the European working class, and to the demarxification in the late 1950s of the programs of the British and West German Socialist parties, which had a large working class constituency. The particular features of the automobile boom further contributed to the deradicalization of the European working class by inducing a shift from community activities to individual consumption.

The growth of the automobile industry was especially rapid and pronounced in the ex-Axis countries of Germany and Italy (and also Japan). Not surprisingly, the liberal domestic economic policies of these three countries in the 1950s and 1960s, the sort of policies natural to a confident capitalism engaged in a great boom, closely resembled the liberal domestic economic policies of the United States in the 1920s, the time of the first great boom in American automobile production.[58] In these countries, working class parties did not participate at all in the governments during the 1950s and 1960s, until in West Germany in 1966 recession brought the Socialists into a "Grand Coalition" with the Christian Democrats.

At the time that Europe underwent its postwar automobile boom, the United States also experienced a renewed expansion, a second wind, in its automobile industry, supported in part by the Keynesian fiscal policies of the Federal government, the Federal highway program, and the Federal home mortgage program which encouraged suburbanization.

By the early 1970s, the ratio of cars to persons in Britain, France, West Germany, and Italy had reached about the American level of 1929, just before the onset of the Great Depression of the 1930s. What happened after these European automobile industries reached the saturation points of their domestic markets? One result contributed to the economic recession and stagnation of 1974–1978. Of course the causes of the economic troubles of the last few years in Europe are many, but the saturation of the automobile market in Britain, France, West Germany, and Italy suggests that there is little basis for a sustained recovery unless, like the French, governments engage in what the Germans have called *strukturpolitik*, that is, the conscious creation of new leading industrial sectors and the consequent recasting of the nation's industrial structure. A product-cycle theorist would predict that the Europeans would adopt as their new (or renewed) sectors those same industries which were the American new sectors a decade or a generation ago, i.e., aerospace, computers, telecommunications, and nuclear power. And this would explain the intensity of the French export drive in aerospace and the French and German export drive in nuclear power since 1975.

The automobile industries of Spain and Brazil (now ranking about seventh and eighth in size) have developed in a rather different way from those in the United States, Britain, France, West Germany, Italy, and Japan. First, in these six earlier automobile industrializers, at least one large automobile corporation was indigenous to the country; indeed, in the United States, Italy, and Japan, foreign corporations have accounted for almost none of the production. In these earlier industrializers, the concept of the "national champion" against foreign competition has been plausible. In Spain and Brazil, in contrast, there has been no such large indigenous automobile corporation. All large producers are foreign multinationals or closely associated with them.

Second, in Britain, France, and West Germany, the multinational presence has been largely American; in Spain and Brazil, it has been multinational, including various European and Japanese corporations. In the 1960s, corporations such as Leyland, Renault, Volkswagen, Fiat, and Toyota entered into the direct foreign investment phase of their own product cycles.

Third, Spain and Brazil have been the first societies to undertake mass production and consumption of automobiles within an authoritarian political system. But the political consequences of coexistence between the auto-industrial age and an authoritarian regime have been different in the two countries.

In Spain, the multinational automobile corporations pushed the governments after Franco's death in 1975 toward the liberalization and even democratization of the political system. The major reason was that automobiles produced in Spain would be very competitive within the European Common Market if Spain were a member. Spain in the late 1970s could be as cost-effective in automobiles as Italy was in the early 1960s, because Spain today holds roughly the relative wage position that Italy held then. But the Common Market would not admit Spain into membership until, in the words of a resolution passed by each of its main institutions in 1975, "freedom and democracy have been established in Spain." (Indeed, given the self-interest of French and Italian farmers, it may not admit Spain even now.)

In Brazil, and in the absence of the special inducements provided by an international organization which is both a common market and a democratic community, the political consequences of the multinational automobile corporations have been in the opposite direction. In the last two years of the Goulart government of the early 1960s, foreign investment in Brazilian manufacturing declined sharply. Among the economic, bureaucratic, and technocratic elites of Brazil, it was a plausible argument that an authoritarian regime was a necessary condition for the renewed flow of foreign investment and *a fortiori* for the expanding flow which was necessary for the leap into the next stage of industrialization. And, in fact, in the years after the military coup of 1964, American and European investment did pour into Brazil; the output of the automobile industry doubled between 1964 and 1970 and doubled again between 1970 and 1974. However, the foreign investment in the

Brazilian automobile industry was somewhat anomalous. Whereas the per capita GNP in other host countries for multinational automobile corporations had been above $1,000, the per capita GNP of Brazil in 1966 was only $340. This made for a rather thin automobile market, despite Brazil's large population. This "premature" foreign investment in the Brazilian automobile industry was clearly induced by the political stability, repression of labor unions, and low wages which were imposed by the authoritarian regime established after the military coup of 1964.

Since Brazil had and continues to have a much lower per capita GNP than other large automobile producers, the greatly-increased consumption of automobiles in Brazil required a special form of income redistribution, that is, redistribution to the middle class from the lower classes. This has been accomplished through government measures which repressed working-class real wages, reduced welfare and public health programs, increased middle-class real salaries, and provided government credit for automobile purchases.[59] These policies, which were necessary for a premature auto-industrial age, could be imposed far more easily by an authoritarian government than by a liberal-democratic one. The calculations of the Brazilian regime were suggested in 1974 by its Finance Minister, Mario Henrique Simsonsen:

> A transfer of income from the richest 20 percent to the poorest 80 percent probably would increase the demand for food, but diminish the demand for automobiles. The result of a sudden redistribution would be merely to generate inflation in the food-producing sector and excess capacity in the car industry.[60]

When the military sought to legitimize its rule, its principal argument was the success of Brazilian industrialization and the greatly-increased consumption of consumer durables, especially automobiles. Of course, even without the multinational automobile industry, there probably would still have been a military coup in Brazil in 1964 and an authoritarian regime. But the *stability* of the authoritarian regime was probably due to the course of the automobile industry.

A product-cycle theorist would also have a ready explanation for the U.S. foreign policy of détente with the Soviet Union during the Nixon and Ford Administrations. It was just at the end of the 1960s that the American automobile corporations, which had recently invested heavily in Southern Europe and the more developed parts of Latin America, were searching for the area with the next highest level of economic development, which, of course, was Eastern Europe and the Soviet Union. The SALT I (1972) and Vladivostok (1974) arms agreements were skillfully designed so as to create simultaneously an atmosphere for détente (desired by the American automobile industry and by American international banks) and a ratification of increased production of strategic missiles (desired by the American aerospace industry, which in the late 1960s also entered into a period of economic decline). Thus Henry Kissinger accomplished his own Reinsurance Treaty with the Russians, as Bismarck had done in 1887; at the same time, Kissinger prevented the disruption of the established foreign policy consensus between autos and aerospace, his own "marriage between iron and rye."

Kissinger's achievement was as brilliant as Bismarck's, but it was even more brief. By 1975, the American automobile industry had rediscovered that operations in communist countries usually entailed problems which outweighed the profits. And by 1977, American and European international banks had loaned some $50 billion to communist countries, and the banks had perceived that this was about the limit of the countries' capacity for orderly repayment. The American industrial and financial interests supporting détente were now much diminished. It is not surprising that the American political figures supporting détente were too.

At about the same time, the great increase in the world price of oil, as a result of OPEC's actions in what has been called the "October Revolution" of 1973, led Soviet authorities to reduce the growth of the Soviet automobile industry. The "auto-industrial age" of the Soviet Union remains on an ever-receding horizon, and the Soviet ideal remains what it has been since the October Revolution of 1917, a great monument to the leading sectors of the Europe of sixty years ago—steel, chemicals, electricity, and armaments.

CONCLUSIONS

It could be argued that the long era during which leading industrial sectors had an impact upon political outcomes has come to its end. For by now the advanced industrial nations are populated with many industrial sectors, and probably never again will one industry alone so dominate these countries as the textile, steel, and automobile industries each did in its time. But our review of the last two centuries also has noted times when political outcomes were shaped not by one sector but by conflicts and coalitions between several, for example, Britain in the 1900s and Germany in the 1920s. The political outcomes of the next decade similarly may be shaped by conflicts between protectionist industries (textiles, steel, recently chemicals) and free trade ones (aerospace, computers, telecommunications), with a swing position being held by the automobile industry, whose interests are divided and conflicting. The long hegemony of the free trade coalition, dating from World War II, may be nearing an end as particular industries and corporations are driven by poor competitiveness in the world market (by phase 4 of Vernon's product cycle), into the protectionist camp. One political consequence would be the eroding of the Atlantic Alliance and of its military organization, NATO, at the very time that the Soviet Union has carried out a large buildup of its military forces in Europe. As the 1890s and the 1930s suggest, a time of protectionist hegemony is unlikely to be an enlightened one.

There is an alternative path and that would be for one country, most probably the United States, to undertake the development of new industrial sectors. Since a new American industry would be likely to create and to dominate for a time an international market for its product, it would be a powerful ally and reinforcement for the now dwindling free trade coalition. And the hegemony of free trade, of "interdependence," might experience a renewal and second wind.

What might be one such new industry in the United States? Here, we might find some clues in the past. Two of our earlier leading sectors, railroads and automobiles, plus another major industry, aerospace, were successive improvements in transportation.[61] But, as the history of the *Concorde* suggests, improvements in transportation may have reached the limits possible within the technological frameworks of the old industries. The next logical leap is to move not bodies but minds, i.e., to improve not transportation but communication. This suggests that an obvious candidate for the next great leap forward is the telecommunications industry. It is an even more obvious candidate since the higher cost of petroleum has in part eroded the economic base of the automobile and aerospace industries. And indeed corporations such as IBM, ITT, and RCA are now poised to undertake a number of significant innovations in visual and computer telecommunications. For such innovations, the main barrier may well be not the lack of capital but the threat of government regulation, which would preserve the sunk investment of the old established corporation in the industry, A.T.&T.[62]

Will the 1980s see a great telecommunications boom fueling a general economic boom like the great railroad, automobile, and aerospace booms of the past? It is not easy to see the shape of such a development, just as it was not easy to see the shapes of the earlier developments on their eve. But a great telecommunications industrial sector would have implications for military power and international politics as well as for international trade. Today, the liberal democracies of the United States and Western Europe find themselves unable to mobilize the vast financial resources required to match the Soviet Union and its European allies tank-for-tank and plane-for-plane, and unwilling to demoralize themselves through a total dependence upon nuclear weapons. But out of a massive telecommunications industry would issue the inventions and innovations for a new kind of weapons systems and military defense, of which existing "precision-guided munitions," "smart bombs," and "automated battlefields" are only premonitions. And these would be weapons systems in which the technologically-advanced liberal democracies of NATO would have both an absolute and a comparative advantage.[63] And once again, innovation of new industrial sectors, "gales of creative destruction," would prove to be the basis, and perhaps the necessary condition, for the conservation of old and worthy political institutions.

NOTES

1. Peter J. Katzenstein, editor, *Between Power and Plenty: Foreign Economic Policies of Advanced Industrial States,* a special issue of *International Organization* 31, 4 (Autumn 1977). A systematic and perceptive review of recent literature on one theme of the new international political economy, the impact of international economics upon domestic politics, is given in Peter Gourevitch, "The Second Image Reversed: The International Sources of Domestic Politics," *International Organization* 32, 4 (Autumn 1978).
2. Joseph A. Schumpeter, *Business Cycles: A Theoretical, Historical, and Statistical Analysis of the Capitalist Process,* two volumes (New York: McGraw-Hill, 1939).
3. Raymond Vernon, *Sovereignty at Bay: The Multinational Spread of U.S. Enterprises* (New York: Basic Books, 1971). An earlier formulation of the idea of certain patterns or cycles in the development of industries can be found in Walther G. Hoffmann, *The Growth of Industrial Economies,* translated by W. O. Henderson and W. H. Chaloner (Manchester: Manchester University Press, 1958).
4. Robert Gilpin, *U.S. Power and the Multinational Corporation: The Political Economy of Foreign Direct Investment* (New York: Basic Books, 1975).
5. E. J. Hobsbawm, *The Age of Revolution: Europe 1789–1848* (London: Weidenfeld and Nicolson, 1962); also the country studies in Carlo M. Cipolla, editor, *The Emergence of Industrial Societies* (London: Collins, Fortana Books, 1973). Statistics on the growth of the textile industry in European countries can be found in B. R. Mitchell, *European*

Historical Statistics, 1750–1970 (New York: Columbia University Press, 1976), pp. 427–436; and in Cipolla, *op. cit.*, pp. 780–788. Three useful overall accounts of European industrialization, from contrasting perspectives, are David S. Landes, *The Unbound Prometheus: Technological Change and Industrial Development in Western Europe from 1750 to the Present* (Cambridge: Cambridge University Press, 1969); Tom Kemp, *Industrialization in Nineteenth Century Europe* (London: Longman, 1969); and W. W. Rostow, *The Stages of Economic Growth* (Cambridge: Cambridge University Press, 1960; second edition, 1971), elaborated in his *The World Economy: History and Prospect* (Austin: University of Texas Press, 1978). In his works, Rostow develops and employs at length the concepts of the leading sector.

6. Frederick B. Artz, *Reaction and Revolution, 1814–1832* (New York: Harper and Row, 1963), Chapters I–III; Hobsbawm, *op. cit.*, Chapter 2.

7. Quoted in Frederick B. Artz, *op. cit.*, pp. 85–86.

8. E. J. Hobsbawm, *Industry and Empire: The Making of Modern Society, Vol. II, 1759 to the Present Day* (New York: Pantheon, 1968), Chapters 3–4; William Langer, *Political and Social Upheaval, 1832–1852* (New York: Harper and Row, 1969), Chapters II–III.

9. Langer, *op. cit.*, Chapters III–IV; Artz, *op. cit.*, Chapters VIII, IX; B. M. Biucchi, "The Industrial Revolution in Switzerland," in Cipolla, *op. cit.*, pp. 627–652.

10. On industrialization in Prussia and Austria, see Knut Borchandt, "The Industrial Revolution in Germany 1700–1914" and N. T. Gross, "The Industrial Revolution in the Habsburg Monarchy 1750–1914," in Cipolla, *op. cit.*, pp. 76–156, 228–276.

11. Langer, *op. cit.*, Chapter IV.

12. The economic basis of the contrast between Britain and Prussia is one theme discussed in Barrington Moore, Jr., *Social Origins of Dictatorship and Democracy: Lord and Peasant in the Making of the Modern World* (Boston: Beacon Press, 1966).

13. On industrialization in Italy and Spain, see Luciano Cafagna, "The Industrial Revolution in Italy 1830–1914" and Jordi Nadal, "The Failure of the Industrial Revolution in Spain 1830–1914," in Cipolla, *op. cit.*, pp. 279–325, 532–620.

14. On Italian politics during the nineteenth century, see Arthur James Whyte, *The Evolution of Modern Italy* (New York: W. W. Norton, 1965); and Denis Mack Smith, *Italy: A Modern History*, revised edition (Ann Arbor: University of Michigan Press, 1969). On Spanish politics, see Gerald Brenan, *The Spanish Labyrinth: An Account of the Social and Political Background of the Civil War* (Cambridge: Cambridge University Press, 1950); and Joan Connolly Ullman, *The Tragic Week: A Study of Anticlericalism in Spain, 1875–1912* (Cambridge, Massachusetts: Harvard University Press, 1968).

15. John Gallagher and Ronald Robinson, "The Imperialism of Free Trade," in George H. Nadel and Perry Curtis, editors, *Imperialism and Colonialism* (New York: Macmillan, 1964).

16. E. J. Hobsbawm, *Industry and Empire*, Chapter 7.

17. Quoted in Michael Edwardes, *The Last Years of British India* (Cleveland: World Publishing, 1963), p. 234.

18. Alexander Gerschenkron, *Economic Backwardness in Historical Perspective* (Cambridge, Massachusetts: Harvard University Press, 1962).

19. Guillermo A. O'Donnell, *Modernization and Bureaucratic–Authoritarianism: Studies in South American Politics* (Berkeley: International Studies, University of California, Berkeley, Politics of Modernization Series No. 9, 1973).

20. Hobsbawm, *Industry and Empire*, Chapters 6 and 7. A useful overall account of the growth and impact of the European iron and steel industries and railroads is Hobsbawm's *The Age of Capital, 1848–1875* (New York: Charles Scribner's Sons, 1975).

21. See, for example, Gerschenkron, *op. cit.*, and Rondo E. Cameron, *France and the Economic Development of Europe, 1800–1914, Conquests of Peace and Seeds of War* (Princeton: Princeton University Press, 1961), Chapter IV.

22. Sanford Elwitt, *The Making of the Third Republic: Class and Politics in France, 1868–1884* (Baton Rouge: Louisiana State University Press, 1975), Introduction and Chapter I.

23. William Woodruff, "The Emergence of an International Economy, 1700–1914," in Cipolla, *op. cit.,* pp. 673–674.

24. See, for example, Gerschenkron, *op. cit.,* and Cameron, *op. cit.,* Chapter IV. A useful and detailed discussion of the relationships between economics and politics in Germany under Bismarck is presented by Fritz Stern, *Gold and Iron: Bismarck, Bleichröder, and the Building of the German Empire* (New York: Alfred A. Knopf, 1977).

25. Cameron, *op. cit.,* W. O. Henderson, *Britain and Industrial Europe: 1750–1870: Studies in British Influence on the Industrial Revolution in Western Europe,* third edition (London: Leicester University Press, 1972).

26. Cafagna, *op. cit.,* pp. 289–290, 302–325.

27. See the comparison between Britain and America drawn by Robert Gilpin, *op. cit.*

28. W. O. Henderson, *op. cit.*

29. W. W. Rostow, *British Economy in the 19th Century* (Cambridge: Cambridge University Press, 1948), p. 88. (Rostow originally developed his argument in 1938.)

30. The connections between the end of railroad expansion and the beginning of the Great Depression are also discussed in Hobsbawm, *Industry and Empire.* An excellent comparative analysis of the politics of the Great Depression is Peter Alexis Gourevitch, "International Trade, Domestic Coalitions, and Liberty: Comparative Responses to the Crisis of 1873–1896," *The Journal of Inter-Disciplinary History,* VIII (Autumn, 1977): 281–313. An earlier classic account is Hans Rosenberg, "Political and Social Consequences of the Great Depression of 1873–1896 in Central Europe," *Economic History Review,* XIII (1943):58–73.

31. Various aspects of imperialism are analyzed in Roger Owen and Bob Sutcliffe, editors, *Studies in the Theory of Imperialism* (London: Longman, 1972).

32. Quoted in J. C. Carr and W. Taplin, *History of the British Steel Industry* (Cambridge, Massachusetts: Harvard University Press, 1962), p. 39.

33. Hobsbawm, *Industry and Empire,* p. 107.

34. Rostow, *The World Economy,* p. 381.

35. Data on the naval budgets of Britain and other European powers are given in Kendall D. Moll, *The Influence of History Upon Seapower, 1865–1914* (Menlo Park, California: Stanford Research Institute, 1969).

36. Quoted in Arthur J. Marder, *The Anatomy of British Sea Power: A History of British Naval Policy in the Pre-Dreadnought Era, 1880–1905* (New York: Alfred A. Knopf, 1940), p. 36.

37. James Morris, "A View of the Royal Navy," *Encounter* XL (March 1973):20.

38. Bernard Semmel, *Imperialism and Social Reform: English Social–Imperial Thought 1895–1914* (Cambridge, Massachusetts: Harvard University Press, 1960).

39. Cameron, *op. cit.,* and François Caron, "French Railroad Investment, 1850–1914," in *Essays in French Economic History,* Rondo Cameron, editor (Homewood, Illinois: Richard D. Irwin, 1970), pp. 315–340.

40. On this coalition between industrialists and Junkers, see Alexander Gerschenkron, *Bread and Democracy in Germany* (Berkeley: University of California Press, 1943); also V. R. Berghahn, *Germany and the Approach of War in 1914* (New York: St. Martin's Press, 1973).

41. Moll, *op. cit.,* The classic analysis of the political economy of German naval procurement is Eckart Kehr, *Battleship Building and Party Politics in Germany 1894–1901* (Chicago: University of Chicago Press, 1975). (Kehr's book was originally published in Germany in 1930.) Also see Berghahn, *op. cit.*

42. W. O. Henderson, *The Rise of German Industrial Power, 1834–1914* (Berkeley: University of California Press, 1975).

43. R. A. Webster, *Industrial Imperialism in Italy, 1908–1915* (Berkeley: University of California Press, 1975).

44. The politics of the German steel industry during the 1920s are discussed in Gerald D. Feldman, *Iron and Steel in the German Inflation, 1916–1923* (Princeton: Princeton University Press, 1977); Charles S. Maier, *Recasting Bourgeois Europe: Stabilization in France, Germany, and Italy in the Decade After World War I* (Princeton: Princeton University Press, 1975); and David Abraham, *Inter-Class Conflict and the Formation of Ruling Class Consensus in Late Weimar Germany* (Doctoral dissertation submitted to the Department of History, University of Chicago, December 1977).

45. On I. G. Farben, see Frank A. Howard, *Buna Rubber: The Birth of an Industry* (New York: D. Van Nostrand, 1947); and Joseph Borkin, *The Crime and Punishment of I. G. Farben* (New York: The Free Press, 1978), an informative and perceptive industrial history, which goes beyond the connotations of its title.

46. The politics of the German chemical and electrical industries during the 1920s are discussed by Maier, *op. cit.*, and Abraham, *op. cit.*

47. Howard, *op. cit.*; Borkin, *op. cit.*, Chapter 2.

48. Abraham, *op. cit.*, presents a thorough and sophisticated demonstration of this argument.

49. Borkin, *op. cit.*, Chapter 3.

50. Abraham, *op. cit.*; Borkin, *op. cit.*, Chapter 3. On the industrial role in the 1932 elections, also see Alan Bullock, *Hitler: A Study in Tyranny,* revised edition (New York: Harper and Row, 1964). An earlier, classic account of the relations between industry and the Nazis is Franz Neumann, *Behemoth: The Structure and Process of National Socialism* (New York: Oxford University Press, 1942).

51. Roland Sarti, *Fascism and the Industrial Leadership in Italy, 1919–1940* (Berkeley: University of California Press, 1971).

52. Donald Winch, *Economics and Politics: A Historical Study* (London: Hodder and Stoughton, 1969).

53. Robert Paul Shay, Jr., *British Rearmament in the Thirties: Politics and Profits* (Princeton: Princeton University Press, 1977).

54. On the early developments of the automobile industry in the United States, see James J. Flink, *The Car Culture* (Cambridge, Massachusetts: The M.I.T. Press, 1975).

55. Useful accounts of the causes of the Great Depression of 1929–1939 are given in Derek H. Aldcroft, *From Versailles to Wall Street, 1919–1929* (Berkeley: University of California Press, 1977); and Charles P. Kindleberger, *The World in Depression, 1929–1939* (Berkeley: University of California Press, 1973).

56. The phrase is from Emma Rothschild, *Paradise Lost: The Decline of the Auto-Industrial Age* (New York: Random House, 1973).

57. W. W. Rostow, *Politics and the Stages of Growth* (Cambridge: Cambridge University Press, 1971), pp. 227–229.

58. European economic policies in the 1950s and 1960s are discussed by Andrew Shonfield, *Modern Capitalism: The Changing Balance of Public and Private Power* (New York: Oxford University Press, 1969).

59. Edmar L. Bacha, "Issues and Evidence on Recent Brazilian Economic Growth" (Cambridge, Massachusetts: Harvard Institute for International Development, Development Discussion Papers, 1976).

60. Quoted in Norman Gall, "The Rise of Brazil," *Commentary* 63 (January 1977):49–50.

61. I have discussed the American aerospace industry in a number of places, including my "Aerospace Production Lines and American Defense Spending," in *American Defense Policy,* Richard G. Head and Ervin J. Rokke, editors, third edition (Baltimore: Johns Hopkins University Press, 1973), pp. 626–640; "Why We Buy the Weapons We Do,"

Foreign Policy 2 (Summer 1973):33–56; and statement and testimony on American defense production in *Defense Industrial Base: DOD Procurement Practices,* Hearings before the Joint Committee on Defense Production, Congress of the United States, 95th Congress (Washington: U.S. Government Printing Office, 1977), pp. 63–90.

62. On the issue of innovation and regulation, see *Competition in the Telecommunications Industry,* Hearings before the Subcommittee on Communications of the Committee on Interstate and Foreign Commerce, House of Representatives, 94th Congress (Washington: U.S. Government Printing Office, 1977).

63. On the implications of these new military technologies, see James Digby, *Precision-Guided Weapons,* Adelphi Papers, no. 118 (London: The International Institute for Strategic Studies, Summer 1975); and Richard Burt, *New Weapons Technologies: Debate and Directions,* Adelphi Papers, no. 126 (London: The International Institute for Strategic Studies, Summer 1976).

Sectoral Conflict and U.S. Foreign Economic Policy, 1914–1940

Jeff Frieden

The period from 1914 to 1940 is one of the most crucial and enigmatic in modern world history and in the history of modern U.S. foreign policy. World War I catapulted the United States into international economic and political leadership, yet in the aftermath of the war, despite grandiose Wilsonian plans, the United States quickly lapsed into relative disregard for events abroad: it did not join the League of Nations, disavowed responsibility for European reconstruction, would not participate openly in many international economic conferences, and restored high levels of tariff protection for the domestic market. Only in the late 1930s and 1940s, after twenty years of bitter battles over foreign policy, did the United States move to center stage of world politics and economics: it built the United Nations and a string of regional alliances, underwrote the rebuilding of Western Europe, almost single-handedly constructed a global monetary and financial system, and led the world in commercial liberalization.

This article examines the peculiar evolution of U.S. foreign economic policy in the interwar years and focuses on the role of domestic socioeconomic and political

Jeff Frieden, "Sectoral Conflict and U.S. Foreign Economic Policy, 1914–1940," *International Organization,* Vol. 42: #1 (Winter 1988). Reprinted by permission of the MIT Press, Cambridge, Massachusetts.

groups in determining foreign policy. The American interwar experience powerfully demonstrates that the country's international position and economic evolution do not sufficiently explain its foreign policy. Indeed, although the contours of the international system and the place of the United States in it changed dramatically during and after World War I, these changes had a very different impact on different sectors of American society. World War I dramatically strengthened the overseas economic interests of many major U.S. banks and corporations, who fought hard for more political involvement by the United States in world affairs. Yet domestically oriented economic groups remained extremely powerful within the United States and sought to maintain a relatively isolated America. Through the 1920s and early 1930s, the two broad coalitions battled to dominate foreign economic policy. The result was an uneasy stand-off in which the two camps entrenched themselves in different portions of the state apparatus, so that policy often ran on two tracks and was sometimes internally contradictory. Only the crisis of the 1930s and the eventual destruction of most of America's overseas competitors led to an "internationalist" victory that allowed for the construction of the American-led post–World War II international political economy.

THE PROBLEM

To virtually all observers then and since, at the end of World War I the United States seemed to dominate the international political economy. It had financed the victorious war effort and provided most of the war matériel that went into it; its industry was by far the world's largest and most productive. Despite its traditional economic insulation, the sheer size of the U.S. economy made the country the world's largest trading power. The center of world finance had shifted from London to New York. The United States clearly had the military, industrial, and financial capacity to impose its will on Europe. Yet after World War I the United States, in the current arcane iconography of the field, did not play the part of international economic hegemon, arbiter, and bank roller of the world economic order. The United States was capable of hegemonic action, and President Woodrow Wilson had hegemonic plans, but they were defeated. The problem was not in Europe, for although the British and French were stronger in 1919 than they would be in 1946, they could hardly have stood in the way of American hegemony. Indeed, European complaints about the United States after World War I were in much the opposite direction: the Europeans bitterly protested America's *refusal* to accept the responsibilities of leadership. The Europeans charged that the United States was stingy with its government finance, hostile in its trade policy, scandalous in its refusal to join the League of Nations, unwilling to get involved in overseeing and smoothing Europe's squabbles. The British and French tried for years to entice and cajole a reluctant America into leadership. America would not be budged, at least until 1940.

The world's most powerful nation pursued a contradictory and shifting set of foreign economic policies. The country both asserted and rejected world leadership, simultaneously initiated and blocked efforts at European stabilization, and began such major cooperative ventures as the League of Nations and the Dawes

Plan only to limit its participation in these American initiatives in ultimately fatal ways. The analytical problem bedevils both economic determinists and political Realists. For those who believe in the primacy of international power politics, it is difficult to explain why a United States able to reconstruct the world political system was unwilling to do so. For those who look at economic affairs first and foremost, America's unchallenged position as the world's leading capital exporter should have accelerated the trend towards trade liberalization and international monetary leadership begun before World War I; instead, the pendulum swung back towards protectionism and little public U.S. government involvement in international monetary issues.

The relevant international relations literature, faced with such analytical anomalies, generally falls back on vague reference to domestic constraints in explaining U.S. foreign economic policy in the interwar period. Charles Kindleberger, whose comparison of the era with the Pax Britannica and Pax Americana is the foundation stone for most international relations thinking on the interwar years, cites E. H. Carr approvingly to the effect that "in 1918, world leadership was offered, by almost universal consent, to the United States . . . [and] was declined," and concludes that "the one country capable of leadership [i.e. the United States] was bemused by domestic concerns and stood aside."[1]

Seen from the perspective of American domestic politics, however, the problem is quite reversed. In the context of traditional American apathy or even hostility toward world affairs, the interwar years saw an amazing flurry of global activity by the country's political, economic, and cultural leaders. Against the backdrop of the long-standing indifference of most of the American political system to events abroad, the level of overseas involvement in the 1920s and 1930s appears both startling and unprecedented.[2]

The contradictory role of the United States in the interwar period can be traced to the extremely uneven distribution of international economic interests within American society. America's international economic position did change during and after World War I, yet overseas assets were accumulated by a very concentrated set of economic actors. This left most of the U.S. economy indifferent to foreign economic affairs, while some of the country's leading economic sectors were both deeply involved and deeply concerned with the international economy. American foreign policy was thus torn between insularity and internationalism; the segments of the foreign-policy bureaucracy that reflected internationally oriented interests tried to use American power to reorganize the world's political economy, while portions of the government tied to domestically oriented sectors insisted on limiting America's international role. The crisis of the 1930s dissolved many of the entrenched interests that had kept policy stalemated and allowed a new group of political leaders to reconstitute a more coherent set of policies.

This article builds on the work of historians investigating the interwar period[3] and on the contributions of other social scientists concerned with the relationship between the international and domestic political economies. The work of Charles Kindleberger and Peter Gourevitch, among many others, has shown the importance of sectoral economic interests in explaining domestic politics and foreign-policy making in advanced industrial societies. Both Gourevitch and Thomas Ferguson have used a sectoral approach to elucidate domestic and international events in the 1930s. The present article is thus an attempt to build on existing sectoral interpretations of modern political economies and an extention of the approach to problems in international relations.[4]

THE ARGUMENT SUMMARIZED

Between 1900 and 1920 the United States went from a position of relative international economic insignificance to one of predominance. A major international borrower and host of foreign direct investment before 1900, by 1920 the United States was the world's leading new lender and foreign direct investor. The development of American overseas investments was in itself unsurprising, and in this the United States simply repeated the experience of other developed countries. Yet the rapidity of the country's shift from a major capital importer and raw-materials exporter to the leading exporter of capital, largely because of the peculiarities of the international economy in the ten years after 1914, was quite extraordinary. Even as a few major American economic actors were catapulted into global economic leadership, most of the economy remained as inward-looking as ever. This division in American economic orientation was at the root of the foreign-policy problems of the 1920s and 1930s.

As American industry and finance matured and the country became richer in capital, many large American corporations and banks looked abroad for markets and investment opportunities. United States overseas investment thus grew gradually from the 1890s until the eve of World War I. As Table 8.1 indicates, American foreign direct investment was appreciable by 1900; it was concentrated in raw materials extraction and agriculture in the Caribbean basin. By 1912 foreign direct investment was quite substantial and overseas lending had become of some importance; the focus was still the Caribbean area.

The gradual expansion of American overseas investment, especially overseas lending, was given a tremendous shove by World War I. The war forced several belligerent countries to borrow heavily from the United States, and previous borrowers from European capital markets now turned to the United States to satisfy their needs for capital. As Table 8.1 shows, American holdings of foreign bonds soared from less than 5 percent of total American holdings of nongovernment bonds in 1912 to nearly 17 percent in 1922. Foreign direct investment also grew rapidly as European preoccupation with war and reconstruction cleared the way for many American corporations to expand further into the Third World and after the war ended in Europe itself. The 1920s saw a continuation of the wartime increase in overseas American lending and investment. American overseas investment in industrial production—especially manufacturing and utilities—and petroleum grew particularly rapidly.

By 1929 American overseas private assets—direct and portfolio investments, along with other assorted long- and short-term assets—were $21 billion. Overseas investments in 1929 were equivalent to over one-fifth of the country's gross national product, a level that was reached again only in 1981.[5]

Table 8.1 INDICATORS OF THE IMPORTANCE OF U.S. FOREIGN INVESTMENT, 1900–1939 (IN MILLIONS OF DOLLARS AND PERCENT)

	1900	1912	1922	1929	1933	1939
1. U.S. foreign direct investment	751	2,476	5,050	7,850	7,000[e]	6,750
2. Domestic corporate and agricultural wealth[a]	37,275	75,100	131,904	150,326	109,375	119,324
3. Row 1 as a percent of Row 2	2.0%	3.3%	3.8%	5.2%	6.4%	5.7%
4. U.S. foreign bondholdings[b]	159[d]	623	4,000	7,375	5,048[f]	2,600[g]
5. U.S. holdings of non-government bonds[c]	5,151	14,524	23,687	38,099	37,748	32,502
6. 4/5, percent	3.1%	4.3%	16.9%	19.4%	13.4%	8.0%

[a] Net reproducible tangible wealth of U.S. corporations and agriculture.

[b] Due to the different sources used, figures here conflict with those in Table 4; those of Table 4 are probably more reliable, but to ensure comparability Goldsmith's figures are used throughout the table.

[c] Excludes only holdings of securities issued by U.S. federal, state, or local governments.

[d] Includes stocks (for 1900 only).

[e] Author's estimates.

[f] Figures are for 1934, from Foreign Bondholders Protective Council, *Annual Report for 1934* (Washington, D.C.: FBPC, 1935), p. 224. This includes only bonds being serviced; a more reasonable measure would include the market value of bonds in default. If this averaged 30% of par value, figures for 1933–34 would be $5,954 million and 15.8% for rows 4 and 6, respectively.

[g] Figures for 1939 holdings of foreign bonds are from Goldsmith and are probably understated.

Source: Foreign investment: Raymond Goldsmith, *A Study of Saving in the United States,* vol. 1 (Princeton, N.J.: Princeton University Press, 1955), p. 1093.

Domestic data: Raymond Goldsmith, Robert Lipsey, and Morris Mendelson, *Studies in the National Balance Sheet of the United States,* vol. 2 (Princeton, N.J.: Princeton University Press, 1963), pp. 72–83.

Although America's overseas investments were substantial by the 1920s, they were very unevenly distributed among important sectors of the U.S. economy. Tables 8.2 and 8.3 illustrate that while overseas investment was extremely important for the financial community and some industrial sectors, most other sectors' foreign assets were insignificant. American foreign investments in mining and petroleum were considerable, both absolutely and relative to capital invested in corresponding activities within the United States. Foreign investment was also of great relative importance to corporations in machinery and equipment (especially electrical appliances), motor vehicles, rubber products, and chemicals. Yet these sectors, which accounted for well over half of all overseas investment in manufacturing, represented barely one-fifth of the country's manufacturing plant; far more American industries were quite uninvolved in overseas production.

Although only a few industries had major foreign operations, foreign lending was a favorite activity on Wall Street. As Table 3 shows, between 1919 and 1929 new foreign capital issues in New York averaged over a billion dollars a year, over one-sixth of all issues (excluding federal, state, and local securities); in a couple of

Table 8.2   FOREIGN DIRECT INVESTMENT AND BOOK VALUE OF FIXED CAPITAL OF SELECTED U.S. INDUSTRIES, 1929 (IN MILLIONS OF DOLLARS AND PERCENT)

Sector	A Foreign direct investment	B Book value of fixed capital	A/B in percent
Mining and petroleum[a,b]	$2,278	$12,886	17.7%
Public utilities, transport, and communications	1,625	41,728[c]	3.9%
Manufacturing	1,534	23,672	6.5%
Machinery and equipment	444	1,907	23.3%
Motor vehicles	184	1,232	14.9%
Rubber products	60	434	13.8%
Chemicals	130	1,497	8.7%
Foodstuffs	222	4,001	5.5%
Lumber and products	69	2,001	3.4%
Metals and products	150	4,788	3.1%
Textiles and products	71	2,932	2.4%
Stone, clay and glass products	23	1,451	1.6%
Leather and products	4	269	1.3%
Agriculture[d]	875	51,033	1.5%

[a] Figures for total manufacturing do not include petroleum refining, which is included under "Mining and petroleum."

[b] Figures for domestic mining and petroleum-invested capital are for the book value of capital including land but excluding working capital.

[c] Value of plant and equipment.

[d] Domestic invested capital is reproducible tangible assets of agricultural sector.

Source: Foreign direct investment: U.S. Department of Commerce, *American Direct Investments in Foreign Countries* (Washington, D.C.: GPO, 1930), pp. 29–36.

Domestic fixed capital: Daniel Creamer, Sergei Dobrovolsky, and Israel Borenstein, *Capital in Manufacturing and Mining* (Princeton, N.J.: Princeton University Press, 1960), pp. 248–51, 317–18; Melville J. Ulmer, *Capital in Transportation, Communications and Public Utilities* (Princeton, N.J.: Princeton University Press, 1960), pp. 235–37; Raymond Goldsmith, Robert Lipsey, and Morris Mendelson, *Studies in the National Balance Sheet of the United States* vol. 2 (Princeton, N.J.: Princeton University Press, 1963), pp. 78–79.

years the proportion approached one-third. The United States was the world's principal long-term lender, and foreign lending was very important to American finance.

The reasons for the uneven pattern of overseas investment are fairly straight forward. It is not surprising that a capital-starved world would turn for loans to the capital-rich United States, especially to the Northeastern financial powerhouses. Foreign direct investment, on the other hand, responded to more specific incentives. Tariff barriers, which proliferated after World War I, forced former or prospective exporters to locate production facilities in overseas markets; often the advantages of local production were great even in the absence of tariffs. Foreign direct investment was thus largely confined to firms with specific technological, managerial, or marketing advantages, such as motor vehicles, electric appliances and utilities, and petroleum, as well as in the extraction of resources available more

Table 8.3　NEW CORPORATE AND FOREIGN CAPITAL ISSUES IN NEW YORK, 1919–1929 (IN MILLIONS OF DOLLARS AND PERCENT)

	A All corporate issues	B Foreign issues	B/A in percent
1919	$2,742	$771	28.1%
1920	2,967	603	20.3%
1921	2,391	692	28.9%
1922	2,775	863	31.1%
1923	2,853	498	17.5%
1924	3,831	1,217	31.8%
1925	6,219	1,316	21.2%
1926	8,628	1,288	14.9%
1927	9,936	1,577	15.9%
1928	9,894	1,489	15.0%
1929	11,604	706	6.1%
Total, 1919–1929	63,840	11,020	17.3%
Annual average, 1919–1929	5,804	1,002	17.3%

Source: United States Department of Commerce, Handbook of American Underwriting of Foreign Securities (Washington, D.C.: GPO, 1930), pp. 32–37.

readily abroad. There was little overseas investment by industries producing such relatively standardized goods as steel, clothing, and footwear; they generally had little exporting experience and few advantages over firms in their lines of business abroad. Thus the major money-center investment and commercial banks were highly international, as were the more technologically advanced manufacturing and extractive industries; traditional labor-intensive industries, which were by far the majority, were little involved in foreign investment.

American industrial export interests were similar to its foreign investments. The major industrial sectors with overseas investments were also the country's leading industrial exporters, as product-cycle theory would predict.[6] Refiners of copper and petroleum and producers of machinery and equipment, motor vehicles, chemicals, and processed food were all major exporters as well as major foreign investors. The only important exceptions to the general congruence of trade and asset diversification were the steel industry and some agricultural interests, especially in the South. Neither steel producers nor, of course, cotton and tobacco farmers had many overseas investments. To a large extent, then, the trade and foreign investment line-ups were complementary.[7]

Sectors with major overseas investment interests would be expected to have a different foreign economic and political outlook than sectors with little or no international production or sales. Internationally oriented banks and corporations would be generally favorable to freer trade, the former to allow debtors to earn foreign exchange and the latter both because intrafirm trade was important to them and because they tended to fear retaliation. Internationally oriented sectors could also be expected to support an extension of American diplomatic commitments abroad, both specifically to safeguard their investments and more generally to provide an international environment conducive to foreign economic growth. Those sectors that sold but did not invest abroad would be sympathetic to American attempts to stabilize foreign markets but might oppose international initiatives that reinforced competing producers overseas. Economic sectors with few foreign assets or sales could be anticipated to support protectionist policies in their industries because they were not importing from overseas subsidiaries, tended to be less competitive, and had few worries about retaliation. Such sectors would be unsupportive of major American international involvement that might strengthen real or potential competitors of U.S. industry.

Two broad blocs on foreign economic policy did indeed emerge after World War I, and their preferences were more or less as might have been predicted. One group of economic interests was "internationalist": it supported American entry into the League of Nations, U.S. financing of European reconstruction, commercial liberalization, and international monetary and financial cooperation. The other cluster of economic interests was the "isolationists": it opposed the league and American financing of Europe, called for renewed trade protection, and was indifferent or hostile to global financial and monetary accords.[8] The two sets of policy preferences were competing rather than complementary, and although there were some actors in a middle ground, the extreme unevenness of American overseas economic expansion meant that preferences tended to harden in their opposition.

The central dilemma of U.S. foreign economic policy for fifteen years after World War I was the great economic strength of two opposing sets of economic and political actors, neither of which was powerful enough to vanquish the other. Among the consequences of interest to the analyst of international relations is that the state *did not* undertake to impose a foreign policy derived from America's international position upon recalcitrant domestic actors; instead, the central state apparatus found itself torn between conflicting interests. The various economic interests entrenched themselves in the political arena and found allies within the government bureaucracy, so that domestic sociopolitical strife was carried out *within* the state apparatus. The Federal Reserve System and the State Department were dominated by economic internationalists, whether of the Wilsonian or Republican variants; the majority of the Congress and the powerful Commerce Department were more closely aligned with the economic nationalists who might support limited measures to encourage American exports but stopped there.

The result was a foreign policy that was eminently contradictory and volatile. The same administration encouraged foreign lending and trade protection against the goods of the borrowers, worked for international monetary cooperation and sought to sabotage it, struggled to reinforce European reconstruction and impeded it at crucial junctures. This was not due to policy stupidity but to the underlying differences in international outlook of powerful domestic socioeconomic groups. The period is thus a useful and illuminating illustration of the interaction of international and domestic sources of foreign policy.

Although it concentrates on the analytical issues of the 1920s and early 1930s, the article shows how after 1933 the world crisis served to thaw some of the policy paralysis that had characterized the postwar Republican administrations. The international and domestic crises both changed the relative strength of important social actors and allowed policy makers to reformulate their relationship to these social actors.

The remainder of this article analyzes the development of American foreign economic policy from 1914 to 1940 in the light of the preceding considerations. The analysis focuses on the interests and activities of America's international bankers. The nation's international financiers were both the most internationally oriented group of economic actors in the United States at the time (as they are today) and the most powerful and prominent members of the internationalist coalition. Their trajectory demonstrates the general lines of the approach taken here quite well, and also clarifies the role of the differentiated state apparatus in the evolution of U.S. foreign economic policy after World War I. The article does not present a complete account of the period in question—this would require a much more detailed discussion of, among other things, overseas events, America's economic nationalists, and institutional and bureaucratic developments—but it does discuss enough of the era to show how a fuller analysis could be developed.

THE EMERGENCE OF AMERICAN ECONOMIC INTERNATIONALISM, 1914–1933

For fifty years before World War I, the American political economy was oriented to the needs of domestic industry. The war accelerated a process already under way, the expansion of international investments by one segment of the U.S. business community. Along with this economic change came the development of a new set of political interests that challenged the previous pattern of foreign economic policy. In the fifteen years after World War I, the economic internationalists developed great, if quite private, influence over foreign policy but lost many public political battles. Until the Depression, American foreign economic policy was divided between measures to support "nationalist" industries and most of agriculture and those preferred by "internationalist" banks, industries, and some export agriculture.

From the Civil War until the early 1900s, however, the country's foreign economic policy was clearly designed to serve domestic industry, mostly home production for the home market and some exportation. The strategy adopted had a number of aims and evolved over time, as David Lake has demonstrated.[9] Raw materials available overseas needed to be developed and imported. Industrial goods, especially the products of basic industry, needed to find overseas markets. American tariffs on raw materials might come down, but the American market was essentially closed to industrial goods.

In this picture America's embryonic international bankers played a subsidiary but important role. They financed overseas raw materials developments and facilitated the transport and sale of raw materials to American industry. They lent dollars to overseas consumers of America's basic industrial products—railways, railroad and subway cars, mining equipment, ships. And of course they financed much of the domestic expansion and merger activity of the industrial combines.

World War I was a turning point in the evolution of American international economic interests. During the war and the period immediately following it, New York became the world's center for long-term lending. American financial supremacy drew America's internationally oriented business people and politicians into world leadership during the war and in the postwar reconstruction of Europe, a role that was to be severely hampered by the strength of economic nationalists within the United States.

The outbreak of hostilities caused financial chaos on European money markets. Panic was only narrowly averted in New York, but by early 1915 the New York market had been stabilized and was the only fully functioning major capital market in the world. Originally the Wilson administration had indicated that it considered the extension of all but short-term loans to the warring powers by American financiers "inconsistent with the true spirit of neutrality." But as the fighting continued, the belligerents began to place major orders in the United States to supply their industries and compensate for their lagging agricultures. American munitions exports went from $40 million in 1914 to nearly $1.3 billion in 1916; all merchandise exports increased from $2.4 billion in 1914 to $5.5 billion in 1916, from about 6 percent to about 12 percent of gross national product. Because imports remained near prewar levels, between 1914 and 1917 the United States averaged an astounding annual trade surplus of $2.5 billion, more than five times the immediate prewar average.[10]

The Allies, who accounted for most of this export expansion (the Central Powers were effectively blockaded), financed some of their American purchases by selling back to United States investors about $2 billion in American securities between the beginning of the war and U.S. entry. This was insufficient, of course, and soon the Wilson administration reversed its earlier financial neutrality. In October 1915 J. P. Morgan and Co. underwrote a $500 million loan to the English and French governments. Because of the opposition of neutralists and anti-Russian, German-American, and Irish-American forces, Morgan was only able to secure the full amount with some difficulty.[11]

Despite widespread hostility to their efforts, the New York bankers continued to finance the Allies. In addition, their long-standing ties with the big industrial combines placed the bankers well to arrange for Allied purchases and shipping. Thus Morgan acted during the war as the purchasing agent in the United States for the British and French, and in the three-year period up to June 1917 these purchases amounted to over one-quarter of all American exports.[12]

The Allies' financial requirements increased as the war dragged on, as did American sympathy for the Allied cause. Morgan led a series of syndicates in a further $250 million loan to England in August 1916, another of $300 million in October 1916, a $250 million issue in January 1917; France floated a $100 million bond in March 1917. All told, between January 1915 and 5 April 1917 the Allies borrowed about $2.6 billion: Great Britain and France $2.11 billion, Canada and Australia $405 million, Russia and Italy $75 million.[13]

Upon American entry into the war, private lending to the belligerents essentially ceased. Instead, between May 1917 and April 1919 the U.S. government issued four Liberty Loans and one postwar Victory Loan and used the proceeds to lend the Allies $9.6 billion.[14] American banks also took the opportunity to establish or drastically expand their branches in France to service the hordes of arriving American troops.[15]

Private lending resumed almost as soon as wartime conditions ended, as Table 3 indicates. Especially after the 1924 Dawes Plan, which symbolized for many the economic stabilization of Europe, lending boomed. As can be seen in Table 8.4 in the early 1920s American lending also shifted away from the wartime allies and toward "non-traditional borrowers": Germany, Canada, Italy, smaller Western European countries, the more commercially important countries of South America, and the Dutch East Indies. United States banks also expanded their branch network overseas from 26 in 1914 to 154 in 1926. As we have mentioned, direct investment abroad by American corporations also rose very rapidly, from $2.7 billion in 1914 to $7.9 billion in 1929.

The rapid overseas expansion of United States businesses after 1914 led to the maturation of an outward-looking internationalist perspective, especially on the part of the international bankers. The leaders of American finance took a new, broader view of the world in which they had invested and decided that as Woodrow Wilson said in 1916, "We have got to finance the world in some important degree, and those who finance the world must understand it and rule it with their spirits and with their minds."[16]

Apart from the general expansion of their lending, the bankers' customers had changed. No longer were the loans going to specific raw-materials projects or railroad development. The new debtors of the 1920s were more advanced nations; many of them, like Germany, were major competitors of U.S. industry. Concern about American tariffs on manufactured goods was thus logical. The debtors were also usually governments, and the close ties the bankers were building with, for example, Central and Eastern European regimes made them especially interested in European economic reconstruction and political harmony. The major international bankers, then, wanted a more internationalist foreign policy for the United States, lower tariffs, and American aid for a European settlement.

The financiers acted on their beliefs, and the postwar period saw the construction of formal and informal institutions and networks that have ever since been at the center of the American foreign policy establishment. The Council on Foreign Relations was formed right after the war: John W. Davis, Morgan's chief counsel and later a Democratic candidate for president, was the council's first president; Alexander Hemphill, chairman of the Guaranty Trust Co., headed the council's finance committee. Thomas W. Lamont of J. P. Morgan and Co. played an active role in the council and brought the founding editor of the council's journal, *Foreign Affairs,* to the job (he was editor of Lamont's *New York Evening Post*). Otto Kahn and Paul Warburg of the investment bank Kuhn, Loeb were founding directors, as was Paul Cravath, the firm's lawyer. Norman H. Davis, another founding director, was a Wall Street banker who served as assistant secretary of the treasury and undersecretary of state under Wilson; he worked closely with Lamont and financier Bernard Baruch in defining the postwar economic settlement in Europe.[17]

Table 8.4 AMERICAN PORTFOLIO OF FOREIGN SECURITIES, 1914–1935 (IN MILLIONS OF DOLLARS; EXCLUDES INTERGOVERNMENT WAR DEBTS)

	1914	1919	1924	1929	1935
Europe	196	1,491	1,946	3,473	2,586
Austria	1	0	27	72	57
Belgium	0	12	181	214	152
Czechoslovakia	—	0	32	32	30
Denmark	0	15	89	165	135
Finland	—	0	29	63	32
France	10	343	449	343	158
Germany	23	2	132	1,019	829
Great Britain	122	891	414	287	42
Hungary	—	0	9	63	57
Italy	0	38	41	365	271
Netherlands	0	0	99	62	132
Norway	3	5	97	185	151
Poland	0	0	30	132	97
Russia	29	127	104	104	104
Sweden	5	20	66	196	213
Switzerland	0	35	116	49	0
Yugoslavia	0	0	18	50	47
Other Europe[a]	3	3	13	72	79
Canada	179	729	1,551	2,003	1,965
South America	43	113	464	1,294	1,241
Argentina	26	58	188	370	344
Bolivia	8	10	38	62	59
Brazil	6	41	146	325	320
Chile	1	1	53	238	237
Colombia	0	1	15	167	146
Peru	2	0	9	77	74
Uruguay	0	2	15	45	51
Venezuela	0	0	0	10	10
Caribbean Region	310	305	390	430	434
Cuba	35	33	76	95	115
Dominican Republic	5	6	15	19	16
Haiti	0	0	17	15	10
Mexico	266	265	270	266	261
Central America	4	2	12	35	32
Asia	217	227	519	926	772
Australia	0	1	24	241	253
China	7	20	23	23	21
Dutch East Indies	0	0	150	175	25
Japan	184	166	234	387	384
Philippines	26	40	88	100	89
Other and international	0	0	0	18	29
Total	945	2,862	4,870	8,144	7,026

Source: Adapted from Cleona Lewis, *America's Stake in International Investments* (Washington, D.C.: Brookings Institution, 1938), pp. 654–55.

[a] In descending order of financial importance in 1929: Greece, Bulgaria, Rumania, Luxemburg, Ireland, Estonia, Danzig, and Lithuania.

The council was the most important such organization, but the internationalist segment of the American business community, headed by the international bankers, also worked with other similar groups. The Foreign Policy Association, the Carnegie Endowment for International Peace (founded 1908), the League of Nations Association, and many others brought scholars, bankers, journalists, politicians, and government officials together in the pursuit of internationalism. In addition to consultation, coordination, and research, the internationalist network aimed to convince average Americans, in the words of the chairman of the Foreign Policy Association, "that their stake in the restoration of normal economic conditions in Europe is in reality as direct and vital as that of the international banker."[18]

More direct was the initiation during World War I of a system of close cooperation between foreign-policy makers, especially those concerned with foreign economic policy, and America's international bankers. It was common for important figures in American international financial circles to serve on policy advisory bodies and sometimes to rotate through positions in government, usually at the State Department and the Federal Reserve Bank of New York. Indeed, during and after the war the State Department and the Federal Reserve Bank of New York established durable working relations with the New York bankers. On every significant foreign policy initiative of the 1920s—from the Versailles Treaty itself to war debts and reparations, to the tariff issue, to the Dawes and Young Plans, to the boom in foreign borrowing and the establishment of the Bank for International Settlements—the international bankers worked together with the like-minded internationalists of the State Department and the Federal Reserve Bank of New York in the evolution of policy.

The financial and other internationalists faced the opposition of extremely powerful forces of economic nationalism in the United States. Senior Morgan partner Thomas Lamont decried "the failure of the American people to understand that the United States of America held a new position in the world" and later reflected on the unfortunate fact that "America entered upon the new decade of the 1920s in full panoply of wealth and power, but possessing little ambition to realize her vast potentialities for strengthening the world in stability and peace."[19]

The stumbling block was the existence of a considerable anti-internationalist political bloc with support from business people who had little interest in foreign affairs, worried about foreign competition, and opposed the export of American capital. The Commerce Department of Herbert Hoover, the prime mover of U.S. economic policy in the 1920s, was closely linked and deeply committed to American domestic industry. In foreign economic affairs its principal concern was thus to promote industrial exports and primary imports, not overseas lending and manufacturing investment. America's domestic industrialists could, like Hoover, agree on some things with the bankers. They all favored expanding American exports, and some kinds of imports. Yet there was little sympathy in domestically oriented industry for freer trade insofar as it meant manufactured imports. Domestic industrialists were also unhappy with American bank loans to foreign competitors, and some of them were wary of capital exports in general. As Hoover put it, "a billion dollars spent upon American railways will give more employment to our people, more advance to our industry, more assistance to our farmers, than twice that sum expended outside the frontiers of the United States."[20]

The United States faced a bewildering array of foreign-policy problems in the 1920s, and in virtually every case the tension between internationalists and nationalists defined the discussion and outcome. There is no need to describe these debates at length, for there is an ample literature on them.[21] Three broad problems—European reconstruction, trade policy, and capital exports—were of special importance, and later I shall summarize the major issues involved in these debates and note the common pattern. In virtually every case internationalist financiers and their allies in the State Department and the Federal Reserve faced the opposition of nationalist forces in Congress and other segments of the executive. The internationalists were almost always defeated, forced to compromise, or forced to adopt some form of semiofficial arrangement that kept the process out of the public eye.

European Reconstruction and War Debts

The general desire of the United States international bankers was for the rapid reconstruction of Europe. Private funds might be used for this purpose, but the financial shakiness of the potential borrowers (especially in Central Europe) made U.S. government involvement preferable. Inasmuch as the debts owed the U.S. government by the Allies were an obstacle to European reconstruction, especially since they encouraged the French to demand larger reparations payments from the Germans, the American financiers favored partial or total cancellation of official war debts.[22] All of this required American leadership: the United States government should help the Europeans back onto the gold standard, arrange for a government-backed bankers' consortium to restore Europe's shattered currencies, regularize and encourage American private capital exports to Europe, force the Europeans to negotiate a reduction of Germany's reparations burden in return for war debts leniency, and combat economic nationalism on the Continent.

This leadership was not forthcoming. Talk of war debt cancellation was quashed by economic nationalists in the cabinet and in Congress, for whom war-debt forgiveness represented a levy on American taxpayers, who would be called upon to make up the Treasury's loss, in favor of the country's European competitors. Although some refunding and reduction did occur, the bankers were forced to retreat. Government-backed loans to the Europeans were also vetoed, as was any official American involvement in the reparations tangle. Only in monetary matters, where the bankers' house organ, the Federal Reserve Bank of New York, was given fairly free rein, was limited progress made.[23]

Opposition to the bankers' plans solidified under President Warren Harding in the early 1920s. Congress and much of the executive branch were intransigent on the war debts and reparations issues. Herbert Hoover's Commerce Department was not generally favorable to financial schemes that might strengthen overseas competitors of American industry or that might allow foreign raw materials producers to raise prices to American manufacturers.[24] Morgan partner Thomas Lamont bitterly blasted "ill-advised steps for the collection of that debt, every penny, principal and interest," while Lamont's New York Evening Post editorialized: "We cannot emphasize too often the mischief for the European situation to-day wrought by Herbert Hoover's assertion that 95 percent of America's claims on the continent are good."[25]

It was not for lack of trying that the bankers were unable to secure government involvement. Benjamin Strong at the Federal Reserve Bank of New York played a major role in European reconstruction planning and implementation. As he said when proposing central-bank cooperation for exchange stabilization to an October 1921 meeting of the Board of Governors of the Federal Reserve System, "whether we want to or not we are going to take some part in this situation abroad. We probably won't do it politically, but we have to do it financially and economically." The governors, far more sympathetic to the desperate straits of European finances than the administration, were strongly in favor, as Governor Norris of Philadelphia indicated:

> I think the three great opportunities that we have had to accomplish the stabilization of foreign exchange were, first, to go into the League of Nations; second, to make a readjustment of our tariff ... and the third was to empower the Secretary of the Treasury to deal in an intelligent way with the refunding of foreign obligations. ... But because we have lost those three it does not follow, of course, that we ought to throw aside and discard all others ... [and] it seems to me that the proposition you have suggested is one that undoubtedly has merit and may reasonably be expected to accomplish some results.[26]

Yet a month later the executive branch refused to allow a central bank conference that Strong and Montagu Norman of the Bank of England had proposed. Strong wrote to Norman at the time, "between the lines I read that there would in fact be no objection if the matter were undertaken privately and without government support or responsibility." Thus when the League of Nations's Financial Committee was supervising an Austrian stabilization program in 1922–1923, the New York bankers were regularly consulted to ensure that the program would meet with the approval of U.S. financial markets—which it did when the U.S. portion of the stabilization loan was floated in June 1923.[27]

Nevertheless, for all intents and purposes the bankers' plans for an American-supervised economic settlement in Europe were foiled. As the Central European economies collapsed in 1923 and 1924, the administration attempted to balance the financiers' insistence on American involvement against equally insistent nationalist demands that the United States stay out of Europe. The State Department, anxious to use American influence and finance to stabilize Europe, began the process that would lead to the Dawes Plan in April 1924. The arrangement worked out was ingenious: negotiations were entrusted to an unofficial delegation of American business people, headed by internationally minded Chicago banker Charles G. Dawes and Owen D. Young, chairman of the board of General Electric. The prominent internationalist bankers and business people at the center of the negotiations consulted closely, if surreptitiously, with the State Department and the Federal Reserve Bank of New York.[28]

The Dawes Plan called for foreign supervision of German public finances, with reparations payments overseen by an American with discreet ties to Morgan's. The German currency was stabilized and investor confidence in Germany restored with a $200 million bond flotation, of which J. P. Morgan and Co. managed $110 million in New York.[29] All things considered, the plan was a reasonable compromise: it used American financial supremacy to settle (at least temporarily) a major European wrangle without committing the U.S. government directly. The only open government involvement was an encouragement to American investors to subscribe to the Dawes loan, and indeed Morgan received over a billion dollars in applications, ten times the amount of the loan. The settlement satisfied most internationalists and most nationalists in the United States temporarily, and even this was quite a feat.[30]

Free Trade and the Tariff

Fundamental domestic differences over U.S. trade policy were harder to paper over. Indeed, the future of America's traditional protectionism was perhaps the most contentious issue in American politics in the 1920s. During World War I, the administration had apparently committed itself to low and flexible tariffs, in line with the bankers' preferences. When the United States became a major lender, foreign borrowers had to be permitted freer access to the U.S. market or loans could not be serviced. Tariff barriers, argued the bankers, were a cause of useless trade rivalries and war. As Morgan partner Dwight Morrow put it, "leadership in world trade is not a thing to be sought by any nation to the exclusion of all others."[31]

But in Congress those American economic actors who demanded protection from foreign imports had the upper hand. In 1921 Congress passed a restrictive Emergency Tariff Act that was followed in 1922 by the Fordney-McCumber tariff.[32] This act had provisions that attempted to satisfy both protectionist industrialists and farmers, and less successfully, internationalist bankers, investors, and traders. The compromise was generally unsatisfactory to both factions, and controversy on the tariff raged throughout the 1920s. Few doubted that traditional American protectionism had returned, and the French Finance Ministry called Fordney-McCumber "the first heavy blow directed against any hope of effectively restoring a world trading system."[33]

Such financiers as Otto Kahn looked with dismay on the continued strength of protectionist sentiment:

> Having become a creditor nation, we have got now to fit ourselves into the role of a creditor nation. We shall have to make up our minds to be more hospitable to imports. We shall have to outgrow gradually certain inherited and no longer applicable views and preconceptions and adapt our economic policies to the changed positions which have resulted from the late war.[34]

Supervision of Foreign Loans

In the early 1920s opposition to the export of American capital mounted. Domestic industrial interests were concerned that the loans were strengthening foreign competitors, especially in Germany, and reducing the capital available to domestic producers. They were also concerned that loans to raw-materials producers might be used to organize producers' cartels that would raise prices charged to U.S. industry.

Hoover and Treasury Secretary Andrew Mellon thus wanted to make new loans contingent on the use of at least part of them for the purchase of American goods, or to a commitment by the borrowers to allow American suppliers to bid on ensuing contracts; they also opposed lending to nations disinclined to service their war debts to the U.S. government and lending that might reinforce the position of suppliers to or competitors with American industry. The bankers, of course, along with Benjamin Strong of the Federal Reserve Bank of New York, opposed any government controls; Secretary of State Charles E. Hughes leaned towards their position.

In 1921 President Harding, Hoover, Hughes, and Mellon met with the leading New York bankers and reached an agreement that the banks would notify the Department of State of all foreign loans and give the department the opportunity to object. Formalized in 1922, the policy was applied as sparingly as possible by a State Department that supported the bankers. Even so, in a number of instances Hoover was able to override the bankers; two prominent successes were blocked loans to a French–German potash cartel and to Brazilian coffee growers. The commerce secretary warned "the American banking community" that "the commissions which might be collected on floating such loans would be no compensation" for the "justifiable criticism . . . from the American potash and coffee consumers when [they] become aware that American capital was being placed at the disposal of these agencies through which prices were being held against our own people." Hoover also threatened to form a pool to break a British rubber cartel, complained about American lending to the German steel trust, and he and Mellon succeeded in stopping several loans for reasons related to war debts or other foreign policy objectives.[35]

Here, again, the conflict between the international interests of financiers and the national concerns of many American business people and politicians clashed. Once more, the outcome was indecisive; the State Department succeeded in blunting most of Hoover's attacks on foreign lending he regarded as excessive, yet pressure never let up.

The deadlock between internationalism and nationalism that formed in the early 1920s remained in place throughout the Coolidge and Hoover administrations. Foreign economic policy retained much of its ambiguity, with government departments and the international bankers cooperating and colliding, depending on the issue and the department involved. Internationalist bankers and business people complained bitterly of the Commerce Department's attempts to restrict their activities and to penalize their overseas clients. As Owen Young wrote to Hoover in 1926, "I am sincerely troubled by our national program, which is demanding amounts from our debtors up to the breaking point, and at the same time excluding their goods from our American markets, except for those few raw materials which we must have."[36]

Although a wide range of issues in American foreign economic policy remained unsolved, the financiers fought continually to implement some form of European economic reconstruction. After the Dawes Plan gave Germany, and by implication other Central European borrowers, the stamp of approval of international finance, loans to Europe exploded. Between 1925 and 1930 Americans lent a total of $5.3 billion to foreigners; $1.3 billion went to Canada, $1.6 billion to Latin America, and $305 million to Japan. Virtually all of the rest—$2.6 billion—

went to Europe, as follows: Germany $1.2 billion (47 percent of the European total), Italy $345 million (13 percent), Eastern and Southeastern Europe $386 million (15 percent), and Scandinavia $385 million (15 percent); the remainder was scattered across a number of lesser borrowers.[37]

The United States had become the world's leading capital exporter, its bankers often acting as leaders in international financial consortia. By far the most important borrower was Germany; by 1929 American portfolio investment there had gone from nearly nothing to over a billion dollars (see Table 4). Germany and Central European prosperity, deemed essential to the political and economic stabilization of Europe, depended largely on injections of United States capital. Between 1925 and 1928 foreigners provided 39 percent of all long-term borrowing by the German public sector and 70 percent of all long-term private borrowing; half of the foreign lending was from America.[38]

Yet it was clear to the financiers that European economic expansion was precarious, and the fundamental division of American foreign economic policy made it more so. The bankers and their allies in the State Department and the Federal Reserve System did what they could to solidify their tenuous attempts at international economic leadership. The curious and often awkward modus vivendi that evolved was illustrated by the financial stabilization programs arranged in a series of European nations between late 1926 and late 1928. In Belgium, Poland, Italy, and Rumania, cooperative central-bank credits—generally put together by the Bank of England and the Federal Reserve Bank of New York—were extended in conjunction with longer-term private loans, of which American banks typically provided at least half. The private bankers were closely involved in the negotiations leading up to the stabilization agreements.[39]

In early 1929 the international bankers who had put together the Dawes Plan—including many who had participated in the financial stabilization programs of the late 1920s—came together again to attempt a further regularization of international financial matters. The United States was represented (unofficially, of course, as at the Dawes Conference) by Owen Young and J. P. Morgan; Thomas Lamont was Morgan's alternate. After dealing with German issues, the conference established the Bank for International Settlements (BIS) to accept continuing German reparations (renamed *annuities*) payments, and more broadly, to manage the international financial system. The BIS, which was the product of the American financiers, was to promote financial stability and take finance out of the hands of unreliable politicians. Indeed, it was founded in such a way as to make congressional approval unnecessary and congressional oversight impossible.[40]

The BIS, however, was powerless to counter the effects of the Great Depression. In May 1931, the Kreditanstalt failure triggered panic throughout Central Europe. President Hoover recognized the inevitable and in late June 1931 declared a moratorium on the payment of war debts in an attempt to stave off, in Treasury Undersecretary Ogden Mills's words, "a major catastrophe of incalculable consequences to the credit structure of the world and to the economic future of all nations."[41] Nevertheless, in 1932 defaults began in Hungary, Greece, Bulgaria, Austria, Yugoslavia, Sweden, and Denmark; in 1933 Germany and Rumania joined the list. By the end of 1934 over 40 percent of American loans to Europe were in default.[42] In the interim, of course, the United States substantially raised tariffs, even though, as Morgan's Thomas Lamont recalled, "I almost went down on my knees to beg Herbert Hoover to veto the asinine Hawley-Smoot Tariff."[43]

The contradictory nature of American foreign economic policy in the 1920s was much noted by financiers and scholars at the time. On the one hand, there was a massive outflow of private capital to Europe, while on the other, European exports to the United States, necessary to debt service, were severely restricted. To top it off, the Harding-Coolidge-Hoover administrations insisted on considering the Allies' war debts to the U.S. government as binding commercial obligations, which further restricted Europe's capacity to service American commercial debts.[44] The reason for this vacillation was that two powerful sets of interests, economic nationalists and economic internationalists, were fighting for power within the United States, and the battle raged through the 1920s and into the 1930s.

The degree to which the contradictions of U.S. foreign economic policy were recognized by the general public is indicated in Franklin Delano Roosevelt's August 1932 campaign-speech explanation of American foreign lending in *Alice in Wonderful* style:

> A puzzled, somewhat skeptical Alice asked the Republican leadership some simple questions:
> "Will not the printing and selling of more stocks and bonds, the building of new plants, and the increase of efficiency produce more goods than we can buy?"
> "No," shouted Humpty Dumpty. "The more we produce the more we can buy."
> "What if we produce a surplus?"
> "Oh, we can sell it to foreign consumers."
> "How can the foreigners pay for it?"
> "Why, we will lend them money."
> "I see," said little Alice, "they will buy our surplus with our money. Of course these foreigners will pay us back by selling us their goods?"
> "Oh, not at all," said Humpty Dumpty. "We set up a high wall called the tariff."
> "And," said Alice at last, "how will the foreigners pay off these loans?"
> "That is easy," said Humpty Dumpty. "Did you ever hear of a moratorium?"
> And so, at last, my friends, we have reached the heart of the magic formula of 1928.[45]

From 1914 on, major overseas investors, led by the international banks, rapidly extended their influence abroad and at home. Yet the battle for control of the state was undecided; instead of a unitary foreign-policy making apparatus with a coherent strategy, the United States had a foreign economic policy in the 1920s and early 1930s that was dualistic and irrational, in the sense that its various parts were in direct conflict with one another.[46] The political ambiguity of American foreign policy left American financial and other internationalists alone with their grandiose plans in a devastated world, determined that they would not again be defeated by forces that did not share their world vision.

THE RISE OF AMERICAN ECONOMIC INTERNATIONALISM, 1933–1940

Just as the shock of World War I dramatically accelerated the extension of American international economic interests, the shock of the 1930s accelerated the demise of America's economic nationalists. During the first two Roosevelt administrations, economic internationalism gradually and haltingly came to dominate U.S. foreign policy, even as policy making became ever more protected from the economic nationalists who continued to dominate the legislature. Faced with international and domestic economic crises of unprecedented depth and scope, the Roosevelt administration, after a brief attempt to rebuild international economic cooperation, retreated into domestic New Deal reforms, then slowly reemerged in the mid- and late-1930s with a series of international economic initiatives that foreshadowed the postwar Bretton Woods system.

The Depression, indeed, had a devastating impact on the traditional economic and political base of the economic nationalists. Industrial production did not regain its 1929 peak until World War II, and in the interim few regarded industry as the dynamo it had been. Agriculture was even more devastated. The banking system, of course, was also hard-hit, but most of the failures were of smaller banks. The big internationally oriented banks remained active both at home and abroad, although their economic and political influence was reduced both by the Depression itself and by Depression-era banking reforms. Table 8.1 demonstrates the continuing importance of international economic interests. Foreign direct investment, as a percentage of total corporate and agricultural invested capital, climbed through the 1930s, largely due to domestic deflation. Foreign bondholdings, of course, dropped because of defaults; this certainly harmed the bondholders but had little effect on the big investment and commercial banks themselves. In any case, holdings of foreign bonds remained substantial, and international bankers continued to hope that pre-1930 levels of lending could be restored.

When Roosevelt took office in March 1933, he hoped to reconcile two major goals: to stabilize international economic relations and to resolve the country's pressing domestic economic problems. Britain had gone off the gold standard in 1931 to devalue the pound and improve Britain's trade position; it had also moved towards trade protection within the empire. By 1933 international monetary, financial, and trade relations were in shambles. At the same time the United States was in the midst of a serious banking crisis, and the agricultural depression that had begun in the late 1920s was deepening. Roosevelt made no secret of the fact that his first priority was domestic, not international, stability.

The administration went into the international economic conference, which began in London in June 1933, willing to discuss some form of monetary cooperation with the British and French but determined that these discussions should not interfere with domestic economic measures. As it turned out, the participants in the London conference were unable to reconcile national economic priorities with internationalism. Early in July Roosevelt effectively wrecked the conference and any hopes for international currency stabilization, saying that "what is to be the value of the dollar in terms of foreign currencies is and cannot be our immediate concern."[47]

With the collapse of international cooperative efforts Roosevelt turned his attention to the domestic economy. In October the U.S. began devaluing the dollar's gold value from $20.67 to $35 an ounce. Although the devaluation was not quite the success its proponents had expected, it did mark the administration's disenchantment with internationally negotiated attempts at stabilization.[48]

Many international bankers approved of Roosevelt's domestic banking decisions and of the dollar devaluation. Yet as 1933 wore on, they were alarmed by his more unorthodox positions. Hostility between the administration and the financiers continued despite the attempts of Roosevelt and some of the bankers to call a truce, and in late 1933 and 1934, a number of financiers and policy makers close to the financial community left the administration or denounced it.[49]

The first two years of the Roosevelt administration were in fact characterized by divisions within the administration and the banking community, as well as a great deal of policy experimentation. Within the administration a running battle was waged between Wilsonian Democrat Cordell Hull as secretary of state, Assistant Secretary Francis Sayre (an international lawyer and Wilson's son-in-law) and other free-trade internationalists on the one hand, and such economic nationalists as Presidential Foreign Trade Advisor and first President of the Export-Import Bank George Peek on the other.[50] To add to the confusion, Treasury Secretary Henry Morgenthau, Roosevelt's closest adviser on economic affairs, was both fascinated by and ignorant of international financial matters.

The nearly desperate economic crisis made the early Roosevelt administration willing to consider politically and ideologically unorthodox policies.[51] Indeed, much of the bankers' distrust of FDR in 1933–1934 stemmed from the belief that he was embracing the notion of national self-sufficiency—economic nationalism with feeling—that was becoming so popular at the time and was often laced with semifascist ideology. For his part, Roosevelt was seriously concerned with the Depression's effect on the nation's social fabric and was convinced that the British and French were insurmountable obstacles to a stabilization agreement that would allow for American economic recovery. Alarmed by the domestic political situation and thoroughly disenchanted with the British and French, Roosevelt enacted emergency measures to stabilize the system. Some financiers approved; most did not.

After the first frenzied phase of crisis management, however, the administration did indeed begin to move in a cautiously internationalist direction. In June 1934 Congress passed Hull's Reciprocal Trade Agreements Act, which was broadly understood as a move towards freer trade. By 1934, too, the value of the dollar had been essentially fixed at $35 an ounce, indicating a renewed commitment to currency stability. In spring 1935 Roosevelt began cooperating with the French (over British objections) to stabilize the franc and pushed for English, American, and French collaboration for exchange-rate stability.[52] In late 1935 George Peek resigned in disgust over Roosevelt's drift to internationalism.

The financiers responded optimistically, if cautiously, to the administration's international initiatives. Early in 1936 Leon Fraser of the First National Bank of New York expressed his general approval of administration policy and his wish that this policy might become wholehearted:

> . . . [A]fter a period of painful trial and harmful error, the authorities have seemingly reached three conclusions, each vital to monetary stabilization at home and abroad. First, they have in fact, but in silence, rejected the proposed elastic dollar and have re-linked the dollar to gold instead of to some commodity index. Second, they have been, and are, practising the gold standard internationally, subject to certain qualifications

deemed to be necessary because of the present chaos. Third, as the logical next step, they stand ready to participate with other countries in the restoration of foreign exchange stabilization . . . Excellent—but a more affirmative stand will become necessary, a more explicit recognition of the responsibility which the advocacy of stabilization implies, and some assurances of a readiness to discharge these responsibilities in order to maintain the reestablished order.[53]

The commitment Fraser sought was indeed forthcoming. Through the summer of 1936 the administration, the British, and the French moved slowly towards a "gentlemen's agreement" to restore their currencies' convertibility to gold and commit themselves to mutual consultations and intervention to avoid exchange-rate fluctuations. On 25 September 1936, the three governments agreed on a scheme embodying these commitments, with a dollar effectively linked to gold. The Tripartite Agreement—soon joined by Belgium, Switzerland, and the Netherlands—was a step towards rebuilding international economic cooperation. As one scholar has noted, "the Tripartite system may be seen as the beginning of an historical evolution that would issue after World War II in a global dollar standard."[54] For the first time the United States participated openly and prominently in leading the way towards international monetary cooperation, and the symbolic importance was more significant than any real accomplishments of the agreement.

By 1937, one prominent banker was able to name three developments that had given hope to those whose greatest fear was economic nationalism:

> First, the tripartite monetary agreement of last September was a challenge to the application of economic nationalism in monetary affairs. Second, our bilateral trade negotiations are a challenge to economic nationalism in trade affairs. . . . Third, some progress is being made in the direction of the re-creation of a normal international capital market in the Western hemisphere by the recent and current negotiations with South America.[55]

Yet the developing internationalism was hardly the same as the bankers' gold-standard liberal orthodoxy. The new system compromised more with domestic countercyclical demand management and with the imperatives of the embryonic "welfare state."[56] Many of the financiers indeed realized that a return to the classical gold standard was unthinkable and with Leon Fraser in 1936 looked forward merely to "a union of what was best in the old gold standard, corrected on the basis of experience to date, and of what seems practicable in some of the doctrines of 'managed currencies'."[57] Yet during the late New Deal, the foreign exchange cooperation of the Trilateral Agreement, the tentative attempts at trade liberalization (by 1939 the reciprocal trade agreements covered 30 percent of American exports and 60 percent of imports[58]) and newfound moderation towards errant debtors all indicated a less ambiguous internationalist course than at any time since Wilson.

THE EPISODE CONSIDERED

Economic nationalism reigned supreme in the U.S. political economy from 1860 until World War I, while since World War II, economic internationalism has dominated; the period considered here marks the transition from a protected home market to full participation in and leadership of world investment and trade. As such, it is of great interest to those who would draw more general conclusions about the origins of state policy in the international arena. The era involved open conflict over the levers of foreign economic policy. In the midst of this conflict the state was unable to derive and implement a unitary foreign economic policy; faced with a fundamentally divided set of domestic economic interests in foreign economic policy, the state and its policies were also divided. Each grouping of economic interests concentrated its forces where it was strongest: economic internationalists built ties with the State Department and the Federal Reserve System, while economic nationalists concentrated their efforts on Congress and a congenial Commerce Department. As socioeconomic interests were split, so too were policy makers and foreign economic policy itself.

The Depression and eventually World War II weakened the economic nationalists and allowed the state to reshape both policies and policy networks. By the late 1930s, economic nationalists were isolated or ignored, and most relevant decisions were placed within the purview of relatively internationalist bureaucracies. As economic internationalism was consolidated, the foreign-policy bureaucracy came to reflect this tendency—even as, in pre-World War I days, the apparatus had been unshakably nationalist in economic affairs.

The evidence examined here provides little support for theories that regard nation-states as rational, unitary actors in the international system. The most serious challenge of the interwar period is to "statist" assertions that foreign-policy makers represent a national interest that they are able to define and defend.[59] By extension, interwar American foreign-policy making calls into question systemic-level approaches that attempt to derive national foreign policies solely from the position of the nation-state in the international structure.[60]

The national interest is not a blank slate upon which the international system writes at will; it is internally determined by the socioeconomic evolution of the nation in question. Some nations aim primarily to expand their primary exports, others to restrict manufactured imports, still others to protect their overseas investments. These goals are set by the constraints and opportunities that various domestic economic interests face in the world arena and by the underlying strength of the various socioeconomic groups. The ability to pursue these "national interests" successfully, and the best strategy to do so, may similarly be determined by international conditions, but the interests themselves are domestically derived and expressed within the domestic political economy. A nation dominated by agro-exporters may respond to a world depression with redoubled efforts to expand exports, while a nation dominated by domestically oriented industry may respond to the same events with a spurt of industrial protectionism.

Nonetheless, underlying socioeconomic interests are mediated through a set of political institutions that can alter their relative influence. Although the relative importance of American overseas investment to the U.S. economy was roughly equal in the 1920s and 1970s, the institutional setting in the first period was far less suited to the concerns of overseas investors than it was in the second period. By the same token, policy makers can at times take the initiative in reformulating the institutional setting and the policies it has produced, as the Roosevelt administration did in the 1930s.

Indeed, one of the questions this survey of interwar American policy raises is the role of major crises in precipitating changes in political institutions, and in policy makers' room to maneuver. The Depression and World War II removed many of the institutional, coalitional, and ideological ties that had bound policy makers in the 1920s. In the United States the result was the defeat of economic nationalism, but of course the crisis had very different effects elsewhere. It would be comforting to regard the victory of economic internationalism in the United States in the 1930s and 1940s as predetermined by the country's previous evolution and experiences, but this is far too facile a solution to a complex problem. A fuller explanation of the forces underlying American foreign-policy making in the 1930s and 1940s is clearly needed, and indeed it is the logical next step for the historians who have added so much to our understanding of the 1919–1933 period or for their followers.

More generally, the interwar period in American foreign economic policy is a fascinating and extreme case of a broader problem, the conflict between domestic and international interests in modern political economies. Virtually all nations have some economic actors for whom the international economy represents primarily opportunities and others for whom it is mostly threats. This tension is especially evident in major capital exporters, since the needs of holders of overseas assets may well conflict with the desires of domestic groups. The twentieth century is full of examples in which the international-domestic divide has been central to political developments in advanced industrial societies: Britain and Germany in the interwar years are perhaps the best-known examples.[61] The American interwar experience is thus an important example of conflict between internationally oriented and domestically based interests. The conditions under which such interaction leads to major sociopolitical clashes or is overcome, and under which the foreign-policy outcome is aggressively nationalistic or internationally cooperative, or some mix of the two, are obviously of great interest to analysts of international politics.

CONCLUSION

This essay has used the evolution of U.S. foreign economic policy from 1914 to 1940 as a benchmark against which to examine the role of international and domestic determinants in the making of foreign economic policy. We have argued that the foreign economic policy of the United States in the interwar period was the result of domestic political struggle between domestic economic actors with conflicting interests in the international economy, and thus different foreign economic policy preferences. After World War I many U.S. banks and corporations saw great opportunities for overseas expansion, and fought for U.S. foreign economic policy to be assertively "internationalist." Other U.S. corporations saw the world economy primarily as a competitive threat and fought for protection and "isolationism." The evolution of the international political and economic environment, the reaction of domestic actors to this evolution, and the unfolding of domestic political struggle combined to determine U.S. foreign economic policy. This essay's effort to specify the interplay of international and domestic forces in the making of foreign policy, raises real questions about approaches that ignore domestic determinants of foreign policy. Between 1914 and 1940 at least, the foreign economic policy of the United States simply cannot be understood without a careful analysis of conflict among the disparate socioeconomic and political forces at work inside the United States itself. Such domestic forces deserve careful, rigorous, and systematic study.

NOTES

1. Charles Kindleberger, *The World in Depression 1929–1939* (Berkeley: University of California Press, 1973), pp. 297–99. The Carr citation is from his *The Twenty Years Crisis, 1919–1930* (London: Macmillan, 1939), p. 234. A popular British satirical history of the 1930s, under the heading, "A Bad Thing," summarized the results of the Great War somewhat more succinctly: "America was thus clearly top nation, and History came to a." Walter Sellar and Robert Yeatman, *1066 And All That* (New York: Dutton, 1931), p. 115.
2. Robert Dallek, *The American Style of Foreign Policy* (New York: Knopf, 1983) is a good survey of traditional American insularity.
3. The historical literature on the period is so enormous that it is feasible only to cite the most recent important additions. Two review essays and a forum are a good start: Kathleen Burk, "Economic Diplomacy Between the Wars," *Historical Journal* 24 (December 1981), pp. 1003–15; Jon Jacobson, "Is There a New International History of the 1920s?" *American Historical Review* 88 (June 1983), pp. 617–45; and Charles Maier, Stephen Schuker, and Charles Kindleberger, "The Two Postwar Eras and the Conditions for Stability in Twentieth-Century Western Europe," *American Historical Review* 86 (April 1981). Other important works include Denise Artaud, *La question des dettes interalliées et la reconstruction de l'Europe* (Paris: Champion, 1979); Frank Costigliola, *Awkward Dominion: American Political, Economic, and Cultural Relations with Europe 1919–1933* (Ithaca, N.Y.: Cornell University Press, 1984); Michael J. Hogan, *Informal Entente: The Private Structure of Cooperation in Anglo-American Economic Diplomacy, 1918–1928* (Columbia: University of Missouri Press, 1977); Melvyn Leffler, *The Elusive Quest: America's Pursuit of European Stability and French Security, 1919–1933* (Chapel Hill: University of North Carolina Press, 1979); William McNeil, *American Money and the Weimar Republic* (New York: Columbia University Press, 1986); Stephen Shucker, *The End of French Predominance in Europe* (Chapel Hill: University of North Carolina Press, 1976); and Dan Silverman, *Reconstructing Europe after the Great War* (Cambridge: Harvard University Press, 1982). Many of the leading scholars in the field summarize their views in Gustav Schmidt, ed., *Konstellationen Internationaler Politik 1924–1932* (Bochum, W. Ger.: Studienverlag Dr. N. Brockmeyer, 1983).
4. Charles Kindleberger, "Group Behavior and International Trade," *Journal of Political Economy* 59 (February 1951), pp. 30–46; Peter Gourevitch, "International Trade, Domestic Coalitions, and Liberty: Comparative Responses to the Crisis of 1873–1896," *Journal of Interdisciplinary History* 8 (Autumn 1977), pp. 281–313; Peter Gourevitch, "Breaking with Orthodoxy: the Politics of Economic Policy Responses to the Depression of the 1930s," *International Organization* 38 (Winter 1984), pp. 95–129; Thomas Ferguson, "From Normalcy to New Deal: Industrial Structure, Party Competition, and American Public Policy in the Great Depression," *International Organization* 38 (Winter 1984), pp. 41–94.

5. For figures on U.S. foreign private assets see Raymond Goldsmith, *A Study of Savings in the United States,* vol. 1 (Princeton, N.J.: Princeton University Press, 1955), p. 1093.

6. The classical explanation of the process is Raymond Vernon, "International Investment and International Trade in the Product Cycle," *Quarterly Journal of Economics* 80 (May 1966), pp. 190–207.

7. On agricultural and industrial trade preferences in the 1920s, see Barry Eichengreen, "The Political Economy of the Smoot-Hawley Tariff," Discussion Paper No. 1244, Harvard Institute for Economic Research, May 1986.

8. Opposition to the league was indeed led by a prominent nationalist Massachusetts senator whose adamant insistence on protecting manufactured goods while allowing the free import of inputs was ably captured by "Mr. Dooley," who noted that "Hinnery Cabin Lodge pleaded f'r freedom f'r th' skins iv cows" in ways that "wud melt th' heart iv th' coldest mannyfacthrer iv button shoes." Cited in John A. Garraty, *Henry Cabot Lodge* (New York: Knopf, 1953), p. 268; the book contains ample, and somewhat weightier, evidence of Lodge's economic nationalism.

9. David Lake, "The State and American Trade Strategy in the Pre-Hegemonic Era," *International Organization* 42 (Winter, 1988).

10. George Edwards, *The Evolution of Finance Capitalism* (London: Longmans, 1938), pp. 204–5, and U.S. Department of Commerce, *Historical Statistics of the United States* (Washington: GPO, 1960), pp. 139, 537. The definitive work on the period is Kathleen Burk, *Britain, America and the Sinews of War, 1914–1918* (Boston: Allen & Unwin, 1985). See also David Kennedy, *Over Here: The First World War and American Society* (New York: Oxford University Press, 1980); John T. Madden, Marcus Nadler, and Harry C. Sauvain, *America's Experience as a Creditor Nation* (New York: Prentice-Hall, 1937), pp. 44–46; Alexander Dana Noyes, *The War Period of American Finance* (New York: Putnam, 1926), pp. 113–18; William J. Schultz and M. R. Caine, *Financial Development of the United States* (New York: Prentice-Hall, 1937), 503–4.

11. Harold Nicolson, *Dwight Morrow* (New York: Macmillan, 1935), pp. 171–75.

12. Cleona Lewis, *America's Stake in International Investments* (Washington, D.C.: Brookings Institution, 1938), p. 352. See for a discussion of the experience Roberta A. Dayer, "Strange Bedfellows: J. P. Morgan and Co., Whitehall, and the Wilson Administration During World War I," *Business History* 18 (July 1976), pp. 127–51.

13. Lewis, *America's Stake,* p. 355; Nicolson, *Dwight Morrow,* pp. 177–82; Vincent P. Carosso, *Investment Banking in America: A History* (Cambridge, Mass.: Harvard University Press, 1970), pp. 205–14. For a thoughtful survey of the political effects, see John Milton Cooper, Jr., "The Command of Gold Reversed: American Loans to Britain, 1915–1917," *Pacific Historical Review* 45 (May 1976), pp. 209–30.

14. This is Lewis's figure; *America's Stake,* p. 362. Others give different amounts. See for example Noyes, *The War Period,* pp. 162–93; Schultz and Caine, *Financial Development,* pp. 525, 533–42; Hiram Motherwell, *The Imperial Dollar* (New York: Brentano's, 1929), p. 85.

15. Charles Kindleberger, "Origins of United States Direct Investment in France," *Business History Review* 48 (Autumn 1974), p. 390.

16. Scott Nearing and Joseph Freeman, *Dollar Diplomacy* (New York: Huebsch, 1925), p. 273.

17. Lawrence H. Shoup and William Minter, *Imperial Brain Trust: The Council on Foreign Relations and United States Foreign Policy* (New York: Monthly Review, 1977), pp. 11–28.

18. Cited in Frank Costigliola, "United States–European Relations and the Effort to Shape American Public Opinion, 1921–1933," in Schmidt, ed., *Konstellationen Internation-*

aler Politik, p. 43. See also Costigliola, *Awkward Dominion*, pp. 56–75 and 140–66, and Robert A. Divine, *Second Chance: The Triumph of Internationalism in America During World War II* (New York: Atheneum, 1972), pp. 6–23.

19. Thomas W. Lamont, *Across World Frontiers* (New York: Harcourt, Brace, 1951), pp. 215, 217–18.

20. Jacob Viner, "Political Aspects of International Finance," *Journal of Business of the University of Chicago* 1 (April 1928), p. 146.

21. See, in addition to works cited above, Paul P. Abrahams, *The Foreign Expansion of American Finance and its Relationship to the Foreign Economic Policies of the United States, 1907–1921* (New York: Arno, 1976); Herbert Feis, *The Diplomacy of the Dollar: First Era 1919–1932* (Baltimore: Johns Hopkins University Press, 1950); Joan Hoff Wilson, *American Business and Foreign Policy, 1920–1933* (Lexington: University Press of Kentucky, 1971); Frank Costigliola, "The United States and the Reconstruction of Germany in the 1920s," *Business History Review* 50 (Winter 1976), pp. 477–502; and Frank Costigliola, "Anglo-American Financial Rivalry in the 1920s," *Journal of Economic History* 38 (December 1977), pp. 911–34. Because the issues are so widely treated, citations will only be given where necessary to confirm a specific fact, controversial interpretation, or direct quotation.

22. On these issues see the articles by Thomas Lamont, James Sheldon, and Arthur J. Rosenthal in *Annals of the American Academy of Political and Social Science* 88 (March 1920), pp. 114–38.

23. See especially Abrahams, *Foreign Expansion of American Finance;* and Costigliola, "Anglo-American Financial Rivalry," pp. 914–20. For an interesting view of one aspect of the war debts tangle, see Robert A. Dayer, "The British War Debts to the United States and the Anglo-Japanese Alliance, 1920–1923," *Pacific Historical Review* 45 (November 1976), pp. S69–95.

24. Joseph Brandes, *Herbert Hoover and Economic Diplomacy* (Pittsburgh: University of Pittsburgh Press, 1962), pp. 170–96; and Melvyn Leffler, "The Origins of Republican War Debt Policy, 1921–1923," *Journal of American History* 59 (December 1972), pp. 585–601.

25. Cited in Silverman, *Reconstructing Europe*, pp. 157 and 189.

26. Cited in U.S. Congress, House of Representatives, Committee on Banking and Currency, Subcommittee on Domestic Finance, *Federal Reserve Structure and the Development of Monetary Policy, 1915–1935: Staff Report* (Washington, D.C.: GPO, 1971), p. 62. I am grateful to Jane D'Arista for bringing these and other documents to my attention.

27. Hogan, *Informal Entente*, pp. 62–66.

28. See, for example, Stephen V. O. Clarke, *Central Bank Cooperation 1924–1931* (New York: Federal Reserve Bank of New York, 1967), pp. 46–57, and Charles G. Dawes, *A Journal of Reparations* (London: Macmillan, 1939), pp. 262–64, for evidence of just how central the bankers were.

29. The agent-general, S. Parker Gilbert, was a close associate of Morgan partner Russell Leffingwell. Costigliola, "The United States and the Reconstruction of Germany," pp. 485–94; Feis, *Diplomacy of the Dollar,* pp. 40–43; Leffler, *Elusive Quest,* pp. 90–112; Nearing and Freeman, *Dollar Diplomacy,* pp. 221–32; Nicolson, *Dwight Morrow,* pp. 272–78; Schuker, *French Predominance in Europe,* pp. 284–89.

30. For Lamont's optimism, see *Proceedings of the Academy of Political Science* 11 (January 1925), pp. 325–32.

31. Nicolson, *Dwight Morrow,* pp. 191–92.

32. Wilson, *American Business,* pp. 70–75.

33. Cited in Silverman, *Reconstructing Europe*, p. 239.

34. Mary Jane Maltz, *The Many Lives of Otto Kahn* (New York: Macmillan, 1963), pp. 204–5. For the similar views of Norman H. Davis, see *Proceedings of the Academy of Political Science* 12 (January 1928), pp. 867–74. See also Wilson, *American Business*, pp. 65–100.

35. Hoover is cited in Joseph Brandes, "Product Diplomacy: Herbert Hoover's Anti-Monopoly Campaign at Home and Abroad," in Ellis Hawley, ed., *Herbert Hoover as Secretary of Commerce* (Iowa City: University of Iowa Press, 1981), p. 193. See also H. B. Elliston, "State Department Supervision of Foreign Loans," in Charles P. Howland, ed., *Survey of American Foreign Relations 1928* (New Haven, Conn.: Yale University Press for the Council on Foreign Relations, 1928), pp. 183–201; John Foster Dulles, "Our Foreign Loan Policy," *Foreign Affairs* 5 (October 1926), pp. 33–48; Brandes, *Herbert Hoover*, pp. 151–96; Feis, *Diplomacy of the Dollar*, pp. 7–17; Leffler, *Elusive Quest*, pp. 58–64.

36. David Burner, *Herbert Hoover: A Public Life* (New York: Alfred A. Knopf, 1979), p. 186.

37. These are recalculated from Lewis, *America's Stake*, pp. 619–29; her aggregate figures are inexplicably inconsistent.

38. McNeil, *American Money*, p. 282.

39. See Richard H. Meyer, *Banker's Diplomacy* (New York: Columbia University Press, 1970).

40. Frank Costigliola, "The Other Side of Isolationism: The Establishment of the First World Bank, 1929–1930." *Journal of American History* 59 (December 1972), and Harold James, *The Reichsbank and Public Finance in Germany 1924–1933* (Frankfurt: Knapp, 1985), pp. 57–94. On BIS attempts at international financial cooperation from 1930 to 1931, see William A. Brown, Jr., *The International Gold Standard Reinterpreted, 1914–1934*, vol. 2 (New York: National Bureau of Economic Research, 1940), pp. 1035–47. For the views of New York bankers see the articles by Shepard Morgan of Chase and Jackson Reynolds of the First National Bank of New York in *Proceedings of the Academy of Political Science* 14 (January 1931), pp. 215–34, and Shepard Morgan, "Constructive Functions of the International Bank," *Foreign Affairs* 9 (July 1931), pp. 580–91. For an excellent overview of this period, see Clarke, *Central Bank Cooperation*.

41. Cited in Leffler, *Elusive Quest*, p. 238. On German-American financial relations after 1930, see Harold James, *The German Slump: Politics and Economics 1924–1936* (Oxford: Clarendon Press, 1986), pp. 398–413.

42. Lewis, *America's Stake*, pp. 400–1; Foreign Bondholders Protective Council, *Annual Report for 1934* (New York: FBPC, 1934), pp. 218–24.

43. Burner, *Herbert Hoover*, p. 298.

44. M. E. Falkus, "United States Economic Policy and the 'Dollar Gap' in the 1920s," *Economic History Review* 24 (November 1972), pp. 599–623, argues that America's enormous balance-of-trade surplus in the 1920s was due more to the structure and composition of U.S. industry and trade than to trade barriers. Whether this is true or not, the fact remains, as Falkus recognizes, that contemporaries on both sides of the tariff wall *perceived* U.S. tariffs to be of major significance in limiting European exports.

45. Feis, *Diplomacy of the Dollar*, p. 14.

46. These conclusions about American foreign policy in the 1920s differ a bit from those of some of the historians upon whose work my analysis is based. Leffler and Costigliola, especially, stress what they see as the unity of American policy, although both emphasize

the importance of domestic constraints on this policy. In my view both scholars, despite their innovations, are too wedded to a modified Open-Door interpretation that overstates the unity and purposiveness of U.S. economic interests, and this methodological overlay colors their conclusions. I believe that the evidence, even as presented by them, warrants my analytical conclusions.

47. Stephen V. O. Clarke, *The Reconstruction of the International Monetary System: The Attempts of 1922 and 1933*, Princeton Studies in International Finance No. 33 (Princeton, N.J.: International Finance Section, Department of Economics, 1973), pp. 19–39; James R. Moore, "Sources of New Deal Economic Policy: The International Dimension," *Journal of American History* 61 (December 1974), pp. 728–44.

48. See especially John Morton Blum, *Roosevelt and Morgenthau* (Boston: Houghton Mifflin, 1970), pp. 45–53, and Ferguson, "Normalcy to New Deal," pp. 82–85. For a sympathetic European view of Roosevelt's policy, see Paul Einzig, *Bankers, Statesmen and Economists* (London: Macmillan, 1935), pp. 121–57.

49. See Blum, *Roosevelt and Morgenthau*, pp. 40–42, and for an interesting example Irving S. Mitchelman, "A Banker in the New Deal: James P. Warburg," *International Review of the History of Banking* 8 (1974), pp. 35–59. For an excellent survey of the period, see Albert Romasco, *The Politics of Recovery: Roosevelt's New Deal* (New York: Oxford University Press, 1983).

50. For details of the Hull-Peek controversy, see Frederick C. Adams, *Economic Diplomacy: The Export-Import Bank and American Foreign Policy 1934–1939* (Columbia: University of Missouri Press, 1976), pp. 81–93 and Robert Dallek, *Franklin D. Roosevelt and American Foreign Policy 1932–1945* (New York: Oxford University Press, 1979), pp. 84–85, 91–93.

51. For a discussion of the impact of crisis on ideologies and institutions, see Judith Goldstein, "Ideas, Institutions and American Trade Policy," *International Organization* 42 (Winter 1988).

52. Blum, *Roosevelt and Morgenthau*, pp. 64–67; Stephen V. O. Clarke, *Exchange Rate Stabilization in the Mid-1930s: Negotiating the Tripartite Agreement*, Princeton Studies in International Finance No. 41 (Princeton, N.J.: International Finance Section, Department of Economics, 1977), pp. 8–21.

53. *Proceedings of the Academy of Political Science* 17 (May 1936), p. 107.

54. Harold van B. Cleveland, "The International Monetary System in the Inter-War Period," in Benjamin Rowland, ed., *Balance of Power or Hegemony: The Interwar Monetary System* (New York: NYU Press, 1976), p. 51. For a lengthier explanation of the ways in which the Tripartite Agreement marked the turning point in the evolution of U.S. economic internationalism, see Charles Kindleberger, *The World in Depression 1929–1939* (Berkeley: University of California Press, 1973), pp. 257–61. See also Blum, *Roosevelt and Morgenthau*, pp. 76–88; and Clarke, *Exchange Rate Stabilization*, pp. 25–58.

55. Robert B. Warren, "The International Movement of Capital," *Proceedings of the Academy of Political Science* 17 (May 1937), p. 71.

56. John G. Ruggie, "International Regimes, Transactions, and Change: Embedded Liberalism in the Postwar Economic Order," *International Organization* 36 (Spring 1982), pp. 379–415, discusses the order that emerged.

57. *Proceedings of the Academy of Political Science* 17 (May 1936), p. 113.

58. Herbert Feis, *The Changing Pattern of International Economic Affairs* (New York: Harper, 1940), p. 95. Stephen Schuker has, in personal communication, insisted that it was not until 1942 or 1943 that Roosevelt moved away from extreme economic nationalism. He marshals important evidence and convincing arguments to this effect, but the

account presented here reflects current scholarly consensus. If, as he has done in the past, Schuker can disprove the conventional wisdom, this analysis of U.S. foreign economic policy in the late 1930s would, of course, need to be revised in the light of new data.

59. See, for example, Stephen D. Krasner, *Defending the National Interest* (Princeton, N.J.: Princeton University Press, 1978).
60. As, for example, David A. Lake, "International Economic Structures and American Foreign Policy, 1887–1934," *World Politics* 35 (July 1983), pp. 517–43.
61. For a survey of each see Frank Longstreth, "The City, Industry and the State," in Colin Crouch, ed., *State and Economy in Contemporary Capitalism* (London: Croom Helm, 1979), and David Abraham, *The Collapse of the Weimar Republic* (Princeton, N.J.: Princeton University Press, 1981). On a related issue see Paul Kennedy, "Strategy *versus* Finance, in Twentieth-Century Britain," in his *Strategy and Diplomacy 1870–1945* (London: Allen & Unwin, 1983).

Economic Instability and Military Strength: The Paradoxes of the 1950 Rearmament Decision

Fred Block

The crisis created by the Soviet invasion of Afghanistan at the end of 1979 bears a striking resemblance to the events almost thirty years before when North Korean forces invaded South Korea and began the Korean War. In both situations, the invasions were widely seen as proof of the Soviet Unions' commitment to a policy of global conquest, and each invasion precipitated an effort by the administration in Washington to increase dramatically U.S. levels of military spending and military preparedness. To be sure, the events in Korea gave rise to direct U.S. military involvement and the loss of thousands of American lives, while it appears likely that U.S. involvement in Afghanistan will be limited to covert support for the various groups resisting the Soviet-backed regime. Yet despite this difference, there is another even more important similarity: in both situations, the invasion precipitated a shift in U.S. policy that appeared to have been in preparation for some time before. The Carter administration had been gradually shifting toward a more anti-

Fred Block, "Economic Instability and Military Strength: The Paradoxes of the 1950 Rearmament Decision," *Politics and Society* 10, 1 (1980): pp. 35–58. Reprinted by permission.

Soviet foreign policy and toward support for increased military spending. Similarly, pressures had been building up for some time for the administration to overcome the weaknesses of the all-volunteer army by restoring the draft. Hence, a number of the post-Afghanistan policy initiatives of the Carter administration had the quality of initiatives that were waiting for a crisis to justify them, rather than being direct responses to a sudden change in the global political military situation.

While the evidence is still not completely in for the Carter administration's recent policy shifts, the documents are available to indicate that this is precisely what happened with the Truman administration and the Korean invasion.[1] Months before the outbreak of the Korean War, the Truman administration had approved a document called NSC (National Security Council)-68, which called for a massive rearmament effort by the United States and Western Europe as the only means to resist Soviet expansion. Despite the worsening of Soviet-American relations in the period from 1947–49, U.S. defense spending had remained in the vicinity of $15 billion a year. The drafters of NSC-68 proposed a rearmament effort that would bring the level of defense spending to $40 billion a year.[2] But given the mood at the time, which included the widespread view that the Soviets were trying to fool the U.S. into spending its way to national bankruptcy, there was no way to gain public and Congressional support for NSC-68. Instead, the Truman administration bided its time, until the coming of the Korean War, particularly the Chinese involvement in the war, created a changed national mood in which the implementation of NSC-68 became possible. As a result, levels of military spending rose dramatically, far in excess of the immediate requirements of the Korean War, so that by 1954, after the Korean truce, military spending was at $41.1 billion a year.[3]

The similarity between the two crises is more than accidental. In a number of important respects, the period of the Korean War rearmament continues to influence the making of U.S. foreign policy. In order to understand these connections, it is necessary to examine more closely the politics of the 1950 rearmament decision. The present paper will do this through a careful analysis of NSC-68 itself and of related documents published in the State Department's *Foreign Relations of the United States* series. This will necessarily fall far short of a full discussion of the complexities of the rearmament decision; such a project would require extensive archival research and probably several book-length manuscripts. My purpose here is more limited—to highlight a number of key aspects of NSC-68 that are important for understanding the concrete legacy it has left for contemporary U.S. policy makers.

THE LOGIC OF NSC-68

The document NSC-68 (which was only declassified in 1975) is a lengthy and careful review of the global situation. It examines the structure of the U.S.-Soviet conflict, outlines the options available to the U.S., and advocates the particular option of extensive rearmament.[4] The scope of the document is broad—it includes the international military situation, the problems of the world economy, and the morale of Western societies. The document grew out of a review of the world situation begun by Truman in late 1949, in the aftermath of the "fall" of China and the first Soviet atomic explosion. One of the key precipitants of the study was the debate over the desirability of U.S. actions to develop the hydrogen bomb and the compatibility of such an effort with the rest of the national defense effort, but the study moved far beyond that specific issue to a broader review of U.S. strategy.

The document bears many of the marks of a bureaucratic product, such as the frequent resort to lists of factors without specifying their relative importance. This device serves as an attempt at bureaucratic log-rolling to gain support among a variety of different agencies. Nevertheless, the document has a high level of internal coherence, indicating that a small number of people were responsible for the actual drafting, so that it is possible to identify a single major logic at work in the document. In short, the document is not simply a hodgepodge of different agency viewpoints. It is a serious effort to develop a coherent strategy.

Ironically, the task of understanding this logic is made easier by some of the current academic discussions about the capitalist world system. It is ironic because it seems that academic discourse, or at least neo-Marxist academic discourse, is only now catching up to the analysis of policy makers thirty years ago. In the debates generated by Immanuel Wallerstein's work on the capitalist world system,[5] a number of writers have insisted on the need to recognize the analytic distinction between the world market and the competitive state system.[6] International competition, in other words, occurs both in the world market and in the international state system. These two types of competition overlap in a variety of ways, and often success in one realm is translated into success in the other, as when an economically powerful nation is able to afford a strong military or when political-military strength results in economic gains. Wallerstein's critics suggest that the analytic distinction must be constantly borne in mind, first, because it is needed to explain those important instances where success in one realm has negative consequences in the other, and second, without the distinction, it is too easy to slip into an economic determinism in which the dynamics of political-military rivalry are not given their due in historical explanation.[7]

In the following passage that appears near the beginning of NSC-68, the drafters of the document show that they clearly understood the distinction between objectives in the international economic realm and objectives in the competitive state system:

> Our overall policy at the present time may be described as one designed to foster a world environment in which the American system can survive and flourish. It therefore rejects the concept of isolation and affirms the necessity of our positive participation in the world community.
>
> This broad intention embraces two subsidiary policies. One is a policy which we would probably pursue even if there were no Soviet threat. It is a policy of attempting to develop a healthy international community. The other is the policy of containing the Soviet system. These two policies are closely interrelated and interact on one another. Nevertheless, the distinction between them is basically valid and contributes to a clearer understanding of what we are trying to do.[8]

For the drafters of NSC-68, a healthy international community meant the restoration of an open world economy in which goods and capital were able to flow across national boundaries in response to market forces. The underlying assumptions linking such an international community to the survival of the American system were spelled out with brutal clarity by Dean Acheson (secretary of state at the time of NSC-68) in Congressional testimony in 1944 that has often been quoted:

> We cannot go through another ten years like the ten years at the end of the Twenties and the beginning of the Thirties, without having the most far-reaching consequences upon our economic and social system. . . . When we look at that problem we may say it is a problem of markets. You don't have a problem of production. The United States has unlimited creative energy. The important thing is markets. We have to see that what the country produces is used and is sold under financial arrangements which make its production possible. . . . You must look to foreign markets.
>
> If you wish to control the entire trade and income of the United States, which means the life of the people, you could probably fix it so that everything produced here would be consumed here, but that would completely change our constitution, our relations of property, human liberty, our very conceptions of law. And nobody contemplates that. Therefore, you find you must look to other markets and those markets are abroad. . . .[9]

Acheson's testimony highlights the close connection between the stability of the domestic U.S. economy in the postwar period and the organization of the international economy. In light of the enormous productiveness of U.S. industry and agriculture and market-imposed limits on domestic purchasing power, the U.S. appeared to face a return to economic depression unless some solution could be found to the problem of creating adequate demand. The solution that required the least change in existing institutions and that had the support of the largest industrial firms and banks was an international one. The United States would run an export surplus for a period of years, exporting substantially more to the rest of the world than it imported.[10] This export surplus would be financed by a dramatic increase in U.S. foreign investment, as U.S. business took advantage of profitable opportunities abroad. This solution would provide markets for U.S. surpluses of agricultural and industrial commodities, supplementing domestic demand with foreign demand, and it would maximize the opportunities available for U.S. business. But its viability depended upon the restoration of a stable international monetary order with a high level of openness to market forces. Without such a stable and open international order, the U.S. would not be able to find markets abroad for its products, nor would overseas investment opportunities be attractive to U.S. firms, since there would be little guarantee that profits could be repatriated. In sum, U.S. policy makers shared the realistic assessment that the strength of the domestic economy was inseparable from the task of stabilizing the international monetary order—creating "a healthy international community."[11]

The drafters of NSC-68 recognized that the creation of an international economic order that was consistent with U.S. economic strength was a problem distinct from the rivalry with the Soviet Union in the international state system. There were nevertheless significant overlaps between the two realms. First, nations that came under Soviet political-military influence were unlikely to cooperate with the U.S. in creating an open world economy. Second, the failure of the U.S. to create a stable international economic order and prevent the return to depression conditions would likely bring to power in Europe leftist regimes that would be more sympathetic to the Soviet Union.[12] Nevertheless, the drafters insisted that the distinction between the two policy areas "is basically valid and contributes to a clearer understanding of what we are trying to do."

This assertion seems strangely out of place. The thrust of the document is to forget the distinction by defining the U.S. global position strictly in political-military terms. The rhetoric of NSC-68 repeatedly proclaims the existence of a political-military conflict that threatens the very existence of the West, so that economic questions pale in comparison. On the first page of NSC-68, the drafters write:

> . . . the Soviet Union, unlike previous aspirants to hegemony, is animated by a new fanatic faith, antithetical to our own, and seeks to impose its absolute authority over the rest of the world. Conflict has, therefore, become endemic and is waged, on the part of the Soviet Union, by violent or non-violent methods in accordance with the dictates of expediency. . . . Any substantial further extension of the area under the domination of the Kremlin would raise the possibility that no coalition adequate to confront the Kremlin with greater strength could be assembled. It is in this context that this Republic and its citizens in the ascendancy of their strength stand in their deepest peril.[13]

And the document's final paragraph begins:

> The whole success of the proposed program hangs ultimately on the recognition by this Government, the American people, and all free peoples, that the cold war is in fact a real war in which the survival of the free world is at stake.[14]

There was good reason for this rhetoric; the drafters of NSC-68 believed that a rearmament policy would solve the problems in both the political-military realm and the economic realm and that a rearmament policy could be sold only through an emphasis on a military threat. More specifically, the drafters were afraid that only in the context of a full militarization of foreign policy would Congress be induced to provide the funds necessary to achieve the critical economic policy objectives.

As we shall see, confusing the distinction between political-military and economic objectives was a tactical expedient designed to solve immediate problems. The brief reference to the importance of the distinction makes sense as a reminder of the sleight of hand that the drafters were performing because they wanted to keep in mind the distinction for long-term strategic purposes. They were aware, in short, of the dangers to a dominant power of overemphasizing one competitive realm at the expense of the other, and they did not want the current expedient to become long-term policy.

THE CONTEXT: INTERNATIONAL ECONOMIC INSTABILITY

To understand why the drafters resorted to this expedient, it is necessary to examine both the international economic context and the international military context. The key economic problem for the United States in the postwar period was that the U.S. enthusiasm for an open world economy was shared by only a tiny fraction of the Western European population, since even many European capitalists were skeptical of the American design.[15] Behind this skepticism lay two concrete realities of Europe's postwar situation: strong inflationary pressures and a deterioration of Europe's international payments position. The inflation was rooted in intense struggles over inadequate supplies of goods. The war had impaired the capacity of the European economies to produce civilian goods, and the end of the war generated tremendous demands on the existing civilian capacity. Capitalists wanted resources to rebuild their plants, while workers wanted more goods and social services as compensation for the long years of war and depression. The results of this conflict were intense inflationary pressures.

No matter whether inflation was held in check by price controls or allowed free reign, the inflationary pressures made any movement toward economic liberalism impractical. In fact, in the immediate postwar years, the movement was entirely in the direction of increased controls over international economic transactions. Exchange controls were carried over from the war to minimize the flow of capital into more stable currencies. Quantitative restrictions were placed on imports so that strong domestic demand would not lead to disastrous trade deficits. Governments also negotiated a series of bilateral trading agreements that made it possible to continue more international trade under conditions where domestic prices were largely irrelevant. Finally, state trading—government centralization of trade in certain commodities—was increasingly resorted to, which also had the effect of severing domestic prices from international prices.

Since the U.S. and Canada did not suffer from the same inflationary pressures, any effort by the Europeans toward international economic liberalization would have led to disastrous outflows of hard currency to these two nations, which had both ample supplies of goods and far more stable currencies. Such an outcome would have been very serious since Europe's international economic position had already deteriorated dramatically from prewar patterns. Before the war, Western Europe was able to finance a trade deficit of some $2.1 billion a year with its earnings from invisibles—shipping, banking, and returns on foreign investments—largely in the Third World. By 1947, Western Europe was running a deficit on those invisibles of some $0.6 billion. The shift occurred because of the liquidation of foreign investments, the accumulation of overseas debts, and the costs of ongoing military efforts in Vietnam, Indonesia, and Malaya. This shift meant that the prewar triangular pattern, in which Europe financed its deficit with the United States with surpluses earned in Asia, could not continue. Since Europe's currency reserves had also declined sharply, there was no obvious way that Europe could finance its trade deficit with the U.S. In the short term, Western Europe had little to export, and in the long term, U.S. protectionism made it unlikely that Western Europe could pay for its dollar imports with exports to the U.S.

The nightmare for U.S. policy makers was that this situation might lead Europe to insulate itself permanently from the U.S. economy. If Europe could not finance its deficit with the U.S., nor risk an economic liberalization that would include the U.S., the Europeans might erect a system of controls that would sharply restrict U.S. exports to Europe. Such controls would also restrict U.S. investment in Europe, since exchange controls would cast doubt on the ability of firms to repatriate profits earned on European investments. Furthermore, if Europe continued down that course, trade between Europe and its former colonies in Asia and Africa would be organized along bilateral lines that would discourage U.S. penetration of those areas. The prospect was of U.S. economic activity largely restricted to the Western hemisphere, leading perhaps to the fundamental institutional changes that Acheson had warned of in 1944.

By 1947 it was clear that without a major American initiative that nightmare would become a reality. Western Europe's imports from the U.S. had already begun to decline because of the lack of means to finance them, and Europe's economic controls appeared likely to harden into a permanent arrangement. It was in this context that the Marshall Plan was devised. The plan represented a multifaceted attack on the various obstacles to Western European participation in an open world economy.

Most obviously, the Marshall Plan provided a means to finance continued Western European imports from the United States at a level of $4 to $5 billion a year. This postponed any chance that Western Europe would close itself off to U.S. exports, and it reversed the decline in the level of U.S. exports. However, the policy makers were keenly aware that Congress was unlikely to approve Marshall Aid for more than a limited number of years. As it was, Congressional resistance to what was widely perceived as a giveaway of U.S. dollars was only overcome through the deliberate creation and exaggeration of Cold War tensions by the Truman administration.[16] From the start, therefore, the problem was how to avoid a reassertion of Western Europe's need to restrict its economic links to the United States once Marshall Aid ended.

The proposed solution was to use the period of the Marshall Plan to strengthen the Western European economies to the point where they could successfully compete in an open world economy. Most immediately this meant squeezing the inflation out of those economies through a combination of deflationary economic policies and political maneuvers designed to weaken the union movements. Additional policies were needed to achieve the long-term goal; great emphasis was placed on encouraging productive investment to strengthen Western Europe's export capacity. Recognizing that the small size of the different European economies could result in needless duplication of capacity, U.S. policy makers supported Western European regionalism as a means to increase the efficiency of new investments. Support for regionalism also made possible a gradualist program of economic liberalization. Since it was impractical to expect nations to move directly from bilateral trading arrangements to full participation in an open world economy, liberalization within Western Europe could be an intermediary step on the road to full liberalization. Finally, Western European regionalism gave legitimacy to the controversial U.S. goal of restoring Germany's industrial strength, which was seen by U.S. policy as indispensable for Western Europe's future participation in an open world economy.[17]

In a number of respects the Marshall Plan was a brilliant success. It provided a temporary solution to the dollar problem, halted the movement toward economic closure, and shifted the European political climate in a pro-American direction. It was also successful in weakening the left and in slowing inflation. Nevertheless, its long-term goals remained elusive. To make Western Europe's economy self-supporting in dollars in an open world economy required major structural changes in the pattern of world trade, which could not be accomplished in a four-year period. It was simply too large a task to alter the practices of European businessmen, to develop efficient mechanisms for planning investments within nations, to achieve a high level of economic coordination across nations, and to overcome Congressional protectionism to expand U.S. markets for European exports. By 1949 it was already clear that when the Marshall Plan came to an end in 1951 the United States would be faced with the same danger—the progressive insulation of the European economies.

But there were also a number of factors that made these concerns even more immediate during the course of 1949. First, there was the continuing possibility that Congress would sharply reduce Marshall Plan appropriations for the third or fourth years of the plan, precipitating a more immediate crisis. Second, Great Britain experienced a serious foreign exchange crisis during 1949. It had been the hope of U.S. policy makers that Great Britain and the British pound would provide a bridge between the U.S. and Western Europe in the constructing of an open world economy. To this end, the U.S. had pressured Britain in 1947 to dismantle many of its exchange controls, so that the pound could again play a role in financing international trade. The results of the experiment were disastrous, and exchange controls were quickly reimposed. Yet in 1949, even with controls and Marshall Plan aid, Great Britain was running an insupportable dollar deficit. The Commonwealth ministers responded by increasing their restrictions on dollar imports and threatened even more severe restrictions if more dollar aid were not forthcoming. And this pressure by Britain for a greater share of Marshall Aid came at a time when there were already fierce conflicts over the distribution of the aid—conflicts that threatened the continuation of European-American cooperation. Third, the U.S. economy slipped into recession in late 1948. Unemployment averaged 5.9 percent during 1949 and reached a peak of 7.6 percent in February of 1950. Since this was the first postwar recession, there was little reason to assume that recovery would occur automatically. It was just as plausible to see the economic downturn as a prelude to the return of the Great Depression. Hence, when U.S. exports began to drop in the second half of 1949, anxiety increased that international factors would intensify deflationary pressures at home. Finally, there were indications of economic slowdown in Western Europe during 1949. While these slowdowns generally originated in deliberate anti-inflationary policies, their continuation could further reduce demand for U.S. exports.

In short, it was relatively easy during the second half of 1949 to construct apocalyptic scenarios in which Britain's problems and economic stagnation on the Continent served to reduce U.S. exports. This reduction, coming on top of a U.S. recession caused by lagging industrial investment, could push the U.S. economy into a downward spiral.

THE CONTEXT: MILITARY STRENGTH

At the same time, the United States faced serious problems in its political-military competition with the Soviet Union. The successful Soviet atomic test came sooner than U.S. policy makers had anticipated, and it meant the loss of the self-confidence that the atomic monopoly had given the U.S.[18] Furthermore, during 1949, there was mounting pressure within Europe for direct negotiations between the United States and the Soviet Union to reduce global tensions. The primary issue to be negotiated was the future of Germany.[19] It was a central tenet of U.S. policy that an economically restored West Germany be strongly oriented toward the West. It was feared by U.S. policy makers that in light of West Germany's strategic location and its economic strength, its neutralization would shift the balance of power in Europe strongly in favor of the Soviets. Without West Germany as an anti-Soviet bulwark—politically, economically, and militarily—France, Italy, and Great Britain would necessarily move closer to the Soviets. This was the threatened "Finlandization" of Western Europe. Just as Finland maintained its independence but was forced to accommodate itself to the Soviet Union in certain areas of policy, so U.S. policy makers feared that all of Western Europe would be Finlandized if Germany were neutralized.

U.S. policy makers believed that if a general European settlement were negotiated during 1949–50, it would be impossible for the U.S. to resist the neutralization of Germany. The problem was that neutralization was an obvious logical solution and it was attractive to those many Europeans who found the idea of an economically and militarily revived Germany abhorrent. Hence, U.S. policy was to avoid negotiation while actively working to incorporate West Germany into a pro-Western alliance. To justify this policy, Dean Acheson used the concept "negotiation from strength" to mean that the United States was eager to negotiate a general European settlement but was only willing to do so when it could come into negotiations from a position of strength.

NSC-68 proposed to create that strength through a massive rearmament effort that would triple U.S. military spending, while also rearming the other members of the Western Alliance. The latter effort would require both dramatic increases in military spending, particularly in France and Britain, and greatly increased U.S. military and economic aid to Western Europe. This rearmament effort was justified by an analysis that stressed the Kremlin's expansionary ambitions and insisted that only through such an effort could liberty and freedom be preserved.

While the rhetoric stressed the political-military necessity of rearmament, it is also clear from the document that rearmament was seen as a solution to the economic weakness of the West. The necessity of continued aid to support Western Europe's rearmament would provide a continuing means to overcome Western Europe's dollar shortage—both immediately and after the Marshall Plan. The advantages of linking aid to rearmament are spelled out in a State Department memo, written in late 1950, that argues for incorporating all aid to Europe into one bill:

> It seems desirable, therefore, if it is feasible, to deal with the European problem in one title. We have been furnishing three kinds of assistance to these areas, (a) military end items, (b) economic aid in support of the military effort abroad [for example, support for the French in Indochina], (c) aid to achieve European economic recovery. The advantages of combining all of these types of aid in one title are as follows. (1) Congress is more likely to be sympathetic toward a program based upon military security than one in which part of the justification is based on continued economic recovery. (2) The

three types of assistance are in effect closely interrelated. Maximum flexibility is needed between funds available for procuring U.S. manufactured end-use items and for the production of such items abroad. *The distinction between aid in support of foreign military effort abroad and aid for economic recovery is largely artificial.*[20]

Furthermore, the rearmament effort was intended to respond to the weakness of demand in both the U.S. and the Western European economies. In NSC-68's assessment of the West's over-all economic situation, the drafters write:

> . . . there are grounds for predicting that the United States and other free nations will within a period of a few years at most experience a decline in economic activity of serious proportions unless more positive governmental programs are developed than are now available.[21]

This is supplemented by another passage that argues:

> With a high level of economic activity, the United States could soon attain a gross national product of $300 billion per year, as was pointed out in the President's Economic Report (January 1950). Progress in this direction would permit, and might itself be aided by, a build-up of the economic and military strength of the United States and the free world; furthermore, if a dynamic expansion of the economy were achieved, the necessary build-up could be accomplished without a decrease in the national standard of living because the required resources could be attained by siphoning off a part of the annual increment in the gross national product.[22]

These passages indicate that the drafters were influenced by Keynesian thought and saw military spending as a way to bolster economic activity. For the United States, rearmament could lead to such a great increase in economic activity that it would be possible to have both guns and butter—a continually rising standard of living. For Western Europe, rearmament would boost economic activity to prevent destabilizing unemployment,[23] and it would expand West Germany's Western markets. The latter was critical in order to reinforce West Germany's pro-Western orientation.

The logic of NSC-68 therefore was to accomplish both objectives of U.S. foreign policy—the containment of the Soviet Union and the creation of an open world economy—through rearmament. Military spending would strengthen the Western Alliance, including West Germany, by adding military interdependence to a precarious economic interdependence, and it would provide the strength that was seen as a precondition for negotiating with the Soviets. At the same time, rearmament would overcome the economic weakness of the West by providing a means to finance Europe's dollar deficit and a means to bolster economic demand.

CRITICISMS AND CONTRADICTIONS

NSC-68's strategy of solving economic problems through military means depended on a rather simple transposition. Instead of honestly confronting the weaknesses of liberal capitalism and the enormous difficulties of creating an open world economy, the drafters chose to transpose Western economic weakness into Soviet military strength. To be sure, the West's economic weakness did greatly enhance the Soviet Union's global strategic position, but this source of strength had nothing to do with Soviet military capacities. The drafters believed, however, that they could provide a justification for rearmament policies by vastly exaggerating Soviet military strength. These rearmament measures would, in turn, strengthen the West militarily and, as we have seen, provide solutions to some of the West's most pressing economic problems. And the success of such a policy would make further use of this transposition unnecessary because the main source of Western weakness would be overcome. In sum, the heart of NSC-68 was the use, as a short-term expedient, of a rhetoric that subordinated all other considerations to the direct confrontation with the Soviet military challenge.

There were voices that objected strenuously to this strategy. No less a figure than George Kennan, an increasingly marginal figure in Acheson's State Department, developed a careful critique of the logic that led to NSC-68. In a memo to Acheson in February of 1950, Kennan sought to show how the logic underlying the Marshall Plan was fundamentally different from the logic of those favoring rearmament:

> Because the Russian attack, ideologically speaking, was a global one, challenging the ultimate validity of the entire non-communist outlook on life, predicting its failure, and playing on the force of that prediction as a main device in the conduct of the cold war, it could be countered only by a movement on our part equally comprehensive, designed to prove the validity of liberal institutions, to confound the predictions of their failure, to prove that a society not beholden to Russian communism could still "work." In this way, the task of combatting communism became as broad as the whole great range of our responsibilities as a world power, and came to embrace all those things which would have had to be done anyway—even in the absence of a communist threat—to assure the preservation and advance of civilization. That Moscow might be refuted, it was necessary that something else should succeed. Thus Moscow's threat gave great urgency to the solution of all those bitter problems of adjustment which in any event would have plagued and tested the countries of the non-communist world in the wake of these two tremendous and destructive world conflicts. And it was not enough, in the face of this fact, to treat the communist attack as purely an outside one, to be dealt with only by direct counter-action. Such an approach was sometimes necessary; but primarily *communism had to be viewed as a crisis of our own civilization, and the principal antidote lay in overcoming the weaknesses of our own institutions.*[24]

For Kennan, the Marshall Plan succeeded because it simultaneously countered the Soviet Union and strengthened liberal institutions in the West. He could not see how the rearmament policy—predicated on the assumption that the threat was strictly external—could solve the problems posed by "the weaknesses of our own institutions." While Kennan could see clearly the transposition involved in the rearmament policy and warn of its limitations, he himself lacked a serious policy alternative. In this period, he campaigned for an economic merger between the United States and Great Britain as a way to bolster Britain's economy and make it an effective bridge between the U.S. and Western Europe.[25] The immense impracticality of this alternative suggests both the enormous seriousness of the West's economic problems and the difficulty of devising a solution that did not rest on the militarization of foreign policy.

In fact, rearmament became official policy largely because of the absence of coherent alternatives. This can be seen by focusing on one particular aspect of the policy—the mechanisms for financing Western Europe's dollar deficit. The rearmament policy provided a number of different ways to funnel dollars into Western European hands. First, dollar aid to support the rearmament effort was far more popular with Congress than simple economic aid, but it could easily be used for many of the same purposes. Second, the stationing of large numbers of U.S. troops in Western Europe and elsewhere added to the outflow of dollars. Finally, offshore procurement of military goods provided an additional form of dollar aid. The U.S. could, for example, buy weapons for France from Great Britain and thus provide Britain with much needed dollars. Together these mechanisms accounted for a substantial and flexible outflow of dollars.

Those attempting to develop an alternative policy to rearmament had to figure a comparable way to provide enough dollars to Western Europe to finance current deficits and discourage any attempts at increased European protectionism. They had only three means available—increased private investment in Europe, increased imports of European goods, or increased government aid. The first was impractical because political and economic instability in Western Europe acted as a major disincentive for business investment. Furthermore, resort to major private (or even public) loans to underwrite European currency stabilization had been discredited by the disastrous experience of the interwar years. Increasing Europe's ability to earn dollars through exports quickly ran into the problem of Congressional protectionism—a powerful force that was unlikely to compromise in the midst of a domestic economic downturn. Finally, any scheme for government aid had to involve some procedure for disarming Congressional skepticism, which is what Kennan sought to do with his improbable idea of a merger between the United States and Great Britain. This skepticism had made it increasingly difficult for the Truman administration to gain Congressional approval for Marshall Plan aid with each passing year. In order to gain such approval, the administration had constantly promised the Congress that the Marshall Plan would succeed in making Western Europe self-sufficient by the program's end. Thus, to preserve the Marshall Plan for its four years, the administration had to bargain away its chance to ask for any continuation of the program.[26] In sum, the seriousness of the problem is indicated by the unlikelihood that even the full militarization of foreign policy could have succeeded in overcoming Congressional resistance to additional aid for Europe, had it not been for the crisis atmosphere created by the Chinese entrance into the Korean War.

The architects of NSC-68 succeeded not because they had a compelling view of the long-term needs of U.S. capitalism, but because they put together a policy that provided solutions to a number of immediate and pressing problems. And moreover, they were provided with an opportunity—in the form of the Korean War—that made their proposals politically practical. The strength of their proposals was that they tended to minimize immediate risks, in contrast, for example, to efforts to reform Western institutions that might have greater long-term benefits but less chance of immediate success. But while the rearmament policy made sense as a five-year plan, its critical flaw was that it biased policy makers toward the militarization of foreign policy for the generation to follow.[27]

THE LEGACY OF NSC-68

Even thirty years later, the legacy of NSC-68 weighs heavily on U.S. foreign policy. It was NSC-68's success in solving short-term problems of U.S. foreign policy that elevated militarization of foreign policy into a paradigmatic solution to foreign policy difficulties. To be sure, the militarization of foreign policy, and the accompanying adoption of Manichean imagery that holds a foreign enemy responsible for all problems, is a temptation with an ancient lineage. The successes that came in the wake of the Truman administration's surrender to this temptation served to make this policy choice even more attractive. Hence, both John Kennedy and Jimmy Carter, when faced with serious obstacles to successful domestic policy initiatives and deteriorating relations within the Western Alliance, moved in the direction of the militarization of foreign policy, opting for increased defense budgets and more belligerent anti-Communist rhetoric. If such tactics succeeded for Truman—both in terms of his own popularity and in easing the economic and political problems of U.S. foreign policy—then surely they might work once again.

Yet the continuing appeal of the paradigm of militarization of foreign policy cannot be explained simply in terms of its earlier success; there are three distinctive structures, created in substantial part by NSC-68, that act to prevent American policy makers from straying too far from the logic of militarization. These structures are the Western military alliance, the military-industrial complex, and the "loss of China" complex.

The Western Alliance

As we have seen, a key component of the strategy of NSC-68 was to overcome Western Europe's tendency to pursue an independent economic course by binding Western Europe to the U.S. with military ties. With the passage of time, this dimension of U.S. policy has become progressively more important, since Western Europe's greater economic power creates multiple interest conflicts between it and the United States. The principal means by which the U.S. has acted to dampen these conflicts and to discourage Western Europe from pursuing the independent policy has been to remind Western Europe of its dependence on the U.S. defense commitment. The great risk for U.S. policy of detente with the Soviet Union is that it would act to sharply reduce Western Europe's fear of the Soviet Union, leading to a weakening of the Western Alliance and increased conflict between the U.S. and Western European governments over such issues as trade, international monetary arrangements, and energy. In this context, periodic resorts to militarization and the revival of Cold War tension between the U.S. and the Soviet Union generate pressures to bring Western Europe back into line.[28]

The Military-Industrial Complex

The rearmament proposed by NSC-68 led to the creation of a large sector of the economy devoted to military production. This sector accounted for a considerable percentage of total corporate profits and total employment in the economy. Once in place, this military-industrial complex tended to be self-perpetuating, since the corporations involved and their employees exerted strong pressure for continuing high levels of military spending. This pressure was effectively transmitted through Congress, as individual senators and representatives acted to maintain stable or increasing levels of employment in their districts. This pressure has been sufficient to prevent any sharp decreases in military spending, except in the immediate aftermath of the Korean and Vietnam Wars.

There have been, however, two periods, 1954–60 and 1971–77, in which the level of military spending remained roughly stable, so that defense spending declined considerably as a percentage of GNP. Yet in the latter part of each of these periods, there was mounting pressure for dramatic new increases in military spending. The pressure derives directly from the military-industrial complex, which stands to gain from higher levels of spending. And in both periods a strong intellectual case could be made for higher levels of defense spending because of the dynamics of a competitive arms race. By the late fifties, for example, the Soviet Union was finally developing the military capacities that the advocates of rearmament in 1950 had foreseen as an immediate threat to the U.S. That the Soviets developed those capacities largely in response to the American rearmament was irrelevant to the case for increased military spending in the early sixties. Similarly, by the late seventies, defense analysts could point with alarm to the Soviet gains that had been made in response to increased American military spending of the sixties.[29] While politicians might be able to resist these pressures for a new round of escalated military spending for a number of years out of a fear of too much stimulus to the economy or out of a commitment to civilian spending, it is difficult to resist the tide indefinitely. The forces for rearmament are persistent and well organized, and the instability of international politics seems bound to provide them with an opportunity to prevail.

Moreover, the structure of the military-industrial complex itself seems to give plausibility to these demands for periodic jumps in the level of military spending. In order to solidify the corporate-government alliance that is at the heart of the military-industrial complex, it was necessary to assure business especially high levels of profits as an exchange for the loss of business autonomy that results from having the government as one's only market for certain goods. This meant institutionalizing certain practices, such as the cost-plus contracts, that guarantee generous corporate profits. The results of such arrangements are that a high degree of waste has been built into the system of military procurement.[30] Added to this is the special attractiveness in military development of unusually large or exotic weapon systems—an attractiveness that derives from the interagency and intercorporate rivalries within the military-industrial complex.

Taken together, these two factors operate against efficient and effective use of military spending at any level. As long as one takes these two factors as given, then a plausible case can always be made that current levels of military preparedness are inadequate and that billions more should be spent both to produce new generations of more basic military weapons and to bring to fruition the large and elaborate systems that are still on the drawing boards.

The "Loss of China" Complex

The final structure is the one that goes furthest to explain why the paradigm of militarization operates so much more strongly on Democratic presidents than on Republicans. The loss-of-China complex operates as a structure precisely because its rests on the special dynamics of the two-party system in the U.S. Here, too, the implementation of NSC-68 created a structure that still shapes policy.

While NSC-68 itself remained classified, its implementation required that the Truman administration adopt in its public rhetoric the Manichean imagery of a world divided between Communist evil and the Western forces of good. This imagery included the notion of a tipping point—any further increase in Communist power anywhere in the world might effectively tip the balance, so that the forces of good would no longer be able to resist the global spread of tyranny.[31] This imagery, of course, had largely been monopolized by the extreme anti-Communist right-wing. In adopting it, the Truman administration gave enormous legitimacy to this extreme anti-Communist viewpoint. In short, by making the defeat of Soviet expansionism the only question of American foreign policy, the Truman administration made itself quite vulnerable to those who felt that insufficient effort had been expended in saving China from the Communists. Within the Manichean framework, the risk of the U.S. being bogged down in a major land war in Asia was certainly less than the dangers involved in increasing the Communist empire by hundreds of millions of Chinese.

Added to this vulnerability was the standard dynamic of a two-party system in which parties out of office move away from the political center. Hence, the position of McCarthy and his allies in the right-wing of the Republican party was enhanced in a period where the normal drift of the party was to the right. The result was the mobilization of large sectors of public opinion against the Truman administration for being soft on communism at precisely the point at which the administration was launching a hard-line anti-Communist foreign policy. Thus Acheson, one of the major architects of NSC-68, was excoriated by McCarthy and others for a host of crimes ranging from his defense of Alger Hiss to the loss of China.[32]

This right-wing attack was doubly costly for the leading figures of the Democratic party. It exposed some of them to a humiliating personal attack that forced them to defend themselves against charges of treason, and it played an important role in the Democratic electoral defeat in 1952. While Eisenhower's victory that year was hardly in doubt, the extent of the Republican landslide certainly owed a good deal to the rhetoric that charged the Democrats with "twenty years of treason."

The lesson that Democratic politicians and policy makers derived from this trauma was not the obvious one. They might well have recognized that adopting the right wing's rhetoric is a dangerous tactic, since the right wing will always be able to find fault with the lack of Democratic party single-mindedness in combating Communism. However, once the genie had been let out of the bottle—once the Democratic party had endorsed the Manichean world view—it was risky for Democratic leaders to repudiate it openly. Instead, the Democrats derived a different lesson—the necessity of avoiding situations where one could be held responsible for the loss of one or another country. The Democrats felt that right-wing charges of insufficient anti-Communist vigilance only became a serious threat when the right-wing could point to a specific country that had been allowed to enter the Communist empire as a result of inaction by a Democratic administration.

The resulting loss-of-China complex explains a great deal of the variation in U.S. imperial foreign policy over the past thirty years. Republican administrations have been far freer to develop a strategy of intervention that took account of the actual specifics of the situation. Hence, Eisenhower was able to decide against American intervention in Vietnam after the defeat of the French at Dienbienphu, since he had little reason to fear a concerted attack on his administration for losing North Vietnam. The Democrats could hardly be persuasive in launching such an attack, and the right wing of the Republican party was a minor threat with the Republican party in office. This meant that Eisenhower could pursue interventions, such as those in Iran, Guatemala, and Lebanon, where the military costs were slight and avoid those that might sap U.S. strength.

In contrast, the loss-of-China complex was a key factor in the Kennedy-Johnson period, making it difficult for those administrations to develop a rational policy of intervention.[33] The resurgence of the Republican right-wing that resulted in the Goldwater nomination in 1964 made the Democrats extremely wary of giving the Republicans an issue that would expand their appeal. This fear operated as a major determinant of the Vietnam policy, since South Vietnam was clearly a prime candidate for the China role. To avoid this danger the Democratic administrations stressed military toughness and gradually escalated the war effort. The key turning point came around 1966 as it became clear that it would take a huge American military effort to defeat the Communist forces and that even such a massive effort might fail. It was at this point that a number of proposals for strategic retreat emerged within high-level policy circles, such as the Gavin plan for a U.S. retreat to coastal enclaves.

The Johnson administration steadfastly resisted such proposals, pursuing instead its policy of continuing escalation, despite severe costs for the domestic economy, further deterioration of the U.S. balance of payments, and growing domestic disorder. The administration's stubbornness was rooted in the anxiety that any policy other than continued escalation was too risky in that it might lead to the collapse of the Saigon government and a Communist victory.[34] Domestic considerations, in short, forced the administration to pursue an extremely dangerous policy rather than take the reasonable risks involved in a strategic retreat that counted on U.S. air power to prevent a Communist military victory. Ironically, it was precisely the latter policy that the Republican administration pursued. It hardly bears repeating that the long-term consequences of the Johnson administration's refusal to make that strategic retreat were enormous for the U.S. global position. It was precisely the ineffectiveness of the U.S. escalation from 1966 to 1968 that created the image of the U.S. as a helpless giant—an image that was important for OPEC's defiance of the U.S. in the seventies. Furthermore, the prolongation of the war undermined the strength of the U.S. army itself and created a popular backlash within the U.S. against an interventionist foreign policy. Finally, the post-1966 escalation rapidly accelerated the tendency toward declining U.S. industrial competitiveness and permanent inflation.

While the Carter administration has avoided direct military intervention in Afghanistan, its definition of the Soviet invasion of that country as the greatest threat since World War II clearly reflects its terror of being held responsible for another strategic loss. Once again, the right wing of the Republican party is dominant and holds the prospect of gaining an electoral victory if it can effectively hang the treason label on the Carter administration. In recognition of this, the Carter administration has sought to undercut the Republicans by borrowing both their rhetoric and their foreign policy—rearmament, revival of the Cold War, and a return to conscription. The Carter administration hopes that by moving quickly to a militarization of foreign policy it can cover itself with the flag before the Republicans have the chance to focus public attention on responsibility for the loss of Afghanistan. Short of directly opposing the right's Manichean world view, this is the only real strategy open to Carter. It is, however, a strategy with considerable risks, since we know that the Republicans' right was successful in attacking the Truman administration just when that administration had fully accepted the militarization of foreign policy. The right's ultimate resource is that it can argue that any specific policy moves are "too little and too late" given the seriousness of the danger—a seriousness that even the Democrats have been forced to acknowledge.

CONCLUSION

It is the combined weight of these three structural realities—each of which was set in motion by NSC-68—that continues to push American foreign policy toward militarization. The tragedy of this is that militarization of foreign policy is an ineffective response to the real dangers posed by Soviet strength. The periodic injections of higher levels of military spending into the American economy have deleterious economic side effects that more than outweigh their marginal contributions to enhanced military security. Further, the resort to militarization of foreign policy consistently involves a diversion for U.S. policy makers from the more difficult tasks of developing diplomatic strategies for responding to the Soviet Union. Just as Truman, at the beginning of the Cold War, relied on the still-secret A-bomb as a substitute for diplomatic skill,[35] so American policy makers have continued to succumb to the fantasy that there exists a technological escape from the problems of great power competition. Finally, in the area where the Soviet threat is perceived to be most serious—the Persian Gulf—the danger arises not from the great strength of the Soviet army, but from the weakness of the feudal regimes with which the U.S. is allied. George Kennan's observation is as true now as it was in 1950: "communism [has] to be viewed as a crisis of our own civilization, and the principal antidote [lies] in overcoming the weaknesses of our own institutions."

NOTES

1. For an analysis of the forces leading up to the Carter policy shifts, see Michael T. Klare, "Resurgent Militarism," Institute for Policy Studies, *Issue Paper,* 1978.
2. Because of internal conflicts within the administration, the drafters of NSC-68 studiously avoided putting a specific dollar figure in the document. However, the $40 bil-

lion figure was used privately by the drafters. On this point, and for a useful overview of the rearmament decision that also emphasizes the parallels with contemporary debates, see Samuel Wells, Jr., "Sounding the Tocsin: NSC-68 and the Soviet Threat," *International Security* (Fall 1979), pp. 116–58.

3. U.S. Department of Commerce, *The National Income and Product Accounts of the United States, 1929–74* (Washington: Government Printing Office), pp. 96–97.

4. For NSC-68, see U.S. Department of State, *Foreign Relations of the United States 1950* (Washington: Government Printing Office, 1977), 1:235–92 (hereafter referred to as *FRUS 1950*).

5. *The Modern World System: Capitalist Agriculture and the Origins of the European World-Economy in the Sixteenth Century* (New York: Academic Press, 1974) and *The Capitalist World Economy* (Cambridge: Cambridge University Press, 1979).

6. See, particularly, Theda Skocpol, "Wallerstein's World System: A Theoretical and Historical Critique," *American Journal of Sociology* 82 (March 1977):1075–90; and Aristide R. Zolberg, "Origins of the Modern World System: A Missing Link" (Paper presented at the American Political Science Association meetings, August 1979).

7. One key use of the analytic distinction is to grasp the process by which an imperial power overinvests in political-military competition, resulting in domestic economic decline.

8. *FRUS 1950*, 1:252.

9. Acheson's testimony before the Special Subcommittee on Postwar Economic Policy and Planning of the House of Representatives is cited in William Appleman Williams, *The Tragedy of American Diplomacy* (New York: Dell, 1962), pp. 235–36.

10. This argument is developed at greater length in Fred Block, *The Origins of International Economic Disorder* (Berkeley: University of California Press, 1977), esp. pp. 33–42.

11. The emphasis on an open world economy also had important ideological dimensions since U.S. policy makers tended to see a close fit between free markets, political liberty, and international peace. These connections are spelled out in Stephen Krasner, "United States Commercial and Monetary Policy: Unraveling the Paradox of External Strength and Internal Weakness," in *Between Power and Plenty*, ed. Peter Katzenstein (Madison: University of Wisconsin Press, 1978), pp. 51–88.

12. A high State Department official wrote in early 1950 of the need to persuade the Soviet Union "*that there will be at least in the near future NO capitalist economic crisis of major proportions. It is of vital importance that we demonstrate domestically, in Western Europe and in the Western world generally, that a free economy is able to produce and distribute generously and continuously. A serious economic depression would obviously be an enormous boon to the Soviets.*" *FRUS 1950*, 1:159 (emphasis in original).

13. *Ibid.*, pp. 237–38.

14. *Ibid.*, p. 292.

15. The next section draws heavily on Block, *Origins*, pp. 70–122.

16. Richard Freeman, *The Truman Doctrine and the Origins of McCarthyism* (New York: Knopf, 1972), Chap. 6.

17. The indispensability derived from West Germany's industrial superiority, which was critical if Western Europe was to improve its over-all trade balance with the rest of the world.

18. In reality, the atomic monopoly was still effective, since the USSR did not develop the means to deliver a nuclear attack on the U.S. until after 1955. Wells, "Sounding the Tocsin," pp. 153–54.

19. On the problem of Germany, see Coral Bell, *Negotiation from Strength* (New York: Knopf, 1963).

20. *FRUS* 1950, 1:409 (emphasis added).

21. *Ibid.*, p. 261.

22. *Ibid.*, p. 258.

23. For evidence of State Department concern with excess industrial capacity in Western Europe and with military spending as a means to stimulate those economies, see *FRUS* 1950, 3:36–40, 45–48.

24. *FRUS* 1950, 1:163–64 (emphasis added). Note that Kennan also clearly distinguishes between political-military rivalry with the Soviet Union on the one hand and the tasks of organizing the world economy on the other.

25. R. B. Manderson-Jones, *The Special Relationship* (London: Weidenfield and Nicolson, 1972), pp. 61–63.

26. On Congressional fears about the length of the program, see William Adams Brown, Jr., and Redvers Opie, *American Foreign Assistance* (Washington: Brookings, 1953), pp. 148–49, 172–76.

27. By militarization of foreign policy I mean the effort to achieve foreign-policy goals through an almost exclusive reliance on military means—from rearmament to actual warfare. Militarization implies a neglect of diplomatic strategies and a failure to balance military concerns with an awareness of the economic costs of particular policies.

28. For an extended discussion of this thesis, see Mary Kaldor, *The Disintegrating West* (New York: Hill & Wang, 1978).

29. For an account of this history, see Alan Wolfe, *The Rise and Fall of the "Soviet Threat"* (Washington: Institute for Policy Studies, 1979).

30. For the classic descriptions of military waste, see Seymour Melman, *Our Depleted Society* (New York: Delta, 1965); and idem, *The Permanent War Economy* (New York: Simon & Schuster, 1974).

31. The tipping point idea is contained in the passage from the first page of NSC-68, quoted above.

32. Freeman, *Truman Doctrine,* pp. 347–60.

33. Political memory operated even more powerfully here because many of the key foreign-policy makers in the Kennedy-Johnson years had served formative apprenticeships in the Truman administration during the rearmament period. Secretary of State Rusk had served in Acheson's State Department and was recommended to Kennedy by Acheson. See Arthur M. Schlesinger, Jr., *A Thousand Days* (Greenwich, Conn.: Fawcett, 1965), pp. 136, 286–91. A more recent example of these continuities was the emergence of Clark Clifford, a veteran of the Truman administration, as a spokesman for the Carter administration's hard-line response to the Soviet invasion of Afghanistan.

34. Daniel Ellsberg makes this argument about the importance of the China analogy at length in *Papers on the War* (New York: Simon and Schuster, 1972), pp. 86–131. Ellsberg was assigned by his superior in the Defense Department the task of imagining alternative ways that "we might come to 'lose Indochina,'" but, he was warned, "you should be clear that you could be signing the death warrant to your career by having anything to do with calculations and decisions like these. A lot of people were ruined for less." *Ibid.*, p. 88.

35. See Martin Sherwin, *A World Destroyed* (New York: Vintage, 1977), Chap. 9.

PART Four

NATIONAL VALUES, DEMOCRATIC INSTITUTIONS, AND FOREIGN POLICY

A distinctive set of values imbues American political culture and gives shape to its political institutions. These values and institutions in turn leave their mark on American foreign policy. In different ways the essays in this section attempt to give meaning to this set of relationships. Samuel Huntington provides the most encompassing examination. Arguing that there is an uneasy relationship between American values and American political institutions, Huntington contends that this gap in normative orientation and practice presents a dynamic of change that can be felt in foreign policy. The pull of American values is manifest in two ways: in attitudes about the institutions that make American foreign policy and in attitudes about changing the institutions and policies of other societies to conform with American values. Huntington argues that in both these areas American history is marked by efforts to close the gap between values of institutions, but that these efforts always embody tensions. The promotion of American liberty abroad often carries with it the need to expand the powers of American government, which in turn conflicts with domestic values of liberty. These tensions present an inevitable "promise of disharmony."

Stephen Krasner argues that the United States has a "weak" political system. The "central decision-making institutions" of the state—the White House and the State Department—are not well positioned to alter their domestic society. In areas such as foreign economic policy this means that American officials often have more limited options than officials in "strong" states. Krasner argues, however, that this does not mean that societal groups dominate American policy. Although highly constrained, American officials can still exercise leadership and manipulate the political agenda.

Michael Doyle explores the relationship between America's democratic institutions and foreign policy. Liberal countries, Doyle observes, tend to maintain peaceful relations with each other. They not only tend to find nonviolent ways to resolve their differences, but they also form an "international liberal community" with deeply rooted and complex interdependent bonds. Doyle argues that this liberal community should be reinforced and extended as a bulwark of American foreign policy.

Michael Mastanduno examines the old orthodoxy that democracies—such as America's—are "decidedly inferior" in the conduct of foreign policy. Do democratic institutions inhibit coherent and effective foreign policy by being more responsive to interest groups than to the imperatives of international politics? Mastanduno finds the American experience to be decidedly mixed and concludes that there are as many advantages and virtues to decentralized and pluralistic institutions in the conduct of foreign policy as there are dangers and liabilities. The old conventional wisdom needs to be rethought.

American Ideals versus American Institutions

Samuel P. Huntington

Throughout the history of the United States a broad consensus has existed among the American people in support of liberal, democratic, individualistic, and egalitarian values. These political values and ideals constitute what Gunnar Myrdal termed "the American Creed," and they have provided the core of American national identity since the eighteenth century. Also throughout American history, political institutions have reflected these values but have always fallen short of realizing them in a satisfactory manner. A gap has always existed between the ideals in which Americans believed and the institutions that embodied their practice. This gap between ideals and institutional practice has generated continuing disharmony between the normative and existential dimensions of American politics. Being human, Americans have never been able to live up to their ideals; being Americans, they have also been unable to abandon them. They have instead existed in a state of national cognitive dissonance, which they have attempted to relieve through various combinations of moralism, cynicism, complacency, and hypocrisy. The "burr under the saddle," as Robert Penn Warren called it, and the efforts to remove that burr have been central features of American politics, defining its dynamics and shape, since at least the eighteenth century and perhaps before. The question now is: Will the gap between ideals and institutional practices and the responses to it continue to play the same role in American politics in the future that they have in the past? Or are there changes taking place or likely to take place in American political ideals, political institutions, and the relation between them that will make their future significantly different from their past?

Three possibilities exist. The relation between ideals and institutions, first, could continue essentially unchanged; second, it could be altered by developments within American society; or third, it could be altered by developments outside American society and by American involvements abroad. Developments within American society or changes in the international environment could alter the relation between American political ideals and institutions in four ways: the content of the ideals could change; the scope of agreement on the ideals could change; the nature of American political institutions could more closely approximate American ideals, thereby reducing the gap between them; or American political institutions could be significantly altered in an illiberal, undemocratic, anti-individualistic direction; or some combination of these developments could take place.

Samuel P. Huntington, "American Ideals versus American Institutions," *Political Science Quarterly*, Vol. 97, No. 1 (Spring 1982). Reprinted with permission.

HISTORY VERSUS PROGRESS?

At various periods in their history Americans have attempted to eliminate or reduce the gap between ideals and institutions by moralistic efforts to reform their
institutions and practices so as to make them conform to the ideals of the American Creed. These periods include the Revolutionary years of the 1760s and 1770s,
the Jacksonian surge of reforms in the 1820s and 1830s, the Progressive era from
the 1890s to 1914, and the latest resurgence of moralistic reform in the 1960s and
early 1970s. These four periods have much in common, and almost always the proponents of reform have failed to realize their goals completely. The relative success
of reform, however, has varied significantly: in particular the goals of reform have
tended to be more widely achieved in the early periods than in the later ones. In
the earlier periods the affirmation of the goals of liberty, equality, democracy, and
popular sovereignty was directed at the destruction or modification of traditional
political and economic institutions; in the later periods, it was directed at the elimination or modification of modern political and economic institutions that had
emerged in the course of historical development. In the earlier periods, in short,
history and progress (in the sense of realizing American ideals) went hand in hand;
in the later periods the achievement of American ideals involved more the restoration of the past than the realization of the future, and progress and history worked
increasingly at cross purposes.

The revolutionaries of the 1770s were the first to articulate the American
Creed on a national basis and were generally successful in effecting major changes
in American institutions: the overthrow of British imperial power, the end of
monarchy, the widespread acceptance of government based on popular consent,
the extension of the suffrage, an end to what remained of feudal practices and privileges, and the substitution of a politics of opinion for a politics of status. In part the
articulation of their goals was conservative; the rights asserted were justified by reference to common law and the rights of Englishmen. But the formulation and public proclamation of those rights was also a revolutionary event in terms of political
theory and political debate.

In the Jacksonian years the American ideology was still new, fresh, and directed toward the elimination of the political restrictions on democracy, the broadening of popular participation in government, the abolition of status and the weakening of specialization—that is, of both ascriptive and achievement norms—in the
public service, and the destruction of the Bank of the United States and other
manifestations of the "money power," so as to open wide the doors of economic opportunity. "Originally a fight against political privilege, the Jacksonian movement
. . . broadened into a fight against economic privilege, rallying to its support a host
of 'rural capitalists and village entrepreneurs.'"[1] Except for the role of blacks and
women in American society, the Jacksonian reforms did complete the virtual elimination of traditional institutions and practices, either inherited from a colonial
past or concocted by the Federalist commercial oligarchy, which deviated from
liberal-democratic values. All this was progressive in the broad sense, but it too
carried with it elements of conservatism. The paradox of the Jacksonians was that
even as they cleared away obstacles to the development of laissez-faire capitalism,

they also looked back politically to ideals of rural republican simplicity.[2] Restoration, not revolution, was their message.

The institutional changes of the Jacksonian years did not, of course, bring political reality fully into accord with Jacksonian principle. Neither property nor power was equally distributed. In the major cities a small number of very wealthy people, most of whom had inherited their position, controlled large amounts of property.[3] As is generally the case, however, income was much more equally distributed than wealth, and both wealth and income were far more evenly distributed in the rural areas, where 90 percent of the population lived, than in the urban areas. In addition there were high levels of social and political equality, which never failed to impress European visitors, whether critical or sympathetic. All in all, money, status, and power were probably more equally distributed among white males in Jacksonian America than at any other time before or since. The other central values of the American Creed—liberty, individualism, democracy—were in many respects even more markedly embodied in American institutions at that time.

For these reasons, Gordon Wood argued, the Jacksonian generation "has often seemed to be the most 'American' of all generations." This "Middle Period" in American history has been appropriately labeled because

> many of the developments of the first two centuries of our history seem to be anticipations of this period, while many of the subsequent developments taking us to the present seem to be recessions from it. In the traditional sense of what it has meant to be distinctly American, this Middle Period of 1820–1860 marks the apogee in the overall trajectory of American history. Americans in that era of individualism, institutional weakness, and boundlessness experienced "freedom" as they rarely have since; power, whether expressed economically, socially, or politically, was as fragmented and diffused as at any time in our history.[4]

After the democratization of government and before the development of industry, the Middle Period is the time when the United States could least well be characterized as a disharmonic society. It was a period when Americans themselves believed that they had "fulfilled the main principles of liberty" and hence were exempt from "further epochal change."[5] All that was needed was to remain true to the achievements of the past.

In the Middle Period, in short, American dream and American reality came close to joining hands even though they were shortly to be parted. The gap between American ideals and institutions was clearly present in Jacksonian America but outside the South probably less so than at any other time in American history. The inequality of social hierarchy and political aristocracy had faded; the inequality of industrial wealth and organizational hierarchy had yet to emerge. Primogeniture was gone; universal (white male) suffrage had arrived; the Standard Oil trust was still in the future.

In the Middle Period and the years following, the only major institutional legacy that was grossly contradictory to the American Creed was slavery and the heritage of slavery, the remnants of which were still being removed a hundred years after the Civil War. With respect to the role of blacks, the creed played a continuingly progressive role, furnishing the basis for challenging the patterns of racial discrimination and segregation that ran so blatantly against the proposition that all men are created equal. Hence, in analyzing the American dilemma in the 1930s, Gunnar Myrdal could take an essentially optimistic attitude toward its eventual resolution. He could see hope in America because his attention was focused on the one area of inequality in American life that was clearly an anachronistic holdover from the past.

More generally, the Middle Period marked a turning point in the nature of progress in America. Prior to that time "progress" in terms of the realization of American ideals of liberty and equality did not conflict with "historical development" in terms of the improvement of economic well-being and security. After the Middle Period, however, progress and history began to diverge. Progress in terms of the "realization of the democratic ideal," in Herbert Croly's phrase, often ran counter to historical trends toward large-scale organization, hierarchy, specialization, and inequality in power and wealth that seemed essential to material improvement. Political progress involves a return to first principles; politically Americans move forward by looking backward, reconsecrating themselves to the ideals of the past as guidelines for the future. Historical development involves pragmatic responses to the increasing scale and complexity of society and economy and demands increasing interaction, both cooperative and competitive, with other societies.

This distinctive character of the Middle Period and its inappropriateness as a foretaste of things to come are well reflected in the observations of the most celebrated foreign observer of the Jacksonian scene. Tocqueville was in a sense half right and half wrong in the two overarching empirical propositions (one static, one dynamic) that he advanced about equality in America. The most distinctive aspect of American society, he argued, is "the general equality of condition among the people." This "is the fundamental fact from which all others seem to be derived and the central point at which all my observations constantly terminated." Second, the tendency toward equality in American and European society constitutes an "irresistible revolution"; the "gradual development of the principle of equality" is a "providential fact"; it is "lasting, it constantly eludes all human interference, and all events as well as all men contribute to its progress."[6] Like other European observers before and since, Tocqueville tended to confuse the values and ideals of Americans with social and political reality. His descriptive hypothesis, nonetheless, still rings true. By and large American society of the Middle Period was characterized by a widespread equality of condition, particularly in comparison to conditions in Europe. Tocqueville's historical projection, in contrast, clearly does not hold up in terms of the distribution of wealth and only in limited respects in terms of the distribution of political power.

In attempting to sum up the diversity and yet common purpose of the Jacksonian age, Joseph L. Blau employs a striking metaphor: "As one drives out of any large city on a major highway, he is bound to see a large signpost, with arrows pointing him to many possible destinations. These arrows have but one thing in common; all alike point away from the city he has just left. Let this stand as a symbol of Jacksonians. Though they pointed to many different possible American futures, all alike pointed away from an America of privilege and monopoly."[7] The Jacksonians were, however, more accurate in pointing to where America should go in terms of its democratic values and ideals than they were in pointing to the actual direction of economic and political development. Industrialization following the Civil War brought into existence new inequalities in wealth, more blatant corruptions of the political process, and new forms of "privilege and monopoly" undreamed of in the Jacksonian years. This divorce of history from progress had two consequences for the reaffirmation of American political values in the Progressive period.

First, during both the revolutionary and Jacksonian years, the articulation of American political ideals was couched to some degree in conservative and backward-looking terms, as a reaffirmation of rights that had previously existed and as an effort to reorder political life in terms of principles whose legitimacy had been previously established. During the Progressive era the backward-looking characteristics of the ideals and vision that were invoked stood out much more sharply. As Richard Hofstadter suggested, the Founding Fathers "dreamed of and planned for a long-term future," the Middle Period generations were absorbed with the present, and the Progressives consciously and explicitly looked to the past: "Beginning with the time of [William Jennings] Bryan, the dominant American ideal has been steadily fixed on bygone institutions and conditions. In early twentieth-century progressivism this backward-looking vision reached the dimension of a major paradox. Such heroes of the progressive revival as Bryan, [Robert M.] La Follette, and [Woodrow] Wilson proclaimed that they were trying to undo the mischief of the past forty years and re-create the old nation of limited and decentralized power, genuine competition, democratic opportunity, and enterprise."[8] The Progressives were reaffirming the old ideals in opposition to large-scale new organizations—economic and political—which were organizing and giving shape to the twentieth century. This was most manifest in William Jennings Bryan, who was, as Croly said, basically "a Democrat of the Middle Period." Bryan, according to Walter Lippmann, "thought he was fighting the plutocracy" but in actuality "was fighting something much deeper than that; he was fighting the larger scale of human life." Bryan was thus a "genuine conservative" who stood for "the popular tradition of America," whereas his enemies were trying to destroy that tradition.[9] But he was also a radical attempting to apply and to realize the ideals of the American Revolution. Bryan was, in fact, just as radical as William Lloyd Garrison, but Garrison was moving with history and Bryan against it. In a similar vein Woodrow Wilson also reacted to the growth of large-scale economic organization with the call to "restore" American politics to their former pristine, individualistic strength and vigor. To achieve this goal Wilson was willing to employ governmental power, thereby, as Lippmann pointed out, creating the inner contradiction that was at the heart of the Progressive outlook. Among the Progressives Theodore Roosevelt was most explicit in arguing that large-scale economic organizations had to be accepted; nonetheless he too held to much of the older ideal; his argument was couched in pragmatic rather than ideological terms: "This is the age of combination, and any effort to prevent all combination will be not only useless, but in the end vicious, because of the contempt for the law which the failure to enforce law inevitably produces."[10]

Second, the reaffirmation of American ideals at the turn of the century could not be as effective as the Revolutionary and Jacksonian affirmations in realizing those ideals in practice. At the extreme Bryan became the Don Quixote of American politics, battling for a vision of American society that could never be realized again. In the Revolutionary and Jacksonian periods the institutional reforms had been substantial and effective. In the Progressive period both economic and political reforms could at best be described as only partly successful. The antitrust laws and other efforts to curb the power of big business made a difference in the development of American business—as any comparison with Europe will demonstrate—but they clearly did not stop or reverse the tendencies toward combination and oligopoly. In the political sphere the introduction of primaries did not bring an end to political machines and bossism, and according to some may even have strengthened them. In Congress the attack on "Czar" Joseph Cannon established the dominance of the seniority system; paternalistic autocracy in effect gave way to gerontocratic oligarchy. The efforts to make government more responsible encouraged the growth of presidential power. That institutional changes were made is indisputable, but so is the fact that by and large they were substantially less successful than the changes of the Revolutionary and Jacksonian years in realizing the hopes and goals of their proponents.

The passion of the 1960s and 1970s was in some respects ideologically purer than the theories of the Progressives. Perhaps for this reason it was also somewhat more effective in eroding political authority. Yet outside of race relations its more specific reforms were little more successful than those of the Progressives. Economic power was assaulted but remained concentrated. Presidential authority was weakened but rebounded. The military and intelligence agencies declined in money, matériel, and morale in the 1970s but were reestablishing themselves on all three fronts by the early 1980s. It seemed likely that the institutional structure and the distribution of power in American society and politics in 1985 would not differ greatly from what they had been in 1960. With the important exception of race relations the gap between ideals and institutions of the early 1980s duplicated that of the early 1960s.

This changing record of success from one creedal passion period to the next reflected the changing nature of reform. In the earlier periods reform generally involved the dismantling of social, political, and economic institutions responsible for the ideals-versus-institutions gap. The disharmony of American politics was thought to be—and in considerable measure was—man-made. Remove the artificial restraints, and society and politics would naturally move in the direction in which they morally should move. In later creedal passion periods, beginning with the Progressive era, this assumption of *natural* congruence of ideal and reality was displaced by the idea of *contrived* congruence. Consciously designed governmental policy and action was necessary to reduce the gap. In the post-World War II period, for instance, "for the first time in American history, equality became a major object of governmental policy."[11] The Progressives created antitrust offices and regulatory commissions to combat monopoly power and promote competition. The reformers of the 1960s brought into existence an "imperial judiciary" in order to eliminate racial segregation and inequalities. To a much greater degree than in the earlier periods, in order to realize American values the reformers of the later periods had to create institutional mechanisms that threatened those values.

In a broader context the actual course of institutional development is the product of the complex interaction of social, political, economic, and ideological forces. In the United States any centralization of power produced by the expansion of governmental bureaucracy is mitigated by pluralistic forces that disperse power among bureaucratic agencies, congressional committees, and interest groups and that undermine efforts to subordinate lower-ranking executive officials to higher-ranking ones. Yet an increasingly sophisticated economy and active involvement in world affairs seem likely to create stronger needs for hierarchy, bureaucracy, centralization of power, expertise, big government specifically, and big organizations generally. In some way or another society will respond to these needs while still attempting to realize the values of the American Creed to which they are so contradictory. If history is against progress, for how long will progress resist history?

Acute tension between the requisites of development and the norms of ideology played a central role in the evolution of the People's Republic of China during its first quarter-century. China can avoid this conflict for as long as its leaders agree on the priority of development over revolution. In the United States, in contrast, no group of leaders can suppress by fiat the liberal values that have defined the nation's identity. The conflict between developmental need and ideological norm that characterized Mao's China in the 1960s and 1970s is likely to be duplicated in the American future unless other forces change, dilute, or eliminate the central ideals of the American Creed.

What is the probability of this happening? Do such forces exist? Several possibilities suggest themselves. First, the core values of the creed are products of the seventeenth and eighteenth centuries. Their roots lie in the English and American revolutionary experiences, in seventeenth-century Protestant moralism and eighteenth-century liberal rationalism. The historical dynamism and appeal of these ideals could naturally begin to fade after two centuries, particularly as those ideals come to be seen as increasingly irrelevant in a complex modern economy and a threatening international environment. In addition, to the extent that those ideals derive from Protestant sources, they must also be weakened by trends toward secularism that exist even in the United States. Each of the four creedal passion periods was preceded or accompanied by a religious "great awakening." These movements of religious reform and revival, however, have successively played less central roles in American society, that of the 1950s being very marginal in its impact compared to that of the 1740s. As religious passion weakens, how likely is the United States to sustain a firm commitment to its traditional values? Would an America without its Protestant core still be America?

Second, the social, economic, and cultural changes associated with the transition from industrial to postindustrial society could also give rise to new political values that would displace the traditional liberal values associated with bourgeois society and the rise of industrialism. In the 1960s and 1970s in both Europe and America social scientists found evidence of the increasing prevalence of "post-bourgeois" or "postmaterialist" values, particularly among younger cohorts. In a somewhat similar vein George Lodge foresaw the displacement of Lockean individualistic ideology in the United States by a "communitarian" ideology, resembling in many aspects the traditional Japanese collectivist approach.[12]

Third, as Hofstadter and others argued, the early twentieth-century immigration of Orthodox, Catholics, and Jews from central, eastern, and southern Europe introduced a different "ethic" into American cities. In the late twentieth century the United States experienced its third major wave of postindependence immigration, composed largely of Puerto Ricans, Mexicans, Cubans, and others from Latin America and the Caribbean. Like their predecessors, the more recent immigrants could well introduce into American society political and social values markedly in contrast with those of Lockean liberalism. In these circumstances the consensus on this type of liberalism could very likely be either disrupted or diluted.

Fourth, the historical function of the creed in defining national identity could conceivably become less significant, and widespread belief in that creed could consequently become less essential to the continued existence of the United States as a nation. Having been in existence as a functioning national society and political entity for over two hundred years, the United States may have less need of these ideals to define its national identity in the future. History, tradition, custom, culture, and a sense of shared experience such as other major nations have developed over the centuries could also come to define American identity, and the role of abstract ideals and values might be reduced. The *ideational* basis of national identity would be replaced by an *organic* one. "American exceptionalism" would wither. The United States would cease to be "a nation with the soul of a church" and would become a nation with the soul of a nation.

Some or all of these four factors could alter American political values so as to reduce the gap between these values and the reality of American institutional practice. Yet the likelihood of this occurring does not seem very high. Despite their seventeenth- and eighteenth-century origins American values and ideals have demonstrated tremendous persistence and resiliency in the twentieth century. Defined vaguely and abstractly, these ideals have been relatively easily adapted to the needs of successive generations. The constant social change in the United States indeed underlies their permanence. Rising social, economic, and ethnic groups need to reinvoke and to reinvigorate those values in order to promote their own access to the rewards of American society. The shift in emphasis among values manifested by younger cohorts in the 1960s and 1970s does not necessarily mean the end of the traditional pattern. In many respects the articulation of these values was, as it had been in the past, a protest against the perceived emergence of new centers of power. The yearning for "belonging and intellectual and esthetic self-fulfillment" found to exist among the younger cohorts of the 1960s and 1970s[13] could in fact be interpreted as "a romantic, Luddite reaction against the bureaucratic and technological tendencies of postindustrialism." This confrontation between ideology and institutions easily fits into the well-established American pattern. Indeed, insofar as "the postindustrial society is more highly educated and more participatory than American society in the past and insofar as American political institutions will be more bureaucratic and hierarchical than before, the conflict between ideology and institutions could be more intense than it has ever been."[14]

Similarly, the broader and longer-term impact of the Latin immigration of the 1950s, 1960s, and 1970s could reinforce the central role of the American Creed both as a way of legitimizing claims to political, economic, and social equality and also as the indispensable element in defining national identity. The children and grandchildren of the European immigrants of the early twentieth century in due course became ardent adherents to traditional American middle-class values. In addition, the more culturally pluralistic the nation becomes, particularly if cultural pluralism encompasses linguistic pluralism, the more essential the political values of the creed become in defining what it is that Americans have in common. At some point traditional American ideals—liberty, equality, individualism, democracy—may lose their appeal and join the ideas of racial inequality, the divine right of kings, and the dictatorship of the proletariat on the ideological scrap heap of history. There is, however, little to suggest that this will be a twentieth-century happening.

If the gap between ideals and institutions remains a central feature of American politics, the question then becomes: What changes, if any, may occur in the traditional pattern of responses to this gap? Three broad possibilities exist. First, the previous pattern of response could continue. If the periodicity of the past prevails, a major sustained creedal passion period will occur in the second and third decades of the twenty-first century. In the interim moralism, cynicism, complacency, and hypocrisy will all be invoked by different Americans in different ways in their efforts to live with the gap. The tensions resulting from the gap will remain and perhaps increase in intensity, but their consequences will not be significantly more serious than they have been in the past. Second, the cycle of response could stabilize to a greater degree than it has in the past. Americans could acquire a greater understanding of their case of cognitive dissonance and through this understanding come to live with their dilemma on somewhat easier terms than they have in the past, in due course evolving a more complex but also more coherent and constant response to this problem. Third, the oscillations among the responses could intensify in such a way as to threaten to destroy both ideals and institutions.

In terms of the future stability of the American political system, the first possibility may be the most likely and the second the most hopeful, but the third is clearly the most dangerous. Let us focus on the third.

Lacking any concept of the state, lacking for most of its history both the centralized authority and the bureaucratic apparatus of the European state, the American polity has historically been a weak polity. It was designed to be so, and traditional inheritance and social environment combined for years to support the framers' intentions. In the twentieth century foreign threats and domestic economic and social needs have generated pressures to develop stronger, more authoritative decision-making and decision-implementing institutions. Yet the continued presence of deeply felt moralistic sentiments among major groups in American society could continue to ensure weak and divided government, devoid of authority and unable to deal satisfactorily with the economic, social, and foreign challenges confronting the nation. Intensification of this conflict between history and progress could give rise to increasing frustration and increasingly violent oscillations between moralism and cynicism. American moralism ensures that government will never be truly efficacious; the realities of power ensure that government will never be truly democratic.

This situation could lead to a two-phase dialectic involving intensified efforts to reform government followed by intensified frustration when those efforts produce not progress in a liberal-democratic direction but obstacles to meeting perceived functional needs. The weakening of government in an effort to reform it could lead eventually to strong demands for the replacement of the weakened and ineffective institutions by more authoritarian structures more effectively designed to meet historical needs. Given the perversity of reform, moralistic extremism in the pursuit of liberal democracy could generate a strong tide toward authoritarian efficiency. "The truth is that," as Plato observed, "in the constitution of society . . . any excess brings about an equally violent reaction. So the only outcome of too much freedom is likely to be excessive subjection in the state or in the individual; which means that the culmination of liberty in democracy is precisely what prepares the way for the cruelest extreme of servitude under a despot."[15]

American political ideals are a useful instrument not only for those who wish to improve American political institutions but also for those who wish to destroy them. Liberal reformers, because they believe in the ideals, attempt to change institutions to approximate those ideals more closely. The enemies of liberalism, because they oppose both liberal ideals and liberal institutions, attempt to use the former to undermine the latter. For them the gap between ideals and institutions is a made-to-order opportunity. The effectiveness of liberal-democratic institutions can be discredited by highlighting their shortcomings compared to the ideals on which they are supposedly modeled. This is a common response of foreigners critical of the American polity, but this approach is not limited to liberalism's foreign enemies. The leading theorists of the American Southern Enlightenment, for instance, took great delight in describing the inequality and repression of the Northern "wage slave" system not because they believed in equality and liberty for all workers but because they wished to discredit the economy that was threatening the future of slavery in the South. "Their obvious purpose [was] to belabor the North rather than to redeem it."[16]

Those who have battered liberal institutions with the stick of liberal ideals have, however, more often been on the left than on the right. There is a reason for this, which is well illustrated by the attitudes of conservatives, liberals, and revolutionaries toward political equality. Traditional conservatives oppose equality. They may perceive American political institutions as embodying more equality than they think desirable. In this case they normally opt out of American society in favor of either internal or external emigration. Traditional conservatives may also perceive and take comfort in the realities of power and inequality that exist in the United States behind the facade and rhetoric of equality. Liberal defenders of American institutions embrace the hypocritical response: they believe that inequality does not exist and that it should not exist. Both the perceptive conservatives and the liberal hypocrites are thus in some sense standpatters, satisfied with the status quo, but only because they have very different perceptions of what that status quo is and very different views about whether equality is good or bad. The ability of traditional conservatives and liberal hypocrites to cooperate in defense of the status quo is hence very limited: neither will buy the others' arguments. In addition, articulate traditional conservatives have been few and far between on the American political landscape, in large part because their values are so contrary to those of the American Creed (see Table 10.1).

Table 10.1   POLITICAL BELIEFS AND POLITICAL EQUALITY

	Traditional conservative	Liberal		Marxist revolutionary
		Hypocrite	Moralist	
Perception of political equality	Does not exist	Does exist	Does not exist	Does not exist
Judgment on political equality	Bad	Good	Good	Good
		Standpatters		Radicals

On the other side of the political spectrum a very different situation exists. Like hypocritical liberals, moralist liberals believe that inequality is bad. Unlike the hypocrites, however, they perceive that inequality exists in American institutions and hence vigorously devote themselves to reform in an effort to eliminate it. To their left, however, the Marxist revolutionaries have views and beliefs that on the surface at least, coincide with those of moralistic liberals. Marxist revolutionaries hold inequality to be bad, see it as pervasive in existing institutions, and attack it and the institutions vigorously. At a deeper and more philosophical level Marxist revolutionaries may believe in the necessity of the violent overthrow of the capitalist order, the dictatorship of the proletariat, and a disciplined Leninist party as the revolutionary vanguard. If they blatantly articulate these beliefs, they are relegated to the outermost fringes of American politics and foreswear any meaningful ideological or political influence. It is, moreover, in the best Leninist tradition to see reform as the potential catalyst of revolution.[17] Consequently, major incentives exist for Marxist revolutionaries to emphasize not what divides them from the liberal consensus but what unites them with liberal reformers, that is, their perception of inequality and their belief in equality. With this common commitment to reform, liberal moralists and Marxist revolutionaries can cooperate in their attack on existing institutions, even though in the long run one group wants to make them work better and the other wants to overthrow them.

The role of Marxism in the consensus of society of America thus differs significantly from its role in the ideologically pluralistic societies of Western Europe. There the differences between liberal and Marxist goals and appeals are sharply delineated, the two philosophies are embraced by different constituencies and parties, and the conflict between them is unceasing. In the United States the prevalence of liberalism means a consensus on the standards by which the institutions of society should be judged, and Marxism has no choice but to employ those standards in its own cause. Philosophical differences are blurred as reform liberalism and revolutionary Marxism blend into a nondescript but politically relevant radicalism that serves the immediate interests of both. This convergence, moreover, exists at the individual as well as the societal level: particular individuals bring together in their own minds elements of both liberal reformism and revolutionary Marxism. American radicals easily perceive the gap between American ideals and American institutions; they do not easily perceive the conflict between reform liberalism and revolutionary Marxism. With shared immediate goals, these two sets of philosophically distinct ideas often coexist in the same mind.

This common ground of liberal reformer and revolutionary Marxist in favor of radical change contrasts with the distance between the liberal hypocrite and the traditional conservative. The hypocrite can defend American institutions only by claiming they are something that they are not. The conservative can defend them only by articulating values that most Americans abhor. The Marxist subscribes to the liberal consensus in order to subvert liberal institutions; the conservative rejects the liberal consensus in order to defend those institutions. The combined effect of both is to strengthen the attack on the established order. For paradoxically, the conservative who defends American institutions with conservative arguments (that they are good because they institutionalize political inequality) weakens those institutions at least as much as the radical who attacks them for the same reason. The net impact of the difficulties and divisions among the standpatters and the converging unity of the liberal and Marxist radicals is to enhance the threat to American political institutions posed by those political ideas whose continued vitality is indispensable to their survival.

Two things are thus clear. American political institutions are more open, liberal, and democratic than those of any other major society now or in the past. If Americans ever abandon or destroy these institutions, they are likely to do so in the name of their liberal-democratic ideals. Inoculated against the appeal of foreign ideas, America has only to fear its own.

AMERICA VERSUS THE WORLD?

The gap between ideals and institutions poses two significant issues with respect to the relations between the United States and the rest of the world. First, what are the implications of the gap for American institutions and processes concerned with foreign relations and national security? To what extent should those institutions and processes conform to American liberal, individualistic, democratic values? Second, what are the implications of the gap for American policy toward other societies? To what extent should the United States attempt to make the institutions and policies of other societies conform to American values? For much of its history when it was relatively isolated from the rest of the world, as it was between 1815 and 1914, the United States did not have to grapple seriously with these problems. In the mid-twentieth century, however, the United States became deeply, complexly, and seemingly inextricably involved with the other countries of the world. That involvement brought to the fore and gave new significance and urgency to these two long-standing and closely related issues. These issues are closely related because efforts to reduce the ideal-versus-institutions gap in the institutions and processes of American foreign relations reduce the ability of the United States to exercise power in international affairs, including its ability to reduce that gap between American values and foreign institutions and policies. Conversely, efforts to encourage foreign institutions and practices to conform to American ideals require the expansion of American power and thus make it more difficult for American institutions and policies to conform to those ideals.

Foreign-Policy Institutions

The relation of its institutions and processes concerned with foreign relations to the ideals and values of its political ideology is a more serious problem for the United States than for most other societies. The differences between the United States and Western Europe in this respect are particularly marked. First, the ideological pluralism of Western European societies does not provide a single set of political principles by which to judge foreign-policy institutions and practices. Those, as well as other institutions and practices, benefit in terms of legitimacy as a result of varied strands of conservative, liberal, Christian Democratic, and Marxist political thought that have existed in Western European societies. Second and more important, in most European societies at least an embryonic national community and in large measure a national state existed before the emergence of ideologies. So also did the need to conduct foreign relations and to protect the security of the national community and the state. National security bureaucracies, military forces, foreign offices, intelligence services, internal security, and police systems were all in existence when ideologies emerged in the eighteenth and nineteenth centuries. Although the ideologies undoubtedly had some implications for and posed some demands on these institutions, their proponents tended to recognize the prior claims of these institutions reflecting the needs of the national community in a world of competing national communities. European democratic regimes thus accept a security apparatus that exists in large part outside the normal process of democratic politics and that represents and defends the continuing interests of the community and the state irrespective of the ideologies that may from one time to another dominate its politics.

In Europe, ideology—or rather ideologies—thus followed upon and developed within the context of an existing national community and state. In America ideology in the form of the principles of the American Creed existed before the formation of a national community and political system. These principles defined the identity of the community when there were no institutions for dealing with the other countries of the world. It was assumed that the foreign-policy institutions, like other political institutions, would reflect the basic values of the preexisting and overwhelmingly preponderant ideology. Yet precisely these institutions—foreign and intelligence services, military and police forces—have functional imperatives that conflict most sharply and dramatically with the liberal-democratic values of the American Creed. The essence of the creed is opposition to power and to concentrated authority. This leads to efforts to minimize the resources of power (such as arms), to restrict the effectiveness of specialized bureaucratic hierarchies, and to limit the authority of the executive in the conduct of foreign policy. This conflict manifests itself dramatically in the perennial issue concerning the role of standing armies and professional military forces in a liberal society. For much of its history the United States was able to avoid the full implications of this conflict because its geographic position permitted it to follow a policy of extirpation—that is, almost abolishing military forces and relegating those that did exist to the distant social and geographic extremities of society.[18] Similarly, the United States did not seem to need and did not have an intelligence service, a professional foreign service, or a national police force.

In the twentieth century the impossibility of sustained isolation led the United States to develop all these institutions. Much more so than those in Western Europe, however, these institutions have coexisted in uneasy and fundamentally incompatible ways with the values of the prevailing ideology. This incompatibility became acute after World War II, when the country's global role and responsibilities made it necessary for the government to develop and to maintain such institutions on a large scale and to accord them a central role in its foreign policy. During the 1950s and early 1960s Americans tended to be blissfully complacent and to ignore the broad gap between ideals and institutions that this created in the foreign-policy and defense sectors of their national life. At the same time, various theories—such as Kennan's ideal of the detached professional diplomat and Huntington's concept of "objective civilian control"—were developed to justify the insulation of these institutions from the political demands of a liberal society.[19] In the end, however, the liberal imperatives could not be avoided, and the late 1960s and 1970s saw overwhelming political pressure to make foreign-policy and security institutions conform to the requirements of the liberal ideology. In a powerful outburst of creedal passion, Americans embarked on crusades against the CIA and FBI, defense spending, the use of military force abroad, the military-industrial complex, and the imperial presidency (to use Arthur Schlesinger, Jr.'s phrase), attempting to expose, weaken, dismantle, or abolish the institutions that protected their liberal society against foreign threats. They reacted with outraged moralistic self-criticism to their government engaging in the type of activities—deception, violence, abuse of individual rights—to protect their society that other countries accept as a matter of course.

This penchant of Americans for challenging and undermining the authority of their political institutions, including those concerned with the foreign relations and security of the country, produces mixed and confused reactions on the part of Europeans and other non-Americans. Their initial reaction to a Pentagon Papers case, Watergate, or investigation of the CIA is often one of surprise, amazement, bewilderment. "What are you Americans up to and why are you doing this to yourselves?" A second reaction, which often follows the first, is grudging admiration for a society that takes its principles so seriously and has such effective procedures for attempting to realize them. This is often accompanied by somewhat envious and wistful comments on the contrast between this situation and the paramountcy of state authority in their own country. Finally, a third reaction often follows, expressing deep concern about the impact that the creedal upheaval will have on the ability of the United States to conduct its foreign policy and to protect its friends and allies.

This last concern over whether its liberal values will permit the United States to maintain the material resources, governmental institutions, and political will to defend its interests in the world becomes more relevant not just as a result of the inextricable involvement of the United States in world affairs but also because of the changes in the countries with which the United States will be primarily involved. During the first part of the twentieth century American external relations were largely focused on Western Europe, where in most countries significant political groups held political values similar to American values. Even more important, lodged deeply in the consciousness of Western European statesmen and intellectuals was the thought, impregnated there by Tocqueville if by no one else, that American political values in some measure embodied the wave of the future, that what America believed in would at some point be what the entire civilized world would believe in. This sympathy, partial or latent as it may have been, nonetheless gave the United States a diplomatic resource of some significance. European societies might resent American moral or moralistic loftiness, but both they and the Americans knew that the moral values set forth by the United States (sincerely or hypocritically) would have a resonance in their own societies and could at times be linked up with internal social and political movements that would be impossible for them to ignore.

In the mid-twentieth century the widespread belief in democratic values among younger Germans and to a lesser degree among younger Japanese provided some support for the convergence thesis. At a more general level, however, the sense that America was the future of Europe weakened considerably. More important, in the late twentieth century the countries with which the United States was having increasing interactions, both competitive and cooperative, were the Soviet Union, China, and Japan. The partial sense of identification and of future convergence that existed between the United States and Europe are absent in American relations with these three countries. Like the United States, these countries have a substantial degree of consensus or homogeneity in social and political values and ideology. The content of each country's consensus, however, differs significantly from that of the United States. In all three societies the stress in one form or another is on the pervasiveness of inequality in human relationships, the "sanctity of authority,"[20] the subordination of the individual to the group and the state, the dubious legitimacy of dissent or challenges to the powers that be. Japan, to be sure, developed a working democracy after World War II, but its long-standing values stressing hierarchy, vertical ranking, and submissiveness leave some degree of disharmony that has resemblances to but is just the reverse of what prevails in American society. The dominant ideas in all three countries stand in dramatic contrast to American ideas of openness, liberalism, equality, individual rights, and freedom to dissent. In the Soviet Union, China, and Japan the prevailing political values and social norms reinforce the authority of the central political institutions of society and enhance the ability of these nations to compete with other societies. In the United States the prevailing norms, insofar as Americans take them seriously, undermine and weaken the power and authority of government and detract, at times seriously, from its ability to compete internationally. In the small world of the West Americans were beguiling cousins; in the larger world that includes the East Americans often seem naïve strangers. Given the disharmonic element in the American political system—the continuing challenge, latent or overt, that lies in the American mind to the authority of American government—how well will the

United States be able to conduct its affairs in this league of powers to whose historical traditions basic American values are almost entirely alien?

Foreign-Policy Goals

In the eyes of most Americans not only should their foreign-policy institutions be structured and function so as to reflect liberal values, but American foreign policy should also be substantively directed to the promotion of those values in the external environment. This gives a distinctive cast to the American role in the world. In a famous phrase Viscount Palmerston once said that Britain did not have permanent friends or enemies, it only had permanent interests. Like Britain and other countries, the United States also has interests, defined in terms of power, wealth, and security, some of which are sufficiently enduring as to be thought of as permanent. As a founded society, however, the United States also has distinctive political principles and values that define its national identity. These principles provide a second set of goals and a second set of standards—in addition to those of national interest—by which to shape the goals and judge the success of American foreign policy.

This heritage, this transposition of the ideals-versus-institutions gap into foreign policy, again distinguishes the United States from other societies. Western European states clearly do not reject the relevance of morality and political ideology to the conduct of foreign policy. They do, however, see the goal of foreign policy as the advancement of the major and continuing security and economic interests of their state. Political principles provide limits and parameters to foreign policy but not to its goals. As a result European public debate over morality versus power in foreign policy has except in rare instances not played the role that it has in the United States. That issue does come up with the foreign policy of Communist states and has been discussed at length, in terms of the conflict of ideology and national interest, in analyses of Soviet foreign policy. The conflict has been less significant there than in the United States for three reasons. First, an authoritarian political system precludes public discussion of the issue. Since the 1920s debate of Trotsky versus Stalin over permanent revolution there has been no overt domestic criticism concerning whether Soviet foreign policy is at one time either too power-oriented or at another time too ideologically oriented. Second, Marxist-Leninist ideology distinguishes between basic doctrine on the one hand and strategy and tactics on the other. The former does not change; the latter is adapted to specific historical circumstances. The twists and turns in the party line can always be justified as ideologically necessary at that particular point in time to achieve the long-run goals of communism, even though those shifts may in fact be motivated primarily by national interests. American political values, in contrast, are usually thought of as universally valid, and pragmatism is seen not as a means of implementing these values in particular circumstances but rather as a means of abandoning them. Third, Soviet leaders and the leaders of other Communist states that pursue their own foreign policies can and do, when they wish, simply ignore ideology when they desire to pursue particular national interest goals.

For most Americans, however, foreign-policy goals should reflect not only the security interests of the nation and the economic interests of key groups within the nation but also the political values and principles that define American identity. If these values do define foreign-policy goals, then that policy is morally justified, the opponents of that policy at home and abroad are morally illegitimate, and all efforts must be directed toward overcoming the opponents and achieving the goals. The prevailing American approach to foreign policy thus has been not that of Stephen Decatur ("Our country, right or wrong!") but that of Carl Schurz ("Our country, right or wrong! When right, to be kept right; when wrong, to be put right!"). To Americans, achieving this convergence between self-interest and morality has appeared as no easy task. Hence the recurring tendencies in American history, either to retreat to minimum relations with the rest of the world and thus avoid the problem of reconciling the pursuit of self-interest with the adherence to principle in a corrupt and hostile environment, or the opposite solution, to set forth on a crusade to purify the world, to bring it into accordance with American principles and in the process to expand American power and thus protect the national interest.

This practice of judging the behavior of one's country and one's government by external standards of right and wrong has been responsible for the often substantial opposition to the wars in which the United States has engaged. The United States will only respond with unanimity to a war in which both national security and political principle are clearly at stake. In the two hundred years after the Revolution, only one war, World War II, met this criterion, and this was the only war to which there was no significant domestic opposition articulated in terms of the extent to which the goals of the war and the way in which it was conducted deviated from the basic principles of the American Creed. In this sense World War II was for the United States the "perfect war"; every other war has been an imperfect war in that certain elements of the American public have objected to it because it did not seem to accord with American principles. As strange as it may seem to people of other societies, Americans have had no trouble conceiving of their government waging an un-American war.

The extent to which the American liberal creed prevails over power considerations can lead to hypocritical and rather absolutist positions on policy. As Seymour Martin Lipset pointed out, if wars should only be fought for moral purposes, then the opponents against which they are fought must be morally evil and hence total war must be waged against them and unconditional surrender exacted from them. If a war is not morally legitimate, then the leaders conducting it must be morally evil and opposition to it in virtually any form is not only morally justified but morally obligatory. It is no coincidence that the country that has most tended to think of wars as crusades is also the country with the strongest record of conscientious objection to war.[21]

The effort to use American foreign policy to promote American values abroad raises a central issue. There is a clear difference between political action to make American political practices conform to American political values and political action to make *foreign* political practices conform to American values. Americans can legitimately attempt to reduce the gap between American institutions and American values, but can they legitimately attempt to reduce the gap between other people's institutions and American values? The answer is not self-evident.

The argument for a negative response to this question can be made on at least four grounds. First, it is morally wrong for the United States to attempt to shape the institutions of other societies. Those institutions should reflect the values and behavior of the people in those societies. To intrude from outside is either imperialism or colonialism, each of which also violates American values. Second, it is difficult practically and in most cases impossible for the United States to influence significantly the institutional development of other societies. The task is simply beyond American knowledge, skill, and resources. To attempt to do so will often be counterproductive. Third, any effort to shape the domestic institutions of other societies needlessly irritates and antagonizes other governments and hence will complicate and often endanger the achievement of other more important foreign-policy goals, particularly in the areas of national security and economic well-being. Fourth, to influence the political development of other societies would require an enormous expansion of the military power and economic resources of the American government. This in turn would pose dangers to the operation of democratic government within the United States.

A yes answer to this question can, on the other hand, also be justified on four grounds. First, if other people's institutions pose direct threats to the viability of American institutions and values in the United States, an American effort to change those institutions would be justifiable in terms of self-defense. Whether or not foreign institutions do pose such a direct threat in any given circumstance is, however, not easily determined. Even in the case of Nazi Germany in 1940 there were widely differing opinions in the United States. After World War II opinion was also divided on whether Soviet institutions, as distinct from Soviet policies, threatened the United States.

Second, the direct-threat argument can be generalized to the proposition that authoritarian regimes in any form and on any continent pose a potential threat to the viability of liberal institutions and values in the United States. A liberal-democratic system, it can be argued, can only be secure in a world system of similarly constituted states. In the past this argument did not play a central role because of the extent to which the United States was geographically isolated from differently constituted states. The world is, however, becoming smaller. Given the increasing interactions among societies and the emergence of transnational institutions operating in many societies, the pressures toward convergence among political systems are likely to become more intense. Interdependence may be incompatible with coexistence. In this case the world, like the United States in the nineteenth century or Western Europe in the twentieth century, will not be able to exist half-slave and half-free. Hence the survival of democratic institutions and values at home will depend upon their adoption abroad.

Third, American efforts to make other people's institutions conform to American values would be justified to the extent that the other people supported those values. Such support has historically been much more prevalent in Western Europe and Latin America than it has in Asia and Africa, but some support undoubtedly exists in almost every society for liberty, equality, democracy, and the rights of the individual. Americans could well feel justified in supporting and helping those individuals, groups, and institutions in other societies who share their belief in these values. At the same time it would also be appropriate for them to be aware that those values could be realized in other societies through institutions significantly different from those that exist in the United States.

Fourth, American efforts to make other people's institutions conform to American values could be justified on the grounds that those values are universally valid and universally applicable, whether or not most people in other societies believe in them. For Americans not to believe in the universal validity of American values could indeed lead to a moral relativism: liberty and democracy are not inherently better than any other political values; they just happen to be those that for historical and cultural reasons prevail in the United States. This relativistic position runs counter to the strong elements of moral absolutism and messianism that are part of American history and culture, and hence the argument for moral relativism may not wash in the United States for relativistic reasons. In addition the argument can be made that some element of belief in the universal validity of a set of political ideals is necessary to arouse the energy, support, and passion to defend those ideals and the institutions modeled on them in American society.

Historically Americans have generally believed in the universal validity of their values. At the end of World War II, when Americans forced Germany and Japan to be free, they did not stop to ask if liberty and democracy were what the German and Japanese people wanted. Americans implicitly assumed that their values were valid and applicable and that they would at the very least be morally negligent if they did not insist that Germany and Japan adopt political institutions reflecting those values. Belief in the universal validity of those values obviously reinforces and reflects those hypocritical elements of the American tradition that stress the United States's role as a redeemer nation and lead it to attempt to impose its values and often its institutions on other societies. These tendencies may, however, be constrained by a recognition that although American values may be universally valid, they need not be universally and totally applicable at all times and in all places.

Americans expect their institutions and policies that are devoted to external relations to reflect liberal standards and principles. So also in large measure do non-Americans. Both American citizens and others hold the United States to standards that they do not generally apply to other countries. People expect France, for instance, to pursue its national self-interests—economic, military, and political—with cold disregard for ideologies and values. But their expectations with respect to the United States are very different: people accept with a shrug actions on the part of France that would generate surprise, consternation, and outrage if perpetrated by the United States. "Europe accepts the idea that America is a country with a difference, from whom it is reasonable to demand an exceptionally altruistic standard of behaviour; it feels perfectly justified in pouring obloquy on shortcomings from this ideal; and also, perhaps inevitably, it seems to enjoy every example of a fall from grace which contemporary America provides."[22]

This double standard is implicit acknowledgment of the seriousness with which Americans attempt to translate their principles into practice. It also provides a ready weapon to foreign critics of the United States, just as it does to domestic ones. For much of its history, racial injustice, economic inequality, and political and religious intolerance were familiar elements in the American landscape, and the contrast between them and the articulated ideals of the American Creed furnished abundant ammunition to generations of European critics. "Anti-Americanism is in this form a protest, not against Americanism, but against its apparent failure."[23] This may be true on the surface. But it is also possible that failure—that is, the persistence of the ideals-versus-institutions gap in American institutions and policies—furnishes the excuse and the opportunity for hostile foreign protest and that the true target of the protest is Americanism itself.

POWER AND LIBERTY: THE MYTH OF AMERICAN REPRESSION

The pattern of American involvement in world affairs has often been interpreted as the outcome of these conflicting pulls of national interest and power on the one hand and political morality and principles on the other. Various scholars have phrased the dichotomy in various ways: self-interest versus ideals, power versus morality, realism versus utopianism, pragmatism versus principle, historical realism versus rationalist idealism, Washington versus Wilson.[24] Almost all, however, have assumed the dichotomy to be real and have traced the relative importance over the years of national interest and morality in shaping American foreign policy. It is, for instance, argued that during the Federalist years realism or power considerations were generally preponderant, whereas during the first four decades of the twentieth century moral considerations and principles came to be uppermost in the minds of American policy makers. After World War II a significant group of writers and thinkers on foreign policy—including Reinhold Niebuhr, George Kennan, Hans Morgenthau, Walter Lippmann, and Robert Osgood—expounded a "new realism" and criticized the moralistic, legalistic, "utopian" Wilsonian approaches, which they claimed had previously prevailed in the conduct of American foreign relations. The new realism reached its apotheosis in the central role played by the balance of power in the theory and practice of Henry Kissinger. A nation's foreign policy, he said, "should be directed toward affecting the foreign policy" of other societies; it should not be "the principal goal of American foreign policy to transform the domestic structures of societies with which we deal."[25]

In the 1970s, however, the new realism of the 1950s and 1960s was challenged by a "new moralism." The pendulum that had swung in one direction after World War II swung far over to the other side. This shift was one of the most significant consequences of American involvement in Vietnam, Watergate, and the democratic surge and creedal passion of the 1960s. It represented the displacement onto the external world of the moralism that had been earlier directed inward against American institutions. It thus represented the first signs of a return to the hypocritical response to the gap between American values and American institutions. The new moralism manifested itself first in congressional action, with the addition to the foreign assistance act of Title IX in 1966 and human rights conditions in the early 1970s. In 1976 Jimmy Carter vigorously criticized President Ford for believing "that there is little room for morality in foreign affairs, and that we must put self-interest above principle."[26] As president, Carter moved human rights to a central position in American foreign relations.

The lines between the moralists and the realists were thus clearly drawn, but on one point they were agreed: they both believed that the conflict between morality and self-interest, or ideals and realism, was a real one. In some respects it was. In other respects, particularly when it was formulated in terms of a conflict between liberty and power, it was not. As so defined, the dichotomy was false. It did not reflect an accurate understanding of the real choices confronting American policy makers in dealing with the external world. It derived rather from the transposition of the assumptions of the antipower ethic to American relations with the rest of the world. From the earliest years of their society Americans have perceived a conflict between imperatives of governmental power and the liberty and rights of the individual. Because power and liberty are antithetical at home, they are also assumed to be antithetical abroad. Hence the pursuit of power by the American government abroad must threaten liberty abroad even as a similar pursuit of power at home would threaten liberty there. The contradiction in American society between American power and American liberty at home is projected into a contradiction between American power and foreign liberty abroad.

During the 1960s and 1970s this belief led many intellectuals to propagate what can perhaps best be termed the myth of American repression—that is, the view that American involvement in the politics of other societies is almost invariably hostile to liberty and supportive of repression in those societies. The United States, as Hans Morgenthau put it, is "repression's friend": "With unfailing consistency, we have since the end of the Second World War intervened on behalf of conservative and fascist repression against revolution and radical reform. In an age when societies are in a revolutionary or prerevolutionary stage, we have become the foremost counterrevolutionary status quo power on earth. Such a policy can only lead to moral and political disaster."[27] This statement, like the arguments generally of those intellectuals supporting the myth of American repression, suffers from two basic deficiencies.

First, it confuses support for the left with opposition to repression. In this respect, it represents another manifestation of the extent to which similarity in immediate objectives can blur the line between liberals and revolutionaries. Yet those who support "revolution and radical reform" in other countries seldom have any greater concern for liberty and human dignity than those who support "conservative and fascist repression." In fact, if it is a choice between rightist and Communist dictatorships, there are at least three good reasons in terms of liberty to prefer the former to the latter. First, the suppression of liberty in right-wing authoritarian regimes is almost always less pervasive than it is in left-wing totalitarian ones. In the 1960s and 1970s, for instance, infringements of human rights in South Korea received extensive coverage in the American media, in part because there were in South Korea journalists, church groups, intellectuals, and opposition political leaders who could call attention to those infringements. The absence of comparable reports about the infringements of human rights in North Korea was evidence not of the absence of repression in that country but of its totality. Right-wing dictatorships moreover are, the record shows, less permanent than left-wing dictatorships;

Portugal, Spain, and Greece are but three examples of right-wing dictatorships that were replaced by democratic regimes. As of 1980, however, no Communist system had been replaced by a democratic regime. Third, as a result of the global competition between the United States and the Soviet Union, right-wing regimes are normally more susceptible to American and other Western influence than left-wing dictatorships, and such influence is overwhelmingly on the side of liberty.

This last point leads to the other central fallacy of the myth of American repression as elaborated by Morgenthau and others. Their picture of the world of the 1960s and 1970s was dominated by the image of an America that was overwhelmingly powerful and overwhelmingly repressive. In effect they held an updated belief in the "illusion of American omnipotence" that attributed the evil in other societies to the machinations of the Pentagon, the CIA, and American business. Their image of America was, however, defective in both dimensions. During the 1960s and 1970s American power relative to that of other governments and societies declined significantly. By the mid-1970s the ability of the United States to influence what was going on in other societies was but a pale shadow of what it had been a quarter-century earlier. When it had an effect, however, the overall effect of American power on other societies was to further liberty, pluralism, and democracy. The conflict between American power and American principles virtually disappears when it is applied to the American impact on other societies. In that case, the very factors that give rise to the consciousness of a gap between ideal and reality also limit in practice the extent of that gap. The United States is in practice the freest, most liberal, most democratic country in the world, with far better institutionalized protections for the rights of its citizens than any other society. As a consequence, any increase in the power or influence of the United States in world affairs generally results—not inevitably, but far more often than not—in the promotion of liberty and human rights in the world. The expansion of American power is not synonymous with the expansion of liberty, but a significant correlation exists between the rise and fall of American power in the world and the rise and fall of liberty and democracy in the world.

The single biggest extension of democratic liberties in the history of the world came at the end of World War II, when stable democratic regimes were inaugurated in defeated Axis countries: Germany, Japan, Italy, and, as a former part of Germany, Austria. In the early 1980s these countries had a population of over two hundred million and included the third and fourth largest economies in the world. The imposition of democracy on these countries was almost entirely the work of the United States. In Germany and Japan in particular the United States government played a major role in designing democratic institutions. As a result of American determination and power the former Axis countries were "forced to be free."[28] Conversely, the modest steps taken toward democracy and liberty in Poland, Czechoslovakia, and Hungary were quickly reversed and Stalinist repression instituted once it became clear that the United States was not able to project its power into Eastern Europe. If World War II had ended in something less than total victory, or if the United States had played a less significant role in bringing about the victory (as was indeed the case east of the Elbe), these transitions to democracy in central Europe and eastern Asia would not have occurred. But—with the partial exception of South Korea—where American armies marched, democracy followed in their train.

The stability of democracy in these countries during the quarter-century after World War II reflected in large part the extent to which the institutions and practices imposed by the United States found a favorable social and political climate in which to take root. The continued American political, economic, and military presence in Western Europe and eastern Asia was, however, also indispensable to this democratic success. At any time after World War II the withdrawal of American military guarantees and military forces from these areas would have had a most unsettling and perhaps devastating effect on the future of democracy in central Europe and Japan.

In the early years of the cold war, American influence was employed to ensure the continuation of democratic government in Italy and to promote free elections in Greece. In both cases, the United States had twin interests in the domestic politics of these countries: to create a system of stable democratic government and to ensure the exclusion of Communist parties from power. Since in both cases the Communist parties did not have the support of anything remotely resembling a majority of the population, the problem of what to do if a party committed to abolishing democracy gains power through democratic means was happily avoided. With American support, democracy survived in Italy and was sustained for a time in Greece. In addition, the American victory in World War II provided the stimulus in Turkey for one of the rarest events in political history: the peaceful self-transformation of an authoritarian one-party system into a democratic competitive party system.

In Latin America, the rise and fall of democratic regimes also coincided with the rise and fall of American influence. In the second and third decades of this century, American intervention in Nicaragua, Haiti, and the Dominican Republic produced the freest elections and the most open political competition in the history of those countries. In these countries, as in others in Central America and the Caribbean, American influence in support of free elections was usually exerted in response to the protests of opposition groups against the repressive actions of their own governments and as a result of American fears that revolution or civil war would occur if significant political and social forces were denied equal opportunity to participate in the political process. The American aim, as Theodore Wright made clear in his comprehensive study, was to "promote political stability by supporting free elections" rather than by strengthening military dictatorships. In its interventions in eight Caribbean and Central American countries between 1900 and 1933 the United States acted on the assumption that "the only way both to prevent revolutions and to determine whether they are justified if they do break out is to guarantee free elections."[29] In Cuba the effect of the Platt Amendment and American interventions was "to pluralize the Cuban political system" by fostering "the rise and entrenchment of opposition groups" and by multiplying "the sources of political power so that no single group, not even the government, could impose its will on society or the economy for very long. . . . The spirit and practices of liberalism—competitive and unregulated political, economic, religious, and social life— overwhelmed a pluralized Cuba."[30] The interventions by United States Marines in

Haiti, Nicaragua, the Dominican Republic, and elsewhere in these years often bore striking resemblances to the interventions by federal marshals in the conduct of elections in the American South in the 1960s: registering voters, protecting against electoral violence, ensuring a free vote and an honest count.

Direct intervention by the American government in Central America and the Caribbean came to at least a temporary end in the early 1930s. Without exception the result was a shift in the direction of more dictatorial regimes. It had taken American power to impose even the most modest aspects of democracy in these societies. When American intervention ended, democracy ended. For the Caribbean and Central America, the era of the Good Neighbor was also the era of the bad tyrant. The efforts of the United States to be the former give a variety of unsavory local characters—Trujillo, Somoza, Batista—the opportunity to be the latter.

In the years after World War II, American attention and activity were primarily directed toward Europe and Asia. Latin America was by and large neglected. This situation began to change toward the later 1950s, and it dramatically shifted after Castro's seizure of power in Cuba. In the early 1960s Latin America became the focus of large-scale economic aid programs, military training and assistance programs, propaganda efforts, and repeated attention by the president and other high-level American officials. Under the Alliance for Progress, American power was to be used to promote and sustain democratic government and greater social equity in the rest of the Western Hemisphere. This high point in the exercise of United States power in Latin America coincided with the high point of democracy in Latin America. This period witnessed the Twilight of the Tyrants: it was the age in which at one point all but one of the ten South American countries (Paraguay) had some semblance of democratic government.[31]

Obviously the greater prevalence of democratic regimes during these years was not exclusively a product of United States policy and power. Yet the latter certainly played a role. The democratic governments that had emerged in Colombia and Venezuela in the late 1950s were carefully nurtured with money and praise. Strenuous efforts were made to head off the attempts of both left-wing guerrillas and right-wing military officers to overthrow Betancourt in Venezuela and to ensure the orderly transition to an elected successor for the first time in the history of that country. After thirty years in which "the U.S. government was less interested and involved in Dominican affairs" than at any other time in history—a period coinciding with Trujillo's domination of the Dominican Republic—American opposition to that dictator slowly mounted in the late 1950s. After his assassination in 1961 "the United States engaged in the most massive intervention in the internal affairs of a Latin American state since the inauguration of the Good Neighbor Policy."[32] The United States prevented a return to power by Trujillo's family members, launched programs to promote economic and social welfare, and acted to ensure democratic liberties and competitive elections. The latter, held in December 1962, resulted in the election of Juan Bosch as president. When the military moved against Bosch the following year, American officials first tried to head off the coup and then, after its success, attempted to induce the junta to return quickly to constitutional procedures. But by that point American "leverage and influence [with the new government] were severely limited," and the only concession the United

States was able to exact in return for recognition was a promise to hold elections in 1965.[33]

Following the military coup in Peru in July 1962, the United States was able to use its power more effectively to bring about a return to democratic government. The American ambassador was recalled; diplomatic relations were suspended; and $81 million in aid was canceled. Nine other Latin American countries were induced to break relations with the military junta—an achievement that could only have occurred at a time when the United States seemed to be poised on the brink of dispensing billions of dollars of largesse about the continent.[34] The result was that new elections were held the following year, and Belaunde was freely chosen president. Six years later, however, when Belaunde was overthrown by a coup, the United States was in no position to reverse the coup or even to prevent the military government that came to power from nationalizing major property holdings of American nationals. The power and the will that had been there in the early 1960s had evaporated by the late 1960s, and with it the possibility of holding Peru to a democratic path. Through a somewhat more complex process, a decline in the American role also helped produce similar results in Chile. In the 1964 Chilean elections, the United States exerted all the influence it could on behalf of Eduardo Frei and made a significant and possibly decisive contribution to his defeat of Salvador Allende. In the 1970 election, the American government did not make any comparable effort to defeat Allende, who won the popular election by a narrow margin. At that point, the United States tried to induce the Chilean Congress to refuse to confirm his victory and to promote a military coup to prevent him from taking office. Both these efforts violated the norms of Chilean politics and American morality, and both were unsuccessful. If on the other hand the United States had been as active in the popular election of 1970 as it had been in that of 1964, the destruction of Chilean democracy in 1973 might have been avoided.

All in all the decline in the role of the United States in Latin America in the late 1960s and early 1970s coincided with the spread of authoritarian regimes in that area. With this decline went a decline in the standards of democratic morality and human rights that the United States could attempt to apply to the governments of the region. In the early 1960s in Latin America (as in the 1910s and 1920s in the Caribbean and Central America), the goal of the United States was democratic competition and free elections. By the mid-1970s that goal had been lowered from the fostering of democratic government to attempting to induce authoritarian governments not to infringe too blatantly on the rights of their citizens.

A similar relationship between American power and democratic government prevailed in Asia. There too the peak of American power was reached in the early and mid-1960s, and there too the decline in this power was followed by a decline in democracy and liberty. American influence had been most pervasive in the Philippines, which for a quarter-century after World War II had the most open, democratic system (apart from Japan) in east and southeast Asia. After the admittedly fraudulent election of 1949 and in the face of the rising threat to the Philippine government posed by the Huk insurgency, American military and economic assistance was greatly increased. Direct American intervention in Philippine politics then played a decisive role not only in promoting Ramon Magsaysay into the presidency but also in assuring that the 1951 congressional elections and 1953 presidential election were open elections "free from fraud and intimidation."[35] In the next three elections the Philippines met the sternest test of democracy: incumbent presidents were defeated for reelection. In subsequent years, however, the American presence and influence in the Philippines declined, and with it one support for Philippine democracy. When President Marcos instituted his martial law regime in 1972, American influence in southeast Asia was clearly on the wane, and the United States held few effective levers with which to affect the course of Philippine politics. In perhaps even more direct fashion, the high point of democracy and political liberty in Vietnam also coincided with the high point of American influence there. The only free national election in the history of that country took place in 1967, when the American military intervention was at its peak. In Vietnam, as in Latin America, American intervention had a pluralizing effect on politics, limiting the government and encouraging and strengthening its political opposition. The defeat of the United States in Vietnam and the exclusion of American power from Indochina were followed in three countries by the imposition of regimes of almost total repression.

The American relationship with South Korea took a similar course. In the late 1940s, under the sponsorship of the United States, U.N.-observed elections inaugurated the government of the Republic of Korea and brought Syngman Rhee to power. During the Korean War (1950–1953) and then in the mid-1950s, when American economic assistance was at its peak, a moderately democratic system was maintained, despite the fact that South Korea was almost literally in a state of siege. In 1956 Rhee won reelection by only a close margin and the opposition party won the vice-presidency and swept the urban centers.

In the late 1950s, however, as American economic assistance to Korea declined, the Rhee regime swung in an increasingly authoritarian direction. The 1960 vice-presidential election was blatantly fraudulent; students and others protested vigorously; and as the army sat on the sidelines, Rhee was forced out of power. A democratic regime under the leadership of John M. Chang came into office but found it difficult to exercise authority and to maintain order. In May 1961 this regime was overthrown by a military coup despite the strong endorsement of the Chang government by the American embassy and military command. During the next two years, the United States exerted sustained pressure on the military government to hold elections and return power to a civilian regime. A bitter struggle took place within the military over this issue; in the end President Park Chung Hee, with American backing and support, overcame the opposition within the military junta, and reasonably open elections were held in October 1963, in which Park was elected president with a 43 percent plurality of the vote. In the struggle with the hard-line groups in the military, one reporter observed, "the prestige and word of the United States have been put to a grinding test"; by insisting on the holding of elections, however, the United States "emerged from this stage of the crisis with a sort of stunned respect from South Koreans for its determination—from those who eagerly backed United States pressures on the military regime and even from officers who were vehemently opposed to it."[36] Thirteen years later, however, the United States was no longer in a position to have the same impact on Korean politics. "You can't talk pure Jefferson to these guys," one American official said. "You've got to have a threat of some kind or they won't listen. . . . There aren't many levers left to pull around here. We just try to keep the civil rights issue before the eyes of Korean authorities on all levels and hope it has some effect."[37] By 1980 American power in Korea had been reduced to the point where there was no question, as there was in 1961 and 1962, of pressuring a new military leadership to hold prompt and fair elections. The issue was simply whether the United States had enough influence to induce the Korean government not to execute Korea's leading opposition political figure, Kim Dae Jung, and even with respect to that, one Korean official observed, "the United States has no leverage."[38] Over the years, as American influence in Korea went down, repression in Korea went up.

The positive impact of American power on liberty in other societies is in part the result of the conscious choices by presidents such as Kennedy and Carter to give high priority to the promotion of democracy and human rights. Even without such conscious choice, however, the presence or exercise of American power in a foreign area usually has a similar thrust. The new moralists of the 1970s maintained that the United States has "no alternative" but to act in terms of the moral and political values that define the essence of its being. The new moralists clearly intended this claim to have at least a normative meaning. But in fact it also describes a historical necessity. Despite the reluctance or inability of those imbued with the myth of American repression to recognize it, the impact of the United States on the world has in large part been what the new moralists say it has to be. The nature of the United States has left it little or no choice but to stand out among nations as the proponent of liberty and democracy. Clearly, the impact of no other country in world affairs has been as heavily weighted in favor of liberty and democracy as has that of the United States.

Power tends to corrupt, and absolute power corrupts absolutely. American power is no exception; clearly it has been used for good purposes and bad in terms of liberty, democracy, and human rights. But also in terms of these values, American power is far less likely to be misused or corrupted than the power of any other major government. This is so for two reasons. First, because American leaders and decision makers are inevitably the products of their culture, they are themselves generally committed to liberal and democratic values. This does not mean that some leaders may not at times take actions that run counter to those values. Obviously this happens: sensibilities are dulled; perceived security needs may dictate other actions; expediency prevails; the immediate end justifies setting aside the larger purpose. But American policy makers are more likely than those of any other country to be sensitive to these trade-offs and to be more reluctant to sacrifice liberal-democratic values. Second, the institutional pluralism and dispersion of power in the American political system impose constraints—unmatched in any other society—on the ability of officials to abuse power and also to ensure that those transgressions that do occur will almost inevitably become public knowledge. The American press is extraordinarily free, strong, and vigorous in its exposure of bad policies and corrupt officials. The American Congress has powers of investigation, legislation, and financial control unequaled by any other national legislature. The ability of American officials to violate the values of their society is therefore highly limited, and the extent to which the press is filled with accounts of how officials have violated those values is evidence not that such behavior is more widespread than it is in other societies but that it is less tolerated than in other societies. The belief that the United States can do no wrong in terms of the values of liberty and democracy is clearly as erroneous abroad as it is at home. But so, alas, is the belief—far more prevalent in American intellectual circles in the 1970s—that the United States could never do right in terms of those values. American power is far more likely to be used to support those values than to counter them, and it is far more likely to be employed on behalf of those values than is the power of any other major country.

The point is often made that there is a direct relation between the health of liberty in the United States and the health of liberty in other societies. Disease in one is likely to infect the other. Thus, on the one hand, Richard Ullman argued that "the quality of political life in the United States is indeed affected by the quality of political life in other societies. The extinction of political liberties in Chile, or their extension in Portugal or Czechoslovakia, has a subtle but nonetheless important effect on political liberties within the United States." Conversely, he also goes on to say, "just as the level of political freedom in other societies affects our own society, so the quality of our own political life has an important impact abroad."[39] This particular point is often elaborated into what is sometimes referred to as the clean hands doctrine—that the United States cannot effectively promote liberty in other countries so long as there are significant violations of liberty within its borders. Let the United States rely on the power of example and "first put our house in order," as Hoffmann phrased it. "Like charity, well-ordered crusades begin at home."[40]

Both these arguments—that of the corrupting environment and that of the shining example—are partial truths. By any observable measure the state of liberty in countries like Chile or Czechoslovakia has in itself no impact on the state of liberty in the United States. Similarly, foreigners usually recognize what Americans tend to forget—that the United States is the most open, free, and democratic society in the world. Hence any particular improvement in the state of liberty in the United States is unlikely to be seen as having much relevance to their societies. Yet these arguments do have an element of truth in them when one additional variable is added to the equation. This element is power.

The impact that the state of liberty in other societies has on liberty in the United States depends upon the power of those other societies and their ability to exercise that power with respect to the United States. What happens in Chile or even Czechoslovakia does not affect the state of liberty in the United States because those are small, weak, and distant countries. But the disappearance of liberty in Britain or France or Japan would have consequences for the health of liberty in the United States, because they are large and important countries intimately involved with the United States. Conversely, the impact of the state of liberty in the United States on other societies depends not upon changes in American liberty (which foreigners will inevitably view as marginal) but rather upon the power and immediacy of the United States to the country in question. The power of example works only when it is an example of power. If the United States plays a strong, confident, preeminent role on the world stage, other nations will be impressed by its power and will attempt to emulate its liberty in the belief that liberty may be the source of power. This point was made quite persuasively in 1946 by Turkey's future premier, Adnan Menderes, in explaining why his country had to shift to democracy:

> The difficulties encountered during the war years uncovered and showed the weak points created by the one-party system in the structure of the country. The hope in the miracles of [the] one-party system vanished, as the one-party system countries were defeated everywhere. Thus, the one-party mentality was destroyed in the turmoil of blood and fire of the second World War. No country can remain unaffected by the great international events and the contemporary dominating ideological currents. This influence was felt in our country too.[41]

In short, no one copies a loser.

The future of liberty in the world is thus intimately linked to the future of American power. Yet the double thrust of the new moralism was paradoxically to advocate the expansion of global liberty and simultaneously to effect a reduction in American power. The relative decline in American power in the 1970s has many sources. One of them assuredly was the democratic surge (of which the new moralism was one element) in the United States in the 1960s and early 1970s. The strong recommitment to democratic, liberal, and populist values that occurred during these years eventually generated efforts to limit, constrain, and reduce American military, political, and economic power abroad. The intense and sustained attacks by the media, by intellectuals, and by congressmen on the military establishment, intelligence agencies, diplomatic officials, and political leadership of the United States inevitably had that effect. The decline in American power abroad weakened the support for liberty and democracy abroad. American democracy and foreign democracy may be inversely related. Due to the mediating effects of power their relationship appears to be just the opposite of that hypothesized by Ullman.

The promotion of liberty abroad thus requires the expansion of American power; the operation of liberty at home involves the limitation of American power. The need in attempting to achieve democratic goals both abroad and at home is to recognize the existence of this contradiction and to assess the trade-offs between these two goals. There is, for instance, an inherent contradiction between welcoming the end of American hegemony in the Western Hemisphere and at the same time deploring the intensification of repression in Latin America. It is also paradoxical that in the 1970s those congressmen who were most insistent on the need to promote human rights abroad were often most active in reducing the American power that could help achieve that result. In key votes in the Ninety-fourth Congress, for instance, 132 congressmen consistently voted in favor of human rights amendments to foreign aid legislation. Seventy-eight of those 132 representatives also consistently voted against a larger military establishment, and another 28 consistent supporters of human rights split their votes on the military establishment. Only 26 of the 132 congressmen consistently voted in favor of both human rights and the military power whose development could help make those rights a reality.

The new realism of the 1940s and 1950s coincided with the expansion of American power in the world and the resulting expansion of American-sponsored liberty and democracy in the world. The new moralism of the 1970s coincided with the relative decline in American power and the concomitant erosion of liberty and democracy around the globe. By limiting American power the new moralism promoted that decline. In some measure, too, the new moralism was a consequence of the decline. The new moralism's concern with human rights throughout the world clearly reflected the erosion in global liberty and democratic values. Paradoxically, the United States thus became more preoccupied with ways of defending human rights as its power to defend human rights diminished. Enactment of Title IX to the foreign assistance act in 1966, a major congressional effort to promote democratic values abroad, came at the mid-point in the steady decline in American foreign economic assistance. Similarly, the various restrictions that Congress wrote into the foreign assistance acts in the 1970s coincided with the general replacement of military aid by military sales. When American power was clearly predominant, such legislative provisions and caveats were superfluous: no Harkin Amendment was necessary to convey the message of the superiority of liberty. The message was there for all to see in the troop deployments, carrier task forces, foreign-aid missions, and intelligence operatives. When these faded from the scene, in order to promote liberty and human rights Congress found it necessary to write more and more explicit conditions and requirements into legislation. These legislative provisions were in effect an effort to compensate for the decline of American power. In terms of narrowing the ideals-versus-institutions gap abroad, they were no substitute for the presence of American power.

Contrary to the views of both "realists" and "moralists," the contradiction arising from America's role in the world is not primarily that of power and self-interest versus liberty and morality in American foreign policy. It is rather the contradiction between enhancing liberty at home by curbing the power of the American government and enhancing liberty abroad by expanding that power.

THE PROMISE OF DISAPPOINTMENT

The term *American exceptionalism* has been used to refer to a variety of characteristics that have historically distinguished the United States from European societies—characteristics such as its relative lack of economic suffering, social conflict, political trauma, and military defeat. "The standing armies, the monarchies, the aristocracies, the huge debts, the crushing taxation, the old inveterate abuses, which flourish in Europe," William Clarke argued in 1881, "can take no root in the New World. The continent of America is consecrated to simple humanity, and its institutions exist for the progress and happiness of the whole people." Yet, as Henry Fairlie pointed out in 1975, "there now *are* standing armies of America; there now *is* something that, from time to time, looks very like a monarchy; there now *is* a permitted degree of inherited wealth that is creating some of the elements of an aristocracy; there now *is* taxation that is crushing."[42] In the same year Daniel Bell came to a similar conclusion by a different path. The "end of American exceptionalism," he argued, is to be seen in "the end of empire, the weakening of power, the loss of faith in the nation's future. . . . Internal tensions have multiplied and there are deep structural crises, political and cultural, that may prove more intractable to solution than the domestic economic problems."[43]

In the late twentieth century, the United States surely seemed to confront many evils and problems that were common to other societies but that it had previously avoided. These developments, however, affected only the incidental elements of American exceptionalism, those of power, wealth, and security. They did not change American political values and they only intensified the gap between political ideals and political institutions that is crucial to American national identity. They thus did not affect the historically most exceptional aspect of the United States, an aspect eloquently summed up and defended by a Yugoslav dissident.

> The United States is not a state like France, China, England, etc., and it would be a great tragedy if someday the United States became such a state. What is the difference? First of all, the United States is not a national state, but a multinational state. Second, the United States was founded by people who valued individual freedom more highly than their own country.
>
> And so the United States is primarily a state of freedom. And this is what is most important. Whole peoples from other countries can say, Our homeland is Germany, Russia, or whatever; only Americans can say, My homeland is freedom.[44]

Americans have said this throughout their history and have lived throughout their history in the inescapable presence of liberal ideals, semiliberal institutions, and the gap between the two. The United States has no meaning, no identity, no political culture or even history apart from its ideals of liberty and democracy and the continuing efforts of Americans to realize those ideals. Every society has its own distinctive form of tension that characterizes its existence as a society. The tension between liberal ideal and institutional reality is America's distinguishing cleavage. It defines both the agony and the promise of American politics. If that tension disappears, the United States of America as we have known it will no longer exist.

The continued existence of the United States means that Americans will continue to suffer from cognitive dissonance. They will continue to attempt to come to terms with that dissonance through some combination of moralism, cynicism, complacency, and hypocrisy. The greatest danger to the gap between ideals and institutions would come when any substantial portion of the American population carried to an extreme any one of these responses. An excess of moralism, hypocrisy, cynicism, or complacency could destroy the American system. A totally complacent toleration of the ideals-versus-institutions gap could lead to the corruption and decay of American liberal-democratic institutions. Uncritical hypocrisy, blind to the existence of the gap and fervent in its commitment to American principles, could lead to imperialistic expansion, ending in either military or political disaster abroad or the undermining of democracy at home. Cynical acceptance of the gap could lead to a gradual abandonment of American ideals and their replacement either by a Thrasymachusian might-makes-right morality or by some other set of political beliefs. Finally, intense moralism could lead Americans to destroy the freest institutions on earth because they believed they deserved something better.

To maintain their ideals and institutions, Americans have no recourse but to temper and balance their responses to the gap between the two. The threats to the future of the American condition can be reduced to the extent that Americans:

- continue to believe in their liberal, democratic, and individualistic ideals and also recognize the extent to which their institutions and behavior fall short of these ideals;
- feel guilty about the existence of the gap but take comfort from the fact that American political institutions are more liberal and democratic than those of any other human society past or present;
- attempt to reduce the gap between institutions and ideals but accept the fact that the imperfections of human nature mean the gap can never be eliminated;
- believe in the universal validity of American ideals but also understand their limited applicability to other societies;
- support the maintenance of American power necessary to protect and promote liberal ideals and institutions in the world arena, but recognize the dangers such power could pose to liberal ideals and institutions at home.

Critics say that America is a lie because its reality falls so far short of its ideals. They are wrong. America is not a lie; it is a disappointment. But it can be a disappointment only because it is also a hope.

NOTES

1. Richard Hofstadter, *The American Political Tradition* (New York: Alfred A. Knopf, 1951), pp. 65–66.
2. Marvin Meyers, *The Jacksonian Persuasion: Politics and Belief* (Stanford, Calif.: Stanford University Press, 1957), p. 8.
3. See Edward Pessen, "The Egalitarian Myth and the American Social Reality: Wealth, Mobility, and Equality in the 'Era of the Common Man,'" *American Historical Review* 76 (October 1971):989–1034, and idem, *Riches, Class, and Power before the Civil War* (Lexington, Mass.: D. C. Heath, 1973). For critical discussions of Pessen's evidence and argument see Whitman Ridgway, "Measuring Wealth and Power in Ante-Bellum America: A Review Essay," *Historical Methods Newsletter* 8 (March 1975):74–78, and Robert E. Gallman, "Professor Pessen on the 'Egalitarian Myth,'" *Social Science History* 2 (Winter 1978):194–207. For Pessen's response, see his "On a Recent Cliometric Attempt to Resurrect the Myth of Antebellum Egalitarianism," *Social Science History* 3 (Winter 1979):208–27.
4. Gordon S. Wood, *History Book Club Review* (June 1975):16–17, commenting on Rush Welter's, *The Mind of America: 1820–1860* (New York: Columbia University Press, 1975).
5. Welter, *The Mind of America: 1820–1860*, pp. 7–10.
6. Alexis de Tocqueville, *Democracy in America*, 2 vols., ed. Phillips Bradley (New York: Vintage Books, 1954), 1:6–17.
7. Joseph L. Blau, ed., *Social Theories of Jacksonian Democracy* (New York: Liberal Arts Press, 1954), pp. xxvii–xxviii.
8. Hofstadter, *American Political Tradition*, p. vi.

9. Herbert Croly, *The Promise of American Life* (New York: Macmillan, 1909), p. 156; and Walter Lippmann, *Drift and Mastery* (Englewood Cliffs, N.J.: Prentice-Hall, 1961), pp. 81–82.

10. Hofstadter, *American Political Tradition,* p. 223.

11. J. R. Pole, *The Pursuit of Equality in American History* (Berkeley: University of California Press, 1978), p. 326.

12. See Ronald Inglehart, *The Silent Revolution: Changing Values and Political Styles among Western Publics* (Princeton, N.J.: Princeton University Press, 1977), and George C. Lodge, *The New American Ideology* (New York: Alfred A. Knopf, 1975).

13. Ronald Inglehart, "The Silent Revolution in Europe: Intergenerational Change in Post-Industrial Societies," *American Political Science Review* 65 (December 1971):991–1017.

14. Samuel P. Huntington, "Postindustrial Politics: How Benign Will It Be?" *Comparative Politics* 6 (January 1974):188–89.

15. Plato, *The Republic,* trans. Francis MacDonald Cornford (New York: Oxford University Press, 1945), p. 290.

16. Louis Hartz, *The Liberal Tradition in America* (New York: Harcourt, Brace, 1955), p. 181.

17. Samuel P. Huntington, *Political Order in Changing Societies* (New Haven, Conn.: Yale University Press, 1968), pp. 362–69.

18. See Samuel P. Huntington, *The Soldier and the State: The Theory and Politics of Civil-Military Relations* (Cambridge: Harvard University Press, 1957), esp. pp. 143–57.

19. George F. Kennan, *American Diplomacy 1900–1950* (Chicago, Ill.: University of Chicago Press, 1951), pp. 93–94; and Huntington, *The Soldier and the State,* pp. 80–97.

20. Lucian W. Pye, *The Spirit of Chinese Politics* (Cambridge, Mass.: MIT Press, 1968), p. 91.

21. Seymour Martin Lipset, "The Banality of Revolt," *Saturday Review,* 18 July 1970, p. 26.

22. Peregrine Worsthorne, "America—Conscience or Shield?" *Encounter,* no. 14 (November 1954):15.

23. Henry Fairlie, "Anti-Americanism at Home and Abroad," *Commentary* 60 (December 1975):35.

24. See for example Hans J. Morgenthau, *In Defense of the National Interest* (New York: Alfred A. Knopf, 1951), and idem, "Another 'Great Debate': The National Interest of the United States," *American Political Science Review* 46 (December 1952):961–88; Reinhold Niebuhr, *Christian Realism and Political Problems* (New York: Charles Scribner's Sons, 1953), and idem, *The Irony of American History* (New York: Charles Scribner's Sons, 1952); Kennan, *American Diplomacy 1900–1950;* Robert E. Osgood, *Ideals and Self-Interest in America's Foreign Relations* (Chicago, Ill.: University of Chicago Press, 1953); and Richard H. Ullman, "Washington versus Wilson," *Foreign Policy,* no. 21 (Winter 1975–76):97–124.

25. Henry A. Kissinger, quoted in Raymond Gastil, "Affirming American Ideals in Foreign Policy," *Freedom at Issue,* no. 38 (November–December 1976):12.

26. Jimmy Carter, address, B'nai B'rith convention, Washington, D.C., 8 September 1976.

27. Hans J. Morgenthau, "Repression's Friend," *New York Times,* 10 October 1974.

28. See John D. Montgomery, *Forced To Be Free: The Artificial Revolution in Germany and Japan* (Chicago, Ill.: University of Chicago Press, 1957).

29. Theodore P. Wright, *American Support of Free Elections Abroad* (Washington, D.C.: Public Affairs Press, 1964), pp. 137–38.

30. Jorge I. Dominguez, *Cuba: Order and Revolution* (Cambridge: Harvard University Press, 1978), p. 13.

31. See Tad Szulc, *The Twilight of the Tyrants* (New York: Henry Holt, 1959).

32. Jerome Slater, *Intervention and Negotiation* (New York: Harper & Row, 1970), p. 7.
33. Abraham F. Lowenthal, *The Dominican Intervention* (Cambridge: Harvard University Press, 1972), p. 16.
34. Jerome Levinson and Juan de Onis, *The Alliance that Lost Its Way* (Chicago, Ill.: Quadrangle Books, 1970), pp. 81–82.
35. H. Bradford Westerfield, *The Instruments of America's Foreign Policy* (New York: Thomas Y. Crowell, 1963), p. 416.
36. A. M. Rosenthal, *New York Times*, 8 April 1963.
37. Quoted by Andrew H. Malcolm, *New York Times*, 11 June 1976.
38. *The Economist*, 30 August 1980, pp. 27–28.
39. Ullman, "Washington versus Wilson," pp. 117, 123.
40. Stanley Hoffmann, "No Choice, No Illusions," *Foreign Policy*, no. 25 (Winter 1976–77): 127.
41. Adnan Menderes, *Cumhuriyef*, 18 July 1946, quoted in Kemal H. Karpat, *Turkey's Politics* (Princeton, N.J.: Princeton University Press, 1959), p. 140, n. 10.
42. Fairlie, "Anti-Americanism at Home and Abroad," p. 34, quoting William Clarke, 1881.
43. Daniel Bell, "The End of American Exceptionalism," in *The American Commonwealth 1976*, eds. Nathan Glazer and Irving Kristol (New York: Basic Books, 1976), p. 197.
44. Mihajlo Mihajlov, "Prospects for the Post-Tito Era," *New America* 17 (January 1980):7.

Policy Making in a Weak State

Stephen D. Krasner

Establishing a set of transitively ordered preferences that persist over time and are related to general societal goals defines the national interest. The existence of such a set of goals does not imply that they will be implemented. Realist approaches to international relations have focused on the ways in which other actors in the international system may frustrate state leaders. The analysis of this study, while sharing the same basic assumptions, emphasizes the domestic constraints that are imposed on the state. In structural approaches to international relations the state is a billiard ball whose internal components are impervious to foreign pressures; here the state is a set of central decision-making institutions and roles that must confront internal as well as external opponents. The central analytic characteristic that determines the ability of a state to overcome domestic resistance is its strength in relation to its own society.[1]

STRONG AND WEAK STATES

The strength of the state in relationship to its own society can be envisioned along a continuum ranging from weak to strong.[2] The weakest kind of state is one that is completely permeated by pressure groups. Central government institutions serve specific interests within the country rather than the general aims of the citizenry as a whole. Lebanon before the civil war of 1975–1976 can be thought of as such a state: public functions and positions were divided between Moslems and Christians; there was little or no agreement on what would constitute the general good or the collective interest of the country. The logical terminus of the weak end of the spectrum is civil war and the complete disintegration of the state.

At the other extreme from a state completely permeated by political pressure groups is one that is able to remake the society and culture in which it exists—that is, to change economic institutions, values, and patterns of interaction among private groups. Such extraordinarily powerful states have only existed immediately after major revolutions. It is not that the state is so strong during such periods but that the society is weak because existing patterns of behavior have been shattered. The clearest examples are the Soviet Union after 1917 and China after 1949. Both countries had suffered many years of war. In China the old regime had been falling apart for a century, unable to cope with pressures from the West. In Russia the First World War had devastated the country and demonstrated the incompetence of the Czarist government. In both countries the regimes that seized power made fundamental changes in economic, cultural, and even familial relationships.

Obviously most states are neither as weak as Lebanon nor as strong as post-revolutionary Communist regimes. Usually the state is able to maintain some autonomy from the society, but at the same time it cannot impose rapid and dramatic structural transformations on the economic or cultural systems. In capitalist or market-economy countries, where there is some autonomy between private and public institutions, three *ideal-typical* relationships between the state and society can be envisioned.

First, the state may be able to resist societal pressure but unable to change the behavior of private actors. For instance, central decision makers may be able to ignore appeals from large corporations but unable to make corporations follow policies that would further the state's goals or create alternative institutions such as state-owned businesses.

Second, the state may be able to resist private pressure and to persuade private groups to follow policies that are perceived as furthering the national interest but be unable to impose structural transformation on its domestic environment. Here public officials have positive power, the ability to change private behavior so that the public interest is better served, and not simply negative power, the ability to prevent the private sector from using public resources to protect private prerogatives. Still, the state must work with existing social structures. In economic affairs these structures can be defined in terms of the juridical nature of the institutions controlling economic activities (for instance, government versus privately owned corporations), the distribution of activity among sectors, and the place of particular firms within sectors.

Finally, a state may have the power to change the behavior of existing private actors and also over a period of time the economic structure itself. The state could create new kinds of economic actors. It could build up certain sectors of the economy through credits, tax relief, or other forms of support. It could favor companies whose activities were perceived as serving the national interest. These possibilities are summed up in Table 11.1.

It is important to recognize that the *weak, moderate, strong,* and *dominant* categories all assume a view of politics that is incompatible with either a liberal or instrumental Marxist approach. All four of these ideal types imply that the state has some autonomy from its own society even if this autonomy is limited, as in the case of weak states, to preventing societal pressure groups from using the instruments of public power for private purposes. Moderate, strong, and dominant states can alter the societal environment in which they act, a phenomenon that is difficult to capture from either a pluralist or instrumental Marxist perspective.

It is very unlikely that any state will fit neatly into one of the classifications, but an ideal-typical taxonomy helps highlight critical distinctions. The weak, moderate, and strong types are the most relevant for polities in advanced market-economy countries. In such countries states may be strong in some issue areas and weak in others. There is no reason to assume *a priori,* that the pattern of strength and weakness will be the same for all policies. One state may be unable to alter the structure of its medical system but be able to construct an efficient transportation network, while another can deal relatively easily with getting its citizens around but cannot get their illnesses cured. States in developed capitalist countries are most likely to fit the moderate pattern of power shown in Table 11.1 in some issue areas and the weak pattern in others. None of these states falls into the nonexistent or the dominant pattern, and only some are strong even in a relatively limited number of issue areas.

Despite variations among issue areas within countries, there are modal differences in the power of the state among the advanced market-economy countries. France and Japan probably have the strongest states. Even in periods of rapidly changing governments, such as the Fourth Republic, the French central administration could exercise public control over private actors. The administrative elite has been able to choose those interest groups that it has preferred to deal with, favoring associations whose views coincided with its preferences. The French state has had a fairly wide range of policy instruments to alter the behavior of private ac-

Table 11.1   POWER OF THE STATE VIS-À-VIS ITS DOMESTIC SOCIETY

	Resist private pressure		Change private behavior		Change social structure	
	Yes	No	Yes	No	Yes	No
Nonexistent		x		x		x
Weak	x			x		x
Moderate	x		x			x
Strong	x		x		x (but slowly)	
Dominant	x		x		x	

tors. The most potent has probably been the control of credit. Because the ratio of self-financing for French firms is low, they must look to the capital market for loans. This market is heavily influenced by the state. The largest bank in France is publicly owned. The French government has very close ties with some private banks. Special funds have been set up to make investments in areas that are perceived as being in the national interest. Such funds have been controlled by the bureaucrats in charge of implementing French economic plans and have been insulated from the legislature. In addition planning officials have signed contracts with individual companies: the private sector has promised to meet certain economic goals, such as production targets and prices; the government has offered tax breaks, changes in import duties, social security payment rebates, favorable provision of capital, guaranteed government purchases, subsidized research, and even free advertising on the government-owned television network. Such arrangements made indicative planning more effective during the 1950s and 1960s.

The French government has also created mixed or wholly government-owned enterprises in certain critical economic sectors such as power generation, nuclear energy, railroads, and airlines. In petroleum the French government became a part owner of the Compagnie Française des Pétroles (CFP) in 1929. After the Second World War intervention in the oil industry was extended. In 1965 the government amalgamated a number of smaller firms to form a second French exploration and development company, ERAP. Oil imports have been closely regulated. Special funds have been provided for oil exploration. Tax rebates have been granted for petroleum development in France or the franc zone. By the 1970s these policies had led to a substantial decline in the amount of oil refined and distributed in France by non-French companies.[3]

The pattern of relationships between the state and the economy in Japan has many similarities with that in France. Intervention at the level of the economic sector or the firm (as opposed to the economy as a whole) has been facilitated by the wide range of policy instruments possessed by the Japanese bureaucracy, particularly the Ministry of International Trade and Industry (MITI) and the Ministry of Finance. MITI has actively coordinated behavior in certain industries by setting goals for output and unit costs. It has been able to grant tax allowances through accelerated depreciation. It has established a system of advisory councils. During the 1950s MITI acted to develop and rationalize the Japanese steel, petrochemical, heavy machinery, automobile, electronics, synthetic rubber, and airplane industries. In dealing with the international economy, Japan has imposed tighter controls than any other advanced capitalist state: through the 1950s the allocation of foreign exchange gave MITI a powerful lever of control over the domestic economy; and MITI has developed close relationships with major trading companies that handle 50 percent to 60 percent of Japanese exports. The Ministry of Finance has pursued a policy of keeping interest rates below levels needed to clear the market. Credit has been allocated through institutional controls. Discrimination among borrowers, rationing, and subsidies have been the rule. The Ministry of Finance's decisions about capital have been used to bolster specific sectors and firms.[4]

In France and Japan, the exercise of state power has been facilitated by political culture. In both countries an activist role for the state is widely accepted. In

France prices and patterns of production are not taken as a given but are regarded as variables that are subject to official control. In Japan a high regard for private enterprise is coupled with a belief that the government should act as a well-intentioned guide. In both countries the bureaucracy is respected. The best graduates from the most elite universities are likely to choose the central administration over the private sector.[5]

This is not to say that in either France or Japan the state always wins, while the private sector plays a merely passive and servile role. Even public ownership has not meant automatic subservience to state preferences in France. The French have recognized that such enterprises must have some autonomy. Firms can bargain with decision makers and even reject official policy. In recent years, as France has become more immeshed in the international economy, precise control has become more difficult. In Japan the Ministry of Finance and MITI have also played a less directive role in recent years, at least in part because of greater exposure to the rest of the world. In at least one dramatic case the Japanese government failed to secure the support of the private sector: in 1969 and 1970 Prime Minister Sato was unable to persuade the Japanese textile industry to accept a secret arrangement with the United States for limiting man-made textile exports, which the Nixon administration had linked with the reversion of Okinawa to Japan.[6] However, in comparison with the United States, the state in France and Japan has more power over its own society. In the terms of Table 11.1, these two countries fall into either the moderate or the strong category for most issue areas.

THE AMERICAN POLITICAL SYSTEM

America has a strong society but a weak state. Within little more than a century after becoming independent the United States had become the world's largest market and leading source of technological innovation. By the end of the Second World War the United States had achieved a position of global dominance unmatched in previous human history.

Through all of this the political system remained weak. The central feature of American politics is the fragmentation and dispersion of power and authority. This has been recognized by pluralists such as Dahl, Polsby, and Truman, who tend to emphasize the system's virtues, as well as by writers such as Huntington, Lowi, McConnell, and Burnham, who see the American polity as gravely flawed. Polsby argues that the different branches of the American government were designed so that they "would be captured by different interests."[7] Truman notes that the "diffusion of leadership and disintegration of policy are not hallucinations."[8] Huntington summarizes the situation as one in which there is a "fusion of functions and division of power."[9] Burnham argues that the political system has been "in domestic matters at any rate—dispersive and fragmented . . . dedicated to the defeat, except temporarily and under the direct pressure of overwhelming crisis, of any attempt to generate domestic sovereignty. . . ."[10]

The Constitution is a document more concerned with limiting than enhancing the power of the state. The Founding Fathers were wary of power; they sought to limit its temptations by dividing power within the government and among societal groups. They preserved the states, gave Congress specific, not unlimited legal powers, established a bicameral legislature, gave the president specific, not unlimited powers, and created an independent judiciary. Although the concept of dividing power among societal groups is not explicitly reflected in the Constitution, it was voiced by Madison at the convention and clearly explicated in *Federalist No. 10*.[11]

The American state—the president and those bureaus relatively insulated from societal pressures, which are the only institutions capable of formulating the national interest—must always struggle against an inherent tendency for power and control to be dissipated and dispersed. They must operate in a political culture that views the activist state with great suspicion. This is particularly true of the business sector. American capitalists have a more negative reaction to public economic activity than their counterparts in other advanced market economies.[12] American central decision makers do not command the policy instruments that are important in countries like France and Japan. It is not clear in the United States where sovereignty rests, if indeed it rests anywhere at all.[13] The jurisdictional boundaries of institutions are unclear. "Dispersed leadership and multiple points of control within one branch reflect and reinforce similar patterns in the other."[14] In trying to promote the national interest the American state often confronts dissident bureaus, recalcitrant Congress, and powerful private actors.

Within the executive branch it cannot be assumed that the president can control all bureaus. Even here the state must struggle against the legislature and the private sector. Many presidential appointments are subject to ratification by the Senate. Budgets require legislative approval. The legal structures of many agencies reflect the desire of Congressional committees to maintain some formal control. Some agencies can get support from Congress against the preferences of the president.[15] Particular public bureaucracies have ties with the private sector. Many federal regulatory agencies are controlled by the groups that they are supposed to regulate. McConnell argues that "a substantial part of government in the United States has come under the influence or control of narrowly based autonomous elites."[16] Agency heads may appeal to societal constituencies. Truman's hesitancy in removing MacArthur during the Korean War can in large part be explained by the general's political popularity and his ties with the right wing of the Republican Party.[17]

More important, for the empirical problems dealt with in this study, is the impact of the Congress on the ability of central decision makers to implement their preferences. Congress presents an inherent problem for two reasons. First, the political needs and constituencies of congressmen are different from those of the president. Second, power within the Congress itself is fragmented and dispersed, offering many points of access for societal groups.

Because congressmen represent geographically specific areas, they are bound to have different concerns from the president's. While the president can be held accountable for the broad effect of policy, rarely can members of the legislature. To get reelected, members of Congress must serve relatively narrow constituencies. They are likely to prefer particularized legislation that allows them to take credit for rendering service to those whose support they need to stay in office. The general tendency in Congress is to appoint members to committees related to the interests of their constituents. Congressmen will service organized groups with disposable political resources. Such groups often keep a close watch on committee activities. Congressmen will try to protect their own bureaucratic clientele from presidential intervention. Cleavages between Congress and the president have often been more salient than those between political parties.[18]

The problems that Congress presents for the implementation of the preferences of central decision makers are exacerbated by the absence of cohesion and centralization in the Congress itself. The American legislature does not confront the president as a unified force. American central decision makers may have to bargain with a number of specific congressional institutions, each capable of blocking state initiatives.

In 1885 Woodrow Wilson wrote about Congress that "power is nowhere concentrated; it is rather deliberately and of set policy scattered amongst many small chiefs."[19] During the twentieth century the dispersal of power in the legislative branch has increased. In both houses the position of the leader of the majority party, the natural focus of centralized authority, has been persistently undermined. From the attack on Speaker Cannon in the House in 1910 until the legislative reforms of the mid-1970s the key element in this trend was the seniority system, which deprived the leadership of the right to select committee chairmen. The Legislative Reorganization Act of 1946 strengthened the position of standing committees and limited the discretion that the leadership could exercise in allocating bills among committees. The Legislative Reform Act of 1970 dispersed power still further by strengthening committee chairmen. Reforms in the Congress from 1970 to 1973 were largely directed at reducing the power of chairmen; in some cases heads of subcommittees have assumed a more prominent role.[20] While recent changes have lessened the importance of seniority, they have not restored any centralized control over individual committees.

The growth of congressional staff and resources since the Second World War has also made it more difficult to achieve coherence. The number of committee staff members increased from 400 in 1946 to 2,000 in 1974. The number of staff assistants for individual members of the Congress had reached 9,000 by 1974. Support institutions such as the General Accounting Office, the Congressional Research Service, the Office of Technology Assessment, and the Congressional Budget Office have all been expanded or created during the last few decades. Congressional perquisites such as franking privileges have been increased. All of these developments have reduced the power of party leaders in the House and the Senate.[21]

Harvey Mansfield has summed up the situation in the following terms: "Dispersion is a formula for producing and encouraging a cadre of miners and sappers like Senator Proxmire and Congressman Les Aspin, skilled in tunneling and penetrating hidden recesses and placing explosive charges in the executive branch—the military-industrial complex, the CIA, Watergate, and domestic surveillance; missionaries like Congressman Drinan seeking converts to their causes; entrepreneurs and brokers putting together the elements of a conglomerate bill that can pass; broken-field runners and players to the grandstand; and, in the Senate, aspirants to the presidency."[22]

The fragmentation of power means that legislation can be blocked at any one of a number of decision-making nodes. In the House these include subcommittees, full committees, the Rules Committee, the full House, the Rules Committee again for a bill going to a conference committee, and the conference committee itself. The situation is similar in the Senate except that there is no direct parallel with the Rules Committee. The Appropriations Committees of both branches can change programs by not approving funds or by issuing reports that tell agencies precisely what to do. Although these reports are not legally binding, an agency jeopardizes its relations with the committees if such instructions are ignored. The jurisdictional authority of individual committees is often not clearly differentiated: the Appropriations and Government Operations Committees, the House Rules Committee, and the Joint Economic Committee all have virtually universal scope in the matters they can consider. There is usually little cooperation between committees with the same jurisdiction in the two houses.[23]

Causes of a Weak Political System

The weakness of the American polity is deeply embedded in the country's history. America has never needed a strong state. The political, social, and economic imperatives that have enhanced the role of the state in Japan and continental Europe have been much less compelling in the United States. First, with one minor exception (the War of 1812), the United States has never been confronted with foreign invasion. Second, American society has been unusually cohesive, and dominant social values have geen congruent with the needs of a modern economy. Third, the American economy has performed extraordinarily well without much direct government intervention, and the abundance generated by economic success has mitigated the demands placed upon the state.

America has not until recently confronted a serious external threat to its territorial and political integrity. On the European continent the great impetus to the centralization of political authority during the sixteenth and seventeenth centuries was the constant threat of war. Fledgling states could not defend themselves without a standing army. To raise and maintain such forces, it was necessary to strengthen the political system.[24] The United States, on the other hand, enjoyed the protection of Britain's maritime dominance during the nineteenth century. By the time America was thrown upon the world scene in the twentieth century, its size and mastery of technology made it possible to create the world's most formidable military force even with a weak government. Curiously, the very weapons that have for the first time made the territorial integrity of the United States vulnerable may also, because of their capital intensity, allow the state to maintain its defenses with a weak political structure. The burdens imposed upon the domestic population by hardened missile sites and nuclear submarines are less than those resulting from large standing armies and extensive reserve corps.

A second reason why a strong state has not developed in America is because dominant social values did not have to be changed to ensure societal cohesion or economic development. America, born modern, did not have to be made modern. Early Americans were favorably disposed to change and to social status based upon achievement rather than ascription. Commitment to social classes was weak. There was never an aristocratic class or feudal institutions that stood in the way of rapid social and economic development. Immigrants absorbed the values held by those who had come before them.[25] Huntington argues that "in Europe the opposition to modernization within society forced the modernization of the political system. In America, the ease of modernization within society precluded the modernization of political institutions."[26] The Founding Fathers' desire to decentralize power led to a viable political system only because their view of American society was wrong. It was not riven with dissension. On the contrary, it was exceptionally cohesive. Checks and balances have offered a workable formula only because the society has been able to perform the kind of integrating functions that fell to the state in most European countries.[27]

Finally, there is a set of economic factors that help explain why the state has been weak in America. Alexander Gerschenkron has pointed to a syndrome associated with the sequence of industrialization. Those countries that underwent the industrial revolution at an earlier period, notably the United States and Great Britain, industrialized more slowly; the scale of industry was smaller; there was less direct intervention from the state because private actors could mobilize their own resources; and slower development did not mean that the country's security would be threatened. Late modernizers—France, Germany, Japan, and Russia—experienced more rapid rates of growth. They relied more on large capital-intensive projects. The state played a direct role in moving the economy from a mercantile and agricultural base to an industrial one, particularly by mobilizing resources and dispensing investment funds.[28]

Furthermore, America has been almost from its inception a relatively wealthy country. It was well endowed with natural resources—most importantly during its formative period, a large amount of land. In terms of per capita income it surpassed Britain in the middle of the nineteenth century, then fell back as a result of immigration and other factors but regained its global lead by the outbreak of the First World War and held it at least through the 1960s. Abundance and rapid growth facilitated equal opportunity and the belief that things would always improve. Social problems were often solved by technological and economic changes rather than political initiatives. All of this good fortune reinforced the myth of social equality and mobility. It was possible to believe that things would always get better, because they usually did for most people. Pressures on the political system were usually relatively modest because the level of social dissatisfaction was mitigated by economic growth. A weak political system could exist because politics was less necessary for a citizenry that perceived itself dividing an expanding rather than stagnant national product. In the words of David Potter, "economic abundance is conducive to political democracy"[29] and, one might add, a democratic system that diffused rather than concentrated power and authority.

Before proceeding, it is well to note, if only briefly, some of the normative consequences of an analytic framework focusing on the strength and weakness of the state. There is an obvious implication that it is better to have a strong state than a weak one: a weak state may be unable to pursue the general interest because it is frustrated by particular societal actors. However, this does not imply that an authoritarian regime is desirable. Democracy is not incompatible with a strong state. The ability to vote political leaders out of office is the critical check on abuse of power. The stalemate system that can frustrate efforts by American central decision makers to take action that would enhance collective societal goals should not be confused with democracy. The ability of individual pressure groups to block government initiatives is not the same as the ability of the citizenry to remove a central decision maker from office. The former makes it difficult for the state to fulfill its purpose of protecting the collective interests of the society; the latter is protection against authoritarianism.

Judgments about the merits of weak and strong political systems cannot be made in an empirical vacuum. America has had a weak state because it has not needed a strong one. And weakness does have its advantages. It probably increases the individual citizen's sense of efficacy, even if attempts to actually influence the government are rare.[30] In addition, as Kenneth Waltz has argued in *Foreign Policy and Democratic Politics,* a political system with many seats of power may enhance debate and ultimately lead to clearer and more responsive policies. A weak state may also offer greater flexibility in the economic sphere. When technology is changing rapidly, flexibility may be critical for economic development, because central decision-making institutions rarely if ever have the capacity to direct such change effectively.[31] Hence, in examining a country's collective economic well-being, any judgment about the relative merits of weak and strong states depends upon the situation the state confronts. Despite the difficulty American central decision makers have in implementing their preferences, American society has still fared extraordinarily well because, on the whole, the private sector has been able to operate with great efficiency. Whether this pattern will continue is a question to which we shall return in the conclusion of this study.

If one looks to critics, supporters, or apologists for the American political system, then, a common thread runs through all of their arguments: in America political power is dispersed and fragmented. This structure rests upon a socioeconomic foundation characterized by shared values, the absence of external threat, internal harmony, equality, and abundance. The implication that some draw, although others ignore, is that the state is weak: it cannot easily penetrate and transform the society. There is an endemic tendency toward ignoring general goals. The system makes obstruction easy, positive action difficult.

STATE LEADERSHIP AND SOCIETAL CONSTRAINTS

The diffusion of power has not, however, had a uniform impact across all political issues. In particular it has not presented severe problems for defending the core goals of foreign policy, territorial and political integrity. Even those analysts most critical of the American political system have been reluctant to include this issue area in their argument.[32] The protection of the territorial and political integrity of the state does not usually lead to disagreements among societal groups. Political elites may argue about how these aims should be secured, but the state rarely has to contend with conflicting interest groups. A state that is weak in relation to its own society can act effectively in the strategic arena because its preferences are not likely to diverge from those of individual societal groups.

There is, however, no reason to assume that foreign economic-policy making is identical with foreign political-policy making. Any economic decision is likely to affect groups within the society differentially, creating the potential for societal conflict. For this reason it is questionable to assume that policy can be understood solely by examining the motivations and perceptions of central decision makers. In a political system where state power is weak and fragmented, foreign as well as domestic economic policy can be influenced or even determined by societal groups.

Private Political Resources

International raw materials policy is an area where the potential for societal frustration of the national interest is great because the major private actors command substantial political resources. The American corporations involved in the international movement of almost all raw materials are very large, especially the oil companies. Table 11.2 lists those handling particular commodities and their rank by sales among all U.S. firms for the year 1976.

In addition the corporations involved in raw materials industries generally operate in fairly concentrated markets at the national and even the global level. Table 11.3 shows levels of concentration for a number of markets within the United States.

Even at the global level many markets have been governed by a relatively small number of firms until recent years, when the influence of host-country governments has risen sharply. Seven companies (five American, one British, one British-Dutch) have dominated the world oil market; three (two Canadian, one French), the nickel market; six (three American, one Canadian, one French, and one Swiss), the aluminum market; three (all American), the banana market. In the iron ore industry, 30 percent of ore traded in 1968 moved within a vertically integrated structure. Although levels of concentration have declined in several markets since 1950, including aluminum, petroleum, lead, and copper, the structure of almost all raw materials industries, even at the global level, has been oligopolistic.[33]

Such large economic units acting in concentrated markets are likely to possess the attributes that confer political power in America. They are usually well represented in Washington through individual lobbyists, law firms, and trade associations. They have large amounts of money. They hold information that public officials cannot procure through other channels. They are competently directed.

Perhaps more than any other societal actor, large corporations are able to appeal to public institutions through all three forms of representation present in the American government: geographic, functional, and national. Because they often employ large numbers of people in geographically specific areas, they are important to particular congressmen. Because they dominate large areas of the economy, they are important to the functional agencies of the executive branch. Because at least some of them are vital for the economy as a whole, they are important to the White House. All of these attributes combine to give most large American corporations direct access to congressional committees, executive departments, and often the White House itself.[34]

Table 11.2 SIZE OF U.S. RAW MATERIALS FIRMS: RANK BY SALES, 1976

Petroleum		Ferrous metals		Nonferrous metals		Tropical foodstuffs		Rubber	
Company	Rank	Company	Rank	Company	Rank	Company	Rank	Company	Rank
Exxon	1	U.S. Steel	14	Alcoa	72	Procter & Gamble	19	Goodyear	23
Texaco	4	Bethlehem	33	Reynolds	108	General Foods	44	Uniroyal	95
Mobil	5	Armco	63	Anaconda	151	United Brands	99	General Tire	111
Socal	6	National	76	AMAX	191	Standard Brands	126	Goodrich	112
Gulf	7	Republic	86	Kennecott	234	Castle and Cook	250		
				Phelps Dodge	240	Hershey	328		
				St. Joe's	251				
				Revere	374				

Source: Fortune 95 (May 1977).

Table 11.3   LEVELS OF CONCENTRATION: PERCENT OF INDUSTRIAL SHIPMENTS, 1972

Product	Four largest companies	Eight largest companies
Primary copper	72	98 (1970)
Primary lead	93	99
Primary zinc	66	90 (1970)
Primary aluminum	79	92
Roasted coffee	65	79
Petroleum refinery products	31	56
Raw cane sugar	44	62
Beet sugar	66	92
Chocolate and cocoa	74	88

Source: U.S. Department of Commerce, Bureau of the Census, Concentration Ratios in Manufacturing.

In some raw materials markets political pressure can come from another source—geographically concentrated groups of domestic owners and workers. Here again the oil industry stands out. In the mid-1960s the value of petroleum and natural gas production accounted for 45 percent of total personal income in Wyoming, 39 percent in Louisiana, 22 percent in New Mexico, 17 percent in Texas, and 15 percent in Oklahoma.[35] Additional sources of energy, especially coal, provide a livelihood for substantial numbers of people in other states. The large membership of such groups can make them particularly telling in influencing Congress because of its geographic system of representation.

In sum, American decision makers face serious constraints in formulating international raw-materials policy. The American political system diffuses and fragments power. In most raw-materials markets they confront societal actors, including large corporations and concentrated groups of domestic producers, that possess substantial political resources. Even when private groups are in disagreement, public initiatives may be frustrated. Political structure and societal interests establish the parameters within which American central decision makers must operate. Yet it would be a mistake to assume that they rigidly determine final outcomes.

Leadership and Decision Arenas

The weakness of the political system and the political resources of private actors do not always lead to frustration for American leaders in their effort to implement the national interest. Obviously, the preferences of societal groups and those of central decision makers may converge without any effort by either side to influence the other. Beyond this analytically simple (but practically important) category, the impediments that a fragmented system imposes on central decision makers can be mitigated in two ways. First, the state can exercise political leadership. In the area of international raw-materials investment the most important manifestations of leadership have involved altering private preferences and exploiting divisions among societal groups. Second, the preferences of political leaders are more likely to be adopted and implemented if decisions are taken by central state institutions such as the White House and the State Department rather than by the Congress or executive bureaus that serve specific domestic interest groups. The arena in which decisions are taken is a function of the way in which an issue is defined, and this definition too can sometimes be altered by political leadership. Both leadership and the ability to make decisions within central state institutions involve situations in which the American polity resembles the moderate pattern of state power described in Table 11.1 rather than the weak one, which is the more typical pattern for the United States.

LEADERSHIP AND CONVERGING PREFERENCES

The preferences of public and private actors may converge for a variety of reasons. The most obvious is that the clearly identified needs of the state can coincide with the economic interests of the firm. In raw-materials markets the state's desire for secure and stable supplies may lead to policies that further the profits, growth, or market control of the firm. In addition private and public preferences may converge because the state can modify the perceptions of societal actors. One way that central decision makers can bring this sort of change about is by offering a compelling interpretation of events that corporate managers are unable to make sense of on their own. By providing a coherent frame of reference the state can alter the way in which private managers define their own interest. Less obviously, preferences may also converge when the state supports policies that have an ambiguous or even moderately negative effect on private actors, because central decision makers can exploit the nonpecuniary motives of corporate officials. This is a much more likely possibility when the state confronts oligopolistic, diversified corporations than when it must deal with sectors composed of large numbers of small owner-operated producing units. Recent developments in the theory of the firm suggest why this should be so.

Classical economic theory expects firms to act as if they were maximizing profits. It assumes perfect competition: each firm acts as if prices and market conditions are given, the entrepreneur has perfect information. Firms fail if they do not equate marginal revenue and marginal cost. This approach is most applicable to small privately owned firms operating in a competitive setting.

In recent years the assumption that profit maximization governs the behavior of business firms has been challenged. Many sectors of the American economy are not characterized by perfect competition. Concentration is high. Firms do not perceive prices as a given. Managers of one firm realize that their decisions partially determine the actions of others. With the diversification of stockholding, owners are no longer managers. Two further approaches, satisficing and behavioral, that take account of these factors have been developed.

The satisficing model focuses on the problem of information. Firms rarely have perfect knowledge of the market. Classical assumptions place unreasonable demands on the choosing organism: payoffs must be associated with each outcome; unexpected results are not considered; outcomes must be ordered and probabilities determined. There is no evidence that these criteria are met in actual situations of any complexity. A more accurate picture emerges if it is assumed that the organism searches for some satisfactory level of payoff and will settle for any outcome that equals or exceeds this level. Business firms, like other complex decision-making organisms, can then be viewed as satisficers rather than maximizers. They attempt to secure one of many satisfactory outcomes based upon past experience and levels of expectation.[36]

Satisficing behavior is characteristic of large business firms. Information costs increase as the complexity of the organization increases. The complexity of the organization is in part a function of its size and diversity. A large firm with many divisions producing, marketing, and distributing different products may find it difficult to arrive at any decision concerning particular government policies.[37] Many corporations are both importers and exporters. Many have extensive foreign investments and at the same time produce import-competing goods domestically. In attempting to adapt themselves to the norms that exist in different countries, central corporate managers may be loath to specify general policy. During the debate over American tariff policies in the late 1950s, for instance, Du Pont and General Electric left their individual division managers to lobby as they saw fit.[38] In the mid-1960s Nestlé's corporate headquarters in Switzerland supported an international cocoa agreement, while its American subsidiary, following the rest of the American industry, opposed it.

Another approach, the behavioral theory of the firm, focuses on the internal needs of the organization rather than on external economic objectives. It analyzes enterprises as coalitions that include managers, workers, suppliers, customers, and stockholders. Organizational survival requires that the firm have enough resources to meet the demands of members of its coalition. In an oligopolistic corporation little attention may be paid to considerations of cost as long as a decision does not affect existing arrangements with regard to the general level of profits, dividends, wages, and output—that is, as long as a decision does not dramatically affect the resources that are used to satisfy the demands of members of the coalition.[39]

Oligopolistic corporate managers have considerable discretion. They make decisions when the actual survival of the organization is not at stake. They coordinate the activity of other coalition members. Managers are likely to avoid risky behavior. If they perform badly, they may find themselves subject to a stockholders' revolt, dismissal by their board of directors, or takeover efforts by outside interests. If they perform well, the owners are not likely to provide them with equivalent rewards. Managers are faced with an asymmetry that induces them to avoid risky endeavors whose failure could threaten their position.[40] They aim at acceptable rather than optimal levels of profits, sales, and growth for their firms.

One kind of risky behavior that corporate managers are not likely to engage in is public conflict with the government. Business leaders are prone to keep a low profile. Direct confrontations with the state may focus attention on the firm that can lead to economic problems or increased government interference.[41] The enormous power possessed by private companies in America has never been fully legitimized by the dominant value system. There has been persistent strain between the economic aims of the company and general social goals.[42] Public exposure al-

ways presents the risk of catalyzing widespread public antipathy that political leaders can mobilize against the autonomy or profitability of the firm. The behavioral
theory of the firm suggests that corporate managers are not likely to place themselves lightly in such an unpredictable and potentially threatening situation.

The behavioral theory also suggests that managers are motivated by nonpecuniary as well as pecuniary considerations. Robert A. Gordon has argued: "The most
important spurs to action by the businessman, other than the desire for goods for
the purpose of direct want satisfaction, are probably the following: the urge for
power, the desire for prestige and the related impulse of emulation, the creative
urge, the propensity to identify oneself with a group and the related feeling of
group loyalty, the desire for security, the urge for adventure and for 'playing the
game' for its own sake, and the desire to serve others."[43]

Chester I. Barnard, in his classic study *The Functions of the Executive,* maintains that nonmaterial rewards are the real cement holding organizations together.
Prestige, personal power, and the attainment of dominating position are, he argues, much more important than material rewards, even in the development of
commercial organizations.[44]

The behavioral theory implies that the government can expect neutrality if its
policies do not threaten the level of resources necessary to satisfy all members of
the coalition composing the firm. Even if official policies have a negative effect on
economic performance, risk-avoiding managers may steer away from confrontations that could raise the saliency of an issue for stockholders, workers, or customers. Furthermore, large diversified firms have a great deal of flexibility. They
can move from one product line to another. They can adjust their production
methods. For such actors consistency of government policy may be more important than its actual substance.[45]

Nonpecuniary objectives open possibilities for the exercise of political leadership: political leaders can manipulate the preferences of private managers. Although the behavioral theory has dealt primarily with intrafirm transactions, there
is no reason why managers cannot get some rewards from outside the firm. To secure nonpecuniary benefits managers may support official policies that are harmful to economic performance so long as resources are adequate to maintain the
firm's internal coalition. If public leaders can cast their policy aims in terms of attitudes that are widely held within the society, uncooperative corporate executives
will experience some cognitive dissonance. As managers come to regard themselves more as trustees of resources meant to serve the whole society and less as
profit maximizers concerned solely with the balance sheet of the firm, the probability of such psychological discomfort increases.[46] Provided that the policy advocated by public decision makers does not threaten the corporation's ability to satisfy its immediate coalition members, managers can eliminate dissonance by
accepting public initiatives.

A similar conclusion can be reached by viewing managers as citizens rather
than private economic actors. David Truman, in a somewhat strained application
of group theory, makes shared social values the central "balance wheel" of the
American polity.[47] "How does a stable policy exist in a multiplicity of interest
groups?" he asks, and answers that "in essence, however, it is that the fact that

membership in organized and potential groups overlap *in the long run* imposes restraints and conformities upon interest groups on pain of dissolution or of failure."[48] The most important "potential interest group" is manifest in the "behavior and the habitual interactions of men" that reflect widely accepted "ideals and traditions."[49] Hans Morgenthau, who writes from a different orientation, comes to a similar conclusion. "Consensus and consent of the governed," he argues, "indispensable for an effective foreign policy in a democracy, flow from the allegiance of a citizen to his nation—its nature, institutions and objectives"—rather than from particular social or economic interests.[50] The existence of such sentiments has recently received some empirical corroboration from a study of the attitudes of American business leaders that concludes that their ideological beliefs are a more important determinant of their general foreign policy outlook than the specific economic interests of their firms.[51]

The problem for the state is to transform these latent loyalties into an active political force, or at least to use them to neutralize potential opposition to state initiatives. This may be done through appeals to individuals or groups. In *War and the Private Investor* Eugene Staley writes:

> Some governments are able to appeal to another powerful non-profit motive which strongly influences more men, and, one may suspect, acts with special effectiveness on those who have already reached the pinnacle of success in finance and business. This is the striving for distinction that is fostered and satisfied by the granting of patents of nobility, order of merit, knighthood. Instances are probably rare where a capitalist has received such recognition as the immediate result of compliance with his government's wishes in the placement of funds abroad, just as direct bribes are relatively unimportant in the influence of investors on governments. Rather, like good jobs with oil companies and banks for former state officials, these distinctions are legitimate prizes, endowed with social approval, which dangle before the eyes of aspirants and supply an incentive to act generally in a seemly and becoming manner.[52]

Obviously, the granting of patents of nobility has not been very salient in the United States. But there are functional equivalents including awards, ambassadorships, and White House dinners.

More important than appeals to specific individuals is the ability of state actors to define issues in ways that touch upon the general concerns of citizens. Foreign policy is distant from the specific experience of most individuals. Even corporate managers engaged in disputes over foreign investment may find it difficult to determine what course of action they should follow. The information they must analyze is political as well as economic. Their long-term economic objectives may not be well defined. Political leaders, on the other hand, may be able to define their own goals more clearly. They may be able to place a specific dispute over a foreign raw material investment in a broader political context. They may be able to feed corporate officials additional information, such as assessments of the political stability of a host-country government, that will lead managers to change their estimates of what action would be best for their firm. The exercise of effective leadership, then, involves changing the perceptions of private actors by defining problems and by appealing to the notion that managers are trustees of social resources, or to their loyalties as citizens, or to their private drives for status and prestige.[53]

In sum, satisficing and behavioral theories of the firm suggest that interests cannot simply be taken as a given. Political leaders may be able to change the goals of private managers. Such leadership will be most difficult when dealing with privately owned economic units operating in a competitive market. Owners of relatively small firms are more likely than the executives of large diversified ones to be able to perceive the impact of government policy. They lack the status and prominence that would give them access to national decision-making arenas. Although some individuals may be capable of acting altruistically even if their sacrifices go unrecognized, they are surely a tiny minority. Purposive kinds of motivations are usually accompanied by solidary ones. Selfless behavior can only rarely be sustained without group recognition.[54] Large corporate managers who accede to the entreaties of public officials are likely to be recognized; the owners of small firms who act in the same way are not.

The probabilities of convergence between the preferences of public and private officials are, then, higher when private units are larger and more complex and issues are identified as being vital to widely held national goals. This convergence is not simply a function of objectively defined economic interests; it is also determined by the general value structure of the society and the ability of political leaders to attach these values to specific policy initiatives. It is, in sum, a function of political leadership as well as material rewards. The presence of large complex corporations presents political opportunities for increasing the coincidence of public and private preferences. The political resources of large corporations may not be mobilized against the state if managerial perceptions are altered by political leaders.

POLICY-MAKING ARENAS

While natural convergence or effective leadership can result in many areas of agreement between public officials and corporate managers, their preferences are obviously not entirely coincident. Political leaders may attempt to implement policies that are opposed by businessmen, and conversely, private managers may press the state to behave in ways that are antithetical to the general aims of stability, security, or greater competition in raw-materials markets. The outcome of such struggles depends in part on the decision-making arena in which they take place. Private firms have often been frustrated in their efforts to secure public support, particularly for foreign investments, because the White House and State Department, where most investment policy is made, are relatively impervious to private pressure. On the other hand, public officials have had great difficulty accomplishing their objectives when such decisions have been taken in Congress or in bureaus that have been penetrated by societal groups.[55]

The degree to which either governmental functions are captured by societal groups or public purposes are frustrated by private interests varies from one issue area to another. Neither the pluralist contention that all interests are automatically represented nor the power-elite argument that narrow socioeconomic groups always prevail, is borne out. There are many examples of laws, such as health, environmental, and antitrust regulations, that impose palpable burdens on powerful and specific economic sectors. On the other hand, there are many attitudes widely held in the society that are never manifest in public law. Rather than treating public-policy making in the United States as a single uniform process, it is necessary to divide it into several separate ones. Different issues are treated in different ways. The inherent fragmentation and decentralization of power in the American political system can be mitigated if decisions are taken by state institutions—the White House, the State Department, and a few other central bureaus—that are insulated from specific societal pressures.

The relevance of issue areas to the policy-making process has its recent origins in the work of E. E. Schattschneider. Even in his first book, which dealt with the 1930 Smoot-Hawley Tariff and focused primarily on interest groups, Schattschneider suggested this line of argument.[56] In *The Semisovereign People,* published twenty-five years later, he contended that the outcome of every political conflict is determined by its scope—that is, the number of people involved in its resolution. The scope determines the setting in which it is decided. Different kinds of actors have different resources that are effective in some settings but not in others. So long as the scope of conflict remains narrow, it is likely to be settled in Congress and particular interest groups are likely to prevail. When the scope of a conflict broadens, however, it is likely to be settled by party rather than committee politics. Special-interest groups do not play a major role in party politics because they cannot decisively contribute to winning elections.[57]

The concept of scope has been further refined by Theodore Lowi and James Q. Wilson. Lowi's typology of policies—distributive, regulative, redistributive—is based upon their incidence. Distributive policies involve resources that are perceived to be unlimited. Decisions can be disaggregated so that all interested parties can get some payoff. The likelihood of government coercion is remote, and the applicability of coercion when it does take place is individual rather than collective. Distributive policies are generally dealt with in legislative committees and even subcommittees. Particular interest groups are powerful. The prime example of distributive politics is tariff setting until 1934, when the passage of the Reciprocal Trade Agreements Act transferred the locus of power over commercial policy from Congress to the president.

Lowi's second major issue area is regulative. Here policy cannot be disaggregated. Large sectors of the public are affected in the same way, and a direct choice must be made as "to who will be indulged and deprived."[58] Peak associations rather than individual firms are involved in bringing pressure on the government. Decisions are made by the whole Congress rather than by individual committees. Examples include laws against unfair competition and for the elimination of substandard goods.

The third major kind of issue is redistributive. Here broad groups of the population, approaching social classes, are affected in the same way. Decisions on such issues are generally taken within the executive rather than the legislative branch. Examples include progressive taxation and social security.[59]

James Q. Wilson has offered an alternative classification of issue areas. He suggests that the basic parameters should be the concentration and diffusion of costs and benefits. Typically a policy that involves concentrated benefits and diffuse costs will lead the potential beneficiaries to organize; particular societal groups are likely to develop symbiotic relations with those government agencies that make decisions directly affecting them. Adversely affected groups are unlikely to be effective because the free-rider problem makes it difficult for them to organize. A similar situation develops when benefits are diffuse but costs concentrated. Here specific groups are likely to organize to oppose government initiatives. Public actors can overcome this resistance, but only by effectively exercising political leadership in the form of mobilizing broadly held sentiments within the general population. Leadership is also necessary in a situation when benefits are diffuse, even if costs are also diffuse. There may be little organized resistance, but political figures must generate their own support. When both costs and benefits are concentrated, there is likely to be a high level of group conflict with shifting coalitions involving public and private actors.[60]

How can these schemata be applied to questions of international raw-materials policy? At a first cut this issue area can be classified as narrow in Schattschneider's terminology, as distributive in Lowi's, and as involving either concentrated costs and diffuse benefits or concentrated benefits and diffuse costs in Wilson's typology. For instance, increasing the price of a particular raw material through the imposition of a tariff or the toleration of oligopolistic practices provides large benefits to particular firms but diffuses cost throughout the society. Failing to protect a foreign concession may have substantial costs for a specific firm but a very modest impact on the general economy. Under such conditions all three formulations suggest that the government will confront well-organized and powerful political interest groups. Decisions are likely to be taken in arenas that maximize the power of these groups, most notably congressional committees or executive departments like agriculture and interior that are responsive to a narrow range of societal groups.

Questions involving the pricing and ownership of raw materials are not, however, invariably decided in such narrow arenas. A second cut at classification is necessary because international politics presents options that are not available for purely domestic issues and because political leaders can themselves redefine a dispute and change both its scope and the arena in which it is decided. Although it has become very fashionable to claim that there is little difference between domestic and international politics, the fact remains that there is no domestic equivalent to war, and there are few analogs to the kinds of solidary appeals that political leaders can make when the state acts in the international system. Politics never really ends, but the claim that it should can only be staked out at the water's edge.

Decisions about the use of military force are taken in arenas, most notably the White House and State Department, that are heavily insulated from particular domestic pressure groups. Central decision makers are not immune to the entreaties or even, as we have too clearly seen in recent years, the purses of major corporations, but they are subject to such pressures to much less a degree than, say, a congressman from Texas voting on oil quotas. The points of access for interest groups "can be hundreds of times greater" for a decision involving tariffs than for one about diplomatic or military action.[61] Most of the resources that presidents need to govern, and to be reelected, cannot be provided by private companies or particular economic sectors.

Of all the executive departments state is least subject to pressure-group tactics. State is charged with defending general interests rather than those of particular domestic groups such as labor (Labor Department), business (Commerce Department), or agriculture (Agriculture Department). It does not make the large expenditures that have so intertwined the Defense Department with particular industries and geographic areas. While this constrains its ability to mobilize societal support, it also limits the pressures that can be placed upon it. When a question involving international raw-materials policy can lead to the use of force or diplomatic confrontation, private corporations are not likely to be able to compel the State Department to defend their interests at the expense of broader national goals.

A second cut at classifying international raw-materials policy is also necessary because the way in which an issue is decided may depend upon the way in which it is defined. The pre-1934 tariff is everyone's favorite example of a policy that was settled through logrolling pressure-group politics. But in 1934 the way in which tariffs were set began to change. At least until the Trade Act of 1974, increasing power was given to the president. The influence of particular groups declined. Logrolling became more difficult. The natural proclivity to protectionism was overcome.

The change in law was itself a reflection of the way in which tariffs were viewed. At least for political leaders such as Secretary of State Hull, the Reciprocal Trade Agreements Act was the product of a vision: the world would be made more prosperous and peaceful through free trade. The Great Depression had given this idea new force. Tariffs were no longer seen simply as a device to provide material benefits for particular sectors of the American economy, but rather as a matter that affected the whole nature of the international system. This change in vision led to a change in policy-making processes, and this change in policy-making processes changed the relative influence of political groups. Political leaders thus can redefine issues and by doing so alter both the process and substance of policy.

In international raw-materials policy the opportunity to redefine issues has been important. The general goals associated with the pricing and ownership of raw materials suggest that these matters involve something other than the economic well-being of particular firms. The nation's ability to make war, the general health of its economy, the stability of its political system, its influence over other states can all be affected by the international availability of unprocessed goods.

This relationship opens possibilities for political leaders. By playing upon these broader themes, they can increase competitiveness and visibility, the two primary means by which the scope of conflict is increased.[62] By increasing the scope of conflict they can change the arena in which the issue is decided. Madison was wrong to suppose in *Federalist No. 10* that the extent of the republic would be an adequate defense against the tyranny of factions. Such tyranny can only be avoided if political leaders are adroit enough to generate effective political pressures that would otherwise remain latent, and in doing so, thrust an issue out of arenas dominated by private corporations and into ones where other groups, both public and private, exercise greater power.

A third reason why raw-materials policies cannot always be viewed as determined by pressure-group politics is that there are often conflicts within the private sector. Small domestic firms do not always share the same objectives as large international producers. Companies that still have hopes of keeping direct investments in a particular country may not support the same policies as those that have been nationalized. Financial institutions that have portfolio investments are more likely to advocate conciliation in the hope of preventing debt repudiation by a foreign state than are direct investors who have already lost their property. Such private disagreements open space for public initiatives. Governmental officials can mobilize support for a course of action even when there is strong opposition from some private actors.

Hence, if there is conflict between the aims of public actors and corporate managers, the former can at times prevail by exercising effective leadership. Such leadership involves appealing to the nonpecuniary motives of the managers of large oligopolistic firms, changing the way in which issues are viewed, and taking advantage of splits among private groups. Because a democratic state must admit the legitimacy of intermediate economic bodies, its leaders must act shrewdly to secure public purposes. The fragmentation of power in the American polity is an endemic disease, but not one that is necessarily fatal to the public interest.

In sum, the United States has a weak political system. The state—that is, central decision-making institutions, most notably the White House and the State Department—cannot directly alter the structure of their domestic society: they cannot establish new kinds of economic units such as state-owned firms or adopt policies that directly benefit some industries or firms at the expense of others, although obviously many macroeconomic policies will indirectly have such an impact.[63] Furthermore, central decision makers may find it difficult to overcome the resistance of specific societal interest groups, because political power in the United States is fragmented and decentralized. There are many points of access to the political system, especially in the Congress and some executive bureaus. Once an issue falls into these decision-making arenas, state preferences can be blocked. The American polity resembles a blackball system. Any major actor, public or private, can often prevent the adoption of a policy. However, as Table 11.1 suggests, even in a weak political system the state is not merely an epiphenomenon: central decision makers can still resist pressures from private groups; they can still formulate preferences related to general societal goals.

The weakness of the American state in relation to its own society does not mean that efforts to implement the national interest (the preferences of central decision makers that are related to enduring general goals) will always be frustrated. Often public and private policy aims converge. Moreover, central decision makers may exercise leadership by altering the preferences of private actors. Satisficing and behavioral theories of the firm suggest that this is most likely when the state is dealing with large oligopolistic companies. The managers of such units have considerable flexibility to adjust the activities of their firm or to satisfy their individual desires for status and prestige. The ability of public leaders to accomplish their goals also depends on the decision-making arena in which an issue is decided. If policy questions are settled in the Congress or executive agencies open to societal pressures, then private actors are likely to be able to block state initiatives. But if they are decided in the White House, the State Department, and other central agencies, it is much more difficult for the private sector to act effectively. The arena in which an issue is decided is partly a function of its inherent nature and partly a function of the way in which it is defined. Rulers can also exercise leadership by changing the way in which societal groups perceive a particular problem, thereby changing the arena in which it is decided and the final policy outcome. In sum, American politics most frequently follows a weak pattern in which the state can resist pressure from societal groups but is unable to overcome societal resistance; but through effective leadership political processes can be amended so that the power of the state follows a moderate pattern in which central decision makers can not only resist societal pressures but also change the behavior of societal groups.

NOTES

1. In developing this analysis I have benefited greatly from the work of Peter Katzenstein. See especially his "International Relations and Domestic Structures" and his "Introduction" and "Conclusion" in the Autumn 1977 issue of *International Organization.*

2. The concept of strength as it is used here is distinct from the increasing scope of governmental activities that has taken place in all countries. The two are related: an increase in scope is likely to mean an increase in state power. However, this is not a logical necessity. For instance, the "capture" thesis of regulatory agencies in the United States contends that increasing scope has enhanced private penetration of public institutions rather than the state's ability to control the private sector. In Britain, where the scope of state activity is greater than in the United States, government agencies still engage in negotiating and conflict resolving rather than autonomously initiating activity. On this last point see Nettl, "The State as a Conceptual Variable," p. 583.

3. Suleiman, *Politics, Power and Bureaucracy in France,* Ch. 12; Shonfield, *Modern Capitalism,* pp. 129–31; Vernon, "Enterprise and Government in Western Europe," pp. 12–14; Katzenstein, "International Relations," pp. 36–37.

4. See the articles on trade, industrial organization, and finance in Patrick and Rosovsky, eds., *Asia's New Giant.*

5. Suleiman, pp. 18–19; Michalet, "France," p. 107; Patrick and Rosovsky, "Japan's Economic Performance: An Overview," in *Asia's New Giant,* p. 53; and Kaplan, *Japan,* p. 10.

6. See Destler et al., *Managing an Alliance,* for a discussion of the Okinawa case, and Zysman, *Political Strategies for Industrial Order,* for French difficulties with the electronics industry.

7. Polsby, *Congress and the Presidency,* pp. 140–41.

8. *The Governmental Process,* p. 529.

9. *Political Order,* p. 110.

10. Burnham, *Critical Elections,* p. 176.

11. Dahl, *Pluralist Democracy,* p. 39.

12. Vogel, "Why Businessmen Distrust Their State."

13. In *Political Order* Huntington argues that one of the characteristics of the American polity is the persistence of the sixteenth-century notion that the law is above the lawmakers—that is, that the state lacks sovereign power.

14. Truman, p. 436.
15. Seidman, *Politics, Position and Power,* pp. 42–47.
16. McConnell, *Private Power and American Democracy,* p. 339.
17. For a discussion of this episode see Neustadt, *Presidential Power.* Neustadt's analysis of bureaucratic politics, with its emphasis on presidential control, is much closer to the perspective of this study than later works from the bureaucratic politics school, which view the president as one actor among many. Even Neustadt tends to exaggerate the autonomous power of the bureaucracy by underemphasizing congressional and societal sources of bureaucratic power.
18. This argument is developed in Mayhew, *Congress.*
19. Quoted in Seidman, p. 38.
20. Huntington, "Congressional Responses," pp. 23–25, and Mansfield, "Dispersion of Authority in Congress," p. 18. Speaker of the House Thomas P. O'Neill did demonstrate effective leadership in ushering the administration's energy bill through the House in 1977. Whether this heralds a new trend remains to be seen, for the program's treatment in the Senate and in the conference committee was a classic example of the ineffectuality resulting from the fragmentation of power.
21. Mansfield, "Dispersion of Authority," pp. 14–16.
22. *Ibid.,* p. 18.
23. See the articles by Fenno and Huitt in Truman, ed., *Congress and America's Future,* and Seidman, pp. 49–50.
24. Huntington, *Political Order,* pp. 122ff.
25. *Ibid.,* p. 126; Burnham, p. 176; and Hartz, *The Liberal Tradition.*
26. Huntington, *Political Order,* p. 129.
27. See Packenham, *Liberal America and the Third World,* pp. 154–55, and Nettl for a general argument along these lines.
28. Gerschenkron, *Economic Backwardness,* Ch. 1.
29. *People of Plenty,* p. 112.
30. See Almond and Verba, *The Civic Culture,* for a discussion of participation and perceptions of efficacy.
31. On the Soviet Union see Leonhard, "The Domestic Politics of the New Soviet Foreign Policy"; on France see Zysman.
32. Lowi, "American Business and Public Policy," and Burnham, p. 176.
33. IBRD, Economic Staff Working Paper No. 15, "The Nickel Outlook Reassessed," Aug. 31, 1972 (mimeo), pp. 2, 4; UNCTAD, Committee on Commodities, "The Marketing and Distribution System for Bananas," TD/B/C.1/162, Dec. 24, 1975 (mimeo); Charles River Associates, "Economic Issues Underlying Supply Access Agreements: A General Analysis and Prospects in Ten Mineral Markets," July 1975 (mimeo), Appendix, pp. 1–2; IBRD, Bank Staff Working Paper No. 160, "The International Market for Iron Ore: Review and Outlook," Aug. 1973 (mimeo), p. 11; Vernon, *Storm over the Multinationals,* p. 81.
34. For a discussion of the attributes of business and other pressure groups see Schattschneider, *Politics, Pressures and the Tariff,* p. 287; Schattschneider, *Semisovereign People,* p. 31; Wilson, *Political Organizations,* pp. 165–66; Truman, pp. 333–34, 506–7; and Huntington, "Congressional Responses," p. 20.
35. Percentages for individual states are derived from data in U.S. Bureau of Mines, *Mineral Yearbook,* 1967, Vol. III.
36. Simon, *Models of Man,* pp. 245–50.
37. See Schelling, "Command and Control," for a discussion of decentralization in the firm, and Chandler, *Strategy and Structure,* for the general evolution of corporate organizational structure.

38. Bauer, Pool, and Dexter, *American Business and Public Policy*, p. 125.
39. Cyert and March, *A Behavioral Theory of the Firm*, p. 53.
40. Williamson, *The Economics of Discretionary Behavior*, and Monson and Downs, "A Theory of Large Managerial Firms," p. 349.
41. Dahl, *Who Governs?* p. 78.
42. McKie, "Changing Views."
43. *Business Leadership in the Large Corporation*, p. 305.
44. *Functions*, p. 145.
45. The chairman of Exxon reportedly said: "We're flexible. We can play the game any way you [the U.S. government] want—if somebody will tell us what the rules are." Quoted in Mikdashi, *The International Politics of Natural Resources*, p. 52.
46. Preston, "Corporation and Society," pp. 434–35.
47. *The Governmental Process*, p. 514.
48. *Ibid.*, p. 168.
49. *Ibid.*, p. 51.
50. "Comments," p. 99.
51. Russett and Hanson, *Interest and Ideology*, pp. 126–27.
52. *War*, pp. 289–90.
53. The concept of leadership as it is used here can be understood in terms of what Parsons has called influence and the activation of commitments. The former refers to the ability of one actor to change the opinions of another, the latter to cashing in on existing norms. These processes are distinct from two other forms of power, physical coercion and bargaining, in which actors exchange resources. The bargaining situation is much more prevalent in France or Japan, where the state can offer loans or other material incentives to private firms. On these general distinctions see Barry, "The Economic Approach to the Analysis of Power and Conflict," pp. 192–95.
54. Wilson, *Political Organizations*, Ch. 3.
55. For a discussion of the impact of decision arenas on U.S. trade and monetary policy see Krasner, "U.S. Commercial and Monetary Policy."
56. Schattschneider, *Politics*, p. 288.
57. Schattschneider, *Semisovereign People*, Ch. 1.
58. Lowi, "American Business," pp. 690–91.
59. *Ibid.*; Lowi, "Decision Making vs. Policy Making"; and Lowi, "Four Systems." Lowi also delineates a fourth category, constituent politics, which is not relevant for this study.
60. Wilson, *Political Organizations*, Ch. 16.
61. Milbrath, "Interest Groups and Foreign Policy," p. 236.
62. Schattschneider, *Semisovereign People*, p. 16, and Wilson, *Political Organizations*, p. 355.
63. For instance, an expansionary monetary policy will benefit debtors and hurt creditors; an open trade policy will benefit export-oriented industries and hurt import-competing ones.

An International Liberal Community

Michael W. Doyle

Americans have always wanted to stand for something in the world. As liberals, we have wanted to stand for freedom, when we could. In recent times, both Republicans and Democrats have joined in this cause. In 1982 President Ronald Reagan announced a "crusade for freedom" and "a campaign for democratic development." In the 1988 presidential campaign, Vice President George Bush endorsed the "Reagan Doctrine." Governor Michael Dukakis repeated President John F. Kennedy's pledge to "pay any price, bear any burden, meet any hardship, support any friend, [and] oppose any foe to assure the survival and success of liberty." Since then, President Bush has ordered an invasion of Panama and announced as a "plain truth: the day of the dictator is over. The people's right to democracy must not be denied."[1] He then justified the invasion as a way to protect U.S. citizens, arrest Manuel Noriega, and bestow democratic freedom to the people of Panama.

Realist skeptics, however, have denounced the pursuit of liberal ideas in foreign affairs as a dangerous illusion that threatens our security. Instead, they say we should focus on employing our national resources to promote our power in a world where nothing but self-help and the balancing of power against power will assure our security.[2] Radical skeptics, on the other hand, have portrayed liberal foreign affairs as little more than a cloak for imperialism.[3] Both sets of critics have identified actual dangers in liberal foreign policy.

What the skeptics miss, however, is the successful establishment of a liberal community of nations, and in missing the liberal community, they miss what appears to be the single best hope for the growth of a stable, just, and secure international order.

In this chapter, I want to examine the legacies of liberalism on foreign affairs and explore their foundations in the liberal community of democratic republican states. After tracing the mixed record of liberal influences on U.S. foreign policy, I will suggest ways in which the United States and its allies in the liberal community can preserve, manage, defend, expand, and (where needed) rescue the community from the threats it now faces.

A LIBERAL COMMUNITY OF PEACE

For almost two centuries liberal countries have tended and, now, liberal democratic countries do tend, to maintain peaceful relations with each other. This is the

Michael W. Doyle, "An International Liberal Community," in Graham Allison and Gregory F. Treverton, eds., *Rethinking America's Security: Beyond Cold War to New World Order* (New York: Norton, 1992), pp. 307–333. Reprinted by permission.

community's first legacy. Other democracies are our natural allies. We tend to respect and accommodate democratic countries. We negotiate rather than escalate disputes.

During the nineteenth century, the United States and Great Britain engaged in nearly continual strife. But after the Reform Bill of 1832 defined actual representation as the formal source of the sovereignty of the British Parliament, Britain and the United States negotiated their disputes despite, for example, severe British grievances against the Northern blockade of the South, with which Britain had close economic ties. Despite severe Anglo-French colonial rivalry, liberal France and liberal Britain formed an entente against illiberal Germany before World War I, and in 1914–15, Italy, the liberal member of the Triple Alliance with Germany and Austria, chose not to fulfill its treaty obligations under the Triple Alliance to support its allies. Instead, Italy joined in an alliance with Britain and France that had the effect of preventing it from having to fight other liberal states, and declared war on Germany and Austria. Despite generations of Anglo-American tension and Britain's wartime restrictions on American trade with Germany, the United States leaned toward Britain and France from 1914 to 1917, before entering World War I on their side.

Liberal states thus appear to exercise peaceful restraint, and a separate peace exists among them. This separate peace provides a political foundation that defines common strategic interests for the United States' crucial alliances with the liberal powers—NATO (North Atlantic Treaty Organization), our Japanese alliance, ANZUS (Australia, New Zealand, United States Treaty Alliance). This foundation resists the corrosive effects of the quarrels with our allies that bedeviled the Carter and Reagan administrations. It also offers the promise of a continuing peace among liberal states and, as the number of liberal states increases, it announces the possibility of global peace this side of the grave and short of a single world empire.

Of course, the outbreak of war, in any given year, between any two given states, is a low-probability event. But the occurrence of a war between any two adjacent states, considered over a long period of time, would be more probable. The apparent absence of war between liberal states, whether adjacent or not, for almost 200 years thus may have significance. Similar claims cannot be made for feudal, Fascist, Communist, authoritarian, or totalitarian forms of rule; nor for pluralistic, or merely similar societies. More significant, perhaps, is that when states are forced to decide on which side of an impending world war they will fight, liberal states wind up all on the same side, despite the complexity of the paths that take them there.

A liberal community of peace has become established among liberal states. (More than forty liberal states currently compose their informal union. Most are in Europe and North America, but they can be found on every continent.) The firm maintenance of their separate peace since the eighteenth century offers the promise of a continuing peace, and a continuation of the unsteady but overall increase in the number of liberal states since that time announces the possibility of an eventual world peace (see Table 12.1).

Although this banner has recently been waved before President Reagan's Republican "crusade for freedom," under President Woodrow Wilson's effort to make the world "safe for democracy" it formed the core vision of the foreign policy of the Democratic party. Wilson's war message of April 2, 1917 expressed this liberal

Table 12.1   THE LIBERAL COMMUNITY (BY DATE "LIBERAL")[a]

Period		Total number
18th century	Swiss Cantons[b]	3
	French Republic 1790–1795	
	United States[b] 1776–	
1800–1850	Swiss Confederation,	8
	United States	
	France 1830–1849	
	Belgium 1830–	
	Great Britain 1932–	
	Netherlands 1848–	
	Piedmont 1848–	
	Denmark 1849–	
1850–1900	Switzerland,	13
	United States,	
	Belgium, Great Britain,	
	Netherlands	
	Piedmont–1861, Italy 1861–	
	Denmark 1866–	
	Sweden 1864–	
	Greece 1864–	
	Canada 1867[c]–	
	France 1871–	
	Argentina 1880–	
	Chile 1891	
1900–1945	Switzerland,	29
	United States,	
	Great Britain,	
	Sweden, Canada	
	Greece–1911,	
1928–1936	Italy–1922	
	Belgium 1940;	
	Netherlands–1940;	
	Argentina–1943	
	France–1940	
	Chile–1924, 1932	
	Australia–1901	
	Norway 1905–1940	
	New Zealand–1907	
	Colombia 1910–1949	
	Denmark 1914–1940	
	Poland 1917–1935	
	Latvia 1922–1934	
	Germany 1918–1932	
	Austria 1918–1934	
	Estonia 1919–1934	
	Finland 1919–	
	Uruguay 1919–	

311

Table 12.1 *(Continued)*

Period	Total number
	Costa Rica 1919–
	Czechoslovakia 1920–1939
	Ireland 1920–
	Mexico 1928–
	Lebanon 1944–
1945[d]–	Switzerland, the United States,
	Great Britain, Sweden
	Canada, Australia, New Zealand,
	Finland, Ireland, Mexico
	Uruguay–1973; 1985–
	Chile–1973;
	Lebanon–1975
	Costa Rica–1948, 1953–
	Iceland 1944–
	France 1945–
	Denmark 1945–
	Norway 1945–
	Austria 1945–
	Brazil 1945–1954, 1955–1964; 1985–
	Belgium 1946–
	Luxemburg 1946–
	Netherlands 1946–
	Italy 1946–
	Philippines 1946–1972; 1987–
	India 1947–1975, 1977–
	Sri Lanka 1948–1961, 1963–1971, 1978–1983
	Ecuador 1948–1963, 1979–
	Israel 1949–
	West Germany 1949–
	Greece 1950–1967, 1975–
	Peru 1950–1962, 1963–1968, 1980–
	El Salvador 1950–1961
	Turkey 1950–1960, 1966–1971; 1984–
	Japan 1951–
	Bolivia 1956–1969, 1982–
	Colombia 1958– 54
	Venezuela 1959–
	Nigeria 1961–1964, 1979–1984
	Jamaica 1962–
	Trinidad and Tobago 1962–
	Senegal 1963–
	Malaysia 1963–
	Botswana 1966–
	Singapore 1965–
	Portugal 1976–
	Spain 1978–

Table 12.1   *(Continued)*

Period	Total number
Dominican Republic 1978–	
Honduras 1981–	
Papua New Guinea 1982–	
Argentina 1983–	
South Korea 1988–	
Taiwan 1988–	

[a] I have drawn up this approximate list of "liberal regimes" (through 1982) according to the four "Kantian" institutions described as essential: market and private property economies; polities that are externally sovereign; citizens who possess juridical rights; and "republican" (whether republican or parliamentary monarchy), representative government. This latter includes the requirement that the legislative branch have an effective role in public policy and be formally and competitively (either inter- or intraparty) elected. Furthermore, I have taken into account whether male suffrage is wide (that is, 30 percent) or, as Kant would have had it, open to "achievement" by inhabitants (for example, to poll tax payers or householders) of the national or metropolitan territory. (This list of liberal regimes is thus more inclusive than a list of democratic regimes, or polyarchies. Female suffrage is granted within a generation of its being demanded by an extensive female suffrage movement; and representative government is internally sovereign (for example, including and especially over military and foreign affairs) as well as stable (in existence for at least three years). (Banks and Overstreet [1983]; U.K. Foreign and Commonwealth Office [1980]; *The Europa Yearbook, 1985;* Langer [1968]; U.S. Department of State [1981]; Gastil [1985]; Freedom House [1991].

[b] There are domestic variations within these liberal regimes. For example, Switzerland was liberal only in certain cantons; the United States was liberal only north of the Mason-Dixon line until 1865, when it became liberal throughout. These lists also exclude ancient "republics," since none appear to fit Kant's criteria (Holmes [1979]).

[c] Canada, as a commonwealth within the British empire, did not have formal control of its foreign policy during this period.

[d] Selected list, excludes liberal regimes with populations less than 1 million. These include all states categorized as "Free" by Freedom House and those "Partly Free" (45 or more free) states with a more pronounced capitalist orientation.

commitment well: "Our object now, as then, is to vindicate the principles of peace and justice in the life of the world as against selfish and autocratic power and to set up amongst the really free and self-governed people of the world such concert of purpose and of action as will henceforth ensure the observance of those principles."

These characteristics do not prove that the peace among liberals is statistically significant, nor that liberalism is the peace's sole valid explanation.[4] But they do suggest that we consider the possibility that liberals have indeed established a separate peace—but only among themselves.

LIBERAL IMPRUDENCE

Liberalism, as the critics note, also carries with it other legacies. Peaceful restraint only seems to work in the liberals' relations with other liberals. Liberal states have fought numerous wars with non-liberal states.

Many of these wars have been defensive, and thus prudent by necessity. Liberal states have been attacked and threatened by nonliberal states that do not exercise any special restraint in their dealings with liberal states. Authoritarian rulers both stimulate and respond to an international political environment in which conflicts of prestige, of interest, and of pure fear of what other states might do all lead states toward war. War and conquest have thus characterized the careers of many authoritarian rulers and ruling parties, from Louis XIV and Napoleon to Mussolini's Fascists, Hitler's Nazis, and Stalin's Communists.

But we cannot simply blame warfare on the authoritarians or totalitarians, as many of our more enthusiastic politicians would have us do.[5] Although most wars arise out of calculations and miscalculations of interest, misunderstandings, and mutual suspicions, such as those that characterized the origins of World War I, aggression by the liberal state has also characterized a large number of wars. Both France and Britain fought expansionist colonial wars throughout the nineteenth century. The United States fought a similar war with Mexico in 1846–48, waged a war of annihilation against the American Indians, and intervened militarily against sovereign states many times before and after World War II. Liberal states invade weak nonliberal states and display striking distrust in dealings with powerful nonliberal states.

We need therefore to remind ourselves that a "freer world" does not automatically mean "a more peaceful world." Trying to make the world safe for democracy does not necessarily make democracies safe for the world.

On the one hand, democracies are prone to being tempted into aggressive crusades to expand overseas the "free world" of mutual security, civil liberties, private property, and democratic rule, and this has led in the past to enormous suffering and only infrequently to successful transplants of democratic rule to previously nondemocratic countries. Furthermore, we distrust nondemocratic countries, sometimes excessively. We regard their domestic oppression as an inherent sign of aggressive intent and downplay the role of error. In the KAL (Korean Airlines) 007 disaster, according to journalist Seymour Hersh, our government pronounced horrible error as evil intent, and we were all too ready to accept that verdict.

On the other hand, democratic majorities sometimes succumb to bouts of isolationism and appeasement, tempting aggressive states to employ strategies of piecemeal conquest (salami tactics). Self-indulgent majorities thus undermine what can be vital collective security interests.

FOUNDATIONS

Neither realist nor Marxist theory accounts well for these two legacies. They can account for aspects of certain periods of international stability.[6] But neither the logic of the balance of power nor of international hegemony explains the separate peace maintained for more than 150 years among states sharing one particular form of governance—liberal principles and institutions. Balance-of-power theory expects, indeed is premised upon, flexible arrangements of geostrategic rivalry that regard foreign capabilities (whether democratically governed or not) as inherently threatening. Realist balancing theory therefore expects rational states to balance against proximate power. It also includes preventive war. But liberal neighbors, such as the United States and Canada, have maintained a long undefended border for over a century. Hegemonic states can police the lesser powers but, as hegemonies wax and wane, the liberal peace still holds. Marxist "ultraimperialists" (Kautsky-ists) expect a form of peaceful rivalry among capitalists, but only liberal capitalists maintain peace. Leninists do expect liberal capitalists to be aggressive toward nonliberal states, but they also (and especially) expect them to be imperialistic toward fellow advanced capitalists, whether liberal or not.

Perpetual Peace, an essay by the eighteenth-century German philosopher Immanuel Kant, helps us understand the effects of democratic republicanism on foreign affairs. In that essay, Kant shows how liberal republics lead to dichotomous international politics: peaceful relations—a "pacific union" among similarly liberal states—and a "state of war" between liberals and nonliberals.

First, Kant argues, republican governments tame the aggressive interests of absolutist monarchies by making government decisions subject to the control of majority representation. They also ingrain the habit of respect for individual rights. Wars then appear as the direct charges on the people's welfare that he and the other liberals thought them to be. Yet these domestic republican restraints do not end war. If they did, liberal states would not be warlike, which is far from the case. They do introduce republican caution, Kant's "hesitation," in place of monarchical caprice. Liberal wars are only fought for popular, liberal purposes. The historical liberal legacy is laden with popular wars fought to promote freedom, protect private property, or support liberal allies against nonliberal enemies.[7]

Second, in order to see how the pacific union removes the occasion of wars among liberal states and not wars between liberal and nonliberal states, we need to shift our attention from constitutional law to international law. Complementing the constitutional guarantee of caution, international law, according to Kant, adds a second source—a guarantee of respect. The separation of nations is reinforced by the development of separate languages and religions. These further guarantee a world of separate states—an essential condition needed to avoid a "global, soul-less despotism." Yet at the same time, they also morally integrate liberal states: "as culture grows and men gradually move towards greater agreement over their principles, they lead to mutual understanding and peace." As republics emerge (the first source) and as culture progresses, an understanding of the legitimate rights of all citizens and of all republics comes into play, and this, now that caution characterizes policy, sets up the moral foundations for the liberal peace.

Correspondingly, international law highlights the importance of Kantian publicity. Domestically, publicity helps ensure that the officials of republics act according to the principles they profess to hold just and according to the interests of the electors they claim to represent. Internationally, free speech and the effective communication of accurate conceptions of the political life of foreign peoples are essential to establish and preserve the understanding on which the guarantee of respect depends.

Domestically just republics, which rest on consent, presume foreign republics to be also consensual, just, and therefore deserving of accommodation. The experience of cooperation helps engender further cooperative behavior when the consequences of state policy are unclear but (potentially) mutually beneficial. At the same time, liberal states assume that nonliberal states, which do not rest on free consent, are not just. Because nonliberal governments are perceived to be in a state of aggression with their own people, their foreign relations become for liberal governments deeply suspect. Wilhelm II of Imperial Germany may or may not have been aggressive (he was certainly idiosyncratic); liberal democracies such as England, France, and the United States, however, assumed that whatever was driving German policy, reliable democratic, constitutional government was not restraining it. They regarded Germany and its actions with severe suspicion—to which the Reich reacted with corresponding distrust. In short, fellow liberals benefit from a presumption of amity; nonliberals suffer from a presumption of enmity. Both presumptions may be accurate. Each, however, may also be self-fulfilling.

Democratic liberals do not need to assume either that public opinion directly rules foreign policy or that the entire governmental elite is liberal. They can also assume a third possibility: that the elite typically manages public affairs but that potentially nonliberal members of the elite have reason to doubt that antiliberal policies would be electorally sustained and endorsed by the majority of the democratic public.

Lastly, "cosmopolitan law" adds material incentives to moral commitments. The cosmopolitan right to hospitality permits the "spirit of commerce" sooner or later to take hold of every nation, thus creating incentives for states to promote peace and to try to avert war. Liberal economic theory holds that these cosmopolitan ties derive from a cooperative international division of labor and free trade according to comparative advantage. Each economy is said to be better off than it would have been under autarky; each thus acquires an incentive to avoid policies that would lead the other to break these economic ties. Since keeping open markets rests upon the assumption that the next set of transactions will also be determined by prices rather than coercion, a sense of mutual security is vital to avoid security motivated searches for economic autarky. Thus, avoiding a challenge to another liberal state's security or even enhancing each other's security by means of alliance naturally follows economic interdependence.

A further cosmopolitan source of liberal peace is that the international market removes difficult decisions of production and distribution from the direct sphere of state policy. A foreign state thus does not appear directly responsible for these outcomes; states can stand aside from, and to some degree above, these inevitably contentious market rivalries and be ready to step in to resolve crises. The interdependence of commerce and the international contacts of state officials also help create crosscutting transnational ties that serve as lobbies for mutual accommodation. According to modern liberal scholars, international financiers and transnational and transgovernmental organizations create interests in favor of accommodation. Moreover, their variety has ensured that no single conflict sours an entire relationship by setting off a spiral of reciprocated retaliation. Conversely, a sense of suspicion, like that characterizing relations between liberal and nonliberal governments, makes transnational contacts appear subversive. Liberal and nonliberal states then mutually restrict the range of contacts between societies, and this can further increase the prospect that a single conflict will determine an entire relationship.

No single constitutional, international, or cosmopolitan source is alone sufficient. Kantian theory is neither solely institutional nor solely ideological, nor solely economic. But together (and only together) the three specific strands of liberal institutions, liberal ideas, and the transnational ties that follow from them, plausibly connect the characteristics of liberal polities and economies with sustained liberal peace.[8] But in their relations with nonliberal states, liberal states have not escaped from the insecurity caused by anarchy in the world political system considered as a whole.[9] Moreover, the very constitutional restraint, international respect for individual rights, and shared commercial interests that establish grounds for peace among liberal states establish grounds for additional conflict in relations between liberal and nonliberal societies.

A NEED FOR NEW THINKING

In our recent past we have often failed to appreciate the significance of the liberal community. So, like the Russians, we stand in need of "new thinking." Our record fits the liberal community, but our debates have failed to understand it. Our failure to understand the opportunities of the liberal community may indeed be an important source of our frequent experience of the imprudent appeasement and crusading imperialism of which conservative and radical skeptics have warned us.

Before our rise to world power in the 1890s, American principles seemed to take a back seat to a series of pressing necessities. Securing our effective independence from England called for a strategy of limited involvement (enunciated in Washington's Farewell Address).[10] Acquiring a secure hold on the preponderance of North America stimulated a doctrine of spheres of influence (the Monroe Doctrine) and a policy of frontier colonialism (Manifest Destiny). Avoiding, succumbing to, then repairing the ravages of civil war reinforced the drive for continental hegemony and isolation from foreign entanglements. None of these dominant strategies was uncontested. Few of our foreign policy debates have been as spirited as the disputes over how best to achieve those goals of national security and economic development, as we can see in the domestic fights over the Jay Treaty (1794), the Tariff (1828), or the Mexican War (1848).

But the principle of freedom followed behind our national strategy. The United States was too weak to export freedom either through force or foreign aid as democratic internationalists such as Thomas Paine had urged and as France and later Britain did. Americans settled upon an international identity as a secularized republican version of the Puritan "City upon a Hill."[11] America would be a model for democratic republicanism, a laboratory of democratic experiment, and a refuge for oppressed liberals from around the world. The American democrats chose "democracy in one country." Defending our existence preempted exporting our essence.

The recent post-1945 cold war period is no better guide to our challenges. Our commitment to freedom was not subordinated to our security or our prosperity; it was, as we then saw it, indistinguishable from them. In 1947 President Truman declared that nearly every nation had to chose between two alternative ways of life: democratic freedom or autocratic oppression. He defined our purposes by announcing that "I believe it must be the policy of the United States to support free peoples who are resisting attempted subjugation by armed minorities or by outside pressures." Following the defeat of the Axis powers, the Communist Soviet Union posed the greatest threat to democratic freedom on a worldwide basis. But in those years national security and economic prosperity pointed in very much the same direction. George Kennan's geopolitical analysis of the five centers of potential global industrial power suggested that as long as the United States prevented any rival from acquiring control over Eurasia, the U.S. would remain secure. Containing the USSR, preventing it from dominating Western Europe and Japan, effectively satisfied this geostrategic imperative.[12] Equally, preserving our prosperity seemed to mean avoiding the spiraling escalation of tariff and investment restrictions, competitive monetary depreciation, and financial expropriation that had accompanied the worldwide economic crisis of the Great Depression. Protectionism, of course, was widespread as the industrial and agrarian economies attempted to readjust to peacetime conditions, but the most serious threat of total restrictions again came from the spread of communism. Having rejected isolationism, we were spared other hard choices. Our principles, our national security, our economic interests all pointed the same way, toward containment of the Communist bloc.

Our last age of intellectually difficult strategic choice was thus the age of our rise to world power, between 1890 and 1940. But it too serves as a poor model for today. Even if we could allow for the significant differences in political and economic environment, the choices made then represent not a positive but a negative model, what we must try to avoid rather than to repeat. We first chose liberal imperialism toward our weaker neighbors in Latin America and the Pacific. Then we chose isolationism in the face of growing demand for our participation in the international organization of international security.

In 1899 President McKinley grandiloquently proclaimed that "our priceless principles undergo no change under the tropical sun. They go with the flag." But from our perspective today, the racism and arrogance that also shaped those policies render them unacceptable, even if the imperial variety of international paternalism were affordable.

The isolationist response to dealings with other powerful states created equally costly results. The United States Senate rejected our participation in the League of Nations, leaving a fatal gap in its membership. As importantly, our reluctance to play a direct and active role in European security complicated the management of the European debt problem (despite the active role played by New York bankers) and in the 1930s raised anew the problem of who or what would contain a reviving Germany. Today, even more clearly, the integration of the world trading system, United States and Third World international debts and deficits, the resource dependence of the major industrial nations of Europe and Japan make an isolationist strategy reckless in the extreme.

We need to go beyond those two historic alternatives in United States national strategy—moralistic isolationism and liberal imperialism.[13] We lack the simple constraints of pre-1898 weakness and post-1945 cold war. Today our economic interests are ambiguous. Can we best revive our sagging productivity through nationalism or multilateralism?[14] President Mikhail Gorbachev's steps toward détente and democratic reform are depriving the original cold war of its purpose.[15] Looming shifts in the balance of resources and productivity suggest to some an increase in Japanese, Chinese, and (if united) European power. But do we really want to regard them as potential enemies and therefore to play multipolar balancing against them?

SECURING AND EXPANDING THE LIBERAL COMMUNITY

An important alternative to the balancing of enemies is thus the cultivation of friends. If the actual history of the liberal community is reliable, a better strategy for our foreign relations lies in the development of the liberal community.

If a concern for protecting and expanding the range of international freedom is to shape our strategic aims, then policy toward the liberal and the nonliberal world should be guided by general liberal principles. At the minimum, this means rejecting the realist balance of power as a general strategy by trusting the liberal community and therefore refusing to balance against the capabilities of fellow democratic liberals. At its fullest, this also means going beyond the standard provisions of international law. Membership in the liberal community implies accepting a positive duty to defend other members of the liberal community, to discriminate in certain instances in their favor, and to override in some (hopefully rare) circumstances the domestic sovereignty of states in order to rescue fellow human beings from intolerable oppression. Authentically liberal policies should, furthermore, attempt to secure personal and civil rights, to foster democratic government, and to expand the scope and effectiveness of the world market economy as well as to meet those basic human needs that make the exercise of human rights possible.

In order to avoid the extremist possibilities of its abstract universalism, however, U.S. liberal policy should be constrained by a geopolitical budget. Strategy involves matching what we are prepared to spend to what we want to achieve. It identifies our aims, resources, threats, and allies. While liberal democracy thus can identify our natural allies abroad, we must let our actual enemies identify themselves.

One reason for this is that we cannot embark upon the "crusades" for democracy that have been so frequent within the liberal tradition. In a world armed with nuclear weapons, crusading is suicidal. In a world where changes in regional balances of power could be extremely destabilizing for ourselves and our allies, indiscriminate provocations of hostility (such as against the People's Republic of China) could create increased insecurity (for Japan and ourselves). In a world of global interdependence, common problems require multilateral solutions. We simply do not have the excess strength that would free us from a need to economize on dangers or to squander opportunities for negotiated solutions.

A second reason why we should let our enemies identify themselves is that our liberal values require that we should reject an indiscriminate "crusade for democracy." If we seek to promote democracy because it reflects the rights of all to be treated with equal respect, irrespective of race, religion, class, or nationality, then equal respect must guide both our aims and our means. A strategy of geopolitical superiority and liberal imperialism, for example, would both require increased arms expenditures and international subversion and have little or (more likely) a retrogressive effect on human rights in the countries that are our targets.

Instead, our strategy should lean toward the defensive. It should strive to protect the liberal community, foster the conditions that might allow the liberal community to grow, and save the use of force for clear emergencies that severely threaten the survival of the community or core liberal values.

Preserving the Community

Above all, liberal policy should strive to preserve the pacific union of similarly liberal societies. It is not only currently of immense strategic value (being the political foundation of both NATO and the Japanese alliance); it is also the single best hope for the evolution of a peaceful world. Liberals should be prepared, therefore, to defend and formally ally with authentically liberal, democratic states that are subject to threats or actual instances of external attack or internal subversion. We must continue to have no liberal enemies and no unconditional alliances with nonliberal states.

We have underestimated the importance of the democratic alliance. Our alliances in NATO, with Japan, ANZUS, and our alignments with other democratic states are not only crucial to our present security, they are our best hopes for long-term peace and the realization of our ideals. We should not treat them as once useful but now purposeless cold war strategic alignments against the power of the USSR.

They deserve our careful investment. Spending $200 million to improve the prospects of President Corazon Aquino's efforts to achieve a transition to stable democracy in the Philippines cannot be considered too large an investment. Placing a special priority on helping the Argentineans and Mexicans manage their international debts is a valuable form of discrimination, if we take into account that financial decompression in those countries might undermine their democratic governance. With the help of West European and Japanese allies, a similar political investment in the economic transition of the fledgling democracies of Eastern Europe merits equivalent attention.

Managing the Community

Much of our success in alliance management has to be achieved on a multilateral basis. The current need to redefine NATO and the increasing importance of the U.S. relationship with Japan offer us an opportunity to broaden the organization of liberal security. Joining all the democratic states together in a single democratic security organization would secure an important forum for the definition and coordination of common interests that stretch beyond the regional concerns of Europe and the Far East. As the cold war fades, pressures toward regionalism are likely to become increasingly strong. In order to avoid the desperate responses that might follow regional reactions to regional crises such as those of the 1920s and 1930s, a wider alliance of liberal democracies seems necessary. It could reduce pressures on Japan and Germany to arm themselves with nuclear weapons, mitigate the strategic vulnerabilities of isolated liberal states such as Israel, and allow for the complementary pooling of strategic resources (combining, for example, Japanese and German financial clout with American nuclear deterrence and American, British, and French expeditionary thrust).

Much of the success of multilateral management will rest, however, on shoring up economic supports. Reducing the U.S. budget and trade deficits will especially require multilateral solutions. Unilateral solutions (exchange rate depreciation, increased taxation) are necessary but not sufficient, and some (protectionism) are neither. Avoiding a costly economic recession calls for trade liberalization and the expansion of demand abroad to match the contraction of governmental and private spending in the United States. But we will also need to create a diplomatic atmosphere conducive to multilateral problem solving. A national strategy that conveys a commitment to collective responsibility in United States diplomacy will go far in this direction.

Discovering ways to manage global interdependence will call for difficult economic adjustments at home and institutional innovations in the world economy. Under these circumstances, liberals will need to ensure that those suffering losses, such as from market disruption or restriction, do not suffer a permanent loss of income or exclusion from world markets. Furthermore, to prevent these emergency measures from escalating into a spiral of isolationism, liberal states should undertake these innovations only by international negotiation and only when the resulting agreements are subject to a regular review by all the parties.[16]

Protecting the Community

The liberal community needs to be protected. Two models could fit liberal national strategy designed to protect against the international power of nonliberal states.[17]

If faced with severe threats from the nonliberal world, the liberal community might simply balance the power of nonliberal states by playing divide and rule within the nonliberal camp, triangulating, for example, between Russia and China as the United States did during the 1970s.

If, on the other hand, the liberal community becomes increasingly predominant (or collectively unipolar) as it now appears to be becoming, the liberal community could adopt a more ambitious grand strategy. Arms exports, trade, and aid could reflect the relative degrees of liberal principle that nonliberal domestic and foreign policies incorporate. Liberal foreign policy could be designed to create a ladder of rewards and punishments—a set of balanced incentives, rewarding liberalization and punishing oppression, rewarding accommodation and punishing aggression. This strategy would both satisfy liberal demands for publicity—consistent public legitimation—and create incentives for the progressive liberalization of nonliberal states.

Expanding the Community

There are few direct measures that the liberal world can take to foster the stability, development, and spread of liberal democratic regimes. Many direct efforts, including military intervention and overt or covert funding for democratic movements in other countries, discredit those movements as the foreign interference backfires through the force of local nationalism. (The democratic movement in Panama denounced U.S. political aid before the invasion and today suffers at home and abroad from its overt dependence on the United States.)

Much of the potential success of a policy designed to foster democracy rests therefore on an ability to shape an economic and political environment that indirectly supports democratic governance and creates pressures for the democratic reform of authoritarian rule.

Politically, there are few measures more valuable than an active human rights diplomacy, which enjoys global legitimacy and (if successful) can assure a political environment that tolerates the sort of dissent that can nourish an indigenous democratic movement. There is reason to pay special attention to those countries entering what Samuel Huntington has called the socioeconomic "transition zone" —countries having the economic development that has typically been associated with democracy.[18] For them, more direct support in the form of electoral infrastructure (from voting machines to battalions of international observers) can provide the essential margin persuading contentious domestic groups to accept the fairness of the crucial first election.

Economically, judging from the historical evidence of the 1920s and 1930s, democratic regimes seem to be more vulnerable to economic depression than authoritarian regimes. (This is why economic aid should be targeted at the margin toward fledgling democracies.) But in periods of stable economic growth, democratic regimes seem to accommodate those social groups that are newly mobilized by economic growth better over the long run than do authoritarian regimes. Democracies expand participation better. They also allow for the expression of nonmaterial goals more easily, it seems, than do the more functionally legitimated authoritarian regimes. Economic growth thus may be the liberals' best long-run strategy.

Following World War II, the allied occupation and remaking of Germany and Japan and the Marshall Plan's successful coordination and funding of the revival of Europe's prewar industrial economies and democratic regimes offer a model of how much can be achieved with an extraordinary commitment of resources and the most favorable possible environment. Practically, today, short of those very special circumstances, there are few direct means to stimulate economic growth and democratic development from abroad. But liberals should persevere in attempts to keep the world economy free from destabilizing protectionist intrusions. Although intense economic interdependence generates conflicts, it also helps to sustain the material well-being underpinning liberal societies and to promise avenues of development to Third World states with markets that are currently limited by low income.[19] To this should be added mutually beneficial measures designed to improve Third World economic performance. Export earnings insurance, international debt management assistance, export diversification assistance, and technical aid are some of these. In the case of the truly desperate poor, the condition of some of the populations of Africa, more direct measures of international aid and relief from famine are required, both as a matter of political prudence and of moral duty.

Rescuing the Community

Liberal principles can also help us think about whether liberal states should attempt to rescue individuals oppressed by their own governments. Should a respect for the rights of individuals elicit our help or even military rescue? Historically, liberals have been divided on these issues,[20] and the U.S. public today has no clear answer to these questions. It supported the "rescue" of Grenada and the purge in Panama, but as many rejected "another Vietnam" in Nicaragua.[21]

Traditionally, and in accord with current international law, states have the right to defend themselves, come to the aid of other states aggressed against, and, where necessary, take forcible measures to protect their citizens from wrongful injury and release them from wrongful imprisonment.[22] But modern international law condemns sanctions designed to redress the domestic oppression of states. The United Nations Charter is ambiguous on this issue, since it finds human rights to be international concerns and permits the Security Council to intervene to prevent "threats" to "international peace and security." Given the ambiguity of the charter and the political stalemate of the Security Council, difficult moral considerations thus must become a decisive factor in considering policy toward domestic oppression in foreign countries.[23]

Nonintervention also has important moral foundations. It helps encourage order—stable expectations—in a confusing world without international government. It rests on a respect for the rights of individuals to establish their own way of life free from foreign interference.

The basic moral presumption of liberal thought is that states should not be subject to foreign intervention, by military or other means. Lacking a global scheme of order or global definition of community, foreign states have no standing to question the legitimacy of other states other than in the name and "voice" of the individuals who inhabit those other states. States therefore should be taken as representing the moral rights of individuals unless there is clear evidence to the contrary. Although liberals and democrats have often succumbed to the temptation to intervene to bring "civilization," metropolitan standards of law and order, and democratic government to foreign peoples expressing no demand for them, these interventions find no justification in a conception of equal respect for individuals. This is simply because it is to their sense of their own self-respect and not our sense of what they should respect that we must accord equal consideration.

What it means to respect their own sense of self-determination is not always self-evident. Ascertaining what it might mean can best be considered as an attempt at both subjective and objective interpretation.

One criterion is subjective. We should credit the voice of their majority. Obviously, this means not intervening against states with apparent majority support. In authoritarian states, however, determining what are the wishes of the majority is particularly difficult. Some states will have divided political communities with a considerable but less than a majority of the population supporting the government, a large minority opposing, and many indifferent. Some will be able to suppress dissent completely. Others will not. Widespread armed resistance sustained by local resources and massive street demonstrations against the state (and not just against specific policies) therefore can provide evidence of a people standing against their own government. Still, one will want to find clear evidence that the dissenters actually want a foreign intervention to solve their oppression.

The other criterion is objective. No group of individuals, even if apparently silent, can be expected to consent to having their basic rights to life, food, shelter, and freedom from torture systematically violated. These sorts of rights clearly crosscut wide cultural differences.

Whenever either or both of these violations take place, one has (1) a prima facie consideration favoring foreign intervention.[24] But even rescuing majorities suffering severe oppression or individuals suffering massive and systematic violations of human rights is not sufficient grounds to justify military intervention. We must also have (2) some reasonable expectation that the intervention will actually end the oppression. We need to expect that it will end the massacre or address starvation (as did India's intervention in East Pakistan and Tanzania's in Uganda). Or, if prodemocratic, it should have a reasonable chance of establishing authentic self-determination, rather than (as J. S. Mill warned) merely introducing new rulers who, dependent on outside support, soon begin to replicate the oppressive behavior of the previous rulers. (The U.S. invasion of Grenada and the covert push in the Philippines seem to qualify; the jury is still out on Haiti and Panama.)

Moreover, (3) the intervention must be a proportional response to the suffering now endured and likely to be endured without an intervention. Countries cannot, any more than villages, be destroyed in order to be saved. We must consider whether means other than military intervention could achieve the liberation from oppression, and we must ensure that the intervention, if necessary, is conducted in a way that minimizes casualties, most particularly noncombatant casualties. In short, we must be able morally to account for the expected casualties of an invasion both to our own soldiers and to the noncombatant victims.

And (4) a normal sense of fallibility, together with a decent respect for the opinions of the entire community of nations, recommends a resort wherever feasible to multilateral organizations to guide and legally legitimate a decision to violate the autonomy of another state.

A LIBERAL FUTURE

If, as is likely, liberal principles and institutions continue to influence the formulation of United States foreign policy in the 1990s, what opportunities and dangers might arise?

Where liberal internationalism among liberal states has been deficient is in preserving its basic preconditions under changing international circumstances, and particularly in supporting the liberal character of its constituent states. It has failed on occasion, as it did in regard to Germany in the 1920s, to provide international economic support for liberal regimes whose market foundations were in crisis. It failed in the 1930s to provide military aid or political mediation to Spain, which was challenged by an armed minority, or to Czechoslovakia, which was caught in a dilemma of preserving national security or acknowledging the claims (fostered by Hitler's Germany) of the Sudeten minority to self-determination. Far-sighted and constitutive measures have only been provided by the liberal international order when one liberal state stood preeminent among the rest, prepared and able to take measures, as did the United States following World War II, to sustain economically and politically the foundations of liberal society beyond its borders. Then measures such as the British Loan, the Marshall Plan, NATO, the General Agreement on Tariffs and Trade, the International Monetary Fund, and the liberalization of Germany and Japan helped construct buttresses for the international liberal order.[25]

Thus the decline of U.S. hegemonic leadership in the 1990s may pose dangers for the liberal world. The danger is not that today's liberal states will permit their economic competition to spiral into war, nor that a world economic crisis is now likely, but that the societies of the liberal world will no longer be able to provide the mutual assistance they might require to sustain liberal domestic orders if they were to be faced with mounting economic crises.

Yet liberals may have escaped from the single greatest traditional danger of international change—the transition between hegemonic leaders. Historically, when one great power begins to lose its preeminence and to slip into mere equality, a warlike resolution of the international pecking order became exceptionally likely. New power challenges old prestige, excessive commitments face new demands; so Sparta felt compelled to attack Athens, France warred Spain, England and Holland fought with France (and with each other), and Germany and England struggled for the mastery of Europe in World War I.[26] But here liberals may again be an exception, for despite the fact that the United States constituted Britain's greatest challenger along all the dimensions most central to the British maritime hegemony, Britain and the United States accommodated their differences. After the defeat of Germany, Britain eventually, though not without regret, accepted its replacement by the United States as the commercial and maritime hegemon of the liberal world. The promise of a peaceable transition from one liberal hegemon to the next liberal hegemon thus may be one of the factors helping to moderate economic and political rivalries among Europe, Japan, and the United States.

CHOICES IN LIBERAL FOREIGN POLICY

In the years ahead we will need to chart our own national strategy as a liberal democracy faced with threats, but now also with opportunities for new thinking. In order to fulfill the promise of liberal internationalism, we must ensure a foreign policy that tries to reconcile our interests with our principles.

We will need to address the hard choices that no government truly committed to the promotion of human rights can avoid. Acknowledging that there may arise circumstances where international action—even force—is needed, we need strategic thinking that curbs the violent moods of the moment.

We will also need to keep our larger purposes in view. Those committed to freedom have made a bargain with their governments. We need only to live up to it. The major costs of a liberal strategy are borne at home. Not merely are its military costs at the taxpayers' expense, but a liberal foreign policy requires adjustment to a less controlled international political environment—a rejection of the status quo in favor of democratic choice. Tolerating more foreign change requires more domestic change. Avoiding an imperial presence in the Persian Gulf may require a move toward energy independence. Allowing for the economic development of the world's poor calls for an acceptance of international trade adjustment. The home front thus becomes the front line of liberal strategy.

The promises of successful liberal internationalism, however, are large and can benefit all. The pursuit of freedom does not guarantee the maintenance of peace. Indeed, the very invocation of "crusade" as a label for President Reagan's democratic initiative of the 1980s warns us otherwise. But the peaceful intent and restraint to which liberal institutions, principles, and interests have led in relations among liberal democracies suggest the possibility of world peace this side of the grave. They offer the promise of a world peace established by the expansion of the separate peace among liberal societies.

NOTES

1. *Department of State Bulletin,* June 1989.
2. For an eloquent polemic defending this view, see the fine essay by Mearsheimer (1990a). For a thoughtful and thorough critique of the position and prescription, see Ullman (1991), Chapter 7.
3. An important account of the many ways in which liberal ideology has served as a cloak for imperialism in U.S. foreign policy can be found in Williams (1962).
4. See the discussion of Kant's international politics and the evidence for the liberal peace in Doyle (1986). Babst (1972) did make a preliminary test of the significance of the distribution of alliance partners in World War I. He found that the possibility that the actual distribution of alliance partners could have occurred by chance was less than 1 percent (p. 56), but this assumes that there was an equal possibility that any two nations could have gone to war with each other; and this is a strong assumption. Rummel (1983) has a further discussion of significance as it applies to his libertarian thesis.
5. There are, however, serious studies that show that Marxist regimes have higher military spending per capita than non-Marxist regimes. But this should not be interpreted as a sign of the inherent aggressiveness of authoritarian or totalitarian governments or—with even greater enthusiasm—the inherent and global peacefulness of liberal regimes. Marxist regimes, in particular, represent a minority in the current international system; they are strategically encircled, and, due to their lack of domestic legitimacy, they might be said to "suffer" the twin burden of needing defenses against both external and internal enemies.
6. See Aron (1986), pp. 151–54, and Russett (1985).
7. Kant regards these wars as unjust and warns liberals of their susceptibility to them. At the same time, he argues that each nation "can and ought to" demand that its neighboring nations enter into the pacific union of liberal states.
8. For a more extensive description and analysis of the liberal community, see Doyle (1983a). Streit (1939), pp. 88, 90–92, seems to have been the first to point out (in contemporary foreign relations) the empirical tendency of democracies to maintain peace

among themselves, and he made this the foundation of his proposal for a (non-Kantian) federal union of the fifteen leading democracies of the 1930s. Recent work by Russett, Maoz, Ray, and Modelski has extended this field into considerations of wider strategies of international reform and the evolution of the international system.

9. For evidence, see Doyle (1983b).

10. Neo-Washingtonians (to coin a label) such as John Gaddis propose a similar strategy for the 1990s. See his "Toward the Post–Cold War World: Structure, Strategy, and Security" (forthcoming in *Foreign Affairs*).

11. See Baritz (1964) and discussion in Davis and Lynn-Jones (1987), p. 22.

12. See the evidence and argument in Gaddis (1982) and (1977).

13. Our record indicates a tendency to succumb to these alternatives, as has been well demonstrated in Ullman (1975–76).

14. See the informative debate between Laura Tyson and Robert Reich in *The American Prospect* (Winter 1991), and for a thorough background to the issues, see Gilpin (1987).

15. George Kennan, America's premier Sovietologist, told the Senate Foreign Relations Committee on April 4, 1989, that the break-up of the system of power through which the Soviet Union has been ruled since 1917 indicates that the time "has clearly passed for regarding the Soviet Union primarily as a possible, if not probable, military opponent."

16. These and similar policies are developed by Bergsten et al. (1978) and Cooper et al. (1978).

17. For a discussion of strategy toward once-enemies now in a transition zone toward potential friends, see Allison (1988).

18. See the comments of Larry Diamond on some suggestions made by Juan Linz in Diamond (1989).

19. Liberal democrats should consider that two serious rival democratic political economies might emerge. The East Asian national corporatist strategy is immensely successful (e.g., Singapore). It is a crucial minor key in Japanese development, it is the major key in Taiwan and South Korea, and it is spreading as a developmental ideal. Another is social democracy. Social insurance and egalitarianism are too deeply rooted in Eastern Europe (witness Walesa's trouncing of Mazowiecki and Yeltsin's defeat in the Russian legislature on land ownership) to allow a happy accommodation with the heavily capitalist element in Western democracy. Furthermore, there are the not as yet very democratic Third World variants, such as Islamic fundamentalism.

20. Liberals also give mixed advice on these matters. Kant argued that the "preliminary articles" from this treaty of perpetual peace required extending nonintervention by force in internal affairs of other states to nonliberal governments and maintaining a scrupulous respect for the laws of war. Yet he thought that liberal states could demand that other states become liberal. J.S. Mill said that intervention was impermissible except to support states threatened by external aggression and by foreign intervention in civil wars. Yet he justified British imperialism in India.

21. See the *ABC/Washington Post* poll reported in *Time,* November 21, 1983, and the *Washington Post,* October 24, 1984.

22. Cutler (1985).

23. Reisman (1984) suggests a legal devolution of Security Council responsibilities to individual states. Schachter (1984) argues that such rights to intervene would be abused by becoming self-serving. For a carefully reasoned revival of moral arguments for just war criteria, see Walzer (1977). The policy of sanctions against South Africa, designed to undermine the domestic system of apartheid, is an earlier instance of these efforts.

24. Lesser violations of human rights (various lesser forms of majority tyranny, for example) can warrant foreign diplomatic interference. The two severe abuses of liberal respect

call for something more. The two severe abuses, of course, also tend to go together. Democratic resistance to authoritarian or totalitarian governments tends to result in the government inflicting severe abuses of human rights on the democratic resistance. Governments that systematically abuse the rights of their citizens rarely have widespread popular support. But they need not go together, hence their independence as criteria. There is one further constraint. Although the only popular movements for which one might justly intervene need not be democratically liberal, it would by these standards clearly be wrong to intervene in favor of a popular movement committed to a political program that would involve the systematic abuse of basic, "objective" human rights.

25. Kindleberger (1973), Gilpin (1975), and Hirsch and Doyle (1977).
26. The popular classic making these arguments is Kennedy (1987).

The United States Political System and International Leadership: A "Decidedly Inferior" Form of Government?

Michael Mastanduno

INTRODUCTION: THE DEMOCRATIC DILEMMA

The framers of the U.S. Constitution created, by conscious design, a constrained government. They were more concerned to avoid the abuse of political power than to create circumstances under which it could be easily exercised. Thus, instead of concentrating power they sought to disperse it, and created the familiar system of "checks and balances" to assure that no part of government accumulated enough influence to threaten the integrity of democracy.

Foreign policy did not constitute an exception to this principle, and the framers assured that the Executive and Congress shared power and decision-making authority. Indeed, in enumerating the powers of each branch they were ar-

Michael Mastanduno, "The United States Political System and International Leadership: A 'Decidedly Inferior' Form of Government?" Paper prepared for background and discussion at the Dartmouth College-International House of Japan Conference. "The United States and Japan on the Eve of the 21st Century: Prospects for Joint Leadership," held at Dartmouth College, June 27–29, 1994. Reprinted with permission.

guably more generous to the legislature than to the president. On the crucial issue of war-making authority, for example, the president was named Commander-in-Chief, but Congress was given the authority to raise and support an army, provide and maintain a navy, and most importantly, to commit the nation to armed struggle by declaring war. The president, with the advice and consent of the Senate, was granted appointment and treaty-making powers. However, the all-important power to collect taxes and appropriate funds was given to the Congress, as was the equally crucial authority to regulate the commerce of the United States with other countries.

The design of a constrained government and the sharing of foreign policy authority created a dilemma, the core of which remains with the United States to this day. On the one hand, the dispersal of political power has the *internal advantage* of helping to promote and protect American democracy. On the other hand, the dispersal of power has an *external disadvantage*, in that it poses a potential constraint on the ability of the United States to conduct effective foreign policy.[1] To survive or flourish in an international system characterized by anarchy, or the lack of a central governing authority, often requires speed, secrecy, and decisiveness in foreign policy decision-making. Governments must be able to seize opportunities, respond to threats and challenges, and make and honor commitments. They must pursue a set of core objectives with consistency, and at the same time manage conflicts among these objectives, make tactical compromises where necessary, and adjust to changing international circumstances. These qualities are more likely to be maximized in more centralized, rather than decentralized, political systems. Alexis de Tocqueville, in his classic appraisal of the United States, recognized this dilemma in concluding that "especially in their conduct of foreign relations, democracies appear to me decidedly inferior to other governments." They "obey impulse rather than prudence," have a propensity to "abandon a mature design for the gratification of a momentary passion," and in general are deficient in the qualities demanded by effective foreign policy.[2]

America's early statesmen were similarly cognizant of the so-called democratic dilemma, and they found a way to resolve it in the *substance* of U.S. foreign policy. By adopting an isolationist foreign policy, they reasoned, the internal benefits of democratic governance would be preserved while the external disadvantages would be minimized. If decentralized, deliberative government handicapped the United States in the age-old game of European power politics, the United States could choose not to play. Geography facilitated and reinforced this choice, since the Atlantic ocean provided a physical barrier that could not be overcome easily by the technologies of the day. The classic statement of the new nation's strategy was articulated by Washington in his Farewell Address, as he admonished his fellow citizens to "steer clear of permanent alliances" and counseled that "[t]he great rule of conduct for us in regard to foreign nations is . . . to have with them as little *political* connection as possible."[3]

The isolationist solution to the democratic dilemma was feasible for over one hundred years, but by the early part of the twentieth century, as U.S. economic power and political influence increased rapidly, strains were apparent. A return to isolationism following U.S. involvement in World War I resulted in an unmitigated disaster for world politics and the global economy. U.S. officials drew the appropriate lessons, and following World War II they abandoned isolationism and sought to exercise international leadership.[4] In the postwar era, U.S. officials were forced to confront directly the dilemma that had been so deftly avoided in earlier times.

DOMESTIC CONSTRAINTS AND U.S. LEADERSHIP

The view that the U.S. political system is "decidedly inferior," or a significant constraint on the ability of the United States to lead internationally approaches conventional wisdom among students and practitioners of U.S. foreign policy. George Kennan once made an unflattering comparison between the foreign policy of American democracy and the behavior of a dinosaur with a huge body and pinsized brain: the beast is slow to rouse, but when it finally recognizes threats to its interests, it flails about indiscriminantly, wrecking its native habitat while attempting to destroy its adversary.[5] Theodore Lowi has claimed that America's decentralized decision-making system creates incentives for leaders to adopt foreign policy strategies that compromise effectiveness, such as the inflation of foreign policy threats and the "overselling" of foreign policy opportunities. He argues that the domestic political system is an "anachronism in foreign affairs," and that it is "the system itself that has so often made our international relations so inimical to our own best interests."[6] In the context of international political economy, Stephen Krasner has popularized the conception of the United States as a "weak state" whose domestic institutions placed it at a considerable disadvantage in the conduct of commercial diplomacy—a disadvantage only offset by the fact that the United States has been extraordinarily powerful internationally.[7] In a 1984 book entitled *Our Own Worst Enemy,* I. M. Destler, Leslie Gelb, and (current Clinton National Security Advisor) Anthony Lake contended that "not only our government but our whole society has been undergoing a systemic breakdown when attempting to foster a coherent, consistent approach to the world."[8] More recently, the distinguished columnist David Broder, reflecting on the first year experience of the Clinton administration, argued that the "decayed condition of our vital institutions" has "damaged the capacity of our system to develop and sustain coherent policy."[9]

What is it about the U.S. political system that so handicaps foreign policy and international leadership? The answer is found in an analysis of the relationship between Executive and Congress: of the institutions of and relationships within the Executive: and of the role played by interest groups and the media in the foreign policy process.

Executive vs. Congress

The power-sharing arrangements stipulated by the U.S. Constitution invite the president and Congress to conduct an ongoing struggle over the control of foreign policy. For the first two decades after World War II, however, that struggle was held in abeyance. The two branches worked out an arrangement in which Congress delegated authority and deferred politically to the Executive, on the grounds that only the presidency possessed the institutional resources, intelligence capability, and decision-making qualities—speed, steadiness, resolve, and flexibility—required to conduct the cold war effectively and lead a global coalition in the struggle against the Soviet Union and communism. The eagerness of Congress to defer might also be attributed to its desire to atone for its contributions to the foreign policy disasters of the interwar period, such as the Smoot-Hawley tariff and the failure of the Versailles Treaty and the League of Nations. In any event, Congress took a secondary and in some cases peripheral role as presidents confronted the Soviet Union in a series of cold war crises, intervened covertly and overtly in the third world, and enmeshed the United States in an array of entangling alliances around the globe. In commercial policy, Congress delegated tariff-cutting authority to the president and passed export control legislation enabling him to restrict trade to any destination for reasons of national security or foreign policy. The great symbol of congressional acquiescence was the Tonkin Gulf Resolution of 1964, which President Johnson took as a green light to expand dramatically America's role in the Vietnam war.

The Vietnam experience shattered this interbranch arrangement and renewed the foreign policy struggle. Out of that debacle emerged the "new" Congress of the 1970s, 1980s, and 1990s—a Congress that was more assertive politically, less inclined to defer to an "imperial" presidency that had squandered U.S. international leadership, and in possession of greater resources and expertise in foreign affairs. Members of Congress have sought to reclaim or expand their authority over the direct use of force, covert intervention, weapons sales, intelligence oversight, trade policy, economic and security assistance, and numerous other aspects of the substance and process of foreign policy. They have increased the size of their personal and committee staffs and have strengthened the capacity of and their reliance upon collective resources such as the General Accounting Office, Congressional Budget Office, and Office of Technology Assessment. Members of Congress are now less reliant on the Executive for sources of foreign policy information and expertise, and possess the administrative resources to facilitate involvement—and potentially to contest the Executive—across a range of foreign policy issues.

Unfortunately, the new Congress has become less coherent institutionally as it has become more assertive. Reforms undertaken in the aftermath of Watergate and Vietnam created greater decentralization, with less emphasis on seniority and with the erosion of committee discipline. As a result, there are now 535 would-be secretaries of state (or commerce, or defense), each with more resources and political influence at his or her disposal. At the same time, these representatives remain beholden to their local constituencies and retain their tendency to approach foreign affairs from a more parochial, as opposed to national, perspective. In short, the Executive shares power with a Congress whose individual members demand and play a greater role in foreign policy, but without necessarily coordinating their initiatives or framing them in terms of a consistent national strategy. As a former member of the Senate, John Tower, has noted, "Five hundred and thirty-five Congressmen with different philosophies, regional interests, and objectives in mind cannot forge a unified foreign policy that reflects the interests of the United States as a whole."[10]

There are numerous examples of the Executive and newly-assertive Congress working at cross-purposes, to the detriment of coherent foreign policy and effective international leadership. With the passage of the Jackson-Vanik Amendment to the Trade Act of 1974, Congress made its mark on foreign policy by linking most-favored-nation (MFN) status to the human rights practices of communist countries. Unfortunately, the Nixon administration had already completed a trade agreement with the Soviet Union and committed itself to granting MFN without any explicit human rights conditions attached. The Amendment made the United States appear unreliable, and helped to destroy the detente strategy of Nixon and Kissinger.[11] Congress and the Executive clashed later in the decade over the SALT II Treaty, and once again the United States came across as an unreliable negotiating partner.

During the 1980s, the Reagan administration and Congress could not agree on the utility or desirability of aiding the Nicaraguan contras. The result was incoherent policy and the sending of mixed signals to allies and adversaries. The administration's foreign policy was ultimately driven into crisis as executive officials sought in frustration and poor judgment to evade congressional prohibitions through extra-legal means. In trade policy, the exposure of members of Congress to protectionist interests and their tendency to blame foreigners for the U.S. trade deficit led to initiatives—most notably the Super 301 provision of the Omnibus Trade and Competitiveness Act of 1988—that significantly complicated the task of the Executive as it attempted to move forward multilateral negotiations to liberalize international trade.[12]

Relations Within the Executive

One important reason the Executive is presumed to enjoy a "comparative advantage" over the Congress in the conduct of foreign policy is that the president has at his disposal an enormous bureaucratic machine to assist in the formulation and implementation of policy. The foreign policy bureaucracy was expanded greatly after World War II to provide the necessary resources and expertise to wage the cold war. State Department personnel multiplied in Washington and abroad, and the National Security Act of 1947 led to the development of parallel institutions—a permanent Department of Defense led by civilians, and a centralized intelligence establishment under the direction of the CIA.[13] In addition, postwar presidents could draw upon the foreign policy resources of the Commerce Department, the Treasury, the Department of Labor, the Office of the U.S. Trade Representative, and numerous other more specialized offices and agencies.

This very structure that provides advantages, however, also poses a potential constraint on foreign policy. Bureaucracies obviously are not passive instruments; they develop and defend their own institutional interests. Their interests come into conflict because they share jurisdiction over so many areas of U.S. foreign policy, and not surprisingly they compete with each other to control the agenda and the substance of policy. In the absence of central direction, the result is often stalemate or vacillation in foreign policy. The turbulent postwar history of U.S. export control policy, in which the Defense, Commerce, and State Departments have struggled over whether to liberalize or restrict trade in advanced technology often without clear guidance from the White House serves as an apt example.[14]

The president obviously needs to control and coordinate the various parts of the foreign policy bureaucracy, and in 1947 Congress provided the institutional means through the creation of the National Security Council (NSC). Eventually, this solution created new problems, as the staff of the NSC transcended its coordinating role and became yet another combatant in the inter-agency struggle to control foreign policy. This process began with President Kennedy, who desired an activist National Security Advisor to offset the inherent incrementalism of the State Department, and reached its zenith under President Nixon, whose National Security Advisor Henry Kissinger sought to neutralize the State Department and to run foreign policy directly from the White House with the assistance of a small staff.[15] The Nixon-Kissinger system produced significant accomplishments—the opening to China, detente with the Soviet Union, extrication from the Vietnam war—but also caused significant problems. Important issues were left unattended until they reached crisis proportions (e.g., international economic policy and the eventual "Nixon shocks" of August 1971), and the overall foreign policy was difficult to legitimate since much of it was conducted in behind-the-scenes negotiations by officials who were neither elected by the public nor accountable to members of Congress.[16]

The problem took a new form during the 1970s and 1980s, as secretaries of state and national security advisors battled to control U.S. foreign policy. During the Carter administration, Cyrus Vance and Zbigniew Brzezinski clashed over arms control, human rights, and policy towards Africa. Their debates were often public, exacerbating the incoherence and lack of direction in U.S. policy. During the Reagan administration, Alexander Haig and William Clark engaged in similar struggles over intervention in Lebanon and the U.S. response to energy trade between the Soviet Union and Western Europe. Although public conflict between the State Department and White House was more muted during Reagan's second term, the NSC staff contributed prominently to the turmoil in U.S. foreign policy created by the Iran-Contra initiatives. Congressional and other critics expressed concern that the NSC staff had moved beyond its traditional coordinating function and had usurped "operational control" of U.S. policy from other executive departments. In fact, the Reagan NSC was continuing, in more extreme fashion, the tradition of NSC control established during the Kennedy administration.[17]

The overall point should be clear. The Executive has been plagued to a significant degree by the same institutional weaknesses attributed to Congress—parochial interests, decentralization, and the lack of effective coordination. Even in the absence of congressional "interference," foreign policy by the Executive may tend to lack consistency or direction. With both branches engaged, the problems are multiplied.

The difficulties raised by the NSC in security policy are also found in foreign economic policy. There, too, interagency struggles are commonplace, usually involving the Departments of State, Treasury, Commerce, and Labor, the Council of Economic Advisors (CEA), the Office of Management and Budget, and several other agencies. The Office of the U.S. Trade Representative (USTR), lodged within the White House, takes on the job of coordinating agency positions and interests in trade policy. Like the NSC, however, USTR is a player as well as a coordinator, with its own set of institutional interests. USTR officials have clashed in recent years with their counterparts in Treasury over the Europe 1992 project, and with officials at the State Department, CEA, and OMB over U.S. trade policy toward Japan.

Two other issues that bear on the ability of the Executive to conduct effective foreign policy are worthy of note. First, although U.S. economic policy and security policy are each plagued by problems of coordination, the problems are far more profound when one considers the need for coordination *across* the two types of policies. As Destler has argued, the economic and security decision-making "complexes" within the executive are self-contained units and almost totally separate from each other in their day to day operations.[18] A President who focuses on one side of the foreign policy house may find it difficult to master or mobilize effectively the bureaucracy on the other side. Bill Clinton has devoted considerable energies to economic policy, and his foreign policy has been criticized as half-hearted, incoherent, and lacking in leadership.[19] In contrast, George Bush sought to master security policy, and often found himself handcuffed in economic policy—as demonstrated by ill-fated trip to Japan in January 1992.

Issues that fall at the intersection of the two policy complexes are often handled poorly. The FSX dispute provides a clear example: the security complex (the State and Defense Departments) negotiated that agreement with Japan in isolation from the economic complex (the Commerce Department and USTR). The former believed the agreement was in the national security interest, while the latter saw it as violating the national economic interest. The resulting bureaucratic battle and decision to reconsider the agreement left America's most important Pacific ally to question the reliability and credibility of its alliance partner. In post-cold war foreign policy, as economic and security issues becoming increasingly intertwined and the United States grows more concerned about "economic security," the institutional divide between the two spheres of policy-making is likely to prove more troublesome. The latest institutional innovation—Clinton's creation of a National Economic Council to mirror the National Security Council and to coordinate economic policy—may reinforce rather than rectify the divide.

Second, the U.S. government has appropriately been called a "government of strangers."[20] The political appointments of each new administration reach far down into the executive bureaucracy. Although this has the advantage of enabling a new administration to put a distinctive stamp on policy, it leaves the United States with a deficit in experience and institutional memory, particularly in contrast to states characterized by "permanent government" such as Japan. Former U.S. negotiators often lament the disadvantage posed to U.S. commercial diplomacy by the fact that Japanese (and other negotiators) often have greater experience and knowledge of the United States than U.S. officials have of foreign countries.[21]

Interest Groups and the Media

Not only is the U.S. government fragmented and decentralized: it also affords ready access to private actors seeking to manipulate government policy to serve their particular interests. If, for government officials, the rule of bureaucratic politics is "where you stand depends on where you sit," the rule of interest group politics is "which way you lean depends on who is pushing you." A former U.S. Senator, Charles Mathias, noted recently in an assessment of U.S. Middle East policy that "as a result of the activities of the [Israeli] lobby, Congressional conviction has been measurably reinforced by the knowledge that political sanctions will be applied to any who fail to deliver."[22]

Interest groups hoping to influence U.S. foreign policy have a variety of channels through which to exert political pressure. They can "push" on members of the House and Senate, on the White House, and on the different agencies of the Executive. The decentralized structure also enables interest groups to play off one branch of government or agency against another, and thereby enhance their potential influence. This point has not been lost on U.S. firms seeking protection or market access abroad—the rule is if the State Department is unsympathetic, try Commerce or USTR; if the Executive as a whole is unresponsive, try the Congress, which may be able to solve your problem by itself, or at least can help to pressure the executive. In trade with Japan, the dogged determination of firms such as Motorola or Toys R Us to "work the system" has been rewarded by special negotiating efforts by U.S. government officials to achieve market access.

The U.S. government often responds more readily to principles that pragmatism, and thus the more powerful or skillful interest groups, can "capture" foreign policy by appealing to broad principles that transcend their narrow self-interest. During the cold war, firms frequently exploited the fear of communism to prod the government to use foreign policy to serve their corporate interests. The interventions in Guatemala in 1954 and Iran in 1953, in the interest of United Fruit and U.S. oil companies, respectively, serve as prominent examples.[23] Others have appealed more recently to "national security" or "fair trade" to bolster their case for protection or special treatment. The machine tool industry's efforts were rewarded by the Reagan administration's negotiation of a voluntary restraint agreement in 1986, and in that same year the semiconductor industry obtained a commitment to market access through the by now infamous U.S.-Japan Semiconductor Arrangement.

Interest groups do not always push in the same direction, and, since the government tends to be receptive, the result can be immobility or stalemate in foreign policy. Jeff Frieden has traced the ambivalence of the United States government toward international economic leadership during the interwar years to the conflict at the societal level between nationalist and internationalist coalitions.[24] Domestically-oriented industry and agriculture "captured" Congress and the Commerce Department, while internationally-oriented industry and finance held sway over the State and Treasury Departments. U.S. foreign policy, reflecting the industry group struggle, bounced back and forth incoherently between engagement and insularity. A similar problem appears to have plagued the Clinton administration's China policy prior to the May 1994 decision to delink trade and human rights. While Secretary of State Christopher lectured the Chinese on their human rights practices, high Commerce officials and large U.S. firms such as General Electric and AT&T conducted their own diplomacy to strengthen economic ties. Industry officials complained publicly that their economic interests were being jeopardized by the State Department, while State contended that its credibility and leverage as an enforcer of U.S. human rights principles had been undermined by the activities of Commerce and U.S. firms. The United States failed to speak with one voice, affording China the opportunity to exploit the divisions.[25]

It is important to note that access to the U.S. political system is readily available not only to domestic groups, but to *foreign* interest groups and governments as well. Foreign lobbying, of course, takes place in all countries and is a standard feature of international relations. The U.S. system is distinctive, however, in that it is especially accommodating to foreign influence. The same multiple channels of influence that are open to domestic groups are open to foreigners as well. And, since political appointments penetrate deeply into the government structure and high officials frequently stay in government for short periods of time and then return to lucrative careers in the private sector, there is a readily available stream of influential individuals for hire by foreign (as well as domestic) interests.

Over the past several years, as U.S.-Japanese economic frictions have intensified, Japanese lobbying efforts in the United States have become particularly contentious. Critics contend that Japanese firms and foundations have undertaken a systematic financial campaign to tip the U.S. political debate in a direction more sympathic to Japan's point of view, by generously endowing universities and think tanks, and by hiring influential former officials of the U.S. government.[26] There is ample evidence to support this view of a Japanese corporate effort: whether and to what extent that effort has been successful is less certain. Where Japanese firms have succeeded (e.g., in the Toshiba incident of 1987, or in keeping semiconductors off the Super 301 list in 1989), they have done so not by overturning a U.S. consensus on their own, but by throwing support behind one side or another in an on-going U.S. political debate either within the U.S. Executive or between the Executive and Congress.[27] This reinforces the main point—the decentralized and fragmented U.S. system allows ready access to powerful and skilled interest groups, whether they be domestic or foreign.

Like the role of Congress, the role of the *media* in foreign policy was affected profoundly by Vietnam and Watergate. Prior to those events, the media tended to act as a conduit for the executive's foreign policy by interpreting, amplifying, and often supporting official positions. After Vietnam, it became far more assertive and adversarial. Some argue that the media played a dominant role in the war itself, in that its critical stance helped to turn the U.S. public against the war effort.[28]

The new, more assertive media, like the new Congress, helps to preserve the integrity of American democracy. It provides a check on the imperial tendencies of the presidency by subjecting official policy to critical scrutiny and by assuring that voices other than that of the president and his inner circle are heard. Yet what is good for democracy may not necessarily be good for foreign policy. Although the media by itself hardly can be held responsible for incoherence in U.S. foreign policy, it clearly exacerbates any lack of coherence by consistently publicizing and dwelling on disputes among high officials and the contradictions and failures of administration policy. As David Broder has noted:

> Reporters are instinctively fight promoters. Consensus-building is not our forte—or our job. Carrying through policy requires sustained effort. The press in all its forms is

episodic. We flit from topic to topic. We hate repetition. Our attitude toward institutions is cavalier.[29]

The media do not simply react to official initiatives, but increasingly have the power to help set the foreign policy agenda by shaping the public and official response to foreign events. Television has replaced print as the principal source of news information for Americans, and one consequence, in the words of Lloyd Cutler, is that foreign policy has been placed "on deadline."[30] Government officials react to the pressure of publicity, and the result is often hasty, ill-conceived policies that play to the immediate impulses of the public rather than to the long-term interests of the country. U.S. policy toward Somalia provides a striking example: the Bush administration's last minute decision to send the U.S. military on a humanitarian mission was driven in part by the strong public reaction to the images of starving children conveyed by evening news programs. Similarly, the Clinton administration's subsequent and rather abrupt decision to abandon the military commitment was influenced by the visceral public reaction of outrage to the image of captured U.S. service personnel being dragged through the streets of Mogadishu. At the time, Secretary of State Christopher and other high officials cautioned against conducting "foreign policy by CNN," but that is precisely what the administration seemed to be doing.

LEADERSHIP IN SPITE OF DOMESTIC CONSTRAINTS?

The post-Vietnam Congress is assertive yet ineffective in foreign policy. The Executive has problems coordinating policy even within its own institutional setting, much less with the Congress. Domestic and foreign interest groups have easy access to government and can distort policy to suit their needs. The media prey on the incoherence of it all and distort policy further through their control of the information that reaches the public most quickly and directly.

This institutional landscape poses a forbidding constraint on the exercise of U.S. leadership. Or does it? In this section I argue, contrary to the conventional wisdom, that the extent to which the domestic political system frustrates or constrains U.S. leadership has been significantly exaggerated. First, the overall record of postwar U.S. foreign policy has been reasonably strong in terms of consistency, flexibility, and the ability to achieve major objectives.[31] Second, the record also indicates that the President has the means and capability to manage domestic constraints and minimize their detrimental impact on leadership. Third, the President can actually turn the domestic system into an asset, or source of strength, in the conduct of foreign policy and the exercise of leadership. A final point, made in a concluding section, is that power and purpose are at least as important as the structure of the domestic political system in determining the effectiveness of U.S. leadership.

The Postwar Record

"International leadership" was defined earlier as the ability to develop and sustain foreign policies that significantly affect the structure and substance of international relations and that contribute significantly to the solution of collective problems or the realization of collective opportunities. One way to approach the question of leadership capacity is to examine the performance record of the United States in the era in which it sought to exercise leadership. Notwithstanding the democratic dilemma and constraints of the domestic system, the postwar U.S. record is quite strong. U.S. officials managed to develop and pursue a set of policies that had a profound impact on the international system. They pursued these policies with consistency over an extended period of time and across administrations, and achieved a large measure of success. Moreover, U.S. policy has been flexible in adjusting to changes in the international environment, and in responding to crises that threaten core foreign policy objectives.

An obvious example of a foreign policy pursued with consistency and systemic effect was containment of the Soviet Union. From Kennan's long telegram in 1946 to the collapse of the Berlin Wall in 1989 (and the subsequent collapse of the Soviet Union itself), U.S. officials across nine administrations led the non-communist world in an effort to prevent the expansion of Soviet political and military influence. As Gaddis notes, different administrations may have pursued different "strategies" of containment.[32] Yet all agreed on the priority of the core objective of containment, irrespective of whether the party in power was Democratic or Republican, whether Congress was assertive or acquiescent, or whether the era was pre- or post-Vietnam. Deviations from containment were sometimes initiated but never pursued seriously as policy alternatives. In this category one might place the Eisenhower/Dulles exploration of rollback, the Carter administration's interest in shifting foreign policy from an "East-West" to a "North-South" emphasis, and the Reagan administration's half-hearted attempt at rollback symbolized by the Reagan Doctrine. The basic objective of containment remained intact and for the most part achieved success.

A corollary to containment was the formation and maintenance of a set of security alliances with non-Communist powers. Here, too, U.S. officials pursued a policy consistently over time that had a major impact on the international system. Notwithstanding discontent over burden-sharing, several major crises (e.g., Suez in 1956, the pipeline in 1982), and occasional domestic attempts to reconsider the core policy (e.g., the Mansfield Amendment), America's basic alliance commitments were not called into question, and in fact thus far have outlived the cold war.

Another core, postwar objective of the United States has been the creation and expansion of an open world economy and multilateral trading system. That objective has been pursued across administrations and has been institutionalized in international institutions such as the IMF and the GATT. The United States has remained the prime mover in the GATT as that institution first took on the tariff barriers that developed during the war and depression years, then attacked non-tariff barriers, and most recently has accepted the challenge of bringing excluded sectors and issues (e.g., agriculture, textiles, services) into the multilateral regime. As U.S. power has declined in relative terms, domestic pressure has built for protection and a reconsideration of the GATT commitment. U.S. officials have tried to resist the pressure, have not abandoned GATT, and instead have worked to strengthen its efficacy and credibility.

Other examples of core U.S. foreign policy objectives pursued with consistency and effectiveness might include the maintenance of a "zone of peace" that incorporated the aggressors of the last major war, and decolonization and the integration of less developed countries into the liberal world economy.[33] The main point should be clear—in terms of the main policies and objectives of postwar U.S. leadership, pursued over the long term, the domestic political system did *not* result in uncertainty, incoherence, or vacillation. Either the domestic constraints were modest, or executive officials apparently found ways to overcome them quite consistently.

The U.S. record also indicates a reasonable degree of *flexibility* in responding to structural changes in the global environment. The Nixon administration's opening to China, in the interest of exploiting the Sino-Soviet split, reversed decades of ideological hostility that was deeply embedded in public and elite sentiment. The opening was not a one-shot deal, as the commitment normalizing relations with China has been sustained through the Ford, Carter, Reagan, Bush, and Clinton administrations. Second, when faced during the early decades of the cold war with the choice between support for democracy or for anti-communist authoritarianism, U.S. officials consistently chose the latter. After Vietnam, U.S. officials began to rethink this approach, and gradually a "pro-democracy" emphasis came to replace uncritical support for right-wing dictators as a core foreign policy objective. The end of the cold war obviously has accelerated this development, but the initial thrust was quite apparent in both the Carter and Reagan administrations. In international monetary policy, the United States moved during the 1970s from supporting a fixed to a floating exchange rate system when it was clear (due in large part to America's own economic policies) that the fixed system was no longer viable. With the glaring exception of the first Reagan administration, U.S. officials have sought in the floating system to coordinate exchange rate and macroeconomic policies with other advanced industrial states in order to recapture the stability and predictability in international economic transactions achieved in the era of fixed rates.[34]

Finally, the democratic dilemma suggests that the nature of the domestic political system will make it difficult for the United States to respond with the necessary speed, secrecy, and decisiveness in times of foreign policy crisis. Again, the record suggests otherwise. Whether one considers threats to national security such as the Cuban Missile Crisis, threats to alliance stability such as the Suez crisis of 1956 or the 1973 Middle East war, or threats to international economic stability such as the Mexican debt crisis of 1982 or the extreme pressures for protection that accompanied record U.S. trade deficits during the mid-1980s, the domestic political system did not prevent U.S. officials from responding quickly and decisively to preserve core foreign policy objectives.

Managing Domestic Constraints

An important reason for the strength of the U.S. postwar record is that an administration with a clear sense of foreign policy purpose has the wherewithal to manage and deflect the potentially detrimental constraints of the domestic political system. Administration officials have at their disposal a variety of instruments and techniques. They can mobilize previously uninvolved domestic actors to support their preferred positions on a given issue. They can appeal to national security and exploit the "rally around the flag" effect as a way to centralize power and gain public support. They can enlist the support of international actors. They can bind the United States to pursue certain policies through international commitments, and then use the existence of those commitments to overcome domestic opposition to the policies. In short, administration officials can exploit their unique position at the intersection of the domestic system and the international system to further their objectives in each arena.[35] Several examples are useful to illustrate these points.

During the Korean war, the Truman and Eisenhower administrations had a severe disagreement with Congress over West European and Japanese trade with Communist countries.[36] Executive officials wanted to curtail that trade, yet recognized that it would be politically difficult and economically costly for America's allies to sever it altogether. To demand and expect full compliance would likely do more damage to the alliance than to the Communist bloc, and thus executive officials were willing to compromise and tolerate some level of continued East-West trade. Congress was unwilling to compromise, believing that with U.S. soldiers dying in Korea it was incumbent upon America's allies, who were receiving U.S. financial assistance, to abandon their Eastern trade. To enforce this preference, members of Congress passed a controversial law (known as the Battle Act), which required America's allies to give up either their Eastern trade or their American economic and military aid.

Executive officials, caught between their domestic constraint and their interest in maintaining alliance cohesion, responded creatively. They lobbied for a loophole in the law that would allow exceptions to be made on national security grounds, and they negotiated a change in the alliance export control regime (CoCom) that enabled the allies to comply with the letter of the law without necessarily having to sever their trade completely. The Executive, not Congress, ultimately controlled negotiations with other non-communist states, and used that control to deflect congressional pressure and to achieve its objectives—to maintain as comprehensive an embargo as possible while preserving alliance cohesion.

A second example concerns the critical ability to commit the nation's armed forces to overseas conflict. After Vietnam, Congress sought to reassert its constitutional prerogative in this area with the passage of the War Powers Resolution in 1973. The Resolution helped to restore Congress' appropriate role, but also had the potential to frustrate the credibility and effectiveness of U.S. military statecraft. By imposing specific time limits on the deployment of U.S. troops and other requirements, the Resolution gives America's adversaries the opportunity to exploit divisions between the Executive and Congress when the former contemplates or threatens the use of force.[37]

Since 1973, Presidents have responded to these requirements in a way that allows Congress some role, but without compromising their ability to use force as necessary to further national or collective goals. As a matter of principle, no President has been willing to concede the constitutionality of the Resolution, but most have been willing to placate Congress by observing in practice at least some of its provisions some of the time. Presidents have been prepared to neglect the consultation or time limit provisions of the Resolution if they believed that to be necessary to protect national security or maintain diplomatic discretion. Even in the case where Congress played its most prominent role, the Persian Gulf conflict, the Bush administration devoted far more energy to gaining international support than to gaining congressional approval. The latter was sought and obtained very late in the process, after an international coalition had been mobilized and an ultimatum delivered to Saddam Hussein.

Third, throughout the postwar era successive administrations have had to defend the liberal trading order against interest groups and members of Congress more inclined toward economic nationalism and protectionism. Executive officials have relied upon delegations of authority from Congress to engage in international negotiations, have channeled demands for protection into the executive bureaucracy, and have cut special deals for interests (e.g., agriculture, textiles) too powerful politically to ignore.[38] Perhaps the most distinctive tactic adopted during the 1980s was the effort to "externalize" the demand for protection at home by focusing on market access abroad. This tactic was employed by the Reagan administration in 1985, as it mobilized export interests by initiating the Uruguay Round, utilizing Section 301 of U.S. trade law, and providing export subsidies in competition for agricultural markets.

The Bush administration similarly adopted a strategy for deflecting illiberal interests. By 1989, large and persistent bilateral trade deficits generated open hostility toward Japan and demands for "managed trade." The administration utilized Super 301, but more sparingly than Congress preferred. It compensated by working with Japan to launch the Structural Impediments Initiative, an ambitious attempt to get at the root causes of market access problems, and a plausible alternative to managed trade. In the face of intense congressional and industry scrutiny, the administration brought both Super 301 and SII negotiations to completion in the middle of 1990, deflecting congressional pressure and leaving Executive officials to focus full attention of their primary trade policy priority—the completion of the Uruguay Round and strengthening of GATT.

These examples suggest that even though Congress and interest groups play a prominent role, the result is not necessarily stalemate, ineffective policy, and the abdication of U.S. leadership. It may require time, effort, and the expense of political capital, but a determined President with a sense of foreign policy purpose can manage the constraints of the domestic political system.

The Domestic System as an Asset to Leadership

Foreign policy officials can do more than merely manage constraints or "limit the damage" of the domestic political system. That system itself can actually be an asset, which Presidents can use to further international leadership.

For example, the pressure exerted by Congress on the Executive can be turansformed by the Executive into bargaining leverage. As Pastor has noted, "a president who is sensitive to the public mood that stimulates congressional concern can turn Congress into an incomparable bargaining asset in international negotiations."[39] Congressional pressure helps the Executive to negotiate more forcefully, by lending credibility to Executive demands while allowing Executive officials to appear moderate and reasonable. This dynamic is most readily apparent in trade policy, and is all-too-familiar to Japanese negotiators. U.S. negotiators hoping to open Japanese or other foreign markets have been able to claim, in effect, with a reasonable degree of plausibility, that "it's best for you to make a deal with us now, for if you wait, Congress will be far more unreasonable and harder on you that we are being." This tactic has also proven useful to presidents in other areas, such as the promotion of human rights.[40] The intense concern of Congress in this area and its willingness to tie U.S. economic and military assistance conditionally to the human rights record of foreign governments has given executive officials the potential to extract concessions in this area while still maintaining a focus on broader geopolitical and security concerns.

Presidents are also subject to the constraint of public opinion, but this, too, can actually be an asset to international leadership. The need for public support creates incentives for executive officials to develop policies that can command a public consensus—or that reflect one already in existence. Foreign policies and international commitments that reflect a public consensus are more likely to be sustained over the long run than are those which do not.

Until recently, the conventional view among political scientists and policy analysts was that on matters of foreign policy, public opinion tended to be impulsive, erratic, and ill-informed. Foreign policy required public consensus, but the public was moodish, unpredictable, and incapable of sound judgment—creating yet one more constraint on effective international leadership. Presidents, by implication, needed to "find a way around" public opinion. However, recent work by Shapiro and Page, among others, has challenged this view and developed what is, from the perspective of international leadership, a far more optimistic view of the public's role in and impact on foreign policy.[41] They find, tracing through decades of survey data, that public opinion on foreign policy issues is "coherent, consistent, and reflective of values that endure over long periods of time."[42] Public opinion is stable and constructive: it signals quite clearly the kind of policies and initiatives that are (or are not likely) to command enduring support. For example, a strong aversion to the direct use of military force—unless there is a clear threat to U.S. interests and no viable alternative—runs through decades of survey data, and was only reinforced by the Vietnam experience. On the other hand, since 1942 there has been high and stable support for an active U.S. role in world affairs, including support for the significant presence of U.S. troops in Europe and Asia. Surveys conducted through the 1970s and 1980s suggest some public sympathy for protectionism: yet, when questions were framed to emphasize reciprocity and the opportunities for U.S. exports, the postwar public consensus in favor of free trade resurfaced.

Although stable, public opinion is not immutable. Shapiro and Page find that public opinion "responds to new information and to objective changes in ways that are regular, predictable, and generally sensible."[43] The collective public is responsive to and can be educated by a President willing to devote the political energy and lay the groundwork for new or changed foreign policy priorities. The postwar shift in public opinion from isolationism to internationalism, and the more recent shift from viewing the Soviet Union as an "unfriendly enemy" to viewing Russia as a country worthy of economic assistance (despite the general and enduring aversion of the public to foreign aid) illustrate the point. The upshot of this revisionist view is that instead of something to be feared or evaded, the impact of public opinion on foreign policy should be welcomed and cultivated by executive officials.

Similarly, an administration with a sensitivity to public opinion can turn the media into an asset as well. One does not have to believe that U.S. public support for the Persian Gulf war was the result of a conspiracy between George Bush and the "punditocracy," to appreciate that the President did use the media effectively to convey his belief that Saddam Hussein represented a profound threat to U.S. interests and to the values of the international community.[44] Yet, administrations can miss opportunities as well. With regard to Japan, the Bush administration worked hard to defend liberal policies against economic nationalism, but did not always speak forcefully at the public level in favor of this preference. The rhetorical ground was left to the critics of administration policy, who were more inclined, for example, to depict Japanese foreign investment as part of a "Japanese invasion" than as an important contributor to the revitalization of the U.S. economy.

A crucial component of leadership is the ability to enter into and sustain international commitments. The United States has made a host of such commitments in the postwar era, and recently Peter Cowhey has argued that the structure of the U.S. political system actually helps U.S. officials to sustain them.[45] He finds that in systems where power is divided, once international commitments are made they are hard to reverse, since reversal requires the acquiescence of more than one center of power. Moreover, the fact that the U.S. system is open and transparent makes it easier for America's negotiating partners to monitor U.S. compliance with commitments. Since the willingness of other states to maintain commitments depends in part on their assessment of whether the United States will keep to the bargain, the transparency of the U.S. political system helps to increase the prospects for enduring international cooperation. Ironically, the "foreign penetration" of the U.S. political system, viewed by some as a weakness or threat, may actually enhance leadership by helping others to track U.S. adherence to international commitments.[46]

CONCLUSION: POWER, PURPOSE, AND LEADERSHIP

The postwar U.S. leadership record, the fact that administrations have techniques to manage domestic constraints, and the fact that the domestic system can actually be turned to international advantage all suggest that as the United States enters the post-cold war era, the foreign policy process need not be viewed as a serious impediment to the exercise of U.S. leadership. The domestic process, however, is only one possible determinant of international leadership. Two other important ones are international power and foreign policy purpose. Although widely debated of late, the United States retains sufficient international power to lead in a post-cold war world. Whether the United States also possesses the foreign policy purpose, however, is more uncertain.

Is the United States a great power in decline? If "power" is defined in terms of relative position over time, and operationalized as control over economic resources, the answer seems clear. The U.S. share of world trade, of financial reserves, and of global output of commodities such as steel and petroleum decreased sharply between 1950 and the 1980s. During the 1980s, the United States shifted from creditor to debtor status as its international financial position deteriorated sharply and rapidly. At the same time, it faced serious competition in world markets and a challenge to its pre-eminence in advanced technology from Japan.[47]

In absolute terms, however, the United States just as clearly remains a dominant power. Its economy remained the largest in terms of GNP, and its market is either the largest or second largest, depending on whether one aggregates the members of the European Union. U.S. productivity stagnated after 1973 but recently has rebounded, and although the United States does not lead in every sector, across manufacturing as a whole it retains its position as the most productive of the advanced industrial states.[48] Widespread concern during the mid-1980s that the United States was "de-industrializing" seems to have abated, and by the early 1990s attention was focused instead on the striking export performance of U.S. firms. A favorable exchange rate, generous amounts of foreign investment, and a concerted effort by U.S. firms to cut costs and improve quality all seemed to contribute to the renewed prowess of U.S. firms in international competition.[49]

Equally important, economic is not the sole form of international power. With the collapse of the Soviet Union, the United States is unambiguously the world's leading military power and is increasingly dominant in the production (and export) of sophisticated weaponry.[50] The United States also possesses the "soft" power resources of culture and ideology; as Russett and Nye argue, to the extent American values (e.g., anti-authoritarianism, liberal economies, individual rights) have become widespread, the United States has been able to retain control over international outcomes without having to exercise overt power over others.[51]

The point is not that United States enjoys complete mastery over international outcomes, or that it will always prevail in international disputes. It never enjoyed that degree of influence, even at the peak of its postwar power. Rather, the point is that despite its relative decline, the United States clearly retains sufficient power to contemplate seriously a leadership role internationally.

The United States may possess the power—does it also possess the foreign policy purpose? The cold war era was distinctive in that it witnessed the combination of U.S. power and purpose. The elements of U.S. foreign policy purpose are well-known: containment of the Soviet Union, permanent alliances with non-Communist states, a willingness to intervene using direct force if necessary to prevent Communist takeovers, and the pursuit of multilateralism in the international economy. With the end of the cold war, the U.S. purpose is no longer clear. There is no central enemy, and despite the best efforts of some officials, a collection of "nasty little states" such as Iraq and North Korea cannot substitute for the big nasty one. There is no consensus on when the United States should intervene, and for what reason. There is both support for, and suspicion of, joining with the United Nations in collective security efforts. The consensus in favor of economic liberalism and multilateralism has been challenged by advocates of industrial policy, managed trade, aggressive unilateralism, regionalism, and by those who view "geo-economic competition" as the principal source of great power rivalry in the years ahead.

The absence of foreign policy purpose is largely a function of the fact that the cold war ended rather abruptly and the adjustment to a new order is still taking place. Yet the problem has been exacerbated by the Clinton administration, which has been strikingly unsuccessful at providing purpose to U.S. policy. It has been noted often that President Clinton seems to wish for the world to stay still while he handles domestic problems, and that the world is clearly not cooperating. The *Economist* recently editorialized that Clinton's "undisguised disinterest in foreign policy, together with his administration's utter absence of a framework for thinking about America's place in the world, have convinced many of America's friends that their worst nightmare may be coming true: a one-superpower world in which the superpower does not have the faintest idea how to perform its central role of preserving peace through preserving the balance of power."[52]

In the absence of clear purpose, foreign policy tends to be reactive, episodic, and directionless. And this is precisely the context within which the potentially *negative* aspects of the U.S. political system weigh most heavily on foreign policy. When there is a lack of consensus at the top, bureaucratic battles within the executive develop and usually become public, as evidenced by the struggles between Brzezinski and Vance during the Carter years over how to deal with the Soviet Union. When the executive is perceived as weak or uncertain, Congress attempts to fill the void, even though it is institutionally incapable of doing so. When neither the executive nor Congress provide direction, the media and to some extent interest groups tend to fill the void, and the administration finds itself—as in recent policy toward Somalia, Bosnia, and NAFTA—catching up with and reacting to events rather than setting the foreign policy agenda, domestically and internationally.

In these circumstances, it is tempting to find fault with the process, and to retreat into the logic of the democratic dilemma. That, however, is to mistake the symptom for the cause. International leadership requires purpose, and when it exists, the system can be made to work.

NOTES

1. See, for example, John W. Spanier and Eric M. Uslaner, *American Foreign Policy Making and the Democratic Dilemmas* (New York: Macmillan Publishing Company, sixth edition, 1994), pp. 17–23.
2. Alexis De Tocqueville, *Democracy in America*, vol. I. trans. by Henry Reeve (Boston: John Allyn, 1882), pp. 299–300.
3. Washington is quoted in *ibid.*, pp. 296–97, emphasis in original.
4. By "international leadership" I mean the ability of a country to develop and sustain foreign policies that have a profound effect on the structure and substance of international relations. I would also include the ability to identify common problems and opportunities, and to take the initiative in mobilizing resources and coalitions to address them.
5. Kennan is quoted in Robert Pastor, "The President Versus Congress," in Robert J. Art and Seyom Brown, eds., *U.S. Foreign Policy: The Search for a New Role* (New York:

Macmillan, 1993), p. 12. Pastor's essay is one of a small handful in the literature that challenges the conventional wisdom directly and effectively.

6. See Lowi, "Making Democracy Safe for the World: On Fighting the Next War," in G. John Ikenberry, ed., *American Foreign Policy: Theoretical Essays* (New York: HarperCollins, 1989), pp. 258–292, quotations at 288.

7. See Krasner, "United States Commercial and Monetary Policy: Unravelling the Paradox of External Strength and Internal Weakness," in Peter Katzenstein, ed., *Between Power and Plenty* (Madison: University of Wisconsin Press, 1978), pp. 51–88; *Defending the National Interest* (Princeton: Princeton University Press, 1978); and "Domestic Constraints on International Economic Leverage," in Klaus Knorr and Frank Trager, *Economic Issues and National Security* (Lawrence: University of Kansas Press, 1977), pp. 160–181.

8. Destler, Gelb, and Lake, *Our Own Worst Enemy: The Unmaking of American Foreign Policy* (New York: Simon and Schuster, 1984), p. 11.

9. Broder, "Can We Govern? Our Weakened Political System Sets Us Up For Failure," in *The Washington Post* (National Weekly Edition), January 31, 1994, p. 23.

10. Tower is quoted in James M. McCormick, *American Foreign Policy and Process,* 2nd ed. (Itasca, Illinois: F. E. Peacock Publishers, 1992), p. 341.

11. The Soviets abrogated the trade agreement after the Jackson-Vanik Amendment passed. See Paula Stern, *Water's Edge: Domestic Politics and the Making of Foreign Economic Policy* (Westport, Conn.: Greenwood Press, 1979).

12. Most of the world trading community viewed Super 301 as contrary to the spirit and possibly the letter of GATT, at a time when the United States was seeking to strengthen GATT and international adherence to it. See, for example, Jagdish Bhagwati, *Aggressive Unilateralism: America's 301 Trade Policy and the World Trading System* (Ann Arbor: University of Michigan Press, 1990).

13. See James A. Nathan and James K. Oliver, *Foreign Policy Making and the American Political System,* 2nd ed. (Boston: Little, Brown, 1987), pp. 24–25.

14. See Michael Mastanduno, *Economic Containment: CoCom and the Politics of East-West Trade* (Ithaca: Cornell University Press, 1992).

15. See Henry A. Kissinger, *White House Years* (Boston: Little, Brown, 1979).

16. Alexander L. George, "Domestic Constraints on Regime Change in U.S. Foreign Policy: The Need for Policy Legitimacy," in Ikenberry, ed., *American Foreign Policy,* pp. 583–608.

17. See John Canham-Clyne, "Business as Usual: Iran-Contra and the National Security State," in Eugene R. Wittkopf, ed., *The Domestic Sources of American Foreign Policy,* 2nd ed. (New York: St. Martin's, 1994), pp. 236–246, at 240–241.

18. I. M. Destler, "A Government Divided: The Security Complex and the Economic Complex," in David A. Deese, ed., *The New Politics of American Foreign Policy* (New York: St. Martin's, 1994), pp. 132–147.

19. For example, Dan Williams and Ann Devroy, "Buckling Under the Weight of the World: The White House Appears Weak and Wavering in Foreign Affairs," *Washington Post,* National Weekly Edition, May 2, 1994, p. 14.

20. Hugh Heclo, *A Government of Strangers* (Washington, D.C.: The Brookings Institution, 1976).

21. For example, Clyde V. Prestowitz, Jr., *Trading Places: How We Are Giving Our Future to Japan and How to Reclaim It,* 2nd ed. (New York: Basic Books, 1989).

22. See Mitchell G. Bard, "The Influence of Ethnic Interest Groups on American Middle East Policy," in Wittkopf, ed., *The Domestic Sources of American Foreign Policy,* p. 79, 86.

23. See Krasner, *Defending the National Interest*.

24. Jeff Frieden, "Sectoral Conflict and U.S. Foreign Economic Policy, 1914–1940," in Ikenberry, ed., *American Foreign Policy*, pp. 133–161.

25. See Robert S. Greenberger, "Cacophony of Voices Drowns Out Message From U.S. to China," *Wall Street Journal*, March 22, 1994, p. A1.

26. The most prominent articulation of this argument is Pat Choate, *Agents of Influence: How Japanese Lobbyists in the United States Manipulate America's Political and Economic System* (New York: Knopf, 1990).

27. See John B. Judis, "The Japanese Megaphone: Foreign Influences on Foreign Policy-making," in Wittkopf, ed., *The Domestic Sources of American Foreign Policy*, p. 102.

28. See, for example, Spanier and Uslaner, *American Foreign Policy and the Democratic Dilemmas*, pp. 233–36.

29. Broder, "Can We Govern?," p. 23.

30. Lloyd Cutler, "Foreign Policy on Deadline." *Foreign Policy*, no. 56 (Fall 1984), pp. 113–128.

31. In his assessment of the interbranch relationship, Robert Pastor similarly argues that the U.S. performance record has been better than it is usually given credit for in terms of consistency and flexibility. See Pastor, "The President Versus Congress," pp. 16–22.

32. John Lewis Gaddis, *Strategies of Containment: A Critical Appraisal of Postwar American National Security Policy* (New York: Oxford University Press, 1982).

33. See Bruce Russett, "The Mysterious Case of Vanishing Hegemony; or, Is Mark Twain Really Dead?," *International Organization*, vol. 39, no. 2 (Spring 1985), pp. 207–231.

34. See John Odell, *U.S. International Monetary Policy* (Princeton: Princeton University Press, 1982), and Yoichi Funabashi, *From the Plaza to the Louvre* (Washington, D.C.: Institute for International Economics, 1989).

35. For an elaboration and illustration of these arguments, see John Ikenberry, David Lake, and Michael Mastanduno, ed., *The State and American Foreign Economic Policy* (Ithaca: Cornell University Press, 1988).

36. For full discussion, see Mastanduno, *Economic Containment*, Ch. 3.

37. A good discussion is McCormick, *American Foreign Policy and Process*, pp. 313–325.

38. See I. M. Destler, *U.S. Trade Politics: System Under Stress* (Washington, D.C.: Institute for International Economics, 1986).

39. Pastor, "The President versus Congress," p. 16.

40. *Ibid.*, p. 17.

41. See, for example, Robert Y. Shapiro and Benjamin J. Page, "Foreign Policy and Public Opinion," and Thomas W. Graham, "Public Opinion and U.S. Foreign Policy Decision-Making," in Deese, ed., *The New Politics of American Foreign Policy*, pp. 190–235. The shifting consensus in the literature is reviewed by Ole Holsti, "Public Opinion and Foreign Policy: Challenges to the Almond-Lippmann Consensus," *International Studies Quarterly*, vol. 36, no. 4 (December 1992), pp. 439–466.

42. Shapiro and Page, "Foreign Policy and Public Opinion," p. 217.

43. *Ibid.*, p. 226.

44. See Eric Alterman, "Operation Pundit Storm: The Media, Political Commentary, and Foreign Policy," in Wittkopf, *The Domestic Sources of American Foreign Policy*, pp. 120–131.

45. Peter Cowhey, "Domestic Institutions and the Credibility of International Commitments: Japan and the United States," *International Organization*, vol. 47, no. 2 (Spring 1993), pp. 299–326.

46. *Ibid.*, p. 314. Interestingly, Cowhey finds in comparative terms that the Japanese political system is less well-equipped for international leadership. The electoral system re-

wards private rather than public goods, reducing incentives for leaders to make international commitments; the parliamentary system makes it easier to reverse commitments; and the system is less transparent, making Japanese compliance with agreements harder to monitor.

47. The "declinist" argument has been made most forcefully by Robert Gilpin, *U.S. Power and the Multinational Corporation* (New York: Basic Books, 1975) and *The Political Economy of International Relations* (Princeton: Princeton University Press, 1987); Robert Keohane and Joseph Nye, *Power and Interdependence* (Boston: Little, Brown, 1977); and Paul Kennedy, *The Rise and Fall of the Great Powers* (New York: Random House, 1987).

48. A well-publicized report by McKinsey and Company in 1993 documented the overall superiority of the United States in manufacturing productivity relative to its primary competitors, Japan and Germany. See Sylvia Nasar, "The American Economy, Back on Top," *New York Times,* February 27, 1994, Sec. 3, p. 1, 6, and "Why US is Indeed Productive," *New York Times,* October 22, 1993, p. D1.

49. See "Who's Sharper Now?," and "Ready to Take on the World," *The Economist,* January 15, 1994, pp. 15, 65–66.

50. Ethan Kapstein, "America's Arms-Trade Monopoly," *Foreign Affairs,* vol. 73, no. 3 (May/June 1994), pp. 13–19.

51. Russett, "The Mysterious Case of Vanishing Hegemony," pp. 228–230, and Joseph Nye, *Bound to Lead* (New York: Basic Books, 1990).

52. "Cornered by His Past," June 4, 1994, pp. 13–14.

Five

PUBLIC OPINION, POLICY LEGITIMACY, AND SECTIONAL CONFLICT

*T*hese next three essays focus on the influence of the diffuse pressures of public opinion, reigning political images, and societal interests on American foreign policy. As such they share elements of several of the approaches in other sections. They share a general view that periods of American foreign policy are punctuated by crystallized sets of images and publicly held views about the proper direction of American foreign policy. Yet each provides a distinctive analytical cut into these domestic structures and processes.

Michael Roskin focuses on shifting generational views or "paradigms" of foreign policy. Each generation, Roskin argues, carries with it a set of "strategic conventional wisdoms" that are formed by a decisive historical event and that guide public orientations toward policy. The Pearl Harbor paradigm, according to Roskin, was interventionist. This view had many sources but took form in the traumatic events of Pearl Harbor and the Second World War. The paradigm reflected an imagery of the international system and a set of lessons to which American leaders must attend. Most important was the lesson that aggression must be met head on and not appeased. The imagery of Pearl Harbor took deep root and was not dislodged, Roskin argues, until the failures of Vietnam seemingly discredited its interventionist orientation. With Vietnam came a new set of lessons, wrapped in a paradigm of nonintervention. One is left to speculate about the mechanisms by which these changes occur and the lessons become entrenched.

Alexander L. George also focuses on diffuse sets of public views on foreign policy as powerful forces that set the terms of choice within government. George argues that government officials are not free to conduct foreign policy as they choose. Officials can sustain foreign policy only when it is developed within a consensus. Consequently, government officials build support for their policy. In analyzing the importance of domestic support George advances the notion of "policy legitimacy," a measure of the degree to which the president has convinced Congress and the public of the soundness of his policy goals. The legitimation of policy, according to George, requires the president to persuade the public of the feasibility and desirability of that policy. These imperatives of domestic legitimacy set limits on what government officials can propose and sustain in the realm of foreign policy. In invoking the notion of legitimacy, therefore, George has focused on a particular mechanism in which a democratic society exerts an influence on the conduct of foreign policy.

Peter Trubowitz looks at the sources of political conflict in American foreign policy. Most analysts look to ideological or institutional cleavages at the national level as the most important sources of conflict over foreign policy. Taking a different approach, Trubowitz looks at geographically based sources of conflict. In an examination of Congressional voting on a variety of foreign policy issues, Trubowitz finds that sectional interests—particularly between the Northeast and South—featured prominently in Congressional debates during the Cold War. At their root, these conflicts were grounded in interregional struggles for political and economic advantage.

From Pearl Harbor to Vietnam: Shifting Generational Paradigms and Foreign Policy

Michael Roskin

United States foreign policy can be seen as a succession of strategic conventional wisdoms, or *paradigms,* on whether the country's defense should start on the near or far side of the oceans. An interventionist paradigm favors the latter, a noninterventionist paradigm, the former. This article argues that each elite American generation comes to favor one of these orientations by living through the catastrophe brought on by the application ad absurdum of the opposite paradigm at the hands of the previous elite generation. Thus the bearers of the "Pearl Harbor paradigm" (themselves reacting to the deficiencies of the interwar "isolationism") eventually drove interventionism into the ground in Vietnam, giving rise to a noninterventionist "Vietnam paradigm." These paradigms seem to shift at approximately generational intervals, possibly because it takes that long for the bearers of one orientation, formed by the dramatic experiences of their young adulthood, to come to power and eventually misapply the lessons of their youth.

Recently much foreign-policy discussion has focused on economic interpretation of United States actions, bureaucratic politics and malfunctions, and executive-legislative relations. While such approaches have made interesting contributions to the field, none have been able to gather together seemingly disparate elements of foreign policy into an overall view that explains this behavior over several decades. The reason is that these popular approaches consistently downplay or even ignore the key element to such an overall view: the strategic assumptions held by decision-making elites—that is, who defines what as strategic; why; and when.[1] In other words, these approaches failed to consider that in certain periods United States policy makers deem much of the globe to be worth fighting for, while at other times they regard most of the world with indifference.

THE CONCEPT OF *PARADIGM*

The concepts of *paradigm* and *paradigm shift* are borrowed from Thomas Kuhn, who used them to describe intellectual growth in the natural sciences. Kuhn called paradigms "universally recognized scientific achievements that for a time provide

Michael Roskin, "From Pearl Harbor to Vietnam: Shifting Generational Paradigms and Foreign Policy." *Political Science Quarterly* 89 (Fall 1974):563–588. Reprinted with permission.

model problems and solutions to a community of practitioners."[2] A paradigm is the basic assumption of a field; acceptance of it is mandatory for practitioners (e.g., those who do not accept the conservation of energy are not physicists; those who do not accept the gas laws are not chemists). Practitioners, having accepted the paradigm, then typically engage in "normal science," that is, the interpretation and detailing of the basic paradigm, which itself is not open to question.[3]

The importance of Kuhn's framework for our purposes is that it is a dynamic view: the paradigms shift. When researchers, operating under their old paradigm, begin to notice that their empirical findings do not come out the way they are supposed to, disquiet enters into the profession. Anomalies or counter-instances crop up in the research and throw the old paradigm into doubt. Then an innovator looks at the data from another angle, reformulates the basic framework, and introduces a new paradigm. Significantly, these innovators tend to be younger men who, "being little committed by prior practice to the traditional rules of normal science, are particularly likely to see that those rules no longer define a playable game and to conceive another set that can replace them."[4] The new paradigm does not triumph immediately and automatically. Now there are two competing, antithetical paradigms; each demands its separate world view. The discussants "are bound partly to talk through each other" because they are looking at the same data from differing angles.[5] The new paradigm makes progress, however, because it claims it "can solve the problems that have led the old one to a crisis."[6] The new paradigm makes particular headway among younger workers. The old practitioners may be beyond conversion; they simply die out. This "paradigm shift" is what Kuhn calls a "scientific revolution," and these "revolutions close with a total victory for one of the two opposing camps."[7]

There is one more point we must include from Kuhn. Which paradigm, the old or the new, is the "truth"? The answer is neither. The new paradigm is at best merely a closer approximation to reality. It seems to explain the data better and offers better paths to future research; it is never the last word. Wide areas of uncertainty remain, especially during the changeover period, when the data can be interpreted ambiguously. It is impossible to say when—or even if—the holders of the old paradigm are completely wrong. The profession merely comes to turn its back on them, ignoring them, leaving them out in the cold.[8]

Kuhn has suggested a theory of the innovation and diffusion of knowledge applicable to all fields, including foreign policy. The crucial difference with foreign-policy paradigms is that they are far less *verifiable* than natural-science paradigms. Students of foreign policy have only the crudest sort of verification procedure: the perception that the old paradigm has given rise to a catastrophe. More subtle perceptions of marginal dysfunctionality tend to go unnoticed (by all but a handful of critics) until the general orientation produces an unmistakable disaster.

How, then, can we adapt the Kuhnian framework to the study of United States foreign policy? The community of practitioners is an elite of persons relevant to foreign policy—both in and out of government, the latter including such opinion leaders as professors and journalists—who structure the debate for wider audiences.[9] While the relationship between mass and elite opinion in foreign policy is well beyond our scope here, most scholarly opinion holds that the mass public has only low or intermittent interest in foreign affairs. One study, for example, found more "isolationism" as one moves down the educational ladder.[10] Foreign aid has never been popular with American voters; only elite opinion sustains it. When the elite ceases to define overseas situations as threats to United States security, the mass public soon loses interest. Major American participation abroad is sustainable only when the elite has been mobilized to support it. Lose this support, and America stays home.

The content of the foreign-policy paradigm varies in detail but is generally reducible to the question of whether overseas areas "matter" to United States security. That is, should the defense of America start on the far or near side of the ocean? The Yale scholar of geopolitics Nicholas Spykman recognized the question as "the oldest issue in American foreign policy" and posed it in 1942 as well as anyone has ever done: "Shall we protect our interests by defense on this side of the water or by active participation in the lands across the oceans?"[11] The former view constitutes what we shall call a "noninterventionist" paradigm; the latter is an "interventionist" paradigm. These antithetical views shift under the impact of catastrophes which seem to prove that the old paradigm was wrong and its adherents mistaken. At that point the previous outsiders (gadflies, radicals, revisionists, etc.) find many of their views accepted as mainstream thinking; their critique becomes the new framework.

Our model resembles Kuhn's but with the important provision that neither old nor new foreign-policy paradigms have much intrinsic validity because neither can be objectively verified in an indeterminate world. Instead of verified, a new foreign-policy paradigm is merely internalized. Counterinstances are ignored; the range of conceivable strategic situations is narrowed to exclude possible alternate paradigms. It may be impossible to distinguish whether this process is emotional or rational, affective or cognitive. The acrimony accompanying foreign-policy paradigm shifts, however, suggests a strong emotional component. Chances are that a member of the American elite who as a young person witnessed the events leading up to Pearl Harbor has developed a very definite orientation to foreign policy, an interventionist one, the assumptions of which are not open for discussion. Similarly, by the early 1970s the interventionist views of Walt Rostow, Dean Rusk, and William Bundy produced mostly irritation (if not outright vituperation) on the part of younger foreign-policy thinkers.

It is here that we add the concept of generation to the Kuhnian model. Political scientists have not looked much at generations in their analyses. Some hold that to separate out a "political generation" is to reify an abstract and nebulous concept. People are born every day and constitute more of a continuum than a segment. The German sociologist Karl Mannheim agreed that generation is a reification, but no more so than the concept of social class, which is indispensable for much modern analysis.[12]

An elite generation freezes upon either an interventionist or noninterventionist paradigm usually after some foreign-policy catastrophe wrought by the application of the opposite paradigm. During a transition period the two paradigms clash. Because they are antithetical, compromise is impossible. The two generations with their different assumptions talk past each other. Eventually the new paradigm wins because it gains more younger adherents, while the advocates of the old paradigm retire and die off. The new paradigm triumphs not so much on an intellectual basis as on an actuarial one.

THE PEARL HARBOR PARADIGM

It may be profitable to look at the foreign-policy paradigm as having a natural life—a birth, a period of growth, and a death. The birth is characterized by a mounting criticism of the old paradigm and then by the conversion of a large portion of the elite to the new paradigm. An event "proves" the old paradigm wrong, as it did to Senator Arthur H. Vandenburg, a staunch isolationist whose turning to interventionism "took firm form on the afternoon of the Pearl Harbor attack. That day ended isolationism for any realist."[13] In honor of Vandenburg's conversion we can label this interventionist orientation the "Pearl Harbor paradigm."

Pearl Harbor, of course, was merely the culmination of an increasingly heated argument in the interwar period between the dominant noninterventionists and interventionist Cassandras. We could also call the latter view the Munich paradigm, the Ethiopian paradigm, or even the Manchurian paradigm.[14] But the Pearl Harbor attack clinched the interventionists' argument by demonstrating they were "right" in warning that an isolated America was impossible. The isolationists either shut up or quickly changed sides.[15] The handful of holdouts, such as those who charged Roosevelt with dragging the country into war, were by and large simply ignored.

The most clearly visible starting point for the rise of the Pearl Harbor paradigm was Secretary of State Stimson's 1932 "nonrecognition" of Japanese expansion into Manchuria. Thereafter concern slowly grew among the American elite that aggressive powers abroad could eventually threaten America. The growth of this concern among younger persons is important for two reasons: First, people who were in their twenties during the late 1930s were less committed to the then-prevailing noninterventionism of the older generation. Accordingly, more of the younger group were open to formulate a new paradigm—an interventionist one. Second, although some older elite members may have been similarly alarmed at overseas threats, it was mostly the younger generation that would staff foreign-policy positions in future decades.

By the time war broke out in Europe in 1939, elite opinion was starting to split. The formation of two committees expressed this division: the isolationist America First and the increasingly interventionist Committee to Defend America by Aiding the Allies. On December 7, 1941, the interventionists could (and did) say, "I told you so," and then enshrined their argument—permanently, they thought—as the basic assumption of American foreign policy: If we do not nip aggression in the bud, it will eventually grow and involve us. By not stopping aggressors immediately, you encouraged them. Apart from the moral issue of helping a victim of aggression, you are also setting up the first line of defense of your own country. Accordingly, altruism and self-interest merge.

The discredited "isolationists" could only meekly retort that in principle at least, the defense of the United States did not start on the other side of the globe, for that merely guarantees American participation in wars that were not intrinsically hers. The last gasps of the remaining noninterventionism came in the 1951 debate to limit troops in Europe and the 1954 Bricker amendment to restrict executive agreements. Occasional whiffs of preinterventionist views could be sensed in debates over foreign aid.

The interesting aspect of the Pearl Harbor paradigm, however, was its duration long past World War II. The interventionist orientation had been so deeply internalized in the struggle with the isolationists that it did not lapse with the Allied victory. By that time almost all sections of the globe now "mattered" to American security, particularly as a new hostile power—the Soviet Union—seemed bent on territorial and ideological aggrandizement. In the 1930s the fate of East Europe bothered Washington very little, but in the span of a decade East Europe became a matter of urgent American concern.[16] Not only had the Soviets inflicted brutal Hitlerlike dictatorships upon the nations of East Europe, it was taken for granted that they were preparing to do the same to West Europe and other areas. But this time America was smarter and stood prepared to stop aggression. In the span of one decade, 1945–1955, the United States committed itself to the defense of more than seventy nations.

A few quotes might suffice to demonstrate the persistence of the Pearl Harbor paradigm into the Vietnam era. Warning of a "new isolationism," Senator Thomas J. Dodd, in a 1965 floor speech, explained:

> The situation in Viet-Nam today bears many resemblances to the situation just before Munich. . . .
>
> In Viet-Nam today we are again dealing with a faraway land about which we know very little.
>
> In Viet-Nam today we are again confronted by an incorrigible aggressor, fanatically committed to the destruction of the free world, whose agreements are as worthless as Hitler's. . . .
>
> If we fail to draw the line in Viet-Nam, in short, we may find ourselves compelled to draw a defense line as far back as Seattle and Alaska, with Hawaii as a solitary outpost in mid-Pacific.[17]

Defense Secretary Robert McNamara, in commenting on Lin Piao's 1965 statement on the universal applicability of "people's war," said, "It is a program of aggression. It is a speech that ranks with Hitler's *Mein Kampf*."[18]

President Johnson too was immersed in the World War II imagery. In his 1965 Johns Hopkins speech he warned:

> The central lesson of our time is that the appetite of aggression is never satisfied. To withdraw from one battlefield means only to prepare for the next. We must say in Southeast Asia—as we did in Europe—in the words of the Bible: "Hitherto shalt thou come, but no further."[19]

In a 1966 speech to NATO parliamentarians, Senator Henry M. Jackson put it this way:

> Analogies with the past may be misleading and I would not argue that this is the 30's all over again. But looking back we think, as I am sure many of you do, that it is wise to

stop aggression before the aggressor becomes strong and swollen with ambition from small successes. We think the world might have been spared enormous misfortunes if Japan had not been permitted to succeed in Manchuria, or Mussolini in Ethiopia, or Hitler in Czechoslovakia or in the Rhineland. And we think that our sacrifices in this dirty war in little Vietnam will make a dirtier and bigger war less likely.[20]

President Johnson said in a 1966 talk in New Hampshire:

Few people realize that world peace has reached voting age. It has been twenty-one years since that day on the U.S.S. *Missouri* in Tokyo Bay when World War II came to an end. Perhaps it reflects poorly on our world that men must fight limited wars to keep from fighting larger wars; but that is the condition of the world. . . .

We are following this policy in Vietnam because we know that the restrained use of power has for twenty-one years prevented the wholesale destruction the world faced in 1914 and again in 1939.[21]

The Pentagon Papers are replete with the World War II analogy. Among these, in a 1966 memo, Walt Rostow explained how his experience as an OSS major plotting German bomb targets taught him the importance of cutting the enemy's POL—petroleum, oil, and lubricants:

With an understanding that simple analogies are dangerous, I nevertheless feel it is quite possible the military effects of a systematic and sustained bombing of POL in North Vietnam may be more prompt and direct than conventional intelligence analysis would suggest.[22]

Rostow seems to have retained a petroleum version of the Pearl Harbor paradigm and to have assumed that Hanoi had *Panzers* and a *Luftwaffe* that could be knocked out.

THE SPECIAL ROLE OF KENNEDY

One member of the foreign-policy elite deserves to be examined at greater length. John F. Kennedy not only internalized what we are calling the Pearl Harbor paradigm, he helped install it.[23] His 1940 best seller, *Why England Slept,* originally written [when] he was twenty-one to twenty-two, was his Harvard senior thesis. The book concerned not only Britain's interwar somnolence in the face of the German threat but posited America in the same position. Kennedy's position at that time, it is interesting to note, was in marked contrast to the isolationism of his father, who was then the United States ambassador to Britain.[24]

The *Why England Slept* of Kennedy's youth laid down a remarkably full-blown view of national security, one that Senator and later President Kennedy retained practically intact. The following were some of the important themes which first appeared in *Why England Slept* and then in his senatorial and presidential speeches:

1. Peace-loving democracy is weak in the face of expansionist totalitarianism.[25]
2. The democratic leader's role is to teach the population that isolated events form an overall pattern of aggression against them.[26]

3. Defense preparedness must be kept up, even if this means increasing defense expenditures.[27]
4. Reliance on a single-weapon defense system is dangerous; a country must have several good defense systems for flexibility.[28]
5. Civil defense measures must be instituted in advance to protect the population in case of war.[29]
6. The nation must be willing actually to go to war in the final crunch; bluffing will not suffice.[30]

In the case of Britain in the late 1930s, argued the young Kennedy, democracy simply did not take the Nazi menace seriously, and British leaders failed to point out the danger and build up defenses. British defense was overconcentrated on the fleet at the expense of the army and most importantly of the air force. Britain's civil defense was weak, particularly in antiaircraft batteries. And finally, British leaders had been so hesitant to actually apply force when needed that Hitler could not take them seriously.

Representative and later Senator Kennedy found these arguments highly applicable to the Eisenhower period, which he often compared to interwar Britain, as in this 1959 speech:

> Twenty-three years ago, in a bitter debate in the House of Commons, Winston Churchill charged the British government with acute blindness to the menace of Nazi Germany, with gross negligence in the maintenance of the island's defenses, and with indifferent, indecisive leadership of British foreign policy and British public opinion. The preceding years of drift and impotency, he said, were "the years the locusts have eaten."
>
> Since January 1953 this nation has passed through a similar period. . . .[31]

America in the 1950s, said Kennedy, refused to see the "global challenge" of Soviet penetration of the Third World. Eisenhower had let United States defense preparedness slide; a "missile gap" had appeared. America must spend more on defense: "Surely our nation's security overrides budgetary considerations. . . . Then why can we not realize that the coming years of the gap present us with a peril more deadly than any wartime danger we have ever known?"[32] The country relied on "massive retaliation" when it needed a flexible response of many options, including counterinsurgency. Kennedy accordingly opposed Republican cuts in our ground troops. And, in a 1959 interview, he emphasized that the United States must be willing to fight for Berlin:

> If we took the view which some Englishmen took, that Prague or the Sudentendeutsch were not worth a war in '38—if we took that view about Berlin, my judgment is that the West Berliners would pass into the communist orbit, and our position in West Germany and our relations with West Germany would receive a fatal blow. . . . They're fighting for New York and Paris when they struggle over Berlin.[33]

One might be tempted to dismiss Senator Kennedy's views as campaign rhetoric. But once in the presidency, Kennedy proceeded to implement them: bigger defense budgets, larger ground forces, "flexible response" (including counterinsurgency), civil defense (especially the 1961 fallout-shelter panic), and finally overt warfare in Southeast Asia. Throughout his presidency, Kennedy and his advisers stuck to the image of the Pearl Harbor paradigm. In his dramatic 1962 television address on the Soviet arms buildup in Cuba, Kennedy used his favorite analogy: "The 1930s taught us a clear lesson: aggressive conduct, if allowed to go unchecked and unchallenged, ultimately leads to war."[34] Vice-President Johnson, in a 1961 memo to Kennedy on Vietnam, wrote:

> The battle against Communism must be joined in South-east Asia with strength and determination to achieve success there—or the United States, inevitably, must surrender the Pacific and take up our defenses on our own shores.[35]

One wonders if Johnson or one of his assistants had read Spykman. Further perusal of the Pentagon Papers shows much the same evaluation of the alleged strategic importance of Vietnam; its fall was defined as a major setback to United States security.[36]

We do not here argue that Vietnam is important or unimportant to the defense of America. That is indeterminate, although within the last decade a considerable portion of elite opinion has switched from the former view to the latter. What interests us is the inability of Kennedy and his advisers to define Southeast Asia as anything but strategic.

Kennedy's age surely contributed to his highly interventionist orientation. He retained what we are calling the Pearl Harbor paradigm as a young man in his early twenties. Eisenhower, by way of contrast, was twenty-seven years older and witnessed the events that led up to American involvement in World War II as a man in his forties. It seems likely, then, that the impact of the events of the late 1930s and early 1940s was far stronger in forming Kennedy's foreign-policy orientation than Eisenhower's.

This perhaps partially explains why the Pearl Harbor paradigm eventually was applied to an extreme and why this process took about a generation. A generation of the United States elite experienced as relatively young people the momentous events leading up to Pearl Harbor. Kennedy was of this generation, which gradually surfaced into public life.[37] Each year there were more members of this generation in positions of foreign-policy leadership. The older generation retired and the proportion of this new generation increased. After about twenty years there were few members of the older generation left in the political machinery. By the time Kennedy assumed the presidency, there were few countervailing views to dilute and moderate a policy of thoroughgoing interventionism. In this sense, we can say that the Pearl Harbor paradigm "blossomed" under Kennedy, who applied it more completely than did Eisenhower.

But while Kennedy was applying the wisdom learned in his youth to its full extent—the Green Berets, the Peace Corps, the Agency for International Development, the Counterinsurgency Committee—the real world was going its own way, becoming less and less relevant to the mental constructs of American foreign-policy planners. We have then a "dysfunction" growing between policy and reality. On the one hand, we have a foreign orientation essentially frozen since the 1940s, and on the other hand, a world which defied pigeonholing into the compartments of the 1940s.

The most conspicuous indicator of this discrepancy was the persistent American inability to evaluate "communism" as no longer monolithic. Here, as with Kuhn's scientific paradigms, the data can be interpreted ambiguously in transitional periods. One side reads the data as still showing essentially a monolith, the other as a badly fractured movement. But at what point in time did it become unreasonable for United States foreign-policy planners to continue to hold the former view? Scholars had been emphasizing the Sino-Soviet split since the early 1960s,[38] but it was not until the early 1970s—after the trauma of Vietnam had set in—that reality was incorporated into policy. When communism became perceivable as nonmonolithic, under President Nixon, it perforce lost its most threatening attribute. Thus redefined, Indochina was no longer worth evaluating as a strategic prize, and American withdrawal became possible. The paradigm had shifted: Vietnam was no longer part of a gigantic pincer movement enveloping us.

After the Vietnam debacle was over, few voices could be heard advocating a return to "business as usual," that is, to continuing the interventionist paradigm. Nixon introduced a policy markedly different from that of his predecessors. It differed rhetorically in announcing to America's allies that they would have to bear primary responsibility for their defense,[39] and it differed physically in reducing United States ground forces to the point where few were available to send abroad. (Total U.S. armed forces fell from 3.5 million in 1968 to 2.2 million in 1974; especially hard hit were the army and the marines, without whom there can be no overseas intervention.)

Just as Pearl Harbor brought with it a massive and general shift in the foreign-policy orientation of the United States elite, so did Vietnam. Pearl Harbor and Vietnam were the points in time at which critics could say, "I told you so," and win widespread if grudging agreement from the old guard. The Pearl Harbor paradigm, applied for three decades to a world from which it was increasingly alienated, eventually was "shipwrecked" on Vietnam.

THE VIETNAM PARADIGM

What follows? It is not difficult to discern an emerging noninterventionist orientation which can be termed the "Vietnam paradigm." Varying in emphasis and nuance, the bearers of the new view all urge *limitation* of American activity (above all, military activity) overseas, particularly in the Third World. John Kenneth Galbraith, for example, wants

> and even more positive commitment to coexistence with the Communist countries. It means a much more determined effort to get military competition with the Soviets under control. . . . It means abandoning the Sub-Imperial ambitions in the Third World and recognizing instead that there is little we can do to influence political development in this part of the world and less that we need to do.[40]

Arthur Schlesinger, Jr., believes the "lessons of Vietnam" show:

> *First, that everything in the world is not of equal importance to us.* Asia and Africa are of vital importance for Asians and Africans . . . but they are not so important for us. . . .

> *Second, that we cannot do everything in the world.* The universalism of the older generation was spacious in design and noble in intent. Its flaw was that it overcommitted our country—it overcommitted our policy, our resources, and our rhetoric. . . .[41]

The critics of only a few years ago might reflect with satisfaction on how much of their critique (not all, to be sure) has been absorbed by the Nixon doctrine.

A deluge of foreign-policy criticism has appeared in the last several years. If we were to boil down the new conventional wisdom and compare it with the old, it might look like this:[42]

Pearl Harbor Paradigm	Vietnam Paradigm
Communism is a monolithic threat.	Communism is a divided spastic.
If we don't intervene overseas, we may get dragged into a war.	If we do intervene overseas, we are sure to get into a war.
We must nip aggression in the bud.	We are not the world's policeman.
The dominoes are falling. Quick, let's do something!	The dominoes are falling. So what?
United States aid and technology will develop backward countries.	Backward countries will develop themselves or not at all.

The catastrophe that each generation experienced implanted viewpoints which, based on the importance for United States security accorded to overseas events, are flatly antithetical. Rational discussion between the two paradigms tends to be impossible, not for want of "facts" but for how they are structured. The structure, or paradigm, is imparted by a traumatic foreign-policy experience. Without such a trauma the inadequacies of the old paradigm might have gone unnoticed. Unfortunately, the indiscriminate application of one paradigm to increasingly changed circumstances tends to produce just that mishap. Given many interventions, it is likely that one will misfire. The adventures which do not misfire conspicuously—Lebanon, the Congo airlifts, Berlin, the Taiwan Straits, Santo Domingo—can be shrugged off or even used to justify continuing interventionism ("It worked there, didn't it?"). In this manner a foreign-policy paradigm actuates a built-in self-destruct mechanism: its eventual application *ad absurdum* by its elite generation.

THE FOREIGN-POLICY PARADIGMS OF YESTERYEAR

Is the above a comparison of just the two most recent epochs in United States diplomatic history, or might the approach be extended backward in time to validate the generational-paradigm approach as a more general tool of analysis? The author wishes to attempt the latter by dividing American foreign policy into periods on the basis of alternating interventionist and noninterventionist paradigms. To do this it is necessary to ask how the elite of a given period answered Spykman's old question of where the defense of America should start—on the near or far side of the oceans. If the answer is "far," then the lands across the seas "matter" to United States security. If the answer is "near," the lands across the seas "do not matter" so much to the security of the United States. In the former case, we have an interventionist period; in the latter, we have a noninterventionist period.

Let us examine United States diplomatic history, looking at periods first in reverse chronology and then by functional categories. As previously stated, the bearers of the Pearl Harbor paradigm were themselves reacting to what they believed were the gross deficiencies of the interwar "isolationism." The 1920 to 1940 period can be called the "Versailles paradigm"; its bearers were condemned as blind for failing to recognize the obvious threat from abroad in 1939–1941. Who were these people? Prominent among them were senators Borah, Hiram Johnson, Nye, and La Follette, the same "battalion of irreconcilables," who opposed the Versailles Treaty and League Covenant in 1919–1920.[43] For such persons World War II was a conflict the United States must and could—through rigorous application of the Neutrality Acts—avoid. Their great lesson was the aftermath of World War I, which, they believed, had achieved nothing: Europe stayed fractious, and even worse, refused to pay its war debts. American participation in that war had been a mistake. As with the Pearl Harbor paradigm, in their arguments self-interest and morality were intertwined. Versailles had been unfair to various nations (the demands of ethnic groups played a role here); the treaty enshrined the victors in positions of superiority; and the League of Nations's Covenant would then entangle America in the next European crisis. The depth of the interwar bitterness probably was not reached until the 1934–1936 Nye Committee hearings, which, in part, sought to blame munitions manufacturers for United States involvement. Out of the Nye hearings grew the Neutrality Acts of 1935–1937. Like the Pearl Harbor paradigm, the Versailles paradigm seems also to have reached full flowering shortly before its demise, exaggerating its increasing irrelevance to the world situation.

It took the critics of the Versailles paradigm at least half a decade to dislodge it. The "isolationists" fought the growing interventionism every inch of the way. Strong emotions came to the surface. "I could scarcely proceed further without losing my self-control," wrote Secretary of State Cordell Hull of a 1939 confrontation with Senator Borah in which the latter disparaged State Department cables on an impending war in Europe.[44] Other sources said that Hull actually wept at the meeting. It took the catastrophe at Pearl Harbor to squelch the obdurate bearers of the Versailles paradigm.

Was this Versailles paradigm a reaction to a previous orientation—an interventionist one? That there was a previous period, sometimes called imperialistic, from the 1890s extending into the next century cannot be doubted. The problem with labeling the period from 1898 (the Spanish-American War) through 1919 (the aftermath of World War I) an "imperial paradigm" is that the continuity of an interventionist policy between the two wars is not clear. With the Pearl Harbor paradigm we can show a consistent propensity for United States intervention over three decades, but with the 1898–1919 period we have interventions, mostly clustered at the beginning and end. In 1898 the United States occupied Cuba, Puerto Rico, the Philippines, Hawaii, and Wake (and part of Samoa in 1899). Then, mostly relating to World War I, the United States occupied or had troops in Mexico, the Virgin Islands, France, and Russia. In between there were only the relatively minor Caribbean occupations. Thus, if this was an imperial paradigm, it sagged in the middle. It may be further objected that two distinct lines of thought accompanied respectively the beginning and end of this period. The earlier thinking favored unilateral colony grabbing, in recognition of the fact that the great European powers were carving up the globe and leaving America without colonies or areas of influence. The later thinking, accompanying World War I, was much more internationalistic, stressing cooperation rather than unilateralism. Some figures, like Senator Albert J. Beveridge, were imperialists at the turn of the century and isolationists about World War I.[45]

The author agrees that such an imperial paradigm is not nearly so consistent as the later interventionist epoch, the Pearl Harbor paradigm. Nonetheless there is a good deal of unity in the three decades of the 1890s, 1900s, and 1910s, and the period generally was an interventionistic one. In the first place, it was a time of almost continual United States naval growth. Starting with Secretary of the Navy Benjamin Tracy's 1889 plans for a vast American fleet and pushed by Theodore Roosevelt (both as assistant secretary of the navy and as president), the U.S. Navy rose from sixth to fourth place in 1990, to third place in 1906, and to second place (to Britain) in 1907. The naval budget went from $21 million in 1885, to $31 million in 1891, to $79 million in 1902, to $104 million in 1906, and to $137 million in 1909. Wilson, although initially cutting the naval budget somewhat, ended up with a $2.2 billion one in 1919.[46] In respect to naval expenditures then, the imperial paradigm did not "sag in the middle."

Further, although some of the foreign-policy elite of this period moved from unilateral imperialism at the turn of the century to equally unilateral withdrawal from Europe's war, there was also a good deal of consistency in positing a need for a major United States role abroad. Woodrow Wilson, for example, after some uncertainty, endorsed both the war with Spain and the annexation of Hawaii and the Philippines. His motives, to be sure, differed from the imperialists; Wilson wanted to prepare Puerto Rico and the Philippines for self-government.[47] But we are less interested in motive than in general orientation, and in this Wilson was unmistakably an interventionist. Indeed, as president, Wilson "carried out more armed interventions in Latin America than any of his predecessors."[48] In 1898 the twenty-seven-year-old Cordell Hull even raised his own infantry company and went with his men as their captain to Cuba (although they requested the Philippines).[49] Liberalism by no means precludes interventionism, as Waltz has pointed out.[50]

We might even consider the imperial paradigm as a sort of training period for the senior staffers of the later Pearl Harbor paradigm: Congressman Hull as ardent Wilson supporter; Franklin D. Roosevelt as enthusiastic assistant secretary of the navy under Wilson; and Stimson as secretary of war under Taft. This helps explain why the Pearl Harbor period was not staffed exclusively by young converts to the growing interventionism of the late 1930s. There was on hand a much older age cohort who had internalized an interventionist framework some forty years earlier and who were eclipsed by the militant noninterventionism of the 1920s and 1930s. This group formed a countertrend subculture which sat out the interwar isolationism until called back into power for the higher positions during World War II. By the 1950s, however, they had mostly been replaced by the younger interventionists of the Kennedy generation.

Can we discern a period still further back out of which grew the imperial paradigm? The 1870s and 1880s are commonly considered the "nadir of diplomacy." The period was marked by massive indifference to overseas affairs, anglophobia (over Britain's aid to the Confederacy) preoccupation with filling out the presumably self-sufficient United States. We might therefore label this epoch the "Continental paradigm." As with later periods, a minority critique starts in the middle of it on the strategic assumptions of the established orientation. In this case there was a growing strategic insecurity and the efforts of navalists—of whom Admiral Mahan was not the first—to rebuild the decrepit United States Navy. The year 1889 was a turning point; the Harrison administration began to discard the passive, inert policies which had characterized the previous two decades and to start actively making policy for the first time since the Civil War.[51] One need only compare the relatively weak American reactions to the bloodshed of the Cuba uprising of 1868–1878 to the much firmer stand of the 1890s.

It is not necessary to go further back than this. Our principal analytical distinctions—a near or far defense, interventionism or noninterventionism, few or many troops overseas—do not readily apply to nineteenth-century America. The United States was too busy, in a Turnerian sense, with filling out its own frontiers. Further, America had little to fear from Europe or Asia, especially with the British fleet ruling the waves.

COMPARING PARADIGMS

While this division of United States diplomatic history into periods is admittedly an artificial construct, we can compare the periods or the "paradigms" that accompany the periods. (This comparison is summarized in Table 14.1.) The concrete expression of an interventionist or noninterventionist view is the number of United States troops overseas. During the imperial and Pearl Harbor periods America had relatively many troops abroad, and they were abroad not merely because of World Wars I and II, respectively. Long before our entry into World War I, there were American soldiers in Cuba, the Philippines, and throughout the Caribbean, including Mexico. During the intervening Versailles period the troops came home not only from Europe but from the Caribbean as well. Only in Nicaragua and Haiti did United States occupation continue past the 1920s. The Philippines were lightly garrisoned and almost forgotten in the interwar period. During the Pearl Harbor period there were troops overseas not only during World War II but long after it. The United States foreign-policy elite during this time was disposed to consider an overseas defense as the only reasonable American strategy. With President Nixon, this strategy seems to be changing, and there are fewer troops overseas.

Much of United States foreign policy hinges on the relationship between the executive and the legislative branches of government. If the Congress follows the president's lead and delivers what he wants, the United States is then able to engage in interventionist moves. When the Congress, specifically the Senate, tires of such activity and starts resenting strong presidential leadership, the possibilities for

Table 14.1 PARADIGMS IN COMPARISON

	Continental 1870s, 1880s	Imperial 1890s–1910s	Versailles 1920s, 1930s	Pearl Harbor 1940s–1960s	Vietnam 1970s–?
General view of foreign areas	"Don't matter"	"Matters"	"Don't matter"	"Matters"	"Don't matter"
View of Europe	Indifference (Anglophobia)	Imitation (Anglophilia)	Irritation	Salvation	Irritation
Losers		Anti-imperialists	Wilsonian internationalists	Isolationists	Globalists
Troops overseas	Almost none	Carribbean, Philippines, China, West Europe, Russia, Mexico	Few in Caribbean, Philippines	Europe, Asia, Latin America, Africa	Decreasing
Congress	Obstructive	Cooperative	Obstructive	Cooperative	Obstructive
Funds for overseas	None	War loans	Begrudging of war debts, anticancellationists, Johnson Act	Marshall Plan, Point Four, AID, arms-sales credits	Begrudging of aid, balance of payments force cutback
Commitments	None	Open Door, Caribbean protectorates, Associated Power in World War I, Philippine defense	Continued Open Door, reduction of Caribbean protectorates	U.N., NATO, SEATO, (CENTO), Congressional resolutions on Formosa, Middle East, Cuba, Berlin, Vietnam	Senate res. 85, War Powers Bill, attempt to repeal resolutions

intervention are reduced. We would therefore expect to find an assertive Congress during noninterventionist periods, particularly at the beginning of these periods. It is for this reason that we get dramatic showdowns between key senators and the president. Especially important is the Senate Foreign Relations Committee, whose chairmen appear "irascible and contentious" when they engage in limiting executive initiatives in foreign affairs. Ranting anglophobe Charles Sumner defeated President Grant's scheme to annex Santo Domingo in 1870. Henry Cabot Lodge (and William Borah) stopped America's entry into President Wilson's beloved League. J. William Fulbright (and Mike Mansfield) cut down President Nixon's foreign-aid program and tried to put the executive on a leash by means of the 1973 War Powers Bill.

There are also, to be sure, executive-legislative difficulties when the paradigm shifts the other way, from noninterventionist to interventionist, which are perhaps not quite as dramatic because in this case the congressional opponents are the "losers"(see below). From 1898 to 1900 there was the bitter but unsuccessful rear guard of those protesting the war with Spain and the Philippines annexation, such as George F. Hoar and George G. Vest in the Senate and Thomas B. Reed, Speaker of the House.[52] In 1939 to 1941 there was a similar rear guard (discussed earlier), of those demanding United States neutrality. One characteristic of a paradigm shift in either direction, then, is a serious fight between the White House and Capitol Hill over who will have the upper hand in foreign policy. When the paradigm is established, conflict between the two branches subsides because there is relative consensus and the acquiescence of one branch to the other; a spirit of "cooperation" and "bipartisanship" then prevails.

The shift from one paradigm to another also involves a rather clearly identifiable group of "losers"—those whose orientation is repudiated. This is not a happy process and much rancor accompanies the displacement of the bearers of the old paradigm and their consignment to obscurity. The anti-imperialists of 1898–1900 sought to preserve a more limited, continental America. Their arguments—strategic, moral, constitutional, and economic—bear a striking resemblance to some of the arguments used to oppose the Vietnam war.[53] The anti-imperialists were condemned by the interventionists of their day; Theodore Roosevelt called them "simply unhung traitors." The losers of twenty years later, the Wilsonian internationalists, also did not go down without a vituperative fight. The isolationists were the clear and unhappy losers as the Pearl Harbor paradigm replaced the Versailles paradigm. One is not yet certain what to call the present crop of losers, but perhaps "globalists" is a label that will stick.[54] Those who defend the dying paradigm appear as obdurate fools who are unable to come to grips with the new realities and who must therefore be ignored. The losers, who stick with the old paradigm while the new one triumphs, gradually cease to be practitioners.

Another characteristic of noninterventionist periods is the begrudging to friends and allies of United States aid, which flowed rather freely during the preceding interventionist period. The failure of the European powers to pay their World War I debts created both a public and congressional furor in the 1920s and culminated in the 1934 Johnson Act prohibiting debtor nations from raising funds in the United States. The "anticancellationists" helped spread the feeling that America had been cheated by tricky and unreliable ex-partners. In the late 1960s a critique of United States foreign aid developed along similar lines: billions have been wasted; they'll never be repaid; we've been much too generous; the recipients are ungrateful; etc. The interesting point here is that the critique came not only from conservatives, but from liberals who previously spoke in favor of foreign aid.

Arms and munitions appear as a minor but interesting point in noninterventionist periods. Arms sales abroad are viewed with great suspicion, as a possible avenue by which the country could get dragged into foreign wars. The Nye Committee hearings and the ensuing Neutrality Acts in the 1930s were attempts to prevent a repetition of America's gradual entanglement in another European war. It can be argued that precisely such an entanglement was repeated under Roosevelt with "cash and carry," Lend Lease, and the destroyers-for-bases deal with Britain. It indeed led to de facto war in the North Atlantic between the United States and Germany months before Pearl Harbor. But, it is interesting to note, in the interventionist Pearl Harbor period there was practically no regret that the Neutrality Acts had thus been circumvented. The problem of arms sales again flared as the Pearl Harbor paradigm came under question. As a result of a 1967 Senate debate, arms sales by means of Export-Import Bank financing and Pentagon loan guarantees were stopped. Nixon's program to supply military hardware instead of United States troops was severely trimmed in the Senate.

The movement away from interventionism seems also to include the congressional and popular scapegoating of manufacturers of munitions. While Senator Nye had his "merchants of death," Senator Proxmire has his "military-industrial complex." In both cases it was alleged that armaments programs take on a life of their own and weapons makers manipulate public spending to their own advantage. The Nye Committee even "began to attack the war-making potential of the executive branch of the government," records Wayne Cole, and "also began to see the president as part of the compound."[55]

In interventionist periods there is a willingness to enter into arrangements that pledge the country to military action overseas. Admittedly, this was slow in coming during World War I, which the United States entered belatedly and only as an "associate" of the Entente. During the Pearl Harbor period, however, the United States carpeted the globe with commitments.

Following these times of generous pledges have come periods of limiting or discarding commitments. In addition to the already-mentioned League rejection and the Neutrality Acts there was the interesting Ludlow Amendment (shelved in the House in 1937 by a vote of 209–188) to require a national referendum to declare war except for actual invasion. As the Vietnam paradigm took hold there was the National Commitments Resolution (without force of law) in 1969 expressing the sense of the Senate that America should fulfill no commitment without specific legislation. In 1973 a War Powers Bill to permit the president only ninety days to use troops abroad without additional legislation overrode Nixon's veto. Further conflict over commitments seemed inevitable as Senator Mansfield continued his efforts to prune United States forces in Europe.

On a more general level, in the noninterventionist periods there is a lessened interest in Europe and in the interventionist periods a heightened interest. During the Continental period there was aloof indifference to Europe buttressed by a sharp anglophobia in the wake of Britain's aid to the Confederacy. As American leaders adopted imperial views, there was an imitation of Europe (colony grabbing) and some cooperation, as in the Peking expedition in 1900. There was also a marked anglophilia starting in the Spanish-American War. After Versailles there was disgust at European greed and squabbling and regret that America had ever become involved in Europe's war. During the Pearl Harbor period there was the virtual United States occupation of West Europe and an almost crusading American involvement in European recovery, rearmament, and unification. By the early 1970s the devalued dollar and pressure to withdraw our forces marked the beginning of a diminished American role in Europe, a trend that was heightened in 1973 and 1974 by differing United States and European approaches to the Middle East and the petroleum shortage. Again the view surfaced that the Europeans were selfish and hopelessly fractious.

On a more general level still, in the noninterventionist periods the lands abroad "do not matter" much to the United States elite; in the interventionist periods foreign lands "matter" a great deal. (Professors in foreign-area and international studies, as well as of foreign languages, have recently noticed the former view among students.) We may also note that the last three periods each began with a catastrophe of overseas origin. Versailles appeared to demonstrate that American participation in a European war had been futile and a profound mistake. Pearl Harbor appeared to demonstrate that the interwar "isolationism" had been absurd and had led to a disaster. And Vietnam appeared to demonstrate that the long-standing interventionist policy had been "wrong" and had led to a disaster.

CYCLICAL THEORIES REVISITED

The approach to diplomatic history, of course, is not completely new or unique. Several writers have advanced views that United States foreign policy tends to swing like a pendulum (an image used by both President Nixon and Senator Fulbright) from extremes of overinvolvement to underinvolvement. Stanley Hoffmann, for example, discerned "the two *tempi* of America's foreign relations," alternating "from phases of withdrawal (or, when complete withdrawal is impossible, priority to domestic concerns) to phases of dynamic, almost messianic romping on the world stage."[56] Hans Morgenthau saw United States policy moving "back and forth between the extremes of an indiscriminate isolationism and an equally indiscriminate internationalism or globalism."[57]

Getting more specific, historian Dexter Perkins divided American foreign relations into cycles of "relatively pacific feeling," followed by "rising bellicosity and war," followed by "postwar nationalism," and then back to "relatively pacific feeling."[58] Getting even more specific, a behaviorally inclined political scientist, Frank L. Klingberg, using such indicators as naval expenditures, annexations, armed expeditions, diplomatic pressures, and attention paid to foreign matters in presidential speeches and party platforms, discovered alternating phases of "introversion" (averaging twenty-one years) and "extroversion" (averaging twenty-seven years). Klingberg added: "If America's fourth phase of extroversion (which began around 1940) should last as long as the previous extrovert phases, it would not end until well into the 1960s."[59] As social scientists, of course, we do not accept the notion that God plays numbers games with United States foreign policy. The most fruitful approach to this cyclical phenomenon, the author believes, is the generationally linked paradigm, which helps explain both the changes in orientation and their spacing in time.

Other writers have found a roughly generational interval of about twenty-five years between upsurges of world violence. (Klingberg too mentioned generations as one possible explanation for his foreign-policy cycles.) Denton and Phillips suggest what we might term a "forgetting" theory to explain their twenty-five-year cycles of violence: That generation, and particularly its decision makers, that experienced an intensive war tends to remember its horrors and avoid similar conflicts. The following generation of decision makers may forget the horrors and remember the heroism; this generation is more likely to engage in violence.[60] This explanation helps account for our Versailles paradigm, but it is flatly at odds with our Pearl Harbor paradigm, during which a generation, virtually all of whom experienced World War II firsthand, displayed little reluctance to apply force overseas. This generation was of course repelled by the violence of World War II but used it to explain why aggression must be "nipped in the bud" to prevent another large conflagration. Walt Rostow, for example, continued to insist that Vietnam *prevented* a large war. "If we had walked away from Asia or if we walk away from Asia now, the consequences will not be peace," said Rostow in 1971. "The consequence will be a larger war and quite possibly a nuclear war."[61]

This author subscribes to a cyclical theory of United States foreign policy only in the most general terms—namely, that if there are alternating orientations of interventionism and noninterventionism, then logically the former will produce more "action" and this will show up as intermittent peaks in statistical tabulations. The question of cycles falls behind the question of the conventional wisdom of foreign-policy thinkers.

In searching for explanations of any cyclical theory, of course, we cannot rule out purely external factors such as threats or challenges from abroad. It may be that such external forces have impinged upon the United States at roughly generational intervals and that we have merely reacted to them. This then dumps the generation question onto the offending land across the sea. The problem here is that during one epoch American foreign-policy thinkers may largely ignore threats and in another epoch they may take threats very seriously. As we have already considered, the Cuban uprising of the 1870s elicited relatively little response from the United States compared to our response to the Cuban uprising of the 1890s. America paid little attention to East Europe in the 1930s and a great deal of attention in the 1940s and 1950s. In 1948 the Soviet-Yugoslav split was seen as an anomaly; in the 1970s the Sino-Soviet dispute is seen as natural, the almost inevitable collision of two nationalisms. *Quisquid recipitur recipitur secundum modum recipiensis.* The world changes, of course, but it takes a changed set of American attitudes to perceive the new situation.

The problem is one of perception catching up with reality not on a continual and incremental basis, but delayed and in spurts. May we hazard that Vietnam will leave behind it a continuation of this pattern? The immediate impact of Vietnam on United States foreign policy is already apparent: the Senate's restorative revolt, demoralized armed forces, international economic difficulties, and skeptical allies. The longer-term effects may be far deeper. If the above generational-paradigm hypothesis is even approximately correct, we can expect persons who witnessed Vietnam while they were in their twenties to retain a noninterventionist orientation. As the elite of this generation gradually surfaces into policy-relevant positions, we can expect them to implement their views. The most important reactions to Vietnam, then, may be yet to come. We might remember in this regard that the depths of interwar isolationism did not come immediately after Versailles but rather a full decade and a half later, with the Neutrality Acts. Will the foreign-policy elite of the 1980s and 1990s still be slaying their long-dead foes?

NOTES

1. This formulation owes something to John Kenneth Galbraith's 1962 query to President Kennedy apropos of Vietnam: "Incidentally, who is the man in your administration who decides what countries are strategic?" Galbraith, *Ambassador's Journal* (Boston, 1969), p. 311.
2. Thomas S. Kuhn, *The Structure of Scientific Revolutions*, 2d ed. (Chicago, 1970), p. viii.
3. *Ibid.*, pp. 19–20.
4. *Ibid.*, p. 90.
5. *Ibid.*, p. 148.
6. *Ibid.*, p. 153.
7. *Ibid.*, p. 166.
8. *Ibid.*, p. 159.
9. The role of the elite in foreign policy should need little elaboration here. See Gabriel A. Almond, *The American People and Foreign Policy*, 2d ed. (New York, 1960), pp. 138–139; James N. Rosenau, *Public Opinion and Foreign Policy* (New York, 1961), pp. 35–36; James N. Rosenau, *National Leadership and Foreign Policy* (Princeton, N.J., 1963), pp. 6–10.
10. Herbert McCloskey, "Personality and Attitude Correlates of Foreign Policy Orientation," in James N. Rosenau (ed.), *Domestic Sources of Foreign Policy* (New York, 1967), pp. 51–109. As Almond put it: "There is some value in recognizing that an overtly interventionist and 'responsible' United States hides a covertly isolationist longing." Almond, *The American People*, p. 67. An attempt to refute Almond's "instability of mood" theory was marred by having all its data drawn from the peak years of the cold war. William R. Caspary, "The 'Mood Theory': A Study of Public Opinion and Foreign Policy," *American Political Science Review*, LXIV (June 1970), 536–647.
11. Nicholas John Spykman, *America's Strategy in World Politics* (New York, 1942), pp. 5, 7.
12. Karl Mannheim, *Essays on the Sociology of Knowledge*, ed. by Paul Kecskemeti (London, 1952), p. 291. Samuel P. Huntington has recently stressed the importance of generations in American political change. See "Paradigms of American Politics: Beyond the One, the Two, and the Many," *Political Science Quarterly*, 89, no. 1 (March 1974).
13. Arthur H. Vandenburg, Jr. (ed.), *The Private Papers of Senator Vandenburg* (Boston, 1952), p. 1.

14. Paul Seabury and Alvin Drischler called it "the Manchurian assumption" and saw it as the basis for our postwar alliances. Seabury and Drischler, "How to Decommit without Withdrawal Symptoms," *Foreign Policy*, 1 (Winter 1970–1971), 51.

15. It is surprising to learn, for example, that liberal internationalist Chester Bowles served on the national committee of America First. See Wayne S. Cole, *America First: The Battle Against Intervention* (Madison, Wis., 1953), p. 22.

16. Historian Norman Graebner poses the following as the key question in the debate over the origins of the cold war: "Why did the United States after 1939 permit the conquest of eastern Europe by Nazi forces, presumably forever, with scarcely a stir, but refused after 1944 to acknowledge any primary Russian interest or right of hegemony in the same region on the heels of a closely won Russian victory against the German invader?" The shift of foreign-policy paradigms helps answer this question. Graebner, "Cold War Origins and the Continuing Debate: A Review of the Literature," *Journal of Conflict Resolution*, 13 (March 1969), 131.

17. U.S., *Congressional Record*, 89th Cong., 1st Sess. (1965), CXI, Pt. 3, 3350–3351.

18. *New York Times*, October 3, 1965 (supplement), p. 5.

19. U.S., President, *Public Papers of the Presidents of the United States* (Washington, D.C.: Office of the *Federal Register*, National Archives and Records Service, 1945–19), Lyndon B. Johnson, 1965, p. 395.

20. U.S., Congress, Senate, Committee on Foreign Relations and Committee on Armed Services, *United States Troops in Europe*, Report, 90th Cong., 2d Sess. October 15, 1968 (Washington, D.C., 1968), p. 18.

21. *Public Papers of the Presidents*, Johnson, 1966, Book II, p. 861.

22. *The Pentagon Papers, as Published by the New York Times* (New York, 1971, paper ed.), p. 499.

23. A parallel figure in the field of journalism was Kennedy's friend Joseph Alsop, who also published a book in 1940 that established his views for decades. See Joseph Alsop and Robert Kintner, *American White Paper* (New York, 1940).

24. Such items raise the possibility that some of the paradigm shift may be explicable in terms of father-son conflict on the psychoanalytic plane. But that approach tends to minimize the substantive issue of strategic assumptions, which is the one that concerns us here. The elder Kennedy's isolationism is from Arthur Schlesinger, Jr., *A Thousand Days: John F. Kennedy in the White House* (Greenwich, Conn., 1967, paper ed.), pp. 85, 125.

25. John F. Kennedy, *Why England Slept*, 2d ed. (New York, 1961), p. 222.

26. *Ibid.*, p. 186.

27. *Ibid.*, p. 223.

28. *Ibid.*, p. 171.

29. *Ibid.*, pp. 169–170.

30. *Ibid.*, pp. 229–230.

31. John F. Kennedy, *The Strategy of Peace*, ed. by Allan Nevins (New York, 1960), p. 193.

32. U.S., *Congressional Record*, 85th Cong., 2d Sess. (1958), CIV, 17571.

33. Kennedy, *Strategy of Peace*, p. 213.

34. *Public Papers of the Presidents*, Kennedy, 1962, p. 807.

35. *Pentagon Papers*, p. 128.

36. *Ibid.*, pp. 27, 35–36, 148–149, 284.

37. For a good exposition of this "age-cohort hypothesis," in this case on the attitudes of European youth toward regional integration, see Ronald Inglehart, "An End to European Integration?" *American Political Science Review*, LXI (March 1967), 94–99.

38. See, for example, G. F. Hudson, Richard Lowenthal, and Roderick MacFarquhar, *The Sino-Soviet Dispute* (New York, 1961); Donald S. Zagoria, *The Sino-Soviet Conflict*,

1956–1961 (Princeton, N.J., 1962); and Leopold Labedz and G. R. Urban (eds), *The Sino-Soviet Conflict* (London, 1964).

39. The Nixon doctrine was first enunciated on Guam, July 25, 1969, to this effect. See *Public Papers of the Presidents,* Nixon, 1969, p. 552.

40. John Kenneth Galbraith, "The Decline of American Powers," *Esquire,* March 1972, p. 163.

41. Arthur Schlesinger, Jr., "Vietnam and the End of the Age of Superpowers," *Harper's,* March 1969, p. 48.

42. Graham Allison came up with a similar but longer comparison of his foreign-policy "axioms" from interviews with more than a hundred elite young Americans. Allison, "Cool It: The Foreign Policy of Young America," *Foreign Policy,* 1 (Winter 1970–1971), 150–154.

43. Jean-Baptiste Duroselle, *From Wilson to Roosevelt: Foreign Policy of the United States, 1913–1945* (New York, 1968), p. 260.

44. Cordell Hull, *The Memoirs of Cordell Hull* (New York, 1948), Vol. 1, pp. 650–651.

45. Selig Adler, *The Isolationist Impulse: Its Twentieth Century Reaction* (New York, 1966), pp. 28–29.

46. Duroselle, *From Wilson to Roosevelt,* pp. 8–9.

47. Harley Notter, *The Origins of the Foreign Policy of Woodrow Wilson* (New York, 1965), pp. 106–129.

48. Thomas A. Bailey, *A Diplomatic History of American People,* 8th ed. (New York, 1969), p. 553.

49. Hull, *Memoirs,* pp. 33–36.

50. Kenneth N. Waltz, *Man, the State and War: A Theoretical Analysis* (New York, 1959), pp. 95–114.

51. Robert L. Beisner, *From the Old to the New Diplomacy, 1865–1900* (New York, forthcoming 1975).

52. Robert L. Beisner, *Twelve Against Empire: The Anti-Imperialists, 1898–1900* (New York, 1968), pp. 139–164, 203–211.

53. Robert L. Beisner, "1898 and 1968: the Anti-Imperialists and the Doves," *Political Science Quarterly,* LXXXV, no. 2 (June 1970).

54. See, for example, Stephen E. Ambrose, *Rise to Globalism: American Foreign Policy 1938–1970* (Baltimore, 1971); and Gary Porter, "Globalism—The Ideology of Total World Involvement," in Marcus G. Raskin and Bernard B. Fall (eds.), *The Vietnam Reader* (New York, 1965), pp. 322–327.

55. Wayne S. Cole, *An Interpretive History of American Foreign Relations* (Homewood, Ill., 1968), p. 443.

56. Stanley Hoffmann, *Gulliver's Troubles, Or the Setting of American Foreign Policy* (New York, 1969), p. 19.

57. Hans J. Morgenthau, *A New Foreign Policy for the United States* (New York, 1969), p. 15.

58. Dexter Perkins, *The American Approach to Foreign Policy,* 2d ed. (Cambridge, Mass., 1962), pp. 146–147.

59. Frank L. Klingberg, "The Historical Alternation of Moods in American Foreign Policy," *World Politics,* IV (January 1952).

60. Frank H. Denton and Warren Phillips, "Some Patterns in the History of Violence," *Journal of Conflict Resolution,* XII (June 1968), 193.

61. *Washington Post,* July 12, 1971, p. A14.

The "Operational Code": A Neglected Approach to the Study of Political Leaders and Decision Making

Alexander L. George

In the past two decades the field of international-relations studies has become increasingly diversified and is now marked by sharp differences over questions of scope, method, and theory. This heterogeneity, however, should not be allowed to obscure broad agreement on some fundamental propositions of overriding importance. One of these is the feeling shared by traditionalists and scientifically oriented investigators alike, and by many academic scholars as well as sophisticated policy makers, that the way in which leaders of nation-states view each other and the nature of world political conflict is of fundamental importance in determining what happens in relations among states.

Reflecting the perspective of the policy maker, for example, Louis Halle, a former State Department planner, writes that the foreign policy of a nation addresses itself not to the external world, as is commonly stated, but rather to "the image of the external world" that is in the minds of those who make foreign policy. Halle concludes his book on American foreign policy with a sober warning: "In the degree that the image is false, actually and philosophically false, no technicians, however proficient, can make the policy that is based on it sound."[1] Essentially the same point has emerged from the work of many scientifically oriented scholars who, influenced by psychological theories of cognition, have been struck by the role that the subjective perceptions and beliefs of leaders play in their decision making in conflict situations.

Convergence on this fundamental point provides an opportunity, therefore, for establishing a more fruitful dialogue among academic scholars of various persuasions and policy-oriented researchers. To call attention to this opportunity and to help structure some of the central research questions, I decided a few years ago to reexamine an older study that had pioneered in the analysis of elite belief systems. I refer to Nathan Leites's concept of "operational code." It must be said im-

Alexander L. George, "The 'Operational Code': A Neglected Approach to the Study of Political Leaders and Decision-Making," *International Studies Quarterly*, 13, 2 (June 1969). Reprinted by permission of International Studies Association.

mediately that this term is a misnomer insofar as it implies incorrectly a set of recipes or repertoires for political action that an elite applies mechanically in its decision making.

A closer examination of what Leites had in mind indicates that he was referring to a set of general beliefs about fundamental issues of history and central questions of politics as these bear in turn on the problem of action. The actor's beliefs and premises that Leites singled out have a relationship to decision making that is looser and more subtle than the term "operational code" implies. They serve, as it were, as a prism that influences the actor's perceptions and diagnoses of the flow of political events, his definitions and estimates of particular situations. These beliefs also provide norms, standards, and guidelines that influence the actor's choice of strategy and tactics, his structuring and weighing of alternative courses of action. Such a belief system influences but does not unilaterally determine decision making; it is an important but not the only variable that shapes decision-making behavior. With this caveat in mind, let me recall briefly the origins, nature, and impact of Leites's study before proceeding to indicate how his approach can be codified into a more explicit and usable research model.

I. BACKGROUND

It is now over fifteen years since Nathan Leites published A *Study of Bolshevism*,[2] which broke important ground in the newly emerging behavioral approach to the study of political elites. During and after World War II many students of world politics turned their attention to the ways in which different elites approached problems of international conflict and cooperation. They posed questions for research that could not be satisfactorily answered by traditional approaches, such as systematic biographical analysis of a ruling group according to the social origins, education, training, and other background characteristics of its members. Biographical profiles of this kind often suggested factors that helped account for the emergence and formation of leadership groups, but they did not illuminate adequately the political orientations, styles of calculation, and behavior of the ruling groups in question.[3]

Leites's book was by no means universally acclaimed. But there were those who welcomed it not merely for its insights into Bolshevik mentality; some thought it introduced a new genre of elite study that might fill some of the needs for a behavioral approach to studies of political leadership.

Thus the eminent anthropologist Clyde Kluckhohn praised A *Study of Bolshevism* as being "a work of gigantic stature that is likely to *faire école* in politics and the other behavioral sciences for many years to come."[4] This expectation has not materialized. A *Study of Bolshevism* inspired few efforts at similar research on other leadership groups.[5]

Among the reasons for this, I believe, is the unusually complex nature of Leites's work, which is not one but several interrelated studies that are subtly interwoven. While the complexity of the work adds to its richness and intellectual appeal, it has also made it unusually difficult for readers to grasp its structure or to describe its research mode.[6]

I wish to call particular attention in this paper to that portion of *A Study of Bolshevism* known as the "operational code." Leites employed this phrase to refer to the precepts or maxims of political tactics and strategy that characterized the classical Bolshevik approach to politics. Leites initially published this portion of his larger treatise separately, and in abbreviated form, as *The Operational Code of the Politburo.*[7] Two years later his more detailed statement of the "operational code" appeared in the full-scale *A Study of Bolshevism* (1953), but now several new dimensions were added and interwoven with it. Hence, the "operational code" became embedded in a much more ambitious sociopsychological account of the historical origins and meanings of Bolshevism. The reader was provided not only with the "operational code," but as Daniel Bell noted, also with a special kind of history of the changing moral temper of an important element of the radical reform-minded Russian intelligentsia. A third component of the study, in some ways the most ambitious, was Leites's delineation of the "Bolshevik character," which he suggested constituted in some respects a distinct type in social history in the sense that any individual is unique though resembling others in important respects.[8]

Hence *A Study of Bolshevism* emerges as far more than a list of maxims of political strategy. Rather, the "operational code" blends and merges at many points with the discussion of "Bolshevik character." The maxims of political strategy that comprise the "operational code" take on the character of *rules of conduct* held out for good Bolsheviks and *norms of behavior* that ideally are internalized by the individual, who thereby acquires a new and different character structure—that of the reliable "hard-core" Bolshevik. In the terminology of modern ego psychology, the individual who succeeds in internalizing this preferred character structure thereby accomplishes an "identity transformation."

Leites dealt briefly, and necessarily speculatively, with the origins of the "Bolshevik character." He saw it as being in part a *reaction* to those qualities of the reform-minded Russian intelligentsia of the nineteenth century that had in Lenin's judgment proven to be quite unsuitable for the task of making a successful revolution.

In dealing with the origins of the Bolshevik character and in particular with its "reactive" aspects, Leites employed a method that drew in part, but only in part, on psychoanalytic theory. This has further complicated the task of understanding the research model on which his complex study is based. Since the question is germane to the task of "disentangling" the operational code portion of the work, some clarification of the role psychoanalytic theory played in Leites's study is necessary before proceeding.

It is true that Leites felt that the full significance of important elements of the emergent Bolshevik character could be better understood by regarding them as "reaction formations" (and other ego defense mechanisms) to powerful unconscious wishes that had helped to shape the older character structure of Russian reform-minded intellectuals.[9] But, according to Leites, the Bolshevik character also represented a *conscious* effort by Lenin and his associates to reverse certain traditional aspects of Russian character. Leites therefore employed psychoanalytic theory to illuminate the unconscious significance of Bolshevik beliefs; but he noted explicitly that his "delineation of the preconscious and conscious content" of Bolshevik doctrine and the operational code did not require the reader either to accept the theory of psychoanalysis or to agree with the particular use Leites made of it in his admittedly speculative attempt to illuminate the possible unconscious significance of some of these Bolshevik beliefs.[10]

What emerges from this is that the set of beliefs about politics associated with the concept "operational code" can be investigated without reference to psychoanalytic hypotheses. These beliefs, implicitly or explicitly held by the political actor, can be inferred or postulated by the investigator on the basis of the kinds of data, observational opportunities, and methods generally available to political scientists. In this respect the "operational code" approach does not differ from research efforts to identify many other beliefs, opinions, and attitudes of political actors. Leites's use of psychoanalytic theory, therefore, offers no impediment to "factoring out" the operational code part of his study.

At the same time, it is one of the attractive features of the operational code construct for behaviorally inclined political scientists that it can serve as a useful "bridge" or "link" to psychodynamic interpretations of unconscious dimensions of belief systems and their role in behavior under different conditions.[11] Thus, once an actor's approach to political calculation has been formulated by the researcher, he can proceed—if he so wishes and is able to do so—to relate some of the beliefs in question to other motivational variables of a psychodynamic character. With the belief system of the political actor in hand, the investigator can move more easily than would otherwise be possible into the sphere of unconscious motives and defenses against them that affect the strength and operation of these beliefs in the actor's political behavior in different circumstances, and to an assessment of the extent to which these beliefs are subject to reality tests of various kinds. An elite's fundamental beliefs about politics are probably resistant to change for various reasons, of which unconscious motivations are but one factor.[12]

Another shortcoming of the *Study* should be mentioned. Leites did not structure and synthesize the various beliefs, rules, and maxims about politics associated with his concept of "operational code." The relationship of the different elements of the Bolshevik view of politics to each other and to the problem of making specific choices of action remained somewhat obscure.[13] That is, he did not clarify sufficiently the order, hierarchy, and interrelationships among the various elements of the "code." I will attempt to redress this by reinterpreting various components of the so-called code and restructuring it into a more tightly knit set of beliefs about fundamental issues and questions associated with the classical problem of political action. To repeat, it is in this sense—as a set of premises and beliefs about politics and not as a set of rules and recipes to be applied mechanically to the choice of action—that the "operational code" construct is properly understood.

II. THE "OPERATIONAL CODE" AND COGNITIVE LIMITS ON RATIONAL DECISION MAKING

A political leader's beliefs about the nature of politics and political conflict, his views regarding the extent to which historical developments can be shaped, and his notions of correct strategy and tactics—whether these beliefs be referred to as "operational code," "weltanschauung," "cognitive map," or an "elite's political culture"—are among the factors influencing that actor's decisions. The "operational code" is a particularly significant portion of the actor's entire set of beliefs about political life.[14] Not all the beliefs and attitudes that influence a political actor's behavior, then, will be considered here. A comprehensive model of decision-making behavior, for example, would also consider the actor's ethical and normative beliefs.[15]

It is widely recognized that there are important cognitive limits on the possibility of rational decision making in politics, as in other sectors of life.[16] In contrast to models of "pure" rationality in statistical decision theory and formal economics, efforts at rational decision making in political life are subject to constraints of the following kind: (1) The political actor's information about situations with which he must deal is usually incomplete; (2) his knowledge of ends-means relationships is generally inadequate to predict reliably the consequences of choosing one or another course of action; and (3) it is often difficult for him to formulate a single criterion by means of which to choose which alternative course of action is "best."[17]

Political actors have to adapt to and try to cope with these cognitive limits or "boundaries" to rational decision making. There are, no doubt, a variety of ways in which different political leaders deal with this problem in similar or different political settings. This is indeed an aspect of comparative political research that has received little systematic attention.[18] How do political leaders in varying political cultures and institutional structures approach the task of making calculations, of deciding what objectives to select, and how to deal with uncertainty and risk—that is, more generally, how to relate means and ends, etc.? What styles of political calculation and strategies are developed for this purpose by different leaders? This has to do, of course, with the familiar problem of the relation of knowledge to action on which many observers and practitioners of politics have reflected. What is proposed here is that this classical problem be conceptualized more rigorously and studied more systematically than in the past.[19]

The issues and questions referred to in the preceding paragraph comprise one part of the "operational code" construct. We shall refer to the "answers" given by a political actor to these questions as his "instrumental beliefs," that is, his beliefs about ends-means relationships in the context of political action.

There is another set of more general issues and questions that are part of an operational code. These are what may be called the political actor's "philosophical" beliefs, since they refer to assumptions and premises he makes regarding the fundamental nature of politics, the nature of political conflict, the role of the individual in history, etc.[20]

It is in terms of these two sets of beliefs—the specific contents of which will be discussed shortly—that I have redefined and restructured the concept of "operational code." What emerges is a research construct for empirical work on decision making that focuses more clearly than did *A Study of Bolshevism* on the interrelated set of beliefs about the nature of political conflict and an effective approach to calculation of political strategy and tactics.

A Study of Bolshevism emphasized the "answers" that in Leites's judgment the old Bolsheviks gave to these central questions about politics and the relation of knowledge to action. However, he did not explicitly state all the issues and questions themselves. This I shall attempt to do here in order to facilitate similar studies of other leaders and other leadership groups, and thereby lead to systematic comparative studies.

There are, of course, difficult problems in employing knowledge of a leader's "operational code," or belief system about politics, for purposes of explaining or predicting his behavior in specific instances.[21] The investigator's knowledge of the actor's general belief system can assist but not substitute for analysis of specific situations and assessment of institutional and other pressures on the political actor's decisions. Knowledge of the actor's approach to calculating choice of action does *not* provide a simple key to explanation and prediction; but it can help the researcher and the policy planner to "bound" the alternative ways in which the subject may perceive different types of situations and approach the task of making a rational assessment of alternative courses of action. Knowledge of the actor's beliefs helps the investigator to clarify the general criteria, requirements, and norms the subject attempts to meet in assessing opportunities that arise to make desirable gains, in estimating the costs and risks associated with them, and in making utility calculations.

Whether it be from the standpoint of philosophy, history, psychology, sociology, economics, or political science, students of human behavior have long agreed that any individual must necessarily simplify and structure the complexity of his world in order to cope with it. In everyday life as in the laboratory, problem solving often requires deliberate or unwitting simplification of a more complex reality. This applies also to the political actor, for he too must somehow comprehend complex situations in order to decide how best to deal with them.[22] In doing so, the actor typically engages in a "definition of the situation," i.e., a cognitive structuring of the situation that will clarify for him the nature of the problem, relate it to his previous experience, and make it amenable to appropriate problem-solving activities. The political actor perceives and simplifies reality partly through the prism of his "cognitive map" of politics. This includes the belief system that has been referred to in the past as the "operational code" of a political actor.

We turn now to the content of an operational code. I have identified a number of questions about politics that together hopefully cover most of the central issues connected with the problem of knowledge and action. The "answers" a political actor gives to these questions serve to define his fundamental orientation towards the problem of leadership and action. Before proceeding we take note of the possibility that in some non-Western cultures the problem of knowledge and its relation to the calculation of political action may be approached differently, and hence the list of fundamental questions identified here may not be entirely applicable.

Most of the observations Leites made about the classical Bolshevik approach to political calculation can be subsumed under one or another of these questions. We will not take up here whether Leites's construction of the classical Bolshevik belief system was valid in all respects. But we shall consider later the question of the extent to which some of the old Bolshevik beliefs have since changed. And we shall suggest some of the ways in which knowledge of this belief system relates to the task of explaining or predicting Soviet behavior.

The immediate objective of this paper—to explicate in detail the nature of the belief system associated with the concept of operational code—does not require us to delve deeply into these additional questions. Of more immediate concern is the adequacy of our explication and restructuring of the code. One useful way of assessing this is to see whether the Bolshevik beliefs described in the *Study* can be subsumed under the various philosophical and instrumental questions we have formulated. We need deal only summarily with Leites's study for this purpose; we shall ignore those dimensions of his multifaceted study that do not constitute the operational code *per se* but comprise related questions concerning the "Bolshevik character," the social-psychological origins of the Bolshevik belief system, and the underlying psychodynamic processes about which Leites speculated.

III. THE PHILOSOPHICAL CONTENT OF AN OPERATIONAL CODE

1. What Is the "Essential" Nature of Political Life? Is the Political Universe Essentially One of Harmony or Conflict? What Is the Fundamental Character of One's Political Opponents?[23]

A political actor's belief system about the nature of politics is shaped particularly by his orientation to other political actors. Most important of these are one's opponents. The way in which they are perceived—the characteristics the political actor attributes to his opponents—exercises a subtle influence on many other philosophical and instrumental beliefs in his operational code.[24]

In the classical Bolshevik belief system the "image of the opponent" was perhaps the cornerstone on which much of the rest of their approach to politics was based. The old Bolsheviks perceived the capitalist opponent as thoroughly hostile at bottom, whatever facade he might display, and possessed of great shrewdness and determination to annihilate his class opponent.

Accordingly, for the old Bolsheviks the political universe was one of acute conflict. The fundamental question of politics and history, as formulated by the Bolsheviks, was "who [will destroy] whom?" This conflict between communists and their class enemies was viewed as fundamental and irreconcilable. It was not attributable to particular historical personages but sprang from the "objective" historical conditions described by Marxist dialectics.

Consistent with these views was another Bolshevik belief regarding the instability of any "intermediate" historical position between being annihilated or achieving world hegemony. So long as the Bolsheviks had not yet achieved world hegemony, the danger of being annihilated by the enemy would remain an ever-present one.

Other answers to the first question posed here are possible and have been given by different elites. For example, the traditional "idealist" conception of international affairs postulates a fundamental harmony of interests among peoples and nations that is only temporarily disrupted because of the wickedness or weakness of certain individuals and the lack of adequate institutions, a view with which "realists" have increasingly taken issue.[25]

It is important to recognize that on this issue as on other elements of the belief system, not all members of a ruling group will necessarily agree; moreover, beliefs can change significantly over a period of time. Thus, in research since the publication of *A Study of Bolshevism* Nathan Leites noted various indications of an important modification in this basic Bolshevik belief, which in turn has potentially far-reaching implications for the Soviet style of political behavior.

2. What Are the Prospects for the Eventual Realization of One's Fundamental Political Values and Aspirations? Can One be Optimistic, or Must One be Pessimistic On This Score; and in What Respects the One and/or the Other?[26]

The conventional Bolshevik position was optimistic, drawing as it did upon ideological-doctrinal premises regarding the eventual triumph of communism on a worldwide scale. Yet it was an optimism tinged with conditional pessimism, i.e., an underlying belief that catastrophe could not be excluded and was an ever-present danger. One had to be constantly aware of the possibility of catastrophe and avoid contributing to its actualization by defective calculations and inept political behavior.

3. Is the Political Future Predictable? In What Sense and To What Extent?[27]

The classical Bolshevik position on this issue reflected the strong "determinist" streak in the Marxist view of history; but this view was balanced by strong "indeterminist" conceptions. Thus, the Bolsheviks believed that while the direction and final outcome of the major historical development from capitalism to communism are predictable, nonetheless the rate of this development and its particular paths are not. At many junctures or branch points of historical development, therefore, more than one outcome is "objectively possible."

This general belief has had important implications for the way in which Bolsheviks approached the problem of "action." The passive orientation to action that was logically and psychologically implicit in the "determinist" view of history was counterbalanced by the "indeterminist" conception of the many zig-zags that historical developments could take prior to reaching their predictable final outcome. From an operational standpoint the latter, "indeterminist," component of the belief dominated in that it emphasized the importance of intelligent, well-calculated action as a means of expediting the historical process. As a result the Bolshevik answer to this question encouraged, and when reinforced by the other beliefs already referred to, even drove its adherents towards "voluntarism" and initiative rather than fatalism and passivity.

Elaborating on this philosophical theme, the Bolsheviks believed that "objective conditions" from time to time create certain "opportunities" for the party to advance its interests at the expense of its opponents. However, it was regarded as not predictable and by no means certain that the party would succeed in "utilizing" these opportunities for advance and in transforming them into realities.

4. How Much "Control" or "Mastery" Can One Have Over Historical Development? What Is One's Role in "Moving" and "Shaping" History in the Desired Direction?[28]

The classical Bolshevik answer to this question follows from beliefs held with respect to the preceding issues. Thus, in the Bolshevik view the party is obliged to seize and utilize any "opportunity" for advance, for men can determine within fairly wide limits the cost and duration of an "inevitable" social change. The answer to this question, therefore, emphasizes the role that dedicated, disciplined and intelligent political actors can play in "moving" history in the desired direction.

5. What Is the Role of "Chance" in Human Affairs and in Historical Development?[29]

The classical Bolshevik answer was that all politically important events are explainable by the laws of Marxism-Leninism; therefore, that history can be importantly shaped by "accidental" events is rejected.

Consistent with this general belief was the Politburo's tendency, often noted by Western observers, to perceive connections between events where we see none; to regard unrelated details as symptomatic of major political trends; and to believe there is complicated planning behind events which we know to be fortuitous. Bolshevik thought minimized the role of chance—with all its unsettling implications for their belief system—by distorting the image of the opponent and perceiving him as preternaturally calculating and powerful, which in turn had other unsettling implications.

Related to this was the emphatic negative the Bolsheviks gave to the question: Can one "muddle through"?[30] It is not only not possible to "muddle through," they believed, but extremely dangerous to try to do so. Accompanying this was the related belief that there is in every situation just one "correct" line or policy. All other policies or choices of action may result in or tend to lead to ruin—i.e., the "catastrophe" held to be an ever-present possibility, as noted above. In the Bolshevik belief system, moreover, political mistakes were rarely harmless or anything less than acutely dangerous. ("Every small step has to be carefully weighed.")

As the preceding discussion has suggested, these beliefs about the major philosophical issues concerning politics are related to each other. This set of beliefs, in turn, is logically and psychologically related to a set of "instrumental" beliefs that refer more specifically to key aspects of the problem of knowledge and action. What should be stressed before proceeding is that the answers different political leaders or elite groups give to the basic questions implicit in the traditional problem of knowledge and action are affected by their philosophical beliefs about the nature of politics.

IV. THE INSTRUMENTAL BELIEFS IN AN OPERATIONAL CODE

1. What Is the Best Approach for Selecting Goals or Objectives for Political Action?[31]

The classical Bolshevik answer to the question of how best to set one's goals in embarking upon action was influenced by two of the general philosophical beliefs already alluded to: the mixture of determinist and indeterminist conceptions regarding future historical developments and the view of one's role in "moving" history in the right direction. Recall in this connection, too, the general injunction implicit in the Bolshevik answer to the third and fourth of the philosophical beliefs noted earlier, namely that the party is obliged to seize all "opportunities" that arise for making advances. How, then, did the Bolsheviks orient themselves more specifically to the critical question of determining what one should strive for, and what the goals and objectives of action should be when an "opportunity" to make gains arises?

The classical Bolshevik "answer" (perhaps partly at the preconscious level) was along the following lines:

(a) One should *not* approach the task of setting the objective or goal of political action by trying first to calculate precisely the probability of achieving each of the alternative objectives that might be pursued in a given situation.

(b) Further, one should not limit the objective one strives for in a particular situation to that which on the basis of such calculations appears to be quite likely or rather certain of being achieved by the means of one's disposal. (Note here the Bolshevik admonition against the tendency to allow assessments of available means and their presumed limited efficacy to unduly circumscribe and limit the magnitude of the objective or goal to be pursued.)

(c) In setting one's goals, therefore, one must counter tendencies towards an overly conservative approach to political action: a reluctance to push for useful gains against seemingly difficult odds, and the related tendency to "pare down" the goals of action to those that seem highly feasible and likely to be achieved.

(d) Against this conservative approach to calculation of ends-means relationships to politics, the Bolsheviks argued on behalf of a strategy of attempting to optimize or maximize the gains that might be derived in a given situation. (Note here the Bolshevik tendency to reject what has been called the "satisficing" strategy that many other decision makers often prefer to an "optimizing" one.)[32]

Let us consider now how some of the familiar cognitive limits on rational decision making are dealt with in support of the preference for an optimizing strategy rather than a more conservative approach. In Bolshevik thinking on this central issue the problem of uncertain or incomplete knowledge relevant to choice of action is "bounded" in a special way. In behalf of the preferred optimizing approach, the Bolshevik code argues—not unrealistically, it may be said—in the following vein:

(a) Political action often has to begin with incomplete knowledge about possible outcomes; it is action itself and only action that will increase knowledge.

(b) What can be achieved in a particular situation cannot be predicted in advance—it can only become known in the process of "struggle," in which one attempts to get the most out of a situation.

(c) In choosing the goals or objectives of a particular course of action, therefore, one should limit them only by assessing what is "objectively possible" in that situation—i.e., not impossible to achieve by intelligent use of resources at one's disposal.

The operative belief, restated, is that in initiating an action the party must be concerned only with ascertaining that the goals it sets are "objectively possible" (in the general and somewhat vague sense already indicated)—not that they can be achieved with high probability. For what can be achieved cannot be predicted in advance; it depends on the "relationship of forces" which can be known only in the process of "struggle" carried out "to the end." What is important, therefore, is that the limited knowledge available to assess the likely consequences of alternative courses of action should not lead the political actor who engages in ends-means calculations to make an overly conservative choice of what to strive for.

Applying these beliefs to the problem of action, the Bolsheviks developed *a special kind of optimizing strategy.* In undertaking an initiative to advance their interests, they often set for themselves not a single objective but a set of graduated objectives. The standard task faced by all decision makers—namely, that of attempting to reconcile what is desirable with what is thought to be feasible—is not overdetermined in this optimizing strategy. Rather, action is oriented in a specific situation to a series of objectives embracing payoffs that are graduated (but perhaps inversely related) in degree of utility and feasibility. The optimizing strategy calls for striving simultaneously for a maximum payoff—even though the probability of achieving it appears to be low—and the more modest payoffs, which appear to be less difficult and more probable. There seems to be an implicit assumption that such a strategy not only provides an opportunity to achieve the maximum payoff in a given situation but should that prove infeasible or emerge as too costly or risky, it will enable one to settle, if necessary, for one of the lesser of the graduated objectives that will constitute the largest payoff that could have been squeezed out of the "opportunity" the situation afforded. The contrast here is with "adventures" where there are no lesser objectives, but only a maximum payoff or a severe loss. (See below.)

Such an optimizing strategy, therefore, is consonant with the general philosophical belief alluded to earlier: namely, that what can be achieved in a particular situation cannot be predicted in advance, that action must begin with incomplete knowledge and a measure of uncertainty regarding possible outcomes, and that it is only through "struggle" that one can find out how much a given "opportunity" to advance will yield.[33]

It should not be assumed that resort to an optimizing strategy of this kind necessarily implies neglect of risk and cost calculations. On the other hand, adherents of this strategy may not give due recognition to the possibility that striving for the maximum possible payoff in a given situation may well entail special costs and risks. Thus, if the optimizing strategy is not correctly perceived as such by the opponent, it may well unduly arouse his sense of danger and mobilize his potential for resistance and counteraction in a way that pursuit of more modest objectives might avoid doing.[34]

We shall shortly discuss Bolshevik beliefs about calculation, control, and acceptance of risks. Here we note that the general Bolshevik answer to the question under discussion proclaimed the need for important limits to this preferred optimizing strategy. Thus, the injunction to optimize was "bounded" by the somewhat contradictory maxim: "Avoid adventures." This maxim, or rule of action, conveys several different imperatives:

(a) A generalized injunction not to embark on forward operations against an opponent that are not carefully calculated in advance to exclude complacent overestimates of one's own strength and underestimates of his strength. Complacent miscalculations of this kind reflect a failure to assess properly whether the "objective conditions" permit a responsible effort to make gains of any kind, and, if so, what the range of objectives should be that one can safely pursue in the given situation.

(b) A generalized injunction against undertaking action that has an uncertain chance of yielding any payoff but is coupled at the same time with a large risk of severe loss if it fails. Actions to advance one's interests should be avoided when they cannot utilize the optimizing strategy noted above in which graduated objectives and payoffs are pursued. An action is "adventuristic" if it has no lesser objectives and no possibility of lesser payoffs—i.e., one for which the expected outcomes are limited to a maximum payoff or a severe loss.

(c) A generalized injunction against permitting one's calculations and choice of action to be dominated by prospects of immediate or short-term gains while ignoring the possibility of the longer-range costs and risks attached to the same action.

We may summarize our discussion of the first instrumental belief in the Bolshevik code as follows: Choose an optimizing strategy that pursues graduated objectives, but "avoid adventures."

The fact that not one but several graduated objectives may serve to orient Soviet action in conflict situations is particularly important in the sphere of world politics. The optimizing strategy that lies behind Soviet initiatives in foreign policy from time to time has evidently complicated the task of Western governments in trying to assess Soviet intentions and to devise appropriate countermeasures. On various occasions in the past unfamiliarity with this aspect of the Soviet operational code seems to have resulted in unnecessary perplexity, confusion, and alarm in attempts to assess Soviet intentions. Western observers have responded to Soviet initiatives (such as the Berlin blockade of 1948) on the assumption that Soviet leaders were pursuing a single objective. Equivocal indications of what the Soviets were after were variously interpreted in terms of what "the" Soviet intention really was, as if the Soviets were pursuing only a single objective rather than a set of graduated objectives. Some Western interpretations focused on indications that the Soviets were pursuing an extremely ambitious objective, thus heightening apprehensions regarding the aggressive bent of Soviet policy, the "risks" Soviet leaders were willing to take, and the "danger" of war. Other interpretations focused on indications that the Soviets were pursuing only a quite modest, even "defensive" objective, thus encouraging the belief that the crisis could be quickly and easily terminated if only the Western policies that had "provoked" the Soviets were altered and concessions made to satisfy them.[35]

It is not possible to discuss in detail here the consequences of Western responses based upon misperception of the nature of Soviet optimizing strategy. One might assume that Western responses in such situations would be more effective if based on awareness that the opponent is pursuing a set of graduated objectives ranging from relatively modest to quite ambitious goals, and that he relies heavily on feedback in deciding how far to go. But we must also consider the possibility that Western responses to Soviet initiatives have occasionally been more effective precisely because they focused on the most ambitious gains the Soviets may have had in mind in pursuing this kind of optimizing strategy.

2. How Are the Goals of Action Pursued Most Effectively?

The classical Bolshevik answer to this question can be summarized in three maxims: "push to the limit," "engage in pursuit" of an opponent who begins to retreat or make concessions, *but* "know when to stop."[36]

The first part of the answer, "push to the limit," enjoins that maximum energy be exerted to attain the objectives of action The "struggle" to attain them should not be curtailed prematurely; pressure should be maintained against the opponent even though he doesn't give signs of buckling and even though it seems to stiffen his resistance at first.

The second part of the answer invokes the principle of "pursuit." Once some progress, some weakening of the opponent's position has been achieved, it is imperative not to yield to the temptation of relaxing pressure. When an opponent begins to talk of making some concessions or offers them, it should be recognized that this is a sign of weakness on his part. Additional and perhaps major gains can be made by continuing to press the opponent under these circumstances.

Once again, however, the Bolshevik operational code set important limits, though of a generalized character, to the preceding two maxims. These limits are, characteristically, embodied in a general injunction, "know when to stop," which is directed against the psychological danger of being carried away by one's success to the point of failing to calculate soberly and rationally the costs and risks of continuing efforts to press forward. Once again, a general injunction of this type lacks operational content; it does not suggest how the maxim is to be applied meaningfully in specific situations; but it is presumably a valuable part of the cognitive and affective makeup of a good Bolshevik.

It has been of considerable value on occasion to Western leaders to understand that their Soviet counterparts structure the problem of action with a set of beliefs and maxims that seem to contradict, or rather, oppose one another. There is as a result what might be called a "tension of opposites" in their cognitive structuring of the problem of action. We saw this already in the beliefs held with respect to the first of the instrumental issues: attempt to optimize gains, but don't engage in "adventures." And we see it again here with reference to the second instrumental issue: "push to the limit" and "pursue" a retreating opponent, but "know when to stop."[37]

Another "tension of opposites" may be discussed at this point that applies to situations in which a Bolshevik leader feels himself put on the defensive by some action of the opponent. The maxims which "bound" this problem of action and create a tension are "resist from the start" any encroachment by the opponent, no matter how slight it appears to be; *but* "don't yield to enemy provocations" and "retreat before superior force."[38]

"Yielding" to an opponent is so worrisome a danger in the classical Bolshevik code (and, presumably, so anxiety-arousing a fantasy in the old Bolshevik psyche) that it gave rise to a strong injunction to be ultrasensitive to encroachments of any kind. No matter how trivial they seem, the opponent's encroachments are to be opposed because failure to "resist from the start" may encourage him to step up his attack. (This is related to fears associated with the second of the philosophical beliefs in which ideological/doctrinal optimism regarding the final triumph of communism is mixed with a certain pessimism, i.e., an underlying belief that nonetheless catastrophe and major setbacks cannot be excluded.)

3. How Are the Risks of Political Action Calculated, Controlled, and Accepted?

The Bolsheviks' answer to this question was importantly influenced by their experience in struggling against vastly stronger, dangerous opponents—first the tsarist government and then, after the revolution, the leading capitalist powers. If we recall the Bolshevik answer to the earlier question on choosing one's objectives in embarking in political action, the present question can be reformulated as follows: *How does one pursue an optimizing strategy while at the same time knowing how to calculate and control its risks?*

(a) The Bolsheviks recognized that it was of course possible, in principle, to "provoke" a strong opponent into a major attack designed to crush the Bolshevik party (or later the Soviet Union). Behavior that might have this effect upon the opponent, therefore, was to be avoided. Nonetheless, it was believed that considerable scope was left short of this for lesser, well-calculated efforts to advance at the stronger opponent's expense. The opponent, it was believed, would be deterred by various constraints from lashing back in an effort to crush the Bolsheviks. The opponent's evaluation of his overall self-interest would keep him from translating his basic hostility—always present—into an operational plan for liquidating the Bolshevik party (and later the Soviet Union).

(b) It is often safe to pursue even quite major objectives at the expense of a stronger opponent (as in the Berlin blockade of 1948–1949 and in the Cuban missile crisis). In the Soviet view the risks of offensive actions of this kind can often be controlled by *limiting the means* they employ on behalf of their ambitious objectives. In the Soviet view it is possible to pursue quite large gains at an enemy's expense in this fashion without triggering a strong, undesired reaction.

We digress briefly at this point to take note of an important difference that often characterized Soviet and U.S. approaches to the calculation and acceptance of risks during the period of the cold war. The question of how to keep conflicts between them safely limited was answered somewhat differently in the "limitations" theories of the two sides. The U.S. theory, strongly reinforced by our reading of the lessons of the Korean War, has been that a limitation on one's objectives is essential to keep limited conflicts from expanding dangerously.[39] This seemed to be borne out by the consequences—i.e., Chinese Communist intervention—of our failure to keep the U.S. objective limited in the Korean War. After defeating the

North Koreans, we enlarged our war aims to include unification of North Korea and South Korea by force of arms, which triggered the Chinese Communist intervention.

The Soviet theory of limitations, on the other hand, holds that it is often safe to pursue even large, far-reaching objectives in limited conflicts without immediate danger or undue risk of their expanding. What is critical in the Soviet view is not so much the limitation of one's objectives but rather limitation of the means one employs on their behalf. (Examples of this theory of limitations are Soviet behavior in the Berlin blockade and Chinese behavior in the Quemoy crisis of 1958. In both cases far-reaching objectives were evidently among those being pursued, but the risks of doing so were controlled by limiting the means employed against the two Western outposts.)

(c) It is a Soviet belief that the fact that risks of high magnitude are in some sense present in a conflict situation—e.g., the danger of war between the Soviet Union and the United States—is less important than (1) whether that undesired consequence is immediately at hand or at some remove in time, and (2) whether the Soviet leaders believe themselves able to control the intermediate events of the sequence that could result in war. Soviet leaders have displayed considerable confidence in their ability to control and avoid quite unacceptable, more distant risks in this way. Their approach to risk calculation is often more sophisticated than that of Western leaders in that Soviet leaders distinguish not only the magnitude of risks but also between risks that are immediate and those which are more remote.

Hence Soviet leaders believe, and often act on the premise, that in a struggle to make important gains one can accept seemingly high risks so long as the undesired event is several steps removed in a possible temporal sequence and so long as, in addition, they believe they can control the sequence of events leading to it. In a number of cases (the North Korean attack on South Korea, some of the Berlin crises, the Cuban missile crisis) the Soviets acted in ways that seemed to indicate to Western leaders and publics that Soviet leaders were prepared to risk and indeed were risking general war. The risk of general war, however, was in fact several steps removed; and Soviet leaders could well believe that they retained the possibility of calling off the crisis or redirecting it into safer channels if necessary.

In other words, Soviet leaders do not settle for a single probability estimate of unwanted risks that may develop in the future; rather, they attempt to subject such estimates of probability to sequential analysis. We may contrast this style of risk calculation with the tendency of Western leaders and publics to blur the time component of the different risks created by a Soviet initiative, or by their own actions, a tendency which disposes Westerners in some situations to magnify their estimates of the prevailing risks and to greater conservatism in risk acceptance.

In this respect, therefore, as in others previously noted, Soviet and U.S. approaches to risk calculation and risk acceptance have often differed. Soviet understanding of the ways in which undesired risks could be calculated and controlled often constituted an advantage. As for Western leaders and publics, their tendency to perceive and interpret Soviet risk-acceptance behavior erroneously from the standpoint of their own approach to risk calculation inclined them to make distorted judgments regarding Soviet intentions and the riskiness and significance of Soviet cold war initiatives. (One may note briefly that over time Western leaders have perhaps come to understand better the Soviet approach to risk calculation and risk acceptance.)

4. What Is the Best "Timing" of Action to Advance One's Interest?[40]

Once again the Bolshevik answer displays a tendency to state the matter in terms of opposites (excluding middle positions). Thus, the Bolshevik code says, somewhat enigmatically or tritely: "There must be neither procrastination nor precipitate action." The party must be able to bide its time indefinitely if need be. But it is forbidden to defer an advance that is feasible now (even though difficult) in the necessarily uncertain expectation that advance would be easier at some later date. Action, therefore, tends to be either required or impermissible; there is nothing in between.

5. What Is the Utility and Role of Different Means for Advancing One's Interests?

Of a number of Bolshevik views about the utility of different means, mention will be made here of one that has been rather unfamiliar to Westerners and is perhaps more idiosyncratic than other Bolshevik beliefs about means. This is the belief that in order to deter a powerful enemy "it often pays to be rude."[41] Rude and even violent language, which may or may not be accompanied by small damaging actions, is expected to serve this purpose by heightening the opponent's estimates of one's strength and determination and/or by weakening the mass support for his policies. The tactic of rudeness was believed to be not overly risky because in Bolshevik thought a "serious" powerful opponent is expected not to allow himself to become emotionally aroused by such tactics.

V. CHANGES IN THE BELIEF SYSTEM

Even a belief system that reflects well-considered evaluations of past political experience is subject to change under certain conditions. Resistance to changing beliefs may be accentuated by personality rigidities, which may be greater in some members of a ruling group than in others; but a variety of other factors may be operative.

Some political elites have a pronounced tendency to perceive and to deal with present problems in the light of authoritative diagnoses they have made of past experiences. They attach considerable importance to making correct diagnoses of past events which they feel provide usable "lessons" of history in the form of models and precedents. The tendency to approach calculation of present policy in this manner is particularly pronounced in radically oriented elites, such as the Marxists, who claim to have a special understanding of history and historical development. As a result a body of general beliefs develops about the nature of political conflict and basically correct or incorrect approaches to dealing with opponents that takes on a doctrinal character. Special precautions may be taken to safeguard the content of such beliefs from arbitrary, unauthorized changes. Beliefs about politics, then, become part of the sacred political culture of the elite that is systematically transmitted to new leaders. Change in such an elite's belief system, then, does not follow simply from the fact that the composition of the top leadership changes.

As noted earlier, indications are available that some changes in important elements of the classical Bolshevik operational code took place or became noticeable in the Khrushchev era. I believe that the restructuring and synthesis in this paper of the major elements of this kind of belief system facilitates inquiry into the possibility of changes in its content and of their implications. Thus, as was suggested earlier, the first philosophical belief in our list appears to be of critical importance in shaping the character of the belief system as a whole and in regulating its impact on the actor's political behavior. Particularly close attention should be given, therefore, to possible shifts in the political actor's image of his opponent, and related to this, his view of the fundamental nature of political conflict.[42]

Let us look briefly now at Leites's more recent research on the Soviet elite from this standpoint. Leites studied statements by Khrushchev and other contemporary Soviet leaders in order to establish whether they held the same set of beliefs regarding the nature of political conflict and the same image of the opponent as Lenin and Stalin had earlier held. He noted various indications that a somewhat more moderate view had emerged of the basic "who-whom" problem that Lenin had so starkly formulated . . . and that the related fear of annihilation had softened. The hypothesis of a change in these beliefs was stated cautiously by Leites.

> When one strikes a balance . . . it would seem that Bolshevik fears of annihilation have declined, which presumably decreases the urgency of total victory as an antidote against extinction.[43]

Such change would be of considerable significance, since as Leites noted, the aggressiveness and expansionist drive in the older variant of Bolshevism had probably been motivated to a significant extent by this basic view of the nature of political conflict and the related fear of annihilation.[44]

If this fundamental belief was attenuated over time, one would expect that such a change would influence other components of the belief system as well. Leites found indications that this was the case. Examining evidence bearing on the question: "Are They Relaxing?" Leites concluded, again cautiously: "Despite the Cuban affair, it cannot be excluded that they are relaxing, to some limited extent."[45] Posing another question: "Are They Mellowing?" and reviewing relevant statements by Khrushchev and other leaders. Leites concluded:

> Thus it would seem that the Bolshevik fear of yielding has, after all, declined, and the insistence on "utilizing possibilities" weakened. . . . contemporary Soviet leaders probably feel less constrained to push forward into any possible accessible space without regard for delayed and indirect consequences. They may even have gained for themselves some slight liberty to concede without an immediate concession in return.[46]

We turn briefly now to the task of accounting for an amelioration in elements of the older Bolshevik belief system. This task is admittedly formidable; the following remarks are by no means intended as an authoritative explanation. Any effort to explain such a change should probably consider several factors and the interactions among them. Changes in top Soviet leadership following Stalin's death in 1953 were undoubtedly of great importance. As Leites noted, Stalin had bent some of the Bolshevik beliefs of Lenin's time in a harsher direction. Even before the accentuation of Stalin's paranoid tendencies in his later years, idiosyncratic elements of his personality had probably rendered his adherence to the Bolshevik belief system relatively impervious to reality testing.[47] Khrushchev's mind was apparently less "closed" in this respect than Stalin's; he was more receptive to recognizing relevant experiences and historical changes as being in some sense "critical tests" of basic components of the belief system and also more capable of cautiously modifying some of these beliefs.

While the difference between Stalin's and Khrushchev's personalities was perhaps critical in this respect, other factors also must be taken into account. The growth of Soviet power may have contributed to Khrushchev's reassessment of the "danger of annihilation." Perhaps of greater importance was the fact that historical experience demonstrated, more during Khrushchev's rule than in Stalin's, that perhaps after all the United States would not engage in an unprovoked war with the Soviet Union. U.S. leaders had not only failed to wage preventive war while the Soviet Union was weak in the immediate post–World War II period, they also seemed prepared to allow it to approach parity with the United States. Well might these historic developments encourage post-Stalin leaders to alter somewhat the earlier image of the U.S. elite as an overwhelmingly hostile, shrewd, determined opponent and to permit themselves to feel a somewhat greater sense of security.[48]

In accounting for changes in the Soviet belief system, therefore, it appears necessary to give weight not only to changes in personality variables but also to the impact of significant historical developments. In addition to those already mentioned, reference should be made to events such as the emergence of greater independence and conflict within the international Communist movement after Stalin's death. It is probably the case that changes in top leadership made it easier to reconsider older beliefs in the light of new developments.

Changes in the belief system that manifested themselves during Khrushchev's period are indeed of considerable significance for world politics. But it is necessary to note that they evidently constituted modifications of the classical Bolshevik belief system, not its abandonment or radical transformation. There remained substantial elements of continuity with the past in the belief system and political culture of post-Stalin Soviet leadership.[49]

VI. CONCLUSION

This paper has formulated and illustrated the set of beliefs about basic issues concerning the nature of politics and political action that have been heretofore implied by the term "operational code." This term is a misnomer in important respects; it should probably be replaced by some other way of referring to these beliefs, such as "approaches to political calculation." I have tried in this paper to codify the general issues and questions around which such a belief system is structured in the hope that it will encourage and facilitate systematic efforts to apply this research approach to a variety of other ruling groups and individual political leaders as well. The possibility emerges of a useful new dimension for comparative studies of different leaders and elite groups.

I have argued in this paper that knowledge of this belief system provides one of the important inputs needed for behavioral analyses of political decision making and leadership styles. The "operational-code" construct does this insofar as it encompasses that aspect of the political actor's perception and structuring of the political world to which he relates, and within which he attempts to operate to advance the interests with which he is identified. This approach should be useful for studying an actor's decision-making "style," and its application in specific situations.

As noted earlier . . . this paper focuses on the political actor's orientation towards opponents (domestic and international) rather than towards other types of political actors. I believe this focus is justified; a belief system about politics is influenced particularly by the actor's assumptions about the nature of political conflict and by his image of opponents.

Of course, the image of the opponent may play a less central and a somewhat different role in the belief systems of elites who do not attribute (as did the Bolsheviks) an irreconcilable hostility to their political enemies. When political opponents are perceived as limited (and perhaps temporary) adversaries, important consequences may be expected to follow for other elements in the belief system. Particularly in such cases is it desirable to supplement attention to the actor's image of the opponent with observations about his orientation towards political friends and followers.

There remain, of course, important questions concerning data and methods to be employed for research directed towards constructing a political actor's belief system about politics. These problems are not taken up in this paper; I would suggest here merely that questions of data and methods be approached in an eclectic and pragmatic spirit. Even provisional answers to the research questions encompassed by the operational code are likely to be useful. Opportunities for research of this kind vary considerably, depending on the particular leaders or elite groups that happen to be of interest. Different research methods may be employed for using materials that are already available, and when opportunities permit, for acquiring new data more systematically. Data relevant to the operational code may be obtained from various kinds of content analysis—both via qualitative analysis of texts (as in Leites's study) or more rigorous quantitative analysis (as by Professor Ole Holsti in his study of John Foster Dulles' image of the Soviet opponent).[50] Similarly, when interviewing is possible, several variants of open-ended, in-depth, or structured interview techniques might be employed. Useful data and inferences on these matters are likely to be obtained also by those who have opportunities to engage in "participant observation," whether as researchers, political journalists, or political participants. Finally, inferences about various aspects of an actor's operational code are possible from case studies of his behavior in particular situations.[51]

NOTES

1. *American Foreign Policy* (London: G. Allen, 1960) pp. 316, 318.
2. (Glencoe, Illinois: The Free Press, 1953), hereafter cited as *Study*.
3. For a useful critique of the systematic multibiographical study of elite groups, see Morris Janowitz, "The Systematic Aspects of Political Biography," *World Politics* 6 (April 1954). A comprehensive critical appraisal of elite theories and related empirical researches is provided in Dankwart A. Rustow, "The Study of Elites," *World Politics* 18 (July 1966).
4. In his review article "Politics, History, and Psychology," *World Politics,* 8 (October 1955), p. 117.
5. An early attempt was made by Theodore Chen to apply the "operational code" approach to Communist Chinese leaders. More recently, in December 1966, Robert North organized a conference of Chinese area specialists at Stanford University to consider again the utility and feasibility of doing a study of the Chinese Communist operational code. Other studies pursue similar research objectives, though not modeled on the operational code: See, for example, Davis B. Bobrow, "The Chinese Communist Conflict System," *Orbis,* 9 (Winter 1966); Howard L. Boorman and Scott A. Boorman, "Strategy and National Psychology in China," *The Annals,* 370 (March 1967); Tang Tsou and Morton H. Halperin, "Mao Tse-tung's Revolutionary Strategy and Peking's International Behavior," *American Political Science Review,* 59 (March 1965).
6. A helpful effort to identify the several components of *A Study of Bolshevism* is provided by Daniel Bell, "Bolshevik Man, His Motivations: A Psychoanalytic Key to Communist Behavior," *Commentary,* 19 (1955), pp. 179–87; much of this essay was reproduced in the same author's "Ten Theories in Search of Reality: The Prediction of Soviet Behavior in the Social Sciences," *World Politics,* 10 (April 1958).
7. (New York: McGraw-Hill, 1951).
8. In this connection see for example Michael Walzer's study of the origins of modern radical politics in the sixteenth century and his effort to construct a general model of radical politics that encompasses Bolshevism as well as Puritanism. *The Revolution of Saints* (Cambridge, Mass.: Harvard University Press, 1965).
9. The psychoanalytic hypotheses employed by Leites were touched upon at various points in *A Study of Bolshevism* and discussed more fully in his article "Panic and Defenses Against Panic in the Bolshevik View of Politics," in *Psychoanalysis and the Social Sciences,* Vol. 4 (New York: International Universities Press, 1955), pp. 135–44.
10. *Study* p. 22. Daniel Bell, *op. cit.,* also called attention to the fact that Leites regards Bolshevik character as both a conscious and unconscious reaction to features of the earlier pre-Bolshevik character.
11. I have suggested elsewhere ("Power As a Compensatory Value for Political Leaders," *Journal of Social Issues,* 24 (July 1968) that political scientists interested in applying personality theories to the study of political leaders need to build a number of conceptual "bridges" that reflect the problems, theoretical interests, and available data of their discipline in order to make more effective use of personality theories rooted in psychoanalysis. The "operational code" construct is one such "bridge." The belief system about politics is part of the cognitive and affective portion of the ego structure of personality; as such it serves an adaptive function for coping with reality. But at the same time the emergence of a belief system may be affected by developmental problems encountered in personality formation; if so, beliefs may then also serve ego defensive functions *vis-à-vis* unconscious wishes and anxieties.
12. In this connection Leites argued that the fact that beliefs comprising the operational code appeared to be held with unusual stubbornness, exaggeration, and intensity raised

the presumption that adherence to them was reinforced by defenses against strong unconscious wishes or fears and hence that they were relatively impervious to many kinds of rational tests.

13. This point was well made recently by John Weakland in a perceptive and balanced appraisal of *A Study of Bolshevism*. Weakland notes that Leites's work is "remarkably simple in overall organization, and for a work aiming to present a code, it gives little attention to synthesis and systematization. . . . We are presented with a list of themes, but these parts of the code are not interrelated. . . . And there is even less attention given to questions of more complex structure, such as possible relationships between themes or principles of different levels. . . ." John H. Weakland, "Investigating the Operational Code of the Chinese Communist Leadership," an unpublished paper written for the Politburo Feasibility Study Conference, Stanford University, 16–18 December 1966.

14. For a more general discussion of political belief systems, see Lucian W. Pye and Sidney Verba (eds.), *Political Culture and Political Development* (Princeton, N.J.: Princeton University Press, 1965), particularly the "Introduction" by L. Pye and "Conclusion: Comparative Political Culture" by S. Verba.

15. These were considered by Leites in *Study*, especially pp. 99–144.

16. In recent years a number of social scientists have attempted to draw upon the field of cognitive psychology in order to elaborate better decision-making models for studies of world politics. While cognitive theory is relevant and suggestive, it does not lend itself readily to the task. Considerable adaption and development is needed. In particular, investigators will have to articulate the substantive beliefs and cognitive problems that are relevant in decision making in political settings, and they will also have to define more specifically the special contexts in which these political beliefs originate, operate in decision making, and change. For a useful discussion and statement of a still quite general model, see Richard A. Brody, "Cognition and Behavior: A Model of International Relations," in O. G. Harvey (ed.), *Experience, Structure, and Adaptability* (New York: Springer, 1966).

17. For useful discussions of these cognitive limits and some of their implications in the arena of political decision making, see James G. March and Herbert A. Simon, *Organizations* (New York: John Wiley, 1958); and Charles E. Lindblom, "The Science of 'Muddling Through,'" *Public Administration Quarterly*, 29 (Spring 1959), pp. 79–88. Lindblom's views have been elaborated in subsequent publications.

18. For interesting developments in this direction, however, see Albert Hirschman's effort to identify some characteristic features of the problem-solving and decision-making styles of Latin American reform leaders, in his *Journeys Toward Progress* (New York: Twentieth Century Fund, 1963); and the research by Wendell Bell and James Mau on "images of the future" as a key variable in social change in developing countries.

19. For insightful essays on some of these questions see for example David S. McLelland, "The Role of Political Style: A Study of Dean Acheson," in Roger Hilsman and Robert C. Good (eds.), *Foreign Policy in the Sixties* (Baltimore: Johns Hopkins University Press, 1965); Peter Gourevitch, "Political Skill: A Case Study," in John D. Montgomery and Arthur Smithies (eds.), *Public Policy* (Cambridge, Mass.: Harvard University Press, 1965), especially pp. 266–68; Erwin C. Hargrove, *Presidential Leadership: Personality and Political Style* (New York: Macmillan, 1966).

Michael Brecher, "Elite Images and Foreign Policy Choices: Kirshna Menon's View of the World," *Pacific Affairs*, 40 (Spring and Summer, 1967). Systematic research on presidential leadership styles is currently being undertaken by Professor James David Barber, Department of Political Science, Yale University.

20. I have borrowed here and adapted the general distinction between "epistemological" and "instrumental" beliefs made by O. G. Brim, D. C. Glass, D. E. Lavin, and N. Goodman, *Personality and Decision Processes: Studies in the Social Psychology of Thinking* (Stanford: Stanford University Press, 1962). In attempting to apply their useful distinction to the subject matter of the "operational code" I have found it necessary to formulate differently the specific issues and questions related to the problem of political action.

21. Leites himself did not overlook these problems or oversimplify the task of utilizing the operational code, with its ambiguous and inconsistent prescriptions, for explaining or predicting Soviet behavior. See *Study,* pp. 16–18.

22. This point has been emphasized particularly in the writings of Charles E. Lindblom. See also March and Simon, *op. cit.,* pp. 139, 151.

23. The summary presented here is drawn from *Study,* pp. 27–30 ("Politics Is War") and pp. 429–41 ("Who-Whom?").

24. For this reason it is of particular interest that in his more recent work Leites has found indications of an amelioration in the Soviet leaders' image of their opponent.

25. On this point see for example Robert E. Osgood, *Ideals and Self-Interest in America's Foreign Relations* (Chicago: University of Chicago Press, 1953); and Kenneth Waltz, *Man, the State and War* (New York: Columbia University Press, 1959).

26. The summary which follows draws from *Study,* pp. 404–16 ("The Incessant Danger of Attack," and "The Uncertainty of Survival Before Victory").

27. The summary presented here draws from *Study,* pp. 32, 77–85 ("Unpredictable Aspects of the Future").

28. See *Study,* pp. 85–92 ("Transforming Opportunities Into Realities").

29. See *Study,* pp. 67–73 ("The Denial of Accidents").

30. See *Study,* pp. 49, 264–68.

31. The discussion of this question draws from and freely interprets materials in *Study,* pp. 32, 47–49, 77–92, 514–24.

32. On this point see for example March and Simon, *op. cit.,* pp. 140–41, 169.

33. During the course of efforts to assess Soviet intentions in placing missiles in Cuba, Charles Bohlen, a leading U.S. specialist on the Soviet Union, cited one of Lenin's adages which compared national expansion to a bayonet drive: If you strike steel, pull back; if you strike mush, keep going. Theodore C. Sorensen, *Kennedy* (New York: Harper and Row, 1965), p. 677.

34. For a discussion of the possibility that the Bolshevik tendency to push to the limit led to an underestimation of the undesired consequences of such conduct, see Leites, *Study,* pp. 33–34, 36–37, 39.

35. In the Cuban missile crisis U.S. policy makers at first entertained various theories, partly overlapping and partly divergent, as to Soviet intentions. They seem to have settled on an interpretation that avoided attributing to the Soviet leaders a single motive in favor of a theory that the Soviets expected that the deployment of missiles would give them prospects for a variety of specific gains in foreign policy. See particularly Roger Hilsman, *To Move a Nation* (New York: Doubleday, 1967), pp. 161–65, 201–02; and Theodore C. Sorensen, *op. cit.,* pp. 676–78.

36. See *Study,* pp. 30–34, 52–53, 442–49, 505–12, 514–24.

37. A similar "tension of opposites" has been noted in the Chinese Communist approach to the problem of strategy and action. See Tang Tsou and Morton H. Halperin, *op. cit.,* p. 89.

38. For a discussion of these maxims, see *Study,* pp. 55–57, 449–61, 46–47, 57–60, 475–503. See also N. Leites, *Kremlin Thoughts: Yielding, Rebuffing, Provoking, Retreating,* The RAND Corporation, RM–3618-ISA (May 1963).

39. See, for example, R. E. Osgood, *Limited War* (Chicago: University of Chicago Press, 1957); W. W. Kaufmann, "Limited Warfare," in Kaufmann (ed.) *Military Policy and National Security* (Princeton: Princeton University Press, 1956); Morton H. Halperin, *Limited War in the Nuclear Age* (New York: John Wiley, 1963).

40. See *Study*, p. 34.

41. See *Study*, pp. 34–42.

42. This would appear to apply also to the Chinese Communist leadership. (See the forthcoming report by Robert C. North on the Stanford University conference which considered the feasibility of research on the Chinese politburo.) Among those scholars who have examined the problem of evaluating and changing beliefs about the opponent are Morton Deutsch, William Gamson, Andréa Modigliani, John Kautsky, Charles E. Osgood, Amitai Etzioni, Ralph K. White, Milton Rokeach and Joseph deRivera.

43. *Kremlin Moods*, The RAND Corporation, RM–3535-ISA (January 1964), p. 126.

44. *Ibid.*, p. 91.

45. *Ibid.*, pp. 164–66.

46. *Ibid.*, p. 211.

47. The importance of Stalin's personality for his political behavior has been emphasized particularly by Robert Tucker. See his "The Dictator and Totalitarianism," *World Politics* (July 1965), and his earlier analysis, "Stalinism and the World Conflict," *Journal of International Affairs*, 8, No. 1 (1954).

48. Interestingly, Khrushchev's period also saw the emergence of a less favorable image of the United States as an opponent. There was both less idealization of, and less respect for the U.S. elite than in the old Bolshevik view. The historic class enemy was now perceived as an "aging," "declining" elite, one which was weaker, less intelligent, less determined than in the past. The changed characteristics imputed to the United States leadership, however, were seen as making it in some respects possibly more dangerous. (See *Kremlin Moods*, pp. 91–126, 1–13).

49. This point was emphasized in Leites's *Kremlin Moods*. There is in [my] knowledge no similar study of further changes in the belief system that may have emerged in the post-Khrushchev era. However, Vernon V. Aspaturian is studying Soviet images of the Kennedy administration.

50. Ole Holsti, "Cognitive Dynamics and Images of the Enemy," in D. J. Finlay, O. R. Holsti, and R. R. Fagen, *Enemies in Politics* (Chicago: Rand McNally, 1967).

51. For example, Arnold Horelick, "The Cuban Missile Crisis: Analysis of Soviet Calculations and Behavior," *World Politics* 16 (April 1964).

Political Conflict and Foreign Policy in the United States: A Geographical Interpretation

Peter Trubowitz

INTRODUCTION

During the quarter-century that followed World War II, American leaders were able to mobilize broad domestic support for their foreign policies. While the conventional wisdom that 'politics stopped at the water's edge' was at best a half-truth, the fact remains that political leaders enjoyed considerable latitude in the making of foreign policy. No one would characterize more recent American foreign policy-making in these terms. From the early 1970s onward, America's leaders experienced great difficulty in articulating a vision of the national interest that inspired broad support in Congress and the polity at large. The foreign policy consensus gave way to bitter and politically divisive conflicts over America's role in the world. Debates took on strongly emotional and symbolic overtones. The Cold War ended, but deep divisions over the ends and means of foreign policy persist. At a time when America's leaders need to make wise choices about the future, doubts remain about their ability to resolve the conflicts that have produced political gridlock and paralysis.

Practitioners, commentators and scholars recognize that American leaders no longer enjoy the freedom or autonomy in managing the nation's foreign policy that they once did. Disagreements arise when it comes to explaining this change. Some analysts locate the source of the problem in the electoral arena, and attribute the change to partisan politics and divided party government (McCormick and Wittkopf, 1990; Winik, 1991). Other observers stress the impact that the dispersion of power in Congress in the 1970s has had on the foreign policy-making process (Destler, 1981; Huntington, 1988; Warburg, 1989). They argue that the breakdown of the seniority system, the proliferation of subcommittees, and the expansion in staff and research resources has made it easier for individual members to pursue their own paths on foreign-policy matters and more difficult for the White House to control Congress. Still others emphasize divisions in élite and mass opinion (Holsti and Rosenau, 1984; Schneider, 1992). Such fragmentation, they contend, makes it harder for national leaders to mobilize consent and act strategically in the international arena.

Peter Trubowitz, "Political Conflict and Foreign Policy in the United States: A Geographical Interpretation," *Political Geography*, 12,2 (March 1993):121–135.

This paper offers an alternative argument about why consensus-building in the area of foreign policy became more difficult. It is argued that since the early 1970s, conflict over foreign policy has been part-and-parcel of a larger, regionally-based struggle for national wealth and power. For over two decades, the fight over America's overseas ambitions and objectives has split the nation along regional lines, pitting the Northeast against the South. Support for the expansive and expensive foreign policy agenda that crystallized after World War II has remained strongest in the South where state and local economies benefit disproportionately from policies that require large federal defense outlays. In the Northeast, where the domestic costs of an expansionist foreign policy now outweigh the benefits, politicians have favored a more restrained and cost-conscious approach to foreign policy. The seemingly intractable divisions over foreign policy are the result of this competition between two regionally-based coalitions which have distinct—and often conflicting—interests.

This argument has two implications for understanding contemporary debates over American foreign policy. The first is that place matters. Sectionalism remains a fundamental feature of American politics, and the politics of foreign policy is no exception. Like other periods in American history when ideological conflicts over foreign policy were shaped by deeper conflicts of interests, today's conflicts between 'liberals' and 'conservatives' over the purposes of American power are fueled by conflicting sectional political imperatives. The second implication follows from this: there is no single national interest. Analysts who assume that America has a unique and discernible national interest, and that this interest should or can determine its relations with other nations, are unable to explain the persistent failure to achieve domestic consensus on international objectives. A regional framework which focuses on the struggle among domestic coalitions for control over the foreign policy agenda reveals how politically-contingent competing definitions of 'the' national interest actually are.

This argument is developed through an analysis of the patterns of regional conflict in the House of Representatives. Using Congress as a proxy for the national polity, the patterns of political alignment over foreign policy are reconstructed from 'key' legislative roll-call votes. The primary empirical task is to demonstrate that the conflicts over foreign policy that first arose in the late 1960s and early 1970s—when the Cold War consensus collapsed—are grounded in a regionally-based struggle that has split the nation's oldest and newest industrial regions into opposing camps. A full explanation of this pattern of regional alignment lies beyond the scope of this paper. For present purposes, a large literature on America's changing geography is drawn on to interpret and explain the pattern of regional competition over foreign policy that is revealed by the data analysis. The conclusion comprises a discussion of the broader implications of the analysis for American foreign policy in the post-Cold War era.

REGIONAL INTERESTS AND FOREIGN POLICY

The geographical diversity of the national economy and the spatially decentralized nature of political representation have made regionalism a distinctive and enduring feature of American political life. Geographical disparities in sectoral concentration, technological advancement and international competitiveness mean that the costs and benefits of public policies are often distributed unequally across the nation. The extreme localism of political representation in the US ensures that these regional differences find political expression at the national level. At the national level, the dispersal of decision-making power and competition between the national parties for regional electoral advantage magnifies the role of regional interests, economic needs and political imperatives in shaping the national agenda. Institutional decentralization provides various channels for elected officials to levy claims on the federal government's resources, initiate or obstruct policy change, and build policy coalitions with political élites from other parts of the country through logrolling, vote-trading, ideological appeals and the like. Regional political competition is the result. This is well understood by political geographers who study the regional bases of political conflict over domestic policy matters.

Regionalism also emerges as a consistent dimension of political competition over foreign policy. Often depicted as contests between competing visions of America's role in the world, conflicts over foreign policy are also conflicts of interest. They have a geographical dimension. To a large extent, this reflects the regionally uneven nature of American involvement in the world economy. During the 1890s, for example, the great debate between the 'imperialists' and the 'continentalists' over overseas expansion pitted the industrial and commercial Northeast against the agrarian South (Hays, 1957; Bensel, 1984; Baack and Ray, 1988). The West played a decisive swing role in the conflict. The Northeast favored a neomercantile strategy combining maritime power, territorial expansion and the bargaining tariff to penetrate and 'capture' underdeveloped markets in Latin America and Asia. The South, in many respects still a colonial appendage of the North, supported a less expansive, *laissez-faire* approach to commercial expansion. Southern interests stressed the advantages of free trade with industrialized nations in Europe and did not require overseas holdings or a large military establishment to achieve its commercial objectives.

A quarter of a century later, conflicting regional imperatives once again shaped debates over foreign policy. At issue this time were the causes of the Great Depression and how America should respond to it. The key question was whether America should assume an active role in promoting global economic recovery and preventing the emergence of closed spheres of influence in Europe and Asia. Politicians who came from parts of the country that had the most to gain from an open, interdependent world economy—the Northeast and South—generally favored policies designed to promote commercial liberalization, global monetary cooperation and collective security (Grassmuck, 1951; Schatz, 1972; Cole, 1983; Frieden, 1988). These 'internationalists' waged a fierce battle against their 'nationalist' rivals from the West. The nationalists, who represented areas of the country that were less competitive in the world economy, called for renewed trade protection and opposed attempts to stabilize global commercial and monetary relations, arguing that such policies granted the White House too much authority in the area of foreign policy and threatened republican ideals at home.

In each of these periods, politicians from different parts of the country sought to equate regional interests with the national interest. Foreign policy issues were debated in terms of their immediate impact on regional prosperity and their longer-range consequences for the social and political arrangements which sustained regional economies. The choices politicians made over foreign policy reflected the fact that decisions over the nation's strategic objectives, market orientation and military posture were not geographically neutral. There were regional winners and regional losers. In each period, politicians who championed a 'strong state' were those best-placed to exercise influence over and benefit from the centralization of power and authority that would accompany an active foreign policy. Competing foreign policy agendas were grounded in interests, and the institutional conflicts that arose between the executive and legislative branches reflected patterns of competition that were grounded in these broader societal conflicts.

Explaining deep and persistent conflict over US foreign policy requires some mapping of the nation's economic geography. Functional position alone, however, is too blunt an instrument to explain fully how regional competition over foreign policy is played out in the national political arena. Party politics also plays a role. American party leaders have a long if inglorious record of playing politics with the national interest (Varg, 1963; Terrill, 1973; Divine, 1974; Nincic, 1992). Within the structures of a two-party system, they have often used foreign policies to mobilize electoral support and marginalize political opponents. During the 1890s, Republican leaders used the lure of new markets in Latin America and Asia to attract agrarian interests in the West to their cause and thus to consolidate Republican hegemony at the national level. In the 1930s, the Democrats used tariff reform to exploit regional tensions within the Republican party and broaden the regional base of the New Deal coalition. These cases underscore the fact that regional foreign policy coalitions are forged in the electoral arena. This means that alternative visions of the national interest are shaped by partisan struggles for political advantage.

SPATIAL ANALYSIS OF HOUSE VOTING

The kind of sectional strife that structured the foreign policy debates of the 1890s and 1930s has not disappeared with time. This paper claims that today's foreign policy conflicts are also structured along regional lines. This proposition is tested by examining how members of the House of Representatives vote on key foreign policy issues from the Nixon through Reagan years. The analysis is based on roll-call votes defined as 'key' votes by groups that monitor political activity in the Congress. These groups are: Americans for Democratic Action, Americans for Constitutional Action, and *Congressional Quarterly*.[1] Each group publishes an annual list of votes on important national issues, foreign as well as domestic. These votes constitute a test of members' policy preferences and their positions on issues whose political significance is unlikely to be lost on elected officials. The data set includes all of the major foreign policy initiatives undertaken by a President that required approval by the House, and votes on all major foreign policy issues that reached the House floor. All of the votes included in the analysis were weighted equally.

The data set was broken down and organized by presidency.[2] For each of the presidencies from Nixon through Reagan, voting similarity or agreement scores were calculated for all pairs of state delegations using a modified version of the pairwise agreement index where state delegations (not individual members) are the unit of analysis.[3] Each state delegation's position on a vote was based on the majority position in the delegation voting yea or nay.[4] The voting index measures the percentage of agreement between state delegations on all of the key foreign policy votes during a presidency. The score is 100 when there is perfect agreement between the majority position of two state delegations; it is 0 if there is perfect disagreement. The number of key votes used to compute the agreement index between delegations varied across presidencies. In part, this reflects differences in the numbers of years Presidents were in office. It also reflects variations in the number of votes selected annually by the various organizations.

Multi-dimensional scaling (MDS) was used to capture the political geography of voting over foreign policy. The basic goal of MDS is to describe the empirical relationships between some set of objects in a space of fixed dimensionality. Others have used this technique to recover patterns in congressional voting (MacRae, 1970; Hoadley, 1980; Easterling, 1987). Here, the simplest, non-metric version is used to provide a spatial display of the voting alignments among congressional or state delegations over foreign policy at different points in time. The states (i.e. state delegations) are represented as points in the space, and distance is an analog for similarity (or dissimilarity). The goal is to find the configuration of interpoint distances between state delegations that corresponds as closely as possible to the similarities among the voting behavior of these delegations. Those state delegations which agree most often in voting are closest to each other in the resulting configuration of points. Those which disagree most are farthest apart in the space.

The most important and difficult stage in MDS analysis involves interpretation. First, the quality of a solution, or the fit between the data and the spatial configuration, must be determined. In the program used here, ALSCAL, the quality of a solution is defined by RSQ. Second, the appropriate dimensionality must be determined with respect to RSQ. In principle, a solution can be derived in any number of dimensions, and RSQ will always be higher when a higher dimensionality is allowed. Since MDS works in a space of fixed dimensionality, it is necessary to determine the most appropriate dimensionality, recognizing that there is a trade-off between the quality of fit (high RSQ) and parsimony (a small number of dimensions). Finally, the interpretation involves searching for meaningful patterns, usually defined as clusters or dimensions. While dimensional structure is often emphasized by analysts, it is equally valid to focus on clusters and search for areas or neighborhoods of the space that have meaning associated with other shared characteristics.[5] This is the approach adopted here.

MDS Results

The results of the scaling analysis are summarized in Table 16.1. Configurations were generated in one, two and three dimensions using ALSCAL. The two-dimensional configuration was selected as the best representation of voting patterns in each of the four presidencies. On average, the two-dimensional solutions account for 94.6 percent of the variance. A third dimension improves the fit by only 1.9 percent on

Table 16.1   SUMMARY OF MULTI-DIMENSIONAL SCALING SOLUTIONS

Presidency	RSQ dimensions			STRESS dimensions		
	1	2	3	1	2	3
Nixon	0.843	0.928	0.957	0.233	0.130	0.090
Ford	0.944	0.966	0.979	0.142	0.094	0.067
Carter	0.854	0.924	0.948	0.221	0.133	0.099
Reagan	0.929	0.966	0.974	0.156	0.097	0.077

Source: Derived from recorded roll-call votes in US Congress.

average. (ALSCAL also generates a 'badness of fit' function, known as STRESS, which is also presented in Table 16.1.) The configurations are presented in Figures 16.1–4. The vertical and horizontal axes are not labelled and should not be interpreted in terms of two linear, orthogonal dimensions. The configurations should be interpreted as clusterings of states in a two-dimensional space. A closely grouped cluster of states indicates a cohesive voting bloc. States from the Northeast are un-

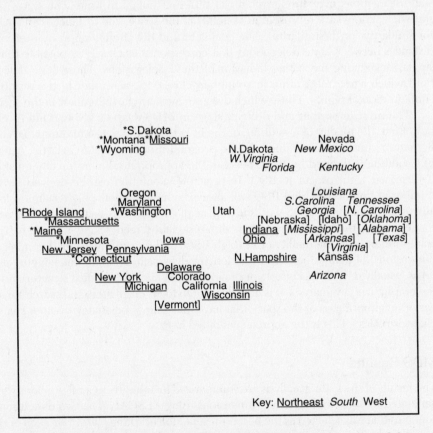

Figure 16.1 Foreign policy alignment during Nixon years. *Source:* derived from multi-dimensional scaling of key roll-call votes in US Congress.

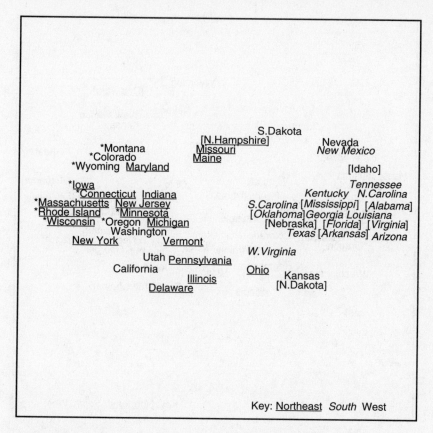

Figure 16.2 Foreign policy alignment during Ford years. *Source:* derived from multi-dimensional scaling of key roll-call votes in US Congress.

derlined. Those from the South are in italics. States from the West are in regular typeface. See the Appendix for a listing of the states in each section.

A visual examination of the MDS configurations reveals that the voting alignment is regional in nature. In each of the spatial maps, the pattern of alignment is defined by discrete clusters or blocs of states. While the cohesion of these voting blocks varies over time, it is apparent that a large proportion of the states consistently cluster on opposite sides of the configurations. During each of the four administrations, the pattern of alignment breaks down along north–south lines and falls along lines others have defined as rustbelt–sunbelt, snowbelt–sunbelt, or core–periphery (Phillips, 1969; Sale, 1975; Weinstein and Firestine, 1978; Bensel, 1984). States from the Northeast tend to cluster together on the left side of the voting spaces. Most of those from the South coalesce on the right side of the configurations. By contrast, the pattern of voting among states from the West is much more mixed. Some states—like California, Oregon and Washington—cluster with those from the Northeast. Others—like Idaho, Kansas and Nebraska—generally align with states from the South. The analysis indicates that there is little consensus over foreign policy.

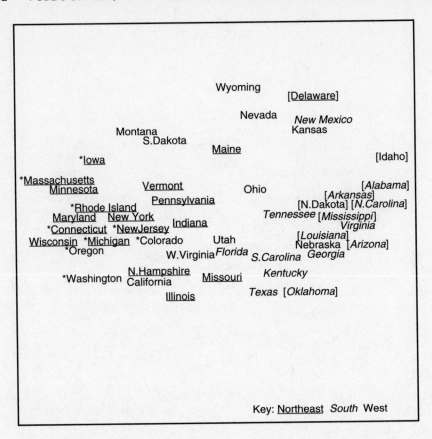

Figure 16.3 Foreign policy alignment during Carter years. *Source:* derived from multi-dimensional scaling of key roll-call votes in US Congress.

Since the Nixon years, the foreign policy agenda in Congress has been dominated by national security issues. While foreign economic policy issues became increasingly important during the Reagan years, the vast majority of the votes in the 1970s and 1980s concerned issues such as defense spending, arms control, war powers, covert operations, military aid, arms sales and overseas alliances. The common and divisive theme that linked these issues was the rising domestic opportunity cost of the *Pax Americana* built after World War II. Critics challenged the *status quo* on two fronts. First, they argued that the ends of American foreign policy outstripped the country's means. Collective energies and resources were being spent unwisely on an expansionist and sometimes misguided foreign policy at the expense of urgent domestic needs and problems. Second, they argued that the method used by national leaders to promote American power overseas threatened republican ideals at home by concentrating political power in the White House.

A number of methods may be used to determine how place-specific these political sentiments are. For present purposes, an index measuring state support for 'strategic retrenchment' was constructed using the votes described above. A vote

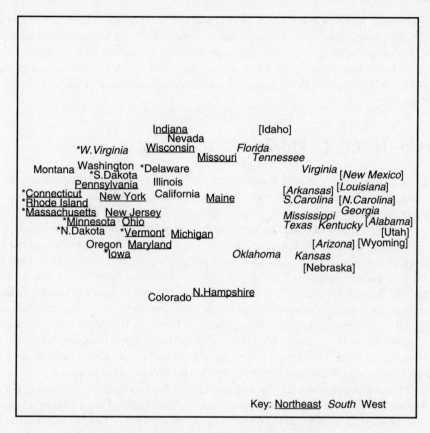

Figure 16.4 Foreign policy alignment during Reagan years. *Source:* derived from multi-dimensional scaling of key roll-call votes in US Congress.

against any of the following was considered a vote in favor of strategic retrenchment: defense spending, foreign aid, arms sales, military bases, overseas alliances, military intervention, international institutions and presidential prerogative in the making of foreign policy. Votes for arms control were treated as a vote in favor of a policy of strategic retrenchment. The position of each member of Congress on these votes was identified. A mean support score for a strategy of retrenchment was calculated by averaging across the votes during each of the four administrations. A state mean was then formed by averaging the scores for all members of a congressional delegation.

In each of the figures, the 10 state delegations that scored highest on the index are marked with an asterisk. The 10 congressional delegations that scored lowest on the index are in brackets. Support for a policy of strategic retrenchment is clearly strongest among states that cluster on the left side of the voting space. Since the early 1970s, this coalition has lobbied for cuts in the defense budget, reductions in America's military presence overseas, and limits on presidential prerogative in the making of foreign policy (e.g war powers, covert operations, executive agreements). Many of these states are located in the Northeast. A few are from the West. By contrast, states that cluster on the right side of the voting spaces have favored a more expansive and expensive conception of the nation's strategic interests, one that has placed a premium on military power. Most of those states that have strongly opposed efforts to scale-back America's role in world affairs are from the South.

THE RUSTBELT VERSUS THE SUNBELT

Why did the foreign policy debates of the 1970s and 1980s divide the nation along regional lines? Why did the pattern of regional cleavage that arose in the 1970s persist into the 1980s? This section provides an interpretation that locates the source of this conflict in America's changing geography. Drawing on the work of political and economic geographers, it is argued that the conflicts over foreign policy cannot be viewed in isolation from regionally-based struggles over domestic policy. The declining economic fortunes of the Northeast led politicians from this region to seek ways of reducing the costs of the nation's foreign policies in order to devote greater resources to domestic problems and needs. These efforts to redefine the nation's political priorities intensified existing tensions between the Northeast and South over domestic policy and provided fertile ground for political leaders who sought to exploit this regional cleavage for electoral gain. The failure of American leaders to forge a broad and stable foreign policy consensus is one consequence.

It has been apparent for some time that the national political economy is undergoing a process of regional restructuring. Older centers of industrial production in the Northeast have been losing much of their economic base to other parts of the country (Agnew, 1987; Markusen, 1987). The migration of industries, jobs and people from the manufacturing belt to the sunbelt since the 1960s is one indication of this shift in economic activity. While many states located in the industrial core experienced sluggish growth rates and economic stagnation, many in the South and West became more prosperous and diversified (Rostow, 1977; Norton and Rees, 1979). The process of regional restructuring is reflected in the political arena. Shifts in regional populations have led to shifts in political power at the national level as the Northeast has lost congressional seats to the South and West through reapportionment (Stanley and Niemi, 1990). At the same time, the growing strength of the South and West in the electoral college has made these regions decisive battle grounds in national electoral campaigns.

Analysts identify a number of factors that have contributed to this process. The relative decline of the manufacturing belt has been linked to reductions in transport costs, the diffusion of large-scale, high-technology production, and regional disparities in labor costs, energy prices and local tax rates (Weinstein and Firestine, 1978; Rees, 1983). No less important are the uneven consequences of the erosion of American commercial power in the international economy (Glickman and Glasmeier, 1989; Markusen and Carlson, 1989). Since the 1960s, the manufacturing belt has suffered disproportionately from the migration of American firms overseas and the rise of Western Europe and Japan as industrial competitors. Spatial disparities in federal spending and federal tax policies have also played a role in accelerating, if not encouraging, regional restructuring (Advisory Commission on Intergovernmental Relations, 1980). Federal expenditures and tax policies are often cited as forces that have spurred the growth of sunbelt states while exacerbating economic difficulties in the manufacturing belt.

The erosion of the manufacturing belt's position in both the national economy and the world economy contributed decisively to the emergence of a new and intense debate over the nation's priorities. At the center of this debate lie questions of regional equity or fairness, and specifically, the issue of purported transfers of economic wealth and power from the manufacturing belt to the sunbelt (Dilger, 1982; Bensel, 1984; Markusen, 1987).[6] In the domestic arena, the re-emergence of sectional strife has colored a broad range of issues. In most accounts, the 1960s mark the beginning of this process, when regional divisions found expression in debates over civil rights, entitlement programs and unionization. By the 1970s, the scope of these debates expanded and gained notoriety as politicians from these regions locked horns over rising energy costs, capital flight to the sunbelt, and regional bias in federal tax and spending policies. The pattern of conflict between the manufacturing belt and the sunbelt continued through the 1980s, finding expression in a wide variety of issues ranging from 'deregulation' to 'industrial policy' to the 'Reagan deficit'.

The struggle between the manufacturing belt and the sunbelt was not limited to domestic policy matters. The widespread belief in the Northeast that federal spending and tax policies favored the South and West made the military budget an attractive target for criticism in the 1970s (Bensel, 1984; Malecki and Stark, 1988). In an era when much of the Northeast was experiencing hard economic times, elected officials and interest groups found it politically advantageous to emphasize the domestic opportunity costs of military intervention, military spending and military aid to the Third World (McCormick, 1989). Such concerns figured prominently in the debates over the Vietnam War. In the 1980s, this 'guns versus butter' controversy grew even sharper in response to the Reagan military build-up (Trubowitz and Roberts, 1992; Wirls, 1992). Many of those who opposed the military build-up believed that it disproportionately benefited the South and West. What some viewed as an unintended consequence of the administration's efforts to make America's military presence overseas more visible, others saw as an industrial policy veiled in the garb of national security.

Similar tensions surfaced in the area of foreign economic policy. The growing vulnerability of many of America's key industrial sectors to global competition in the 1970s led to growing disenchantment with free-trade policies in the Northeast. Free trade has proven to be a more attractive economic strategy in the South and West (Sanders, 1986; Wade and Gates, 1990). Conflicting regional interests also appear to have shaped political attitudes toward overseas investment. The rapid expansion of American firms overseas in the 1960s and 1970s penalized areas in the manufacturing belt where a disproportionate share of the nation's unionized work force resided (Gilpin, 1975; Bluestone and Harrison 1982). As early as 1970, labor unions like the AFL–CIO and the UAW began sending out distress signals, pointing to the consequences of 'capital flight' for the nation's traditional manufacturing sectors. In an effort to protect jobs, labor pursued a dual strategy: lobbying for common wage standards at home and tighter controls on the outflow of capital abroad. This strategy has struck a far more responsive chord in the Northeast than it has in the South.

The decline of America's industrial core does not fully explain these conflicts over foreign policy. Sectionally-based conflicts over foreign policy have also been fueled by partisan competition. In the 1970s, as northern Democrats gained greater control over the party's national agenda, party leaders pressed for cuts in the military budget, a larger role for Congress in foreign policy-making, and reductions in the size of US forces overseas. These efforts helped the Democratic party expand its political base in the Northeast. At the same time, however, they exacerbated tensions between the northern and southern wings of the party that had arisen over issues such as civil rights, social welfare and the Vietnam War (Sundquist, 1983; Bensel, 1984; Gillon, 1987; Black and Black, 1987). The emergence of this fault line in the Democratic party became increasingly difficult to paper over as a growing number of political organizations, like the Americans for Democratic Action and the Northeast–Midwest Institute, began to mobilize political and economic interests in the manufacturing belt to redress perceived regional inequities in federal spending, labor costs and energy prices.

This regional schism within the Democratic party provided new political opportunities for a Republican party that was also undergoing change. Over the course of the 1970s, the center of political gravity in the Republican party moved from East to West. The rise of the 'Reagan Right' in the late 1970s and early 1980s marked the culmination of a process that began in the 1960s with the divisive nomination of Goldwater for President. This process gradually eroded the power of the 'eastern' wing of the Republican party (Reinhard, 1983; Rae, 1989; Himmelstein, 1990). Touting the virtues of 'laissez-faire', 'law and order', and a 'strong national defense', the Republican party began to penetrate the once-solid Democratic South. This tactical shift is evident in the so-called southern strategy embraced by every Republican candidate for the White House since Nixon. Like Republicans in the 1890s who used the issue of tariff reform to divide the South and West, Republican party leaders in the current era have used defense policy to exploit regional tensions between the Northeast and South.

CONCLUSION

Since the early 1970s, the conflicts between the manufacturing belt and the sunbelt over national priorities have made it extremely difficult for national leaders to mobilize broad national support for their foreign policies. Like other eras in American history marked by protracted domestic struggles over 'the national interest', issues of foreign policy have been defined and debated in terms of their impact on regional growth, stability and power. This fundamental fact is obscured by accounts which identify ideological or institutional cleavages at the national level as the source of domestic political competition and conflict over the foreign policy agenda. What recedes from view are the regional political imperatives that structure the possibilities for building the clearly dominant and stable coalitions that give political leaders wide latitude in conducting foreign policy. The sectional cleavages of the 1970s and 1980s did not afford national leaders this possibility.

The present study suggests that sectionalism remains a persistent force in American political life, and in the foreign policy arena in particular. Contrary to what is now conventional wisdom among foreign policy analysts, sectionalism is not a relic of the past. The findings also speak to debates among political geographers. Some analysts now argue that the political salience of large macro-level cleavages—north versus south, core versus periphery—is fading (Garreau, 1981; Agnew, 1988; Martis, 1988). This study, however, follows the work of others (Bensel, 1984; Archer, 1988; Earle, 1992) in underscoring the enduring significance of macro-level or sectional cleavages in explaining political behavior (e.g. national elections, congressional voting, social movements) in the American context. Sectionalism may not be as salient a political force today as it was a century ago, but it continues to exert a powerful influence on how politicians interpret and respond to changes in America's position in the world.

This means that sectionalism will shape the politics of American foreign policy in the post-Cold War era. Such forces are already at play in the current debate over the 'peace dividend'. Like the debate over the Reagan military build-up in the 1980s, the debate over the 'military build-down' in the 1990s is breaking down along familiar regional lines. At issue is not just how much to cut the Pentagon's budget but perhaps more importantly, how the savings should be spent (Trubowitz, 1992). The stakes are high. The choices politicians face raise fundamental questions about the distribution of national resources, the locus of political power at the federal level and, last but not least, who will benefit and who will not. At a time when there is little consensus over how to revitalize the American economy, and where foreign policy issues are increasingly entering the political arena as economic issues, domestic political competition over foreign policy is likely to intensify. If the recent past is any guide to the future, debates over foreign policy will continue to be shaped by conflicting sectional interests.

ACKNOWLEDGMENTS

I wish to thank Catherine Boone, John O'Loughlin and anonymous reviewers of *Political Geography* for their comments and suggestions. Erik Devereux provided valuable assistance in the data collection and data analysis. The study was supported by a research fellowship from the Center for International Studies at Princeton University. The roll-call data were provided by the Inter-University Consortium for Political and Social Research. An earlier version of this paper was presented at Princeton's Center for International Studies.

NOTES

1. The author was unable to obtain key votes for the 99th Congress (1985–86) from the Americans for Constitutional Action. For this Congress, the list of votes from *Congressional Quarterly* and the Americans for Democratic Action was supplemented by those used by the *National Journal* in rating legislators.
2. The following time-frames were used to classify the votes by presidency: Nixon (1969–74); Ford (1975–76); Carter (1977–80); Reagan (1981–86). The voting records for the House during the 100th Congress (1987–88) were not available in time for this study.

3. The historical scope of the analysis makes it necessary to use a unit of analysis that is stable over time. States are a logical choice for such purposes. The boundaries of legislative districts change; state boundaries do not. Alaska and Hawaii were not included in the data analysis.
4. Following convention, paired votes and announced positions were treated as formal votes.
5. For a good discussion of this issue see Kruskal and Wish (1978).
6. This controversy gained notoriety in the mid-1970s with the publication of articles in the *New York Times, Business Week* and the *National Journal* on the regional flow of federal funds.

REFERENCES

Advisory Commission on Intergovernmental Relations (1980). *Regional Growth: Historic Perspective.* Washington, DC: ACIR.

Agnew, J. (1987). *The United States in the World-Economy: A Regional Geography.* Cambridge: Cambridge University Press.

Agnew, J. (1988). Beyond core and periphery: the myth of regional political-economic restructuring and sectionalism in contemporary American politics. *Political Geography Quarterly* 7, 127–139.

Archer, J. C. (1988). Macrogeographical versus microgeographical cleavages in American presidential elections: 1940–1984. *Political Geography Quarterly* 7, 111–125.

Baack, B. and Ray, E. (1988). Special interests and the nineteenth-century roots of the US military-industrial complex. *Research in Economic History* 11, 153–169.

Bensel, R. F. (1984). *Sectionalism and American Political Development: 1880–1980.* Madison, WI: University of Wisconsin Press.

Black, E. and Black, M. (1987). *Politics and Society in the South.* Cambridge, MA: Harvard University Press.

Bluestone, B. and Harrison, B. (1982). *The Deindustrialization of America: Plant Closings, Community Abandonment, and the Dismantling of Basic Industry.* New York: Basic Books.

Cole, W. S. (1983). *Roosevelt and the Isolationists: 1932–45.* Lincoln, NE: University of Nebraska Press.

Destler, I. M. (1981). Executive–congressional conflict in foreign policy. In *Congress Reconsidered,* 2nd edn (L. C. Dodd and B. I. Oppenheimer eds.) pp. 342–363. Washington, DC: Congressional Quarterly Press.

Dilger, R. (1982). *The Sunbelt/Snowbelt Controversy: The War Over Federal Funds.* New York: New York University Press.

Divine, R. A. (1974). *Foreign Policy and US Presidential Elections, 1940–1948.* New York: New Viewpoints.

Earle, C. (1992). *Geographical Inquiry and American Historical Problems.* Stanford, CA: Stanford University Press.

Easterling, D. (1987). Political science: using the general Euclidean model to study ideological shifts in the US Senate. In *Multidimensional Scaling: History, Theory, and Applications* (F. Young and R. Hamer eds.) pp. 221–256. London: Lawrence Erlbaum Associates.

Frieden, J. (1988). Sectoral conflict and US foreign economic policy, 1914–1940. *International Organization* 42, 59–90.

Garreau, J. (1981). *The Nine Nations of North America.* Boston, MA: Houghton Mifflin.

Gillon, S. M. (1987). *Politics and Vision: The ADA and American Liberalism, 1947–1985.* Oxford: Oxford University Press.

Gilpin, R. (1975). *US Power and the Multinational Corporation: The Political Economy of Foreign Direct Investment.* New York: Basic Books.

Glickman, N. J. and Glasmeier, A. K. (1989). The international economy and the American South. In *Deindustrialization and Regional Economic Transformation: The Experience of the United States* (L. Rodwin and H. Sazanami eds.) pp. 60–80. Boston, MA: Unwin Hyman.

Grassmuck, G. L. (1951). *Sectional Biases in Congress on Foreign Policy.* Baltimore, MD: Johns Hopkins Press.

Hays, S. P. (1957). *The Response to Industrialism: 1885–1914.* Chicago, IL: University of Chicago Press.

Himmelstein, J. L. (1990). *To the Right: The Transformation of American Conservatism.* Berkeley, CA: University of California Press.

Hoadley, J. (1980). The emergence of political parties in Congress, 1789–1803. *American Political Science Review* 74, 757–779.

Holsti, O. R. and Rosenau, J. N. (1984). *American Leadership in World Affairs: Vietnam and the Breakdown of Consensus.* Boston, MA: Allen and Unwin.

Huntington, S. P. (1988). Foreign policy and the constitution. In *Crisis and Innovation: Constitutional Democracy in America* (F. Krinsky ed.) pp. 77–87. Oxford: Basil Blackwell.

Kruskal, J. B. and Wish, M. (1978). *Multidimensional Scaling.* Beverly Hills, CA: Sage Publications.

MacRae, D., Jr. (1970). *Issues and Parties in Legislative Voting.* New York: Harper and Row.

McCormick, J. M. and Wittkopf, E. R. (1990). Bipartisanship, partisanship, and ideology in congressional–executive foreign policy relations, 1947–1988. *Journal of Politics* 52, 1077–1100.

McCormick, T. J. (1989). *America's Half-Century: United States Foreign Policy in the Cold War.* Baltimore, MD: The Johns Hopkins University Press.

Malecki, E. J. and Stark, L. M. (1988). Regional and industrial variation in defence spending: some American evidence. In *Defence Expenditure and Regional Development* (M. J. Breheny ed.) pp. 67–101. London: Mansell Publishing Ltd.

Markusen, A. R. (1987). *Regions: The Economics and Politics of Territory.* Totowa, NJ: Rowman and Littlefield.

Markusen, A. R. and Carlson, V. (1989). Deindustrialization in the American Midwest: causes and responses. In *Deindustrialization and Regional Economic Transformation: The Experience of the United States* (L. Rodwin and H. Sazanami eds.) pp. 29–59. Boston, MA: Unwin Hyman.

Martis, K. C. (1988). Sectionalism and the United States Congress. *Political Geography Quarterly* 7, 99–109.

Nincic, M. (1992). *Democracy and Foreign Policy: The Fallacy of Political Realism.* New York: Columbia University Press.

Norton, R. D. and Rees, J. (1979). The product cycle and the spatial decentralization of American manufacturing. *Regional Studies* 13, 141–151.

Phillips, K. (1969). *The Emerging Republican Majority.* New York: Doubleday.

Rae, N. (1989). *The Decline of Liberal Republicans from 1952 to the Present.* Oxford: Oxford University Press.

Rees, J. (1983). Regional economic decentralization processes in the United States and their policy implications. In *Contemporary Studies in Sociology,* 2 (D. A. Hicks and N. Glickman eds.) pp. 241–278. Greenwich, CT: JAI Press.

Reinhard, D. W. (1983). *The Republican Right Since 1945.* Lexington, KY: The University Press of Kentucky.

Rostow, W. W. (1977). Regional change in the fifth Kondratieff upswing. In *The Rise of the Sunbelt Cities* (D. C. Perry and A. J. Watkins eds.) pp. 83–103. Beverly Hills, CA: Sage Publications.

Sale, K. (1975). *Power Shift: The Rise of the Southern Rim and its Challenge to the Eastern Establishment.* New York: Vintage Books.

Sanders, E. (1986). The regulatory surge of the 1970s in historical perspective. In *Public Regulation: New Perspectives on Institutions and Policies* (E. E. Bailey ed.) pp. 117–150. Cambridge; MA: The MIT Press.

Schatz, A. W. (1972). The reciprocal trade agreements program and the 'farm vote': 1934–1940. *Agricultural History* 46, 498–514.

Schneider, W. (1992). The old politics and the new world order. In *Eagle in a New World: American Grand Strategy in the Post-Cold War Era* (K. Oye, R. J. Lieber and D. Rothchild eds.) pp. 35–68. New York: HarperCollins.

Stanley, H. W. and Niemi, R. G. (1990). *Vital Statistics on American Politics,* 2nd edn. Washington, DC: Congressional Quarterly Press.

Sundquist, J. L. (1983). *Dynamics of the Party System: Alignment and Realignment of Political Parties in the United States.* Washington, DC: Brookings Institution.

Terrill, T. E. (1973). *The Tariff, Politics, and American Foreign Policy: 1874–1901.* Westport, CT: Greenwood Press.

Trubowitz, P. (1992). Déjà vu all over again: regional struggles over America's foreign policy agenda. Paper presented at the American Political Science Association, Chicago, Illinois.

Trubowitz, P. and Roberts, B. E.(1992). Regional interests and the Reagan military build-up. *Regional Studies* 26, 555–567.

Varg, P. A. (1963). *Foreign Policies of the Founding Fathers.* Lansing, MI: Michigan State University Press.

Wade, L. L. and Gates, J. B. (1990). A new tariff map of the United States (House of Representatives). *Political Geography Quarterly* 9, 284–304.

Warburg, G. F. (1989). *Conflict and Consensus: The Struggle between Congress and the President over Foreign Policymaking.* New York: Harper and Row.

Weinstein, B. L. and Firestine, R. E. (1978). *Regional Growth and Decline in the United States.* New York: Praeger.

Winik, J. (1991). The quest for bipartisanship: a new beginning for a new world order. *The Washington Quarterly* 14, 115–130.

Wirls, D. (1992). *Build-up: The Politics of Defense in the Reagan Era.* Ithaca, NY: Cornell University Press.

APPENDIX

Sectional division of states

NORTHEAST: Connecticut, Delaware, Illinois, Indiana, Iowa, Maine, Maryland, Massachusetts, Michigan, Minnesota, Missouri, New Hampshire, New Jersey, New York, Ohio, Pennsylvania, Rhode Island, Vermont, Wisconsin.

SOUTH: Alabama, Arizona, Arkansas, Florida, Georgia, Kentucky, Louisiana, Mississippi, New Mexico, North Carolina, Oklahoma, South Carolina, Tennessee, Texas, Virginia, West Virginia.

WEST: California, Colorado, Idaho, Kansas, Montana, Oregon, Nebraska, Nevada, North Dakota, South Dakota, Utah, Washington, Wyoming.

PART
Six

BUREAUCRATIC POLITICS AND ORGANIZATIONAL CULTURE

During the 1970s the role of bureaucracy and organizational process was brought squarely into the study of American foreign policy. The basic insight is straightforward: foreign-policy officials sit atop huge bureaucracies, and the organizational politics and processes that produce decisions often color those decisions. The study of policy, in other words, cannot be separated from the process of creating it. A huge literature has emerged that extends and critiques the claims of this tradition.

The seminal contribution to this approach is Graham T. Allison's study of the Cuban missile crisis. Most studies of foreign policy, Allison argues, are based on rational models of decision making. Scholars attempt to understand policy in terms of the purposive actions of government; explanation involves reconstructing the rationality of the decision. Alongside this model, Allison places two additional models: bureaucratic politics and organizational process. These models highlight the bureaucratic operations within the "black box" of government. In using these models to reconstruct decision making during the Cuban missile crisis, Allison argues that the additional models help reveal decisions less explicable in terms of the rational model.

Stephen Krasner and David Welch each present an important critique of the literature of bureaucratic politics. Both critics question the argument that the president is simply a victim of the huge organizations he commands. When the issues are sufficiently important, Krasner argues, top officials can overcome the vagaries of parochial bureaucratic interests and politics. Welch argues that the

413

virtues of the bureaucratic-politics model should not obscure the larger forces that impinge on foreign policy.

James C. Thomson, Jr. provides some additional insights concerning the workings of bureaucracy as it shaped policy during the Vietnam War. Although not elaborated as a model, Thomson's article details the influence of bureaucratic culture on decision making, suggesting the importance of nonanalytical factors on policy choice.

Conceptual Models and the Cuban Missile Crisis

Graham T. Allison

The Cuban missile crisis is a seminal event. For thirteen days of October 1962 there was a higher probability that more human lives would end suddenly than ever before in history. Had the worst occurred, the death of 100 million Americans, over 100 million Russians, and millions of Europeans as well would make previous natural calamities and inhumanities appear insignificant. Given the probability of disaster—which President Kennedy estimated as "between 1 out of 3 and even"— our escape seems awesome.[1] This event symbolizes a central if only partially thinkable fact about our existence. That such consequences could follow from the choices and actions of national governments obliges students of government as well as participants in governance to think hard about these problems.

Improved understanding of this crisis depends in part on more information and more probing analyses of available evidence. To contribute to these efforts is part of the purpose of this study. But here the missile crisis serves primarily as grist for a more general investigation. This study proceeds from the premise that marked improvement in our understanding of such events depends critically on more self-consciousness about what observers bring to the analysis. What each analyst sees and judges to be important is a function not only of the evidence about what happened but also of the "conceptual lenses" through which he looks at the evidence. The principal purpose of this essay is to explore some of the fundamental assumptions and categories employed by analysts in thinking about problems of governmental behavior, especially in foreign and military affairs.

The general argument can be summarized in three propositions:

1. Analysts think about problems of foreign and military policy in terms of largely implicit conceptual models that have significant consequences for the content of their thought.[2]

Though the present product of foreign policy analysis is neither systematic nor powerful, if one carefully examines explanations produced by analysts, a number of fundamental similarities emerge. Explanations produced by particular analysts display quite regular, predictable features. This predictability suggests a substructure. These regularities reflect an analyst's assumptions about the character of puzzles, the categories in which problems should be considered, the types of evidence that

Graham T. Allison, "Conceptual Models of the Cuban Missile Crisis," *American Political Science Review,* 63, No. 3 (September 1969), 689–718. Reprinted with permission of the author and the American Political Science Association.

are relevant, and the determinants of occurrences. The first proposition is that clusters of such related assumptions constitute basic frames of reference or conceptual models in terms of which analysts both ask and answer the question: What happened? Why did the event happen? What will happen?[3] Such assumptions are central to the activities of explanation and prediction, for in attempting to explain a particular event, the analyst cannot simply describe the full state of the world leading up to that event. The logic of explanation requires that he single out the relevant, important determinants of the occurrence.[4] Moreover, as the logic of prediction underscores, the analyst must summarize the various determinants as they bear on the event in question. Conceptual models both fix the mesh of the nets that the analyst drags through the material in order to explain a particular action or decision and direct him to cast his net in select ponds, at certain depths, in order to catch the fish he is after.

   2. Most analysts explain (and predict) the behavior of national governments in terms of various forms of one basic conceptual model, here entitled the rational policy model (model I).[5]

In terms of this conceptual model, analysts attempt to understand happenings as the more or less purposive acts of unified national governments. For these analysts the point of an explanation is to show how the nation or government could have chosen the action in question, given the strategic problem that it faced. For example in confronting the problem posed by the Soviet installation of missiles in Cuba, rational-policy-model analysts attempt to show how this was a reasonable act from the point of view of the Soviet Union, given Soviet strategic objectives.

   3. Two "alternative" conceptual models, here labeled an organizational-process model (model II) and a bureaucratic-politics model (model III) provide a base for improved explanation and prediction.

Although the standard frame of reference has proved useful for many purposes, there is powerful evidence that it must be supplemented, if not supplanted, by frames of reference which focus upon the large organizations and political actors involved in the policy process. Model I's implication that important events have important causes, i.e., that monoliths perform large actions for big reasons, must be balanced by an appreciation of the facts (a) that monoliths are black boxes covering various gears and levers in a highly differentiated decision-making structure, and (b) that large acts are the consequences of innumerable and often conflicting smaller actions by individuals at various levels of bureaucratic organizations in the service of a variety of only partially compatible conceptions of national goals, organizational goals, and political objectives. Recent developments in the field of organization theory provide the foundation for the second model. According to this organizational-process model, what model I categorizes as "acts" and "choices" are instead *outputs* of large organizations functioning according to certain regular patterns of behavior. Faced with the problem of Soviet missiles in Cuba, a model II analyst identifies the relevant organizations and displays the patterns of organizational behavior from which this action emerged. The third model focuses on the internal politics of a government. Happenings in foreign affairs are understood, according to the bureaucratic-politics model, neither as choices nor as outputs. Instead, what happens is categorized as *outcomes* of various overlapping bargaining games among players arranged hierarchically in the national government. In confronting the problem posed by Soviet missiles in Cuba, a model III analyst displays the perceptions, motivations, positions, power, and maneuvers of principal players from which the outcome emerged.[6]

A central metaphor illuminates differences among these models. Foreign policy has often been compared to moves, sequences of moves, and games of chess. If one were limited to observations on a screen upon which moves in the chess game were projected without information as to how the pieces came to be moved, he would assume—as model I does—that an individual chess player was moving the pieces with reference to plans and maneuvers toward the goal of winning the game. But a pattern of moves can be imagined that would lead the serious observer, after watching several games, to consider the hypothesis that the chess player was not a single individual but rather a loose alliance of semi-independent organizations, each of which moved its set of pieces according to standard operating procedures. For example, movement of separate sets of pieces might proceed in turn, each according to a routine, the king's rook, bishop, and their pawns repeatedly attacking the opponent according to a fixed plan. Furthermore, it is conceivable that the pattern of play would suggest to an observer that a number of distinct players, with distinct objectives but shared power over the pieces, were determining the moves as the resultant of collegial bargaining. For example, the black rook's move might contribute to the loss of a black knight with no comparable gain for the black team, but with the black rook becoming the principal guardian of the "palace" on that side of the board.

The space available does not permit full development and support of such a general argument.[7] Rather, the sections that follow simply sketch each conceptual model, articulate it as an analytic paradigm, and apply it to produce an explanation. But each model is applied to the same event: the U.S. blockade of Cuba during the missile crisis. These "alternative explanations" of the same happening illustrate differences among the models—*at work*.[8] A crisis decision by a small group of men in the context of ultimate threat, this is a case of the rational policy model par excellence. The dimensions and factors that models II and III uncover in this case are therefore particularly suggestive. The concluding section of this paper suggests how the three models may be related and how they can be extended to generate predictions.

MODEL I: RATIONAL POLICY

Rational-Policy Model Illustrated

Where is the pinch of the puzzle raised by the *New York Times* over Soviet deployment of an antiballistic missile system?[9] The question, as the *Times* states it, concerns the Soviet Union's objective in allocating such large sums of money for this weapon system while at the same time seeming to pursue a policy of increasing détente. In former President Johnson's words, "the paradox is that this [Soviet deployment of an antiballistic missile system] should be happening at a time when there is abundant evidence that our mutual antagonism is beginning to ease."[10] This question troubles people primarily because Soviet antiballistic missile deployment, and evidence of Soviet actions towards détente, when juxtaposed in our implicit model, produce a question. With reference to what objective could the Soviet government have rationally chosen the simultaneous pursuit of these two courses of actions? This question arises only when the analyst attempts to structure events as purposive choices of consistent actors.

How do analysts attempt to explain the Soviet emplacement of missiles in Cuba? The most widely cited explanation of this occurrence has been produced by two RAND sovietologists, Arnold Horelick and Myron Rush.[11] They conclude that "the introduction of strategic missiles into Cuba was motivated chiefly by the Soviet leaders' desire to overcome . . . the existing large margin of U.S. strategic superiority."[12] How do they reach this conclusion? In Sherlock Holmes' style, they seize several salient characteristics of this action and use these features as criteria against which to test alternative hypotheses about Soviet objectives. For example, the size of the Soviet deployment and the simultaneous emplacement of more expensive, more visible intermediate-range missiles as well as medium-range missiles, it is argued, exclude an explanation of the action in terms of Cuban defense— since that objective could have been secured with a much smaller number of medium-range missiles alone. Their explanation presents an argument for one objective that permits interpretation of the details of Soviet behavior as a value-maximizing choice.

How do analysts account for the coming of the First World War? According to Hans Morgenthau, "the first World War had its origin exclusively in the fear of a disturbance of the European balance of power.[13] In the period preceding World War I, the Triple Alliance precariously balanced the Triple Entente. If either power combination could gain a decisive advantage in the Balkans, it would achieve a decisive advantage in the balance of power. "It was this fear," Morgenthau asserts, "that motivated Austria in July 1914 to settle its accounts with Serbia once and for all, and that induced Germany to support Austria unconditionally. It was the same fear that brought Russia to the support of Serbia, and France to the support of Russia."[14] How is Morgenthau able to resolve this problem so confidently? By imposing on the data a "rational outline."[15] The value of this method, according to Morgenthau, is that "it provides for rational discipline in action and creates astounding continuity in foreign policy which makes American, British, or Russian foreign policy appear as an intelligent, rational continuum . . . regardless of the different motives, preferences, and intellectual and moral qualities of successive statesmen."[16]

Stanley Hoffmann's essay "Restraints and Choices in American Foreign Policy" concentrates, characteristically, on "deep forces": the international system, ideology, and national character—which constitute restraints, limits, and blinders.[17] Only secondarily does he consider decisions. But when explaining particular occurrences, though emphasizing relevant constraints, he focuses on the choices of nations. American behavior in Southeast Asia is explained as a reasonable choice of "downgrading this particular alliance (SEATO) in favor of direct U.S. involvement," given the constraint: "one is bound by one's commitments; one is committed by one's mistakes."[18] More frequently Hoffmann uncovers confusion or contradiction in the nation's choice. For example, U.S. policy towards underdeveloped countries is explained as "schizophrenic."[19] The method employed by Hoffman in producing these explanations as rational (or irrational) decisions, he terms "imaginative reconstruction."[20]

Deterrence is the cardinal problem of the contemporary strategic literature. Thomas Schelling's *Strategy of Conflict* formulates a number of propositions focused upon the dynamics of deterrence in the nuclear age. One of the major propositions concerns the stability of the balance of terror: in a situation of mutual deterrence the probability of nuclear war is reduced not by the "balance" (the sheer equality of the situation) but rather by the *stability* of the balance, i.e., the fact that neither opponent in striking first can destroy the other's ability to strike back.[21] How does Schelling support this proposition? Confidence in the contention stems not from an inductive canvass of a large number of previous cases, but rather from two calculations. In a situation of "balance" but vulnerability, there are values for which a rational opponent could choose to strike first, e.g., to destroy enemy capabilities to retaliate. In a "stable balance," where no matter who strikes first, each has an assured capability to retaliate with unacceptable damage, no rational agent could choose such a course of action (since that choice is effectively equivalent to choosing mutual homicide). Whereas most contemporary strategic thinking is driven *implicitly* by the motor upon which this calculation depends, Schelling explicitly recognizes that strategic theory does assume a model. The foundation of a theory of strategy is, he asserts: "the assumption of rational behavior—not just of intelligent behavior, but of behavior motivated by conscious calculation of advantages, calculation that in turn is based on an explicit and internally consistent value system."[22]

What is striking about these examples from the literature of foreign policy and international relations are the similarities among analysts of various styles when they are called upon to produce explanations. Each assumes that what must be explained is an action, i.e., the realization of some purpose or intention. Each assumes that the actor is the national government. Each assumes that the action is chosen as a calculated response to a strategic problem. For each, explanation consists of showing what goal the government was pursuing in committing the act and how this action was a reasonable choice, given the nation's objectives. This set of assumptions characterizes the rational-policy model. The assertion that model I is the standard frame of reference implies no denial of highly visible differences among the interests of sovietologists, diplomatic historians, international relations theorists, and strategists. Indeed, in most respects differences among the work of Hans Morgenthau, Stanley Hoffmann, and Thomas Schelling could not be more pointed. Appreciation of the extent to which each relies predominantly on model I, however, reveals basic similarities among Morgenthau's method of "rational reenactment," Hoffmann's "imaginative reconstruction," and Schelling's "vicarious problem solving;" family resemblances among Morgenthau's "rational statesman," Hoffmann's "roulette player," and Schelling's "game theorist."[23]

Most contemporary analysts (as well as laymen) proceed predominantly—albeit most often implicitly—in terms of this model when attempting to explain happenings in foreign affairs. Indeed, that occurrences in foreign affairs are the *acts of nations* seems so fundamental to thinking about such problems that this underlying model has rarely been recognized: to explain an occurrence in foreign policy simply means to show how the government could have rationally chosen that action.[24] These brief examples illustrate five uses of the model. To prove that most analysts think largely in terms of the rational policy model is not possible. In this limited space it is not even possible to illustrate the range of employment of the framework. Rather my purpose is to convey to the reader a grasp of the model and a challenge: let the reader examine the literature with which he is most familiar and make his judgment.

The general characterization can be sharpened by articulating the rational-policy model as an "analytic paradigm" in the technical sense developed by Robert K. Merton for sociological analyses.[25] Systematic statement of basic assumptions, concepts, and propositions employed by model I analysts highlights the distinctive thrust of this style of analysis. To articulate a largely implicit framework is of necessity to caricature. But caricature can be instructive.

Rational Policy Paradigm

I. Basic Unit of Analysis: Policy as National Choice

Happenings in foreign affairs are conceived as actions chosen by the nation or national government.[26] Governments select the action that will maximize strategic goals and objectives. These "solutions" to strategic problems are the fundamental categories in terms of which the analyst perceives what is to be explained.

II. Organizing Concepts

A. National Actor   The nation or government, conceived as a rational unitary decision maker, is the agent. This actor has one set of specified goals (the equivalent of a consistent utility function), one set of perceived options, and a single estimate of the consequences that follow from each alternative.

B. The Problem   Action is chosen in response to the strategic problem which the nation faces. Threats and opportunities arising in the "international strategic marketplace" move the nation to act.

C. Static Selection   The sum of activity of representatives of the government relevant to a problem constitutes what the nation has chosen as its "solution." Thus the action is conceived as a steady-state choice among alternative outcomes (rather than, for example, a large number of partial choices in a dynamic stream).

D. Action as Rational Choice   The components include:

1. Goals and Objectives   National security and national interests are the principal categories in which strategic goals are conceived. Nations seek security and a range of further objectives. (Analysts rarely translate strategic goals and objectives into an explicit utility function; nevertheless, analysts do focus on major goals and objectives and trade off side effects in an intuitive fashion.)

2. Options   Various courses of action relevant to a strategic problem provide the spectrum of options.

3. Consequences   Enactment of each alternative course of action will produce a series of consequences. The relevant consequences constitute benefits and costs in terms of strategic goals and objectives.

4. Choice   Rational choice is value-maximizing. The rational agent selects the alternative whose consequences rank highest in terms of his goals and objectives.

III. Dominant Inference Pattern

This paradigm leads analysts to rely on the following pattern of inference: if a nation performed a particular action, that nation must have had ends towards which the action constituted an optimal means. The rational policy model's explanatory power stems from this inference pattern. Puzzlement is relieved by revealing the purposive pattern within which the occurrence can be located as a value-maximizing means.

IV. General Propositions

The disgrace of political science is the infrequency with which propositions of any generality are formulated and tested. "Paradigmatic analysis" argues for explicitness about the terms in which analysis proceeds and seriousness about the logic of explanation. Simply to illustrate the kind of propositions on which analysts who employ this model rely, the formulation includes several.

The basic assumption of value-maximizing behavior produces propositions central to most explanations. The general principle can be formulated as follows: the likelihood of any particular action results from a combination of the nation's (1) relevant values and objectives, (2) perceived alternative courses of action, (3) estimates of various sets of consequences (which will follow from each alternative), and (4) net valuation of each set of consequences. This yields two propositions.

A. An increase in the cost of an alternative, i.e., a reduction in the value of the set of consequences which will follow from that action, or a reduction in the probability of attaining fixed consequences, reduces the likelihood of that alternative being chosen.

B. A decrease in the costs of an alternative, i.e., an increase in the value of the set of consequences which will follow from that alternative, or an increase in the probability of attaining fixed consequences, increases the likelihood of that action being chosen.[27]

V. Specific Propositions

A. Deterrence   The likelihood of any particular attack results from the factors specified in the general proposition. Combined with factual assertions, this general proposition yields the propositions of the subtheory of deterrence.

1. A stable nuclear balance reduces the likelihood of nuclear attack. This proposition is derived from the general proposition plus the asserted fact that a second-strike capability affects the potential attacker's calculations by increasing the likelihood and the costs of one particular set of consequences which might follow from attack—namely, retaliation.
2. A stable nuclear balance increases the probability of limited war. This proposition is derived from the general proposition plus the asserted fact that though increasing the costs of a nuclear exchange, a stable nuclear balance nevertheless produces a more significant reduction in the probability that such consequences would be chosen in response to a limited war. Thus this set of consequences weighs less heavily in the calculus.

B. Soviet Force Posture   The Soviet Union chooses its force posture (i.e., its weapons and their deployment) as a value-maximizing means of implementing Soviet strategic objectives and military doctrine. A proposition of this sort underlies Secretary of Defense Laird's inference from the fact of two hundred SS-9s (large intercontinental missiles) to the assertion that "the Soviets are going for a first-strike capability, and there's no question about it."[28]

Variants of the Rational-Policy Model

This paradigm exhibits the characteristics of the most refined version of the rational model. The modern literature of strategy employs a model of this sort. Problems and pressures in the "international strategic marketplace" yield probabilities of occurrence. The international actor, which could be any national actor, is simply a value-maximizing mechanism for getting from the strategic problem to the logical solution. But the explanations and predictions produced by most analysts of foreign affairs depend primarily on variants of this "pure" model. The point of each is the same: to place the action within a value-maximizing framework, given certain constraints. Nevertheless, it may be helpful to identify several variants, each of which might be exhibited similarly as a paradigm. The first focuses upon the national actor and his choice in a particular situation, leading analysts to further constrain the goals, alternatives, and consequences considered. Thus, (1) national propensities or personality traits reflected in an "operational code," (2) concern with certain objectives, or (3) special principles of action narrow the "goals" or "alternatives" or "consequences" of the paradigm. For example, the Soviet deployment of ABMs is sometimes explained by reference to the Soviet's "defense-mindedness." Or a particular Soviet action is explained as an instance of a special rule of action in the Bolshevik operational code.[29] A second related cluster of variants focuses on the individual leader or leadership group as the actor whose preference function is maximized and whose personal (or group) characteristics are allowed to modify the alternatives, consequences, and rules of choice. Explanations of the U.S. involvement in Vietnam as a natural consequence of the Kennedy-Johnson administration's axioms of foreign policy rely on this variant. A third more complex variant of the basic model recognizes the existence of several actors within a government, for example, hawks and doves or military and civilians, but attempts to explain (or predict) an occurrence by reference to the objectives of the victorious actor. Thus, for example, some revisionist histories of the cold war recognize the forces of light and the forces of darkness within the U.S. government but explain American actions as a result of goals and perceptions of the victorious forces of darkness.

Each of these forms of the basic paradigm constitutes a formalization of what analysts typically rely upon implicitly. In the transition from implicit conceptual model to explicit paradigm much of the richness of the best employments of this model has been lost. But the purpose in raising loose, implicit conceptual models to an explicit level is to reveal the basic logic of analysts' activity. Perhaps some of the remaining artificiality that surrounds the statement of the paradigm can be erased by noting a number of the standard additions and modifications employed by analysts who proceed *predominantly* within the rational policy model. First, in the course of a document analysts shift from one variant of the basic model to another, occasionally appropriating in an ad hoc fashion aspects of a situation which are logically incompatible with the basic model. Second, in the course of explaining a number of occurrences, analysts sometimes pause over a particular event about which they have a great deal of information and unfold it in such detail that an impression of randomness is created. Third, having employed other assumptions and categories in deriving an explanation or prediction, analysts will present their product in a neat, convincing rational policy model package. (This accommodation is a favorite of members of the intelligence community whose association with the details of a process is considerable but who feel that by putting an occurrence in a larger rational framework, it will be more comprehensible to their audience.) Fourth, in attempting to offer an explanation—particularly in cases where a prediction derived from the basic model has failed—the notion of a "mistake" is invoked. Thus, the failure in the prediction of a "missile gap" is written off as a Soviet mistake in not taking advantage of their opportunity. Both these and other modifications permit model I analysts considerably more variety than the paradigm might suggest. But such accommodations are essentially appendages to the basic logic of these analyses.

The U.S. Blockade of Cuba: A First Cut[30]

The U.S. response to the Soviet Union's emplacement of missiles in Cuba must be understood in strategic terms as simple value-maximizing escalation. American nuclear superiority could be counted on to paralyze Soviet nuclear power; Soviet transgression of the nuclear threshold in response to an American use of lower levels of violence would be wildly irrational, since it would mean virtual destruction of the Soviet Communist system and Russian nation. American local superiority was overwhelming: it could be initiated at a low level while threatening with high credibility an ascending sequence of steps short of the nuclear threshold. All that was required was for the United States to bring to bear its strategic and local superiority in such a way that American determination to see the missiles removed would be demonstrated, while at the same time allowing Moscow time and room to retreat without humiliation. The naval blockade—euphemistically named a quarantine in order to circumvent the niceties of international law—did just that.

The U.S. government's selection of the blockade followed this logic. Apprised of the presence of Soviet missiles in Cuba, the president assembled an executive committee (ExCom) of the National Security Council and directed them to "set aside all other tasks to make a prompt and intense survey of the dangers and all possible courses of action."[31] This group functioned as "fifteen individuals on our own, representing the President and not different departments."[32] As one of the participants recalls, "The remarkable aspect of those meetings was a sense of complete equality."[33] Most of the time during the week that followed was spent canvassing all the possible tracks and weighing the arguments for and against each. Six major categories of action were considered.

1. Do Nothing   U.S. vulnerability to Soviet missiles was no new thing. Since the U.S. already lived under the gun of missiles based in Russia, a Soviet capability to strike from Cuba too made little real difference. The real danger stemmed from the possibility of U.S. overreaction. The U.S. should announce the Soviet action in a calm, casual manner, thereby deflating whatever political capital Khrushchev hoped to make of the missiles.

This argument fails on two counts. First, it grossly underestimates the military importance of the Soviet move. Not only would the Soviet Union's missile capability be doubled and the U.S. early warning system outflanked, the Soviet Union would have an opportunity to reverse the strategic balance by further installations, and indeed, in the longer run, to invest in cheaper, shorter-range rather than more expensive longer-range missiles. Second, the political importance of this move was undeniable. The Soviet Union's act challenged the American president's most solemn warning. If the U.S. failed to respond, no American commitment would be credible.

2. Diplomatic Pressures   Several forms were considered: an appeal to the U.N. or OAS for an inspection team, a secret approach to Khrushchev, and a direct approach to Khrushchev, perhaps at a summit meeting. The United States would demand that the missiles be removed, but the final settlement might include neutralization of Cuba, U.S. withdrawal from the Guantanamo base, and withdrawal of U.S. Jupiter missiles from Turkey or Italy.

Each form of the diplomatic approach had its own drawbacks. To arraign the Soviet Union before the U.N. Security Council held little promise, since the Russians could veto any proposed action. While the diplomats argued, the missiles would become operational. To send a secret emissary to Khrushchev demanding that the missiles be withdrawn would be to pose untenable alternatives. On the one hand, this would invite Khrushchev to seize the diplomatic initiative, perhaps committing himself to strategic retaliation in response to an attack on Cuba. On the other hand, this would tender an ultimatum that no great power could accept. To confront Khrushchev at a summit would guarantee demands for U.S. concessions, and the analogy between U.S. missiles in Turkey and Russian missiles in Cuba could not be erased.

But why not trade U.S. Jupiters in Turkey and Italy, which the president had previously ordered withdrawn, for the missiles in Cuba? The U.S. had chosen to withdraw these missiles in order to replace them with superior, less vulnerable

Mediterranean Polaris submarines. But the middle of the crisis was no time for concessions. The offer of such a deal might suggest to the Soviets that the West would yield and thus tempt them to demand more. It would certainly confirm European suspicions about American willingness to sacrifice European interests when the chips were down. Finally, the basic issue should be kept clear. As the president stated in reply to Bertrand Russell, "I think your attention might well be directed to the burglars rather than to those who have caught the burglars."[34]

3. A Secret Approach to Castro   The crisis provided an opportunity to separate Cuba and Soviet Communism by offering Castro the alternatives, "split or fall." But Soviet troops transported, constructed, guarded, and controlled the missiles. Their removal would thus depend on a Soviet decision.

4. Invasion   The United States could take this occasion not only to remove the missiles but also to rid itself of Castro. A navy exercise had long been scheduled in which Marines, ferried from Florida in naval vessels, would liberate the imaginary island of Vieques.[35] Why not simply shift the point of disembarkment? (The Pentagon's foresight in planning this operation would be an appropriate antidote to the CIA's Bay of Pigs!)

Preparations were made for an invasion, but as a last resort. American troops would be forced to confront twenty thousand Soviets in the first cold war case of direct contact between the troops of the super powers. Such brinksmanship courted nuclear disaster, practically guaranteeing an equivalent Soviet move against Berlin.

5. Surgical Air Strike   The missile sites should be removed by a clean, swift conventional attack. This was the effective counteraction which the attempted deception deserved. A surgical strike would remove the missiles and thus eliminate both the danger that the missiles might become operational and the fear that the Soviets would discover the American discovery and act first.

The initial attractiveness of this alternative was dulled by several difficulties. First, could the strike really be "surgical"? The air force could not guarantee destruction of all the missiles.[36] Some might be fired during the attack; some might not have been identified. In order to assure destruction of Soviet and Cuban means of retaliating, what was required was not a surgical but rather a massive attack—of at least five hundred sorties. Second, a surprise air attack would of course kill Russians at the missile sites. Pressures on the Soviet Union to retaliate would be so strong that an attack on Berlin or Turkey was highly probable. Third, the key problem with this program was that of advance warning. Could the President of the United States, with his memory of Pearl Harbor and his vision of future U.S. responsibility, order a "Pearl Harbor in reverse"? For 175 years unannounced Sunday morning attacks had been an anathema to our tradition.[37]

6. Blockade   Indirect military action in the form of a blockade became more attractive as the ExCom dissected the other alternatives. An embargo on military shipments to Cuba enforced by a naval blockade was not without flaws, however. Could the U.S. blockade Cuba without inviting Soviet reprisal in Berlin? The likely solution to joint blockades would be the lifting of both blockades, restoring the new status quo, and allowing the Soviets additional time to complete the missiles. Second, the possible consequences of the blockade resembled the drawbacks which disqualified the air strike. If Soviet ships did not stop, the United States would be forced to fire the first shot, inviting retaliation. Third, a blockade would deny the traditional freedom of the seas demanded by several of our close allies and might be held illegal, in violation of the U.N. charter and international law, unless the United States could obtain a two-thirds vote in the OAS. Finally, how could a blockade be related to the problem, namely, some seventy-five missiles on the island of Cuba, approaching operational readiness daily? A blockade offered the Soviets a spectrum of delaying tactics with which to buy time to complete the missile installations. Was a fait accompli not required?

In spite of these enormous difficulties the blockade had comparative advantages: (1) It was a middle course between inaction and attack, aggressive enough to communicate firmness of intention but nevertheless not so precipitous as a strike. (2) It placed on Khrushchev the burden of choice concerning the next step. He could avoid a direct military clash by keeping his ships away. His was the last clear chance. (3) No possible military confrontation could be more acceptable to the U.S. than a naval engagement in the Caribbean. (4) This move permitted the U.S., by flexing its conventional muscle, to exploit the threat of subsequent nonnuclear steps in each of which the U.S. would have significant superiority.

Particular arguments about advantages and disadvantages were powerful. The explanation of the American choice of the blockade lies in a more general principle, however. As President Kennedy stated in drawing the moral of the crisis:

> Above all, while defending our own vital interests, nuclear powers must avert those confrontations which bring an adversary to a choice of either a humiliating retreat or a nuclear war. To adopt that kind of course in the nuclear age would be evidence only of the bankruptcy of our policy—of a collective death wish for the world.[38]

The blockade was the United States' only real option.

MODEL II: ORGANIZATIONAL PROCESS

For some purposes governmental behavior can be usefully summarized as action chosen by a unitary rational decision maker: centrally controlled, completely informed, and value-maximizing. But this simplification must not be allowed to conceal the fact that a "government" consists of a conglomerate of semifeudal loosely allied organizations, each with a substantial life of its own. Government leaders do sit formally and to some extent in fact on top of this conglomerate. But governments perceive problems through organizational sensors. Governments define alternatives and estimate consequences as organizations process information. Governments act as these organizations enact routines. Government behavior can therefore be understood according to a second conceptual model, less as deliberate choices of leaders and more as *outputs* of large organizations functioning according to standard patterns of behavior.

To be responsive to a broad spectrum of problems, governments consist of large organizations among which primary responsibility for particular areas is divided. Each organization attends to a special set of problems and acts in quasi independence on these problems. But few important problems fall exclusively within the domain of a single organization. Thus government behavior relevant to any important problem reflects the independent output of several organizations, partially coordinated by government leaders. Government leaders can substantially disturb but not substantially control the behavior of these organizations.

To perform complex routines the behavior of large numbers of individuals must be coordinated. Coordination requires standard operating procedures: rules according to which things are done. Assured capability for reliable performance of action that depends upon the behavior of hundreds of persons requires established "programs." Indeed, if the eleven members of a football team are to perform adequately on any particular down, each player must not "do what he thinks needs to be done" or "do what the quarterback tells him to do." Rather each player must perform the maneuvers specified by a previously established play which the quarterback has simply called in this situation.

At any given time a government consists of *existing* organizations, each with a *fixed* set of standard operating procedures and programs. The behavior of these organizations—and consequently of the government—relevant to an issue in any particular instance is therefore determined primarily by routines established in these organizations prior to that instance. But organizations do change. Learning occurs gradually, over time. Dramatic organizational change occurs in response to major crises. Both learning and change are influenced by existing organizational capabilities.

Borrowed from studies of organizations, these loosely formulated propositions amount simply to *tendencies*. Each must be hedged by modifiers like "other things being equal" and "under certain conditions." In particular instances tendencies hold—more or less. In specific situations the relevant question is: more or less? But this is as it should be. For on the one hand, "organizations" are no more homogeneous a class than "solids." When scientists tried to generalize about "solids," they achieved similar results. Solids tend to expand when heated, but some do and some don't. More adequate categorization of the various elements now lumped under the rubric *organizations* is thus required. On the other hand, the behavior of particular organizations seems considerably more complex than the behavior of solids. Additional information about a particular organization is required for further specification of the tendency statements. In spite of these two caveats, the characterization of government action as organizational output differs distinctly from model I. Attempts to understand problems of foreign affairs in terms of this frame of reference should produce quite different explanations.[39]

Organizational Process Paradigm[40]

I. Basic Unit of Analysis: Policy as Organizational Output

The happenings of international politics are in three critical senses outputs of organizational processes. First, the actual occurrences are organizational outputs. For example, Chinese entry into the Korean War—that is, the fact that Chinese soldiers were firing at U.N. soldiers south of the Yalu in 1950—is an organizational action: the action of men who are soldiers in platoons which are in companies, which in turn are in armies, responding as privates to lieutenants who are responsible to captains and so on to the commander, moving into Korea, advancing against enemy troops, and firing according to fixed routines of the Chinese army. Government leaders' decisions trigger organizational routines. Government leaders can trim the edges of this output and exercise some choice in combining outputs. But the mass of behavior is determined by previously established procedures. Second, existing organizational routines for employing present physical capabilities constitute the effective options open to government leaders confronted with any problem. Only the existence of men, equipped and trained as armies and capable of being transported to North Korea, made entry into the Korean War a live option for the Chinese leaders. The fact that fixed programs (equipment, men, and routines which exist at the particular time) exhaust the range of buttons that leaders can push is not always perceived by these leaders. But in every case it is critical for an understanding of what is actually done. Third, organizational outputs structure the situation within the narrow constraints of which leaders must contribute their "decision" concerning an issue. Outputs raise the problem, provide the information, and make the initial moves that color the face of the issue that is turned to the leaders. As Theodore Sorensen has observed: "Presidents rarely, if ever, make decisions—particularly in foreign affairs—in the sense of writing their conclusions on a clean slate . . . The basic decisions, which confine their choices, have all too often been previously made."[41] If one understands the structure of the situation and the face of the issue—which are determined by the organizational outputs—the formal choice of the leaders is frequently anticlimactic.

II. Organizing Concepts
A. Organizational Actors   The actor is not a monolithic nation or government but rather a constellation of loosely allied organizations on top of which government leaders sit. This constellation acts only as component organizations perform routines.[42]

B. Factored Problems and Fractionated Power   Surveillance of the multiple facets of foreign affairs requires that problems be cut up and parceled out to various organizations. To avoid paralysis, primary power must accompany primary responsibility. But if organizations are permitted to do anything, a large part of what they do will be determined within the organization. Thus each organization perceives problems, processes information, and performs a range of actions in quasi independence (within broad guidelines of national policy). Factored problems and fractionated power are two edges of the same sword. Factoring permits more specialized attention to particular facets of problems than would be possible if government leaders tried to cope with these problems by themselves. But this additional attention must be paid for in the coin of discretion for *what* an organization attends to and *how* organizational responses are programmed.

C. Parochial Priorities, Perceptions, and Issues   Primary responsibility for a narrow set of problems encourages organizational parochialism. These tendencies are enhanced by a number of additional factors: (1) selective information available to the organization, (2) recruitment of personnel into the organization, (3) tenure of individuals in the organization, (4) small group pressures within the organization, and (5) distribution of rewards by the organization. Clients (e.g., interest groups), government allies (e.g., congressional committees), and extranational counterparts (e.g., the British Ministry of Defense for the Department of Defense, ISA, or the British Foreign Office for the Department of State, EUR) galvanize this parochialism. Thus organizations develop relatively stable propensities concerning operational priorities, perceptions, and issues.

D. Action as Organizational Output   The preeminent feature of organizational activity is its programmed character: the extent to which behavior in any particular case is an enactment of preestablished routines. In producing outputs the activity of each organization is characterized by:

1. Goals: Constraints, Defining Acceptable Performance   The operational goals of an organization are seldom revealed by formal mandates. Rather each organization's operational goals emerge as a set of constraints defining acceptable performance. Central among these constraints is organizational health, defined usually in terms of bodies assigned and dollars appropriated. The set of constraints emerges from a mix of expectations and demands of other organizations in the government, statutory authority, demands from citizens and special interest groups, and bargaining within the organization. These constraints represent a quasi resolution of conflict—the constraints are relatively stable, so there is some resolution. But conflict among alternative goals is always latent; hence it is a quasi resolution. Typically the constraints are formulated as imperatives to avoid roughly specified discomforts and disasters.[43]

2. Sequential Attention to Goals   The existence of conflict among operational constraints is resolved by the device of sequential attention. As a problem arises, the subunits of the organization most concerned with that problem deal with it in terms of the constraints they take to be most important. When the next problem arises, another cluster of subunits deals with it, focusing on a different set of constraints.

3. Standard Operating Procedures   Organizations perform their "higher" functions, such as attending to problem areas, monitoring information, and preparing relevant responses for likely contingencies, by doing "lower" tasks, for example, preparing budgets, producing reports, and developing hardware. Reliable performance of these tasks requires standard operating procedures (hereafter SOPs). Since procedures are "standard," they do not change quickly or easily. Without these standard procedures, it would not be possible to perform certain concerted tasks. But because of standard procedures, organizational behavior in particular instances often appears unduly formalized, sluggish, or inappropriate.

4. Programs and Repertoires   Organizations must be capable of performing actions in which the behavior of large numbers of individuals is carefully coordinated. Assured performance requires clusters of rehearsed SOPs for producing specific actions, e.g., fighting enemy units or answering an embassy's cable. Each cluster comprises a "program" (in the terms both of drama and computers) which the organization has available for dealing with a situation. The list of programs relevant to a type of activity, e.g., fighting, constitutes an organizational repertoire. The number of programs in a repertoire is always quite limited. When properly triggered, organizations execute programs; programs cannot be substantially changed in a particular situation. The more complex the action and the greater the number of individuals involved, the more important are programs and repertoires as determinants of organizational behavior.

5. Uncertainty Avoidance   Organizations do not attempt to estimate the probability distribution of future occurrences. Rather, organizations avoid uncertainty. By arranging a *negotiated environment,* organizations regularize the reactions of other actors with whom they have to deal. The primary environment, relations with other organizations that comprise the government, is stabilized by such arrangements as agreed budgetary splits, accepted areas of responsibility, and established conventional practices. The secondary environment, relations with the international world, is stabilized between allies by the establishment of contracts (alliances) and "club relations" (U.S. State and U.K. Foreign Office or U.S. Treasury and U.K. Treasury). Between enemies contracts and accepted conventional practices perform a similar function, for example the rules of the "precarious status quo" which President Kennedy referred to in the missile crisis. Where the international environment cannot be negotiated, organizations deal with remaining uncertainties by establishing a set of *standard scenarios* that constitute the contingencies for which they prepare. For example, the standard scenario for Tactical Air Command of the U.S. air force involves combat with enemy aircraft. Planes are designed and pilots trained to meet this problem. That these preparations are less relevant to more probable contingencies, e.g., provision of close-in ground support in limited wars like Vietnam, has had little impact on the scenario.

6. Problem-Directed Search   Where situations cannot be construed as standard, organizations engage in search. The style of search and the solution are largely determined by existing routines. Organizational search for alternative courses of action is problem-oriented: it focuses on the atypical discomfort that must be avoided. It is simple-minded: the neighborhood of the symptom is searched first; then the neighborhood of the current alternative. Patterns of search reveal biases which in turn reflect such factors as specialized training or experience and patterns of communication.

7. Organizational Learning and Change   The parameters of organizational behavior mostly persist. In response to nonstandard problems organizations search and routines evolve, assimilating new situations. Thus learning and change follow in large part from existing procedures. But marked changes in organizations do sometimes occur. Conditions in which dramatic changes are more likely include: (1) Periods of budgetary feast. Typically, organizations devour budgetary feasts by purchasing additional items on the existing shopping list. Nevertheless, if committed to change, leaders who control the budget can use extra funds to effect changes. (2) Periods of prolonged budgetary famine. Though a single year's famine typically results in few changes in organizational structure but a loss of effectiveness in performing some programs, prolonged famine forces major retrenchment. (3) Dramatic performance failures. Dramatic change occurs (mostly) in response to major disasters. Confronted with an undeniable failure of procedures and repertoires, authorities outside the organization demand change, existing personnel are less resistant to change, and critical members of the organization are replaced by individuals committed to change.

E. Central Coordination and Control   Action requires decentralization of responsibility and power. But problems lap over the jurisdictions of several organizations. Thus the necessity for decentralization runs headlong into the requirement for coordination. (Advocates of one horn or the other of this dilemma—responsive action entails decentralized power vs. coordinated action requires central control—account for a considerable part of the persistent demand for government reorganization.) Both the necessity for coordination and the centrality of foreign policy to national welfare guarantee the involvement of government leaders in the procedures of the organizations among which problems are divided and power shared. Each organization's propensities and routines can be disturbed by government leaders' intervention. Central direction and persistent control of organizational activity, however, is not possible. The relation among organizations and between organizations and the government leaders depends critically on a number of structural variables, including: (1) the nature of the job, (2) the measures and information available to government leaders, (3) the system of rewards and punishments for organizational members, and (4) the procedures by which human and material resources get committed. For example, to the extent that rewards and punishments for the members of an organization are distributed by higher authorities, these authorities can exercise some control by specifying criteria in terms of which organizational output is to be evaluated. These criteria become constraints within which organizational activity proceeds. But constraint is a crude instrument of control.

Intervention by government leaders does sometimes change the activity of an organization in an intended direction. But instances are fewer than might be expected. As Franklin Roosevelt, the master manipulator of government organizations, remarked:

> The Treasury is so large and far-flung and ingrained in its practices that I find it is almost impossible to get the action and results I want. . . . But the Treasury is not to be compared with the State Department. You should go through the experience of trying to get any changes in the thinking, policy, and action of the career diplomats and then you'd know what a real problem was. But the Treasury and the State Department put together are nothing compared with the na-a-vy . . . To change anything in the na-a-vy is like punching a feather bed. You punch it with your right and you punch it with your left until you are finally exhausted, and then you find the damn bed just as it was before you started punching.[44]

John Kennedy's experience seems to have been similar: "The State Department," he asserted, "is a bowl full of jelly."[45] And lest the McNamara revolution in the Defense Department seem too striking a counterexample, the navy's recent rejection of McNamara's major intervention in naval weapons procurement, the F-111B, should be studied as an antidote.

F. Decisions of Government Leaders   Organizational persistence does not exclude shifts in governmental behavior. For government leaders sit atop the conglomerate of organizations. Many important issues of governmental action require that these leaders decide what organizations will play out which programs where. Thus stability in the parochialisms and SOPs of individual organizations is consistent with some important shifts in the behavior of governments. The range of these shifts is defined by existing organizational programs.

III. Dominant Inference Pattern

If a nation performs an action of this type today, its organizational components must yesterday have been performing (or have had established routines for performing) an action only marginally different from this action. At any specific point in time, a government consists of an established conglomerate of organizations, each with existing goals, programs, and repertoires. The characteristics of a government's action in any instance follows from those established routines and from the choice of government leaders—on the basis of information and estimates provided by existing routines—among existing programs. The best explanation of an organization's behavior at t is $t - 1$; the prediction of $t + 1$ is t. Model II's explanatory power is achieved by uncovering the organizational routines and repertoires that produced the outputs that comprise the puzzling occurrence.

IV. General Propositions

A number of general propositions have been stated above. In order to illustrate clearly the type of proposition employed by model II analysts, this section formulates several more precisely.

A. Organizational Action   Activity according to SOPs and programs does not constitute far-sighted, flexible adaptation to "the issue" (as it is conceived by the analyst). Detail and nuance of actions by organizations are determined predominantly by organizational routines, not government leaders' directions.

1. SOPs constitute routines for dealing with *standard* situations. Routines allow large numbers of ordinary individuals to deal with numerous instances, day after day, without considerable thought, by responding to basic stimuli. But this regularized capability for adequate performance is purchased at the price of standardization. If the SOPs are appropriate, average performance, i.e., performance averaged over the range of cases, is better than it would be if each instance were approached individually (given fixed talent, timing, and resource constraints). But specific instances, particularly critical instances that typically do not have "standard" characteristics, are often handled sluggishly or inappropriately.

2. A program, i.e., a complex action chosen from a short list of programs in a repertoire, is rarely tailored to the specific situation in which it is executed. Rather, the program is (at best) the most appropriate of the programs in a previously developed repertoire.

3. Since repertoires are developed by parochial organizations for standard scenarios defined by that organization, programs available for dealing with a particular situation are often ill-suited.

B. Limited Flexibility and Incremental Change   Major lines of organizational action are straight, i.e., behavior at one time is marginally different from that behavior at $t - 1$. Simple-minded predictions work best: Behavior at $t + 1$ will be marginally different from behavior at the present time.

1. Organizational budgets change incrementally—both with respect to totals and with respect to intraorganizational splits. Though organizations could divide the money available each year by carving up the pie anew (in the light of changes in objectives or environment), in practice, organizations take last year's budget as a base and adjust incrementally. Predictions that require large budgetary shifts in a single year between organizations or between units within an organization should be hedged.
2. Once undertaken, an organizational investment is not dropped at the point where "objective" costs outweigh benefits. Organizational stakes in adopted projects carry them quite beyond the loss point.

C. Administrative Feasibility   Adequate explanation, analysis, and prediction must include administrative feasibility as a major dimension. A considerable gap separates what leaders choose (or might rationally have chosen) and what organizations implement.

1. Organizations are blunt instruments. Projects that require several organizations to act with high degrees of precision and coordination are not likely to succeed.
2. Projects that demand that existing organization units depart from their accustomed functions and perform previously unprogrammed tasks are rarely accomplished in their designed form.
3. Government leaders can expect that each organization will do its part in terms of what the organization knows how to do.
4. Government leaders can expect incomplete and distorted information from each organization concerning its part of the problem.
5. Where an assigned piece of a problem is contrary to the existing goals of an organization, resistance to implementation of that piece will be encountered.

V. Specific Propositions
A. Deterrence   The probability of nuclear attack is less sensitive to balance and imbalance or stability and instability (as these concepts are employed by model I strategists) than it is to a number of organizational factors. Except for the special case in which the Soviet Union acquires a credible capability to destroy the U.S. with a disarming blow, U.S. superiority or inferiority affects the probability of a nuclear attack less than do a number of organizational factors.

First, if a nuclear attack occurs, it will result from organizational activity: the firing of rockets by members of a missile group. The enemy's *control system,* i.e., physical mechanisms and standard procedures which determine who can launch rockets when, is critical. Second, the enemy's programs for bringing his strategic forces to *alert status* determine probabilities of accidental firing and momentum. At the outbreak of World War I, if the Russian tsar had understood the organizational processes which his order of full mobilization triggered, he would have realized that he had chosen war. Third, organizational repertoires fix the range of effective choice open to enemy leaders. The menu available to Tsar Nicholas in 1914 has two entrees: full mobilization and no mobilization. Partial mobilization was not an organizational option. Fourth, since organizational routines set the chessboard, the training and deployment of troops and nuclear weapons is crucial. Given that the outbreak of hostilities in Berlin is more probable than most scenarios for nuclear war, facts about deployment, training, and tactical nuclear equipment of Soviet troops stationed in East Germany—which will influence the face of the issue seen by Soviet leaders at the outbreak of hostilities and the manner in which choice is implemented—are as critical as the question of "balance."

B. Soviet Force Posture   Soviet force posture, i.e., the fact that certain weapons rather than others are procured and deployed, is determined by organizational factors such as the goals and procedures of existing military services and the goals and processes of research and design labs, within budgetary constraints that emerge from the government leader's choices. The frailty of the Soviet air force within the Soviet military establishment seems to have been a crucial element in the Soviet failure to acquire a large bomber force in the 1950s (thereby faulting American intelligence predictions of a "bomber gap"). The fact that missiles were controlled until 1960 in the Soviet Union by the Soviet ground forces, whose goals and procedures reflected no interest in an intercontinental mission, was not irrelevant to the slow Soviet buildup of ICBMs (thereby faulting U.S. intelligence predictions of a "missile gap"). These organizational factors (Soviet ground forces' control of missiles and that service's fixation with European scenarios) make the Soviet deployment of so many MRBMs that European targets could be destroyed three times over more understandable. Recent weapon developments, e.g., the testing of a fractional orbital bombardment system (FOBS) and multiple warheads for the SS-9, very likely reflect the activity and interests of a cluster of Soviet research and development organizations rather than a decision by Soviet leaders to acquire a first-strike weapon system. Careful attention to the organizational components of the Soviet military establishment (strategic rocket forces, navy, air force, ground forces, and national air defense), the missions and weapons systems to which each component is wedded (an independent weapon system assists survival as an independent service), and existing budgetary splits (which probably are relatively stable in the Soviet Union as they tend to be everywhere) offer potential improvements in medium- and longer-term predictions.

The U.S. Blockade of Cuba: A Second Cut

Organizational Intelligence

At 7:00 P.M. on October 22, 1962, President Kennedy disclosed the American discovery of the presence of Soviet strategic missiles in Cuba, declared a "strict quarantine on all offensive military equipment under shipment to Cuba," and demanded that "Chairman Khrushchev halt and eliminate this clandestine, reckless, and provocative threat to world peace."[46] This decision was reached at the pinnacle of the U.S. government after a critical week of deliberation. What initiated that precious week were photographs of Soviet missile sites in Cuba taken on October 14. These pictures might not have been taken until a week later. In that case, the President speculated, "I don't think probably we would have chosen as prudently as we finally did."[47] U.S. leaders might have received this information three weeks earlier—if a U-2 had flown over San Cristobal in the last week of September.[48] What determined the context in which American leaders came to choose the blockade was the discovery of missiles on October 14.

There has been considerable debate over alleged American intelligence failures in the Cuban missile crisis.[49] But what both critics and defenders have neglected is the fact that the discovery took place on October 14, rather than three weeks earlier or a week later, as a consequence of the established routines and procedures of the organizations which constitute the U.S. intelligence community. These organizations were neither more nor less successful than they had been the previous month or were to be in the months to follow.[50]

The notorious "September estimate," approved by the United States Intelligence Board (USIB) on September 19, concluded that the Soviet Union would not introduce offensive missiles into Cuba.[51] No U-2 flight was directed over the western end of Cuba (after September 5) before October 4.[52] No U-2 flew over the western end of Cuba until the flight that discovered the Soviet missiles on October 14.[53] Can these "failures" be accounted for in organizational terms?

On September 19, when USIB met to consider the question of Cuba, the "system" contained the following information: (1) shipping intelligence had noted the arrival in Cuba of two large-hatch Soviet lumber ships, which were riding high in the water; (2) refugee reports of countless sightings of missiles, but also a report that Castro's private pilot, after a night of drinking in Havana, had boasted: "We will fight to the death and perhaps we can win because we have everything, including atomic weapons"; (3) a sighting by a CIA agent of the rear profile of a strategic missile; (4) U-2 photos produced by flights of August 29, September 5, and 17 showing the construction of a number of SAM sites and other defensive missiles.[54] Not all of this information was on the desk of the estimators, however. Shipping intelligence experts noted the fact that large-hatch ships were riding high in the water and spelled out the inference: the ships must be carrying "space-consuming" cargo.[55] These facts were carefully included in the catalogue of intelligence concerning shipping. For experts sensitive to the Soviets' shortage of ships, however, these facts carried no special signal. The refugee report of Castro's private pilot's remark had been received at Opa Locka, Florida, along with vast reams of inaccurate reports generated by the refugee community. This report and a thousand others had to be checked and compared before being sent to Washington. The two weeks required for initial processing could have been shortened by a large increase in resources, but the yield of this source was already quite marginal. The CIA agent's sighting of the rear profile of a strategic missile had occurred on September 12; transmission time from agent sighting to arrival in Washington typically took nine to twelve days. Shortening this transmission time would impose severe cost in terms of danger to subagents, agents, and communication networks.

On the information available, the intelligence chiefs who predicted that the Soviet Union would not introduce offensive missiles into Cuba made a reasonable and defensible judgment.[56] Moreover, in the light of the fact that these organizations were gathering intelligence not only about Cuba but about potential occurrences in all parts of the world, the informational base available to the estimators involved nothing out of the ordinary. Nor, from an organizational perspective, is there anything startling about the gradual accumulation of evidence that led to the formulation of the hypothesis that the Soviets were installing missiles in Cuba and the decision on October 4 to direct a special flight over western Cuba.

The ten-day delay between that decision and the flight is another organizational story.[57] At the October 4 meeting the Defense Department took the opportunity to raise an issue important to its concerns. Given the increased danger that a U-2 would be downed, it would be better if the pilot were an officer in uniform rather than a CIA agent. Thus the air force should assume responsibility for U-2 flights over Cuba. To the contrary the CIA argued that this was an intelligence operation and thus within the CIA's jurisdiction. Moreover, CIA U-2s had been modified in certain ways which gave them advantages over Air Force U-2s in averting Soviet SAMs. Five days passed while the State Department pressed for less risky alternatives such as drones and the air force (in Department of Defense guise) and CIA engaged in territorial disputes. On October 9 a flight plan over San Cristobal was approved by COMOR, but to the CIA's dismay, air force pilots rather than CIA agents would take charge of the mission. At this point details become sketchy, but several members of the intelligence community have speculated that an air force pilot in an air force U-2 attempted a high-altitude overflight on October 9 that "flamed out", i.e., lost power, and thus had to descend in order to restart its engine. A second round between air force and CIA followed, as a result of which air force pilots were trained to fly CIA U-2s. A successful overflight took place on October 14.

This ten-day delay constitutes some form of "failure." In the face of well-founded suspicions concerning offensive Soviet missiles in Cuba that posed a critical threat to the United States's most vital interest, squabbling between organizations whose job it is to produce this information seems entirely inappropriate. But for each of these organizations, the question involved the issue: "*Whose* job was it to be?" Moreover, the issue was not simply which organization would control U-2 flights over Cuba, but rather the broader issue of ownership of U-2 intelligence activities—a very long-standing territorial dispute. Thus though this delay was in one sense a "failure," it was also a nearly inevitable consequence of two facts: many jobs do not fall neatly into precisely defined organizational jurisdictions; and vigorous organizations are imperialistic.

Organizational Options

Deliberations of leaders in ExCom meetings produced broad outlines of alternatives. Details of these alternatives and blueprints for their implementation had to be specified by the organizations that would perform these tasks. These organizational outputs answered the question: What, specifically, *could* be done?

Discussion in the ExCom quickly narrowed the live options to two: an air strike and a blockade. The choice of the blockade instead of the air strike turned on two points: (1) the argument from morality and tradition that the United States could not perpetrate a "Pearl Harbor in reverse"; (2) the belief that a "surgical" air strike was impossible.[58] Whether the United States *might* strike first was a question not of capability but of morality. Whether the United States *could* perform the surgical strike was a factual question concerning capabilities. The majority of the members of the ExCom, including the president, initially preferred the air strike.[59] What effectively foreclosed this option, however, was the fact that the air strike they wanted could not be chosen with high confidence of success.[60] After having tentatively chosen the course of prudence—given that the surgical air strike was not an option—Kennedy reconsidered. On Sunday morning, October 21, he called the air force experts to a special meeting in his living quarters, where he probed once more for the option of a "surgical" air strike.[61] General Walter C. Sweeny, Commander of Tactical Air Forces, asserted again that the air force could guarantee no higher than 90 percent effectiveness in a surgical air strike.[62] That "fact" was false.

The air strike alternative provides a classic case of military estimates. One of the alternatives outlined by the ExCom was named *air strike*. Specification of the details of this alternative was delegated to the air force. Starting from an existing plan for massive U.S. military action against Cuba (prepared for contingencies like a response to a Soviet Berlin grab), air force estimators produced an attack to guarantee success.[63] This plan called for extensive bombardment of all missile sites, storage depots, airports, and in deference to the navy, the artillery batteries opposite the naval base at Guantanamo.[64] Members of the ExCom repeatedly expressed bewilderment at military estimates of the number of sorties required, likely casualties, and collateral damage. But the "surgical" air strike that the political leaders had in mind was never carefully examined during the first week of the crisis. Rather this option was simply excluded on the grounds that since the Soviet MRBMs in Cuba were classified "mobile" in U.S. manuals, extensive bombing was required. During the second week of the crisis careful examination revealed that the missiles were mobile in the sense that small houses are mobile: that is, they could be moved and reassembled in six days. After the missiles were reclassified "movable" and detailed plans for surgical air strikes specified, this action was added to the list of live options for the end of the second week.

Organizational Implementation   ExCom members separated several types of blockade: offensive weapons only, all armaments, and all strategic goods including POL (petroleum, oil, and lubricants). But the *"details"* of the operation were left to the navy. Before the president announced the blockade on Monday evening, the first stage of the navy's blueprint was in motion, and a problem loomed on the horizon.[65] The navy had a detailed plan for the blockade. The president had several less precise but equally determined notions concerning what should be done, when, and how. For the navy the issue was one of effective implementation of the navy's blockade—without the meddling and interference of political leaders. For the president the problem was to pace and manage events in such a way that the Soviet leaders would have time to see, think, and blink.

A careful reading of available sources uncovers an instructive incident. On Tuesday the British ambassador, Ormsby-Gore, after having attended a briefing on the details of the blockade, suggested to the president that the plan for intercepting Soviet ships far out of reach of Cuban jets did not facilitate Khrushchev's hard decision.[66] Why not make the interception much closer to Cuba and thus give the Russian leader more time? According to the public account and the recollection of a number of individuals involved, Kennedy "agreed immediately, called McNamara, and over emotional navy protest, issued the appropriate instructions."[67] As Sorensen records, "in a sharp clash with the Navy, he made certain his will prevailed."[68] The navy's plan for the blockade was thus changed by drawing the blockade much closer to Cuba.

A serious organizational orientation makes one suspicious of this account. More careful examination of the available evidence confirms these suspicions, though alternative accounts must be somewhat speculative. According to the public chronology, a quarantine drawn close to Cuba became effective on Wednesday morning, the first Soviet ship was contacted on Thursday morning, and the first boarding of a ship occurred on Friday. According to the statement by the Department of Defense, boarding of the *Marcula* by a party from the *John R. Pierce* "took place at 7:50 A.M., E.D.T., 180 miles northeast of Nassau."[69] The *Marcula* had been trailed since about 10:30 the previous evening.[70] Simple calculations suggest that the *Pierce* must have been stationed along the navy's original arc, which extended five hundred miles out to sea from Cape Magsi, Cuba's easternmost tip.[71] The blockade line was *not* moved as the president ordered and the accounts report.

What happened is not entirely clear. One can be certain, however, that Soviet ships passed through the line along which American destroyers had posted themselves before the official "first contact" with the Soviet ship. On October 26 a Soviet tanker arrived in Havana and was honored by a dockside rally for "running the blockade." Photographs of this vessel show the name *Vinnitsa* on the side of the vessel in Cyrillic letters.[72] But according to the official U.S. position, the first tanker to pass through the blockade was the *Bucharest*, which was hailed by the navy on the morning of October 25. Again simple mathematical calculation excludes the possibility that the *Bucharest* and the *Vinnitsa* were the same ship. It seems probable that the navy's resistance to the president's order that the blockade be drawn in closer to Cuba forced him to allow one or several Soviet ships to pass through the blockade after it was officially operative.[73]

This attempt to leash the navy's blockade had a price. On Wednesday morning, October 24, what the president had been awaiting occurred. The eighteen dry cargo ships heading towards the quarantine stopped dead in the water. This was the occasion of Dean Rusk's remark, "We are eyeball to eyeball and I think the other fellow just blinked."[74] But the navy had another interpretation. The ships had simply stopped to pick up Soviet submarine escorts. The president became quite concerned lest the navy—already riled because of presidential meddling in its affairs—blunder into an incident. Sensing the president's fears, McNamara became suspicious of the navy's procedures and routines for making the first interception. Calling on the Chief of Naval Operations in the navy's inner sanctum, the navy flag plot, McNamara put his questions harshly.[75] Who would make the first interception? Were Russian-speaking officers on board? How would submarines be dealt with? At one point McNamara asked Anderson what he would do if a Soviet ship's captain refused to answer questions about his cargo. Picking up the Manual of Navy Regulations, the navy man waved it in McNamara's face and shouted, "It's all in there." To which McNamara replied, "I don't give a damn what John Paul Jones would have done; I want to know what you are going to do, now."[76] The encounter ended on Anderson's remark: "Now, Mr. Secretary, if you and your deputy will go back to your office, the navy will run the blockade."[77]

MODEL III: BUREAUCRATIC POLITICS

The leaders who sit on top of organizations are not a monolithic group. Rather each is in his own right a player in a central competitive game. The name of the game is bureaucratic politics: bargaining along regularized channels among players positioned hierarchically within the government. Government behavior can thus be understood according to a third conceptual model not as organizational outputs but as outcomes of bargaining games. In contrast with model I, the bureaucratic politics model sees no unitary actor but rather many actors as players, who focus not on a single strategic issue but on many diverse intranational problems as well, in terms of no consistent set of strategic objectives but rather according to various conceptions of national, organizational, and personal goals, making government decisions not by rational choice but by the pulling and hauling that is politics.

The apparatus of each national government constitutes a complex arena for the intranational game. Political leaders at the top of this apparatus plus the men who occupy positions on top of the critical organizations form the circle of central players. Ascendancy to this circle assures some independent standing. The necessary decentralization of decisions required for action on the broad range of foreign policy problems guarantees that each player has considerable discretion. Thus power is shared.

The nature of problems of foreign policy permits fundamental disagreement among reasonable men concerning what ought to be done. Analyses yield conflicting recommendations. Separate responsibilities laid on the shoulders of individual personalities encourage differences in perceptions and priorities. But the issues are of first-order importance. What the nation does really matters. A wrong choice could mean irreparable damage. Thus responsible men are obliged to fight for what they are convinced is right.

Men share power. Men differ concerning what must be done. The differences matter. This milieu necessitates that policy be resolved by politics. What the nation does is sometimes the result of the triumph of one group over others. More often, however, different groups pulling in different directions yield a resultant distinct from what anyone intended. What moves the chess pieces is not simply the reasons which support a course of action, nor the routines of organizations which enact an alternative, but the power and skill of proponents and opponents of the action in question.

This characterization captures the thrust of the bureaucratic-politics orientation. If problems of foreign policy arose as discrete issues and decisions were determined one game at a time, this account would suffice. But most issues, e.g., Vietnam or the proliferation of nuclear weapons, emerge piecemeal, over time, one lump in one context, a second in another. Hundreds of issues compete for players' attention every day. Each player is forced to fix upon his issues for that day, fight them on their own terms, and rush on to the next. Thus the character of emerging issues and the pace at which the game is played converge to yield government "decisions" and "actions" as collages. Choices by one player, outcomes of minor games, outcomes of central games, and "foul-ups"—these pieces, when stuck to the same canvas, constitute government behavior relevant to an issue.

The concept of national security policy as political outcome contradicts both public imagery and academic orthodoxy. Issues vital to national security, it is said, are too important to be settled by political games. They must be "above" politics. To accuse someone of "playing politics with national security" is a most serious charge. What public conviction demands, the academic penchant for intellectual elegance reinforces. Internal politics is messy; moreover, according to prevailing doctrine, politicking lacks intellectual content. As such, it constitutes gossip for journalists rather than a subject for serious investigation. Occasional memoirs, anecdotes in historical accounts, and several detailed case studies to the contrary, most of the literature of foreign policy avoids bureaucratic politics. The gap between academic literature and the experience of participants in government is nowhere wider than at this point.

Bureaucratic Politics Paradigm[78]

I. Basic Unit of Analysis: Policy as Political Outcome

The decisions and actions of governments are essentially intranational political outcomes: outcomes in the sense that what happens is not chosen as a solution to a problem but rather results from compromise, coalition, competition, and confusion among government officials who see different faces of an issue; political in the sense that the activity from which the outcomes emerge is best characterized as bargaining. Following Wittgenstein's use of the concept of a "game," national behavior in international affairs can be conceived as outcomes of intricate and subtle, simultaneous, overlapping games among players located in positions the hierarchical arrangement of which constitutes the government.[79] These games proceed neither at random nor at leisure. Regular channels structure the game. Deadlines force issues to the attention of busy players. The moves in the chess game are thus to be explained in terms of the bargaining among players with separate and unequal power over particular pieces and with separable objectives in distinguishable subgames.

II. Organizing Concepts

A. Players in Positions The actor is neither a unitary nation nor a conglomerate of organizations, but rather a number of individual players. Groups of these players constitute the agent for particular government decisions and actions. Players are men in jobs.

Individuals become players in the national security policy game by occupying a critical position in an administration. For example, in the U.S. government the players include "Chiefs": the President, Secretaries of State, Defense, and Treasury, Director of the CIA, Joint Chiefs of Staff, and, since 1961, the Special Assistant for National Security Affairs;[80] "Staffers": the immediate staff of each Chief; "Indians": the political appointees and permanent government officials within each of the departments and agencies; and "*Ad Hoc* Players": actors in the wider government game (especially "Congressional Influentials"), members of the press, spokesmen for important interest groups (especially the "bipartisan foreign policy establishment" in and out of Congress), and surrogates for each of these groups. Other members of the Congress, press, interest groups, and public form concentric circles around the central arena—circles which demarcate the permissive limits within which the game is played.

Positions define what players both may and must do. The advantages and handicaps with which each player can enter and play in various games stems from his position. So does a cluster of obligations for the performance of certain tasks. The two sides of this coin are illustrated by the position of the modern Secretary of State. First, in form and usually in fact, he is the primary repository of political judgment on the political-military issues that are the stuff of contemporary foreign policy; consequently, he is a senior personal advisor to the President. Second, he is the colleague of the President's other senior advisers on the problems of foreign policy, the Secretaries of Defense and Treasury, and the Special Assistant for National Security Affairs. Third, he is the ranking U.S. diplomat for serious negotiation. Fourth, he serves as an Administration voice to Congress, the country, and the world. Finally, he is "Mr. State Department" or "Mr. Foreign Office," "leader of officials, spokesman for their causes, guardian of their interests, judge of their disputes, superintendent of their work, master of their careers."[81] But he is not first one, and then the other. All of these obligations are his simultaneously. His performance in one affects his credit and power in the others. The perspective stemming from the daily work which he must oversee—the cable traffic by which his department maintains relations with other foreign offices—conflicts with the president's requirement that he serve as a generalist and coordinator of contrasting perspectives. The necessity that he be close to the President restricts the extent to which, and the force with which, he can front for his department. When he defers to the Secretary of Defense rather than fighting for his department's position—as he often must—he strains the loyalty of his officialdom. The Secretary's resolution of these conflicts depends not only upon the position, but also upon the player who occupies the position.

For players are also people. Men's metabolisms differ. The core of the bureaucratic politics mix is personality. (How each man manages to stand the heat in his kitchen, each player's basic operating style, and the complementarity or contradiction among personalities and styles in the inner circles are irreducible pieces of the policy blend.) Moreover, each person comes to his position with baggage in tow, including sensitivities to certain issues, commitments to various programs, and personal standing and debts with groups in the society.

B. Parochial Priorities, Perceptions, and Issues Answers to the questions: "What is the issue?" and "What must be done?" are colored by the position from which the questions are considered. For the factors which encourage organizational parochialism also influence the players who occupy positions on top of (or within) these organizations. To motivate members of his organization, a player must be sensitive to the organization's orientation. The games into which the player can enter and the advantages with which he plays enhance these pressures. Thus propensities of perception stemming from position permit reliable prediction about a player's stances in many cases. But these propensities are filtered through the baggage which players bring to positions. Sensitivity to both the pressures and the baggage is thus required for many predictions.

C. Interests, Stakes, and Power   Games are played to determine outcomes. But outcomes advance and impede each player's conception of the national interest, specific programs to which he is committed, the welfare of his friends, and his personal interests. These overlapping interests constitute the stakes for which games are played. Each player's ability to play successfully depends upon his power. Power, i.e., effective influence on policy outcomes, is an elusive blend of at least three elements: bargaining advantages (drawn from formal authority and obligations, institutional backing, constituents, expertise, and status), skill and will in using bargaining advantages, and other players' perceptions of the first two ingredients. Power wisely invested yields an enhanced reputation for effectiveness. Unsuccessful investment depletes both the stock of capital and the reputation. Thus each player must pick the issues on which he can play with a reasonable probability of success. But no player's power is sufficient to guarantee satisfactory outcomes. Each player's needs and fears run to many other players. What ensues is the most intricate and subtle of games known to man.

D. The Problem and the Problems   "Solutions" to strategic problems are not derived by detached analysts focusing coolly on *the* problem. Instead deadlines and events raise issues in games and demand decisions of busy players in contexts that influence the face the issue wears. The problems for the players are both narrower and broader than *the* strategic problem. For each player focuses not on the total strategic problem but rather on the decision that must be made now. But each decision has critical consequences not only for the strategic problem but for each player's organizational, reputational, and personal stakes. Thus the gap between the problems the player was solving and the problem upon which the analyst focuses is often very wide.

E. Action-Channels   Bargaining games do not proceed randomly. Action-channels, i.e., regularized ways of producing action concerning types of issues, structure the game by preselecting the major players, determining their points of entrance into the game, and distributing particular advantages and disadvantages for each game. Most critically, channels determine "who's got the action," that is, which department's Indians actually do whatever is chosen. Weapon procurement decisions are made within the annual budgeting process; embassies' demands for action cables are answered according to routines of consultation and clearance from State to Defense and White House; requests for instructions from military groups (concerning assistance all the time, concerning operations during war) are composed by the military in consultation with the Office of the Secretary of Defense, State, and White House; crisis responses are debated among White House, State, Defense, CIA, and ad hoc players; major political speeches, especially by the president but also by other chiefs, are cleared through established channels.

F. Action as Politics   Government decisions are made and government actions emerge neither as the calculated choice of a unified group nor as a formal summary of leaders' preferences. Rather the context of shared power but separate judgments concerning important choices determines that politics is the mechanism of choice. Note the *environment* in which the game is played: inordinate uncertainty about what must be done, the necessity that something be done, and crucial consequences of whatever is done. These features force responsible men to become active players. The *pace of the game*—hundreds of issues, numerous games, and multiple channels—compels players to fight to "get others' attention," to make them "see the facts," to assure that they "take the time to think seriously about the broader issue." The *structure of the game*—power shared by individuals with separate responsibilities—validates each player's feeling that "others don't see my problem," and "others must be persuaded to look at the issue from a less parochial perspective." The *rules of the game*—he who hesitates loses his chance to play at that point, and he who is uncertain about his recommendation is overpowered by others who are sure—pressures players to come down on one side of a 51:49 issue and play. The *rewards of the game*—effectiveness, i.e., impact on outcomes, as the immediate measure of performance—encourages hard play. Thus, most players come to fight to "make the government do what is right." The strategies and tactics employed are quite similar to those formalized by theorists of international relations.

G. Streams of Outcomes   Important government decisions or actions emerge as collages composed of individual acts, outcomes of minor and major games, and foul-ups. Outcomes which could never have been chosen by an actor and would never have emerged from bargaining in a single game over the issue are fabricated piece by piece. Understanding of the outcome requires that it be disaggregated.

III. Dominant Inference Pattern

If a nation performed an action, that action was the *outcome* of bargaining among individuals and groups within the government. That outcome included *results* achieved by groups committed to a decision or action, *resultants* which emerged from bargaining among groups with quite different positions and *foul-ups*. Model III's explanatory power is achieved by revealing the pulling and hauling of various players, with different perceptions and priorities, focusing on separate problems, which yielded the outcomes that constitute the action in question.

IV. General Propositions
1. Action and Intention   Action does not presuppose intention. The sum of behavior of representatives of a government relevant to an issue was rarely intended by any individual or group. Rather, separate individuals with different intentions contributed pieces which compose an outcome distinct from what anyone would have chosen.

2. Where You Stand Depends on Where You Sit[82]   Horizontally, the diverse demands upon each player shape his priorities, perceptions, and issues. For large classes of issues, e.g., budgets and procurement decisions, the stance of a particular player can be predicted with high reliability from information concerning his seat. In the notorious B-36 controversy, no one was surprised by Admiral Radford's testimony that "the B-36 under any theory of war is a bad gamble with national security," as opposed to Air Force Secretary Symington's claim that "a B-36 with an A-bomb can destroy distant objectives which might require ground armies years to take."[83]

3. Chiefs and Indians   The aphorism "where you stand depends on where you sit" has vertical as well as horizontal application. Vertically, the demands upon the president, chiefs, staffers, and Indians are quite distinct.

The foreign policy issues with which the president can deal are limited primarily by his crowded schedule: the necessity of dealing first with what comes next. His problem is to probe the special face worn by issues that come to his attention, to preserve his leeway until time has clarified the uncertainties, and to assess the relevant risks.

Foreign-policy chiefs deal most often with the hottest issue *de jour,* though they can get the attention of the president and other members of the government for other issues which they judge important. What they cannot guarantee is that "the president will pay the price" or that "the others will get on board." They must build a coalition of the relevant powers that be. They must "give the president confidence" in the right course of action.

Most problems are framed, alternatives specified, and proposals pushed, however, by Indians. Indians fight with Indians of other departments; for example, struggles between International Security Affairs of the Department of Defense and Political-Military of the State Department are a microcosm of the action at higher levels. But the Indian's major problem is how to get the *attention* of chiefs, how to get an issue decided, how to get the government "to do what is right."

In policy making then, the issue looking *down* is options: how to preserve my leeway until time clarifies uncertainties. The issue looking *sideways* is commitment: how to get others committed to my coalition. The issue looking *upwards* is confidence: how to give the boss confidence in doing what must be done. To paraphrase one of Neustadt's assertions which can be applied down the length of the ladder, the essence of a responsible official's task is to induce others to see that what needs to be done is what their own appraisal of their own responsibilities requires them to do in their own interests.

V. Specific Propositions
1. Deterrence   The probability of nuclear attack depends primarily on the probability of attack emerging as an outcome of the bureaucratic politics of the attacking government. First, which players can decide to launch an attack? Whether the effective power over action is controlled by an individual, a minor game, or the central game is critical. Second, though model I's confidence in nuclear deterrence stems from an assertion that in the end governments will not commit suicide,

model III recalls historical precedents. Admiral Yamamoto, who designed the Japanese attack on Pearl Harbor, estimated accurately: "In the first six months to a year of war against the U.S. and England I will run wild, and I will show you an uninterrupted succession of victories; I must also tell you that, should the war be prolonged for two or three years, I have no confidence in our ultimate victory."[84] But Japan attacked. Thus, three questions might be considered. One: could any member of the government solve his problem by attack? What patterns of bargaining could yield attack as an outcome? The major difference between a stable balance of terror and a questionable balance may simply be that in the first case most members of the government appreciate fully the consequences of attack and are thus on guard against the emergence of this outcome. Two: what stream of outcomes might lead to an attack? At what point in that stream is the potential attacker's politics? If members of the U.S. government had been sensitive to the stream of decisions from which the Japanese attack on Pearl Harbor emerged, they would have been aware of a considerable probability of that attack. Three: how might miscalculation and confusion generate foul-ups that yield attack as an outcome? For example, in a crisis or after the beginning of conventional war, what happens to the information available to and the effective power of members of the central game.

The U.S. Blockade of Cuba: A Third Cut

The Politics of Discovery

A series of overlapping bargaining games determined both the *date* of the discovery of the Soviet missiles and the *impact* of this discovery on the administration. An explanation of the politics of the discovery is consequently a considerable piece of the explanation of the U.S. blockade.

Cuba was the Kennedy administration's "political Achilles' heel."[85] The months preceding the crisis were also months before the congressional elections, and the Republican Senatorial and Congressional Campaign Committee had announced that Cuba would be "the dominant issue of the 1962 campaign."[86] What the administration billed as a "more positive and indirect approach of isolating Castro from developing, democratic Latin America," Senators Keating, Goldwater, Capehart, Thurmond, and others attacked as a "do-nothing" policy.[87] In statements on the floor of the House and Senate, campaign speeches across the country, and interviews and articles carried by national news media, Cuba—particularly the Soviet program of increased arms aid—served as a stick for stirring the domestic political scene.[88]

These attacks drew blood. Prudence demanded a vigorous reaction. The president decided to meet the issue head on. The administration mounted a forceful campaign of denial designed to discredit critics' claims. The president himself manned the front line of this offensive, though almost all administration officials participated. In his news conference on August 19, President Kennedy attacked as "irresponsible" calls for an invasion of Cuba, stressing rather "the totality of our obligations" and promising to "watch what happens in Cuba with the closest attention."[89] On September 4 he issued a strong statement denying any provocative Soviet action in Cuba.[90] On September 13 he lashed out at "loose talk" calling for an invasion of Cuba.[91] The day before the flight of the U-2 which discovered the missiles, he campaigned in Capehart's Indiana against those "self-appointed generals and admirals who want to send someone else's sons to war."[92]

On Sunday, October 14, just as a U-2 was taking the first pictures of Soviet missiles, McGeorge Bundy was asserting:

> I *know* that there is no present evidence, and I think that there is no present likelihood that the Cuban government and the Soviet government would, in combination, attempt to install a major offensive capability.[93]

In this campaign to puncture the critics' charges, the administration discovered that the public needed positive slogans. Thus Kennedy fell into a tenuous semantic distinction between "offensive" and "defensive" weapons. This distinction originated in his September 4 statement that there was no evidence of "offensive ground to ground missiles" and warned "were it to be otherwise, the gravest issues would arise."[94] His September 13 statement turned on this distinction between "defensive" and "offensive" weapons and announced a firm commitment to action if the Soviet Union attempted to introduce the latter into Cuba.[95] Congressional committees elicited from administration officials testimony which read this distinction and the president's commitment into the *Congressional Record*.[96]

What the president least wanted to hear, the CIA was most hesitant to say plainly. On August 22 John McCone met privately with the president and voiced suspicions that the Soviets were preparing to introduce offensive missiles into Cuba.[97] Kennedy heard this as what it was: the suspicion of a hawk. McCone left Washington for a month's honeymoon on the Riviera. Fretting at Cap Ferrat, he bombarded his deputy, General Marshall Carter, with telegrams, but Carter, knowing that McCone had informed the president of his suspicions and received a cold reception, was reluctant to distribute these telegrams outside the CIA.[98] On September 9 a U-2 "on loan" to the Chinese Nationalists was downed over mainland China.[99] The Committee on Overhead Reconnaissance (COMOR) convened on September 10 with a sense of urgency.[100] Loss of another U-2 might incite world opinion to demand cancellation of U-2 flights. The president's campaign against those who asserted that the Soviets were acting provocatively in Cuba had begun. To risk downing a U-2 over Cuba was to risk chopping off the limb on which the president was sitting. That meeting decided to shy away from the western end of Cuba (where SAMs were becoming operational) and modify the flight pattern of the U-2s in order to reduce the probability that a U-2 would be lost.[101] USIB's unanimous approval of the September estimate reflects similar sensitivities. On September 13 the president had asserted that there were no Soviet offensive missiles in Cuba and committed his administration to act if offensive missiles were discovered. Before congressional committees, administration officials were denying that there was any evidence whatever of offensive missiles in Cuba. The implications of a national intelligence estimate which concluded that the Soviets were introducing offensive missiles into Cuba were not lost on the men who constituted America's highest intelligence assembly.

The October 4 COMOR decision to direct a flight over the western end of Cuba in effect "overturned" the September estimate, but without officially raising that issue. The decision represented McCone's victory, for which he had lobbied with the president before the September 10 decision, in telegrams before the September 19 estimate, and in person after his return to Washington. Though the politics of the intelligence community is closely guarded, several pieces of the story can be told.[102] By September 27 Colonel Wright and others in DIA believed that the Soviet Union was placing missiles in the San Cristobal area.[103] This area was marked suspicious by the CIA on September 29 and certified top priority on October 3. By October 4 McCone had the evidence required to raise the issue officially. The members of COMOR heard McCone's argument but were reluctant to make the hard decision he demanded. The significant probability that a U-2 would be downed made overflight of western Cuba a matter of real concern.[104]

The Politics of Issues   The U-2 photographs presented incontrovertible evidence of Soviet offensive missiles in Cuba. This revelation fell upon politicized players in a complex context. As one high official recalled, Khrushchev had caught us "with our pants down." What each of the central participants saw, and what each did to cover both his own and the administration's nakedness, created the spectrum of issues and answers.

At approximately 9:00 A.M. Tuesday morning, October 16, McGeorge Bundy went to the president's living quarters with the message: "Mr. President, there is now hard photographic evidence that the Russians have offensive missiles in Cuba."[105] Much has been made of Kennedy's "expression of surprise,"[106] but *"surprise"* fails to capture the character of his initial reaction. Rather it was one of startled anger, most adequately conveyed by the exclamation: "He can't do that to *me!"*[107] In terms of the president's attention and priorities at that moment, Khrushchev had chosen the most unhelpful act of all. Kennedy had staked his full presidential authority on the assertion that the Soviets would not place offensive weapons in Cuba. Moreover, Khrushchev had assured the president through the most direct and personal channels that he was aware of the president's domestic political problem and that nothing would be done to exacerbate this problem. The chairman had *lied* to the president. Kennedy's initial reaction entailed action. The missiles must be removed.[108] The alternatives of "doing nothing" or "taking a diplomatic approach" could not have been less relevant to *his* problem.

These two tracks—doing nothing and taking a diplomatic approach—were the solutions advocated by two of his principal advisers. For Secretary of Defense McNamara the missiles raised the specter of nuclear war. He first framed the issue as a straightforward strategic problem. To understand the issue one had to grasp two obvious but difficult points. First, the missiles represented an inevitable occurrence: narrowing of the missile gap. It simply happened sooner rather than later. Second, the United States could accept this occurrence, since its consequences were minor: "seven-to-one missile 'superiority,' one-to-one missile 'equality,' one-to-seven missile 'inferiority'—the three postures are identical." McNamara's statement of this argument at the first meeting of the ExCom was summed up in the phrase "a missile is a missile."[109] "It makes no great difference," he maintained, "whether you are killed by a missile from the Soviet Union or Cuba."[110] The implication was clear. The United States should not initiate a crisis with the Soviet

Union, risking a significant probability of nuclear war over an occurrence which had such small strategic implications.

The perceptions of McGeorge Bundy, the president's assistant for national security affairs, are the most difficult of all to reconstruct. There is no question that he initially argued for a diplomatic track.[111] But was Bundy laboring under his acknowledged burden of responsibility in Cuba I? Or was he playing the role of devil's advocate in order to make the president probe his own initial reaction and consider other options?

The president's brother, Robert Kennedy, saw most clearly the political wall against which Khrushchev had backed the president. But he, like McNamara, saw the prospect of nuclear doom. Was Khrushchev going to force the president to an insane act? At the first meeting of the ExCom he scribbled a note, "Now I know how Tojo felt when he was planning Pearl Harbor."[112] From the outset he searched for an alternative that would prevent the air strike.

The initial reaction of Theodore Sorensen, the president's special counsel and "alter ego," fell somewhere between that of the president and his brother. Like the president, Sorensen felt the poignancy of betrayal. If the president had been the architect of the policy which the missiles punctured, Sorensen was the draftsman. Khrushchev's deceitful move demanded a strong countermove. But like Robert Kennedy, Sorensen feared lest the shock and disgrace lead to disaster.

To the Joint Chiefs of Staff the issue was clear. *Now* was the time to do the job for which they had prepared contingency plans. Cuba I had been badly done; Cuba II would not be. The missiles provided the *occasion* to deal with the issue: cleansing the Western Hemisphere of Castro's communism. As the president recalled on the day the crisis ended, "An invasion would have been a mistake—a wrong use of our power. But the military are mad. They wanted to do this. It's lucky for us that we have McNamara over there."[113]

McCone's perceptions flowed from his confirmed prediction. As the Cassandra of the incident, he argued forcefully that the Soviets had installed the missiles in a daring political probe which the United States must meet with force. The time for an air strike was now.[114]

The Politics of Choice   The process by which the blockade emerged is a story of the most subtle and intricate probing, pulling, and hauling; leading, guiding, and spurring. Reconstruction of this process can only be tentative. Initially the president and most of his advisers wanted the clean surgical air strike. On the first day of the crisis, when informing Stevenson of the missiles, the president mentioned only two alternatives: "I suppose the alternatives are to go in by air and wipe them out or to take other steps to render them inoperable."[115] At the end of the week a sizable minority still favored an air strike. As Robert Kennedy recalled: "The fourteen people involved were very significant. . . . If six of them had been president of the U.S., I think that the world might have been blown up."[116] What prevented the air strike was a fortuitous coincidence of a number of factors—the absence of any one of which might have permitted that option to prevail.

First, McNamara's vision of holocaust set him firmly against the air strike. His initial attempt to frame the issue in strategic terms struck Kennedy as particularly inappropriate. Once McNamara realized that the name of the game was a strong response, however, he and his deputy Gilpatric chose the blockade as a fallback. When the Secretary of Defense—whose department had the action, whose reputation in the cabinet was unequaled, in whom the president demonstrated full confidence—marshalled the arguments for the blockade and refused to be moved, the blockade became a formidable alternative.

Second, Robert Kennedy—the president's closest confidant—was unwilling to see his brother become a "Tojo." His arguments against the air strike on moral grounds struck a chord in the president. Moreover, once his brother had stated these arguments so forcefully, the president could not have chosen his initially preferred course without in effect agreeing to become what RFK had condemned.

The president learned of the missiles on Tuesday morning. On Wednesday morning, in order to mask our discovery from the Russians, the president flew to Connecticut to keep a campaign commitment, leaving RFK as the unofficial chairman of the group. By the time the president returned on Wednesday evening, a critical third piece had been added to the picture. McNamara had presented his argument for the blockade. Robert Kennedy and Sorensen had joined McNamara. A powerful coalition of the advisers in whom the president had the greatest confidence, and with whom his style was most compatible, had emerged.

Fourth, the coalition that had formed behind the president's initial preference gave him reason to pause. *Who* supported the air strike—the Chiefs, McCone, Rusk, Nitze, and Acheson—as much as *how* they supported it, counted. Fifth, a piece of inaccurate information, which no one probed, permitted the blockade advocates to fuel (potential) uncertainties in the president's mind. When the president returned to Washington Wednesday evening, RFK and Sorensen met him at the airport. Sorensen gave the president a four-page memorandum outlining the areas of agreement and disagreement. The strongest argument was that the air strike simply could not be surgical.[117] After a day of prodding and questioning, the air force had asserted that it could not guarantee the success of a surgical air strike limited to the missiles alone.

Thursday evening, the president convened the ExCom at the White House. He declared his tentative choice of the blockade and directed that preparations be made to put it into effect by Monday morning.[118] Though he raised a question about the possibility of a surgical air strike subsequently, he seems to have accepted the experts' opinion that this was no live option.[119] (Acceptance of this estimate suggests that he may have learned the lesson of the Bay of Pigs—"Never rely on experts"—less well than he supposed.)[120] But this information was incorrect. That no one probed this estimate during the first week of the crisis poses an interesting question for further investigation.

A coalition, including the president, thus emerged from the president's initial decision that something had to be done; McNamara, Robert Kennedy, and Sorensen's resistance to the air strike; incompatibility between the president and the air strike advocates; and an inaccurate piece of information.[121]

CONCLUSION

This essay has obviously bitten off more than it has chewed. For further developments and synthesis of these arguments the reader is referred to the larger study.[122]

In spite of the limits of space, however, it would be inappropriate to stop without spelling out several implications of the argument and addressing the question of relations among the models and extensions of them to activity beyond explanation.

At a minimum the intended implications of the argument presented here are four. First, formulation of alternative frames of reference and demonstration that different analysts, relying predominantly on different models, produce quite different explanations should encourage the analyst's self-consciousness about the nets he employs. The effect of these "spectacles" in sensitizing him to particular aspects of what is going on—framing the puzzle in one way rather than another, encouraging him to examine the problem in terms of certain categories rather than others, directing him to particular kinds of evidence, and relieving puzzlement by one procedure rather than another—must be recognized and explored.

Second, the argument implies a position on the problem of "the state of the art." While accepting the commonplace characterization of the present condition of foreign-policy analysis—personalistic, noncumulative, and sometimes insightful—this essay rejects both the counsel of despair's justification of this condition as a consequence of the character of the enterprise, and the "new frontiersmen's" demand for *a priori* theorizing on the frontiers and *ad hoc* appropriation of "new techniques."[123] What is required as a first step is noncasual examination of the present product: inspection of existing explanations, articulation of the conceptual models employed in producing them, formulation of the propositions relied upon, specification of the logic of the various intellectual enterprises, and reflection on the questions being asked. Though it is difficult to overemphasize the need for more systematic processing of more data, these preliminary matters of formulating questions with clarity and sensitivity to categories and assumptions so that fruitful acquisition of large quantities of data is possible are still a major hurdle in considering most important problems.

Third, the preliminary, partial paradigms presented here provide a basis for serious reexamination of many problems of foreign and military policy. Model II and model III cuts at problems typically treated in model I terms can permit significant improvements in explanation and prediction.[124] Full model II and III analyses require large amounts of information. But even in cases where the information base is severely limited, improvements are possible. Consider the problem of predicting Soviet strategic forces. In the mid-1950s, model I style calculations led to predictions that the Soviets would rapidly deploy large numbers of long-range bombers. From a model II perspective both the frailty of the air force within the Soviet military establishment and the budgetary implications of such a build-up would have led analysts to hedge this prediction. Moreover, model II would have pointed to a sure, visible indicator of such a build-up: noisy struggles among the services over major budgetary shifts. In the late 1950s and early 1960s model I calculations led to the prediction of immediate massive Soviet deployment of ICBMs. Again, a model II cut would have reduced this number because in the earlier period strategic rockets were controlled by the Soviet ground forces rather than an independent service, and in the later period this would have necessitated massive shifts in budgetary splits. Today, model I considerations lead many analysts both to recommend that an agreement not to deploy ABMs be a major American objective in upcoming strategic negotiations with the USSR and to predict success. From a model II vantage point the existence of an ongoing Soviet ABM program, the strength of the organization (National Air Defense) that controls ABMs, and the fact that an agreement to stop ABM deployment would force the virtual dismantling of this organization make a viable agreement of this sort much less likely. A model III cut suggests that (a) there must be significant differences among perceptions and priorities of Soviet leaders over strategic negotiations, (b) any agreement will affect some players' power bases, and (c) agreements that do not require extensive cuts in the sources of some major players' power will prove easier to negotiate and more viable.

Fourth, the present formulation of paradigms is simply an initial step. As such it leaves a long list of critical questions unanswered. Given any action, an imaginative analyst should always be able to construct some rationale for the government's choice. By imposing and relaxing constraints on the parameters of rational choice (as in variants of model I) analysts can construct a large number of accounts of any act as a rational choice. But does a statement of reasons why a rational actor would choose an action constitute an explanation of the *occurrence* of that action? How can model I analysis be forced to make more systematic contributions to the question of the determinants of occurrences? Model II's explanation of t in terms of $t - 1$ is explanation. The world is contiguous. But governments sometimes make sharp departures. Can an organizational process model be modified to suggest where change is likely? Attention to organizational change should afford greater understanding of why particular programs and SOPs are maintained by identifiable types of organizations and also how a manager can improve organizational performance. Model III tells a fascinating "story." But its complexity is enormous, the information requirements are often overwhelming, and many of the details of the bargaining may be superfluous. How can such a model be made parsimonious? The three models are obviously not exclusive alternatives. Indeed, the paradigms highlight the partial emphasis of the framework—what each emphasizes and what it leaves out. Each concentrates on one class of variables, in effect relegating other important factors to a ceteris parabus clause. Model I concentrates on "market factors:" pressures and incentives created by the "international strategic marketplace." Models II and III focus on the internal mechanism of the government that chooses in this environment. But can these relations be more fully specified? Adequate synthesis would require a typology of decisions and actions, some of which are more amenable to treatment in terms of one model and some to another. Government behavior is but one cluster of factors relevant to occurrences in foreign affairs. Most students of foreign policy adopt this focus (at least when explaining and predicting). Nevertheless, the dimensions of the chess board, the character of the pieces, and the rules of the game—factors considered by international systems theorists—constitute the context in which the pieces are moved. Can the major variables in the full function of determinants of foreign policy outcomes be identified?

Both the outline of a partial *ad hoc* working synthesis of the models and a sketch of their uses in activities other than explanation can be suggested by generating predictions in terms of each. Strategic surrender is an important problem of international relations and diplomatic history. War termination is a new, developing area of the strategic literature. Both of these interests lead scholars to address a central question: *Why* do nations surrender *when?* Whether implicit in explanations or more explicit in analysis, diplomatic historians and strategists rely upon propositions which can be turned forward to produce predictions. Thus at the risk of being timely—and in error—the present situation (August 1968) offers an interesting test case: Why will North Vietnam surrender when?[125]

In a nutshell, analysis according to model I asserts: nations quit when costs outweigh the benefits. North Vietnam will surrender when she realizes "that continued fighting can only generate additional costs without hope of compensating gains, this expectation being largely the consequence of the previous application of force by the dominant side."[126] U.S. actions can increase or decrease Hanoi's strategic costs. Bombing North Vietnam increases the pain and thus increases the probability of surrender. This proposition and prediction are not without meaning. That—"other things being equal"—nations are more likely to surrender when the strategic cost-benefit balance is negative is true. Nations rarely surrender when they are winning. The proposition specifies a range within which nations surrender. But over this broad range the relevant question is: why do nations surrender?

Models II and III focus upon the government machine through which this fact about the international strategic marketplace must be filtered to produce a surrender. These analysts are considerably less sanguine about the possibility of surrender *at the point* that the cost-benefit calculus turns negative. Never in history (i.e., in none of the five cases I have examined) have nations surrendered at that point. Surrender occurs sometime thereafter. *When* depends on process of organizations and politics of players within these governments—as they are affected by the opposing government. Moreover, the effects of the victorious power's action upon the surrendering nation cannot be adequately summarized as increasing or decreasing strategic costs. Imposing additional costs by bombing a nation may increase the probability of surrender. But it also may reduce it. An appreciation of the impact of the acts of one nation upon another thus requires some understanding of the machine which is being influenced. For more precise prediction, models II and III require considerably more information about the organizations and politics of North Vietnam than is publicly available. On the basis of the limited public information, however, these models can be suggestive.

Model II examines two subproblems. First, to have lost is not sufficient. The government must know that the strategic cost-benefit calculus is negative. But neither the categories nor the indicators of strategic costs and benefits are clear. And the sources of information about both are organizations whose parochial priorities and perceptions do not facilitate accurate information or estimation. Military evaluation of military performance, military estimates of factors like "enemy morale," and military predictions concerning when "the tide will turn" or "the corner will have been turned" are typically distorted. In cases of highly decentralized guerrilla operations, like Vietnam, these problems are exacerbated. Thus strategic costs will be underestimated. Only highly *visible* costs can have direct impact on leaders without being filtered through organizational channels. Second, since organizations define the details of options and execute actions, surrender (and negotiation) is likely to entail considerable bungling in the early stages. No organization can define options or prepare programs for this treasonous act. Thus, early overtures will be uncoordinated with the acts of other organizations, e.g., the fighting forces, creating contradictory "signals" to the victor.

Model III suggests that surrender will not come at the point that strategic costs outweigh benefits, but that it will not wait until the leadership group concludes that the war is lost. Rather the problem is better understood in terms of four additional propositions. First, strong advocates of the war effort, whose careers are closely identified with the war, rarely come to the conclusion that costs outweigh benefits. Second, quite often from the outset of a war, a number of members of the government (particularly those whose responsibilities sensitize them to problems other than war, e.g., economic planners or intelligence experts) are convinced that the war effort is futile. Third, surrender is likely to come as the result of a political shift that enhances the effective power of the latter group (and adds swing members to it). Fourth, the course of the war, particularly actions of the victor, can influence the advantages and disadvantages of players in the loser's government. Thus, North Vietnam will surrender not when its leaders have a change of heart, but when Hanoi has a change of leaders (or a change of effective power within the central circle). How U.S. bombing (or pause), threats, promises, or action in the South affect the game in Hanoi is subtle but nonetheless crucial.

That these three models could be applied to the surrender of governments other than North Vietnam should be obvious. But that exercise is left for the reader.

NOTES

1. Theodore Sorensen, *Kennedy* (New York, 1965), p. 705.
2. In attempting to understand problems of foreign affairs, analysts engage in a number of related, but logically separable enterprises: (a) description, (b) explanation, (c) prediction, (d) evaluation, and (e) recommendation. This essay focuses primarily on explanation (and by implication, prediction).
3. In arguing that explanations proceed in terms of implicit conceptual models, this essay makes no claim that foreign-policy analysts have developed any satisfactory empirically tested theory. In this essay the use of the term *model* without qualifiers should be read *conceptual scheme.*
4. For the purpose of this argument we shall accept Carl G. Hempel's characterization of the logic of explanation: an explanation "answers the question, '*Why* did the ex-planadum-phenomenon occur?' by showing that the phenomenon resulted from particular circumstances, specified in C_1, C_2, ... C_k, in accordance with laws L_1, L_2, ... L_r. By pointing this out, the argument shows that given the particular circumstances and the laws in question, the occurrence of the phenomenon was to be *expected;* and it is in this sense that the explanation enables us to understand why the phenomenon occurred." *Aspects of Scientific Explanation* (New York, 1965), p. 337. While various patterns of explanation can be distinguished, *viz.,* Ernest Nagel, *The Structure of Science: Problems in the Logic of Scientific Explanation,* New York, 1961), satisfactory scientific explanations exhibit this basic logic. Consequently prediction is the converse of explanation.
5. Earlier drafts of this argument have aroused heated arguments concerning proper names for these models. To choose names from ordinary language is to court confusion as well as familiarity. Perhaps it is best to think of these models as I, II, and III.

6. In strict terms the "outcomes" which these three models attempt to explain are essentially actions of national governments, i.e., the sum of activities of all individuals employed by a government relevant to an issue. These models focus not on a state of affairs, i.e., a full description of the world, but upon national decision and implementation. This distinction is stated clearly by Harold and Margaret Sprout, "Environmental Factors on the Study of International Politics," in James Rosenau (ed.), *International Politics and Foreign Policy* (Glencoe, Illinois, 1961), p. 116. This restriction excludes explanations offered principally in terms of international systems theories. Nevertheless, this restriction is not severe, since few interesting explanations of occurrences in foreign policy have been produced at that level of analysis. According to David Singer, "The nation state—our primary actor in international relations . . . is clearly the traditional focus among Western students and is the one which dominates all of the texts employed in English-speaking colleges and universities." David Singer, "The Level-of-Analysis Problem in International Relations," Klaus Knorr and Sidney Verba (eds.), *The International System* (Princeton, 1961). Similarly, Richard Brody's review of contemporary trends in the study of international relations finds that "scholars have come increasingly to focus on acts of nations. That is, they all focus on the behavior of nations in some respect. Having an interest in accounting for the behavior of nations in common, the prospects for a common frame of reference are enhanced."

7. For further development and support of these arguments see the author's larger study, *Bureaucracy and Policy: Conceptual Models and the Cuban Missile Crisis* (forthcoming). In its abbreviated form the argument must at some points appear overly stark. The limits of space have forced the omission of many reservations and refinements.

8. Each of the three "case snapshots" displays the work of a conceptual model as it is applied to explain the U.S. blockade of Cuba. But these three cuts are primarily exercises in hypothesis generation rather than hypothesis testing. Especially when separated from the larger study, these accounts may be misleading. The sources for these accounts include the full public record plus a large number of interviews with participants in the crisis.

9. *New York Times*, February 18, 1967.

10. *Ibid.*

11. Arnold Horelick and Myron Rush, *Strategic Power and Soviet Foreign Policy* (Chicago, 1965). Based on A. Horelick, "The Cuban Missile Crisis: An Analysis of Soviet Calculations and Behavior," *World Politics* (April, 1964).

12. Horelick and Rush, *Strategic Power and Soviet Foreign Policy*, p. 154.

13. Hans Morgenthau, *Politics Among Nations* (3rd ed.; New York, 1960), p. 191.

14. *Ibid.*, p. 192.

15. *Ibid.*, p. 5.

16. *Ibid.*, pp. 5–6.

17. Stanley Hoffmann, *Daedalus* (Fall, 1962); reprinted in *The State of War* (New York, 1965).

18. *Ibid.*, p. 171.

19. *Ibid.*, p. 189.

20. Following Robert MacIver; see Stanley Hoffmann, *Contemporary Theory in International Relations* (Englewood Cliffs, 1960), pp. 178–179.

21. Thomas Schelling, *The Strategy of Conflict* (New York, 1960), p. 232. This proposition was formulated earlier by A. Wohlstetter, "The Delicate Balance of Terror," *Foreign Affairs* (January, 1959).

22. Schelling, *op. cit.*, p. 4.

23. See Morgenthau, *op. cit.*, p. 5; Hoffmann, *Contemporary Theory*, pp. 178–179; Hoffmann, "Roulette in the Cellar," *The State of War*; Schelling, *op. cit.*

24. The larger study examines several exceptions to this generalization. Sidney Verba's excellent essay "Assumptions of Rationality and Non-Rationality in Models of the International System" is less an exception than it is an approach to a somewhat different problem. Verba focuses upon models of rationality and irrationality of *individual* statesmen: in Knorr and Verba, *The International System.*

25. Robert K. Merton, *Social Theory and Social Structures* (Revised and Enlarged Edition; New York, 1957), pp. 12–16. Considerably weaker than a satisfactory theoretical model, paradigms nevertheless represent a short step in that direction from looser, implicit conceptual models. Neither the concepts nor the relations among the variables are sufficiently specified to yield propositions deductively. "Paradigmatic Analysis" nevertheless has considerable promise for clarifying and codifying styles of analysis in political science. Each of the paradigms stated here can be represented rigorously in mathematical terms. For example, model I lends itself to mathematical formulation along the lines of Herbert Simon's "Behavioral Theory of Rationality," *Models of Man* (New York, 1957). But this does not solve the most difficult problem of "measurement and estimation."

26. Though a variant of this model could easily be stochastic, this paradigm is stated in non-probabilistic terms. In contemporary strategy a stochastic version of this model is sometimes used for predictions; but it is almost impossible to find an explanation of an occurrence in foreign affairs that is consistently probabilistic.

   Analogies between model I and the concept of explanation developed by R. G. Collingwood, William Dray, and other revisionists among philosophers concerned with the critical philosophy of history are not accidental. For a summary of the revisionist position see Maurice Mandelbaum, "Historical Explanation: The Problem of Covering Laws," *History and Theory* (1960).

27. This model is an analogue of the theory of the rational entrepreneur which has been developed extensively in economic theories of the firm and the consumer. These two propositions specify the substitution effect. Refinement of this model and specification of additional general propositions by translating from the economic theory is straightforward.

28. *New York Times,* March 22, 1969.

29. See Nathan Leites, *A Study of Bolshevism* (Glencoe, Illinois, 1953).

30. As stated in the introduction, this "case snapshot" presents, without editorial commentary, a model I analyst's explanation of the U.S. blockade. The purpose is to illustrate a strong, characteristic rational policy model account. This account is (roughly) consistent with prevailing explanations of these events.

31. Theodore Sorensen, *op. cit.,* p. 675.

32. *Ibid.,* p. 679.

33. *Ibid.,* p. 679.

34. Elie Abel, *The Missile Crisis* (New York, 1966), p. 144.

35. *Ibid.,* p. 102.

36. Sorensen, *op. cit.,* p. 684.

37. *Ibid.,* p. 685. Though this was the formulation of the argument, the facts are not strictly accurate. Our tradition against surprise attack was rather younger than 175 years. For example President Theodore Roosevelt applauded Japan's attack on Russia in 1904.

38. *New York Times,* June, 1963.

39. The influence of organizational studies upon the present literature of foreign affairs is minimal. Specialists in international politics are not students of organization theory. Organization theory has only recently begun to study organizations as decision makers and has not yet produced behavioral studies of national security organizations from a deci-

sion-making perspective. It seems unlikely, however, that these gaps will remain unfilled much longer. Considerable progress has been made in the study of the business firm as an organization. Scholars have begun applying these insights to government organizations, and interest in an organizational perspective is spreading among institutions and individuals concerned with actual government operations. The "decision making" approach represented by Richard Snyder, R. Bruck, and B. Sapin, *Foreign Policy Decision-Making* (Glencoe, Illinois, 1962), incorporates a number of insights from organization theory.

40. The formulation of this paradigm is indebted both to the orientation and insights of Herbert Simon and to the behavioral model of the firm stated by Richard Cyert and James March, *A Behavioral Theory of the Firm* (Englewood Cliffs, 1963). Here, however, one is forced to grapple with the less routine, less quantified functions of the less differentiated elements in government organizations.

41. Theodore Sorensen, "You Get to Walk to Work," *New York Times Magazine,* March 19, 1967.

42. Organizations are not monolithic. The proper level of disaggregation depends upon the objectives of a piece of analysis. This paradigm is formulated with reference to the major organizations that constitute the U.S. government. Generalization to the major components of each department and agency should be relatively straightforward.

43. The stability of these constraints is dependent on such factors as rules for promotion and reward, budgeting and accounting procedures, and mundane operating procedures.

44. Marriner Eccles, *Beckoning Frontiers* (New York, 1951), p. 336.

45. Arthur Schlesinger, *A Thousand Days* (Boston, 1965), p. 406.

46. U.S. Department of State, *Bulletin,* XLVII, pp. 715–720.

47. Schlesinger, *op. cit.,* p. 803.

48. Theodore Sorensen, *Kennedy,* p. 675.

49. See U.S. Congress, Senate, Committee on Armed Services, Preparedness Investigation Subcommittee, *Interim Report on Cuban Military Build-up,* 88th Congress, 1st Session, 1963, p. 2; Hanson Baldwin, "Growing Risks of Bureaucratic Intelligence," *The Reporter* (August 15, 1963), 48–50; Roberta Wohlstetter, "Cuba and Pearl Harbor," *Foreign Affairs* (July, 1965), 706.

50. U.S. Congress, House of Representatives, Committee on Appropriations, Subcommittee on Department of Defense Appropriations, *Hearings,* 88th Congress, 1st Session, 1963, 25 ff.

51. R. Hilsman, *To Move a Nation* (New York, 1967), pp. 172–173.

52. Department of Defense Appropriations, *Hearings,* p. 67.

53. *Ibid.,* pp. 66–67.

54. For (1) Hilsman, *op. cit.,* p. 186; (2) Abel, *op. cit.,* p. 24; (3) Department of Defense Appropriations, *Hearings,* p. 64; Abel, *op. cit.,* p. 24; (4) Department of Defense Appropriations, *Hearings,* pp. 1–30.

55. The facts here are not entirely clear. This assertion is based on information from (1) "Department of Defense Briefing by the Honorable R. S. McNamara, Secretary of Defense, State Department Auditorium, 5:00 p.m., February 6, 1963." A verbatim transcript of a presentation actually made by General Carroll's assistant, John Hughes; and (2) Hilsman's statement, *op. cit.,* p. 186. But see R. Wohlstetter's interpretation, "Cuba and Pearl Harbor," p. 700.

56. See Hilsman, *op. cit.,* pp. 172–174.

57. Abel, *op. cit.,* pp. 26 ff; Weintal and Bartlett, *Facing the Brink* (New York, 1967), pp. 62 ff; *Cuban Military Build-up;* J. Daniel and J. Hubbell, *Strike in the West* (New York, 1963), pp. 15 ff.

58. Schlesinger, *op. cit.,* p. 804.

59. Sorensen, *Kennedy,* p. 684.

60. *Ibid.,* pp. 684 ff.

61. *Ibid.,* pp. 694–697.

62. *Ibid.,* p. 697; Abel, *op. cit.,* pp. 100–101.

63. Sorensen, *Kennedy,* p. 669.

64. Hilsman, *op. cit.,* p. 204.

65. See Abel, *op. cit.,* pp. 97 ff.

66. Schlesinger, *op. cit.,* p. 818.

67. *Ibid.*

68. Sorensen, *Kennedy,* p. 710.

69. *New York Times,* October 27, 1962.

70. Abel, *op. cit.,* p. 171.

71. For the location of the original arc see Abel, *op. cit.,* p. 141.

72. *Facts on File,* Vol. XXII, 1962, p. 376, published by Facts on File, Inc., New York, yearly.

73. This hypothesis would account for the mystery surrounding Kennedy's explosion at the leak of the stopping of the *Bucharest.* See Hilsman, *op. cit.,* p. 45.

74. Abel, *op. cit.,* p. 153.

75. See *ibid.,* pp. 154 ff.

76. *Ibid.,* p. 156.

77. *Ibid.*

78. This paradigm relies upon the small group of analysts who have begun to fill the gap. My primary source is the model implicit in the work of Richard E. Neustadt, though his concentration on presidential action has been generalized to a concern with policy as the outcome of political bargaining among a number of independent players, the president amounting to no more than a "superpower" among many lesser but considerable powers. As Warner Schilling argues, the substantive problems are of such inordinate difficulty that uncertainties and differences with regard to goals, alternatives, and consequences are inevitable. This necessitates what Roger Hilsman describes as the process of conflict and consensus building. The techniques employed in this process often resemble those used in legislative assemblies, though Samuel Huntington's characterization of the process as "legislative" overemphasizes the equality of participants as opposed to the hierarchy which structures the game. Moreover, whereas for Huntington foreign policy (in contrast to military policy) is set by the executive, this paradigm maintains that the activities which he describes as legislative are characteristic of the process by which foreign policy is made.

79. The theatrical metaphor of stage, roles, and actors is more common than this metaphor of games, positions, and players. Nevertheless, the rigidity connotated by the concept of *role* both in the theatrical sense of actors reciting fixed lines and in the sociological sense of fixed responses to specified social situations makes the concept of games, positions, and players more useful for this analysis of active participants in the determination of national policy. Objections to the terminology on the grounds that *game* connotes nonserious play overlook the concept's application to most serious problems both in Wittgenstein's philosophy and in contemporary game theory. Game theory typically treats more precisely structured games, but Wittgenstein's examination of the "language game" wherein men use words to communicate is quite analogous to this analysis of the less specified game of bureaucratic politics. See Ludwig Wittgenstein, *Philosophical Investigations,* and Thomas Schelling, "What is Game Theory?" in James Charlesworth, *Contemporary Political Analysis.*

80. Inclusion of the President's Special Assistant for National Security Affairs in the tier of "Chiefs" rather than among the "Staffers" involves a debatable choice. In fact he is both super-staffer and near-chief. His position has no statutory authority. He is especially de-

pendent upon good relations with the President and the Secretaries of Defense and State. Nevertheless, he stands astride a genuine action-channel. The decision to include this position among the Chiefs reflects my judgment that the Bundy function is becoming institutionalized.

81. Richard E. Neustadt, Testimony, United States Senate, Committee on Government Operations, Subcommittee on National Security Staffing, *Administration of National Security*, March 26, 1963, pp. 82–83.

82. This aphorism was stated first, I think, by Don K. Price.

83. Paul Y. Hammond, "Super Carriers and B-36 Bombers," in Harold Stein (ed.), *American Civil-Military Decisions* (Birmingham, 1963).

84. Roberta Wohlstetter, *Pearl Harbor* (Stanford, 1962), p. 350.

85. Sorensen, *Kennedy*, p. 670.

86. *Ibid.*

87. *Ibid.*, pp. 670 ff.

88. *New York Times*, August, September, 1962.

89. *New York Times*, August 20, 1962.

90. *New York Times*, September 5, 1962.

91. *New York Times*, September 14, 1962.

92. *New York Times*, October 14, 1962.

93. Cited by Abel, *op. cit.*, p. 13.

94. *New York Times*, September 5, 1962.

95. *New York Times*, September 14, 1962.

96. Senate Foreign Relations Committee; Senate Armed Services Committee; House Committee on Appropriation; House Select Committee on Export Control.

97. Abel, *op. cit.*, pp. 17–18. According to McCone he told Kennedy, "The only construction I can put on the material going into Cuba is that the Russians are preparing to introduce offensive missiles." See also Weintal and Bartlett, *op. cit.*, pp. 60–61.

98. Abel, *op. cit.*, p. 23.

99. *New York Times*, September 10, 1962.

100. See Abel, *op. cit.*, pp. 25–26; and Hilsman, *op. cit.*, p. 174.

101. Department of Defense Appropriation, *Hearings*, 69.

102. A basic but somewhat contradictory account of parts of this story emerges in the Department of Defense Appropriations, *Hearings*, 1–70.

103. Department of Defense Appropriations, *Hearings*, 71.

104. The details of the ten days between the October 4 decision and the October 14 flight must be held in abeyance.

105. Abel, *op. cit.*, p. 44.

106. *Ibid.*, pp. 44 ff.

107. See Richard Neustadt, "Afterword," *Presidential Power* (New York, 1964).

108. Sorensen, *Kennedy*, p. 676; Schlesinger, *op. cit.*, p. 801.

109. Hilsman, *op. cit.*, p. 195.

110. *Ibid.*

111. Weintal and Bartlett, *op. cit.*, p. 67; Abel, *op. cit.*, p. 53.

112. Schlesinger, *op. cit.*, p. 803.

113. *Ibid.*, p. 831.

114. Abel, *op. cit.*, p. 186.

115. *Ibid.*, p. 49.

116. Interview, quoted by Ronald Steel, *New York Review of Books*, March 13, 1969, p. 22.

117. Sorensen, *Kennedy*, p. 686.

118. *Ibid.*, p. 691.

119. *Ibid.*, pp. 691–692.

120. Schlesinger, *op. cit.*, p. 296.

121. Space will not permit an account of the path from this coalition to the formal government decision on Saturday and action on Monday.

122. *Bureaucracy and Policy* (forthcoming, 1969).

123. Thus my position is quite distinct from both poles in the recent "great debate" about international relations. While many "traditionalists" of the sort Kaplan attacks adopt the first posture and many "scientists" of the sort attacked by Bull adopt the second, this third posture is relatively neutral with respect to whatever is in substantive dispute. See Hedly Bull, "International Theory: The Case for a Classical Approach," *World Politics* (April, 1966); and Morton Kaplan, "The New Great Debate: Traditionalism vs. Science in International Relations," *World Politics* (October, 1966).

124. A number of problems are now being examined in these terms both in the Bureaucracy Study Group on Bureaucracy and Policy of the Institute of Politics at Harvard University and at the Rand Corporation.

125. In response to several readers' recommendations, what follows is reproduced *verbatim* from the paper delivered at the September 1968 Association meetings (Rand P-3919). The discussion is heavily indebted to Ernest R. May.

126. Richard Snyder, *Deterrence and Defense* (Princeton, 1961), p. 11. For a more general presentation of this position see Paul Kecskemeti, *Strategic Surrender* (New York, 1964).

Are Bureaucracies Important? (Or Allison Wonderland)

Stephen D. Krasner

Who and what shapes foreign policy? In recent years analyses have increasingly emphasized not rational calculations of the national interest or the political goals of national leaders but rather bureaucratic procedures and bureaucratic politics. Starting with Richard Neustadt's *Presidential Power,* a judicious study of leadership published in 1960, this approach has come to portray the American president as trapped by a permanent government more enemy than ally. Bureaucratic theorists imply that it is exceedingly difficult if not impossible for political leaders to control the organizational web which surrounds them. Important decisions result from numerous

Stephen D. Krasner, "Are Bureaucracies Important? (Or Allison Wonderland)," *Foreign Policy* 7 (Summer 1971). Copyright 1972 by the Carnegie Endowment for International Peace. Reprinted with permission.

smaller actions taken by individuals at different levels in the bureaucracy who have partially incompatible national, bureaucratic, political, and personal objectives. They are not necessarily a reflection of the aims and values of high officials.

Presidential Power was well received by John Kennedy, who read it with interest, recommended it to his associates, and commissioned Neustadt to do a private study of the 1962 Skybolt incident. The approach has been developed and used by a number of scholars—Roger Hilsman, Morton Halperin, Arthur Schlesinger, Richard Barnet, and Graham Allison—some of whom held subcabinet positions during the 1960s. It was the subject of a special conference at the Rand Corporation, a main theme of a course at the Woodrow Wilson School at Princeton, and the subject of a faculty seminar at Harvard. It is the intellectual paradigm which guides the new public policy program in the John F. Kennedy School of Government at Harvard. Analyses of bureaucratic politics have been used to explain alliance behavior during the 1956 Suez crisis and the Skybolt incident, Truman's relations with MacArthur, American policy in Vietnam, and now most thoroughly the Cuban missile crisis in Graham Allison's *Essence of Decision: Explaining the Cuban Missile Crisis,* published in 1971 (Little, Brown & Company). Allison's volume is the elaboration of an earlier and influential article on this subject. With the publication of his book this approach to foreign policy now receives its definitive statement. The bureaucratic interpretation of foreign policy has become the conventional wisdom.

My argument here is that this vision is misleading, dangerous, and compelling: misleading because it obscures the power of the president; dangerous because it undermines the assumptions of democratic politics by relieving high officials of responsibility; and compelling because it offers leaders an excuse for their failures and scholars an opportunity for innumerable reinterpretations and publications.

The contention that the chief executive is trammelled by the permanent government has disturbing implications for any effort to impute responsibility to public officials. A democratic political philosophy assumes that responsibility for the acts of governments can be attributed to elected officials. The charges of these men are embodied in legal statutes. The electorate punishes an erring official by rejecting him at the polls. Punishment is senseless unless high officials are responsible for the acts of government. Elections have some impact only if government, that most complex of modern organizations, can be controlled. If the bureaucratic machine escapes manipulation and direction even by the highest officials, then punishment is illogical. Elections are a farce not because the people suffer from false consciousness, but because public officials are impotent, enmeshed in a bureaucracy so large that the actions of government are not responsive to their will. What sense to vote a man out of office when his successor, regardless of his values, will be trapped in the same web of only incrementally mutable standard operating procedures?

THE RATIONAL-ACTOR MODEL

Conventional analyses that focus on the values and objectives of foreign policy, what Allison calls the rational-actor model, are perfectly coincident with the ethical assumptions of democratic politics. The state is viewed as a rational unified actor. The behavior of states is the outcome of a rational decision-making process. This process has three steps. The options for a given situation are spelled out. The consequences of each option are projected. A choice is made which maximizes the values held by decision makers. The analyst knows what the state did. His objective is to explain why by imputing to decision makers a set of values which are maximized by observed behavior. These values are his explanation of foreign policy.

The citizen, like the analyst, attributes error to either inappropriate values or lack of foresight. Ideally the electorate judges the officeholder by governmental performance, which is assumed to reflect the objectives and perspicacity of political leaders. Poor policy is made by leaders who fail to foresee accurately the consequences of their decisions or attempt to maximize values not held by the electorate. Political appeals, couched in terms of aims and values, are an appropriate guide for voters. For both the analyst who adheres to the rational-actor model and the citizen who decides elections, values are assumed to be the primary determinant of government behavior.

The bureaucratic-politics paradigm points to quite different determinants of policy. Political leaders can only with great difficulty overcome the inertia and self-serving interests of the permanent government. What counts is managerial skill. In *Essence of Decision* Graham Allison maintains that "the central questions of policy analysis are quite different from the kinds of questions analysts have traditionally asked. Indeed, the crucial questions seem to be matters of planning for management." Administrative feasibility, not substance, becomes the central concern.

The paradoxical conclusion—that bureaucratic analysis with its emphasis on policy guidance implies political nonresponsibility—has most clearly been brought out by discussions of American policy in Vietnam. Richard Neustadt on the concluding page of *Alliance Politics,* his most recent book, muses about a conversation he would have had with President Kennedy in the fall of 1963 had tragedy not intervened. "I considered asking whether, in the light of our machine's performance on a British problem, he conceived that it could cope with South Vietnam's. . . . [I]t was a good question, better than I knew. It haunts me still." For adherents of the bureaucratic-politics paradigm Vietnam was a failure of the "machine," a war in Arthur Schlesinger's words "which no president . . . desired or intended."[1] The machine dictated a policy which it could not successfully terminate. The machine, not the cold war ideology and hubris of Kennedy and Johnson, determined American behavior in Vietnam. Vietnam could hardly be a tragedy, for tragedies are made by choice and character, not fate. A knowing electorate would express sympathy, not levy blame. Machines cannot be held responsible for what they do, nor can the men caught in their workings.

The strength of the bureaucratic web has been attributed to two sources: organizational necessity and bureaucratic interest. The costs of coordination and search procedures are so high that complex organizations *must* settle for satisfactory rather than optimal solutions. Bureaucracies have interests defined in terms of budget allocation, autonomy, morale, and scope which they defend in a game of political bargaining and compromise within the executive branch.

The imperatives of organizational behavior limit flexibility. Without a division of labor and the establishment of standard operating procedures it would be impossible for large organizations to begin to fulfill their statutory objectives, that is to perform tasks designed to meet societal needs rather than merely to perpetuate the organization. A division of labor among and within organizations reduces the job of each particular division to manageable proportions. Once this division is made, the complexity confronting an organization or one of its parts is further reduced through the establishment of standard operating procedures. To deal with each problem as if it were *sui generis* would be impossible given limited resources and information-processing capacity and would make intraorganizational coordination extremely difficult. Bureaucracies are then unavoidably rigid; but without the rigidity imposed by division of labor and standard operating procedures, they could hardly begin to function at all.

However, this rigidity inevitably introduces distortions. All of the options to a given problem will not be presented with equal lucidity and conviction unless by some happenstance the organization has worked out its scenarios for that particular problem in advance. It is more likely that the organization will have addressed itself to something *like* the problem with which it is confronted. It has a set of options for such a hypothetical problem, and these options will be presented to deal with the actual issue at hand. Similarly, organizations cannot execute all policy suggestions with equal facility. The development of new standard operating procedures takes time. The procedures which would most faithfully execute a new policy are not likely to have been worked out. The clash between the rigidity of standard operating procedures which are absolutely necessary to achieve coordination among and within large organizations and the flexibility needed to spell out the options and their consequences for a new problem and to execute new policies is inevitable. It cannot be avoided even with the best of intentions of bureaucratic chiefs anxious to faithfully execute the desires of their leaders.

THE COSTS OF COORDINATION

The limitations imposed by the need to simplify and coordinate indicate that the great increase in governmental power accompanying industrialization has not been achieved without some costs in terms of control. Bureaucratic organizations and the material and symbolic resources which they direct have enormously increased the ability of the American president to influence the international environment. He operates, however, within limits set by organizational procedures.

A recognition of the limits imposed by bureaucratic necessities is a useful qualification of the assumption that states always maximize their interest. This does not, however, imply that the analyst should abandon a focus on values or assumptions of rationality. Standard operating procedures are rational given the costs of search procedures and need for coordination. The behavior of states is still determined by values, although foreign policy may reflect satisfactory rather than optimal outcomes.

An emphasis on the procedural limits of large organizations cannot explain nonincremental change. If government policy is an outcome of standard operating procedures, then behavior at time t is only incrementally different from behavior at time $t - 1$. The exceptions to this prediction leap out of events of even the last year—the Nixon visit to China and the new economic policy. Focusing on the needs dictated by organizational complexity is adequate only during periods when policy is altered very little or not at all. To reduce policy makers to nothing more than the caretakers and minor adjustors of standard operating procedures rings hollow in an era rife with debates and changes of the most fundamental kind in America's conception of its objectives and capabilities.

Bureaucratic analysts do not, however, place the burden of their argument on standard operating procedures but on bureaucratic politics. The objectives of officials are dictated by their bureaucratic position. Each bureau has its own interests. The interests which bureaucratic analysts emphasize are not clientalistic ties between government departments and societal groups or special relations with congressional committees. They are, rather, needs dictated by organizational survival and growth—budget allocations, internal morale, and autonomy. Conflicting objectives advocated by different bureau chiefs are reconciled by a political process. Policy results from compromises and bargaining. It does not necessarily reflect the values of the president, let alone of lesser actors.

The clearest expression of the motivational aspects of the bureaucratic politics approach is the by now well-known aphorism—where you stand depends upon where you sit. Decision makers, however, often do not stand where they sit. Sometimes they are not sitting anywhere. This is clearly illustrated by the positions taken by members of the ExCom during the Cuban missile crisis, which Allison elucidates at some length. While the military, in Pavlovian fashion, urged the use of arms, the secretary of defense took a much more pacific position. The wise old men such as Acheson, imported for the occasion, had no bureaucratic position to defend. Two of the most important members of the ExCom, Robert Kennedy and Theodore Sorensen, were loyal to the president, not to some bureaucratic barony. Similarly, in discussions of Vietnam in 1966 and 1967, it was the secretary of defense who advocated diplomacy and the secretary of state who defended the prerogatives of the military. During Skybolt McNamara was attuned to the president's budgetary concerns, not those of the air force.

Allison, the most recent expositor of the bureaucratic-politics approach, realizes the problems which these facts present. In describing motivation he backs off from an exclusive focus on bureaucratic position, arguing instead that decision makers are motivated by national, organizational, group, and personal interests. While maintaining that the "propensities and priorities stemming from position are sufficient to allow analysts to make reliable predictions about a player's stand" (a proposition violated by his own presentation), he also notes that "these propensities are filtered through the baggage that players bring to positions." For both the missile crisis and Vietnam it was the "baggage" of culture and values, not bureaucratic position, which determined the aims of high officials.

Bureaucratic analysis is also inadequate in its description of how policy is made. Its axiomatic assumption is that politics is a game with the preferences of players given and independent. This is not true. The president chooses most of the important players and sets the rules. He selects the men who head the large bureaucracies. These individuals must share his values. Certainly they identify with his beliefs to a greater extent than would a randomly chosen group of candidates. They also feel some personal fealty to the president who has elevated them from positions of corporate or legal to ones of historic significance. While bureau chiefs are undoubtedly torn by conflicting pressures arising either from their need to protect their own bureaucracies or from personal conviction, they must remain the president's men. At some point disagreement results in dismissal. The values which bureau chiefs assign to policy outcomes are not independent. They are related through a perspective shared with the president.

The president also structures the governmental environment in which he acts through his impact on what Allison calls "action-channels." These are decision-making processes which describe the participation of actors and their influence. The most important "action-channel" in the government is the president's ear. The president has a major role in determining who whispers into it. John Kennedy's reliance on his brother, whose bureaucratic position did not afford him any claim to a decision-making role in the missile crisis, is merely an extreme example. By allocating tasks, selecting the White House bureaucracy, and demonstrating special affections, the president also influences "action-channels" at lower levels of the government.

The president has an important impact on bureaucratic interests. Internal morale is partially determined by presidential behavior. The obscurity in which Secretary of State Rogers languished during the China trip affected both State Department morale and recruitment prospects. Through the budget the president has a direct impact on that most vital of bureaucratic interests. While a bureau may use its societal clients and congressional allies to secure desired allocations, it is surely easier with the president's support than without it. The president can delimit or redefine the scope of an organization's activities by transferring tasks or establishing new agencies. Through public statements he can affect attitudes towards members of a particular bureaucracy and their functions.

THE PRESIDENT AS "KING"

The success a bureau enjoys in furthering its interests depends on maintaining the support and affection of the president. The implicit assumption of the bureaucratic-politics approach that departmental and presidential behavior are independent and comparably important is false. Allison, for instance, vacillates between describing the president as one "chief" among several and as a "king" standing above all other men. He describes in great detail the deliberations of the ExCom, implying that Kennedy's decision was in large part determined by its recommendations, and yet notes that during the crisis Kennedy vetoed an ExCom decision to bomb a SAM base after an American U-2 was shot down on October 27. In general bureaucratic analysts ignore the critical effect which the president has in choosing his advisers, establishing their access to decision making, and influencing bureaucratic interests.

All of this is not to deny that bureaucratic interests may sometimes be decisive in the formulation of foreign policy. Some policy options are never presented to the president. Others he deals with only cursorily, not going beyond options presented by the bureaucracy. This will only be the case if presidential interest and attention are absent. The failure of a chief executive to specify policy does not mean that the government takes no action. Individual bureaucracies may initiate policies which suit their own needs and objectives. The actions of different organizations may work at cross-purposes. The behavior of the state, that is, of some of its official organizations, in the international system appears confused or even contradictory. This is a situation which develops, however, not because of the independent power of government organizations but because of failures by decision makers to assert control.

The ability of bureaucracies to independently establish policies is a function of presidential attention. Presidential attention is a function of presidential values. The chief executive involves himself in those areas which he determines to be important. When the president does devote time and attention to an issue, he can compel the bureaucracy to present him with alternatives. He may do this, as Nixon apparently has, by establishing an organization under his special assistant for national security affairs, whose only bureaucratic interest is maintaining the president's confidence. The president may also rely upon several bureaucracies to secure proposals. The president may even resort to his own knowledge and sense of history to find options which his bureaucracy fails to present. Even when presidential attention is totally absent, bureaus are sensitive to his values. Policies which violate presidential objectives may bring presidential wrath.

While the president is undoubtedly constrained in the implementation of policy by existing bureaucratic procedures, he even has options in this area. As Allison points out, he can choose which agencies will perform what tasks. Programs are fungible and can be broken down into their individual standard operating procedures and recombined. Such exercises take time and effort, but the expenditure of such energies by the president is ultimately a reflection of his own values and not those of the bureaucracy. Within the structure which he has partially created himself he can, if he chooses, further manipulate both the options presented to him and the organizational tools for implementing them.

Neither organizational necessity nor bureaucratic interests are the fundamental determinants of policy. The limits imposed by standard operating procedures as well as the direction of policy are a function of the values of decision makers. The president creates much of the bureaucratic environment which surrounds him through his selection of bureau chiefs, determination of "action-channels," and statutory powers.

THE MISSILE CRISIS

Adherents of the bureaucratic-politics framework have not relied exclusively on general argument. They have attempted to substantiate their contentions with detailed investigations of particular historical events. The most painstaking is Graham Allison's analysis of the Cuban missile crisis in his *Essence of Decision*. In a superlative heuristic exercise Allison attempts to show that critical facts and relationships are ignored by conventional analysis that assumes states are unified rational actors. Only by examining the missile crisis in terms of organizational necessity and bureaucratic interests and politics can the formulation and implementation of policy be understood.

The missile crisis, as Allison notes, is a situation in which conventional analysis would appear most appropriate. The president devoted large amounts of time to policy formulation and implementation. Regular bureaucratic channels were short-circuited by the creation of an executive committee which included representatives of the bipartisan foreign-policy establishment, bureau chiefs, and the president's special aides. The president dealt with details which would normally be left to bureaucratic subordinates. If under such circumstances the president could not effectively control policy formulation and implementation, then the rational-actor model is gravely suspect.

In his analysis of the missile crisis Allison deals with three issues: the American choice of a blockade, the Soviet decision to place MRBMs and IRBMs on Cuba, and the Soviet decision to withdraw the missiles from Cuba. The American decision is given the most detailed attention. Allison notes three ways in which bureaucratic procedures and interests influenced the formulation of American policy: first in the elimination of the nonforcible alternatives; second through the collection of information; third through the standard operating procedures of the air force.

In formulating the U.S. response the ExCom considered six alternatives. These were:

1. Do nothing
2. Diplomatic pressure
3. A secret approach to Castro
4. Invasion
5. A surgical air strike
6. A naval blockade

The approach to Castro was abandoned because he did not have direct control of the missiles. An invasion was eliminated as a first step because it would not have been precluded by any of the other options. Bureaucratic factors were not involved.

The two nonmilitary options of doing nothing and lodging diplomatic protests were also abandoned from the outset because the president was not interested in them. In terms of both domestic and international politics this was the most important decision of the crisis. It was a decision which only the president had authority to make. Allison's case rests on proving that this decision was foreordained by bureaucratic roles. He lists several reasons for Kennedy's elimination of the nonforcible alternatives. Failure to act decisively would undermine the confidence of members of his administration, convince the permanent government that his administration lacked leadership, hurt the Democrats in the forthcoming election, destroy his reputation among members of Congress, create public distrust, encourage American allies and enemies to question American courage, invite a second Bay of Pigs, and feed his own doubts about himself. Allison quotes a statement by Kennedy that he feared impeachment and concludes that the "nonforcible paths—avoiding military measures, resorting instead to diplomacy—could not have been more irrelevant to *his* problems." Thus Allison argues that Kennedy had no choice.

Bureaucratic analysis, what Allison calls in his book the governmental-politics model, implies that any man in the same position would have had no choice. The elimination of passivity and diplomacy was ordained by the office and not by the man.

Such a judgment is essential to the governmental-politics model, for the resort to the "baggage" of values, culture, and psychology which the president carries with him undermines the explanatory and predictive power of the approach. To adopt, however, the view that the office determined Kennedy's action is both to underrate his power and to relieve him of responsibility. The president defines his own role. A different man could have chosen differently. Kennedy's *Profiles in Courage* had precisely dealt with men who had risked losing their political roles because of their "baggage" of values and culture.

Allison's use of the term *intragovernmental balance of power* to describe John Kennedy's elimination of diplomacy and passivity is misleading. The American government is not a balance-of-power system; at the very least it is a loose hierarchical one. Kennedy's judgments of the domestic, international, bureaucratic, and personal ramifications of his choice were determined by *who* he was as well as *what* he was. The central mystery of the crisis remains why Kennedy chose to risk nuclear war over missile placements which he knew did not dramatically alter the strategic balance. The answer to this puzzle can only be found through an examination of values, the central concern of conventional analysis.

The impact of bureaucratic interests and standard operating procedures is reduced then to the choice of the blockade instead of the surgical air strike. Allison places considerable emphasis on intelligence gathering in the determination of this choice. U-2 flights were the most important source of data about Cuba; their information was supplemented by refugee reports, analyses of shipping, and other kinds of intelligence. The timing of the U-2 flights, which Allison argues was determined primarily by bureaucratic struggles, was instrumental in determining Kennedy's decision:

> Had a U-2 flown over the western end of Cuba three weeks earlier, it could have discovered the missiles, giving the administration more time to consider alternatives and to act before the danger of operational missiles in Cuba became a major factor in the equation. Had the missiles not been discovered until two weeks later, the blockade would have been irrelevant, since the Soviet missile shipments would have been completed . . . An explanation of the politics of the discovery is consequently a considerable piece of the explanation of the U.S. blockade.

The delay, however, from September 15 to October 14, when the missiles were discovered reflected presidential values more than bureaucratic politics. The October 14 flight took place ten days after COMOR, the interdepartmental committee which directed the activity of the U-2s, had decided the flights should be made. "This ten-day delay constitutes some form of 'failure,'" Allison contends. It was the result, he argues, of a struggle between the Central Intelligence Agency and the air force over who would control the flights. The air force maintained that the flights over Cuba were sufficiently dangerous to warrant military supervision; the Central Intelligence Agency, anxious to guard its own prerogatives, maintained that its U-2s were technically superior.

However, the ten-day delay after the decision to make a flight over western Cuba was not entirely attributable to bureaucratic bickering. Allison reports an attempt to make a flight on October 9, which failed because the U-2 flamed out. Further delays resulted from bad weather. Thus the inactivity caused by bureaucratic infighting amounted to only five days (October 4 to October 9) once the general decision to make the flight was taken. The other five days' delay caused by engine failure and the weather must be attributed to some higher source than the machinations of the American bureaucracy.

However, there was also a long period of hesitation before October 4. John McCone, director of the Central Intelligence Agency, had indicated to the president on August 22 that he thought there was a strong possibility that the Soviets were preparing to put offensive missiles on Cuba. He did not have firm evidence, and his contentions were met with skepticism in the administration.

INCREASED RISKS

On September 10 COMOR had decided to restrict further U-2 flights over western Cuba. This decision was based upon factors which closely fit the rational-actor model of foreign policy formulation. COMOR decided to halt the flights because the recent installation of SAMs in western Cuba coupled with the loss of a Nationalist Chinese U-2 increased the probability and costs of a U-2 loss over Cuba. International opinion might force the cancellation of the flights altogether. The absence of information from U-2s would be a national, not simply a bureaucratic, cost. The president had been forcefully attacking the critics of his Cuba policy, arguing that patience and restraint were the best course of action. The loss of a U-2 over Cuba would tend to undermine the president's position. Thus, COMOR's decision on September 10 reflected a sensitivity to the needs and policies of the president rather than the parochial concerns of the permanent government.

The decision on October 4 to allow further flights was taken only after consultation with the president. The timing was determined largely by the wishes of the president. His actions were not circumscribed by decisions made at lower levels of the bureaucracy of which he was not aware. The flights were delayed because of conflicting pressures and risks confronting Kennedy. He was forced to weigh the potential benefits of additional knowledge against the possible losses if a U-2 were shot down.

What if the missiles had not been discovered until after October 14? Allison argues that had the missiles been discovered two weeks later, the blockade would have been irrelevant, since the missile shipments would have been completed. This is true, but only to a limited extent. The blockade was irrelevant even when it was put in place, for there were missiles already on the island. As Allison points out in his rational-actor cut at explaining the crisis, the blockade was both an act preventing the shipment of additional missiles and a signal of American firmness. The missiles already on Cuba were removed because of what the blockade meant and not because of what it did.

An inescapable dilemma confronted the United States. It could not retaliate until the missiles were on the island. Military threats or action required definitive proof. The United States could only justify actions with photographic evidence. It could only take photos after the missiles were on Cuba. The blockade could only be a demonstration of American firmness. Even if the missiles had not been discovered until they were operational, the United States might still have begun its response with a blockade.

Aside from the timing of the discovery of the missiles, Allison argues that the standard operating procedures of the air force affected the decision to blockade rather than to launch a surgical air strike. When the missiles were first discovered, the air force had no specific contingency plans for dealing with such a situation. They did, however, have a plan for a large-scale air strike carried out in conjunction with an invasion of Cuba. The plan called for the air bombardment of many targets. This led to some confusion during the first week of the ExCom's considerations because the air force was talking in terms of an air strike of some five hundred sorties, while there were only some forty known missile sites on Cuba. Before this confusion was clarified, a strong coalition of advisers was backing the blockade.

As a further example of the impact of standard operating procedures, Allison notes that the air force had classified the missiles as mobile. Because this classification assumed that the missiles might be moved immediately before an air strike, the commander of the air force would not guarantee that a surgical air strike would be completely effective. By the end of the first week of the ExCom's deliberations, when Kennedy made his decision for a blockade, the surgical air strike was presented as a "null option." The examination of the strike was not reopened until the following week, when civilian experts found that the missiles were not in fact mobile.

This incident suggests one caveat to Allison's assertion that the missile crisis is a case which discriminates against bureaucratic analysis. In crises, when time is short, the president may have to accept bureaucratic options which could be amended under more leisurely conditions.

NOT ANOTHER PEARL HARBOR

The impact of the air force's standard operating procedures on Kennedy's decision must, however, to some extent remain obscure. It is not likely that either McNamara, who initially called for a diplomatic response, or Robert Kennedy, who was partially concerned with the ethical implications of a surprise air strike, would have changed their recommendations even if the air force had estimated its capacities more optimistically. There were other reasons for choosing the blockade aside from the apparent infeasibility of the air strike. John Kennedy was not anxious to have the Pearl Harbor analogy and applied to the United States. At one of the early meetings of the ExCom his brother had passed a note saying, "I now know how

Tojo felt when he was planning Pearl Harbor." The air strike could still be considered even if the blockade failed. A chief executive anxious to keep his options open would find a blockade a more prudent initial course of action.

Even if the air force had stated that a surgical air strike was feasible, this might have been discounted by the president. Kennedy had already experienced unrealistic military estimates. The Bay of Pigs was the most notable example. The United States did not use low-flying photographic reconnaissance until after the president had made his public announcement of the blockade. Prior to the president's speech on October 22, twenty high-altitude U-2 flights were made. After the speech there were eighty-five low-level missions, indicating that the intelligence community was not entirely confident that U-2 flights alone would reveal all of the missile sites. The Soviets might have been camouflaging some missiles on Cuba. Thus, even if the immobility of the missiles had been correctly estimated, it would have been rash to assume that an air strike would have extirpated all of the missiles. There were several reasons, aside from the air force's estimate, for rejecting the surgical strike.

Thus in terms of policy formulation it is not clear that the examples offered by Allison concerning the timing of discovery of the missiles and the standard operating procedures of the air force had a decisive impact on the choice of a blockade over a surgical air strike. The ultimate decisions did rest with the president. The elimination of the nonforcible options was a reflection of Kennedy's values. An explanation of the Cuban missile crisis which fails to explain policy in terms of the values of the chief decision maker must inevitably lose sight of the forest for the trees.

The most chilling passages in *Essence of Decision* are concerned not with the formulation of policy but with its implementation. In carrying out the blockade the limitations on the president's ability to control events become painfully clear. Kennedy did keep extraordinarily close tabs on the workings of the blockade. The first Russian ship to reach the blockade was allowed to pass through without being intercepted on direct orders from the president. Kennedy felt it would be wise to allow Khrushchev more time. The president overrode the ExCom's decision to fire on a Cuban SAM base after a U-2 was shot down on October 27. A spy ship similar to the *Pueblo* was patrolling perilously close to Cuba and was ordered to move further out to sea.

Despite concerted presidential attention coupled with an awareness of the necessity of watching minute details which would normally be left to lower levels of the bureaucracy, the president still had exceptional difficulty in controlling events. Kennedy personally ordered the navy to pull in the blockade from eight hundred miles to five hundred miles to give Khrushchev additional time in which to make his decision. Allison suggests that the ships were not drawn in. The navy, being both anxious to guard its prerogatives and confronted with the difficulty of moving large numbers of ships over millions of square miles of ocean, failed to promptly execute a presidential directive.

There were several random events which might have changed the outcome of the crisis. The navy used the blockade to test its antisubmarine operations. It was forcing Soviet submarines to surface at a time when the president and his advisers were unaware that contact with Russian ships had been made. A U-2 accidentally strayed over Siberia on October 22. Any one of these events, and perhaps others still unknown, could have triggered escalatory actions by the Russians.

Taken together, they strongly indicate how much caution is necessary when a random event may have costly consequences. A nation like a drunk staggering on a cliff should stay far from the edge. The only conclusion which can be drawn from the inability of the chief executive to fully control the implementation of a policy in which he was intensely interested and to which he devoted virtually all of his time for an extended period is that the risks were even greater than the president knew. Allison is more convincing on the problems concerned with policy implementation than on questions relating to policy formulation. Neither bureaucratic interests nor organizational procedures explain the positions taken by members of the ExCom, the elimination of passivity and diplomacy, or the choice of a blockade instead of an air strike.

CONCLUSION

A glimpse at almost any one of the major problems confronting American society indicates that a reformulation and clarification of objectives, not better control and direction of the bureaucracy, is critical. Conceptions of man and society long accepted are being undermined. The environmentalists present a fundamental challenge to the assumption that man can control and stand above nature, an assumption rooted both in the successes of technology and industrialization and Judeo-Christian assertions of man's exceptionalism. The nation's failure to formulate a consistent crime policy reflects in part an inability to decide whether criminals are freely willing rational men subject to determinations of guilt or innocence or the victims of socioeconomic conditions or psychological circumstances over which they have no control. The economy manages to defy accepted economic precepts by sustaining relatively high inflation and unemployment at the same time. Public officials and economists question the wisdom of economic growth. Conflicts exist over what the objectives of the nation should be and what its capacities are. On a whole range of social issues the society is torn between attributing problems to individual inadequacies and social injustice.

None of these issues can be decided just by improving managerial techniques. Before the niceties of bureaucratic implementation are investigated, it is necessary to know what objectives are being sought. Objectives are ultimately a reflection of values, of beliefs concerning what man and society ought to be. The failure of the American government to take decisive action in a number of critical areas reflects not so much the inertia of a large bureaucratic machine as a confusion over values which afflicts the society in general and its leaders in particular. It is in such circumstances too comforting to attribute failure to organizational inertia, although nothing could be more convenient for political leaders who having either not formulated any policy or advocated bad policies can blame their failures on the governmental structure. Both psychologically and politically, leaders may find it advantageous to have others think of them as ineffectual rather than evil. But the facts are otherwise—particularly in foreign policy. There the choices—and the responsibility—rest squarely with the president.

NOTE

1. Quoted in Daniel Ellsberg, "The Quagmire Myth and the Stalemate Machine," *Public Policy* (Spring 1971):218.

The Organizational Process and Bureaucratic Politics Paradigms: Retrospect and Prospect

David A. Welch

1991 marked the twentieth anniversary of the publication of Graham Allison's *Essence of Decision: Explaining the Cuban Missile Crisis.*[1] The influence of this work has been felt far beyond the study of international politics. Since 1971, it has been cited in over 1,100 articles in journals listed in the *Social Sciences Citation Index,* in every periodical touching political science, and in others as diverse as *The American Journal of Agricultural Economics* and *The Journal of Nursing Administration.* The book continues to sell thousands of copies every year, reflecting its widespread use in university curricula. To those familiar with it, none of this will be surprising, particularly in view of its genesis: as Allison notes in the preface (*ED,* p. ix), it "represents to a large extent the most recent but still unfinished 'Evolving Paper'" of the Research Seminar on Bureaucracy, Politics, and Policy at Harvard University's Institute of Politics, a group that included Ernest May, Morton Halperin, Stanley Hoffmann, Fred Iklé, William Kaufmann, Andrew Marshall, Richard Neustadt, Don Price, Harry Rowen, Thomas Schelling, James Q. Wilson, and Adam Yarmolinski—the kind of gathering that would have prompted Presi-

David A. Welch, "The Organizational Process and Bureaucratic Politics Paradigms: Retrospect and Prospect," *International Security,* Vol. 17, No. 2, Fall 1992.

dent Kennedy to quip, "Never has so much talent been gathered in one room since Thomas Jefferson dined alone."[2]

It was Jefferson who advocated a fundamental reconsideration of prevailing institutions once every generation.[3] Thus the twentieth anniversary of this seminal work seems an appropriate time to reflect on the achievements and the prospects of the revolution that it wrought. My aim is not to review the book *per se;* little can be added now to the perceptive critiques it received at the time of publication.[4] Rather, my aim is to use the book as a vehicle for assessing the contribution to our understanding of international politics of that which it spawned: the bureaucratic politics approach, broadly construed.[5] Allison himself represented *Essence of Decision* as experimental, exploratory, and preliminary; his purpose was to chart a course for others to follow (*ED*, p. 273). Fidelity to his project requires that we periodically take a bearing and, if necessary, make mid-course corrections. Such is the intent of this paper.[6]

ALLISON'S PROJECT

In the preface to *Essence of Decision,* Allison writes that the book had two main aims: to try to solve certain puzzles about the Cuban missile crisis, and to explore the influence of the analyst's unrecognized assumptions upon his or her thinking about events of that kind. "Answers to questions like why the Soviet Union tried to sneak strategic offensive missiles into Cuba must be affected by basic assumptions we make, categories we use, our angle of vision," Allison writes. "But what kind of assumptions do we tend to make? How do these assumptions channel our thinking? What alternative perspectives are available?" (*ED*, p. v).

The dominant frame of reference most analysts of world politics use is the rational actor model (Allison's "Model I"), which conceives of states as unitary and purposive, making consistent, value-maximizing choices within specified constraints (*ED*, p. 30). The major contribution of *Essence of Decision* is to elucidate two alternative frameworks, the organizational process model (or Model II) and the governmental (or bureaucratic) politics model (Model III). Each is developed in one theoretical chapter, and applied to the case of the Cuban missile crisis in another. For the political scientists, Allison maintains, "the theoretical chapters constitute the contribution" (*ED*, p. vi), presenting relatively rigorously-formulated paradigms that "provide a basis for improved explanations and predictions" (*ED*, p. 5). In other words, Allison claims that the organizational process and bureaucratic politics paradigms perform *better* than the rational actor paradigm in the tasks paradigms are meant to fulfill. Do they?

To answer this question, I briefly describe the nature and function of "analytic paradigms"; I comment on Allison's specification of Models II and III; and I examine the performance of each on three crucial dimensions. I reach two negative conclusions, and one positive one. First, students of international politics have largely failed to take up Allison's challenge to build and to test theory at the intragovernmental level of analysis. Second, despite the dearth of rigorous tests, there are convincing reasons to believe that neither Model II nor Model III is as useful as, let alone analytically superior to, Model I. Nevertheless, Allison's motivating intuition that bureaucracies are important may yet be vindicated since there are strong *prima facie* grounds to believe that *some* paradigm concentrating the analyst's attention on organizational characteristics or processes other than those on which Models II and III focus might yield significant analytical gains. While I stop well short of specifying such a paradigm in detail, I make a few preliminary remarks intended to be suggestive in this regard.

THE NATURE AND PURPOSE OF A PARADIGM

Allison works with the conception of a paradigm developed by Robert Merton for sociological analyses: "a systematic statement of the basic assumptions, concepts, and propositions employed by a school of analysis." The components of Allison's paradigms include the basic unit of analysis, the organizing concepts, the dominant inference pattern, and several purely illustrative propositions (*ED,* p. 32). None of Allison's three models is a fully-specified causal model relating dependent and independent variables; instead, each is meant to be pretheoretical, or, better, "metatheoretical," since it merely invites the reader to "think about X as if it were Y."[7]

By themselves, metatheories have no explanatory or predictive power; they are neither testable nor falsifiable, since no expectations or predictions follow directly from them. Consequently, their performance cannot be judged by direct empirical test. Instead, they must be assessed on the basis of how well they perform what Merton calls "at least five closely related functions":

1. Paradigms serve a "notational function. . . . They provide a compact parsimonious arrangement of the central concepts and their interrelations as these are utilized for description and analysis."
2. The explicit statement of an analytic paradigm "lessens the likelihood of inadvertently importing hidden assumptions and concepts, since each new assumption and each new concept must be either logically *derivable* from the previous terms of the paradigm or explicitly *incorporated* in it. The paradigm thus supplies a pragmatic and logical guide for the avoidance of ad hoc (i.e., logically irresponsible) hypotheses."
3. Paradigms "advance the *cumulation* of theoretical interpretation. In this connection, we can regard the paradigm as the foundation upon which the house of interpretations is built. If a new story cannot be built directly upon the paradigmatic foundations, if it cannot be derived from the foundations, then it must be considered a new wing of the total structure, and the foundations (of concepts and assumptions) must be extended to support the new wing. Moreover, each new story which *can* be built upon the original foundations strengthens our confidence in their substantial quality just as every new extension, precisely because it requires additional foundations, leads us to suspect the soundness of the original substructure."
4. Paradigms, "by their very arrangement, suggest the *systematic* cross-tabulation of presumably significant concepts and may thus sensitize the analyst

to types of empirical and theoretic problems which might otherwise be overlooked. They promote *analysis* rather than concrete description."

5. Paradigms "make for the codification of methods of *qualitative* analysis in a manner approximating the logical, if not the empirical, rigor of *quantitative* analysis."[8]

Of these, the third and fourth functions provide the clearest criteria for assessing the performance of paradigms. While paradigms themselves have no explanatory or predictive power, theories derived from them do, and it is by assessing the performance of these theories that we ultimately judge the value of the paradigms. This is what Allison means when he suggests that Models II and III provide a *basis* for improved explanations and predictions. Useful paradigms, therefore, facilitate the development of successful theories that permit general causal inferences, provide cogent explanations, and improve predictions. In contrast, unproductive paradigms generate theories that perform poorly, or result only in a proliferation of atheoretical concrete descriptions. Judgments about the worth of paradigms are always relative, however. As Thomas Kuhn notes, "Paradigms gain their status because they are more successful than their competitors in solving a few problems that the group of practitioners has come to recognize as acute. To be more successful is not, however, to be either completely successful with a single problem or notably successful with any large number."[9]

THE SPECIFICATION OF THE PARADIGMS

Allison introduces the organizational process paradigm (Model II) by contrasting it with Model I, the rational actor model:

> For some purposes, governmental behavior can be usefully summarized as action chosen by a unitary, rational decisionmaker: centrally controlled, completely informed, and value maximizing. But this simplification must not be allowed to conceal the fact that a government consists of a conglomerate of semi-feudal, loosely allied organizations, each with a substantial life of its own. Government leaders do sit formally and, to some extent, in fact, on top of this conglomerate. But governments perceive problems through organizational sensors. Governments define alternatives and estimate consequences as their component organizations process information; governments act as these organizations enact routines. Governmental behavior can therefore be understood, according to a second conceptual model, less as deliberate choices and more as *outputs* of large organizations functioning according to standard patterns of behavior. . . . To perform complex routines, the behavior of large numbers of individuals must be coordinated. Coordination requires standard operating procedures: rules according to which things are done. . . . At any given time, a government consists of *existing* organizations, each with a *fixed* set of standard operating procedures and programs. . . . Existing organizational routines for employing present physical capabilities constitute the range of effective choice open to government leaders confronted with any problem. . . . The fact that the fixed programs . . . exhaust the range of buttons that leaders can push is not always perceived by these leaders. But in every case it is critical for an understanding of what is actually done (*ED*, pp. 67–68, 79).

The crucial respect in which Model II represents a revision of Model I, therefore, is its understanding that governmental behavior is constrained by the routines of the organizations of which the government is composed. Belying the title of the book, Model II does not operate at the moment of decision; rather, it explains deviations from ideal rationality at the moment of decision by highlighting the ways in which organizational routines constrain the *formation of options,* and it explains deviations from perfect instrumentality after decisions are made by revealing how routines affect implementation. Within those constraints, however, Model II has nothing to say about the decisions themselves, which by default may be analyzed in terms of bounded rationality, the operation of bureaucratic politics, or some other conceptual framework highlighting such factors as the influence of cognitive and perceptual biases, the role of affect, the dynamics of small-group decision-making processes, and so forth.

According to Model III, "The 'leaders' who sit on top of organizations are not a monolithic group. Rather, each individual in this group is, in his own right, a player in a central, competitive game. The name of the game is politics: bargaining along regularized circuits among players positioned hierarchically within the government." Players "make governmental decisions not by a single rational choice but by the pulling and hauling that is politics" (*ED,* p. 144). Model III therefore explains deviations from ideal rationality by revealing the political gamesmanship behind them. Unlike organizational routines, these games may operate during the moment of decision itself as well as in the option-formation stage or during implementation, rendering Model III broader in scope, more ambitious in its goals, and potentially more fruitful than Model II. Note that Model III does not suppose that the individual players behave irrationally in the games in which they participate, merely that the net effect of those games is to deflect state behavior from the course that would have been chosen by a unitary rational actor.[10]

It is unfortunate that Allison's successors have focused overwhelmingly on Model III, all but ignoring Model II. Allison himself contributed to this tendency in a later article with Morton Halperin that conflated the two models, relegating organizational processes to the status of "constraints" within the bureaucratic politics paradigm.[11] In reality, while the two may well operate synergistically, they postulate fundamentally different constraints on rationality and are worthy of the distinct development they received in *Essence of Decision.*[12] The temptation to conflate the two models may have stemmed from errors in the original specification of the paradigms. For example, among the organizing concepts Allison includes in his specification of Model II are the parochial priorities and perceptions of organizations (*ED,* p. 81), which, in fact, have nothing to do with routines and which properly belong to the bureaucratic politics paradigm. Likewise, in elaborating the crucial Model II concept of "action as organizational output," Allison writes that, in producing outputs, the activity of an organization is characterized by its goals, or "constraints defining acceptable performance," for example, the imperative to defend one's turf against rival organizations. While this may well be true of organizational behavior (and for some issues, such as budget allocations, most certainly *is* true), the goals of organizations also properly belong to Model III, for while they define interests (and thus the structure of the "game"), they are logically distinct from routines.[13]

THE PERFORMANCE OF THE PARADIGMS

It is obvious that Model I is, in important senses, wrong; states are not unitary, purposive, rational actors. As Allison puts it, "We are forced to recognize that in treating happenings as actions, and national governments as unitary purposive actors, we are 'modeling.' The fact that the assumptions and categories of this model neglect important factors such as organizational processes and bureaucratic politics suggests that the model is inadequate" (*ED*, p. 254). Nevertheless, as Allison argues, the criticism that Model I is unrealistic—while true—does not provide a basis for assessing its performance as a paradigm.[14] Newton assumed wrongly that mass concentrates at a point, but he could not have relinquished this assumption without jeopardizing his prodigious accomplishments in specifying theoretical relationships between physical objects. While it may be, as David Kozak insists, that "recognizing bureaucratic politics leads to a realistic understanding of the U.S. policy process" and that "ignoring bureaucratic politics can only lead to ignorance and naiveté," only someone seeking mere concrete description will consider the point important.[15]

Allison's claim that Models II and III represent improvements on Model I hinges not on their superior realism, but on their potentially greater power and fruitfulness as paradigms. To determine how well paradigms perform, and hence to judge their relative worth, we must gauge the productivity of the "normal science" that they permit.[16] Normal science is the activity of articulating theory, determining significant facts, and matching facts with theory.[17] A productive paradigm paves the way for a normal science capable of solving a good proportion of the puzzles drawn to the analyst's attention. Let us look closely at the performance of Models II and III in these terms.

Articulating Theory

Since students of international politics have paid comparatively little attention to Model II, or have conflated it with Model III, they have made little attempt to develop theories of state behavior in which organizational routines play a central role. In *Essence of Decision,* however, Allison advances several theoretical propositions derivable from Model II: (1) existing organizational routines limit the range of available options in a given situation; (2) organizational routines resist change; (3) existing organizational routines determine the course of implementation; and (4) organizational routines systematically induce instrumental irrationalities in state behavior. These are sound theoretical propositions, in that they are clear, plausible, and (with perhaps the exception of the fourth, as I discuss below), testable.

Ironically, despite the considerably greater attention analysts have paid to Model III, the body of theory it has spawned is far less clear, far less plausible, and more difficult to test. The central difficulty revolves around the hypothesized relationship between a player's bureaucratic position and his or her preferences. The tightest theoretical proposition is captured by Miles's Law: "Where you stand depends upon where you sit."[18] Allison writes: "For large classes of issues—e.g., budgets and procurement decisions—the stance of a particular player can be predicted with high reliability from information about his seat."[19] In addition, Allison suggests that bureaucratic position determines a player's perception of an issue: "Where you sit influences what you see as well as where you stand (on any issue)."[20] But Allison confuses matters by insisting that "Each player pulls and hauls with the power at his discretion for outcomes that will advance his conception of *national,* organizational, *group,* and *personal* interests,"[21] and that "each person comes to his position with baggage in tow. His bags include sensitivities to certain issues, commitments to various projects, and personal standing with and debts to groups in society" (*ED,* p. 166). Moreover, "individuals' perceptions of the issue will differ radically. These differences will be partially predictable from the pressure of their position plus their personality" (*ED,* pp. 180–181). It is not clear, therefore, whether, or on what issues, we should expect bureaucratic position to be determinative. As Stephen Krasner puts it, bureaucratic analysis implies that the office—not its occupant—determines how players behave.[22] Indeed, at points Allison seems actively to deny any theoretical relationship between a player's position and his or her preferences and perceptions. "The peculiar preferences and stands of individual players can have a significant effect on governmental action," Allison writes. "Had someone other than Paul Nitze been head of the Policy Planning Staff in 1949, there is no reason to believe that there would have been an NSC 68. Had [Douglas] MacArthur not possessed certain preferences, power, and skills, U.S. troops might never have crossed the narrow neck [of Korea]" (*ED,* p. 174). If the idiosyncracies of particular individuals determined these important actions and policies, specifically bureaucratic determinants can hardly have played an important role.

A second and related difficulty concerns the theoretical relationship between bureaucratic position and influence in the decision-making process. "What determines each player's impact on results?" Allison asks; "*1. Power.* Power (i.e., effective influence on government decisions and actions) is an elusive blend of at least three elements: bargaining advantages, skill and will in using bargaining advantages, and other players' perceptions of the first two ingredients" (*ED,* p. 168). But bargaining skills and advantages, and the will to use them, are idiosyncratic. They are not necessarily linked to bureaucratic positions *per se.* Again, Allison himself is his clearest critic on this point: "The hard core of the bureaucratic politics mix is personality," he writes. "How each man manages to stand the heat in *his* kitchen, each player's basic operating style, and the complementarity or contradiction among personalities and styles in the inner circles are irreducible pieces of the policy blend."[23]

The third major element in Allison's theoretical articulation of the bureaucratic politics paradigm is the conceptualization of the manner in which decisions are made: through a bargaining process characterized by the "pulling and hauling that is politics," the net result of which is action rarely intended by any player in particular (*ED,* p. 175). This third conceptualization would seem to present no theoretical difficulties.

Determining Significant Facts and Matching Facts with Theory

Despite being clear and plausible, the four theoretical propositions Allison advances in his presentation of Model II do not match up well with the facts of the Cuban missile crisis as they presently appear, which demonstrate that existing organizational routines neither exhaust the range of available options, nor resist change, nor necessarily determine the course of implementation, nor systematically induce instrumental irrationalities in state behavior.

The deployment of Soviet missiles to Cuba itself clearly illustrates that existing organizational routines do not exhaust the range of available options to decision-makers. The Soviet Union had never deployed nuclear missiles outside its borders before and had no set procedures for so doing. On short notice, the various branches of the Soviet military put together a massive redeployment of missiles already operational in Central Europe, demonstrating the remarkable ability of organizations to respond to political directives issued essentially without concern for the available set of routines.[24] Nor was the list of possible responses to the Soviet deployment generated by the ExComm (President Kennedy's executive committee) wholly dependent upon existing organizational routines. Certain options—such as a quiet diplomatic *démarche*—could have been arranged ad hoc and implemented immediately. It seems likely that if President Kennedy had chosen this option, his preferred channel would have been a secret approach to Ambassador Anatoly Dobrynin by his brother, Robert Kennedy.[25] This would have been neither bureaucratic nor routine; but the fact that it was one channel among several possibilities indicates that organizational rigidities did not constitute a serious constraint on the range of diplomatic options. Even the range of military options was little constrained by organizational routines. Some pre-existing plans were inherently flexible in the choice of missions and targets.[26] Other military options could have been worked up over a period of time.[27] Of course, the existing repertoire of organizational routines *can* restrict the range of available options prior to a decision in special circumstances: namely, when complex operations are involved, and when time is particularly short. As Glenn Snyder and Paul Diesing note, the July Crisis of 1914 might well have unfolded differently if, in addition to the Schlieffen Plan, the German General Staff had prepared a plan for a deterrent show of force in the east.[28] But a spectacular example such as this does not establish a general theoretical point;[29] such a constraint is always a matter of degree, and generally affects only a portion of the range of options available to national leaders (namely, immediate large-scale military options).

The power of an appeal to organizational rigidities as a constraint on rational action seems further weakened by the observation that routines can be quite flexible, and are often modified or overridden (cf. *ED*, pp. 94–95). The annals of military history are full of examples of this. Few organizations are as thoroughly "scripted" as military forces, yet in every war they have achieved spectacular results by modifying or overriding standard operating procedures. Jimmy Doolittle's April 1942 raid on Tokyo was made possible by launching land-based bombers from an aircraft carrier; Sherman's march through the Carolinas was made possible by innovations to standard fording techniques.[30] In the Cuban missile crisis, national leaders repeatedly and effectively modified organizational routines whenever they felt it necessary to do so. The creation and operation of the ExComm itself short-circuited regular bureaucratic channels.[31] President Kennedy monitored naval activities on the quarantine line through a direct channel to the commander, Vice Admiral Alfred G. Ward, bypassing the normal chain of command.[32] The president also countermanded a preauthorized retaliatory strike on the surface-to-air missile site responsible for downing an American U-2 on October 27.[33] Attorney General Robert Kennedy succeeded in canceling the planned sabotage operations in Cuba of Operation Mongoose's Task Force W when he found out about them.[34] In one case, a subordinate brought potentially counterproductive aspects of routines to the attention of national leaders precisely so that they *could* modify them: NATO Supreme Allied Commander General Lauris Norstad, fearing that a highly-visible unilateral alert of American forces in Europe might undercut the allies' support for Kennedy's stand on Cuba, in view of the fact that he had not consulted them on military contingencies, requested and received permission to modify the nature of the alert in Europe. Raymond Garthoff calls it "a wise move, and a good example of political-military 'feedback' in decision-making."[35] It is also a good demonstration that Model II errs in conceiving implementation as essentially mechanical once a decision is made.

This leaves the claim that organizational routines systematically degrade instrumentality. One respect in which we might believe they do so is by constraining decision-makers' access to information. As Allison puts it, "information about Soviet missiles in Cuba came to the attention of the President on October 14 rather than three weeks earlier, or a week later, as a consequence of the routines and procedures of the organizations that make up the U.S. intelligence community. These 'eyes and ears' of the government function less as integral parts of a unitary head that entertains preconceptions and theories than as organs that perform their tasks in a habitual fashion" (*ED*, p. 118). Roger Hilsman notes that intelligence-gathering procedures in 1962 resulted in a lag of ten days to two weeks between the time an informant in Cuba noticed something unusual and the time the report reached Washington.[36] While this may seem an inordinately long period of time, the discovery of the missiles was actually an impressive accomplishment, in view of the volume of information the Central Intelligence Agency (CIA) had to process and the fact that the Soviets were taking pains to prevent it.[37] The key point is that without routines, the government would not have discovered the missiles in time, and would not have been able to react. Routines are instrumentally rational given the opportunity costs of doing without them.[38]

Moreover, during the Cuban missile crisis, some of the greatest dangers to successful crisis management stemmed from the *breakdown* of routines, not from their normal operation. Consider three examples:

First, when President Kennedy ordered the Strategic Air Command (SAC) to a higher state of alert, General Thomas Power, SAC commander-in-chief, ordered the alert sent out in the clear, rather than in code, as would have been standard procedure. Power's intention was to make the Soviets feel vulnerable to American nuclear might; but this was far from the president's desire at the time, and under other circumstances might have prompted an adverse reaction from the Soviet Union.[39]

Second, at the height of the crisis on October 27, 1962, Soviet air defense forces in Cuba—much to Khrushchev's shock and chagrin—shot down an American U-2 reconnaissance plane without requesting permission from their superiors.[40] Under other circumstances, this might have been the first step on a ladder of escalation.

Third, also on October 27, an American U-2 violated standing orders to stay clear of Soviet territory and inadvertently strayed into Siberian air space, heightening Khrushchev's fear of nuclear attack at a crucial point in the confrontation.[41] This could have provided the spark that ignited the powder keg.

As these three examples show, we must ask in any given case whether organizational routines are more of a help or more of a hindrance to the promotion of national goals. *Violations* of standard procedures can represent constraints on ideally rational action at least as powerful as blind, mechanical adherence to routines. Organizational routines thus cannot be said to have a *uniformly* negative effect on instrumentality. While it may be possible to argue that they have a *net* negative effect on instrumentality, no study presently exists substantiating such a claim.[42]

Nonetheless, Model II draws to the analyst's attention the undeniable fact that from time to time organizations *do* perform in blind accordance with routines, with results that national leaders would not have chosen deliberately. One reason for the failure of President Carter's mission to rescue American hostages in Teheran, for example, was the fact that incompatible equipment and procedures prevented Marine helicopter pilots from communicating with their Air Force support planes at Desert One.[43] In the Cuban missile crisis on October 27, American fighters attached to Alaska Air Command scrambled to escort the stray U-2 safely back to base in response to its distress call. This was normal procedure. It is conceivable that those planes could have become involved in hostilities with the Soviet fighters that had scrambled to intercept the U-2; but neither the ExComm nor the president was aware of this danger, because neither had authorized the escort.[44] What these examples demonstrate is that if decision-makers are *unaware* of routines, they will be unable to modify them as necessary.[45] Decision-makers are never omniscient; they cannot know or control all aspects of organizational behavior. This fact may be relatively innocuous in the normal course of events, but in situations of acute danger such as the Cuban missile crisis, its implications can be profound. Model I's relative insensitivity to organizational complexity suggests that some paradigm focusing attention on organizational behavior might well be useful; but *routines* are not a helpful analytic category, because they cannot be said to have the uniform characteristics or pervasive and systematic effects upon which to build powerful theories of state behavior.

How well does Model III perform at determining significant facts and matching fact with theory? Given the evident confusion in Model III theory, the question would seem difficult to answer. Let us concentrate on the theoretical propositions that most analysts associate with Model III:

Proposition 1: Player preferences correlate highly with bureaucratic positions.

Proposition 2: Player perceptions correlate highly with bureaucratic positions.

Proposition 3: A player's influence in a decision-making process flows from his or her bureaucratic position.

Proposition 4: A decision-making process may be understood as a bargaining situation in which players "pull" and "haul" to promote their organizational interests, with the net result that governmental decisions do not reflect the intentions of any player in particular.

Let us begin by considering the first two propositions.[46] Allison and Halperin noted their hope that the bureaucratic politics paradigm would prove "sufficiently general to apply to the behavior of most modern governments in industrialized nations."[47] Without controlled, cross-national studies, it is impossible to judge how strongly players' preferences and perceptions correlate with their positions.[48] Anecdotal evidence is far from conclusive. It is not difficult to find examples that support propositions 1 and 2 strongly. As First Lord of the Admiralty, Winston Churchill was a staunch defender of the Royal Navy's interests and of its extremely costly building programs; later, as Chancellor of the Exchequer, he was an effective cost-cutter who rebuffed the Navy at almost every turn.[49] Similarly, as the State of California's Director of Finance under Governor Ronald Reagan, Caspar Weinberger earned the moniker "Cap the Knife" for his budget-slashing prowess; as President Reagan's Secretary of Defense, however, his single-minded promotion of military spending prompted Senator Mark Hatfield (R-Ore.) to declare him "a draft dodger in the war on the federal deficit."[50] But for every Winston Churchill or Caspar Weinberger there is a James Watt or an Anne Burford whose attitudes and actions prove to be antithetical to the interests and preferences of the organizations they represent.[51]

Similarly inconclusive are the many case studies that attempt to assess the power of bureaucratic affiliation as a predictor of preferences and perceptions in particular circumstances. Richard Head found no evidence of bureaucratic politics at work in his study of the 1976 crisis in the Korean demilitarized zone.[52] In contrast, Steve Smith's study of the Iran hostage rescue mission purports to bear out propositions 1 and 2, because key players took positions that seemed to reflect their locations in the bureaucratic structure.[53] But even in that case, the crucial role of Zbigniew Brzezinski raises important questions about what preferences a national security adviser should be expected to have simply by virtue of holding the office, and whether his strong advocacy of the military option cannot be explained more simply and more accurately by appeal to the hawkishness he himself brought to it. The vast majority of cases lead to indecisive verdicts. The debate within the Eisenhower administration following the fall of Dienbienphu is typical in this respect: the hawks included the vice president (Richard Nixon), the secretary of state (John Foster Dulles), and the chairman of the joint chiefs of staff (Admiral Arthur W. Radford), while the most passionate of the doves was a military man, chief of staff of the U.S. Army General Matthew B. Ridgway.[54] It is impossible to identify any clear bureaucratic pattern in this distribution of preferences. Some studies purportedly offering strong support for propositions 1 and 2 turn out on closer inspection to offer no support at all, such as Jiri Valenta's attempt to explain the 1968 Soviet decision to invade Czechoslovakia in bureaucratic-political terms.[55] Still other case studies that purport to demonstrate the power of the bureaucratic politics paradigm actually end up strongly supporting the rational actor model. For example, while the TFX competition was influenced in various ways by bureaucratic parochialism, the actual decision to award the TFX contract to General Dynamics and Grumman rather than to Boeing was made consensually by four men—Secretary of Defense Robert McNamara, Deputy Secretary of Defense Roswell Gilpatric, Air Force Secretary Eugene Zuckert, and Air Force Undersecretary Joseph Charyk—on the basis of a systematic comparison of the pros and cons of the two proposals, and against the backdrop of a very clear conception of interests. Indeed, two of the four men represented the Air Force, yet endorsed the proposal favored by the Navy.[56]

Somewhat more suggestive are studies that demonstrate at least a weak correlation between organizational affiliation and certain attitudes and dispositions. Career military officers' perceptions of risk, for example, apparently tend to be lower than those of civilians.[57] In postwar crises, American military leaders have also tended to be willing to apply greater force than their civilian counterparts once a decision to use force has been made (although they have *not* been appreciably more willing to resort to force in the first place).[58] An extensive study of senior Canadian officials revealed that members of the Department of National Defence had the most positive attitudes toward American foreign policy and U.S.-Canadian relations, while members of the Canadian International Development Agency had the least.[59] None of these studies is cross-national, and all demonstrate that a wide spectrum of attitudes and dispositions can be present in any organization; nevertheless, they do suggest that preferences and perceptions can correlate to some degree with positions.

It remains to be shown, however, whether these correlations are strong enough to be important, particularly in serious cases. If the Cuban missile crisis is representative, the answer seems to be negative. As Krasner puts it, decision-makers "often do not stand where they sit. Sometimes they are not sitting anywhere. This is clearly illustrated by the positions taken by members of the ExComm during the Cuban missile crisis, which Allison elucidates at some length."[60] If preferences and positions correlate strongly with positions only on such issues as budget allocations and turf battles, then Model III's explanatory power would seem to be extremely limited.

What of proposition 3? Again, it is difficult to assess the extent to which a player's influence in a decision-making process flows from his or her bureaucratic position since no serious attempt has been made to gauge it. Anecdotal evidence suggests an equivocal judgment. For example, some American secretaries of state have been enormously influential in policy-making (Dean Acheson, John Foster Dulles, James Baker), while others have not (Christian Herter, Dean Rusk, William Rogers). Clearly the office of secretary of state does not in itself carry with it influence; as Henry Kissinger puts it, "presidents listen to advisers whose views they think they need, not to those who insist on a hearing because of the organizational chart."[61] On the other hand, one position that clearly carries with it an enormous amount of influence—whether or not its holder is a forceful personality—is that of the president of the United States. As the Cuban missile crisis demonstrates, the president is all but unfettered in his ability to make decisions and to shape the decision-making process.[62] Kennedy was constrained neither by Congress nor by his advisers. Indeed, when disagreements between the president and the ExComm became acute, Kennedy simply bypassed the ExComm.[63] One is tempted to draw the unremarkable conclusion that a player's influence in a given situation flows from his or her office only where there is hierarchical differentiation of authority, and only at the top. In all other cases, influence may well be fully determined by such intangible factors as personality, preference congruity, and access to superiors.[64]

Finally, the extent to which a decision-making process may be understood as a bargaining situation in which players "pull" and "haul" to promote their organizational interests, with the net result that governmental decisions do not reflect the intentions of any player in particular, would seem to be quite small, except in those few cases where authority structures do not define *a priori* who will have the final say. The ExComm, for example, engaged in no "bargaining" of any kind; never did one player assent to X only on condition of receiving Y as a *quid pro quo.* This was because authority was not evenly distributed among the members of the group; the president held all of it. The "pulling and hauling" that went on took the form of normal debate in which players argued for and against various options; the name of the game was persuasion, and the only player who had to be persuaded was the president (cf. *ED,* p. 200).

Since many decision-making situations involve hierarchical distributions of authority, the process by which decisions are made should not normally be expected to result in a choice unintended by any player in particular.[65] During the Cuban missile crisis, the *decisions* of the ExComm or the Soviet Presidium may certainly be said to have reflected the intentions of President Kennedy and Chairman Khrushchev, respectively, although many actions of the organizations responsible for implementing those decisions clearly did not. That they failed to do so was not the result of bargaining or pulling and hauling, but of insubordination, incompetence, honest mistakes, technical difficulties, and even on occasion the uncritical execution of routines. None of these factors falls within the purview of Model III.

It cannot be denied that governments often make decisions that reflect bureaucratic interests, as Model III would have us expect. During the invasion of Grenada, for example, American military planners assigned a role to a battalion of Rangers for bureaucratic rather than military reasons: namely, to increase Congressional support for a third Ranger battalion (which was subsequently authorized in November 1984).[66] In the case of the Iran hostage rescue mission, planners decided to allow Marine pilots to fly the helicopters primarily so that every service would have a role in the operation—a decision that "may have been the single greatest mistake of the planning staff."[67] Clearly, bureaucratic factors such as interservice rivalries often do have an effect on decision-making and implementation, and can degrade instrumentality.[68] Sometimes this may be explained by the fact that top decision-makers are unaware of the details of implementation and are therefore effectively barred by ignorance from eliminating bureaucratically-induced irrationalities; sometimes it may reflect a set of preferences in which bureaucratic harmony is valued more highly than optimum efficiency. Understanding the role of bureaucratic interests can illuminate decision-making in such cases; but Model III does not capture either of these dynamics. The former is most fruitfully analyzed in terms of an organizational complexity paradigm of the kind sketched in the final section below, while the latter is most fruitfully analyzed as a special case of the rational actor model applied at both the inter- and intra-national levels of analysis.

Solving Puzzles

The acid test of a paradigm is its ability to solve puzzles other paradigms prove incapable of handling. The most engaging chapter of *Essence of Decision* is Chapter 4, in which Allison applies Model II to a large number of puzzles that seem to resist a Model I analysis. A reconsideration of these puzzles, however, reveals the limited explanatory utility of routines, as Model II's difficulties matching fact with theory might lead us to expect. Upon review, Allison's Model II puzzles may be grouped into three categories: (type I) those that emerge from a straw-man Model I analysis; (type II) those that resist a Model I analysis but for which other equally plausible or preferable explanations are available; and (type III) those based on factual errors. Here I will provide one example of each; the reader will find a more thorough accounting in Table 19.1.

A straw-man Model I analysis (type I) is evident in the following puzzle: Why did the Soviets ship more than one missile to Cuba for each launcher under construction when the launchers themselves were "soft" and could not reasonably be expected to survive an American response long enough to fire a second salvo? Allison's Model II explanation is that the Soviets routinely equipped their launchers with two missiles each, and normally made no attempt to harden them; the Soviet military merely followed its scripts for installing missile sites, and consequently wasted considerable effort shipping unnecessary missiles to Cuba (*ED*, pp. 108–109, 111). Recent information, however, suggests that the Soviets intended to supply extra missiles and warheads purely as spares to offset reliability problems.[69] This was a fully rational provision. What therefore seems to be a puzzle from a Model I perspective if one makes a faulty assumption (namely, that extra missiles indicate an intention to have a refire capability) is easily resolved within Model I when we correct that assumption.

Certain aspects of Soviet and American behavior during the crisis, however, cannot be explained in rational-actor terms at all (type II). For example, even though the Soviets intended to deploy missiles to Cuba secretly, they failed to camouflage the missile sites until *after* the Americans announced their discovery. Allison's Model II explanation is that Soviet standard operating procedures for installing medium-range ballistic missiles did not call for camouflage, and the construction crews in Cuba merely followed standard procedures (*ED*, p. 111). Yet the question of camouflage had been considered by Soviet planners, and the Soviet-Cuban agreement governing the deployment reportedly assigned responsibility for camouflage to the Soviets.[70] Someone somewhere in the Soviet chain of command failed to pass the word. Why should we blame the routines for the failure, rather than (for example) a breakdown of communications or incompetence?[71]

The puzzle with which Allison opens Chapter 4 is an example of a puzzle based on a factual error (type III): Why did the State Department fail to follow through on President Kennedy's order to remove the Jupiter missiles from Turkey? Allison's answer is that the State Department, operating according to its own procedures and relying on its own judgment, decided that U.S.-Turkish harmony would not permit the withdrawal of weapons only recently deployed (*ED*, pp. 101, 141–143). But in fact President Kennedy had not issued an order to remove the Jupiter missiles from Turkey prior to the crisis; consequently, there is no puzzle to explain.[72] Moreover, if there were such a puzzle, it would be a type II puzzle; if the State Department had failed to follow through on a presidential order, it would not have been a matter of routine, but an act of insubordination.

Standing in marked contrast to Chapter 4 is Allison's Chapter 6, in which he persuasively argues that the behavior of both Kennedy and Khrushchev reflected

Table 19.1 ORGANIZATIONAL ROUTINES AND BEHAVIORAL PUZZLES IN THE CUBAN MISSILE CRISIS (FROM *ED*, CH. 4).

Allison's puzzle	Model II explanation	Reclassification & Commentary
Why did the State Department fail to follow through on JFK's order to remove the Jupiter missiles from Turkey?	The State Department exercised its own judgment that the missiles should not be withdrawn.	Type III (based on factual error): JFK did not order the removal of Jupiter missiles from Turkey until after the crisis.[1]
Why did the Soviet SAM network and radar system only begin to operate after construction on the Soviet missile sites had begun, increasing the likelihood that U.S. reconnaissance would discover the MRBMs and IRBMs?	Separate organizations within the Soviet military were charged with installing SAMs, radars, and MRBMs/IRBMs. Coordination was not a matter of routine.	Type I (based on straw-man Model I analysis) or Type II (alternative or preferable explanation available): The Soviets could have deployed air defenses and MRBMs sequentially if they had wanted to. Either they did not choose to do so, valuing speed over security, or unforeseen technical problems prevented it.
Why did the Soviets fail to camouflage the missiles until after the Americans discovered them?	Soviet standard operating procedures (SOPs) for installing MRBMs did not call for camouflage.	Type II: The Soviets originally intended to camouflage the missiles; a communications failure occurred somewhere in the chain of command. Incompetence, not routines, account for this failure. After the discovery of the missiles, camouflage retained some value (complicating U.S. monitoring, air strike planning, etc.).[2]
Why did the Soviets work on the missile sites only during the day until after they had been discovered?	Construction crews followed their routines, which did not call for construction at night.	Type I: Round-the-clock construction was unnecessary, because the deployment proceeded on schedule; lights added an extra layer of complexity to the operation; lights posed additional risks of discovery.
Why did the Soviets build SAM, MRBM, and IRBM sites in established patterns that enabled U.S. intelligence to identify the nature of the deployment?	Soviet missile sites are routinely built according to standard specifications.	Type I or Type II: Established SAM pattern provided optimal coverage. In any case, since the missile sites were supposed to be camouflaged, established patterns should have posed no unacceptable risk of discovery.
Why did the Soviets assemble the Il-28 trainers before the Il-28 bombers?	Trainers are routinely assembled before bombers.	Type I: The Il-28s were intended to play a coastal defense role against American infiltrations; they

Table 19.1 *(Continued)*

Allison's puzzle	Model II explanation	Reclassification & Commentary
		were never intended to be part of a Soviet nuclear deterrent. The Soviets (and Cubans) believed them to be extrinsic to the crisis. This fact also helps explain why securing the withdrawal of the Il-28s was such a difficult problem for the Soviets after the crisis.[3]
Why did the Soviets attempts to deploy MRBMs and IRBMs simultaneously?	When the order came down to "place missiles in Cuba," the responsible organization—the Strategic Rocket Forces—chose the weapons mix it believed best fulfilled its organizational mission.	Type I: Nuclear missiles were meant to serve two main functions: to deter an American invasion and to redress the strategic nuclear imbalance. The chosen mix served both objectives adequately.[4]
Why did the Soviets ship two missiles for each launcher when the launchers were "soft" and could not reasonably be expected to survive more than one salvo?	Soviet launchers were routinely equipped with two missiles each, and no attempt was normally made to harden them.	Type I: Extra missiles and warheads were spares to offset reliability problems. The launchers were never intended to have a refire capability.[5]
Why did Soviet military personnel in Cuba take such pains to disguise their identities (e.g., by never wearing uniforms, yet displayed unit insignia in their barracks and otherwise behaved like soldiers (e.g., by forming in ranks of fours and moving in truck convoys)?	Standard procedures of Soviet military units.	Type II: Soviet troops were poorly briefed on concealment techniques. The fact that Soviet troops made some effort at concealment (e.g., by wearing civilian sport shirts) indicates that they were capable of transcending their routines (e.g., wearing uniforms). Incompetence seems to have prevented more thorough concealment.
Why did the Soviets ship such a wide variety of equipment to Cuba, including tanks, SNAPPER missiles, FROG tactical rockets, etc.?	The equipment sent was standard issue for the units deployed.	Type I: The equipment sent was sent deliberately; the Soviets intended to deploy a full, battle-capable force in Cuba to defend the island against an American invasion.
Why did the Soviets attempt so many complicated operations simultaneously?	Each organization performed its actions according to its routines, without central control.	Type I: The Soviets sought to serve a range of goals, and placed a premium on speed. The simultaneous pursuit of several complicated actions was necessary, although not without its risks.

487

Table 19.1 *(Continued)*

Allison's puzzle	Model II explanation	Reclassification & Commentary
Why did American intelligence fail to discover the missiles before October 14?	The routines and procedures of the American intelligence community prevented earlier discovery.	Type I: Discovery of the missiles was a success, not a failure. In the absence of routines and procedures, the American intelligence community would not have discovered the missiles at all.
Why did the U.S. Air Force fail to examine and present to the ExComm a surgical air strike option in the first week of deliberations?	The Air Force planning unit took an existing air strike plan off the shelf and presented it to the ExComm. The existing plan was designed with a different objective in view (destroying Castro's military capability).	Type II: The ExComm failed to communicate to the Air Force the purposes for which it was considering a surgical air strike, and did not insist clearly that the Air Force present a plan for one. Had the ExComm been clearer on what it wanted, the Air Force could have delivered; but it would still have argued against a small strike.[6]
Why did the Air Force incorrectly estimate the prospects that an air strike would succeed in knocking out the Soviet missiles?	Air Force manuals indicated that SS-4 MRBMs were "mobile, 'field-type' missiles," and concluded that they might be moved before U.S. planes could hit them.	Type III: The Air Force did not err when it refused to guarantee the Soviet missiles would be destroyed; this is an assessment that it would have made *whether or not it believed the missiles to be mobile.* In any event, what the ExComm really wanted to know was whether the Soviet missiles could be launched under attack; this was not communicated clearly to the Air Force.
Why did the Navy fail to execute the president's order to draw the quarantine line closer to Cuba until 500 miles?	Institutionally-based resistance on the part of the Navy. (This does not appear to be related to any matter of organizational routine.)	Type III: The president did not order the quarantine line moved closer to Cuba until October 30, whereupon the Navy moved the line.[7]
Why did the SAC bomber force disperse to civilian airports—some of which were within range of operational MRBMs in Cuba—especially in view of the "no cities" doctrine?	SAC merely executed its pre-programmed alert procedures.	Type I or Type II: SAC had more than a week to alter its dispersal program if it felt doing so was necessary, or if the ExComm had ordered it. SAC was confident of U.S. strategic nuclear superiority, and would not have seen the need to alter its dispersal program.[8] This puzzle illustrates how

Table 19.1 *(Continued)*

Allison's puzzle	Model II explanation	Reclassification & Commentary
		organizations behave according to their own preferences in the absence of political direction, and also illustrates that political leaders have finite resources of knowledge and attention.
Why were American aircraft in Florida lined up wing-to-wing, increasing their vulnerability to attack, when the Air Force assured the president they were not?	The Air Force arranged aircraft on the apron in the standard pattern.	Type II: Either the order to keep the aircraft dispersed had not been transmitted to the air bases, or someone had overlooked issuing the order.
Why was a U.S. intelligence ship so close to the Cuban coast during the crisis?	The ship was engaged in routine surveillance.	Type II: Someone neglected to move the ship until Robert Kennedy noticed it. This puzzle illustrates both the role of organizational complexity and of the ability of decision-makers to intervene in standard procedures once they become aware of their potential consequences.
Why did an American U-2 stray into Soviet air space at the height of the crisis?	The aircraft was on a routine mission.	Type II: Had the U-2 correctly followed its routines, it would not have strayed off-course. Had the ExComm known about the mission, it could have canceled it. Illustrates the dangers when routines break down, and also illustrates the impact of organizational complexity.

1. See note 72 in text.
2. Blight and Welch, *On the Brink*, p. 335.
3. See *Ibid.*, pp. 345–346.
4. *Ibid.*, pp. 327–329; see also Garthoff, *Reflections*, p. 18; Hilsman, *To Move a Nation*, p. 164; *ED*, pp. 237–244.
5. See note 69 in the text.
6. See note 27 in the text.
7. See Bouchard, *Command in Crisis*, pp. 111–112.
8. See note 39 in the text.

their sensitivity to the awesome responsibility they shared for resolving the crisis peacefully.[73] This is a thesis that has been strongly confirmed by evidence and testimony that have come to light since *Essence of Decision* was written.[74] It is interesting to note that the responsibilities they felt were in large measure to humanity as a whole, not solely to their respective national interests, nor to their personal political fortunes. Thus Khrushchev agreed to a settlement that avoided war at the cost of considerable damage to his (and his country's) prestige, while Kennedy for his part was apparently prepared to resort to a public trade of Jupiter missiles in Turkey for Soviet missiles in Cuba in order to avoid a war. Such a trade might well have damaged NATO irreparably and triggered a firestorm of controversy in the United States, threatening Kennedy's political career.[75] While this does not necessarily contradict Model III theory, sustaining a Model III analysis in this case would seem to require the inference that, at least in the case of national leaders, the interests and preferences that attach to bureaucratic positions may be cosmopolitan in nature (see *ED*, pp. 211–212). This would seem to doom the project of inferring interests and preferences from bureaucratic positions, and thus of determining correlations, in all but the most mundane cases.

The most interesting feature of Allison's discussion in Chapter 6, however, is the fact that it makes no attempt to solve puzzles in Model III terms at all. Perhaps this should not be surprising, given the ambiguity of Model III theory and the evident lack of fit between fact and theory in the case of the Cuban missile crisis, where few players stood where they sat, where the decision-making processes contained no "bargaining," where pulling and hauling was limited to the realm of persuasion and debate, and where the president and Khrushchev held all the cards in their respective "games." What Chapter 6 does contain, however, is an account of the ways in which decisions unfolded with particular reference to the identification of players, the description of their interests and preferences, and an assessment of their influence. In short, it offers a glimpse into decision-making at the intra-governmental level of analysis. And this is precisely the field in which bureaucratic politics has germinated and borne fruit. The overwhelming majority of studies invoking the bureaucratic politics paradigm as their particular "conceptual lens" have as their objective the elucidation of the ways in which different players and organizations *actually interact* in a given circumstance.[76] Indeed, in response to criticisms about the poor performance of Model III theory, advocates and practitioners of bureaucratic analysis typically resort to a call for "better theories" tailored for specific situations—for example, theories of *Soviet* decision-making, or theories of Soviet decision-making *during the Brezhnev period*, and so on.[77] This is to identify the bureaucratic politics paradigm with the governmental level of analysis broadly understood; it is to forsake the quest for universally valid theoretical propositions and to embrace concrete description.

Concrete descriptions of bureaucratic politics have their value. They enable us to understand how and why governments make decisions in particular cases. But concrete descriptions by themselves do not constitute theoretical progress. To date it would appear that the bureaucratic politics paradigm, which more than twenty years ago promised to bring order and insight to an untidy field, has not lived up to expectations, because the project it heralded never got off the ground.

CONCLUSIONS

Considerable care must be taken in drawing conclusions from the above discussion, because it is easily misconstrued. For example, casting doubt upon the accomplishments of the organizational process and bureaucratic politics paradigms does not impugn Allison's twin projects of bringing greater rigor to the study of international politics and attempting to move beyond traditional rational-actor analysis, both of which have been duly hailed.[78] Nor does it call into question the validity of developing analytic paradigms that focus attention at the intra-governmental level of analysis. Instead, it merely suggests that the particular paradigms Allison developed in his early work may not be the best possible candidates. A corollary of this conclusion is that, for the time being, those who seek useful general propositions about international politics should think twice about abandoning rational actor analysis, which is comparatively well-developed, and whose advantages in clarity, parsimony, and operationalization are obvious. Indeed, astute observers quickly noted how well rational-actor analysis held up in *Essence of Decision* itself.[79] Perhaps this should have been expected, given Allison's methodologically-commendable choice to develop his alternative paradigms with reference to a case where Model I could be expected to perform particularly well.[80]

However, Model I's usefulness should not be permitted to obscure the fact that rationality *is* constrained in various important ways by factors that are either determined or strongly influenced by organizational or bureaucratic considerations. The Cuban missile crisis provides several thought-provoking illustrations. One such factor is intra-governmental failures of communication. The ExComm, for example, deemed the status of the Soviet missiles in Cuba to be a crucial consideration in their deliberations. If the missiles were operational, many of its members believed, then the risks of a launch from Cuba either during or in response to an American air strike would have been unacceptably high. This strongly inclined many of them against the air strike option.[81] The main source of their concern was uncertainty as to whether Soviets warheads had arrived in Cuba. At each day's intelligence briefing, the president's first question was, "What about the *warheads?* Are they there or not?"[82] There was no evidence of Soviet warheads in Cuba; but the CIA continued to report increasing numbers of Soviet missiles as "operational." The term "operational" had a technical meaning in the intelligence community (that the missiles could be fired, but not, as the ExComm thought, that they were armed with warheads), and the CIA was using the term correctly in its briefs. But the ExComm did not understand what it meant.[83] The fact that different organizations speak different languages clearly constrained decision-making in this instance. In fact, the CIA had information to suggest that warheads were in transit, aboard the freighter *Poltava,* and that the shipment was interdicted by the quarantine.[84] The CIA appears never to have communicated this important information to the ExComm. Had communications with the White House been clearer, the CIA could have flagged this information and rushed it through the system.

The danger of a launch-under-attack from Cuba—warheads or no warheads— was, in any case, negligible, and information existed that would have enabled military planners to demonstrate this fact to the ExComm.[85] But here again a communications failure prevented the ExComm from appreciating this. The president asked the Air Force if they could guarantee that an air strike would *destroy* all of the Soviet missiles in Cuba; he did not ask if an air strike could *prevent a launch-under-attack*, for which destroying the missiles was unnecessary and disrupting firing procedures sufficient. General Sweeney, commander-in-chief of the Tactical Air Command, properly said no. The president lacked the military expertise to ask the right question; Sweeney, who was not a party to the ExComm's deliberations, answered the question the president had asked, not the one he would have asked had he known more about first-generation liquid-fueled ballistic missiles. In modern governments, organizations and roles are highly differentiated by function and expertise. This differentiation may prevent useful information that is actually in the system from reaching the people who need it in order to make a fully-informed decision.[86]

Another important constraint in the Cuban missile crisis was the sheer complexity of the apparatus both Kennedy and Khrushchev were attempting to manipulate, with limited success. As I noted above, direct control of organizational behavior is possible where decision-makers know what to worry about and how to go about controlling it. But no leader of a modern power is capable of monitoring and controlling the activities of even a small portion of the people and organizations over which he or she has nominal authority. The danger is not necessarily one of blind adherence to routines, although this is among the possible dangers; I noted cases where the *breakdown* of routines posed serious threats to successful crisis management, as well as one case where a clear-thinking subordinate brought potentially perilous aspects of routines to the attention of national leaders who otherwise would have been unaware of them. But organizational complexity represents a constraint on rational action because it generates noise and results in behavior of which national leaders are unaware, which they cannot control, and which they do not intend.[87]

Still other constraints flow from the ways in which organizations process and store information. For example, the Committee on Overhead Reconnaissance (COMOR) paid strict attention to the details of U-2 flights over Cuba, but paid virtually no attention to U-2s on polar flights, one of which strayed into Soviet air space at the height of the crisis as the result of a navigational error. Another U-2 on a similar mission had accidentally flown into Soviet airspace as recently as August 30, 1962.[88] But for some reason, that fact did not register on October 27. Poor organizational memory, the inability to assimilate past experience to present circumstances in constructive ways, or inadequate resources prevented COMOR from drawing the conclusion that it would be prudent to cancel all unnecessary polar air-sampling missions at this time of acute national danger.

Considerations such as these suggest that it may well be useful to develop a paradigm that concentrates the analyst's attention on the effects of organizational complexity and that permits the formulation and testing of a body of theory that specifies (for example) relationships between language-congruity (the degree to which the meanings that two organizations attach to words match) and the ability of two organizations to communicate or cooperate effectively, between the number of organizations implicated in a decision and the degree to which their behavior reflects the intentions and serves the purposes of national leaders, and between the attention leaders pay to details of implementation and the degree to which organizational behavior reflects their intent.[89] Allison's efforts may well be credited with drawing to our attention the fact that there is room for creative theory-building at the intra-governmental level of analysis, even though routines and the diversity of bureaucratic interests are not the only interesting elements of intra-governmental decision-making processes, nor are they necessarily the most salient aspects of the undeniably important fact that governments are not unitary rational actors.

It remains to be seen whether the most fruitful challengers to Model I will prove to be paradigms concentrating the analyst's attention at the intra-governmental level of analysis, or on cultural, societal, cognitive, or affective factors—or perhaps some combination of these. In time, it may be possible to reach stronger conclusions about the relative performance of various approaches to the study of foreign-policy decision-making than seem possible at the moment; alternative paradigms have had comparatively little chance to stake their claims.[90] It should be clear, however, that certain judgments will always be inappropriate, such as the oft-heard criticism that the *real* forces behind international politics are systemic, and that students of decision-making processes "look at real or potential international crises from the wrong end of the telescope."[91] *Ex cathedra* condemnations of one paradigm from within another are epistemologically sterile, and have the unfortunate effect of obscuring the fact that light can be shed on the same object from many angles at once. The greater complexity and comparative difficulty of organizational, bureaucratic, or psychological approaches to international politics may well perpetuate the "theory gap" that currently favors systemic approaches built upon the foundations of rational-actor analysis, just as they perpetuate a similar gap between the natural and the social sciences. But Allison's reasons for looking at old problems through new lenses are as valid now as they were more than two decades ago. And although this paper argues that mid-course corrections are in order, there is little doubt that twenty years from now, *Essence of Decision* will continue to be hailed as a critical turning point in the study of international politics.

NOTES

1. Graham T. Allison, *Essence of Decision: Explaining the Cuban Missile Crisis* (Boston: Little, Brown, 1971). (Subsequent references to this book appear as *ED*, within parentheses in the text.) The book expands upon an earlier article: Graham T. Allison, "Conceptual Models and the Cuban Missile Crisis," *American Political Science Review*, Vol. 63, No. 3 (September 1969), pp. 689–718.
2. Lawrence Martin, *The Presidents and the Prime Ministers* (Toronto: Doubleday, 1982), pp. 196–197.
3. Adrienne Koch and William Peden, eds., *The Life and Selected Writings of Thomas Jefferson* (New York: Modern Library, 1972), pp. 413, 436, 440.
4. The best of these are Robert J. Art, "Bureaucratic Politics and American Foreign Policy: A Critique," *Policy Sciences*, Vol. 4, No. 4 (December 1973), pp. 467–490; and Stephen D. Krasner, "Are Bureaucracies Important? (Or Allison Wonderland)," *For-*

eign Policy, No. 7 (Summer 1972), pp. 159–179. A useful review of reviews containing some original insights may be found in Desmond J. Ball, "The Blind Men and the Elephant: A Critique of Bureaucratic Politics Theory," *Australian Outlook,* Vol. 28, No. 1 (April 1974), pp. 71–92.

5. My evaluation is strictly confined to the field of international politics. Specialists in other disciplines (e.g., agricultural economics) are better positioned than I to judge the impact of these paradigms on their own fields.

6. An excellent analysis with a similar goal from a complementary perspective appeared as this article was in press; see Jonathan Bendor and Thomas H. Hammond, "Rethinking Allison's Models," *American Political Science Review,* Vol. 86, No. 2 (June 1992), pp. 301–322.

7. See Davis S. Bobrow, "The Relevance Potential of Different Products," in Raymond Tanter and Richard H. Ullman, eds., *Theory and Policy in International Relations* (Princeton, N.J.: Princeton University Press, 1972), pp. 206–207. See also Allison, "Conceptual Models and the Cuban Missile Crisis," p. 690n. Allison freely employs a variety of synonyms for the word "paradigm," such as "model," "approach," "perspective," "frame of reference," "framework," "conceptual lens," and "conceptual scheme." These are also useful synonyms for the less familiar term "metatheory."

8. Robert K. Merton, *Social Theory and Social Structure,* rev. and enl. ed. (New York: Free Press, 1965), pp. 12–16 (emphasis in the original).

9. Thomas S. Kuhn, *The Structure of Scientific Revolutions,* 2d ed., enl. (Chicago: University of Chicago Press, 1970), p. 23.

10. Graham T. Allison and Morton H. Halperin, "Bureaucratic Politics: A Paradigm and Some Policy Implications," in Tanter and Ullman, *Theory and Policy in International Relations,* p. 43.

11. *Ibid.,* pp. 40–79; 43, 54–56.

12. Allison seems later to have reconsidered the conflation, faulting Roger Hilsman's political-process model for being "an amalgamation of the bureaucratic model and the organizational process model (Model II)." Graham T. Allison, "Review Essay of Roger Hilsman, *The Politics of Policy Making in Defense and Foreign Affairs: Conceptual Models and Bureaucratic Politics* [Englewood Cliffs, N.J.: Prentice-Hall, 1987]," *Political Science Quarterly,* Vol. 102, No. 3 (Fall 1987), p. 524.

13. *ED,* pp. 81–82. Mis-specifications such as these lead to the inclusion of "imperialism" on the list of general propositions suggested by Model II, when it undoubtedly falls under the rubric of Model III: "Most organizations define the central goal of 'health' in terms of growth in budget, manpower, and territory." *ED,* p. 93. Allison's specification of the bureaucratic politics paradigm does not seem to include any elements that properly belong to Model II, although it does include certain superfluities. For example, under Model III's specific propositions, Allison writes, "In a nuclear crisis, the central decisions will be hammered out *not* in the formal forums, e.g., the National Security Council, but rather by an *ad hoc* group that includes the President, the heads of the major organizations involved, plus individuals in whom the President has special confidence." *ED,* p. 180. Nothing in the paradigm logically warrants such a proposition. The same may be said of Allison's inclusion of misperception, misexpectation, and miscommunication under the heading of Model III general propositions (pp. 178–179).

14. "This objection stems from a basic misconception of the function of theoretical models in explanation and prediction. The regularity with which this error is resurrected in the social sciences is disheartening. The natural sciences and the philosophy of science have relegated it to an appropriate methodological dump." *ED,* pp. 286–288 n. 93.

15. David C. Kozak, "The Bureaucratic Politics Approach: The Evolution of the Paradigm," in David C. Kozak and James M. Keagle, eds., *Bureaucratic Politics and National Security: Theory and Practice* (Boulder, Colo.: Lynne Rienner, 1988), p. 13.

16. These comparisons are rarely seriously attempted in political science, where paradigms proliferate but never die. Consider, for example, the interminable debates between realists and idealists in the field of international politics; the debates between liberals, Marxists, and statists in comparative politics; and the debates between Straussians and non-Straussians in political theory. Possible explanations for the interminability of these paradigm debates include (a) poor specifications of the paradigms (each is a moving target); (b) insensitivity to fundamental incommensurabilities; (c) the uniformly poor quality of theory; (d) the possibility that political phenomena are too indeterminate to permit any one paradigm to enjoy more than marginal success; and (e) the possibility that the political scientists are too wedded to their paradigms to recognize the advantages competing paradigms may offer.

17. Kuhn, *The Structure of Scientific Revolutions*, p. 34.

18. Arnold Miles, a senior civil servant in the Federal Budget Bureau in the 1940s, was the first to formulate this oft-repeated aphorism. Richard E. Neustadt and Ernest R. May, *Thinking in Time: The Uses of History for Decision-Makers* (New York: Free Press, 1986), p. 157.

19. *ED*, p. 176; see also *ED*, p. 165. As David Kozak puts it, "policy positions are determined by or are a function of an actor's perspective as developed by his or her bureaucratic culture." Kozak, "The Bureaucratic Politics Approach: The Evolution of the Paradigm," p. 7.

20. *ED*, pp. 178, 166; Allison and Halperin, "Bureaucratic Politics," p. 44.

21. *ED*, p. 171, emphasis added. Cf. Allison and Halperin, "Bureaucratic Politics," p. 48, who maintain that the interests pursued by players in games include national security interests, organizational interests, domestic interests, and personal interests.

22. Krasner, "Are Bureaucracies Important?" p. 171. See also Art, "Bureaucratic Politics and American Foreign Policy," pp. 472–473. Art notes that what he calls the "first wave" of scholars studying the relationship between bureaucratic politics and foreign policy (such as Warner Schilling) generally treated pre-existing mindsets as more important than bureaucratic processes, and refrained from formulating general theory along the lines of Miles's Law as a result. See *ibid.*, p. 471. Art goes further to suggest that the "second wave," of which Allison is the most prominent, should have been at least as circumspect: "If you cannot specify in what issue areas other than budgetary and procurement decisions stance correlates highly with position, instead merely stating that this works 'in many cases,' then why claim something for your paradigm that your own analysis does not bear out? By asking these questions of the position-perception proposition, we begin to see in microcosm one of the central difficulties with the bureaucratic politics paradigm: we must qualify it with so many amendments before it begins to work that when it does, we may not be left with a bureaucratic paradigm, but may in reality be using another one quite different." *Ibid.*, p. 473.

23. *ED*, p. 166. A serious attempt to mediate Models I and III by introducing a notion of *role* that permits two-way causal inferences between the preferences of particular players and the positions they occupy in the bureaucratic structure—while avoiding altogether leaning on the idiographic variable "personality"—may be found in Martin Hollis and Steve Smith, "Roles and Reasons in Foreign Policy Decision Making," *British Journal of Political Science*, Vol. 16, No. 3 (July 1986), pp. 269–286. This may well be a theoretical track worth exploring. The adjustment can work either on the supposition

that roles constrain personalities, or that for any given role only certain personality types will, as a matter of fact, be admitted. It would therefore be possible, if this track were followed, to concede that preferences and perceptions depend in crucial respects on personalities, without weakening the hypothesized correlation between preferences or perceptions and bureaucratic positions. In any event, what is necessary is to be clear that what the bureaucratic politics paradigm seems to require here is correlation, not causation. Interpreting Miles's Law in this fashion would seem an adequate theoretical response to the difficulties Allison's discussion presents.

24. As Allison notes, several aspects of the redeployment were undoubtedly done "by the book." Others, however, were not. Roger Hilsman notes, for example, that the concrete arches for the nuclear storage sheds were pre-cast in the Soviet Union and shipped all the way to Cuba, which according to a Model I analysis would suggest that the Soviets placed a premium on speed. Roger Hilsman, *To Move a Nation: The Politics of Foreign Policy in the Administration of John F. Kennedy* (Garden City, N.Y.: Doubleday, 1967), p. 165.

25. See, e.g., the discussion in James G. Blight and David A. Welch, *On the Brink: Americans and Soviets Reexamine the Cuban Missile Crisis,* 2d ed. (New York: Noonday, 1990), pp. 337–338, 340–342.

26. E.g., Operational Plan 312–62. Admiral Robert L. Dennison, *CINCLANT Historical Account of Cuban Crisis—1963 (U)* (Washington, D.C.: National Security Archive, Cuban Missile Crisis File), p. 17.

27. It is correct, as Allison maintains, that the Air Force failed in the first instance to brief the president on a surgical air strike option, instead presenting for consideration a much larger-scale attack on Cuban military installations more appropriate to the early stages of an invasion. But as Allison's own discussion indicates, this was because the president had failed to make clear what it was that interested him. A truly surgical air strike could have been planned and executed on short notice; the Air Force's failure to present one was the result of a miscommunication compounded by the Air Force's judgment that a truly surgical air strike would not be militarily effective. *ED,* pp. 124–126. Moreover, as Allison argues, the president and his advisers did not understand that, contrary to the military's judgment, a large-scale air strike was unnecessary for the intended purpose; "Pure foul-up and confusion are sufficient to account for the fact that most of the civilian members of the ExCom failed to see this point." *ED,* p. 205. Foul-ups and confusion are extrinsic to Model II.

28. Glenn H. Snyder and Paul Diesing, *Conflict Among Nations: Bargaining, Decision Making, and System Structure in International Crises* (Princeton, N.J.: Princeton University Press, 1977), p. 373.

29. It is interesting to note that the First World War is the only war in history whose outbreak analysts have been tempted to explain in Model II terms.

30. "My engineers . . . reported that it was absolutely impossible for an army to march across the lower portions of the State in winter," Confederate General Joseph E. Johnston remarked in reference to the latter feat. "I made up my mind that there had been no such army in existence since the days of Julius Caesar." James M. McPherson, *Battle Cry of Freedom* (New York: Oxford University Press, 1988), pp. 827–828.

31. Krasner, "Are Bureaucracies Important?" p. 170.

32. Cf. Raymond L. Garthoff, *Reflections on the Cuban Missile Crisis,* 2d ed. (Washington, D.C.: Brookings, 1989), p. 67, and Joseph F. Bouchard, *Command in Crisis: Four Case Studies* (New York: Columbia University Press, 1991), pp. 96–97, 115–116. Allison remarks that "for the first time in U.S. military history, local commanders received repeated orders about the details of their military operations directly from political lead-

ers—contrary to two sacred military doctrines." The claim that "this circumvention of the *chain of command* and the accompanying countermand of the *autonomy of local commanders* created enormous pain and serious friction," however, overstates the importance of one sharp exchange between Secretary of Defense Robert McNamara and Chief of Naval Operations Admiral George Anderson. In any case, no matter how much resentment the Navy might have felt, the direct manipulation of procedure nevertheless worked. See *ED*, p. 128.

33. *ED*, p. 140; Garthoff, *Reflections*, pp. 98–99n.

34. Scott D. Sagan, "Nuclear Alerts and Crisis Management," *International Security*, Vol. 9, No. 4 (Spring 1985), pp. 121–122.

35. Garthoff, *Reflections*, pp. 60–61n.

36. Hilsman, *To Move a Nation*, p. 168.

37. *Ibid.*, p. 191. Allison's argument that a struggle between the Air Force and the CIA for control of the U-2 flights over Cuba contributed to delays in discovering the Soviet missiles (a Model III argument that does not actually belong in a discussion of Model II, since it involves pulling and hauling, not routines), is seriously flawed. *ED*, pp. 122–123. As Allison notes, the Stennis Report concluded that there was "no evidence whatsoever to suggest that any conflict between the CIA and SAC existed or that there was any delay in photographic coverage of the island because of the fact that the U-2 program was being operated by the CIA prior to October 14. Likewise there is no evidence whatsoever of any deadlock between the two agencies or any conflict or dispute with respect to the question of by whom the flights should be flown." *ED*, p. 307 n. 90. In any case— *contra ED*, p. 187—it is unlikely that the Soviet missile bases would have been identifiable from the air much earlier, simply because of the rapidity with which they were being constructed. See Blight and Welch, *On the Brink*, p. 44.

38. Krasner, "Are Bureaucracies Important?" p. 164.

39. See Sagan, "Nuclear Alerts and Crisis Management," p. 108; Garthoff, *Reflections*, pp. 61–62; Blight and Welch, *On the Brink*, pp. 207–209.

40. Blight and Welch, *On the Brink*, pp. 338–340. Khrushchev and others evidently believed that such a request would have been a matter of routine. The actual wording of the air defense crews' standing orders is not known, but some Soviet commentators believe that the orders were ambiguous, and that the officers involved might well have believed that they had pre-delegated authority. See *ibid.*, p. 339.

41. Sagan, "Nuclear Alerts and Crisis Management," pp. 119–120.

42. The foregoing discussion presupposes that it is possible to imagine a well-behaved utility function for any given state (or, at least, a well-ordered set of "national goals" that a unitary, instrumentally-rational actor would pursue), and that it is possible to gauge with confidence the utilities of foregone alternatives. The practical and theoretical difficulties of both tasks cast further doubt on the claim that organizational routines systematically degrade instrumentality. See, e.g. Kenneth J. Arrow, *Social Choice and Individual Values*, 2d ed. (New York: Wiley, 1963).

43. Richard A. Gabriel, *Military Incompetence: Why the American Military Doesn't Win* (New York: Hill and Wang, 1985), pp. 107–108.

44. Sagan, "Nuclear Alerts and Crisis Management," pp. 121–122. It has been reported that American ships on anti-submarine duty in the Atlantic, without presidential knowledge uncritically employed textbook procedures for forcing Soviet submarines to surface, damaging at least one. See *ibid.*, pp. 112–118, and *ED*, p. 138. But Joseph Bouchard demonstrates that this was not the case: "contrary to what the organizational model would predict, the Navy readily adapted to a civilian-inspired modification to its ASW procedures. . . . There were no significant incidents between U.S. Navy ASW forces and

Soviet submarines during the Cuban Missile Crisis." Bouchard, *Command in Crisis,* pp. 117–128, 123, 125.

45. As a corollary, dangers arise when leaders believe they have a degree of awareness and control that they do not in fact have. See Peter D. Feaver, *Guarding the Guardians* (Ithaca, N.Y.: Cornell University Press, forthcoming).

46. Note that propositions 1 and 2 are phrased in terms of correlation rather than causation; while the proposition that a player's preferences are *determined* by his or her position is plausible and testable, a specifically bureaucratic analysis of decision-making does not require such a strong claim.

47. Allison and Halperin, "Bureaucratic Politics," p. 43.

48. The most impressive effort of this kind is Snyder and Diesing's study of crisis decision making. Snyder writes in a personal note that the bureaucratic politics model can be reduced to "a theory of coalition formation," and that the proposition that attitudes are "determined" (*sic*) by bureaucratic role "does not survive our analysis." *Conflict Among Nations,* p. 408n.

49. See, e.g., Henry Pelling, *Winston Churchill,* 2d ed. (London: Macmillan, 1989), pp. 147–162, 298–325; and Arthur J. Marder, *From the Dreadnought to Scapa Flow: The Royal Navy in the Fisher Era, 1904–1919,* Vol. 2 (London: Oxford University Press, 1965), pp. 292–293.

50. Barry M. Blechman, *The Politics of National Security: Congress and U.S. Defense Policy* (New York: Oxford University Press, 1990), pp. 36–37.

51. See, e.g., George Cameron Coggins and Doris K. Nagel, " 'Nothing Beside Remains': The Legal Legacy of James G. Watt's Tenure as Secretary of the Interior on Federal Land Law and Policy," *Boston College Environmental Affairs Law Review,* Vol. 17 (Spring 1990), pp. 473–550; Gwen Kinkead, "James Watt's Self-Made Storm," *Fortune,* Vol. 104 (November 30, 1981), pp. 138–139, 142, 146–147, 150; "EPA: Toxic Agency," *Economist,* Vol. 286 (February 19, 1983), pp. 26, 31.

52. Richard Head, "Crisis Decisionmaking: Bureaucratic Politics and the Use of Force," in Kozak and Keagle, eds., *Bureaucratic Politics and National Security,* pp. 72–90.

53. See Steve Smith, "Policy Preferences and Bureaucratic Position: The Case of the American Hostage Rescue Mission," in *ibid.,* pp. 122–143.

54. Hilsman, *The Politics of Policy Making in Defense and Foreign Affairs,* p. 30.

55. Jiri Valenta, "The Bureaucratic Politics Paradigm and the Soviet Invasion of Czechoslovakia," *Political Science Quarterly,* Vol. 94, No. 1 (Spring 1979), pp. 55–76; and Valenta, *Soviet Intervention in Czechoslovakia, 1968: Anatomy of a Decision* (Baltimore: Johns Hopkins University Press, 1979). Karen Dawisha demonstrates that differences of opinion on the desirability of invasion within the Soviet military establishment were at least as great as within the Soviet Communist Party. Karen Dawisha, "The Limits of the Bureaucratic Politics Model: Observations on the Soviet Case," *Studies in Comparative Communism,* Vol. 13, No. 4 (Winter 1980), pp. 306–307; cf. also Dawisha, "Soviet Strategic Concerns and the Role of the Military," *British Journal of Political Science,* Vol. 10, No. 3 (July 1980), pp. 341–363; and Dawisha, "The Soviet Union and Czechoslovakia," *The Jerusalem Journal of International Relations,* Special Issue on Studies in Crisis Behavior, Vol. 3, Nos. 2–3 (Winter/Spring 1978), pp. 143–171.

56. Richard Austin Smith, "TFX: The $7-Billion Contract That Changed the Rules," in Morton H. Halperin and Arnold Kanter, eds., *Readings in American Foreign Policy: A Bureaucratic Perspective* (Boston: Little, Brown, 1973), pp. 213–235, esp. pp. 234–235.

57. Stephen T. Hosmer, *Constraints on U.S. Strategy in Third World Conflicts* (New York: Crane, Russak, 1987), pp. 14–15.

58. Richard K. Betts, *Soldiers, Statesmen, and Cold War Crises* (Cambridge, Mass.: Harvard University Press, 1977), Appendix A, pp. 215–221.

59. Peyton V. Lyon and David Leyton-Brown, "Image and Policy Preference: Canadian Elite Views on Relations with the United States," *International Journal*, Vol. 32, No. 3 (Summer 1977), pp. 654, 659.

60. Krasner, "Are Bureaucracies Important?" 165. See also David A. Welch and James G. Blight, "The Eleventh Hour of the Cuban Missile Crisis: An Introduction to the ExComm Transcripts," *International Security*, Vol. 12, No. 3 (Winter 1987/88), pp. 23–24.

61. Henry A. Kissinger, *White House Years* (Boston: Little, Brown, 1979), p. 31.

62. See, e.g., Krasner, "Are Bureaucracies Important?" pp. 168–169.

63. The clearest example of this is the "Cordier Maneuver," Kennedy's decision to lay the groundwork through the UN for a public trade of Soviet missiles in Cuba for American Jupiter missiles in Turkey. See Welch and Blight, "The Eleventh Hour of the Cuban Missile Crisis," pp. 12–18.

64. Allison as much as acknowledges this himself: "Arguments in the ExCom for and against the nonmilitary tracks involved difficult estimates, interpretations, and matters of judgment. Indeed, in retrospect, an analyst weighing all the available arguments could decide either way. But, as Sorensen's record of these events reveals, the rapid abandonment of the nonmilitary path resulted less from the balance of argument than from the intra-governmental balance of power. 'The President had rejected this course from the outset.'. . . The coalition that had formed behind the President's initial preference [an air strike] gave him reason to pause. *Who* supported the air strike—the Chiefs, McCone, Rusk, Nitze, and Acheson—counted as much as *how* they supported it. This *entente cordiale* was not composed of the President's natural allies." *ED*, pp. 202–204; citing Theodore Sorensen, *Kennedy* (New York: Harper and Row, 1965), p. 683.

65. See Art, "Bureaucratic Politics and American Foreign Policy," pp. 471, 474.

66. Gabriel, *Military Incompetence*, p. 179.

67. *Ibid.*, p. 111.

68. In addition, parochial bureaucratic interests can affect broad policy directions. The interests of the various services, for example, were apparently among the most powerful determinants of the counterforce strategy. See Charles-Philippe David, *Debating Counterforce: A Conventional Approach in a Nuclear Age* (Boulder, Colo.: Westview Press, 1987), pp. 209–215.

69. It appears that the Soviets actually planned to deploy 1.5 missiles and warheads per launcher, rather than two, although Allison's factual error is inconsequential to the present point. See James G. Blight, Bruce J. Allyn, and David A. Welch, *Cuba on the Brink: Fidel Castro, The Missile Crisis, and the Collapse of Communism* (New York: Pantheon, forthcoming).

70. Blight and Welch, *On the Brink*, p. 335.

71. Allison himself notes that "some of the anomalies in the Soviet build-up must be traced to errors and blunders of specific individuals in the Soviet Union" (*ED*, p. 109); this would seem to be one of them.

72. Barton J. Bernstein, "The Cuban Missile Crisis: Trading the Jupiters in Turkey?" *Political Science Quarterly*, Vol. 95, No. 1 (Spring 1980), pp. 104–117; Welch and Blight, "The Eleventh Hour of the Cuban Missile Crisis," pp. 16–18. Kennedy did order the Department of Defense to explore the question of removing the Jupiters from Turkey in NSAM 181, but did not order that they be so removed until after the crisis. *National Security Action Memorandum (NSAM)* No. 181, August 23, 1962 (Washington, D.C.: National Security Archive, Cuban Missile Crisis File).

73. "This nuclear crisis seems to have magnified both rulers' conceptions of the consequences of nuclear war, and each man's awareness of his responsibility for these consequences." *ED*, p. 212.

74. See generally Blight and Welch, *On the Brink*, esp. pp. 319–321.

75. Welch and Blight, "The Eleventh Hour of the Cuban Missile Crisis," pp. 12–18; cf. *ED*, p. 195.

76. See, e.g., Halperin and Kanter, *Readings in American Foreign Policy;* and Morton Halperin, *Bureaucratic Politics and American Foreign Policy* (Washington, D.C.: Brookings, 1974).

77. See, e.g., the comments by Allison, Fred H. Eidlin, and Jiri Valenta, as well as the rejoinder by Karen Dawisha, in *Studies in Comparative Communism,* Vol. 13, No. 4 (Winter 1980), pp. 327–346.

78. See, e.g., David Lloyd Larson, "Review Essay on *Essence of Decision,*" *American Political Science Review,* Vol. 67, No. 4 (December 1973), pp. 1431–1432.

79. E.g., Stephen J. Cimbala, "Review Essay on *Essence of Decision,*" *Journal of Politics,* Vol. 34, No. 2 (May 1972), pp. 683–685.

80. "In the context of ultimate danger to the nation, a small group of men, unhitched from the bureaucracy, weighed the options and decided. Such central, high-level, crisis decisions would seem to be the type of outcome for which Model I analysis is most suited. Model II and Model III are forced to compete on Model I's home ground." *ED*, pp. 8–9. One might well counter, however, that the unusual urgency of the Cuban missile crisis should have increased decision-makers' reliance on organizational routines, restricted their ability to improvise, and bolstered organizational bargaining leverage (because of the premium on interorganizational harmony in times of acute national danger). In short, it is possible to argue that in the Cuban missile crisis, Model I had to compete on Model II and Model III's home ground, not vice versa.

81. See, e.g., Marc Trachtenberg, "White House Tapes and Minutes of the Cuban Missile Crisis," *International Security,* Vol. 10, No. 1 (Summer 1985), pp. 173–174.

82. Welch and Blight, "The Eleventh Hour of the Cuban Missile Crisis," p. 26.

83. David A. Welch, ed., *Proceedings of the Hawk's Cay Conference on the Cuban Missile Crisis,* CSIA Working Paper 88-1 (Cambridge, Mass.: Center for Science and International Affairs, 1988), pp. 71–74.

84. Garthoff, *Reflections,* p. 38.

85. For a detailed argument, see Blight and Welch, *On the Brink,* pp. 209–212.

86. Important asymmetries in knowledge *between* governments may also be explained by inter-organizational information flows and communications failure *within* governments. For example, the Jupiter missiles in Turkey actually became operational in April 1962, and the first Jupiter launch position was formally transferred to the Turks on October 22. The president and his advisers were unaware of these events, because they were details of implementation stemming from decisions made years before—during the Eisenhower administration. However, Khrushchev may well have been aware of both events, and they could have played an important role in shaping his behavior before and during the crisis. See Garthoff, *Reflections,* p. 60.

87. Some of those actions may be the result of pernicious ambiguities in the roles and responsibilities of organizations and their personnel. The U-2 shoot-down of October 27 provides a clear demonstration of Model I's lack of realism; but neither routines nor bureaucratic politics played a role. The real culprit in this case, it seems, was the dangerous ambiguity of the standing orders under which Soviet anti-aircraft forces in Cuba operated in a context resembling war fever. See Blight and Welch, *On the Brink,* p. 339.

88. Sagan, "Nuclear Alerts and Crisis Management," pp. 119–120.

89. Art, "Bureaucratic Politics and American Foreign Policy," pp. 476–480.

90. Steve Chan notes that studies of cognitive mapping, propaganda analysis, operational code, and "culture at a distance" suggest that decision-makers in different countries operate on the basis of distinctive belief systems that bear directly on their assessments and behavior. These belief systems tend to be both more durable and more comprehensive than particular issues, institutions, and leaders, and may therefore prove to be extremely useful in the quest for general theories of decision-making. In any case, rational-actor and bureaucratic approaches both require an understanding of decision-makers' belief systems. Steve Chan, "Rationality, Bureaucratic Politics and Belief System: Explaining the Chinese Policy Debate, 1964–66," *Journal of Peace Research,* Vol. 16, No. 4 (1979), p. 346, and citations therein. At the individual level of analysis, psychological approaches to decision-making shed considerable light on events such as the Cuban missile crisis. These include Irving Janis's work on "groupthink," the dynamics of small-group decision-making processes in Irving Janis, *Groupthink: Psychological Studies of Policy Decisions* (New York: Houghton Mifflin, 1982); the work of Robert Jervis, Richard Ned Lebow, and Janice Gross Stein on cognitive processes and misperceptions, in Robert Jervis, *Perception and Misperception in International Politics* (Princeton: Princeton University Press, 1976); Richard Ned Lebow, *Between Peace and War: The Nature of International Crisis* (Baltimore: Johns Hopkins, 1981); Robert Jervis, Richard Ned Lebow, and Janice Gross Stein, *Psychology and Deterrence* (Baltimore: Johns Hopkins, 1985); and James Blight's phenomenological examination of the role of affect in James G. Blight, *The Shattered Crystal Ball: Fear and Learning in the Cuban Missile Crisis* (Totowa, N.J.: Rowman and Littlefield, 1990). Whether these approaches can or will yield testable, general propositions about foreign-policy decision-making remains to be seen, but each has identified an important type of constraint on ideally-rational action. Indeed, most of the interesting phenomena Allison discusses in his presentation of Model III easily fit under the rubric of one or more of these approaches, and may fruitfully be examined in terms of them. Zeev Maoz makes a credible case for a synthetic, multi-layered "bottom-up" approach, concentrating on the ways in which individual preferences and perceptions combine and interact to produce foreign policy outcomes. Maoz argues that bureaucratic dynamics are themselves susceptible to rational-actor, cybernetic, or cognitive analyses. Maoz, *National Choices and International Processes* (Cambridge: Cambridge University Press, 1990), includes a superb and comprehensive critical literature review.

91. Edward A. Kolodziej, "Raymond Aron: A Critical Retrospective and Prospective," *International Studies Quarterly,* Vol. 29, No. 1 (March 1985), p. 11.

How Could Vietnam Happen? An Autopsy*

James C. Thomson, Jr.

As a case study in the making of foreign policy, the Vietnam War will fascinate historians and social scientists for many decades to come. One question that will certainly be asked: How did men of superior ability, sound training, and high ideals—American policy makers of the 1960s—create such costly and divisive policy?

As one who watched the decision-making process in Washington from 1961 to 1966 under presidents Kennedy and Johnson, I can suggest a preliminary answer. I can do so by briefly listing some of the factors that seemed to me to shape our Vietnam policy during my years as an East Asian specialist at the State Department and the White House. I shall deal largely with Washington as I saw or sensed it, and not with Saigon, where I have spent but a scant three days, in the entourage of the vice-president, or with other decision centers, the capitals of interested parties. Nor will I deal with other important parts of the record: Vietnam's history prior to 1961, for instance, or the overall course of America's relations with Vietnam.

Yet a first and central ingredient in these years of Vietnam decisions does involve history. The ingredient was *the legacy of the 1950s*—by which I mean the so-called "loss of China," the Korean War, and the Far East policy of Secretary of State Dulles.

This legacy had an institutional by-product for the Kennedy administration: in 1961 the U.S. government's East Asian establishment was undoubtedly the most rigid and doctrinaire of Washington's regional divisions in foreign affairs. This was especially true at the Department of State, where the incoming administration found the Bureau of Far Eastern Affairs the hardest nut to crack. It was a bureau that had been purged of its best China expertise and of farsighted, dispassionate men as a result of McCarthyism. Its members were generally committed to one policy line: the close containment and isolation of mainland China, the harassment

*From the beginning of John Kennedy's administration into this fifth year of Lyndon Johnson's presidency, substantially the same small group of men have presided over the destiny of the United States. In that time they have carried the country from a limited involvement in Vietnam into a war that is brutal, probably unwinnable, and to an increasing body of opinion, calamitous and immoral. How could it happen? Many in government or close to it will read the following article with the shock of recognition. Those less familiar with the processes of power can read it with assurance that the author had a first-hand opportunity to watch the slide down the slippery slope during five years (1961–1966) of service in the White House and Department of State.

of "neutralist" nations which sought to avoid alignment with either Washington or Peking, and the maintenance of a network of alliances with anticommunist client states on China's periphery.

Another aspect of the legacy was the special vulnerability and sensitivity of the new Democratic administration on Far East policy issues. The memory of the McCarthy era was still very sharp, and Kennedy's margin of victory was too thin. The 1960 Offshore Islands TV debate between Kennedy and Nixon had shown the president-elect the perils of "fresh thinking." The administration was inherently leery of moving too fast on Asia. As a result the Far East Bureau (now the Bureau of East Asian and Pacific Affairs) was the last one to be overhauled. Not until Averell Harriman was brought in as assistant secretary in December 1961 were significant personnel changes attempted, and it took Harriman several months to make a deep imprint on the bureau because of his necessary preoccupation with the Laos settlement. Once he did so, there was virtually no effort to bring back the purged or exiled East Asia experts.

There were other important by-products of this legacy of the 1950s:

The new administration inherited and somewhat shared *a general perception of China-on-the-march*—a sense of China's vastness, its numbers, its belligerence; a revived sense, perhaps, of the Golden Horde. This was a perception fed by Chinese intervention in the Korean War (an intervention actually based on appallingly bad communications and mutual miscalculation on the part of Washington and Peking; but the careful unraveling of that tragedy, which scholars have accomplished, had not yet become part of the conventional wisdom).

The new administration inherited and briefly accepted *a monolithic conception of the Communist bloc.* Despite much earlier predictions and reports by outside analysts, policy makers did not begin to accept the reality and possible finality of the Sino-Soviet split until the first weeks of 1962. The inevitably corrosive impact of competing nationalisms on communism was largely ignored.

The new administration inherited and to some extent shared *the "domino theory" about Asia.* This theory resulted from profound ignorance of Asian history and hence ignorance of the radical differences among Asian nations and societies. It resulted from a blindness to the power and resilience of Asian nationalisms. (It may also have resulted from a subconscious sense that since "all Asians look alike," all Asian nations will act alike.) As a theory the domino fallacy was not merely inaccurate but also insulting to Asian nations; yet it has continued to this day to beguile men who should know better.

Finally, the legacy of the 1950s was apparently compounded by an uneasy sense of a worldwide communist challenge to the new administration after the Bay of Pigs fiasco. A first manifestation was the president's traumatic Vienna meeting with Khrushchev in June 1961; then came the Berlin crisis of the summer. All this created an atmosphere in which President Kennedy undoubtedly felt under special pressure to show his nation's mettle in Vietnam—if the Vietnamese, unlike the people of Laos, were willing to fight.

In general the legacy of the 1950s shaped such early moves of the new administration as the decisions to maintain a high-visibility SEATO (by sending the secretary of state himself instead of some underling to its first meeting in 1961), to back away from diplomatic recognition of Mongolia in the summer of 1961, and most important, to expand U.S. military assistance to South Vietnam that winter on the basis of the much more tentative Eisenhower commitment. It should be added that the increased commitment to Vietnam was also fueled by a new breed of military strategists and academic social scientists (some of whom had entered the new administration) who had developed theories of counter-guerrilla warfare and were eager to see them put to the test. To some counterinsurgency seemed a new panacea for coping with the world's instability.

So much for the legacy and the history. Any new administration inherits both complicated problems and simplistic views of the world. But surely among the policy makers of the Kennedy and Johnson administrations there were men who would warn of the dangers of an open-ended commitment to the Vietnam quagmire?

This raises a central question at the heart of the policy process: Where were the experts, the doubters, and the dissenters? Were they there at all, and if so, what happened to them?

The answer is complex but instructive.

In the first place the American government was sorely *lacking in real Vietnam or Indochina expertise.* Originally treated as an adjunct of Embassy Paris, our Saigon embassy and the Vietnam desk at State were largely staffed from 1954 onward by French-speaking Foreign Service personnel of narrowly European experience. Such diplomats were even more closely restricted than the normal embassy officer—by cast of mind as well as language—to contacts with Vietnam's French-speaking urban elites. For instance, Foreign Service linguists in Portugal are able to speak with the peasantry if they get out of Lisbon and choose to do so; not so the French speakers of Embassy Saigon.

In addition the *shadow of the "loss of China"* distorted Vietnam reporting. Career officers in the department, and especially those in the field, had not forgotten the fate of their World War II colleagues who wrote in frankness from China and were later pilloried by senate committees for critical comments on the Chinese Nationalists. Candid reporting on the strengths of the Viet Cong and the weaknesses of the Diem government was inhibited by the memory. It was also inhibited by some higher officials, notably Ambassador Nolting in Saigon, who refused to sign off on such cables.

In due course, to be sure, some Vietnam talent was discovered or developed. But a recurrent and increasingly important factor in the decision-making process was *the banishment of real expertise.* Here the underlying cause was the "closed politics" of policy making as issues become hot: the more sensitive the issue, and the higher it rises in the bureaucracy, the more completely the experts are excluded, while the harassed senior generalists take over (that is, the secretaries, undersecretaries, and presidential assistants). The frantic skimming of briefing papers in the back seats of limousines is no substitute for the presence of specialists; furthermore, in times of crisis such papers are deemed "too sensitive" even for review by the specialists. Another underlying cause of this banishment, as Vietnam became more critical, was the replacement of the experts, who were generally and increasingly pessimistic, by men described as "can-do guys," loyal and energetic fixers unsoured by expertise. In early 1965, when I confided my growing policy doubts to an older colleague on the NSC staff, he assured me that the smartest thing both of us could do was to "steer clear of the whole Vietnam mess"; the gentleman in question had the misfortune to be a "can-do guy," however, and is now highly placed in Vietnam, under orders to solve the mess.

Despite the banishment of the experts, internal doubters and dissenters did indeed appear and persist. Yet as I watched the process, such men were effectively neutralized by a subtle dynamic: *the domestication of dissenters.* Such domestication arose out of a twofold clubbish need: on the one hand, the dissenter's desire to stay aboard; and on the other hand, the nondissenter's conscience. Simply stated, dissent when recognized was made to feel at home. On the lowest possible scale of importance I must confess my own considerable sense of dignity and acceptance (both vital) when my senior White House employer would refer to me as his "favorite dove." Far more significant was the case of the former undersecretary of state, George Ball. Once Mr. Ball began to express doubts, he was warmly institutionalized: he was encouraged to become the in-house devil's advocate on Vietnam. The upshot was inevitable: the process of escalation allowed for periodic requests to Mr. Ball to speak his piece; Ball felt good, I assume (he had fought for righteousness); the others felt good (they had given a full hearing to the dovish option); and there was minimal unpleasantness. The club remained intact; and it is of course possible that matters would have gotten worse faster if Mr. Ball had kept silent or left before his final departure in the fall of 1966. There was also, of course, the case of the last institutionalized doubter, Bill Moyers. The president is said to have greeted his arrival at meetings with an affectionate "Well, here comes Mr. Stop-the-Bombing . . ." Here again the dynamics of domesticated dissent sustained the relationship for a while.

A related point—and crucial, I suppose, to government at all times—was *the "effectiveness" trap,* the trap that keeps men from speaking out as clearly or often as they might within the government. And it is the trap that keeps men from resigning in protest and airing their dissent outside the government. The most important asset that a man brings to bureaucratic life is his "effectiveness," a mysterious combination of training, style, and connections. The most ominous complaint that can be whispered of a bureaucrat is: "I'm afraid Charlie's beginning to lose his effectiveness." To preserve your effectiveness, you must decide where and when to fight the mainstream of policy; the opportunities range from pillow talk with your wife to private drinks with your friends to meetings with the secretary of state or the president. The inclination to remain silent or to acquiesce in the presence of the great men—to live to fight another day, to give on this issue so that you can be "effective" on later issues—is overwhelming. Nor is it the tendency of youth alone; some of our most senior officials, men of wealth and fame whose place in history is secure, have remained silent lest their connection with power be terminated. As for the disinclination to resign in protest: while not necessarily a Washington or even American specialty, it seems more true of a government in which ministers have no parliamentary back bench to which to retreat. In the absence of such a refuge it is easy to rationalize the decision to stay aboard. By doing so one may be able to prevent a few bad things from happening and perhaps even make a few good things happen. To exit is to lose even those marginal chances for "effectiveness."

Another factor must be noted: as the Vietnam controversy escalated at home, there developed *a preoccupation with Vietnam public relations as opposed to Vietnam policy making*. And here, ironically, internal doubters and dissenters were heavily employed. For such men, by virtue of their own doubts, were often deemed best able to "massage" the doubting intelligentsia. My senior East Asia colleague at the White House, a brilliant and humane doubter who had dealt with Indochina since 1954, spent three-quarters of his working days on Vietnam public relations: drafting presidential responses to letters from important critics, writing conciliatory language for presidential speeches, and meeting quite interminably with delegations of outraged Quakers, clergymen, academics, and housewives. His regular callers were the late A. J. Muste and Norman Thomas; mine were members of the Women's Strike for Peace. Our orders from above: keep them off the backs of busy policy makers (who usually happened to be nondoubters). Incidentally, my most discouraging assignment in the realm of public relations was the preparation of a White House pamphlet entitled *Why Vietnam,* in September 1965; in a gesture toward my conscience, I fought—and lost—a battle to have the title followed by a question mark.

Through a variety of procedures, both institutional and personal, doubt, dissent, and expertise were effectively neutralized in the making of policy. But what can be said of the men "in charge"? It is patently absurd to suggest that they produced such tragedy by intention and calculation. But it is neither absurd nor difficult to discern certain forces at work that caused decent and honorable men to do great harm.

Here I would stress the paramount role of *executive fatigue.* No factor seems to me more crucial and underrated in the making of foreign policy. The physical and emotional toll of executive responsibility in State, the Pentagon, the White House, and other executive agencies is enormous; that toll is of course compounded by extended service. Many of today's Vietnam policy makers have been on the job from four to seven years. Complaints may be few, and physical health may remain unimpaired, though emotional health is far harder to gauge. But what is most seriously eroded in the deadening process of fatigue is freshness of thought, imagination, a sense of possibility, a sense of priorities and perspective—those rare assets of a new administration in its first year or two of office. The tired policy maker becomes a prisoner of his own narrowed view of the world and his own clichéd rhetoric. He becomes irritable and defensive—short on sleep, short on family ties, short on patience. Such men make bad policy and then compound it. They have neither the time nor the temperament for new ideas or preventive diplomacy.

Below the level of the fatigued executives in the making of Vietnam policy was a widespread phenomenon: *the curator mentality* in the Department of State. By this I mean the collective inertia produced by the bureaucrat's view of his job. At State the average "desk officer" inherits from his predecessor our policy toward Country X; he regards it as his function to keep that policy intact—under glass, untampered with, and dusted—so that he may pass it on in two to four years to his successor. And such curatorial service generally merits promotion within the system.

(Maintain the status quo, and you will stay out of trouble.) In some circumstances the inertia bred by such an outlook can act as a brake against rash innovation. But on many issues this inertia sustains the momentum of bad policy and unwise commitments—momentum that might otherwise have been resisted within the ranks. Clearly, Vietnam is such an issue.

To fatigue and inertia must be added the factor of internal confusion. Even among the "architects" of our Vietnam commitment there has been persistent *confusion as to what type of war we were fighting* and as a direct consequence, *confusion as to how to end that war.* (The "credibility gap" is in part a reflection of such internal confusion.) Was it for instance a civil war, in which case counterinsurgency might suffice? Or was it a war of international aggression? (This might invoke SEATO or UN commitment.) Who was the aggressor—and the "real enemy"? The Viet Cong? Hanoi? Peking? Moscow? International Communism? Or maybe "Asian Communism"? Differing enemies dictated differing strategies and tactics. And confused throughout, in like fashion, was the question of American objectives; your objectives depended on whom you were fighting and why. I shall not forget my assignment from an assistant secretary of state in March 1964: to draft a speech for Secretary McNamara which would, *inter alia,* once and for all dispose of the canard that the Vietnam conflict was a civil war. "But in some ways, of course," I mused, "it *is* a civil war." "Don't play word games with me!" snapped the assistant secretary.

Similar confusion beset the concept of "negotiations"—anathema to much of official Washington from 1961 to 1965. Not until April 1965 did "unconditional discussions" become respectable via a presidential speech; even then the secretary of state stressed privately to newsmen that nothing had changed, since "discussions" were by no means the same as "negotiations." Months later that issue was resolved. But it took even longer to obtain a fragile internal agreement that negotiations might include the Viet Cong as something other than an appendage to Hanoi's delegation. Given such confusion as to the whos and whys of our Vietnam commitment, it is not surprising, as Theodore Draper has written, that policy makers find it so difficult to agree on how to end the war.

Of course one force—a constant in the vortex of commitment—was that of *wishful thinking.* I partook of it myself at many times. I did so especially during Washington's struggle with Diem in the autumn of 1963, when some of us at State believed that for once in dealing with a difficult client state the U.S. government could use the leverage of our economic and military assistance to make good things happen instead of being led around by the nose by men like Chiang Kai-shek and Syngman Rhee (and in that particular instance, by Diem). If we could prove that point, I thought, and move into a new day, with or without Diem, then Vietnam was well worth the effort. Later came the wishful thinking of the air-strike planners in the late autumn of 1964; there were those who actually thought that after six weeks of air strikes, the North Vietnamese would come crawling to us to ask for peace talks. And what, someone asked in one of the meetings of the time, if they don't? The answer was that we would bomb for another four weeks, and that would do the trick. And a few weeks later came one instance of wishful thinking that was symptomatic of good men misled: in January 1965 I encountered one of the very highest figures in the administration at a dinner, drew him aside, and told him of my worries about the air-strike option. He told me that I really shouldn't worry; it was his conviction that before any such plans could be put into effect, a neutralist government would come to power in Saigon that would politely invite us out. And finally, there was the recurrent wishful thinking that sustained many of us through the trying months of 1965–1966 after the air strikes had begun: that surely, somehow, one way or another, we would "be in a conference in six months," and the escalatory spiral would be suspended. The basis of our hope: "It simply can't go on."

As a further influence on policy makers I would cite the factor of *bureaucratic detachment.* By this I mean what at best might be termed the professional callousness of the surgeon (and indeed medical lingo—the *surgical strike* for instance—seemed to crop up in the euphemisms of the times). In Washington the semantics of the military muted the reality of war for the civilian policy makers. In quiet air-conditioned thick-carpeted rooms such terms as *systematic pressure, armed reconnaissance, targets of opportunity,* and even *body count* seemed to breed a sort of games-theory detachment. Most memorable to me was a moment in the late 1964 target planning when the question under discussion was how heavy our bombing should be, and how extensive our strafing, at some midpoint in the projected pattern of systematic pressure. An assistant secretary of state resolved the point in the following words: "It seems to me that our orchestration should be mainly violins, but with periodic touches of brass." Perhaps the biggest shock of my return to Cambridge, Massachusetts, was the realization that the young men, the flesh and blood I taught and saw on these university streets, were potentially some of the numbers on the charts of those faraway planners. In a curious sense Cambridge is closer to this war than Washington.

There is an unprovable factor that relates to bureaucratic detachment: the ingredient of *cryptoracism.* I do not mean to imply any conscious contempt for Asian loss of life on the part of Washington officials. But I do mean to imply that bureaucratic detachment may well be compounded by a traditional Western sense that there are so many Asians, after all; that Asians have a fatalism about life and a disregard for its loss; that they are cruel and barbaric to their own people; and that they are very different from us (and all look alike?). And I *do* mean to imply that the upshot of such subliminal views is a subliminal question whether Asians, and particularly Asian peasants, and most particularly Asian communists, are really people—like you and me. To put the matter another way: would we have pursued quite such policies—and quite such military tactics—if the Vietnamese were white?

It is impossible to write of Vietnam decision making without writing about language. Throughout the conflict words have been of paramount importance. I refer here to the impact of *rhetorical escalation* and to the *problem of oversell.* In an important sense Vietnam has become of crucial significance to us *because we have said that it is of crucial significance.* (The issue obviously relates to the public relations preoccupation described earlier.)

The key here is domestic politics: the need to sell the American people, press, and Congress on support for an unpopular and costly war in which the objectives themselves have been in flux. To sell means to persuade, and to persuade means rhetoric. As the difficulties and costs have mounted, so has the definition of the stakes. This is not to say that rhetorical escalation is an orderly process; executive prose is the product of many writers, and some concepts—North Vietnamese infiltration, America's "national honor," Red China as the chief enemy—have entered the rhetoric only gradually and even sporadically. But there is an upward spiral nonetheless. And once you have *said* that the American Experiment itself stands or falls on the Vietnam outcome, you have thereby created a national stake far beyond any earlier stakes.

Crucial throughout the process of Vietnam decision making was a conviction among many policy makers: that Vietnam posed a *fundamental test of America's national will*. Time and again I was told by men reared in the tradition of Henry L. Stimson that all we needed was the will, and we would then prevail. Implicit in such a view, it seemed to me, was a curious assumption that Asians lacked will, or at least that in a contest between Asian and Anglo-Saxon wills, the non-Asians must prevail. A corollary to the persistent belief in will was a *fascination with power* and an awe in the face of the power America possessed as no nation or civilization ever before. Those who doubted our role in Vietnam were said to shrink from the burdens of power, the obligations of power, the uses of power, the responsibility of power. By implication such men were soft-headed and effete.

Finally, no discussion of the factors and forces at work on Vietnam policy makers can ignore the central fact of *human ego investment*. Men who have participated in a decision develop a stake in that decision. As they participate in further related decisions, their stake increases. It might have been possible to dissuade a man of strong self-confidence at an early stage of the ladder of decision; but it is infinitely harder at later stages, since a change of mind there usually involves implicit or explicit repudiation of a chain of previous decisions.

To put it bluntly: at the heart of the Vietnam calamity is a group of able, dedicated men who have been regularly and repeatedly wrong—and whose standing with their contemporaries, and more important, with history, depends, as they see it, on being proven right. These are not men who can be asked to extricate themselves from error.

The various ingredients I have cited in the making of Vietnam policy have created a variety of results, most of them fairly obvious. Here are some that seem to me most central:

Throughout the conflict there has been *persistent and repeated miscalculation* by virtually all the actors in high echelons and low, whether dove, hawk, or something else. To cite one simple example among many: in late 1964 and early 1965 some peace-seeking planners at State who strongly opposed the projected bombing of the North urged that instead American ground forces be sent to South Vietnam; this would, they said, increase our bargaining leverage against the North— our "chips"—and would give us something to negotiate about (the withdrawal of our forces) at an early peace conference. Simultaneously the air-strike option was urged by many in the military who were dead set against American participation in "another land war in Asia"; they were joined by other civilian peace seekers who wanted to bomb Hanoi into early negotiations. By late 1965 we had ended up with the worst of all worlds: ineffective and costly air strikes against the North, spiraling ground forces in the South, and no negotiations in sight.

Throughout the conflict as well there has been *a steady give-in to pressures for a military solution* and only minimal and sporadic efforts at a diplomatic and political solution. In part this resulted from the confusion (earlier cited) among the civilians—confusion regarding objectives and strategy. And in part this resulted from the self-enlarging nature of military investment. Once air strikes and particularly ground forces were introduced, our investment itself had transformed the original stakes. More air power was needed to protect the ground forces; and then more ground forces to protect the ground forces. And needless to say, the military mind develops its own momentum in the absence of clear guidelines from the civilians. Once asked to save South Vietnam, rather than to "advise" it, the American military could not but press for escalation. In addition, sad to report, assorted military constituencies, once involved in Vietnam, have had a series of cases to prove: for instance the utility not only of air power (the air force) but of supercarrier-based air power (the navy). Also, Vietnam policy has suffered from one ironic by-product of Secretary McNamara's establishment of civilian control at the Pentagon: in the face of such control, interservice rivalry has given way to a united front among the military—reflected in the new but recurrent phenomenon of JCS unanimity. In conjunction with traditional congressional allies (mostly Southern senators and representatives) such a united front would pose a formidable problem for any president.

Throughout the conflict there have been *missed opportunities, large and small, to disengage ourselves from Vietnam on increasingly unpleasant but still acceptable terms.* Of the many moments from 1961 onward I shall cite only one, the last and most important opportunity that was lost: in the summer of 1964 the president instructed his chief advisers to prepare for him as wide a range of Vietnam options as possible for postelection consideration and decision. He explicitly asked that all options be laid out. What happened next was in effect Lyndon Johnson's slow-motion Bay of Pigs. For the advisers so effectively converged on one single option—juxtaposed against two other, phony options (in effect blowing up the world or scuttle-and-run)—that the president was confronted with unanimity for bombing the North from all his trusted counselors. Had he been more confident in foreign affairs, had he been deeply informed on Vietnam and Southeast Asia, and had he raised some hard questions that unanimity had submerged, this president could have used the largest electoral mandate in history to deescalate in Vietnam in the clear expectation that at the worst a neutralist government would come to power in Saigon and politely invite us out. Today, many lives and dollars later, such an alternative has become an elusive and infinitely more expensive possibility.

In the course of these years another result of Vietnam decision making has been *the abuse and distortion of history.* Vietnamese, Southeast Asian, and Far Eastern history has been rewritten by our policy makers and their spokesmen to conform with the alleged necessity of our presence in Vietnam. Highly dubious analogies from our experience elsewhere—the "Munich" sellout and "containment" from Europe, the Malayan insurgency and the Korean War from Asia—have been imported in order to justify our actions. And more recent events have been fitted to the Procrustean bed of Vietnam. Most notably the change of power in Indonesia in 1965–1966 has been ascribed to our Vietnam presence; and virtually all progress in the Pacific region—the rise of regionalism, new forms of cooperation, and mounting growth rates—has been similarly explained. The Indonesian allegation is undoubtedly false (I tried to prove it during six months of careful investigation at the White House and had to confess failure); the regional allegation is patently unprovable in either direction (except, of course, for the clear fact that the economies of both Japan and Korea have profited enormously from our Vietnam-related procurement in these countries; but that is a costly and highly dubious form of foreign aid).

There is a final result of Vietnam policy I would cite that holds potential danger for the future of American foreign policy: *the rise of a new breed of American ideologues who see Vietnam as the ultimate test of their doctrine.* I have in mind those men in Washington who have given a new life to the missionary impulse in American foreign relations: who believe that this nation, in this era, has received a threefold endowment that can transform the world. As they see it, that endowment is composed of first, our unsurpassed military might; second, our clear technological supremacy; and third, our allegedly invincible benevolence (our "altruism," our affluence, our lack of territorial aspirations). Together, it is argued, this threefold endowment provides us with the opportunity and the obligation to ease the nations of the earth toward modernization and stability: toward a full-fledged *Pax Americana Technocratica.* In reaching toward this goal Vietnam is viewed as the last and crucial test. Once we have succeeded there, the road ahead is clear. In a sense these men are our counterpart to the visionaries of communism's radical left: they are technocracy's own Maoists. They do not govern Washington today. But their doctrine rides high.

Long before I went into government, I was told a story about Henry L. Stimson that seemed to me pertinent during the years that I watched the Vietnam tragedy unfold—and participated in that tragedy. It seems to me more pertinent than ever as we move toward the election of 1968.

In his waning years Stimson was asked by an anxious questioner, "Mr. Secretary, how on earth can we ever bring peace to the world?" Stimson is said to have answered: "You begin by bringing to Washington a small handful of able men who believe that the achievement of peace is possible."

"You work them to the bone until they no longer believe that it is possible."

"And then you throw them out—and bring in a new bunch who believe that it is possible."

Seven

PERCEPTIONS, PERSONALITY, AND SOCIAL PSYCHOLOGY

*T*hese next five essays are concerned with the cognitive and social psychological limitations and patterns of decision making in foreign policy. Rather than focus on societal constraints or bureaucratic constraints on policy making, these writers focus on the role of the individual making choices. In a trail-blazing essay Robert Jervis presents a series of hypotheses that specify types of misperception in foreign-policy decision making. Decision makers tend to fit incoming information into existing theories and images. Decision makers tend to be closed to new information and to resist new theories or expectations. Jervis also explores the sources of these theories or images of other actors and the international system. Further hypotheses are developed about the way decision makers misperceive opposing actors and their processes of decision making. Taken together, Jervis presents a complex array of cognitive biases that decision makers are prone to exhibit and that constitute an interlocking web of misperceptions in foreign policy.

Philip Tetlock and Charles McGuire present a more general statement of the cognitive approach to foreign policy. What unites this approach is a set of assumptions about foreign policy decision makers and their environment: that the environment is overflowing with information and policy makers must inevitably deal with problems of incomplete and unreliable information. The central research question is to understand the "cognitive strategies" that policy makers rely on to make sense of their environment.

Yuen Foong Khong looks a one particularly powerful device that policy makers often use to make sense of the foreign policy circumstances they confront—the historical analogy. He argues that analogies are attractive to foreign policy officials for a variety of reasons: they make a new situation look familiar; they provide a normative assessment of the situation; they provide a convenient path to policy action; and they suggest what might happen in the future.

David Winter and his colleagues stress the role of personality in foreign policy, doing so by examining the personalities and policies of recent American and Soviet leaders—Bush and Gorbachev. They note the circumstances under which personality factors might matter: when leaders occupy strategic locations; when events are new or ambiguous; when other forces impinging on policy are conflicting and balanced; and when action is required. The authors examine the two leaders' beliefs, operational codes, and other personality traits, and they conclude that the two leaders have compatible personality characteristics that tend toward conciliation.

Irving Janis presents a different approach to misperception in foreign policy making by focusing on dynamics of group decision. Most important decisions in American foreign policy are made within a group setting. Within such a setting, Janis argues, pressure for conformity consistently appears. When one member of the group appears to deviate from the group's norms, efforts are made to tone down or change the view of the dissident. If this fails, the ideas of the deviant member tend to be ignored. It is this general set of findings from studies in group psychology that Janis labels *groupthink.* Misperception occurs when the "members' striving for unanimity overrides their motivation to realistically appraise alternative courses of action." Janis uses this working argument to examine a variety of cases of failures in American foreign policy, including the 1965 Vietnam escalation decision.

Hypotheses on Misperception

Robert Jervis

In determining how he will behave, an actor must try to predict how others will act and how their actions will affect his values. The actor must therefore develop an image of others and of their intentions. This image may, however, turn out to be an inaccurate one; the actor may for a number of reasons misperceive both others' actions and their intentions. In this research note I wish to discuss the types of misperceptions of other states' intentions which states tend to make. The concept of intention is complex, but here we can consider it to comprise the ways in which the state feels it will act in a wide range of future contingencies. These ways of acting usually are not specific and well developed plans. For many reasons a national or individual actor may not know how he will act under given conditions, but this problem cannot be dealt with here.

I. PREVIOUS TREATMENTS OF PERCEPTION IN INTERNATIONAL RELATIONS

Although diplomatic historians have discussed misperception in their treatments of specific events, students of international relations have generally ignored this topic. However, two sets of scholars have applied content analysis to the documents that flowed within and between governments in the six weeks preceding World War I. But the data have been put into quantitative form in a way that does not produce accurate measures of perceptions and intentions and that makes it impossible to gather useful evidence on misperception.[1]

The second group of theorists who have explicitly dealt with general questions of misperception in international relations consists of those, like Charles Osgood, Amitai Etzioni, and to a lesser extent Kenneth Boulding and J. David Singer, who have analyzed the cold war in terms of a spiral of misperception.[2] This approach grows partly out of the mathematical theories of L. F. Richardson[3] and partly out of findings of social and cognitive psychology, many of which will be discussed in this research note.

These authors state their case in general if not universal terms but do not provide many historical cases that are satisfactorily explained by their theories. Furthermore, they do not deal with any of the numerous instances that contradict

Robert Jervis, "Hypotheses on Misperception," *World Politics* 20, no. 3 (April 1968). Copyright © 1968 by Princeton University Press. Reprinted with permission of Princeton University Press.

their notion of the self-defeating aspects of the use of power. They ignore the fact that states are not individuals and that the findings of psychology can be applied to organizations only with great care. Most important, their theoretical analysis is for the most part of reduced value because it seems largely to be a product of their assumption that the Soviet Union is a basically status-quo power whose apparently aggressive behavior is a product of fear of the West. Yet they supply little or no evidence to support this view. Indeed, the explanation for the differences of opinion between the spiral theorists and the proponents of deterrence lies not in differing general views of international relations, differing values and morality,[4] or differing methods of analysis,[5] but in differing perceptions of Soviet intentions.

II. THEORIES—NECESSARY AND DANGEROUS

Despite the limitations of their approach, these writers have touched on a vital problem that has not been given systematic treatment by theorists of international relations. The evidence from both psychology and history overwhelmingly supports the view (which may be labeled hypothesis 1) that decision makers tend to fit incoming information into their existing theories and images. Indeed, their theories and images play a large part in determining what they notice. In other words, actors tend to perceive what they expect. Furthermore (hypothesis 1a), a theory will have greater impact on an actor's interpretation of data (a) the greater the ambiguity of the data and (b) the higher the degree of confidence with which the actor holds the theory.[6]

For many purposes we can use the concept of differing levels of perceptual thresholds to deal with the fact that it takes more, and more unambiguous, information for an actor to recognize an unexpected phenomenon than an expected one. An experiment by Bruner and Postman determined "that the recognition threshold for . . . incongruous playing cards (those with suits and colors reversed) is significantly higher than the threshold for normal cards."[7] Not only are people able to identify normal (and therefore expected) cards more quickly and easily than incongruous (and therefore unexpected) ones, but also they may at first take incongruous cards for normal ones.

However, we should not assume, as the spiral theorists often do, that it is necessarily irrational for actors to adjust incoming information to fit more closely their existing beliefs and images. (*Irrational* here describes acting under pressures that the actor would not admit as legitimate if he were conscious of them.) Abelson and Rosenberg label as "psycho-logic" the pressure to create a "balanced" cognitive structure—i.e., one in which "all relations among 'good elements' [in one's attitude structure] are positive (or null), all relations among 'bad elements' are positive (or null), and all relations between good and bad elements are negative (or null)." They correctly show that the "reasoning [this involves] would mortify a logician."[8] But those who have tried to apply this and similar cognitive theories to international relations have usually overlooked the fact that in many cases there are important logical links between the elements and the processes they describe which cannot be called "psycho-logic." (I am here using the term *logical* not in the narrow sense of drawing only those conclusions that follow necessarily from the premises, but rather in the sense of conforming to generally agreed-upon rules for the treating of evidence.) For example, Osgood claims that psycho-logic is displayed when the Soviets praise a man or a proposal and people in the West react by distrusting the object of this praise.[9] But if a person believes that the Russians are aggressive, it is logical for him to be suspicious of their moves. When we say that a decision maker "dislikes" another state, this usually means that he believes that that other state has policies conflicting with those of his nation. Reasoning and experience indicate to the decision maker that the "disliked" state is apt to harm his state's interests. Thus in these cases there is no need to invoke "psycho-logic," and it cannot be claimed that the cases demonstrate the substitution of "emotional consistency for rational consistency."[10]

The question of the relations among particular beliefs and cognitions can often be seen as part of the general topic of the relation of incoming bits of information to the receivers' already-established images. The need to fit data into a wider framework of beliefs, even if doing so does not seem to do justice to individual facts, is not, or at least is not only, a psychological drive that decreases the accuracy of our perceptions of the world, but is "essential to the logic of inquiry."[11] Facts can be interpreted and indeed identified only with the aid of hypotheses and theories. Pure empiricism is impossible, and it would be unwise to revise theories in the light of every bit of information that does not easily conform to them.[12] No hypothesis can be expected to account for all the evidence, and if a prevailing view is supported by many theories and by a large pool of findings, it should not be quickly altered. Too little rigidity can be as bad as too much.[13]

This is as true in the building of social and physical science as it is in policy making.[14] While it is terribly difficult to know when a finding throws serious doubt on accepted theories and should be followed up and when instead it was caused by experimental mistakes or minor errors in the theory, it is clear that scientists would make no progress if they followed Thomas Huxley's injunction to "sit down before fact as a mere child, be prepared to give up every preconceived notion, follow humbly wherever nature leads, or you will learn nothing."[15]

As Michael Polanyi explains, "It is true enough that the scientist must be prepared to submit at any moment to the adverse verdict of observational evidence. But not blindly. . . . There is always the possibility that as in [the cases of the periodic system of elements and the quantum theory of light], a deviation may not affect the essential correctness of a proposition. . . . The process of explaining away deviations is in fact quite indispensable to the daily routine of research," even though this may lead to the missing of a great discovery.[16] For example, in 1795 the astronomer Lalande did not follow up observations that contradicted the prevailing hypotheses and could have led him to discover the planet Neptune.[17]

Yet we should not be too quick to condemn such behavior. As Thomas Kuhn has noted, "There is no such thing as research without counterinstances."[18] If a set of basic theories—what Kuhn calls a paradigm—has been able to account for a mass of data, it should not be lightly trifled with. As Kuhn puts it: "Life-long resistance, particularly from those whose productive careers have committed them to an older tradition of normal science [i.e., science within the accepted paradigm], is not a violation of scientific standards but an index to the nature of scientific research itself. The source of resistance is the assurance that the older paradigm will ultimately solve all its problems, that nature can be shoved into the box the paradigm provides. Inevitably, at times of revolution, that assurance seems stubborn and pigheaded as indeed it sometimes becomes. But it is also something more. That same assurance is what makes normal science or puzzle-solving science possible."[19]

Thus it is important to see that the dilemma of how "open" to be to new information is one that inevitably plagues any attempt at understanding in any field. Instances in which evidence seems to be ignored or twisted to fit the existing theory can often be explained by this dilemma instead of by illogical or nonlogical psychological pressures toward consistency. This is especially true of decision makers' attempts to estimate the intentions of other states, since they must constantly take account of the danger that the other state is trying to deceive them.

The theoretical framework discussed thus far, together with an examination of many cases, suggests hypothesis 2: scholars and decision makers are apt to err by being too wedded to the established view and too closed to new information, as opposed to being too willing to alter their theories.[20] Another way of making this point is to argue that actors tend to establish their theories and expectations prematurely. In politics, of course, this is often necessary because of the need for action. But experimental evidence indicates that the same tendency also occurs on the unconscious level. Bruner and Postman found that "perhaps the greatest single barrier to the recognition of incongruous stimuli is the tendency for perceptual hypotheses to fixate after receiving a minimum of confirmation. . . . Once there had occurred in these cases a partial confirmation of the hypothesis . . . it seemed that nothing could change the subject's report."[21]

However, when we apply these and other findings to politics and discuss kinds of misperception, we should not quickly apply the label of cognitive distortion. We should proceed cautiously for two related reasons. The first is that the evidence available to decision makers almost always permits several interpretations. It should be noted that there are cases of visual perception in which different stimuli can produce exactly the same pattern on an observer's retina. Thus for an observer using one eye the same pattern would be produced by a sphere the size of a golf ball which was quite close to the observer, by a baseball-sized sphere that was further away, or by a basketball-sized sphere still further away. Without other clues the observer cannot possibly determine which of these stimuli he is presented with, and we would not want to call his incorrect perceptions examples of distortion. Such cases, relatively rare in visual perception, are frequent in international relations. The evidence available to decision makers is almost always very ambiguous, since accurate clues to others' intentions are surrounded by noise[22] and deception. In most cases, no matter how long, deeply, and "objectively" the evidence is analyzed, people can differ in their interpretations, and there are no general rules to indicate who is correct.

The second reason to avoid the label of cognitive distortion is that the distinction between perception and judgment, obscure enough in individual psychology, is almost absent in the making of inferences in international politics. Decision makers who reject information that contradicts their views—or who develop complex interpretations of it—often do so consciously and explicitly. Since the evidence available contains contradictory information, to make any inferences requires that much information be ignored or given interpretations that will seem tortuous to those who hold a different position.

Indeed, if we consider only the evidence available to a decision maker at the time of decision, the view later proved incorrect may be supported by as much evidence as the correct one—or even by more. Scholars have often been too unsympathetic with the people who were proved wrong. On closer examination it is frequently difficult to point to differences between those who were right and those who were wrong with respect to their openness to new information and willingness to modify their views. Winston Churchill, for example, did not open-mindedly view each Nazi action to see if the explanations provided by the appeasers accounted for the data better than his own beliefs. Instead, like Chamberlain, he fitted each bit of ambiguous information into his own hypotheses. That he was correct should not lead us to overlook the fact that his methods of analysis and use of theory to produce cognitive consistency did not basically differ from those of the appeasers.[23]

A consideration of the importance of expectations in influencing perception also indicates that the widespread belief in the prevalence of "wishful thinking" may be incorrect, or at least may be based on inadequate data. The psychological literature on the interaction between affect and perception is immense and cannot be treated here, but it should be noted that phenomena that at first were considered strong evidence for the impact of affect on perception often can be better treated as demonstrating the influence of expectations.[24] Thus, in international relations, cases like the United States' misestimation of the political climate in Cuba in April 1961, which may seem at first glance to have been instances of wishful thinking, may instead be more adequately explained by the theories held by the decision makers (e.g., Communist governments are unpopular). Of course desires may have an impact on perception by influencing expectations, but since so many other factors affect expectations, the net influence of desires may not be great.

There is evidence from both psychology[25] and international relations that when expectations and desires clash, expectations seem to be more important. The United States would like to believe that North Vietnam is about to negotiate or that the USSR is ready to give up what the United States believes is its goal of world domination, but ambiguous evidence is seen to confirm the opposite conclusion, which conforms to the United States' expectations. Actors are apt to be especially sensitive to evidence of grave danger if they think they can take action to protect themselves against the menace once it has been detected.

III. SAFEGUARDS

Can anything then be said to scholars and decision makers other than "Avoid being either too open or too closed, but be especially aware of the latter danger"? Although decision makers will always be faced with ambiguous and confusing evidence and will be forced to make inferences about others which will often be inaccurate, a number of safeguards may be suggested which could enable them to minimize their errors. First and most obvious, decision makers should be aware that they do not make "unbiased" interpretations of each new bit of incoming information, but rather are inevitably heavily influenced by the theories they expect to be verified. They should know that what may appear to them as a self-evident and unambiguous inference often seems so only because of their preexisting beliefs. To someone with a different theory the same data may appear to be unimportant or to support another explanation. Thus many events provide less independent support for the decision makers' images than they may at first realize. Knowledge of this should lead decision makers to examine more closely evidence that others believe contradicts their views.

Second, decision makers should see if their attitudes contain consistent or supporting beliefs that are not logically linked. These may be examples of true psycho-logic. While it is not logically surprising, nor is it evidence of psychological pressures, to find that people who believe that Russia is aggressive are very suspicious of any Soviet move, other kinds of consistency are more suspect. For example, most people who feel that it is important for the United States to win the war in Vietnam also feel that a meaningful victory is possible. And most people who feel defeat would neither endanger U.S. national security nor be costly in terms of other values also feel that we cannot win. Although there are important logical linkages between the two parts of each of these views (especially through theories of guerrilla warfare), they do not seem strong enough to explain the degree to which the opinions are correlated. Similarly, in Finland in the winter of 1939, those who felt that grave consequences would follow Finnish agreement to give Russia a military base also believed that the Soviets would withdraw their demand if Finland stood firm. And those who felt that concessions would not lead to loss of major values also believed that Russia would fight if need be.[26] In this country those who favored a nuclear test ban tended to argue that fallout was very harmful, that only limited improvements in technology would flow from further testing, and that a test ban would increase the chances for peace and security. Those who opposed the test ban were apt to disagree on all three points. This does not mean, of course, that the people holding such sets of supporting views were necessarily wrong in any one element. The Finns who wanted to make concessions to the USSR were probably correct in both parts of their argument. But decision makers should be suspicious if they hold a position in which elements that are not logically connected support the same conclusion. This condition is psychologically comfortable and makes decisions easier to reach (since competing values do not have to be balanced off against each other). The chances are thus considerable that at least part of the reason why a person holds some of these views is related to psychology and not to the substance of the evidence.

Decision makers should also be aware that actors who suddenly find themselves having an important shared interest with other actors have a tendency to overestimate the degree of common interest involved. This tendency is especially strong for those actors (e.g., the United States, at least before 1950) whose beliefs about international relations and morality imply that they can cooperate only with "good" states and that with those states there will be no major conflicts. On the other hand, states that have either a tradition of limited cooperation with others (e.g., Britain) or a strongly held theory that differentiates occasional from permanent allies[27] (e.g., the Soviet Union) find it easier to resist this tendency and need not devote special efforts to combating its danger.

A third safeguard for decision makers would be to make their assumptions, beliefs, and the predictions that follow from them as explicit as possible. An actor should try to determine, before events occur, what evidence would count for and against his theories. By knowing what to expect he would know what to be surprised by, and surprise could indicate to that actor that his beliefs needed reevaluation.[28]

A fourth safeguard is more complex. The decision maker should try to prevent individuals and organizations from letting their main task, political future, and identity become tied to specific theories and images of other actors.[29] If this occurs, subgoals originally sought for their contribution to higher ends will take on value of their own, and information indicating possible alternative routes to the original goals will not be carefully considered. For example, the U.S. Forest Service was unable to carry out its original purpose as effectively when it began to see its distinctive competence not in promoting the best use of lands and forests but rather in preventing all types of forest fires.[30]

Organizations that claim to be unbiased may not realize the extent to which their definition of their role has become involved with certain beliefs about the world. Allen Dulles is a victim of this lack of understanding when he says, "I grant that we are all creatures of prejudice, including CIA officials, but by entrusting intelligence coordination to our central intelligence service, which is excluded from policy making and is married to no particular military hardware, we can avoid to the greatest possible extent the bending of facts obtained through intelligence to suit a particular occupational viewpoint."[31] This statement overlooks the fact that the CIA has developed a certain view of international relations and of the cold war which maximizes the importance of its information gathering, espionage, and subversive activities. Since the CIA would lose its unique place in the government if it were decided that the "back alleys" of world politics were no longer vital to U.S. security, it is not surprising that the organization interprets information in a way that stresses the continued need for its techniques.

Fifth, decision makers should realize the validity and implications of Roberta Wohlstetter's argument that "a willingness to play with material from different angles and in the context of unpopular as well as popular hypotheses is an essential ingredient of a good detective, whether the end is the solution of a crime or an intelligence estimate."[32] However, it is often difficult psychologically and politically for any one person to do this. Since a decision maker usually cannot get "unbiased" treatments of data, he should instead seek to structure conflicting biases into the decision-making process. The decision maker, in other words, should have devil's advocates around. Just as, as Neustadt points out,[33] the decision maker will want to create conflicts among his subordinates in order to make appropriate choices, so he will also want to ensure that incoming information is examined from many different perspectives with many different hypotheses in mind. To some extent this kind of examination will be done automatically through the divergence of goals, training, experience, and information that exists in any large organization. But in many cases this divergence will not be sufficient. The views of those analyzing the data will still be too homogeneous, and the decision maker will have to go out of his way not only to cultivate but to create differing viewpoints.

While all that would be needed would be to have some people examining the data trying to validate unpopular hypotheses, it would probably be more effective if they actually believed and had a stake in the views they were trying to support. If in 1941 someone had had the task of proving the view that Japan would attack Pearl Harbor, the government might have been less surprised by the attack. And only a person who was out to show that Russia would take objectively great risks would have been apt to note that several ships with especially large hatches going to Cuba were riding high in the water, indicating the presence of a bulky but light cargo that was not likely to be anything other than strategic missiles. And many people who doubt the wisdom of the administration's Vietnam policy would be somewhat reassured if there were people in the government who searched the statements and actions of both sides in an effort to prove that North Vietnam was willing to negotiate and that the official interpretation of such moves as the communist activities during the Tet truce of 1967 was incorrect.

Of course all these safeguards involve costs. They would divert resources from other tasks and would increase internal dissension. Determining whether these costs would be worth the gains would depend on a detailed analysis of how the suggested safeguards might be implemented. Even if they were adopted by a government, of course, they would not eliminate the chance of misperception. However, the safeguards would make it more likely that national decision makers would make conscious choices about the way data were interpreted rather than merely assuming that they can be seen in only one way and can mean only one thing. Statesmen would thus be reminded of alternative images of others just as they are constantly reminded of alternative policies.

These safeguards are partly based on hypothesis 3: actors can more easily assimilate into their established image of another actor information contradicting that image if the information is transmitted and considered bit by bit than if it comes all at once. In the former case each piece of discrepant data can be coped with as it arrives and each of the conflicts with the prevailing view will be small enough to go unnoticed, to be dismissed as unimportant, or to necessitate at most a slight modification of the image (e.g., addition of exceptions to the rule). When the information arrives in a block, the contradiction between it and the prevailing view is apt to be much clearer and the probability of major cognitive reorganization will be higher.

IV. SOURCES OF CONCEPTS

An actor's perceptual thresholds—and thus the images that ambiguous information is apt to produce—are influenced by what he has experienced and learned about.[34] If one actor is to perceive that another fits in a given category he must first have, or develop, a concept for that category. We can usefully distinguish three levels at which a concept can be present or absent. First, the concept can be completely missing. The actor's cognitive structure may not include anything corresponding to the phenomenon he is encountering. This situation can occur not only in science fiction but also in a world of rapid change or in the meeting of two dissimilar systems. Thus China's image of the Western world was extremely inaccurate in the mid-nineteenth century, her learning was very slow, and her responses were woefully inadequate. The West was spared a similar struggle only because it had the power to reshape the system it encountered. Once the actor clearly sees one instance of the new phenomenon, he is apt to recognize it much more quickly in the future.[35] Second, the actor can know about a concept but not believe that it reflects an actual phenomenon. Thus communist and Western decision makers are each aware of the other's explanation of how his system functions but do not think that the concept corresponds to reality. Communist elites, furthermore, deny that anything *could* correspond to the democracies' description of themselves. Third, the actor may hold a concept but not believe that another actor fills it at the present moment. Thus the British and French statesmen of the 1930s held a concept of states with unlimited ambitions. They realized that Napoleons were possible, but they did not think Hitler belonged in that category. Hypothesis 4 distinguishes these three cases: misperception is most difficult to correct in the case of a missing concept and least difficult to correct in the case of a recognized but presumably unfilled concept. All other things being equal (e.g., the degree to which the concept is central to the actor's cognitive structure), the first case requires more cognitive reorganization than does the second, and the second requires more reorganization than the third.

However, this hypothesis does not mean that learning will necessarily be slowest in the first case, for if the phenomena are totally new, the actor may make such grossly inappropriate responses that he will quickly acquire information clearly indicating that he is faced with something he does not understand. And the sooner the actor realizes that things are not—or may not be—what they seem, the sooner he is apt to correct his image.[36]

Three main sources contribute to decision makers' concepts of international relations and of other states and influence the level of their perceptual thresholds for various phenomena. First, an actor's beliefs about his own domestic political system are apt to be important. In some cases, like that of the USSR, the decision makers' concepts are tied to an ideology that explicitly provides a frame of reference for viewing foreign affairs. Even where this is not the case, experience with his own system will partly determine what the actor is familiar with and what he is apt to perceive in others. Louis Hartz claims, "It is the absence of the experience of social revolution which is at the heart of the whole American dilemma. . . . In a whole series of specific ways it enters into our difficulty of communication with the rest of the world. We find it difficult to understand Europe's 'social question.'. . . We are not familiar with the deeper social struggles of Asia and hence tend to interpret even reactionary regimes as 'democratic.'"[37] Similarly, George Kennan argues that in World War I the Allied powers, and especially America, could not understand the bitterness and violence of others' internal conflicts: ". . . The inability of the Allied statesmen to picture to themselves the passions of the Russian civil war [was partly caused by the fact that] we represent . . . a society in which the manifestations of evil have been carefully buried and sublimated in the social behavior of people, as in their very consciousness. For this reason, probably, despite our widely traveled and outwardly cosmopolitan lives, the mainsprings of political behavior in such a country as Russia tend to remain concealed from our vision."[38]

Second, concepts will be supplied by the actor's previous experiences. An experiment from another field illustrates this. Dearborn and Simon presented business executives from various divisions (e.g., sales, accounting, production) with the same hypothetical data and asked them for an analysis and recommendations from the standpoint of what would be best for the company as a whole. The executives' views heavily reflected their departmental perspectives.[39] William W. Kaufmann shows how the perceptions of Ambassador Joseph Kennedy were affected by his past: "As befitted a former chairman of the Securities Exchange and Maritime Commissions, his primary interest lay in economic matters. . . . The revolutionary character of the Nazi regime was not a phenomenon that he could easily grasp. . . . It was far simpler, and more in accord with his own premises, to explain German aggressiveness in economic terms. The Third Reich was dissatisfied, authoritarian, and expansive largely because her economy was unsound."[40] Similarly it has been argued that Chamberlain was slow to recognize Hitler's intentions partly because of the limiting nature of his personal background and business experiences.[41] The impact of training and experience seems to be demonstrated when the background of the appeasers is compared to that of their opponents. One difference stands out: "A substantially higher percentage of the anti-appeasers (irrespective of class origins) had the kind of knowledge which comes from close acquaintance, mainly professional, with foreign affairs."[42] Since members of the diplomatic corps are responsible for meeting threats to the nation's security before these grow to major proportions, and since they have learned about cases in which aggressive states were not recognized as such until very late, they may be prone to interpret ambiguous data as showing that others are aggressive. It should be stressed that we cannot say that the professionals of the 1930s were more apt to make accurate judgments of other states. Rather, they may have been more sensitive to the chance that others were aggressive. They would then rarely take an aggressor for a status-quo power, but would more often make the opposite error.[43] Thus in the years before World War I the permanent officials in the British Foreign Office overestimated German aggressiveness.[44]

A parallel demonstration in psychology of the impact of training on perception is presented by an experiment in which ambiguous pictures were shown to both advanced and beginning police-administration students. The advanced group perceived more violence in the pictures than did the beginners. The probable explanation is that "the law enforcer may come to accept crime as a familiar personal experience, one which he himself is not surprised to encounter. The acceptance of crime as a familiar experience in turn increases the ability or readiness to perceive violence where clues to it are potentially available."[45] This experiment lends weight to the view that the British diplomats' sensitivity to aggressive states was not totally a product of personnel selection procedures.

A third source of concepts, which frequently will be the most directly relevant to a decision maker's perception of international relations, is international history. As Henry Kissinger points out, one reason why statesmen were so slow to recognize the threat posed by Napoleon was that previous events had accustomed them only to actors who wanted to modify the existing system, not overthrow it.[46] The other side of the coin is even more striking: historical traumas can heavily influence future perceptions. They can either establish a state's image of the other state involved or can be used as analogies. An example of the former case is provided by the fact that for at least ten years after the Franco-Prussian War most of Europe's statesmen felt that Bismarck had aggressive plans when in fact his main goal was to protect the status quo. Of course the evidence was ambiguous. The post-1871 Bismarckian maneuvers, which were designed to keep peace, looked not unlike the pre-1871 maneuvers designed to set the stage for war. But that the post-1871 maneuvers were seen as indicating aggressive plans is largely attributable to the impact of Bismarck's earlier actions on the statemen's image of him.

A state's previous unfortunate experience with a type of danger can sensitize it to other examples of that danger. While this sensitivity may lead the state to avoid the mistake it committed in the past, it may also lead it mistakenly to believe that the present situation is like the past one. Santayana's maxim could be turned around: "Those who remember the past are condemned to make the opposite mistakes." As Paul Kecskemeti shows, both defenders and critics of the unconditional surrender plan of the Second World War thought in terms of the conditions of World War I.[47] Annette Baker Fox found that the Scandinavian countries' neutrality policies in World War II were strongly influenced by their experiences in the previous war, even though vital aspects of the two situations were different. Thus "Norway's success [during the First World War] in remaining nonbelligerent though pro-Allied gave the Norwegians confidence that their country could again stay out of war." [48] And the lesson drawn from the unfortunate results of this policy was an important factor in Norway's decision to join NATO.

The application of the Munich analogy to various contemporary events has been much commented on, and I do not wish to argue the substantive points at stake. But it seems clear that the probabilities that any state is facing an aggressor who has to be met by force are not altered by the career of Hitler and the history of the 1930s. Similarly the probability of an aggressor's announcing his plans is not increased (if anything, it is decreased) by the fact that Hitler wrote *Mein Kampf*. Yet decision makers are more sensitive to these possibilities, and thus more apt to perceive ambiguous evidence as indicating they apply to a given case, than they would have been had there been no Nazi Germany.

Historical analogies often precede, rather than follow, a careful analysis of a situation (e.g., Truman's initial reaction to the news of the invasion of South Korea was to think of the Japanese invasion of Manchuria). Noting this precedence, however, does not show us which of many analogies will come to a decision maker's mind. Truman could have thought of nineteenth-century European wars that were of no interest to the United States. Several factors having nothing to do with the event under consideration influence what analogies a decision maker is apt to make. One factor is the number of cases similar to the analogy with which the decision maker is familiar. Another is the importance of the past event to the political system of which the decision maker is a part. The more times such an event occurred and the greater its consequences were, the more a decision maker will be sensitive to the particular danger involved and the more he will be apt to see ambiguous stimuli as indicating another instance of this kind of event. A third factor is the degree of the decision maker's personal involvement in the past case—in time, energy, ego, and position. The last-mentioned variable will affect not only the event's impact on the decision maker's cognitive structure, but also the way he perceives the event and the lesson he draws. Someone who was involved in getting troops into South Korea after the attack will remember the Korean War differently from someone who was involved in considering the possible use of nuclear weapons or in deciding what messages should be sent to the Chinese. Greater personal involvement will usually give the event greater impact, especially if the decision maker's own views were validated by the event. One need not accept a total application of learning theory to nations to believe that "nothing fails like success."[49] It also seems likely that if many critics argued at the time that the decision maker was wrong, he will be even more apt to see other situations in terms of the original event. For example, because Anthony Eden left the government on account of his views and was later shown to have been correct, he probably was more apt to see as Hitlers other leaders with whom he had conflicts (e.g., Nasser). A fourth factor is the degree to which the analogy is compatible with the rest of his belief system. A fifth is the absence of alternative concepts and analogies. Individuals and states vary in the amount of direct or indirect political experience they have had which can provide different ways of interpreting data. Decision makers who are aware of multiple possibilities of states' intentions may be less likely to seize on an analogy prematurely. The perception of citizens of nations like the United States, which have relatively little history of international politics, may be more apt to be heavily influenced by the few major international events that have been important to their country.

The first three factors indicate that an event is more apt to shape present perceptions if it occurred in the recent rather than the remote past. If it occurred recently, the statesman will then know about it at first hand even if he was not involved in the making of policy at the time. Thus if generals are prepared to fight the last war, diplomats may be prepared to avoid the last war. Part of the Anglo-French reaction to Hitler can be explained by the prevailing beliefs that the First World War was to a large extent caused by misunderstandings and could have been avoided by farsighted and nonbelligerent diplomacy. And part of the Western perception of Russia and China can be explained by the view that appeasement was an inappropriate response to Hitler.[50]

V. THE EVOKED SET

The way people perceive data is influenced not only by their cognitive structure and theories about other actors but also by what they are concerned with at the time they receive the information. Information is evaluated in light of the small part of the person's memory that is presently active—the "evoked set." My perceptions of the dark streets I pass walking home from the movies will be different if the film I saw had dealt with spies than if it had been a comedy. If I am working on aiding a country's education system and I hear someone talk about the need for economic development in that state, I am apt to think he is concerned with education, whereas if I had been working on, say, trying to achieve political stability in that country, I would have placed his remarks in that framework.[51]

Thus hypothesis 5 states that when messages are sent from a different background of concerns and information than is possessed by the receiver, misunderstanding is likely. Person A and person B will read the same message quite differently if A has seen several related messages that B does not know about. This difference will be compounded if, as is frequently the case, A and B each assume that the other has the same background he does. This means that misperception can occur even when deception is neither intended nor expected. Thus Roberta Wohlstetter found not only that different parts of the United States government had different perceptions of data about Japan's intentions and messages partly because they saw the incoming information in very different contexts, but also that officers in the field misunderstood warnings from Washington: "Washington advised General Short [in Pearl Harbor] on November 27 to expect 'hostile action' at any moment, by which it meant 'attack on American possessions from without,' but General Short understood this phrase to mean 'sabotage.'"[52] Washington did not realize the extent to which Pearl Harbor considered the danger of sabotage to be primary, and furthermore it incorrectly believed that General Short had received the intercepts of the secret Japanese diplomatic messages available in Washington which indicated that surprise attack was a distinct possibility. Another implication of this hypothesis is that if important information is known to only part of the government of state A and part of the government of state B, international messages may be misunderstood by those parts of the receiver's government that do not match, in the information they have, the part of the sender's government that dispatched the message.[53]

Two additional hypotheses can be drawn from the problems of those sending messages. Hypothesis 6 states that when people spend a great deal of time drawing up a plan or making a decision, they tend to think that the message about it they wish to convey will be clear to the receiver.[54] Since they are aware of what is to them the important pattern in their actions, they often feel that the pattern will be equally obvious to others, and they overlook the degree to which the message is apparent to them only because they know what to look for. Those who have not participated in the endless meetings may not understand what information the sender is trying to convey. George Quester has shown how the German and to a lesser extent the British desire to maintain target limits on bombing in the first eighteen months of World War II was undermined partly by the fact that each side knew the limits it was seeking and its own reasons for any apparent "exceptions" (e.g., the German attack on Rotterdam) and incorrectly felt that these limits and reasons were equally clear to the other side.[55]

Hypothesis 7 holds that actors often do not realize that actions intended to project a given image may not have the desired effect because the actions themselves do not turn out as planned. Thus even without appreciable impact of different cognitive structures and backgrounds, an action may convey an unwanted message. For example, a country's representatives may not follow instructions and so may give others impressions contrary to those the home government wished to convey. The efforts of Washington and Berlin to settle their dispute over Samoa in the late 1880s were complicated by the provocative behavior of their agents on the spot. These agents not only increased the intensity of the local conflict but led the decision makers to become more suspicious of the other state because they tended to assume that their agents were obeying instructions and that the actions of the other side represented official policy. In such cases both sides will believe that the other is reading hostility into a policy of theirs which is friendly. Similarly, Quester's study shows that the attempt to limit bombing referred to above failed partly because neither side was able to bomb as accurately as it thought it could and thus did not realize the physical effects of its actions.[56]

VI. FURTHER HYPOTHESES FROM THE PERSPECTIVE OF THE PERCEIVER

From the perspective of the perceiver several other hypotheses seem to hold. Hypothesis 8 is that there is an overall tendency for decision makers to see other states as more hostile than they are.[57] There seem to be more cases of statesmen incorrectly believing others are planning major acts against their interest than of statesmen being lulled by a potential aggressor. There are many reasons for this which are too complex to be treated here (e.g., some parts of the bureaucracy feel it is their responsibility to be suspicious of all other states; decision makers often feel they are "playing it safe" to believe and act as though the other state were hostile in questionable cases; and often, when people do not feel they are a threat to others, they find it difficult to believe that others may see them as a threat). It should be noted, however, that decision makers whose perceptions are described by this hypothesis would not necessarily further their own values by trying to correct for this tendency. The values of possible outcomes as well as their probabilities must be considered, and it may be that the probability of an unnecessary arms-tension cycle arising out of misperceptions, multiplied by the costs of such a cycle, may seem less to decision makers than the probability of incorrectly believing another state is friendly, multiplied by the costs of this eventuality.

Hypothesis 9 states that actors tend to see the behavior of others as more centralized, disciplined, and coordinated than it is. This hypothesis holds true in related ways. Frequently too many complex events are squeezed into a perceived pattern. Actors are hesitant to admit or even see that particular incidents cannot be explained by their theories.[58] Those events not caused by factors that are important parts of the perceiver's image are often seen as though they were. Further, actors see others as more internally united than they in fact are and generally overestimate the degree to which others are following a coherent policy. The degree to which the other side's policies are the product of internal bargaining,[59] internal misunderstandings, or subordinates' not following instructions is underestimated.

This is the case partly because actors tend to be unfamiliar with the details of another state's policy-making processes. Seeing only the finished product, they find it simpler to try to construct a rational explanation for the policies, even though they know that such an analysis could not explain their own policies.[60]

Familiarity also accounts for hypothesis 10: because a state gets most of its information about the other state's policies from the other's foreign office, it tends to take the foreign office's position for the stand of the other government as a whole. In many cases this perception will be an accurate one, but when the other government is divided or when the other foreign office is acting without specific authorization, misperception may result. For example, part of the reason why in 1918 Allied governments incorrectly thought "that the Japanese were preparing to take action [in Siberia], if need be, with agreement with the British and French alone, disregarding the absence of American consent,"[61] was that Allied ambassadors had talked mostly with Foreign Minister Motono, who was among the minority of the Japanese favoring this policy. Similarly, America's NATO allies may have gained an inaccurate picture of the degree to which the American government was committed to the MLF because they had greatest contact with parts of the government that strongly favored the MLF. And states that tried to get information about Nazi foreign policy from German diplomats were often misled because these officials were generally ignorant of or out of sympathy with Hitler's plans. The Germans and the Japanese sometimes purposely misinformed their own ambassadors in order to deceive their enemies more effectively.

Hypothesis 11 states that actors tend to overestimate the degree to which others are acting in response to what they themselves do when the others behave in accordance with the actor's desires; but when the behavior of the other is undesired, it is usually seen as derived from internal forces. If the *effect* of another's action is to injure or threaten the first side, the first side is apt to believe that such was the other's *purpose.* An example of the first part of the hypothesis is provided by Kennan's account of the activities of official and unofficial American representatives who protested to the new Bolshevik government against several of its actions. When the Soviets changed their position, these representatives felt it was largely because of their influence.[62] This sort of interpretation can be explained not only by the fact that it is gratifying to the individual making it, but also, taking the other side of the coin mentioned in hypothesis 9, by the fact that the actor is most familiar with his own input into the other's decision and has less knowledge of other influences. The second part of hypothesis 11 is illustrated by the tendency of actors to believe that the hostile behavior of others is to be explained by the other side's motives and not by its reaction to the first side. Thus Chamberlain did not see that Hitler's behavior was related in part to his belief that the British were weak. More common is the failure to see that the other side is reacting out of fear of the first side, which can lead to self-fulfilling prophecies and spirals of misperception and hostility.

This difficulty is often compounded by an implication of hypothesis 12: when actors have intentions that they do not try to conceal from others, they tend to assume that others accurately perceive these intentions. Only rarely do they believe that others may be reacting to a much less favorable image of themselves than they think they are projecting.[63]

For state A to understand how state B perceives A's policy is often difficult because such understanding may involve a conflict with A's image of itself. Raymond Sontag argues that Anglo-German relations before World War I deteriorated partly because "the British did not like to think of themselves as selfish or unwilling to tolerate 'legitimate' German expansion. The Germans did not like to think of themselves as aggressive or unwilling to recognize 'legitimate' British vested interest."[64]

Hypothesis 13 suggests that if it is hard for an actor to believe that the other can see him as a menace, it is often even harder for him to see that issues important to him are not important to others. While he may know that another actor is on an opposing team, it may be more difficult for him to realize that the other is playing an entirely different game. This is especially true when the game he is playing seems vital to him.[65]

The final hypothesis, hypothesis 14, is as follows: actors tend to overlook the fact that evidence consistent with their theories may also be consistent with other views. When choosing between two theories, we have to pay attention only to data that cannot be accounted for by one of the theories. But it is common to find people claiming as proof of their theories data that could also support alternative views. This phenomenon is related to the point made earlier that any single bit of information can be interpreted only within a framework of hypotheses and theories. And while it is true that "we may without a vicious circularity accept some datum as a fact because it conforms to the very law for which it counts as another confirming instance, and reject an allegation of fact because it is already excluded by law,"[66] we should be careful lest we forget that a piece of information seems in many cases to confirm a certain hypothesis only because we already believe that hypothesis to be correct and that the information can with as much validity support a different hypothesis. For example, one of the reasons why the German attack on Norway took both that country and England by surprise, even though they had detected German ships moving toward Norway, was that they expected not an attack but an attempt by the Germans to break through the British blockade and reach the Atlantic. The initial course of the ships was consistent with either plan, but the British and Norwegians took this course to mean that their predictions were being borne out.[67] This is not to imply that the interpretation made was foolish, but only that the decision makers should have been aware that the evidence was also consistent with an invasion and should have had a bit less confidence in their views.

The longer the ships would have to travel the same route, whether they were going to one or another of two destinations, the more information would be needed to determine their plans. Taken as a metaphor, this incident applies generally to the treatment of evidence. Thus as long as Hitler made demands for control only of ethnically German areas, his actions could be explained either by the hypothesis that he had unlimited ambitions or by the hypothesis that he wanted to unite all the Germans. But actions against non-Germans (e.g., the takeover of Czechoslovakia in March 1938) could not be accounted for by the latter hypothesis. And it was this action that convinced the appeasers that Hitler had to be stopped. It is interesting to speculate on what the British reaction would have been had Hitler left Czechoslovakia alone for a while and instead made demands on Poland similar to those he eventually made in the summer of 1939. The two paths would then still not have diverged, and further misperception could have occurred.

NOTES

1. See for example Ole Holsti, Robert North, and Richard Brody, "Perception and Action in the 1914 Crisis," in J. David Singer, ed., *Quantitative International Politics* (New York, 1968). For a fuller discussion of the Stanford content analysis studies and the general problems of quantification, see my "The Costs of the Quantitative Study of International Relations," in Klaus Knorr and James N. Rosenau, eds., *Contending Approaches to International Politics* (forthcoming).

2. See, for example, Osgood, *An Alternative to War or Surrender* (Urbana, 1962); Etzioni, *The Hard Way to Peace* (New York, 1962); Boulding, "National Images and International Systems," *Journal of Conflict Resolution,* III (June 1959), 120–31; and Singer, *Deterrence, Arms Control, and Disarmament* (Columbus, 1962).

3. *Statistics of Deadly Quarrels* (Pittsburgh, 1960) and *Arms and Insecurity* (Chicago, 1960). For nonmathematicians a fine summary of Richardson's work is Anatol Rapoport's "L. F. Richardson's Mathematical Theory of War," *Journal of Conflict Resolution,* I (September 1957), 249–99.

4. See Philip Green, *Deadly Logic* (Columbus, 1966); Green, "Method and Substance in the Arms Debate," *World Politics,* XVI (July 1964), 642–67; and Robert A. Levine, "Fact and Morals in the Arms Debate," *World Politics,* XIV (January 1962), 239–58.

5. See Anatol Rapoport, *Strategy and Conscience* (New York, 1964).

6. Floyd Allport, *Theories of Perception and the Concept of Structure* (New York, 1955), 382; Ole Holsti, "Cognitive Dynamics and Images of the Enemy," in David Finlay, Ole Holsti, and Richard Fagen, *Enemies in Politics* (Chicago, 1967), 70.

7. Jerome Bruner and Leo Postman, "On the Perceptions of Incongruity: A Paradigm," in Jerome Bruner and David Krech, eds., *Perception and Personality* (Durham, N.C., 1949), 210.

8. Robert Abelson and Milton Rosenberg, "Symbolic Psycho-logic," *Behavioral Science,* III (January 1958), 4–5.

9. p. 27.

10. *Ibid.,* 26.

11. I have borrowed this phrase from Abraham Kaplan, who uses it in a different but related context in *The Conduct of Inquiry* (San Francisco, 1964), 86.

12. The spiral theorists are not the only ones to ignore the limits of empiricism. Roger Hilsman found that most consumers and producers of intelligence felt that intelligence should not deal with hypotheses but should only provide the policy makers with "all the facts" (*Strategic Intelligence and National Decisions* [Glencoe, 1956], 46). The close interdependence between hypotheses and facts is overlooked partly because of the tendency to identify "hypotheses" with "policy preferences."

13. Karl Deutsch interestingly discusses a related question when he argues, "Autonomy . . . requires both intake from the present and recall from memory, and selfhood can be seen in just this continuous balancing of a limited present and a limited past. . . . No further self-determination is possible if either openness or memory is lost. . . . To the extent that [systems cease to be able to take in new information], they approach the behavior of a bullet or torpedo: their future action becomes almost completely determined by their past. On the other hand, a person without memory, an organization without values or policy . . . —all these no longer steer, but drift: their behavior depends little on their past and almost wholly on their present. Driftwood and the bullet are thus each the epitome of another kind of loss of self-control . . ." (*Nationalism and Social Communication* [Cambridge, Mass., 1954], 167–68). Also see Deutsch's *The Nerves of Government* (New York, 1963), 98–109, 200–256. A physicist makes a similar argument: "It is clear that if one is too attached to one's preconceived model, one will miss all radical discoveries. It is amazing to what degree one may fail to register mentally an observa-

tion which does not fit the initial image. . . . On the other hand, if one is too open-minded and pursues every hitherto-unknown phenomenon, one is almost certain to lose oneself in trivia" (Martin Deutsch, "Evidence and Inference in Nuclear Research," in Daniel Lerner, ed., *Evidence and Inference* [Glencoe, 1958], 102).

14. Raymond Bauer, "Problems of Perception and the Relations Between the U.S. and the Soviet Union," *Journal of Conflict Resolution*, V (September 1961), 223–29.

15. Quoted in W. I. B. Beveridge, *The Art of Scientific Investigation*, 3rd ed. (London, 1957), 50.

16. *Science, Faith, and Society* (Chicago, 1964), 31. For a further discussion of this problem, see *ibid.*, 16, 26–41, 90–94; Polanyi, *Personal Knowledge* (London, 1958), 8–15, 30, 143–68, 269–98, 310–11; Thomas Kuhn, *The Structure of Scientific Revolution* (Chicago, 1964); Kuhn, "The Function of Dogma in Scientific Research," in A. C. Crombie, ed., *Scientific Change* (New York, 1963), 344–69; the comments on Kuhn's paper by Hall, Polanyi, and Toulmin, and Kuhn's reply, *ibid.*, 370–95. For a related discussion of these points from a different perspective, see Norman Storer, *The Social System of Science* (New York, 1960), 116–22.

17. "He found that the position of one star relative to others . . . had shifted. Lalande was a good astronomer and knew that such a shift was unreasonable. He crossed out his first observation, put a question mark next to the second observation, and let the matter go" (Jerome Bruner, Jacqueline Goodnow, and George Austin, *A Study of Thinking* [New York, 1962], 105).

18. *The Structure of Scientific Revolution,* 79.

19. *Ibid.,* 150–51.

20. Requirements of effective political leadership may lead decision makers to voice fewer doubts than they have about existing policies and images, but this constraint can only partially explain this phenomenon. Similar calculations of political strategy may contribute to several of the hypotheses discussed below.

21. p. 221. Similarly, in experiments dealing with his subjects' perception of other people, Charles Dailey found that "premature judgment appears to make new data harder to assimilate than when the observer withholds judgment until all data are seen. It seems probable . . . that the observer mistakes his own inferences for facts" ("The Effects of Premature Conclusion Upon the Acquisition of Understanding of a Person," *Journal of Psychology*, XXX [January 1952], 149–50). For other theory and evidence on this point, see Bruner, "On Perceptual Readiness," *Psychological Review*, LXIV (March 1957), 123–52; Gerald Davidson, "The Negative Effects of Early Exposure to Suboptimal Visual Stimuli," *Journal of Personality*, XXXII (June 1964), 278–95; Albert Myers, "An Experimental Analysis of a Tactical Blunder," *Journal of Abnormal and Social Psychology*, LXIX (November 1964), 493–98; and Dale Wyatt and Donald Campbell, "On the Liability of Stereotype or Hypothesis," *Journal of Abnormal and Social Psychology*, XLIV (October 1950), 496–500. It should be noted that this tendency makes "incremental" decision making more likely (David Braybrooke and Charles Lindblom, *A Strategy of Decision* [New York, 1963]), but the results of this process may lead the actor further from his goals.

22. For a use of this concept in political communication, see Roberta Wohlstetter, *Pearl Harbor* (Stanford, 1962).

23. Similarly, Robert Coulondre, the French ambassador to Berlin in 1939, was one of the few diplomats to appreciate the Nazi threat. Partly because of his earlier service in the USSR, "he was painfully sensitive to the threat of a Berlin-Moscow agreement. He noted with foreboding that Hitler had not attacked Russia in his *Reichstag* address of April 28. . . . So it went all spring and summer, the ambassador relaying each new evidence of the impending diplomatic revolution and adding to his admonitions his pleas for decisive counteraction" (Franklin Ford and Carl Schorske, "The Voice in the Wilderness: Robert

Coulondre," in Gordon Craig and Felix Gilbert, eds., *The Diplomats,* Vol. III [New York, 1963] 573–74). His hypotheses were correct, but it is difficult to detect differences between the way he and those ambassadors who were incorrect, like Neville Henderson, selectively noted and interpreted information. However, to the extent that the fear of war influenced the appeasers' perceptions of Hitler's intentions, the appeasers' views did have an element of psycho-logic that was not present in their opponents' position.

24. See for example Donald Campbell, "Systematic Error on the Part of Human Links in Communications Systems," *Information and Control,* I (1958), 346–50; and Leo Postman, "The Experimental Analysis of Motivational Factors in Perception," in Judson S. Brown, ed., *Current Theory and Research in Motivation* (Lincoln, Neb., 1953), 59–108.

25. Dale Wyatt and Donald Campbell, "A Study of Interviewer Bias as Related to Interviewer's Expectations and Own Opinions," *International Journal of Opinion and Attitude Research,* IV (Spring 1950), 77–83.

26. Max Jacobson, *The Diplomacy of the Winter War* (Cambridge, Mass., 1961), 136–39.

27. Raymond Aron, *Peace and War* (Garden City, 1966), 29.

28. Cf. Kuhn, *The Structure of Scientific Revolution,* 65. A fairly high degree of knowledge is needed before one can state precise expectations. One indication of the lack of international-relations theory is that most of us are not sure what "naturally" flows from our theories and what constitutes either "puzzles" to be further explored with the paradigm or "anomalies" that cast doubt on the basic theories.

29. See Philip Selznick, *Leadership in Administration* (Evanston, 1957).

30. Ashley Schiff, *Fire and Water: Scientific Heresy in the Forest Service* (Cambridge, Mass., 1962). Despite its title, this book is a fascinating and valuable study.

31. *The Craft of Intelligence* (New York, 1963), 53.

32. p. 302. See Beveridge, 93, for a discussion of the idea that the scientist should keep in mind as many hypotheses as possible when conducting and analyzing experiments.

33. *Presidential Power* (New York, 1960).

34. Most psychologists argue that this influence also holds for perception of shapes. For data showing that people in different societies differ in respect to their predisposition to experience certain optical illusions and for a convincing argument that this difference can be explained by the societies' different physical environments, which have led their people to develop different patterns of drawing inferences from ambiguous visual cues, see Marshall Segall, Donald Campbell, and Melville Herskovits, *The Influence of Culture on Visual Perceptions* (Indianapolis, 1966).

35. Thus when Bruner and Postman's subjects first were presented with incongruous playing cards (i.e., cards in which symbols and colors of the suits were not matching, producing red spades or black diamonds), long exposure times were necessary for correct identification. But once a subject correctly perceived the card and added this type of card to his repertoire of categories, he was able to identify other incongruous cards much more quickly. For an analogous example—in this case changes in the analysis of aerial reconnaissance photographs of an enemy's secret weapons-testing facilities produced by the belief that a previously unknown object may be present—see David Irving, *The Mare's Nest* (Boston, 1964), 66–67, 274–75.

36. Bruner and Postman, 220.

37. *The Liberal Tradition in America* (New York, 1955), 306.

38. *Russia and the West Under Lenin and Stalin* (New York, 1962), 142–43.

39. DeWitt Dearborn and Herbert Simon, "Selective Perception: A Note on the Departmental Identification of Executives," *Sociometry,* XXI (June 1958), 140–44.

40. "Two American Ambassadors: Bullitt and Kennedy," in Craig and Gilbert, 358–59.

41. Hugh Trevor-Roper puts this point well: "Brought up as a business man, successful in municipal politics, [Chamberlain's] outlook was entirely parochial. Educated Conserva-

tive aristocrats like Churchill, Eden, and Cranborne, whose families had long been used to political responsibility, had seen revolution and revolutionary leaders before, in their own history, and understood them correctly; but the Chamberlains, who had run from radical imperialism to timid conservatism in a generation of life in Birmingham, had no such understanding of history or the world: to them the scope of human politics was limited by their own parochial horizons, and Neville Chamberlain could not believe that Hitler was fundamentally different from himself. If Chamberlain wanted peace, so must Hitler" ("Munich—Its Lessons Ten Years Later," in Francis Loewenheim, ed., *Peace or Appeasement?* [Boston, 1965], 152–53). For a similar view see A. L. Rowse, *Appeasement* (New York, 1963), 117.

But Donald Lammers points out that the views of many prominent British public figures in the 1930s do not fit this generalization (*Explaining Munich* [Stanford, 1966], 13–140). Furthermore, arguments that stress the importance of the experiences and views of the actors' ancestors do not explain the links by which these influence the actors themselves. Presumably Churchill and Chamberlain read the same history books in school and had the same basic information about Britain's past role in the world. Thus what has to be demonstrated is that in their homes aristocrats like Churchill learned different things about politics and human nature than did middle-class people like Chamberlain and that these experiences had a significant impact. Alternatively, it could be argued that the patterns of child-rearing prevalent among the aristocracy influenced the children's personalities in a way that made them more likely to see others as aggressive.

42. *Ibid.*, 15.

43. During a debate on appeasement in the House of Commons, Harold Nicolson declared, "I know that those of us who believe in the traditions of our policy, . . . who believe that one great function of this country is to maintain moral standards in Europe, to maintain a settled pattern of international relations, not to make friends with people who are demonstrably evil . . . —I know that those who hold such beliefs are accused of possessing the Foreign Office mind. I thank God that I possess the Foreign Office mind" (quoted in Martin Gilbert, *The Roots of Appeasement* [New York, 1966], 187). But the qualities Nicolson mentions and applauds may be related to a more basic attribute of "the Foreign Office mind"—suspiciousness.

44. George Monger, *The End of Isolation* (London, 1963). I am also indebted to Frederick Collignon for his unpublished manuscript and several conversations on this point.

45. Hans Toch and Richard Schulte, "Readiness to Perceive Violence as a Result of Police Training," *British Journal of Psychology*, LII (November 1961), 392 (original italics omitted). It should be stressed that one cannot say whether or not the advanced police students perceived the pictures "accurately." The point is that their training predisposed them to see violence in ambiguous situations. Whether on balance they would make fewer perceptual errors and better decisions is very hard to determine. For an experiment showing that training can lead people to "recognize" an expected stimulus even when that stimulus is in fact not shown, see Israel Goldiamond and William F. Hawkins, "Vexierversuch: The Log Relationship Between Word-Frequency and Recognition Obtained in the Absence of Stimulus Words," *Journal of Experimental Psychology*, LVI (December 1958), 457–63.

46. *A World Restored* (New York, 1964), 2–3.

47. *Strategic Surrender* (New York, 1964), 215–41.

48. *The Power of Small States* (Chicago, 1959), 81.

49. William Inge, *Outspoken Essays*, First Series (London, 1923), 88.

50. Of course, analogies themselves are not "unmoved movers." The interpretation of past events is not automatic and is informed by general views of international relations and complex judgments. And just as beliefs about the past influence the present, views

about the present influence interpretations of history. It is difficult to determine the degree to which the United States' interpretation of the reasons it went to war in 1917 influenced American foreign policy in the 1920s and 1930s and how much the isolationism of that period influenced the histories of the war.

51. For some psychological experiments on this subject see Jerome Bruner and A. Leigh Minturn, "Perceptual Identification and Perceptual Organization," *Journal of General Psychology,* LIII (July 1955), 22–28; Seymour Feshbach and Robert Singer, "The Effects of Fear Arousal and Suppression of Fear Upon Social Perception," *Journal of Abnormal and Social Psychology,* LV (November 1957), 283–88; and Elsa Sippoal, "A Group Study of Some Effects of Preparatory Sets," *Psychology Monographs,* XLVI, No. 210 (1935), 27–28. For a general discussion of the importance of the perceiver's evoked set, see Postman, 87.

52. pp. 73–74.

53. For example, Roger Hilsman points out, "Those who knew of the peripheral reconnaissance flights that probed Soviet air defenses during the Eisenhower administration and the U-2 flights over the Soviet Union itself . . . were better able to understand some of the things the Soviets were saying and doing than people who did not know of these activities" (*To Move a Nation* [Garden City, 1967], 66). But it is also possible that those who knew about the U-2 flights at times misinterpreted Soviet messages by incorrectly believing that the sender was influenced by, or at least knew of, these flights.

54. I am grateful to Thomas Schelling for discussion on this point.

55. *Deterrence Before Hiroshima* (New York, 1966), 105–22.

56. *Ibid.*

57. For a slightly different formulation of this view, see Holsti, 27.

58. The Soviets consciously hold an extreme version of this view and seem to believe that nothing is accidental. See the discussion in Nathan Leites, *A Study of Bolshevism* (Glencoe, 1953), 67–73.

59. A. W. Marshall criticizes Western explanations of Soviet military posture for failing to take this into account. See his "Problems of Estimating Military Power," a paper presented at the 1966 Annual Meeting of the American Political Science Association, 16.

60. It has also been noted that in labor-management disputes both sides may be apt to believe incorrectly that the other is controlled from above, either from the international union office or from the company's central headquarters (Robert Blake, Herbert Shepard, and Jane Mouton, *Managing Intergroup Conflict in Industry* [Houston, 1964], 182). It has been further noted that both Democratic and Republican members of the House tend to see the other party as the one that is more disciplined and united (Charles Clapp, *The Congressman* [Washington, 1963], 17–19).

61. George Kennan, *Russia Leaves the War* (New York, 1967), 484.

62. *Ibid.,* 404, 408, 500.

63. Herbert Butterfield notes that these assumptions can contribute to the spiral of "Hobbesian fear. . . . You yourself may vividly feel the terrible fear that you have of the other party, but you cannot enter into the other man's counterfear or even understand why he should be particularly nervous. For you know that you yourself mean him no harm and that you want nothing from him save guarantees for your own safety; and it is never possible for you to realize or remember properly that since he cannot see the inside of your mind, he can never have the same assurance of your intentions that you have" (*History and Human Conflict* [London, 1951], 20).

64. *European Diplomatic History 1871–1932* (New York, 1933), 125. It takes great mental effort to realize that actions which seem only the natural consequence of defending your vital interests can look to others as though you are refusing them any chance of increasing their influence. In rebutting the famous Crowe "balance of power" memoran-

dum of 1907, which justified a policy of "containing" Germany on the grounds that she was a threat to British national security, Sanderson, a former permanent undersecretary in the Foreign Office, wrote, "It has sometimes seemed to me that to a foreigner reading our press the British Empire must appear in the light of some huge giant sprawling all over the globe, with gouty fingers and toes stretching in every direction, which cannot be approached without eliciting a scream" (quoted in Monger, 315). But few other Englishmen could be convinced that others might see them this way.

65. George Kennan makes clear that in 1918 this kind of difficulty was partly responsible for the inability of either the Allies or the new Bolshevik government to understand the motivations of the other side: "There is . . . nothing in nature more egocentrical than the embattled democracy. . . . It . . . tends to attach to its own cause an absolute value which distorts its own vision of everything else. . . . It will readily be seen that people who have got themselves into this frame of mind have little understanding for the issues of any contest other than the one in which they are involved. The idea of people wasting time and substance on any *other* issue seems to them preposterous" (*Russia and the West,* 11–12).

66. Kaplan, 89.

67. Johan Jorgen Holst, "Surprise, Signals, and Reaction: The Attack on Norway," *Cooperation and Conflict,* No. 1 (1966), 34. The Germans made a similar mistake in November 1942 when they interpreted the presence of an Allied convoy in the Mediterranean as confirming their belief that Malta would be resupplied. They thus were taken by surprise when landings took place in North Africa (William Langer, *Our Vichy Gamble* [New York, 1966], 365).

Cognitive Perspectives on Foreign Policy[*]

Philip E. Tetlock and Charles B. McGuire, Jr.

The last fifteen years have witnessed an impressive expansion of cognitive research on foreign policy—on both methodological and theoretical fronts. On the methodological front, investigators have shown skill in drawing insights from a variety of research techniques, including laboratory experiments (reviewed by Holsti and George, 1975; Jervis, 1976); historical case studies (George and Smoke, 1974; Janis, 1982; Lebow, 1981); content analyses of archival documents (Axelrod, 1976; Falkowski, 1979; Hermann, 1980a, 1980b; Tetlock, 1983c), interview and questionnaire studies (Bonham, Shapiro, and Trumble, 1979; Heradstveit, 1974, 1981);

[*]Philip E. Tetlock and Charles B. McGuire, Jr., "Cognitive Perspectives on Foreign Policy." Excerpted from S. Long, ed., *Political Behavior Annual* (Boulder, Colo.: Westview Press, 1985).

and computer simulations of belief systems (Abelson, 1968; Anderson and Thorson, 1982). There are, moreover, numerous examples of multimethod convergence in the research literature: investigators from different methodological traditions have often arrived at strikingly similar conclusions concerning the roles that cognitive variables play in the foreign policymaking process. The theoretical diversity is equally impressive and healthy. In developing hypotheses linking cognitive and foreign policy variables, investigators have drawn upon a variety of intellectual traditions, including work on attribution theory (Heradstveit, 1981; Jervis, 1976; Tetlock, 1983b); cognitive-consistency theory (Jervis, 1976); behavioral decision theory (Fischhoff, 1983; Jervis, 1982); the effects of stress on information processing (Holsti and George, 1975; Janis and Mann, 1977; Suedfeld and Tetlock, 1977), organizational principles underlying political belief systems (George, 1969; Holsti, 1977; Walker, 1983); and individual differences in cognitive styles (Bonham and Shapiro, 1977; Hermann, 1980a; Tetlock, 1981, 1983a, 1984). Each of these approaches has borne at least some empirical fruit.

We believe careful appraisal is now needed of what has been accomplished and of the directions in which theoretical and empirical work appears to be developing. We have divided our review chapter into four sections: "The Cognitive Research Program in Foreign Policy," "Representational Research," "Process Research," and "Conclusions."

I. THE COGNITIVE RESEARCH PROGRAM IN FOREIGN POLICY

Cognitive research on foreign policy can be viewed as an incipient research program. The hard core of the cognitive research program is difficult to specify with confidence. (What fundamental assumptions do the overwhelming majority of investigators who work at this level of analysis share?) We believe, however, that the hard core consists of two key assumptions which deserve to be spelled out in detail:

1. The international environment imposes heavy information-processing demands upon policymakers. It is very difficult to identify the best or utility-maximizing solutions to most foreign policy problems. Policymakers must deal with incomplete and unreliable information on the intentions and capabilities of other states. The range of response options is indeterminate. The problem consequences of each option are shrouded in uncertainty. Policymakers must choose among options that vary on many, seemingly incommensurable value dimensions (e.g., economic interests, international prestige, domestic political advantages, human rights, even lives). Finally, to compound the difficulty of the task, policymakers must sometimes work under intense stress and time pressure.
2. Policymakers (like all human beings) are limited-capacity information processors who resort to simplifying strategies to deal with the complexity, uncertainty, and painful trade-offs with which the world confronts them (cf. Abelson and Levi, in press; Einhorn and Hogarth, 1981; George, 1980; Jervis, 1976; Nisbett and Ross, 1980; Simon, 1957; Taylor and Fiske, 1984).

The foreign policy of a nation addresses itself, not to the external world per se, but to the simplified image of the external world constructed in the minds of those who make policy decisions (Axelrod, 1976; George, 1980; Holsti, 1976; Jervis, 1976). Policymakers may behave "rationally" (attempt to maximize expected utility) but only within the context of their simplified subjective representations of reality.

Implicit in these hard-core assumptions is the central research objective of the cognitive research program: to understand *the cognitive strategies that policymakers rely upon to construct and maintain their simplified images of the environment*. We find it useful to distinguish two basic types of cognitive strategies, both of which have received substantial attention: (a) reliance on cognitive or knowledge structures that provide frameworks for assimilating new information and choosing among policy options (belief systems, operational codes, cognitive maps, scripts); (b) reliance on low-effort judgmental and choice heuristics that permit policymakers to make up their minds quickly and with confidence in the correctness of their positions (e.g., "satis-ficing" decision rules, the availability, representativeness, and anchoring heuristics).

These two (by no means mutually exclusive) coping strategies correspond closely to the distinction cognitive psychologists have drawn between declarative knowledge (first category) and procedural knowledge (second category) of mental functioning (cf. Anderson, 1978, 1980). Research on declarative knowledge in the foreign policy domain—which we call representational research—is concerned with clarifying *what* policymakers think. What assumptions do they make about themselves, other states, the relationships among states, the goals or values underlying foreign policy, and the types of policies most instrumental to attaining those goals or values? Can typologies or taxonomies of foreign policy belief systems be developed? To what extent and in what ways do policymakers' initial beliefs or assumptions guide—even dominate—the interpretation of new evidence and the making of new decisions? The best-known examples of representational research are studies of the operational codes and cognitive maps of political elites (Axelrod, 1976; George, 1969, 1980; Heradstveit, 1981; Holsti, 1977). Research on procedural knowledge—which we call process research—is concerned with identifying abstract (content-free) laws of cognitive functioning that focus on *how* policymakers think about issues (the intellectual roots of process research can be directly traced to experimental cognitive and social psychology). The best-known examples of process research are studies of perception and misperception in international relations: the rules or heuristics that policymakers use in seeking causal explanations for the behavior of other states, in drawing lessons from history or in choosing among courses of action (cf. George, 1980; Jervis, 1976, 1982; Tetlock, 1983b).

Reasonable challenges can be raised to the hard-core premises of the program. One can question, for instance, the causal importance of policymakers' cognitions about the environment. Correlations between cognitions and actions are not sufficient to establish causality. The beliefs, perceptions, and values that people express may merely be justifications for policies they have already adopted as a result of other processes (e.g., psychodynamic needs and conflicts, bureaucratic role demands, domestic political pressures, international exigencies).

II. REPRESENTATIONAL RESEARCH

Psychologists and political scientists have invented an intimidatingly long list of terms to describe the cognitive structures that perceivers rely upon in encoding new information. These terms include "scripts" (Abelson, 1981; Schank and Abelson, 1977); "operational codes" (George, 1969; Holsti, 1977); "cognitive maps" (Axelrod, 1976); "stereotypes" (Allport, 1954; Hamilton, 1979); "frames" (Minsky, 1975); "nuclear scenes" (Tompkins, 1979); "prototypes" (Cantor and Mischel, 1979); as well as the more traditional and inclusive term "schemas" (Nisbett and Ross, 1980). We do not propose a detailed classification of all possible cognitive structures in this chapter (for preliminary efforts in this area see Nisbett and Ross, 1980; Schank and Abelson, 1977; Taylor and Fiske, 1984). Our goals are more modest. We shall focus only on cognitive research specifically concerned with foreign policy. Within that domain, we further restrict our attention to two issues likely to be central to future theoretical developments in the field:

1. What theoretical and methodological tools are at our disposal to describe the cognitive structures that influence foreign policy?
2. To what extent is information processing in the foreign policy domain theory-driven (dominated by existing cognitive structures) as opposed to data-driven (responsive to external reality)?

Describing Foreign Policy Belief Systems

In principle, people can subscribe to an infinite variety of images of their own states, of other states, and of the relationships among states. We use the term "idiographic representational research" to describe case studies which present detailed descriptions of the foreign policy belief systems of individual decision makers. We use the term "nomothetic representational" research to describe studies in which the primary goal is the development and testing of general theoretical statements that apply to large populations of individuals. The focus thus shifts from the uniqueness of particular policymakers to underlying similarities or themes that permit cross-individual and cross-situational comparisons. We discuss three lines of nomothetic representational research: the work on operational codes, cognitive mapping, and personality correlates of foreign policy belief systems.

Operational Code Research

Operational codes impose badly needed cognitive order and stability on an ambiguous and complex international environment (George, 1969). They do so in multiple ways: by providing norms, standards, and guidelines that influence (but do not unilaterally determine) decision makers' choices of strategy and tactics in dealings with other nations. George proposed that the essence of an operational code can be captured in its answers to a number of "philosophical" questions concerning the "nature of the political universe" and a number of "instrumental" questions concerning the types of policies most likely to achieve important objectives (see also Holsti, 1977).

Operational codes are organized hierarchically such that central or core beliefs exert more influence on peripheral beliefs than vice versa. One strong "belief candidate" for a central organizing role in operational codes is whether the decision maker believes the political universe to be essentially one of conflict or one of harmony (Holsti, 1977). People who view the world in Hobbesian, zero-sum terms (a war of all against all) are likely to differ on a variety of belief dimensions from those who see the world as potentially harmonious. These two groups will tend to appraise the motives and goals of opponents differently and disagree on the best strategies for pursuing policy goals. Another strong candidate for a central organizing role in operational codes is the decision-maker's belief concerning the root causes of international conflict. People who attribute conflict to different root causes (e.g., human nature, attributes of nations, the international system) will tend to have different views on the likelihood of, and necessary conditions for, long-term peace.

Tetlock (1983b) notes that both sides seem to possess an unlimited capacity to view international events in ways that support their initial positions ("aggressive" Soviet acts can always be construed as defensive responses to external threats; "conciliatory" Soviet acts can always be construed as deceptive maneuvers designed to weaken Western resolve). This is consistent with the "principle of least resistance" in the attitude change literature (McGuire, in press). Those beliefs most likely to "give in" to contradictory evidence are beliefs that have the fewest connections to other beliefs in the cognitive system.

Cognitive Mapping

Cognitive mapping is a methodological technique for capturing the causal structure of policymakers' cognitive representations of policy domains (Axelrod, 1976). Cognitive maps consist of two key elements: concept variables, which are represented as points, and causal beliefs linking the concepts, represented as arrows between points. A concept variable is defined simply: something that can take on different values (e.g., defense spending, American national security, balance of trade). Causal beliefs exist whenever decision makers believe that change in one concept variable leads to change in another variable.

Axelrod and other investigators have constructed a number of cognitive maps based on detailed content analyses of archival documents (e.g., Hitler-Chamberlain negotiations at Munich, the British Far Eastern Committee deliberations on Persia) and interviews with policymakers (e.g., State Department officials, energy experts). These studies demonstrate, at minimum, that: (1) cognitive mapping can be done with acceptable levels of intercoder reliability; (2) policymaking deliberations are saturated with causal arguments and that maps of these deliberations tend to be large and elaborate (in the sense that many different concept variables are causally connected with each other). (See Axelrod, 1976; Bonham and Shapiro, 1976; Bonham, Shapiro, and Trumble, 1979; Levi and Tetlock, 1980; Ross, 1976.)

Systematic analysis of cognitive maps has, however, provided more than descriptive information; it has also deepened our understanding of the cognitive bases of foreign policy. For instance, although cognitive maps are large and causally elaborate, they also tend to be simple, in that maps do not usually include trade-off relationships. Preferred policies usually have only positive consequences; rejected policies, only negative ones (cf. Jervis, 1976). This obviously makes decision making much easier; competing, difficult-to-quantify values do not have to be weighed against each other. Maps also rarely include reciprocal causal relationships (feedback loops) among variables: causality flows in only one direction. Axelrod summarizes the cognitive portrait of the decision-maker that emerges from his work in this way:

> one who has more beliefs than he can handle, who employs a simplified image of the policy environment that is structurally easy to operate with, and who then acts rationally within the context of his simplified image. (1976)

Our confidence in this summary portrait is reinforced by the very similar conclusions that have emerged from laboratory research on judgment and decision making (Abelson and Levi, in press; Einhorn and Hogarth, 1981; Kahneman, Slovic, and Tversky, 1981).

Individual Difference Research on Belief Systems

Even the most prominent advocate of the realist school of international politics— Henry Kissinger—concedes that foreign policymakers "work in darkness"; they make choices not only without knowledge of the future but usually even without adequate knowledge of what is happening in the present (Kissinger, 1979). This "structural uncertainty" (Steinbruner, 1974) of foreign policy problems has led many analysts to propose an analogy between international politics and projective tests used in personality assessment: the international scene, in much the same way as a good projective test, evokes different psychologically important response themes from national leaders. Foreign policy belief systems do not emerge in a psychological vacuum; they emerge as plausible self-expressive responses to the situations in which policymakers find themselves (Etheredge, 1978). From this standpoint, it is essential to study the personality background or context out of which belief systems evolve.

Evidence on relations between personality and foreign policy preferences comes from the full range of methodological sources, including laboratory experiments, surveys, content analyses of archival documents, expert ratings of policymakers, and case studies (Christiansen, 1959; Eckhardt and Lentz, 1967; Etheredge, 1978; Lasswell, 1930; McClosky, 1967; Terhune, 1970; Tetlock, 1981; Tetlock, Crosby, and Crosby, 1981). The similarity in results across methodologies is, moreover, impressive.

These lines of research remind us that foreign policy belief systems do not exist in isolation from broader dimensions of individual differences in interpersonal style, cognitive style, and basic motivational variables. To paraphrase Lasswell (1930), foreign policy beliefs may sometimes serve as rationalizations for psychological needs and tendencies that have been displaced onto the international scene. A critical challenge for future theory will be to resolve the tension between purely cognitive analyses of foreign policy (which grant "functional autonomy" to belief systems) and motivational analyses of foreign policy (which view belief systems as subservient to other psychological variables and systems).

A Comment on Theory-Driven versus Data-Driven Processing

We turn from the nature of foreign policy belief systems to the impact of belief systems on the policymaking process. A casual reader of the literature might easily walk away with the impression that foreign policy is overwhelmingly "theory-driven" (i.e., that the preconceptions policymakers bring to decision-making situations are much more important determinants of the actions taken than is the objective evidence). Both experimental and case study evidence appear to support this conclusion. The laboratory evidence comes from multiple sources, including research on primary effects in impression formation, the resistance of political attitudes and stereotypes to change (Hamilton, 1979; Lord, Ross, and Lepper, 1979); rigidity or set effects in problem solving (Luchins, 1942); and the persistence of causal attributions even after the discrediting of the information on which the attributions were initially based (Nisbett and Ross, 1980). The evidence from actual foreign policy settings comes most importantly from the pioneering work of Jervis (1976). He notes that the historical record contains many references to government leaders who have treated belief-supportive information uncritically while simultaneously searching for all possible flaws in belief-challenging information.

We need to be careful, however, in discussing the theory-driven nature of foreign policy. Reliance on prior beliefs and expectations is not irrational per se (one would expect it from a "good Bayesian"); it becomes irrational only when perseverance and denial dominate openness and flexibility. Cognitive models of foreign policy—like cognitive models generally—must acknowledge the coexistence of theory-driven and data-driven processing. Each is necessary; neither will suffice alone (see Bennett, 1981).

III. PROCESS RESEARCH

The previous section examined representational research on the beliefs and assumptions decision makers bring to policy problems and on the impact of those beliefs and assumptions on foreign policy. In this section, we focus on the rules or procedures that people may use in making policy decisions: the rules vary widely in form, in complexity, and in the "mental effort" required for their execution (Newell and Simon, 1972; Payne, 1982).

In practice, however, the laboratory and field evidence of the last ten years indicates that people do not rely equally on effort-demanding and top-of-the-head procedural rules. People appear to be "cognitive misers"—effort savers who show a marked preference for simple, low-effort heuristics that permit them to make up their minds quickly, easily, and with confidence in the correctness of the stands they have taken (see Abelson and Levi, in press; Einhorn and Hogarth, 1981; Fischhoff, 1981; Nisbett and Ross, 1980; Taylor and Fiske, 1984).

This "cognitive miser" theme helps to unify research on cognitive processes in foreign policy. We examine here five lines of research: work on the fundamental attribution error, extracting lessons from history, avoidance of value trade-offs, the policy-freezing effects of commitment, and crisis decision making. In each case, the cognitive miser image of the decision maker serves as leitmotif: policymakers often seem unwilling or unable to perform the demanding information-processing tasks required by normative models of judgment and choice.

The "Fundamental Attribution Error"

The fundamental attribution error has been described as a pervasive bias in social perception (Jones, 1979; Nisbett and Ross, 1980; Ross, 1977). Numerous experiments indicate that, in explaining the actions of others, people systematically underestimate the importance of external or situational causes of behavior and overestimate the importance of internal or dispositional causes (Kelley and Michela, 1980; Jones, 1979; Nisbett and Ross, 1980). The most influential explanation for the fundamental attribution error focuses on people's tendency to rely on low-effort judgmental heuristics (as opposed to more demanding procedural rules) in interpreting events. Jones (1979), for instance, argues that in many settings the most cognitively available (first-to-come-to-mind) explanation for behavior is some intrinsic property or disposition of the person who performed the behavior.

Do the laboratory studies describe judgmental processes that also operate in foreign policy settings? Our answer is a tentative yes. Two important qualifications should, however, be noted. First, the natural unit of causal analysis for foreign policymakers is often the nation-state, not the individual human actor used in laboratory experiments. With this caveat, though, much seems to fall into place. Jervis (1976) argues that policymakers tend to see the behavior of other states as more centralized, planned, and coordinated than it is. He notes, for instance, a number of historical situations in which national leaders have ascribed far too much significance to movements of military forces that were routine, accidental, or responses to immediate situational variables (e.g., the North Vietnamese interpretation of reduced American air attacks on Hanoi and Haiphong in 1966 as support for a peace initiative, not a reaction to inclement weather). Jervis also notes historical situations in which policymakers have seriously overestimated the internal coherence of the foreign policies of states. National policies are not always the result of long-term planning; sometimes they are reactions to immediate opportunities or setbacks or the products of miscalculation, miscommunication, bureaucratic infighting, or domestic political pressures. Observers often attribute Machiavellian intentions to policies that are the cumulative result of many unrelated causes (e.g., the Allies exaggerated the coordination among German, Italian, and Japanese moves in the late 1930s and early 1940s; the Soviets saw the failure of the Western powers to invade France in 1943 as part of a well-calculated effort to make the Soviet Union bear the brunt of the war against Nazi Germany).

A second qualification is also, however, necessary to our discussion of the fundamental attribution error. As with belief perseverance, we should refrain from strong normative judgments. We rarely know the true causes of the behavior of other states. In a world in which policymakers are motivated to make or misrepresent their intentions (Heuer, 1981), the truth tends to emerge slowly and rarely completely.

Extracting Lessons from History

Analogical reasoning can be defined as "the transfer of knowledge from one situation to another by a process of mapping—finding a set of one-to-one correspondences (often incomplete) between aspects of one body of information and other" (Gick and Holyoak, 1983, p. 2). Many psychologists regard analogical reasoning as fundamental to human intelligence and problem solving (e.g., Newell and Simon, 1972; Sternberg, 1982). People try to categorize and structure unfamiliar problems in terms of familiar ones.

Students of foreign policy have also paid attention to analogical reasoning—in particular, to how policymakers use historical precedents to justify current policies (George, 1980; Jervis, 1976; May, 1973). Case studies of foreign policy decisions are filled with references to policymakers who were determined to profit from what they think were the lessons of the past (e.g., Stanley Baldwin, Adolf Hitler, Harry Truman, Charles de Gaulle, John F. Kennedy, Lyndon Johnson). For instance, when the Korean War broke out unexpectedly in 1950, Harry Truman perceived parallels with totalitarian aggression in the 1930s and quickly concluded that the North Korean invasion had to be repelled (Paige, 1968). Similarly, Lyndon Johnson's fear of "another Castro" shaped his perceptions of the unrest in the Dominican Republic in 1965 and his judgment of the need for American intervention (Lowenthal, 1972).

There is nothing wrong with trying to learn from the past. Unfortunately, policymakers often draw simplistic, superficial, and biased lessons from history. Various lines of evidence are revealing in this connection:

1. One's political perspective heavily colors the conclusions one draws from history. In a survey of American opinion leaders, Holsti and Rosenau (1979) examined the lessons that supporters and opponents of American involvement drew from the Vietnam War. Prominent lessons for hawks were that the Soviet Union is expansionist and that the United States should avoid graduated escalation and honor alliance commitments. Prominent lessons for doves were that the United States should avoid guerrilla wars (e.g., Angola), that the press is more truthful on foreign policy than the administration, and the civilian leaders should be wary of military advice. Interestingly, *no one lesson* appeared on both the hawk and dove lists (cf. Zimmerman and Axelrod, 1981).

2. If contending states learn anything from one crisis experience to the next, it may be simply to become more belligerent in their dealings with adversaries. Lessons of history are often assimilated into Realpolitik belief systems that emphasize the importance of resolve and toughness when "vital interests" are at stake (Leng, 1983).

3. Policymakers rarely consider a broad range of historical analogies before deciding which one best fits the problem confronting them. They rely on

the most salient or cognitively available precedent (usually a precedent that policymakers have experienced at firsthand or that occurred early in their adult lives).

4. Policymakers often draw sweeping generalizations from preferred histori-cal analogies and are insensitive to differences between these analogies and current situations (history, after all, never repeats itself exactly). One rarely hears policymakers, privately or publicly, conceding the partial relevance of several analogies to a problem and then attempting to draw contingent rather than universal generalizations. For example, instead of "If a military buildup (or appeasement), then a nuclear holocaust," one could ask, "Under what conditions will one or the other policy increase or decrease the likelihood of war?"

Avoidance of Value Trade-Offs

In many decision-making situations, there are no clear right or wrong answers. Each policy option has both positive and negative features (e.g., lower inflation is accompanied by higher unemployment; greater military strength is accompanied by greater budget deficits). Available experimental and historical evidence indi-cates that decision makers find trade-offs unpleasant and tend to avoid them (Abel-son and Levi, in press; Einhorn and Hogarth, 1981; Gallhofer and Saris, 1979; George, 1980; Jervis, 1976; Slovic, 1975; Steinbruner, 1974). Trade-offs are un-pleasant for cognitive reasons (it is very difficult to "net out" the positive and neg-ative features of alternatives—What common units can be used to compare the value of human lives and one's national credibility as an ally?) and for motivational reasons (it is very difficult to justify to oneself and to others that one has sacrificed one basic value in favor of another). To avoid trade-offs, decision makers rely on a variety of "noncompensatory choice heuristics" (Montgomery and Svenson, 1976). For instance, according to Tversky's (1972) elimination-by-aspects rule, people compare response alternatives on one value dimension at a time, with the values being selected with a probability proportional to their perceived importance. All alternatives not having satisfactory loadings on the first (most important) value are eliminated. A second value is then selected with a probability proportional to its importance, and the process continues until only one option remains.

Experimental data have repeatedly demonstrated the importance of noncom-pensatory choice heuristics in decision making (Bettman, 1979; Montgomery and Svenson, 1976; Payne, 1976; Tversky, 1972; Wallsten, 1980). In the words of Ham-mond and Mumpower (1979): "We are not accustomed to presenting the rationale for the choice between values. . . . When our values conflict, we retreat to a singu-lar emphasis on our favorite value."

Research in foreign policy settings supports this generalization. As already noted, cognitive maps of policymaking deliberations make few references to value trade-offs (i.e., policy options typically are not seen as having contradictory effects on "utility"). Similarly, Jervis (1976) has used the term "belief system overkill" to describe the tendency of policymakers in historical situations to avoid trade-offs by generating a plethora of logically independent reasons in support of the stands they have taken. Jervis (1976, p. 137) describes the phenomenon in this way: "decision-makers do not simultaneously estimate how a policy will affect many values. Instead, they look at only one or two most salient values. As they come to favor a policy that seems best on these restricted dimensions, they alter their earlier beliefs and establish new ones so that as many reasons as possible support their choice." (See also George, 1980).

The Freezing Effects of Commitment

Once people have committed themselves to a course of action, they find it very difficult to retreat from that commitment. These "attitude-freezing" effects of commitment have been studied extensively in experimental social psychology and organizational behavior (e.g., Deutsch and Gerard, 1955; Helmreich and Collins, 1968; Janis and Mann, 1977; Kiesler, 1971; Staw, 1980). Public announcement of an attitudinal position increases later resistance to persuasive attacks on the attitude and motivates people to generate cognitions supportive of the attitude. The more irreversible the commitment, the stronger the effects tend to be (Janis and Mann, 1977; Staw, 1980). The most influential explanation for these findings is in terms of cognitive dissonance theory (Festinger, 1964). People seek to justify their commitments (and their self-images as rational, moral beings) by protraying actions they have freely chosen as reasonable and fair.

In addition to the laboratory evidence, many foreign policy examples exist of the "freezing" effects of commitment on the attitudes of national leaders. Jervis (1976) has offered the most comprehensive analysis of such effects. He identifies many plausible examples, including: the unwillingness of the pre-World War II Japanese government to compromise the gains achieved as a result of its large military losses in China, President Wilson's abandonment of his serious reservations about entering World War I after making the crucial decision, and the reluctance of American officials committed to the Diem regime in South Vietnam to acknowledge the regime's shortcomings. To some extent, such postcommitment bolstering of decisions is adaptive (little would be accomplished if we abandoned commitments in the face of the first setback). Postcommitment bolstering becomes "irrational" only when the desire of decision makers to justify their commitments (and to recoup "sunk costs"—Staw, 1980) blinds them to alternative policies with higher expected payoffs. Assessing exactly when postcommitment bolstering becomes irrational is, of course, a tricky judgment call.

Crisis Decision Making

Policymakers fall prey to the previously discussed biases and errors even under favorable information-processing conditions. Policymakers do not, however, always work under favorable conditions. They must sometimes function in highly stressful crisis environments in which they need to analyze large amounts of ambiguous and inconsistent evidence under severe time pressure, always with the knowledge that miscalculations may have serious consequences for their own careers and vital national interests (Brecher, 1979; C. Hermann, 1969; Holsti, Brody and North, 1969; Holsti and George, 1975; Lebow, 1981).

Converging evidence—from laboratory experiments and simulations, historical case studies, and content analyses of decision makers' statements—supports this "disruptive-stress" hypothesis. The experimental literature on the effects of stress is enormous (for reviews, see Janis and Mann, 1977; Staw, Sandelands, and Dutton, 1981). There is basic agreement, though, that high levels of stress reduce the complexity and quality of information processing. The impairment includes a lessened likelihood of accurately identifying and discriminating among unfamiliar stimuli (Postman and Bruner, 1948); rigid reliance on old, now inappropriate problem-solving strategies (Cowen, 1952); reduced search for new information (Schroder, Driver, and Streufert 1967); and heightened intolerance for inconsistent evidence (Streufert and Streufert, 1978).

Case studies and content analyses of historical records point to similar conclusions. As crises intensify, particularly crises that culminate in war, images of environment and policy options appear to simplify and rigidify. Policymakers are more likely to ignore alternative interpretations of events, to attend to a restricted range of options, and to view possible outcomes of the conflict in terms of absolute victory or defeat (C. Hermann, 1972; Holsti, 1972; Holsti and George, 1975; Lebow, 1981; Raphael, 1982; Suedfeld and Tetlock, 1977; Tetlock, 1979, 1983b, 1983c).

Simplification effects are not, however, an automatic reaction to international crises (see Tanter, 1978, for a detailed review). We need a theory—similar to the Janis and Mann (1977) conflict model of decision making—that allows for the possibility that threats to important values do not always disrupt, and sometimes even facilitate, complex information processing. The effects of crises may depend on many factors: individual difference variables (self-image as effective coper, track record of performance in previous crises) and situational variables (the reversibility and severity of existing threats).

IV. CONCLUDING REMARKS

How successful has the cognitive research program been? Many positive signs exist. There is no shortage of theoretical speculation and hypotheses on how cognitive variables influence foreign policy. Considerable research has been done. There are impressive indications of multimethod convergence in the work to date. A cumulative body of knowledge appears to be developing. Perhaps most important, the research program continues to be "heuristically provocative" in the sense of suggesting new avenues of empirical and theoretical exploration.

But all is not well within the cognitive research program. Current theory is seriously fragmented. Consensus is lacking on the extent to which and the ways in which cognitive variables influence foreign policy. Contradictory examples can be identified for most, if not all, of the theoretical generalizations offered earlier on the role that cognitive variables play in foreign policy. Consider the following claims:

- Policymakers are too slow in revising their initial impressions of an event.
- Policymakers overestimate the importance of long-term planning and underestimate the importance of chance and immediate situational pressures as causes of the behavior of other states.
- Policymakers avoid difficult value trade-offs.
- Policymakers draw simple and biased lessons from history.
- Policymakers rigidly defend and bolster past commitments.
- Policymakers analyze information in especially simplistic and superficial ways under high-stress crisis conditions.

Although the preponderance of the evidence is consistent with the above generalizations, the exceptions cannot be glibly dismissed. One can point to laboratory and historical situations in which the generalizations do not hold up well (e.g., Abelson and Levi, in press; Janis, 1982; Jervis, 1976; Maoz, 1981; McAllister, Mitchell, and Beach, 1979; Payne, 1982; Tetlock, 1983b).

The cognitive research program must ultimately come to grips with these anomalies. We believe a viable cognitive theory will have to take the form of a "contingency theory" of political information processing—one that acknowledges the capacity of people to adopt different modes of information processing in response to changing circumstances. From a contingency theory perspective, the search for immutable laws of cognitive functioning is misguided (Jenkins, 1981; McAllister et al., 1979; Payne, 1982; Tetlock, 1984). The appropriate question is not "What kind of machine is the human information processor?" but rather "What kinds of machines do people become when confronted with particular types of tasks in particular types of environments?" No single cognitive portrait of the policymaker is possible. Under some conditions, people rely on complex information-processing rules that approximate those prescribed by normative models of judgment and choice. Under other conditions, policymakers rely on simple top-of-the-head rules that minimize mental effort and strain. The major objective of the positive heuristic of the research program should not be to arrive at a global characterization of the information processor; rather, it should be to identify the personality and situational boundary conditions for the applicability of different characterizations of the information processor.

REFERENCES

Abelson, R. P. (1968). "Psychological Implication." In R. P. Abelson et al., eds., *Theories of Cognitive Consistency: A Sourcebook*. Chicago: Rand-McNally.

—— (1973). "The Structure of Decision." In R. C. Schank, and K. M. Colby, eds., *Computer Models of Thought and Language*. San Francisco: Freeman.

—— (1981). "Psychological Status of the Script Concept." *American Psychologist* 36: 715–29.

Abelson, R. P., and Levi, A. (3d ed., in press). "Decision-Making and Decision Theory." In G. Lindzey and E. Aronson, eds., *Handbook of Social Psychology*. Reading, MA: Addison-Wesley.

Allison, G. (1972). *Essence of Decision*. Boston: Little, Brown.

Aliport, G. W. (1943). "The Ego in Contemporary Psychology," *Psychological Review* 50: 451–78.

—— (1954). *The Nature of Prejudice*. Garden City, NY: Doubleday/Anchor.

Anderson, J. (1976). *Language, Memory and Thought*. Hillsdale, NJ: Erlbaum.

—— (1978). "Arguments Concerning Representations for Mental Imagery." *Psychological Review* 85:249–77.

—— (1980). *Cognitive Psychology and Its Implications*. San Francisco: Freeman.

Anderson, P. A., and Thorson, S. J. (1982). "Systems Simulation: Artificial Intelligence Based Simulations of Foreign Policy Decision Making." *Behavioral Science* 27:176–93.

Axelrod, R. (1976). *Structure of Decision*. Princeton: Princeton University Press.

Bennett, W. L. (1981). "Perception and Cognition: An Information Processing Framework for Politics." In S. Long, ed., *Handbook of Political Behavior*. NY: Plenum.

Bellman, J. R. (1979). *An Information Processing Theory of Consumer Choice*. Reading, MA: Addison-Wesley.

Bonham, G. M., and Shapiro, M. J. (1976). "Explanation of the Unexpected: The Syrian Intervention in Jordan in 1970." In R. P. Axelrod, ed., *Structure of Decision*. Princeton: Princeton University Press.

—— (1977). "Foreign Policy Decision Making in Finland and Austria: The Application of a Cognitive Process Model." In G. M. Bonham and M. J. Shapiro, eds., *Thought and Action in Foreign Policy*. Basel: Birkhauser Verlag.

Bonham, G. M.; Shapiro, M.; and Trumble, T. (1979). "The October War: Changes in Cognitive Orientation Toward the Middle East Conflict." *International Studies Quarterly* 23:3–44.

Brecher, M. (1979). "State Behavior in a Crisis: A Model." *Journal of Conflict Resolution* 23:446–80.

Cantor, N., and Mischel, W. (1979). "Prototypes in Person Perception." In L. Berkowitz, ed., *Advances in Experimental Social Psychology*. Vol. 2, NY: Academic Press.

Cantril, H. (1967). *The Human Dimension: Experiences in Policy Research*. New Brunswick: Rutgers University Press.

Christiansen, B. (1959). *Attitudes Toward Foreign Affairs as a Function of Personality*. Oslo: Oslo University Press.

Converse, P. E. (1964). "The Nature of Belief Systems in Mass Publics." In D. Apter, ed., *Ideology and Discontent*. NY: The Free Press.

Cowen, E. L. (1952). "Stress Reduction and Problem Solving Rigidity." *Journal of Consulting Psychology* 16:425–28.

Deutsch, M., and Gerard, H. (1955). "A Study of Normative and Informational Social Influences upon Individual Judgment." *Journal of Abnormal and Social Psychology* 15: 629–36.

Dollard, J.; Doob, L.; Miller, N.; Mowrer, O. H.; and Sears, R. (1939). *Frustration and Aggression*. New Haven: Yale University Press.

Eckhardt, W., and Lentz, T. (1967). "Factors of War/Peace Attitudes." *Peace Research Reviews* 1:1–22.

Einhorn, H., and Hogarth, R. M. (1981). "Behavioral Decision Theory." *Annual Review of Psychology* 31:53–88.

Etheredge, L. S. (1978). *A World of Men: The Private Sources of American Foreign Policy.* Cambridge: MIT Press.

—— (1981). "Government Learning: An Overview." In S. Long, ed., *Handbook of Political Behavior.* NY: Plenum.

Falkowski, L. S., ed. (1979). *Psychological Models in International Politics.* Boulder, CO: Westview Press.

Feifer, G. (February 1981). "Russian Disorders: The Sick Man of Europe." *Harpers.* pp. 41–55.

Festinger, L. (1964). *Conflict, Decision and Dissonance.* Stanford: Stanford University Press.

Fischhoff, B. (1975). "Hindsight and Foresight: The Effects of Outcome Knowledge on Judgment Under Uncertainty." *Journal of Experimental Psychology: Human Perception and Performance* 1:288–99.

—— (1981). "For Those Condemned to Study the Past: Heuristics and Biases in Hindsight." In D. Kahneman, P. Slovic, and A. Tversky, eds., *Judgment Under Uncertainty.* Cambridge: Cambridge University Press.

—— (1983). "Strategic Policy Preferences: A Behavioral Decision Theory Perspective." *Journal of Social Issues* 39:133–60.

Gallhofer, I. N., and Saris, W. E. (1979). "Strategy Choices of Foreign Policy-Makers." *Journal of Conflict Resolution* 23:425–45.

George, A. L. (1969). "The 'Operational Code': A Neglected Approach to the Study of Political Leaders and Decision-Making." *International Studies Quarterly* 13:190–222.

—— (1980). *Presidential Decisionmaking in Foreign Policy: The Effective Use of Information and Advice.* Boulder, CO: Westview Press.

George, A. L., and Smoke, R. (1974). *Deterrence in American Foreign Policy: Theory and Practice.* NY: Columbia University Press.

Gick, M., and Holyoak, K. (1983). "Schema Induction and Analogical Transfer." *Cognitive Psychology* 15:1–38.

Hamilton, D. (1979). "A Cognitive-Attributional Analysis of Stereotyping." In L. Berkowitz, ed., *Advances in Experimental Social Psychology.* Vol. 12. NY: Academic Press.

Hammond, D., and Mumpower, J. (1979). "Risks and Safeguards in the Formation of Social Policy." *Knowledge: Creation, Diffusion, Utilization* 1:245–58.

Helmreich, R., and Collins, B. (1968). "Studies in Forced Compliance: Commitment and Magnitude of Inducement to Comply as Determinants of Opinion Change." *Journal of Personality and Social Psychology* 10:75–81.

Heradstveit, D. (1974). *Arab and Israeli Elite Perceptions.* Oslo: Universitatforlaget.

—— (1981). *The Arab-Israeli Conflict: Psychological Obstacles to Peace.* Oslo: Universitatforlaget.

Hermann, C. (1969). *Crises in Foreign Policy.* Indianapolis: Bobbs-Merrill.

—— (1972). *International Crises: Insights from Behavioral Research.* NY: The Free Press.

Hermann, M. G. (1980a). "Assessing the Personalities of Soviet Politburo Members." *Personality and Social Psychology Bulletin* 6:332–52.

—— (1980b). "Explaining Foreign Policy Behavior Using the Personal Characteristics of Political Leaders." *International Studies Quarterly* 24:7–46.

Heuer, R. (1981). "Strategic Deception and Counter-Deception." *International Studies Quarterly* 25:294–327.

Hitch, C., and McKean, R. (1965). *The Economics of Defense in the Nuclear Age.* NY: Atheneum.

Holsti, O. R. (1972). *Crisis Escalation War.* Montreal: McGill-Queen's University Press.

—— (1976). "Foreign Policy Formation Viewed Cognitively." In R. Axelrod, ed., *Structure of Decision.* Princeton: Princeton University Press.

—— (1977). "The 'Operational Code' as an Approach to the Analysis of Belief Systems." *Final Report to the National Science Foundation.* Grant No. SOC 75–15368. Duke University.

Holsti, O. R.; Brody, R. A.; and North, R. C. (1969). "The Management of International Crisis: Affect and Action in American-Soviet Relations:" In D. G. Pruitt and R. C. Snyder, eds., *Theory and Research on the Causes of War.* Englewood Cliffs, NJ: Prentice-Hall.

Holsti, O. R., and George, A. L. (1975). "Effects of Stress Upon Foreign Policymaking." In C. P. Cotter, ed., *Political Science Annual.* Indianapolis: Bobbs-Merrill.

Holsti, O. R., and Rosenau, J. (1979). "Vietnam, Consensus, and the Belief Systems of American Leaders." *World Politics* 32:1–56.

Janis, I. (2d ed., 1982), *Groupthink.* Boston: Houghton Mifflin.

Janis, I., and Mann, L. (1977). *Decision Making.* NY: The Free Press.

Jenkins, J. (1981). "Can We Have a Fruitful Cognitive Psychology?" In J. H. Flowers, ed., *Nebraska Symposium on Motivation.* Lincoln: University of Nebraska Press.

Jervis, R. (1976). *Perception and Misperception in International Politics.* Princeton: Princeton University Press.

—— (1982). "Perception and Misperception in International Politics: An Updating of the Analysis." Paper presented at the Annual Meeting of the International Society of Political Psychology, Washington, D. C., June 24–27, 1982.

Jones, E. E. (1979). "The Rocky Road from Acts to Dispositions." *American Psychologist* 34:107–17.

Kahn, H. (1961). *On Thermonuclear War.* Princeton: Princeton University Press.

Kahneman, D.; Slovic, P.; and Tversky, A., eds. (1981). *Judgment Under Uncertainty: Heuristics and Biases.* Cambridge: Cambridge University Press.

Kaiser, R. (1981). "U.S.-Soviet Relations: Goodbye to Detente." *Foreign Affairs.* Special issue, "America and the World, 1980" 59 (3):500–21.

Kelley, H. H., and Michela, J. (1980). "Attribution Theory and Research." *Annual Review of Psychology* 31:457–501.

Kiesler, C., ed. (1971). *The Psychology of Commitment.* NY: Academic Press.

Kissinger, H. A. (1979). *White House Years.* NY: Knopf.

Lakatos, I. (1970). "Falsification and the Methodology of Scientific Research Programs." In I. Lakatos and A. Musgrave, eds., *Criticism and the Growth of Knowledge.* Cambridge: Cambridge University Press.

Lasswell, H. (1930). *Psychopathology and Politics.* Chicago: University of Chicago Press.

Lebow, R. N. (1981). *Between Peace and War.* Baltimore: Johns Hopkins University Press.

Leng, R. J. (1983). "When Will They Ever Learn?: Coercive Bargaining in Recurrent Crises." *Journal of Conflict Resolution* 27:379–419.

Levi, A., and Tetlock, P. E. (1980). "A Cognitive Analysis of the Japanese Decision to Go to War." *Journal of Conflict Resolution* 24:195–212.

Lord, C.; Ross, L.; and Lepper, M. (1979). "Biased Assimilation and Attitude Polarization: The Effects of Prior Theory on Subsequently Considered Evidence." *Journal of Personality and Social Psychology* 37:2098–2108.

Lowenthal, A. F. (1972). *The Dominican Intervention*. Cambridge: Harvard University Press.

Luchins, A. S. (1942). "Mechanization in Problem-Solving: The Effects of Einstellung." *Psychological Monographs* 54:1–95.

Lyons, E. (1954). *Our Secret Allies*. NY: Duell, Sloan and Pearce.

Maoz, Z. (1981). "The Decision to Raid Entebbe." *Journal of Conflict Resolution* 25:677–707.

May, E. (1973). *Lessons of the Past*. NY: Oxford University Press.

McAllister, P. W.; Mitchell, T. R.; and Beach, L. R. (1979). "The Contingency Model for the Selection of Decision Strategies: An Empirical Test of the Effects of Significance, Accountability, and Reversibility." *Organizational Behavior and Human Performance* 24:228–44.

McClosky, H. (1967). "Personality and Attitude Correlates of Foreign Policy Orientation." In J. N. Rosenau, ed., *Domestic Sources of Foreign Policy*. NY: The Free Press.

McGuire, W. J. (3d ed., in press). "The Nature of Attitudes and Attitude Change." In G. Lindzey and E. Aronson, eds., *Handbook of Social Psychology*. Reading, MA: Addison-Wesley.

Minsky, M. (1975). "A Framework for Representing Knowledge." In P. H. Winston, ed., *Psychology of Computer Vision*. NY: McGraw-Hill.

Montgomery, H., and Svenson, O. (1976). "On Decision Rules and Information Processing Strategies for Choice Among Multiattribute Alternatives." *Scandinavian Journal of Psychology* 17:283–91.

Newell, A., and Simon, H. A. (1972). *Human Problem Solving*. Englewood Cliffs, NJ: Prentice-Hall.

Niebuhr, R. (1960). *Moral Man and Immoral Society*. NY: Scribner's.

Nisbett, R., and Ross, L. (1980). *Human Inference: Strategies and Shortcomings of Social Judgment*. Englewood Cliffs, NJ: Prentice-Hall.

Paige, G. D. (1968). *The Korean Decision*. NY: The Free Press.

Payne, J. W. (1976). "Task Complexity and Contingent Processing in Decision-Making: An Information Search and Protocol Analysis." *Organizational Behavior and Human Performance* 16:366–87.

—— (1982). "Contingent Decision Behavior." *Psychological Bulletin* 92:382–402.

Postman, L., and Bruner, J. S. (1948). "Perception Under Stress." *Psychological Review* 55:314–23.

Putnam, R. (1971). *The Beliefs of Politicians*. New Haven: Yale University Press.

Raphael, T. D. (1982). "Integrative Complexity Theory and Forecasting International Crises: Berlin 1946–1962." *Journal of Conflict Resolution* 26:423–50.

Ross, L. (1977). "The Intuitive Psychologist and His Shortcomings: Distortions in the Attribution Process." In L. Berkowitz, ed., *Advances in Experimental Social Psychology*. Vol. 10, NY: Academic Press.

Ross, S. (1976). "Complexity and the Presidency: Gouverneur Morris in the Constitutional Convention." In R. Axelrod, ed., *Structure of Decision.* Princeton: Princeton University Press.

Schank, R. C., and Abelson, R. P. (1977). *Scripts, Plans, Goals and Understanding: An Inquiry into Human Knowledge Structures.* Hillsdale, NJ: Erlbaum.

Schelling, T. (1963). *The Strategy of Conflict.* Cambridge: Harvard University Press.

Schroder, H. M.; Driver, M.; and Streufert, S. (1967). *Human Information Processing.* NY: Holt, Rinehart and Winston.

Simon, H. A. (1957). *Models of Man: Social and Rational.* NY: Wiley.

Slovic, P. (1975). "Choice Between Equally Valued Alternatives." *Journal of Experimental Psychology: Human Perception and Performance* 1:280–87.

Staw, B. M. (1980). "Rationality and Justification in Organizational Life." In B. M. Staw and L. Cummings, eds., *Research in Organizational Behavior.* Vol. 2. Greenwich, CT: JAI Press.

Staw, B. M.; Sandelands, L. E.; and Dutton, J. E. (1981). "Threat-Rigidity Effects in Organizational Behavior: A Multilevel Analysis." *Administrative Science Quarterly* 26:501–24.

Steinbruner, J. (1974). *The Cybernetic Theory of Decision.* Princeton: Princeton University Press.

Steinbruner, J., and Carter, B. (1975). "The Organizational Dimension of the Strategic Posture: The Case for Reform." *Daedalus* (Summer) Issued as Vol. 4, No. 3, of *The Proceedings of the American Academy of Arts and Sciences.*

Sternberg, R. J. (1982). *Handbook of Human Intelligence.* NY: Cambridge University Press.

Streufert, S., and Streufert, S. (1978). *Behavior in the Complex Environment.* Washington, D.C.: Winston and Sons.

Suedfeld, P., and Tetlock, P. E. (1977). "Integrative Complexity of Communications in International Crises." *Journal of Conflict Resolution* 21:168–78.

Tanter, R. (1978). "International Crisis Behavior: An Appraisal of the Literature." In M. Brecher, ed., *Studies of Crisis Behavior.* New Brunswick, NJ: Transaction.

Taylor, S., and Fiske, S. (1984). *Social Cognition.* Reading, MA: Addison-Wesley.

Terhune, K. (1970). "The Effects of Personality on Cooperation and Conflict." In R. G. Swingle, ed., *The Structure of Conflict.* NY: Academic Press.

Tetlock, P. E. (1979). "Identifying Victims of Groupthink from Public Statements of Decision Makers." *Journal of Personality and Social Psychology* 37:1314–24.

—— (1981). "Personality and Isolationism: Content Analysis of Senatorial Speeches." *Journal of Personality and Social Psychology* 41:737–43.

—— (1983a). "Accountability and Complexity of Thought." *Journal of Personality and Social Psychology* 45:74–83.

—— (1983b). "Policy-Makers' Images of International Conflict." *Journal of Social Issues* 39:67–86.

—— (1983c). "Psychological Research on Foreign Policy: A Methodological Overview." In L. Wheeler, ed., *Review of Personality and Social Psychology.* Vol. 4, Beverly Hills, CA: Sage.

—— (1984). "Accountability: The Neglected Social Context of Judgment and Choice." In B. Staw and L. Cummings, eds., *Research in Organizational Behavior.* Vol. 6, Greenwich, CT: JAI Press.

Tetlock, P. E.; Crosby, F.; and Crosby, T. (1981). "Political Psychobiography." *Micropolitics* 1:193–213.

Tompkins, S. S. (1979). "Script Theory: Differential Magnification of Affects." In H. E. Howe and R. A. Dienstbier, eds., *Nebraska Symposium on Motivation.* Vol. 26. Lincoln: University of Nebraska Press.

Tuchman, B. (1962). *The Guns of August.* NY: Macmillan.

Tversky, A. (1972). "Elimination by Aspects: A Theory of Choice." *Psychological Review* 79:281–99.

Walker, S. (1983). "The Motivational Foundations of Political Belief Systems: A Re-analysis of the Operational Code Construct." *International Studies Quarterly* 27:179–201.

Wallsten, T. (1980). "Processes and Models to Describe Choice and Inference." In T. Wallsten, ed., *Cognitive Processes in Choice and Behavior.* Hillsdale, NJ: Erlbaum.

White, R. K. (1965). "Soviet Perceptions of the U.S. and the U.S.S.R." In H. C. Kelman, ed., *International Behavior.* NY: Holt, Rinehart and Winston.

—— (1969). "Three Not-so-Obvious Contributions of Psychology to Peace." Lewin Memorial Address, *Journal of Social Issues* 25 (4):23–29.

—— (rev. ed., 1970). *Nobody Wanted War: Misperception in Vietnam and Other Wars.* NY: The Free Press.

—— (1977). "Misperception in the Arab-Israeli Conflict." *Journal of Social Issues* 33 (1):190–221.

Wohlstetter, A. (1959). "The Delicate Balance of Terror." *Foreign Affairs* 37:211–35.

Zimmerman, W., and Axelrod, R. P. (1981). "The Lessons of Vietnam and Soviet Foreign Policy." *World Politics* 34:1–24.

Seduction by Analogy in Vietnam: The Malaya and Korea Analogies

Yuen Foong Khong

At the beginning of Herzog's *Aguirre the Wrath of God,* a troop of Spanish conquistadors is seen debating about whether to continue the dangerous search for El Dorado. The leader of the expedition urged the troop to turn back but lost out to

Yuen Foong Khong, "Seduction by Analogy in Vietnam: The Malaya and Korea Analogies," in Kenneth Thompson, ed., *Institutions and Leadership: Prospects for the Future.* (Lanham: University Press of America, 1987).

his assistant Aguirre, who, through argument and intimidation, persuaded the en-
tourage to continue. Aguirre invoked the Mexico analogy twice—Cortez founded
Mexico against all odds and survived to reap the fortune—to bolster his argument.
What he and his entourage did not know was that El Dorado, that "Lost City of
Gold," was a fiction invented by the weak Peruvians to trick them. There was no El
Dorado. Only death and destruction awaited them.

Analogies have not played quite so decisive a role in convincing America's leaders to fight communism in Greece, Korea or Vietnam. But they did inform the thinking of successive Presidents, Secretaries, Undersecretaries and others who formulated America's post-war foreign policy. As Paul Kattenburg, former chairman of the
Interdepartmental Working Group on Vietnam in the early 1960's, puts it, "Reasoning by historical analogy became a virtual ritual in the United States under Secretaries of State Acheson (1949–52), Dulles (1953–58) and Rusk (1961–68). . . ." (1980,
p. 98). Dean Acheson, for example, helped convince Congressional leaders to support Truman's request for $400 million in aid to Greece and Turkey in 1947 by em-
phasizing the drastic consequences of abdicating this responsibility: like apples in a
barrel infected by one rotten one, he prophesized, the corruption of Greece would
infect Iran and everything east. Truman's decision to defend South Korea in 1950
was strongly influenced by the lessons of the past. He saw North Korea's actions as
analogous to those of Hitler's, Mussolini's and Japan's in the 1930s. These events
taught that failure to check aggression early on only brought about a world war later
(May, 1973, pp. 80–83). If the stakes were so high and the prevention of world war
so worthy a goal, it should not come as a surprise that Truman approved MacArthur's
march North to roll back totalitarianism (álá Germany and Japan) in the fall of 1950.
Four years later, Eisenhower invoked the same analogies to persuade Churchill to
join America to prevent the fall of Dien Bien Phu:

> If I may refer again to history; we failed to halt Hirohito, Mussolini and Hitler by not
> acting in unit and in time. That marked the beginning of many years of stark tragedy
> and desperate peril. May it not be that our nations have learned something from that
> lesson? . . . (cited in Pentagon Papers, 1971, v. 1, p. 99)

Churchill rejected the analogy; he feared that joint intervention by the United
States and Britain "might well bring the world to the verge of a major war" (cited in
Schlesinger, 1966, p.7). John F. Kennedy saw great similarities between Malaya and
Vietnam—the New Villages of Malaya became Strategic Hamlets in Vietnam, the
major difference being the New Villages worked whereas the Strategic Hamlets did
not. In meetings with his advisers, Lyndon Johnson repeatedly voiced worries about
Chinese intervention álá Korea if the United States pushed Hanoi too hard; United
States intelligence then guessed and we now know that it was improbable that the
Chinese would have intervened short of a United States invasion of North Vietnam
(Pentagon Papers, v. 4, p. 63; Karnow, 1983, pp. 329, 452–53). More recent and
even more dubious uses of analogies include seeing the Nicaraguan contras as the
"moral equal of our Founding Fathers," as well as the claim that failure to aid the
contras is tantamount to a Munich-like "self-defeating appeasement."

What makes historical analogies so attractive, despite their obvious limitations? I want to argue that historical analogies possess four properties which make

them especially endearing to policy makers. One, they explain a new situation to us in terms we are familiar with. This is the "what is" or descriptive property of the analogy. Two, they provide a normative assessment of the situation. This is the "what ought to be" aspect. Three, analogies also prescribe a strategy to get from "what is" to "what ought to be." This is the prescriptive component of the analogy. Four, analogies also suggest what is likely to occur in the future. In other words, they also have predictive abilities. Not all historical analogies exhibit all four characteristics; when they do, however, they become especially potent, and perhaps in the last analysis, mischievous.

I hope to make the above points by examining two of the most important analogies used by policy makers in thinking about Vietnam: Malaya and Korea. Malaya and Korea have also been chosen because they succeed one another as the most important analogies: Malaya being especially relevant from 1961–63, Korea for the crucial years of 1964–66. The structural properties of these two analogies only partially illuminate why they were so popular despite being so imprecise; I am aware that there are cognitive, psychological and historical reasons which also account for their attractiveness. Cognitive explanations, for example, will stress the information processing value of analogies—they allow the policy maker to simplify and assess the vast amount of information out there. Historical-psychological explanations, on the other hand, will stress the degree to which direct experience with the events of the 1930's or 50's conditions policy makers to see future events along those lines. I deal with the cognitive and historical explanations in my research-in-progress; the focus in this paper shall be on the structural properties of analogies.

MALAYA AND THE NEW INSURGENCIES

John F. Kennedy and his New Frontiersmen came into office convinced that China and the Soviet Union formed a monolithic bloc bent on expanding the area under their control. Only containment by the United States—especially in Greece, Turkey and most of all, Korea—have kept the communists at bay. Despite the failure to "integrate" South Korea into the communist bloc, China and the Soviet Union remained inherently expansionist. Their new strategy, however, relied neither on missiles nor conventional troops. "Non-nuclear wars, and sub-limited or guerrilla warfare," Kennedy believed, "have since 1945 constituted the most active and constant threat to Free World security" (Public Papers, 1961, p. 229). National Security Action Memorandum 132, signed by Kennedy in February 1962, reiterated this theme. Kennedy directed Fowler Hamilton, the Administrator of the Agency for International Development, to "give utmost attention and emphasis to programs designed to counter Communist indirect aggression, which I regard as a grave threat during the 1960s" (Pentagon Papers, 1971, v. 2, p. 666). The key word here is indirect, for it was this new communist strategy which called for an appropriate U.S. response.

Kennedy's address to the graduating class of the U.S. Military Academy in the spring of 1962 is worth quoting at length because it spelled out his beliefs more concretely:

> Korea has not been the only battle ground since the end of the Second World War. Men have fought and died in Malaya, in Greece, in the Philippines, in Algeria and Cuba, and Cyprus and almost continuously on the Indo-China Peninsula, No nuclear weapons have been fired. No massive nuclear retaliation has been considered appropriate. This is another type of war, new in its intensity, ancient in its origin—war by guerrillas, subversives, insurgents, assassins, war by ambush instead of by combat; by infiltration, instead of aggression, seeking victory by eroding and exhausting the enemy instead of engaging him. It requires in those situations where we must counter it . . . a whole new kind of strategy, a wholly different kind of force, and therefore a new and wholly different kind of military training (Public Papers, 1962, p. 453).

Quite apart from the problem of telling the new graduates that their training might have been obsolete, this speech exemplified the thinking of the New Frontiersmen. The historian Ernest May found it surprising that documents of the Vietnam debate in 1961 contained few references to the Korean analogy whereas documents of 1964 contained many (May, 1973, p. 96). The diagnosis implied in the above speech explains this "surprise": Malaya, Greece, the Philippines, not Korea, were the models for thinking about Vietnam in the early 1960s. The Korea analogy illustrated the aggressive tendencies of communist regimes well but it had one shortcoming. In 1950, North Korea attempted a conventional invasion of the South; the U.S. U.N. response was also conventional. In 1961–62, the situation in Vietnam was different. Ngo Dinh Diem's South Vietnam was not threatened by an outright invasion of regular North Vietnamese units but by communist guerrillas who were mostly Southerners. Malaya and the other "indirect aggression" analogies were more useful in explaining the new kind of war brewing in South Vietnam and in thinking about the appropriate response to such threats.

The parallels between Malaya and Vietnam are striking. A British colony until 1957, Malaya was occupied by the Japanese during the Second World War. The Malayan Communist Party, reorganized as the Malayan People's Anti-Japanese Army (MPAJA) was the only domestic group to cooperate with the British to mount an armed resistance against the Japanese. MPAJA members, mostly ethnic Chinese, mounted guerrilla operations against the Japanese army. Although they succeeded in making life difficult for the Japanese, they were unable to dislodge them.

The MPAJA, however, attracted a substantial number of recruits and with their anti-imperialists credentials enhanced towards the end of the war, they emerged as a viable contender for power after Japan's surrender. Unlike Ho Chi Minh's Communist Party which took over Hanoi in the aftermath of Japan's defeat, the communists in Malaya did not or were unable to take over. While they did enjoy some support from Chinese peasants and workers, they did not really command the support of most Malays, the majority group in Malaya. When the British returned to Malaya, they quickly and ruthlessly surpressed the communist and the urban organizations (e.g. trade unions) controlled by them. Fighting for their political survival and also reasoning that they did not fight against an imperialist power only to bring back another, the Malayan Communist Party launched a major insurrection in 1948. The insurrection began with the ambush-murder of three European rubber estate managers; assassinations of government officials, terrorizing of uncooperative peasants—the kind of violence which Kennedy alluded to above—were common. The conflict dragged on for twelve years but in the end the guerrillas lost (Short, 1975).

Robert K. G. Thompson is the man most often credited for defeating the guerrillas in Malaya. Initially, the British saw the insurrection as a military problem. They launched large-scale military operations and bombed suspected jungle bases. Two years later, they were worse off than when they began (Hilsman, p. 429). Thompson concluded that so long as the guerrillas had the support—voluntary or involuntary—of the peasants, it was impossible to defeat them. He came up with the idea of "New Villages," secure hamlets where the peasants were isolated from the guerrillas. Civic action teams would visit to provide simple government services and the police would train the peasants in the use of firearms and win their confidence so that the communist sympathizers could be identified. The switch from a "search and destroy" strategy to a "clear and hold" strategy contributed greatly to the successful containment of communism in Malaya.

The Malaya analogy is helpful in making sense of the war in South Vietnam. Those familiar with the case of Malaya can identify similar forces at work: a legitimate government, supported by the majority, is threatened by local communist insurgents bent on seizing power at the behest of China and the Soviet Union. Related to, but distinct from, this description is a normative assessment of the parties in conflict in Malaya-South Vietnam: the cause of the guerrillas is unjust, as are the means—infiltration, assassination, terror—they employ. As such, the guerrillas ought to be defeated in South Vietnam as they were defeated in Malaya.

But the Malaya analogy does more than designate the end of defeating the communist guerrillas as good. It also prescribes a morally acceptable means of countering indirect aggression. By morally acceptable I mean a proportional response. In moral discourse, it is not enough to have a moral end, the means chosen to realize that end must also not incur disproportionate costs relative to the benefits conferred by achieving the end. In other words, a just end can be tarnished by unjust—i.e. disproportionate—means.

The proportional response suggested by the Malaya analogy is the construction of New Villages to physically isolate the guerrilla's potential supporters from the guerrillas. As conceived and executed by Robert K. G. Thompson in Malaya, this response to guerrilla insurgency passes the proportionality test because it leaves the rest of the population in peace and the costs of relocation are imposed on likely supporters. Weighed against the end of preserving a government supported by the majority, the costs do not appear disproportionate. The Kennedy administration encouraged Diem to follow this strategy and provided much of the material (Strategic Hamlet Kits) and money necessary to construct the Strategic Hamlets. It is of course not possible to say that Kennedy and his advisers (especially Roger Hilsman) believed in the Strategic Hamlet program because it was morally sound but it is possible to say that the Malaya analogy did not prescribe a strategy which might have exacted disproportionate costs. The idea of proportional response, with or without its moral dimension, would have appealed to the Kennedy administration. It fitted right in with the strategy of "flexible response," the attempt by Kennedy and his advisers to tailor the amount of force the U.S. should apply to the requirements of any given situation.

The Malaya analogy went beyond prescribing a proportional response, it also suggested that such a response could work. Again, in moral discourse, effectiveness is a critical consideration. Pursuing the most noble goal does not make one's actions morally sound if they are unlikely to achieve the goals. The Malaya analogy predicts a high probability of success: if the problem in Vietnam is like the problem in Malaya and if the New Villages worked in Malaya, then they or their equivalent—the Strategic Hamlets—are likely to work in South Vietnam as well. Thus Roger Hilsman, Assistant Secretary for Far Eastern Affairs, believed that the best way to "pull the teeth of the Viet Cong terrorist campaign" was not by killing them but by protecting the peasants in Strategic Hamlets. "[T]his technique," according to Hilsman, "was used successfully in Malaya against the Communist movement there" (*Department of State Bulletin,* July 8, 1963, p. 44). By suggesting that the prescribed means is able to attain the desired end (defeating the communist guerrillas), the predictive component of the Malaya analogy reinforces the normative weight of Kennedy's policy towards South Vietnam.

KOREA AND THE CHANGING CHARACTER OF THE VIETNAM WAR

By 1965 Malaya was no longer the dominant analogy. Its place was taken by the Korea analogy. The descriptive, normative, prescriptive and predictive elements found in the Malaya analogy are also present in the Korea analogy.

The Korea analogy was invoked primarily to show that the war in Vietnam was a war of aggression by the North against the South. This is in contrast to the Malaya analogy, which, while implying external support, saw the war primarily in terms of Southern guerrillas fighting against the army of South Vietnam (ARVN). The Korean analogy emphasized the more prominent role, if not the direct participation, of North Vietnamese soldiers. Thus Secretary of State Dean Rusk equated the infiltration of North Vietnamese material and men into South Vietnam with the overt aggression of North Korea against South Korea (*DOSB,* June 28, 1965, p. 1032). Lyndon Johnson did the same in his public speeches as well as his private conversations. Years after the he made the fateful decisions of 1965, Johnson admonished Doris Kearns, his biographer, for seeing the Vietnam conflict as a civil war:

> How . . . can you . . . say that South Vietnam is not a separate country with a traditionally recognized boundary? . . . Oh sure, there were some Koreans in both North and South Korea who believed their country was one country, yet was there any doubt that North Korean aggression took place? (Kearns, 1976, p. 328)

For William Bundy, perhaps the most consistent proponent of the Korea analogy, Korea forced the relearning of the lessons of the 1930s—"aggression of any sort must be met early and head-on or it will be met later and in tougher circumstances" (*DOSB,* February 8, 1965, p. 168). Adlai Stevenson's United Nation address titled "Aggression from the North" best captures the Johnson administration's position. Stevenson, reversing Kennedy's slighting of the Korea analogy, questioned the relevance of the Malaya, Greece and Philippine analogies and went on to emphasize the parallel between Vietnam and Korea: "North Vietnam's commitment to seize control of the South is no less total than was the commitment of the regime in North Korea in 1950" (*DOSB*, March 22 1965, p. 404).

What is interesting about the descriptive component of the Korea analogy is that it does provide a better description of "what is" in 1964–66. By the fall of 1964, the U.S. was finding "more and more 'bona fide' North Vietnamese soldiers among the infiltrees" (Pentagon Papers, v. 3, p. 207). An estimated ten thousand North Vietnamese troops went South in 1964 (Pentagon Papers, v. 3, p. 207; Cf. Karnow, 1983, p. 334). As the perceived and actual nature of the war changed from guerrilla warfare to a mixture of guerrilla as well as conventional assaults, there was also a shift from reliance on the Malaya to the Korea analogy. Both the Malaya and Korea analogies explained the nature of the Vietnam conflict in terms we are familiar with; the Korea analogy, however, captured the changing nature of the conflict more successfully.

If one accepts the description of the North-South relationship—i.e., a case of the North trying to conquer the South—given by the Korea analogy, the actions of the North clearly become unjustifiable. Regardless of how it is put, the normative invocation is clear: aggression ought to be stopped, South Vietnam should not be allowed to fall, the United States ought to come to the help of the South.

The Korea analogy does more than merely invoke these normative ends, it also prescribes the means to realize them: through the introduction of U.S. troops. I am not claiming that when policy makers relied on the Korea analogy throughout 1965 in thinking about Vietnam, they were decisively influenced by the Korean strategy of using U.S. troops to halt aggression. However, if one believes that the problem in Vietnam is like the problem in Korea 1950, one is likely to consider quite seriously the ready-made answer supplied by the Korea analogy, namely, the introduction of U.S. troops. In this sense, the introduction of U.S. ground forces as the appropriate response is part and parcel of the Korea analogy.

Like the Malaya analogy, the Korea analogy also prescribed a proportional response. That is, if one accepts the description, provided by the Korea analogy, that the North was attacking the South. Introducing U.S. troops is proportional in the sense that it falls short of more drastic measures (e.g., invading North Vietnam or using nuclear weapons, see Pentagon Papers, v. 3, p. 623) and it is a step beyond merely advising and training the ARVN. If Kennedy's interest in not replying with overwhelming force had to do with the dictates of flexible response and the attempt to calibrate force to meet a given threat, Johnson's reluctance to consider a vastly disproportionate response had to do with the fear of bringing about a general war.

Evidence of Johnson's concern about proportionality can be found in a crucial meeting he had with his Joint Chiefs in July 1965, a few days before his decision to grant McNamara's request for 100 thousand combat troops. Johnson probed the JCS for North Vietnamese and Chinese reactions to the proposed U.S. action. The President was worried: "If we come in with hundreds of thousands of men and billions of dollars, won't this cause China and Russia to come in?" General Johnson, Army

Chief of Staff, replied that they would not, to which Johnson retorted: "MacArthur didn't think they would come in either" (cited in Berman, 1982, pp. 117–18). It is well known that Johnson was always careful about not going beyond like MacArthur did. Consequently the use of nuclear weapons, the invasion of North Vietnam, destruction of the latter's dyke system and bombing the North Vietnamese civilians were never even proposed (Gelb and Betts, 1979, pp. 264–65).

Beyond proportionality is the issue of likelihood of success. Here again, the Korea analogy, like the Malaya and virtually all analogies used in thinking about Vietnam, predicts a high probability of success. If the problem in Korea and Vietnam are essentially similar, it stands to reason that the strategy which proved ultimately successful in Korea, namely U.S. intervention, will also be successful in Vietnam. And probability of success, we have argued earlier, adds moral weight to the policy. By providing an optimistic prediction of the likely outcome of introducing U.S. troops, the Korea analogy makes this policy prescription all the more attractive.

MALAYA, KOREA AND VIETNAM: THE IGNORED DIFFERENCES

Having explored the features of the Malaya and Korea analogies which made them attractive to policy makers, it is necessary to point out that there were those who were suspicious of these analogies, in part and in whole. General L.L. Lemnitzer, Chairman of the Joint Chiefs of Staff in the first two years of Kennedy's administration, was highly skeptical of the Malaya analogy. In a memorandum to General Maxwell Taylor, Kennedy's handpicked personal adviser and soon-to-be successor to Lemnitzer, the latter complained that "The success of the counter-terrorist police organization in Malaya has had considerable impact" on the Kennedy administration's approach to Vietnam. Given the "considerable impact" of the Malaya analogy, General Lemnitzer felt obliged to point out its defects. He pointed to five "major differences between the situations in Malaya and South Vietnam." His analysis is prescient and important enough to be cited in full:

a. Malayan borders were far more controllable in that Thailand cooperated in refusing the Communists an operational safe haven.
b. The racial characteristics of the Chinese insurgents in Malaya made identification and segregation a relatively simple matter as compared to the situation in Vietnam where the Viet Cong cannot be distinguished from the loyal citizen.
c. The scarcity of food in Malaya versus the relative plenty in South Vietnam made the denial of food to the Communist guerrillas a far more important and readily usable weapon in Malaya.
d. Most importantly, in Malaya the British were in actual command, with all of the obvious advantages this entails, and used highly trained Commonwealth troops.
e. Finally, it took the British nearly 12 years to defeat an insurgency which was less strong than the one in South Vietnam. (Pentagon Papers, v. 2, p. 650).

Lemnitzer's critique of the Malaya analogy is interesting because it appreciated the on-the-ground differences between Malaya and South Vietnam. He took issue with the description, prescription and prediction provided by the Malaya analogy. The latter implied that sanctuaries for the guerrillas was not a major issue, Lemnitzer believed that such a description did not conform to the situation in South Vietnam, where the guerrillas could have "safe haven[s]" in Laos and Cambodia. Lemnitzer also found the prescription—emphasis on counter-terrorist police and hence political measures instead of emphasis on military measures—suggested the Malaya analogy wanting. He preferred the Philippine experience, where "the military framework used was highly successful" (Pentagon Papers, v. 2, p. 650). Finally, Lemnitzer was less sanguine about the prediction of eventual success than Kennedy's civilian advisers. The implication of Lemnitzer's analysis was that the Vietnamese communists would be hard to beat.

History proved Lemnitzer right. Even with American troops and command, the National Liberation Front could not be subdued. Uncontrollable borders, namely sanctuaries and infiltration routes in Laos and Cambodia, also partially explain the difficulty. So does the difficulty of distinguishing loyal from disloyal peasants in Vietnam. There was also the character of the government being helped, a crucial difference omitted in Lemnitzer's analysis. Malaya had a relatively stable and popular government both as a British colony and as a newly independent country; it was apparent even by 1961 that the South Vietnamese government was neither popular nor stable. Within the Diem regime, there was constant infighting and jockeying for power, so much so that the only principals Diem could trust were his brothers and their wives; without, Diem did not encourage the setting up of institutions which could have channeled the political participation of the religious sects, nationalist political parties and students.

The other interesting point about Lemnitzer's critique is that it was ignored. The Kennedy administration continued to believe in the relevance of the Malaya analogy. Thus in April 1963, U. Alexis Johnson, Deputy Under Secretary of State suggested that the post war insurgencies in Burma, Indonesia, Malaya, Indochina and the Philippines were coordinated by China but singled out Malaya as the struggle which "provided valuable lessons which are now being applied in VietNam" (*DOSB*, April 29, 1963, p. 636). Similarly, Roger Hilsman, Kennedy's major adviser on communist insurgencies, claimed that the best way to defeat the Viet Cong was not by killing them but by protecting them in strategic hamlets, a "technique used successfully in Malaya against the Communist movement there." (*DOSB*, July 8, 1963, p. 44).

The Strategic Hamlet program failed. Formally initiated as "Operation SUNRISE" in Bin Duong Province in early 1962, it died with the Ngos in late 1963. The failure of the strategic hamlet does not necessarily mean that the error lay in misapplying the lessons of Malaya to Vietnam but it does make the analogy suspect. It is, however, always necessary to point out the differences which account for the dissimilar outcomes. General Lemnitzer's memorandum—written in late 1961—is a first step in this direction. To be sure Lemnitzer was not addressing himself to the Strategic Hamlet program, but his observations, if correct, could help explain why a similar program was successful in Malaya but not in Vietnam.

The Korea analogy, on the other hand, found its antagonist in George Ball, Under Secretary of State. In an October 1964 memorandum to Dean Rusk, Robert McNamara and McGeorge Bundy, Ball sought to question "the assumptions of our Viet-Nam policy," before deciding in "the next few weeks" between a number of options, including bombing North Vietnam and introducing substantial U.S. ground forces in South Vietnam (Ball, Atlantic Monthly, July 1972, p. 36). Ball wrote:

> . . . I want to emphasize one key point at the outset: The problem of South Viet-Nam is *sui generis.* South Vietnam is not Korea, and in making fundamental decisions it would be a mistake for us to rely too heavily on the Korean analogy (Ball, 1972, p. 37).

Ball, like Lemnitzer, found five differences. Most of them, in this memorandum at least, dealt with the descriptive deficiencies of the Korean analogy: the U.S. had a clear United Nations mandate in Korea but not in South Vietnam; fifty-three other countries provided troops to fight in Korea while the U.S. was "going it alone" in Vietnam. More importantly, Syngman Rhee's government was stable and enjoyed wide support whereas South Vietnam was characterized by "governmental chaos." Perhaps the most important difference Ball identified was over the nature of the war: the Korean War was a classical case of invasion whereas in South Vietnam "there has been no invasion—only slow infiltration. . . . The Viet Cong insurgency does have substantial indigenous support" (Ball, 1972, p. 37). Whether Ball intended it or not, and I think he intended it, spelling out these differences raises questions about the normative assessment as well as the predictions provided by the Korean analogy. If the insurgency enjoyed substantial support and if the South Vietnamese government was incompetent, should and could the South Vietnamese regime be preserved?

Ball received better treatment from his superiors than Lemnitzer did from his. After reading the memorandum, Rusk, McNamara and Bundy debated the arguments with Ball on two successive Saturday afternoons (Atlantic Monthly, July 1972, p. 33). Ball failed to convince his superiors. The lessons of Korea continued to haunt the principal policy makers, almost to a man. Johnson could not forget "the withdrawal of our forces from South Korea and then our immediate reaction to the Communist aggression of 1950" and he worried about "repeating the same sharp reversal" in Vietnam (Johnson, 1971, p. 152). For Dean Rusk, the war in Vietnam, like Korea, was not a civil war but a case of aggression of one state against another across national boundaries. William Bundy argued that it took a war to beat back aggression in Korea and that it might take another to beat back the North Vietnamese and Chinese in Southeast Asia (*DOSB*, June 21, 1965).

If in retrospect some of Lyman Lemnitzer's and George Ball's objections to the Malaya and Korea analogy seem prescient and sound, one needs to remember that their advice was heard but not taken. This was so partly because the descriptive, normative, prescriptive and predictive components of the respective analogies combined to form an internally consistent and remarkably wholesome way to look at Vietnam. Together with the cognitive and historical-psychological reasons alluded to earlier but not discussed in this paper, these structural properties of historical analogies help explain why policy makers hold on to their analogies despite warnings about their limitations.

REFERENCES

Ball, George. "Top Secret: The Prophecy the President Rejected." *Atlantic Monthly*, July 1972.

Berman, Larry. *Planning A Tragedy*. New York: W. W. Norton, 1982.

Gelb, Leslie and Betts, Richard. *The Irony of Vietnam: The System Worked*. Washington D.C.: Brookings, 1979.

Hilsman, Roger. *To Move A Nation*. New York: Doubleday, 1967.

Karnow, Stanley. *Vietnam: A History*. New York: Viking, 1983.

Kattenburg, Paul. *The Vietnam Trauma*. New Jersey: Transaction, 1980.

Kearns, Doris. *Lyndon Johnson and the American Dream*. New York: Harper and Row, 1976.

May, Ernest. *Lessons of the Past: The Use and Misuse of History in American Foreign Policy*. New York: Oxford, 1973.

The Pentagon Papers: The Defense Department History of United States Decision Making on Vietnam. Senator Gravel edition. v. 1–4. Boston: Beacon Press, 1971.

Public Papers of the Presidents: John F. Kennedy.

Public Papers of the Presidents: Lyndon B. Johnson.

Schlesinger, Arthur. *The Bitter Heritage: Vietnam and American Democracy 1941–1966*. Boston: Houghton Mifflin, 1966.

Short, Anthony. *The Communist Insurrection in Malaya 1948–1960*. London: Frederick Muller, 1975.

United States Department of State. *Department of State Bulletin*. 1961–1966.

The Personalities of Bush and Gorbachev Measured at a Distance: Procedures, Portraits, and Policy

David G. Winter,
Margaret G. Hermann,
Walter Weintraub,
and Stephen G. Walker

INTRODUCTION

In recent months, internal developments within the Soviet Union, and between the Soviet Union and the United States, have raised the possibility of a new era in relations between the superpowers. In 1981, for example, who would have predicted that Ronald Reagan would cap his presidency, against the background of the Statue of Liberty, by exchanging smiles, handshakes, and waves with the leader of the Soviet Union? Or that newspaper headlines would speak of genuinely contested elections within the USSR (even mentioning the familiar democratic electoral paraphernalia of "exit polls")? With the inauguration of George Bush, each country now has a leader of whom much is expected, yet about whom surprisingly little is known. What is George Bush really like? And who is the "real" Mikhail Gorbachev? How should we interpret their actions? What can we expect when they come together to negotiate?

ON STUDYING BUSH AND GORBACHEV

The Leader as "Projective Screen"

So far, each leader's actions, and even the "manifest" or policy content of their words, are an ambiguous stimulus (not unlike a Rorschach inkblot) in which different observers can read their own interpretations. With his hand initially ex-

David G. Winter, Margaret G. Hermann, Walter Weintraub, and Stephen G. Walker, "The Personalities of Bush and Gorbachev Measured at a Distance: Procedures, Portraits, and Policy," *Political Psychology* 12, 2 (1991):215–245. Reprinted with permission.

tended to Congress in cooperation (after a negative campaign filled with innu-endo), President Bush has confused liberal opponents and troubled his conserva-tive supporters (Dionne, 1989). Yet in the first 18 months, Bush's administration seemed off to a slow start in terms of defining policy and filling positions, and echos of innuendo still emanated from the Republican National Committee. Events seem to confirm the words of *Time* magazine back during the campaign: "Many who know him find it difficult to imagine what he would do [as president]. . . . Could Bush show the decisiveness, the moral authority and necessary sense of command to guide the country . . . ?"

In the case of Gorbachev, opinion and analysis have been even more sharply divided. Many students of Soviet politics suggest that Gorbachev has chosen peace over socialism—"cooperation with the West over the search for unilateral advan-tage" (Holloway, 1989, pp. 67, 70); "not the struggle between classes but the com-mon plight of man" (Legvold, 1989, p. 85). In sharp contrast, however, are the words of columnist William Safire (1989): "They're [Soviet leaders] all headed the same way—toward fixing the Soviet economy until it becomes strong enough to feed itself and afford the arms to dominate its neighbors." Richard Nixon's analysis runs along similar lines. Beneath the "fashionably tailored suits, the polished man-ners and the smooth touch in personal encounters," he suggests, the "new Gor-bachev" is mainly motivated toward such familiar Soviet goals: "to erode the strength of the [NATO] alliance" and "to lull the West into a false sense of secu-rity," thus to create "a stronger Soviet Union and an expanding Soviet empire" (Nixon, 1989, pp. 207, 211, 218). Vice-President Quayle echos Nixon's doubts: "For although the Soviet leadership professes to adhere to 'new thinking,' it is still quite capable of 'old thinking,' as well" (1989, p. 6). One columnist even argued bluntly that "Gorbachev is on [a] power trip" (Charen, 1990). Finally, as we write, a respected authority on Soviet matters concluded that Gorbachev "is in truth a puzzling and enigmatic figure, and is becoming more so as his troubles deepen" (Shulman, 1990, p. 5).

Thus although Bush's career in government service spans several decades, and although Gorbachev has been in office for 6 years, we do not have consensus in the West about the "real" personalities of the two men—their motives, beliefs, opera-tional codes, self-concept, and styles. (They are not unique in this respect. Previ-ous behavior and the manifest content of campaign rhetoric are often of little use in forecasting American presidential behavior, as students of the surprising admin-istrations of Chester Arthur, Harry Truman, and Lyndon Johnson can attest.)

The Importance of Leaders' Personalities

Are the answers to these questions important? Obviously personality is not the only predictor of political behavior, and sometimes it is not even a major predictor. (On December 8, 1941, for example, Franklin D. Roosevelt's personality was largely irrelevant to whether the United States declared war on Japan.) Whatever Bush's and Gorbachev's personalities, their political behavior will be strongly shaped and constrained by situational factors such as budget deficits and economic-organization difficulties, respectively. Still, conditions in both countries do embody many of Greenstein's (1969, Chap. 2) classic criteria for identifying occasions when personalities of single actors can have an important influence on events: (1) First, Gorbachev and Bush occupy strategic locations in their respective political systems; (2) The present situation contains many new or ambiguous elements and is open to restructuring; (3) Internally and internationally, opposed forces are delicately balanced; (4) The important issues and problems demand active effort rather than routine role performance.

Thus in the 1990s we have, as it were, an equation in two unknowns. Perhaps psychological interpretations of the personalities of both leaders, drawing on systematic theory and research, could guide our understanding of events and even suggest answers to questions of policy. Yet we lack direct access to either leader, and so analysis and interpretation must be carried out at a distance. We intend this paper as a first step. Though drawn from diverse disciplines, each of the present authors is experienced in studying personality at a distance. We have applied our individual techniques to the study of Bush and Gorbachev, using both a common data set and individually selected additional materials. Drawing on the rather striking convergence of our separate results, we then construct personality profiles for both leaders. We conclude with some predictions and suggest a few broad policy implications.

We are acutely aware of the perils of prediction. What we write, during a time of nationalist ferment in the Baltic republics and negotiations for German unification, will appear in print only after many months. We run the risk of being dramatically wrong. [Indeed, the final draft of this paper was finished in June 1990, when the Iraqi invasion of Kuwait was only a gleam in Saddam Hussein's eye; and revisions were completed even as one columnist pronounced that "the Gorbachev era ends"; see Rosenthal (1990).] Yet if personality assessment at a distance is worth doing, it is worth doing boldly—suggesting answers that go beyond the obvious, to questions that are important.

ASSESSING PERSONALITY AT A DISTANCE

How can psychologists assess the motives of people whom they have never met and cannot study directly? In recent years, personality researchers have developed a variety of objective methods of measuring motives and other personality characteristics "at a distance," through systematic content analysis of speeches, interviews, and other spontaneous verbal material (Hermann, 1977, 1980a, 1980b, 1987; Walker, 1983; Weintraub, 1981, 1989; Winter, 1991; Winter and Stewart, 1977). These techniques have often been used in aggregate studies of political leaders—for example, in predicting foreign policy orientation or propensity for violence (Hermann, 1980a, b; Winter, 1980). Sometimes, though, at-a-distance techniques have been used to construct systematic portraits of particular leaders: Hermann assessed the motives and other personal characteristics of Ronald Reagan (1983) and Syrian leader Hafez Al-Assad (1988); Walker (1986) analyzed Woodrow

Wilson's operational code; Weintraub (1989) studied the verbal behavior of seven recent American presidents; and Winter and Carlson (1988) used the motive scores of Richard Nixon's first inaugural address to resolve several paradoxes of his political career, while seeking validation of these scores from a systematic review of Nixon's public and private life.

When prepared speeches and even "spontaneous" interview responses are scored for any psychological characteristic, skeptical readers often ask whether the resulting scores reflect the motives or other characteristics of the leader or of the speechwriters, or whether the scores are affected by efforts at positive self-presentation (even disinformation). Of course, speechwriters are generally selected for their ability to express what the leader wants to say, especially in the case of important speeches. In most cases, American presidents are involved in the preparation of important speeches [see Safire (1975, pp. 24, 25, 529, 530) and Price (1977, pp. 42–50) regarding Richard Nixon; and Noonan (1990, pp. 68–92, 186–200) regarding Reagan].

Using more spontaneous interview material may reduce (though it does not fully eliminate) this problem. Yet in a larger sense, it may not matter whether the source was the leader or a speech writer, or whether the speeches reflect "real personality" or self-presentation. Whatever their status, they exist as, are taken as, and have effects as the leader's words.

The major assumption of the present at-a-distance study, then, is that a leader's words and the scores based on them are a reasonable guide to the speaker's personality. More specifically, we assume that the personality variables we have measured, using the procedures we have followed, are sufficiently robust to override any effects of authorship, impression management, disinformation, and ego defensiveness. We further assume that the effects of the particular topics discussed and the situation in which the leader speaks are adequately controlled by the comparison groups that we have used for interpreting the raw scores we obtained (see below). Obviously, these assumptions are debatable; but for us their usefulness rests on the pragmatic criterion of whether the scores are useful in predicting or interpreting interesting and significant political behavior and outcomes.

In the present paper, we apply our various techniques to a comparative study of Bush and Gorbachev. We then suggest some likely trends, opportunities, issues, problems, and pitfalls confronting each leader, both separately and in joint interaction.

PERSONALITY VARIABLES ASSESSED

Taken together, our methods cover quite a range of personality variables, including the major personality domains of motivation, cognition, styles, and traits and defenses, drawn from many different personality theories. In this section, we introduce each variable, describing its theoretical antecedents and how it is measured in verbal behavior, indicating who was responsible for its measurement in the present study, and noting the major references in the personality and political psychology literature. Table 24.1 summarizes this information.

Table 24.1 MAJOR PERSONALITY VARIABLES ASSESSED AT A DISTANCE FOR BUSH AND GORBACHEV

Variable	Scoring description and major references
Motives (Hermann, 1987; Winter, 1991)	
Achievement	Concern with excellence, success in competition, or unique accomplishment.
Affiliation	Concern with warm, friendly relationships; friendly, convivial activity; nurturant help.
Power	Concern with impact or effect on others, prestige, or reputation.
Beliefs and styles (Hermann, 1980b, 1987)	
Beliefs	
Nationalism	Identification with or favorable reference to own nation; nonidentification with or unfavorable reference to other nations.
Events controllable	Accepts responsibility for planning or initiating action.
Self-confidence	Self seen as instigator of activity, authority figure, or recipient of positive feedback.
Cognitive and interpersonal styles	
Conceptual complexity	Ratio of high complexity words to low complexity words.
Distrust	Doubts, misgivings, or expectation of harm from groups not identified with.
Task emphasis	Ratio of task words to interpersonal words.
Operational code (George, 1969; Walker, 1983, 1990)	
Self-attributions	
Friendly/hostile	Political life seen as harmonious vs. conflicted: relationship with opponents seen as friendly vs. hostile.
Optimistic/pessimistic	Optimism vs. pessimism about realizing values and aspirations.
High/low control	History seen as shaped by people vs. chance.
Comprehensive/limited goals	Articulates goals that are comprehensive and long-range vs. piecemeal and limited.
Self-scripts	
Methods of reaching goals	Verbal (promises, threats) versus action (reward, sanctions); politics (rewards, promises) vs. conflict (sanctions, threats); positive (appeals for support, gives support) vs. negative resists, opposes).
Verbal style (reflecting traits and defenses) (Weintraub, 1981, Chap. 2; 1989, Chap. 1)	
I/we ratio	Ratio of "I" pronouns to "we" pronouns.
Expressions of feeling	Self-described as experiencing some feeling.
Evaluators	Judgments of good/bad, useful/useless, right/wrong, correct/incorrect, proper/improper, pleasant/unpleasant, and exclamations of opinion.

Table 24.1 *(Continued)*

Variable	Scoring description and major references
Direct references to audience	Direct references to the audience, the situation, or the physical surroundings.
Adverbial intensifiers	Adverbs that increase the force of a statement.
Rhetorical questions	Questions meant to arouse and engage the audience.
Retractors	Partial or complete retraction of an immediately preceeding statement.
Negatives	All negating words such as "not," "no," "never," "nobody," "nothing," etc.
Explainers	Reasons or justifications for actions; causal connections.
Qualifiers	Expressions of uncertainty, modifiers that weaken assertions, and phrases contributing vagueness or looseness.
Creative expressions	Novel words or combinations of words; metaphors.

Motives

Motivation involves goals and goal-directed actions. Drawing on the classic theoretical insights of Freud (1915–1917/1961–1963), Jung (1910), and Murray (1938), personality psychologists have in recent decades developed methods of measuring several important human motives through content analysis of fantasy productions or other imaginative verbal material (see Atkinson, 1958). The *achievement motive* involves a concern for excellence and unique accomplishment, and is associated with restless activity, moderate risk-taking, using feedback or knowledge of results, and entrepreneurial activity (see McClelland, 1961). The *affiliation motive* involves a concern for close relations with others. Sometimes it predicts interpersonal warmth and self-disclosure, but under conditions of threat or stress, it can produce a "prickly," defensive orientation to others (see Boyatzis, 1973; McAdams, 1982). The *power motive,* a concern for impact and prestige, leads both to formal social power and also to profligate, impulsive actions such as aggression, drinking, and taking extreme risks (see Winter, 1973; Winter and Stewart, 1978). These three motives are selected from Murray's (1938) comprehensive taxonomy as involving some of the most common and important human goals and concerns. In the present study, power and affiliation motives were scored in two different ways: (a) by Hermann's computer-based adaptation of the original scoring systems, which focuses particularly on verb phrases, and (b) by Winter's (1991) integrated "running text" scoring system, which was also used to score achievement motivation.

Beliefs and Styles

These variables, scored by Hermann, reflect some of the most widely studied beliefs and dimensions of cognitive and interpersonal style, as emphasized in the personality theories of Kelly (1955), Rotter (1990), Rogers (1959) and others. *Nation-*

alism (or ethnocentrism), a belief in the superiority of one's own group or nation and the inferiority of others, and *distrust,* or suspicion of other people and institutions, are two key belief and stylistic components of authoritarianism, arguably the single most studied personality variable (see Adorno *et al.,* 1950; Brown, 1965, Chap. 10; Meloen *et al.,* 1988; and Tucker, 1965).

Belief in the Controllability of Events   This belief captures the ancient distinction between will and fate as determinants of outcomes, as in the famous words of Cassius to Brutus, in Shakespeare's *Julius Caesar* (I, ii, 140–141):

> The fault, dear Brutus, is not in our stars
> But in ourselves, that we are underlings.

In modern personality research, this belief has been variously conceptualized as internal versus external locus of control (Strickland, 1977) and more recently as facilitating versus debilitating attributional style (Weiner, 1980; Zullow *et al.,* 1988). Among leaders, the belief that events can be controlled is associated with effective action and adaptation.

Self-Confidence   The sense that one is both effective and loved reflects self-esteem and related aspects of the self-concept. Its theoretical roots go back to the psychoanalytic concept of narcissism. Ziller *et al.* (1977) have demonstrated its importance in leader behavior. Self-confident leaders tend to be active rather than reactive; however, leaders who are less self-confident may be better listeners and more responsive to others.

Conceptual Complexity   Conceptual complexity, or the ability to differentiate aspects or dimensions of the environment, derives from Kelly's theory of personality (1955; see also Bieri, 1961; and Ziller *et al.,* 1977). As a cognitive style, it is negatively related to the "intolerance of ambiguity" (black-and-white thinking) component of authoritarianism. Among leaders, high nationalism and distrust and low conceptual complexity are associated with an aggressive, autocratic, and often simplistic political style.

Task Versus Social-Emotional Emphasis   This variable reflects two different kinds of leadership or interpersonal style, derived from early social psychological studies of experimental small groups [Bales (1958), see Byars (1973) for an extension of this distinction to specifically political material].[1] Task-focused leaders have an "agenda," whether relating to economic affairs or national security. Social-emotional leaders, lower in task emphasis, are more attuned to the subtle nuances, interpersonal structures, and shifting alignments of the political process.

Overall Personality Orientations

Recently Hermann (1987) has elaborated a series of six broad "orientations," each consisting of different combinations of the motivational and cognitive variables that she had previously studied as separate variables. For example, the "expansionist" orientation involves controlling more territory, resources, and people. It involves a combination of power motivation, nationalism and distrust, belief that events can be controlled, self-confidence, and a strong task emphasis. In contrast, the "developmental" orientation (composed of affiliation motivation, nationalism, cognitive complexity, self-confidence, and an interpersonal emphasis) involves improvement (with the help of on other countries) rather than expansion. Table 24.2 lists these orientations along with their component variables.

Operational Codes and "Self-Scripts"

In contrast to the broad, abstract cognitive elements discussed above, which are drawn from psychological theories of personality, the concept of operational code was developed by political scientists to describe structures of specifically political beliefs. Originated by Leites (1951), the operational code construct has been developed by George (1969), Holsti (1970), and later Walker (1983, 1990). As reformulated by George, a political leader's operational code beliefs can be described as the "answers" (phrased as a choice from among two or more alternatives) to a series of philosophical and instrumental questions such as the following: What is the essential nature of political life (friendly or hostile)? What are the prospects for realizing one's fundamental political aspirations? How much control can one have over history? How can political goals be pursued effectively? What is the best timing? What is the usefulness of different means?

In the present study, Walker conceptualized the answers to George's philosophical questions as a series of "self-attributions" describing the individual's relationship to the political universe (friendly versus hostile, optimistic versus pessimistic, high versus low control, and comprehensive versus limited goals), and conceptualized the answers to the instrumental questions as a series of "self-scripts" (promises, rewards, threats, sanctions, appeals, giving support, opposition and resistance). Specific self-attributions and self-scripts coded in the present study are shown in Table 24.1. Taken together, these two kinds of codes act as cognitive heuristics, mediating or filtering the day-to-day flow of information about the situation and other political actors. Because the operational code construct is currently undergoing development and refinement (see Walker, 1990), the specific variables actually coded for Bush and Gorbachev are slightly different and the Gorbachev coding is more elaborate, as will be seen in Table VII. For example, the Bush coding emphasized his view of the political universe, while the later Gorbachev coding focused more on his view of self, or how the self was located in relation to that political universe.

Traits and Defenses

Traits are the everyday language of personality description: the enduring ways in which people interact with others and appear to them, as described in the writings of Jung (1921/1971), Eysenck (see Eysenck and Eysenck, 1985), and Allport (1961), among others. On the basis of numerous clinical experimental studies and at-a-distance research, Weintraub (1981, 1986, 1989) has measured several features of verbal style that are indicators of different traits and their characteristic

Table 24.2   PERSONALITY ORIENTATIONS AND THEIR COMPONENT VARIABLES[a]

Orientation	Definition	Component variables
Expansionist	Interest in gaining control over more territory, resources, or people	Power motivation Nationalism Belief in own ability to control events Self-confidence Distrust Task emphasis
Active independent	Interest in participating in the international community, but on one's own terms and without engendering a dependent relationship with another country	Affiliation motivation Nationalism Belief in own ability to control events Cognitive complexity Self-confidence Task emphasis
Influential	Interest in having an impact on other nations' foreign policy behavior, in playing a leadership role in regional or international affairs	Power motivation Belief in own ability to control events Cognitive complexity Self-confidence Interpersonal emphasis
Mediator/Integrator	Concern with reconciling differences between other nations, with resolving problems in the international arena	Affiliation motivation Belief in own ability to control events Cognitive complexity Interpersonal emphasis
Opportunist	Interest in taking advantage of present circumstances, in dealing effectively with the demands and opportunities of the moment, in being expedient	Cognitive complexity Interpersonal emphasis
Developmental	Commitment to be continued improvement of one's own nation with the best help available from other countries or international organizations	Affiliation motivation Nationalism Cognitive complexity Self-confidence Interpersonal emphasis

[a]Adapted from Hermann (1987, pp. 170–173).

defensive styles (as originally developed in the theoretical work of Anna Freud, 1946). Table 24.3 shows how the different verbal style measures, described in Table 24.1, are combined to assess these traits and defenses (see Weintraub, 1989, pp. 95–102).

Recent personality research (see Eysenck and Eysenck, 1985; Norman, 1963) suggests that many of these traits can be further grouped into two major factors: introversion–extraversion and stability–neuroticism.

Table 24.3   COMPONENT VERBAL STYLE FEATURES OF TRAITS AND DEFENSE

Trait or defense	Component features of verbal behavior
Interpersonal style	
Engaging (vs. aloof)	Direct references
	Rhetorical questions
Passivity	Frequency of "me"
Oppositional	Negatives
Emotional style	
Emotional expressiveness	High I/we ratio
	Low nonpersonal references
	Expressions of feeling
	Evaluators
	Adverbial intensifiers
	Direct references
	Rhetorical questions
Anxiety	Negatives
	Explainers
	Qualifiers
Depression	High I/we ratio
	Low nonpersonal references
	Direct references
Anger	Negatives
	Frequency of "I" and "we"
Sensitivity to criticism	Adverbial intensifiers
	Negatives
	Evaluators
Decision-making style	
Decisiveness	High ratio of (I + we)/me
Dogmatic	Low qualifiers, low retractors
Impulsive	Low or moderate qualifiers, high retractors
Paranoid	High qualifiers, low retractors
Obsessive	High qualifiers, high retractors

A Common Theoretical Conception of Personality

While we each have our own conceptions of personality, the present study reflects a shared theoretical view of personality that is eclectic and diverse, with special emphases on (a) motives or goals, (b) adaptive or defensive transformations of these goals, and (c) cognitive characteristics or "algorithms" that filter or process information from the environment.

SELECTING MATERIAL TO BE SCORED

All four methods of assessing personality at a distance are based on content analysis of verbal material, typically transcripts of speeches and press conference responses. In an effort to provide common databases for the present study, the second author assembled two collections of documents: (a) For Bush, there were transcripts of his "stump speech," several television interviews, and the New Hampshire Republican candidates' debate, all from the 1988 presidential election campaign. Comparison materials were available from the two other major candidates, Michael Dukakis and Jesse Jackson. (b) For Gorbachev, there were transcripts of 20 speeches and 27 interviews during the period December 10, 1984 through December 7, 1988. These two collections are referred to as the "standard samples."

The methods employed by each author, however, vary in the kinds and amounts of verbal material they customarily use, in the ways this material is analyzed, and in the nature and amount of material from other persons needed for making comparisons. Motive imagery scores, for example, are usually standardized within a sample of similar material from as many as 30 other people. In the present study, therefore, some authors selected from the standard samples and added extra material in ways that reflected their customary procedures. Table 24.4 summarizes the materials used to score each category of personality variables.

In measuring Bush's motives, Winter used two sources: (a) scores from the October 12, 1987, speech announcing his candidacy for president, interpreted in comparison to similar speeches by 13 other major 1988 candidates (see Winter, 1988); and (b) his January 20, 1989 Inaugural Address, interpreted in comparison to all previous first inaugural addresses from George Washington through Ronald Reagan (see Winter, 1987, Table 1; 1990). Gorbachev's motive scores were also based on two sources: (a) From the standard sample, four interviews from the period April–October 1985 (his first year in office), and two interviews from December 1987–June 1988, by which time the main lines of his policy were established, were scored. These were interpreted in comparison to scores from similar interviews with 22 world leaders (see Winter, 1990). (b) To compare Gorbachev with previous Soviet leaders, his first speech ("report") to a Congress of the Communist Party of the Soviet Union, after assuming the position of General Secretary, was scored along with equivalent speeches by Lenin, Stalin, Khrushchev, and Brezhnev.[2]

Hermann measured beliefs, cognitive and interpersonal styles, and affiliation and power motivation from the full standard samples. Bush's raw scores were interpreted in comparison with those of Dukakis and Jackson; Gorbachev's, in comparison with those of a sample of 53 world leaders. [See Hermann (1980b) for a detailed description of this sample.]

Walker measured Bush's operational code by examining campaign statements on foreign policy topics such as the Middle East, South Africa, U.S.–Soviet relations and arms control, and communist insurgency in the Western hemisphere; as compared to similar statements by Dukakis and Jackson (providing at least an ordinal comparison). For Gorbachev, he examined a random subset of 107 paragraphs (stratified by occasion and topic) from the standard sample. Gorbachev's scores were directly interpreted without comparisons to others because at the time this latter coding was done each element of self-attribution or self-script had been elaborated into a pair of binary alternatives (see Walker, 1990).

Weintraub scored traits and defenses from a 6000-word subset of the standard sample for Bush, and from six interviews of the standard sample for Gorbachev. In

Table 24.4   MATERIALS USED TO SCORE AND COMPARE PERSONALITY VARIABLES

Variable	Material used for	
	Scoring	Comparison
Bush		
Motives	(a) Standard campaign sample (MGH)	(a) 1988 Standard campaign sample; also sample of 53 world leaders
	(b) Candidacy announcement speech (DGW)	(b) Other 1988 announcement speeches
	(c) Inaugural address (DGW)	(c) Other inaugurals
Beliefs and styles	Standard campaign sample	Standard campaign sample; also sample of 53 world leaders
Operational code	Foreign policy statements from standard campaign sample	Foreign policy statements from standard campaign sample
Traits and defenses	Selections from standard campaign sample	Selections from standard campaign sample; also selections from recent U.S. presidents
Gorbachev		
Motives	(a) Standard sample (MGH)	(a) Sample of 53 world leaders
	(b) Selected interviews from standard sample (DGW)	(b) Interviews from 22 world leaders
	(c) First "report" to CPSU Congress (DGW)	(c) Similar reports by Lenin through Brezhnev
Beliefs and styles	Standard sample	Sample of 53 world leaders
Operational code	Selected paragraphs from standard sample	No explicit comparison
Traits and defenses	Selections from standard sample	Selections from recent U.S. presidents; also (implicitly) selections from other Slavic leaders

both cases, scores were interpreted by comparison with those of seven postwar U.S. presidents (see Weintraub, 1989); Bush was also compared with Dukakis and Jackson, and Gorbachev with a sample of Slavic political leaders.

Methodological Issues

We intend this study as an approach to the goal of a standardized taxonomy for describing personality at a distance. Obviously the variation in materials used across (and sometimes within) each of the authors of this study means that this goal is not yet realized. While such variation creates a certain methodological "looseness" and possible difficulties, we believe that the convergence of results across methods and materials is sufficiently robust in the present case.

Two more specific methodological issues need to be addressed. Procedures for assessing interscorer reliability vary across the different techniques (see the references listed in Table 24.1 for details). For the motive, belief, and style variables, category agreement between scorers and experts and among scorers is usually calculated formally, with a standard of 0.85 or higher required for all variables [see Winter (1973, p. 248) for details of category agreement calculation]. While the verbal-style measures of traits are objectively defined (see Weintraub, 1989, pp. 11–16), formal measures of interscorer agreement are not routinely calculated. Operational code analysis involves more holistic interpretation of the speaker's entire line of argument. No formal measures of inter-scorer agreement are calculated.

The Gorbachev material, of course, had been translated from Russian into English (in some interviews, by way of some other intermediate language). Previous research (Hermann, 1980a, p. 352, n. 2; Winter, 1973, pp. 92–93) suggests that little bias on these scoring systems is introduced by this translation process.

RESULTS

Tables 24.5 through 24.8 present the results of the scoring and analysis of data for each of the main domains and variables of personality described in Tables 24.1 through 24.4. For each variable, the tables give scores both in raw form and then in comparison to the appropriate other groups, as discussed above. We will proceed domain by domain, presenting results, drawing conclusions and making predictions on the basis of previous research. In the final selection, we will bring all of our results, conclusions, and predictions together into integrated personality portraits of Bush and Gorbachev.

Motives

Table 24.5 presents motive scores for Bush and Gorbachev. Affiliation and power motives were measured in two different ways (Hermann's and Winter's procedures), using different samples of interviews and speeches, and making comparisons to several different groups of other political leaders. To facilitate comparisons of these different estimates, Table V presents the means and standard deviations for all estimates of each motive. Despite the differences of method, the results suggest reasonably clear and consistent motive profiles for each leader. Bush scores high in the achievement and affiliation motives, but only a little above average in power. (Compared with other Americans—1988 candidates or previous presidents—he is average; compared with leaders from other countries, he is high.) Gorbachev's motive profile—high achievement, high affiliation, and average power—is remarkably similar. As with Bush, the power comparison score depends on the comparison group used. Compared with other Soviet leaders, Gorbachev is low in power motivation; but compared with other world leaders, he is average (Winter) or high (Hermann).[3] This suggests that as a group, Soviet and American leaders may be more power-motivated than the world average.

Comparison to Other United States Presidents and Other World Leaders   Winter (1987, 1988) suggested that achievement, affiliation, and power motives could be conceptualized as three orthogonal dimensions, and that the more

Table 24.5 MOTIVES OF BUSH AND GORBACHEV

Motive	Study	Bush			Gorbachev		
		Speech or Comp[a]	Raw[b]	Comparison[c]	Speech or Comp[a]	Raw[b]	Comparison[c]
Achievement	DGW	ACS	8.76	61	SS	3.82	59
	DGW	IA	7.85	58	CPSU	5.45	60
Mean				60 H			60 H
SD				1.5			0.5
Affiliation	MGH	WL	0.18	66	WL	0.20	68
		C88		53	BPM		58
	DGW	ACS	4.04	62	SS	3.91	69
		IA	10.81	83	CPSU	1.27	50
Mean				66 H			61 H
SD				10.9			7.8
Power	MGH	WL	0.44	72	WL	0.50	77
		C88		48	BPM		38
	DGW	ACS	8.76	51	SS	5.15	47
		IA	6.92	53	CPSU	1.88	39
Mean				56 M			50 M
SD				9.4			15.8

[a]Speech and/or comparison group for this score: For MGH analysis: SS = Standard sample; WL = Compared to 53 world leaders; BPM = Compared to Brezhnev-era Politburo members; C88 = compared to 1988 candidates. For DGW analysis: ACS = Announcement of candidacy speech (compared to other 1988 candidates); IA = Inaugural address (compared to other first inaugural addresses); SS = Standard sample (compared to 22 other world leaders); CPSU = First report after assuming leadership to a Communist Party Congress (compared to first reports of other leaders).

[b]Proportion of verb phrases scored for imagery in MGH analysis; images per 1000 words in DGW analysis.

[c]Standard score (based on comparison group as in note a); M = 50, SD = 10. For averaged scores, H = high (one SD or more above comparison mean); M = medium (within SD of comparison mean).

similar the motive profiles of any two leaders, the less the Pythagorean distance between the two "points" representing the motive scores of those leaders. By this criterion,[4] Bush and Gorbachev are very similar to each other, and each is more similar to Richard Nixon than to any other United States president. Compared to other world leaders (see Winter, 1990), Gorbachev most closely resembles King Hussein of Jordan, Enrico Berlinguer (leader of the Italian Communist party from 1972 until his death in 1984), Argentine general (later president from 1976 to 1981) Jorge Videla, and Brazilian general (later president from 1974 to 1979) Ernesto Giesel. He is *least* like Ayatollah Khomeini and SWAPO leader Sam Nujoma.

What is the use of such comparisons? Characterizing Bush as a "preppy Nixon" or Mikhail Gorbachev as a "socialist Nixon" may be an entertaining statistical game, but do these comparisons have any broader practical purpose? Similarities of motive profile may draw our attention to deeper similarities of style and performance. Thus Gorbachev, like Nixon, extricated his country from a disastrous "third world" war, and sought rapprochement with long-standing enemies. Like Hussein and Berlinguer, and in contrast to Khomeini, Gorbachev is charting a pragmatic course of realistic compromise through the minefields of militant ideological–theological dispute. Like Nixon, Bush reacts negatively to personalized criticism; also like Nixon, he walks a narrow line between suspicion and the desire to negotiate arms reduction.

These comparisons may also alert us to possible problems and dangers. Would Bush and Gorbachev, like Nixon, be vulnerable to scandal? And if their remarkable flexibility ever fails them, would they rigidly dig in to support a failing line of policy? Thus generals Videla and Geisel both set out to dismantle constricting bureaucracies and expand economic growth; but intractable problems, dissatisfaction, and opposition eventually led them toward authoritarian solutions—"dirty wars" against their own people if not outright attacks on a foreign enemy.

Predictions Based on Motive Scores   In terms of previous at-a-distance research on motives (see Terhune, 1968a, 1968b; Winter, 1980, 1991), the motive profiles of Bush and Gorbachev suggest that they will be *rationally cooperative* (high achievement and affiliation), interested in maximizing joint outcomes rather than exploiting the other (low power). They will *seek arms limitation agreements* (high affiliation) and will be *unlikely to use aggression* in the pursuit of policy (average power). On the other hand, they are sensitive to the nuances of friendship-versus-rejection (high affiliation). Under stress they may become prickly and defensive, especially if they perceive the other side as threatening or exploitative. If backed into an extreme corner in this way, they might even strike out with ill-conceived and inchoate hostility.

Beliefs and Styles

Table 24.6 presents scores for the cognitive variables measured by Hermann's techniques. Again, the results vary somewhat according to which comparison groups are used. Considering the world leaders' comparison scores (which are based on the larger sample), Bush and Gorbachev both score high in nationalism, distrust, and conceptual complexity.[5] Their high complexity scores suggest that Bush and Gorbachev are both able to differentiate among alternative principles, policies, and points of view, and then to integrate these disparate elements into complex higher-order generalizations. Bush and Gorbachev both have strongly nationalist orientations and tend to distrust others. (This distrust may be a sign of the prickly defensiveness that affiliation-motivated people display when they are in uncomfortable situations). In most people, suspicious nationalism goes along with simplistic, black-or-white thinking [see Brown (1965, Chap. 10) on these cognitions as features of the authoritarian personality]. In Bush and Gorbachev, however, these tendencies should be mitigated by their high conceptual complexity. Thus they may be able to defuse competitive, "patriotic" issues by making subtle distinctions and complex integrations——in short, by intellectualization.

Gorbachev's average scores on the belief that events are controllable, self-confidence, and task emphasis all suggest a leader who is reasonably capable of sus-

Table 24.6 BELIEFS AND STYLES OF BUSH AND GORBACHEV

	Bush			Gorbachev		
		Comparison scores[b]			Comparison scores[b]	
Variable	Raw score[a]	World leaders	1988 candidates	Raw score[a]	World leaders	Brezhnev Politburo members
Beliefs						
Nationalism	0.40	76 H	50 M	0.38	74 H	37 L
Events controllable	0.33	35 L	48 M	0.42	41 M	42 M
Self-confidence	0.60	31 L	48 M	0.84	48 M	75 H
Styles						
Conceptual complexity	0.54	64 H	48 M	0.54	64 H	74 H
Distrust	0.29	59 M	49 M	0.39	66 H	69 H
Task emphasis	0.47	37 L	47 M	0.61	48 M	20 L

[a]Proportion of time during which a characteristic that could have been exhibited was in fact exhibited.

[b]Standardized score (based on comparison group noted at the top of the column); M = 50, SD = 10. H = Relatively high (one SD or more above comparison mean; M = medium (within one SD of comparison mean); L = relatively low (one SD or more below comparison mean).

tained, optimistic work. (For a Soviet leader, however, Gorbachev gives much greater emphasis to the *interpersonal* dimension of leadership than to task issues.) Bush's low scores on these three variables, in contrast, suggest a slightly more interpersonally focused leader, who is vulnerable to fatalistic drift (or distraction through affiliative conviviality), at least under stress.

Overall Personality Orientations Scores on these cognitive variables (as well as scores on their affiliation and power motives) combine to suggest that Gorbachev has a *developmental orientation* to the political process. Previous research (see Hermann, 1987) shows that leaders with this orientation are intent on improving their nations, either economically or militarily, or both. But because they are uncertain that they or their nations can govern events, they are constantly trying to see what others can do to help them and through persuasion to get these others to be of aid. With constant vigilance, such leaders seek out those who appear able to shape events; indeed, they often seem aware of potentially rewarding relationships before most other actors in the international or domestic political system become aware.

Developmentally oriented leaders engage in "controlled dependence": they use others but do not become symbiotic with these others, nor do they try to control or dominate others. Through an attitude of friendliness and collaboration, they make others feel good but do so while committing only a moderate amount of their own resources. By taking the initiative, leaders with this orientation perceive they can work with others to create opportunities for themselves. The ultimate goal is improvement of the condition of the nation, and like a "dog with a bone," these leaders keep maneuvering their governments toward actions that will have some payoff toward that goal. They are not very tolerant of problems or events that take away from this ultimate goal, or of people who do not "pull their weight" in working toward the regime's goal.

Bush also has many aspects of the developmental orientation; but his primary political orientation is that of *integrator* or consensus-builder, concerned with morale and the cohesiveness of the groups with which he works (see Hermann, 1989). Leaders with this orientation see themselves as agents of the people, reflecting their needs and wishes, reconciling differences, and minimizing conflict. They are reactive, working on the policies and programs that their followers want addressed. As an integrator or mediator, Bush would seek to forge compromise and consensus among his constituents, letting them define the agenda rather than imposing one himself. For this orientation, the "best" policy is that which brings together the broadest base of support. Thus these leaders are driven by popularity ratings. For developmental leaders, in contrast, the "best" policy is whatever will solve the problem and improve the condition of the nation. They are driven by vision, thus, in the process, by the need for information, and finally by results.

Operational Codes

Table 24.7 gives the operational code characterizations of each leader. As an incrementalist with limited goals, Bush sees the world as potentially dangerous, calling for a variety of responses but initially emphasizing the paths of conflict (threats, sanctions). In a world perceived to be less dangerous and more friendly, Gorbachev has a comprehensive perspective and goals. While he can take either the path of politics (praise, reward) or the path of conflict, his choice of response emphasizes positive reactions rather than negative ones and words rather than action. In simplest terms, Bush employs *specific threats*, while Gorbachev is more likely to make broader *exhortations to virtue*. Both leaders express an optimistic sense of being able to control foreign policy outcomes.

Traits

Table 24.8 presents the scores on the verbal characteristics that Weintraub (1981, 1989) uses to construct trait ratings. Both Bush and Gorbachev have an engaging interpersonal style (high direct references and rhetorical questions). Bush's higher scores on negatives and "me" pronouns, however, suggest that his engaging style is tinged with oppositional and passive tendencies. In terms of emotional style, Bush and Gorbachev are both highly expressive, but in different ways. Bush shows personally expressive verbal characteristics (high I/we ratio, expressions of feeling, and low nonpersonal references). Gorbachev's expressivity, in contrast, is based on less personal verbal characteristics that suggest intensification and thus perhaps calculation (evaluators, adverbial intensifiers, direct references, and rhetorical questions). Gorbachev thus appears to engage in controlled expression of feelings; he is, in short, an accomplished actor-politician.

Neither Bush nor Gorbachev is especially high in anxiety (average negatives, explainers, and qualifiers), but Bush is perhaps prone to depression (high I/we ra-

Table 24.7 OPERATIONAL CODES OF BUSH AND GORBACHEV[a]

Component	Bush characterization	Gorbachev characterization
Self-attributions		
Friendly/hostile	Dangerous (potentially hostile relations with others; varied kinds of opponents)	Friendly (13:0)[b]
Optimistic/pessimistic	Optimistic	Optimistic (9:1)
High/low control	High Control	Moderately high control (5:2)
Comprehensive/limited	Limited goals	Comprehensive goals (8:0)
Self-script		
Methods of reaching goals	Conflict	Mixed politics/conflict (9:8); Positive vs. negative (15:5); Verbal vs. action (12:5)

[a]The conceptualizations and measurement of some variables were slightly different for Bush and Gorbachev; see text.

[b]Ratio of frequency of first alternative to frequency of second alternative.

Table 24.8 TRAITS AND DEFENSES OF BUSH AND GORBACHEV

Comparison[b] Variable	Postwar U.S. presidents Raw score[a]	Bush Raw score[a]	Comparisons[b] C88	USP	Gorbachev Raw score[a]	USP
Use of "I"	25.0	47.8	H	H	11.8	L
Use of "we"	18.0	10.4	L	L	19.3	M
I/we ratio	1.4	4.6	H	H	0.6	L
Use of "me"	2.0	3.5	H	H	0.9	L
Expressions of feeling	3.0	4.0	H	M	1.8	L
Evaluators	9.0	15.0	M	H	12.4	H
Direct references to audience	2.0	4.2	H	H	3.1	M
Adverbial intensifiers	13.0	12.9	M	M	21.4	H
Rhetorical questions	1.0	2.5	H	H	2.5	H
Retractors	7.0	10.9	H	M	7.4	M
Negatives	12.0	15.2	M	M	13.1	M
Explainers	5.0	3.5	L	L	5.1	M
Qualifiers	11.0	9.0	M	M	6.3	L
Nonpersonal references	750.0	543.5	L	L	854.1	L
Creative expressions	2.0	4.0	M	M	1.3	L

[a]Frequency per 1000 words.

[b]Comparison groups: C88 = 1988 candidates; USP = postwar U.S. presidents.

tio, direct references, low nonpersonal references). Both leaders are especially sensitive to criticism (high negatives and evaluators, and for Gorbachev, high adverbial intensifiers). In such cases, Bush is especially likely to show anger (high I, we, and negatives), while Gorbachev, in contrast, tends to take control of the challenge (frequent interruptions and direct engagement).

In terms of decision style, Bush appears rather impulsive (low qualifiers and high retractors). Sometimes leaders with this pattern can become paralyzed with indecision in crisis situations. Gorbachev shows a more balanced flexibility (moderate retractors). His low qualifiers score may suggest impulsive tendencies, although this may be in part an artifact of using some interviews in which he answered previously submitted questions. Bush scores moderate on creativity, while Gorbachev scores low. This suggests that Gorbachev draws on others for new ideas and solutions to problems.

Overall, both leaders are engaging, expressive, and perhaps impulsive and prone to anger. Neither is anxious, although Bush may be depressed on occasion. In terms of the broader factors of introversion-extraversion and neuroticism-stability, each leader could therefore be classified as a stable extravert, with Gorbachev a little more so and Bush a little less so on both dimensions.

DISCUSSION: PERSONALITY PORTRAITS, PREDICTIONS, AND POLICY

Personality Portraits of Bush and Gorbachev

Table 24.9 draws together the scores presented in the last section into brief personality portraits of Bush and Gorbachev. Both are motivated primarily for achievement and affiliation—for standards of excellence, improvement, and innovation, as well as for friendly cooperation—rather than for impact, power, and exploitation. At heart, both are somewhat suspicious and nationalistic, characteristics which under threat could be defensively exacerbated by their high affiliation motives. Under most circumstances, however, both are able to recognize and deal with complexity, which keeps their suspicious nationalism under control.

Bush expresses his own emotions openly. He may be somewhat unpredictable, with episodes of impulsive behavior alternating with periods of depression and drift. In these circumstances, his conflict self-script may be engaged. Gorbachev is also expressive, but in a more calculated way. With greater emotional control, he is optimistic and capable of sustained effort, involving mostly positive verbal self-scripts that balance politics and conflict. Both leaders are reasonably stable extraverts.

Gorbachev, with his developmental orientation, is concerned with solving national problems and seeking national improvement; to accomplish this he would seek out information and approach others for help. While Bush shares some of the characteristics of this developmental orientation, his stronger integrator/mediator orientation would lead him more to reconciling the feelings and opinions of others than to shaping his own agenda.

Table 24.9 PERSONALITY PORTRAITS OF BUSH AND GORBACHEV

Personality domain	Bush	Gorbachev
Motives	Achievement and affiliation; only moderate power	Achievement and affiliation; low to moderate power
Beliefs	Distrustful nationalist, but high on cognitive complexity	Distrustful nationalist, but high on cognitive complexity
	Events only seen as partly controllable	Events seen as controllable
	Low-self-confidence	High self-confidence
Style	Tends to emphasize people rather than task	Tends to emphasize people and task
Operational code	Sees world as dangerous	Sees world as friendly
	Sets limited goals	Sets comprehensive goals
	Uses conflict	Uses politics (positive words) as well as conflict
Traits	Emotionally expressive	Emotionally expressive, in a calculated way
	Not anxious	Not anxious
	Vulnerable to depression, indecision	Not vulnerable to depression
	Sensitive to criticism	Sensitive to criticism
	Reacts with anger	Reacts by taking control of situation
	Impulsive	Somewhat impulsive
	Reasonably stable extravert	Stable extravert
Overall	*Integrator/mediator orientation (with secondary developmental/ improvement orientation)*	*Developmental/improvement orientation*

Predicting Political Outcomes

Cooperation Considering these portraits in the light of previous at-a-distance research on political leaders, we can characterize both Bush and Gorbachev as leaders who want to be *peacemakers, concerned with development and not prone to seek political ends through violence and war.* They are likely to pursue interdependent rather than independent foreign policies. This conclusion is supported by their motive profiles, their cognitions or beliefs, and their patterns of traits.

With respect to Gorbachev, this analysis supports the "cooperative" view put forward by Holloway (1989) and Legvold (1989), rather than the traditionalist interpretations by Nixon, Quayle, and others quoted at the beginning of this paper.

Much of the Bush presidential record supports a similarly cooperative view. An apparent exception, such as the December 1989 invasion of Panama, would on this interpretation be understood as an expression of Bush's impulsivity rather than any enduring desire for power and conquest. Actually, the whole sequence of Bush's inaction during the October 1989 attempted coup in Panama and his invasion two months later may reflect his alternating tendencies toward passive drift and impulsive action. Our results are also consistent with phrases used by Duffy (1989, pp. 16, 22) to describe Bush's style: "very loyal to people, more than to ideas" and "reactive" (high affiliation motive); "gambles . . . only after carefully researching the odds," "lack of ideological conviction," and "regards almost anything . . . as negotiable" (high achievement motive); and "working his will among fellow [leaders] rather than through appeals to public opinion" (high affiliation motive, only moderate power motive).

Negotiation   Given this predisposition toward cooperation, what will happen when Bush and Gorbachev actually negotiate with each other? Of course, high-level negotiations are carefully orchestrated by policy planning staffs, with only limited scope for any effects of leaders' personalities. Nevertheless, it is interesting to extrapolate from several laboratory studies of motivation and negotiation behavior (see Schnackers and Kleinbeck, 1975; Terhune, 1968a,b) in order to estimate what these limited, marginal effects might be.

Under almost all bargaining conditions, achievement-motivated people are consistently the most cooperative negotiators. In international-relations simulation games, they have the highest ratio of cooperative acts to conflict acts. They are low in "military effort"; and while they may lie in simulation game "newspapers," they are likely to tell the truth in direct messages. These tendencies would be reinforced by their overall "developmental" orientations. (Power-motivated people, in contrast, are the most exploitative and conflict-prone.) Extrapolating (perhaps excessively) from these laboratory studies, then, we may expect that *Bush and Gorbachev will be predisposed by their personality dispositions toward cooperative negotiations for mutual advantage and toward maximizing joint outcomes.* Affiliation motivation, on the other hand, plays a much more variable role in negotiation, depending on the degree of threat in the "payoff matrix" and the perceived similarity of the counterplayer. Under low threat, and when surrounding others are similar in attitude and friendly in style (i.e., "friends"), affiliation-motivated people are genuinely warm and cooperative. Under higher threat, or when faced with strangers or dissimilar, unfriendly others ("enemies"), they can become suspicious and defensive, perhaps reflecting their fear of rejection, as well as their nationalistic distrust and sensitivity to criticism.

Achievement and affiliation-motivated negotiators tend to articulate "strategic" and "mutual" reasons (rather than "greed") for their choices. They tend to view their partner as a "cooperator" or "fellow worker" rather than a "competitor," "yielder," or "gambler"—but with also occasional negative overtones of "opportunist."

Finally, their overall orientations of developmental (Gorbachev) and mediator (Bush) seem almost perfect foils for each other: Bush seeks a broader consensus; Gorbachev is willing to give that consensus in exchange for developmental help.

Change and Reform   Both leaders are faced with rapidly changing international and (for Gorbachev especially) domestic situations, creating a need for reforms and new policies. Their high achievement motive scores suggest both an opportunity and a possible problem. First, the evidence from laboratory and field studies suggests that people high in achievement motivation are more *likely to change policies that are not working.* For example, achievement-motivated people are more likely to pick up new information and, as a result, to modify their performance on the basis of results [Sinha and Mehta (1972); see also the general discussion in McClelland (1961, pp. 231–233, and 1985, pp. 237–238, 247–249)]. An earlier political example would be the dramatic changes introduced by achievement-motivated Richard Nixon in American foreign policy (the opening to China and detente with the Soviet Union) and domestic policy (the "New Economic Policy" of 1971). This *capacity for conceptual breakthrough* seems evident in Gorbachev's words and deeds since 1985.

Among 20th-century American presidents, however, achievement motivation is significantly correlated with Barber's (1977) classification of "active-negative"[6]— that is, showing *under stress a self-defeating "rigidification"* or reluctance to give up an obviously failing policy. Barber's examples include Wilson, Hoover, Johnson, and Nixon, each of whom scored high in achievement motivation. Jimmy Carter, also high in achievement motivation, showed a similar pattern of rigidification and "malaise." These five leaders certainly did not lack the capacity for vision—that is, the ability to size up situations and forecast consequences.

Yet if these five leaders had the vision associated with achievement motivation, why did they sometimes ignore the gathering signs of failure, rigidly pursuing discredited policies? I suggest that their rigidity can be explained by their *sense of limited control over policy implementation.* Actual policy change involves the political process: compromising on a "less-than-the-best" alternative (in Simon's terms, "satisficing" rather than "optimizing"); repeated negotiating to secure approval from diffuse and decentralized groups; and delegating authority to people of doubtful competence, whom one did not choose and may not trust. Taken together, these steps all reflect the leader's limited control over policy implementation.

To leaders high in achievement motivation but low in power motivation, such lack of personal control over the achievement process would be aversive because they naturally tend to assume personal responsibility for outcomes.[7] To preserve a sense of personal control over outcomes, therefore, they may do one of three things: (1) make demagogic appeals to "the people" over the heads of "the politicians" (as did Wilson), (2) take ethical shortcuts (as did Nixon), or (3) become too deeply involved in minor details or "micromanaging" (as did Carter). Their perspective becomes foreshortened, their frustration mounts, and they become trapped. On the basis of their motive scores, the *problems of frustration and the temptations to popular demagoguery, shortcuts or micromanagement* might be potential problems for Bush and Gorbachev.

Political visions, once articulated, can only be achieved through the political process, success at which is likely to call for power motivation. To a power-motivated leader, building alliances through compromise, negotiating, calculating support, and careful monitoring of delegated authority are the very stuff of power— pleasures in themselves rather than painful distractions from a larger vision. If leaders scoring low or average in power motivation cannot be expected to enjoy these necessary functions, perhaps they can delegate them to a more power-motivated lieutenant. In that case, it becomes important to assess the motives of those around Bush and Gorbachev—people such as James Baker and Aleksandr Yakovlev, whom Legvold has termed "Gorbachev's alter ego" (1989, p. 85).

Another part of the political process involves articulating a political vision to the people. Initially, this involves arousing popular enthusiasm. But no vision is achieved overnight; and so leaders must sustain popular energy, bridging the inevitable times of deprivation and difficulty with continued commitment and sacrifice. These are the situations that call for charismatic leaders—Franklin Roosevelt and Churchill are vivid historical examples—whose high power motives lead them to seek impact on others, as part of "expansionist" or "influential" orientations (see Table 24.2).

Considering the situations and leadership orientations of Bush and Gorbachev, then, we might speculate that any serious future erosion of consensus, or continuing difficulty and failure of development goals, could set the conditions for the emergence of alternative, power-motivated leaders who are better able to articulate (in Bush's words) "the vision thing" and thereby arouse popular enthusiasm and kindle popular energy. In history, the danger of charisma is that enthusiasm, once aroused, often overflows its visionary channels and spills over into aggression toward others.

Policy Implications

Perhaps it is always important to structure negotiations so that both parties like each other. *In negotiations between two affiliation-motivated leaders (each prone to distrust and nationalism), however, it becomes especially critical to insure that initial impressions are favorable:* (1) that the other is perceived as similar, and (2) that agreements on minor matters be used to build the impression of broader underlying agreement that will generate further momentum. For this reason it is probably wise to proceed slowly and cautiously. On each side, the reason for caution is not so much the question of whether the other side is "really" trustworthy, but rather whether they will be *perceived* as trustworthy. Ironically, these policy prescriptions for affiliation-motivated leaders in negotiation are aptly reflected in the advisory words of Richard Nixon—another leader very high in the affiliation motive, and known for being prickly and defensive in the presence of his "enemies"—whose doubts about Gorbachev were quoted at the beginning of this paper:

> The people of the United States and the people of the Soviet Union can be friends. *Because of our profound differences, the governments of our two nations cannot be friends.* . . . Gorbachev's historic challenge is to implement reforms that will *remove those differences* (1989, p. 219, emphasis added).

Given the importance of these symbolic first steps, and the constant mutual potential for prickly defensiveness, some early 1989 exchanges in the U.S.-Soviet dialogue seem unfortunate. In May, for example, defense secretary Cheney predicted, on television, that Gorbachev "would ultimately fail; that is to say, that he will not be able to reform the Soviet economy. . . . And when that happens, he's likely to be replaced by somebody who will be far more hostile. . . ." ("Rethinking a gloomy view,"

1989). Two weeks later, presidential spokesperson Fitzwater described a Gorbachev weapons reduction proposal as "throwing out, in a kind of drugstore cowboy fashion, one arms control proposal after another" (Hoffman, 1989, p. A30).

On the other hand, an incident from the 1989 Malta summit meeting illustrates a more positive way of dealing with sensitivities of this sort (see Maynes, 1990). On the first day of the summit, Gorbachev complained about Bush's repeated statements that changes within the Soviet Union represented an acceptance of "western" democratic values. Democracy, Gorbachev argued, is a "universal" value; Bush's use of "western" had overtones that were humiliating both to himself and to the Soviet people. Bush replied that he had never thought about this; since that time, he has omitted the adjective "western" when speaking of "democratic values."

Since both leaders have the capacity for conceptualizing and articulating change, but also have possible problems with implementing that change, each leader would do well to cultivate implementation "back-up," in the form of associates whose power motivation would enable them to enjoy the political process in its own terms and for its own sake. Ideally, these associates should be immune from distrustful nationalism, be deliberative instead of impulsive, and be decisive (for Bush) and creative (for Gorbachev).

SUMMARY

Based on previous research with other political leaders and laboratory studies of ordinary people, there is reason to be optimistic about the impact of the personalities of Bush and Gorbachev on world peace and international cooperation, at least between the superpowers. Their motives seem benign. Their political orientations seem complementary—almost ideally so. To get the reconciliation, integration and wider consensus that he seeks, Bush seems willing to give the development help that Gorbachev wants and needs. Their beliefs and operational codes are largely compatible, with any problems (such as nationalism, or a low sense that events are controllable) being overcome by their traits and cognitive and interpersonal styles.

The biggest problem for both leaders is likely to be a sense of frustration and possible malaise if new ideas, structural reforms, and emerging reconciliations become bogged down in the mire of political opposition. Given the situation of the Soviet economy and nationalities, these are likely to be especially acute problems for Gorbachev, although long-term United States economic vulnerabilities could pose the same problem for Bush. In those circumstances, their personalities could make them vulnerable to frustration and depression; in an extreme case, even to impulsive and inchoate violence. Moreover, their low power motivation, in combination with latent sensitivity and distrust, could jeopardize their continuation in office.

So far at least, the 1989 and 1990 summit meetings between Bush and Gorbachev support the analyses suggested in this paper, demonstrating that with a positive start and especially strong efforts to minimize the mutual sense of threat, negotiations can proceed cooperatively toward a new structure of superpower peace.

ACKNOWLEDGMENTS

This paper is based on two symposia in which all four authors participated: "Assessing the personality characteristics of the current presidential candidates," at the July 1988 annual meeting of the International Society of Political Psychology, and "How Gorbachev's personality shapes Soviet foreign policy behavior," at the March 1989 annual meeting of the International Studies Association.

NOTES

1. Parsons and Bales (1955) suggest that these two kinds of leaders reflect the even more basic distinction between "instrumental" and "expressive" functions.
2. We are grateful to David Schmitt (1990) for assembling this speech material, and to Janet E. Malley for scoring it. Malenkov, Andropov, and Chernenko were not included because they did not, as party leaders, give such a speech to a CPSU Congress. It is difficult to know whether Stalin's 1924 "Organizational Report," and even more, Lenin's 1918 "Political Report," can be properly compared with the later reports, which were given in a much different organizational setting and political climate. For standardization purposes, however, they were included because it was desirable to use as large a sample as possible.
3. One final source of data can be used to estimate Gorbachev's motive profile. His December 7, 1988, speech to the United Nations, when compared with the average of John F. Kennedy's two United Nations addresses, shows similar achievement and affiliation motivation levels, and a much lower power motive. Compared with other American presidents, Kennedy's Inaugural Address was about average in achievement and very high in affiliation and power (see Winter, 1987). Assuming that Kennedy's UN speeches were really similar to his inaugural (for which we have standardized scores), this would at least suggest that Gorbachev is relatively high in affiliation and low in power.
4. These comparisons were made using Bush's inaugural scores and Gorbachev's interview scores ("IA" and "SS," respectively, in Table IV).
5. Tetlock and Boettger (1989) found that Gorbachev scores high on a different but related measure of integrative complexity. Tetlock also found (personal communication) that Bush scored low during his vice-presidential years, but has increased to moderate as president.
6. Barber (1977) argues the reverse: that active-negative presidents are power-driven, while active-positives want to achieve. Since his analysis refers to manifest actions and results, rather than to latent motives, there is no necessary conflict with the present results. In addition, Barber's use of "achievement" and "power" motives is probably different from the scoring definitions.
7. To illustrate: In response to the disarmingly simple question, "Why not the best?" that Jimmy Carter used as the title of his campaign autobiography, a seasoned politician can suggest several "realpolitik" answers: (1) because members of Congress, foreign leaders, and others with veto power may have different ideas about what *is* "best;" (2) because "the best" might not benefit powerful constituencies; (3) because getting to "the best" may involve delays and detours—a "Pilgrim's Progress" through the quagmire of politics; (4) because "the best" costs too much; and (5) because reaching "the best" requires reliance on lower-level officials who are themselves far from being "the best."

REFERENCES

Adorno, T. W., Frenkel-Brunswik, E., Levinson, D. J., and Sanford, R. N. (1950). *The authoritarian personality.* New York: Harper.

Allport, G. W. (1961). *Pattern and growth in personality.* New York: Holt, Rinehart, & Winston.

Atkinson, J. W. (Ed.). (1958). *Motives in fantasy, action, and society.* Princeton NJ: Van Nostrand.

Bales, R. F. (1958). Task roles and social roles in problem-solving groups. In E. E. Maccoby, T. M. Newcomb, and E. L. Hartley (Eds.), *Readings in social psychology* (3rd ed., pp. 437–447). New York: Holt, Rinehart, & Winston.

Barber, J. D. (1977). *Presidential character: Predicting performance in the White House.* 2nd ed. Englewood Cliffs, NJ: Prentice-Hall.

Bieri, J. (1961). Complexity-simplicity as a personality variable in cognitive and preferential behavior. In D. W. Fiske and S. R. Maddi (Eds.), *Functions of varied experience* (pp. 355–379). Homewood, IL: Dorsey.

Boyatzis, R. (1973). Affiliation motivation. In D. C. McClelland & R. S. Steele (Eds.), *Human motivation* (pp. 252–276). Morristown, NJ: General Learning Press.

Brown, R. W. (1965). *Social psychology.* New York: Free Press.

Byars, R. S. (1973). Small-group theory and shifting styles of political leadership. *Comparative Political Studies, 5,* 443–469.

Charen, M. (1990, February 13). Gorbachev is on power trip. *Ann Arbor News,* p. All.

Dionne, E. J., Jr. (1989, May 14). Conservatives find Bush troubling. *New York Times,* section I, p. 24.

Duffy, M. (1989, August 21). Mr. Consensus. *Time,* 134, 16–22.

Eysenck, H. J., and Eysenck, M. W. (1985). *Personality and individual differences: A natural science approach.* New York: Plenum.

Freud, A. (1946). *The ego and the mechanisms of defense.* New York: International Universities Press.

Freud, S. (1961–1963). *Introductory lectures on psychoanalysis.* In J. Strachey (Ed.), *Standard edition of the complete psychological works of Sigmund Freud* (Vols. 15, 16). London: Hogarth Press. (Original work published 1915–1917).

George, A. L. (1969). The "operational code:" A neglected approach to the study of political leaders and decision-making. *International Studies Quarterly* 13, 190–222.

Greenstein, F. I. (1969). *Personality and politics.* Chicago: Markham.

Hermann, M. G. (Ed.) (1977). *A psychological examination of political leaders.* New York: Free Press.

Hermann, M. G. (1980a). Assessing the personalities of Soviet Politburo members. *Personality and Social Psychology Bulletin,* 6, 332–352.

Hermann, M. G. (1980b). Explaining foreign policy behavior using the personal characteristics of political leaders. *International Studies Quarterly,* 24, 7–46.

Hermann, M. G. (1983). Assessing personality at a distance: A portrait of Ronald Reagan. *Mershon Center Quarterly Report,* 7(6). Columbus, OH: Mershon Center of the Ohio State University.

Hermann, M. G. (1987). Assessing the foreign policy role orientations of sub-Saharan African leaders. In S. G. Walker (Ed.), *Role theory and foreign policy analysis* (pp. 161–198). Durham, NC: Duke University Press.

Hermann, M. G. (1988). Syria's Hafez Al-Assad. In B. Kellerman and J. Rubin (Eds.), *Leadership and negotiation in the Middle East* (pp. 70–95). New York: Praeger.

Hermann, M. G. (1989, Spring). Defining the Bush presidential style. *Mershon Memo.* Columbus OH: Ohio State University.

Hoffman, D. (1989, May 17). Gorbachev's gambits challenged. *Washington Post,* p. A1, A30.

Holloway, D. (1989). Gorbachev's new thinking. *Foreign Affairs,* 68(1), 66–81.

Holsti, O. (1970). The "Operational Code" approach to the study of political Leaders: John Foster Dulles' philosophical and instrumental beliefs. *Canadian Journal of Political Science,* 3, 123–157.

Jervis, R. (1976). *Perception and misperception in international politics.* Princeton, NJ: Princeton University Press.

Jung, C. J. (1910). The association method. *American Journal of Psychology,* 21, 219–240.

Jung, C. J. (1971). *Psychological types.* In *The collected works of C. G. Jung* (Vol. 6). Princeton, NJ: Princeton University Press. (Original work published 1921)

Kelly, G. A. (1955). *A theory of personality.* New York: Norton.

Legvold, R. (1989). The revolution in Soviet foreign policy. *Foreign Affairs,* 68, 82–98.

Leites, N. (1951). *The operational code of the Politburo.* New York: McGraw-Hill.

McAdams, D. P. (1982). Intimacy motivation. In A. J. Stewart, (Ed.), *Motivation and society* (pp. 133–171). San Francisco: Jossey-Bass.

McClelland, D. C. (1961). *The achieving society.* Princeton, NJ: Van Nostrand.

Maynes, C. W. (1990). America without the Cold War. *Foreign Policy,* 78, 3–26.

Meloen, J. D., Hagendoorn, L., Raaijmakers, Q., and Visser, L. (1988). Authoritarianism and the revival of political racism: Reassessment in the Netherlands of the reliability and validity of the concept of authoritarianism by Adorno *et al. Political Psychology,* 9, 413–429.

Murray, H. A. (1938). *Explorations in personality.* New York: Oxford University Press.

Nixon, R. M. (1989). American foreign policy: The Bush agenda. *Foreign Affairs,* 68, 199–219.

Noonan, P. (1990). *Present at the revolution.* New York: Random House.

Norman, W. (1963). Toward an adequate taxonomy of personality attributes: Replicated factor structure in peer nomination personality ratings. *Journal of Abnormal and Social Psychology,* 60, 574–583.

Parsons, T., and Bales, R. F. (1955). *Family: Socialization and interaction process.* Glencoe, IL: Free Press.

Price, R. (1977). *With Nixon.* New York: Viking Press.

Quayle, J. D. (1989, June 9). Text of remarks by the Vice President at the Conference on Atlantic Community. Washington, DC: Office of the Vice President.

Rethinking a gloomy view on perestroika. (1989, May 2). *New York Times,* p. 1.

Rogers, C. R. (1959). A theory of therapy, personality, and interpersonal relationships, as developed in the client-centered framework. In S. Koch (Ed.), *Psychology: A study of a science,* Vol. 3. (pp. 184–256). New York: McGraw-Hill.

Rosenthal, A. M. (1990, September 21). The Gorbachev era ends. *New York Times,* p. A13.

Rotter, J. B. (1990). Internal versus external control of reinforcement: A case history of a variable. *American Psychologist,* 45, 489–493.

Safire, W. (1975). *Before the fall: An inside view of the pre-Watergate White House.* New York: Belmont Tower Books.

Safire, W. (1989, March 27). Taking the crabby view of the grinning Russkies. *New York Times,* section I, p. 17.

Schmitt, D. (1990, July). *Measuring the motives of Soviet leaders and Soviet society: Congruence created or congruence reflected?* Paper presented at the annual meeting of the International Society of Political Psychology, Washington, D.C.

Schnackers, U., and Kleinbeck, U. (1975). Machmotiv und machtthematisches Verhalten in einem Verhandlungsspiel [Power motivation and power-related behavior in a bargaining game]. *Archiv für Psychologie,* 127, 300–319.

Shulman, M. D. (1990, June 17). How well do we know this man? Review of D. Doder and L. Branson, *Gorbachev: Heretic in the Kremlin. New York Times Book Review,* p. 5.

Sinha, B. P., and Mehta, P. (1972). Farmers' need for achievement and change-proneness in acquisition of information from a farm telecast. *Rural Sociology,* 37, 417–427.

Strickland, B. (1977). Internal-external control of reinforcement. In T. Blass, (Ed.), *Personality variables in social behavior* (pp. 219–279). Hillsdale, NJ: Erlbaum.

Terhune, K. W. (1968a). Motives, situation, and interpersonal conflict within prisoners' dilemma. *Journal of Personality and Social Psychology Monograph Supplement,* 8, part 2.

Terhune, K. W. (1968b). Studies of motives, cooperation, and conflict within laboratory microcosms. *Buffalo Studies,* 4, 29–58.

Tetlock, P. E., and Boettger, R. (1989). Cognitive and rhetorical styles of traditionalist and reformist Soviet politicians: A content analysis study. *Political Psychology,* 10, 209–232.

Tucker, R. C. (1965). The dictator and totalitarianism. *World Politics,* 17, 55–83.

Walker, S. (1983). The motivational foundations of political belief systems: A re-analysis of the operational code construct. *International Studies Quarterly,* 27, 179–201.

Walker, S. (1986, July). *Woodrow Wilson's operational code.* Paper presented at the meeting of the International Society of Political Psychology, Amsterdam.

Walker, S. (1990). The evolution of operational code analysis. *Political Psychology,* 11, 403–418.

Weiner, B. (1980). *Human motivation.* New York: Holt, Rinehart and Winston.

Weintraub, W. (1981). *Verbal behavior: Adaptation and psychopathology.* New York: Springer.

Weintraub, W. (1986). Personality profiles of American presidents as revealed in their public statements: The presidential news conferences of Jimmy Carter and Ronald Reagan. *Political Psychology,* 7, 285–295.

Weintraub, W. (1989). *Verbal behavior in everyday life.* New York: Springer.

Winter, D. G. (1973). *The power motive.* New York: Free Press.

Winter, D. G. (1979). *Psychological characteristics of selected world leaders assessed at a distance.* Unpublished paper, Wesleyan University.

Winter, D. G. (1980). Measuring the motive patterns of southern Africa political leaders at a distance. *Political Psychology,* 2, 75–85.

Winter, D. G. (1987). Leader appeal, leader performance, and the motive profiles of leaders and followers: A study of American presidents and elections. *Journal of Personality and Social Psychology, 52*, 196–202.

Winter, D. G. (1988, July). What makes Jesse run? [Motives of the 1988 candidates]. *Psychology Today*, pp. 20 ff.

Winter, D. G. (1990). *Inventory of motive scores of persons, groups, and societies measured at a distance*, Ann Arbor: University of Michigan Department of Psychology.

Winter, D. G. (1991). Measuring personality at a distance: Development of an integrated system for scoring motives in running text. In A. J. Stewart, J. M. Healy, Jr., and D. J. Ozer, (Eds.), *Perspectives in personality: Approaches to understanding lives*. London: Jessica Kingsley.

Winter, D. G., and Carlson, L. (1988). Using motive scores in the psychobiographical study of an individual: The case of Richard Nixon. *Journal of Personality, 56*, 75–102.

Winter, D. G., and Stewart, A. J. (1977). Content analysis as a method of studying political leaders. In M. G. Hermann (Ed.). *A psychological examination of political leaders* (pp. 27–61). New York: Free Press.

Winter, D. G., and Stewart, A. J. (1978). The power motive. In H. London, and J. Exner (Eds.), *Dimensions of personality* (pp. 391–447). New York: Wiley.

Ziller, R. C., Stone, W. F., Jackson, R. M., and Terbovic, N. J. (1977). Self-other orientations and political behavior. In M. G. Hermann (Ed.), *A psychological examination of political leaders* (pp. 176–204). New York: Free Press.

Zullow, H. M., Oettingen, G., Peterson, C., and Seligman, M. E. P. (1988). Pessimistic explanatory style in the historical record: CAVing LBJ, presidential candidates, and East versus West Berlin. *American Psychologist, 43*, 673–682.

Escalation of the Vietnam War: How Could It Happen?

Irving L. Janis

All observers agree that a stable group of policy advisers met regularly with President Johnson to deliberate on what to do about the war in Vietnam. Fragmentary evidence now at hand gives some clues about how and why the group's policy of escalating the war was so assiduously pursued during the period from 1964 through

1967. The escalation decisions were made despite strong warnings from intelligence experts within the United States government, as well as from leaders of the United Nations, from practically all of America's allies, and from influential sectors of the American public. Even if the members of Johnson's advisory group were willing to pay a high price to attain their economic and political objectives in Vietnam, they apparently ignored until too late the mounting signs that their decisions to escalate the war were having devastating political repercussions within the United States and that these repercussions were threatening to destroy the president's chances of being reelected. Accounts in the Pentagon Papers about the group's meetings and private statements made by individual members expose what seem to be gross miscalculations and blatant symptoms of groupthink. The evidence now available is far from complete, and conclusions will have to be drawn quite tentatively. Nevertheless, it is worthwhile to grapple with the main questions that need to be answered to discover if the groupthink hypothesis applies to these recent, notoriously ill-conceived decisions.

WHAT NEEDS TO BE EXPLAINED?

More than a mere exercise in the psychological analysis of recent foreign policy decisions, showing how group dynamics may have influenced America's Vietnam policy may help us to understand how conscientious statesmen could ignore the impressive voices of so many reputable Americans concerning the immorality as well as the adverse political consequences of their military actions. Perhaps even more important, an analysis of the shared illusions of Johnson's inner circle may give us insights that help explain how such men could still the inner voices of their own consciences. As Ithiel Pool, one of the few American professors of political science who supported the Johnson administration's basic Vietnam policy, points out: "It is hard to understand how intelligent men could believe that aerial bombardment, harassment and interdiction artillery fire, defoliation, and population displacement could be effective means to win a population, or how moral men could believe them appropriate means of action among the population we are defending." After all, the policy makers in the Johnson administration were sincere democrats who prided themselves on their humanitarian outlook. How could they justify their decisions to authorize search-and-destroy missions, fire-free zones, and the use of "whatever violent means are necessary to destroy the enemy's sanctuaries"—all of which set the stage, the normative background, for the Mylai massacre and other acts of violence by the United States military forces against Vietnamese villagers?

The most thorough analysis of the Johnson administration's Vietnam War decisions is in the Department of Defense's study known as the Pentagon Papers, which was declassified and published in twelve volumes by the United States government in 1971, after *The New York Times* and other newspapers had revealed the main contents to the American public. In restrained but unambiguous terms, the historians and political analysts who prepared this secret study call attention time and again to the poor quality of the decision-making procedures used by the policy makers who met regularly with President Johnson. They emphasize in particular the group's failure to canvass the full range of alternative courses of action and their superficial assessment of the pros and cons of the military recommendations under consideration during 1964 and 1965. For example, at a major strategy meeting on September 7, 1964, according to the Department of Defense analysts, "a rather narrow range of proposals was up for consideration." Neil Sheehan, in *The New York Times* book on the Pentagon Papers, adds that "the study indicates no effort on the part of the President and his most trusted advisers to reshape their policy along the lines of . . . [the] analysis" prepared jointly by experts from the three leading intelligence agencies of the government toward the end of 1964. According to that analysis, bombing North Vietnam had little chance of breaking the will of Hanoi. The vital decision made on February 13, 1965, to launch the previously planned air strikes against North Vietnam, the Defense Department study states, "seems to have resulted *as much from the lack of alternative proposals as from any compelling logic in their favor.*"

After leaving the government, Bill Moyers, an articulate member of Johnson's in-group, admitted: "With but rare exceptions we always seemed to be calculating the short-term consequences of each alternative at every step of the [policy-making] process, but not the long-term consequences. And with each succeeding short-range consequence we became more deeply a prisoner of the process."

Who were the prisoners and why couldn't they escape?

PRESIDENT JOHNSON'S INNER CIRCLE

During the Johnson administration the major Vietnam decisions were made by a small inner circle of government officials, most of whom remained for a few years and then were replaced, one at a time. In addition to the president, the in-group included special White House assistant McGeorge Bundy (later replaced by Walt Rostow), Secretary of Defense Robert McNamara (replaced during the last year of the Johnson administration by Clark Clifford), and Secretary of State Dean Rusk (who managed to remain in Johnson's advisory group from the bitter beginning to the bitter end). For several years press secretary Bill Moyers and Undersecretary of State George Ball also participated in the meetings. The group also included General Earl Wheeler, chairman of the Joint Chiefs of Staff from 1964 on, and Richard Helms, director of the Central Intelligence Agency from 1966 on.

President Johnson consulted this small group on all major policy decisions concerning the Vietnam War. Although most individual members of the inner circle were replaced before the Johnson administration came to an end, "its work was distinctively continuous because new men joined it only infrequently and always one at a time." The members sometimes called themselves "the Tuesday lunch group," and others have referred to the group as "the Tuesday cabinet." At their Tuesday noon meetings, the members deliberated about the next steps to be taken in the Vietnam War and often dealt with purely military matters, such as the targets in North Vietnam to be bombed next.

Before discussing symptoms of groupthink, we must consider whether Johnson's inner circle was unified by bonds of mutual friendship and loyalty, an essential precondition for the emergence of the groupthink syndrome. Some journalists depict Lyndon B. Johnson as an extraordinarily aggressive and insensitive leader, who made such excessive and humiliating demands on everyone who came in frequent contact with him that he was cordially disliked, if not hated. With these alleged attributes in mind, we are led to wonder if perhaps the apparent unity of Johnson's inner circle was simply superficial conformity and polite deference out of a sense of expediency, with each member inwardly feeling quite detached from the leader and perhaps from the group as a whole. But if this were the case, it was not detected by Chester Cooper, J. Townsend Hoopes, Bill Moyers, James Thomson, Jr., and other observers in the Johnson administration who were in contact with members of the inner circle. Rather, the picture we get from those who observed from close at hand is that the group was highly cohesive.

Most explicit on this point is Henry Graff, who had the opportunity to conduct private interviews with President Johnson and with each of his principal advisers on four different occasions between mid-1965 and the end of 1968. Graff was repeatedly impressed by what appeared to him to be genuine friendship and mutual support among the members of the Tuesday cabinet, which he felt characterized the group up until early 1968. Later in 1968 he noted a tone of querulousness in the comments the men made about the mounting barrage of criticisms directed against Johnson's war policy, as the increasingly obvious signs of its failure began to take their toll. But before that final phase, according to Graff:

> The men of the Tuesday cabinet were loyal to each other, with a devotion compounded of mutual respect and common adversity. They soon learned, as all congenial committeemen learn, to listen selectively and to talk harmoniously even when in disagreement. Familiarity with one another's minds became an asset as well as a handicap in the years they conferred and labored. And their facility with words (laced with the Pentagonese all spoke so fluently) made the sessions memorable for the participants week in and week out.

Even in early 1968, when outstanding officials like Deputy Secretary of Defense Paul Nitze were submitting their resignations and it was hard to avoid bickering within the inner circle about whether the Vietnam War policy could be salvaged, Graff was still impressed by the "loyalty with which the men around the President defended him and the decisions they had helped him reach, regardless of any private misgivings they may have increasingly entertained." During the preceding year or two, as the members "felt increasingly beleaguered," Graff surmises, "they turned toward one another for reassurance" and became "natural friends" of their chief. He adds that the Tuesday cabinet exerted an extraordinarily powerful influence over its leader, perhaps more than any other presidential advisory group in American history.

Bill Moyers, from his personal observation as a member of Johnson's inner circle, has corroborated Graff's conclusion that the group was highly cohesive. Directly in line with the groupthink hypothesis, Moyers mentions the concurrence-seeking tendency of the members as part of his explanation for the lack of critical debate about Vietnam War policies:

> one of the significant problems in the Kennedy and Johnson administrations was that the men who handled national security affairs became too close, too personally fond of each other. They tended to conduct the affairs of state almost as if they were a gentle-

men's club, and the great decisions were often made in that warm camaraderie of a small board of directors deciding what the club's dues are going to be for the members next year. . . . So you often dance around the final hard decision which would set you against . . . men who are very close to you, and you tend to reach a consensus.

DANIEL ELLSBERG'S CRITIQUE OF THE "QUAGMIRE MYTH"

The points just discussed lead one to suspect that groupthink was one of the causes of the Vietnam War fiascoes perpetrated by the Johnson administration. But there are, of course, other ways of interpreting the available observations, including some that provide an explanation solely in terms of political considerations. An extreme position of this type is taken by political analyst Daniel Ellsberg. In June 1971 he turned over to *The New York Times* and other newspapers the secret Pentagon Papers, which stunned the nation. Only a few weeks before Ellsberg had published a scholarly article in which he presented his own opinions on the causes of the Vietnam War, based on his study of the secret documents.

Ellsberg challenges what he calls the "quagmire myth," which depicts the American presidents and their advisers as stumbling into the Vietnam War during the 1950s and 1960s by taking one little step after another, without being aware of the deep quicksand lying ahead. Ellsberg denies that United States escalation decisions stemmed from unrealistic presidential hopes or failures to foresee the consequences. Each major escalation decision by President Johnson and his predecessors, he claims, was made with full awareness that either larger military steps would almost certainly have to be taken or else retreat and a Communist victory would have to be accepted. American policy makers, according to Ellsberg, regarded the measures taken not as "last steps" but rather as "holding actions, adequate to avoid defeat in the short run but long shots so far as ultimate success was concerned." Their essential purpose was to "buy time," to postpone defeat in Vietnam, with all its accompanying "political and personal consequences of charges of 'softness on Communism.'" In brief, America's Vietnam policy was largely determined by one fundamental political rule; "This is not a good year for this administration to lose Vietnam to communism." Every year there were important programs to push through Congress, and congressional elections were always coming up within a year or so, even if presidential elections were not close at hand.

The power of this fundamental rule, Ellsberg claims, derived from a mixture of motives originating primarily from deeply ingrained memories of the defeatist charges to which the Truman administration had been subjected by Senator Joseph McCarthy and other right-wing Republicans after General MacArthur was removed from command during the Korean War stalemate. Those right-wingers had "tattooed on the skins of politicians and bureaucrats alike some vivid impressions of what could happen to a liberal administration that chanced to be in office the day a red flag rose over Saigon."

Ellsberg adds that a subsidiary rule (another legacy of the humiliations of the Korean War) was also in the minds of the policy makers: Avoid committing United

States ground troops to a land war in Asia. This second rule, he believes, accounts for the policy makers' reluctance to use truly powerful military means against the North Vietnamese except in a dire crisis to avert defeat.

All the main escalation decisions, in Ellsberg's view, were made in periods of deep pessimism and were intended only to restore the stalemate in order to postpone a possible Communist victory. In each instance the president and his principal advisers allegedly knew what the costs would be and were willing to pay them, even though in their public statements they were saying that only one more small step was needed for victory.

Ellsberg claims that his explanation accounts for all the Vietnam War decisions made by five presidents—Truman, Eisenhower, Kennedy, Johnson, and Nixon. It certainly has the aesthetic beauty of supplying a relatively simple formula to explain the United States government's sorry record of involvement in Vietnam over a period of more than twenty years. But how well does it fit the available evidence?

Although Ellsberg argues that the policy makers were generally quite realistic, he admits that there are some sticky facts concerning "buoyant hopes" during the Johnson administration: "When U.S. combat units flooded into Vietnam from 1965 on, the pessimism of later 1964 gave way increasingly to buoyant hopes, by 1967, of an essentially military victory." Moreover, in essential agreement with the observations reported by James Thomson, Jr., and other "insiders" in the Johnson administration, Ellsberg says that yes, there was a great deal of "self-deception," "inadvertance," "inattention," "lack of realistic planning," "over-ambitious aims for means used," and "over-optimistic expectations." He acknowledges that all these "flaws and limitations increasingly do characterize the executive decision-making process." But Ellsberg tries to explain away all the overoptimism as the consequence of implementing the chosen policy: The deception of Congress and the public gave rise to a tendency for the policy makers' expectations gradually to "drift in the direction of the public optimism expressed constantly from the outset . . . eventually replacing phony and invalid optimism with genuine invalid optimism."

Thus, Ellsberg leaves open the possibility that President Johnson and his advisers were making miscalculations about their Vietnam policies as a result of wishful thinking during 1967 and perhaps before that, "from 1965 on." In addition he suggests that when all the major escalation decisions were made, well before 1967, the policy makers' adherence to the fundamental rule may itself have been based on a miscalculation concerning political reaction in the United States to the alternative policy of withdrawal from Vietnam: "Fear of . . . McCarthyism's power at the polls may always have been *overdrawn*. . . . Yet, what matters, of course, is what . . . officials *believe* their risks to be."

Ellsberg mentions some observations suggesting that during 1965 the fundamental rule, whether based on miscalculations or not, was used as a kind of slogan and that social pressure was put on the president to act in accordance with the slogan in a way that would deflect attention away from other serious risks:

> In the spring of 1965 President Johnson is reported to have received calls almost daily from one of his closest advisers telling him (what no one had to tell him): "Lyndon, don't be the first American President to lose a war." It is true that such advisers omitted warnings of other deadly errors.

Ellsberg adds that Johnson's advisers neglected to call his attention to the dangers of bypassing Congress, of allowing official military statements that describe the enemy forces as defeated to be issued during a lull in the fighting when those forces were readying for a major offensive, and of accepting recommendations from the Pentagon to "draft and spend and kill and suffer casualties at the rate . . . [the] military will propose."

In short, this portion of Ellsberg's account of what was going on in 1965 does not offer such convincing arguments in support of his purely political explanation that an explanation based on the groupthink hypothesis should be discarded. In contrast to more global statements he makes elsewhere in his paper, these passages certainly do not preclude the possibility that the members of Johnson's advisory group were collectively overlooking or remaining silent about some of the most unfavorable consequences of their policy recommendations.

A "COLOSSAL MISJUDGMENT" AND SUBSEQUENT MISCALCULATIONS

As for the alleged "pessimism of later 1964," the available evidence does not show an impressive degree of fit with Ellsberg's hypothesis that the president and his advisers had a realistic view of what their escalation decisions would accomplish. When we look into the Pentagon Papers, we find that the conferees sometimes did talk about the possibility that the war might last for years, but we also find a number of direct contradictions of Ellsberg's statement that unrealistic hopes were not a prominent factor in the major escalation decisions of late 1964 and early 1965. These decisions involved accepting a military plan, known as Operation Rolling Thunder, to launch massive air attacks against North Vietnam. According to the Department of Defense study, the original purpose of the plan was "to break the will of North Vietnam." The Department of Defense study also asserts: "The idea that destroying, or threatening to destroy, North Vietnam's industry would pressure Hanoi into calling it quits, seems, in retrospect, a *colossal misjudgment.*" In the spring of 1965, when the air assaults were started, according to the study, "official hopes were high that the Rolling Thunder program . . . would rapidly convince Hanoi that it should agree to negotiate a settlement to the war in the South. After a month of bombing with no response from the North Vietnamese, optimism began to wane."

According to the Pentagon Papers, the escalation of the air war was planned secretly during the election campaign in the fall of 1964. The decision to authorize the first phase of the plan was made one month *after* Johnson's election victory; the decision to authorize the second phase was made only about two months later. In this period the administration did not need to be very concerned about the prospects of defeat of its program in Congress, and the next election was a long way off. The landslide victory itself must have shown the astute political minds in Washington that the failure of Goldwater's aggressive anticommunist campaign meant that at least for the time being there was little realistic basis for worry about the power of the right-wing Republicans to mobilize public support. Yet precisely during the months when the election victory was still fresh in mind, President Johnson and his advisers made the major decisions to authorize the Rolling Thunder program.

Tom Wicker, *New York Times* associate editor and columnist, reports that he was informed by several officials close to the president in 1964 that the same type of elated self-confidence that had pervaded the thinking of Kennedy's ingroup prior to the Bay of Pigs fiasco was reexperienced following the 1964 election victory, at the time Johnson and his advisers committed themselves to escalating the air war in Vietnam:

> Several officials who were close to Johnson at that time . . . recall the sheer *ebullience* of the moment. One of them had also served Kennedy and remembers the same *sense of omnipotence* in the White House in early 1961. . . . [He said,] *"We thought we had the golden touch. It was just like that with Johnson after sixty-four."*

These observations, if accurate, suggest that when Johnson and his principal advisers were deliberating about the escalation decisions, they shared a staunch faith that somehow everything would come out right despite all the gloomy predictions in the intelligence reports prepared by their underlings.

By the summer of 1965 the complete failure of the air war could not be denied, especially when the Vietcong successfully carried out a major offensive and took over large amounts of territory in South Vietnam. Washington began to receive urgent requests from General Westmoreland, the United States military commander in Vietnam, for more and more ground troops. At the end of July, when the decision was made to approve a huge increase in ground forces, Washington officials had become extremely pessimistic, just as Ellsberg says. They realized the war would be long and hard and would require even more troops in the future. But even so, the conferees' intentions and expectations, described in the Pentagon Papers, only partially corresponded to the pattern described by Ellsberg. True, "the major participants in the decision . . . *understood* the consequences." But we are also told that the choice as they saw it

> was *not* whether to hold on for a while or let go—the choice was viewed as *winning* or losing South Vietnam. . . .
> Instead of simply denying the enemy victory and convincing him that he would not win, the thrust became *defeating* the enemy in the South.

The Department of Defense study suggests that when the decision was made to increase American forces in 1965, perhaps "no one really foresaw what the troop needs in Vietnam would be," and the enemy forces may have been "consistently underrated." This could hardly be called an instance in which the decision makers definitely foresaw the consequences.

All during the summer and fall of 1965 the air war against North Vietnam was continued. But because Operation Rolling Thunder was not achieving its original purpose of breaking the will of the North Vietnamese, its purpose was redefined. The new objective of the operation was to reduce the flow of men and supplies from the north. This change for the first time brought the policy makers' internal rationale into line with the alleged purpose that had been told to Congress and to the public during the preceding months. In deciding to continue the Rolling Thunder program to attain this much more modest objective, however, the Washington officials were making still another misjudgment. The Pentagon Papers quote a Department of Defense document dated January 18, 1966, that states: "The program [Rolling Thunder] so far has not successfully interdicted infiltration of men and material into South Vietnam."

Here again, as in the case of the decision to increase ground troops, we see that a decision made when the policy makers were gloomy is not necessarily free of miscalculations. In general the mere fact that conferees find themselves in a crisis and realize they are facing the possibility of defeat does not preclude a strong element of wishful thinking and even a strong dose of overoptimism about limited hopes such as escaping with their skins intact, successfully postponing defeat indefinitely, and holding out long enough for a lucky break to turn the tide in their favor.

A major part of Ellsberg's argument about the lack of a sizable gap between expectations and reality hinges on the fact that when the major escalation decisions were made, reports from intelligence experts in the CIA, the State Department, and the Defense Department showed a "persistent skepticism . . . about proposals for improving [the long-run prospects of anti-Communist forces] . . . a pessimism almost unrelieved, often stark—yet in retrospect, credibly realistic, frank, cogent." The Pentagon Papers bear out Ellsberg's contention that the policy makers were aware of at least some of the pessimistic estimates contained in these reports. But there is no evidence to show that President Johnson and his principal advisers personally accepted the invariably pessimistic estimates in the intelligence reports or took seriously the likelihood that further major escalations of the type outlined in the contingency plans prepared by assistant secretaries and other lower-echelon officials would actually be needed. The Pentagon Papers indicate that on some important occasions the dire forecasts were simply ignored. In the late fall of 1964, for example, the high hopes of President Johnson and his principal advisers that Operation Rolling Thunder would break the will of North Vietnam were evidently not diminished by the fact that the entire intelligence community, according to the Department of Defense study, "tended toward a pessimistic view." About a year and a half later the CIA repeatedly estimated that stepping up the bombing of North Vietnam's oil-storage facilities would not "cripple Communist military operations," and the policy makers were aware of this prediction. Instead of accepting it, however, they apparently accepted the optimistic estimates from the Pentagon, which asserted that the bombing would "bring the enemy to the conference table or cause the insurgency to wither from lack of support." Thus the Pentagon Papers do not support Ellsberg's contention but instead corroborate statements of the inside observers who say that President Johnson and his inner circle of advisers paid little attention to the pessimistic forecasts from experts in the government's intelligence agencies.

The cogency and validity of Ellsberg's explanation remain an open question. The evidence shows that even if his main arguments against the quagmire myth are subsequently verified by fresh evidence about the deliberations of the policy makers, his analysis of the major escalation decisions made by the Johnson administration still leaves open the possibility that the President's advisory group made serious miscalculations and that the errors arose from group pressures of the type postulated by the groupthink hypothesis. Ellsberg's impressive case that the policy makers gave high priority to the decision rule "this is not the year to allow a red flag to rise over Saigon" may prove to be well substantiated, but the evidence may also show that Johnson's inner circle used this rule in just the way that a group suffering from groupthink uses any shared ideological slogan or stereotype. Furthermore, Ellsberg's own critique of the quagmire myth presents a number of observations and inferences concerning errors of judgment, overoptimism, and wishful thinking that are essentially the same as those contained in reports made by inside observers who were located in the White House (James Thomson and Bill Moyers), in the Department of Defense (Townsend Hoopes), and in the State Department (Chester Cooper) during the Johnson administration. Nevertheless, the challenge posed by Ellsberg's analysis highlights the need to postpone drawing any definitive conclusions until we have further evidence about what the members of the policy-making group believed and what they said to each other when they were deliberating about their escalation decisions.

MAJOR SOURCES OF ERROR

James Thomson, Jr., a historian who was a member of McGeorge Bundy's staff in the White House, has attempted to explain the poor quality of the escalation decisions, which he calls "Lyndon Johnson's slow-motion Bay of Pigs." He addresses himself to the paradox that although the members of the policy-making group had all the attributes of well-qualified and well-intentioned leaders—sound training, high ability, and humanitarian ideals—they persistently ignored the major consequences of practically all their Vietnam War policy decisions. They repeatedly gave in to pressures for a military rather than a diplomatic or political solution; they took little account of the destructive impact of their policies on the Vietnamese people, whom they were supposedly helping; they badly bungled or sabotaged every opportunity to negotiate disengagement of the United States from Vietnam. What could cause a group of responsible policy makers to persist in a course of action that was producing so much suffering to the people of Vietnam and so much havoc within their own nation?

In attempting to answer this question, Thomson discusses a large number of causal factors. Some are historical and political considerations, such as institutional constraints in the State Department against sponsoring policies that could be construed as "soft on communism" in the Far East; these were the legacy of America's Asia policy of the 1950s. Thomson also points out that the policy advisory group was insulated from political expertise in the government, and as the Vietnam decisions progressively involved more and more military force, it was essential for the policy makers to consult more and more with military experts, who almost always proposed escalating the war. Still, being exposed to strong pressures from the military establishment should not necessarily cause high-level civilians who preside over their country's foreign policy to move consistently in the direction of military escalation. Surely hardheaded policy makers in the Johnson administration could raise critical questions, insist on full political briefings, assess the unfortunate consequences of military escalation, and work out alternative ways of settling the problems of United States involvement in Vietnam.

What happened to the critical evaluators, the doubters, the dissenters? Thomson answers this crucial question, again on the basis of his personal observations and experiences within the White House, by citing a number of psychological factors that he believes influenced decision making by the group of men who shaped America's Vietnam policy. He lists about two dozen specific factors, which can be classified into six major categories: (1) excessive time pressures, (2) bureaucratic detachment, (3) stereotyped views of Communists and Orientals, (4) overcommitment to defeating the enemy, (5) domestication of dissenters, and (6) avoidance of opposing views. I shall try to show how Thomson's seemingly diverse points may be brought together into a single psychological explanation by giving an interpretation in terms of the groupthink hypothesis.

APPLYING THE GROUPTHINK HYPOTHESIS

Because we do not yet have well-authenticated details of the way the president and his inner circle carried out their policy deliberations from 1964 to 1968, the available observations must be used mainly to point up the new questions that need to be answered in order to determine whether the groupthink hypothesis offers at least a partial explanation of the ill-fated escalation decisions made by the Johnson administration. Thomson's account of the defective ways Johnson's in-group arrived at its Vietnam policy decisions are fairly well corroborated by other inside observers (Cooper, Hoopes, and Moyers) and hint at small-group processes. But neither Thomson nor any other observer explicitly discusses any aspect of group dynamics (except for the few sentences quoted from Bill Moyers concerning the group's tendency to seek consensus instead of debating the issues). Thomson confines his discussion to two different types of causes, both of which may have played an important role in the Vietnam escalation policy. One type involves the sociological features of the large organization—the social patterns and pressures that arise in a government bureaucracy. The other type pertains to individual psychology, focusing on the way the individual decision maker reacts to the tasks and pressures imposed upon him. Do these two types of causal factors tell the whole story?

The groupthink hypothesis, when added to the sociological and the individual psychological factors, may contribute a more complete explanation and may help us understand how and why the various patterns of behavior described by Thomson became dominant reactions. The groupthink hypothesis can encompass the psychological factors he discusses but points to a different source of trouble from that of explanations focusing either on the bureaucratic organization or on the individual. Rather than assuming that each policy maker is responding to the demands of the bureaucracy and to other pressures in his own way and that it so happens that each of them ends up by becoming detached, biased, overcommitted to his past decisions and prone to ignore challenging intelligence reports, we shall pursue the possibility that the commonality of the responses of the key policy makers may arise from their interaction in a small group, which generates norms that all the members strive to live up to.

EFFECTS OF STRESS ON GROUP COHESIVENESS

The first factor derived from Thomson's analysis—excessive time pressure—is likely to affect the mental efficiency of any individual, whether he is functioning alone or in a group. Time pressure is, of course, one of the sources of stress that besets any group of executives in a crisis, especially if the members are required to take prompt action when they are confronted with contradictory political pressures from many different interested parties. Whenever a decision has to be made that vitally affects the security of his nation, the government executive is likely to undergo a variety of severe stresses. He realizes that a great deal is at stake for his country and for the rest of the world and that it also may be a crucial moment in his personal career. If he chooses the wrong course of action, he may lose his status, face public humiliation, and suffer a profound loss of self-esteem. These political and personal threats can have a cumulative effect, especially when the decision maker is under constant time pressure and has little opportunity to study even the most important proposals. (Washington bureaucrats quipped that the reason McNamara looked so good in comparison to the others who participated in the White House meetings was that the long drive from the Pentagon gave him eight extra minutes to do his homework in the back of his limousine.) All members of a government policy-making group share these common sources of stress whenever they have to make an important foreign policy decision. Even if the president alone is officially responsible, each of his close advisers knows that if the group makes a serious error and the prestige of the administration is badly damaged, every member may in one way or another be held accountable. Any member of the inner circle might become a scapegoat and be pilloried by investigating committees or the news media. The members of Johnson's advisory group were subjected to a mounting spiral of severe stress as the threats of public humiliation and loss of prestige gradually began to materialize.

Field studies of infantry platoons, air crews, and disaster control teams bear out the findings of social psychological experiments with college students that show that external sources of stress produce a heightened need for affiliation. In times of crisis, a natural tendency arises among the harassed members of a preestablished group to meet together more often and to communicate more than ever with each other, to find out what the others know about the dangers confronting them, to exchange ideas about how the threats might best be dealt with, and to gain reassurance. The heightened need for affiliation, which leads to greater dependency upon one's primary work group and increased motivation to adhere to the group's norms, can have beneficial effects on morale and stress tolerance. But the increase in group cohesiveness will have adverse effects if it leads, as the groupthink hypothesis predicts, to an increase in concurrence-seeking at the expense of critical thinking. An executive committee like Johnson's Tuesday lunch group would be expected to show both the positive and the negative effects of increased cohesiveness during periods of crisis.

We can view the excessive time pressures described by Thomson as a causal factor that adversely affects the quality of the policy makers' decisions in at least two different ways. First, overwork and fatigue generally impair each decision maker's mental efficiency and judgment, interfering with his ability to concentrate on complicated discussions, to absorb new information, and to use his imagination to anticipate the future consequences of alternative courses of action. (This is a matter of individual psychology and is the aspect emphasized by Thomson.) The additional aspect to be considered is this: Excessive time pressure is a source of stress that along with the even more severe sources of stress that generally arise in a crisis will have the effect of inducing a policy-making group to become more cohesive and more likely to indulge in groupthink. Thus, in order to pursue the groupthink hypothesis, we are led to raise this question: *Did the members of Johnson's advisory group display signs of an increase in group cohesiveness and a corresponding increase in manifestations of concurrence-seeking during crisis periods, when they had relatively little time off from their jobs?* We shall return to this question shortly.

EFFECTS OF COMMITMENT TO PRIOR GROUP DECISIONS

Bureaucratic detachment and stereotyped views of communists and Asians involve attitudes that affect the deliberations preceding each new decision. From the beginning most members of Johnson's inner circle probably shared similar ideological viewpoints on basic issues of foreign policy and domestic politics. However, all of them probably did not start with the same attitude of detachment toward the human suffering inflicted by the war and the same unsophisticated stereotypes concerning world communism and the peoples of the Orient. As a historian Thomson was shocked to realize the extent to which crudely propagandistic conceptions entered the group's plans and policy statements. He indicates that Johnson's inner circle uncritically accepted the domino theory, which simplistically assumes that all Asian countries will act alike, so that if the communists were permitted to gain control over one country in the Far East, all neighboring countries would promptly become vulnerable and fall under communist domination. As for the Vietcong and the North Vietnamese, the dominant stereotypes made these "Communist enemies" into the embodiment of evil and thus legitimized the destruction of countless human lives and the burning of villages. In support of Thomson's analysis psychologist Ralph K. White has shown how consistently the public statements of Johnson, Rusk, McNamara, and others in the Tuesday lunch group reveal the pervasiveness of the policy maker's black-and-white picture of the Vietnam War, which always contrasts an image of the diabolical opponents with an image of the invariably moral and virile American government.

When Johnson's Tuesday lunch group was formed, some members probably held these attitudes strongly and others probably had somewhat different views. In the course of interaction the former may have influenced the latter. For example, as Thomson suggests, the few members who had spent many years participating in military planning conferences at the Pentagon may have introduced to the rest of the group a detached dehumanizing attitude toward the Vietnam War, using the euphemistic vocabulary of *body counts, surgical air strikes,* and *pacification.* The members of the group who began with a more humanistic way of thinking and talking about the evils of war may have followed the lead of the military men. But why would the members holding detached attitudes succeed in getting the others to adopt their dehumanizing outlook? Why not the other way around?

One of the main psychological assumptions underlying the groupthink hypothesis is that when a policy-making group becomes highly cohesive, a homogenization of viewpoints takes place, helping the group to preserve its unity by enabling all the members to continue to support the decisions to which the group has become committed. When one of the main norms is being committed to pursuing a war policy, as in this case, we expect that commitment will be bolstered by subsidiary norms that reduce disputes and disharmony within the group. In this context detachment toward the use of military means and dehumanization of the victims of war, as well as negative stereotypes of the enemy, have functional value for a group committed to military escalation. Sharing such attitudes tends to minimize the likelihood that any member will challenge the group's policy by raising moral and humanitarian considerations, which would stimulate bickering, recriminations, and discord. It follows from the same psychological assumption that if the same group were to commit itself to a nonviolent peace-seeking course of action, a reverse trend would appear: The members who personally think in terms of moral and humanitarian values would no longer suppress such considerations but rather would take the lead in setting a new fashion for using a humanizing vocabulary that bolsters the new group norm.

Additional historical evidence is obviously needed in order to pursue the suggestion that the attitude of detachment toward the victims of war and the stereotyped conceptions of the North Vietnamese Communists expressed by Johnson's Tuesday lunch group might be interpreted as symptoms of groupthink. Among the main questions to be answered are those having to do with when, in the sequence of decisions, these adverse attitudes were manifested by most or all members of the group. *Were attitudes of detachment and stereotyped views of communists and Asians expressed relatively rarely by members of the in-group before their first major decisions to escalate the war? Does the emergence of a dehumanizing vocabulary and stereotyped terms in the group's discussions fit the pattern of a subsidiary group norm that follows the militaristic decisions the members had previously agreed upon?*

Overcommitment to defeating the enemy—another factor described by Thomson—involves a well-known human weakness that makes it hard for anyone to correct the errors he has made in the past. The men in Johnson's inner circle, according to Thomson, ultimately convinced themselves that the Vietnam War was of crucial significance for America's future—a conviction that grew directly out of their own explanations and justifications. It became essential to the policy makers to continue the costly and unpopular war, Thomson surmises, because they had *said* it was essential.

Instead of reevaluating their policy in response to clear-cut setbacks, their energetic proselytizing led them to engage in "rhetorical escalation" that matched the military escalation, deepening their commitment to military victory rather than a political solution through negotiation with the government of North Vietnam. The members of Johnson's inner circle, according to another inside observer, remained "united both in their conviction about the rightness of present policy and the fact that all were implicated in the major [escalation] decisions since 1964."

We know that most individuals become heavily ego-involved in maintaining their commitment to any important decision for which they feel at least partly responsible. Once a decision maker has publicly announced the course of action he has selected, he is inclined to avoid looking at evidence of the unfavorable consequences. He tries to reinterpret setbacks as victories, to invent new arguments to convince himself and other that he made the right decision, clinging stubbornly to unsuccessful policies long after everyone else can see that a change is needed. Each policy maker, whether he has made the crucial decisions by himself or as a member of a group, is thus motivated to perpetuate his past errors—provided, of course, that his nose is not rubbed in inescapable evidence.

Like attitudes of detachment and derogatory stereotypes, the tendency to recommit oneself to prior decisions can be greatly augmented by social pressures that arise within a cohesive group. From time to time setbacks induce a policy maker to doubt the wisdom of past decisions in which he has participated. But what a man does about his doubts, if he is a member of an in-group of policy makers, depends in large part on the norms of the group. If the members agree that loyalty to their group and its goals requires rigorous support of the group's primary commitment to open-minded scrutiny of new evidence and willingness to admit errors (as in a group committed to the ideals of scientific research), the usual psychological tendency to recommit themselves to their past decisions after a setback can give way to a careful reappraisal of the wisdom of their past judgments. The group norm in such a case inclines them to compare their policy with alternative courses of action and may lead them to reverse their earlier decisions. On the other hand, if, as often happens, the members feel that loyalty to the group requires unwavering support of the group's past policy decisions, the usual psychological tendency to bolster past commitments is reinforced. Following a series of escalation decisions, every member is likely to insist that the same old military drumbeat is the right one and that sooner or later everyone who matters will want to be in step with it.

Did President Johnson's group of policy makers show signs of adhering to a norm requiring the members to continue supporting the group's past escalation decisions? Many of the characteristics mentioned by Thomson and other observers suggest a positive answer. In elaborating on the group's commitment to its past decisions, Thomson describes the group's tendency to evolve a set of shared rationalizations to justify the militant Vietnam policy. He mentions a closely related symptom that also carries a strong taint of groupthink—mutual agreement to rewrite recent history in a way that would justify the Vietnam escalation policy:

> another result of Vietnam decision making has been *the abuse and distortion of history*. Vietnamese, Southeast Asian, and Far Eastern history has been rewritten by our

policy makers and their spokesmen to conform with the alleged necessity of our presence in Vietnam. Highly dubious analogies from our experience elsewhere—the "Munich" sellout and "containment" from Europe, the Malayan insurgency and the Korean War from Asia—have been imported in order to justify our actions. And more recent events have been fitted to the Procrustean bed of Vietnam. Most notably, the change of power in Indonesia in 1965–1966 has been ascribed to our Vietnam presence; and virtually all progress in the Pacific region—the rise of regionalism, new forms of cooperation, the mounting growth rates—has been similarly explained. The Indonesian allegation is undoubtedly false (I tried to prove it during six months of careful investigation at the White House and had to confess failure); the regional allegation is patently unprovable in either direction.

We cannot avoid recollecting how the bureaucrats in Orwell's *1984* rewrote their own history and were able to make their new versions quite acceptable to those who remembered what really happened by requiring all loyal followers of Big Brother to practice "doublethink"—knowing and at the same time not knowing the truth. How did the policy makers in the Johnson administration handle this problem within their own ranks? *Were the insiders who could not accept the new rationalized version of East Asian history silenced by the rest of the group?*

CONFORMITY PRESSURES

Similar questions need to be answered about the way in which the policy makers handled the "loyal opposition," the government officials, Vietnam experts, and Congressmen who were arguing in favor of the alternative policy of negotiating a peace settlement. Did the members of Johnson's policy-making group consider the eminent members of their own political party who advocated alternative policies to be transmitters of potentially important ideas about how the problems of Vietnam might be solved? Or *did they gravitate toward the groupthink view that advocates of a negotiated peace were disloyal and had to be kept out of their high counsels? Did they privately brand the leading doves as despicable "isolationists" who were a threat to American security?*

We can see from the foregoing questions that from the standpoint of a groupthink interpretation, the phenomena resulting from the group's commitment to its past policy decisions include the remaining types of factors extracted from Thomson's analysis—domestication of dissenters and avoidance of opposing views from critics inside and outside the government. Both of these may be manifestations of a group process involving a constant striving for homogeneous beliefs and judgments among all members of the in-group, in line with their past commitments. Striving for consensus, which helps the members achieve a sense of group unity and esprit de corps, is, of course, the psychological basis for all the symptoms of groupthink.

We learn from Thomson that during the Johnson administration everyone in the hierarchy, including every senior official, was subjected to conformity pressures, which took the form of making those who openly questioned the escalation policy the butt of an ominous epithet: "I am afraid he's losing his effectiveness."

This "effectiveness trap"—the threat of being branded a "has-been" and losing access to the seats of power—inclines its victims to suppress or tone down their criticisms. In a more subtle way, it makes any member who starts to voice his misgivings ready to retreat to a seemingly acquiescent position in the presence of quizzical facial expressions and crisp retorts from perturbed associates and superiors.

Thomson also informs us that during Johnson's administration, whenever members of the in-group began to express doubts—as some of them certainly did—they were treated in a rather standardized way that effectively "domesticated" them through subtle social pressures. The dissenter was made to feel at home, providing he lived up to two restrictions: first, that he did not voice his doubts to outsiders and thus play into the hands of the opposition; and second, that he kept his criticisms within the bounds of acceptable deviation, not challenging any of the fundamental assumptions of the group's prior commitments. One "domesticated dissenter" was Bill Moyers, a close adviser of President Johnson. When Moyers arrived at a meeting, Thomson tells us, the president greeted him with, "Well, here comes Mr. Stop-the-Bombing." Undersecretary of State George Ball, who became a critic of the escalation decisions, was similarly domesticated for a time and became known as "the in-house devil's advocate on Vietnam." From time to time he was encouraged to "speak his piece . . . and there was minimal unpleasantness." The upshot, Thomson says, was that "the club remained intact."

From the standpoint of reducing tension and bolstering morale within "the club," the subtle domestication process may work well, both for the dissenter and for the rest of the group. The nonconformist can feel that he is still accepted as a member in good standing. Unaware of the extent to which he is being influenced by the majority, he has the illusion that he is free to speak his mind. If on occasion he goes too far, he is warned about his deviation in an affectionate or joking way and is reminded only indirectly of his potentially precarious status by the labels the others give him ("Mr. Stop-the-Bombing," "our favorite dove"). The others in the group, as Thomson says, feel satisfied about giving full consideration to the opposing position and can even pat themselves on the back for being so democratic about tolerating open dissent. Nevertheless, the domesticated dissenter repeatedly gets the message that there is only a very small piece of critical territory he can tread safely and still remain a member in good standing. He knows that if he is not careful he will reach the boundary beyond which he risks being branded as having lost his "effectiveness."

In this connection, we wonder why two of the domesticated dissenters within Johnson's in-group—George Ball and Bill Moyers—unexpectedly resigned from their posts and left Washington in 1966. A similar question arises about the departure of McGeorge Bundy in 1967 and Robert McNamara in 1968. Did these men leave for purely personal reasons that had nothing to do with their criticisms of the escalation policy? Were they perhaps fired by President Johnson—without the consent of his other advisers—because he was dissatisfied with their work or because he was offended by their criticisms? *Or was the departure of any of these formerly domesticated dissenters a result of a group process, involving collective pressures from most or all other members of the in-group because of violations of a group norm—the taboo against challenging the war policies to which the group had previously committed itself?* If the evidence points to an affirmative answer to the last question, indicating that one or more of the dissenters became casualties of group pressures, we shall have some strong support for the groupthink hypothesis.

These are not rhetorical questions. Several alternative hypotheses could account for the departure of the domesticated dissenters. The groupthink hypothesis, though one plausible explanation, cannot yet be evaluated as being more valid than (for example) the possibility that the President got rid of these men not as the leader acting on behalf of the group but solely on his own initiative, without the support of the majority of his close advisers. It is even conceivable that the inner circle was split into factions and that a coalition of (for example) the Joint Chiefs of Staff and Walt Rostow won the support of the president at the expense of an opposing faction that was pushing for deescalation. We cannot expect to be in a position to evaluate the applicability of the groupthink hypothesis to the handling of dissenters among Johnson's advisers until more candid observations become available from the men who left the group and from the core insiders such as Johnson, Rusk, Rostow, Wheeler, and Helms. Even more valuable would be detailed minutes of their meetings, specifying who said what about each of the issues raised by the domesticated dissenters. In the meantime, we have to make do with the observations already at hand.

THE WAYS OF A TRANSGRESSOR: EXIT ROBERT McNAMARA

Fortunately, a detailed account has been published of how Secretary of Defense McNamara was precipitously removed from his position as the second most powerful member of the Johnson administration. The story comes from Townsend Hoopes, whose position as undersecretary of the air force brought him in frequent contact with McNamara during the secretary's last months in office. Hoopes was in a position to make firsthand observations of events at the Pentagon, but regrettably, he does not inform us about his sources of information concerning what McNamara and others said at high-level meetings of the president's advisory group, in which the undersecretary was not a participant. If Hoopes's statements prove to be accurate, we shall be led to conclude that McNamara was a domesticated dissenter who despite desperate attempts to remain a loyal member of Johnson's team was eliminated from the government because his repeated efforts to bring about a policy change in the direction of deescalation of the Vietnam War could not be tolerated by what Hoopes calls the "gathering of homogeneous hawks."

In the spring of 1967, according to Hoopes, the inner group of advisers was nearly unanimous in supporting the Vietnam War policy, the one dissenter being McNamara. The book on the Pentagon Papers prepared by *The New York Times* contains a considerable amount of documentary evidence of McNamara's dissent:

> Mr. McNamara's disillusionment with the war has been reported previously, but the depth of his dissent from established policy is fully documented for the first time in the Pentagon study, which he commissioned on June 17, 1967.

The study details how this turnabout by Mr. McNamara—originally a leading advocate of the bombing policy and, in 1965, a confident believer that American intervention would bring the Vietcong insurgency under control—opened a deep policy rift in the Johnson Administration.

The study does not specifically say, however, that his break with established policy led President Johnson to nominate him on November 28, 1967, as president of the World Bank and to replace him as Secretary of Defense.

There are many indications that throughout the spring of 1967 McNamara went through considerable turmoil after he had concluded that the others in the group were wrong in assuming that the North Vietnamese could be bombed into coming to the negotiating table. According to some reports, supposedly originating with his wife, he was at war with himself and up half the night trying to decide what he ought to do.

A highly revealing episode occurred shortly after McNamara had presented some impressive facts about the ineffectiveness of the bombings to a Senate investigating committee. President Johnson was displeased by McNamara's statement and made bitter comments about his giving this information to the senators. The president complained to one senator, "that military genius, McNamara, has gone dovish on me." To someone on his staff in the White House the President spoke more heatedly, accusing the secretary of defense of playing right into the hands of the enemy, on the grounds that his statement would increase Hanoi's bargaining power. "Venting his annoyance to a member of his staff, he drew the analogy of a man trying to sell his house while one of the sons of the family went to the prospective buyer to point out that there were leaks in the basement." This line of thought strongly suggests that in his own mind Johnson regarded his in-group of policy advisers as a family and its leading dissident member as an irresponsible son who was sabotaging the family's interests. Underlying this revealing imagery seem to be two implicit assumptions that epitomize groupthink: We are a good group, so any deceitful acts we perpetrate are fully justified. Anyone in the group who is unwilling to distort the truth to help us is disloyal.

Hoopes describes how with each passing month McNamara was gradually eased out of his powerful position, finding himself less and less welcome at the White House, until finally he was removed from his high office in "a fast shuffle" by the president, who was "confident that he would go quietly and suffer the indignity in silence." Once McNamara was removed from the group, Hoopes concludes, the members could once again enjoy complete unity and relatively undisturbed confidence in the soundness of their war policy. During the months following McNamara's nonvoluntary departure, increasing numbers of intelligence specialists and other experts were urging a reappraisal on the basis of new evidence following the surprise Tet offensive by the supposedly defeated Vietcong in early 1968. But, according to Hoopes, the in-group, having become temporarily homogeneous once again, avoided calling them in for consultations and apparently did not study their reports.

The members' sense of confidence may have been maintained for a time by Rostow's effective mind guarding, which went far beyond the call of duty. Hoopes claims that during the last year of Johnson's administration, as discontent with the

Vietnam War was growing throughout America and even within the military bureaucracy, Rostow cleverly screened the inflow of information and used his power to keep dissident experts away from the White House. This had the intended effect of preventing the president and some of his advisers from becoming fully aware of the extent of disaffection with the war and of the grounds for it. The group managed to discount all the strong pressures from prestigious members of their own political party and even from former members of the White House group (such as McGeorge Bundy) until after a new member of the Tuesday lunch group—Clark Clifford, who replaced McNamara as Secretary of Defense—unexpectedly became convinced of the soundness of the deescalation position. (Clifford had been brought in as a dependable hawk who would restore unity to the group.) Relatively unhampered by loyalties to the old group, Clifford reported to Hoopes and the rest of his revitalized staff at the Pentagon that at the daily meetings on Vietnam in the White House he was outnumbered 8 to 1. But Clifford fought hard and well, according to Hoopes. During this period other powerful influences may also have been at work to induce Secretary of State Rusk and others in the group to take account, belatedly, of the numerous persuasive reasons for modifying their policy. The transformation culminated in the unprecedented speech from the White House on March 31, 1968, when, with tears in his eyes, President Johnson announced that he was deescalating the war in Vietnam and would not seek reelection.

If Hoopes's account of the way McNamara and other nonconformists were dealt with is corroborated by subsequent testimony from other observers and by documentary records, we shall have strong evidence that at least during the last half of 1967 the failure of Johnson's in-group to take account of the growing signs that its Vietnam policy required drastic revision was a product of groupthink. The hypothesis leads us to ask questions about other symptoms of groupthink, such as striving for unanimous agreement and willingness to take serious risks on the basis of a shared illusion of invulnerability.

UNANIMITY WITHIN THE GROUP

In the Pentagon Papers the Department of Defense analysts say that "from the September [1964] meeting forward, there was little basic disagreement among the principals [the term the study uses for the senior policy makers] on the need for military operations against the North." Lyndon B. Johnson, however, says in his memoirs that sometimes there were marked disagreements among his advisers. But the instances he describes seem limited to periods when more than one member of the group was proposing a temporary halt in the bombing as a move toward peace. For example, at a meeting on December 18, 1965, when McNamara, Rusk, and Bundy argued for a bombing pause in order to pursue Soviet Ambassador Dobrynin's proposal for diplomatic discussions with Hanoi, the military men and others gave opposing arguments that were "equally persuasive," according to Johnson, and it was "another of those 51:49 decisions that . . . keep [the president] awake late at night." In contrast Johnson emphasizes the unanimous agreement of the group in his descriptions of six meetings at which major escalation decisions were recommended—on September 9, 1964; February 6 and 8, 1965; July 27, 1965; January 31, 1966; and September 28, 1967. On the last of these dates, for example, the issue was whether to speed deployment of American troops to Vietnam, as requested by General Westmoreland. Johnson's only comment is, "All my advisers agreed that we should carry out this acceleration."

Henry Graff, when interviewing members of the Tuesday lunch group, was impressed by the repeated emphasis on unanimity expressed by each of them. George Ball, when asked in 1966 about his opposition to bombing North Vietnam, took pains to affirm his basic agreement with the rest of the group. "The one thing we have to do," Ball resolutely told Graff, "is to win this damned war." He added that until the commitment of a large number of troops was made six months earlier, other options may have been open, but now "there is no longer any useful argument to be made about current policies." Ball seems to have become so domesticated at the time of the interview that we can hardly believe he was still a dissenter.

Confidence in ultimate victory despite repeated setbacks and failures was another theme in the interviews. For example, in January 1968 Rostow told his fellow historian with complete certainty, "History will salute us." On this point Graff's interviews bear out an admission made by Bill Moyers after he had resigned from his post in the White House: "There was a confidence," Moyers said, "it was never bragged about, it was just there—a residue, perhaps of the confrontation over the missiles in Cuba—that when the chips were really down, the other people would fold."

OVERLOOKING THE RISKS

The Department of Defense study, in disagreement with Ellsberg's claim that the administration was never optimistic when major escalation decisions were made, indicates that the members of the policy-making group were overoptimistic about defeating North Vietnam by means of bombing raids during 1964 and early 1965. In the book on the Pentagon Papers published by *The New York Times*, Neil Sheehan's summary of the Defense Department study states that in November 1964 the air war against North Vietnam was expected "to last two to six months, during which Hanoi was apparently expected to yield." Despite momentary periods of pessimism and gloom about setbacks, according to Chester Cooper, a great deal of overoptimism was manifested from 1964 up until the last several months of the Johnson administration:

> The optimistic predictions that flowered from time to time . . . reflected genuinely held beliefs. While occasional doubts crossed the minds of some, perhaps all [senior policy makers], the conviction that the war would end "soon" and favorably was clutched to the breast like a child's security blanket. Views to the contrary were not favorably received. . . . We thought we could handle Vietnam without any noticeable effect on our economy or society. . . .
>
> Because the war was likely to be over "soon," there was also a reluctance to make any substantial changes in the bureaucratic structure. There would be no special institutional arrangements for staffing the war, for implementing or following up decisions.

We know, of course, that Johnson's Tuesday lunch group did not have a care-free attitude about the dangers of extending the Vietnam War to the point where China or Russia might become directly involved. During certain periods, especially before 1966, the members were so keenly aware of the vulnerability of America's forces in Vietnam and of the possible fall of the government of South Vietnam that they wanted to avoid engaging in peace negotiations for fear of having little or no bargaining power. The members of the group continued to be aware of the precariousness of South Vietnam's cooperation with America's anticommunist efforts throughout the entire Johnson administration. Thus it certainly cannot be said that they maintained grossly overoptimistic illusions about the overall security of the American military enterprise in Vietnam. Yet at times there may have been a more limited type of illusion that inclined the policy makers to be willing to take long-shot gambles. Many observations suggest that the group experienced some temporary lapses in realism about the grave material, political, and moral risks of escalation. The lapses were caused by shared illusions that "everything will go our way, none of the dangers will seriously affect us."

Observations bearing directly on the risky decisions made by Johnson's Tuesday lunch group during 1966 are reported by David Kraslow and Stuart Loory, two well-known journalists who made a careful study of the public record of the Vietnam War and interviewed more than forty United States officials who knew something about the inside story. In their account of what went on behind the scenes when Johnson's Tuesday lunch group was making its crucial decisions, we can identify many clear indications of a sense of unwarranted complacency about the ultimate success of the group's chosen policy. If their account proves to be substantially verified by subsequent historical analysis, it will raise a number of additional questions concerning the role of groupthink in the policy makers' willingness to take extreme risks with regard to provoking an all-out war with China and Russia, presumably on the basis of a shared assumption that events were bound to come out the way they hoped.

Throughout 1966 the Tuesday lunch group was primarily concerned about selecting bombing targets in North Vietnam. Kraslow and Loory describe how the group attempted to evaluate every proposed target by following a special procedure, which the members felt would enable them to take account of all the relevant criteria:

> As a result of all the staff work in the Pentagon and at the State Department, the authorization requests for each target were reduced to a single sheet of paper—a kind of report card—on which the suggested strikes were described in summary. Each individual sheet contained a checklist for four items:
>
> 1. The military advantage of striking the proposed target.
> 2. The risk of American aircraft and pilots in a raid.
> 3. The danger that the strike might widen the war by forcing other countries into the fighting.
> 4. The danger of heavy civilian casualties.
>
> At the Tuesday lunch President Johnson and his advisers worked over each of the target sheets like schoolteachers grading examination papers. Each of the men graded each of the targets in the four categories.
>
> The decisions were made on the basis of averaged-out grades. . . .

In this manner the president and his principal advisers, working over a lunch table in the White House, showed their intense concern with individual road junctions, clusters of trucks and structures down to small buildings in a land thousands of miles away. Their obvious concern lent great weight to the contention that never has more care been taken in making sure that limited-war-making objectives were not being exceeded.

Did the group's ritualistic adherence to a standardized procedure for selecting targets induce the members to feel justified in their destructive way of dealing with the Vietnamese people? After all, the danger of heavy civilian casualties from United States air attacks was being taken into account on their checklists. Did they allow the averaging to obscure the fact that they were giving the greatest weight to military objectives, with relatively little regard for humanitarian considerations or for political effects that could have serious consequences for United States national security? *Did the members of the group share the illusion that they were being vigilant about all aspects of United States policy in Vietnam, while confining their efforts almost solely to the routines of selecting bombing targets?*

The great need for vigilance, of course, derived from the danger that a bombing attack would provoke Russia or China to transform the Vietnam War into the third world war. Although this risk was on the members' checklist, on at least one occasion, according to Kraslow and Loory, this consideration was given less importance than the supposed advantages of striking the target. In the late spring of 1966, the Tuesday lunch group authorized for the first time the bombing of the large petroleum-storage depot in the Hanoi-Haiphong area, even though the members were informed that Soviet ships were located dangerously close to the target area in the harbor at Haiphong. The rationale for this risky decision was that the bombing might push the government of North Vietnam to begin negotiations under conditions favorable to the United States. Throughout the spring of 1966 American government officials had repeatedly tried to find out if the enemy was ready to work out a peace settlement. Ambassador Lodge reported from Saigon that he had some indications that the bombing raids and supply difficulties were creating a strong desire in Hanoi for peace talks. With this information in mind and with full awareness that Soviet ships might accidentally be sunk, the Tuesday lunch group decided that the time was ripe for a severe blow in the vicinity of the enemy's major harbor. This decision must have involved much more than mere wishful thinking about the ultimate military and political success of bombing North Vietnam. If Kraslow and Loory are reporting accurately, all members of the group knew the venture was precarious and could bring America to the brink of war with the Soviet Union. The Defense Department analysts who prepared the Pentagon Papers say that the execution message sent to the commander in chief of Pacific forces was "a remarkable document, attesting in detail to the political sensitivity of the strikes."

If the air attack was so politically sensitive, why was it authorized in the first place? *Was this decision to carry out the bombing raid (despite the risk of provoking the Soviet Union to enter the war) based on a flimsy sense of invulnerability shared by the members of the group while they were conferring?*

We are not informed about how complacent or perturbed the members felt when they were making the decision, but we are told that subsequently the leading participant, when he was alone, became deeply agitated as he thought about the riskiness of the decision: President Johnson on the night the raid was to be executed (June 29, 1966) was too upset to sleep:

> For months afterward President Johnson would tell occasional visitors how he worried that night that the raids would somehow go wrong and an errant bomb would strike a Soviet ship in Haiphong harbor and start World War III.
>
> He worried so much that his daughter, Luci, returning home from a date with her fiance, Pat Nugent, urged the President to pray. She . . . urged her father to seek solace in the [Catholic] church [to which she belonged]. . . . At 10:30 P.M. a waiting Dominican monk saw two black limousines drive up to the entrance of the neo-Gothic building. The President, Mrs. Johnson, Luci and Nugent stepped out of one car; a detail of Secret Service men, from the other.
>
> The entire group entered the dim, empty church. The presidential party dropped to its knees and prayed silently.
>
> Back in the White House, the President remained awake most of the night, awaiting the final reports on the raids. At 4:30 A.M., satisfied that no great mishap had occurred, he went to sleep.

Did the president's anxiety about the risks arise only when he was alone, when the members of the group were not available to reassure him about the dangerous action they had collectively authorized? During the day or so preceding the scheduled bombing (when it could have been called off) did he set aside his deep concerns about the danger of provoking the outbreak of World War III out of a sense of commitment to the group? Did he abstain from using his presidential powers to cancel the dangerous mission or to call another meeting of the group to reconsider the decision because he felt that any move toward reversal might be regarded as a violation of the group's taboo against raising doubts about its prior decisions? Unfortunately, Lyndon B. Johnson is less than candid in his memoirs, *The Vantage Point*. He makes no mention of the episode. Perhaps these questions will be answered later in a more revealing biography.

DESTROYING THE ELUSIVE FLOWERS OF PEACE

Johnson does mention in his memoirs a series of abortive efforts to end the war in Vietnam through negotiations. His comments pose some related questions about the Tuesday lunch group's willingness to take serious risks with regard to sabotaging peace negotiations and losing the United States government's credibility at home and in the world community. One such abortive effort described by Johnson was the Marigold plan, which fleetingly occupied the attention of United States policy makers toward the end of 1966, when they were assured that Hanoi for once would not demand a cessation of the bombings of North Vietnam until *after* an agreement was reached:

> In the summer of 1966 Ambassador Lodge was approached in Saigon by Janusz Lewandowski, the Polish member of the International Control Commission, who had

just visited Hanoi. Talks began. Those exchanges, reported in secret cables under the code name Marigold, continued for six months. . . . After receiving assurance from Lodge [concerning the bombing halt] . . . we authorized him to tell the Polish representative on December 3 that we were ready to meet with the North Vietnamese in Warsaw on December 6, using the Lewandowski draft as the basis for discussion. . . .

. . . [But] the North Vietnamese failed to show up for the critical meeting the Poles had promised to arrange in Warsaw on December 6, 1966.

The code name Marigold was assigned to this potential peace move by William P. Bundy, an assistant secretary of state in close contact with the policy-making members of the White House group, who was in charge of all such developments. He gave them flower names as a satirical reference to "flower children" and other supposedly disreputable elements in American society who stood for peace—perhaps in deference to the policy makers' commitment to a hard-nosed military approach in Vietnam.

Chester Cooper, another State Department official and an active Marigolder, told a bitter story in his memoirs, *The Lost Crusade* (1970). According to Cooper, the Marigold peace initiative was destroyed as a result of a decision by Johnson's Tuesday lunch group to resume bombing within the city limits of Hanoi just when the opening sessions were being held in Warsaw with Polish officials who were expected to function as go-betweens with the North Vietnamese government. Essentially the same story had been told two years earlier by Kraslow and Loory on the basis of their interviews of unnamed government officials, one of whom may have been Chester Cooper. One small part of the story is acknowledged by Johnson in his memoirs: "The Poles claimed that the North Vietnamese had failed to appear because we had bombed targets near Hanoi two days before the suggested meeting." Johnson argues that whether the Poles had any definite commitment from Hanoi was uncertain and that the bombings should not have made any difference: "If Lewandowski had reported accurately to Hanoi, the North Vietnamese knew perfectly well that the bombing would not end before the talks began." What Johnson leaves out of his account is that United States negotiations with Polish officials continued for more than a week after the first scheduled meeting date and that while those meetings were going on the United States launched two additional air attacks against Hanoi. According to the account in the Pentagon Papers, "The major result of the raids close to Hanoi on Dec. 2, 4, 13, and 14—all inside a previously established 30-mile sanctuary around the capital—'was to undercut what appeared to be a peace feeler from Hanoi.'"

Johnson also fails to mention that he and his policy advisers had received repeated warnings that renewal of the bombing would damage the prospects of the Marigold plan. The warning messages came from the United States ambassador in Warsaw, from a leading Polish diplomat in Saigon who had been instrumental in initiating the peace move, and from the Italian ambassador to the United States, who was also one of the originators of the Marigold peace plan. At the same time, a group of influential officials in the United States State Department who were deeply involved in planning the peace talks—including Nicholas Katzenbach, acting as secretary of state in Rusk's absence, and Averell Harriman, the official United States ambassador given a special mandate to seek peace—strongly recommended to the president and his key advisers that the Hanoi bombing program not be continued while the talks were going on in Warsaw.

Cooper does not believe that the Marigold plan was deliberately sabotaged by Johnson and his advisers; rather, the Johnson administration's search for a way out of the war at the end of 1966 was genuine, although not always "whole-hearted" and "marked by groping and fumbling." One of the main reasons for fumbling this peace initiative and other negotiations later on, Cooper suggests, was that Johnson's in-group was adhering to a norm of being tough and belligerent toward the enemy, maintaining a strong virile stance whenever the opportunity for a give-and-take political settlement arose:

> Stopping or moderating the bombing, even temporarily and even as a logical or necessary accompaniment to a diplomatic initiative, was regarded as an American admission of weakness and failure. . . . It was no great mystery why, despite American protestations in favor of a political rather than a military solution, the North Vietnamese were wary and skeptical. And to compound their suspicions, many of Washington's plans for a "political solution" involved, for all practical purposes, a negotiated surrender by the North Vietnamese.

Perhaps the group norm of avoiding conciliatory acts that could be construed as signs of softness and a lack of virility accounts for the fact that during the period when the Marigold plan was germinating, "the issue of negotiations was very much a residual claimant on the time of the President's 'Tuesday Lunch' group; it was the military track, and especially the bombing targets, that virtually dominated the discussions."

Whether the United States policy makers were sincere or insincere in their efforts to start peace talks in December 1966, they overlooked the foreseeable consequences of their decision to bomb Hanoi at that particular time, when diplomats in many different countries knew that a peace move was supposed to be getting under way. A number of influential foreign diplomats who had worked hard to bring the contending nations to the peace table in Warsaw were astounded and spoke heatedly to Secretary General U Thant and others in the United Nations about America's ruthless destruction of the frail Marigold plan, which they had so carefully nurtured for six months. Furthermore, practically all high-ranking officials in the Italian and Polish governments knew that the first steps of the secret Marigold plan were being taken, for their ambassadors were functioning as mediators. After each of the four bombings of the Hanoi area representatives of both governments expressed their shock and did not hesitate to openly question United States representatives about their government's alleged sincerity in seeking a peaceful settlement. Thus, the Hanoi bombings had the effect of inducing distrust, unnecessarily putting a strain on relations with Italian representatives who had been allies, and creating bitter feelings of alienation in the Polish government, which may have undermined years of United States effort to wean that country away from Soviet influence.

Probably less embittered but no less demoralized than the foreign diplomats who functioned as mediators were their counterparts in the United States State Department, the officials who were given the task of pursuing the elusive flowers of peace. They could hardly be expected to continue to work assiduously on their assigned mission of trying to arrange for peace talks when their own urgent requests for a temporary halting of the air war against North Vietnam to allow the carefully planned peace negotiations to get under way were completely disregarded.

Resumption of the bombings against Hanoi in December 1966 evoked an outcry of protest and recriminations against the United States in the world press, which at that time still knew nothing about the peace initiative. Mass protest meetings were held in England and in other countries allied with the United States. Many responsible American commentators for the first time began to attack the United States war effort in Vietnam as senseless. Only one month earlier President Johnson had promised, in what he called a "declaration of peace," to try to arrange for a withdrawal of American troops from Vietnam. Again we are reminded of Orwell's *1984* "doublethink" vocabulary, in which "war is peace." Johnson's November peace statements were not forgotten when the air war against Hanoi was resumed a month later. The credibility gap widened and continued to haunt the president throughout the remainder of his administration.

If United States policy makers sincerely intended to pursue the peace negotiations, their failure to call off the bombing of the Hanoi area resulted in a complete fiasco. It utterly ruined all chances for fulfilling that intention. We must await the declassification of the relevant documents before we can expect to find out whether the group members shared the belief that they were conscientiously pursuing opportunities for peace negotiations by denying that their militaristic decision to step up the bombing of North Vietnam would undermine the peace talks.

Even if subsequent historical research were to show that United States policy makers were insincere—for example, that they were deliberately prolonging the war in the expectation that later they might obtain a favorable peace settlement—their decision to ignore the warnings would still have to be rated as foolish because the members overlooked the undesirable political consequences. They could have foreseen that all those who knew about the Marigold plan would point to United States leaders as the saboteurs of the attempted peace move because of their ill-timed bombing attacks. If the policy makers were being deceitful, they should have realized that they would be exposing their disreputable intentions of prolonging the war unless they postponed the raids against Hanoi for a short time, until it became apparent that the conferees who were trying to implement the Marigold peace plan could not come to any agreement. *Did the members of Johnson's advisory group ignore the obvious risks because of their overconfidence in the military policy to which they were committed, sharing the overoptimistic belief that the renewed bombing attacks against Hanoi would succeed at long last in forcing a weakened enemy to seek peace on America's terms?*

When we consider the credibility gap in terms of the groupthink hypothesis, we are led to raise the following additional question: *Did the president and other members of the group make the mistake of destroying public confidence in their statements about the war because they were mutually supporting each other in discounting mounting evidence of the failure of the military policy to which they had committed themselves?* The plausibility of an affirmative answer is suggested by Hoopes's assertion that President Johnson repeatedly issued unwarranted, optimistic statements to the press, not just because he was temperamentally inclined to oversell his policies but because he was also constantly "buoyed by the stream of glad tidings coming from his advisers." The president, during his last year in office, according to Hoopes, became

> the victim of (1) Rostow's "selective briefings"—the time-honored technique of under-lining, within a mass of material, those particular items that one wishes to draw to the special attention of a busy chief—and (2) the climate of cozy implicit agreement on fundamentals which had so long characterized discussions within the inner circle on Vietnam, where never was heard a discouraging word.

If historical research on the Johnson administration proves Hoopes to be right, we shall have strong evidence that the president, like other members of the inner circle, was a victim of groupthink. But any definitive judgment of whether this conclusion is correct will have to await the release of secret documents from the White House files and the publication of candid memoirs that provide dependable answers to the questions just posed.

LIMITATIONS OF THE GROUPTHINK HYPOTHESIS

Suppose the historical evidence supports the groupthink hypothesis. Will we then be led to conclude that there was really nothing wrong with the Johnson administration's foreign policy toward Southeast Asia that couldn't be cured simply by avoiding groupthink? Certainly not. Even if the policy makers had not indulged in groupthink, the Vietnam War policies might have been essentially the same because of the political and economic values of the men who held power positions in the United States government. Still, it is probable that if they were indulging in groupthink, they were prevented from becoming fully aware of the futility of their ill-conceived escalation decisions and from correcting some of their most fallacious assumptions soon enough to reconsider the alternatives open to them. It is conceivable that group dynamic factors influenced their deliberations to such a degree that if the Johnson administration had been able to set up the appropriate conditions for avoiding groupthink, the policy makers might have renounced some of their original war aims and might at least have become willing to negotiate a peace settlement in 1966, when the Marigold plan was being pursued, if not earlier.

Careful historical analysis of United States government documents and memoirs should sooner or later yield some definitive answers to the queries raised in this chapter. The answers might prove to be negative, of course, in which case the groupthink interpretation of the Johnson administration's errors in its Vietnam War policies will have to be discarded. For example, the decisions may have largely reflected the influence of just one man, the president himself. It seems improbable, however, that his advisers exerted no real influence over him and that when they said they agreed to his policy of escalation, they secretly disagreed. Men of the caliber of McNamara, Rusk, Rostow, and Bundy are not likely to be mere sycophants, like those who surround a dictator. If the alleged facts as presented by Cooper, Hoopes, Moyers, Thomson, and other analysts are essentially correct, it seems highly probable that group dynamics exerted considerable influence on the decisions of the policy makers who escalated the war in Vietnam.

The Vietnam case study, even though sufficient evidence is not yet at hand for evaluating alternative interpretations, shows better than any other the potential contemporary relevance of the groupthink hypothesis. It reveals the type of inquiries that will need to be made when the historical records become more complete in order to test the validity of the groupthink hypothesis. The questions asked in this chapter are not those that historians and political analysts typically ask. Perhaps if social scientists take seriously the potential influence of group dynamics on high-level policy decisions, they will ferret out the evidence necessary to answer those questions.

PART
Eight

THEORETICAL DEBATES AFTER THE COLD WAR

The dramatic end of the Cold War has triggered interesting new theoretical debates and reconsiderations about American foreign policy. The Cold War was a major inspiration for foreign policy theory, so it would be surprising if its end did not also stimulate new debates and research agendas. Reconsiderations are already underway, and the theoretical center of gravity is shifting.

Deudney and Ikenberry take up the question of "Who won the Cold War?" This is a debate that is not just of historical interest—it has major implications about what lessons policymakers should draw about the future and the most effective instruments of American foreign policy. The conventional view, according to Deudney and Ikenberry, is that American containment policy and "peace through strength" were the decisive factors that altered Soviet policy. Some even argue that the Reagan administration's military build-up, Star Wars, and its ideological offensive were the key source of the Cold War's end. Deudney and Ikenberry argue that this interpretation is misleading. Other factors unrelated to military strength mattered, including peace, human rights movements, and the benign "face" that Western democracies presented to the Soviet Union. They also argue that the remarkable convergence of thinking by Reagan and Gorbachev on a form of radical antinuclearism also mattered. Their piece signals the beginning of a new debate over what factors triggered the great historical turn of events—and they suggest that the debate should include not just the impact of "policy" but also the impact of the American and Western "polity."

Gaddis and Cumings are each engaged in another debate that is brought on by the end of the Cold War, one that is being carried on primarily between diplomatic historians. Gaddis wants to use our new knowledge about the Cold War as a completed historical event and new historical evidence about the Soviet Union to reflect on the old debate about Cold War origins. Gaddis argues that our new awareness of the Soviet Union's corrupt and repressive past should give pause to diplomatic historians (who he calls "orthodox" but others call "revisionist") who bought into a sort of "moral equivalency" assumption about Soviet–American competition. The Soviet Union's fundamental illegitimacy was not fully acknowledged by these diplomatic historians, and so they found themselves questioning whether the United States had undertaken sufficient efforts to "get along" with the Soviet Union.

Cumings provides a spirited critique of Gaddis and other diplomatic historians who have attempted to mold a postrevisionist account of the origins of the Cold War. Cumings defends the main thrust of the revisionist account, arguing that economic interests were the deep source of American foreign policy after the war. The exchange reveals that diplomatic historians are not only rethinking the origins of the Cold War, but they are also rearguing it.

Who Won the Cold War?

Daniel Deudney and G. John Ikenberry

The end of the Cold War marks the most important historical divide in half a century. The magnitude of those developments has ushered in a wide-ranging debate over the reasons for its end—a debate that is likely to be as protracted, controversial, and politically significant as that over the Cold War's origins. The emerging debate over why the Cold War ended is of more than historical interest: At stake is the vindication and legitimation of an entire world view and foreign policy orientation.

In thinking about the Cold War's conclusion, it is vital to distinguish between the domestic origins of the crisis in Soviet communism and the external forces that influenced its timing and intensity, as well as the direction of the Soviet response. Undoubtedly, the ultimate cause of the Cold War's outcome lies in the failure of the Soviet system itself. At most, outside forces hastened and intensified the crisis. However, it was not inevitable that the Soviet Union would respond to this crisis as it did in the late 1980s—with domestic liberalization and foreign policy accommodation. After all, many Western experts expected that the USSR would respond to such a crisis with renewed repression at home and aggression abroad, as it had in the past.

At that fluid historic juncture, the complex matrix of pressures, opportunities, and attractions from the outside world influenced the direction of Soviet change, particularly in its foreign policy. The Soviets' field of vision was dominated by the West, the United States, and recent American foreign policy. Having spent more than 45 years attempting to influence the Soviet Union, Americans are now attempting to gauge the weight of their country's impact and, thus, the track record of U.S. policies.

In assessing the rest of the world's impact on Soviet change, a remarkably simplistic and self-serving conventional wisdom has emerged in the United States. This new conventional wisdom, the "Reagan victory school," holds that President Ronald Reagan's military and ideological assertiveness during the 1980s played the lead role in the collapse of Soviet communism and the "taming" of its foreign policy. In that view the Reagan administration's ideological counter-offensive and military buildup delivered the knock-out punch to a system that was internally bankrupt and on the ropes. The Reagan Right's perspective is an ideologically pointed version of the more broadly held conventional wisdom on the end of the Cold War that emphasizes the success of the "peace-through-strength" strategy manifest in four decades of Western containment. After decades of waging a costly "twilight

Daniel Deudney and G. John Ikenberry, "Who Won the Cold War?" *Foreign Policy* 87 (Summer 1992): 123–138; 90 (Spring 1993): 171–176. Reprinted with permission.

struggle," the West now celebrates the triumph of its military and ideological resolve.

The Reagan victory school and the broader peace-through-strength perspectives are, however, misleading and incomplete—both in their interpretation of events in the 1980s and in their understanding of deeper forces that led to the end of the Cold War. It is important to reconsider the emerging conventional wisdom before it truly becomes an article of faith on Cold War history and comes to distort the thinking of policymakers in America and elsewhere.

The collapse of the Cold War caught almost everyone, particularly hardliners, by surprise. Conservatives and most analysts in the U.S. national security establishment believed that the Soviet-U.S. struggle was a permanent feature of international relations. As former National Security Council adviser Zbigniew Brzezinski put it in 1986, "the American-Soviet contest is not some temporary aberration but a historical rivalry that will long endure." And to many hardliners, Soviet victory was far more likely than Soviet collapse. Many ringing predictions now echo as embarrassments.

The Cold War's end was a baby that arrived unexpectedly, but a long line of those claiming paternity has quickly formed. A parade of former Reagan administration officials and advocates has forthrightly asserted that Reagan's hard-line policies were the decisive trigger for reorienting Soviet foreign policy and for the demise of communism. As former Pentagon officials like Caspar Weinberger and Richard Perle, columnist George Will, neoconservative thinker Irving Kristol, and other proponents of the Reagan victory school have argued, a combination of military and ideological pressures gave the Soviets little choice but to abandon expansionism abroad and repression at home. In that view, the Reagan military buildup foreclosed Soviet military options while pushing the Soviet economy to the breaking point. Reagan partisans stress that his dramatic "Star Wars" initiative put the Soviets on notice that the next phase of the arms race would be waged in areas where the West held a decisive technological edge.

Reagan and his administration's military initiatives, however, played a far different and more complicated role in inducing Soviet change than the Reagan victory school asserts. For every "hardening" there was a "softening": Reagan's rhetoric of the "Evil Empire" was matched by his vigorous anti-nuclearism; the military buildup in the West was matched by the resurgence of a large popular peace movement; and the Reagan Doctrine's toughening of containment was matched by major deviations from containment in East-West economic relations. Moreover, over the longer term, the strength marshaled in containment was matched by mutual weakness in the face of nuclear weapons, and efforts to engage the USSR were as important as efforts to contain it.

THE IRONY OF RONALD REAGAN

Perhaps the greatest anomaly of the Reagan victory school is the "Great Communicator" himself. The Reagan Right ignores that his anti-nuclearism was as strong as his anticommunism. Reagan's personal convictions on nuclear weapons were profoundly at odds with the beliefs of most in his administration. Staffed by officials who considered nuclear weapons a useful instrument of statecraft and who were openly disdainful of the moral critique of nuclear weapons articulated by the arms control community and the peace movement, the administration pursued the hardest line on nuclear policy and the Soviet Union in the postwar era. Then vice president George Bush's observation that nuclear weapons would be fired as a warning shot and Deputy Under Secretary of Defense T. K. Jones's widely quoted view that nuclear war was survivable captured the reigning ethos within the Reagan administration.

In contrast, there is abundant evidence that Reagan himself felt a deep antipathy for nuclear weapons and viewed their abolition to be a realistic and desirable goal. Reagan's call in his famous March 1983 "Star Wars" speech for a program to make nuclear weapons impotent and obsolete was viewed as cynical by many, but actually it expressed Reagan's heartfelt views, views that he came to act upon. As *Washington Post* reporter Lou Cannon's 1991 biography points out, Reagan was deeply disturbed by nuclear deterrence and attracted to abolitionist solutions. "I know I speak for people everywhere when I say our dream is to see the day when nuclear weapons will be banished from the face of the earth," Reagan said in November 1983. Whereas the Right saw anti-nuclearism as a threat to American military spending and the legitimacy of an important foreign policy tool, or as propaganda for domestic consumption, Reagan sincerely believed it. Reagan's anti-nuclearism was not just a personal sentiment. It surfaced at decisive junctures to affect Soviet perceptions of American policy. Sovietologist and strategic analyst Michael MccGwire has argued persuasively that Reagan's anti-nuclearism decisively influenced Soviet-U.S. relations during the early Gorbachev years.

Contrary to the conventional wisdom, the defense buildup did not produce Soviet capitulation. The initial Soviet response to the Reagan administration's buildup and belligerent rhetoric was to accelerate production of offensive weapons, both strategic and conventional. That impasse was broken not by Soviet capitulation but by an extraordinary convergence by Reagan and Mikhail Gorbachev on a vision of mutual nuclear vulnerability and disarmament. On the Soviet side, the dominance of the hardline response to the newly assertive America was thrown into question in early 1985 when Gorbachev became general secretary of the Communist party after the death of Konstantin Chernenko. Without a background in foreign affairs, Gorbachev was eager to assess American intentions directly and put his stamp on Soviet security policy. Reagan's strong antinuclear views expressed at the November 1985 Geneva summit were decisive in convincing Gorbachev that it was possible to work with the West in halting the nuclear arms race. The arms control diplomacy of the later Reagan years was successful because, as *Washington Post* journalist Don Oberdorfer has detailed in *The Turn: From the Cold War to a New Era* (1991), Secretary of State George Shultz picked up on Reagan's strong convictions and deftly side-stepped hard-line opposition to agreements. In fact, Schultz's success at linking presidential unease about nuclear weapons to Soviet overtures in the face of right-wing opposition provides a sharp contrast with John Foster Dulles's refusal to act on President Dwight Eisenhower's nuclear doubts and the opportunities presented by Nikita Khrushchev's détente overtures.

Reagan's commitment to anti-nuclearism and its potential for transforming the U.S. -Soviet confrontation was more graphically demonstrated at the October 1986 Reykjavík summit when Reagan and Gorbachev came close to agreeing on a comprehensive program of global denuclearization that was far bolder than any seriously entertained by American strategists since the Baruch Plan of 1946. The sharp contrast between Reagan's and Gorbachev's shared skepticism toward nuclear weapons on the one hand, and the Washington security establishment's consensus on the other, was showcased in former secretary of defense James Schlesinger's scathing accusation that Reagan was engaged in "casual utopianism." But Reagan's anomalous anti-nuclearism provided the crucial signal to Gorbachev that bold initiatives would be reciprocated rather than exploited. Reagan's anti-nuclearism was more important than his administration's military buildup in catalyzing the end of the Cold War.

Neither anti-nuclearism nor its embrace by Reagan have received the credit they deserve for producing the Soviet-U.S. reconciliation. Reagan's accomplishment in this regard has been met with silence from all sides. Conservatives, not sharing Reagan's anti-nuclearism, have emphasized the role of traditional military strength. The popular peace movement, while holding deeply antinuclear views, was viscerally suspicious of Reagan. The establishment arms control community also found Reagan and his motives suspect, and his attack on deterrence conflicted with their desire to stabilize deterrence and establish their credentials as sober participants in security policy making. Reagan's radical anti-nuclearism should sustain his reputation as the ultimate Washington outsider.

The central role of Reagan's and Gorbachev's anti-nuclearism throws new light on the 1987 Treaty on Intermediate-range Nuclear Forces, the first genuine disarmament treaty of the nuclear era. The conventional wisdom emphasizes that this agreement was the fruit of a hard-line negotiating posture and the U.S. military buildup. Yet the superpowers' settlement on the "zero option" was not a vindication of the hard-line strategy. The zero option was originally fashioned by hardliners for propaganda purposes, and many backed off as its implementation became likely. The impasse the hard line created was transcended by the surprising Reagan-Gorbachev convergence against nuclear arms.

The Reagan victory school also overstates the overall impact of American and Western policy on the Soviet Union during the 1980s. The Reagan administration's posture was both evolving and inconsistent. Though loudly proclaiming its intention to go beyond the previous containment policies that were deemed too soft, the reality of Reagan's policies fell short. As Sovietologists Gail Lapidus and Alexander Dallin observed in a 1989 *Bulletin of the Atomic Scientists* article, the policies were "marked to the end by numerous zigzags and reversals, bureaucratic conflicts, and incoherence." Although rollback had long been a cherished goal of the Republican party's right wing, Reagan was unwilling and unable to implement it.

The hard-line tendencies of the Reagan administration were offset in two ways. First, and most important, Reagan's tough talk fueled a large peace movement in the United States and Western Europe in the 1980s, a movement that put significant political pressure upon Western governments to pursue far-reaching arms control proposals. That mobilization of Western opinion created a political climate in which the rhetoric and posture of the early Reagan administration was a significant political liability. By the 1984 U.S. presidential election, the administration had embraced arms control goals that it had previously ridiculed. Reagan's own anti-nuclearism matched that rising public concern, and Reagan emerged as the spokesman for comprehensive denuclearization. Paradoxically, Reagan administration policies substantially triggered the popular revolt against the nuclear hardline, and then Reagan came to pursue the popular agenda more successfully than any other postwar president.

Second, the Reagan administration's hardline policies were also undercut by powerful Western interests that favored East-West economic ties. In the early months of Reagan's administration, the grain embargo imposed by President Jimmy Carter after the 1979 Soviet invasion of Afghanistan was lifted in order to keep the Republican party's promises to Midwestern farmers. Likewise, in 1981 the Reagan administration did little to challenge Soviet control of Eastern Europe after Moscow pressured Warsaw to suppress the independent Polish trade union Solidarity, in part because Poland might have defaulted on multibillion dollar loans made by Western banks. Also, despite strenuous opposition by the Reagan administration, the NATO allies pushed ahead with a natural gas pipeline linking the Soviet Union with Western Europe. That a project creating substantial economic interdependence could proceed during the worst period of Soviet-U.S. relations in the 1980s demonstrates the failure of the Reagan administration to present an unambiguous hard line toward the Soviet Union. More generally, NATO allies and the vocal European peace movement moderated and buffered hard-line American tendencies.

In sum, the views of the Reagan victory school are flawed because they neglect powerful crosscurrents in the West during the 1980s. The conventional wisdom simplifies a complex story and ignores those aspects of Reagan administration policy inconsistent with the hard-line rationale. Moreover, the Western "face" toward the Soviet Union did not consist exclusively of Reagan administration policies, but encompassed countervailing tendencies from the Western public, other governments, and economic interest groups.

Whether Reagan is seen as the consummate hardliner or the prophet of anti-nuclearism, one should not exaggerate the influence of his administration, or of other short-term forces. Within the Washington beltway, debates about postwar military and foreign policy would suggest that Western strategy fluctuated wildly, but in fact the basic thrust of Western policy toward the USSR remained remarkably consistent. Arguments from the New Right notwithstanding, Reagan's containment strategy was not that different from those of his predecessors. Indeed, the broader peace-through-strength perspective sees the Cold War's finale as the product of a long-term policy, applied over the decades.

In any case, although containment certainly played an important role in blocking Soviet expansionism, it cannot explain either the end of the Cold War or the direction of Soviet policy responses. The West's relationship with the Soviet Union was not limited to containment, but included important elements of mutual vulnerability and engagement. The Cold War's end was not simply a result of Western strength but of mutual weakness and intentional engagement as well.

Most dramatically, the mutual vulnerability created by nuclear weapons overshadowed containment. Nuclear weapons forced the United States and the Soviet Union to eschew war and the serious threat of war as tools of diplomacy and created imperatives for the cooperative regulation of nuclear capability. Both countries tried to fashion nuclear explosives into useful instruments of policy, but they came to the realization—as the joint Soviet-American statement issued from the 1985 Geneva summit put it—that "nuclear war cannot be won and must never be fought." Both countries slowly but surely came to view nuclear weapons as a common threat that must be regulated jointly. Not just containment, but also the overwhelming and common nuclear threat brought the Soviets to the negotiating table. In the shadow of nuclear destruction, common purpose defused traditional antagonisms.

A second error of the peace-through-strength perspective is the failure to recognize that the West offered an increasingly benign face to the communist world. Traditionally, the Soviets' Marxist-Leninist doctrine held that the capitalist West was inevitably hostile and aggressive, an expectation reinforced by the aggression of capitalist, fascist Germany. Since World War II, the Soviets' principal adversaries had been democratic capitalist states. Slowly but surely, Soviet doctrine acknowledged that the West's behavior did not follow Leninist expectations, but was instead increasingly pacific and cooperative. The Soviet willingness to abandon the Brezhnev Doctrine in the late 1980s in favor of the "Sinatra Doctrine"—under which any East European country could sing, "I did it my way"—suggests a radical transformation in the prevailing Soviet perception of threat from the West. In 1990, the Soviet acceptance of the de facto absorption of communist East Germany into West Germany involved the same calculation with even higher stakes. In accepting the German reunification, despite that country's past aggression, Gorbachev acted on the assumption that the Western system was fundamentally pacific. As Russian foreign minister Andrei Kozyrev noted subsequently, that Western countries are pluralistic democracies "practically rules out the pursuance of an aggressive foreign policy." Thus the Cold War ended despite the assertiveness of Western hardliners, rather than because of it.

THE WAR OF IDEAS

The second front of the Cold War, according to the Reagan victory school, was ideological. Reagan spearheaded a Western ideological offensive that dealt the USSR a death blow. For the Right, driving home the image of the Evil Empire was a decisive stroke rather than a rhetorical flourish. Ideological warfare was such a key front in the Cold War because the Soviet Union was, at its core, an ideological creation. According to the Reagan Right, the supreme vulnerability of the Soviet Union to ideological assault was greatly underappreciated by Western leaders and publics. In that view, the Cold War was won by the West's uncompromising assertion of the superiority of its values and its complete denial of the moral legitimacy of the Soviet system during the 1980s. Western military strength could prevent defeat, but only ideological breakthrough could bring victory.

Underlying that interpretation is a deeply ideological philosophy of politics and history. The Reagan Right tended to view politics as a war of ideas, an orientation that generated a particularly polemical type of politics. As writer Sidney Blumenthal has pointed out, many of the leading figures in the neoconservative movement since the 1960s came to conservatism after having begun their political careers as Marxists or socialists. That perspective sees the Soviet Union as primarily an ideological artifact, and therefore sees struggle with it in particularly ideological terms. The neoconservatives believe, like Lenin, that "ideas are more fatal than guns."

Convinced that Bolshevism was quintessentially an ideological phenomenon, activists of the New Right were contemptuous of Western efforts to accommodate Soviet needs, moderate Soviet aims, and integrate the USSR into the international system as a "normal" great power. In their view, the *realpolitik* strategy urged by George Kennan, Walter Lippmann, and Hans Morgenthau was based on a misunderstanding of the Soviet Union. It provided an incomplete roadmap for waging the Cold War, and guaranteed that it would never be won. A particular villain for the New Right was Secretary of State Henry Kissinger, whose program of détente implied, in their view, a "moral equivalence" between the West and the Soviet Union that amounted to unilateral ideological disarmament. Even more benighted were liberal attempts to engage and co-opt the Soviet Union in hopes that the two systems could ultimately reconcile. The New Right's view of politics was strikingly globalist in its assumption that the world had shrunk too much for two such different systems to survive, and that the contest was too tightly engaged for containment or Iron Curtains to work. As James Burnham, the ex-communist prophet of New Right anticommunism, insisted in the early postwar years, the smallness of our "one world" demanded a strategy of "rollback" for American survival.

The end of the Cold War indeed marked an ideological triumph for the West, but not of the sort fancied by the Reagan victory school. Ideology played a far different and more complicated role in inducing Soviet change than the Reagan school allows. As with the military sphere, the Reagan school presents an incomplete picture of Western ideological influence, ignoring the emergence of ideological common ground in stimulating Soviet change.

The ideological legitimacy of the Soviet system collapsed in the eyes of its own citizens not because of an assault by Western ex-leftists, but because of the appeal of Western affluence and permissiveness. The puritanical austerity of Bolshevism's "New Soviet Man" held far less appeal than the "bourgeois decadence" of the West. For the peoples of the USSR and Eastern Europe, it was not so much abstract liberal principles but rather the Western way of life—the material and cultural manifestations of the West's freedoms—that subverted the Soviet vision. Western popular culture—exemplified in rock and roll, television, film, and blue jeans—seduced the communist world far more effectively than ideological sermons by anti-communist activists. As journalist William Echikson noted in his 1990 book *Lighting the Night: Revolution in Eastern Europe,* "instead of listening to the liturgy of Marx and Lenin, generations of would-be socialists tuned into the Rolling Stones and the Beatles."

If Western popular culture and permissiveness helped subvert communist legitimacy, it is a development of profound irony. Domestically, the New Right battled precisely those cultural forms that had such global appeal. V. I. Lenin's most potent ideological foils were John Lennon and Paul McCartney, not Adam Smith and Thomas Jefferson. The Right fought a two-front war against communism abroad and hedonism and consumerism at home. Had it not lost the latter struggle, the West may not have won the former.

The Reagan victory school argues that ideological assertiveness precipitated the end of the Cold War. While it is true that right-wing American intellectuals were assertive toward the Soviet Union, other Western activists and intellectuals were building links with highly placed reformist intellectuals there. The Reagan victory school narrative ignores that Gorbachev's reform program was based upon "new thinking"—a body of ideas developed by globalist thinkers cooperating across the East-West divide. The key themes of new thinking—the common threat of nuclear destruction, the need for strong international institutions, and the importance of ecological sustainability—built upon the cosmopolitanism of the Marxist tradition and officially replaced the Communist party's class-conflict doctrine during the Gorbachev period.

It is widely recognized that a major source of Gorbachev's new thinking was his close aide and speechwriter, Georgi Shakhnazarov. A former president of the Soviet political science association, Shakhnazarov worked extensively with Western globalists, particularly the New York-based group known as the World Order Models Project. Gorbachev's speeches and policy statements were replete with the language and ideas of globalism. The Cold War ended not with Soviet ideological capitulation to Reagan's anticommunism but rather with a Soviet embrace of globalist themes promoted by a network of liberal internationalists. Those intellectual influences were greatest with the state elite, who had greater access to the West and from whom the reforms originated.

Regardless of how one judges the impact of the ideological struggles during the Reagan years, it is implausible to focus solely on recent developments without accounting for longer-term shifts in underlying forces, particularly the widening gap between Western and Soviet economic performance. Over the long haul, the West's ideological appeal was based on the increasingly superior performance of the Western economic system. Although contrary to the expectation of Marx and Lenin, the robustness of capitalism in the West was increasingly acknowledged by Soviet analysts. Likewise, Soviet elites were increasingly troubled by their economy's comparative decline.

The Reagan victory school argues that the renewed emphasis on free-market principles championed by Reagan and then British prime minister Margaret Thatcher led to a global move toward market deregulation and privatization that the Soviets desired to follow. By rekindling the beacon of laissez-faire capitalism, Reagan illuminated the path of economic reform, thus vanquishing communism.

That view is misleading in two respects. First, it was West European social democracy rather than America's more free-wheeling capitalism that attracted Soviet reformers. Gorbachev wanted his reforms to emulate the Swedish model. His vision was not of laissez-faire capitalism but of a social democratic welfare state.

Second, the Right's triumphalism in the economic sphere is ironic. The West's robust economies owe much of their relative stability and health to two generations of Keynesian intervention and government involvement that the Right opposed at every step. As with Western popular culture, the Right opposed tendencies in the West that proved vital in the West's victory.

There is almost universal agreement that the root cause of the Cold War's abrupt end was the grave domestic failure of Soviet communism. However, the Soviet response to this crisis—accommodation and liberalization rather than aggression and repression—was significantly influenced by outside pressures and opportunities, many from the West. As historians and analysts attempt to explain how recent U.S. foreign policy helped end the Cold War, a view giving most of the credit to Reagan-era assertiveness and Western strength has become the new conventional wisdom. Both the Reagan victory school and the peace-through-strength perspective on Western containment assign a central role in ending the Cold War to Western resolve and power. The lesson for American foreign policy being drawn from those events is that military strength and ideological warfare were the West's decisive assets in fighting the Cold War.

The new conventional wisdom, in both its variants, is seriously misleading. Operating over the last decade, Ronald Reagan's personal anti-nuclearism, rather than his administration's hardline, catalyzed the accommodations to end the Cold War. His administration's effort to go beyond containment and on the offensive was muddled, counter-balanced, and unsuccessful. Operating over the long term, containment helped thwart Soviet expansionism but cannot account for the Soviet domestic failure, the end of East-West struggle, or the direction of the USSR's reorientation. Contrary to the hard-line version, nuclear weapons were decisive in abandoning the conflict by creating common interests.

On the ideological front, the new conventional wisdom is also flawed. The conservatives' anticommunism was far less important in delegitimating the Soviet system than were that system's internal failures and the attraction of precisely the Western "permissive culture" abhorred by the Right. In addition, Gorbachev's attempts to reform communism in the late-1980s were less an ideological capitulation than a reflection of philosophical convergence on the globalist norms championed by liberal internationalists. And the West was more appealing not because of its laissez-faire purity, but because of the success of Keynesian and social welfare innovations whose use the Right resisted.

Behind the debate over who "won" the Cold War are competing images of the forces shaping recent history. Containment, strength, and confrontation—the trinity enshrined in conventional thinking on Western foreign policy's role in ending the Cold War—obscure the nature of these momentous changes. Engagement and interdependence, rather than containment, are the ruling trends of the age. Mutual vulnerability, not strength, drives security politics. Accommodation and integration, not confrontation, are the motors of change.

That such encouraging trends were established and deepened even as the Cold War raged demonstrates the considerable continuity underlying the West's support today for reform in the post-Soviet transition. Those trends also expose as one-sided and self-serving the New Right's attempt to take credit for the success of forces that, in truth, they opposed. In the end, Reagan partisans have been far more successful in claiming victory in the Cold War than they were in achieving it.

To the Editor:

To judge from informal conversations I have had with citizens of Eastern Europe and the former Soviet Union over the past two years, the conviction that Ronald Reagan won the Cold War by being tough on the communists is nigh-universal in those areas. It is ironic to observe the contortions that Western academics will go through trying to explain away that obvious historical reality. Daniel Deudney and John Ikenberry's "Who Won the Cold War?" in Foreign Policy #87 (Summer 1992) is probably the most valiant such attempt to date; but it resembles a complex, deftly argued mathematical treatise boldly demonstrating that two plus two does not equal four.

If, as the authors assert, Reagan's anti-nuclearism, rather than his toughness, was the main factor in the Soviets' defeat, then the question arises why Jimmy Carter—whose anti-nuclearism was at least as strong as and far more public than Reagan's—did not have better luck with his Soviet interlocutors. Nuclear fears were more or less at the basis of U.S. policy toward the Soviets from the time of Robert McNamara on. But throughout the 1970s, the overriding U.S. emphasis on nuclear arms control coincided with a series of Western defeats in Africa, Southeast Asia, and Southwest Asia (Afghanistan), as well as some political close calls in Europe. It was only after three to four years of unremittingly tough policies under Reagan—both public and private statements of Soviet officials at the time characterized them as such—that the desired sea-change in Soviet leadership opinion took place. That, we now know, was Reagan's simple plan—to negotiate, but to do so from a position of strength. He reestablished a position of strength through a massive arms buildup, through deliberately tough talk (culminating in the "evil empire" line), through uncompromising (and widely criticized) positions on arms control, through active harassment of Soviet imperial efforts in the Third World (including Grenada), through a tightening of technological export controls, and through (for the Soviets) the frightening prospect of the Strategic Defense Initiative (SDI).

What is particularly annoying is that the same crowd that now denies Reagan credit for that achievement railed against his policies in the early 1980s. Time's Strobe Talbott, who similarly dismisses the Reagan victory, lambasted the Reagan administration in 1984 for foolishly believing that "it could influence the composition and orientation of the post-Brezhnev leadership." But that is precisely what Reagan set out to do, and what he did. (Mikhail Gorbachev came to power in 1985.) Deudney and Ikenberry fail to answer the critical question of why an innovator like Gorbachev was given the reins. The evident answer is that the Soviet leadership was desperate enough. Like a chess player being cornered by his opponent, the Soviets sought deliverance under Gorbachev through bold, and ultimately self-destructive, diplomatic and political gambits. Under softer U.S. policies in the 1970s, by contrast, the Soviets were complacent, uncompromising, and steadily more aggressive, believing (as they sometimes publicly stated) that the correlation of forces was shifting in their favor.

Yes, of course, there were countercurrents in Western opinion during the 1980s, such as the antinuclear movement. There is always debate in democracies. But Deudney and Ikenberry overlook who won the debate. The British general election, the West German election, the deployment of intermediate-range nuclear force missiles—all showed that the antinuclearists could not be used, as the Soviets had successfully used them before, to undercut resurgent U.S. power.

That the main disintegrative forces in the Soviet empire were internal is also undeniable. But those forces had to be nurtured and turned against the leadership by Western strength and Western rhetoric. The Jimmy Carter–Cyrus Vance approach of rewarding the Soviet buildup with one-sided arms control treaties, opening Moscow's access to Western capital markets and technologies, and condoning Soviet imperial expansion was perfectly designed to preserve the Brezhnev-style approach, delivering the Soviets from any need to reevaluate (as they did under Gorbachev) or change their policies. Had the basic Carter-Vance approach been continued (perhaps the only meritorious aspect of that policy was Carter's anti-Soviet human rights rhetoric), the Cold War and the life of the Soviet Union would almost certainly have been prolonged.

There is a grain of truth in most arguments, and the grain of truth in Deudney and Ikenberry's is that Reagan, unlike his hardest-line followers, was wisely willing, once a position of strength had been secured, to negotiate and draw Gorbachev along. But even in the later stages, Reagan kept up tough human rights rhetoric (Gorbachev almost canceled the 1988 Moscow summit over it) and proved uncompromising on a host of issues, including SDI. Reagan knew what all the most effective democratic statesmen of the twentieth century—Winston Churchill, Dean Acheson, John Foster Dulles, Henry Jackson—knew: namely, that the only way to moderate or change policies of a dictatorship is to meet its challenge with courage, firmness, and unshakable resolve (victory may then permit magnanimity). It is precisely that simple truth, so often driven home by the multiple horrors of this century's history, that liberal academia has forgotten.

Patrick Glynn
Resident Scholar
The American Enterprise Institute
Washington, D.C.

The Authors' Reply:

Despite the ambitions of ideologues with Manichean world views, attempts to reduce the complexity and ironies of international politics to mathematical simplicity and certainty are doomed to fail. Patrick Glynn's argument that Reagan's military buildup and ideological assertiveness won the Cold War is pervasive, self-serving, and wrong.

First, for Reagan to have restored America's strength presumes that America had been weak. But the image of American weakness in the late 1970s was largely fabricated by right-wing activists and bore little relation to military and geopolitical realities. The most ominous strategic American vulnerability during the Carter years—the so-called "window of vulnerability"—had conveniently disappeared by the time of the Scowcroft Commission in the early Reagan administration. America *was not weak, but its image was weakened by extremist rhetoric that disappeared when the right wing came to power.*

Second, the view that the Soviet Union was gaining in places like Afghanistan and Angola betrays the same illusion that inspired America's Vietnam adventure. Those countries were not the West's to lose, and Soviet intervention turned into a costly quagmire because of local resistance rather than because of the force of American policy. The Soviet misadventures in the Third World in the 1970s were an object lesson in geopolitical realities that the American Right refused to recognize. Soviet overextension was a reflection of Soviet rather than American weakness, and the Soviet termination of those interventions had little to do with American reassertiveness.

Third, Glynn's conventional wisdom misunderstands Reagan's and Gorbachev's anti-nuclearism and its catalytic role in ending the Cold War. The Reagan administration did not have a simple two-point plan to rebuild and negotiate from strength. Rather, the administration was profoundly schizophrenic about the role of nuclear weapons in statecraft. Reagan's personal anti-nuclearism seems to have been far more radical and deeply held than Carter's. At the Geneva and Reykjavik summits, Reagan and Gorbachev bonded on radical anti-nuclearism, and from that common ground sought to defuse the relationship of antagonism. Had Reagan actually held a nuclear hard line, the Cold War might have ended in a hot war rather than in accommodation.

Fourth, the other pillar of the Right's conventional view is that Reagan's ideological reassertion of Western values was decisive. Most basically, the appeal of the Western way of life and human rights had little to do with inspirational speeches. The reorientation of Soviet elites was a longer process that involved Western liberal efforts to break down the Iron Curtain and subvert the Stalinist state and East-West antagonism through joint enterprises and exchanges. Further, the Helsinki accords, condemned by the Right as sell-outs, played a role, as did Carter's human rights policy. The credibility of the West's commitment to human rights was reinforced by the Carter administration's willingness to condemn all antiliberal regimes rather than only those that were geopolitically convenient targets.

In conclusion, it is vital not to overconcentrate on the events of the late 1970s and 1980s in ending the Cold War. The ultimate reason for its end was the internal crisis of the Soviet system—a crisis that external pressure, at most, intensified. Moreover, the West's interaction with the Soviet Union during that conflict was a mixture of a relatively consistent willingness to counterbalance and a relative willingness to accommodate. Glynn's conventional wisdom misses the ironies of recent events, plays down the deeper forces and long-term consistencies, and ignores the importance of Western moderation and accommodation in taming the great Soviet bear.

Daniel Deudney
University of Pennsylvania
Philadelphia

G. John Ikenberry
Carnegie Endowment for International Peace
Washington, D.C.

The Tragedy of Cold War History*

John Lewis Gaddis

I

It has been well over three decades, now, since William Appleman Williams first called for "a searching review of the way America has defined its own problems and objectives, and its relationship with the rest of the world." In one of the most influential books ever written about the history of United States foreign relations, Williams rejected the celebratory tone that had characterized the work of an earlier generation of American diplomatic historians, insisting that the record of this nation's foreign policy had been a "tragedy" because of the gap we had allowed to develop between our aspirations and accomplishments in world affairs. We had preached self-determination but objected when others sought to practice it; we had proclaimed the virtues of economic freedom even as we sought to impose economic control. The result, Williams concluded, was that "America's humanitarian urge to assist other people is undercut—even subverted—by the way it goes about helping them."[1]

The classical definition of "tragedy" is greatness brought low through some fundamental flaw in one's own character. When one considers the difficulties the United States created for itself in the world through its own hubris and arrogance during the 1960s and early 1970s, it is hardly surprising that Williams's tragic view of American diplomatic history seemed, to a great many people at the time, to make sense. To a good many people even today, it still does.

Therein, however, lies a danger. Any view held by a considerable number of people risks becoming an orthodoxy, and the members of our profession are no more exempt than others from that tendency. I only met Bill Williams once, but I gather that he was, if anything, a profoundly unorthodox character.[2] I suspect that the last thing he would have wanted would be to see his own ideas—or anybody else's, for that matter—become conventional wisdom.[3] As he himself put it in *The Tragedy of American Diplomacy*, "history is a way of learning, of getting closer to the truth. It is only by abandoning the clichés that we can even define the tragedy."[4]

What I would like to do here is to question some clichés and then try to redefine a tragedy. For if we mean what we say when we enjoin one another—in a way that has become, in itself, almost an orthodoxy—to transform diplomatic history into a truly international history,[5] then surely Williams's tragic view of the Ameri-

*SHAFR presidential address delivered at Washington, 29 December 1992.

John Lewis Gaddis, "The Tragedy of Cold War History," *Diplomatic History* 17, 4 (Fall 1993). Reprinted by permission.

can experience in world affairs is a good place to start. How well does it hold up when placed within an international context? How does an interpretation that has influenced the writing of so much Cold War history look today, now that the Cold War is over? And how might we apply Williams's habit of asking creatively irritating questions as we seek to understand the post-Cold War world?

The end of the Cold War has obliged most of us, after all, to jettison quite a number of clichés, orthodoxies, and long-cherished pearls of conventional wisdom: in this sense, we are all well on the way to becoming post-Cold War revisionists. It is all the more important, then, that we take another look into what Williams called the "mirror" of history, "in which, if we are honest enough, we can see ourselves as we are as well as the way we would like to be."[6]

II

Let us begin with an issue our students are already beginning to raise with us, which is what the Cold War was all about in the first place. Given what we now know about the internal fragility of the Soviet Union; given what has long been clear about the economic absurdity of Marxism-Leninism; given the persuasive evidence that an international Communist "monolith" never really existed; given all of these things, exactly what was the threat to American interests anyway? Whatever could have justified the massive expenditures on armaments, the violations of human rights abroad and civil liberties at home, the neglect of domestic priorities, the threats to blow up the world—whatever could have excused all the deplorable things the United States did during the Cold War if no genuine threat ever existed? Does not this record only confirm what Williams suspected: that the American system has a built-in propensity to fight cold wars, and that if the Soviet Union had not provided the necessary adversary, someone else would have?

Few historians would deny, today, that the United States did expect to dominate the international scene after World War II, and that it did so well before the Soviet Union emerged as a clear and present antagonist. Woodrow Wilson years earlier had provided the rationale, with his call for a collective security organization to keep the peace, and for self-determination and open markets as a way of simultaneously removing the causes of war.[7] It took the fall of France and the surprise attack at Pearl Harbor to bring Wilson's ideas into the policy arena, to be sure, but the country's leadership, if not yet the country as a whole, was thoroughly committed to them long before World War II ended.[8]

This vision of the future assumed a strong military role for the United States:[9] Americans would hardly have been prepared, even under the best of circumstances, to turn the entire task of peacekeeping over to the United Nations, however enthusiastically they endorsed that organization.[10] And there is no question but that careful calculations of material advantage lay behind all of this. After all, no one had ever combined the fact of self-interest with the appearance of disinterest more skillfully than Woodrow Wilson, and that aspect of his legacy was still very much around as influential Americans, inside and outside the government, set out to design the postwar world.[11]

But let us be fair to those designers: they also assumed that the Great Powers would act *in concert rather than in competition* with one another. That presupposition had been the basis for Franklin D. Roosevelt's early and somewhat crude concept of the "four policemen," and it carried over into the more sophisticated planning for the United Nations and the organization of the postwar international economy that went on during the last two years of World War II.[12] It is certainly true that the United States expected to lead the new world order; it alone was in a position to set the rules and to provide the resources without which that system could hardly function. But the system was to have been based, we need to remember, upon the principle of what we would today call *common* security. It was to have operated, at least insofar as the Great Powers were concerned, within a framework of consent, not coercion; and most Americans expected, perhaps naively, that this relatively open and relaxed form of hegemony could be made to coincide with their own security interests.[13]

Let us recall, as well, that the United States plan for the postwar world was never fully put into effect. Part of the reason was its failure to take into account the extent of wartime devastation in Europe, and the consequent improbability that a return to open markets alone could solve that problem.[14] But the main difficulty lay more in the realm of geopolitics than economics: it was that Washington's conception of common security ran up against another one, emanating from Moscow, that was of a profoundly different character.

There was nothing relaxed, or open, or "consensual" about Josef Stalin's vision of an acceptable international order; and the more we reconsider Soviet history now that the Soviet Union itself has become history, the harder it becomes to separate any aspect of it from the baleful and lingering influence of this remarkable but sinister figure. One need hardly accept a "great man" theory of history to recognize that in the most authoritarian government the world has ever seen, the authoritarian who ran it did make a difference.[15]

Stalin was, above all else, a Great Russian nationalist, a characteristic very much amplified by his non-Russian origins.[16] His ambitions followed those of the old princes of Muscovy, with their determination to "gather in" and to dominate the lands that surrounded them. That Stalin cloaked this goal within an ideology of proletarian internationalism ought not to conceal its real origins and character: Stalin's most influential role models, as his most perceptive biographer, Robert Tucker, has now made clear, were not Lenin, or even Marx, but Peter the Great and ultimately Ivan the Terrible.[17] His rule replicated the pattern of earlier tsarist autocracies identified by the great pre-revolutionary Russian historian, V. O. Kliuchevskii: "Exhausting the resources of the country, they only bolstered the power of the state without elevating the self-confidence of the people. . . . The state swelled up; the people grew lean."[18]

Now, if the Soviet Union had occupied, let us say, the position of Uruguay in the post-World War II international system, this kind of autocracy certainly would have oppressed those who had to live under it, but it would hardly have caused a Cold War. If the Soviet Union had been the superpower that it actually was, but with a system of checks and balances that could have constrained Stalin's authoritarian tendencies, a Cold War might have happened, but it would probably not have been as dangerous or as protracted a conflict. If the Soviet Union had been a superpower *and* an authoritarian state, but if someone other than Stalin had been running it—a Bukharin, for example, or perhaps even a Trotsky—then its government could have been in the hands of a Kremlin leader who, although by no means a democrat, would at least have known the outside world,[19] and might have found it easier than Stalin did to deal with on a basis of wary cooperation instead of absolute distrust.

But none of these counterfactuals became fact. Stalin was Stalin, and the people of the Soviet Union, together with the rest of the world, were stuck with him at the end of World War II. That was a tragedy, if not in a classical sense, then in an all too modern one. Let me try to illustrate why with a series of vignettes based on some of the new information we have about the great autocrat's life:

Stalin, we are told, once kept a parrot in a cage in his Kremlin apartment. The Soviet leader had the habit of pacing up and down in his rooms for long periods of time, smoking his pipe, brooding about God knows what, and occasionally spitting on the floor. One day the parrot, having observed this many times, tried to mimic Stalin's spitting. Stalin immediately responded by reaching into the cage and crushing the parrot's head with his pipe, instantly killing it.[20]

Stalin once was on vacation in the Crimea, and was kept awake during the night by a barking dog. "Shoot it," he told his guards. "But Josef Vissarionovich," they reported the next morning, "the dog is a seeing-eye dog, and it belongs to a blind peasant." "Shoot the dog," Stalin commanded, "and send the peasant to the Gulag."[21]

Stalin once had a wife—actually his second wife—who had an independent mind, and who was becoming concerned about the repressiveness of his policies. After she argued with him about this one night, either he shot and killed her, or she shot and killed herself.[22]

Stalin once had a rival, whose name was Trotsky. Stalin not only outmaneuvered him, exiled him, and eventually had him killed; he also killed everyone he could who had ever been associated with Trotsky or any other potential rival, as well as hundreds of thousands of other people who had never had anything at all to do with Trotsky or with anyone else who could conceivably have challenged Stalin's rule. Some three million Soviet citizens died, it is estimated, as a result of these purges.[23]

Stalin once had an idea: that in order to finance the industrialization that Marxist theory said had to take place before there could be a Marxist state, the Soviet government had to ensure a reliable supply of grain for export by forcibly collectivizing agriculture.[24] The best estimate is that over fourteen million Soviet citizens died from the famine, exiles, and executions that resulted.[25]

Stalin once presided over the fighting of a great war, in which at least another twenty-six million Soviet citizens were killed.[26] When it was over, he congratulated himself not only on a great victory, but on the impressive territorial gains victory had brought. Wars, he told his foreign minister, V. M. Molotov, were a progressive force in history: "The First World War ripped one country out of the grips of capitalist slavery. The Second created a socialist system. The Third will finish off imperialism forever."[27]

My purpose, in reciting this litany, is to make the point that the United States and its allies, at the end of World War II, were not dealing with a normal, everyday, run-of-the-mill, statesmanlike head of government. They confronted instead a psychologically disturbed but fully functional and highly intelligent dictator[28] who had projected his own personality not only onto those around him but onto an entire nation and had thereby, with catastrophic results, remade it in his image.[29] And he had completed that task, I might add, long before the Cold War policies of the United States could possibly have given him an excuse to do so. The twentieth century has been full of tragedies, but what Stalin did to the Soviet Union and, let us not forget, to its neighbors as well, must surely rank as among the greatest of them.

III

One might justifiably ask at this point, though: so what? Were not Stalin's sins fully apparent decades ago; and indeed did they not figure prominently in the earliest "orthodox" accounts of Cold War origins? Is not raising this issue now a matter of beating a horse that has not only long been dead, but is mummified, possibly even petrified? There are several reasons why I think this is not the case, why the nature of Stalinism is an issue to which American diplomatic historians will need to return.[30]

First, archives are important, even if all they do is to confirm old arguments. The new Soviet sources, however, may well do more than that: the evidence we are getting suggests strongly that conditions inside the U.S.S.R., not just under Stalin but also under Lenin and several of Stalin's successors, were worse than most outside experts on that country had ever suspected. Whether one is talking about the death toll from collectivization, or from the purges, or from the war; whether one considers the brutality with which the survivors were treated; whether one evaluates the economic and ecological damage inflicted on the territories in which they lived; whether one looks at what the Soviet system meant for other countries that got sucked into the Soviet sphere of influence—whatever dimensions of Soviet history one looks at, what is emerging from the archives are horror stories more horrifying than most of the images put forward, without the benefit of archives, by the Soviet Union's most strident critics while the Cold War was still going on.[31] That seems to me, in itself, to be significant.

But there is a second reason why I think a reconsideration of Stalinism is in order, and it has to do with the way American diplomatic historians have for too long thought about the Cold War. Reflecting one of the most curious intellectual habits to grow out of that conflict, we have tended to divide the world, rather like ancient Gaul, into three parts. We have preoccupied ourselves primarily, as one might have expected, with the "first" world, where most of the archives have long been open. We have frequently challenged each other, quite correctly in my view, to extend our horizons to include the "third" world, and to give full attention to the often intrusive impact the United States has had on the regions that made it up. It is very odd, though, that with all of our emphasis on "border crossings" and on the need for a genuinely international perspective, American diplomatic historians have made so little effort to understand what was really happening in—and what the impact of American policies was on—the "second" world.

This omission resulted in part, of course, from inaccessibility. It was difficult to find out much because governments in the Soviet Union, China, Eastern Europe, and other Marxist states kept so much so carefully hidden. Part of the problem also had to do, I suspect, with the lingering effects of McCarthyism on our profession. The ideological excesses of the late 1940s and the early 1950s so traumatized American academics that for decades afterward we avoided looking seriously at the possibility that communism might indeed have influenced the behavior of communist states. Because some charges of Soviet espionage were exaggerated, we assumed too easily that all of them had been, that the spies were simply figments of right-wing imaginations. Because we regarded gestures like Congressional "captive nations" resolutions as a form of pandering to ethnic constituencies, we tended to lose sight of the fact that there really were "captive nations."[32] And perhaps we also worried that if we talked too explicitly about these kinds of things, we would wind up sounding too much like John Foster Dulles, or, for a more recent generation, Ronald Reagan.

There was another problem as well, though, that got in the way of an accurate assessment of what was happening in the "second" world. It had to do with an unfortunate tendency, imported from international relations theory, to lock ourselves into a view of the world that accorded equal legitimacy, and therefore more or less equal respectability, to each of the major states within it, while ignoring the circumstances that had brought them into existence and the means by which they remained in power.[33] Because all nations seek power and influence, or so "realist" theory tells us,[34] we fell into the habit of assuming that they did so for equally valid reasons; that in turn led to a kind of "moral equivalency" doctrine in which the behavior of autocracies was thought to be little different from that of democracies.

This was not, to be sure, a universal tendency. Many members of our profession have long argued that certain "third world" autocracies held power illegitimately, and have vigorously condemned American foreign policy for putting up with them. But not everyone who took this view was willing to grant equal attention to what those few citizens of the "second" world who were free to speak had been telling us all along during the Cold War, which was that communism as it was practiced in the Soviet Union really was, and had always been, at least as illegitimate and repressive a system. Now that they are free to speak—and to act—the people of the former Soviet Union appear to have associated themselves more closely with President Reagan's famous indictment of that state as an "evil empire"[35] than with our own more balanced academic assessments. The archives, as noted earlier, are providing documentary evidence for such an interpretation. And yet, these developments have not yet visibly altered our field's actual preoccupation with the "first" world, our periodic exhortations to give greater emphasis to the "third" world, and our corresponding neglect of the "second" world, which badly needs the historiographical equivalent of an affirmative action policy.

A truly international approach to diplomatic history, I should think, would be one fully prepared to look into the "mirror" that Williams wrote about to see whether we have given adequate attention to a tragedy that has had the most profound consequences—extending over more than seven decades—for the largest nation on the face of the earth, and for most of the other nations that surrounded it.

IV

What would that mean, though, for the writing of American diplomatic history? The most persistent issue historians of the Cold War's origins have had to wrestle with is a variation on what we would today call the "Rodney King" question: "Couldn't we all have gotten along if we had really tried?" We answered that question long ago with respect to another great twentieth-century dictator, Adolf Hitler: few of us have any difficulty whatever with the proposition that Nazi Germany really did represent absolute evil, and that there was never any possibility that, if only we had tried, we could have "gotten along" with so odious a regime.

Nevertheless, many American diplomatic historians have made, and still make, the argument that the United States should have undertaken a greater effort than it did at the beginning of the Cold War to "get along" with the Soviet Union.[36] We have tended to reject the notion, popular early in the late 1940s and early 1950s, that Stalin was another Hitler, that what we were witnessing in the U.S.S.R. and Eastern Europe was not communism at all, but rather "Red Fascism."[37] It is quite true, of course, that the Soviet autocrat did differ from his German counterpart in several important ways, not the least of which was that Stalin was more cautious than Hitler and would back down if confronted with the fact or at least the plausible prospect of resistance.[38] Nor did Stalin ever seek the systematic extermination of an entire people: the Holocaust was, and remains, unique.[39]

But as both Robert Tucker and Alan Bullock have recently made clear,[40] the similarities between Stalin and Hitler far outweigh the differences. These were both remarkably single-minded men, driven to dominate all those around them. They combined narcissism with paranoia in a way that equipped them superbly for the task of obtaining, and holding onto, power. They persisted even in the most unpromising of circumstances; and although capable of tactical retreats, they were not to be swayed from their ultimate objectives. They were extraordinarily crafty, prepared to take miles when inches were given them. And, most important, they both had visions of security for themselves that meant complete insecurity for everyone else: we have long known that Hitler killed millions in pursuit of his vision, but we now know that Stalin killed many more.[41] It is really quite difficult, after reading careful studies like those of Tucker, Bullock, and also the Russian historian Dimitri Volkogonov, to see how there could have been any long-term basis for coexistence—for "getting along"—with either of these fundamentally evil dictators. One was dealing here with states that had been reshaped to reflect individuals; but these individuals, in turn, were incapable of functioning within the framework of mutual cooperation, indeed mutual coexistence, that any political system has to have if it is to ensure the survival of all of the parts that make it up.

The tragedy of Cold War history, then, is that although fascism was defeated in World War II, authoritarianism—as it had been nurtured and sustained by Marxism-Leninism—was not. That form of government was at the apex of its influence during the last half of the 1940s, even as the Soviet Union itself lay physically dev-astated:[42] material conditions alone do not explain everything that happens in the world.[43] As a result, Stalin was able to create or inspire imitators whose influence extended well past his own demise in 1953.

Stalin's clones appeared first in Eastern Europe, where he installed regimes that were so scrupulous in following his example that they conducted their own set of purge trials during the late 1940s, a decade after the "Leader of Progressive Mankind" had shown the way.[44] His influence was still present in that part of the world four decades later, as the careers of Erich Honecker, Nicolai Ceausescu, and their counterparts abundantly illustrate. Stalin certainly provided a model for the third great autocrat of the twentieth century, Mao Zedong, who it now appears had no interest in any form of cooperation with the United States when he took power in China in 1949.[45] Despite his differences with Stalin's successors, Mao was still emulating Stalin himself when he launched the ill-conceived "Great Leap For-ward" in 1957, a program of crash industrialization that is now believed to have cost the lives of between twenty and forty-six million Chinese, a civilian death toll that may be higher than what Stalin and Hitler together managed to achieve.[46] And then there were all the little Stalins and Maos who appeared elsewhere in the world during the Cold War: Kim Il-sung, Ho Chi Minh, Pol Pot, Fidel Castro, Haile Mengistu, Babrak Karmal, and many others, each of whom, like their teach-ers, promised liberation for their people but delivered repression.

Now, tyrants—even well-intentioned tyrants–are nothing new in history. Cer-tainly the United States associated itself with its own share of repressive dictators throughout the Cold War, and had been doing so long before that conflict began. But there was something special about the Marxist-Leninist authoritarians, and it is going to be important for post-Cold War historians to understand what it was.[47] They were all, like Hitler, murderous idealists, driven to apply all of the energies they and the countries they ruled could command in an effort to implement a set of concepts that were ill conceived, half-baked, and ultimately unworkable.[48] They believed that, by sheer force of will, all obstacles could be overcome, and they were willing to pay whatever price was necessary in terms of lives to overcome them.[49] There was little sense among them of the need to balance ends and means; rather, in such systems, as George Orwell noted long ago, ends justified means, which meant that means corrupted ends.[50] These were not hard-nosed realists but rather brutal romantics; that does not justify us, though, in romanticizing any of them.

V

But just what was it about the twentieth century that allowed such romantics to gain such power during its first eight decades, and then so abruptly, at the end of the ninth, to lose it? After all, the great authoritarians were not alien visitors: they obviously sprang from circumstances not of their own making, and they rose to preeminence by taking advantage—with astonishing skill and persistence—of the circumstances that surrounded them. History, for a long time, was on their side; and then it ceased to be. We need to understand why.

One way we might find out would be to follow another piece of advice from William Appleman Williams, which is that we rediscover Karl Marx.[51] It was Marx, more than anyone else, who alerted us to the fact that there are long-term, "substructural" forces in history, and that they do shape modes of economic production, forms of political organization, and even social consciousness.[52] To use a metaphor from much more recent discoveries in the geological sciences, Marx exposed the underlying "tectonic" processes that drive history forward, in much the same way that comparable processes push the continents around on the face of the earth.[53] These forces by no means determine the actions of individuals, but they do establish the environment within which they function. "Men make their own history," Marx emphasized in his famous 1852 essay, *The Eighteenth Brumaire of Louis Bonaparte,* "but they do not make it just as they please; they do not make it under circumstances chosen by themselves, but under circumstances directly found, given and transmitted from the past."[54]

We have neglected Marx's approach to history, I believe, for several reasons. First, we too easily confused Marxism with Marxism-Leninism, which was as thorough a perversion of Marx's own thinking as one can imagine.[55] Second, Marx's incompetence as an economist, which was considerable, obscured his strengths as a historian. Third, Marx himself weakened his historical analysis, though, by falling victim to what we now recognize as the Fukuyama fallacy:[56] this is the curious tendency of those who think that they have identified the ultimate "engine" of history to assume that history will stop with them. Marx insisted that the progression from feudalism through capitalism to socialism and communism was irreversible, but that it would then for some reason end at that point.

What really appears to have happened is that one set of tectonic forces—industrialization, the emergence of class-consciousness, and the alienation that flowed from it—undermined liberal democratic bourgeois market capitalism late in the nineteenth and early in the twentieth centuries, thus paving the way for fascism, communism, and the authoritarianism that accompanied them. But during the second half of the twentieth century these tectonic forces evolved into something else—post-industrialization, the emergence of communications consciousness, and the alienation that flowed from it—which then undermined the foundations of authoritarianism and brought us around to our next historically determined phase, which turned out to be liberal, democratic, bourgeois market capitalism all over again. Marx, it seems, had mixed up linear with cyclical processes in history,[57] and that was a substantial error indeed. But it does not invalidate his larger insight into the existence of tectonic forces and the role they play in human affairs. That insight might well serve as a starting point for a reconsideration, not just of the Cold War, but of the twentieth century as a whole.

The great authoritarians of this century arose, from this perspective, because they turned historical tectonics to their own advantage: they were able to align their own actions with deep sub-structural forces, and thus convey an appearance of inevitability—of having history on their side—in most of what they did. Nothing more quickly demoralizes one's opposition, after all, than the impression that history itself has turned against it.[58] With the passage of time, though, the historical tectonics shifted, the authoritarians' successors were unable to adapt, and they themselves became demoralized, with the result that their regimes collapsed very much as the dinosaurs did once the environment within which they had flourished no longer existed. One might even conclude from this that the Cold War's outcome was predetermined all along, and that the real tragedy of Cold War history was all the wasted effort the opponents of authoritarianism put into trying to bring about what was going to happen anyway.[59]

It is most unlikely, though, that Marx would have taken this position, because despite all of his emphasis on underlying historical forces, he was no historical determinist.[60] The authoritarians arose, he might well have argued, because a few key individuals made their own history by exploiting the circumstances that confronted them, circumstances that, at the time, presented them with immense possibilities. It was the *intersection* of action with environment that produced results, not action alone or environment alone. But once one admits that possibility, one also has to allow that the resistance to authoritarianism may have made a difference. It would make no sense to claim that dictators can exploit tectonic forces, but that their opponents can never do so. So let us consider the resistance to authoritarianism, and that gets us back to the actions the United States—and its allies—have taken in the affairs of this century.

If, as seems likely, the twentieth century is remembered as one whose history was very largely shaped by the rise and fall of authoritarian regimes, then historians will have no choice but to debate the role the United States played in resisting them. They may conclude that that role was an active one: that the Americans themselves harnessed tectonic forces even more successfully than the authoritarians did, and that after a protracted struggle the Wilsonian vision prevailed over those of Lenin, Stalin, Hitler, Mao, and their respective imitators for that reason. Or historians may see the American contribution as a more passive one: that it was one of holding the line, of providing evidence that authoritarianism need not be the only path to the future, until such time as the underlying tectonic forces shifted, thus undermining authoritarianism's foundations and bringing about the events we have recently witnessed. Or historians may take the position that the truth lay somewhere in between.

But whatever the direction these lines of interpretation eventually take, the role of the United States in resisting authoritarianism will be at the center of them. It would seem most appropriate, therefore, for historians of American foreign relations to be at the center of that debate. I see little evidence that that is happening, though, and I wonder if this is not because we have allowed Williams's "tragic" view of American diplomacy to obscure our vision. We have turned a set of criticisms that might have been appropriate for particular policies at a particular time and place into something approaching a universal frame of reference. We have transformed what was, in its day, a profoundly unorthodox criticism of conventional wisdom into an orthodoxy that has now become conventional wisdom. Like most orthodoxies, it does not wear particularly well; it distorts our understanding of our place in the world, and also of ourselves.

How often do we ask the question: "tragedy" as compared to what? Gaps exist, after all, between the aspirations and the accomplishments of all states, just as they do in the lives of all individuals; if they alone are to be our criteria for defining "tragedy," then that is a characteristic inseparable from human existence, which rather weakens its analytical usefulness. If one defines "tragedy" according to the *extent* of the gap between aspirations and accomplishments, it becomes a more fruitful concept. But if one then *compares* gaps in terms of their extent, setting the American "tragedy" against those of other Great Powers in the twentieth century, ours appears more to fade out than to stand out. Perhaps that is why the United States is still the country of choice for those who seek to leave their own countries in the hope of finding better lives. The truly oppressed normally flee *away* from their oppressor, not toward it. If we are to take the voices of the oppressed seriously in doing history, we will need to listen to everything they are telling us, not just those parts of it that fit our preconceptions.

That raises an additional reason, though, for rediscovering Karl Marx. One of his most powerful insights was that even the most successful and beneficial institutions carry within them the seeds of their own destruction. We have seen the authoritarians destroy themselves—with an arguable amount of help from us and from our friends—in a way that might not have surprised Marx and would surely have gratified him, given the extent to which his own philosophy had as its objective the liberation, not the enslavement, of the individual.[61] But the passage of time respects no state and no system, and from a Marxian perspective it is not too difficult to see where the internal contradictions in our own system—the "fault lines" along which tectonic forces intersect, if you will—may lie.

Go back to Woodrow Wilson, whose Fourteen Points speech anticipates, better than any other document I know, what is likely to be the central dilemma of the post-Cold War world. For is not the logic of open markets really economic integration, and is not the logic of self-determination really political fragmentation? And is this not a contradiction of such depth and such significance that Marx himself would have found it memorable? Can we really expect to abandon control of our economic lives—as market theory suggests we must—and at the same time take control of our political lives—as democratic theory suggests we should? Did Marx not teach us that economics and politics cannot be separated when it comes to human lives, however easily we may separate these categories in our minds? The fault line separating the forces of integration and fragmentation, not just in our own society but through much of the rest of the world as well, may turn out to be at least as long, as deep, and as dangerous as the one between democratic and authoritarian government that preoccupied us through so much of the twentieth century.[62] These considerations too, it seems to me, ought to fall within the scope of a truly international approach to American diplomatic history.

Americans are no more likely to be exempted from tragic processes in history than anyone else is; but American diplomatic historians have treated these processes in a shallow, shortsighted, and curiously antiseptic way. We need to regain a clearer sense of what real tragedy, in this less than perfect world, is all about. That means placing our concept of tragedy within an international context. It means comparing the American "tragedy" with the others that surrounded it. It means using history as a genuine way of learning, not simply as a convenient platform from which we hold forth, either in self-condemnation or self-congratulation. It means, in the most fundamental sense, meeting our obligations as historians, which involve being honest not only about ourselves but about the environment in which we have had to live. And it means according equal respect, as I fear we have not yet done, to *all* of the survivors, and to *all* of the dead.

NOTES

1. William Appleman Williams, *The Tragedy of American Diplomacy*, rev. ed. (New York, 1988), 15. The first edition of Williams's book appeared in 1959. For two excellent assessments of Williams's influence see Bradford Perkins, "The Tragedy of American Diplomacy: Twenty-Five Years After," in *Redefining the Past: Essays in Diplomatic History in Honor of William Appleman Williams*, ed. Lloyd C. Gardner (Corvallis, OR, 1986), 21–34; and Gary R. Hess, "After the Tumult: The Wisconsin School's Tribute to William Appleman Williams," *Diplomatic History* 12 (Fall 1988):483–99.

2. See William G. Robbins, "William Appleman Williams: 'Doing History Is Best of All. No Regrets,'" in Gardner, ed., *Redefining the Past*, 3–19.

3. Gardner makes this point in *ibid.*, vii.

4. Williams, *The Tragedy of American Diplomacy*, 13.

5. See, for example, Christopher Thorne, "After the Europeans: American Designs for the Remaking of Southeast Asia," *Diplomatic History* 12 (Spring 1988):201–8; Michael H. Hunt, "Internationalizing U.S. Diplomatic History: A Practical Agenda," *ibid.* 15 (Winter 1991):1–11; idem, "The Long Crisis in U.S. Diplomatic History: Coming to Closure," *ibid.* 16 (Winter 1992): esp. 128–35; as well as essays by Robert J. McMahon, Emily S. Rosenberg, and Akira Iriye in *Explaining the History of American Foreign Relations*, ed. Michael J. Hogan and Thomas G. Paterson (New York, 1991).

6. Williams, *The Tragedy of American Diplomacy*, 16.

7. The best discussion of this Wilsonian synthesis is still N. Gordon Levin, Jr., *Woodrow Wilson and World Politics: America's Response to War and Revolution* (New York, 1968).

8. Robert A. Divine, *Second Chance: The Triumph of Internationalism in America during World War II* (New York, 1967); John Lewis Gaddis, *The United States and the Origins of the Cold War, 1941–1947* (New York, 1972), 1–31; Thomas G. Paterson, *Soviet-American Confrontation: Postwar Reconstruction and the Origins of the Cold War* (Baltimore, 1973), 1–29; Melvyn P. Leffler, *A Preponderance of Power: National Security, the Truman Administration, and the Cold War* (Stanford, 1992), 1–24.

9. Michael S. Sherry, *Preparing for the Next War: American Plans for Postwar Defense, 1941–45* (New Haven, 1977), and *The Rise of American Air Power: The Creation of Armageddon* (New Haven, 1987), makes this point effectively.

10. See Thomas M. Campbell, *Masquerade Peace: America's UN Policy, 1944–1945* (Tallahassee, 1973), esp. 197–200.

11. I have discussed the American habit of linking self-interest with disinterest at greater length in *The United States and the End of the Cold War: Implications, Reconsiderations, Provocations* (New York, 1992), 9–11.

12. The best discussion of Roosevelt's thinking on this matter is Warren F. Kimball, *The Juggler: Franklin Roosevelt as Wartime Statesman* (Princeton, 1991), 83–105. But see also G. John Ikenberry, "Rethinking the Origins of American Hegemony," *Political Science Quarterly* 104 (Fall 1989): esp. 380–81; and, for a good analysis of the prerequisites for such a concert, Charles A. Kupchan and Clifford A. Kupchan, "Concerts, Collective Security, and the Future of Europe," *International Security* 16 (Summer 1991):116–25.

13. See Leffler, *A Preponderance of Power,* 19; Ikenberry, "Rethinking the Origins of American Hegemony," 381–82. This vision of the postwar world, as Arthur Schlesinger has recently reminded us, was not too different from what the "new world order" of the post-Cold War era was supposed to look like. Arthur M. Schlesinger, Jr., "Franklin D. Roosevelt and U.S. Foreign Policy" (Address delivered at the Society for Historians of American Foreign Relations Annual Convention, Poughkeepsie, New York, 18 June 1992). See also, on this point, Kimball, *The Juggler,* 105.

14. Ikenberry, "Rethinking the Origins of American Hegemony," 384–85; also Henry R. Nau, *The Myth of America's Decline: Leading the World Economy into the 1990s* (New York, 1990), 87–92. The definitive account, of course, is Michael J. Hogan, *The Marshall Plan: America, Britain, and the Reconstruction of Western Europe, 1947–1952* (New York, 1987).

15. It has long been understood that Hitler's Germany was surprisingly loosely administered. See, on this point, Alan Bullock, *Hitler and Stalin: Parallel Lives* (New York, 1992), 424–29, 434–35.

16. Napoleon and Hitler provide two other striking examples of transplanted nationalism.

17. Robert C. Tucker, *Stalin in Power: The Revolution from Above, 1928–1941* (New York, 1990), 17–23, 60–64, 276–82, 482–86. See also Bullock, *Hitler and Stalin,* 632–35.

18. Quoted in Bullock, *Hitler and Stalin,* 633.

19. For Stalin's provincialism see *ibid.,* 31–32.

20. Tucker, *Stalin in Power,* 147.

21. I was told this tale by Stalin's wartime interpreter, Valentin Berezhkov.

22. Tucker, *Stalin in Power,* 215–17. See also Dimitri Volkogonov, *Stalin: Triumph and Tragedy,* ed. and trans. Harold Shukman (New York, 1991), 514.

23. Robert Conquest, *The Great Terror: A Reassessment* (New York, 1990), 486.

24. *Ibid.,* 70–71.

25. Robert Conquest, *The Harvest of Sorrow: Soviet Collectivization and the Terror-Famine* (New York, 1986), 306.

26. Volkogonov, *Stalin,* 505.

27. Quoted in Woodford McClellan, "Molotov Remembers," Cold War International History Project *Bulletin* 1 (Spring 1992): 19. This comment echoes one quoted long ago by Milovan Djilas: "The war shall soon be over. We shall recover in fifteen or twenty years, and then we'll have another go at it." *Conversations with Stalin,* trans. Michael B. Petrovich (New York, 1962), 114–15.

28. Bullock, *Hitler and Stalin,* 360–62, provides a clear explanation, based on psychiatric literature, of why paranoia need not be functionally disabling. For Stalin's intelligence see Volkogonov, *Stalin,* 225–36.

29. Tucker, *Stalin in Power,* esp. 130, 174–81, 425–31, 443–52, 473, is particularly good on the degree to which Stalinist methods extended down through all levels of the Soviet government.

30. Bradford Perkins has pointed out that by the 1970s "[a]lmost no historian any longer wrote on the Cold War with the purpose of holding Joseph Stalin guilty before the bar of history." "The Tragedy of American Diplomacy," 32.

31. I owe this point to my Ohio University colleague, Steven Miner. See also "Revelations from the Russian Archives," *IREX News in Brief* 3 (July/August 1992): 1, 4, an account of a recent exhibition of Soviet archival documents held at the Library of Congress. The *Bulletin* of the new Cold War International History Project at the Woodrow Wilson Center is an invaluable source of information on Soviet and East European archives.

32. Books such as Allen Weinstein, *Perjury: The Hiss-Chambers Case* (New York, 1978); Ronald Radosch and Joyce Milton, *The Rosenberg File: A Search for the Truth* (New York, 1983); and Robert Chadwell Williams, *Klaus Fuchs: Atom Spy* (Cambridge, MA, 1987),

have long since made it clear that Soviet espionage was no myth. But it is remarkable that Bennett Kovrig's *Of Walls and Bridges: The United States and Eastern Europe* (New York, 1991) is the only comprehensive history of United States policy toward Eastern Europe during the Cold War, and that apart from Bernard S. Morris, *Communism, Revolution, and American Policy* (Durham, 1987), almost nothing has been done on American attitudes toward communism as an ideology. For a convincing argument emphasizing the importance of ideology in Cold War history see John Mueller, "Quiet Cataclysm: Some Afterthoughts on World War III," in *The End of the Cold War: Its Meaning and Implications,* ed. Michael J. Hogan (New York, 1992), 40–41.

33. Hunt, "The Long Crisis in U.S. Diplomatic History," 117–21, makes this point in the course of criticizing what he describes as the "realist" school in the writing of American diplomatic history. But he then goes on to suggest that "progressive" historians, among whom he includes the corporatists, "share an antagonism toward realism" (p. 123). That may be, but this group by no means rejects "realism's" emphasis on the primacy of *interests;* indeed if anything, the "progressives" have reduced historical explanation to matters of material interest more determinedly than Hunt's "realists" have, as he subsequently comes close to acknowledging (p. 127). Part of the problem here may be that Hunt has confused the "realism" of international relations theorists like Hans Morgenthau and Kenneth Waltz, which is indeed reductionist in its emphasis on the primacy of states and interests, with a considerably more heterogenous group of American diplomatic historians.

34. Hans J. Morgenthau, *Politics among Nations: The Struggle for Power and Peace* (New York, 1948), along with its five subsequent editions, is of course the classic text. For a critique of "realist" theory by one of Hunt's "realist" historians see John Lewis Gaddis, "International Relations Theory and the End of the Cold War," *International Security* 17 (Winter 1992/93):5–58.

35. Speech to the National Association of Evangelicals, Orlando, Florida, 8 March 1983, *Public Papers of the Presidents: Ronald Reagan, 1983* (Washington, 1984), 363–64. It is often forgotten that the larger context of this speech was an attack, based on the theological arguments of C. S. Lewis, on the idea of "moral equivalency."

36. The most recent major study to take this view—even as it acknowledges the repressiveness of Stalin's regime—is Leffler, *A Preponderance of Power,* esp. 98–99. Leffler subsequently makes the point that "U.S. policymakers, like officials in other times and places, chose to deter and contain rather than reassure the enemy" (p. 121). But that, of course, assumes an "enemy" capable of being reassured. I have seen nothing in the recent biographical studies of Stalin to suggest that he met that standard.

37. See Les K. Adler and Thomas G. Paterson, "Red Fascism: The Merger of Nazi Germany and Soviet Russia in the American Image of Totalitarianism, 1930's–1950's," *American Historical Review* 75 (April 1970):1046–64.

38. It is difficult to imagine Hitler tolerating the continued independence of Finland in the way Stalin did after the Russo-Finnish War, for example, or agreeing to withdraw from northern Iran as readily as Stalin did after being challenged by the Americans in 1946, or behaving with the same circumspection that Stalin showed *after* he had authorized the 1948 Berlin blockade and the 1950 North Korean invasion of South Korea. For more on Stalin's cautiousness see Bullock, *Hitler and Stalin,* 856–57; also Vojtech Mastny, *Russia's Road to the Cold War: Diplomacy, Warfare, and the Politics of Communism, 1941–1945* (New York, 1979), esp. 311.

39. Bullock, *Hitler and Stalin,* 974. See also Charles S. Maier, *The Unmasterable Past: History, Holocaust, and German National Identity* (Cambridge, MA, 1988).

40. This paragraph summarizes several of the major arguments of Tucker's *Stalin in Power* and Bullock's *Hitler and Stalin.* Tucker makes the similarities explicit on pp. 591–92 of his book; Bullock's entire book deals with them, but see especially pp. 347–52 and 726.

41. Charles Maier estimates 20 million state-sanctioned deaths not resulting directly from military operations in the Soviet Union and its occupied territories between 1926 and 1953. His comparable figure for Germany and its occupied territories between 1933 and 1945 is 7.8 million, which includes 4.5 million Jews killed in the Holocaust. Maier, *The Unmasterable Past*, 74–75. Alan Bullock gives the figure of eighteen million "victims of Nazi brutality in the whole of Europe," including between 5.6 and 6.9 million Jews. Bullock, *Hitler and Stalin*, 808–9, 989. But Bullock's total presumably includes the direct victims of German military operations; Maier's does not. Robert Conquest's estimate of Soviet citizens who died as a result of collectivization and the purges is 17.5 million. Conquest, *The Harvest of Sorrow*, 306; and idem, *The Great Terror*, 485–86. But his figures do not include, as Maier's do, deaths in Soviet-occupied territories after 1939. Dimitri Volkogonov places the total for Stalin's victims, excluding all war losses, somewhat higher, at from 19.5 to 22 million. Volkogonov, *Stalin*, 824. A maximum estimate of Hitler's noncombatant victims, then, would fall well short of half the minimum estimate of Stalin's.

42. Adam B. Ulam, *The Communists: The Story of Power and Lost Illusions, 1948–1991* (New York, 1992), 1–9, makes this point effectively.

43. Consider the circumstances in which the Soviet sphere of influence, and then the Soviet Union itself, collapsed between 1989 and 1991. The military power of the Soviet state had never been greater, but unlike the situation in 1945, its authority—a psychological and not a material condition—was non-existent.

44. *Ibid.*, 25–27, 116. The encomium is from Georgii Malenkov's tribute to Stalin on his seventieth birthday in 1949, as quoted in Bullock, *Hitler and Stalin*, 958.

45. See, on this point, Yang Kuisong, "The Soviet Factor and the CCP's Policy toward the United States in the 1940s," *Chinese Historians* 5 (Spring 1992):17–34.

46. Harrison Salisbury, *The New Emperors: China in the Era of Mao and Deng* (Boston, 1992), 166.

47. It obviously was *not* Jeane Kirkpatrick's famous 1979 distinction between "authoritarian" and "totalitarian" regimes, with its claim that authoritarians, who tended to be on the right, might someday give up power, but that totalitarians, who were Marxist-Leninists, never would. Jeane J. Kirkpatrick, "Dictatorships and Double Standards," *Commentary* 68 (November 1979):34–45. After all, most of them just have, and Kirkpatrick has now reconsidered. See her *The Withering Away of the Totalitarian State . . . and Other Surprises* (Washington, 1990), esp. 274–75.

48. "It is a fact of major tragicomical proportions," Jon Elster noted in 1986, commenting on the influence of Friedrich Engels, "that a third of mankind professes these naive, amateurish speculations as its official philosophy." Jon Elster, *An Introduction to Karl Marx* (New York, 1986), 11. The origins of this tendency to force unworkable ideas on unwilling people are eloquently discussed in Richard Pipes, *The Russian Revolution* (New York, 1990), 121–52.

49. See Bullock, *Hitler and Stalin*, 293, 352, 551, 769.

50. I take this to have been the point of Orwell's providentially *un*prophetic novel *1984* (New York, 1949).

51. William Appleman Williams, *The Great Evasion: An Essay on the Contemporary Relevance of Karl Marx and on the Wisdom of Admitting the Heretic into the Dialogue about America's Future* (Chicago, 1964).

52. For a succinct overview see Ernst Breisach, *Historiography: Ancient, Medieval, & Modern* (Chicago, 1983), 292–95. Elster, *An Introduction to Karl Marx*, 103–21, provides a sharp critique.

53. I have developed this "tectonic" metaphor more fully in *The United States and the End of the Cold War*, 155–67.

54. Quoted in Robert C. Tucker, ed., *The Marx-Engels Reader*, 2d ed. (New York, 1978), 595.

55. See, on this point, Elster, *An Introduction to Karl Marx*, 13–14.
56. Named, of course, for Francis Fukuyama, who inappropriately chose the summer of 1989 to publish a widely read article entitled "The End of History?" *The National Interest* 16 (Summer 1989):3–18.
57. What happened to Marx might best be described with a fable. Once upon a time there was a historically conscious flea who lived inside a very large hula hoop. This flea believed strongly in historical progress, in marching smartly forward—to the extent that fleas can march—toward historically determined ends. "Almost there," the flea would say to himself, as he huffed and puffed along the inside of the hula hoop. "Any moment now." But of course the moment never came, and after flea-years of effort, having grown old in the pursuit of the ultimate end, the flea suddenly noticed one day that the landscape around him was beginning to look familiar. "It's *déjà vu* all over again!" the flea gasped, quoting Hegel, at which point he promptly fell over dead not far from the place at which he had begun. The moral of this story is that you can be just as surprised, in life, by facing forward without looking back as you can by facing backward without looking ahead. Or, to put it another way, curved surfaces often appear flat to those with limited horizons.
58. A point made with great clarity in Arthur Koestler's classic novel about the Moscow purge trials, *Darkness at Noon* (New York, 1940).
59. I am indebted to Philip Nash for suggesting this point.
60. Williams, *The Great Evasion*, 27–28, is particularly good on Marx's nondeterministic view of history.
61. Elster, *An Introduction to Karl Marx*, 25, 35, 43, 48–49.
62. For more on these tendencies see Gaddis, *The United States and the End of the Cold War*, 193–216.

"Revising Postrevisionism," or, the Poverty of Theory in Diplomatic History

Bruce Cumings

In spite of the title, this is not another essay about how badly read and provincial are American diplomatic historians; in fact, my temperature reading indicates a lot of good and interesting work out there. The title would have been unwieldy had I made my intent perfectly clear: This is an essay about how badly read and provincial are the keepers of the field—those who clean out the barnyard, get the cattle back into their cubbyholes, rake out the old, rake in the new, plant shoots, root out

Bruce Cumings, "'Revising Postrevisionism,' or, the Poverty of Theory in Diplomatic History," *Diplomatic History,* 17 (Winter 1993).

weeds, forecast crises and watersheds, sow discord, reap textbooks, pocket the rutabaga, and scold the rest of us for our lack of theory. My focus is on what is sometimes called "postrevisionism," an odd season coming after the shimmering summer of orthodoxy and the dusky winter of heterodoxy.

Rather than recite the Farmer's Almanac of postrevisionism, however, after some initial observations I will focus on one textbook, on the work of one self-described postrevisionist and one postrevisionist in spite of himself, and finally, on a postrevisionism that I can recommend highly—even if it is not our solution, but still part of the problem. I offer my critique in the spirit of Carl Becker's radical idea that a professor's purpose is "to think otherwise."[1]

ORTHODOXY AND REVISION: PERFECT, IMPERFECT, OR PLUPERFECT?

The most elemental act of "theory" is to name things: "x is y" might be the simplest summary of Heidegger's theme in *What Is Called Thinking?* Without comparing this to that, we cannot think. Without naming or "calling" we cannot think— "thinking *qua* thinking, is essentially a call," Heidegger wrote.[2] But there are better and worse names, better and worse calls, as the ancient Chinese philosophers knew. So we need another fillip to our "thinking": the rectification of names, another term for classification, or even dialogue and debate. And finally there is the problem Nietzsche posed, and that also became Heidegger's concern: "What things are called is incomparably more important than what they are."[3]

With this paragraph, we crank open a can of worms, true, but we retrieve it from a darkened pantry that the literature in question rarely if ever opened. The literature is suffused with "naming" and "calling" to be sure (a "Babel of labels," as we will see), but it barely gets us to the second level of rectification and debate. Furthermore, the names can barely stand the light of day.

The formulation that wishes to reign can be put simply: There is the orthodox literature on the Cold War, which was followed by the revisionist literature, which was then followed by the postrevisionist literature. What is called orthodoxy is usually assumed (something no self-respecting Chinese scholar would ever have done), but we recognize it in its solidity, its respectability, its immanent power. Revisionism then appears like a bucking bronco needing a saddle: unconfined, not reputable (if not disreputable), of fleeting influence. Postrevisionism is the wagon claiming to tether these two horses, taking energy from both. If this were "thesis: antithesis: synthesis," it might work. But it turns out that we do not know the thesis (what is the orthodox view?), the antithesis is badly understood, and the synthesis struts forth as a Whig attempt on a Chinese menu (to mix several metaphors), choosing one from Column A and one from Column B only to produce a dish that resuscitates "orthodoxy" for a new generation.

The proof of this pudding will come later. For now let us return to the phrase, "what things are called is incomparably more important than what they are." *What they are* is a phrase expressing the historian's *point d'honneur*: objectivity. The past "as it really was," the historian as the objective recorder of primary sources, history not as *a* pursuit of truth but as *the* pursuit of truth. Rankean method, which still holds sway in many history departments (albeit with a strong admixture of Anglo-Saxon positivism),[4] assumed that the historian could be trained to the objective standard of a camera lens, achieving results identical to the popular notion of the innocent eye of the camera: the historian's "eye" is merely there to record "the facts." The historian then performs the linguistic magician's trick of letting them "speak for themselves."

So, *what things are called* cannot be more important than what they *are;* to suggest so leads straight to a hell of nihilism and irrationality.[5] Is this Nietzsche's position?

It is not. He did not, of course, believe in positivist objectivity. He found in it an "unscrupulous benevolence": "The objective man is indeed a mirror," he wrote, "accustomed to submitting before whatever wants to be known."[6] But neither is this rejection of objectivity an act of nihilism and irrationality. The act of naming is, to paraphrase Heidegger, a "call" for the memory, a procedure of memory.[7] Historians are the custodians of memory, true, but Nietzsche has a different point. He takes us back to the barnyard.

Memory is precisely what distinguishes human beings from animals: "Consider the cattle," Nietzsche begins—they graze, munch grass, ingest and digest, buck snort into the ozone layer, and leap about with no sign of pleasure or melancholy. "This is a hard sight for man to see. . . . He cannot help envying them their happiness." The human wonders why the cow does not speak to him of his happiness (or not); the cow "would like to answer, and say: 'The reason is I always forget what I was going to say'—but then he forgot this answer too."[8]

Humans are not like that: man "clings relentlessly to the past: however far and fast he may run, this chain runs with him." And this is "a matter for wonder": "A moment, now here and then gone, nothing before it came, again nothing after it has gone, nonetheless returns as a ghost and disturbs the peace of a later moment. A leaf flutters from the scroll of time, floats away—and suddenly floats back again and falls into a man's lap. Then the man says 'I remember' and envies the animal."[9]

The barnyard animal, Nietzsche says, "lives *unhistorically,*" like the child playing "in blissful blindness between the hedges of past and future." But unlike the cow, the child's play will be disturbed: "Then it will learn to understand the phrase 'it was': that password which gives conflict, suffering, and satiety access to man . . . *an imperfect tense that can never become a perfect one.*"[10]

What things are called is how memory establishes its categories: Herbert Feis and Arthur Schlesinger, Jr., occupy a place in diplomatic history's mind as orthodox historians of the Cold War. William Appleman Williams locates in the memory as a "revisionist." But what does it mean, this term "revisionist"? Does it mean he revised earlier views? Or does it function semiotically for something else?

The orthodox school supplied an early and pithy answer: Williams is a Communist. Not a revisionist, not a neo-Marxist, but a Communist. In a letter to the executive secretary of the American Historical Association in 1954 (the apogee of McCarthyism), Schlesinger termed Williams a "pro-Communist scholar." The archly orthodox Feis, usually one to mince words, was not so inclined when referring to Cold War revisionists: He castigated the editor of the *New York Times Book*

Review in 1971 for having the temerity to substitute "Marxian" for "Communist" in a letter he wrote to the *Review:* "I meant Communist, not merely Marxian. . . . Most of the writings and analyses of the historians of the New Left seemed to me poor imitations of Communist official doctrine."[11] Indeed, what things are called seems to be more important than what they are.

Unconvinced? Then identify the author of these words: "The intense quest for exports . . . was inadvisable and always an impending source of conflict. . . . [I deplore] the fanaticism with which from the time of Secretary Hull, Will Clayton and Dean Acheson the American Government had made itself the exponent of trade expansion." This person went on to say that Stalin had not, in fact, supported the Greek guerrillas and that the invitation to the Soviets to join the Marshall Plan was just for show, framed precisely to elicit rejection. Is it Beard? Probably not, considering that he died in 1947. Williams? His ideas, but not his language. Gabriel Kolko or Harry Elmer Barnes? Too mild. It is Feis, in a letter mailed to Schlesinger within a month of the letter to the *Times Book Review.*[12]

No innocent bystander, no one uninvolved in our peculiarly American debates, would believe that truth, rather than naming, labeling, and stigmatizing, is at stake here: a hermeneutics of censure and exclusion. One observant foreigner, Mary Kaldor, dissects our Cold War debates with a few flourishes of her scalpel, coming to the conclusion that the real issue seems to be who started the Cold War, and little more than that—a question she rightly sees as moral or political, not historical.[13]

There is a historical method that can account for this American dissensus, however, and lead us to truth. It is Nietzsche's—made popular by Foucault as *genealogy.* "What then is truth?" Nietzsche asked in 1873: "A mobile army of metaphors, metonyms, anthropomorphisms, a sum, in short, of human relationships which . . . come to be thought of, after long usage by a people, as fixed, binding, and canonical. Truths are illusions which we have forgotten are illusions." Or as Alasdaire MacIntyre puts Nietzsche's broader point, truth is "an unrecognized motivation serving an unacknowledged purpose."[14]

There is not truth, but many claims to truth: to do history is to grasp the origins of a particular truth-claim. This is what Nietzsche did brilliantly in *The Genealogy of Morals,* thus to reconstruct the genealogy of Judeo-Christian morality. This is a better way of thinking about the *descent* of Cold War debate from 1945 to the present—it "explains more of the variance," to use the language of a political scientist.[15]

Nietzsche wrote that words like "meaning" and "purpose" are only signs that some master has imposed upon history, an assessment: What we know as history is always "a fresh interpretation . . . through which any previous 'meaning' and 'purpose' are necessarily obscured and even obliterated." History is thus "a continuous sign-chain of ever new interpretations" (incessant "revisionism" in our terms), expressing a genealogy of moral valence.[16]

Foucault took this argument up in a famous essay, "Nietzsche, Genealogy, History." Genealogy "opposes itself to the search for 'origins'"; for historians, origins means "that which was already there," as if it does not require a human being to determine "what was there," but can simply be "found." Instead, history "is the concrete body of a development, with its moments of intensity, its lapses, its extended periods of feverish agitation, its fainting spells; and only a metaphysician would seek its soul in the distant ideality of the origin."[17]

If there is truth in history, it does not reside in the shifting debates of historians, or in what statesmen say about their policies, or in what historians find in primary documents observed "pristine" in the archives, in the positivist sense that a transparent weathervane registers these documents correctly, without necessary recourse to a frame of reference, a set of assumptions, a theory. History with a capital *H* is not truth but a descent through various interpretations.

If we accept Foucault's arguments about "discourse," perhaps truth must be reconnoitered in some "prediscursive" structure, something prior to language and interpretation. What Foucault meant by the "prediscursive" is subject to sharp debate, but my sense of his and Nietzsche's thought is that they would see something like "class struggle" as discursive, something like a steel mill or an oil field, or perhaps a world market economy, as prediscursive.[18] If this is the case, the oil field remains uncomprehended without knowledge of what it is good for, without a conception of oil's relationship to something else: oil's value, perhaps, or a variant of the same thing, its uses for an industrial machine.

In this sense, the House of Saud, without a divining rod or a clue, ensconced itself on top of the prediscursive: the largest oil pools in the world. During World War II, the mammoth dimensions of the prediscursive disclosed themselves or, more properly, were discovered by people with the proper divining rods—but to do that you needed a theory (although not much of one).[19] Whereupon the House of Saud entered the industrial discursive . . . and Washington came to "a wholesale redefinition of the importance of the Middle East."[20]

Let us return to MacIntyre's rendering of Nietzsche's method of discovering truth through genealogy: Truth is "an unrecognized motivation serving an unacknowledged purpose." A Freudian idea perhaps, but also an Achesonian idea, a "Wise Men" idea. I was struck in Acheson's finely crafted memoirs to see him refer to the stillness that fell upon U.S.-Japanese relations in the days before Pearl Harbor by reference to "the apprehension of imponderables." As I wrote in my recent book,[21] he appeared to say that through his actions and those of others in the Roosevelt administration, a field of choice had corraled the Japanese, and that the only thing to do was wait and see which choice they made (attack—and lose; submit—and lose). Acheson went to chop trees in Archibald MacLeish's field on that Sunday morning, and before he was done chopping he got his answer—the one he appeared to want . . . a motivation unrecognized *by others* serving an unacknowledged purpose *of Acheson's*.

In Kai Bird's new book on John J. McCloy, we find this same seemingly indeterminate phrase reappearing, this time via Felix Frankfurter—who credited Bismarck with putting "'imponderables' into the vocabulary of affairs." McCloy also liked to use the term.[22] Then again, it might simply be that men like McCloy and Robert Lovett reserved their real thoughts (ponderables?) for people like Russell Leffingwell, chairman of the House of Morgan, when they were not sharing them with the Rockefellers.[23]

There seems to be something in the prediscursive that the Wise Men did not want to talk about with the rest of us, however, but merely wanted to "represent." Maybe oil is the answer, here, too. "Who says national security says Western Europe and oil" might be the simplest formulation of McCloy's 1940s viewpoint. Two weeks after Pearl Harbor he "startled" Henry Stimson by backing a campaign against Hitler in North Africa—"it must constantly be borne in mind that the greatest oil deposits in the world are in this area," he wrote.[24]

In early 1947, petroleum policy in the State Department was in Paul Nitze's hands, supervised by Dean Acheson (no doubt it is mere coincidence that these names keep popping up). The issue was how to erase the famous "Red Line" that Calouste Gulbenkian had drawn on the map in 1928, how now to divide Persian Gulf oil between American, British, and French companies, and even more, how to divvy up Saudi Arabia's vast new discoveries among American companies and find distributors capable of absorbing the tidal wave of oil about to slosh onto the world market, without destroying the world oil regime. The answer? Form a cartel with Socony, Socal, Standard of New Jersey, and Texaco and sell the oil to Western Europe and Japan—just then being reconstituted industrially by the United States. The four companies signed the historic agreement on 12 March 1947, which just happened to be the day that Truman spoke to a joint session of Congress about the defense of Greece and Turkey.[25]

Now loping into the field comes William S. Borden, to show how Japan and Germany were posted as industrial workshops in the late 1940s, linked to regional spheres of economic influence, and fueled by cheap oil from the Middle East—something he calls "capitalist-bloc multilateralism" (not a bad name, that). Industrial revival would create markets for American goods, particularly if cheap energy kept the costs of production down. (Getting Europe and Japan off coal and onto oil would also weaken the power of left-wing miners' unions.) All this, of course, meant restoring colonial relationships "to the south," now viewed as "natural economies" functioning according to the doctrine of comparative advantage, no longer exclusive to the colonizers but "open" to American influence. The "reverse course" in Japan was thus not a product of the Cold War so much as a rearrangement of the world economy. (Alfred Chandler was once asked how Japan and West Germany "did it": "improved institutional arrangements and cheap oil" was his answer.) None of it really got working smoothly, however, until the Korean War came along, solving (with its military procurements and the pump-priming of NSC-68-style military Keynesianism) the "dollar gap" problem.[26]

With Borden's fine book, we move forward to the apprehension of ponderables, to motivations recognized and serving acknowledged purposes: that is, the truth of the early Cold War period. And lo and behold, the declassified discursive finds the orthodox Kennan fretting about how Japan might "reopen some sort of Empire toward the South."[27]

In my recent book, I sought, in the most careful language I could muster, to suggest that Acheson's thinking about the unmentionable, signified by "the apprehension of imponderables," might also have had something to do with his famed "Press Club speech" in January 1950. The general reaction has been this: "you must subscribe to a conspiracy theory." "Conspiracy theory" in the American context, as we will see, connotes a theory, the capitalist clique/plot as the only way of thinking about the generalized interest that Acheson and McCloy represented (and *said* they represented, not to mention being *paid* to represent).

With this discussion as preface, we now seek to demonstrate our points from the literature of orthodoxy and revisionism.

HISTORY IN THE PLUPERFECT[28] TENSE: WHO WILL EDUCATE THE EDUCATORS?

I now wish to lasso three representative examples of naming, cubbyholing, and theorizing from the field of American diplomatic history. The first is a representative textbook; the second, the work of arch-postrevisionist John Lewis Gaddis; and the third, arch-cubbyholer and devotee of theory, Michael H. Hunt.

We begin with Jerald A. Combs's *American Diplomatic History*,[29] a taxonomic effort useful for my task on three counts: (1) Professor Combs assumes that we all know what we mean when we say "orthodox" and "revisionist"; (2) he recapitulates Schlesinger's and Feis's concerns with "naming"; (3) Michael Hunt's backcover endorsement enthusiastically calls it "detailed, scrupulous, fair-minded." (The reader should keep in mind that this is a textbook, designed to introduce students to the field, and that therefore many of my criticisms of Dr. Combs are better directed at the field he tills.)

Although "orthodoxy" is never quite specified, we deduce from chapter fourteen ("The Cold War") that it is solid and mainstream and that the correct position was first inscribed by George Kennan, Louis Halle, Hans Morgenthau, Samuel Flagg Bemis, Winston Churchill, Robert Murphy, and Herbert Feis. Only one of these names a historian (Bemis). Revisionism's meaning is also assumed. It first sallies forth with the Wilsonian D. F. Fleming, thence with "neo-Marxist" William Appleman Williams and his prominent students (Thomas J. McCormick, Walter LaFeber, Lloyd Gardner—p. 256), and finally with "hard-line economic determinist" Gabriel Kolko (p. 314). Kolko's appearance begets adjectival distinction, and we now learn of "moderate" and "radical" revisionists.[30]

Williams and his group appear at first to belong to the "moderate" camp. We learn (and they learn) that "their critique was based on Lenin's theory that imperialism was an inevitable consequence of capitalism." Still, according to Combs, they do not treat American policy as "a vicious plot by an evil capitalist clique but as a product of general American ideology" (p. 257). Unpacking this particular rectification of names is taxing, but it appears to mean this: (1) "radical" revisionists treat American policy as a vicious plot by evil capitalist cliques; (2) "moderate" revisionists, to the contrary, follow in the van of Vladimir Ilyich who—based on the above evidence—thought imperialism was an inevitable consequence of capitalism, that is, a product of general American ideology. Or perhaps it means that by focusing on "ideology," the "moderates" avoid the pitfall of conjuring evil capitalist clique plots (which the "radicals" do not). But then further on Combs speaks of "Kolko and other socialists of strong economic determinist leanings like the William Appleman Williams group" (p. 315); on the same page LaFeber is specifically included in the "radical revisionist" category for making the (empirical) observation that it was Roosevelt rather than Truman who accepted French reoccupation of Indochina. As we turn the page, the now-seamless unanimity of the revisionists is illustrated with a quote from Noam Chomsky. The first nonhistorian to intrude the revisionist circle in Combs's account, Chomsky is chided for asking how historians could "regard America's leaders as merely mistaken, 'noble and virtuous, bewildered and victimized but not responsible, never responsible.'"

At the end of this same paragraph, however, Combs quite inadvertently says what he really thinks: that during the Vietnam years, "the revisionist view had acquired respectability, and historians found themselves compelled to deal with it in earnest." Later on (p. 333) he makes the same point: "The revisionist voice was never more than a minority voice in the historical community [*sic*], but . . . it could be ignored no longer by the leading diplomatic historians as it had been in the previous era."

That is, there are revisionists, and then there are historians. We found but one academic historian in the orthodox column and only one nonhistorian in the revisionist, but nonetheless there are people—"leading historians" would be a good guess—who decide what to ignore and what not to, what to respect and what not to. By a rhetorical inversion, made no less impressive to eager students by Combs's unconscious sleight of hand, the orthodox (non-) historian now strides forth as solid, respectable, and powerful; the revisionist (historian) as wild (Leninist when not "vehement and relentless in [his] Marxism," like Kolko—p. 327), not reputable (the revisionist is not really a historian), and of fleeting influence (destined to be ignored in any but an unusual era like Vietnam). Postrevisionism is barely a murmur in Combs's account, but encomiums to John Lewis Gaddis close chapter nineteen: he (together with Alonzo Hamby) did not do much to alter "the overall perspective" of a Kennan or a Lippmann, to be sure; instead, in Combs's view, "they simply elaborated upon it and *placed it more accurately in historical context*" (my emphasis).

To summarize Professor Combs's rectification of names: American officials are the authors of the orthodox historical position. Revisionists are people who reject this position, drawing on Marx and Lenin. Historians are the people who ignore the revisionists while elaborating upon and placing in historical perspective the orthodox view.

If this procedure exemplifies the thinking in a cubbyholing "book on the field," it also serves as an unwritten rule of politics and discourse in academe. The truth of the matter is—and I do not say this to single out Professor Combs, but to single out the profession—that all these labels (radical, revisionist, determinist, not to mention neo-Marxist or Leninist) signify not an intellectual approach to the subject, but a politics of censure. They signify not thinking, but fear. They signify exclusion.

In Heidegger's terms, these names "call" people for our memory, where they reside in a category called stigma. They connote Peter Novick's observation: "By aggregating a carefully selected list of writers—including the most vulnerable, and omitting the most circumspect, all Cold War revisionists could be tarred . . . and made collectively responsible" for the work of all those so designated.[31] They signify Chomsky's original, devastating insight in his famous article in 1966,[32] that most scholars do not wish to speak truth to power, they do not wish to hold our public servants responsible for their acts, but busy themselves instead in apologetics, in succoring the powerful and ignoring or blaming the victims. They tell us, in short, what a blight on the mind was the Cold War struggle.

For this essay I reread Lloyd Gardner's *Architects of Illusion,* to see if I still thought it was the fine book I did when I first read it in 1970. I noticed some scribbling in the margins by a young graduate student who wondered if Gardner had really read Kolko. Other than that, I would not change a word in the light of more than two decades passing, and I doubt that Lloyd would either.

Disciple of the "Leninist" Williams that he was, Gardner cited Vladimir Ilyich exactly twice: first to show Lenin's affinity with William Bullitt's views on Germany; second to show his affinity with Listian political economy—according to Lord Keynes. Gardner's brilliant chapter on Kennan led me to reflect on what a masterful name George Frost brought to his doctrine: containment! Imagine, for an America to march outward and inherit Britain's role, and you mark it up for the *defense.* Imagine, a doctrine defining hegemony by what it *opposes,* obviating the necessity to explain to the American people what it *is,* and what its consequences will be for them.

Here is what Gardner says about the "orthodox" Cold War histories (p. 301): "Early books on the origins of the Cold War were little more than annotated collective memoirs of Americans who participated in that transition period. The historian's facts and conclusions had already been chosen for him before he began." What was the Cold War about, according to Gardner? When all was said and done, Eugene Meyer, head of the World Bank in 1947, got it right (p. 318): Meyer had "one conception," "the idea of America's having succeeded to the world power which was once Britain's."

JOHN LEWIS GADDIS AS EDUCATOR

We begin with my well-thumbed and annotated copy of John Gaddis's first book.[33] I see by the furious marginal scribblings that I could write fifty pages on his first chapter. So let me be brief: By 1972, that is, two decades ago, Gaddis's postrevisionism was already well advanced, even if not yet named. The orthodox school no longer reigned: Schlesinger appears only in the bibliography, Feis comes in for mild criticism (p. 266n), Kennan comes in for long discussion and nuanced appreciation, but not without some demurrals (for example, p. 323). Orthodoxy is not questioned, it merely disappears; Gaddis has no sustained account of how his work differs from the old school.

We do come to know that he differs from revisionists, however. Such people, we learn on the second page of the preface, have "performed a needed service," but alas, "their focus has been too narrow." Gaddis, to the contrary, has "tried to convey the full diversity" of the many other forces that helped determine American policy.

Kolko gets his dismissal in a footnote (pp. 50–51): He was wrong about the United States "deliberately set[ting] out to counteract" the Left on a world scale (in fact, when American authorities disarmed local resistance groups, according to Gaddis, they did so to secure communications and restore civilian governments);

Kolko also "focuses too narrowly on economic factors." The conclusion has a some-what longer discussion (pp. 357–58), emphasizing again the narrowness of an economic focus, the assumption (just like Combs) that a host of disparate revisionists subscribe to "the basic elements of the Williams thesis" (Barton Bernstein, Gardner, Kolko, LaFeber, Gar Alperovitz, David Horowitz). All neglect "the profound impact of the domestic political system on the conduct of American foreign policy." Yet Gaddis's book mostly lacks the evidence to make this last point, his central one: an unsystematic, nearly random survey of articles in the popular press, sermons by Fulton J. Sheen, speeches in the *Congressional Record*, etc., is no way to judge how "profound" was the impact of domestic politics.

Shortly we get this sentence: "One might, of course, argue that the political system reflected the economic substructure, and that American officials were un-witting tools of capitalism, but it is difficult to justify this assumption [*sic*] without resorting to the highly questionable techniques of economic determinism." Lest anyone fail to get the point, the next sentence begins. "At times, it seems as if revisionists do employ this approach."

Translated: Some people argue that the American political system reflected the economic substructure. What that means is that American officials were unwitting tools of capitalism. It is difficult to justify this assumption. (Untranslatable: justify Gaddis's attributed assumption? Which one? Or does he mean prove or disprove the relationships just posited?) To justify that highly questionable assumption you need to resort to the highly questionable "techniques" (methods, presumably) of "economic determinism" (not explained; it is assumed we all know what that is).

If my angst shows through, perhaps it is because we assign these books to young students. And here is the logic a student would pick up: revisionists are people who focus narrowly on economics and believe in the capitalist clique/plot theory, which can only be justified by the highly questionable methods of the capitalist clique/plot methodology. And with that, you can dismiss a book like *The Politics of War*—which has at least one substantive (and often empirical or evidential) alternative judgment per page to Gaddis's book.

Rather than structure a debate (in which case a fair presentation of your opponent's ideas is obligatory) or try to refute the revisionist account with evidence (in which case Kolko merits a chapter, not a footnote), Gaddis's treatment is purely discursive, designed rhetorically to malign the enemy, close off debate, warn readers away, and, perhaps most important in 1972, return a generation of young people to the fold.

Having said all that, Gaddis's first book was a useful, thoughtful contribution to the debate on the Cold War, one that I always suggest to students. It just is not as good as Kolko's, which still stands today as the best single account of the origins of the Cold War.[34]

By 1983, "postrevisionism" had pushed up roots as such, with Gaddis's influential article—although, as he acknowledges, he did not invent the term.[35] It would be a fruitless exercise for me to indicate my points of disagreement with this text, because Lloyd Gardner and Warren Kimball did that so well at the time.[36] But I would remind readers of Kimball's conclusion: Postrevisionism is "orthodoxy plus archives." It is also revisionism minus archives.

For much of the article, Gaddis cites recent work presumably proving this and disproving that about the origins of the Cold War, while calling for more "sophisticated" analysis of imperialism (for example, the work of Wolfgang Mommsen), and better understanding of the balance of power, the role of bureaucracies, internal "determinants" of foreign policy, comparative history, and "the impact of United States policies on foreign societies."[37] Gaddis seems to have grown more sophisticated himself by this time, writing freely of "the American empire."

In fact, the hermeneutics of censure and exclusion had not changed, and Gaddis's reading of the revisionists had become worse, more malevolent—akin to the Schlesinger and Feis position (these are Communists). The synonym for revisionists used throughout the text is "New Left." It was not only Combs in 1983 but also Gaddis in 1983 who lumped Williams together with other revisionists as those utilizing "the classical [sic] Leninist model of imperialism" (p. 172; see also pp. 175, 183).[38] While granting that revisionists were never monolithic, Gaddis proceeded to make them sound very much so, once again rounding up the usual suspects: Alperovitz, Bernstein, Gardner, LaFeber, Kolko, Williams (p. 173n). But as with Combs, Kolko begat distinction: "militantly revisionist" (p. 181n). The revisionist theory, according to Gaddis, had to do with an American "crisis of capitalism" necessitating exports and foreign markets, an "internally motivated drive for empire."[39] And, of course, the clique/plot soon trots along: Americans, the revisionists say, were "tricked by cynical but skillful leaders into supporting this policy of imperialism" (p. 173).

By the end of the article (p. 189) we learn that revisionists were tempted by the siren song of turning "history into an instrument of politics" and genuflected "as if by reflex, to the changing ideological fashions of the day." But now, Gaddis wrote, it was time to remember the impact historians have on society generally, thereby imposing "an obligation to get our history as straight as we can at the beginning." This was now being done by people who "put childish things away," by mature historians who had marched into the archives. Translation: Revisionists did not do history and do not use archives.[40]

Somehow the image of Bill Williams trimming his coat to the "ideological fashions of the day" in the late 1950s is almost as funny as the idea that Cold War historians ought to have gotten their history as straight as they could "at the beginning"—presumably 1947, when Beard scolded Truman for his new doctrine and Schlesinger fashioned "the vital center" while judging James Burnham's new book (calling for a unilateral American global empire) to be brilliant and perceptive. I prefer this formulation, recalling Gardner's reference to Eugene Meyer: "The beginning is, rather, the veil that conceals the origin."[41]

Postrevisionism has the same hermeneutics as the orthodox school: Schlesinger and Feis and Gaddis agree on what to call the revisionists. But perhaps they disagree on what constitutes orthodoxy. For Schlesinger, orthodoxy meant adherence to the position that the Cold War (for Americans) was "the brave and essential response of free men to Communist aggression." The minute he says it, of course, we recognize it as unhistorical: not a statement of fact, nor an idea, but a moral position that can function from 1776 to the Gulf war. It was "brave." These were "free men." Passive and inert, they responded to "aggression," modified and made more threatening by the adjective "Communist." ("Essential" can have at least two meanings in this context, so I leave it uninterpreted.)[42] By the late 1960s, "Communist aggression" had become, at least for a younger generation, a signifier for Dean Rusk lying about Vietnam. And by 1983, *a fortiori,* no ambitious historian-of-the-field seeking consensus would be caught dead saying something quite so revealing.

So: an agreement on names, on "what things are called," but not on substance now characterized orthodoxy and postrevisionism. Why? Is it a matter of new primary materials, yielding new knowledge? Perhaps—but if so, that would explain 1983, but not 1993, when diplomatic historians tack to a zeitgeist now willing, in the face of the collapse of Western communism, to read the historical judgment of 1989–1993 back into the origins of the Cold War, thereby dusting off Schlesinger's position for a new generation.

It might be a matter of theory, in that Feis, Schlesinger, and Gaddis truly must have no idea what the multivariate school they call revisionism is talking about; to give a student *The Tragedy of American Diplomacy* and get back the notion that Williams uses Lenin's theories, or is a Communist, would merit an *F*. Perhaps for Feis at least, any theory linking American expansion to economic motivation sent him scurrying to the shelf where he kept Stalin's speeches (unless he was castigating Cordell Hull privately to Schlesinger). But even so, the grade is *F;* this is not theoretical debate so much as theory confronting a tabula rasa, theory against atheory, the failure of orthodoxy and postrevisionism to grasp theory (let alone present one themselves).

Nor can the disagreement on substance be a matter of truth, that what was "true" in 1955 became "false" in 1967, partially true in 1983, and fully true in 1989. Merely to formulate this sequence is to conjure with "relativism," another bogeyman for historians. For the orthodox school, then, there must have been truth followed by the interruption of passion, whereupon truth outed again: precisely what Allan Bloom manifestly thought, for example, in his best-selling book where everything connoted by "the 60s" functions as foolish passion, when it is not original sin.[43] It is also what Gaddis thinks: Put your childish things away.

Gaddis found another "synthesis" in 1986, with a new name: "corporatism." Again, I cannot offer a better defense of corporatism than its advocates have put forth.[44] I merely want to replay one part of one paragraph (Gaddis, p. 358):

> At this point, I must confess to a certain perplexity as to just what corporatism is. . . . It is clearly not the Marxist-Leninist view of capitalism, because in the corporatist scheme of things the state is not solely the puppet of economic interests, but exerts some degree of control over them. At the same time, though, neither is corporatism a system of absolute state control, as is found in the Soviet Union today. . . . Corporatism does not connote simply the interest of the business community, because it includes as well the concerns of labor and agriculture.

In 1986 the literature on the relative autonomy of the capitalist state was all the rage, Thomas Ferguson had spelled out his theory on which industrial firms accommodated labor and which did not, and students of communism were beginning to understand the imbedded character of socialist states (for example, China's "iron rice bowl"). If we cannot expect Gaddis to have read that literature, let alone Marx or Lenin on the state (grotesquely caricatured here), we might expect him to have read Beard, who, in *The Open Door at Home,* understood that American capitalism had not one but two broad tendencies (which he grouped under the industrial and the agrarian "theses"), each having a differential relationship to the state. Gaddis's perplexity, though, is surely American: If you look up "corporatism" in the *Encyclopedia of the Social Sciences,* you will find this: "See fascism." This perplexity did not keep Gaddis from finding a new wagon with which to tether two broncos (revisionism and corporatism): "reductionism."

We find this term in Gaddis's next attempt to till the field, his 1990 critique of the "parochialism," "American exceptionalism," and "systematic innocence" of American historians who try to understand foreign relations.[45] "Our generalizations have not been as sophisticated as they might have been," he says, and then leaps to the attack against—are you ready?—Bill Williams! As if animated by some hidden reflex (to use his metaphor), Gaddis begins just as he did two decades earlier, just as he did a decade earlier: hiving off after the revisionists, now lumped under a new rubric: "reductionists." Williams, Gardner, LaFeber, McCormick—the whole gang tried to explain American behavior "almost exclusively in economic terms" (p. 407). If these horses were not in the barnyard, Gaddis would have to buy them at auction, so intent is he on flogging them yet again (which is not to suggest they are in any sense "dead," quite the contrary). It is possible that the entire field of diplomatic history would have nothing to talk about if Bill Williams had stayed in the United States Navy?

True to hermeneutic form, Kolko also gets his licks, disguised as praise: He had the "strength" to provide "an explicit methodological justification for reductionism" (p. 409). When I looked up the reference in *Politics of War* I could not imagine what Gaddis referred to, but then I understood that his comment was mimetic of the earlier claim that those who theorize the capitalist clique/plot use capitalist clique/plot methods.

There are new books, however, that "go beyond the reductionism of Williams and the corporatists" (the new conflation). Michael Hunt's *Ideology and United States Foreign Policy* is Gaddis's example, which we treat below. But alas, Hunt also wanders into reductionist pastures, by putting "race" at the center of the American worldview. (This is the part of his book that I particularly liked.) So, how to get beyond those who think in single categories—"whether economic, corporatist, or racist"?

Gaddis suggests "eclecticism," while noting its demerits (p. 409). If "ours is, after all, a *social* science," can we not be as content as scientists doing quantum mechanics with "imperfect explanations"? Did Einstein now allow for a four-dimensional universe? Returning us to the corn field, Gaddis then discovers the "cropduster" approach to history, which certainly is not one-dimensional, even if it does get applied "in an indiscriminate way." Here (p. 410) the example is Emily Rosenberg's *Spreading the American Dream,* a good book he says, but weakened by adherence to "what she calls 'liberal-developmentalism'," arguing that there could be (quoting Rosenberg) "no truly enlightened dissent against the ultimate acceptance of American ways, and this faith bred an intolerance, a narrowness, that was the very opposite of liberality."

True perhaps of the American role in Guatemala or Vietnam, Gaddis allows, but what about South Korea (he also mentions Japan and West Germany)? Here I must pass, if not pass out (history as Foucault's "fainting spell"), because forty years of American-supported state terror in South Korea is not sufficient evidence to make Professor Rosenberg's point. Soon Gaddis is back to flaying Williams (this time as an American exceptionalist) and assaying another brand of reductionism: dependency theory ("dependency theory . . . combine[s] the worst features of the 'reductionist' and 'crop-duster' approaches"—pp. 414–15). The first book illustrating this discussion is LaFeber's *Inevitable Revolutions*—and by now I imagine that LaFeber is ready to strap himself into that cropduster in *North By Northwest* and take a flyer over some Ohio cornfields.[46]

The most recent of Gaddis's essays (at this writing), his 1992 SHAFR Presidential Address,[47] arrived perfectly timed and miraculously appropriate for my conclusions on his work. As if I had scripted the essay, he begins again with Williams (first sentence). Even the title is taken from Williams. And then come the labels. But a dialectical reversal has occurred: Gaddis is the revisionist, Williams the champion of orthodoxy. *Tragedy* had now become "the conventional wisdom." The end of the Cold War, however, must cause historians "to jettison . . . orthodoxies, and long-cherished pearls of conventional wisdom" and become instead "post-Cold War revisionists" (p. 2).

The rest of the essay dwells mainly on what a monster Stalin was, how much citizens of the former Soviet Union now agree with Ronald Reagan that theirs was an "evil empire," how all the world's Communist leaders were just like Stalin ("Stalin's clones"), and just like Hitler ("murderous idealists"). Gaddis then executes another reversal, opining that "we have neglected Marx's approach to history."

The essay concludes by suggesting that at the dawn of the Cold War only the United States stood between civilization and mass murder, but that we still fail to see this because "we have allowed Williams's 'tragic' view of American diplomacy to obscure our vision" (p. 15). It is now our "universal frame of reference," our new "orthodoxy" and "conventional wisdom." Gaddis closes with this missive: "We need to regain a clearer sense of what real tragedy, in this less than perfect world, is all about. . . . [This] means, in the most fundamental sense, meeting our obligations as historians, which involve being honest not only about ourselves but about the environment in which we had to live. And it means according equal respect, as I fear we have not yet done, to *all* of the survivors, to *all* of the dead."

Thus, Bill Williams gets flogged whether he is a pro-Communist, a revisionist, a reductionist, an American exceptionalist, the author of the new orthodoxy in diplomatic history, or, by implication, a dishonest historian who ignored the millions who died at the hands of world-historical monsters. And we still wait, through two decades of writing, for John Lewis Gaddis to take one of his arguments seriously and try to refute it.

This latest essay struck me as an exercise in fiction. (No serious person can claim that Williams or his school represent orthodoxy.) It is akin to what I wrote about Schlesinger—we recognize the viewpoint as unhistorical: not a statement of fact, nor an idea, but a moral position, a political point, Gaddis getting his licks in on Williams again.

Of course, Hegel was right: There is a cunning to history, it has its utterly unexpected reversals and inversions. One of them is happening in 1993: We can now see that the end of the Cold War was not the victory of democracy and the market, the death knell of the Beard/Williams critique, the occasion for a definitive reckoning with "tragedy," the finale for monsters profligate in taking lives, or the end of history. It was a return, in the Old Testament sense: to history, to the imperial overstretch Beard warned against, and to the ethnic and racial barbarism that was Hitler's distinctive form of evil.

But we can now take stock of Gaddis's critique and, as 1992 presidential candidate Ross Perot liked to say, clean out the barn. We can rectify names. Professor Gaddis is not a postrevisionist. He is an anti-revisionist, every bit as determined as 1950s historians like Schlesinger and Samuel Eliot Morison to plow their furrow and call it "mainstream," and to put Beard out to pasture:[48] It is just that Bill Williams is Gaddis's Beard. But Gaddis is not anti-orthodox.[49] The corpus of his work is entirely bereft of "thinking otherwise" about our leaders and their policies, or speaking truth to power (to cite a realist named Morgenthau). "Postrevisionism" in this case connotes not a synthesis, but a vain attempt at post-Indochina War consensus, marred continuously by the habits of stigma and exclusion. Fortunately, it has not worked, and we may say of Williams in the 1990s what Hartz said of Beard in the 1950s, that when all is said and done "Beard somehow stays alive, and the reason for this is that, as in the case of Marx, you merely demonstrate your subservience to a thinker when you spend your time attempting to disprove him."[50]

MICHAEL HUNT AS EDUCATOR

Professor Hunt is another keeper of the field, and may also be called a postrevisionist even if he does not use the term. His *Ideology and United States Foreign Policy*[51] seeks to show how both Kennan (orthodox) and Williams (revisionist) were acts in a long-running American drama. The curtain went up with Thomas Paine and his likes (1776 and all that), and the way Americans think about the world has not changed much since. This is a good and useful book, like Hunt's others.[52] It has an excellent chapter showing how Anglo-Saxon males from Ben Franklin to Dean Acheson discoursed authoritatively on the manifold demerits of every (other) racial and ethnic group in the world and often despised the American mass democracy that they purported to champion.[53]

Hunt is good at revealing the moral side to Kennan's vaunted realpolitik, and the discussion of Williams and his students has better aim than the Combs/Gaddis buckshot. After a reasonable summary of Williams's account of "informal open door imperialism," Hunt says rightly that Williams "also drew, in a free-wheeling way, on Marxist theory" (pp. 9–10) and later notes the many differences among Williams's students (p. 200). Shortly, however, a fly buzzes into the ointment (p. 11):

> Though he claimed that the open-door ideology was the product of objective economic forces, little of *Tragedy* is devoted to demonstrating the link between the requirements of the economy and the concerns of policymakers. Indeed, Williams has

on occasion seemingly rejected a clear-cut economic determinism. Ideas, he noted in a 1966 essay, may "originate as instruments of specific interests" only in time to "break their narrow bounds and emerge as broad, inclusive conceptions of the world."

Thus, Hunt finds Williams guilty of an "interpretive ambiguity": "*Tragedy* insists on the centrality of the connection, but . . . having made this concession, [Williams] leaves us wondering how central economic self-interest is." This lapse, Hunt thinks, "deserves attention for the limitations it reveals about any conception of ideology that is tied tightly to economic self-interest." What is the source of Williams's confusion? It is his "excessively narrow conception of ideology colliding with his sensitivity to historical complexity."

Let me summarize Hunt's point: Williams rejected "a clear-cut economic determinism." Williams thereby escapes being hoisted on that petard. But this makes his theory confusing, in Hunt's understanding. Why is that? Because Williams's "excessively narrow conception of ideology" (which Hunt just said he did not have) has bumped into "historical complexity." Hunt goes on in the next paragraph to reject definitions of ideology that are "either dismissive [Kennan] or reductionist [Williams]." In sum: Williams is reductionist whether he is reductionist or not.

Hunt now invokes Clifford Geertz, Gabriel Almond, and Sidney Verba to make perfectly clear things ideological (p. 12). They help us to understand that ideology "is much more than simply a tool wielded in the self-interest of . . . calculating capitalists." Ideologies, as they show, are "coherent systems of symbols, values and beliefs." At the heart of their approach is, first, "a refusal to posit a single, simple reason for the origins and persistence of a particular ideology," for example, "the existence of a 'base' that determines the 'superstructure.'" Again, an inquiring student would conclude that with Williams you really get, when all is said and done, the capitalist clique/plot. Hunt, however, associates his own definition of ideology with Geertz and "culture."

Terry Eagleton's recent study entitled *Ideology* lists sixteen different meanings of this term in circulation at the moment and suggests that ideology is like halitosis: it is "what the other person has."[54] The notion that Marxist ideology is narrow, determinist, rigid, and susceptible to the capitalist clique/plot tendency, Eagleton argues (p. 4), "was elevated in the post-war period from a piece of popular wisdom to an elaborate [American] sociological theory." (Eagleton's catalog of the myriad ways in which Marxists use "ideology" might help to educate the educators, if they would consent to read it.) The idea that ideology equals culture, he writes, is "the most general of all meanings of ideology," "unworkably broad and suspiciously silent on the question of political conflict" (p. 28). He locates Geertz's conception[55] not in Parsonian structural/functionalism as Hunt does, but in Hegel's lineage, kin to Althusser's structuralism (p. 151).

Perhaps of most interest for the orthodox/revisionist/postrevisionist discourse is Eagleton's observation that "exactly the same piece of language may be ideological in one context and not in another" (p. 9). When Hunt discusses Williams, he seeks to be fair and merely indicates his own misunderstanding. When we turn the page and arrive at Geertz, his implicit comparisons with Williams are purely ideological (in Eagleton's sense), and fully consonant with early postwar structural/functionalism—which postulated that the Soviets were "in the grip of ideology while the United States sees things as they really are."[56] Thus, although Hunt's brand of postrevisionism is far more nuanced and critical of American diplomacy than Gaddis's, conceptually and genealogically he ends up where Gaddis does: Mainstream historians do history, and revisionists do something else.

Curiously, Louis Hartz nowhere intrudes Hunt's book. Yet Hartz's class analysis (no feudalism = no socialism, a nation born free in an unfree world) predicts America's inability to understand social revolutions, the subject of Hunt's chapter four. Instead, Hunt recommends Packenham's *Liberal America and the Third World* (pp. 2, 211), a Hartzian derivative distinctly inferior to the original. In his concluding chapter, Hunt begins with a quote from Marx ("men make their own history, but . . . they do not make it under circumstances chosen by themselves") and says "we would do well to accept the young Marx's promptings" (p. 171). This is the first time I have seen the young Marx located post-*Manifesto* (1852). But why not take the old Marx, of the *Grundrisse,* on America?

> . . . a country where bourgeois society did not develop on the foundation of the feudal system, but developed rather from itself; where this society appears not as the surviving result of a centuries-old movement, but rather as the starting-point of a new movement; where the state, in contrast to all earlier national formations, was from the beginning subordinate to bourgeois society, to its production, and never could make the pretence of being an end-in-itself; where, finally, bourgeois society itself, linking up the productive forces of an old world with the enormous natural terrain of a new one, has developed to hitherto unheard-of dimensions . . . and where, finally, even the antitheses of bourgeois society itself appear only as vanishing moments.[57]

Jean Baudrillard's recent book, entitled *America,* is merely a "postmodern" embroidering of Marx's brilliant theme here, and of Hartz's idea that North America is not "exceptional" so much as fully bourgeois, the most advanced capitalist society, spinning out its telos in a vacuum called North America and in a time called the future. Fredric Jameson is correct to say that in the *Grundrisse* Marx understood the world market as "the ultimate horizon of capitalism,"[58] with the United States occupying that horizon since the mid-nineteenth century (Perry "discovering" Japan in 1853, etc.). Here too, I might add, is an old Marx who does not seem to be speaking of capitalist clique/plots. Nay, he seems to be an American exceptionalist! In any case, he helps us see how classically *American* Hunt's book is.

Hunt is also a determined stabletender and sower of articles (usually in this journal) that seek to fertilize the field. His most recent missive announces the closure of a "long crisis" in diplomatic history, a crisis signified primarily by other historians pointing out the atheoretical, state-centric, archive-dependent and conservative nature of the field.[59] If the crisis is not fully overcome, diplomatic history nonetheless "has reached a watershed whose significance justifies yet another act of introspection." If we have not perhaps reached a watershed, nonetheless such "stock-taking" (I like that metaphor) can supply "a clear and accessible picture of the major tendencies and developments" in the field for graduate students now in "training" (pp. 116–17). That is, the educator will now educate.

Although the footnotes indicate attention to social and cultural history, state theory, and the problems of language in the doing of history (Hunt is the one who criticizes the "Babel of labeling" in the field), the major thrust of the article is that the field has "fragmented" into "three fairly distinct yet interdependent realms of inquiry." We are assured that all are of "primary and equal importance." The next paragraph implies that some are more equal than others, however, because the "most imposing domain" remains U.S. foreign policy, and "the leading citizens" (no longer Combs's "leading historians," but close) are "realists." The leading "elder" in the domain? Kennan. This breathtaking departure is then followed by a standard rundown on the assumptions of the realists (pp. 117–18).

The second major fragmentation? You guessed it: well, not revisionists this time, but "progressives"—Beard to Williams to Gardner/LaFeber/McCormick, but a term also roping in the corporatists. Hunt lauds the postwar drivers for restarting the progressive wagontrain and the corporatists for reformulating and extending the progressive position—not without Hunt's sympathy and care for nuance. Nonetheless, the progressives ought to do better at "establishing greater congruence between economic developments and structure on the one hand and elite perspectives and policy on the other," and (like Gaddis) Hunt suggests that they ought to read more "neo-Marxist theory"—the footnote drawing us to Hunt's *Ideology*, work by Emily Rosenberg and Rosemary Foot, and Craig Murphy's Gramscian analysis of American hegemony (p. 127—only the latter qualifies as remotely neo-Marxist).

What is the third domain that resolved the crisis of diplomatic history? It is not postrevisionism, but "international history" done multiarchivally. Those who have led the way here include trailblazers Archibald Cary Coolidge, Dexter Perkins, and William Langer, followed by John Fairbank and Ernest May (p. 130). Some might see this flock as suspiciously Cambridge-centric, but in any case the trailblazers for this new third path did most of their multiarchival work in the interwar period, except for May. A major postwar accomplishment, Hunt writes, was the introduction of "area studies." This is something dear to my heart, but it is perhaps the most atheoretical of scholarly fields (by definition), and atheoretical certainly does not mean apolitical: We now have a stunning and disturbing book on area studies at Harvard and its complicity with the CIA and the FBI, focusing on the Russian Research Center, which served as model for other area studies programs.[60] This book will curl the hair of uninitiates and hardly make the case for a nonstate-centric international history.

When all is said and done, the new Harvard international history seems to mean multiarchival diplomatic history. Hunt goes beyond the Langer/Fairbank tradition, however, to suggest that international historians need better conceptualizations of "the notion of an 'American empire'" and recommends that we consult Mommsen's *Theories of Imperialism* for "conceptual orientation." He also argues for including "previously marginalized actors" and "ordinary people" in our work (pp. 133–34). If the latter is a welcome suggestion (one acted upon by many historians in recent years), Mommsen is no help: Far from conceptualizing American imperialism (on which he has only a handful of pages—and then only to talk about Williams's influence in Germany), he provides a text useful at best for undergraduates. Concerned with making distinctions between this theory and that, from Hobson to W. W. Rostow, Mommsen's book cannot compare to recent texts like Giovanni Arrighi's *Geometry of Imperialism*. The discussion of Marx is weak, "New

Left" theories of imperialism are conflated with Maoist theories, and his grasp of Maoism is about as bad as any I have come across.[61]

For someone who recommends area studies approaches, Hunt leaves the issue of language curiously unexamined—and here I mean foreign languages, for how else can one do multiarchival research? He does at one point (p. 139) ask why we need "some half dozen accounts of the origins of U.S. involvement in Vietnam when we have so little talent within our own ranks devoted to *translating the Vietnamese experience*" (emphasis added). Otherwise, the problem is not discussed—and yet it is crucial to any decent "international history," both as a matter of theory and practice.

If a personal note is not out of bounds in examining Professor Hunt as educator, my *Origins of the Korean War* is the lead example in footnote 32 of . . . of what? "The cultural-systems and social-structure orientations, with their strong anthropological and sociological points of view so appealing to those in Asian studies." This is one stable I never thought I would find myself roped into: I use the word "culture" as infrequently as anyone I know. I do not read many anthropologists, and the main "social-structural" interpretations in my work come from political economists like Barrington Moore, Karl Polanyi, and Charles Beard. But I do read Korean, and early on determined that there was absolutely no legitimate reason for privileging Americans at the expense of Koreans or vice versa: something that diplomatic history as a field in the United States must do as a matter of method, because (except for the European countries, and even here there are many exceptions) most practitioners cannot read the languages of the countries they study in relation to American diplomacy, and all rely mostly on American documentation. The practice of using materials written by the objects of American policy cannot be separated from the theory of not privileging one group of human beings as against another. Finally, note Hunt's words: We need people to *translate* the Vietnamese experience. Translate it into what? English, as a service to diplomatic historians?[62] Into American conceptions of the world?

The conclusion to Hunt's article, that the theoretical crisis is now "transformed" by the new "three-realm field" (pp. 138–39) cannot be sustained: Michael Hunt is still part of the problem. Hunt's work is also part of the solution, however, because it is not given to censure and exclusion, is admirably multiarchival and multilingual, and mostly restricts itself to what ought to be our only realm of activity: thought.

HISTORY IN THE IMPERFECT TENSE

We do have a good example of a proper "postrevisionist" text in Melvyn P. Leffler's new book.[63] Showing no concern whatsoever for the debates over orthodoxy and revisionism and not claiming to be postrevisionist, Leffler nonetheless seeks a synthesis that overcomes both, while summing up their insights: a big leap, this attempted *aufhebung*, and I will have some criticism. But few other books so aptly reflect what historians and political scientists have learned about the Cold War in the past quarter-century. A *Preponderance of Power* is testimony to the potential of cumulation as a way to knowledge in diplomatic history, and it is difficult to categorize in our earlier genealogy—although Leffler supports Gaddis's arguments about economics serving national security, not vice versa.[64]

Deeply researched and clearly written, Leffler's account is reasonably free of bias: He takes good work where he finds it. Furthermore, his biases come, as they ought to, from his approach to the subject, his interpretation, his worldview. He is averse to labeling and cubbyholing, just as his own contributions in this book cannot readily be summarized in a pithy phrase.

If we disinter the labels for a moment, the orthodox school will find little comfort in Leffler's account. Comfort comes only with his agreement on American goals in Western Europe and Japan, and with his somewhat dewy-eyed and distinctly timebound conclusion.[65] Otherwise, he argues, Truman administration officials consistently distorted Soviet behavior, refused to negotiate, ignored Stalin's conservatism, and deployed an inflated Soviet threat for its uses in getting the other things they wanted (just as Mary Kaldor has argued, although he does not cite her work).[66] Soviet actions, he concludes, were "contradictory," "reactive," "defensive," and "cautious" (except in the 1948 Berlin crisis); their capabilities were "limited" and the United States always knew that—as was reflected in continuous judgments from 1945 through 1952 that the USSR was not ready for war (pp. 513–15). Truman's policies ranged from the wise and prudent to the regrettable in the First World, and to the foolish and disastrous in the Third World—where Truman and his advisers misconstrued anticolonial movements as Soviet tools, leading to the interventions in Korea and Vietnam and to odious associations with one dictator after another.

Revisionists will be happy with many of Leffler's substantive points, besides those above: that containment arrived early, "before Kennan," and that officials quickly extended it to global dimensions; that the United States sought to reform rather than demolish European colonialism, and that it utterly misconstrued revolutionary nationalism; that the United States tolerated any sort of fascist collaborator or reactionary dictator as long as he was reliably anti-Communist; and that the road to Korea and Vietnam was paved with bad intentions to revive Japan's economic relationship with its Asian periphery.

Democracy and the American public play barely any role in Truman administration deliberations; this structured absence in Leffler's book will stun many readers—if not revisionists—the moment they think about it. The Truman Doctrine, the Marshall Plan, NATO, Korea—all these decisions went forward with remarkable ease, with domestic opposition almost always exaggerated in the literature (according to Leffler). "Postrevisionism" à la John Gaddis is evident throughout the account, but Gaddis also comes in for significant criticism (mostly in the footnotes).

Revisionists are honored in a time-lapse breach, however. Much of Leffler's evidence comes from historians who have toiled in the archives on one regional conflict or another and who have published in the 1970s and 1980s; the central figures who created what is called "revisionism" and whose ideas stimulated much of this research are mostly absent. Fleming, Williams, Gardner, LaFeber, and Kolko are not in the index; Kolko and Gardner are in the bibliography but Fleming and Williams are not, and from LaFeber we find but two articles. While synthesizing the empirical insights of a generation of younger historians, Leffler whites out the conceptions that lay behind them, the theoretical searchlights that enabled them to discover and interpret the documents they found in the archives. This turns out to be a significant absence, going to the heart of why *A Preponderance of Power* is not yet our solution, but also remains part of the problem.[67] However learned Leffler is in the newer literature—and he is very much so, an excellent reader—he is atheoretical and depends on discursive techniques to advance his argument. He is also ahistorical, in the specific sense that he has taken a slice of time, called it the origins of the Cold War, and thus isolated it from what went before and came after.[68]

What is his argument? That Truman's policymakers sought a "preponderance of power" in the postwar world, driven by geostrategic conceptions of the relationship of national power to "control of resources, industrial infrastructure, and overseas bases" (p. 12). These conceptions were deeply influenced by fears and uncertainties about the postwar world, leading to prudent action here, foolish action there. "Economic interests often reinforced geostrategic imperatives and ideological predilections," he writes in a key passage (pp. 14–15), but were still subordinate to "concerns about correlations of power ... [that] far exceeded" worries about "the well-being of the American economy." Nor were "organizational imperatives" the mainspring of national security policies; they merely "buttressed" them. Partisan politics reinforced rather than divided Washington (liberal anticommunism was just as "fierce" as the conservative variety, if more discriminating), and the public was "malleable."

So, there we have it—a concise statement farming out other interpretations: it was not economics, it was not ideology, it was not bureaucracy, it was not democracy or partisan conflict that shaped Truman's policies. All these things were present, but geostrategic imperatives and inchoate fears were more important. The narrative structure reinforces these ideas with frequent constructions of apprehension, frustration, anxiety, fear, alarm, fright, dread, and horror. The theme is reified throughout the text, making the reader think that Acheson was just as apprehensive about Europe's survival in 1952 as Kennan was in 1945.

I have sought to articulate my position on these questions in my recent book, but suffice it to say that I would exactly reverse the sequence: "Geostrategic imperatives and ideological predilections often reinforced economic interests." It is as simple as Acheson saying "defense perimeter" in public and "great crescent" in private, as complex as "economic interest" being irreducible to "the well-being of the American economy" or the percentage of exports in U.S. production (Leffler, pp. 160–61, 316–17). That may have been true of early and vulgar revisionist accounts, but the sophisticated work is about world economy, not the American economy. Was the health of the world economy less important to Acheson, Lovett, and McCloy than geostrategy and their fears about the Soviets? I do not see how they can be read this way.

Leffler is not sure either. Although his theme is firm at beginning and end, many readers will find parts of his account indistinguishable from those that place world economy first (for example the discussion of an open world and loans to Britain—pp. 61–62). An early restatement of his theme inadvertently elides the economic ("Fear and power—not unrelenting Soviet pressure, not humanitarian impulses, not domestic political considerations, not British influence—were the key factors shaping American policies toward the Kremlin"—p. 51). Take this causal statement, about Russia's place in the postwar world economy: "Fear inspired American officials to prod the Kremlin to accept an open sphere" (p. 54). Why fear and not access to Eastern markets or opposition to state-controlled economies or a desire to link semi-peripheral Eastern Europe with industrial Western Europe (all of which are mentioned in the text)?

Whether geostrategy or world economy were more important can also be posed as whether Kennan or Acheson was more important. Leffler's conception is very close to Kennan's: Advanced industrial structure is central to war-making power, and war-making power is the source of realpolitik conflict, which can only be resolved through strategies seeking a balance of power. But, as I have argued, Kennan never understood his boss, who had a Wall Street internationalist's conception of what made the world go 'round—money, investment, a hidden hegemonic hand.

For Acheson, the leitmotiv of the 1940s was the long cycle of British decline and American advance, with "the fifteen weeks" in 1947 marking not the defense of free peoples against Soviet aggression so much as the final passage of the baton from London to Washington. Korea—to take something close to my heart—was, for Acheson, not Kennan's suppurating black hole, but something useful to Japanese industrial revival, a twinkling star in a "great crescent" linking Tokyo with Alexandria. The Korean War was not North Korea's response to the great crescent, but something useful for NSC-68 and military Keynesianism, the pump Acheson found in 1950 that finally primed not the American economy, but the allied economies—and thus the world economy. The Vietnam War was important to shore up the periphery throughout the world, but not more important than the run on the dollar in 1968: So, Acheson decided, the war ought to be shut down.

Kennan the realist was to Acheson, what Henry Kissinger the realist was to Nelson Rockefeller and then Richard Nixon, what Zbigniew Brzezinski was to David Rockefeller and then Jimmy Carter: realpolitik engineer for an architecture never fully articulated. So was the elected president: As Leffler notes, Acheson "almost never discussed fundamental objectives with the President." Not for Harry Truman, the apprehension of imponderables.

Acheson had an easy and hearty contempt for definitions of security policy that ignored world economy, most of which came from an American military that, in the early postwar period, destroyed several forests to produce the endless reams of strategic surveys, requirements estimates, redefinitions of vital interests, position papers, departmental and interdepartmental committee reports, etc., that now clutter the archives and that seem to have elicited inordinate attention from Mel Leffler. Acheson's papers are a clear, polished lens that illumines the postwar world; Kennan's papers give you that world through a glass darkly; the Pentagon still has not come to a conclusion on its nature.

The competing doctrines of the Cold War period are just so much cut forest, unless they are linked to constituencies within and without the state: constituencies generate doctrines, and doctrines generate constituencies (this was Franz Schurmann's insight). Rollback was the strategy generated by a dying isolationism and an always-strong American unilateralism and nationalism. NSC-68 was about military Keynesianism, it was about generating constituencies that came to make up the national security state, the required "system maintenance" (to speak structural-functionally) for the extraordinary and unprecedented commitments that the Truman administration had taken upon itself. NSC-68 was about the end of the atomic monopoly, it was about the absence of bipartisanship in the wake of the victory of the Chinese revolution, it was about how to jumpstart the advanced economies, it embodied the year-long debate in Washington over containment and rollback, and finally, it was about fear. (It was not about geostrategy, for there was none worthy of the name in that overblown document.)

Leffler's lack of concern for hegemonic advance and decline is part of the ahistoricity of his text. It is the same with his argument about the Marshall Plan. Whereas Michael J. Hogan makes World War II into an ellipsis, an interruption in the continuity of corporate capitalist innovation since Hoover in the 1920s, the word capitalism barely intrudes Leffler's text—let alone different ways to organize it. In his implicit refutation of Hogan (pp. 160–61), he says that the "economic motivations behind the Marshall Plan were secondary" but "not unimportant." Economic motivation, however, is reduced to whether the U.S. economy had to export to ensure prosperity. Missed is the substance of the corporatist thesis: for Ferguson, the political coalition at the top of high-technology and labor-accommodating multinational firms that made the second New Deal and took the world as its oyster; for Hogan, the new, organized capitalism of technocratic instrumentality, transnational coordination, bureaucratic planning, associative politics, and state regulation that straddled both sides of World War II.

Leffler gives us the world according to Truman's advisers, without the theoretical underpinning and with, in my view, almost no sense of the obstacles that they faced at home—remnant isolationism, a restive right wing, strong and recalcitrant labor, Republicans out of power for a generation, the nationalism of firms producing for the American market, conflicting strategies for dealing with communism at home and abroad, expansionist Asia-firstism with its deep roots in the body politic, Eastern Establishment internationalism with its correspondingly shallow political roots. There is little politics in the book: Truman's advisers generally get their way. As for the obstacles they faced abroad, it is difficult to figure them out if you visit no foreign archives.[69] Thus, we get little sense of the true dimensions of the crisis that gripped Washington beginning in 1949 and that I have written much about elsewhere. The result is a book that does not tell us much that specialists on the Cold War did not already know, while frequently reinterpreting many disputes in the literature in a manner far more conservative, I think, than was Leffler's original intent.[70]

Tom McCormick did not go into the archives to figure out this period, but did some reading through the lenses of world system theory. He came out with a better rendering of the 1949–50 crisis than we find in Leffler, one that interrogates the idea that evidence is only found in the archives. But let us stop here with Mel Leffler's book, and then go on with McCormick. *Preponderance of Power* is a very good book. It is immensely informative. It is a postrevisionist success. It is worthy of a much longer appreciation and critique than I can bring to bear here. I fling no Montana frisbees. It needed more theory.

It seems to me that the end of the Cold War in Europe demolishes a number of academic theories: most of all the theory of totalitarianism, certainly game theory as applied to international relations, even the sanctified realpolitik doctrine of rationally known national interest, which utterly fails to explain Gorbachev turning a global superpower into a regional basket case—perhaps our most extraordinary example of a world ending not with a bang but a whimper. But the demise of the Cold War leaves world system theory reasonably intact, I think, and therefore—Gaddis notwithstanding—leaves Williams intact.[71] Indeed, Immanuel Wallerstein predicted the crisis of "actually-existing" socialism and its future dependency on Western Europe at least as far back as 1984—it was the wrong system, in the wrong place, at the wrong time.[72]

To return to the origins of the Cold War and McCormick, however, if 1947 was the critical watershed year, then all the West had to do was hold Kennan's containment lines long enough (until the 1980s let us say), whereupon the other side would collapse and the United States and its allies would win. But 1947 was only the end of the beginning. Containment was unstable, both in the world and at home (in the United States). The period 1947–1950 was the determining "crisis of the new order" (McCormick's words),[73] because vast reaches of the globe were in the turmoil of decolonization, the core industrial economies needed primary resources, and therefore the passive/active dialectic of containment and rollback in Soviet-American competition had to be extended to the Third World. Here the much-maligned Mao (I refer to his 1947 ideas on bloc conflict in the "intermediate zone") was a superior theorist to Kennan or Acheson or Stalin, all of whom expressed disdain for and caution about Third World entanglement (but only Kennan escaped it, by hiving off to Princeton in 1950).

The years 1947–1950 were also the determining period for the American home front. The turn to the periphery necessitated permanent empire, what Harry Elmer Barnes called "perpetual war for perpetual peace," what Charles Beard in 1947 called "an unlimited program of underwriting, by money and military 'advice,' poverty-stricken, feeble and instable [*sic*] governments around the edges of the gigantic and aggressive Slavic Empire"—whereby, in the process, "the domestic affairs of the American people became appendages to an aleatory expedition in the management of the world." Beard counseled "a prudent recognition and calculation of the limits on power," lest the United States suffer "a terrible defeat in a war"—like the "wrecks of overextended empires scattered through the centuries."[74] (Presumably that has nothing to say to us in 1993.)

NSC-68 and the Korean War exemplified the new strategy and the First-Third World struggle reinterpreted as East-West crisis that made the strategy appear correct and that got Congress and the American people to hold still for Beard's "expedition." Thus arose the national security state and the military-industrial complex at home and a far-flung imperial structure abroad.

I would also assert that the crisis of 1949–50 can make sense of some mysteries that have long gripped the field of American history: orientations toward the Old World and the New, New England versus the frontier, "Europe-first" versus "Asia-first," and that subject no historian of the United States seems ever to tire of discussing, "exceptionalism." A recent issue of the *American Historical Review* carries a lead article in which Ian Tyrrel argues that a transnational or world system perspective can help American historians overcome their addiction to exceptionalism, and a commentary in which Michael McGerr responds that Tyrrel got it all wrong.[75] I found it rather amazing that the *AHR* should find this debate worthy of prominent feature, because the "new transnational history," as it is called, has been "new" since at least 1974, when Wallerstein and Schurmann published their books: and if I may say so, Tyrrel's discussion of both the "new history" and American exceptionalism seemed to me quite pedestrian.

Tyrrel nonetheless has a point, and the way I would put it is that a world economy perspective can do for American history what the study of America's role in the world did for Bill Williams: "Williams discovering America, almost like Columbus," in Warren Susman's brilliant observation.[76] Williams reading America from the outside in, to put it another way. But to see Louis Hartz as the grand American exceptionalist, as Tyrrel and others do, is to get things exactly backwards: Hartz was a *European* exceptionalist, that is, a devotee of what Allan Bloom and others have exalted as "The West" who just happened to grow up in Omaha. He spent his life trying but failing to find Europe's replication in America—could not even find it in Harvard yard (in spite of the brilliance of its international historians), and ended up roaming the British museum.

Louis Hartz had the idea, in other words, that the New World was not Europe: To him the United States was a fragment and an implant that had only a partial understanding of the European project; likewise, the states of South America were a new amalgam of Iberian and indigenous influences. A Lockean liberalism never fully known, understood, or realized—now there is an idea that can help us explain the genealogy of American diplomatic history: its atheoretical character, its lack of intellectualism, its unconscious affinity for state interpretations, its peculiarly American lack of connectedness to what European intellectuals think about. It is also typically American in being ahistorical: not about America, of course, but about America in the world, and the world in America. Nietzsche, just after talking about the cattle,[77] linked ahistoricity to a childlike state, to the "plastic power" of people, to human creativity, to the very capacity of those unencumbered by the past *to act,* in a passage full of meaning for this unhistorical nation we live in. But that is where I started, in the barnyard.

My purpose in this essay was not to revisit the shootout at the OK Corral, but to rustle up the sagebrush and stir up the chickencoop. In fact, I do not believe in revisionism, let alone postrevisionism, let alone antirevisionism masquerading as postrevisionism. Michael Hunt is right: This is a Babel of labels. These terms merely give us the genealogy, the descent, and the moral and political valence of Cold War scholarship.

History is not a narrative of the *it was*—"what actually happened"; nor is it a Jack Webb quest after "the facts"—which never speak for themselves; it is a discipline dedicated to the eternal recurrence of revision: arguments, debates, and controversies about "what exactly did happen, why it happened, and what would be an adequate account of its significance."[78] If diplomatic history was the most conservative tendency in the history profession before the Vietnam debates, its subject— America's role in a non-American world—remains the most vulnerable to conflating objective truth with patriotic homily. Of all branches of history it is closest to the state, particularly in a state/empire. Therefore, the diplomatic historian's code ought always to be this: "The state never has any use for truth as such, but only for truth which is useful to it."[79] That code implies a commitment "to think otherwise," while living in the imperfect tense of history.

NOTES

1. Quoted in Walter LaFeber, "Fred Harvey Harrington," *Diplomatic History* 9 (Fall 1985):313.
2. Martin Heidegger, *What Is Called Thinking?* trans. J. Glenn Gray (New York, 1968), 161.
3. Friedrich Nietzsche, *The Gay Science*, trans. Walter Kaufmann (New York, 1974), 121.
4. Peter Novick has an excellent passage on how Ranke was misinterpreted in England and American in *That Noble Dream: The "Objectivity Question" and the American Historical Profession* (New York, 1988), 25–31.
5. Novick has many examples of this assumption in practice among historians, particularly those who see themselves as guardians of the discipline. See *Noble Dream*, 606–9.
6. The full passage, beautiful and pregnant with meaning, reads as follows:

   [The objective man] is accustomed to submitting before whatever wants to be known, without any other pleasure than that found in knowing and "mirroring"; he waits until something comes, and then spreads himself out tenderly lest light footsteps and the quick passage of spiritlike beings should be lost on his plane and skin. Whatever still remains in him of a "person" strikes him as accidental, often arbitrary, still more often disturbing: to such an extent has he become a passageway and reflection of strange forms and events even to himself.

   Nietzsche, *Beyond Good and Evil: Prelude to a Philosophy of the Future*, trans. Walter Kaufmann (New York, 1966), 126–27.
7. "What is it that is named with the words 'think,' 'thinking,' 'thought'? Toward what sphere of the spoken word do they direct us? A thought—where is it, where does it go? Thought is in need of memory, the gathering of thought." Heidegger, *What Is Called Thinking?* 138.
8. "On the Uses and Disadvantages of History for Life," in Nietzsche, *Untimely Meditations*, trans. R. J. Hollingdale, intro. J. P. Stern (New York, 1983), 60–61.
9. *Ibid.*, 61. This passage had influence on thinkers as dissimilar as Freud and Walter Benjamin.
10. *Ibid.* (emphasis added).
11. Novick, *Noble Dream*, 450. Schlesinger's letter to Boyd Shafer was dated 1 July 1954; Feis's to John Leonard, 15 April 1971. "Pro-Communist scholar" is an interesting McCarthyite wrinkle: pro-Communist, yes, but also a scholar. It reminds me of Donald Zagoria's reference to me as a "leftist scholar" when my first book was blurbed in *Foreign Affairs* in 1982. To academics, this would make a difference, just as it would in a courtroom. But to students? For them, Schlesinger had called Williams a Communist, Zagoria had called Cumings a leftist.
12. Feis to Schlesinger, 7 May 1971, cited in *ibid.*, 449.
13. Kaldor, *The Imaginary Conflict* (New York, 1990), 35–48. For a broader inquiry into the provincialism of American diplomatic history that in the text, but especially in the foot-

notes, also gives a good sense of the vibrance of international history that I mentioned at the start of this essay see Christopher Thorne, *Border Crossings: Studies in International History* (New York, 1988).

14. *Three Rival Versions of Moral Enquiry: Encyclopaedia, Genealogy, and Tradition* (Notre Dame, 1990), 35.

15. Several of my friends who like to read Marx have chided me for my interest in Nietzsche. They would do well to ponder Adorno's statement that *The Genealogy of Morals* is far better Marxism than the texts in the *ABCs of Communism* genre, or Benjamin's forays into dialectical materialism. See Theodor Adorno to Walter Benjamin, 10 November 1938, in Adorno et al., *Aesthetics and Politics* (London, 1977), 132.

16. Nietzsche, *On the Genealogy of Morals*, ed. and trans. Walter Kaufmann (New York, 1969), 15–23, 77–78.

17. "Nietzsche, Genealogy, History," in Michel Foucault, *Language, Counter-Memory, Practice: Selected Essays and Interviews*, trans. Donald F. Bouchard and Sherry Simon (Ithaca, 1977).

18. MacIntyre argues that Foucault consistently denied any "fundamental sets or structures" that create explanation or understanding (*Rival Versions*, p. 52), whereas Gary Gutting says Foucault never was explicit (see his *Michel Foucault's Archaeology of Scientific Reason* [New York, 1989]). Gutting notes that *L'Archeologie du Savoir* provided "no serious discussion of the nature of the nondiscursive factors and of the influence they exert"; "there is no elucidation of the fundamental nature and ultimate significance of the link between the discursive and the nondiscursive" (p. 259). Unless a remove into Berkeleyean phenomenalism is proposed, I think the industrial installations of the past two hundred years, if not necessarily their relationships, represent a "fundamental set or structure" that cannot be deconstructed, that can be apprehended by human senses like eyesight, and that do create relationships that require explanation and understanding, that is, humans trying to comprehend their meaning (for example they generate interests). Nietzsche rarely comments on this problem, because he was mostly concerned with moral and philosophical discourse, but occasionally he condemned the "money economy" of his time and clearly recognized an entity called the state.

19. Daniel Yergin, *The Prize: The Epic Quest for Oil, Money and Power* (New York, 1991), 439–43. J. Paul Getty reached the pinnacle of billionaire status (enabling him to increase his contributions to the Democratic party, if not to enjoy better restaurants because "he made it a point to chew each mouthful of food thirty-three times") by virtue of paying a young geologist named Paul Walton to fly over the Saudi desert in a DC-3. Walton noticed a saucer-shaped mound pushing up the sand and thought that might be a good place to drill a hole. Thus was brought in an oil field described by *Fortune* as "somewhere between colossal and history-making."

20. *Ibid.*, 395. Rather like the famous territorial division between Churchill and Stalin, in 1944 Roosevelt drew "a rough sketch" of the Middle East for British ambassador Lord Halifax: "Persian oil," he told the Ambassador, "is yours. We share the oil of Iraq and Kuwait. As for Saudi Arabian oil, it is ours." (*Ibid.*, 401).

21. Bruce Cumings, *The Origins of the Korean War*, vol. 2, *The Roaring of the Cataract, 1947–1950* (Princeton, 1990), 408–38.

22. Kai Bird, *The Chairman: John J. McCloy and the Making of the American Establishment* (New York, 1992), 154.

23. In 1947, McCloy and Leffingwell had long discussions on the World Bank, reflecting back on the errors of the 1920s; in the same year, Leffingwell warned Lovett—his "Locust Valley neighbor"—that Europe was "drifting toward catastrophe" unless the United States provided loans and grants "on a great scale." He then tutored Lovett on how

to keep the Russians out of the Marshall Plan, without seeming to do so. See their discussions in Ron Chernow, *The House of Morgan: An American Banking Dynasty and the Rise of Modern Finance* (New York, 1990), 486–89. At an early meeting of the World Bank, with McCloy in charge, the British Director Sir James Grigg remarked, "here goes a meeting of the Chase Bank," whereupon McCloy set about organizing bank affairs in a house Nelson Rockefeller lent him on Georgetown's Foxhall Road. Bird, *The Chairman,* 289; see also p. 387 for McCloy as "a Rockefeller man." When Eisenhower suggested that McCloy be named high commissioner of Germany, Robert Morgenthau told Harry Hopkins "McCloy isn't the man to go. . . . After all, his clients are people like General Electric, Westinghouse, General Motors"—in other words, the high-technology, labor-accommodating multinational firms Tom Ferguson writes about (Bird, *The Chairman,* 225).

24. Bird, *The Chairman,* 143, 178.

25. Yergin, *The Prize,* 413–16. There was the irksome problem of antitrust, because three of the four firms were fashioned out of John D. Rockefeller's Standard Oil. But Truman's attorney general did not think that was a problem and okayed the agreement. This was followed in September 1947 by huge deals involving Anglo-Iranian, Gulf, and Shell, and thus "the mechanisms, capital and marketing systems were in place to move vast quantities of Middle Eastern oil into the European market" and to move Europe off coal and onto oil (*Ibid.,* 422–24).

26. William S. Borden, *The Pacific Alliance: United States Foreign Economic Policy and Japanese Trade Recovery, 1947–54* (Madison, 1984), 1–17.

27. Cumings, *Origins* 2:57.

28. As in Eisenhower's rumored comment, "Why in pluperfect hell do we have to worry so much about that little teat of a country? [Korea]"

29. University of California Press, 1983.

30. Sometimes the distinction is worthy of a contortionist, as in Combs's judgment on Barton Bernstein: "radical revisionist . . . somewhat harsher in tone than Ronald Steel, a moderate revisionist" (p. 333n).

31. Novick, *Noble Dream,* 450–51. That is, LaFeber's finely crafted history is no different than the rantings and near-plagiarism (apparent if you first read D. F. Fleming and I. F. Stone and then read him) of David Horowitz in *The Free World Collosus: A Critique of American Foreign Policy in the Cold War* (New York, 1965).

32. "The Responsibility of the Intellectuals," *New York Review of Books,* December 1966, reprinted in Chomsky, *American Power and the New Mandarins* (New York, 1967).

33. John Lewis Gaddis, *The United States and the Origins of the Cold War, 1941–1947* (New York, 1972).

34. Gabriel Kolko, *The Politics of War: The World and United States Foreign Policy. 1943–1945* (New York, 1968). Merely to read Kolko's nine-page introduction is to behold a superior historian, whose views could only be reduced to "economic determinism" with great violence to his argument—one I fully share—that knowing the Cold War begins with "the history of the great shifting and reintegration of the world political system that occurred between 1943 and 1949."

35. John Lewis Gaddis, "The Emerging Post-Revisionist Synthesis on the Origins of the Cold War," *Diplomatic History* 7 (Summer 1983):171–90. Gaddis says J. Samuel Walker first coined the term. Meanwhile I do not know whether to put a pluperfect hyphen in the middle or not: Gaddis's title is "Post-Revisionist," but in the text it is "postrevisionist."

36. "Responses to John Lewis Gaddis," *ibid.,* 191–93, 198–200. Gardner placed before readers Robert A. Divine's masterful portrait of "the internationalists" (from his *Second*

Chance: The Triumph of Internationalism in America during World War II), which ought to be read over and over to Gaddis, Leffler, and anyone else who thinks "national security" came before world economy.

37. Here (p. 187n) is where I come in for honorable mention, for having made "a start" in that direction with my first book, *The Origins of the Korean War,* vol. 1, *Liberation and the Emergence of Separate Regimes* (Princeton, 1981).

38. I do not know which would upset Bill Williams more—to be called New Left or Leninist. Probably the former.

39. Whereas, as we have just seen (footnote 34), Kolko located the crisis in the world system.

40. This judgment is also reflected in Gaddis's statement that "Revisionism in one form or another will always be with us, and that is no bad thing, because the writing of history would be much less interesting without it." See Gaddis, "Emerging Post-Revisionist Synthesis," 189. Coming right after the sentence about revisionists turning history into an instrument of politics, the connotation is the same as Combs's: Historians do history, revisionists do something else; sometimes the revisionists cannot be ignored, most of the time they can.

41. Heidegger, *What Is Called Thinking?* 152.

42. As Novick notes, Schlesinger characterized this as the orthodox view, while allowing that he did not see the Cold War as "a 'pure' case of Russian aggression and American response" in his influential 1967 article. *Noble Dream,* 448. For the article see Arthur Schlesinger, Jr., "Origins of the Cold War," *Foreign Affairs* 46 (October 1967):22–52. Today it reads like a pure exercise in discursive politics.

43. Allan David Bloom, *The Closing of the American Mind* (New York, 1987), builds toward the penultimate chapter, "The Sixties," where the world-historical event of his (and presumably) our life takes place, in isolated, weatherbeaten Ithaca, New York.

44. See Gaddis, "The Corporatist Synthesis: A Skeptical View," and Michael J. Hogan. "Corporatism: A Positive Appraisal," *Diplomatic History* 10 (Fall 1986):357–72.

45. John Lewis Gaddis, "New Conceptual Approaches to the Study of American Foreign Relations: Interdisciplinary Perspectives," *Diplomatic History* 14 (Summer 1990): 405–23.

46. There are, let it be said, lots of good suggestions in this essay for what diplomatic historians ought to do to acquire theory; I assign the article to my students and have noticed them taking Gaddis to heart.

47. John Lewis Gaddis, "The Tragedy of Cold War History," *Diplomatic History* 17 (Winter 1993):1–16.

48. See Novick, *Noble Dream,* 332–48.

49. And getting more orthodox all the time: see chapter two in *The Long Peace: Inquiries into the History of the Cold War* (New York, 1987); and Gaddis's (re-)discovery that the Cold War was about freedom vs. tyranny after all, in Michael J. Hogan, ed., *The End of the Cold War: Its Meaning and Implications* (New York, 1992), 24. The very idea of "a long peace" in the post-1945 period is obscene, given the millions of lives lost in Korea, Vietnam, and elsewhere. But I have criticized this notion in my contribution to the Hogan volume (87–89), and will say no more here.

50. Louis Hartz, *The Liberal Tradition in America* (New York, 1955), 28.

51. Michael H. Hunt, *Ideology and U.S. Foreign Policy* (New Haven, 1955), 28.

52. Michael H. Hunt, *The Making of a Special Relationship: The United States and China to 1914* (New York, 1983), for example, has an excellent account of the "open door constituency."

53. Even Germans and Swedes were too "swarthy" for Franklin—"Palantine boors," he hoped they would go back where they came from. Only Saxons entered his hallowed

realm of "not swarthy" (p. 46). As for Acheson, "If you truly had a democracy and did what the people wanted, you'd go wrong every time" (p. 180).

54. Terry Eagleton, *Ideology: An Introduction* (London, 1991), 1–2.

55. Hunt at first cites Geertz's "Thick Description: Toward an Interpretive Theory of Culture" (p. 215) and later (p. 227) the same text Eagleton uses, "Ideology as a Cultural System."

56. Eagleton, *Ideology*, 4.

57. Karl Marx, "Bastiat and Carey," in *Grundrisse: Foundations of the Critique of Political Economy*, trans. Martin Nicolaus (New York, 1973), 883–88.

58. Fredric Jameson, *Postmodernism, or, The Cultural Logic of Late Capitalism* (Durham, 1991), xix.

59. Michael H. Hunt, "The Long Crisis in U.S. Diplomatic History: Coming to Closure," *Diplomatic History* 16 (Winter 1992):115–40.

60. Sigmund Diamond, *Compromised Campus: The Collaboration of Universities with the Intelligence Community, 1945–1955* (New York, 1992). Harvard takes up the first half of the book, whereupon Diamond moves on to Yale.

61. As soon as Mommsen quotes Marx from *The German Ideology* on the ever-widening scope of the world market, Mommsen says Marx "interpreted capitalism as a closed system" (p. 31). Mommsen has recourse to Karl Wittfogel on the superficiality of Maoism as a type of Marxism (p. 58), and then examines Mao's views on imperialism in the most cursory and even silly fashion, citing two 1930s texts and one broadside (not authored by Mao) from the *Beijing Review* circa 1963, ignoring the substantial work on Mao's worldview by John Gittings, Franz Schurmann, Stuart Schram, and many others whose books were available when this passage was written. When Mommsen finally gets to a few comments on Williams, it is to criticize his theory as narrow, by which he means that Williams locates imperial policy "chiefly in the economic field" (p. 93)—that is, Hunt's much-reiterated point. See Wolfgang J. Mommsen, *Theories of Imperialism*, trans. S. Falla (New York, 1977).

62. Paradoxically, it is unfair to single out Hunt here, even though these are his words, because he is one of the few diplomatic historians who reads Chinese fluently. My comment is apt for the field as a whole, but not at all for him.

63. Melvyn P. Leffler, *A Preponderance of Power: National Security, the Truman Administration, and the Cold War* (Stanford, 1992).

64. See Gaddis, "Emerging Post-Revisionist Synthesis," 173–75, for comparison.

65. That is, it could only have been written in the immediate aftermath of the events of 1989 and 1990, before the Gulf war, Yugoslavia, and the mounting evidence that the United States wants to continue the military-industrial complex that sustained containment—but directed this time against Third World "renegades" and, implicitly, Germany and Japan. The conclusion also strikes one as perhaps written for another book—for example in the "Wise Men" section (pp. 499–502), where Leffler sums up what he takes to be wise policy: "Truman administration officials grasped the nature of the Soviet threat," had "a shrewd understanding of Soviet weaknesses," etc., which directly contradicts much of what he said earlier.

66. See in particular Leffler's excellent account of the famed Clifford-Elsey report of 1946—"a totally misleading rendition of Soviet capabilities," combined with "incredibly disingenuous" judgments about Soviet perceptions (pp. 130–38).

67. Professor Leffler, in his critique of this essay (Melvyn Leffler to Bruce Cumings, 6 August 1992), found it preposterous that I would accuse him of ignoring Williams, Kolko, and the others, because their work has informed his throughout his career. His earlier work certainly shows their influence, but in *Preponderance* he fails to point out that they

etched the agenda for the more recent Cold War history that he frequently cites. Furthermore, the basic thrust of *Preponderance* is to grant that they were right on a number of crucial issues, while denying that they were right about the basic motivations of American foreign policy.

68. Dr. Leffler also complained mightily in his letter to me about this criticism, as perhaps any historian would. He argued that given his earlier work on the interwar years, it was a cheap shot. That he is a fine historian who knows the interwar period is beyond doubt, but that does not relieve *Preponderance* of my criticism.

69. I am indebted to Walter LaFeber for pointing out to me that Leffler used not one foreign archive or manuscript source.

70. I am indebted to Michael Hogan for a discussion on this point.

71. Williams was, of course, not a formal "world systems" theorist, but every chapter of *Tragedy* has some grist for the world system mill.

72. I refer to his formal remarks at a panel at the Annual Meeting of the American Political Science Association, Washington, 1984; Tom Ferguson and I shared the platform with him.

73. Thomas J. McCormick, *America's Half-Century: United States Foreign Policy in the Cold War* (Baltimore, 1989), 72–98.

74. Charles Austin Beard, *Roosevelt and the Coming of the War* (New York, 1947) 580, 592–93, 597.

75. Ian Tyrrel, "American Exceptionalism in an Age of International History," and Michael McGerr, "The Price of the 'New Transnational History'," *American Historical Review* 96 (October 1991):1031–55, 1056–67.

76. Warren Susman, "The Smoking Room School of History," in *History and the New Left: Madison, Wisconsin, 1950–1970*, ed. Paul Buhle (Philadelphia, 1990), 44.

77. Nietzsche, *Untimely Meditations*, 62–63.

78. Ian Jarvie, quoted in Robert A. Rosenstone, "History in Images/History in Words: Reflections on the Possibility of Really Putting History onto Film," *American Historical Review* 93 (December 1988):1176.

79. Nietzsche continues, "more precisely for anything whatever useful to it whether it be truth, half-truth, or error." See "Schopenhauer as Educator," in *Untimely Meditations*, 190.